Conference of the North American Chapter of the Association for Computational Linguistics: Human Language Technologies (NAACL HLT 2018)

Short Papers

New Orleans, Louisiana, USA
1 – 6 June 2018

ISBN: 978-1-5108-6347-7

NAACL HLT 2018

**The 2018 Conference of the
North American Chapter of the
Association for Computational Linguistics:
Human Language Technologies**

**Proceedings of the Conference
Volume 2 (Short Papers)**

June 1-June 6, 2018
New Orleans, Louisiana

Diamond Sponsors

Platinum Sponsors

Gold Sponsors

Silver Sponsors

Bronze Sponsors

Message from the General Chair

Welcome to New Orleans and to NAACL HLT 2018 – the biggest NAACL to date. Natural Language Processing and Computational Linguistics is constantly growing and changing with a constant flow of new methods and topics. Every year also sees an even more exciting and diverse research community, with a steadily increasing number researchers, companies both large and small, and a vibrant community of practitioners and students who are excited at the prospect of taking on the newest challenges of the discipline. This year's NAACL HLT conference reflects what an exciting time this is for our field, and highlights the vibrancy and vitality of our community.

I feel extremely lucky to be able to work with a fantastic program committee, especially the two extremely dedicated, creative and resourceful program chairs: Amanda Stent and Heng Ji. Their innovations include a new review form, intended to elicit higher quality reviews, the opportunity for authors to review the reviewers, the Test-of-Time awards, and a program where poster and demo sessions run consistently in parallel to the oral sessions, in order to allow the conference to reflect the ever increasing diversity of research topics and the corresponding volume of accepted papers. I am especially excited about the new Test-of-Time papers award session, and hope to see this new innovation become a regular part of ACL conferences.

We have named the Test-of-Time award in memory of Aravind Joshi, who left us this year, after having a huge lifetime impact on our community. We will always remember him for his gentle conversational style, sharp focus, interest in linguistic, computational and mathematical properties of language, and his lifetime commitment to mentoring women in NLP. I feel extremely lucky to have been one of his Ph.D. students.

This year we also introduced an industrial track, with the aim of featuring papers that focus on scalable, interpretable, reliable and customer facing methods for industrial applications of Natural Language Processing. The idea of having such a track was proposed by Yunyao Li who strongly advocated for it: this proposal was then discussed and approved by the NAACL board. After that, it was all go, with an incredible amount of work to promote and organize it by the industrial track chairs: Jennifer Chu-Carroll, Yunyao Li and Srinivas Bangalore.

The overall program looks amazing and reflects the cooperative way that everyone on the committee worked together. What a team! I am so grateful for getting to be a part of this community of people, and I really appreciate the enthusiasm and attention to detail reflected in their hard work: Amanda Stent and Heng Ji (program chairs); Jennifer Chu-Carroll, Yunyao Li and Srinivas Bangalore (industrial track chairs); Ying Lin (website chair); Marie Meteer and Jason Williams (workshop co-chairs); Mohit Bansal and Rebecca Passonneau (tutorial co-chairs); Yang Liu, Tim Paek, and Manasi Patwardhan (demo co-chairs); Chris Callison-Burch and Beth Hockey (Family-Friendly Program Co-Chairs) Stephanie Lukin and Meg Mitchell (publication co-chairs); Jonathan May (handbook chair); Silvio Ricardo Cordeiro, Shereen Oraby, Umashanthi Pavalanathan, and Kyeongmin Rim (student cochairs) along with Swapna Somasundaran and Sam Bowman (Faculty Advisors) for the student research workshop; Lena Reed (student volunteer coordinator); Kristy Hollingshead, Kristen Johnson, and Parisa Kordjamshidi (local sponsorships and exhibits cochairs); Yonatan Bisk and Wei Xu (publicity and social media chairs); David Yarowsky and Joel Tetreault (treasurers) and Alexis Palmer and Jason Baldridge (the NAACL international Sponsorship Team). Also thanks to Rich at SoftConf for his speedy response to questions and his willingness to help us innovate with our new review form. And thanks to Julia Hockenmaier and the whole NAACL Executive Board for always being willing to consult on any issue.

The program highlights three keynote speakers in the main track: Dilek Hakkani-Tür, Kevin Knight, and Charles Yang. We also have two keynote speakers in the industry track: Mari Ostendorf and Daniel Marcu. These talks promising to be interesting across a range of issues from language acquisition in children to the commercial possibilities of conversational agents. The industry track will also feature two panels, one on careers in industry (as compared to academia) and the other on ethics in NLP. The program also includes six tutorials featuring topics of current interest and sources of innovation in the field. We have sixteen workshops plus the student research workshop: some of these workshops have become events in themselves with many of them repeated each year. We will also have plenary sessions for the outstanding paper awards and the new Test-Of-Time papers award session.

Any event of this scale can only happen with the the hard work of a wonderful group of people. I especially want to thank the NAACL board for being willing to consult on a range of different issues and Priscilla Rasmussen for taking care of all the millions of details that need to be looked after every single day to make sure the logistical aspects of the conference come together. I want to especially thank Priscilla for her hard work and creativity organizing our social event: we first will go to Mardi Gras World to see the world of wonders created each year for the Mardi Gras. From there we go to the river, to the dockside River City Plaza and River City Ballroom for New Orleans' famous cuisine and libations and dancing to live Zydeco, funk, soul and R&B.

ACL has been working for several years to increase diversity at our conferences and in our community. So, taking inspiration from ACL 2017, we aimed to make NAACL family friendly, by providing childcare at the conference, and encouraging people to bring their families to the social events and breakfasts. Diversity can also be a consequence of the support for students to attend the conference that we receive from the NSF, CRA-CCC and CRA-W: this subsidizes student travel to the student research workshop as well as their registration and ACL memberships. When combined with the support we are able to give to our student volunteers, we aim to make it possible for students from all over the world to come to the conference and be part of our community. We also decided, in consultation with the NAACL board, to provide subsidies to the Widening NLP workshop, which is only being held for the second time at this year's NAACL (last year called the Women in NLP workshop). These subsidies enable participation from students and young researchers from developing countries to attend the conference.

I am grateful to our sponsors for their generous contributions, which add so much to what we can do at the conference. Our Diamond sponsors are Bloomberg, Google, and Toutiao AI Lab (ByteDance). The Platinum sponsor is Amazon. The Gold Sponsors are Ebay, Grammarly, IBM Research, KPMG, Oracle, Poly AI, Tulane University, Capital One and Two Sigma. The Silver sponsors are Nuance and Facebook, and the Bronze sponsors are iMerit and USC/ISI.

Finally, there are many more people who through their hard work and dedication have contributed to make this conference a success: the area chairs, workshop organizers, tutorial presenters, student mentors, and reviewers. And of course you all, the attendees without whom there would be no conference: you are the life and spirit of the conference and the NAACL community. I hope you all have a fun and exciting time at NAACL HLT 2018!

NAACL HLT 2018 General Chair
Marilyn Walker, University of California Santa Cruz

Message from the Program Co-Chairs

We welcome you to New Orleans for the 16th Annual Conference of the North American Chapter of the Association for Computational Linguistics: Human Language Technologies (NAACL HLT 2018)! We had three primary goals for NAACL HLT 2018: construct a great program; manage the integrity and quality of the publication process; and ensure broad participation.

Construct a great program: NAACL HLT 2018 does have a great program, thanks to all of you! We will have three exciting keynotes, from Charles Yang, Kevin Knight and Dilek Hakkani-Tür. 331 research track papers (205 long, 125 short), accepted following peer review, will be presented[1]. Four of these papers have been identified as outstanding papers, and one will be named best paper. We will also feature a "Test of Time" session with retrospectives (from the authors) on three influential papers from ACL venues. We thank the committees who nominated and voted on these paper awards.

The main program at NAACL HLT 2018 also includes 16 TACL paper presentations, 20 demos, a student research workshop and an industry track. Keynotes from both the research and industry tracks are plenary. In a change from previous years of NAACL HLT, and motivated by EMNLP 2017, poster and oral presentation sessions will be held in parallel during the day. All posters are grouped thematically (including posters from the industry track and student research workshop and demos) and assigned to poster sessions so as to not be against oral presentation sessions with the same theme.

Manage the integrity and quality of the publication process: To manage load, we decided that each area chair should be responsible for no more than 30 submissions and that reviewers should be responsible for reviewing no more than 3 submissions. To help reviewers, we and the ACL program co-chairs constructed a more structured review form, with questions related to the new ACL guidelines on publication and reviewing, as well as to contribution types, experimental methods (thank you, Bonnie Webber!), software and handling of data.

We recruited an excellent group of 72 area chairs; we thank them for their leadership, and for nominating and voting on outstanding papers, outstanding reviewers and test of time papers. 1372 individuals reviewed papers for the conference (as program committee members, ad hoc reviewers or secondary reviewers); all but 49 reviewers had no more than 3 submissions to review overall, and the 49 reviewers who took on a heavier load did so voluntarily. We thank all our reviewers, especially the ad-hoc reviewers who provided last minute reviews and the outstanding reviewers identified by the area chairs.

Submissions were assigned to area chairs and reviewers using a combination of area chair expertise, Toronto Paper Matching System (TPMS) scores and reviewer bids. Both long and short paper submissions received 3 reviews each. Long paper authors had an opportunity to respond to reviews. Accept/reject suggestions were made by area chairs working in small groups of 2-3 and discussing with reviewers as necessary; final decisions were made by the program chairs. Where there was disagreement or discussion, one area chair wrote a short meta review that was shared with the authors.

This year, if the authors of a NAACL HLT 2018 submission and the author of a review for that submission both consented, then we will include the review in a review corpus to be released jointly with the program chairs of ACL, Iryna Gureyvich and Yusuke Miyao. We also asked authors of accepted papers to upload the source code for their papers. Both of these corpora will be released in the coming months.

The health of our field as a science is dependent on a scalable peer review process, which in turn depends on (a) conscientious effort from a broad pool of expert reviewers, and (b) tools, processes and policies that can structure and facilitate reviewing. As a field we are at a breaking point: we are growing rapidly,

---

[1]We received 1122 research track submissions (664 long, 458 short). 33 were rejected without review and 85 were withdrawn by the authors either before, during or after review.

with corresponding heavy load on experienced reviewers; and we lack good tools to manage the process. Peer review involves several tasks that we, as NLP researchers, ought to be uniquely qualified to address, including expertise sourcing, network analysis and text mining. We have written a proposal with other members of the ACL community about ways the ACL can improve our peer review infrastructure. We have also written a collection of "how to" documents that we will pass on to future conference organizers.

Ensure broad participation: To ensure broad participation, we recruited program committee members using a similar method to that used for NAACL HLT 2016: we invited anyone who had published repeatedly in ACL sponsored venues, who had a PhD or significant experience in the field spanning more than 5 years, and whose email address was up to date in START. We thank Dragomir Radev for giving us a list of names from the ACL anthology.

We also kept a blog where we discussed and attempted to "demystify" each stage of the publication process. This blog can be found at the conference website, `http://naacl2018.org`. We are very grateful to the researchers who wrote guest blog posts, including Justine Cassell, Barbara Plank, Preslav Nakov, Omer Levy, Gemma Boleda, Emily Bender, Nitin Madnani, David Chiang, Kevin Knight, Dan Bikel and Joakim Nivre.

On our blog, we reported on the diversity of our area chair, reviewer and author pools in terms of years of experience, affiliation type and geography, and gender. We will include these details in our report to the NAACL Executive Committee. We hope that future years' chairs will make similar reports.

The excellence of the overall NAACL HLT 2018 program is thanks to all the chairs and organizers. We especially thank the following people: Margaret Mitchell and Stephanie Lukin, the publication chairs; Jonathan May, the handbook chair; Yonatan Bisk and Wei Xu, the publicity and social media chairs; Ying Lin, the tireless website chair; and Marilyn Walker, the NAACL HLT 2018 general chair. We thank the chairs of NAACL HLT 2016 and ACL 2017 for their informative blogs, and the program chairs of NAACL HLT 2016, Owen Rambow and Ani Nenkova, for their advice. We thank the program co-chairs of ACL 2018, Iryna Gurevych and Yusuke Miyao, who have been very collaborative on matters related to reviewing. We thank Shuly Winter, who helped fix a serious START bug. We thank Julia Hockenmaier and the NAACL Executive Committee for their support. We are grateful for the professional work of Rich Gerber and his colleagues at SoftConf (START), and of Priscilla Rasmussen from the ACL.

It has been an enormous privilege for us to see the scientific advances that will be presented at this conference. We would like to close with some advice for you, the conference attendees.

- The presenters have made valuable contributions to our science; their oral, poster and demo presentations are worth your time and attention.
- Talk to some people you haven't previously met. They may be your future collaborators!
- You can follow the conference on social media; we have a conference app and website where we will post any updates to the program, and our twitter handle is @naaclhlt.
- This event is run by a professional organization with a code of conduct[2]. If you observe or are the recipient of unprofessional behavior, you may contact any current member of the ACL or NAACL Executive Committees, the NAACL HLT general chair (Marilyn Walker), us (the program chairs), or Priscilla Rasmussen (acl@aclweb.org). We will hold your communications in strict confidence and consult you before taking any action.

We look forward to a wonderful conference!

NAACL HLT 2018 Program Co-Chairs
Heng Ji, RPI
Amanda Stent, Bloomberg

---

[2] `https://www.aclweb.org/adminwiki/index.php?title=Anti-Harassment_Policy`

Organizing Committee

General Chair

Marilyn Walker, University of California, Santa Cruz

Program Co-Chairs

Heng Ji, Rensselaer Polytechnic Institute
Amanda Stent, Bloomberg

Industry Track Co-Chairs

Srinivas Bangalore, Interactions
Jennifer Chu-Carroll, Elemental Cognition
Yunyao Li, IBM

Demonstration Co-Chairs

Yang Liu, University of Texas at Dallas
Tim Paek, Apple
Manasi Patwardhan, Tata Consultancy Services Research, India

Student Research Workshop Co-Chairs

Chairs:
> Silvio Ricardo Cordeiro, Aix-Marseille Université
> Shereen Oraby, University of California, Santa Cruz
> Umashanthi Pavalanathan, Georgia Institute of Technology
> Kyeongmin Rim, Brandeis University

Faculty Advisors:
> Swapna Somasundaran, ETS Princeton
> Sam Bowman, New York University

Workshop Co-Chairs

Marie Meteer, Brandeis University
Jason Williams, Microsoft Research

Tutorial Co-Chairs

Mohit Bansal, University of North Carolina
Rebecca Passonneau, Pennsylvania State University

Publications Co-Chairs

Stephanie Lukin, U.S. Army Research Laboratory
Margaret Mitchell, Google

Handbook Chair

Jonathan May, University of Southern California Information Sciences Institute

Local Arrangements Chair

Priscilla Rasmussen, ACL

Family-Friendly Program Co-Chairs

Chris Callison-Burch, University of Pennsylvania
Beth Hockey, Intel

International Sponsorships Co-Chairs

Alexis Palmer, University of North Texas
Jason Baldridge, Google

Local Sponsorships and Exhibits Co-Chairs

Kristy Hollingshead, Florida Institute for Human & Machine Cognition
Kristen Johnson, Purdue University
Parisa Kordjamshidi, Tulane University / Florida Institute for Human and Machine Cognition

Publicity and Social Media Co-Chairs

Yonatan Bisk, University of Washington
Wei Xu, Ohio State University

Website Chair

Ying Lin, Rensselaer Polytechnic Institute

Student Volunteer Coordinator

Lena Reed, University of California, Santa Cruz

Program Committee, Research Track

Area Chairs

Cognitive Modeling/Psycholinguistics
    Morteza Dehghani, University of Southern California
    Kristy Hollingshead, Institute for Human & Machine Cognition
Dialogue and Interactive Systems
    Yun-Nung (Vivian) Chen, National Taiwan University
    Gabriel Skantze, KTH Royal Institute of Technology
Discourse and Pragmatics
    Jacob Eisenstein, Georgia Institute of Technology
    Junyi (Jessy) Li, University of Texas at Austin
    Annie Louis, University of Edinburgh
    Yi Yang, Bloomberg
Generation
    Dimitra Gkatzia, Edinburgh Napier University
    Shashi Narayan, University of Edinburgh
    Michael White, Ohio State University
Information Extraction
    Mausam, Indian Institute of Technology Delhi
    Dan Bikel, Google
    Chia-Hui Chang, National Central University
    Bonan Min, BBN
    Aurélie Névéol, CNRS

Marius Pasca, Google
Hinrich Schütze, Ludwig Maximilian University of Munich
Avirup Sil, IBM Research AI
Michael Strube, HITS gGmbH

Machine Learning for NLP
Chris Dyer, Google DeepMind
Ozan Irsoy, Bloomberg
Tie-Yan Liu, Microsoft Research
Raymond Mooney, University of Texas at Austin

Machine Translation
Marine Carpuat, University of Maryland
Kyunghyun Cho, New York University
Daniel Marcu, Amazon
Taro Watanabe, Google
Deyi Xiong, Soochow University

NLP Applications
Jinho Choi, Emory University
Joel Tetreault, Grammarly

Phonology, Morphology and Word Segmentation
Jennifer Foster, Dublin City University
Barbara Plank, University of Groningen

Question Answering
Eugene Agichtein, Emory University
Hannaneh Hajishirzi, University of Washington
Idan Szpektor, Google

Semantics
Yoav Artzi, Cornell University
Mona Diab, George Washington University
Kevin Duh, Johns Hopkins University
Jonathan May, University of Southern California
Preslav Nakov, Qatar Computing Research Institute
Roi Reichart, Technion - Israel Institute of Technology
Dan Roth, University of Pennsylvania
Scott Wen-tau Yih, Allen Institute for Artificial Intelligence

Sentiment Analysis
Smaranda Muresan, Columbia University
Swapna Somasundaran, ETS Princeton

Social Media Analysis and Computational Social Science
Mark Dredze, Johns Hopkins University
Miles Osborne, Bloomberg
Alan Ritter, Ohio State University
Sara Rosenthal, IBM
William Yang Wang, University of California, Santa Barbara

Speech
Eric Fosler-Lussier, Ohio State University
Dilek Hakkani-Tur, Google
Mari Ostendorf, University of Washington

Summarization
George Giannakopoulos, NCSR "Demokritos"
Xiaojun Wan, Peking University
Lu Wang, Northeastern University

Tagging, Chunking, Syntax and Parsing
    Michael Collins, Columbia University
    Yoav Goldberg, Bar Ilan University
    Daisuke Kawahara, Kyoto University
    Emily Pitler, Google
    Anders Søgaard, University of Copenhagen
    Aline Villavicencio, University of Essex / Federal University of Rio Grande do Sul
Text Mining
    Kai-wei Chang, University of Virginia
    Jing Jiang, Singapore Management University
    Zornitsa Kozareva, Google
    Chin-Yew Lin, Microsoft Research Asia
Theory and Formalisms
    David Chiang, University of Notre Dame
    Daniel Gildea, University of Rochester
    Giorgio Satta, University of Padua
Vision, Robotics and Other Grounding
    Joyce Chai, Michigan State University
    Vicente Ordonez, University of Virginia

Reviewers

Reviewers who are acknowledged by the program committee for providing one or more outstanding reviews are listed in bold. Individuals who (also) served as secondary reviewers are marked with † and those who (also) served as ad-hoc reviewers with *.

Mourad Abbas
Ahmed Abdelali
Asad Abdi
Muhammad Abdul-Mageed
Anne Abeille
Omri Abend
Abhishek Abhishek
Mohamed Abouelenien
José Abreu
Sallam Abualhaija
Amjad Abu-Jbara
Lasha Abzianidze
Oliver Adams
Gilles Adda
Yvonne Adesam
Stergos Afantenos
Naveed Afzal
Apoorv Agarwal
Swati Agarwal
Željko Agić
Eugene Agichtein
Manex Agirrezabal
Lars Ahrenberg
Salah Ait-Mokhtar

Yamen Ajjour†
Alan Akbik
Ahmet Aker
Cem Akkaya*
Ahmad Al Sallab
Özge Alacam
Domagoj Alagić†
Sameh Alansary
Iñaki Alegria
Nikolaos Aletras
Beatrice Alex
Theodora Alexopoulou
Enrique Alfonseca
Ahmed Ali
Dimitris Alikaniotis
Hend Al-Khalifa
Mehdi Allahyari
Miltiadis Allamanis
James Allan
Alexandre Allauzen
Miguel A. Alonso
Omar Alonso
Laura Alonso Alemany
Abdulrahman Alosaimy

Rami Al-Rfou
Edgar Altszyler
Nora Al-Twairesh
Bharat Ram Ambati
Waleed Ammar*
Dimitra Anastasiou
Tim Anderson
Jacob Andreas
Nicholas Andrews
Ion Androutsopoulos
Anietie Andy
Gabor Angeli*
Marianna Apidianaki
Emilia Apostolova
Jun Araki
Masahiro Araki
Shlomo Argamon
Piyush Arora
Raman Arora
Sanjeev Arora
Masayuki Asahara
Elliott Ash
Nicholas Asher
Giuseppe Attardi

Aitziber Atutxa Salazar[†]
Isabelle Augenstein
Michael Auli
AiTi Aw
Amittai Axelrod
Wilker Aziz
Homa B. Hashemi
Collin Baker
Omid Bakhshandeh
Niranjan Balasubramanian
Timothy Baldwin
Tyler Baldwin
Kalika Bali
Miguel Ballesteros
Ramy Baly
David Bamman
Rafael E. Banchs
Ritwik Banerjee
Mohit Bansal
Libby Barak
Denilson Barbosa
Alistair Baron
Marco Baroni
Alberto Barrón-Cedeño
Valerio Basile
Roberto Basili
Tanmay Basu
Daniel Bauer
Timo Baumann
Anshul Bawa[†]
John Bear
Frédéric Béchet
Barend Beekhuizen
Beata Beigman Klebanov
Yonatan Belinkov
Charley Beller
Anja Belz
Michael Bendersky
Jonathan Berant
Raffaella Bernardi
Delphine Bernhard
Yevgeni Berzak
Steven Bethard
Rahul Bhagat
Chandra Bhagavatula
Aditya Bhargava[†]
Pushpak Bhattacharyya
Chris Biemann
Ann Bies
Or Biran
Yonatan Bisk

Prakhar Biyani
Yuri Bizzoni[†]
Anders Björkelund
Philippe Blache
Alan W Black
Eduardo Blanco
Roi Blanco
Nate Blaylock
Reihane Boghrati*
Bernd Bohnet
Piotr Bojanowski
Ondřej Bojar
Danushka Bollegala
Marcel Bollmann
Kalina Bontcheva
Benjamin Börschinger
Florian Boudin
Fethi Bougares
Pierrette Bouillon
Gosse Bouma
Johan Boye
Kristy Boyer
David Bracewell
Ellen Breitholz
Chris Brew
Ted Briscoe
Chris Brockett
Julian Brooke
Pawel Budzianowski[†]
Paul Buitelaar
Harry Bunt
Wray Buntine
David Burkett
Jill Burstein
Miriam Butt
Donna Byron
José G. C. de Souza
Aoife Cahill
Deng Cai[†]
Ruket Cakici
Iacer Calixto*
Chris Callison-Burch
Nicoletta Calzolari
Jose Camacho-Collados
Leonardo Campillos Llanos*[†]
Marie Candito
Kai Cao*
Liangliang Cao
Yuan Cao
Ziqiang Cao
Cornelia Caragea

Giuseppe Carenini
Mark Carman
Xavier Carreras
Vitor Carvalho
Francisco Casacuberta
Taylor Cassidy
Vittorio Castelli
Damir Cavar
Asli Celikyilmaz
Daniel Cer
Özlem Çetinoğlu*
Soumen Chakrabarti
Tanmoy Chakraborty
Yllias Chali
Nathanael Chambers
Yee Seng Chan
Muthu Kumar Chandrasekaran
Angel Chang
Franklin Chang
Yin-Wen Chang
Yung-Chun Chang
Lidia S. Chao
Snigdha Chaturvedi
Wanxiang Che
Ciprian Chelba
Berlin Chen
Bin Chen
Boxing Chen
Changyou Chen
Chen Chen
Cheng Chen
Hsin-Hsi Chen
Jianfu Chen
John Chen
Kehai Chen[†]
Kuan-Yu Chen
Ping Chen
Qian Chen
Qingcai Chen
Wenliang Chen
Xinchi Chen
Yubo Chen
Zhiyuan Chen
Jianpeng Cheng
Pengxiang Cheng[†]
Weiwei Cheng
Hadda Cherroun
Colin Cherry
Emmanuele Chersoni[†]
Sean Chester
Jackie Chi Kit Cheung

Niyati Chhaya
Lianhua Chi
Hai Leong Chieu
Manoj Chinnakotla
Laura Chiticariu
Martin Chodorow
Eunsol Choi
Jinho D. Choi
Key-Sun Choi
Shamil Chollampatt
Monojit Choudhury
Christos Christodoulopoulos
Jason Chuang
Junyoung Chung
Tagyoung Chung
Kenneth Church
Philipp Cimiano
Alina Maria Ciobanu
Stephen Clark
Mathieu Cliche
Martin Cmejrek
Kevin Cohen
Shay B. Cohen
William Cohen
Michael Collins*
Çağrı Çöltekin*
John Conroy
Matthieu Constant
Paul Cook
Matthew Coole[†]
Robin Cooper
Silvio Cordeiro*
Mark Core
Marta R. Costa-jussà
Ryan Cotterell
Aaron Courville
Benoit Crabbé
Josep Crego
Dan Cristea
Danilo Croce
Paul Crook
Scott Crossley
Heriberto Cuayáhuitl
Lei Cui
Xiaodong Cui
Yiming Cui
Aron Culotta
Giovanni Da San Martino
Walter Daelemans
Andrew Dai
Bo Dai*

Beatrice Daille
Bhavana Dalvi
Marco Damonte
Falavigna Daniele
Kareem Darwish
Dipanjan Das
Pradipto Das
Sarthak Dash
Hal Daumé III
Johannes Daxenberger
Adrià de Gispert
Eric De La Clergerie
Marie-Catherine de Marneffe
Gerard de Melo
Renato de Mori
Edward Dearden[†]
Luciano Del Corro
Louise Deléger
Rodolfo Delmonte
Dina Demner-Fushman
Steve DeNeefe
John DeNero
Lingjia Deng
Zhi-Hong Deng
Pascal Denis
Michael Denkowski
Tejaswini Deoskar
Nina Dethlefs
Luis Fernando D'Haro
Giuseppe Di Fabbrizio
Weicong Ding
Stefanie Dipper
Nemanja Djuric
Simon Dobnik
Ellen Dodge
Jesse Dodge
Daxiang Dong
Li Dong
Bonnie Dorr
Doug Downey
Eduard Dragut
Mark Dras
Markus Dreyer
Aleksandr Drozd
Jinhua Du
Lan Du
Nan Duan
Ewan Dunbar
Long Duong
Nadir Durrani
Greg Durrett

Ondřej Dušek
Marc Dymetman
Seth Ebner[†]
Richard Eckart de Castilho
Judith Eckle-Kohler
Steffen Eger
Markus Egg
Koji Eguchi
Patrick Ehlen
Vladimir Eidelman
Andreas Eisele
Asif Ekbal
Layla El Asri
Roxanne El Baff[†]
Ahmed El Kholy
Shady Elbassuoni
Michael Elhadad
Mahmoud El-Haj
Hady Elsahar[†]
Tamer Elsayed
Micha Elsner
Akiko Eriguchi
Katrin Erk
Arash Eshghi
Ramy Eskander
Maxine Eskenazi
Keelan Evanini
Roger Evans
David Fagnan[†]
James Fan
Lisa Fan
Hao Fang
Stefano Faralli
Richárd Farkas
Noura Farra*
Manaal Faruqui
Nicolas R Fauceglia
Marcello Federico
Christian Federmann
Wes Feely[†]
Anna Feldman
Minwei Feng
Yansong Feng
Elisa Ferracane[†]
Francis Ferraro
Olivier Ferret
Oliver Ferschke
Simone Filice
Denis Filimonov
Katja Filippova
Andrew Finch

Gregory Finley
Nicholas FitzGerald
Eileen Fitzpatrick
Jeffrey Flanigan
Lucie Flekova
Michael Flor*
Radu Florian*
José A. R. Fonollosa
Mikel L. Forcada
George Foster
James Foulds
Anette Frank
Diego Frassinelli
Jesse Freitas
Lea Frermann
Annemarie Friedrich
Guohong Fu
Xiao Fu
Atsushi Fujii
Akinori Fujino
Atsushi Fujita
Sanae Fujita
Fumiyo Fukumoto
Richard Futrell
Robert Gaizauskas
Byron Galbraith
Michel Galley
Björn Gambäck
Michael Gamon
Kuzman Ganchev
Ashwinkumar Ganesan[†]
Debasis Ganguly
Yuze Gao[†]
Jesús Miguel García[†]
Marcos Garcia
Miguel A. García-Cumbreras
Claire Gardent
Matt Gardner
Dan Garrette
Guillermo Garrido
Justin Garten*
Milica Gašić
Tao Ge*
Kallirroi Georgila
Abbas Ghaddar[†]
Debanjan Ghosh*
Kevin Gimpel
Filip Ginter
Roxana Girju
James Glass
Michael Glass

Alfio Gliozzo[†]
Koldo Gojenola
Yoav Goldberg
Dan Goldwasser
Carlos Gómez-Rodríguez
Hugo Gonçalo Oliveira*
Hila Gonen
Samuel González-López
Kyle Gorman
Genevieve Gorrell
Isao Goto
Amit Goyal
Kartik Goyal
Pawan Goyal
Vishal Goyal
Thomas Graf
Yvette Graham
Floriana Grasso
Christophe Gravier
Nancy Green
Spence Green
Stephan Greene
Gregory Grefenstette
Eleni Gregoromichelaki
Ralph Grishman
Stig-Arne Grönroos[†]
Cyril Grouin
Jiatao Gu*
Anupam Guha
Curry Guinn
Hongyu Guo
Jiang Guo
Weiwei Guo
Xiaoxiao Guo
Yufan Guo
Nitish Gupta
Sonal Gupta
Suchin Gururangan[†]
Joakim Gustafson
Francisco Guzmán
Nizar Habash
Yaakov HaCohen-Kerner
Barry Haddow
Christian Hadiwinoto[†]
Matthias Hagen
Udo Hahn
Hannaneh Hajishirzi
Hazem Hajj
Kishaloy Halder
John Hale
David Hall

Keith Hall*
Michael Hammond
Thierry Hamon
Xianpei Han*
Mark Hansen
Jiangang Hao
Sanda Harabagiu
Christian Hardmeier
Sadid A. Hasan
Mohammed Hasanuzzaman
Mark Hasegawa-Johnson
Kazuma Hashimoto[†]
Eva Hasler
Hany Hassan
Helen Hastie
Bradley Hauer[†]
Catherine Havasi
Hangfeng He[†]
Hua He
Lihong He[†]
Wei He
Yifan He
Zhongjun He
Kenneth Heafield
Peter Heeman
Michael Heilman
Benjamin Heinzerling*
James Henderson
John Henderson
Matthew Henderson
James Hendler
Iris Hendrickx
Aurélie Herbelot
Ulf Hermjakob
Teresa Herrmann
Jonathan Herzig
Jack Hessel
Chris Hidey[†]
Felix Hieber
Ryuichiro Higashinaka
Derrick Higgins
Tsutomu Hirao
Keikichi Hirose
Graeme Hirst
Chris Hokamp[†]
Eric Holgate[†]
Nils Holzenberger[†]
Yu Hong
Enamul Hoque
Chiori Hori
Takaaki Hori

Veronique Hoste
Yufang Hou
Julian Hough
Dirk Hovy
Christine Howes
Shu-Kai Hsieh
Chun-Nan Hsu
Wen-Lian Hsu
Zhiting Hu
Xinyu Hua
Hen-Hsen Huang
Minlie Huang
Po-Sen Huang
Ruihong Huang
Shujian Huang
Xiaojiang Huang
Xiaolei Huang[†]
Xuanjing Huang
Zhongqiang Huang
Matthias Huck
Matt Huenerfauth
Mans Hulden
Rebecca Hwa
Mei-Yuh Hwang
Seung-won Hwang
Irina Illina[†]
Kenji Imamura
Kentaro Inui
Hitoshi Isahara
Alexei V. Ivanov
Mohit Iyyer
Sharmistha Jat[†]
Donghong JI
Yangfeng Ji
Di Jiang
Hui Jiang
Ridong Jiang
Xin Jiang
Charles Jochim[†]
Anders Johannsen
Richard Johansson
Michael Johnston
Kristiina Jokinen
Gareth Jones
Aditya Joshi
Mahesh Joshi
Shafiq Joty
Armand Joulin
Marcin Junczys-Dowmunt
David Jurgens
Kyo Kageura

Nobuhiro Kaji
Rasoul Kaljahi*
Hidetaka Kamigaito[†]
Hetunandan Kamisetty
Min-Yen Kan
Masahiro Kaneko[†]
Katharina Kann
Pinar Karagoz
Dimitri Kartsaklis
Lauri Karttunen
David Kauchak
Anna Kazantseva
Arefeh Kazemi
Mark Keane
Chris Kedzie
Andrew Kehler
Simon Keizer
John Kelleher
Ruth Kempson
Casey Kennington
Kian Kenyon-Dean
Kristian Kersting
Shahram Khadivi
Mitesh M. Khapra
Daniel Khashabi
Tushar Khot
Emre Kiciman
Douwe Kiela
Gunhee Kim
Jin-Dong Kim
Joo-Kyung Kim[†]
Jung-Jae Kim
Young-Bum Kim
Tracy Holloway King
Brian Kingsbury
Katrin Kirchhoff
Svetlana Kiritchenko
Julia Kiseleva
Dietrich Klakow
Guillaume Klein[†]
Jan Kleindienst
Alexandre Klementiev
Julien Kloetzer
Kevin Knight
Alistair Knott
Hayato Kobayashi
Philipp Koehn*
Rob Koeling
Jean-Pierre Koenig
Arne Köhn[†]
Varada Kolhatkar

Thomas Kollar
Alexander Koller
Mamoru Komachi
Kazunori Komatani
Alexandros Komninos[†]
Rik Koncel-Kedziorski
Grzegorz Kondrak
Lingpeng Kong
Ioannis Konstas
Mikhail Kopotev
Stefan Kopp
Valia Kordoni
Yannis Korkontzelos
Leila Kosseim
Katsunori Kotani
Mikhail Kozhevnikov
Emiel Krahmer
Martin Krallinger
Jayant Krishnamurthy
Vincent Kríž
Canasai Kruengkrai
Udo Kruschwitz
Germán Kruszewski
Lun-Wei Ku
Marco Kuhlmann
Roland Kuhn
Wu Kui[†]
Vivek Kulkarni
Shankar Kumar
Vaibhav Kumar
Jonathan Kummerfeld*
Gourab Kundu
Mikko Kurimo
Sadao Kurohashi
Robin Kurtz[†]
Mucahid Kutlu[†]
Tom Kwiatkowski
Oi Yee Kwong
Shibamouli Lahiri
Alice Lai
Wai Lam
Mathias Lambert
Patrik Lambert
Vasileios Lampos
Phillippe Langlais
Ni Lao
Guy Lapalme
Mirella Lapata
Shalom Lappin
Staffan Larsson
Jey Han Lau

Alberto Lavelli
Julia Lavid-López
Joseph Le Roux
Claudia Leacock
Chong Min Lee
Honglak Lee
Jihwan Lee[†]
John Lee
Kenton Lee
Moontae Lee
Sungjin Lee
Taesung Lee
Yoong Keok Lee
Young-Suk Lee
Fabrice Lefevre
Tao Lei
Alessandro Lenci
Chee Wee (Ben) Leong
Yves Lepage
James Lester
Johannes Leveling
Tomer Levinboim
Rivka Levitan
Sarah Ita Levitan
Gina-Anne Levow
Omer Levy
Mike Lewis
Binyang Li
Bofang Li[†]
Chen Li
Fangtao Li
Haizhou Li
Junhui Li
Lihong Li
Mu Li
Peifeng Li
Peng Li
Sheng Li
Sujian Li
Wenjie Li
Xiang Li*
Xiaoli Li
Xiaoqing Li[†]
Xiujun Li
Yanran Li
Yingyu Liang[†]
Constantine Lignos
Chu-Cheng Lin
Jimmy Lin
Junyang Lin[†]
Xiao Ling

Pierre Lison
Marina Litvak
Bing Liu*
Bing Liu
Can Liu
Changsong Liu
Jing Liu[†]
Kang Liu
Lemao Liu
Qi Liu[†]
Qun Liu
Shujie Liu
Ting Liu
Xiaodong Liu
Xueqing Liu[†]
Yang Liu
Karen Livescu
Elena Lloret*
Lajanugen Logeswaran[†]
Nikhil Londhe
José Lopes*
Oier Lopez de Lacalle
Adrian Pastor López Monroy
Aurelio López López
Anastassia Loukina
Di Lu*
Qin Lu
Wei Lu
Yi Luan
Nichola Lubold[†]
Michal Lukasik
Stephanie Lukin
Rebecca Lunsford
Weihua Luo
Minh-Thang Luong
Veronica Lynn[†]
Ji Ma
Mingbo Ma
Wei-Yun Ma
Xuezhe Ma
Andrew Maas
Brian Mac Namee
Klaus Macherey
Wolfgang Macherey
Nitin Madnani
Bernardo Magnini
Debanjan Mahata
Wolfgang Maier
Adam Makarucha
Nikolaos Malandrakis*
Andreas Maletti

Igor Malioutov
Fragkiskos Malliaros
Rob Malouf
Liliana Mamani Sanchez
Suresh Manandhar
Inderjeet Mani
Christopher D. Manning
Saab Mansour
Ramesh Manuvinakurike
Junhua Mao
Mitchell Marcus
Anna Margolis
Benjamin Marie
Erwin Marsi
David Martinez
Héctor Martínez Alonso*
André F. T. Martins
Bruno Martins
David Martins de Matos
Yuval Marton
Luis Marujo
Shigeki Matsubara
Yoichi Matsuyama
Yevgen Matusevych
Chandler May[†]
James Mayfield
Karen Mazidi
David McAllester
Andrew McCallum
Diana McCarthy
David McClosky
Bridget McInnes
Kathy McKeown
Brian McMahan
Louise McNally
Paul McNamee
Michael McTear
Julie Medero
Philipp Meerkamp
Oren Melamud
Gábor Melis
Arul Menezes
Fandong Meng
Helen Meng
Wolfgang Menzel
Angeliki Metallinou
Haitao Mi
Lisa Michaud
Stuart Middleton
Juliana Miehle[†]
Tomas Mikolov

Timothy Miller
Shachar Mirkin
Anand Mishra[†]
Teruko Mitamura
Jeff Mitchell*[†]
Prasenjit Mitra
Makoto Miwa
Daichi Mochihashi
Marie-Francine Moens
Abdelrahman Mohamed
Saif Mohammad*
Abidalrahman Moh'd
Behrang Mohit
Karo Moilanen
Diego Molla
Simonetta Montemagni
Andres Montoyo
Taesun Moon
Nafise Sadat Moosavi
Roser Morante
Véronique Moriceau
Emmanuel Morin
Hajime Morita
Alessandro Moschitti
Nasrin Mostafazadeh
Lili Mou
Danielle L Mowery
Matthew Mulholland*
Philippe Muller
Dragos Munteanu
Yugo Murawaki
Elena Musi
Seung-Hoon Na[†]
Seema Nagar
Masaaki Nagata
Ajay Nagesh
Saeed Najafi[†]
Satoshi Nakamura
Mikio Nakano
Yukiko Nakano
Ndapa Nakashole
Courtney Napoles
Jason Naradowsky
Karthik Narasimhan
Shrikanth Narayanan
Alexis Nasr
Vivi Nastase*
Roberto Navigli
Hamada Nayel
Claire Nédellec
Mark-Jan Nederhof

Arvind Neelakantan
Matteo Negri
Guenter Neumann
Dominick Ng
Hwee Tou Ng
Jun-Ping Ng
Vincent Ng
Axel-Cyrille Ngonga Ngomo
Dat Quoc Nguyen
Dong Nguyen*
Thien Huu Nguyen*
Viet-An Nguyen
Jian Ni
Garrett Nicolai
Massimo Nicosia
Vlad Niculae
Jian-Yun Nie
Jan Niehues
Rodney Nielsen
Takashi Ninomiya
Nobal Bikram Niraula
Hitoshi Nishikawa
Zheng-Yu Niu
Joakim Nivre
Chikashi Nobata
Hiroshi Noji
Pierre Nugues
Diarmuid Ó Séaghdha
Mick O'Donnell
Brendan O'Connor
Timothy O'Donnell
Stephan Oepen
Nir Ofek
Kemal Oflazer
Alice Oh
Jong-Hoon Oh
Kiyonori Ohtake
Naoaki Okazaki
Manabu Okumura
Hiroshi G. Okuno
Eda Okur[†]
Shereen Oraby*
Naoki Otani
Myle Ott
Jessica Ouyang[†]
Cecilia Ovesdotter Alm
Lilja Øvrelid
Gözde Özbal[†]
Ankur Padia[†]
Ulrike Pado
Sebastian Padó

Alexis Palmer
Alessio Palmero Aprosio
Sinno Jialin Pan
Alexander Panchenko[†]
Patrick Pantel
Aasish Pappu
Ivandré Paraboni
Ankur Parikh
Sunghyun Park[†]
Rebecca J. Passonneau
Siddharth Patwardhan
Michael J. Paul
Umashanthi Pavalanathan
Adam Pease
Pavel Pecina
Stephan Peitz
Jing Peng[†]
Xiaochang Peng
Gerald Penn
Alicia Pérez[†]
Laura Perez-Beltrachini
Verónica Pérez-Rosas
Bryan Perozzi
Matthew Peters
Slav Petrov
Volha Petukhova
Nghia The Pham
Maria Pia di Buono[†]
Scott Piao
Olivier Pietquin
Mohammad Taher Pilehvar
Yuval Pinter
Tommi Pirinen
Nikiforos Pittaras
Paul Piwek
Benjamin Piwowarski
Lahari Poddar[†]
Christian Pölitz
Massimo Poesio
Thierry Poibeau
Adam Poliak[†]
Heather Pon-Barry
Simone Paolo Ponzetto
Hoifung Poon
Ana-Maria Popescu
Marius Popescu
Andrei Popescu-Belis
Maja Popović
Fred Popowich
Rebecca Portnoff
Christopher Potts

Vinodkumar Prabhakaran*
Animesh Prasad
Adithya Pratapa†
Daniel Preoţiuc-Pietro
Patti Price
Emily Prud'hommeaux
Matthew Purver
Ashequl Qadir
Behrang QasemiZadeh
Tao Qin
Long Qiu
Minghui Qiu
Xipeng Qiu
Preethi Raghavan
Altaf Rahman
Rohan Ramanath
Carlos Ramisch
Nitin Ramrakhiyani†
Vivek Kumar Rangarajan Sridhar
Peter A. Rankel
Jinfeng Rao
Sudha Rao
Ari Rappoport
Mohammad Sadegh Rasooli
Antoine Raux
Sujith Ravi*
Kyle Rawlins
Manny Rayner
Paul Rayson
Marta Recasens
Siva Reddy
Sravana Reddy
Marek Rei
Ehud Reiter
David Reitter
Steve Renals
Ludovic Rheault
Giuseppe Riccardi
Matthew Richardson
Mark Riedl
Martin Riedl
Jason Riesa
Arndt Riester
German Rigau
Mattia Rigotti
Laura Rimell
Fabio Rinaldi
Eric Ringger
Michael Rist†
Alan Ritter
Brian Roark

Kirk Roberts
Melissa Roemmele
Marcus Rohrbach
Lina M. Rojas Barahona
Oleg Rokhlenko
Stephen Roller
Laurent Romary
Salvatore Romeo†
Marc-Antoine Rondeau
Eric Rosen
Andrew Rosenberg
Sophie Rosset*
Paolo Rosso
Benjamin Roth
Michael Roth
Johann Roturier
Aku Rouhe†
Salim Roukos
Bryan Routledge
Andrew Roxburgh†
Alla Rozovskaya
Nicholas Ruiz
Anna Rumshisky
Josef Ruppenhofer
Alexander Rush
Irene Russo
Attapol Rutherford
Kugatsu Sadamitsu
Markus Saers
Kenji Sagae
Benoît Sagot
Saurav Sahay
Hassan Sajjad
Keisuke Sakaguchi
Peña Saldarriaga†
Avneesh Saluja
Rajhans Samdani
Magali Sanches Duran
Enrico Santus
Murat Saraclar
Ruhi Sarikaya
Anoop Sarkar
Yutaka Sasaki
Ryohei Sasano
Prasanna Sattigeri
Nikunj Saunshi†
Christina Sauper
Asad Sayeed
Christian Scheible
Frank Schilder
Michael Schlichtkrull†

Natalie Schluter*
Allen Schmaltz
Helmut Schmid
Andrew Schneider†
Jodi Schneider
Alexandra Schofield
William Schuler
Sabine Schulte im Walde
Hannes Schulz
H. Andrew Schwartz
Lane Schwartz
Roy Schwartz*
Stephanie Schwartz
Holger Schwenk
Donia Scott
Pascale Sébillot
Natalia Segal†
Satoshi Sekine
Jean Senellart
Rico Sennrich
Chandramohan Senthilkumar
Minjoon Seo
Izhak Shafran
Cui Shaobo†
Vasu Sharma†
Serge Sharoff
Lanbo She*
Baoxu Shi
Shuming Shi
Yangyang Shi
Hiroyuki Shindo
Chaitanya Shivade
Ekaterina Shutova
Maryam Siahbani
Advaith Siddharthan
Carina Silberer
Miikka Silfverberg†
Fabrizio Silvestri
Michel Simard
Patrick Simianer†
Kiril Simov
Serra Sinem Tekiroglu†
Abhishek Singh†
Sameer Singh
Kairit Sirts
Sunayana Sitaram
Steve Skiena
Kevin Small
Ronnie Smith
Jan Šnajder
Artem Sokolov

Youngseo Son[†]
Hyun-Je Song
Linfeng Song
Radu Soricut
Michael Spranger
Richard Sproat
Vivek Srikumar
Somayajulu Sripada
Manfred Stede
Pontus Stenetorp
Amanda Stent*
Mark Stevenson
Brandon Stewart
Matthew Stone
Svetlana Stoyanchev
Veselin Stoyanov*
Carlo Strapparava
Karl Stratos
Kristina Striegnitz
Jannik Strötgen
Sara Stymne
Jinsong Su
Keh-Yih Su*
Katsuhito Sudoh
Elior Sulem[†]
Ming Sun
Xu Sun
Peter Sutton
Hisami Suzuki
Jun Suzuki
Yoshimi Suzuki
John Sylak-Glassman
György Szarvas
Stan Szpakowicz
Oscar Täckström
Hiroya Takamura
David Talbot
Partha Talukdar
Akihiro Tamura
Chenhao Tan
Takaaki Tanaka
Niket Tandon
Duyu Tang
Xavier Tannier
Yuka Tateisi
Rachael Tatman
Tatiane Tavares
Kapil Thadani
Mariët Theune
Paul Thompson
Sam Thomson

Christoph Tillmann
Ivan Titov
Erik Tjong Kim Sang
Takenobu Tokunaga
Marc Tomlinson
Sara Tonelli
Antonio Toral
Kentaro Torisawa
Marwan Torki
Samia Touileb
Trang Tran
David Traum
Adam Trischler[†]
Chen-Tse Tsai*
Richard Tzong-Han Tsai
Reut Tsarfaty
Ling Tsou[†]
Oren Tsur
Yoshimasa Tsuruoka
Yulia Tsvetkov
Zhaopeng Tu
Gökhan Tür*
Marco Turchi
Ferhan Ture
Martin Tutek[†]
Kiyotaka Uchimoto
Stefan Ultes
Lyle Ungar
Shyam Upadhyay
Masao Utiyama
Takehito Utsuro
Ozlem Uzuner
Naushad UzZaman
Raghuram Vadapalli
Alessandro Valitutti
Andreas van Cranenburgh
Rogier van Dalen
Tim Van de Cruys
Kees van Deemter
Lonneke van der Plas
Benjamin Van Durme
Emiel van Miltenburg
Rik van Noord[†]
Marten van Schijndel
Vincent Vandeghinste
David Vandyke
Vasudeva Varma
Sumithra Velupillai
Deepak Venugopal
Marc Verhagen
Yannick Versley

Karin Verspoor
Marc Vilain
David Vilar
David Vilares
Jesús Vilares
Martin Villalba
Veronika Vincze
Andreas Vlachos
Svitlana Volkova*
Clare Voss
Piek Vossen
Atro Voutilainen
Ivan Vulić
Yogarshi Vyas
V.G. Vinod Vydiswaran
Henning Wachsmuth
Joachim Wagner*
Byron Wallace
Matthew Walter
Xiaojun Wan
Baoxun Wang
Chang Wang
Chi Wang*
Jiang Wang
Jingjing Wang
Jinpeng Wang
Rui Wang
Tong Wang
Yanshan Wang
Yiou Wang
Yue Wang[†]
Zhiguo Wang
Zhongqing Wang
Leo Wanner
Nigel Ward
Shinji Watanabe
Taro Watanabe*
Christopher Waterson*
Bonnie Webber
Wouter Weerkamp
David Weir
Michael Wiegand
Rodrigo Wilkens*
Theresa Wilson
Shuly Wintner
Sam Wiseman
Guillaume Wisniewski
Travis Wolfe
Lawrence Wolf-Sonkin[†]
Kam-Fai Wong
Hua Wu

Jian Wu
Joern Wuebker†
Min Xiao
Shasha Xie
Wenduan Xu
Nianwen Xue
Adam Yala
Ikuya Yamada
Bishan Yang
Diyi Yang
Min Yang
Qian Yang
Yaqin Yang
Yi Yang
Yinfei Yang†
Roman Yangarber
Tae Yano
Jin-ge Yao
Mark Yatskar*
James Yifei Yang†
Wenpeng Yin*
Ding Ying
Dani Yogatama
Su-Youn Yoon
Naoki Yoshinaga
Dian Yu
Dianhai Yu

Jianfei Yu
Liang-Chih Yu
Mo Yu
François Yvon
Nasser Zalmout†
Roberto Zamparelli
Fabio Massimo Zanzotto
Klaus Zechner
Luke Zettlemoyer
Deniz Zeyrek
Feifei Zhai
Biao Zhang†
Boliang Zhang*
Dakun Zhang†
Hao Zhang
Jiajun Zhang
Jianwen Zhang
Lei Zhang
Longtu Zhang†
Meishan Zhang
Min Zhang
Qi Zhang
Sheng Zhang†
Tong Zhang
Wei Zhang
Wei Zhang
Yongfeng Zhang

Yue Zhang
Dongyan Zhao
Hai Zhao
Jun Zhao
Ran Zhao
Tiejun Zhao
Xiaoqing Zheng
Zilong Zheng†
Alisa Zhila
Dong Zhou
Jie Zhou
Junsheng Zhou
Nina Zhou
Xuanyu Zhou†
Muhua Zhu
Xiaodan Zhu
Andrea Zielinski
Heike Zinsmeister
Imed Zitouni
Michael Zock
Chengqing Zong
Bowei Zou
Arkaitz Zubiaga*
Ingrid Zukerman

Outstanding Paper Award Committee

Joyce Chai
Michael Collins

Jennifer Foster
Smaranda Muresan

Joel Tetreault (Chair)

Test-of-Time Paper Expert Award Committee

Marilyn Walker (Chair)
Antal van den Bosch
Chris Callison-Burch
Claire Cardie
Joyce Chai
Walter Daelemans
Katrin Erk
Pascale Fung

Iryna Gurevych
Katrin Kirchhoff
Yuji Matsumoto
Yusuke Miyao
Alessandro Moschitti
Massimo Poesio
Owen Rambow
Anoop Sarkar

Amanda Stent
Michael Strube
Lucy Vanderwende
Hua Wu
Chengqing Zong

Student Volunteers

Akhtar Shad
Amorim Evelin
Amplayo Reinald Kim
Basu Roy Chowdhury Somnath
Chatterjee Rajen
Chinnappa Dhivya
Choubey Prafulla
Cocos Anne
Dai Zeyu
Ezeani Ignatius
Fu Yao
Gella Spandana
Goo Chih-Wen
Gu Jiatao
Hao Shudong

Jiang Chao
Jiang Jyun-Yu
Jiang Youxuan
Juraska Juraj
Keith Katherine
Kenyon-Dean Kian
Kriz Reno
Kumar Vishwajeet
Maharjan Suraj
Mokhtari Shekoofeh
Nangia Nikita
Paula Felipe
Poddar Shivani
Rahgooy Taher
Schneider Andrew

Shen Yanyao
Srivastava Shashank
Strubell Emma
Su Shang-Yu
Szubert Ida
Tran Trang
Vempala Alakananda
Wiegreffe Sarah
Xiao Liqiang
Yasunaga Michihiro
Ye Hai
Yu Tao
Zhao Jieyu

Outstanding Papers

For NAACL HLT 2018 we recognize four outstanding research track papers (one of these will be named best paper). These four papers were selected by a committee composed of Joyce Chai (Michigan State University), Michael Collins (Columbia University), Jennifer Foster (Dublin City University), Smaranda Muresan (Columbia University) and Joel Tetreault (Grammarly; chair), all NAACL HLT 2018 area chairs with no conflicts with the candidate outstanding papers. The nine candidate papers were selected by the program chairs from nineteen papers nominated by the area chairs. These papers will be presented in a plenary session on the last day of the conference. Congratulations to the authors!

- *Deep Contextualized Word Representations*, by Matthew Peters, Mark Neumann, Mohit Iyyer, Matt Gardner, Christopher Clark, Kenton Lee and Luke Zettlemoyer

- *Learning to Map Context-Dependent Sentences to Executable Formal Queries*, by Alane Suhr, Srinivasan Iyer and Yoav Artzi

- *Neural Text Generation in Stories using Entity Representations as Context*, by Elizabeth Clark, Yangfeng Ji and Noah A. Smith

- *Recurrent Neural Networks as Weighted Language Recognizers*, by Yining Chen, Sorcha Gilroy, Andreas Maletti, Jonathan May and Kevin Knight

Test of Time Papers

For NAACL HLT 2018 we recognize three influential and inspiring Computational Linguistics (CL) papers which were published between 2002-2012 at the Association for Computational Linguistics (ACL) conferences (including ACL, NAACL, EACL, EMNLP and CONLL), workshops and journals (including TACL and CL), to recognize research that has had long-lasting influence until today, including positive impact on a subarea of CL, across subareas of CL, and outside of the CL research community. These papers may have proposed new research directions and new technologies, or released results and resources that have greatly benefit the community. Nineteen candidate test of time papers were nominated by our area chairs. Separate votes on these papers were held separately by two committees: an expert award committee consisting of all ACL and NAACL general chairs and program chairs and NAACL board members from 2013-2018 who did not have a conflict with the nominated papers, and a community award committee consisting of the 1000 authors who have published the most papers at ACL venues and who did not have a conflict with the nominated papers. These papers will be re-presented by the authors in a plenary session on the second day of the conference. Congratulations to the authors!

- *BLEU: a Method for Automatic Evaluation of Machine Translation*, by Kishore Papineni, Salim Roukos, Todd Ward and Wei-Jing Zhu

- *Discriminative Training Methods for Hidden Markov Models: Theory and Experiments with Perceptron Algorithms*, by Michael Collins

- *Thumbs up?: Sentiment Classification using Machine Learning Techniques*, by Bo Pang, Lillian Lee and Shivakumar Vaithyanathan

Keynote Talk: Why 72?
Charles Yang
University of Pennsylvania

Biography

Charles is a Professor of Linguistics, Computer Science, and Psychology at the University of Pennsylvania and directs the Program in Cognitive Science. He has spent a long time to work out the tricks children use to learn languages and is now ready to try them out on machines. His most recent book, The Price of Linguistic Productivity, is the winner of the 2017 LSA Leonard Bloomfield award.

Keynote Talk: The Moment When the Future Fell Asleep
Kevin Knight
University of Southern California / Information Sciences Institute

Biography

Kevin is a professor of computer science at the University of Southern California and fellow of the Information Sciences Institute. He is a 2014 fellow of the ACL for foundational contributions to machine translation, to the application of automata for NLP, to decipherment of historical manuscripts, to semantics and to generation.

Keynote Talk: Google Assistant or My Assistant? Towards Personalized Situated Conversational Agents
Dilek Hakkani-Tür
Google Research

Abstract

Interacting with machines in natural language has been a holy grail since the beginning of computers. Given the difficulty of understanding natural language, only in the past couple of decades, we started seeing real user applications for targeted/limited domains. More recently, advances in deep learning based approaches enabled exciting new research frontiers for end-to-end goal-oriented conversational systems. However, personalization (i.e., learning to take actions from users and learning about users beyond memorizing simple attributes) remains a research challenge. In this talk, I'll review end-to-end situated dialogue systems research, with components for situated language understanding, dialogue state tracking, policy, and language generation. The talk will highlight novel approaches where dialogue is viewed as a collaborative game between a user and an agent in the presence of visual information. The situated conversational agent can be bootstrapped using user simulation (crawl), improved through interactions with crowd-workers (walk), and iteratively refined with real user interactions (run).

Biography

Dilek is a research scientist at Google Research Dialogue Group and has previously held positions at Microsoft Research, ICSI, and AT&T Labs – Research. She is a fellow of the IEEE and of ISCA. Her research interests include conversational AI, natural language and speech processing, spoken dialogue systems, and machine learning for language processing.

Table of Contents

xxvii

xxx

xxxi

Conference Program

June 2

07:30–08:45 **Breakfast**

08:45–09:00 **Welcome from the Chairs**

09:00–10:00 **Keynote (sponsored by Toutiao AI Lab)**

Why 72?
Charles Yang, University of Pennsylvania

10:00–10:30 **Morning Coffee**

10:30–11:30 **Information Extraction 1**

10:30–11:30 **Phonology, Morphology and Word Segmentation 1**

10:30–11:30 **Speech 1**

10:30–12:00 **Discourse and Pragmatics 1**

Enhanced Word Representations for Bridging Anaphora Resolution
Yufang Hou

Gender Bias in Coreference Resolution
Rachel Rudinger, Jason Naradowsky, Brian Leonard and Benjamin Van Durme

Gender Bias in Coreference Resolution: Evaluation and Debiasing Methods
Jieyu Zhao, Tianlu Wang, Mark Yatskar, Vicente Ordonez and Kai-Wei Chang

Integrating Stance Detection and Fact Checking in a Unified Corpus
Ramy Baly, Mitra Mohtarami, James Glass, Lluís Màrquez, Alessandro Moschitti
and Preslav Nakov

10:30–12:00   NLP Applications 1

A Corpus of Non-Native Written English Annotated for Metaphor
Beata Beigman Klebanov, Chee Wee (Ben) Leong and Michael Flor

A Simple and Effective Approach to the Story Cloze Test
Siddarth Srinivasan, Richa Arora and Mark Riedl

An Annotated Corpus for Machine Reading of Instructions in Wet Lab Protocols
Chaitanya Kulkarni, Wei Xu, Alan Ritter and Raghu Machiraju

Annotation Artifacts in Natural Language Inference Data
Suchin Gururangan, Swabha Swayamdipta, Omer Levy, Roy Schwartz, Samuel Bowman and Noah A. Smith

Humor Recognition Using Deep Learning
Peng-Yu Chen and Von-Wun Soo

Leveraging Intra-User and Inter-User Representation Learning for Automated Hate Speech Detection
Jing Qian, Mai ElSherief, Elizabeth Belding and William Yang Wang

Reference-less Measure of Faithfulness for Grammatical Error Correction
Leshem Choshen and Omri Abend

June 2 (continued)

11:30–12:30	**Machine Learning 1**

11:30–12:30	**Information Extraction 2**

11:30–12:30	**Machine Translation 1**

12:30–14:00	**Lunch**

14:00–15:00	**Industry Track Keynote**

15:00–15:30	**Afternoon Coffee**

15:30–17:00	**Machine Learning 2**

15:48–16:06   *Training Structured Prediction Energy Networks with Indirect Supervision*
Amirmohammad Rooshenas, Aishwarya Kamath and Andrew McCallum

15:30–17:00	**Social Media and Computational Social Science 1**

16:06–16:24   *Si O No, Que Penses? Catalonian Independence and Linguistic Identity on Social Media*
Ian Stewart, Yuval Pinter and Jacob Eisenstein

June 2 (continued)

15:30–17:00   Vision, Robotics and Other Grounding 1

15:30–17:00   Semantics 1

A Transition-Based Algorithm for Unrestricted AMR Parsing
David Vilares and Carlos Gómez-Rodríguez

Analogies in Complex Verb Meaning Shifts: the Effect of Affect in Semantic Similarity Models
Maximilian Köper and Sabine Schulte im Walde

Character-Based Neural Networks for Sentence Pair Modeling
Wuwei Lan and Wei Xu

Determining Event Durations: Models and Error Analysis
Alakananda Vempala, Eduardo Blanco and Alexis Palmer

Diachronic Usage Relatedness (DURel): A Framework for the Annotation of Lexical Semantic Change
Dominik Schlechtweg, Sabine Schulte im Walde and Stefanie Eckmann

Directional Skip-Gram: Explicitly Distinguishing Left and Right Context for Word Embeddings
Yan Song, Shuming Shi, Jing Li and Haisong Zhang

Discriminating between Lexico-Semantic Relations with the Specialization Tensor Model
Goran Glavaš and Ivan Vulić

Evaluating bilingual word embeddings on the long tail
Fabienne Braune, Viktor Hangya, Tobias Eder and Alexander Fraser

Frustratingly Easy Meta-Embedding – Computing Meta-Embeddings by Averaging Source Word Embeddings
Joshua Coates and Danushka Bollegala

Introducing Two Vietnamese Datasets for Evaluating Semantic Models of (Dis-)Similarity and Relatedness
Kim Anh Nguyen, Sabine Schulte im Walde and Ngoc Thang Vu

15:30–17:00 Sentiment Analysis 1

Knowledge-Enriched Two-Layered Attention Network for Sentiment Analysis
Abhishek Kumar, Daisuke Kawahara and Sadao Kurohashi

Letting Emotions Flow: Success Prediction by Modeling the Flow of Emotions in Books
Suraj Maharjan, Sudipta Kar, Manuel Montes, Fabio A. Gonzalez and Thamar Solorio

Modeling Inter-Aspect Dependencies for Aspect-Based Sentiment Analysis
Devamanyu Hazarika, Soujanya Poria, Prateek Vij, Gangeshwar Krishnamurthy, Erik Cambria and Roger Zimmermann

Multi-Task Learning Framework for Mining Crowd Intelligence towards Clinical Treatment
Shweta Yadav, Asif Ekbal, Sriparna Saha, Pushpak Bhattacharyya and Amit Sheth

Recurrent Entity Networks with Delayed Memory Update for Targeted Aspect-Based Sentiment Analysis
Fei Liu, Trevor Cohn and Timothy Baldwin

17:00–18:30 NLP Applications 2

18:12–18:30 *Near Human-Level Performance in Grammatical Error Correction with Hybrid Machine Translation*
Roman Grundkiewicz and Marcin Junczys-Dowmunt

June 2 (continued)

17:00–18:30   Question Answering 1

17:54–18:12   *Strong Baselines for Simple Question Answering over Knowledge Graphs with and without Neural Networks*
Salman Mohammed, Peng Shi and Jimmy Lin

17:00–18:30   SRW Highlights

June 3

07:45–08:45   Breakfast

08:45–09:00   Announcements

09:00–10:00   Keynote 2 (sponsored by Google)

The Moment When the Future Fell Asleep
Kevin Knight, University of Southern California / Information Sciences Institute

10:00–10:30   Morning Coffee

10:30–11:30   Cognitive Modeling and Psycholinguistics 1

11:06–11:24   *Looking for Structure in Lexical and Acoustic-Prosodic Entrainment Behaviors*
Andreas Weise and Rivka Levitan

Semi-Supervised Event Extraction with Paraphrase Clusters
James Ferguson, Colin Lockard, Daniel Weld and Hannaneh Hajishirzi

Structure Regularized Neural Network for Entity Relation Classification for Chinese Literature Text
Ji Wen, Xu Sun, Xuancheng Ren and Qi Su

Syntactic Patterns Improve Information Extraction for Medical Search
Roma Patel, Yinfei Yang, Iain Marshall, Ani Nenkova and Byron Wallace

Syntactically Aware Neural Architectures for Definition Extraction
Luis Espinosa Anke and Steven Schockaert

10:30–12:00   Tagging, Chunking, Syntax and Parsing 1

A Dynamic Oracle for Linear-Time 2-Planar Dependency Parsing
Daniel Fernández-González and Carlos Gómez-Rodríguez

Are Automatic Methods for Cognate Detection Good Enough for Phylogenetic Reconstruction in Historical Linguistics?
Taraka Rama, Johann-Mattis List, Johannes Wahle and Gerhard Jäger

Automatically Selecting the Best Dependency Annotation Design with Dynamic Oracles
Guillaume Wisniewski, Ophélie Lacroix and François Yvon

Consistent CCG Parsing over Multiple Sentences for Improved Logical Reasoning
Masashi Yoshikawa, Koji Mineshima, Hiroshi Noji and Daisuke Bekki

Exploiting Dynamic Oracles to Train Projective Dependency Parsers on Non-Projective Trees
Lauriane Aufrant, Guillaume Wisniewski and François Yvon

Improving Coverage and Runtime Complexity for Exact Inference in Non-Projective Transition-Based Dependency Parsers
Tianze Shi, Carlos Gómez-Rodríguez and Lillian Lee

Towards a Variability Measure for Multiword Expressions
Caroline Pasquer, Agata Savary, Jean-Yves Antoine and Carlos Ramisch

15:30–17:00   **Text Mining 1**

15:30–17:00   **Semantics 3**

15:30–17:00   **Tagging, Chunking, Syntax and Parsing 2**

15:30–17:00   **Machine Learning 4**

Contextual Augmentation: Data Augmentation by Words with Paradigmatic Relations
Sosuke Kobayashi

Cross-Lingual Learning-to-Rank with Shared Representations
Shota Sasaki, Shuo Sun, Shigehiko Schamoni, Kevin Duh and Kentaro Inui

Self-Attention with Relative Position Representations
Peter Shaw, Jakob Uszkoreit and Ashish Vaswani

Text Segmentation as a Supervised Learning Task
Omri Koshorek, Adir Cohen, Noam Mor, Michael Rotman and Jonathan Berant

What's in a Domain? Learning Domain-Robust Text Representations using Adversarial Training
Yitong Li, Timothy Baldwin and Trevor Cohn

June 3 (continued)

15:30–17:00   Phonology, Morphology and Word Segmentation 2

Are All Languages Equally Hard to Language-Model?
Ryan Cotterell, Sebastian J. Mielke, Jason Eisner and Brian Roark

The Computational Complexity of Distinctive Feature Minimization in Phonology
Hubie Chen and Mans Hulden

Unsupervised Disambiguation of Syncretism in Inflected Lexicons
Ryan Cotterell, Christo Kirov, Sebastian J. Mielke and Jason Eisner

17:00–18:30   Test of Time Session (in honor of Aravind Joshi)

17:00–17:15   *Awards and Remembrances*

17:15–17:40   *BLEU: a Method for Automatic Evaluation of Machine Translation (Test of Time)*
Kishore Papineni, Salim Roukos, Todd Ward and Wei-Jing Zhu, IBM Research

17:40–18:05   *Discriminative Training Methods for Hidden Markov Models: Theory and Experiments with Perceptron Algorithms (Test of Time)*
Michael Collins, Columbia University

18:05–18:30   *Thumbs up?: Sentiment Classification using Machine Learning Techniques (Test of Time)*
Bo Pang, Lillian Lee, Shivakumar Vaithyanathan, Cornell University, IBM Research

June 4 (continued)

Simple and Effective Semi-Supervised Question Answering
Bhuwan Dhingra, Danish Danish and Dheeraj Rajagopal

TypeSQL: Knowledge-Based Type-Aware Neural Text-to-SQL Generation
Tao Yu, Zifan Li, Zilin Zhang, Rui Zhang and Dragomir Radev

10:30–12:00 Social Media and Computational Social Science 3

Community Member Retrieval on Social Media Using Textual Information
Aaron Jaech, Shobhit Hathi and Mari Ostendorf

Cross-Domain Review Helpfulness Prediction Based on Convolutional Neural Networks with Auxiliary Domain Discriminators
Cen Chen, Yinfei Yang, Jun Zhou, Xiaolong Li and Forrest Sheng Bao

Predicting Foreign Language Usage from English-Only Social Media Posts
Svitlana Volkova, Stephen Ranshous and Lawrence Phillips

10:30–12:00 Summarization 2

A Discourse-Aware Attention Model for Abstractive Summarization of Long Documents
Arman Cohan, Franck Dernoncourt, Doo Soon Kim, Trung Bui, Seokhwan Kim, Walter Chang and Nazli Goharian

A Mixed Hierarchical Attention Based Encoder-Decoder Approach for Standard Table Summarization
Parag Jain, Anirban Laha, Karthik Sankaranarayanan, Preksha Nema, Mitesh M. Khapra and Shreyas Shetty

Effective Crowdsourcing for a New Type of Summarization Task
Youxuan Jiang, Catherine Finegan-Dollak, Jonathan K. Kummerfeld and Walter Lasecki

Key2Vec: Automatic Ranked Keyphrase Extraction from Scientific Articles using Phrase Embeddings
Debanjan Mahata, John Kuriakose, Rajiv Ratn Shah and Roger Zimmermann

Learning to Generate Wikipedia Summaries for Underserved Languages from Wikidata
Lucie-Aimée Kaffee, Hady Elsahar, Pavlos Vougiouklis, Christophe Gravier, Frederique Laforest, Jonathon Hare and Elena Simperl

Multi-Reward Reinforced Summarization with Saliency and Entailment
Ramakanth Pasunuru and Mohit Bansal

Objective Function Learning to Match Human Judgements for Optimization-Based Summarization
Maxime Peyrard and Iryna Gurevych

Pruning Basic Elements for Better Automatic Evaluation of Summaries
Ukyo Honda, Tsutomu Hirao and Masaaki Nagata

Unsupervised Keyphrase Extraction with Multipartite Graphs
Florian Boudin

Where Have I Heard This Story Before? Identifying Narrative Similarity in Movie Remakes
Snigdha Chaturvedi, Shashank Srivastava and Dan Roth

11:30–12:30   **Dialogue and Interactive Systems 1**

11:30–12:30   **Information Extraction 5**

11:30–12:30   **Generation 3**

12:30–14:00   **Lunch**

13:00–14:00   *NAACL Business Meeting*
Julia Hockenmaier, University of Illinois at Urbana-Champaign

14:00–15:30   **Sentiment Analysis 2**

15:12–15:30   *Multimodal Emoji Prediction*
Francesco Barbieri, Miguel Ballesteros, Francesco Ronzano and Horacio Saggion

14:00–15:30   **Discourse and Pragmatics 2**

15:12–15:30   *Higher-Order Coreference Resolution with Coarse-to-Fine Inference*
Kenton Lee, Luheng He and Luke Zettlemoyer

14:00–15:30   **Tagging, Chunking, Syntax and Parsing 3**

14:54–15:12   *Non-Projective Dependency Parsing with Non-Local Transitions*
Daniel Fernández-González and Carlos Gómez-Rodríguez

14:00–15:30   **Cognitive Modeling and Psycholinguistics 2**

Detecting Linguistic Characteristics of Alzheimer's Dementia by Interpreting Neural Models
Sweta Karlekar, Tong Niu and Mohit Bansal

14:00–15:30   **Dialogue and Interactive Systems 2**

Deep Dungeons and Dragons: Learning Character-Action Interactions from Role-Playing Game Transcripts
Annie Louis and Charles Sutton

Feudal Reinforcement Learning for Dialogue Management in Large Domains
Iñigo Casanueva, Paweł Budzianowski, Pei-Hao Su, Stefan Ultes, Lina M. Rojas Barahona, Bo-Hsiang Tseng and Milica Gasic

14:00–15:30   Text Mining 2

Evaluating Historical Text Normalization Systems: How Well Do They Generalize?
Alexander Robertson and Sharon Goldwater

Gated Multi-Task Network for Text Classification
Liqiang Xiao, Honglun Zhang and Wenqing Chen

Natural Language to Structured Query Generation via Meta-Learning
Po-Sen Huang, Chenglong Wang, Rishabh Singh, Wen-tau Yih and Xiaodong He

Smaller Text Classifiers with Discriminative Cluster Embeddings
Mingda Chen and Kevin Gimpel

14:00–15:30   Speech 2

Role-specific Language Models for Processing Recorded Neuropsychological Exams
Tuka Al Hanai, Rhoda Au and James Glass

Slot-Gated Modeling for Joint Slot Filling and Intent Prediction
Chih-Wen Goo, Guang Gao, Yun-Kai Hsu, Chih-Li Huo, Tsung-Chieh Chen, Keng-Wei Hsu and Yun-Nung Chen

June 4 (continued)

14:00–15:30   **Vision, Robotics and Other Grounding 3**

An Evaluation of Image-Based Verb Prediction Models against Human Eye-Tracking Data
Spandana Gella and Frank Keller

Learning to Color from Language
Varun Manjunatha, Mohit Iyyer, Jordan Boyd-Graber and Larry Davis

Punny Captions: Witty Wordplay in Image Descriptions
Arjun Chandrasekaran, Devi Parikh and Mohit Bansal

The Emergence of Semantics in Neural Network Representations of Visual Information
Dhanush Dharmaretnam and Alona Fyshe

Visual Referring Expression Recognition: What Do Systems Actually Learn?
Volkan Cirik, Louis-Philippe Morency and Taylor Berg-Kirkpatrick

Visually Guided Spatial Relation Extraction from Text
Taher Rahgooy, Umar Manzoor and Parisa Kordjamshidi

Watch, Listen, and Describe: Globally and Locally Aligned Cross-Modal Attentions for Video Captioning
Xin Wang, Yuan-Fang Wang and William Yang Wang

June 4 (continued)

15:30–16:00   Afternoon Coffee

17:00–18:15   Outstanding Paper Session (sponsored by Amazon)

Enhanced Word Representations for Bridging Anaphora Resolution

Yufang Hou
IBM Research Ireland
yhou@ie.ibm.com

Abstract

Most current models of word representations
(e.g., *GloVe*) have successfully captured fine-
grained semantics. However, semantic similarity exhibited in these word embeddings is
not suitable for resolving bridging anaphora,
which requires the knowledge of associative
similarity (i.e., relatedness) instead of semantic similarity information between synonyms
or hypernyms. We create word embeddings
(*embeddings_PP*) to capture such relatedness
by exploring the syntactic structure of noun
phrases. We demonstrate that using *embed-
dings_PP* alone achieves around 30% of accuracy for bridging anaphora resolution on the
ISNotes corpus. Furthermore, we achieve a
substantial gain over the state-of-the-art system (Hou et al., 2013b) for bridging antecedent
selection.

1 Introduction

Bridging (Clark, 1975; Prince, 1981; Gundel et al.,
1993) establishes entity coherence in a text by
linking anaphors and antecedents via various non-
identity relations. In Example 1, the link between
the bridging anaphor (**the chief cabinet secretary**) and the antecedent (*Japan*) establish local
(entity) coherence.

(1) Yet another political scandal is racking *Japan*.
On Friday, **the chief cabinet secretary** an-
nounced that **eight cabinet ministers** had received five million yen from the industry.

Choosing the right antecedents for bridging
anaphors is a subtask of bridging resolution. For
this substask, most previous work (Poesio et al.,
2004; Lassalle and Denis, 2011; Hou et al., 2013b)
calculate semantic relatedness between an anaphor
and its antecedent based on word co-occurrence
count using certain syntactic patterns.

Most recently, word embeddings gain a lot popularity in NLP community because they reflect human intuitions about semantic similarity and relatedness. Most word representation models explore the distributional hypothesis which states
that words occurring in similar contexts have
similar meanings (Harris, 1954). State-of-the-
art word representations such as word2vec skip-
gram (Mikolov et al., 2013) and GloVe (Pennington et al., 2014) have been shown to perform well
across a variety of NLP tasks, including textual entailment (Rocktäschel et al., 2016), reading comprehension (Chen et al., 2016), and information
status classification (Hou, 2016). However, these
word embeddings capture both "genuine" similarity and relatedness, and they may in some cases
be detrimental to downstream performance (Kiela
et al., 2015). Bridging anaphora resolution is one
of such cases which requires lexical association
knowledge instead of semantic similarity information between synonyms or hypernyms. In Example 1, among all antecedent candidates, "*the chief
cabinet secretary*" is the most similar word to the
bridging anaphor "**eight cabinet ministers**" but
obviously it is not the antecedent for the latter.

In this paper, we explore the syntactic structure
of noun phrases (NPs) to derive contexts for nouns
in the GloVe model. We find that the prepositional
structure (e.g., X *of* Y) and the possessive structure (e.g., Y'*s* X) are a useful context source for
the representation of nouns in terms of relatedness
for bridging relations.

We demonstrate that using our word embeddings based on PP contexts (*embeddings_PP*)
alone achieves around 30% of accuracy on bridging anaphora resolution in the ISNotes corpus,
which is 12% better than the original GloVe word
embeddings. Moreover, adding an additional feature based on *embeddings_PP* leads to a significant
improvement over a state-of-the-art system on

Proceedings of NAACL-HLT 2018, pages 1–7
New Orleans, Louisiana, June 1 - 6, 2018. ©2018 Association for Computational Linguistics

bridging anaphora resolution (Hou et al., 2013b).

2   Related Work

Bridging anaphora resolution. Anaphora plays an important role in discourse comprehension. Different from *identity anaphora* which indicates that a noun phrase refers back to the same entity introduced by previous descriptions in the discourse, *bridging anaphora* links anaphors and antecedents via lexico-semantic, frame or encyclopedic relations.

Bridging resolution has to recognize bridging anaphors and find links to antecedents. There has been a few works tackling full bridging resolution (Hahn et al., 1996; Hou et al., 2014). In recent years, various computational approaches have been developed for bridging anaphora recognition (Markert et al., 2012; Hou et al., 2013a) and for bridging antecedent selection (Poesio et al., 2004; Hou et al., 2013b). This work falls into the latter category and we create a new lexical knowledge resource for the task of choosing antecedents for bridging anaphors.

Previous work on bridging anaphora resolution (Poesio et al., 2004; Lassalle and Denis, 2011; Hou et al., 2013b) explore word co-occurence count in certain syntactic preposition patterns to calculate word relatedness. These patterns encode associative relations between nouns which cover a variety of bridging relations. Our PP context model exploits the same principle but is more general. Unlike previous work which only consider a small number of prepositions per anaphor, the PP context model considers all prepositions for all nouns in big corpora. It also includes the possessive structure of NPs. The resulting word embeddings are a general resource for bridging anaphora resolution. In addition, it enables efficient computation of word association strength through low-dimensional matrix operations.

Enhanced word embeddings. Recently, a few approaches investigate different ways to improve the vanilla word embeddings. Levy and Goldberg (2014) explore the dependency-based contexts in the Skip-Gram model. The authors replace the linear bag-of-words contexts in the original Skip-Gram model with the syntactic contexts derived from the automatically parsed dependency trees. They observe that the dependency-based embeddings exhibit more functional similarity than the original skip-gram embeddings. Heinzerling et al.

(2017) show that incorporating dependency-based word embeddings into their selectional preference model slightly improve coreference resolution performance. Kiela et al. (2015) try to learn word embeddings for similarity and relatedness separately by utilizing a thesaurus and a collection of psychological association norms. The authors report that their relatedness-specialized embeddings perform better on document topic classification than similarity embeddings. Schwartz et al. (2016) demonstrate that symmetric patterns (e.g, X *or* Y) are the most useful contexts for the representation of verbs and adjectives. Our work follows in this vein and we are interested in learning word representations for bridging relations.

3   Approach

3.1   Asymmetric Prepositional and Possessive Structures

The syntactic prepositional and possessive structures of NPs encode a variety of bridging relations between anaphors and their antecedents. For instance, *the rear door of that red car* indicates the part-of relation between "door" and "car", and *the company's new appointed chairman* implies the employment relation between "chairman" and "company". We therefore extract noun pairs *door–car, chairman–company* by using syntactic structure of NPs which contain prepositions or possessive forms.

It is worth noting that bridging relations expressed in the above syntactic structures are asymmetric. So for each noun pair, we keep the head on the left and the noun modifier on the right. However, a lot of nouns can appear on both positions, such as "***travelers** in the train station*", "***travelers** from the airport*", "*hotels for **travelers***", "*the destination for **travelers***". To capture the differences between these two positions, we add the postfix "_PP" to the nouns on the left. Thus we extract the following four pairs from the above NPs: *travelers_PP–station, travelers_PP–airport, hotels_PP–travelers, destination_PP–travelers*.

3.2   Word Embeddings Based on PP Contexts (*embeddings_PP*)

Our PP context model is based on GloVe (Pennington et al., 2014), which obtains state-of-the-art results on various NLP tasks. We extract noun pairs as described in Section 3.1 from the automatically parsed Gigaword corpus (Parker et al., 2011;

Target Word	*embeddings_PP*	*GloVe_Giga*
president	minister, mayor, governor, clinton bush	vice, presidency, met, former presidents
president_PP	vice-president_PP, federation, republic usa, corporation	—
residents	villagers, citizens, inhabitants, families participants	locals, villagers, people, citizens homes
residents_PP	resident_PP, neighborhood, shemona[1] ashraf, suburbs	—
members	participants, leaders, colleagues, officials lawmakers	member, representatives, others, leaders groups
members_PP	member_PP, representatives_PP, basij[2] leaders_PP, community	—
travelers	travellers, thirsts_PP, shoppers quarantines_PP, needle-sharing_PP	travellers, passengers, vacationers tourists, shoppers
travelers_PP	e-tickets, travellers_PP, cairngorms[3] flagstaffs_PP, haneda[4]	—

[1] Shemona is a city in Israel.   [2] Basij is a paramilitary group in Iran.
[3] Cairngorms is mountain range in Scotland.   [4] Haneda is an airport in Japan.

Table 1: Target words and their top five nearest neighbors in *embeddings_PP* and *GloVe_Giga*

Napoles et al., 2012). We treat each noun pair as a sentence containing only two words and concatenate all 197 million noun pairs in one document. We employ the GloVe tookit[1] to train the PP context model on the above extracted noun pairs. All tokens are converted to lowercase, and words that appear less than 10 times are filtered. This results in a vocabulary of around 276k words and 188k distinct nouns without the postfix "_PP". We set the context window size as two and keep other parameters the same as in Pennington et al. (2014). We report results for 100 dimension embeddings, though similar trends were also observed with 200 and 300 dimensions.

For comparison, we also trained a 100 dimension word embeddings (*GloVe_Giga*) on the whole Gigaword corpus, using the same parameters reported in Pennington et al. (2014).

Table 1 lists a few target words and their top five nearest neighbors (using cosine similarity) in *embeddings_PP* and *GloVe_Giga* respectively. For the target words "residents" and "members", both *embeddings_PP* and *GloVe_Giga* yield a list of similar words and most of them have the same semantic type as the target word. For the "travelers" example, *GloVe_Giga* still presents the similar words with the same semantic type, while *embed-dings_PP* generates both similar words and related words (words containing the postfix "_PP"). More importantly, it seems that *embeddings_PP* can find reasonable semantic roles for nominal predicates (target words containing the postfix "_PP"). For instance, "president_PP" is mostly related to countries or organizations, and "residents_PP" is mostly related to places.

The above examples can be seen as qualitative evaluation for our PP context model. We assume that *embeddings_PP* can be served as a lexical knowledge resource for bridging antecedent selection. In the next section, we will demonstrate the effectiveness of *embeddings_PP* for the task of bridging anaphora resolution.

4 Quantitative Evaluation

For the task of bridging anaphora resolution, we use the dataset ISNotes[2] released by Hou et al. (2013b). This dataset contains around 11,000 NPs annotated for information status including 663 bridging NPs and their antecedents in 50 texts taken from the WSJ portion of the OntoNotes corpus (Weischedel et al., 2011). It is notable that bridging anaphors in ISNotes are not limited to definite NPs as in previous work (Poesio et al., 1997, 2004; Lassalle and Denis, 2011).

---

[1] https://github.com/stanfordnlp/GloVe

[2] http://www.h-its.org/english/research/nlp/download

The semantic relations between anaphor and antecedent in the corpus are quite diverse: only 14% of anaphors have a part-of/attribute-of relation with the antecedent and only 7% of anaphors stand in a set relationship to the antecedent. 79% of anaphors have "other" relation with their antecedents, without further distinction. This includes encyclopedic relations such as **the waiter** – *restaurant* as well as context-specific relations such as **the thieves** – *palms*.

We follow Hou et al. (2013b)'s experimental setup and reimplement *MLN model II* as our baseline. We first test the effectiveness of *embeddings_PP* alone to resolve bridging anaphors. Then we show that incorporating *embeddings_PP* into *MLN model II* significantly improves the result.

4.1 Using *embeddings_PP* Alone

For each anaphor a, we simply construct the list of antecedent candidates E_a using NPs preceding a from the same sentence as well as from the previous two sentences. Hou et al. (2013b) found that globally salient entities are likely to be the antecedents of all anaphors in a text. We approximate this by adding NPs from the first sentence of the text to E_a. This is motivated by the fact that ISNotes is a newswire corpus and globally salient entities are often introduced in the beginning of an article. On average, each bridging anaphor has 19 antecedent candidates using this simple antecedent candidate selection strategy.

Given an anaphor a and its antecedent candidate list E_a, we predict the most related NP among all NPs in E_a as the antecedent for a. The relatedness is measured via cosine similarity between the head of the anaphor (plus the postfix "_PP") and the head of the candidate.

This simple deterministic approach based on *embeddings_PP* achieves an accuracy of 30.32% on the ISNotes corpus. Following Hou et al. (2013b), accuracy is calculated as the proportion of the correctly resolved bridging anaphors out of all bridging anaphors in the corpus.

We found that using *embeddings_PP* outperforms using other word embeddings by a large margin (see Table 2), including the original GloVe vectors trained on Gigaword and Wikipedia 2014 dump (*GloVe_GigaWiki14*) and GloVe vectors that we trained on Gigaword only (*GloVe_Giga*). This confirms our observation in Section 3.2 that *em-*

	acc
GloVe_GigaWiki14	18.10
GloVe_Giga	19.00
embeddings_wo_PPSuffix	22.17
embeddings_PP	**30.32**

Table 2: Results of *embeddings_PP* alone for bridging anaphora resolution compared to the baselines. Bold indicates statistically significant differences over the baselines using randomization test ($p < 0.01$).

biddings_PP can capture the relatedness between anaphor and antecedent for various bridging relations.

To understand the role of the suffix "_PP" in *embeddings_PP*, we trained word vectors *embeddings_wo_PPSuffix* using the same noun pairs as in *embeddings_PP*. For each noun pair, we remove the suffix "_PP" attached to the head noun. We found that using *embeddings_wo_PPSuffix* only achieves an accuracy of 22.17% (see Table 2). This indicates that the suffix "_PP" is the most significant factor in *embeddings_PP*. Note that when calculating cosine similarity based on the first three word embeddings in Table 2, we do not add the suffix "_PP" to the head of an bridging anaphor because such words do not exist in these word vectors.

4.2 *MLN model II + embeddings_PP*

MLN model II is a joint inference framework based on Markov logic networks (Domingos and Lowd, 2009). In addition to modeling the semantic, syntactic and lexical constraints between the anaphor and the antecedent (local constraints), it models that:

- semantically or syntactically related anaphors are likely to share the same antecedent (joint inference constraints);

- a globally salient entity is preferred to be the antecedent of all anaphors in a text even if the entity is distant to the anaphors (global salience constraints);

- several bridging relations are strongly signaled by the semantic classes of the anaphor and the antecedent, e.g., a job title anaphor such as *chairman* prefers a GPE or an organization antecedent (semantic class constraints).

4

	acc
MLN model II	41.32
MLN model II + GloVe_GigaWiki14	39.52
MLN model II + embeddings_wo_PPSuffix	40.42
MLN model II + embeddings_PP	**45.85**

Table 3: Results of integrating *embeddings_PP* into *MLN model II* for bridging anaphora resolution compared to the baselines. Bold indicates statistically significant differences over the baselines using randomization test ($p < 0.01$).

Due to the space limit, we omit the details of *MLN model II*, but refer the reader to Hou et al. (2013b) for a full description.

We add one constraint into *MLN model II* based on *embeddings_PP*: each bridging anaphor a is linked to its most related antecedent candidate using cosine similarity. We use the same strategy as in the previous section to construct the list of antecedent candidates for each anaphor. Unlike the previous section, which only uses the vector of the NP head to calculate relatedness, here we include all common nouns occurring before the NP head as well because they also represent the core semantic of an NP (e.g., *"earthquake victims"* and *"the state senate"*).

Specifically, given an NP, we first construct a list N which consists of the head and all common nouns appearing before the head, we then represent the NP as a vector v using the following formula, where the suffix "_PP" is added to each n if the NP is a bridging anaphor:

$$v = \frac{\sum_{n \in N} embeddings\_PP_n}{|N|} \quad (1)$$

Table 3 shows that adding the constraint based on *embeddings_PP* improves the result of *MLN model II* by 4.5%. However, adding the constraint based on the vanilla word embeddings (*GloVe_GigaWiki14*) or the word embeddings without the suffix "_PP" (*embeddings_wo_PPSuffix*) slightly decreases the result compared to *MLN model II*. Although *MLN model II* already explores preposition patterns to calculate relatedness between head nouns of NPs, it seems that the feature based on *embeddings_PP* is complementary to the original preposition pattern feature. Furthermore, the vector model allows us to represent the meaning of an NP beyond its head easily.

5   Conclusions

We present a PP context model based on GloVe by exploring the asymmetric prepositional structure (e.g., **X** *of* **Y**) and possessive structure (e.g., **Y**'s **X**) of NPs. We demonstrate that the resulting word vectors (*embeddings_PP*) are able to capture the relatedness between anaphor and antecedent in various bridging relations. In addition, adding the constraint based on *embeddings_PP* yields a significant improvement over a state-of-the-art system on bridging anaphora resolution in ISNotes (Hou et al., 2013b).

For the task of bridging anaphora resolution, Hou et al. (2013b) pointed out that future work needs to explore wider context to resolve context-specific bridging relations. Here we combine the semantics of pre-nominal modifications and the head by vector average using *embeddings_PP*. We hope that our embedding resource[3] will facilitate further research into improved context modeling for bridging relations.

Acknowledgments

The author thanks the anonymous reviewers for their valuable feedback.

References

Danqi Chen, Jason Bolton, and Christopher D. Manning. 2016. A thorough examination of the CNN/Daily mail reading comprehension task. In *Proceedings of the 54th Annual Meeting of the Association for Computational Linguistics,* Berlin, Germany, 7–12 August 2016. pages 2358–2367.

Herbert H. Clark. 1975. Bridging. In *Proceedings of the Conference on Theoretical Issues in Natural Language Processing,* Cambridge, Mass., June 1975. pages 169–174.

---

[3]*embeddings_PP* can be downloaded from `https://doi.org/10.5281/zenodo.1211616`

Pedro Domingos and Daniel Lowd. 2009. *Markov Logic: An Interface Layer for Artificial Intelligence.* Morgan Claypool Publishers.

Jeanette K. Gundel, Nancy Hedberg, and Ron Zacharski. 1993. Cognitive status and the form of referring expressions in discourse. *Language* 69:274–307.

Udo Hahn, Michael Strube, and Katja Markert. 1996. Bridging textual ellipses. In *Proceedings of the 16th International Conference on Computational Linguistics,* Copenhagen, Denmark, 5–9 August 1996. volume 1, pages 496–501. http://www. aclweb.org/anthology/C96-1084.pdf.

Zellig S. Harris. 1954. Distributional structure. *Word* 10:146–162.

Benjamin Heinzerling, Nafise Sadat Moosavi, and Michael Strube. 2017. Revisiting selectional preferences for coreference resolution. In *Proceedings of the 2017 Conference on Empirical Methods in Natural Language Processing,* Copenhagen, Denmark, 7–11 November 2017. pages 1332–1339.

Yufang Hou. 2016. Incremental fine-grained information status classification using attention-based LSTMs. In *Proceedings of the 26th International Conference on Computational Linguistics,* Osaka, Japan, 11–16 December 2016. pages 1880–1890.

Yufang Hou, Katja Markert, and Michael Strube. 2013a. Cascading collective classification for bridging anaphora recognition using a rich linguistic feature set. In *Proceedings of the 2013 Conference on Empirical Methods in Natural Language Processing,* Seattle, Wash., 18–21 October 2013. pages 814–820. http://aclweb.org/ anthology/D13-1077.pdf.

Yufang Hou, Katja Markert, and Michael Strube. 2013b. Global inference for bridging anaphora resolution. In *Proceedings of the 2013 Conference of the North American Chapter of the Association for Computational Linguistics: Human Language Technologies,* Atlanta, Georgia, 9–14 June 2013. pages 907–917. http://aclweb.org/ anthology/N13-1111.pdf.

Yufang Hou, Katja Markert, and Michael Strube. 2014. A rule-based system for unrestricted bridging resolution: Recognizing bridging anaphora and finding links to antecedents. In *Proceedings of the 2014 Conference on Empirical Methods in Natural Language Processing,* Doha, Qatar, 25–29 October 2014. pages 2082–2093. http://aclweb. org/anthology/D13-1077.pdf.

Douwe Kiela, Felix Hill, and Stephen Clark. 2015. Specializing word embeddings for similarity or relatedness. In *Proceedings of the 2015 Conference on Empirical Methods in Natural Language Processing,* Lisbon, Portugal, 17–21 September 2015. pages 2044–2048.

Emmanuel Lassalle and Pascal Denis. 2011. Leveraging different meronym discovery methods for bridging resolution in French. In *Proceedings of the 8th Discourse Anaphora and Anaphor Resolution Colloquium (DAARC 2011),* Faro, Algarve, Portugal, 6–7 October 2011. pages 35–46.

Omer Levy and Yoav Goldberg. 2014. Dependency-based word embeddings. In *Proceedings of the 52st Annual Meeting of the Association for Computational Linguistics,* Baltimore, USA, 22–27 June 2014.

Katja Markert, Yufang Hou, and Michael Strube. 2012. Collective classification for fine-grained information status. In *Proceedings of the 50th Annual Meeting of the Association for Computational Linguistics,* Jeju Island, Korea, 8–14 July 2012. pages 795–804. http://www.aclweb.org/ anthology/P12-1084.pdf.

Tomas Mikolov, Ilya Sutskever, Kai Chen, Gregory S. Corrado, and Jeffrey Dean. 2013. Distributed representations of words and phrases and their compositionality. In *Advances in Neural Information Processing Systems 26 (NIPS 2013),* pages 3111–3119.

Courtney Napoles, Matthew Gormley, and Benjamin Van Durme. 2012. Annotated Gigaword. In *Proceedings of the Joint Workshop on Automatic Knowledge Base Construction & Web-scale Knowledge Extraction (AKBC-WEKEX)* Montréal, Québec, Canada, 7-8 June 2012. pages 95–100.

Robert Parker, David Graff, Junbo Kong, Ke Chen, and Kazuaki Maeda. 2011. English Gigaword Fifth Edition. LDC2011T07.

Jeffrey Pennington, Richard Socher, and Christopher D. Manning. 2014. Glove: Global vectors for word representation. In *Proceedings of the 2014 Conference on Empirical Methods in Natural Language Processing,* Doha, Qatar, 25–29 October 2014. pages 1532–1543.

Massimo Poesio, Rahul Mehta, Axel Maroudas, and Janet Hitzeman. 2004. Learning to resolve bridging references. In *Proceedings of the 42nd Annual Meeting of the Association for Computational Linguistics,* Barcelona, Spain, 21–26 July 2004. pages 143–150.

Massimo Poesio, Renata Vieira, and Simone Teufel. 1997. Resolving bridging references in unrestricted text. In *Proceedings of the ACL Workshop on Operational Factors in Practical, Robust Anaphora Resolution for Unrestricted Text, Madrid, Spain, July 1997.* pages 1–6.

Ellen F. Prince. 1981. Towards a taxonomy of given-new information. In P. Cole, editor, *Radical Pragmatics*, Academic Press, New York, N.Y., pages 223–255.

Tim Rocktäschel, Edward Grefenstette, Karl Moritz
Hermann, Tomas Kocisky, and Phil Blunsom. 2016.
Reasoning about entailment with neural attention.
In *Proceedings of the 4th International Confer-
ence on Learning Representations,* San Juan, Puerto
Rico, 2-4 May 2016.

Roy Schwartz, Roi Reichart, and Ari Rappoport. 2016.
Symmetric patterns and coordinations: Fast and en-
hanced representations of Verbs and Adjectives. In
*Proceedings of the 2016 Conference of the North
American Chapter of the Association for Computa-
tional Linguistics: Human Language Technologies,*
San Diego, California, 12–17 June 2016. pages 499–
505.

Ralph Weischedel, Martha Palmer, Mitchell Marcus,
Eduard Hovy, Sameer Pradhan, Lance Ramshaw,
Nianwen Xue, Ann Taylor, Jeff Kaufman, Michelle
Franchini, Mohammed El-Bachouti, Robert Belvin,
and Ann Houston. 2011. OntoNotes release 4.0.
LDC2011T03, Philadelphia, Penn.: Linguistic Data
Consortium.

Gender Bias in Coreference Resolution

Rachel Rudinger, Jason Naradowsky, Brian Leonard, and Benjamin Van Durme
Johns Hopkins University

Abstract

We present an empirical study of gender bias in coreference resolution systems. We first introduce a novel, Winograd schema-style set of minimal pair sentences that differ only by pronoun gender. With these *Winogender schemas*, we evaluate and confirm systematic gender bias in three publicly-available coreference resolution systems, and correlate this bias with real-world and textual gender statistics.

1 Introduction

There is a classic riddle: *A man and his son get into a terrible car crash. The father dies, and the boy is badly injured. In the hospital, the surgeon looks at the patient and exclaims, "I can't operate on this boy, he's my son!"* **How can this be?**

That a majority of people are reportedly unable to solve this riddle[1] is taken as evidence of underlying implicit gender bias (Wapman and Belle, 2014): many first-time listeners have difficulty assigning both the role of "mother" and "surgeon" to the same entity.

As the riddle reveals, the task of coreference resolution in English is tightly bound with questions of gender, for humans and automated systems alike (see Figure 1). As awareness grows of the ways in which data-driven AI technologies may acquire and amplify human-like biases (Caliskan et al., 2017; Barocas and Selbst, 2016; Hovy and Spruit, 2016), this work investigates how gender biases manifest in coreference resolution systems.

There are many ways one could approach this question; here we focus on gender bias with respect to occupations, for which we have corresponding U.S. employment statistics. Our approach is to construct a challenge dataset in

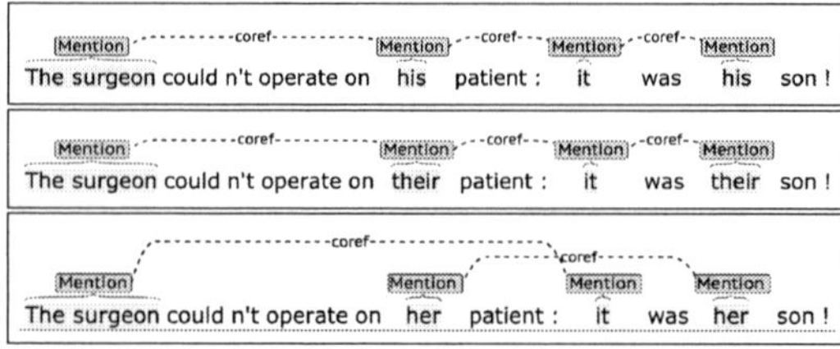

Figure 1: Stanford CoreNLP rule-based coreference system resolves a male and neutral pronoun as coreferent with "The surgeon," but does not for the corresponding female pronoun.

the style of *Winograd schemas*, wherein a pronoun must be resolved to one of two previously-mentioned entities in a sentence designed to be easy for humans to interpret, but challenging for data-driven systems (Levesque et al., 2011). In our setting, one of these mentions is a person referred to by their occupation; by varying only the pronoun's gender, we are able to test the impact of gender on resolution. With these "Winogender schemas," we demonstrate the presence of systematic gender bias in multiple publicly-available coreference resolution systems, and that occupation-specific bias is correlated with employment statistics. We release these test sentences to the public.[2]

In our experiments, we represent gender as a categorical variable with either two or three possible values: female, male, and (in some cases) neutral. These choices reflect limitations of the textual and real-world datasets we use.

2 Coreference Systems

In this work, we evaluate three publicly-available off-the-shelf coreference resolution systems, representing three different machine learning paradigms: rule-based systems, feature-driven

---

[1] The surgeon is the boy's mother.

[2] `https://github.com/rudinger/winogender-schemas`

Proceedings of NAACL-HLT 2018, pages 8–14
New Orleans, Louisiana, June 1 - 6, 2018. ©2018 Association for Computational Linguistics

statistical systems, and neural systems.

Rule-based In the absence of large-scale data for training coreference models, early systems relied heavily on expert knowledge. A frequently used example of this is the Stanford multi-pass sieve system (Lee et al., 2011). A deterministic system, the sieve consists of multiple rule-based models which are applied in succession, from highest-precision to lowest. Gender is among the set of mention attributes identified in the very first stage of the sieve, making this information available throughout the system.

Statistical Statistical methods, often with millions of parameters, ultimately surpassed the performance of rule-based systems on shared task data (Durrett and Klein, 2013; Björkelund and Kuhn, 2014). The system of Durrett and Klein (2013) replaced hand-written rules with simple feature templates. Combinations of these features implicitly capture linguistic phenomena useful for resolving antecedents, but they may also unintentionally capture bias in the data. For instance, for occupations which are not frequently found in the data, an occupation+pronoun feature can be highly informative, and the overly confident model can exhibit strong bias when applied to a new domain.

Neural The move to deep neural models led to more powerful antecedent scoring functions, and the subsequent learned feature combinations resulted in new state-of-the-art performance (Wiseman et al., 2015; Clark and Manning, 2016b). Global inference over these models further improved performance (Wiseman et al., 2016; Clark and Manning, 2016a), but from the perspective of potential bias, the information available to the model is largely the same as in the statistical models. A notable exception is in the case of systems which make use of pre-trained word embeddings (Clark and Manning, 2016b), which have been shown to contain bias and have the potential to introduce bias into the system.

Noun Gender and Number Many coreference resolution systems, including those described here, make use of a common resource released by Bergsma and Lin (2006)[3] ("B&L"): a large list of English nouns and noun phrases with gender and number counts over 85GB of web news. For example, according to the resource, 9.2% of mentions of the noun "doctor" are female. The resource was compiled by bootstrapping coreference information from the dependency paths between pairs of pronouns. We employ this data in our analysis.

3 Winogender Schemas

Our intent is to reveal cases where coreference systems may be more or less likely to recognize a pronoun as coreferent with a particular occupation based on pronoun gender, as observed in Figure 1. To this end, we create a specialized evaluation set consisting of 120 hand-written sentence templates, in the style of the Winograd Schemas (Levesque et al., 2011). Each sentence contains three referring expressions of interest:

1. OCCUPATION , a person referred to by their occupation and a definite article, e.g., "the paramedic."

2. PARTICIPANT , a secondary (human) participant, e.g., "the passenger."

3. PRONOUN , a pronoun that is coreferent with either OCCUPATION or PARTICIPANT.

We use a list of 60 one-word occupations obtained from Caliskan et al. (2017) (see supplement), with corresponding gender percentages available from the U.S. Bureau of Labor Statistics.[4] For each occupation, we wrote two similar sentence templates: one in which PRONOUN is coreferent with OCCUPATION, and one in which it is coreferent with PARTICIPANT (see Figure 2). For each sentence template, there are three PRONOUN instantiations (female, male, or neutral), and two PARTICIPANT instantiations (a specific participant, e.g., "the passenger," and a generic paricipant, "someone.") With the templates fully instantiated, the evaluation set contains 720 sentences: 60 occupations × 2 sentence templates per occupation × 2 participants × 3 pronoun genders.

Validation Like Winograd schemas, each sentence template is written with one intended correct answer (here, either OCCUPATION or PAR-

---

[3] This data was distributed in the CoNLL 2011 and 2012 shared tasks on coreference resolution. (Pradhan et al., 2011, 2012)

[4] 50 are from the supplement of Caliskan et al. (2017), an additional 7 from personal communication with the authors, and three that we added: *doctor, firefighter,* and *secretary.*

(1a) **The paramedic** performed CPR on the passenger even though she/he/they knew it was too late.	

(1a) **The paramedic** performed CPR on the passenger even though she/he/they knew it was too late.

(2a) The paramedic performed CPR on **the passenger** even though she/he/they was/were already dead.

(1b) **The paramedic** performed CPR on someone even though she/he/they knew it was too late.

(2b) The paramedic performed CPR on **someone** even though she/he/they was/were already dead.

Figure 2: A "Winogender" schema for the occupation *paramedic*. Correct answers in bold. In general, OCCUPATION and PARTICIPANT may appear in either order in the sentence.

TICIPANT).[5] We aimed to write sentences where (1) pronoun resolution was as unambiguous for humans as possible (in the absence of additional context), and (2) the resolution would not be affected by changing pronoun gender. (See Figure 2.) Nonetheless, to ensure that our own judgments are shared by other English speakers, we validated all 720 sentences on Mechanical Turk, with 10-way redundancy. Each MTurk task included 5 sentences from our dataset, and 5 sentences from the Winograd Schema Challenge (Levesque et al., 2011)[6], though this additional validation step turned out to be unnecessary.[7] Out of 7200 binary-choice worker annotations (720 sentences × 10-way redundancy), 94.9% of responses agree with our intended answers. With simple majority voting on each sentence, worker responses agree with our intended answers for 718 of 720 sentences (99.7%). The two sentences with low agreement have neutral gender ("they"), and are not reflected in any binary (female-male) analysis.

Correlation (r)	RULE	STAT	NEURAL
B&L	0.87	0.46	0.35
BLS	0.55	0.31	0.31

Table 1: Correlation values for Figures 3 and 4.

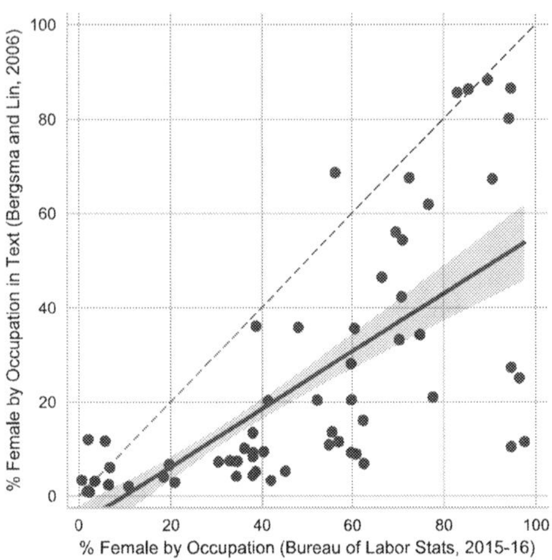

Figure 3: Gender statistics from Bergsma and Lin (2006) correlate with Bureau of Labor Statistics 2015. However, the former has systematically lower female percentages; most points lie well below the 45-degree line (dotted). Regression line and 95% confidence interval in blue. Pearson r = 0.67.

4 Results and Discussion

We evaluate examples of each of the three coreference system architectures described in 2: the Lee et al. (2011) sieve system from the rule-based paradigm (referred to as RULE), Durrett and Klein (2013) from the statistical paradigm (STAT), and the Clark and Manning (2016a) deep reinforcement system from the neural paradigm (NEURAL).

By multiple measures, the Winogender schemas reveal varying degrees of gender bias in all three systems. First we observe that these systems do not behave in a gender-neutral fashion. That is to say, we have designed test sentences where correct pronoun resolution is not a function of gender (as validated by human annotators), but system predictions do exhibit sensitivity to pronoun gender: 68% of male-female minimal pair test sentences are resolved differently by the RULE system; 28% for STAT; and 13% for NEURAL.

Overall, male pronouns are also more likely to be resolved as OCCUPATION than female or neutral pronouns across all systems: for RULE, 72% male vs 29% female and 1% neutral; for STAT, 71% male vs 63% female and 50% neutral; and for NEURAL, 87% male vs 80% female and 36% neutral. Neutral pronouns are often resolved as neither OCCUPATION nor PARTICIPANT, possibly due to the number ambiguity of "they/their/them."

---

[5]Unlike Winograd schemas, we are not primarily concerned with whether these sentences are "hard" to solve, e.g., because they would require certain types of human knowledge or could not be easily solved with word co-occurrence statistics.

[6]We used the publicly-available examples from `https://cs.nyu.edu/faculty/davise/papers/WinogradSchemas/WSCollection.html`

[7]In the end, we did not use the Winograd schemas to filter annotators, as raw agreement on the Winogender schemas was much higher to begin with (94.9% Winogender vs. 86.5% Winograd).

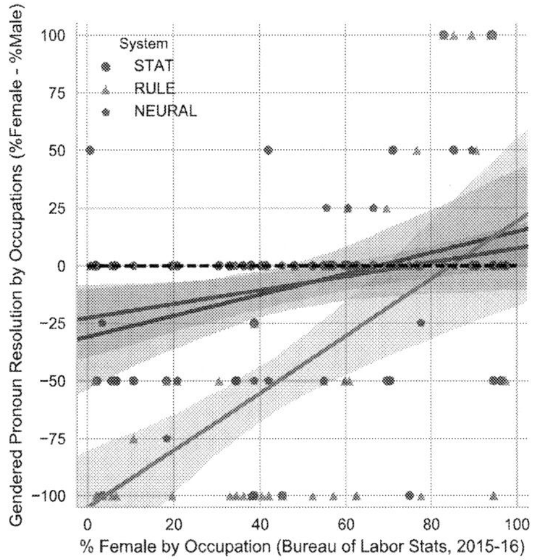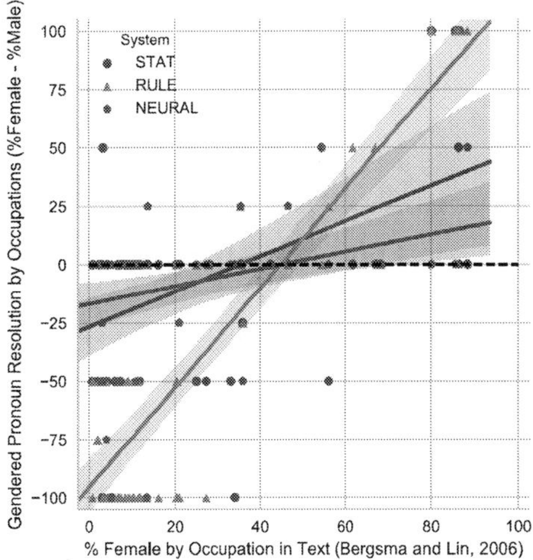

Figure 4: These two plots show how gender bias in coreference systems corresponds with occupational gender statistics from the U.S Bureau of Labor Statistics (left) and from text as computed by Bergsma and Lin (2006) (right); each point represents one occupation. The y-axes measure the extent to which a coref system prefers to match female pronouns with a given occupation over male pronouns, as tested by our Winogender schemas. A value of 100 (maximum female bias) means the system always resolved female pronouns to the given occupation and never male pronouns (100% - 0%); a score of -100 (maximum male bias) is the reverse; and a value of 0 indicates no gender differential. Recall the Winogender evaluation set is gender-balanced for each occupation; thus the horizontal dotted black line (y=0) in both plots represents a hypothetical system with 100% accuracy. Regression lines with 95% confidence intervals are shown.

When these systems' predictions diverge based on pronoun gender, they do so in ways that reinforce and magnify real-world occupational gender disparities. Figure 4 shows that systems' gender preferences for occupations correlate with real-world employment statistics (U.S. Bureau of Labor Statistics) and the gender statistics from text (Bergsma and Lin, 2006) which these systems access directly; correlation values are in Table 1. We also identify so-called "gotcha" sentences in which pronoun gender does not match the occupation's majority gender (BLS) if OCCUPATION is the correct answer; all systems perform worse on these "gotchas."[8] (See Table 2.)

Because coreference systems need to make discrete choices about which mentions are coreferent, percentage-wise differences in real-world statistics may translate into absolute differences in system predictions. For example, the occupation "manager" is 38.5% female in the U.S. according to real-world statistics (BLS); mentions of "manager" in text are only 5.18% female (B&L resource); and finally, as viewed through the behavior of the three coreference systems we tested,

no managers are predicted to be female. This illustrates two related phenomena: first, that data-driven NLP pipelines are susceptible to sequential amplification of bias throughout a pipeline, and second, that although the gender statistics from B&L correlate with BLS employment statistics, they are systematically male-skewed (Figure 3).

System	"Gotcha"?	Female	Male
RULE	no	38.3	51.7
	yes	10.0	37.5
STAT	no	50.8	61.7
	yes	45.8	40.0
NEURAL	no	50.8	49.2
	yes	36.7	46.7

Table 2: System accuracy (%) bucketed by gender and difficulty (so-called "gotchas," shaded in purple). For female pronouns, a "gotcha" sentence is one where either (1) the correct answer is OCCUPATION but the occupation is < 50% female (according to BLS); or (2) the occupation is ≥ 50% female but the correct answer is PARTICIPANT; this is reversed for male pronouns. Systems do uniformly worse on "gotchas."

5 Related Work

Here we give a brief (and non-exhaustive) overview of prior work on gender bias in NLP systems and datasets. A number of papers explore (gender) bias in English word embeddings:

---

[8] "The librarian helped the child pick out a book because he liked to encourage reading." is an example of a "gotcha" sentence; librarians are > 50% female (BLS).

how they capture implicit human biases in modern (Caliskan et al., 2017) and historical (Garg et al., 2018) text, and methods for debiasing them (Bolukbasi et al., 2016). Further work on debiasing models with adversarial learning is explored by Beutel et al. (2017) and Zhang et al. (2018).

Prior work also analyzes social and gender stereotyping in existing NLP and vision datasets (van Miltenburg, 2016; Rudinger et al., 2017). Tatman (2017) investigates the impact of gender and dialect on deployed speech recognition systems, while Zhao et al. (2017) introduce a method to reduce amplification effects on models trained with gender-biased datasets. Koolen and van Cranenburgh (2017) examine the relationship between author gender and text attributes, noting the potential for researcher interpretation bias in such studies. Both Larson (2017) and Koolen and van Cranenburgh (2017) offer guidelines to NLP researchers and computational social scientists who wish to predict gender as a variable. Hovy and Spruit (2016) introduce a helpful set of terminology for identifying and categorizing types of bias that manifest in AI systems, including *overgeneralization*, which we observe in our work here.

Finally, we note independent but closely related work by Zhao et al. (2018), published concurrently with this paper. In their work, Zhao et al. (2018) also propose a Winograd schema-like test for gender bias in coreference resolution systems (called "WinoBias"). Though similar in appearance, these two efforts have notable differences in substance and emphasis. The contribution of this work is focused primarily on schema construction and validation, with extensive analysis of observed system bias, revealing its correlation with biases present in real-world and textual statistics; by contrast, Zhao et al. (2018) present methods of debiasing existing systems, showing that simple approaches such as augmenting training data with gender-swapped examples or directly editing noun phrase counts in the B&L resource are effective at reducing system bias, as measured by the schemas. Complementary differences exist between the two schema formulations: Winogender schemas (this work) include gender-neutral pronouns, are syntactically diverse, and are human-validated; WinoBias includes (and delineates) sentences resolvable from syntax alone; a Winogender schema has one occupational mention and one "other participant" mention; WinoBias has two occupational mentions. Due to these differences, we encourage future evaluations to make use of both datasets.

6   Conclusion and Future Work

We have introduced "Winogender schemas," a pronoun resolution task in the style of Winograd schemas that enables us to uncover gender bias in coreference resolution systems. We evaluate three publicly-available, off-the-shelf systems and find systematic gender bias in each: for many occupations, systems strongly prefer to resolve pronouns of one gender over another. We demonstrate that this preferential behavior correlates both with real-world employment statistics and the text statistics that these systems use. We posit that these systems *overgeneralize* the attribute of gender, leading them to make errors that humans do not make on this evaluation. We hope that by drawing attention to this issue, future systems will be designed in ways that mitigate gender-based overgeneralization.

It is important to underscore the limitations of Winogender schemas. As a diagnostic test of gender bias, we view the schemas as having high *positive predictive value* and low *negative predictive value*; that is, they may demonstrate the presence of gender bias in a system, but not prove its absence. Here we have focused on examples of occupational gender bias, but Winogender schemas may be extended broadly to probe for other manifestations of gender bias. Though we have used human-validated schemas to demonstrate that existing NLP systems are comparatively more prone to gender-based overgeneralization, we do not presume that matching human judgment is the ultimate objective of this line of research. Rather, human judgements, which carry their own implicit biases, serve as a lower bound for equitability in automated systems.

Acknowledgments

The authors thank Rebecca Knowles and Chandler May for their valuable feedback on this work. This research was supported by the JHU HLT-COE, DARPA AIDA, and NSF-GRFP (1232825). The U.S. Government is authorized to reproduce and distribute reprints for Governmental purposes. The views and conclusions contained in this publication are those of the authors and should not be interpreted as representing official policies or endorsements of DARPA or the U.S. Government.

References

Solon Barocas and Andrew D Selbst. 2016. Big data's disparate impact. *California Law Review*, pages 104(3):671–732.

Shane Bergsma and Dekang Lin. 2006. Bootstrapping path-based pronoun resolution. In *Proceedings of the 21st International Conference on Computational Linguistics and 44th Annual Meeting of the Association for Computational Linguistics*, pages 33–40, Sydney, Australia. Association for Computational Linguistics.

Alex Beutel, Jilin Chen, Zhe Zhao, and Ed H. Chi. 2017. Data decisions and theoretical implications when adversarially learning fair representations. *CoRR*, abs/1707.00075.

Anders Björkelund and Jonas Kuhn. 2014. Learning structured perceptrons for coreference resolution with latent antecedents and non-local features. In *Proceedings of the 52nd Annual Meeting of the Association for Computational Linguistics (Volume 1: Long Papers)*, pages 47–57, Baltimore, Maryland. Association for Computational Linguistics.

Tolga Bolukbasi, Kai-Wei Chang, James Y Zou, Venkatesh Saligrama, and Adam T Kalai. 2016. Man is to computer programmer as woman is to homemaker? debiasing word embeddings. In D. D. Lee, M. Sugiyama, U. V. Luxburg, I. Guyon, and R. Garnett, editors, *Advances in Neural Information Processing Systems 29*, pages 4349–4357. Curran Associates, Inc.

Aylin Caliskan, Joanna J. Bryson, and Arvind Narayanan. 2017. Semantics derived automatically from language corpora contain human-like biases. *Science*, 356(6334):183–186.

Kevin Clark and Christopher D. Manning. 2016a. Deep reinforcement learning for mention-ranking coreference models. In *Empirical Methods on Natural Language Processing (EMNLP)*.

Kevin Clark and Christopher D. Manning. 2016b. Improving coreference resolution by learning entity-level distributed representations. In *Association for Computational Linguistics (ACL)*.

Greg Durrett and Dan Klein. 2013. Easy victories and uphill battles in coreference resolution. In *Proceedings of the Conference on Empirical Methods in Natural Language Processing*, Seattle, Washington. Association for Computational Linguistics.

Nikhil Garg, Londa Schiebinger, Dan Jurafsky, and James Zou. 2018. Word embeddings quantify 100 years of gender and ethnic stereotypes. *Proceedings of the National Academy of Sciences*.

Dirk Hovy and Shannon L. Spruit. 2016. The social impact of natural language processing. In *Proceedings of the 54th Annual Meeting of the Association for Computational Linguistics (Volume 2: Short Papers)*, pages 591–598, Berlin, Germany. Association for Computational Linguistics.

Corina Koolen and Andreas van Cranenburgh. 2017. These are not the stereotypes you are looking for: Bias and fairness in authorial gender attribution. In *Proceedings of the First ACL Workshop on Ethics in Natural Language Processing*, pages 12–22, Valencia, Spain. Association for Computational Linguistics.

Brian Larson. 2017. Gender as a variable in natural-language processing: Ethical considerations. In *Proceedings of the First ACL Workshop on Ethics in Natural Language Processing*, pages 1–11, Valencia, Spain. Association for Computational Linguistics.

Heeyoung Lee, Yves Peirsman, Angel Chang, Nathanael Chambers, Mihai Surdeanu, and Dan Jurafsky. 2011. Stanford's multi-pass sieve coreference resolution system at the conll-2011 shared task. In *Conference on Natural Language Learning (CoNLL) Shared Task*.

Hector J. Levesque, Ernest Davis, and Leora Morgenstern. 2011. The winograd schema challenge. In *KR*.

Emiel van Miltenburg. 2016. Stereotyping and bias in the flickr30k dataset. *MMC*.

Sameer Pradhan, Alessandro Moschitti, Nianwen Xue, Olga Uryupina, and Yuchen Zhang. 2012. CoNLL-2012 shared task: Modeling multilingual unrestricted coreference in OntoNotes. In *Proceedings of the Sixteenth Conference on Computational Natural Language Learning (CoNLL 2012)*, Jeju, Korea.

Sameer Pradhan, Lance Ramshaw, Mitchell Marcus, Martha Palmer, Ralph Weischedel, and Nianwen Xue. 2011. Conll-2011 shared task: Modeling unrestricted coreference in ontonotes. In *Proceedings of the Fifteenth Conference on Computational Natural Language Learning (CoNLL 2011)*, Portland, Oregon.

Rachel Rudinger, Chandler May, and Benjamin Van Durme. 2017. Social bias in elicited natural language inferences. In *Proceedings of the First ACL Workshop on Ethics in Natural Language Processing*, pages 74–79, Valencia, Spain. Association for Computational Linguistics.

Rachael Tatman. 2017. Gender and dialect bias in youtube's automatic captions. In *Proceedings of the First ACL Workshop on Ethics in Natural Language Processing*, pages 53–59, Valencia, Spain. Association for Computational Linguistics.

Mikaela Wapman and Deborah Belle. 2014. Undergraduate thesis. https://mikaelawapman.com/category/gender-schemas/.

Sam Wiseman, Alexander M. Rush, Stuart Shieber, and Jason Weston. 2015. Learning anaphoricity and antecedent ranking features for coreference resolution. In *Proceedings of the 53rd Annual Meeting of the Association for Computational Linguistics and the 7th International Joint Conference on Natural Language Processing (Volume 1: Long Papers)*, pages 1416–1426. Association for Computational Linguistics.

Sam Wiseman, Alexander M. Rush, and Stuart M. Shieber. 2016. Learning global features for coreference resolution. In *Proceedings of the 2016 Conference of the North American Chapter of the Association for Computational Linguistics: Human Language Technologies*, pages 994–1004, San Diego, California. Association for Computational Linguistics.

Brian Hu Zhang, Blake Lemoine, and Margaret Mitchell. 2018. Mitigating unwanted biases with adversarial learning. In *Proceedings of the First AAAI/ACM Conference on AI, Ethics, and Society*.

Jieyu Zhao, Tianlu Wang, Mark Yatskar, Vicente Ordonez, and Kai-Wei Chang. 2017. Men also like shopping: Reducing gender bias amplification using corpus-level constraints. In *Proceedings of the 2017 Conference on Empirical Methods in Natural Language Processing*, pages 2979–2989, Copenhagen, Denmark. Association for Computational Linguistics.

Jieyu Zhao, Tianlu Wang, Mark Yatskar, Vicente Ordonez, and Kai-Wei Chang. 2018. Gender bias in coreference resolution: Evaluation and debiasing methods. In *Proceedings of the 2018 Conference of the North American Chapter of the Association for Computational Linguistics: Human Language Technologies*, New Orleans, Louisiana. Association for Computational Linguistics.

Gender Bias in Coreference Resolution:
Evaluation and Debiasing Methods

Jieyu Zhao[§]   **Tianlu Wang**[†]   **Mark Yatskar**[‡]
Vicente Ordonez[†]   **Kai-Wei Chang**[§]
[§]University of California, Los Angeles   {jyzhao, kwchang}@cs.ucla.edu
[†] University of Virginia   {tw8bc, vicente}@virginia.edu
[‡]Allen Institute for Artificial Intelligence   marky@allenai.org

Abstract

We introduce a new benchmark, WinoBias, for coreference resolution focused on gender bias. Our corpus contains Winograd-schema style sentences with entities corresponding to people referred by their occupation (e.g. the nurse, the doctor, the carpenter). We demonstrate that a rule-based, a feature-rich, and a neural coreference system all link gendered pronouns to pro-stereotypical entities with higher accuracy than anti-stereotypical entities, by an average difference of 21.1 in F1 score. Finally, we demonstrate a data-augmentation approach that, in combination with existing word-embedding debiasing techniques, removes the bias demonstrated by these systems in WinoBias without significantly affecting their performance on existing coreference benchmark datasets. Our dataset and code are available at http://winobias.org.

1 Introduction

Coreference resolution is a task aimed at identifying phrases (mentions) referring to the same entity. Various approaches, including rule-based (Raghunathan et al., 2010), feature-based (Durrett and Klein, 2013; Peng et al., 2015a), and neural-network based (Clark and Manning, 2016; Lee et al., 2017) have been proposed. While significant advances have been made, systems carry the risk of relying on societal stereotypes present in training data that could significantly impact their performance for some demographic groups.

In this work, we test the hypothesis that coreference systems exhibit gender bias by creating a new challenge corpus, WinoBias.This dataset follows the winograd format (Hirst, 1981; Rahman and Ng, 2012; Peng et al., 2015b), and contains references to people using a vocabulary of 40 occupations. It contains two types of challenge sentences that require linking gendered pro-

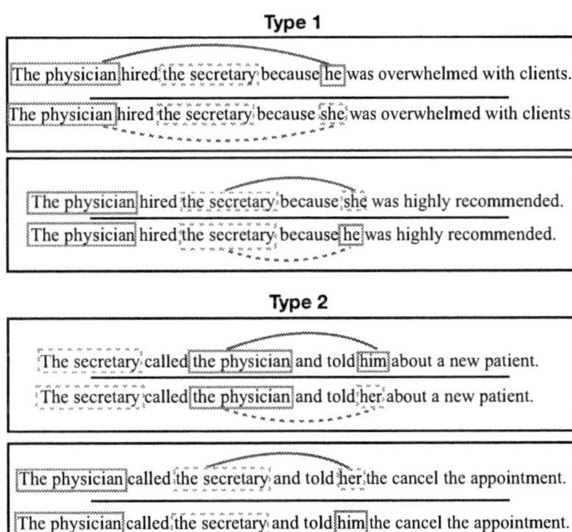

Figure 1: Pairs of gender balanced co-reference tests in the WinoBias dataset. Male and female entities are marked in solid blue and dashed orange, respectively. For each example, the gender of the pronominal reference is irrelevant for the co-reference decision. Systems must be able to make correct linking predictions in pro-stereotypical scenarios (solid purple lines) and anti-stereotypical scenarios (dashed purple lines) equally well to pass the test. Importantly, stereotypical occupations are considered based on US Department of Labor statistics.

nouns to either male or female stereotypical occupations (see the illustrative examples in Figure 1). None of the examples can be disambiguated by the gender of the pronoun but this cue can potentially distract the model. We consider a system to be gender biased if it links pronouns to occupations dominated by the gender of the pronoun (pro-stereotyped condition) more accurately than occupations not dominated by the gender of the pronoun (anti-stereotyped condition). The corpus can be used to certify a system has gender bias.[1]

We use three different systems as prototypi-

---

[1]Note that the counter argument (i.e., systems are gender bias free) may not hold.

15

Proceedings of NAACL-HLT 2018, pages 15–20
New Orleans, Louisiana, June 1 - 6, 2018. ©2018 Association for Computational Linguistics

cal examples: the Stanford Deterministic Coreference System (Raghunathan et al., 2010), the Berkeley Coreference Resolution System (Durrett and Klein, 2013) and the current best published system: the UW End-to-end Neural Coreference Resolution System (Lee et al., 2017). Despite qualitatively different approaches, all systems exhibit gender bias, showing an average difference in performance between pro-stereotypical and anti-stereotyped conditions of 21.1 in F1 score. Finally we show that given sufficiently strong alternative cues, systems can ignore their bias.

In order to study the source of this bias, we analyze the training corpus used by these systems, Ontonotes 5.0 (Weischedel et al., 2012).[2] Our analysis shows that female entities are significantly underrepresented in this corpus. To reduce the impact of such dataset bias, we propose to generate an auxiliary dataset where all male entities are replaced by female entities, and vice versa, using a rule-based approach. Methods can then be trained on the union of the original and auxiliary dataset. In combination with methods that remove bias from fixed resources such as word embeddings (Bolukbasi et al., 2016), our data augmentation approach completely eliminates bias when evaluating on WinoBias , without significantly affecting overall coreference accuracy.

2 WinoBias

To better identify gender bias in coreference resolution systems, we build a new dataset centered on people entities referred by their occupations from a vocabulary of 40 occupations gathered from the US Department of Labor, shown in Table 1.[3] We use the associated occupation statistics to determine what constitutes gender stereotypical roles (e.g. 90% of nurses are women in this survey). Entities referred by different occupations are paired and used to construct test case scenarios. Sentences are duplicated using male and female pronouns, and contain equal numbers of correct coreference decisions for all occupations. In total, the dataset contains 3,160 sentences, split equally for development and test, created by researchers familiar with the project. Sentences were created to follow two prototypical templates but annotators were encouraged to come up with scenar-

Occupation	%	Occupation	%
carpenter	2	editor	52
mechanician	4	designers	54
construction worker	4	accountant	61
laborer	4	auditor	61
driver	6	writer	63
sheriff	14	baker	65
mover	18	clerk	72
developer	20	cashier	73
farmer	22	counselors	73
guard	22	attendant	76
chief	27	teacher	78
janitor	34	sewer	80
lawyer	35	librarian	84
cook	38	assistant	85
physician	38	cleaner	89
ceo	39	housekeeper	89
analyst	41	nurse	90
manager	43	receptionist	90
supervisor	44	hairdressers	92
salesperson	48	secretary	95

Table 1: Occupations statistics used in WinoBias dataset, organized by the percent of people in the occupation who are reported as female. When woman dominate profession, we call linking the noun phrase referring to the job with female and male pronoun as 'pro-stereotypical', and 'anti-stereotypical', respectively. Similarly, if the occupation is male dominated, linking the noun phrase with the male and female pronoun is called, 'pro-stereotypical' and 'anti-steretypical', respectively.

ios where entities could be interacting in plausible ways. Templates were selected to be challenging and designed to cover cases requiring semantics and syntax separately.[4]

Type 1: [entity1] [interacts with] [entity2] [conjunction] [pronoun] [circumstances]. Prototypical WinoCoRef style sentences, where co-reference decisions must be made using world knowledge about given circumstances (Figure 1; Type 1). Such examples are challenging because they contain no syntactic cues.

Type 2: [entity1] [interacts with] [entity2] and then [interacts with] [pronoun] for [circumstances]. These tests can be resolved using syntactic information and understanding of the pronoun (Figure 1; Type 2). We expect systems to do well on such cases because both semantic and syntactic cues help disambiguation.

Evaluation To evaluate models, we split the data in two sections: one where correct co-reference decisions require linking a gendered

---

[2]The corpus is used in CoNLL-2011 and CoNLL-2012 shared tasks, http://www.conll.org/previous-tasks

[3]Labor Force Statistics from the Current Population Survey, 2017. https://www.bls.gov/cps/cpsaat11.htm

[4]We do not claim this set of templates is complete, but that they provide representative examples that, pratically, show bias in existing systems.

pronoun to an occupation stereotypically associated with the gender of the pronoun and one that requires linking to the anti-stereotypical occupation. We say that a model passes the WinoBias test if for both Type 1 and Type 2 examples, pro-stereotyped and anti-stereotyped co-reference decisions are made with the same accuracy.

3 Gender Bias in Co-reference

In this section, we highlight two sources of gender bias in co-reference systems that can cause them to fail WinoBias: training data and auxiliary resources and propose strategies to mitigate them.

3.1 Training Data Bias

Bias in OntoNotes 5.0 Resources supporting the training of co-reference systems have severe gender imbalance. In general, entities that have a mention headed by gendered pronouns (e.g."he", "she") are over 80% male.[5] Furthermore, the way in which such entities are referred to, varies significantly. Male gendered mentions are more than twice as likely to contain a job title as female mentions.[6] Moreover, these trends hold across genres.

Gender Swapping To remove such bias, we construct an additional training corpus where all male entities are swapped for female entities and vice-versa. Methods can then be trained on both original and swapped corpora. This approach maintains non-gender-revealing correlations while eliminating correlations between gender and co-reference cues.

We adopt a simple rule based approach for gender swapping. First, we anonymize named entities using an automatic named entity finder (Lample et al., 2016). Named entities are replaced consistently within document (i.e. "Barak Obama ... Obama was re-elected." would be annoymized to "E1 E2 ... E2 was re-elected."). Then we build a dictionary of gendered terms and their realization as the opposite gender by asking workers on Amazon Mechnical Turk to annotate all unique spans in the OntoNotes development set.[7]

---

[5]To exclude mentions such as "his mother", we use Collins head finder (Collins, 2003) to identify the head word of each mention, and only consider the mentions whose head word is gender pronoun.

[6]We pick more than 900 job titles from a gazetteer.

[7]Five turkers were presented with anonymized spans and asked to mark if it indicated male, female, or neither, and if male or female, rewrite it so it refers to the other gender.

Rules were then mined by computing the word difference between initial and edited spans. Common rules included "she → he", "Mr." → "Mrs.", "mother" → "father." Sometimes the same initial word was edited to multiple different phrases: these were resolved by taking the most frequent phrase, with the exception of "her → him" and "her → his" which were resolved using part-of-speech. Rules were applied to all matching tokens in the OntoNotes. We maintain anonymization so that cases like "John went to his house" can be accurately swapped to "E1 went to her house."

3.2 Resource Bias

Word Embeddings Word embeddings are widely used in NLP applications however recent work has shown that they are severely biased: "man" tends to be closer to "programmer" than "woman" (Bolukbasi et al., 2016; Caliskan et al., 2017). Current state-of-art co-reference systems build on word embeddings and risk inheriting their bias. To reduce bias from this resource, we replace GloVe embeddings with debiased vectors (Bolukbasi et al., 2016).

Gender Lists While current neural approaches rely heavily on pre-trained word embeddings, previous feature rich and rule-based approaches rely on corpus based gender statistics mined from external resources (Bergsma and Lin, 2006). Such lists were generated from large unlabeled corpora using heuristic data mining methods. These resources provide counts for how often a noun phrase is observed in a male, female, neutral, and plural context. To reduce this bias, we balance male and female counts for all noun phrases.

4 Results

In this section we evaluate of three representative systems: rule based, Rule, (Raghunathan et al., 2010), feature-rich, Feature, (Durrett and Klein, 2013), and end-to-end neural (the current state-of-the-art), E2E, (Lee et al., 2017). The following sections show that performance on WinoBias reveals gender bias in all systems, that our methods remove such bias, and that systems are less biased on OntoNotes data.

WinoBias Reveals Gender Bias Table 2 summarizes development set evaluations using all three systems. Systems were evaluated on both types of sentences in WinoBias (T1 and T2), sepa-

Method	Anon.	Resour.	Aug.	OntoNotes	T1-p	T1-a	Avg	Diff	T2-p	T2-a	Avg	Diff
E2E				**67.7**	**76.0**	49.4	62.7	26.6*	**88.7**	75.2	82.0	13.5*
E2E	✓			66.4	73.5	51.2	62.6	21.3*	86.3	70.3	78.3	16.1*
E2E	✓	✓		66.5	67.2	59.3	63.2	7.9*	81.4	82.3	81.9	0.9
E2E	✓		✓	66.2	65.1	59.2	62.2	5.9*	86.5	**83.7**	**85.1**	2.8*
E2E	✓	✓	✓	66.3	63.9	**62.8**	**63.4**	**1.1**	81.3	83.4	82.4	**2.1**
Feature				**61.7**	**66.7**	56.0	61.4	10.6*	**73.0**	57.4	65.2	15.7*
Feature	✓			61.3	65.9	56.8	61.3	9.1*	72.0	58.5	65.3	13.5*
Feature	✓	✓		61.2	61.8	**62.0**	**61.9**	**0.2**	67.1	63.5	65.3	3.6
Feature	✓		✓	61.0	65.0	57.3	61.2	7.7*	72.8	63.2	68.0	9.6*
Feature	✓	✓	✓	61.0	62.3	60.4	61.4	1.9*	71.1	**68.6**	**69.9**	**2.5**
Rule				57.0	76.7	37.5	57.1	39.2*	50.5	29.2	39.9	21.3*

Table 2: F1 on OntoNotes and WinoBias development set. WinoBias results are split between Type-1 and Type-2 and in pro/anti-stereotypical conditions. * indicates the difference between pro/anti stereotypical conditions is significant ($p < .05$) under an approximate randomized test (Graham et al., 2014). Our methods eliminate the difference between pro-stereotypical and anti-stereotypical conditions (Diff), with little loss in performance (OntoNotes and Avg).

Method	Anon.	Resour.	Aug.	OntoNotes	T1-p	T1-a	Avg	Diff	T2-p	T2-a	Avg	Diff
E2E				**67.2**	**74.9**	47.7	61.3	27.2*	**88.6**	77.3	**82.9**	11.3*
E2E	✓	✓	✓	66.5	62.4	**60.3**	**61.3**	**2.1**	78.4	**78.0**	78.2	**0.4**
Feature				**64.0**	**62.9**	58.3	60.6	4.6*	**68.5**	57.8	63.1	10.7*
Feature	✓	✓	✓	63.6	62.2	**60.6**	**61.4**	**1.7**	**70.0**	**69.5**	**69.7**	**0.6**
Rule				58.7	72.0	37.5	54.8	34.5*	47.8	26.6	37.2	21.2*

Table 3: F1 on OntoNotes and Winobias test sets. Methods were run once, supporting development set conclusions.

Model	Original	Gender-reversed
E2E	66.4	65.9
Feature	61.3	60.3

Table 4: Performance on the original and the gender-reversed developments dataset (anonymized).

rately in pro-stereotyped and anti-stereotyped conditions (T1-p vs. T1-a, T2-p vs T2-a). We evaluate the effect of named-entity anonymization (Anon.), debiasing supporting resources[8] (Resour.) and using data-augmentation through gender swapping (Aug.). E2E and Feature were retrained in each condition using default hyperparameters while Rule was not debiased because it is untrainable. We evaluate using the coreference scorer v8.01 (Pradhan et al., 2014) and compute the average (Avg) and absolute difference (Diff) between pro-stereotyped and anti-stereotyped conditions in WinoBias.

All initial systems demonstrate severe disparity between pro-stereotyped and anti-stereotyped conditions. Overall, the rule based system is most biased, followed by the neural approach and feature rich approach. Across all conditions, anonymization impacts E2E the most, while all other debiasing methods result in insignificant loss

in performance on the OntoNotes dataset. Removing biased resources and data-augmentation reduce bias independently and more so in combination, allowing both E2E and Feature to pass WinoBias without significantly impacting performance on either OntoNotes or WinoBias . Qualitatively, the neural system is easiest to de-bias and our approaches could be applied to future end-to-end systems. Systems were evaluated once on test sets, Table 3, supporting our conclusions.

Systems Demonstrate Less Bias on OntoNotes While we have demonstrated co-reference systems have severe bias as measured in WinoBias , this is an out-of-domain test for systems trained on OntoNotes. Evaluating directly within OntoNotes is challenging because sub-sampling documents with more female entities would leave very few evaluation data points. Instead, we apply our gender swapping system (Section 3), to the OntoNotes development set and compare system performance between swapped and unswapped data.[9] If a system shows significant difference between original and gender-reversed conditions, then we would consider it gender biased on OntoNotes data.

Table 4 summarizes our results. The E2E sys-

---

[8]Word embeddings for E2E and gender lists for Feature

[9]This test provides a lower bound on OntoNotes bias because some mistakes can result from errors introduce by the gender swapping system.

tem does not demonstrate significant degradation in performance, while **Feature** loses roughly 1.0-F1.[10] This demonstrates that given sufficient alternative signal, systems often do ignore gender biased cues. On the other hand, WinoBias provides an analysis of system bias in an adversarial setup, showing, when examples are challenging, systems are likely to make gender biased predictions.

5   Related Work

Machine learning methods are designed to generalize from observation but if algorithms inadvertently learn to make predictions based on stereotyped associations they risk amplifying existing social problems. Several problematic instances have been demonstrated, for example, word embeddings can encode sexist stereotypes (Bolukbasi et al., 2016; Caliskan et al., 2017). Similar observations have been made in vision and language models (Zhao et al., 2017), online news (Ross and Carter, 2011), web search (Kay et al., 2015) and advertisements (Sweeney, 2013). In our work, we add a unique focus on co-reference, and propose simple general purpose methods for reducing bias.

Implicit human bias can come from imbalanced datasets. When making decisions on such datasets, it is usual that under-represented samples in the data are neglected since they do not influence the overall accuracy as much. For binary classification Kamishima et al. (2012, 2011) add a regularization term to their objective that penalizes biased predictions. Various other approaches have been proposed to produce "fair" classifiers (Calders et al., 2009; Feldman et al., 2015; Misra et al., 2016). For structured prediction, the work of Zhao et al. (2017) reduces bias by using corpus level constraints, but is only practical for models with specialized structure. Kusner et al. (2017) propose the method based on causal inference to achieve the model fairness where they do the data augmentation under specific cases, however, to the best of our knowledge, we are the first to propose data augmentation based on gender swapping in order to reduce gender bias.

Concurrent work (Rudinger et al., 2018) also studied gender bias in coreference resolution systems, and created a similar job title based, winograd-style, co-reference dataset to demonstrate bias [11]. Their work corroborates our findings of bias and expands the set of systems shown to be biased while we add a focus on debiasing methods. Future work can evaluate on both datasets.

6   Conclusion

Bias in NLP systems has the potential to not only mimic but also amplify stereotypes in society. For a prototypical problem, coreference, we provide a method for detecting such bias and show that three systems are significantly gender biased. We also provide evidence that systems, given sufficient cues, can ignore their bias. Finally, we present general purpose methods for making co-reference models more robust to spurious, gender-biased cues while not incurring significant penalties on their performance on benchmark datasets.

Acknowledgement

This work was supported in part by National Science Foundation Grant IIS-1760523, two NVIDIA GPU Grants, and a Google Faculty Research Award. We would like to thank Luke Zettlemoyer, Eunsol Choi, and Mohit Iyyer for helpful discussion and feedback.

References

Shane Bergsma and Dekang Lin. 2006. Bootstrapping path-based pronoun resolution. In *ACL*.

Tolga Bolukbasi, Kai-Wei Chang, James Zou, Venkatesh Saligrama, and Adam Kalai. 2016. Man is to computer programmer as woman is to homemaker? debiasing word embeddings. In *NIPS*.

Toon Calders, Faisal Kamiran, and Mykola Pechenizkiy. 2009. Building classifiers with independency constraints. In *Data mining workshops, 2009. ICDMW'09. IEEE international conference on*. IEEE, pages 13–18.

Aylin Caliskan, Joanna J Bryson, and Arvind Narayanan. 2017. Semantics derived automatically from language corpora contain human-like biases. *Science* 356(6334):183–186.

Kevin Clark and Christopher D. Manning. 2016. Deep reinforcement learning for mention-ranking coreference models. In *Empirical Methods on Natural Language Processing*.

Michael Collins. 2003. Head-driven statistical models for natural language parsing. *Computational linguistics* 29(4):589–637.

---

[10]We do not evaluate the **Rule** system as it cannot be train for anonymized input.

[11]Their dataset also includes gender neutral pronouns and examples containing one job title instead of two.

Greg Durrett and Dan Klein. 2013. Easy victories and uphill battles in coreference resolution. In *Proceedings of the Conference on Empirical Methods in Natural Language Processing*. Association for Computational Linguistics, Seattle, Washington.

Michael Feldman, Sorelle A Friedler, John Moeller, Carlos Scheidegger, and Suresh Venkatasubramanian. 2015. Certifying and removing disparate impact. pages 259–268.

Yvette Graham, Nitika Mathur, and Timothy Baldwin. 2014. Randomized significance tests in machine translation. In *WMT@ ACL*. pages 266–274.

Graeme Hirst. 1981. Anaphora in natural language understanding. *Berlin Springer Verlag* .

Toshihiro Kamishima, Shotaro Akaho, Hideki Asoh, and Jun Sakuma. 2012. Fairness-aware classifier with prejudice remover regularizer. *Machine Learning and Knowledge Discovery in Databases* pages 35–50.

Toshihiro Kamishima, Shotaro Akaho, and Jun Sakuma. 2011. Fairness-aware learning through regularization approach. In *Data Mining Workshops (ICDMW), 2011 IEEE 11th International Conference on*. IEEE, pages 643–650.

Matthew Kay, Cynthia Matuszek, and Sean A Munson. 2015. Unequal representation and gender stereotypes in image search results for occupations. In *Human Factors in Computing Systems*. ACM, pages 3819–3828.

Matt J Kusner, Joshua Loftus, Chris Russell, and Ricardo Silva. 2017. Counterfactual fairness. In *Advances in Neural Information Processing Systems*. pages 4069–4079.

Guillaume Lample, Miguel Ballesteros, Sandeep Subramanian, Kazuya Kawakami, and Chris Dyer. 2016. Neural architectures for named entity recognition. *arXiv preprint arXiv:1603.01360* .

Kenton Lee, Luheng He, Mike Lewis, and Luke Zettlemoyer. 2017. End-to-end neural coreference resolution. In *EMNLP*.

Ishan Misra, C Lawrence Zitnick, Margaret Mitchell, and Ross Girshick. 2016. Seeing through the human reporting bias: Visual classifiers from noisy human-centric labels. In *CVPR*. pages 2930–2939.

Haoruo Peng, Kai-Wei Chang, and Dan Roth. 2015a. A joint framework for coreference resolution and mention head detection. In *CoNLL*. page 10.

Haoruo Peng, Daniel Khashabi, and Dan Roth. 2015b. Solving hard coreference problems. In *NAACL*.

Sameer Pradhan, Xiaoqiang Luo, Marta Recasens, Eduard Hovy, Vincent Ng, and Michael Strube. 2014. Scoring coreference partitions of predicted mentions: A reference implementation. In *ACL*.

Karthik Raghunathan, Heeyoung Lee, Sudarshan Rangarajan, Nathanael Chambers, Mihai Surdeanu, Dan Jurafsky, and Christopher Manning. 2010. A multipass sieve for coreference resolution. In *EMNLP*. pages 492–501.

Altaf Rahman and Vincent Ng. 2012. Resolving complex cases of definite pronouns: The winograd schema challenge. In *EMNLP*. pages 777–789.

Karen Ross and Cynthia Carter. 2011. Women and news: A long and winding road. *Media, Culture & Society* 33(8):1148–1165.

Rachel Rudinger, Jason Naradowsky, Brian Leonard, and Benjamin Van Durme. 2018. Gender bias in coreference resolution. In *NAACL*.

Latanya Sweeney. 2013. Discrimination in online ad delivery. *Queue* 11(3):10.

Ralph Weischedel, Sameer Pradhan, Lance Ramshaw, Jeff Kaufman, Michelle Franchini, Mohammed El-Bachouti, Nianwen Xue, Martha Palmer, Jena D Hwang, Claire Bonial, et al. 2012. Ontonotes release 5.0 .

Jieyu Zhao, Tianlu Wang, Mark Yatskar, Vicente Ordonez, and Kai-Wei Chang. 2017. Men also like shopping: Reducing gender bias amplification using corpus-level constraints. In *EMNLP*.

Integrating Stance Detection and Fact Checking in a Unified Corpus

Ramy Baly[1], Mitra Mohtarami[1], James Glass[1]
Lluís Màrquez[3*], Alessandro Moschitti[3*], Preslav Nakov[2]
[1]MIT Computer Science and Artificial Intelligence Laboratory, MA, USA
[2]Qatar Computing Research Institute, HBKU, Qatar; [3]Amazon
{baly,mitram,glass}@mit.edu
{lluismv,amosch}@amazon.com; pnakov@qf.org.qa

Abstract

A reasonable approach for fact checking a claim involves retrieving potentially relevant documents from different sources (e.g., news websites, social media, etc.), determining the stance of each document with respect to the claim, and finally making a prediction about the claim's factuality by aggregating the strength of the stances, while taking the reliability of the source into account. Moreover, a fact checking system should be able to explain its decision by providing relevant extracts (rationales) from the documents. Yet, this setup is not directly supported by existing datasets, which treat fact checking, document retrieval, source credibility, stance detection and rationale extraction as independent tasks. In this paper, we support the interdependencies between these tasks as annotations in the same corpus. We implement this setup on an Arabic fact checking corpus, the first of its kind.

1 Introduction

Fact checking has recently emerged as an important research topic due to the unprecedented amount of fake news and rumors that are flooding the Internet in order to manipulate people's opinions (Darwish et al., 2017a; Mihaylov et al., 2015a,b; Mihaylov and Nakov, 2016) or to influence the outcome of major events such as political elections (Lazer et al., 2018; Vosoughi et al., 2018). While the number of organizations performing fact checking is growing, these efforts cannot keep up with the pace at which false claims are being produced, including also clickbait (Karadzhov et al., 2017a), hoaxes (Rashkin et al., 2017), and satire (Hardalov et al., 2016). Hence, there is need for automatic fact checking.

While most previous research has focused on English, here we target Arabic. Moreover, we propose some guidelines, which we believe should be taken into account when designing fact-checking corpora, irrespective of the target language.

Automatic fact checking typically involves retrieving potentially relevant documents (news articles, tweets, etc.), determining the stance of each document with respect to the claim, and finally predicting the claim's factuality by aggregating the strength of the different stances, taking into consideration the reliability of the documents' sources (news medium, Twitter account, etc.). Despite the interdependency between *fact checking* and *stance detection*, research on these two problems has not been previously supported by an integrated corpus. This is a gap we aim to bridge by retrieving documents for each claim and annotating them for stance, thus ensuring a natural distribution of the stance labels.

Moreover, in order to be trusted by users, a fact-checking system should be able to explain the reasoning that led to its decisions. This is best supported by showing extracts (such as sentences or phrases) from the retrieved documents that illustrate the detected stance (Lei et al., 2016). Unfortunately, existing datasets do not offer manual annotation of sentence- or phrase-level supporting evidence. While deep neural networks with attention mechanisms can infer and extract such evidence automatically in an unsupervised way (Parikh et al., 2016), potentially better results can be achieved when having the target sentence provided in advance, which enables supervised or semi-supervised training of the attention. This would allow not only more reliable evidence extraction, but also better stance prediction, and ultimately better factuality prediction. Following this idea, our corpus also identifies the most relevant stance-marking sentences.

* This work was carried out when the authors were scientists at QCRI, HBKU.

21

Proceedings of NAACL-HLT 2018, pages 21–27
New Orleans, Louisiana, June 1 - 6, 2018. ©2018 Association for Computational Linguistics

2   Related Work

The connection between fact checking and stance detection has been argued for by Vlachos and Riedel (2014), who envisioned a system that (*i*) identifies factual statements (Hassan et al., 2015; Gencheva et al., 2017; Jaradat et al., 2018), (*ii*) generates questions or queries (Karadzhov et al., 2017b), (*iii*) creates a knowledge base using information extraction and question answering (Ba et al., 2016; Shiralkar et al., 2017), and (*iv*) infers the statements' veracity using text analysis (Banerjee and Han, 2009; Castillo et al., 2011; Rashkin et al., 2017) or information from external sources (Popat et al., 2016; Karadzhov et al., 2017b; Popat et al., 2017). This connection has been also used in practice, e.g., by Popat et al. (2017); however, different datasets had to be used for stance detection vs. fact checking, as no dataset so far has targeted both.

Fact checking is very time-consuming, and thus most datasets focus on claims that have been already checked by experts on specialized sites such as *Snopes* (Ma et al., 2016; Popat et al., 2016, 2017), *PolitiFact* (Wang, 2017), or *Wikipedia hoaxes* (Popat et al., 2016).[1] As fact checking is mainly done for English, non-English datasets are rare and often unnatural, e.g., translated from English, and focusing on US politics.[2] In contrast, we start with claims that are not only relevant to the Arab world, but that were also originally made in Arabic, thus producing the first publicly available Arabic fact-checking dataset.

Stance detection has been studied so far disjointly from fact checking. While there exist some datasets for Arabic (Darwish et al., 2017b), the most popular ones are for English, e.g., from SemEval-2016 Task 6 (Mohammad et al., 2016) and from the Fake News Challenge (FNC).[3] Despite its name, the latter has no annotations for factuality, but consists of article-claim pairs labeled for stance: *agrees*, *disagrees*, *discusses*, and *unrelated*. In contrast, we retrieve documents for each claim, which yields an arguably more natural distribution of stance labels compared to FNC.

Evidence extraction. Finally, an important characteristic of our dataset is that it provides evidence, in terms of text fragments, for the *agree* and *disagree* labels. Having such supporting evidence annotated enables both better learning for supervised systems performing stance detection or fact checking, and also the ability for such systems to learn to explain their decisions to users. Having this latter ability has been recognized in previous work on rationalizing neural predictions (Lei et al., 2016). This is also at the core of recent research on machine comprehension, e.g., using the SQuAD dataset (Rajpurkar et al., 2016). However, such annotations have not been done for stance detection or fact checking before.

Finally, while preparing the camera-ready version of the present paper, we came to know about a new dataset for Fact Extraction and VERification, or FEVER (Thorne et al., 2018), which is somewhat similar to ours as it it about both factuality and stance, and it has annotation for evidence. Yet, it is also different as (*i*) the claims are artificially generated by manually altering Wikipedia text, (*ii*) the knowledge base is restricted to Wikipedia articles, and (*iii*) the stance and the factuality labels are identical, assuming that Wikipedia articles are reliable to be able to decide a claim's veracity. In contrast, we use real claims from news outlets, we retrieve articles from the entire Web, and we keep stance and factuality as separate labels.

3   The Corpus

Our corpus contains claims labeled for factuality (*true* vs. *false*). We associate each claim with several documents, where each claim-document pair is labeled for stance (*agree, disagree, discuss,* or *unrelated*) similar to the FakeNewsChallenge (FNC) dataset. Overall, the process of corpus creation went through several stages – *claim extraction, evidence extraction* and *stance annotation* –, which we describe below.

Claim Extraction   We consider two websites as the source of our claims. VERIFY[4] is a project that was established to expose false claims made about the war in Syria and other related Middle Eastern issues. It is an independent platform that debunks claims made by all parties to the conflict. To the best of our knowledge, this is the only platform that publishes fact-checked claims in Arabic.

---

[1]Annotating from scratch is needed in some cases, e.g., in the context of question answering (Mihaylova et al., 2018), or when targeting credibility (Castillo et al., 2011).

[2]See for example the CLEF-2018 lab on Automatic Identification and Verification of Claims in Political Debates, which features US political debates translated to Arabic: http://alt.qcri.org/clef2018-factcheck/

[3]http://www.fakenewschallenge.org/

[4]http://www.verify-sy.com

It is worth noting that the VERIFY website only shows claims that were debunked as false and misleading, and hence we used it to extract only the *false* claims for our corpus (we extracted the *true* claims from a different source; see below).

We thoroughly preprocessed the original claims. First, we manually identified and excluded all claims discussing falsified multimedia (images or video), which cannot be verified using textual information and NLP techniques only, e.g.

(1) *Pro-regime pages have circulated pictures of fighters fleeing an explosion.*

نشرت صفحَاتٍ موَالية لِلنظَام صور لقَاتلين يهربون من انفجَار

Note that the claims in VERIFY were written in a form that presents the *corrected* information after debunking the original false claim. For instance, the original false claim in example 2a is corrected and published in VERIFY as shown in example 2b. We manually rendered these corrected claims to their original false form, which we used for our corpus.

(2a) (original false claim) *FIFA intends to investigate the game between Syria and Australia.*

الفيفَا تعتزم التحقيق في المبَارَاة بين سوريَا وَاستَرَاليَا

(2b) (corrected claim in VERIFY) *FIFA does not intend to investigate the game between Syria and Australia, as pro-regime pages claim.*

الفيفَا لَا تعتزم التحقيق في المبَارَاة بين سوريَا وَاستَرَليَا، كمَا تدّعِي صفحَات موَالية لِلنظَام.

After extracting the false claims from VERIFY, we collected the true claims of our corpus from REUTERS[5] by extracting headlines of news documents. We used a list of manually selected keywords to extract claims with the same topics as those extracted from VERIFY.

Then, we manually excluded claims that contained political rhetorical statements (see example 3 below), multiple facts, accusations or denials, and ultimately we only kept those claims that discuss factual events, i.e., that can be verified.

(3) *Presidents Vladimir Putin and Recep Tayyip Erdogan hope that Astana talks will lead to peace.*

الرئِيسَان فِلَادِيمير بوتين ورجب طيّب اردوغَان يَأملان بَأن محَادثاتٍ استَانة سوف تُؤدي الَى السلَام.

Overall, starting with 1,381 claims, we ended up with 422 worth-checking claims: 219 *false* claims from VERIFY, and 203 *true* claims from REUTERS.

Evidence Extraction Following the assumption that identifying stance towards claims can help predict their veracity, we want to associate each claim with supporting and opposing pieces of textual evidence. We used the Google custom search API for document retrieval, and we performed the following steps to increase the likelihood of retrieving relevant documents. First, as in (Karadzhov et al., 2017b), we transformed each claim into sub-queries by selecting named entities, adjectives, nouns and verbs with the highest TF.DF score, calculated on a collection of documents from the claims' sources. Then, we used these sub-queries with the claim itself as input to the search API and retrieved the first 20 returned links, from which we excluded those directing to VERIFY and REUTERS, and social media websites that are mostly opinionated. Finally, we calculated two similarity measures between the links' content (documents) and the claims: the tri-gram containment (Lyon et al., 2001) and the cosine distance between average word embeddings of both texts.[6]. We only kept documents with non-zero values for both measures, yielding 3,042 documents: 1,239 for false claims and 1,803 for true claims.

---

[6]Word embeddings were generated by training the GloVe (Pennington et al., 2014) model on the Arabic Gigaword (Parker et al., 2011)

Stance Annotation: We used CrowdFlower to recruit Arabic speakers to annotate the claim-document pairs for stance. Each pair was assigned to 3–5 annotators, who were asked to assign one of the following standard labels (also used at FNC): *agree*, *disagree*, *discuss* and *unrelated*. First, we conducted small-scale pilot tasks to fine-tune the guidelines and to ensure their clarity. The annotators were also asked to focus on the stance of the document towards the claim, regardless of the factuality of either text. This ensures that stance is captured without bias, so it can be used later with other information (e.g., time, website's credibility, author reliability) to predict factuality. Finally, the annotators were asked to specify segments in the documents representing the *rationales* that made them assign *agree* or *disagree* as labels. For quality control purposes, we further created a small hidden test set by annotating 50 pairs ourselves, and we used it to monitor the annotators' performance, keeping only those who maintained an accuracy of over 75%.

Ultimately, we used majority voting to aggregate stance labels for each pair, using the annotators' performance scores to break ties. On average, 77% of the annotators for each claim-document pair agreed on its label, thus allowing proper majority aggregation for most pairs. A total of 133 pairs with significant annotation disagreement required us to manually check and correct the proposed annotations. We further automatically refined the documents by (*i*) excluding sentences with more than 200 words, and (*ii*) limiting the size of a document to 100 sentences. Such extra-long documents tend to originate from crawling ill-structured websites, or from parsing some specific types of websites such as web forums.

Table 1 shows the distribution over the stance labels,[7] which turns out to be very similar to that for the FNC dataset. We can see that there are very few documents disagreeing with *true* claims (about 0.5%), which suggests that stance is positively correlated with factuality. However, the number of documents agreeing with *false* documents is larger than the number of documents disagreeing with them, which illustrates one of the main challenges when trying to predict the factuality of news based on stance.

---

[7]The corpus is available at http://groups.csail. mit.edu/sls/downloads/
and also at http://alt.qcri.org/resources/

Claims	Annotated Documents	Stance (document-to-claim)			
		Agree	*Disagree*	*Discuss*	*Unrelated*
False: 219	1,239	103	82	159	895
True: 203	1,803	371	5	250	1,177
Total: 402	3,042	474	87	409	2,072

Table 1: Statistics about stance and factuality labels.

4 Experiments and Evaluation

We experimented with our Arabic corpus, after preprocessing it with ATB-style segmentation using MADAMIRA (Pasha et al., 2014), using the following systems:

- FNC BASELINE SYSTEM. This is the FNC organizers' system, which trains a gradient boosting classifier using hand-crafted features reflecting polarity, refute, similarity and overlap between the document and the claim.

- ATHENE. It was second at FNC (Hanselowski et al., 2017), and was based on a multi-layer perceptron with the baseline system's features, word n-grams, and features generated using latent semantic analysis and other factorization techniques.

- UCL. It was third at FNC (Riedel et al., 2017), training a softmax layer using similarity features.

- MEMORY NETWORK. We also experimented with an end-to-end memory network that showed state-of-the-art results on the FNC data (Mohtarami et al., 2018).

The evaluation results are shown in Table 2. We use 5-fold cross-validation, where all claim-document pairs for the same claim are assigned to the same fold. We report *accuracy*, macro-average F_1-*score*, and *weighted accuracy*, which is the official evaluation metric of FNC.

Overall, our corpus appears to be much harder than FNC. For instance, the FNC baseline system achieves weighted accuracy of 75.2 on FNC vs. 55.6 (up to 64.8) on our corpus. We believe that this is because we used a realistic information retrieval approach (see Section 3), whereas the FNC corpus contains a significant number of totally unrelated document–claim pairs, e.g., about 40% of the *unrelated* examples have no word overlap with the claim (even after stemming!), which makes it much easier to correctly predict the *unrelated* class (and this class is also by far the largest).

Model	document Content Used	Weigh. Acc.	Acc.	F_1 (macro)	F_1 (*agree, disagree, discuss, unrelated*)
Majority class	—	34.8	68.1	20.3	0 / 0 / 0 / 81
FNC baseline system	full document (default)	55.6	72.4	41.0	60.4 / 9.0 / 10.4 / 84
	best sentence	50.5	70.6	37.2	50.3 / 5.4 / 10.3 / 82.9
	best sentence **+rationale**	60.6	75.6	45.9	73.5 / 13.2 / 11.3 / 85.5
	full document **+rationale**	64.8	78.4	53.2	84.4 / 32.5 / 8.4 / 87.5
UCL (*#3rd in FNC*)	full document (default)	49.3	66.0	37.1	47.0 / 7.8 / 13.4 / 80
	best sentence	46.8	66.7	34.7	44.3 / 3.5 / 11.4 / 79.8
	best sentence **+rationale**	58.5	71.9	44.8	71.6 / 12.6 / 12.4 / 82.6
	full document **+rationale**	63.7	76.3	51.6	84.2 / 21.4 / 15.3 / 85.3
Athene (*#2rd in FNC*)	full document (default)	55.1	70.5	41.3	59.1 / 9.2 / 14.1 / 82.3
	best sentence	48.0	67.5	36.1	43.9 / 4.00 / 15.7 / 80.7
	best sentence **+rationale**	60.6	74.3	48.0	73.5 / 18.2 / 15.9 / 84.6
	full document **+rationale**	65.5	80.2	55.8	85.0 / 36.6 / 12.8 / 88.8
Memory Network	full document (default)	55.3	70.9	41.6	60.0 / 15.0 / 8.5 / 83.1
	best sentence	52.4	71.0	38.2	58.1 / 8.1 / 4.1 / 82.6
	best sentence **+rationale**	60.1	75.5	46.4	72.5 / 23.1 / 4.1 / 85.7
	full document **+rationale**	65.8	79.7	55.2	86.9 / 31.3 / 14.9 / 87.6

Table 2: Performance of some stance detection models from FNC when applied to our Arabic corpus.

Table 2 allows us to study the utility of having gold rationales for the stance (for the *agree* and *disagree* classes only) under different scenarios. First, we show the results when using the full document along with the claim, which is the default representation. Then, we use the best sentence from the document, i.e., the one that is most similar to the claim as measured by the cosine of their average word embeddings. This performs worse, which can be attributed to sometimes selecting the wrong sentence. Next, we experiment with using the rationale instead of the best sentence when applicable (i.e., for *agree* and *disagree*), while still using the best sentence for *discuss* and *unrelated*. This yields sizable improvements on all evaluation metrics, compared to using the best sentence (5-12 point absolute) or the full document (3-9 points absolute). We further evaluate the impact of using the rationales, when applicable, but using the full document otherwise. This setting performed best (80.2% accuracy with ATHENE, and 3-8 points of improvement over best+rationale), as it has access to most information: full document + rationale.

Overall, the above experiments demonstrate that having a gold rationale can enable better learning. However, the results should be considered as a kind of upper bound on the expected performance improvement, since here we used gold rationales at *test* time, which would not be available in a real-world scenario. Still, we believe that sizable improvements would still be possible when using the gold rationales for training only.

Finally, we built a simple fact-checker, where the factuality of a claim is determined based on aggregating the predicted stances (using FNC's baseline system) of the documents we retrieved for it. This yielded an accuracy of 56.2 when using the full documents, and 59.7 when using the best sentence + rationale (majority baseline of 50.5), thus confirming once again the utility of having a rationale, this time for a downstream task.

5 Conclusion and Future Work

We have described a novel corpus that unifies stance detection, stance rationale, relevant document retrieval, and fact checking. This is the first corpus to offer such a combination, not only for Arabic but in general. We further demonstrated experimentally that these unified annotations, and the gold rationales in particular, are beneficial both for stance detection and for fact checking.

In future work, we plan to extend the annotations to cover other important aspects of fact checking such as source reliability, language style, and temporal information, which have been shown useful in previous research (Castillo et al., 2011; Lukasik et al., 2015; Ma et al., 2016; Mukherjee and Weikum, 2015; Popat et al., 2017).

Acknowledgment

This research was carried out in collaboration between the MIT Computer Science and Artificial Intelligence Laboratory (CSAIL) and the HBKU Qatar Computing Research Institute (QCRI).

References

Mouhamadou Lamine Ba, Laure Berti-Equille, Kushal Shah, and Hossam M. Hammady. 2016. VERA: A platform for veracity estimation over web data. In *Proceedings of the 25th International Conference Companion on World Wide Web*. Montréal, Canada, WWW '16, pages 159–162.

Protima Banerjee and Hyoil Han. 2009. Answer credibility: A language modeling approach to answer validation. In *Proceedings of the Annual Conference of the North American Chapter of the Association for Computational Linguistics*. Boulder, CO, USA, NAACL-HLT '09, pages 157–160.

Carlos Castillo, Marcelo Mendoza, and Barbara Poblete. 2011. Information credibility on Twitter. In *Proceedings of the 20th International Conference on World Wide Web*. Hyderabad, India, WWW '11, pages 675–684.

Kareem Darwish, Dimitar Alexandrov, Preslav Nakov, and Yelena Mejova. 2017a. Seminar users in the Arabic Twitter sphere. In *Proceedings of the 9th International Conference on Social Informatics*. Oxford, UK, SocInfo '17, pages 91–108.

Kareem Darwish, Walid Magdy, and Tahar Zanouda. 2017b. Improved stance prediction in a user similarity feature space. In *Proceedings of the Conference on Advances in Social Networks Analysis and Mining*. Sydney, Australia, ASONAM '17, pages 145–148.

Pepa Gencheva, Preslav Nakov, Lluís Màrquez, Alberto Barrón-Cedeño, and Ivan Koychev. 2017. A context-aware approach for detecting worth-checking claims in political debates. In *Proceedings of the International Conference on Recent Advances in Natural Language Processing*. Varna, Bulgaria, RANLP '17, pages 267–276.

Andreas Hanselowski, Avinesh PVS, Benjamin Schiller, and Felix Caspelherr. 2017. Team Athene on the fake news challenge. https://medium.com/@andre134679/team-athene-on-the-fake-news-challenge-28a5cf5e017b.

Momchil Hardalov, Ivan Koychev, and Preslav Nakov. 2016. In search of credible news. In *Proceedings of the 17th International Conference on Artificial Intelligence: Methodology, Systems, and Applications*. Varna, Bulgaria, AIMSA '16, pages 172–180.

Naeemul Hassan, Chengkai Li, and Mark Tremayne. 2015. Detecting check-worthy factual claims in presidential debates. In *Proceedings of the 24th ACM International Conference on Information and Knowledge Management*. Melbourne, Australia, CIKM '15, pages 1835–1838.

Israa Jaradat, Pepa Gencheva, Alberto Barrón-Cedeño, Lluís Màrquez, and Preslav Nakov. 2018. ClaimRank: Detecting check-worthy claims in Arabic and English. In *Proceedings of the 16th Annual Conference of the North American Chapter of the Association for Computational Linguistics*. New Orleans, LA, USA, NAACL-HLT '18.

Georgi Karadzhov, Pepa Gencheva, Preslav Nakov, and Ivan Koychev. 2017a. We built a fake news & clickbait filter: What happened next will blow your mind! In *Proceedings of the International Conference on Recent Advances in Natural Language Processing*. Varna, Bulgaria, RANLP '17, pages 334–343.

Georgi Karadzhov, Preslav Nakov, Lluís Màrquez, Alberto Barrón-Cedeño, and Ivan Koychev. 2017b. Fully automated fact checking using external sources. In *Proceedings of the Conference on Recent Advances in Natural Language Processing*. Varna, Bulgaria, RANLP '17, pages 344–353.

David M.J. Lazer, Matthew A. Baum, Yochai Benkler, Adam J. Berinsky, Kelly M. Greenhill, Filippo Menczer, Miriam J. Metzger, Brendan Nyhan, Gordon Pennycook, David Rothschild, Michael Schudson, Steven A. Sloman, Cass R. Sunstein, Emily A. Thorson, Duncan J. Watts, and Jonathan L. Zittrain. 2018. The science of fake news. *Science* 359(6380):1094–1096.

Tao Lei, Regina Barzilay, and Tommi Jaakkola. 2016. Rationalizing neural predictions. In *Proceedings of the Conference on Empirical Methods in Natural Language Processing*. Austin, TX, USA, EMNLP '16, pages 107–117.

Michal Lukasik, Trevor Cohn, and Kalina Bontcheva. 2015. Point process modelling of rumour dynamics in social media. In *Proceedings of the 53rd Annual Meeting of the Association for Computational Linguistics and the 7th International Joint Conference on Natural Language Processing*. Beijing, China, ACL-IJCNLP '15, pages 518–523.

Caroline Lyon, James Malcolm, and Bob Dickerson. 2001. Detecting short passages of similar text in large document collections. In *Proceedings of Conference on Empirical Methods in Natural Language Processing*. Pittsburgh, PA, USA, EMNLP '01, pages 118–125.

Jing Ma, Wei Gao, Prasenjit Mitra, Sejeong Kwon, Bernard J. Jansen, Kam-Fai Wong, and Meeyoung Cha. 2016. Detecting rumors from microblogs with recurrent neural networks. In *Proceedings of the 25th International Joint Conference on Artificial Intelligence*. New York, NY, USA, IJCAI '16, pages 3818–3824.

Todor Mihaylov, Georgi Georgiev, and Preslav Nakov. 2015a. Finding opinion manipulation trolls in news community forums. In *Proceedings of the Nineteenth Conference on Computational Natural Language Learning*. Beijing, China, CoNLL '15, pages 310–314.

Todor Mihaylov, Ivan Koychev, Georgi Georgiev, and Preslav Nakov. 2015b. Exposing paid opinion manipulation trolls. In *Proceedings of the International Conference Recent Advances in Natural Language Processing*. Hissar, Bulgaria, RANLP '15, pages 443–450.

Todor Mihaylov and Preslav Nakov. 2016. Hunting for troll comments in news community forums. In *Proceedings of the 54th Annual Meeting of the Association for Computational Linguistics*. Berlin, Germany, ACL '16, pages 399–405.

Tsvetomila Mihaylova, Preslav Nakov, Lluis Marquez, Alberto Barron-Cedeno, Mitra Mohtarami, Georgi Karadzhov, and James Glass. 2018. Fact checking in community forums. In *Proceedings of the Thirty-Second AAAI Conference on Artificial Intelligence*. New Orleans, LA, USA, AAAI '18.

Saif Mohammad, Svetlana Kiritchenko, Parinaz Sobhani, Xiao-Dan Zhu, and Colin Cherry. 2016. SemEval-2016 task 6: Detecting stance in tweets. In *Proceedings of the International Workshop on Semantic Evaluation*. Berlin, Germany, SemEval '16, pages 31–41.

Mitra Mohtarami, Ramy Baly, James Glass, Preslav Nakov, Lluís Màrquez, and Alessandro Moschitti. 2018. Automatic stance detection using end-to-end memory networks. In *Proceedings of the 16th Annual Conference of the North American Chapter of the Association for Computational Linguistics*. New Orleans, LA, USA, NAACL-HLT '18.

Subhabrata Mukherjee and Gerhard Weikum. 2015. Leveraging joint interactions for credibility analysis in news communities. In *Proceedings of the 24th ACM Conference on Information and Knowledge Management*. Melbourne, Australia, CIKM '15, pages 353–362.

Ankur Parikh, Oscar Täckström, Dipanjan Das, and Jakob Uszkoreit. 2016. A decomposable attention model for natural language inference. In *Proceedings of the Conference on Empirical Methods in Natural Language Processing*. Austin, TX, USA, EMNLP '16, pages 2249–2255.

Robert Parker, David Graff, Ke Chen, Junbo Kong, and Kazuaki Maeda. 2011. Arabic Gigaword Fifth Edition, LDC2011T11. Web Download. Philadelphia: Linguistic Data Consortium.

Arfath Pasha, Mohamed Al-Badrashiny, Mona T Diab, Ahmed El Kholy, Ramy Eskander, Nizar Habash, Manoj Pooleery, Owen Rambow, and Ryan Roth. 2014. MADAMIRA: A Fast, Comprehensive Tool for Morphological Analysis and Disambiguation of Arabic. In *Proceedings of the Conference on Language Resources and Evaluation*. Reykjavik, Iceland, LREC '14, pages 1094–1101.

Jeffrey Pennington, Richard Socher, and Christopher Manning. 2014. Glove: Global Vectors for Word Representation. In *Proceedings of the conference on empirical methods in natural language processing*. Doha, Qatar, EMNLP '14, pages 1532–1543.

Kashyap Popat, Subhabrata Mukherjee, Jannik Strötgen, and Gerhard Weikum. 2016. Credibility assessment of textual claims on the web. In *Proceedings of the International on Conference on Information and Knowledge Management*. Indianapolis, IN, USA, CIKM '16, pages 2173–2178.

Kashyap Popat, Subhabrata Mukherjee, Jannik Strötgen, and Gerhard Weikum. 2017. Where the truth lies: Explaining the credibility of emerging claims on the web and social media. In *Proceedings of the Conference on World Wide Web Companion*. Perth, Australia, WWW '17, pages 1003–1012.

Pranav Rajpurkar, Jian Zhang, Konstantin Lopyrev, and Percy Liang. 2016. SQuAD: 100,000+ questions for machine comprehension of text. In *Proceedings of the 2016 Conference on Empirical Methods in Natural Language Processing*. Austin, TX, USA, EMNLP '16, pages 2383–2392.

Hannah Rashkin, Eunsol Choi, Jin Yea Jang, Svitlana Volkova, and Yejin Choi. 2017. Truth of varying shades: Analyzing language in fake news and political fact-checking. In *Proceedings of the Conference on Empirical Methods in Natural Language Processing*. EMNLP '17, pages 2931–2937.

Benjamin Riedel, Isabelle Augenstein, Georgios P Spithourakis, and Sebastian Riedel. 2017. A simple but tough-to-beat baseline for the Fake News Challenge stance detection task. *ArXiv:1707.03264* .

Prashant Shiralkar, Alessandro Flammini, Filippo Menczer, and Giovanni Luca Ciampaglia. 2017. Finding streams in knowledge graphs to support fact checking. In *Proceedings of the IEEE International Conference on Data Mining*. New Orleans, LA, USA, ICDM '17.

James Thorne, Andreas Vlachos, Christos Christodoulopoulos, and Arpit Mittal. 2018. Fever: A large-scale dataset for fact extraction and verification. In *Proceedings of the Annual Conference of the North American Chapter of the Association for Computational Linguistics*. New Orleans, LA, USA, NAACL-HLT '18.

Andreas Vlachos and Sebastian Riedel. 2014. Fact checking: Task definition and dataset construction. In *Proceedings of the ACL 2014 Workshop on Language Technologies and Computational Social Science*. Baltimore, MD, USA, pages 18–22.

Soroush Vosoughi, Deb Roy, and Sinan Aral. 2018. The spread of true and false news online. *Science* 359(6380):1146–1151.

William Yang Wang. 2017. "Liar, liar pants on fire": A new benchmark dataset for fake news detection. In *Proceedings of the 55th Annual Meeting of the Association for Computational Linguistics*. Vancouver, Canada, ACL '17, pages 422–426.

Is Something Better than Nothing? Automatically Predicting Stance-based Arguments using Deep Learning and Small Labelled Dataset.

Pavithra Rajendran[1], Danushka Bollegala[1], Simon Parsons[2]
University of Liverpool[1], King's College London[2]

Abstract

Online reviews have become a popular portal among customers making decisions about purchasing products. A number of corpora of reviews have been widely investigated in NLP in general, and, in particular, in argument mining. This is a subset of NLP that deals with extracting arguments and the relations among them from user-based content. A major problem faced by argument mining research is the lack of human-annotated data. In this paper, we investigate the use of weakly supervised and semi-supervised methods for automatically annotating data, and thus providing large annotated datasets. We do this by building on previous work that explores the classification of opinions present in reviews based on whether the stance is expressed explicitly or implicitly. In the work described here, we automatically annotate stance as implicit or explicit and our results show that the datasets we generate, although noisy, can be used to learn better models for implicit/explicit opinion classification.

1 Introduction

Sentiment analysis and opinion mining are widely researched NLP sub-fields that have extensively investigated opinion-based data such as online reviews (Pang et al., 2008; Cui et al., 2006). Reviews contain a wide range of opinions posted by users, and are useful for customers in deciding whether to buy a product or not. With abundant data available online, analysing online reviews becomes difficult, and tasks such as sentiment analysis are inadequate to identify the reasoning behind a user's review. Argument mining is an emerging research field that attempts to solve this problem by identifying arguments and the relation between them using ideas from argumentation theory (Palau and Moens, 2009).

An argument can be defined in two different ways — (1) abstract arguments which do not refer to any internal structure (Dung, 1995) and (2) structured arguments where an argument is a collection of premises leading to a conclusion. One major problem that is faced by argument mining researchers is the variation in the definition of an argument, which is highly dependent on the data at hand. Previous work in argument mining has mostly focussed on a particular domain (Grosse et al., 2015; Villalba and Saint-Dizier, 2012; Ghosh et al., 2014; Boltuzic and Snajder, 2014; Park and Cardie, 2014; Cabrio and Villata, 2012). Furthermore, an argument can be defined in a variety of ways depending on the problem being solved. As a result, we focus on the specific domain of opinionated texts such as those found in online reviews.

Prior work (Carstens et al., 2014; Rajendran et al., 2016a) in identifying arguments in online reviews has considered sentence-level statements to be arguments based on abstract argumentation models. However, to extract arguments at a finer level based on the idea of structured arguments is a harder task, requiring us to manually annotate argument components such that they can be used by supervised learning techniques. Because of the heterogenous nature of user-based content, this labelling task is time-consuming and expensive (Khatib et al., 2016; Habernal and Gurevych, 2015) and often domain-dependent.

Here, we are interested in analysing the problem of using supervised learning where the quantity of human-annotated or labelled data is small, and investigating how this issue can be handled by using weakly-supervised and semi-supervised techniques. We build on our prior work (Rajendran et al., 2016b), which created a small manually annotated dataset for the supervised binary classification of opinions present in online reviews, based

Proceedings of NAACL-HLT 2018, pages 28–34
New Orleans, Louisiana, June 1 - 6, 2018. ©2018 Association for Computational Linguistics

Opinion	Stance	Aspect	Annotation
Great *hotel*!	direct	hotel	Explicit
don't get fooled by book reviews and movies, this *hotel* is not a five star luxury experience, it dosen't even have sanitary standards!	direct and indirect	hotel	Explicit
another annoyance was the *internet* access, for which you can buy a card for 5 dollars and this is supposed to give you 25 mins of access, but if you use the card more than once, it debits an access charge and rounds minutes to the nearest five.	indirect	internet	Implicit
the other times that we contacted front desk/guest services (very difficult to tell them apart) we were met by unhelpful unknowledgable staff for very straightforward requests verging on the sarcastic and rude	indirect	staff	Implicit
the attitude of all the staff we met was awful, they made us feel totally unwelcome	direct and indirect	staff	Explicit

Table 1: Examples of opinions along with the following information: whether the stance is directly (and) or indirectly expressed, the aspect present and whether the opinion is annotated explicit or implicit.

on how the stance is expressed linguistically in the structure of these opinions. One disadvantage of that work is the lack of a large labelled dataset, but there is a large amount of unannotated (unlabelled) online reviews available from the same source, TripAdvisor.

Our aim in this paper is to investigate whether automatically labelling a large set of unlabelled opinions as implicit/explicit can assist in creating deep learning models for the implicit/explicit classification task and also for other related tasks that depend on this classification. In our investigation, we are interested in automatically labelling such a dataset using the previously proposed supervised approach described in (Rajendran et al., 2016b).

We report experiments that are carried out using two different approaches — weakly-supervised and semi-supervised learning (Section. 4). In the weakly-supervised approach, we randomly divide the manually annotated implicit/explicit opinions into different training sets that are used to train SVM classifiers for automatically labelling unannotated opinions. The unannotated opinions are labelled based on different voting criteria — *Fully-Strict*, *Partially-Strict* and *No-Strict*. In the semi-supervised approach, an SVM classifier is either trained on a portion of the annotated implicit/explicit opinions or using the entire data. The resulting classifier is then used to predict the unannotated opinions and those with highest confidence are appended to the training data. This process is repeated for m iterations.

All the approaches give us a set of automatically labelled opinions. A Long Short-Term Memory (LSTM) (Hochreiter and Schmidhuber, 1997) model is trained on this data and tested on the original manually-annotated dataset. Results show that the maximum overall accuracy of 0.84 on the annotated dataset is obtained using an LSTM model trained using the labelled data generated by the weakly-supervised approach using the *Partially-Strict* voting criterion.

2 Related work

Research in argument mining attempts to automatically identify arguments and their relations that are present in natural language texts. Lippi and Torroni (2016) present a detailed survey of existing work in argument mining. This is carried out on different domains such as debates (Cabrio and Villata, 2012; Habernal and Gurevych, 2016), reviews (Wyner et al., 2012; Gabbriellini and Santini, 2015), tweets (Bosc et al., 2016), and dialogues (Biran and Rambow, 2011). Amgoud et al. (2015) find arguments in such texts as not formally structured with most of the content left implicit. An argument, in general, is treated as a set of premises that are linked to a claim or conclusion and, those arguments in which the major premises are left implicit are termed as enthymemes. It is important to understand whether the content that is left implicit in natural language texts are to be dealt as enthymemes or not. In our earlier work (Rajendran et al., 2016b), we propose an approach for reconstructing structures similar to enthymemes in opinions that are present in online reviews. However, the annotated dataset used in our approach was small and not useful for deep learning models. Recent work in argument mining is able to achieve better performance for the argument identification task using neural network models with the availability of a large corpus of annotated arguments (Habernal et al., 2018; Eger et al., 2017). Annotating a large corpus by hand is a tedious task and little existing work in argument mining has explored alternative ways to do it. Naderi and Hirst (2014) propose a frame-based approach for dealing with arguments present in parliamentary discourse and suggest that using a semi-supervised approach can help in developing their dataset into a large corpus. Habernal and Gurevych (2015) have proposed a semi-supervised based approach for identifying arguments using a clustering based approach on unlabelled data. Their results outperform several baselines and provide a way of developing their corpus without having to manually annotate the entire dataset. In this paper, we show that a small labelled dataset trained using an existing SVM-based classifer with the best features can help in automatically labelling a large dataset and we also evaluate its usefulness for modelling deep learning models.

3 Implicit/Explicit classification

Our prior work (Rajendran et al., 2016b) defines a sentence-level statement that is of a positive/negative sentiment and talks about a target as being a stance-containing opinion. Biber and Finegan (1988) define stance as the expression of the user's attitude and judgement in their message to convince the audience towards the standpoint taken by them. This is different from the definition used for stance detection in NLP, in which, a given piece of text is classified as being for or against a given claim. Based on the definition given in Biber and Finegan (1988), we take stance-containing opinions to be classified as being implicit or explicit based on how the stance or the standpoint of the reviewer towards the target is expressed in the linguistic structure of the opinion. This definition of what we term implicit or explicit may depend on the audience interpretation and may vary for evey individual. In order to make the human annotation task less subjective, Rajendran et al. (2016b) use the following cues to label the opinions as implicit or explicit. These opinions are extracted from hotel reviews present in the ArguAna corpus (Wachsmuth et al., 2014). Some examples from Rajendran et al. (2016b) are given in Table. 1.

Explicit opinion

1. Direct approval/disapproval is expressed by the reviewer. Few examples are: *I do not like the hotel, I would definitely recommend this hotel*

2. Strong intensity of expression. Certain words or clauses have a strong positive/negative intensity towards a particular target. For example, *worst staff!* has a strong negative intensity in comparison to *the staff were not helpful.*

Implicit opinion

1. Words or clauses indicate positive/negative expression but do not express it with a strong intensity. For example, *the staff were friendly and helped us with our baggages.*

2. Opinions that are expressed as personal facts. Few examples are *small room, carpets are dirty* etc.

3. Opinions that express a form of justification such as describing an incident that indirectly is meant to imply the reviewer's satisfaction or dissatisfaction. For example, *they made us wait for a long time for the check-in and the staff completely ignored us.*

To overcome the data imbalance for the two classes, the original dataset annotated by a single annotator was undersampled in (Rajendran et al., 2016b) into 1244 opinions (495 explicit and 749 implicit). Next, two annotators were asked to independently annotate this undersampled dataset, and the inter-annotator agreement for this task is 0.70, measured using Cohen's κ (Cohen, 1960).

4 Methodology

4.1 Weakly-supervised Approach

Our first experiment uses a method that is similar to bagging (Breiman, 1996). Starting from a randomly selected subset of the undersampled annotated data, we first create three different training sets, T_1, T_2 and T_3. These training sets are then each used to train an SVM classifier which uses the highest discriminative features (Rajendran et al., 2017) identified for predicting implicit and explicit stance:

Unigrams and Bigrams Each word present in an opinion and each pair of consecutive words present in an opinion are considered as features.

Noun-Adjective pattern Let us consider $\mathcal{N}$ to represent the list of k nouns in an opinion and $\mathcal{A}$ to represent the list of l adjectives. The combination of each noun with an adjective is considered as a Noun tag + Adjective tag

Dataset	Labelled Data		Average-based		Fully-Strict		Partially-Strict		No-Strict	
	Exp	Imp	Size	Acc	Size	Acc	Size	Acc	Size	Acc
D1	100	749	4931	73.95	4376	72.99	4541	75.56	4931	67.76
D2	200	749	4931	79.5	4310	75.64	4575	82.07	4931	71.66
D3	300	749	4931	80.99	4427	79.50	4655	83.36	4931	73.71
D4	400	749	4931	81.50	4541	78.13	4726	84.08	4931	76.36
D5	495	100	4931	76.41	3411	76.20	4113	75.32	4931	82.23
D6	495	200	4931	81.72	3742	83.52	4276	80.30	4931	83.19
D7	495	300	4931	83.01	4054	83.36	4409	83.44	4931	79.90
D8	495	400	4931	82.42	4054	83.60	4498	84.08	4931	82.31
D9	495	500	4931	83.54	4501	83.44	4762	84.00	4931	82.63
D10	495	600	4931	83.75	4484	83.52	4762	83.52	4931	82.39
D11	495	700	4931	82.15	4678	83.19	4797	84.00	4931	82.55

Table 2: Datasets vary in the number of explicit and implicit opinions that are randomly sampled from the labelled data to be trained by the SVM classifier. For each of the weakly supervised approach, we give *size*, the number of the predicted labels that are used to train an LSTM-based model. This model was then tested on the entire labelled data, and the accuracy of this LSTM model is reported.

feature. Thus there are $k.l$ combined Noun + Adjective features in total for each opinion.

Average-based sentence embedding We compute the mean of the 300-dimensional pre-trained word embedding vectors trained using GloVe (Pennington et al., 2014) to create a sentence embedding, and use each dimension in the sentence embedding as a feature in the classifier.

$$\mathbf{v} = \frac{1}{|\mathbf{S}|} \sum_{i=1}^{|\mathbf{S}|} \mathbf{s}_i \qquad (1)$$

where $|\mathbf{S}|$ represents the size of the opinion and $\mathbf{s}_i$ represents the pre-trained word embedding for the ith word in the opinion.

The three resulting SVM classifiers are then used to annotate 4931 unannotated opinions, and these newly annotated opinions are then used to train an LTSM classifier. We generate the annotated opinions in two different ways — what we call the average-based method and the voting-based method — and for each method we use the resulting annotated opinions differently as described next.

Average-Based Each training set T_1, T_2 and T_3 is used to train separate SVM classifiers, which are used to label the unlabelled opinions, giving corresponding annotated opinion sets U_1, U_2 and U_3. Separate LSTM models are trained on each of U_1, U_2 and U_3, and tested on the original set of annotated data. Finally, the averaged performance across the three LSTMs is reported.

Iterations	Self-training		Reserved	
	Size	Accuracy	Size	Accuracy
1	22	49.43	511	67.68
5	2110	80.86	1717	68.24
10	2574	81.83	2194	70.25
15	3600	82.71	3152	70.98
20	3613	82.71	3708	68.81
25	4931	82.71	4931	64.22

Table 3: Accuracy of the LSTM model on annotated data using a set of automatically labelled unannotated opinions of *Size*.

Voting-Based Again, each training set T_1, T_2 and T_3 is used to train separate SVM classifiers, which are used to label the unlabelled opinions, giving corresponding annotated opinion sets U_1, U_2 and U_3. We then followed an approach that is similar to Ng and Cardie (2003) to combine the opinions in U_1, U_2 and U_3 into a single set, denoted by U_F, using the following voting criteria:

Fully-Strict An opinion is included in U_F if all three SVM classifiers predict the same stance label.

Partially-Strict An opinion is included in U_F if all three SVM classifiers identify it as explicit, or if at least two of them classify it as implicit.

No-Strict An opinion is included in U_F as implicit if at least one of the classifiers predict it to be implicit, otherwise it is included in U_F as explicit.

U_F was then used to train an LSTM classifier and this was tested on the original annotated data.

Note that moving from Fully-strict $\rightarrow$ Partially-Strict $\rightarrow$ No-Strict relaxes the requirement on including an opinion in U_F so that the number of opinions in the training data increases.

4.2 Semi-supervised approach

We conduct a second experiment to test the combination of both labelled (1244 opinions) and unlabelled (4931 opinions) data using the following popular semi-supervised learning methods.

Self-training method We train an SVM using the labelled data D and use this to annotate the unannotated data U. The annotated opinions from U which are labelled with the highest probability are then added to D. This process is repeated m times.

Reserved method Here we use the method of Liu et al. (2013), where a portion of the training data R is reserved, and the remainder is used for training the SVM. The resulting classifier is run on the combination of U and R. The annotated opinions from U with the highest probability and the opinions from R that have the lowest probability of having a correct label generated by the SVM are appended to the training dataset. This operation is repeated m times. We chose 222 explicit opinions and 287 implicit opinions as the training data, and took 273 explicit opinions and 462 implicit opinions as the reserved portion.

After the final iteration, the final set of annotations of the opinions in U is used to train an LSTM model. The resulting classifier is then tested on the original set of annotated data.

5 Experiment and Results

We used Keras[1] to implement an LSTM model with an embedding layer using pre-trained 300 dimensional GloVe embeddings, followed by an LSTM layer of size 100 with a dropout rate of 0.5 and a sigmoid output layer. The input length is padded to 50. Parameter optimisation is done using Adam (Kingma and Ba, 2014). For the semi-supervised approaches, we consider the number of iterations, $m = 1 - 25$.

Table. 2 reports under *Size* the number of unannotated data that is automatically labelled using the weakly-supervised approaches. The corresponding columns *Exp* and *Imp* contain the number of manually annotated opinions that are used to train the SVM classifier used in the first-step of the proposed method. The *Acc* column denotes the accuracy for predicting the labels of the annotated dataset using the LSTM model trained on the automatically labelled, unannotated data.

Looking at the performance of the weakly-supervised approach in Table. 2, we observe the effect of varying the size of the explicit and the implicit opinion sets that are used to train the SVM-based classifier (see columns *Emp* and *Imp* in Table. 2). Comparing these with the accuracy scores, we find that using the largest set of explicit opinions in training the initial SVMs gives new annotated data that can train classifiers that perform best on the original annotated data. Overall, using the entire undersampled data for training the SVMs and using the *Partially-Strict* voting based method gives the best performance with an accuracy of 0.84.

Table. 3 reports the results obtained using the self-training method and the reserved method. These show how the size of the labelled unannotated dataset increases at each iteration and these newly annotated opinions are added to the training data. The accuracy of the LSTM model in predicting the labels of annotated opinions improves with the size of the automatically labelled dataset. However, the accuracy of the reserved method decreases in performance after 20 iterations[2]. Of the two methods, the self-training method performs best, showing that using training data with the lowest confidence does not help in this task.

Overall, the results are positive, showing a range of methods that can create automatically labelled data which is accurate enough to be useful for deep-learning methods. The dataset is publicly available at `https://goo.gl/Bym2Vz`.

6 Conclusion

This work investigated a particular task related to argument mining where we have a small annotated dataset. Our results show that using a semi-supervised method with the available small annotated dataset is sufficient to label a larger unlabelled dataset so it can be used to train a deep learning LSTM model for argument mining.

References

Leila Amgoud, Philippe Besnard, and Anthony Hunter. 2015. Representing and reasoning about arguments mined from texts and dialogues. In *ECSQARU*. pages 60–71.

Douglas Biber and Edward Finegan. 1988. Adverbial

---

[1] `https://keras.io/`

[2] This is typical of such methods as less reliable examples are added to the training data.

stance types in english. In *Discourse Processes*. volume 11, pages 1–34.

Or Biran and Owen Rambow. 2011. Identifying justifications in written dialogs. In *ICSE*. pages 162–168.

Filip Boltuzic and Jan Snajder. 2014. Back up your stance: Recognizing arguments in online discussions. In *ACL*. pages 49–58.

Tom Bosc, Elena Cabrio, and Serena Villata. 2016. Dart: a dataset of arguments and their relations on twitter. In *LREC*. pages 1258–1263.

Leo Breiman. 1996. Bagging predictors. *Machine learning* 24(2):123–140.

Elena Cabrio and Serena Villata. 2012. Combining textual entailment and argumentation theory for supporting online debates interactions. In *ACL*. pages 208–212.

Lucas Carstens, Francesca Toni, and Valentinos Evripidou. 2014. Argument mining and social debates. In *COMMA*. pages 451–452.

Jacob Cohen. 1960. A coefficient of agreement for nominal scales. *Educational and Psychological Measurement* 20(1):37–46.

Hang Cui, Vibhu Mittal, and Mayur Datar. 2006. Comparative experiments on sentiment classification for online product reviews. In *AAAI*. pages 1265–1270.

P. M. Dung. 1995. On the acceptability of arguments and its fundamental role in nonmonotonic reasoning, logic programming and n-person games. *Artif. Intell.* 77:321–357.

Steffen Eger, Johannes Daxenberger, and Iryna Gurevych. 2017. Neural end-to-end learning for computational argumentation mining. In *ACL*. pages 11–22.

Simone Gabbriellini and Francesco Santini. 2015. A micro study on the evolution of arguments in amazon. coms reviews. In *PRIMA*. pages 284–300.

Debanjan Ghosh, Smaranda Muresan, Nina Wacholder, Mark Aakhus, and Matthew Mitsui. 2014. Analyzing argumentative discourse units in online interactions. In *ACL*. pages 39–48.

Kathrin Grosse, Maria P Gonzalez, Carlos I Chesnevar, and Ana G Maguitman. 2015. Integrating argumentation and sentiment analysis for mining opinions from twitter. *AI Communications* 28:387–401.

Ivan Habernal and Iryna Gurevych. 2015. Exploiting debate portals for semi-supervised argumentation mining in user-generated web discourse. In *EMNLP*. pages 2127–2137.

Ivan Habernal and Iryna Gurevych. 2016. Which argument is more convincing? analyzing and predicting convincingness of web arguments using bidirectional lstm. In *ACL*. pages 1589–1599.

Ivan Habernal, Henning Wachsmuth, Iryna Gurevych, and Benno Stein. 2018. The argument reasoning comprehension task: Identification and reconstruction of implicit warrants. In *NAACL-HLT*. page (to appear).

Sepp Hochreiter and Jürgen Schmidhuber. 1997. Long short-term memory. *Neural computation* 9(8):1735–1780.

Khalid Al Khatib, Henning Wachsmuth, Matthias Hagen, Jonas Kohler, and Benno Stein. 2016. Cross-domain mining of argumentative text through distant supervision. In *NAACL-HLT*. pages 1395–1404.

Diederik P. Kingma and Jimmy Ba. 2014. Adam: A method for stochastic optimization. *CoRR* abs/1412.6980.

Marco Lippi and Paolo Torroni. 2016. Argumentation mining: State of the art and emerging trends. *TOIT* 16(2):10.

Zhiguang Liu, Xishuang Dong, Yi Guan, and Jinfeng Yang. 2013. Reserved self-training: A semi-supervised sentiment classification method for chinese microblogs. In *IJCNLP*. pages 455–462.

Nona Naderi and Graeme Hirst. 2014. Argumentation mining in parliamentary discourse. In *PRIMA*. pages 16–25.

Vincent Ng and Claire Cardie. 2003. Weakly supervised natural language learning without redundant views. In *NAACL-HLT*. pages 94–101.

Raquel Mochales Palau and Marie-Francine Moens. 2009. Argumentation mining: the detection, classification and structure of arguments in text. In *ICAIL*. pages 98–107.

Bo Pang, Lillian Lee, et al. 2008. Opinion mining and sentiment analysis. *Foundations and Trends in Information Retrieval* 2(1–2):1–135.

Joonsuk Park and Claire Cardie. 2014. Identifying appropriate support for propositions in online user comments. In *ACL*. pages 29–38.

Jeffrey Pennington, Richard Socher, and Christopher D. Manning. 2014. Glove: Global vectors for word representation. In *EMNLP*. pages 1532–1543.

Pavithra Rajendran, Danushka Bollegala, and Simon Parsons. 2016a. Assessing weight of opinion by aggregating coalitions of arguments. In *COMMA*. pages 431–438.

Pavithra Rajendran, Danushka Bollegala, and Simon Parsons. 2016b. Contextual stance classification of opinions: A step towards enthymeme reconstruction in online reviews. In *ArgMining@ACL*. pages 32–39.

Pavithra Rajendran, Danushka Bollegala, and Simon Parsons. 2017. Identifying argument based relation properties in opinions. In *PACLING*.

Maria Paz Garcia Villalba and Patrick Saint-Dizier. 2012. A framework to extract arguments in opinion texts. *IJCINI* 6:62–87.

Henning Wachsmuth, Martin Trenkmann, Benno Stein, Gregor Engels, and Tsvetomira Palakarska. 2014. A review corpus for argumentation analysis. In *CICLing*. pages 115–127.

Adam Wyner, Jodi Schneider, Katie Atkinson, and Trevor J. M. Bench-Capon. 2012. Semi-automated argumentative analysis of online product reviews. In *COMMA*. pages 43–50.

Multi-Task Learning for Argumentation Mining in Low-Resource Settings

Claudia Schulz, Steffen Eger, Johannes Daxenberger, Tobias Kahse, Iryna Gurevych
Ubiquitous Knowledge Processing Lab (UKP-TUDA)
Department of Computer Science
Technische Universität Darmstadt
www.ukp.tu-darmstadt.de

Abstract

We investigate whether and where multi-task learning (MTL) can improve performance on NLP problems related to argumentation mining (AM), in particular argument component identification. Our results show that MTL performs particularly well (and better than single-task learning) when little training data is available for the main task, a common scenario in AM. Our findings challenge previous assumptions that conceptualizations across AM datasets are divergent and that MTL is difficult for semantic or higher-level tasks.

1 Introduction

Computational argumentation mining (AM) deals with the automatic identification of argumentative structures within natural language. This can be beneficial in many applications such as summarizing arguments in texts to improve comprehensibility for end-users, or information retrieval and extraction (Persing and Ng, 2016). A common task is to segment a text into argumentative and non-argumentative components and identify the type of argumentative components. As an illustration, consider the (simplified) example from Eger et al. (2017): "Since [it killed many marine lives]$_{Premise}$ [tourism has threatened nature]$_{Claim}$." Here, the non-argumentative token "Since" is followed by two argumentative components: a premise that supports a claim.

Argumentation is highly subjective and conceptualized in different ways (Peldszus and Stede, 2013; Al-Khatib et al., 2017). On the one hand, this implies that creating reliable ground-truth datasets for AM is costly, as it requires trained annotators. However, even trained annotators have problems identifying and classifying arguments

reliably in texts (Habernal and Gurevych, 2017). To tackle AM in a new domain or develop new AM tasks, it may thus not be possible to create large datasets as required by most state-of-the-art machine learning approaches. On the other hand, the different conceptualizations of argumentation resulted in AM corpora with different argument component types, with very little conceptual overlap between some of these corpora (Daxenberger et al., 2017). This distinguishes AM from more established NLP tasks like discourse parsing (Braud et al., 2016) and makes it particularly challenging. Therefore, a natural question is how to handle new AM datasets in a new domain and with sparse data.

Here, we investigate how existing AM datasets from different domains and with different conceptualizations of arguments can be leveraged to tackle these challenges. More precisely, we study whether conceptually diverse AM datasets from different domains can help deal with new AM datasets when data is limited. A promising direction to incorporate existing datasets as "auxiliary knowledge" is by means of *multi-task learning* (MTL), a paradigm that dates back to the 1990s (Caruana, 1993, 1996), but has only recently gained large attention (Collobert et al., 2011; Søgaard and Goldberg, 2016; Hashimoto et al., 2017). The idea behind MTL is to learn several tasks jointly, similarly to human learning, so that tasks serve as mutual sources of "inductive bias" for one another. MTL has been reported particularly beneficial when tasks exhibit "natural hierarchies" (Søgaard and Goldberg, 2016) or when the amount of training data for the main task is sparse (Benton et al., 2017; Augenstein and Søgaard, 2017), where the auxiliary tasks may act as regularizers to prevent overfitting (Ruder et al., 2017). The latter is precisely the scenario most relevant to us.

In this paper, we (1) investigate to which de-

35

Proceedings of NAACL-HLT 2018, pages 35–41
New Orleans, Louisiana, June 1 - 6, 2018. ©2018 Association for Computational Linguistics

gree training a system to solve several conceptually different AM tasks jointly improves performance over learning in isolation, (2) compare performance gains across different dataset sizes, and (3) do so across various domains. Our findings show that MTL is helpful for AM—particularly in data sparsity settings—when treating other AM tasks as auxiliary.[1]

2   Related Work

AM is a relatively new field in NLP. Hence, a lot of related work revolves around creating new corpora. We use six such corpora, described in more detail in Section 3. On the modeling side, Stab and Gurevych (2017) and Persing and Ng (2016) rely on pipeline approaches for AM, combining parts of the pipeline using integer linear programming (ILP). Eger et al. (2017) propose neural end-to-end models for AM. While Daxenberger et al. (2017) show that there is little consensus on the conceptualization of a claim across AM corpora, Al-Khatib et al. (2016) use distant supervision to overcome domain gaps for identifying (non-)argumentative text.

MTL has been applied in many different settings. Bollmann and Søgaard (2016) and Peng and Dredze (2017) use data from different domains as different tasks and thereby improve historical spelling normalization and Chinese word segmentation and NER, respectively. Plank et al. (2016) apply an MTL setup to POS tagging across 22 different languages, where the auxiliary task is to predict token frequency. Eger et al. (2017) explore sub-tasks (such as component identification) of a complex AM tagging problem (including relations between components) as auxiliaries and find that this improves performances. However, they stay within one single domain and dataset, and thus their approach does not address the question how new AM datasets with sparse data can profit from existing AM resources. Conceptually closest to our work, Braud et al. (2017) leverage data from different languages as well as different domains in order to improve discourse parsing. While MTL was shown effective for syntactic tasks under certain conditions (Søgaard and Goldberg, 2016), Alonso and Plank (2017) find that MTL does not improve performances in four

out of five semantic (i.e., higher level) tasks that they study. We are among the first to perform a structured investigation of MTL for higher-level pragmatic tasks, which are thought to be much more challenging than syntactic tasks (Alonso and Plank, 2017), and in particular, explore it for AM in cross-domain settings.

3   Experiments

Data   We experiment with six datasets for *argument component identification*, i.e. the token-level segmentation and typing of components. These datasets are all of different sizes, have different average text lengths, and different argument component types and label distributions, as summarized in Table 1. We only choose datasets containing both argumentative components and non-argumentative text. Claims are available in five of six datasets, and all datasets have premises (resp. "justification"), although it is unclear how large the conceptual overlap is across datasets. Further component types are idiosyncractic. `hotel` has the largest number of types, namely, six. Most datasets also come with further information, e.g. relations between argument components, which are not considered here.

Approach   Due to the difference in annotations used in the different datasets, we consider each dataset as a separate AM task. We treat all of them as sequence tagging problems, where predicting BIO tags (argument segmentation) and argument component types (component classification) is framed as a joint task. This is achieved through token-level BIO tagging with the label set $\{O\} \cup \{B, I\} \times T$, where T is a dataset specific set of argument component types, e.g. $T = \{\text{claim}, \text{premise}, \ldots\}$. Thus, the overall number of tags in each dataset is twice the number of non-"O" component types plus one $(2 \cdot |T| + 1)$. We use the state-of-the-art framework by Reimers and Gurevych (2017) for both single-task learning (STL) and MTL. It employs a bidirectional LSTM (BILSTM) model with a CRF layer over individual LSTM outputs to account for label dependencies. We use *nadam* as optimizer. For MTL, the recurrent layers of the deep BILSTM are shared by all tasks, with a separate CRF layer for each task. All tasks terminate at the same level. The main task determines the number of mini-batches used for training, i.e. in every iteration the main task is trained on all its mini-batches and all other

---

Dataset	Domain	#Docs	Tokens	Component Types
Reed et al. (2008)	various (Araucaria)	507	120	C (16), P (46), O (38)
Biran and Rambow (2011)	wikipedia discussions	118	1592	C (9), justification (23), O (68)
Liu et al. (2017), Gao et al. (2017)	hotel reviews	194	185	C (39), P (22), major C (7), implicit P (8), background (7), recommendation (5), O (12)
Habernal and Gurevych (2017)	web discourse	340	250	C (4), P (25), backing (13), rebuttal (3), refutation (1), O (54)
Habernal et al. (2017)	news comments	1927	108	P (53), O (47)
Stab and Gurevych (2017)	persuasive essays	402	366	C (15), P (45), major C (8), O (32)

Table 1: AM datasets: C – claim, P – premise, O – non-argumentative; numbers in parentheses are label distributions in %; 'tokens' is the average in each document.

(auxiliary) tasks are trained on the same number of (randomly drawn) mini-batches.

To simulate data sparsity, we experiment with different sizes of training data for the main task. We first draw a "sparse" training set of 21K tokens[2] for each of the six AM datasets and a dev set of 9K to simulate a sparse scenario with 30K given tokens. The remaining data of each specific dataset is used as its test set (at least 5K tokens). We then randomly draw a subset of the training data to create three more 'sparsity scenarios' with 12K, 6K, and 1K tokens, respectively. Both dev and test set remain the same as in the 21K scenario. It is worth emphasizing how little data is used in the 1K scenario—only 1-10 documents (or roughly 50 sentences). We train a separate STL system for each of the six datasets and each of the four sparsity scenarios. In the MTL setup, the respective sparsity data is used as the main task, all other (auxiliary) AM datasets, each considered a separate task, are trained on all their available data. To measure the effect of MTL as opposed to a mere increase of training data, we furthermore train for each main task (i.e. each dataset and sparsity scenario) an STL system on the union of (training data of) main and auxiliary task, and evaluate it on the main task's test data.

Hyperparameter optimization For each sparsity scenario and dataset we train 50 STL/MTL systems using GloVe embeddings (Pennington et al., 2014) and 50 using the embeddings by Komninos and Manandhar (2016). For each run we randomly choose a layout with either one hidden layer of $h \in \{50, 100, 150\}$ units or two layers of 100 units as well as variational dropout rates between 0.2 and 0.5 for the input layer and for the hidden units.

4 Results

Note that we experiment with artificially shrunk datasets, which makes our results incomparable with those reported for the full datasets in other works. Nevertheless, it is to be expected that our STL model is on par with results obtained in recent works also using neural models for argument component identification, since our state-of-the-art BILSTM has the same architecture as the one by Eger et al. (2017).

Overall trends Table 2 reports the average macro-F1[3] test scores over the respective ten best (according to the macro-F1 dev scores) hyperparameter configurations. We compare STL on each task, MTL with all remaining datasets as auxiliary tasks, and the union baseline. For three of the six datasets, MTL yields a significant improvement in all sparsity scenarios. Interestingly, these are the datasets with only one or two types of argument components. For the other three datasets, MTL only yields an improvement in the sparser data scenarios. The union baseline generally performs (considerably) worse than STL in all scenarios. This implies that the domains and component types (label spaces) used in the different AM datasets are too diverse to model them as one single task and that the improvement of MTL over STL cannot be attributed to more available data.

Figure 1 shows the general trends of our results. For each dataset, the figure plots the difference between normalized MTL and normalized STL macro-F1 scores ($\mathrm{MTL}_{\mathrm{norm}}(k) - \mathrm{STL}_{\mathrm{norm}}(k)$) for $k = $ 1K, 6K, 12K, 21K training data points for the main task. For each specific dataset, the normalized macro-F1 score is defined as $\sigma_{\mathrm{norm}}(k) = \frac{\sigma(k)}{\mathrm{STL}(1\mathrm{K})}$, where $\sigma(k)$ is the original macro-F1 score and STL(1K) denotes the STL score for 1K train-

---

[2]Or more, since whole documents are added to the training set until the sum of tokens is at least 21K. Similarly for smaller training and dev sets.

[3]As implemented in scikit-learn (Pedregosa et al., 2011).

Dataset	21K	12K	6K	1K
var – STL	43.34	42.85	38.89	31.30
var – MTL	**47.39**	**45.63**	**42.14**	**37.10**
var – BL	30.45	27.35	26.75	26.62
wiki – STL	23.37	22.57	20.93	19.74
wiki – MTL	**32.50**	**31.99**	**28.03**	**20.17**[*]
wiki –BL	18.34	18.12	17.49	20.47
news – STL	56.49	54.61	54.21	49.67
news – MTL	**57.76**	**56.34**	**55.41**[*]	**52.43**
news – BL	32.63	40.63	36.54	35.51
essays – STL	60.54	56.35	49.68	24.60
essays – MTL	60.55	**57.90**[*]	**52.14**	**32.55**
essays – BL	48.38	31.58	21.13	12.39
web – STL	23.43	22.33	19.71	11.28
web – MTL	23.27	22.97	**21.73**	**15.31**
web – BL	15.21	14.94	12.09	10.80
hotel – STL	47.91	47.78	45.64	29.82
hotel – MTL	46.44	46.78	46.60	**39.45**
hotel – BL	45.69	43.61	42.56	20.39

Table 2: Macro-F1 for AM component identification, comparing MTL, STL (significant differences in bold with $p < 0.01$, $p < 0.05$ if [*] using Mann-Whitney U Test) and union baseline (BL).

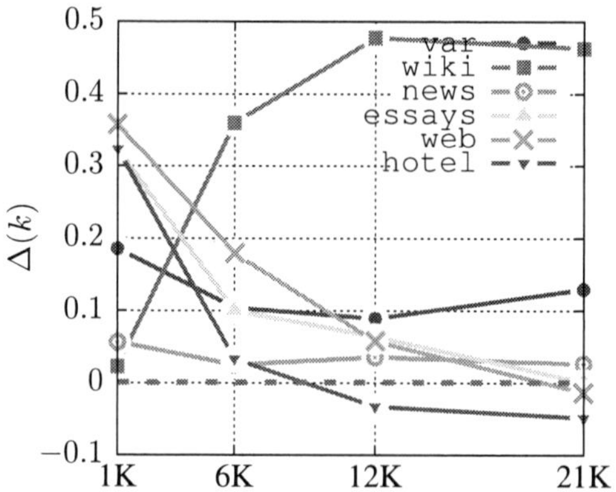

Figure 1: MTL versus STL: curves $\Delta(k) = \mathrm{MTL}_{\mathrm{norm}}(k) - \mathrm{STL}_{\mathrm{norm}}(k)$ as a function of size k of main task.

ing data. Using this normalization, all scores are directly comparable and have the interpretation of improvement over the STL scenario with 1K tokens. It is noteworthy that MTL always improves over STL when the main task is very sparse (1K) and gains are sometimes substantial (between 30 and 40% for web, essays, and hotel).

We observe three different patterns with respect to the main task: (i) for essays, web, and hotel, MTL is considerably better than STL when the main task is sparse, but for 21K tokens we observe either minimal gains or losses from MTL compared to STL. (ii) The var and news datasets are stable, with consistent small gains from MTL over STL for all sizes of the main task. Finally, (iii) wiki displays an unusual pattern in that MTL gains are increasing with the amount of training data. We attribute this to the large label imbalance in wiki, where nearly 70% of the data is 'O'. When training data is very sparse, STL predicts 99% of all tokens as 'O', which results in a high F1 score for this component type but very low F1 scores (below 1%) for the two other component types. The macro-F1 is thus lower than that of MTL, where 'claim' and 'premise' have a higher F1 score. Even though STL improves on the identification of 'premise' and 'claim' in the 21k scenario, the trend remains, since MTL also improves

on these labels.

Detailed analysis Upon closer inspection, we find that across all datasets MTL generally improves performance for class labels with low frequency as compared to STL. The more training data becomes available, the better STL gets in predicting such class labels, thus closing the gap to MTL. However, for wiki even 21K does not seem sufficient for STL to learn the two infrequent class labels, predicting 87% as 'O', so MTL still yields more than 10pp higher F1 for these infrequent classes.

Further analysis of our results reveals that the increase in the overall F1 score for MTL over STL is both due to improved component segmentation (BIO labeling) and better type prediction. For example, in the 21K and 6K data settings, the BIO labeling improves by 1-4pp macro-F1 for nearly all datasets and even by up to 17% for wiki. Unsurprisingly, in most cases, MTL also reduces invalid BIO sequences ('O' followed by 'I'). Regarding the F1 scores of argument component types, we observe an improvement of MTL over STL for claims or major claims in all datasets containing these types and for premises in all but one dataset. It is further interesting that for the hotel dataset, MTL confuses premises mainly with the semantically similar implicit premises, whereas STL confuses premises with claims. Moreover, in both hotel and essays, claims are rarely predicted to be major claims, but major claims are predicted to be claims (both STL and MTL).

These results indicate that, despite the different domains and label spaces of the six datasets, MTL appears to learn generalized cross-domain representations of argument components, which aid argument component identification in sparse data scenarios and across domains.

5 Concluding Remarks

We showed that MTL improves performance over STL on AM tasks (particularly) when training data is sparse. More precisely, argument component identification on a small AM dataset improves when treating other AM datasets as auxiliary tasks, even if these include different component types, coming from diverse domains. Overall, our results challenge the view that MTL is only infrequently effective for semantic or higher-level tasks (Alonso and Plank, 2017). We attribute the success of MTL over STL to a few factors in our setting: (1) Alonso and Plank (2017) used syntactic auxiliary tasks for semantic main tasks, whereas we choose only higher-level auxiliary tasks for higher-level main tasks. (2) The label spaces of all our tasks are relatively small, so that generalized representations can be learned in the LSTMs' hidden layers without suffering from *label* sparsity. (3) The AM tasks considered here apparently do share common ground, a finding worth mentioning in itself given the contrary evidence in related work (Daxenberger et al., 2017).

Our findings cannot be readily anticipated by previous research, which has reached mixed conclusions regarding the effectiveness of MTL overall and particular aspects, such as the size of main task. For example, while Luong et al. (2016) suggest that success of MTL requires that the auxiliary task does not swamp the main task data, Benton et al. (2017) and Yang et al. (2017) come to the opposite conclusion that MTL is particularly effective when the data of the main task is small, and Bingel and Søgaard (2017) find a low correlation between size of the main task and MTL success. Our curves in Figure 1 appear to *prefer* the view that MTL is effective when the main task training data is sparse.

The scope for future work is vast. For example, it would be interesting to investigate whether standard low-level tasks, such as POS tagging or chunking, are effective for AM. Furthermore, other architectures for multi-task learning that apply soft parameter sharing, such as sluice networks (Ruder et al., 2017), will be investigated.

Acknowledgments

Calculations for this research were conducted on the Lichtenberg high performance cluster of Technische Universität Darmstadt. This work has been supported by the German Federal Ministry of Education and Research (BMBF) under the promotional references 16DHL1040 (FAMULUS), 01UG1816B (CEDIFOR), and 03VP02540 (ArgumenText).

References

Khalid Al-Khatib, Henning Wachsmuth, Matthias Hagen, Jonas Köhler, and Benno Stein. 2016. Cross-Domain Mining of Argumentative Text through Distant Supervision. In *Proceedings of the 15th Conference of the North American Chapter of the Association for Computational Linguistics: Human Language Technologies*. pages 1395–1404.

Khalid Al-Khatib, Henning Wachsmuth, Matthias Hagen, and Benno Stein. 2017. Patterns of Argumentation Strategies across Topics. In *Proceedings of the 2017 Conference on Empirical Methods in Natural Language Processing*. pages 1362–1368.

Héctor Martínez Alonso and Barbara Plank. 2017. When is multitask learning effective? Semantic sequence prediction under varying data conditions. In *Proceedings of the 15th Conference of the European Chapter of the Association for Computational Linguistics*. volume 1, pages 44–53.

Isabelle Augenstein and Anders Søgaard. 2017. Multi-Task Learning of Keyphrase Boundary Classification. In *Proceedings of the 55th Annual Meeting of the Association for Computational Linguistics*. volume 2, pages 341–346.

Adrian Benton, Margaret Mitchell, and Dirk Hovy. 2017. Multi-Task Learning for Mental Health using Social Media Text. In *Proceedings of the 15th Conference of the European Chapter of the Association for Computational Linguistics*. volume 1, pages 152–162.

Joachim Bingel and Anders Søgaard. 2017. Identifying beneficial task relations for multi-task learning in deep neural networks. In *Proceedings of the 15th Conference of the European Chapter of the Association for Computational Linguistics*. volume 2, pages 164–169.

Or Biran and Owen Rambow. 2011. Identifying Justifications in Written Dialogs by Classifying Text as Argumentative. *International Journal of Semantic Computing* 5(4):363–381.

Marcel Bollmann and Anders Søgaard. 2016. Improving historical spelling normalization with bidirectional LSTMs and multi-task learning. In *Proceedings of the 26th International Conference on Computational Linguistics*. pages 131–139.

Chloé Braud, Ophélie Lacroix, and Anders Søgaard. 2017. Cross-lingual and cross-domain discourse segmentation of entire documents. In *Proceedings of the 55th Annual Meeting of the Association for Computational Linguistics*. volume 2, pages 237–243.

Chloé Braud, Barbara Plank, and Anders Søgaard. 2016. Multi-view and multi-task training of RST discourse parsers. In *Proceedings of the 26th International Conference on Computational Linguistics*. pages 1903–1913.

Rich Caruana. 1993. Multitask Learning: A Knowledge-Based Source of Inductive Bias. In *Proceedings of the 10th International Conference on Machine Learning*. volume 2, pages 41–48.

Rich Caruana. 1996. Algorithms and Applications for Multitask Learning. In *Proceedings of the 13th International Conference on Machine Learning*. pages 87–95.

Ronan Collobert, Jason Weston, Léon Bottou, Michael Karlen, Koray Kavukcuoglu, and Pavel Kuksa. 2011. Natural Language Processing (Almost) from Scratch. *Journal of Machine Learning Research* 12:2493–2537.

Johannes Daxenberger, Steffen Eger, Ivan Habernal, Christian Stab, and Iryna Gurevych. 2017. What is the Essence of a Claim? Cross-Domain Claim Identification. In *Proceedings of the 2017 Conference on Empirical Methods in Natural Language Processing*. pages 2045–2056.

Steffen Eger, Johannes Daxenberger, and Iryna Gurevych. 2017. Neural End-to-End Learning for Computational Argumentation Mining. In *Proceedings of the 55th Annual Meeting of the Association for Computational Linguistics*. volume 1, pages 11–22.

Yang Gao, Hao Wang, Chen Zhang, and Wei Wang. 2017. Reinforcement Learning Based Argument Component Detection. *arxiv* http://arxiv.org/abs/1702.06239.

Ivan Habernal and Iryna Gurevych. 2017. Argumentation mining in user-generated web discourse. *Computational Linguistics* 43(1):125–179.

Ivan Habernal, Henning Wachsmuth, Iryna Gurevych, and Benno Stein. 2017. The Argument Reasoning Comprehension Task. Technical report. http://arxiv.org/abs/1708.01425.

Kazuma Hashimoto, Caiming Xiong, Yoshimasa Tsuruoka, and Richard Socher. 2017. A Joint Many-Task Model: Growing a Neural Network for Multiple NLP Tasks. In *Proceedings of the 30th Conference on Neural Information Processing Systems*. pages 1–17.

Alexandros Komninos and Suresh Manandhar. 2016. Dependency Based Embeddings for Sentence Classification Tasks. In *Proceedings of the 15th Conference of the North American Chapter of the Association for Computational Linguistics: Human Language Technologies*. pages 1490–1500.

Haijing Liu, Yang Gao, Pin Lv, Mengxue Li, Shiqiang Geng, Minglan Li, and Hao Wang. 2017. Using Argument-based Features to Predict and Analyse Review Helpfulness. In *Proceedings of the 2017 Conference on Empirical Methods in Natural Language Processing*. pages 1358–1363.

Minh-Thang Luong, Quoc V. Le, Ilya Sutskever, Oriol Vinyals, and Lukasz Kaiser. 2016. Multi-task Sequence to Sequence Learning. In *Proceedings of the 2016 International Conference on Learning Representations*.

F. Pedregosa, G. Varoquaux, A. Gramfort, V. Michel, B. Thirion, O. Grisel, M. Blondel, P. Prettenhofer, R. Weiss, V. Dubourg, J. Vanderplas, A. Passos, D. Cournapeau, M. Brucher, M. Perrot, and E. Duchesnay. 2011. Scikit-learn: Machine learning in Python. *Journal of Machine Learning Research* 12:2825–2830.

Andreas Peldszus and Manfred Stede. 2013. From argument diagrams to argumentation mining in texts: A survey. *International Journal on of Cognitive Informatics and Natural Intelligence* 7(1):1–31.

Nanyun Peng and Mark Dredze. 2017. Multi-task Multi-domain Representation Learning for Sequence Tagging. In *Proceedings of the 2nd Workshop on Representation Learning for NLP*. pages 91–100.

Jeffrey Pennington, Richard Socher, and Christopher D Manning. 2014. GloVe: Global Vectors for Word Representation. In *Proceedings of the 2014 Conference on Empirical Methods in Natural Language Processing*. pages 1532–1543.

Isaac Persing and Vincent Ng. 2016. End-to-End Argumentation Mining in Student Essays. In *Proceedings of the 15th Conference of the North American Chapter of the Association for Computational Linguistics: Human Language Technologies*. pages 1384–1394.

Barbara Plank, Anders Søgaard, and Yoav Goldberg. 2016. Multilingual Part-of-Speech Tagging with Bidirectional Long Short-Term Memory Models and Auxiliary Loss. In *Proceedings of the 54th Annual Meeting of the Association for Computational Linguistics*. volume 2, pages 412–418.

Chris Reed, Raquel Mochales Palau, Glenn Rowe, and Marie-Francine Moens. 2008. Language Resources for Studying Argument. In *Proceedings of the 6th Conference on Language Resources and Evaluation*. pages 2613–2618.

Nils Reimers and Iryna Gurevych. 2017. Reporting Score Distributions Makes a Difference: Performance Study of LSTM-networks for Sequence Tagging. In *Proceedings of the 2017 Conference on Empirical Methods in Natural Language Processing*. pages 338–348.

Sebastian Ruder, Joachim Bingel, Isabelle Augenstein, and Anders Søgaard. 2017. Sluice networks: Learning what to share between loosely related tasks. http://arxiv.org/abs/1705.08142.

Anders Søgaard and Yoav Goldberg. 2016. Deep multi-task learning with low level tasks supervised at lower layers. In *Proceedings of the 54th Annual Meeting of the Association for Computational Linguistics*. volume 1, pages 231–235.

Christian Stab and Iryna Gurevych. 2017. Parsing Argumentation Structures in Persuasive Essays. *Computational Linguistics* 43(3):619–659.

Zhilin Yang, Ruslan Salakhutdinov, and William W. Cohen. 2017. Transfer learning for sequence tagging with hierarchical recurrent networks. In *Proceedings of the 2017 International Conference on Learning Representations*.

Neural Models for Reasoning over Multiple Mentions using Coreference

Bhuwan Dhingra[1]   **Qiao Jin**[2]   **Zhilin Yang**[1]
William W. Cohen[1]   **Ruslan Salakhutdinov**[1]

[1]Carnegie Mellon University
[2]University of Pittsburgh
{bdhingra,zhiliny,wcohen,rsalakhu}@cs.cmu.edu, qij9@pitt.edu

Abstract

Many problems in NLP require aggregating information from multiple mentions of the same entity which may be far apart in the text. Existing Recurrent Neural Network (RNN) layers are biased towards short-term dependencies and hence not suited to such tasks. We present a recurrent layer which is instead biased towards coreferent dependencies. The layer uses coreference annotations extracted from an external system to connect entity mentions belonging to the same cluster. Incorporating this layer into a state-of-the-art reading comprehension model improves performance on three datasets – Wikihop, LAMBADA and the bAbi AI tasks – with large gains when training data is scarce.

1 Introduction

A long-standing goal of NLP is to build systems capable of reasoning about the information present in text. One important form of reasoning for Question Answering (QA) models is the ability to aggregate information from multiple mentions of entities. We call this *coreference-based reasoning* since multiple pieces of information, which may lie across sentence, paragraph or document boundaries, are tied together with the help of referring expressions which denote the same real-world entity. Figure 1 shows examples.

QA models which directly read text to answer questions (commonly known as Reading Comprehension systems) (Hermann et al., 2015; Seo et al., 2017a), typically consist of RNN layers. RNN layers have a bias towards *sequential recency* (Dyer, 2017), i.e. a tendency to favor short-term dependencies. Attention mechanisms alleviate part of the issue, but empirical studies suggest RNNs with attention also have difficulty modeling long-term dependencies (Daniluk et al., 2017). We conjecture that when training data

is scarce, and inductive biases play an important role, RNN-based models would have trouble with coreference-based reasoning.

<table>
<tr><td>

Context: [...] **mary** got the football there [...] **mary** went to the <u>bedroom</u> [...] **mary** travelled to the hallway [...]
Question: where was the football before the hallway ?

</td></tr>
<tr><td>

Context: Louis-Philippe Fiset [...] was a local physician and politician in the **Mauricie** area [...] is located in the **Mauricie** region of Quebec, <u>Canada</u> [...]
Question: country of citizenship – louis-philippe fiset ?

</td></tr>
</table>

Figure 1: Example questions which require coreference-based reasoning from the bAbi dataset (top) and Wikihop dataset (bottom). Coreferences are in bold, and the correct answers are underlined.

At the same time, systems for coreference resolution have seen a gradual increase in accuracy over the years (Durrett and Klein, 2013; Wiseman et al., 2016; Lee et al., 2017). Hence, in this work we use the annotations produced by such systems to adapt a standard RNN layer by introducing a bias towards *coreferent recency*. Specifically, given an input sequence and coreference clusters extracted from an external system, we introduce a term in the update equations for Gated Recurrent Units (GRU) (Cho et al., 2014) which depends on the hidden state of the coreferent antecedent of the current token (if it exists). This way hidden states are propagated along coreference chains and the original sequence in parallel.

We compare our Coref-GRU layer with the regular GRU layer by incorporating it in a recent model for reading comprehension. On synthetic data specifically constructed to test coreference-based reasoning (Weston et al., 2015), C-GRUs lead to a large improvement over regular GRUs. We show that the structural bias introduced and coreference signals are both important to reach high performance in this case. On a more re-

42

Proceedings of NAACL-HLT 2018, pages 42–48
New Orleans, Louisiana, June 1 - 6, 2018. ©2018 Association for Computational Linguistics

alistic dataset (Welbl et al., 2017), with noisy coreference annotations, we see small but significant improvements over a state-of-the-art baseline. As we reduce the training data, the gains become larger. Lastly, we apply the same model to a broad-context language modeling task (Paperno et al., 2016), where coreference resolution is an important factor, and show improved performance over state-of-the-art.

2 Related Work

Entity-based models. Ji et al. (2017) presented a generative model for jointly predicting the next word in the text and its gold-standard coreference annotation. The difference in our work is that we look at the task of reading comprehension, and also work in the more practical setting of system extracted coreferences. EntNets (Henaff et al., 2016) also maintain dynamic memory slots for entities, but do not use coreference signals and instead update all memories after reading each sentence, which leads to poor performance in the low-data regime (c.f. Table 1). Yang et al. (2017) model references in text as explicit latent variables, but limit their work to text generation. Kobayashi et al. (2016) used a pooling operation to aggregate entity information across multiple mentions. Wang et al. (2017) also noted the importance of reference resolution for reading comprehension, and we compare our model to their one-hot pointer reader.

Syntactic-recency. Recent work has used syntax, in the form of dependency trees, to replace the sequential recency bias in RNNs with a syntactic recency bias (Tai et al., 2015; Swayamdipta, 2017; Qian et al., 2017; Chen et al., 2017). However, syntax only looks at dependencies within sentence boundaries, whereas our focus here is on longer ranges. Our resulting layer is structurally similar to GraphLSTMs (Peng et al., 2017), with an additional attention mechanism over the graph edges. However, while Peng et al. (2017) found that using coreference did not lead to any gains for the task of relation extraction, here we show that it has a positive impact on the reading comprehension task. **Self-Attention** (Vaswani et al., 2017) models are becoming popular for modeling long-term dependencies, and may also benefit from coreference information to bias the learning of those dependencies. Here we focus on recurrent layers and leave such an analysis to future work.

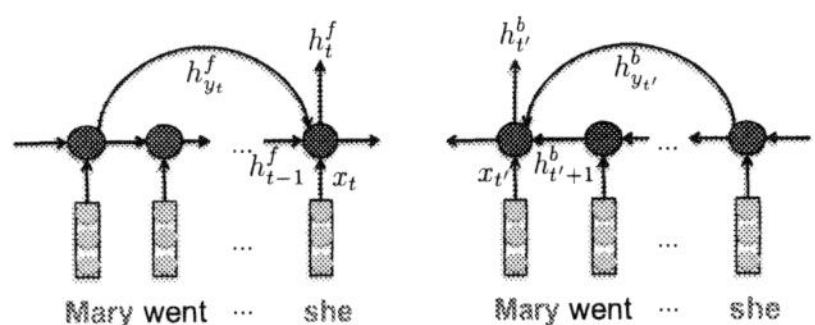

Figure 2: Forward (left) and Backward (right) Coref-GRU layers. **Mary** and **she** are coreferent.

Part of this work was described in an unpublished preprint (Dhingra et al., 2017b). The current paper extends that version and focuses exclusively on coreference relations. We also report results on the WikiHop dataset, including the performance of the model in the low-data regime.

3 Model

Coref-GRU (C-GRU) Layer. Suppose we are given an input sequence $w_1, w_2, \ldots, w_T$ along with their word vectors $x_1, \ldots, x_T$ and annotations for the most recent coreferent antecedent for each token $y_1, \ldots, y_T$, where $y_t \in \{0, \ldots, t-1\}$ and $y_t = 0$ denotes the null antecedent (for tokens not belonging to any cluster). We assume all tokens belonging to a mention in a cluster belong to that cluster, and there are C clusters in total. Our recurrent layer is adapted from GRU cells (Cho et al., 2014), but similar extensions can be derived for other recurrent cells as well. The update equations in a GRU all take the same basic form given by:

$$f(W x_t + U h_{t-1} + b).$$

The bias for sequential recency comes from the second term $U h_{t-1}$. In this work we add another term to introduce a bias towards coreferent recency instead:

$$f(W x_t + \alpha_t U \phi_s(h_{t-1}) + (1 - \alpha_t) U' \phi_c(h_{y_t}) + b),$$

where h_{y_t} is the hidden state of the coreferent antecedent of w_t (with $h_0 = 0$), ϕ_s and ϕ_c are nonlinear functions applied to the hidden states coming from the sequential antecedent and the coreferent antecedent, respectively, and α_t is a scalar weight which decides the relative importance of the two terms based on the current input (so that, for example, pronouns may assign a higher weight for the coreference state). When $y_t = 0$, α_t is set to 1, otherwise it is computed using a key-based addressing scheme (Miller et al., 2016), as $\alpha_t = \text{softmax}(x_t^T k)$, where k is a trainable key vector. In this work we use simple slicing functions $\phi_s(x) = x[1:d/2]$, and $\phi_c(x) = x[d/2:d]$ which decompose the hidden states into a sequential and a coreferent component, respectively. Figure 2 (left) shows an illustration of the layer, and the full update equations are given in Appendix A.

Connection to Memory Networks. We can also view the model as a memory network (Sukhbaatar et al., 2015) with a memory state M_t at each time step which is a $C \times d$ matrix. The rows of this memory matrix correspond to the state of each coreference cluster at time step t. The main difference between Coref-GRUs and a typical memory network such as EntNets (Henaff et al., 2016) lies in the fact that we use coreference annotations to read and write from the memory rather than let model learn how to access the memory. With Coref-GRUs, only the content of the memories needs to be learned. As we shall see in Section 4, this turns out to be a useful bias in the low-data regime.

Bidirectional C-GRU. To extend to the bidirectional case, a second layer is fed the same sequence in the reverse direction, $x_T, \ldots, x_1$ and $y_t \in \{0, t+1, \ldots, T\}$ now denotes the immediately descendent coreferent token from w_t. Outputs from the two layers are then concatenated to form the bi-directional output (see Figure 2).

Complexity. The resulting layer has the same time-complexity as that of a regular GRU layer. The memory complexity increases since we have to keep track of the hidden states for each coreference cluster in the input. If there are C clusters and B is the batch size, the resulting complexity is by $O(BTCd)$. This scales linearly with the input size T, however we leave exploration of more efficient architectures to future work.

Reading comprehension architecture. All tasks we look at involve tuples of the form (p, q, a, C), where the goal is to find the answer a from candidates C to question q with passage p as context. We use the Gated-Attention (GA) reader (Dhingra et al., 2017a) as a base architecture, which computes representations of the passage by passing it through multiple bidirectional GRU layers with an attention mechanism in between layers. We compare the original GA architecture (GA w/ GRU) with one where the bidirectional GRU layers are replaced with bidirectional C-GRU layers (GA w/ C-GRU). Performance is reported in terms of the accuracy of detecting the

correct answer from C, and all models are trained using cross-entropy loss. When comparing two models we ensure the number of parameters are the same in each. Other implementation details are listed in Appendix B.

4 Experiments & Results

Method	Avg	Max	# failed
EntNets (Henaff et al., 2016)	–	0.704	15
QRN (Seo et al., 2017b)	–	**0.901**	7
Bi-GRU	0.727	0.767	13
Bi-C-GRU	0.790	0.831	12
GA w/ GRU	0.764	0.810	10
GA w/ GRU + 1-hot	0.766	0.808	9
GA w/ C-GRU	0.870	0.886	**5**

Table 1: Accuracy on bAbi-1K, averaged across all 20 tasks. Following previous work we run each task for 10 random seeds, and report the **Avg** and **Max** (based on dev set) performance. A task is considered failed if its **Max** performance is < 0.95.

BAbi AI tasks. Our first set of experiments are on the 1K training version of the synthetic bAbi AI tasks (Weston et al., 2015). The passages and questions in this dataset are generated using templates, removing many complexities inherent in natural language, but it still provides a useful testbed for us since some tasks are specifically constructed to test the coreference-based reasoning we tackle here. Experiments on more natural data are described below.

Table 1 shows a comparison of EntNets (Henaff et al., 2016), QRNs (Seo et al., 2017b) (the best published results on bAbi-1K), and our models. We also include the results for a single layer version of GA Reader (which we denote simply as Bi-GRU or Bi-C-GRU when using coreference) to enable fair comparison with EntNets. In each case we see clear improvements of using C-GRU layers over GRU layers. Interestingly, EntNets, which have $>99\%$ performance when trained with $10K$ examples only reach 70% performance with 1K training examples. The Bi-C-GRU model significantly improves on this baseline, which shows that, with less data, coreference annotations can provide a useful bias for a memory network on how to read and write memories.

A break-down of task-wise performance is given in Appendix C. Comparing C-GRU to the GRU based method, we find that the main gains are on tasks 2 (two supporting facts), 3 (three supporting facts) and 16 (basic induction). All these

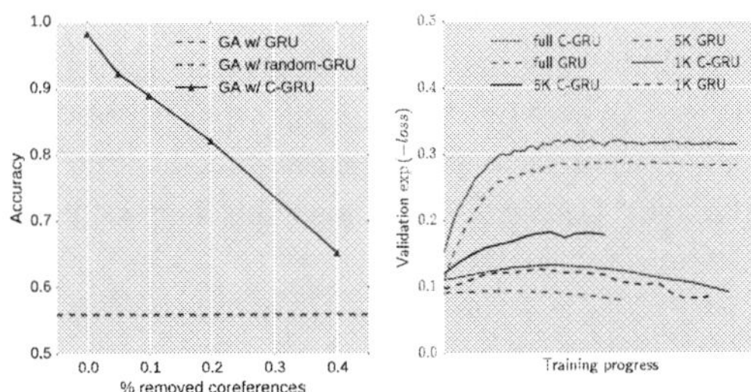

Figure 3: **Left:** Accuracy of GA w/ C-GRU as coreference annotations are removed for bAbi task 3. **Right:** Expected probability of correct answer ($\exp(-loss)$) on Validation set as training progresses on Wikihop dataset for 1K, 5K and the full training datasets.

Method	Follow	Follow +single	Follow +multiple	Overall	
	Dev	Dev	Dev	Dev	Test
1K					
GA w/ GRU	0.307	0.332	0.287	0.263	–
GA w/ C-GRU	0.355	0.370	0.354	0.330	–
5K					
GA w/ GRU	0.382	0.385	0.390	0.336	–
GA w/ C-GRU	0.452	0.454	0.460	0.401	–
full					
BiDAF	–	–	–	–	0.429
GA w/ GRU	0.606	0.615	0.604	0.549	–
GA w/ C-GRU	**0.614**	**0.616**	**0.614**	**0.560**[†]	**0.593**

Table 2: Accuracy on Wikihop. **Follow:** annotated as answer follows from the given passages. **Follow +multiple:** annotated as requiring multiple passages for answering. **Follow +single** annotated as requiring one passage for answering. [†]$p = 0.057$ using Mcnemar's test compared to GA w/ GRU.

tasks require aggregation of information across sentences to derive the answer. Comparing to the QRN baseline, we found that C-GRU was significantly worse on task 15 (basic deduction). On closer examination we found that this was because our simplistic coreference module which matches tokens exactly was not able to resolve "mice" to "mouses" and "cats" to "cat". On the other hand, C-GRU was significantly better than QRN on task 16 (basic induction).

We also include a baseline which uses coreference features as 1-hot vectors appended to the input word vectors (GA w/ GRU + 1-hot). This provides the model with information about the coreference clusters, but does not improve performance, suggesting that the regular GRU is unable to track the given coreference information across long distances to solve the task. On the other hand, in Figure 3 (left) we show how the performance of GA w/ C-GRU varies as we remove gold-standard mentions from coreference clusters, or if we replace them with random mentions (GA w/ random-GRU). In both cases there is a sharp drop in performance, showing that specifically using coreference for connecting mentions is important.

Wikihop dataset. Next we apply our model to the Wikihop dataset (Welbl et al., 2017), which is specifically constructed to test multi-hop reading comprehension across documents. Each instance in this dataset consists of a collection of passages $(p_1, \ldots, p_N)$, and a query of the form (h, r) where h is an entity and r is a relation. The task is to find the tail entity t from a set of provided candidates $\mathcal{C}$. As preprocessing we concatenate all documents in a random order, and extract coreference anno-

tations from the Berkeley Entity Resolution system (Durrett and Klein, 2013) which gets about 62% F1 score on the CoNLL 2011 test set. We only keep the coreference clusters which contain at least one candidate from $\mathcal{C}$ or an entity which co-occurs with the head entity h. We report results in Table 2 when using the full training set, as well as when using a reduced training set of sizes 1K and 5K, to test the model under a low-data regime. In Figure 3 we also show the training curves of $\exp(-loss)$ on the validation set.

We see higher performance for the C-GRU model in the low data regime, and better generalization throughout the training curve for all three settings. This supports our conjecture that the GRU layer has difficulty learning the kind of coreference-based reasoning required in this dataset, and that the bias towards coreferent recency helps with that. However, perhaps surprisingly, given enough data both models perform comparably. This could either indicate that the baseline learns the required reasoning patterns when given enough data, or, that the bias towards corefence-based reasoning hurts performance for some other types of questions. Indeed, there are 9% questions which are answered correctly by the baseline but not by C-GRU, however, we did not find any consistent patterns among these in our analyses. Lastly, we note that both models vastly outperform the best reported result of BiDAf from

(Welbl et al., 2017)[1]. We believe this is because the GA models select answers from the list of candidatees, whereas BiDAF ignores those candidates.

Method	overall	context
Chu et al. (2017)	0.4900	–
GA w/ GRU	0.5398	0.6677
GA w/ GRU + 1-hot	0.5338	0.6603
GA w/ C-GRU	**0.5569**	**0.6888**[†]

Table 3: Accuracy on LAMBADA test set, averaged across two runs with random initializations. **context:** passages for which the answer is in context. **overall:** full test set for comparison to prior work. $^{\dagger}p < 0.0001$ using Mcnemar's test compared to GA w/ GRU.

LAMBADA dataset. Our last set of experiments is on the broad-context language modeling task of LAMBADA dataset (Paperno et al., 2016). This dataset consists of passages 4-5 sentences long, where the last word needs to be predicted. Interestingly, though, the passages are filtered such that human volunteers were able to predict the missing token given the full passage, but not given only the last sentence. Hence, predicting these tokens involves a broader understanding of the whole passage. Analysis of the questions (Chu et al., 2017) suggests that around 20% of the questions need coreference understanding to answer correctly. Hence, we apply our model which uses coreference information for this task.

We use the same setup as Chu et al. (2017) which formulated the problem as a reading comprehension one by treating the last sentence as query, and the remaining passage as context to extract the answer from. In this manner only 80% of the questions are answerable, but the performance increases substantially compared to pure language modeling based approaches. For this dataset we used Stanford CoreNLP to extract coreferences (Clark and Manning, 2015), which achieved 0.63 F1 on the CoNLL test set. Table 3 shows a comparison of the GA w/ GRU baseline and GA w/ C-GRU models. We see a significant gain in performance when using the layer with coreference bias. Furthermore, the 1-hot baseline which uses the same coreference information, but with sequential recency bias fails to improve over the regular GRU

layer. While the improvement for C-GRU is small, it is significant, and we note that questions in this dataset involve several different types of reasoning out of which we only tackle one specific kind. The proposed GA w/ C-GRU layer sets a new state-of-the-art on this dataset.

5 Conclusion

We present a recurrent layer with a bias towards *coreferent recency*, with the goal of tackling reading comprehension problems which require aggregating information from multiple mentions of the same entity. Our experiments show that when combined with a powerful reading architecture, the layer provides a useful inductive bias for solving problems of this kind. In future work, we aim to apply this model to other problems where long-term dependencies at the document level are important. Noise in the coreference annotations has a detrimental effect on the performance (Figure 3), hence we also aim to explore joint models which learn to do coreference resolution and reading together.

Acknowledgments

This work was supported by NSF under grants CCF-1414030 and IIS-1250956 and by grants from Google.

References

Huadong Chen, Shujian Huang, David Chiang, and Jiajun Chen. 2017. Improved neural machine translation with a syntax-aware encoder and decoder. *ACL*.

Kyunghyun Cho, Bart Van Merriënboer, Caglar Gulcehre, Dzmitry Bahdanau, Fethi Bougares, Holger Schwenk, and Yoshua Bengio. 2014. Learning phrase representations using rnn encoder-decoder for statistical machine translation. *arXiv preprint arXiv:1406.1078*.

Zewei Chu, Hai Wang, Kevin Gimpel, and David McAllester. 2017. Broad context language modeling as reading comprehension. *EACL*.

Kevin Clark and Christopher D Manning. 2015. Entity-centric coreference resolution with model stacking. In *Proceedings of the 53rd Annual Meeting of the Association for Computational Linguistics and the 7th International Joint Conference on Natural Language Processing (Volume 1: Long Papers)*, volume 1, pages 1405–1415.

Michał Daniluk, Tim Rocktäschel, Johannes Welbl, and Sebastian Riedel. 2017. Frustratingly short attention spans in neural language modeling. *ICLR*.

---

[1] The official leaderboard at http://qangaroo.cs.ucl.ac.uk/leaderboard.html shows two models with better performance than reported here (as of April 2018). Since we were unable to find publications for these models we omit them here.

Bhuwan Dhingra, Hanxiao Liu, Zhilin Yang, William W Cohen, and Ruslan Salakhutdinov. 2017a. Gated-attention readers for text comprehension. *ACL*.

Bhuwan Dhingra, Zhilin Yang, William W Cohen, and Ruslan Salakhutdinov. 2017b. Linguistic knowledge as memory for recurrent neural networks. *arXiv preprint arXiv:1703.02620*.

Greg Durrett and Dan Klein. 2013. Easy victories and uphill battles in coreference resolution. In *EMNLP*, pages 1971–1982.

Chris Dyer. 2017. Should neural network architecture reflect linguistic structure? CoNLL Keynote.

Mikael Henaff, Jason Weston, Arthur Szlam, Antoine Bordes, and Yann LeCun. 2016. Tracking the world state with recurrent entity networks. *arXiv preprint arXiv:1612.03969*.

Karl Moritz Hermann, Tomas Kocisky, Edward Grefenstette, Lasse Espeholt, Will Kay, Mustafa Suleyman, and Phil Blunsom. 2015. Teaching machines to read and comprehend. In *Advances in Neural Information Processing Systems*, pages 1693–1701.

Yangfeng Ji, Chenhao Tan, Sebastian Martschat, Yejin Choi, and Noah A Smith. 2017. Dynamic entity representations in neural language models. *EMNLP*.

Sosuke Kobayashi, Ran Tian, Naoaki Okazaki, and Kentaro Inui. 2016. Dynamic entity representation with max-pooling improves machine reading. In *Proceedings of the 2016 Conference of the North American Chapter of the Association for Computational Linguistics: Human Language Technologies*, pages 850–855.

Kenton Lee, Luheng He, Mike Lewis, and Luke Zettlemoyer. 2017. End-to-end neural coreference resolution. *EMNLP*.

Alexander Miller, Adam Fisch, Jesse Dodge, Amir-Hossein Karimi, Antoine Bordes, and Jason Weston. 2016. Key-value memory networks for directly reading documents. *arXiv preprint arXiv:1606.03126*.

Denis Paperno, Germán Kruszewski, Angeliki Lazaridou, Quan Ngoc Pham, Raffaella Bernardi, Sandro Pezzelle, Marco Baroni, Gemma Boleda, and Raquel Fernández. 2016. The lambada dataset: Word prediction requiring a broad discourse context. *ACL*.

Nanyun Peng, Hoifung Poon, Chris Quirk, Kristina Toutanova, and Wen-tau Yih. 2017. Cross-sentence n-ary relation extraction with graph lstms. *Transactions of the Association for Computational Linguistics*, 5:101–115.

Jeffrey Pennington, Richard Socher, and Christopher D. Manning. 2014. Glove: Global vectors for word representation. In *Empirical Methods in Natural Language Processing (EMNLP)*, pages 1532–1543.

Feng Qian, Lei Sha, Baobao Chang, Lu-chen Liu, and Ming Zhang. 2017. Syntax aware lstm model for chinese semantic role labeling. *arXiv preprint arXiv:1704.00405*.

Minjoon Seo, Aniruddha Kembhavi, Ali Farhadi, and Hannaneh Hajishirzi. 2017a. Bidirectional attention flow for machine comprehension. *ICLR*.

Minjoon Seo, Sewon Min, Ali Farhadi, and Hannaneh Hajishirzi. 2017b. Query-reduction networks for question answering. *ICLR*.

Sainbayar Sukhbaatar, Jason Weston, Rob Fergus, et al. 2015. End-to-end memory networks. In *Advances in neural information processing systems*, pages 2440–2448.

Swabha Swayamdipta. 2017. *Learning Algorithms for Broad-Coverage Semantic Parsing*. Ph.D. thesis, Carnegie Mellon University Pittsburgh, PA.

Kai Sheng Tai, Richard Socher, and Christopher D Manning. 2015. Improved semantic representations from tree-structured long short-term memory networks. *ACL*.

Ashish Vaswani, Noam Shazeer, Niki Parmar, Jakob Uszkoreit, Llion Jones, Aidan N Gomez, Lukasz Kaiser, and Illia Polosukhin. 2017. Attention is all you need. *NIPS*.

Hai Wang, Takeshi Onishi, Kevin Gimpel, and David McAllester. 2017. Emergent logical structure in vector representations of neural readers. *2nd Workshop on Representation Learning for NLP, ACL*.

Dirk Weissenborn, Georg Wiese, and Laura Seiffe. 2017. Fastqa: A simple and efficient neural architecture for question answering. *CoNLL*.

Johannes Welbl, Pontus Stenetorp, and Sebastian Riedel. 2017. Constructing datasets for multi-hop reading comprehension across documents. *arXiv preprint arXiv:1710.06481*.

Jason Weston, Antoine Bordes, Sumit Chopra, Alexander M Rush, Bart van Merriënboer, Armand Joulin, and Tomas Mikolov. 2015. Towards ai-complete question answering: A set of prerequisite toy tasks. *arXiv preprint arXiv:1502.05698*.

Sam Wiseman, Alexander M Rush, and Stuart M Shieber. 2016. Learning global features for coreference resolution. *NAACL*.

Zichao Yang, Phil Blunsom, Chris Dyer, and Wang Ling. 2017. Reference-aware language models. *EMNLP*.

A C-GRU update equations

For simplicity, we introduce the variable m_t which concatenates ($\|$) the sequential and coreferent hidden states:

$$m_t = \alpha_t \phi_s(h_{t-1}) \| (1 - \alpha_t)\phi_c(h_{y_t})$$

Then the update equations are given by:

$$r_t = \sigma(W^r x_t + U^r m_t + b^r)$$
$$z_t = \sigma(W^z x_t + U^z m_t + b^z)$$
$$\tilde{h}_t = \tanh(W^h x_t + r_t \odot U^h m_t + b^h)$$
$$h_t = (1 - z_t) \odot m_t + z_t \tilde{h}_t$$

The attention parameter α_t is given by:

$$\alpha_t = \frac{\exp x_t^T k_1}{\exp x_t^T k_1 + \exp x_t^T k_2}$$

where k_1 and k_2 are trainable key vectors.

B Implementation details

We use $K = 3$ layers with the GA architecture. We keep the same hyperparameter settings when using GRU or C-GRU layers, which we describe here.

For the **bAbi** dataset, we use a hidden state size of $d = 64$, batch size of $B = 32$, and learning rate 0.01 which is halved after every 120 updates. We also use dropout with rate 0.1 at the output of each layer. The maximum number of coreference clusters across all tasks was $C = 13$. Half of the tasks in this dataset are extractive, meaning the answer is present in the passage, whereas the other half are classification tasks, where the answer is in a list of candidates which may not be in the passage. For the extractive tasks, we use the attention sum layer as described in the GA Reader paper (Dhingra et al., 2017a). For the classification tasks we replace this with a softmax layer for predicting one of the classes.

For the **Wikihop** dataset, we use a hidden state size of $d = 64$, batch size $B = 16$, and learning rate of 0.0005 which was halved every 2500 updates. The maximum number of coreference clusters was set to 50 for this dataset. We used dropout of 0.2 in between the intermediate layers, and initialized word embeddings with Glove (Pennington et al., 2014). We also used character embeddings, which were concatenated with the word embeddings, of size 10. These were output from a CNN layer with 50 filters each of width 5. Following (Weissenborn et al., 2017), we also appended a feature to the word embeddings in the passage which indicated if the token appeared in the query or not.

For the **LAMBADA** dataset, we use a hidden state size of $d = 256$, batch size of $B = 64$, and learning rate of 0.0005 which was halved every 2 epochs. Word vectors were initialized with Glove, and dropout of 0.2 was applied after intermediate layers. The maximum number of coreference clusters in this dataset was 15.

C Task-wise bAbi performance

Task	QRN	GA w/ GRU	GA w/ C-GRU
1: Single Supporting Fact	1.000	0.997	1.000
2: Two Supporting Facts	**0.993**	**0.345**	**0.990**
3: Three Supporting Facts	**0.943**	**0.558**	**0.982**
4: Two Argument Relations	1.000	1.000	1.000
5: Three Argument Relations	0.989	0.989	0.993
6: Yes/No Questions	0.991	0.962	0.976
7: Counting	**0.904**	**0.946**	**0.976**
8: Lists / Sets	0.944	0.947	0.964
9: Simple Negation	1.000	0.991	0.990
10: Indefinite Knowledge	1.000	0.992	0.986
11: Basic Coreference	1.000	0.995	0.996
12: Conjunction	1.000	1.000	0.996
13: Compound Coreference	1.000	0.998	0.993
14: Time Reasoning	**0.992**	**0.895**	**0.849**
15: Basic Deduction	**1.000**	**0.521**	**0.470**
16: Basic Induction	**0.470**	**0.488**	**0.999**
17: Positional Reasoning	0.656	0.580	0.574
18: Size Reasoning	0.921	0.908	0.896
19: Path Finding	0.213	0.095	0.099
20: Agent's Motivation	0.998	0.998	1.000
Average	**0.901**	**0.810**	**0.886**

Table 4: Breakdown of task-wise performance on bAbi dataset. Tasks where C-GRU is significant better / worse than either GRU or QRNs are highlighted.

Automatic Dialogue Generation with Expressed Emotions

Chenyang Huang, Osmar R. Zaïane, Amine Trabelsi, Nouha Dziri
Department of Computing Science, University of Alberta
{chuang8,zaiane,atrabels,dziri}@ualberta.ca

Abstract

Despite myriad efforts in the literature designing neural dialogue generation systems in recent years, very few consider putting restrictions on the response itself. They learn from collections of past responses and generate one based on a given utterance without considering, speech act, desired style or emotion to be expressed. In this research, we address the problem of forcing the dialogue generation to express emotion. We present three models that either concatenate the desired emotion with the source input during the learning, or push the emotion in the decoder. The results, evaluated with an emotion tagger, are encouraging with all three models, but present better outcome and promise with our model that adds the emotion vector in the decoder.

1 Introduction

Automatic dialogue generation (Ritter et al., 2011) aims at generating human-like responses given a human-to-human dialogue history. Most conversational agents are specialized for a specific domain such as travel booking (Xu and Rudnicky, 2000) and are typically finite state-based or template-based. Open domain dialogue systems have seen a growing interest in recent years thanks to neural dialogue generation systems, based on deep learning models. These systems do not encode dialog structure and are entirely data-driven. They learn to predict the maximum-likelihood estimation (MLE) based on a large training corpus. The machine learning-based system basically learns to predict the words and the sentence to respond based on the previous utterances. However, while such a system can generate grammatically correct and human-like answers, the responses are often generic and non-committal instead of being specific and emotionally intelligent. For instance, we can not dictate a particular emotion to express.

In this paper, we consider a model in which the wished emotion to be expressed is injected to direct the response generation. For example, if the user says: "I just missed my deadline." If we want the system to respond with sadness, it could be "I am sorry to hear that.", but we can also force the response to express anger: "You should never do it again!"

There are some challenges to tackle this task.

- The current neural dialogue models are not satisfactory in general.

- There is a lack of dialogue corpora that are labeled with emotions.

- The evaluation is hard because emotion is subjective and sometimes ambiguous.

The idea is to use an emotion mining from text classifier (Yadollahi et al., 2017) to predict the emotion or emotions expressed in the source utterance, then decide based on the detected emotions, which emotion e is expressed in the response. The response is evaluated using the same emotion classifier and is declared successful if e is predicted from the response. The emotion tagger we use is based on the work in (Yadollahi et al., 2017) but uses a deep learning model and trains on 9 emotions: *anger, disgust, fear, guilt, joy, love, sadness, surprise*, and *thankfulness*. These are based on the six basic emotions from Ekman's model (Ekman, 1992), to which we added guilt, love and thankfulness in the context of an open ended conversational agent that we aim to be emotionally intelligent for companionship to elderly users.

In this paper, we proposed three approaches to make our model of our conversational agent generate responses expressing specific emotions. The first two approaches add the emotion as a token with the input during the learning either before the

Proceedings of NAACL-HLT 2018, pages 49–54
New Orleans, Louisiana, June 1 - 6, 2018. ©2018 Association for Computational Linguistics

utterance sentence or after, and the third approach injects the desired emotion directly in the decoder.

2   Related Work

Vinyals and Le (2015) adopted the Sequence-to-sequence (Seq2Seq) model used in machine translation (Sutskever et al., 2014) in the task of automatic response generation. Seq2Seq learns to generate a sequence of words from another sequence of words as input. Since then, many works based on this framework have been conducted to improve the response quality from different points of view. Reinforcement learning has also been adopted to force the model to have longer discussions (Li et al., 2016b). Serban et al. (2017) proposed a hierarchical encoder to generate a response from more utterances. Moreover, there are also attempts to avoid generating dull, short responses (Li et al., 2017a,b).

3   Embed Emotion into Seq2Seq Models

Seq2Seq is a conditional language model which takes as input message-response pairs (X, Y), where $X = x_1, x_2, \cdots, x_m$ and $Y = y_1, y_2, \cdots, y_n$ are sentences consisting of sequences of words. The goal of the model is to minimize the cross entropy loss $\mathcal{L} = \log p(Y|X)$. Despite the variants of Seq2Seq models, they usually consist of two major components: encoder and decoder. The encoder embeds a source message into a vector which is then fed into the decoder. The decoder generates $\hat{Y} = \hat{y_1}, \hat{y_2}, \cdots$ step by step. This procedure can be described as $c = \text{Encoder}(X), Y = \text{Decoder}(c)$. In our case, each (X, Y) pair is assigned with an additional desired response emotion e. Our goal is therefore to minimize $-\log p(Y|X, e)$. We propose two methods to tackle this task based on how to embed e, either concatenating an emotion token to the input message, or injecting the emotion into the decoder.

3.1   Seq2Seq with Attention

The choice of our encoder is LSTM (Hochreiter and Schmidhuber, 1997) and it can be formulated as the following.

$$h_t^{En}, c_t^{En} = \text{LSTM}^{En}(M(x_i), [h_{t-1}^{En}; c_{t-1}^{En}])$$
$$h_0^{En} = c_0^{En} = \mathbf{0} \tag{1}$$

Where h_t^{En} and c_t^{En} are encoder's hidden state and cell state at time t. $M(x)$ is the vector representation of word x (Mikolov et al., 2013). In our experiments, we apply the state-of-the-art *FastText* (Joulin et al., 2016) pre-trained model.

Adapting attention mechanism in sequence generation has shown promising improvement (Bahdanau et al., 2014; Luong et al., 2015). In our case, we use the global attention with general score function (Luong et al., 2015) under the assumption that generated words can be aligned to any of the words in the previous dialogue utterance. We use another LSTM to decode the information, the decoder with attention can be described as:

$$\mathbf{h}^{En} = [h_1^{En}, h_2^{En}, \cdots, h_m^{En}] \tag{2}$$
$$\hat{h}_t = \alpha_t \cdot \mathbf{h}^{En} \tag{3}$$
$$\alpha_t = \text{Softmax}(h_t^{De} W_a \mathbf{h}^{En}) \tag{4}$$
$$h_t^{De}, c_t^{De} = \text{LSTM}^{De}(M(y_i), [\hat{h}_{t-1}; c_{t-1}^{De}]) \tag{5}$$
$$\hat{h}_0 = h_m^{En}, c_0^{De} = c_m^{En} \tag{6}$$

Where h_t^{De} and c_t^{De} are hidden state and cell state. α_t is the attention weights over all hidden states of encoder. W_a is a trainable matrix which is initialized randomly.

3.2   Embedding Emotion

Our first model is inspired by Google's multilingual neural machine translation system (Johnson et al., 2016). Generating different types of emotional responses can be an analogy to translating the same sentence into different languages. The implementation is straight forward; we make each emotion a single token and concatenate it with the input X so that our model has the target of minimizing $\log p(Y|X')$, where $X' = \text{Concat}(e, X)$. This approach reduces the two individual inputs into one so that they can be trained on normal Seq2Seq models. Further more, we consider the concatenation in two ways, before X and after X, as the following.

$$X_1 = \{e, x_1, x_2, \cdots, x_m\} \ (Enc - bef) \tag{7}$$
$$X_2 = \{x_1, x_2, \cdots, x_m, e\} \ (Enc - aft) \tag{8}$$

Both of the methods are embedding the desired emotion into an encoder. We name them *Enc-bef* and *Enc-aft*, respectively. e is the emotion of the generated response and is obtained from Y by an emotion mining classifier. Both models require to change the m in (2) and (6) to $m + 1$.

Li et al. (2016a) proposed a modified Seq2Seq model that allows models to learn the speaking

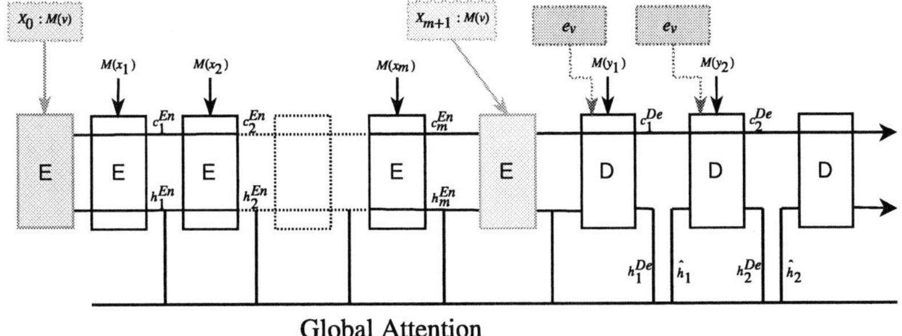

Figure 1: Three models to embed emotion: orange and yellow are the addition emotion tokens to concatenate with the source sentences for model *Enc-bef* and *Enc-aft* respectively. The salmon-colored blocks represent the emotion vectors which need to be feed into decoder of model *Dec* repeatedly.

styles of different people from a movie script corpus. Our third approach adapts their idea but instead of embedding people/speaker into the decoder, we feed the emotion vectors v_e during the decoding. Equation (5) is changed to $h_t^{De}, c_t^{De} =$ LSTM$^{De}(M(y_i), [\hat{h}_{t-1}; c_{t-1}^{De}; v_e])$. v_e is drawn from a trainable embedding layer. We name this model *Dec*. The models are shown in Figure 1.

4 Dataset

To train the dialogue models, we use the Open-Subtitles dataset (lis, 2016). Precisely, we use the pre-processed data by (Li et al., 2016a) and further removed duplicates. The total amount of utterances is 11.3 million, each utterance has a minimal length of 6 words.

Since there is no existing dialogue data set labeled with emotions, we trained our own emotion classifier to tag the corpus. We use the CBET dataset [1] (Yadollahi et al., 2017; Shahraki and Zaiane, 2017), it contains 9 emotions and 81k instances. Each instance is labeled with up to two emotions. The emotions are *anger, surprise, joy, love, sadness, fear, disgust, guilt*, and *thankfulness*. We train a bidirectional LSTM (Graves et al., 2005) model and achieve an F1-score of 68.4% with precision 49.1% and recall 52.9% on these emotions. To tag the target utterances with higher confidence, we use a threshold to separate those utterances that do not express emotion. 34.01% are thus labeled as Non-emotion. 'Non-emotion' is treated as a special emotion when training the dialogue models, but it is not considered in the evaluation.

5 Experiments and Evaluation

5.1 Seq2Seq

With the purpose of comparison, the parameters of the three models are set to be the same. The dimensions of LSTM hidden units are set to 600. Adam optimizer (Kingma and Ba, 2014) with learning rate of 0.0001 is used. The size of the vocabulary space is set to 25,000, which is the same as that in (Li et al., 2016a). We also use *FastText* (Joulin et al., 2016) pre-trained word embedding which is shared by the LSTMs in both encoder and decoder and set to trainable. We held out 50k samples from the whole dataset as test set. 95% of the remaining is used to train the dialogue models, and 5% of it is used for evaluation and preventing overfitting.

5.2 Accuracy of Expressed Emotions

In this research, we tackle the problem of training a generative model that can respond while expressing a specific emotion. Unlike the work by (Li et al., 2016a), expensive human evaluation is not needed. Instead, we evaluate the output using an emotion mining classifier to see whether the intended emotion is among the detected ones. For each input utterance, we let the model generate responses for each of the 9 emotions and check, using the emotion classifier, which emotion is indeed expressed in the output. Hence, the emotions' accuracies of the generated responses are estimated by the emotion classifier. Different from the procedure of tagging, where we put a threshold to enforce a higher precision, the most possible emotion is chosen in the evaluation. The results are shown in Table 1.

---

[1] http://www.cs.ualberta.ca/~zaiane/data/CBET/CBET.csv

Emotion	*Enc-bef*	*Enc-aft*	*Dec*
anger	60.34%	62.44%	68.24%
fear	89.34%	86.46%	87.52%
joy	45.76%	41.36%	48.53%
love	56.96%	55.32%	59.13%
sadness	94.16%	93.93%	94.22%
surprise	84.46%	85.11%	87.22%
thankfulness	87.89%	89.51%	91.06%
disgust	78.06%	76.94%	79.01%
guilt	93.25%	92.16%	91.22%
Average	76.69%	75.91%	78.46%

Table 1: Per class accuracy of generated response

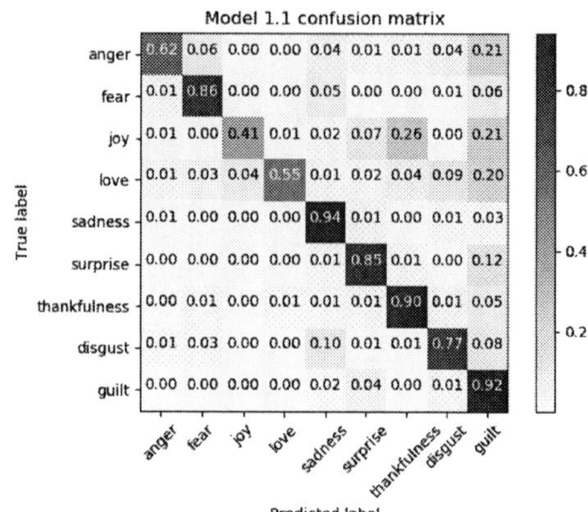

Figure 3: Confusion matrix of model *Enc-aft*

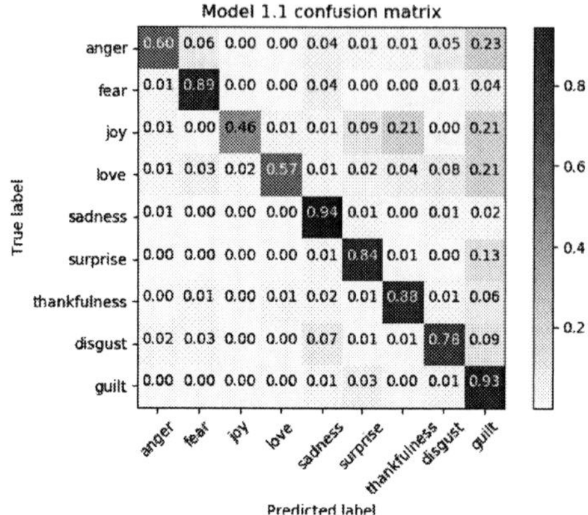

Figure 2: Confusion matrix of model *Enc-bef*

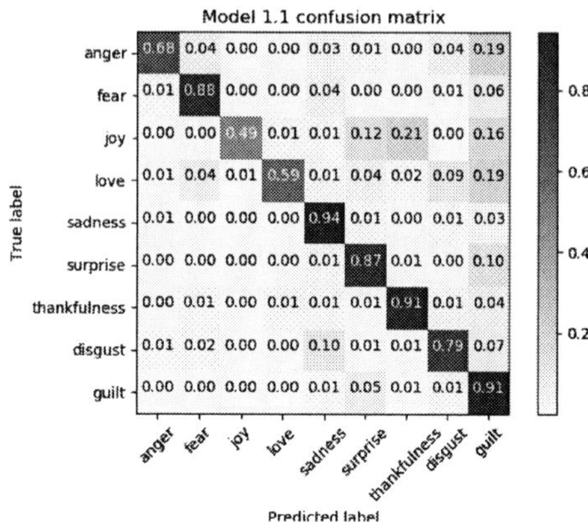

Figure 4: Confusion matrix of model *Dec*

6   Results and Discussion

From Table 1, we can observe that *Dec* has better overall average accuracies than *Enc-bef* and *Enc-aft*. The average accuracies of *Enc-bef* and *Enc-aft* are very close. However, we notice some discrepancies in the individual emotions' accuracies. For instance, *fear* is better captured by *Enc-bef*, while *anger* has a much better accuracy for *Dec*.

To further inspect the results, we also show the normalized confusion matrix of each model respectively, as in Figure 2, 3 and 4. We can notice obvious dark colored diagonals for the three figures. This indicates that all the three proposed models, indeed, have the ability to generate responses with given emotions. From these figures, we find that models tend to generate the responses with *guilt* regardless of the desired emotion. All the three models tend to generate *thankfulness* while they were instructed to express *joy*.

The patterns of confusion matrices of model *Enc-aft*, *Enc-bef* and *Dec* are close to each other. However, Dec model has a slightly better overall performance.

Tables 2 and 3 display examples of generated responses, according to different emotions, given a source utterance extracted from the test set. We can observe that the generated text is: (1) related to the source text; (2) expresses the desired emotions. For instance, when responding to "What is she doing here?", the generated text employs "she" rather than "he". The models are also able to express the emotion of *fear* by generating the word "afraid". When instructed to respond to the previous utterance "I didn't realize you were here", and to express *guilt*, all the models are able to generate "I am sorry". In terms of semantics, while the source is mentioning "here", the *Dec* model is able to answer with "I was just in the garden" which remains coherent with the location context.

Since increasing the diversity is not the target of this work, our models also suffer from this com-

source	what is she doing here ?
target	how do i open this god forsaken window !
anger *Enc-bef*	she 's going to kill herself
anger *Enc-aft*	she 's going to kill you
anger *Dec*	she 's supposed to be in the house
fear *Enc-bef*	i 'm afraid i can 't tell you
fear *Enc-aft*	she 's trying to kill herself
fear *Dec*	i 'm afraid she 's not here
love *Enc-bef*	she wants to see you in the bedroom
love *Enc-aft*	she 's in love with you
love *Dec*	she wants to be with you
disgust *Enc-bef*	she 's not allowed to leave
disgust *Enc-aft*	she 's going to be sick
disgust *Dec*	she 's the one who raped me

Table 2: Examples of generated responses by the three models with emotions *anger*, *fear*, *love* and *disgust*.

source	i didn 't realize you were here
target you	maybe i should leave so can continue
joy *Enc-bef*	i 'm here to make a phone call
joy *Enc-aft*	i 'm so happy for you
joy *Dec*	i was just in the garden house
sadness *Enc-bef*	i thought you were gonna be here
sadness *Enc-aft*	she 's trying to kill herself
sadness *Dec*	i thought i 'd be here
guilt *Enc-bef*	i 'm sorry i didn 't
guilt *Enc-aft* you	i 'm sorry i didn 't know were here
guilt *Dec*	i 'm sorry i didn 't hear you
surprise *Enc-bef*	i 'm here to find out
surprise *Enc-aft*	i thought you were going to be here
surprise *Dec*	i thought you might be here

Table 3: Examples of generated responses by the three models with emotions *joy*, *sadness*, *guilt* and *surprise*.

mon problem of Seq2Seq models. Similar to generating "I don't know" regardless of source sentences, in Seq2Seq models (Sordoni et al., 2015; Serban et al., 2016; Li et al., 2016b), our model tends to generate "I <unk>l be back in a minute" for emotion *anger*. The diversity of words that are used for each emotion are low, e.g., generations for emotion *fear* often have the word "gun" and the responses of emotion "sadness" often start with "I don't want ". This is clearly a side effect from our training data.

7 Conclusion

Emotional intelligence is the ability to monitor interlocutor's emotions and in turn appropriately express emotions in response. In our case, monitoring emotions in utterances is done using an emotion mining classifier. We assume that given some mapping rules, we can decide to express a specific emotion in the response. For instance if the message expresses sadness, the response could express compassion or surprise depending upon context. The work presented herein focuses solely on generating a response that expresses a given desired emotion, and assumes the emotion to be expressed is given via these mapping rules. However, one could automatically learn the emotion to express given the emotion in the message directly from the data by changing the input message-response pairs (X, Y) into $((X, e_X), (Y, e_Y))$ where e_X is the emotion in the message and e_Y is the emotion in the response. In this paper, we show that it is indeed possible to generate fluent responses that express a desired emotion. We present three models to do so. Despite the differences among the models, they are all trained towards minimizing $- \log p(Y|X, e)$ and all converge. The expression of some emotions (*guilt*, *sadness* and *thankfulness*) even reach accuracies over the 90%.

In our early experiments, we tagged each of the target utterance with the most possible emotion regardless of its confidence, wrongly assuming that all target utterances have a significant emotion. Although, our generative models can still be forced to produce the desired emotions, the quality of the generated sentences in terms of expressed emotions is below what is presented in Table 1 where the utterances without emotions (below a certain threshold) were labeled by "Non-Emotion". This shows the importance of learning to express emotions only from the utterances that indeed strongly convey measurable emotions. The other sentences are still kept to contribute in building the language model. We believe that adding reasoning to the mix can further enhance the emotional intelligence of a conversational agent.

References

2016. Opensubtitles2016: Extracting large parallel corpora from movie and tv subtitles.

Dzmitry Bahdanau, Kyunghyun Cho, and Yoshua Bengio. 2014. Neural machine translation by jointly learning to align and translate. *arXiv preprint arXiv:1409.0473* .

Paul Ekman. 1992. An argument for basic emotions. *Cognition and Emotion* 6:169–200.

Alex Graves, Santiago Fernández, and Jürgen Schmidhuber. 2005. Bidirectional lstm networks for improved phoneme classification and recognition. *Artificial Neural Networks: Formal Models and Their Applications–ICANN 2005* pages 753–753.

Sepp Hochreiter and Jürgen Schmidhuber. 1997. Long short-term memory. *Neural computation* 9(8):1735–1780.

Melvin Johnson, Mike Schuster, Quoc V Le, Maxim Krikun, Yonghui Wu, Zhifeng Chen, Nikhil Thorat, Fernanda Viégas, Martin Wattenberg, Greg Corrado, et al. 2016. Google's multilingual neural machine translation system: enabling zero-shot translation. *arXiv preprint arXiv:1611.04558* .

Armand Joulin, Edouard Grave, Piotr Bojanowski, Matthijs Douze, Hérve Jégou, and Tomas Mikolov. 2016. Fasttext.zip: Compressing text classification models. *arXiv preprint arXiv:1612.03651* .

Diederik P Kingma and Jimmy Ba. 2014. Adam: A method for stochastic optimization. *arXiv preprint arXiv:1412.6980* .

Jiwei Li, Michel Galley, Chris Brockett, Georgios Spithourakis, Jianfeng Gao, and Bill Dolan. 2016a. A persona-based neural conversation model. In *Proceedings of the 54th Annual Meeting of the Association for Computational Linguistics (Volume 1: Long Papers)*. volume 1, pages 994–1003.

Jiwei Li, Will Monroe, and Dan Jurafsky. 2017a. Data distillation for controlling specificity in dialogue generation. *arXiv preprint arXiv:1702.06703* .

Jiwei Li, Will Monroe, Alan Ritter, Michel Galley, Jianfeng Gao, and Dan Jurafsky. 2016b. Deep reinforcement learning for dialogue generation. *arXiv preprint arXiv:1606.01541* .

Jiwei Li, Will Monroe, Tianlin Shi, Alan Ritter, and Dan Jurafsky. 2017b. Adversarial learning for neural dialogue generation. *arXiv preprint arXiv:1701.06547* .

Minh-Thang Luong, Hieu Pham, and Christopher D Manning. 2015. Effective approaches to attention-based neural machine translation. *arXiv preprint arXiv:1508.04025* .

Tomas Mikolov, Ilya Sutskever, Kai Chen, Greg S Corrado, and Jeff Dean. 2013. Distributed representations of words and phrases and their compositionality. In *Advances in neural information processing systems*. pages 3111–3119.

Alan Ritter, Colin Cherry, and William B Dolan. 2011. Data-driven response generation in social media. In *Proceedings of the conference on empirical methods in natural language processing*. Association for Computational Linguistics, pages 583–593.

Iulian Vlad Serban, Alessandro Sordoni, Yoshua Bengio, Aaron C Courville, and Joelle Pineau. 2016. Building end-to-end dialogue systems using generative hierarchical neural network models. In *AAAI*. pages 3776–3784.

Iulian Vlad Serban, Alessandro Sordoni, Ryan Lowe, Laurent Charlin, Joelle Pineau, Aaron C Courville, and Yoshua Bengio. 2017. A hierarchical latent variable encoder-decoder model for generating dialogues. In *AAAI*. pages 3295–3301.

Ameneh Gholipour Shahraki and Osmar R Zaiane. 2017. Lexical and learning-based emotion mining from text. In *Proceedings of the International Conference on Computational Linguistics and Intelligent Text Processing*.

Alessandro Sordoni, Michel Galley, Michael Auli, Chris Brockett, Yangfeng Ji, Margaret Mitchell, Jian-Yun Nie, Jianfeng Gao, and Bill Dolan. 2015. A neural network approach to context-sensitive generation of conversational responses. *arXiv preprint arXiv:1506.06714* .

Ilya Sutskever, Oriol Vinyals, and Quoc V Le. 2014. Sequence to sequence learning with neural networks. In *Advances in neural information processing systems*. pages 3104–3112.

Oriol Vinyals and Quoc Le. 2015. A neural conversational model. *arXiv preprint arXiv:1506.05869* .

Wei Xu and Alexander I Rudnicky. 2000. Task-based dialog management using an agenda. In *Proceedings of the 2000 ANLP/NAACL Workshop on Conversational systems-Volume 3*. Association for Computational Linguistics, pages 42–47.

Ali Yadollahi, Ameneh Gholipour Shahraki, and Osmar R Zaiane. 2017. Current state of text sentiment analysis from opinion to emotion mining. *ACM Computing Surveys (CSUR)* 50(2):25.

Guiding Generation for Abstractive Text Summarization based on Key Information Guide Network

Chenliang Li and **Weiran Xu**[*] and **Si Li** and **Sheng Gao**
Beijing University of Posts and Telecommunications, Beijing
`chenliangli,xuweiran,lisi,gaosheng@bupt.edu.cn`

Abstract

Neural network models, based on the attentional encoder-decoder model, have good capability in abstractive text summarization. However, these models are hard to be controlled in the process of generation, which leads to a lack of key information. We propose a guiding generation model that combines the extractive method and the abstractive method. Firstly, we obtain keywords from the text by a extractive model. Then, we introduce a Key Information Guide Network (KIGN), which encodes the keywords to the key information representation, to guide the process of generation. In addition, we use a prediction-guide mechanism, which can obtain the long-term value for future decoding, to further guide the summary generation. We evaluate our model on the *CNN/Daily Mail* dataset. The experimental results show that our model leads to significant improvements.

1 Introduction

Text summarization aims to generate a brief summary from an input document while retaining the key information. There are two broad approaches to summarization: *extractive* and *abstractive*. *Extractive models* (Mihalcea and Tarau, 2004; Yasunaga et al., 2017) usually extract a few sentences or keywords from the source text, while *abstractive models* (Rush et al., 2015; Nallapati et al., 2016) generate new words and phrases that not in the source text to construct the summary.

Recently, inspired by the success of encoder-decoder model (Sutskever et al., 2014), abstractive summarization models (Nallapati et al., 2016; See et al., 2017) are able to generate the summaries with high ROUGE scores. While these models proved to be capable of capturing the regularities of the text summarization, they are hard to be controlled in the process of generation. Without external guidance, these models just get the source

text as input and then output the summary, which certainly leads to a lack of key information.

Zhou et al. (2017) propose a selective gate network to retain more key information in the summary. However, the selective gate network, which is controlled by the representation of the input text, controls the information flow from encoder to decoder for just once. If some key information does not pass the network, it is hard for them to appear in the summary. See et al. (2017) propose a pointer-generator model, which uses the pointer mechanism (Vinyals et al., 2015) to copy words from the input text, to deal with the out-of-vocabulary (OOV) words. Without external guidance, it is hard for the pointer to identify keywords. To address these problems, we combine the extractive model and the abstractive model and use the former one to obtain keywords as guidance for the latter one.

In this paper we propose a guiding generation model for abstractive text summarization. Firstly, we use a extractive method to obtain the keywords from the text. Then, we introduce a Key Information Guide Network (KIGN), which encodes the keywords to the key information representation and integrates it into the abstractive model, to guide the process of generation. The guidance is mainly in two aspects: the attention mechanism (Bahdanau et al., 2014) and the pointer mechanism. In addition, we propose a novel prediction-guide mechanism based on He et al. (2017), which predicts the extent of key information covered in the final summary, to further guide the summary generation. Experiments show that our model achieves significant improvements.

2 Related work

Neural encoder-decoder models. Abstractive models(Rush et al., 2015; Chopra et al., 2016) have been widely used in text summarization. Nallapati et al. (2016) use a pointer network (Vinyals

---

[*] Corresponding Author: Weiran Xu

55

Proceedings of NAACL-HLT 2018, pages 55–60
New Orleans, Louisiana, June 1 - 6, 2018. ©2018 Association for Computational Linguistics

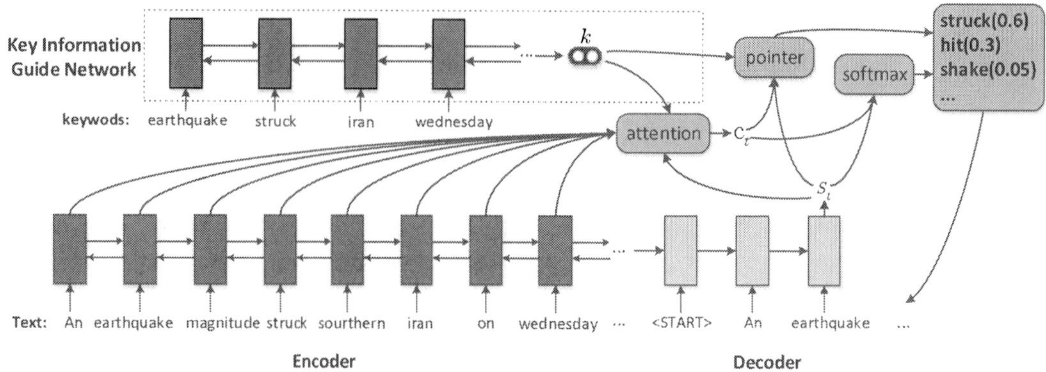

Figure 1: Our key information guide model. It consists of key information guide network, encoder and decoder. In the key information guide network, we encode the keywords to the key information representation k.

et al., 2015) to deal with the unknown word problem.

Keywords extraction. TextRank algorithm (Mihalcea and Tarau, 2004), which extracts keywords from the source text, is unsupervised.

Prediction-guide mechanism. Inspired by the success of AlphaGO, He et al. (2017) propose a prediction network to predict the long-term value of the final summary. Our prediction-guide mechanism is use to guarantee the more key information covered in the final summary.

3 Our Model

In this section, we describe (1) our baseline encoder-decoder model, (2) our key information guide network, and (3) our prediction-guide mechanism.

3.1 Encoder-decoder model based attention

Our baseline model is similar to that of Nallapati et al. (2016). The tokens of the input article $x = \{x_1, x_2, ..., x_N\}$ are fed into the encoder, which maps the text into a sequence of encoder hidden states $\{h_1, h_2, ..., h_n\}$. At each decoding time step t, the decoder reads the previous word embedding w_{t-1} and the previous context vector c_{t-1} as inputs to obtain the decoder hidden state s_t. The context vector c_t is calculated by using the attention mechanism:

$$e_{ti} = v^T tanh(W_h h_i + W_s s_t) \quad (1)$$

$$\alpha_t^e = softmax(e_t) \quad (2)$$

$$c_t = \sum_{i=1}^{N} \alpha_{ti}^e h_i \quad (3)$$

where v, W_h, W_s are learnable parameters, h_i is the hidden state of the input token x_i.

The context vector c_t, which represents what has been read from the source text, is concatenated with the decoder hidden state s_t to predict the next word with a softmax layer over the whole vocabulary:

$$P(y_t|y_1, ..., y_{t-1}) = softmax(f(s_t, c_t)) \quad (4)$$

where f represents a linear function.

3.2 Key information guide network

Most encoder-decoder models (Zhou et al., 2017; See et al., 2017) just get the source text as input and then output the summary, which is hard to be controlled in the process of generation and leads to a lack of key information in the summary. We propose a key information guide network to guide the process of generation from two aspects: the attention mechanism and the pointer mechanism.

In detail, we extract keywords from the text by using TextRank algorithm. As shown in Figure 1, the keywords are fed one-by-one into the key information guide network, and then we concatenate the last forward hidden state $\vec{h}_n$ and backward hidden state $\overleftarrow{h}_1$ as the key information representation k:

$$k = \begin{bmatrix} \overleftarrow{h}_1 \\ \vec{h}_n \end{bmatrix} \quad (5)$$

Attention mechanism: Traditional attention mechanism is hard to identify keywords, which just uses the decoder state as a query to get the attention distribution of the encoder hidden states. We use the key information representation k as extra input to the attention mechanism, changing equation (1) to:

$$e_{ti} = v^T tanh(W_h h_i + W_s s_t + W_k k) \quad (6)$$

where W_k is a learnable parameter. We use the new e_{ti} to obtain new attention distribution α_t^e (Equation 2) and new context vector c_t (Equation 3).

Our key information representation k makes the attention mechanism more focus on the keywords. That is seem like to introduce prior knowledge to the model.

Then, we apply the key information representation k and use the new context vector c_t to calculate a probability distribution over all words in the vocabulary, changing equation (4) to:

$$P_v(y_t|y_1, ..., y_{t-1}) = softmax(f(s_t, c_t, k)) \quad (7)$$

where v represents that y_t is from the target vocabulary.

Pointer mechanism: Due to the limitation of the vocabulary size, some keywords may not be in the target vocabulary, which will certainly lead to a lack of them in the final summary. Therefore we take the key information representation k, the context vector c_t and the decoder hidden state s_t as inputs to calculate a soft switch p_{sw}, which is used to choose between generating a word from the target vocabulary or copying a word from the input text:

$$p_{sw} = \sigma(w_k^T k + w_c^T c_t + w_{s_t}^T s_t + b_{sw}) \quad (8)$$

where w_k^T, w_c^T, w_s^T and b_{sw} are parameters, σ is the sigmoid function.

Our pointer mechanism, which is equipped with the key information representation, has the ability to identify the keywords. We use the new attention distribution α_{ti}^e as the probability of the input token w_i and obtain the following probability distribution to predict the next word:

$$P(y_t = w) = p_{sw} P_v(y_t = w)$$
$$+ (1 - p_{sw}) \sum_{i:w_i=w} \alpha_{ti}^e \quad (9)$$

Note that if w is an out-of-vocabulary word, $P_v(y_t = w)$ is zero.

During training, we minimize a maximum-likelihood loss at each decoding time step, which is most widely used in sequence generation. We

define y_t^* as the target word for the decoding time step t and the overall loss is:

$$L = -\frac{1}{T} \sum_{t=0}^{T} logP(y_t^*|y_1^*, ..., y_{t-1}^*, x) \quad (10)$$

3.3 Prediction-guide mechanism at test time

At test time, when predicting the next word, we consider not only the above probability (Equation 9), but also a long-term value predicted by the prediction-guide mechanism. The prediction-guide mechanism is based on He et al. (2017).

Our prediction-guide mechanism, which is a single-layer feed forward network with sigmoid activation function, predicts the extent of the key information covered in the final summary. At each decoding time step t, we take mean pooling over the decoder hidden states $\bar{s}_t = \frac{1}{t} \sum_{l=1}^{t} s_l$, the encode hidden states $\bar{h}_n = \frac{1}{n} \sum_{i=1}^{n} h_i$ and the key information representation k as inputs to calculate the long-term value.

We sample two partial summaries y_{p1} and y_{p2} for each x with random stop to get $\bar{s}_t$. Then, we finish the generation from y_p to obtain M average decoder hidden states $\bar{s}$ of the completed summaries $S(y_p)$ (using beam search), and compute the average score:

$$AvgCos(x, y_p) = \frac{1}{M} \sum_{\bar{s} \in S(y_p)} cos(\bar{s}, k) \quad (11)$$

where cos is the function of cosine similarity.

We hope the predicted value of $v(x, y_{p1})$ can be larger than $v(x, y_{p2})$ if $AvgCos(x, y_{p1}) > AvgCos(x, y_{p2})$. Therefore, the loss function of the prediction-guide network is as follows:

$$L_{pg} = \sum_{(x,y_{p1},y_{p2})} e^{v(x,y_{p2})-v(x,y_{p1})} \quad (12)$$

where $AvgCos(x, y_{p1}) > AvgCos(x, y_{p2})$.

At test time, we first compute the normalized log probability of each candidate, and then linearly combine it with the value predicted by the prediction-guide network. In detail, given an abstractive model $P(y|x)$ (Equation 9), a prediction-guide network $v(x, y)$ and a hyperparameter $\alpha \in (0, 1)$, the score of partial sequence y for x is computed by:

$$\alpha \times logP(y|x) + (1 - \alpha) \times log\, v(x, y) \quad (13)$$

where $\alpha \in (0, 1)$, is a hyperparameter.

Model	ROUGE-1	ROUGE-2	ROUGE-L
Enc-dec+attn baseline (50k vocab)	31.33	11.81	28.83
Abstractive model (Nallapati et al., 2016)	35.46	13.30	32.65
Baseline+pointer	36.44	15.66	33.42
KIGN	37.76	16.56	34.49
Prediction-guide	37.24	16.27	34.14
KIGN+Prediction-guide	**38.95**	**17.12**	**35.68**

Table 1: ROUGE F1 scores for models on the CNN/Daily Mail test set. All our ROUGE scores have a 95% confidence interval of at most ± 0.25 as reported by the official ROUGE script.

4 Experiments

4.1 Experiment setting

We use the *CNN/Daily Mail* dataset(Nallapati et al., 2016; Hermann et al., 2015) and use scripts supplied by Nallapati et al. (2016) to obtain the same version of the data, which has 28,7226 training pairs, 13,368 validation pairs and 11,490 test pairs. We use two 256-dimensional LSTMs for the bidirectional encoder and one 256-dimensional LSTM for the decoder. In our key information guide network, the approach of encoding keywords is same to the encoder. In addition, we use a vocabulary of 50k words for both source and target and do not pre-train the word embeddings - they are learned from scratch during training. During training and testing, we truncate the text to 400 tokens and limit the length of the summary to 100 tokens. We train using Adagrad (Duchi et al., 2011) with learning rate 0.15 and an initial accumulator value of 0.1. The batch size is set as 16. Following the previous work, our evaluation metric is F-score of ROUGE (Lin and Hovy, 2003).

In addition, for the prediction-guide mechanism, we set the single-layer feed forward network with 800 nodes. For the hyperparameter α, we test the performances of KIGN+Prediction-guide model using different α during decoding. As can be seen from the figure 2, the performance is stable for the α ranging from 0.8 to 0.95. When α is set as 0.9, we can obtain the highest F-score of ROUGE. Besides, we set the M as 8 and adapt mini-batch training with batch size to be 16. The network is trained with AdaDelta (Zeiler, 2012).

During training and at test time we truncate the input tokens to 400 and limit the length of the output summary to 100 tokens for training and 120 tokens at test time, which is similar to See et al. (2017). We trained our keywords network model less than $200,000$ training iterations. Then

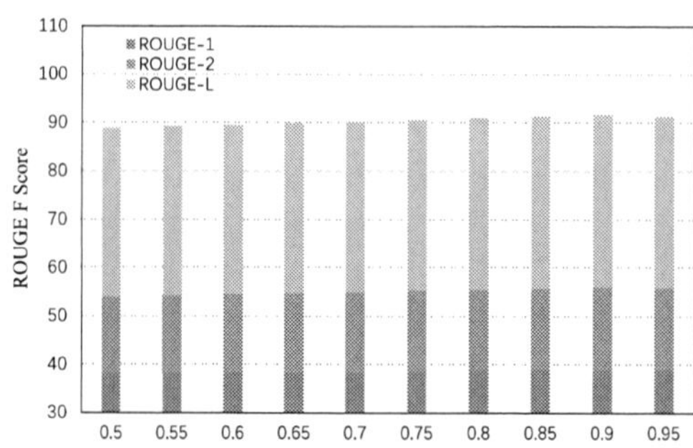

Figure 2: ROUGE-1, ROUGE-2 and ROUGE-L F1 scores of KIGN+Prediction-guide model w.r.t different hyperparameter α.

we trained the single-layer feed forward network based on the KIGN model. Finally, at test time, we combine the KIGN model and the prediction-guide mechanism to generate the summary.

4.2 Results and discussions

We compare our model with the baseline model (enc-dec+attn), hierarchical networks (Nallapati et al., 2016) and the baseline model equipped with pointer-mechanism since we use the pointer mechanism in our model.

Table 1 shows that our key information guide network scores exceed the baseline model equipped with the pointer-mechanism by (+1.3 ROUGE-1, +0.9 ROUGE-2, +1.0 ROUGE-L). In addition, we just add the prediction-guide mechanism on the baseline model equipped with the pointer-mechanism to understand the contribution of each part. The scores of that exceed the baseline model equipped with the pointer-mechanism by (+0.8 ROUGE-1, +0.6 ROUGE-2, +0.7 ROUGE-L). Finally, combining the key information guide network and the prediction-guide mechanism, we achieve a better performance. Our best model scores exceed the baseline model with pointer-

Text(truncated): **google claims** to have cracked a problem that has flummoxed anyone who has tried to read a doctor's note - how to **read anyone's handwriting**. the firm claims the latest update to its **android handsets can under 82 languages in 20 distinct scripts**, and **works with both printed and cursive writing input with or without a stylus**. it even allows users to simply draw emoji they want to send. scroll down for video. the california search giant claims the latest update to its android handsets can understand handwriting in 82 languages in 20 distinct scripts. google says its handwriting recognition works by building on large-scale language modeling, robust multi-language ocr.

Gold: google handwriting input works on android phones and tablets. handsets can under 82 languages in 20 distinct scripts. works with both printed and cursive writing input with or without a stylus.

Baseline+pointer-mechanism: google claims to have cracked a problem that has flummoxed anyone who has tried to read a doctor 's note how to read anyone 's handwriting.

Our model: google claims the latest update to its android handsets can under 82 languages in 20 distinct scripts, and works with both printed and cursive writing input with or without a stylus.

Figure 3: Comparison of the output of two models on a news article. Bold words in text are the key information. (Baseline: enc-dec+attn; Our model: KIGN+prediction-guide)

mechanism by (+2.5 ROUGE-1, +1.5 ROUGE-2, +2.2 ROUGE-L). In this paper, we do not implement coverage mechanism in our model, which can greatly improve the score of ROUGE (See et al., 2017).

4.3 Case study

Figure 3 is an example to show the coverage of the key information between the text and the summary and the bold words are the key information of the text. We compare the output of two models and give the gold summary. It shows that the main idea of the text is about google handwriting input working on android handsets and some function introduction. The baseline model equipped with pointer-mechanism produces the summary, which just shows that google have cracked the problem of reading handwriting, while the summary generated by our model covers almost all the key information of the text.

5 Conclusion

In this work, we propose a guiding generation model for abstractive text summarization. We combine the extractive model and the abstractive model. Firstly, we use the extractive method to obtain keywords from the input text. Then, we introduce a key information guide network, which encodes the keywords to the key information representation, to guide the process of generation. In addition, we propose a prediction-guide mechanism to further guide the generation at test time. Experiments show that our model leads to significant improvements.

Acknowledge

We thank the anonymous reviewers for useful comments. This work was supported by Beijing Natural Science Foundation (4174098), National Natural Science Foundation of China (61702047), National Natural Science Foundation of China (61703234) and the Fundamental Research Funds for the Central Universities (2017RC02).

References

Dzmitry Bahdanau, Kyunghyun Cho, and Yoshua Bengio. 2014. Neural machine translation by jointly learning to align and translate. *CoRR*, abs/1409.0473.

Sumit Chopra, Michael Auli, and Alexander M. Rush. 2016. Abstractive sentence summarization with attentive recurrent neural networks. In *Proceedings of the 2016 Conference of the North American Chapter of the Association for Computational Linguistics: Human Language Technologies*, pages 93–98. Association for Computational Linguistics.

John Duchi, Elad Hazan, and Yoram Singer. 2011. Adaptive subgradient methods for online learning and stochastic optimization. *J. Mach. Learn. Res.*, 12:2121–2159.

Di He, Hanqing Lu, Yingce Xia, Tao Qin, Liwei Wang, and Tieyan Liu. 2017. Decoding with value networks for neural machine translation. In I. Guyon, U. V. Luxburg, S. Bengio, H. Wallach, R. Fergus, S. Vishwanathan, and R. Garnett, editors, *Advances in Neural Information Processing Systems 30*, pages 177–186. Curran Associates, Inc.

Karl Moritz Hermann, Tomas Kocisky, Edward Grefenstette, Lasse Espeholt, Will Kay, Mustafa Suleyman, and Phil Blunsom. 2015. Teaching machines to read and comprehend. In C. Cortes, N. D. Lawrence, D. D. Lee, M. Sugiyama, and R. Garnett, editors, *Advances in Neural Information Processing Systems 28*, pages 1693–1701. Curran Associates, Inc.

Chin-Yew Lin and Eduard Hovy. 2003. Automatic evaluation of summaries using n-gram co-occurrence statistics. In *Proceedings of the 2003 Human Language Technology Conference of the*

North American Chapter of the Association for Computational Linguistics.

Rada Mihalcea and Paul Tarau. 2004. Textrank: Bringing order into texts. In *Proceedings of EMNLP 2004*, pages 404–411, Barcelona, Spain. Association for Computational Linguistics.

Ramesh Nallapati, Bowen Zhou, Cicero dos Santos, Caglar Gulcehre, and Bing Xiang. 2016. Abstractive text summarization using sequence-to-sequence rnns and beyond. In *Proceedings of The 20th SIGNLL Conference on Computational Natural Language Learning*, pages 280–290. Association for Computational Linguistics.

Alexander M. Rush, Sumit Chopra, and Jason Weston. 2015. A neural attention model for abstractive sentence summarization. In *Proceedings of the 2015 Conference on Empirical Methods in Natural Language Processing*, pages 379–389. Association for Computational Linguistics.

Abigail See, Peter J. Liu, and Christopher D. Manning. 2017. Get to the point: Summarization with pointer-generator networks. In *Proceedings of the 55th Annual Meeting of the Association for Computational Linguistics (Volume 1: Long Papers)*, pages 1073–1083. Association for Computational Linguistics.

Ilya Sutskever, Oriol Vinyals, and Quoc V. Le. 2014. Sequence to sequence learning with neural networks. In *Proceedings of the 27th International Conference on Neural Information Processing Systems - Volume 2*, NIPS'14, pages 3104–3112, Cambridge, MA, USA. MIT Press.

Oriol Vinyals, Meire Fortunato, and Navdeep Jaitly. 2015. Pointer networks. In C. Cortes, N. D. Lawrence, D. D. Lee, M. Sugiyama, and R. Garnett, editors, *Advances in Neural Information Processing Systems 28*, pages 2692–2700. Curran Associates, Inc.

Michihiro Yasunaga, Rui Zhang, Kshitijh Meelu, Ayush Pareek, Krishnan Srinivasan, and Dragomir Radev. 2017. Graph-based neural multi-document summarization. In *Proceedings of the 21st Conference on Computational Natural Language Learning (CoNLL 2017)*, pages 452–462. Association for Computational Linguistics.

Matthew D. Zeiler. 2012. ADADELTA: an adaptive learning rate method. *CoRR*, abs/1212.5701.

Qingyu Zhou, Nan Yang, Furu Wei, and Ming Zhou. 2017. Selective encoding for abstractive sentence summarization. In *Proceedings of the 55th Annual Meeting of the Association for Computational Linguistics (Volume 1: Long Papers)*, pages 1095–1104. Association for Computational Linguistics.

Natural Language Generation by
Hierarchical Decoding with Linguistic Patterns

Shang-Yu Su[†]   Kai-Ling Lo[⋆]   Yi-Ting Yeh[⋆]   Yun-Nung Chen[⋆]
[⋆]Department of Computer Science and Information Engineering
[†]Department of Electrical Engineering
National Taiwan University
{r05921117,b04902010,b03902071}@ntu.edu.tw   y.v.chen@ieee.org

Abstract

Natural language generation (NLG) is a critical component in spoken dialogue systems. Classic NLG can be divided into two phases: (1) sentence planning: deciding on the overall sentence structure, (2) surface realization: determining specific word forms and flattening the sentence structure into a string. Many simple NLG models are based on recurrent neural networks (RNN) and sequence-to-sequence (seq2seq) model, which basically contains a encoder-decoder structure; these NLG models generate sentences from scratch by jointly optimizing sentence planning and surface realization using a simple cross entropy loss training criterion. However, the simple encoder-decoder architecture usually suffers from generating complex and long sentences, because the decoder has to learn all grammar and diction knowledge. This paper introduces a hierarchical decoding NLG model based on linguistic patterns in different levels, and shows that the proposed method outperforms the traditional one with a smaller model size. Furthermore, the design of the hierarchical decoding is flexible and easily-extensible in various NLG systems[1].

1   Introduction

Spoken dialogue systems that can help users to solve complex tasks have become an emerging research topic in artificial intelligence and natural language processing areas (Wen et al., 2017; Bordes et al., 2017; Dhingra et al., 2017; Li et al., 2017). A typical dialogue system pipeline contains a speech recognizer, a natural language understanding component, a dialogue manager, and a natural language generator (NLG).

NLG is a critical component in a dialogue system, where its goal is to generate the natural language given the semantics provided by the dialogue manager. As the endpoint of interacting with users, the quality of generated sentences is crucial for user experience. The common and mostly adopted method is the rule-based (or template-based) method (Mirkovic and Cavedon, 2011), which can ensure the natural language quality and fluency. Considering that designing templates is time-consuming and the scalability issue, data-driven approaches have been investigated for open-domain NLG tasks.

Recent advances in recurrent neural network-based language model (RNNLM) (Mikolov et al., 2010, 2011) have demonstrated the capability of modeling long-term dependency by leveraging RNN structure. Previous work proposed an RNNLM-based NLG (Wen et al., 2015) that can be trained on any corpus of dialogue act-utterance pairs without any semantic alignment and hand-crafted features. Sequence-to-sequence (seq2seq) generators (Cho et al., 2014; Sutskever et al., 2014) further offer better results by leveraging encoder-decoder structure: previous model encoded syntax trees and dialogue acts into sequences (Dušek and Jurčíček, 2016) as inputs of attentional seq2seq model (Bahdanau et al., 2015). However, it is challenging to generate long and complex sentences by the simple encoder-decoder structure due to grammar complexity and lack of diction knowledge.

This paper proposes a hierarchical decoder leveraging linguistic patterns, where the decoding hierarchy is constructed in terms of part-of-speech (POS) tags. The original single decoding process is separated into a multi-level decoding hierarchy, where each decoding layer generates words associated with a specific POS set. The experiments show that our proposed method outperforms the

---

The first two authors have equal contributions.

[1]The source code is available at https://github.com/MiuLab/HNLG.

61

Proceedings of NAACL-HLT 2018, pages 61–66
New Orleans, Louisiana, June 1 - 6, 2018. ©2018 Association for Computational Linguistics

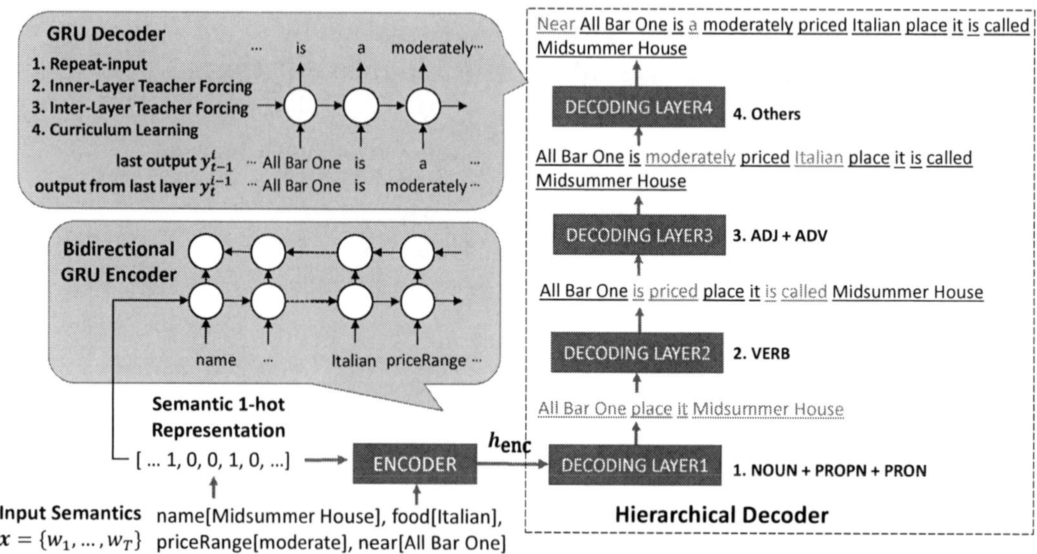

Figure 1: The framework of the proposed semantically conditioned NLG model.

classic seq2seq model with less parameters. In addition, our proposed model allows other word-level or sentence-level characteristics to be further leveraged for better generalization.

2 The Proposed Approach

The framework of the proposed semantically conditioned NLG model is illustrated in Figure 1, where the model architecture is based on an encoder-decoder (seq2seq) design (Cho et al., 2014; Sutskever et al., 2014). In the seq2seq architecture, a typical generation process includes encoding and decoding phases: First, the given semantic representation sequence $\mathbf{x} = \{w_t\}_1^T$ is fed into a RNN-based encoder to capture the temporal dependency and project the input to a latent feature space, and encoded into 1-hot semantic representation as the initial state of the encoder in order to maintain the temporal-independent condition as shown in the left-bottom of Figure 1. The recurrent unit of the encoder is bidirectional gated recurrent unit (GRU) (Cho et al., 2014),

$$\mathbf{h}_{\text{enc}} = \text{BiGRU}(\mathbf{x}). \tag{1}$$

Then the encoded semantic vector, $\mathbf{h}_{\text{enc}}$, flows into an RNN-based decoder as the initial state to generate word sequences by an RNN model shown in the left-top component of the figure.

2.1 Hierarchical Decoder

Despite the intuitive and elegant design of the seq2seq model, it is difficult to generate long, complex, and decent sequences by such encoder-decoder structure, because a single decoder is not capable of learning all diction, grammar, and other related linguistic knowledge. Some prior work applied additional technique such as reranker to select a better result among multiple generated sequences (Wen et al., 2015; Dušek and Jurčíček, 2016). However, the issue still remains unsolved in NLG community.

Therefore, we propose a hierarchical decoder to address the above issue, where the core idea is to separate the decoding process and learn different types of patterns instead of learning all relevant knowledge together. The hierarchical decoder is composed of several decoding layers, each of which is only responsible for learning a portion of the related knowledge. Namely, the linguistic knowledge can be incorporated into the decoding process and divided into several subsets.

In this paper, we use part-of-speech (POS) tags as the additional linguistic features to construct the hierarchy, where POS tags of the words in the target sentence are separated into several subsets and each layer is responsible for decoding the words associated with a specific set of POS patterns. An example is shown in the right part of Figure 1, where the first layer at the bottom is in charge of learning to decode nouns, pronouns, and proper nouns, and the second layer is in charge of verbs, and so on. Our approach is also intuitive from the viewpoint of how humans learn to speak; for example, infants first learn to say the keywords which are often nouns. When an infant says *"Daddy, toilet."*, it actually means *"Daddy, I want to go to the toilet."*. Along with the growth of the age, children learn more grammars and vocabulary and then start adding verbs to the sentences, further adding adverbs, and so on. This process of how humans learn to speak is the core motivation of our proposed method.

In the hierarchical decoder, the initial state of each GRU-based decoding layer i is the extracted feature $\mathbf{h}_{\text{enc}}$ from the encoder, and the input at every step is the last predicted token $\mathbf{y}_{t-1}^i$ concatenated with the output from the previous layer $\mathbf{y}_t^{i-1}$,

$$\mathbf{h}_t^i, \mathbf{o}_t^i = \text{GRU}_{\text{dec}}^i(\mathbf{y}_{t-1}^i, \mathbf{y}_t^{i-1} \mid \mathbf{h}_{\text{enc}}, \mathbf{h}_{t-1}^i), \quad (2)$$

$$\mathbf{y}_t^i = \texttt{argmax}(\mathbf{o}_t), \quad (3)$$

where $\mathbf{h}_t^i$ is the t-th hidden state of the i-th GRU decoding layer and $\mathbf{y}_t^i$ is the t-th outputted word in the i-th layer. The cross entropy loss is used for optimization.

2.2 Inner- and Inter-Layer Teacher Forcing

Teacher forcing (Williams and Zipser, 1989) is a strategy for training RNN that uses model output from a prior time step as an input, and it works by using the expected output at the current time step $\hat{\mathbf{y}}_t$ as the input at the next time step, rather than the output generated by the network. In our proposed framework, an input of a decoder contains not only the output from the last step but one from the last decoding layer. Therefore, we design two types of teacher forcing techniques – inner-layer and inter-layer.

Inner-layer teacher forcing is the classic teacher forcing strategy:

$$\mathbf{h}_t^i, \mathbf{o}_t^i = \text{GRU}_{\text{dec}}^i(\hat{\mathbf{y}}_{t-1}^i, \mathbf{y}_t^{i-1} \mid \mathbf{h}_{\text{enc}}, \mathbf{h}_{t-1}^i). \quad (4)$$

Inter-layer teacher forcing uses the labels instead of the actual output tokens of the last layer:

$$\mathbf{h}_t^i, \mathbf{o}_t^i = \text{GRU}_{\text{dec}}^i(\mathbf{y}_{t-1}^i, \hat{\mathbf{y}}_t^{i-1} \mid \mathbf{h}_{\text{enc}}, \mathbf{h}_{t-1}^i). \quad (5)$$

The teacher forcing techniques can also be triggered only with a certain probability, which is known as the schedule sampling approach (Bengio et al., 2015). In our experiments, the schedule sampling approach is also adopted.

2.3 Repeat-Input Mechanism

The concept of our proposed method is to hierarchically generate the sequence, gradually adding words associated with different linguistic patterns. Therefore, the generated sequences from the decoders become longer as the generating process proceeds to the higher decoding layers, and the sequence generated by a upper layer should contain the words predicted by the lower layers. In order to ensure the output sequences with the constraints, we design a strategy that repeats the outputs from the last layer as inputs until the current decoding layer outputs the same token, so-called repeat-input mechanism. This approach offers at least two merits: (1) Repeating inputs tells the decoder that the repeated tokens are important to encourage the decoder to generate them. (2) If the expected output sequence of a layer is much shorter than the one of the next layer, the large difference in length becomes a critical issue of the hierarchical decoder, because the output sequence of a layer will be fed into the next layer. With the repeat-input mechanism, the impact of length difference can be mitigated.

2.4 Curriculum Learning

The proposed hierarchical decoder consists of several decoding layers, the expected output sequences of upper layers are longer than the ones in the lower layers. The framework is suitable for applying the curriculum learning (Elman, 1993), in which core concept is that a curriculum of progressively harder tasks could significantly accelerate a networks training. The training procedure is to train each decoding layer for some epochs from the bottommost layer to the topmost one.

3 Experiments

3.1 Setup

The experiments are conducted using the E2E NLG challenge dataset (Novikova et al., 2017)[2], which is a crowd-sourced dataset of 50k instances in the restaurant domain. The input is the semantic frame containing specific slots and corresponding values, and the output is the natural language containing the given semantics as shown in Figure 1.

To prepare the labels of each layer within the hierarchical structure of the proposed method,

---

[2] http://www.macs.hw.ac.uk/ InteractionLab/E2E/

	NLG Model	**BLEU**	**ROUGE-1**	**ROUGE-2**	**ROUGE-L**
(a)	Sequence-to-Sequence Model	**44.7**	51.6	19.5	40.6
(b)	+ Hierarchical Decoder	41.1	60.2	31.4	46.2
(c)	+ Hierarchical Decoder, Repeat-Input	41.2	60.5	33.8	48.6
(d)	+ Hierarchical Decoder, Curriculum Learning	40.9	62.9	34.5	50.1
(e)	+ All	44.1	**67.3**	**38.0**	**53.8**
(f)	(e) with High Inner-Layer TF Prob.	36.9	58.5	31.3	45.9
(g)	(e) with High Inter-Layer TF Prob.	42.5	**67.3**	**38.7**	53.3
(h)	(e) with High Inner- and Inter-Layer TF Prob.	41.7	64.5	36.6	52.0

Table 1: The NLG performance reported on BLEU, ROUGE-1, ROUGE-2, and ROUGE-L of models (%).

we utilize spaCy toolkit to perform POS tagging for the target word sequences. Some properties such as names of restaurants are delexicalized (for example, replaced with symbols "RESTAURANT_NAME") to avoid data sparsity. We assign the words with specific POS tags for each decoding layer: **nouns**, **proper nouns**, and **pronouns** for the first layer, **verbs** for the second layer, **adjectives** and **adverbs** for the third layer, and **others** for the forth layer. Note that the hierarchies with more than four levels are also applicable, the proposed hierarchical decoder is a general and easily-extensible concept.

The experimental results are shown in Table 1. Row (a) is the simple seq2seq model as the baseline. The probability of activating inter-layer and inner-layer teacher forcing is set to 0.5 in the rows (a)-(e); to evaluate the impact of teacher forcing, the probability is set to 0.9 (rows (f)-(h)). The probability of teacher forcing is attenuated every epoch, the decay ratio is 0.9. We perform 20 training epochs without early stop; when the curriculum learning approach is applied, only the first layer is trained during first five epochs, the second decoder layer starts to be trained at the sixth epoch, and so on. To evaluate the quality of the generated sequences regarding both precision and recall, the evaluation metrics include BLEU and ROUGE (1, 2, L) scores.

3.2 Results and Analysis

To fairly examine the effectiveness of our proposed approaches, we control the size of the proposed model to be smaller. The baseline seq2seq decoder has 400-dim hidden layer, and the models with the proposed hierarchical decoder (rows (b)-(h)) have four 100-dim decoding layers. Table 1 shows that simply introducing the hierarchical decoding technique without increment of parameters (row (b)) to separate the generation process

into several phases achieves significant improvement in ROUGE scores, 16.7% in ROUGE-1, 61% in ROUGE-2, and 13.8% in ROUGE-L respectively. Applying the proposed repeat-input mechanism (row (c)) and the curriculum learning strategy (row (d)) both offer considerable improvement. Combining all the proposed techniques (row (e)) yields the best performance in ROUGE scores with nearly the same performance in BLEU and achieves 30.4%, 94.8%, and 32.5% improvement in ROUGE-1, ROUGE-2, and ROUGE-L respectively, demonstrating the effectiveness of the proposed approach.

To further verify the impact of teacher forcing, the integrated models (row (e)) with high inter and inner-layer teacher forcing probability (rows (f)-(h)) are also evaluated. Note that when the teacher forcing is activated probabilistically, the strategies are also known as schedule sampling (Bengio et al., 2015). Row (f) shows that high probability of triggering inner-layer teacher forcing results in severe performance degradation, while models with high inter-layer teacher forcing probability (rows (g)-(h)) can avoid the harmful impact. The results are reasonable and reflects the potential issue of error propagation within the proposed hierarchical structure.

Note that the decoding process is a single-path forward generation without any heuristics and other mechanisms (like beam search and reranking), so the effectiveness of the proposed methods can be fairly verified. The experiments show that by considering linguistic patterns in hierarchical decoding, the proposed approaches can significantly improve NLG results with smaller models.

4 Conclusion

This paper proposes a seq2seq-based model with a hierarchical decoder that leverages various linguistic patterns and further designs several corresponding training and inference techniques. The experimental results show that the models applying the proposed methods achieve significant improvement over the classic seq2seq model. By introducing additional word-level or sentence-level labels as features, the hierarchy of the decoder can be designed arbitrarily. Namely, the proposed hierarchical decoding concept is general and easily-extensible, with flexibility of being applied to many NLG systems.

Acknowledgements

We would like to thank reviewers for their insightful comments on the paper. The authors are supported by the Institute for Information Industry, Ministry of Science and Technology of Taiwan, Google Research, Microsoft Research, and MediaTek Inc..

References

Dzmitry Bahdanau, Kyunghyun Cho, and Yoshua Bengio. 2015. Neural machine translation by jointly learning to align and translate. In *Proceedings of ICLR*.

Samy Bengio, Oriol Vinyals, Navdeep Jaitly, and Noam Shazeer. 2015. Scheduled sampling for sequence prediction with recurrent neural networks. In *Advances in Neural Information Processing Systems*. pages 1171–1179.

Antoine Bordes, Y-Lan Boureau, and Jason Weston. 2017. Learning end-to-end goal-oriented dialog. In *Proceedings of ICLR*.

Kyunghyun Cho, Bart Van Merriënboer, Caglar Gulcehre, Dzmitry Bahdanau, Fethi Bougares, Holger Schwenk, and Yoshua Bengio. 2014. Learning phrase representations using RNN encoder-decoder for statistical machine translation. In *Proceedings of EMNLP*. pages 1724–1734.

Bhuwan Dhingra, Lihong Li, Xiujun Li, Jianfeng Gao, Yun-Nung Chen, Faisal Ahmed, and Li Deng. 2017. Towards end-to-end reinforcement learning of dialogue agents for information access. In *Proceedings of ACL*. pages 484–495.

Ondřej Dušek and Filip Jurčíček. 2016. Sequence-to-sequence generation for spoken dialogue via deep syntax trees and strings. In *Proceedings of ACL*. pages 45–51.

Jeffrey L Elman. 1993. Learning and development in neural networks: The importance of starting small. *Cognition* 48(1):71–99.

Xiujun Li, Yun-Nung Chen, Lihong Li, Jianfeng Gao, and Asli Celikyilmaz. 2017. End-to-end task-completion neural dialogue systems. In *Proceedings of IJCNLP*. pages 733–743.

Tomas Mikolov, Martin Karafiát, Lukas Burget, Jan Cernocký, and Sanjeev Khudanpur. 2010. Recurrent neural network based language model. In *Proceedings of Interspeech*.

Tomáš Mikolov, Stefan Kombrink, Lukáš Burget, Jan Černocký, and Sanjeev Khudanpur. 2011. Extensions of recurrent neural network language model. In *Proceedings of ICASSP*. IEEE, pages 5528–5531.

Danilo Mirkovic and Lawrence Cavedon. 2011. Dialogue management using scripts. US Patent 8,041,570.

Jekaterina Novikova, Ondrej Dušek, and Verena Rieser. 2017. The E2E dataset: New challenges for end-to-end generation. In *Proceedings of SIGDIAL*. pages 201–206.

Ilya Sutskever, Oriol Vinyals, and Quoc V Le. 2014. Sequence to sequence learning with neural networks. In *Proceedings of NIPS*. pages 3104–3112.

Tsung-Hsien Wen, Milica Gasic, Dongho Kim, Nikola Mrksic, Pei-Hao Su, David Vandyke, and Steve Young. 2015. Stochastic language generation in dialogue using recurrent neural networks with convolutional sentence reranking. In *Proceedings of SIGDIAL*. pages 275–284.

Tsung-Hsien Wen, Milica Gasic, Nikola Mrksic, Lina M Rojas-Barahona, Pei-Hao Su, Stefan Ultes, David Vandyke, and Steve Young. 2017. A network-based end-to-end trainable task-oriented dialogue system. In *Proceedings of EACL*. pages 438–449.

Ronald J Williams and David Zipser. 1989. A learning algorithm for continually running fully recurrent neural networks. *Neural computation* 1(2):270–280.

A   Dataset Detail

The experiments are conducted using the E2E NLG challenge dataset, which is a crowd-sourced dataset in the restaurant domain, the training set contains 42064 instances while there are 4673 instances in the validation (development) set. In our experiments, we use the validation set to test our models. In the E2E NLG Challenge dataset, the input is the semantics containing slots and their values, and the output is the corresponding natural language. For example, the slot-value pairs `"name[Bibimbap House], food[English], priceRange[moderate], area[riverside], near[Clare Hall]"` correspond to the target sentence

"Bibimbap House is a moderately priced restaurant who's main cuisine is English food. You will find this local gem near Clare Hall in the Riverside area.".

B Parameter Setting

We use mini-batch Adam as the optimizer with the batch size of 32 examples. The baseline seq2seq model (row (a)) sets the encoder's hidden layer size to 200 and the decoder's to 400. The size of the hidden layer in the encoder and the decoder layers of the models based on the proposed hierarchical decoder (rows (b)-(h)) are 200 and 100, respectively. Note that in this setting, the models applied the proposed methods will have less parameters than the baseline seq2seq model. In terms of the models utilized the basic RNN cell, the baseline seq2seq model (row (a)) has 640k parameters whereas the proposed models (rows (b)-(h)) have only 520k parameters.

Neural Poetry Translation

Marjan Ghazvininejad[†], Yejin Choi[‡,♠], and Kevin Knight[†]
[†]Information Sciences Institute & Computer Science Department
University of Southern California
{ghazvini,knight}@isi.edu
[‡]Paul G. Allen School of Computer Science & Engineering, University of Washington
[♠]Allen Institute for Artificial Intelligence
yejin@cs.washington.edu

Abstract

We present the first neural poetry translation system. Unlike previous works that often fail to produce any translation for fixed rhyme and rhythm patterns, our system always translates a source text to an English poem. Human evaluation ranks translation quality as acceptable 78.2% of the time.

1 Introduction

Despite recent improvements in machine translation, automatic translation of poetry remains a challenging problem. This challenge is partially due to the intrinsic complexities of translating a poem. As Robert Frost says "Poetry is what gets lost in translation". Nevertheless, in practice poems have always been translated and will continue to be translated between languages and cultures.

In this paper, we introduce a method for automatic poetry translation. As an example, consider the following French poem:

French poem:
Puis je venais masseoir pr'es de sa chaise
Pour lui parler le soir plus 'a mon aise.

(Literally:
Then I came to sit near her chair
To discuss with her the evening more
at my ease.)

Our goal is to translate this poem into English, but also to obey target rhythm and rhyme patterns specified by the user, such as *2-line rhyming iambic pentameter*, ten syllables per line with alternating stress 0101010101, where 0 represents an unstressed syllable, and 1 represents a stressed syllable. Lines strictly rhyme if their pronunciations match from the final stressed vowel onwards; slant rhyming allows variation. Overall, this is a difficult task even for human translators.

In spite of recent works in automatic poetry generation (Oliveira, 2012; He et al., 2012; Yan et al., 2013; Zhang and Lapata, 2014; Yi et al., 2017; Wang et al., 2016; Ghazvininejad et al., 2016, 2017; Hopkins and Kiela, 2017; Oliveira, 2017), little has been done on automatic poetry translation. Greene et al. (2010) use phrase-based machine translation techniques to translate Italian poetic lines to English-translation lattices. They search these lattices for the best translation that obeys a given rhythm pattern. Genzel et al. (2010) also use phrase-based machine translation technique to translate French poems to English ones. They apply the rhythm and rhyme constraints during the decoding process. Both methods report total failure in generating any translations with a fixed rhythm and rhyme format for most of the poems. Genzel et al. (2010) report that their method can generate translations in a specified scheme for only 12 out of 109 6-line French stanzas.

This failure is due to the nature of the phrase-based machine translation (PBMT) systems. PBMT systems are bound to generate translations according to a learned bilingual phrase table. These systems are well-suited to unconstrained translation, as often the phrase table entries are good translations of source phrases. However, when rhythm and rhyme constraints are applied to PBMT, translation options become extremely limited, to the extent that it is often impossible to generate *any* translation that obeys the poetic constraints (Greene et al., 2010). In addition, literal translation is not always desired when it comes to poetry. PBMT is bound to translate phrase-by-phrase, and it cannot easily add, remove, or alter details of the source poem.

In this paper, we propose the first neural poetry translation system and show its quality in translating French to English poems. Our system is much more flexible than those based on PBMT, and is always able to produce translations into any scheme. In addition, we propose two novel im-

67

Proceedings of NAACL-HLT 2018, pages 67–71
New Orleans, Louisiana, June 1 - 6, 2018. ©2018 Association for Computational Linguistics

provements to increase the quality of the translation while satisfying specified rhythm and rhyme constraints. Our proposed system generates the following translation for the French couplet mentioned above:

French poem:
Puis je venais masseoir pr'es de sa chaise
Pour lui parler le soir plus 'a mon aise.
Our system:
And afterwards I came to sit together.
To talk about the evening at my pleasure.

2 Data

We use a French translation of Oscar Wilde's *Ballad of Reading Gaol* (Wilde, 2001) by Jean Guiloineau[1] as our input poem, and the original Wilde's poem as the human reference. This test set contains 109 6-line stanzas, 29 of which we use for development. For each stanza, we require our machine translation to produce odd lines with iambic tetrameter and even lines with iambic trimeter, with even lines (2, 4, 6) rhyming.

3 Proposed Method

3.1 Model A: Initial Model

Unconstrained Machine Translation. The base of our poetry translation system is an encoder-decoder sequence-to-sequence model (Sutskever et al., 2014) with a two-layer recurrent neural network (RNN) with long short-term memory (LSTM) units (Hochreiter and Schmidhuber, 1997). It is pre-trained on parallel French-English WMT14 corpus.[2] Specifically, we use 2-layer LSTM cells with 1000 hidden cells for each layer. For pre-training, we set the dropout ratio to 0.5. Batch size is set to 128, and the learning rate is initially set as 0.5 and starts to decay by 0.5 when the perplexity of the development set starts to increase. Gradients are clipped at 5 to avoid gradient explosion. We stop pre-training the system after 3 epochs. In order to adapt the translation system to in-domain data, we collect 16,412 English songs with their French translations and 12,538 French songs with their English translations (6M word tokens in total) as our training corpus,[3] and continue training the system (warm start)[4] with this dataset.

---

[1] https://bit.ly/2GN1ZGk

[2] http://www.statmt.org/wmt14/translation-task.html

[3] http://lyricstranslate.com/

[4] We continue training the system while we set dropout ratio to 0.2, and keep the other settings fixed.

This encoder-decoder RNN model is used to generate the unconstrained translation of the poems.

Enforcing Rhythm in Translation. To enforce the rhythm constraint, we adopt the technique of Ghazvininejad et al. (2016). We create a large finite-state acceptor (FSA) that compactly encodes all word sequences that satisfy the rhythm constraint. In order to generate a rhythmic translation for the source poem, we constrain the possible LSTM translations with this FSA. To do so, we alter the beam search of the decoding phase of the neural translation model to only generate outputs that are accepted by this FSA.

Enforcing Rhyme in Translation. Ghazvininejad et al. (2016) fix the rhyme words in advance and build an FSA with the chosen rhyme words in place. Unlike their work, we do not fix the rhyme words in the FSA beforehand, but let the model choose rhyme words during translation. We do so by partitioning the vocabulary into rhyme classes and building one FSA for each class. This FSA accepts word sequences that obey the rhythm pattern and end with any word within the corresponding rhyme class. Then we translate each line of the source poem multiple times, once according to each rhyme class. In the final step, for each set of rhyming lines, we select a set of translations that come from the same rhyme class and have the highest combined translation score. In practice, we just make FSAs for each of the 100 most frequent rhyme classes (out of 1505), which covers 67% of actual rhyming word tokens in our development set.

3.2 Model B: Biased Decoding with Unconstrained Translation

Naive application of rhythm and rhyme constraints to the neural translation system limits the translation options of the system. Sometimes the beam search finds no related translation that satisfies the constraints, forcing the decoder to choose an unrelated target-language token. The system does not have a way to recover from this situation, and continues to generate a totally unrelated phrase. An example is rhythm- and rhyme-constrained translation of "Et buvait lair frais jusquau soir" ("And drinking fresh air until the evening") to "I used to close my hair" by our initial system (Figure 1).

We therefore propose to use the output of *unconstrained* translation as a guideline for the constrained translation process. To do so, we encourage the words that appear in the unconstrained translation during the decoding step of the constrained one. We encourage by multiplying their RNN log probabilities by 5 during beam search. Figure 1 shows how this technique addresses the problem.

French poem:

Sans mains tordues, comme ces hommes,
Ces pauvres hommes sans espoir,
Qui osent nourrir lespérance
Dans le caveau du désespoir:
Il regardait vers le soleil
Et buvait lair frais jusquau soir.

Human reference:

He did not wring his hands, as do
Those witless men who dare
To try to rear the changeling Hope
In the cave of black Despair:
He only looked upon the sun,
And drank the morning air.

Unconstrained machine translation:

Like these men
These poor men without hope,
Who dare to feed the hope.
In the vault of despair
He was looking to the sun
And drinking fresh air until the evening.

**Rhythmic and rhyming translation
by model A:**

Without a crooked hand as men.
These hopeless people there.
Who dare to feed the expectations.
Surrounded by despair.
He only looking at the sun.
I used to close my hair.

**Rhythmic and rhyming translation
by model B:**

Without a crooked hand as men.
These hopeless people there.
Who dare to feed the expectations.
Surrounded by despair.
He only looking at the sun.
Was drinking fresh of air.

Figure 1: An example of poetry translation by models A and B. Biased decoding with unconstrained translation (Model B) produces a better translation compared to the baseline rhythm- and rhyme-constrained system.

3.3 Model C: Biased Decoding with All Potential Translation

Our poetry translation system is also challenged by rare words for which the system has not learned a good translation. The unconstrained system produces a special <UNK> token for these cases, but the FSA does not accept <UNK>, as it is not pronounceable. We can let the system produce its next guess instead, but <UNK> is a sign that the translation system is not sure about the source meaning.

To overcome this problem, we use an idea similar to model B. This time, *in addition to encouraging the unconstrained translated words*, we encourage all potential translations of the foreign words. To get the potential translations, we use the translation table (t-table) extracted from parallel French-English training data using Giza++ (Och and Ney, 2003). This way, the system receives an external signal that guides it toward selecting better translations for the rare foreign word. We run five iterations of each of IBM models 1, 2, HMM, and 4 to get the t-table. An example of how this method improves the poem quality over model B can be observed in the fifth line of the poems in Figure 2.

4 Results

Our first experiment compares model A with model B. These systems generated non-identical translations for 77 (out of 80) of the test stanzas. We ask 154 Amazon mechanical turk judges to compare these translations (each pair of translations was compared twice). We present the judges with the French poem for reference and did not mention that the poems are computer generated. Judges have the option to prefer either of the poems or state they cannot decide. The results in Table 1 clearly show that the model B generates better translations.

In the second experiment, we compare model B with model C. We have 84 judges compare 42 different poems. Table 2 shows that judges preferred the outputs of model C by a 17.7% margin.

We also ask 238 judges to rank translations of all the 80 stanzas of the test set as very bad, bad, ok, good, and very good. Table 3 shows the distribution of this ranking. We see that 78.2% of the judges ranked the output ok or more (49.6% of the poems were ranked good or very good). Figure 3 shows an example of the poems ranked as very good.

5 Conclusion

In this paper we presented the first neural poetry translation system and provided two novel methods to improve the quality of the translations. We conducted human evaluations on generated po-

French poem:

Il ny avait que sable et boue
Où sétait ouverte la tombe.
Le long des murs de la prison
On ne voyait aucune tombe.
Un petit tas de chaux ardente
Servait de linceul à cette ombre.

Human reference:

For where a grave had opened wide,
There was no grave at all:
Only a stretch of mud and sand
By the hideous prison-wall,
And a little heap of burning lime,
That the man should have his pall.

Unconstrained machine translation:

There was only sand and mud
Where the grave opened.
Along the walls of prison
We saw no grave
A little pile of <UNK>
<UNK> to this shadow.

Rhythmic and rhyming translation by model B:

But there was only sand and mud.
To where the grave was laid.
Along the walls of prison wall.
We saw no masquerade.
A little lot of prostitutes.
They used to shroud this shade.

Rhythmic and rhyming translation by model C:

But there was only sand and mud.
To where the grave was laid.
Along the walls of prison wall.
We saw no masquerade.
A little bunch of shiny lime.
They used to shroud this shade.

Figure 2: An example of poetry translation by models B and C. Biased decoding with all potential translation (Model C) produces a better translation compared to Model B.

Method Name	User Preference
Model A	18.2%
Cannot Decide	19.5%
Model B	**62.3%**

Table 1: Users prefer translations generated by model A.

ems and showed that the proposed improvements highly improve the translation quality.

French poem:

Tels des vaisseaux dans la tempête,
Nos deux chemins sétaient croisés,
Sans mîme un signe et sans un mot,
Nous navions mot déclarer ;
Nous nétions pas dans la nuit sainte
Mais dans le jour déshonoré.

Human reference:

Like two doomed ships that pass in storm
We had crossed each others way:
But we made no sign, we said no word,
We had no word to say;
For we did not meet in the holy night,
But in the shameful day.

Translation by our full system (model C):

And like some ships across the storm.
These paths were crossed astray.
Without a signal nor a word.
We had no word to say.
We had not seen the holy night.
But on the shameful day.

Figure 3: A sample poem translated by our full system (Model C).

Method Name	User Preference
Model B	26.7%
Cannot Decide	28.9%
Model C	**44.4%**

Table 2: Users prefer translations generated by model C.

Very Bad	Bad	OK	Good	Very Good
5.9%	15.9%	28.6%	35.3%	14.3%

Table 3: Quality of the translated poems by model C.

Acknowledgments

We would like to thank the anonymous reviewers for their helpful comments. This work was supported in part by DARPA under the CwC program through the ARO (W911NF-15-1-0543), NSF (IIS-1524371), and gifts by Google and Facebook.

References

Dmitriy Genzel, Jakob Uszkoreit, and Franz Och. 2010. Poetic statistical machine translation: rhyme and meter. In _Proceedings of EMNLP_.

Marjan Ghazvininejad, Xing Shi, Yejin Choi, and Kevin Knight. 2016. Generating topical poetry. In _Proceedings of EMNLP_.

Marjan Ghazvininejad, Xing Shi, Jay Priyadarshi, and Kevin Knight. 2017. Hafez: an interactive poetry generation system. In *Proceedings of ACL Demo Track*.

Erica Greene, Tugba Bodrumlu, and Kevin Knight. 2010. Automatic analysis of rhythmic poetry with applications to generation and translation. In *Proceedings of EMNLP*.

Jing He, Ming Zhou, and Long Jiang. 2012. Generating Chinese classical poems with statistical machine translation models. In *Proceedings of AAAI*.

Sepp Hochreiter and Jurgen Schmidhuber. 1997. Long short-term memory. *Neural computation* 9(8).

Jack Hopkins and Douwe Kiela. 2017. Automatically generating rhythmic verse with neural networks. In *Proceedings of ACL*.

Franz Josef Och and Hermann Ney. 2003. A systematic comparison of various statistical alignment models. *Computational linguistics* 29(1).

Hugo Oliveira. 2012. PoeTryMe: a versatile platform for poetry generation. *Computational Creativity, Concept Invention, and General Intelligence* 1.

Hugo Gonçalo Oliveira. 2017. A survey on intelligent poetry generation: Languages, features, techniques, reutilisation and evaluation. In *Proceedings of the 10th International Conference on Natural Language Generation*.

Ilya Sutskever, Oriol Vinyals, and Quoc Le. 2014. Sequence to sequence learning with neural networks. In *proceedings of NIPS*.

Qixin Wang, Tianyi Luo, Dong Wang, and Chao Xing. 2016. Chinese song iambics generation with neural attention-based model. In *Proceedings of IJCAI*.

Oscar Wilde. 2001. *Ballad of Reading Gaol*. Electric Book Company.

Rui Yan, Han Jiang, Mirella Lapata, Shou-De Lin, Xueqiang Lv, and Xiaoming Li. 2013. I, Poet: Automatic Chinese poetry composition through a generative summarization framework under constrained optimization. In *Proceedings of IJCAI*.

Xiaoyuan Yi, Ruoyu Li, and Maosong Sun. 2017. Generating chinese classical poems with RNN encoder-decoder. In *Chinese Computational Linguistics and Natural Language Processing Based on Naturally Annotated Big Data*.

Xingxing Zhang and Mirella Lapata. 2014. Chinese poetry generation with recurrent neural networks. In *Proceedings of EMNLP*.

RankME: Reliable Human Ratings for Natural Language Generation

Jekaterina Novikova, Ondřej Dušek and Verena Rieser
Interaction Lab
Heriot-Watt University
Edinburgh, UK
`j.novikova, o.dusek, v.t.rieser@hw.ac.uk`

Abstract

Human evaluation for natural language generation (NLG) often suffers from inconsistent user ratings. While previous research tends to attribute this problem to individual user preferences, we show that the quality of human judgements can also be improved by experimental design. We present a novel *rank-based magnitude estimation* method (RankME), which combines the use of continuous scales and relative assessments. We show that RankME significantly improves the reliability and consistency of human ratings compared to traditional evaluation methods. In addition, we show that it is possible to evaluate NLG systems according to multiple, distinct criteria, which is important for error analysis. Finally, we demonstrate that RankME, in combination with Bayesian estimation of system quality, is a cost-effective alternative for ranking multiple NLG systems.

1 Introduction

Human judgement is the primary evaluation criterion for language generation tasks (Gkatzia and Mahamood, 2015). However, limited effort has been made to improve the reliability of these subjective ratings (Gatt and Krahmer, 2017). In this research, we systematically compare and analyse a wide range of alternative experimental designs for eliciting intrinsic user judgements for the task of comparing multiple systems. We draw upon previous studies in language generation, e.g. (Belz and Kow, 2010, 2011; Siddharthan and Katsos, 2012), as well as in the related field of machine translation (MT), e.g. (Bojar et al., 2016, 2017). In particular, we investigate the following challenges:

Distinct criteria: Traditionally, NLG outputs are evaluated according to different criteria, such as naturalness and informativeness (Gatt and Krahmer, 2017). Naturalness, also known as fluency or

readability, targets the linguistic competence of the text. Informativeness, otherwise known as accuracy or adequacy, targets the relevance and correctness of the output relative to the input specification. Ideally, we want to measure outputs of NLG systems with respect to these distinct criteria, especially for error analysis. For instance, one system may produce syntactically fluent output but misses important information, while another system, although being less fluent, may generate output that covers the meaning perfectly. Nevertheless, human judges often fail to distinguish between these different aspects, which results in highly correlated scores, e.g. (Novikova et al., 2017a). This is one of the reasons why some more recent research adds a general, overall quality criterion (Wen et al., 2015a,b; Manishina et al., 2016; Novikova et al., 2016, 2017a), or even uses only that (Sharma et al., 2016). In the following, we show that discriminative ratings for different aspects can still be obtained, using distinctive task design.

Consistency: Previous research has identified a high degree of inconsistency in human judgements of NLG outputs, where ratings often differ significantly ($p < 0.001$) for the same utterance (Walker et al., 2007). While this might be attributed to individual preferences, e.g. (Walker et al., 2007; Dethlefs et al., 2014), we also show that consistency (as measured by inter-annotator agreement) can be improved by different experimental setups, e.g. the use of continuous scales instead of discrete ones. Inconsistent user ratings are problematic in many ways, e.g. when developing metrics for automatic evaluation (Dušek et al., 2017; Novikova et al., 2017a).

Relative vs. absolute assessment. Intrinsic human evaluation methods are typically designed to *assess* the quality of a system. However, they are frequently used to *compare* the quality of different NLG systems, which is not necessarily appropriate.

Proceedings of NAACL-HLT 2018, pages 72–78
New Orleans, Louisiana, June 1 - 6, 2018. ©2018 Association for Computational Linguistics

In the following, we show that *relative* assessment methods produce more consistent and more discriminative human ratings than direct assessment methods.

In order to investigate these challenges, we compare several state-of-the-art NLG systems, which are evaluated by human crowd workers using a range of evaluation setups. We show that our newly introduced method, called *rank-based magnitude estimation* (*RankME*), outperforms traditional evaluation methods. It combines advances suggested by previous research, such as continuous scales (Belz and Kow, 2011), magnitude estimation (Siddharthan et al., 2012) and relative assessment (Callison-Burch et al., 2007). All code and data, as well as a more detailed description of the study setup are publicly available at: `https://github.com/jeknov/RankME`

2 Experimental Setup

We were able to obtain outputs of 3 systems from the recent E2E NLG challenge (Novikova et al., 2017b):[1] the *Sheffield NLP* system (Chen et al., 2018) and the *Slug2Slug* system (Juraska et al., 2018), as well as the outputs of the baseline *TGen* system (Dušek and Jurčíček, 2016). We chose these systems in order to assess whether our methods can discriminate between outputs of different quality: Automatic metric scores, including BLEU, METEOR, etc., indicate that the *Slug2Slug* and *TGen* systems show similar performance while *Sheffield*'s is further apart.[1]

All three systems are based on the sequence-to-sequence (seq2seq) architecture with attention (Bahdanau et al., 2015). *Sheffield NLP* and *TGen* both use this basic architecture with LSTM recurrent cells (Hochreiter and Schmidhuber, 1997) and a beam search, *TGen* further adds a reranker to penalize semantically invalid outputs. *Slug2Slug* is an ensemble of three seq2seq models with LSTM recurrent decoders. Two of them use LSTM recurrent encoders and one uses a convolutional encoder. A reranker checking for semantic validity selects among the outputs of all three models.

We use the first one hundred outputs for each system, and we collect human ratings from three independent crowd workers for each output using the CrowdFlower platform. We use three different methods to collect human evaluation data: 6-point Likert scales, plain magnitude estimation

[1]`http://www.macs.hw.ac.uk/ InteractionLab/E2E`

Method	DA	RR	DS	CS
Likert	x		x	
Plain ME	x			x
RankME		x		x

Table 1: Three methods used to collect human evaluation data. Here, DA = direct assessment, RR = relative ranking, DS = discrete scale, CS = continuous scale.

(*plain ME*), and rank-based magnitude estimation (*RankME*). In a magnitude estimation (ME) task (Bard et al., 1996), subjects provide a relative rating of an experimental sentence to a reference sentence, which is associated with a pre-set/fixed number. If the target sentence appears twice as good as the reference sentence, for instance, subjects are to multiply the reference score by two; if it appears half as good, they should divide it in half, etc. Note that ME implies the use of continuous scales, i.e. rating scales without numerical labels, similar to the visual analogue scales used by Belz and Kow (2011) or direct assessment scales of (Graham et al., 2013; Bojar et al., 2017), however, without given end-points. Siddharthan and Katsos (2012) have previously used ME for evaluating readability of automatically generated texts. RankME extends this idea by asking subjects to provide a relative ranking of *all* target sentences. Table 1 provides a summary of methods and scales, and indicates whether relative ranking or direct assessment was used.

3 Judgements of Multiple Criteria

In our experiments, we collect ratings on the following criteria:

- **Informativeness** (= adequacy): *Does the utterance provide all the useful information from the meaning representation?*
- **Naturalness** (= fluency): *Could the utterance have been produced by a native speaker?*
- **Quality:** *How do you judge the overall quality of the utterance in terms of its grammatical correctness, fluency, adequacy and other important factors?*

In order to investigate whether judgements of these criteria are correlated, we compare two experimental setups: In *Setup 1*, crowd workers are shown the input meaning representation (MR) and the corresponding output of one of the NLG systems and are asked to evaluate the output with respect to all three aspects in one task. In *Setup 2*, these aspects are assessed separately, in individual tasks. Furthermore, when crowd workers are asked to assess naturalness, the MR is not shown to them since it is not relevant for the task. Both setups utilise all three data collection methods – Likert scales, plain ME and RankME.

The results in Table 2 show that scores are highly correlated for Setup 1. This is in line with previous research in MT (Callison-Burch et al., 2007; Koehn, 2010). Separate collection (Setup 2), however, decreases correlation between naturalness and quality, as well as naturalness and informativeness to very low levels, especially when using ME methods. Nevertheless, informativeness and quality are still highly correlated. We assume that this is due to the fact that raters see the MR in both cases.

To obtain more insight into informativeness ratings, we asked crowd workers to further distinguish informativeness in terms of added and missed information with respect to the original MR. Crowd workers were asked to select a checkbox for *added information* if the output contained information not present in the given MR, or a checkbox for *missed information* if the output missed some information from the MR. The results of Chi-squared test show that distributions of missed and added information are significantly different (p < 0.01), i.e. systems add or delete information at different rates. Again, this information is valuable for error analysis. In addition, results in Table 4 show that assessing the amount of missed information indeed produces a different overall system ranking to added information. As such, it is worth considering missed information as a separate criterion for evaluation. This can also be approximated automatically, as demonstrated by Wiseman et al. (2017).

4 Consistency and Use of Scales

To assess consistency in human ratings, we calculate the intra-class correlation coefficient (ICC), which measures inter-observer reliability for more than two raters (Landis and Koch, 1977). In our experiments, we compare discrete Likert scales with continuous scales implemented via ME with respect to the resulting reliability of collected human ratings. The results in Table 3 show that the use of ME significantly increases ICC levels for naturalness and quality. This effect is especially pronounced for Setup 2 where ratings are collected separately. Both plain ME and RankME methods show a significant increase in ICC, with the RankME method showing the highest ICC results. This difference is most apparent for naturalness,

where RankME shows an ICC of 0.42 compared to plain ME's 0.27. For informativeness, Likert scales already provide satisfactory agreement.

In previous research, discrete, ordinal Likert scales are the dominant method of human evaluation for NLG, although they may produce results where statistical significance is overestimated (Gatt and Krahmer, 2017). Recent studies show that continuous scales allow subjects to give more nuanced judgements (Belz and Kow, 2011; Graham et al., 2013; Bojar et al., 2017). Moreover, raters were found to strongly prefer continuous scales over discrete ones (Belz and Kow, 2011). In addition to this previous work, our results also show that continuous scales significantly improve reliability of human ratings when implemented via ME.

5 Ranking vs Direct Assessment

Most data collection methods for evaluation, including Likert and plain ME, are designed to directly *assess* the quality of a system. However, these methods are almost always used to *compare* multiple systems *relative* to each other. Recently, the NLP evaluation literature has started to address this issue, mostly using binary comparisons, for example between the outputs of two MT systems (Dras, 2015; Bojar et al., 2016). In our experiments, Likert and plain ME are direct assessment (DA) methods, while RankME is a relative ranking (RR)-based method (see also Table 1). In order to directly compare DA and RR, we generated overall system rankings based on our different methods, using pairwise bootstrap test at 95% confidence level (Koehn, 2004) to establish statistically significant differences.

The results in Table 4 show that both plain ME and RankME methods produce similar rankings of NLG systems, which is in line with previous research in MT (Bojar et al., 2016). It is also apparent that ME methods, by using a continuous scale, provide more distinctive overall rankings than Likert scales. For naturalness scores, no method results in clear system ratings, which possibly reflects in the low ICC of this criterion (cf. Table 3). RankME is the only method to provide a clear ranking with respect to overall utterance quality. However, its ranking of informativeness is less clear than that of plain ME, which might be due to the different results for missed and added information (see Sec. 4). In addition, the results in Table 3 show that RR, in combination with Setup 2, results in more consistent ratings than DA.

		Setup 1	Setup 2
		naturalness	
Likert	quality	0.54*	-0.01
Plain ME		0.44*	-0.03
RankME		0.28*	-0.04

		Setup 1	Setup 2
		informativeness	
Likert	quality	0.00	0.54*
Plain ME		0.48*	0.71*
RankME		0.55*	0.74*

		Setup 1	Setup 2
		naturalness	
Likert	inform.	0.15*	-0.18*
Plain ME		0.03	-0.07
RankME		0.09	-0.08

Table 2: Spearman correlation between ratings of naturalness and quality, collected using two different setups and three data collection methods – Likert, plain ME and RankME. Here, "*" denotes $p < 0.05$.

Method	Rating	Setup 1	Setup 2
Likert	naturalness	0.07	0.12
	quality	0.02	0.41*
	informativeness	0.93*	0.78*
Plain ME	naturalness	-0.03	0.27*
	quality	0.22*	0.60*
	informativeness	0.59*	0.79*
RankME	naturalness	0.11	**0.42***
	quality	0.10	**0.68***
	informativeness	0.72*	**0.82***

Table 3: ICC scores for human ratings of naturalness, informativeness and quality. "*" denotes $p < 0.05$.

Ranking	Rating criterion & method
1. Slug2Slug 2. TGen 3. Sheffield NLP	Plain ME informativeness RankME quality TrueSkill quality added information
1. TGen 2. Slug2Slug 3. Sheffield NLP	missing information
1.–2. Slug2Slug + TGen 3. Sheffield NLP	Plain ME quality RankME informativeness TrueSkill informativeness Likert quality Likert informativeness
1.–2. Slug2Slug + Sheffield NLP 3. TGen	Likert naturalness
1.–3. Slug2Slug + TGen + Sheffield NLP	Plain ME naturalness RankME naturalness TrueSkill naturalness

Table 4: Results of system ranking using different data collection methods with Setup 2 (different ranks are statistically significant with $p < 0.05$).

5.1 Relative comparisons of many outputs

While there are clear advantages to relative rank-based assessment, the amount of data needed for this approach grows quadratically with the number of systems to compare, which is problematic with larger numbers of systems, e.g. in a shared task challenge. Data-efficient ranking algorithms, such as TrueSkill (Herbrich et al., 2006), are therefore applied by recent MT evaluation studies (Sakaguchi et al., 2014; Bojar et al., 2016) to produce overall system rankings based on a sample of binary comparisons. However, TrueSkill has not previously been used for evaluating NLG systems. TrueSkill produces system rankings by gradually updating a Bayesian estimate of each system's capability according to the "surprisal" of pairwise comparisons of individual system outputs. This way, fewer direct comparisons between systems are needed to establish their overall ranking. We computed system rankings using TrueSkill over comparisons collected via RankME and were able to show that it produces exactly the same system rankings for all three criteria as using RankME directly (see Table 4), despite the fact that the comparisons are only used in a "win-loss-tie" fashion. This shows that RankME can be used with TrueSkill to produce consistent rankings of a larger number of systems.

6 Conclusion and Discussion

In this paper, we demonstrate that the experimental design has a significant impact on the reliability as well as the outcomes of human evaluation studies for natural language generation. We first show that correlation effects between different evaluation criteria can be minimised by eliciting them separately. Furthermore, we introduce RankME, which combines relative rankings and magnitude estimation (with continuous scales), and demonstrate that this method results in better agreement amongst raters and more discriminative results. Finally, our results suggest that TrueSkill is a cost-effective alternative for producing overall relative rankings of multiple systems. This framework has the potential to not only significantly influence how NLG evaluation studies are run, but also produce more reliable data for further processing, e.g. for developing more accurate automatic evaluation metrics, which we are currently lacking, e.g. (Novikova et al., 2017a).

In current work, we test RankME with a wider range of systems (*under submission*). We also plan to investigate how this method transfers to related tasks, such as evaluating open-domain dialogue responses, e.g. (Lowe et al., 2017). In addition, we aim to investigate additional NLG evaluation methods, such as extrinsic task contributions, e.g. (Rieser et al., 2014; Gkatzia et al., 2016).

Acknowledgements

This research received funding from the EPSRC projects DILiGENt (EP/M005429/1) and MaDrIgAL (EP/N017536/1). The Titan Xp used for this research was donated by the NVIDIA Corporation.

References

Dzmitry Bahdanau, Kyunghyun Cho, and Yoshua Bengio. 2015. Neural Machine Translation by Jointly Learning to Align and Translate. In *3rd International Conference on Learning Representations (ICLR)*. San Diego, CA, USA. ArXiv: 1409.0473. http://arxiv.org/abs/1409.0473.

Ellen Gurman Bard, Dan Robertson, and Antonella Sorace. 1996. Magnitude estimation of linguistic acceptability. *Language* 72:32–68. https://doi.org/10.2307/416793.

Anja Belz and Eric Kow. 2010. Comparing rating scales and preference judgements in language evaluation. In *Proceedings of the 6th International Natural Language Generation Conference (INLG)*. Trim, Ireland, pages 7–15. http://aclweb.org/anthology/W10-4201.

Anja Belz and Eric Kow. 2011. Discrete vs. continuous rating scales for language evaluation in NLP. In *Proceedings of the 49th Annual Meeting of the Association for Computational Linguistics: Short papers*. Portland, OR, USA, pages 230–235. http://aclweb.org/anthology/P11-2040.

Ondřej Bojar, Rajen Chatterjee, Christian Federmann, Yvette Graham, Barry Haddow, Shujian Huang, Matthias Huck, Philipp Koehn, Qun Liu, Varvara Logacheva, et al. 2017. Findings of the 2017 conference on machine translation (WMT17). In *Proceedings of the Second Conference on Machine Translation (WMT)*. Copenhagen, Denmark, pages 169–214. http://aclweb.org/anthology/W17-4717.

Ondřej Bojar, Rajen Chatterjee, Christian Federmann, Yvette Graham, Barry Haddow, Matthias Huck, Antonio Jimeno Yepes, Philipp Koehn, Varvara Logacheva, Christof Monz, Matteo Negri, Aurelie Neveol, Mariana Neves, Martin Popel, Matt Post, Raphael Rubino, Carolina Scarton, Lucia Specia, Marco Turchi, Karin Verspoor, and Marcos Zampieri. 2016. Findings of the 2016 conference on machine translation (WMT16). In *Proceedings of the First Conference on Machine Translation (WMT), Volume 2: Shared Task Papers*. Berlin, Germany, pages 131–198. http://aclweb.org/anthology/W16-2301.

Chris Callison-Burch, Cameron Fordyce, Philipp Koehn, Christof Monz, and Josh Schroeder. 2007. (Meta-) evaluation of machine translation. In *Proceedings of the Second Workshop on Statistical Machine Translation (WMT)*. Prague, Czech Republic, pages 136–158. http://aclweb.org/anthology/W07-0718.

Mingjie Chen, Gerasimos Lampouras, and Andreas Vlachos. 2018. Sheffield at E2E: structured prediction approaches to end-to-end language generation. In *The E2E NLG Challenge*. To appear.

Nina Dethlefs, Heriberto Cuayáhuitl, Helen Hastie, Verena Rieser, and Oliver Lemon. 2014. Cluster-based prediction of user ratings for stylistic surface realisation. In *Proceedings of the European Chapter of the Association for Computational Linguistics (EACL)*. Gothenburg, Sweden, pages 702–711. http://aclweb.org/anthology/E14-1074.

Mark Dras. 2015. Evaluating human pairwise preference judgements. *Computational Linguistics* 41(2):337–345. https://doi.org/10.1162/COLI_a_00222.

Ondřej Dušek and Filip Jurčíček. 2016. Sequence-to-sequence generation for spoken dialogue via deep syntax trees and strings. In *Proceedings of the 54th Annual Meeting of the Association for Computational Linguistics (Volume 2: Short Papers)*. Berlin, Germany, pages 45–51. arXiv:1606.05491. http://aclweb.org/anthology/P16-2008.

Ondřej Dušek, Jekaterina Novikova, and Verena Rieser. 2017. Referenceless Quality Estimation for Natural Language Generation. In *Proceedings of the 1st Workshop on Learning to Generate Natural Language (LGNL)*. Sydney, Australia. ArXiv: 1708.01759. http://arxiv.org/abs/1708.01759.

Albert Gatt and Emiel Krahmer. 2017. Survey of the state of the art in natural language generation: Core tasks, applications and evaluation. *Journal of Artificial Intelligence Research (JAIR)* 60. https://arxiv.org/abs/1703.09902.

Dimitra Gkatzia, Oliver Lemon, and Verena Rieser. 2016. Natural language generation enhances human decision-making with uncertain information. In *Proceedings of the 54th Annual Meeting of the Association for Computational Linguistics (Volume 2: Short Papers)*. Berlin, Germany, pages 264–268. arXiv:1606.03254. http://aclweb.org/anthology/P16-2043.

Dimitra Gkatzia and Saad Mahamood. 2015. A snapshot of NLG evaluation practices 2005–2014. In *Proceedings of the 15th European Workshop on Natural Language Generation (ENLG)*. Association for Computational Linguistics, Brighton, UK, pages 57–60. https://doi.org/10.18653/v1/W15-4708.

Yvette Graham, Timothy Baldwin, Alistair Moffat, and Justin Zobel. 2013. Continuous Measurement

Scales in Human Evaluation of Machine Translation. In *Proceedings of the 7th Linguistic Annotation Workshop & Interoperability with Discourse*. Sofia, Bulgaria, pages 33–41. http://aclweb.org/anthology/W13-2305.

Ralf Herbrich, Tom Minka, and Thore Graepel. 2006. Trueskill^{TM}: a Bayesian skill rating system. In *Proceedings of the 19th International Conference on Neural Iinformation Processing Systems (NIPS)*. Vancouver, Canada, pages 569–576. http://papers.nips.cc/paper/3079-trueskilltm-a-bayesian-skill-rating-system.pdf.

Sepp Hochreiter and Jürgen Schmidhuber. 1997. Long short-term memory. *Neural computation* 9(8):1735–1780. https://doi.org/10.1162/neco.1997.9.8.1735.

Juraj Juraska, Panagiotis Karagiannis, Kevin K. Bowden, and Marilyn A. Walker. 2018. A Deep Ensemble Model with Slot Alignment for Sequence-to-Sequence Natural Language Generation. In *Proceedings of the North American Chapter of the Association for Computational Linguistics (NAACL)*. To appear.

Philipp Koehn. 2004. Statistical significance tests for machine translation evaluation. In *Proceedings of the 2004 Conference on Empirical Methods in Natural Language Processing (EMNLP)*. Barcelona, Spain, pages 388–395. http://aclweb.org/anthology/W04-3250.

Philipp Koehn. 2010. *Statistical machine translation*. Cambridge University Press, Cambridge; New York. http://dx.doi.org/10.1017/CBO9780511815829.

J. Richard Landis and Gary G. Koch. 1977. The measurement of observer agreement for categorical data. *Biometrics* 33(1):159–174. https://doi.org/10.2307/2529310.

Ryan Lowe, Michael Noseworthy, Iulian Vlad Serban, Nicolas Angelard-Gontier, Yoshua Bengio, and Joelle Pineau. 2017. Towards an automatic turing test: Learning to evaluate dialogue responses. In *Proceedings of the 55th Annual Meeting of the Association for Computational Linguistics (Volume 1: Long Papers)*. Association for Computational Linguistics, pages 1116–1126. https://doi.org/10.18653/v1/P17-1103.

Elena Manishina, Bassam Jabaian, Stéphane Huet, and Fabrice Lefevre. 2016. Automatic corpus extension for data-driven natural language generation. In *Proceedings of the Tenth International Conference on Language Resources and Evaluation (LREC)*. Portorož, Slovenia, pages 3624–3631. http://www.lrec-conf.org/proceedings/lrec2016/pdf/571_Paper.pdf.

Jekaterina Novikova, Ondřej Dušek, Amanda Cercas Curry, and Verena Rieser. 2017a. Why we need new evaluation metrics for NLG. In *Proceedings of the 2017 Conference on Empirical Methods in Natural Language Processing (EMNLP)*. pages 2231–2242. http://aclweb.org/anthology/D17-1237.

Jekaterina Novikova, Ondřej Dušek, and Verena Rieser. 2017b. The E2E dataset: New challenges for end-to-end generation. In *Proceedings of the 18th Annual SIGdial Meeting on Discourse and Dialogue (SIGDIAL)*. pages 201–206. http://aclweb.org/anthology/W17-5525.

Jekaterina Novikova, Oliver Lemon, and Verena Rieser. 2016. Crowd-sourcing NLG data: Pictures elicit better data. In *Proceedings of the 9th International Natural Language Generation conference (INLG)*. Edinburgh, UK, pages 265–273. http://aclweb.org/anthology/W16-6644.

Verena Rieser, Oliver Lemon, and Simon Keizer. 2014. Natural language generation as incremental planning under uncertainty: Adaptive information presentation for statistical dialogue systems. *IEEE/ACM Transactions on Audio, Speech, and Language Processing* 22(5):979–993. https://doi.org/10.1109/TASL.2014.2315271.

Keisuke Sakaguchi, Matt Post, and Benjamin Van Durme. 2014. Efficient elicitation of annotations for human evaluation of machine translation. In *Proceedings of the Ninth Workshop on Statistical Machine Translation (WMT)*. Baltimore, MD, USA, pages 1–11. http://aclweb.org/anthology/W14-3301.

Shikhar Sharma, Jing He, Kaheer Suleman, Hannes Schulz, and Philip Bachman. 2016. Natural language generation in dialogue using lexicalized and delexicalized data. *CoRR* abs/1606.03632. http://arxiv.org/abs/1606.03632.

Advaith Siddharthan, Matthew Green, Kees van Deemter, Chris Mellish, and René van der Wal. 2012. Blogging birds: Generating narratives about reintroduced species to promote public engagement. In *Proceedings of the Seventh International Natural Language Generation Conference (INLG)*. Utica, IL, USA, pages 120–124. http://aclweb.org/anthology/W12-1520.

Advaith Siddharthan and Napoleon Katsos. 2012. Offline sentence processing measures for testing readability with users. In *Proceedings of the NAACL-HLT 2012 Workshop on Predicting and Improving Text Readability (PITR)*. Montréal, Canada, pages 17–24. http://aclweb.org/anthology/W12-2203.

Marilyn Walker, Amanda Stent, François Mairesse, and Rashmi Prasad. 2007. Individual and domain adaptation in sentence planning for dialogue. *Journal of Artificial Intelligence Research*

(JAIR) 30(1):413–456. `https://doi.org/10.1613/jair.2329`.

Tsung-Hsien Wen, Milica Gasić, Dongho Kim, Nikola Mrkšić, Pei-Hao Su, David Vandyke, and Steve Young. 2015a. Stochastic language generation in dialogue using recurrent neural networks with convolutional sentence reranking. In *Proceedings of the 16th Annual Meeting of the Special Interest Group on Discourse and Dialogue (SIGDIAL)*. Association for Computational Linguistics, Prague, Czech Republic, pages 275–284. `http://aclweb.org/anthology/W15-4639`.

Tsung-Hsien Wen, Milica Gašić, Nikola Mrkšić, Pei-Hao Su, David Vandyke, and Steve Young. 2015b. Semantically conditioned LSTM-based natural language generation for spoken dialogue systems. In *Proceedings of the 2015 Conference on Empirical Methods in Natural Language Processing (EMNLP)*. Lisbon, Portugal, pages 1711–1721. `http://aclweb.org/anthology/D15-1199`.

Sam Wiseman, Stuart M. Shieber, and Alexander M. Rush. 2017. Challenges in data-to-document generation. In *Proceedings of the 2017 Conference on Empirical Methods in Natural Language Processing, EMNLP 2017, Copenhagen, Denmark, September 9-11, 2017*. Copenhagen, Denmark, pages 2253–2263. `https://aclweb.org/anthology/D17-1239`.

Sentence Simplification with Memory-Augmented Neural Networks

Tu Vu[1], Baotian Hu[2], Tsendsuren Munkhdalai[3] and Hong Yu[1,2]
[1]University of Massachusetts Amherst, Amherst, MA 01003, USA
`tuvu@cs.umass.edu`
[2]University of Massachusetts Medical School, Worcester, MA 01655, USA
`{baotian.hu,hong.yu}@umassmed.edu`
[3]Microsoft Research, Montréal, QC H3A 3H3, Canada
`tsendsuren.munkhdalai@microsoft.com`

Abstract

Sentence simplification aims to simplify the content and structure of complex sentences, and thus make them easier to interpret for human readers, and easier to process for downstream NLP applications. Recent advances in neural machine translation have paved the way for novel approaches to the task. In this paper, we adapt an architecture with augmented memory capacities called Neural Semantic Encoders (Munkhdalai and Yu, 2017) for sentence simplification. Our experiments demonstrate the effectiveness of our approach on different simplification datasets, both in terms of automatic evaluation measures and human judgments.

1 Introduction

The goal of sentence simplification is to compose complex sentences into simpler ones so that they are more comprehensible and accessible, while still retaining the original information content and meaning. Sentence simplification has a number of practical applications. On one hand, it provides reading aids for people with limited language proficiency (Watanabe et al., 2009; Siddharthan, 2003), or for patients with linguistic and cognitive disabilities (Carroll et al., 1999). On the other hand, it can improve the performance of other NLP tasks (Chandrasekar et al., 1996; Knight and Marcu, 2000; Beigman Klebanov et al., 2004).

Prior work has explored monolingual machine translation (MT) approaches, utilizing corpora of simplified texts, e.g., Simple English Wikipedia (SEW), and making use of statistical MT models, such as phrase-based MT (PBMT) (Štajner et al., 2015; Coster and Kauchak, 2011; Wubben et al., 2012), tree-based MT (TBMT) (Zhu et al., 2010; Woodsend and Lapata, 2011), or syntax-based MT (SBMT) (Xu et al., 2016).

Inspired by the success of neural MT (Sutskever et al., 2014; Cho et al., 2014), recent work has started exploring neural simplification with sequence to sequence (Seq2seq) models, also referred to as encoder-decoder models. Nisioi et al. (2017) implemented a standard LSTM-based Seq2seq model and found that they outperform PBMT, SBMT, and unsupervised lexical simplification approaches. Zhang and Lapata (Zhang and Lapata, 2017) viewed the encoder-decoder model as an agent and employed a deep reinforcement learning framework in which the reward has three components capturing key aspects of the target output: simplicity, relevance, and fluency.

The common practice for Seq2seq models is to use recurrent neural networks (RNNs) with Long Short-Term Memory (LSTM, Hochreiter and Schmidhuber, 1997) or Gated Recurrent Unit (GRU, Cho et al., 2014) for the encoder and decoder (Nisioi et al., 2017; Zhang and Lapata, 2017). These architectures were designed to be capable of memorizing long-term dependencies across sequences. Nevertheless, their memory is typically small and might not be enough for the simplification task, where one is confronted with long and complicated sentences.

In this study, we go beyond the conventional LSTM/GRU-based Seq2seq models and propose to use a memory-augmented RNN architecture called Neural Semantic Encoders (NSE). This architecture has been shown to be effective in a wide range of NLP tasks (Munkhdalai and Yu, 2017). The contribution of this paper is twofold:

(1) First, we present a novel simplification model which is, to the best of our knowledge, the first model that use memory-augmented RNN for the task. We investigate the effectiveness of neural Seq2seq models when different neural architectures for the encoder are considered. Our experiments reveal that the NSELSTM model that uses an

Proceedings of NAACL-HLT 2018, pages 79–85
New Orleans, Louisiana, June 1 - 6, 2018. ©2018 Association for Computational Linguistics

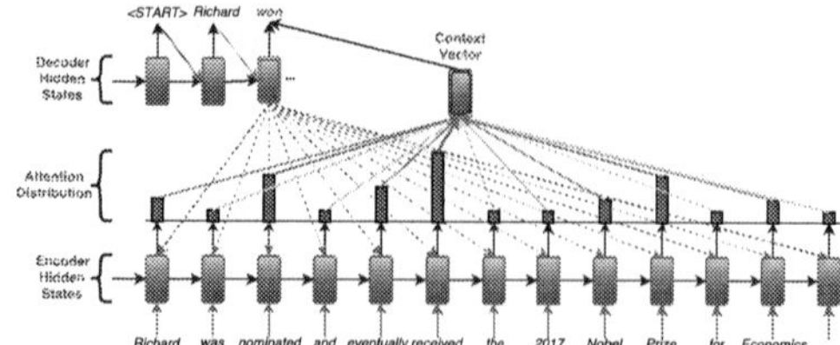

Figure 1: Attention-based encoder-decoder model. The model may attend to relevant source information while decoding the simplification, e.g., to generate the target word *won* the model may attend to the source words *received*, *nominated* and *Prize*.

NSE as the encoder and an LSTM as the decoder performed the best among these models, improving over strong simplification systems. (2) Second, we perform an extensive evaluation of various approaches proposed in the literature on different datasets. Results of both automatic and human evaluation show that our approach is remarkably effective for the task, significantly reducing the reading difficulty of the input, while preserving grammaticality and the original meaning. We further discuss some advantages and disadvantages of these approaches.

2 Neural Sequence to Sequence Models

2.1 Attention-based Encoder-Decoder Model

Our approach is based on an attention-based Seq2seq model (Bahdanau et al., 2015) (Figure 1). Given a complex source sentence $\mathcal{X} = x_{1:T_x}$, the model learns to generate its simplified version $\mathcal{Y} = y_{1:T_y}$. The encoder reads through $\mathcal{X}$ and computes a sequence of hidden states $h_{1:T_x}$:

$$h_t = \mathcal{F}^{enc}(h_{t-1}, x_t),$$

where $\mathcal{F}^{enc}$ is a non-linear activation function (e.g., LSTM), h_t is the hidden state at time t. Each time the model generates a target word y_t, the decoder looks at a set of positions in the source sentence where the most relevant information is located. Specifically, another non-linear activation function F^{dec} is used for the decoder where the hidden state s_t at time t is computed by:

$$s_t = \mathcal{F}^{dec}(s_{t-1}, y_{t-1}, c_t).$$

Here, the context vector c_t is computed as a weighted sum of the hidden vectors $h_{1:T_x}$:

$$c_t = \sum_{i=1}^{T_x} \alpha_{ti} h_i, \qquad \alpha_{ti} = \frac{\exp(s_{t-1} \odot h_i)}{\sum_{j=1}^{T_x} \exp(s_{t-1} \odot h_j)},$$

where $\odot$ is the dot product of two vectors. Generation is conditioned on c_t and all the previously generated target words $y_{1:t-1}$:

$$P(\mathcal{Y}|\mathcal{X}) = \prod_{t=1}^{T_y} P(y_t|\{y_{1:t-1}\}, c_t),$$

$$P(y_t|\{y_{1:t-1}\}, c_t) = \mathcal{G}(y_{t-1}, s_t, c_t),$$

where $\mathcal{G}$ is some non-linear function. The training objective is to minimize the cross-entropy loss of the training source-target pairs.

2.2 Neural Semantic Encoders

An RNN allows us to compute a hidden state h_t of each word summarizing the preceding words $x_{1:t}$, but not considering the following words $x_{t+1:T_x}$ that might also be useful for simplification. An alternative approach is to use a bidirectional-RNN (Schuster and Paliwal, 1997). Here, we propose to use Neural Semantic Encoders (NSE, Munkhdalai and Yu, 2017). During each encoding time step t, we compute a memory matrix $M_t \in \mathbb{R}^{T_x \times D}$ where D is the dimensionality of the word vectors. This matrix is initialized with the word vectors and is refined over time through NSE's functions to gain a better understanding of the input sequence. Concretely, NSE sequentially reads the tokens $x_{1:T_x}$ with its *read* function:

$$r_t = \mathcal{F}^{enc}_{read}(r_{t-1}, x_t),$$

where $\mathcal{F}^{enc}_{read}$ is an LSTM, $r_t \in \mathbb{R}^D$ is the hidden state at time t. Then, a *compose* function is used to compose r_t with relevant information retrieved from the memory at the previous time step, M_{t-1}:

$$c_t = \mathcal{F}^{enc}_{compose}(r_t, m_t),$$

where $\mathcal{F}^{enc}_{compose}$ is a multi-layer perceptron with one hidden layer, $c_t \in \mathbb{R}^{2D}$ is the output vector, and $m_t \in \mathbb{R}^D$ is a linear combination of the memory slots of M_{t-1}, weighted by $\sigma_{ti} \in \mathbb{R}$:

$$m_t = \sum_{i=1}^{T_x} \sigma_{ti} M_{t-1,i}, \qquad \sigma_{ti} = \frac{\exp(r_t \odot M_{t-1,i})}{\sum_{j=1}^{T_x} \exp(r_t \odot M_{t-1,j})}.$$

Here, $M_{t-1,i}$ is the ith row of the memory matrix at time $t-1$, M_{t-1}. Next, a *write* function is used to map c_t to the encoder output space:

$$w_t = \mathcal{F}^{enc}_{write}(w_{t-1}, c_t),$$

where $\mathcal{F}^{enc}_{write}$ is an LSTM, $w_t \in \mathbb{R}^D$ is the hidden state at time t. Finally, the memory is updated accordingly. The retrieved memory content pointed by σ_{ti} is erased and the new content is added:

$$M_{t,i} = (1 - \sigma_{ti}) M_{t-1,i} + \sigma_{ti} w_t.$$

NSE gives us unrestricted access to the entire source sequence stored in the memory. As such, the encoder may attend to relevant words when encoding each word. The sequence $w_{1:T_x}$ is then used as the sequence $h_{1:T_x}$ in Section 2.1.

2.3 Decoding

We differ from the approach of Zhang et al. (2017) in the sense that we implement both a greedy strategy and a beam-search strategy to generate the target sentence. Whereas the greedy decoder always chooses the simplification candidate with the highest log-probability, the beam-search decoder keeps a fixed number (beam) of the highest scoring candidates at each time step. We report the best simplification among the outputs based on automatic evaluation measures.

3 Experimental Setup

3.1 Datasets

Following (Zhang and Lapata, 2017), we experiment on three simplification datasets, namely: (1) *Newsela* (Xu et al., 2015), a high-quality simplification corpus of news articles composed by Newsela[1] professional editors. We used the split of the data in (Zhang and Lapata, 2017), i.e., 94,208/1,129/1,077 pairs for train/dev/test. (2) *WikiSmall* (Zhu et al., 2010), which contains aligned complex-simple sentence pairs from English Wikipedia (EW) and SEW. The dataset has 88,837/205/100 pairs for train/dev/test. (3) *WikiLarge* (Zhang and Lapata, 2017), a larger corpus in which the training set is a mixture of three Wikipedia datasets in (Zhu et al., 2010; Woodsend and Lapata, 2011; Kauchak, 2013), and the development and test sests are complex sentences taken from *WikiSmall*, each has 8 simplifications written by Amazon Mechanical Turk workers (Xu et al., 2016). The dataset has 296,402/2,000/359 pairs for train/dev/test. Table 1 provides statistics on the training sets.

Dataset	vocab size		#tokens/sent	
	src	tgt	src	tgt
Newsela	41,066	30,193	25.94	15.89
WikiSmall	113,368	93,835	24.26	20.33
WikiLarge	201,841	168,962	25.17	18.51

Table 1: Statistics for the training sets: the vocabulary size (vocab size), and the average number of tokens per sentence (#tokens/sent) of the source (src) and target (tgt) language.

3.2 Models and Training Details

We implemented two attention-based Seq2seq models, namely: (1) LSTMLSTM: the encoder

[1] https://newsela.com

is implemented by two LSTM layers; (2) NSELSTM: the encoder is implemented by NSE. The decoder in both cases is implemented by two LSTM layers. For all experiments, our models have 300-dimensional hidden states and 300-dimensional word embeddings. Parameters were initialized from a uniform distribution [-0.1, 0.1]. We used the same hyperparameters across all datasets. Word embeddings were initialized either randomly or with Glove vectors (Pennington et al., 2014) pre-trained on Common Crawl data (840B tokens), and fine-tuned during training. We used a vocabulary size of 20K for Newsela, and 30K for WikiSmall and WikiLarge. Our models were trained with a maximum number of 40 epochs using Adam optimizer (Kingma and Ba, 2015) with step size $\alpha = 0.001$ for LSTMLSTM, and 0.0003 for NSELSTM, the exponential decay rates $\beta_1 = 0.9, \beta_2 = 0.999$. The batch size is set to 32. We used dropout (Srivastava et al., 2014) for regularization with a dropout rate of 0.3. For beam search, we experimented with beam sizes of 5 and 10. Following (Jean et al., 2015), we replaced each out-of-vocabulary token $\langle unk \rangle$ with the source word x_k with the highest alignment score α_{ti}, i.e., $k = \underset{i}{\arg\max}(\alpha_{ti})$.

Our models were tuned on the development sets, either with BLEU (Papineni et al., 2002) that scores the output by counting n-gram matches with the reference, or SARI (Xu et al., 2016) that compares the output against both the reference and the input sentence. Both measures are commonly used to automatically evaluate the quality of simplification output. We noticed that SARI should be used with caution when tuning neural Seq2seq simplification models. Since SARI depends on the differences between a system's output and the input sentence, large differences may yield very good SARI even though the output is ungrammatical. Thus, when tuning with SARI, we ignored epochs in which the BLEU score of the output is too low, using a threshold ς. We set ς to 22 on Newsela, 33 on WikiSmall, and 77 on WikiLarge.

3.3 Comparing Systems

We compared our models, either tuned with BLEU (-B) or SARI (-S), against systems reported in (Zhang and Lapata, 2017), namely DRESS, a deep reinforcement learning model, DRESS-LS, a combination of DRESS and a lexical simplification model (Zhang and Lapata, 2017), PBMT-

R, a PBMT model with dissimilarity-based re-ranking (Wubben et al., 2012), HYBRID, a hybrid semantic-based model that combines a simplification model and a monolingual MT model (Narayan and Gardent, 2014), and SBMT-SARI, a SBMT model with simplification-specific components. (Xu et al., 2016).

3.4 Evaluation

We measured BLEU, and SARI at corpus-level following (Zhang and Lapata, 2017). In addition, we also evaluated system output by eliciting human judgments. Specifically, we randomly selected 40 sentences from each test set, and included human reference simplifications and corresponding simplifications from the systems above[2]. We then asked three volunteers[3] to rate simplifications with respect to *Fluency* (the extent to which the output is grammatical English), *Adequacy* (the extent to which the output has the same meaning as the input sentence), and *Simplicity* (the extent to which the output is simpler than the input sentence) using a five point Likert scale.

4 Results and Discussions

4.1 Automatic Evaluation Measures

The results of the automatic evaluation are displayed in Table 2. We first discuss the results on Newsela that contains high-quality simplifications composed by professional editors. In terms of BLEU, all neural models achieved much higher scores than PBMT-R and HYBRID. NSELSTM-B scored highest with a BLEU score of 26.31. With regard to SARI, NSELSTM-S scored best among neural models (29.58) and came close to the performance of HYBRID (30.00). This indicates that NSE offers an effective means to better encode complex sentences for sentence simplification.

On WikiSmall, HYBRID – the current state-of-the-art – achieved best BLEU (53.94) and SARI (30.46) scores. Among neural models, NSELSTM-B yielded the highest BLEU score (53.42), while NSELSTM-S performed best on SARI (29.75). On WikiLarge[4], again, NSELSTM-B had the highest BLEU score of 92.02. SBMT-SARI – that was

---

² The outputs of comparison systems are available at https://github.com/XingxingZhang/dress.

³ two native English speakers and one non-native fluent English speaker

⁴ Here, BLEU scores are much higher compared to Newsela and WikiSmall since there are 8 reference simplifications for each input sentence in the test set.

Model	Newsela		WikiSmall		WikiLarge	
	BLEU	SARI	BLEU	SARI	BLEU	SARI
PBMT-R	18.19	15.77	46.31	15.97	81.11	38.56
HYBRID	14.46	**30.00**	**53.94**	**30.46**	48.97	31.40
SBMT-SARI	NA		NA		73.08	**39.96**
DRESS	23.21	27.37	34.53	27.48	77.18	37.08
DRESS-LS	24.30	26.63	36.32	27.24	80.12	37.27
LSTMLSTM-B	24.38	27.66	50.53	17.67	88.81	34.22
NSELSTM-B	**26.31**	27.42	53.42	17.47	**92.02**	33.43
LSTMLSTM-S	23.50	28.67	31.32	28.04	81.95	35.45
NSELSTM-S	22.62	29.58	29.72	29.75	80.43	36.88

Table 2: Model performance using automatic evaluation measures (BLEU and SARI).

trained on a huge corpus of 106M sentence pairs and 2B words – scored highest on SARI with 39.96, followed by DRESS-LS (37.27), DRESS (37.08), and NSELSTM-S (36.88).

4.2 Human Judgments

The results of human judgments are displayed in Table 3. On Newsela, NSELSTM-B scored highest on Fluency. PBMT-R was significantly better than all other systems on Adequacy while LSTMLSTM-S performed best on Simplicity. NSELSTM-B did very well on both Adequacy and Simplicity, and was best in terms of Average. Example model outputs on Newsela are provided in Table 4.

On WikiSmall, NSELSTM-B performed best on both Fluency and Adequacy. On WikiLarge, LSTMLSTM-B achieved the highest Fluency score while NSELSTM-B received the highest Adequacy score. In terms of Simplicity and Average, NSELSTM-S outperformed all other systems on both WikiSmall and WikiLarge.

As shown in Table 3, neural models often outperformed traditional systems (PBMT-R, HYBRID, SBMT-SARI) on Fluency. This is not surprising given the recent success of neural Seq2seq models in language modeling and neural machine translation (Zaremba et al., 2014; Jean et al., 2015). On the downside, our manual inspection reveals that neural models learn to perform copying very well in terms of rewrite operations (e.g., copying, deletion, reordering, substitution), often outputting the same or parts of the input sentence.

Finally, as can be seen in Table 3, REFERENCE scored lower on Adequacy compared to Fluency and Simplicity on Newsela. On Wikipedia-based datasets, REFERENCE obtained high Adequacy scores but much lower Simplicity scores compared to Newsela. This supports the assertion by previous work (Xu et al., 2015) that SEW has a large proportion of inadequate simplifications.

Model	Newsela				WikiSmall				WikiLarge			
	F	A	S	Avg.	F	A	S	Avg.	F	A	S	Avg.
REFERENCE	4.58	2.98	3.99	3.85	4.63	3.97	3.59	4.06	4.59	4.43	2.38	3.80
PBMT-R	3.73	**3.90**	1.98	3.20	4.07	4.11	2.28	3.49	4.22	4.09	2.31	3.54
HYBRID	2.77	2.56	2.41	2.58	3.21	3.62	2.56	3.13	2.63	2.48	2.26	2.46
SBMT-SARI	NA				NA				3.89	3.87	2.54	3.43
DRESS	3.98	2.84	2.93	3.25	4.35	3.33	3.49	3.72	4.56	3.66	2.63	3.62
DRESS-LS	3.99	2.90	2.98	3.29	4.43	3.33	3.56	3.77	4.68	3.88	2.63	3.73
LSTMLSTM-B	3.95	2.93	3.14	3.34	4.42	3.88	2.65	3.65	**4.80**	4.47	1.89	3.72
NSELSTM-B	**4.26**	3.13	3.39	**3.59**	**4.74**	**4.22**	2.49	3.82	4.73	**4.58**	1.94	3.75
LSTMLSTM-S	4.24	3.03	**3.45**	3.57	4.59	3.40	3.42	3.80	4.73	4.23	2.21	3.72
NSELSTM-S	3.83	2.78	3.01	3.21	4.57	3.28	**3.81**	**3.89**	4.65	3.95	**2.90**	**3.83**

Table 3: Average human ratings (Fluency (F), Adequacy (A), Simplicity (S), and Average (Avg.)).

COMPLEX: Another parent , Mike Munson , sits on the bench with a tablet and uses an app to track and analyze the team 's shots .
REFERENCE: **Basketball** parent Mike Munson sits on the bench with a tablet , **like an iPad** .
PBMT-R: Another parent , Mike Munson **is** on the bench with a tablet and uses an app to track and analyze the team 's shots .
HYBRID: another parent , mike munson sits uses an app to track and analyze shots .
DRESS: Another parent , Mike Munson , sits on the bench with a **computer** .
DRESS-LS: Another parent , Mike Munson , sits on the bench with a **computer** .
LSTMLSTM-B: **He starts** on the bench with a tablet and uses an app to track .
NSELSTM-B: Another parent , Mike Munson , sits on the bench with a tablet and uses an app to track .
LSTMLSTM-S: **She** sits on the bench with a tablet and uses an app to track and **study** the team 's shots .
NSELSTM-S: **He** sits on the bench with a tablet .
COMPLEX: Stowell believes that even documents about Lincoln 's death will give people a better understanding of the man who was assassinated 150 years ago this April .
REFERENCE: Stowell **thinks** that even **information** about Lincoln 's death will **help** people **understand him** .
PBMT-R: Stowell **thinks** that even documents about Lincoln 's death will give people a better understanding of the man who was killed 150 years ago this April .
HYBRID: documents **that** will give people a understanding the man was assassinated 150 years ago .
DRESS: Stowell **thinks** that even documents about Lincoln 's death will give people a better understanding of the man .
DRESS-LS: Stowell **thinks** that even documents about Lincoln 's death will give people a better understanding of the man .
LSTMLSTM-B: Stowell believes that **only** documents about Lincoln 's death will give people a better understanding .
NSELSTM-B: Stowell believes that **the discovery** about Lincoln 's death will give people a better understanding of the man .
LSTMLSTM-S: Stowell **thinks** that even documents about Lincoln 's death will give people a better understanding of the man .
NSELSTM-S: Stowell **thinks** that even **papers** about Lincoln 's death will give people a better understanding of the man .

Table 4: Example model outputs on Newsela. Substitutions are shown in bold.

4.3 Correlations

Table 5 shows the correlations between the scores assigned by humans and the automatic evaluation measures. There is a positive significant correlation between Fluency and Adequacy (0.69), but a negative significant correlation between Adequacy and Simplicity (-0.64). BLEU correlates well with Fluency (0.63) and Adequacy (0.90) while SARI correlates well with Simplicity (0.73). BLEU and SARI show a negative significant correlation (-0.54). The results reflect the challenge of managing the trade-off between Fluency, Adequacy and Simplicity in sentence simplification.

	Adequacy	Simplicity	BLEU	SARI
Fluency	0.69**	-0.03	0.63**	-0.48**
Adequacy		-0.64**	0.90**	-0.81**
Simplicity			-0.56**	0.73**
BLEU				-0.54**

Table 5: Pearson correlation between the scores assigned by humans and the automatic evaluation measures. Scores marked ** are significant at $p < 0.01$.

5 Conclusions

In this paper, we explore neural Seq2seq models for sentence simplification. We propose to use an architecture with augmented memory capacities which we believe is suitable for the task, where one is confronted with long and complex sentences. Results of both automatic and human evaluation on different datasets show that our model is capable of significantly reducing the reading difficulty of the input, while performing well in terms of grammaticality and meaning preservation.

6 Acknowledgements

We would like to thank Emily Druhl, Jesse Lingeman, and the UMass BioNLP team for their help with this work. We also thank Xingxing Zhang and Sergiu Nisioi for valuable discussions, and the anonymous reviewers for their thoughtful comments and suggestions.

References

Dzmitry Bahdanau, Kyunghyun Cho, and Yoshua Bengio. 2015. Neural machine translation by jointly learning to align and translate. In *Proceedings of the International Conference on Learning Representations (ICLR)*, Curran Associates, Inc., San Diego, CA, USA, pages 3104–3112.

Beata Beigman Klebanov, Kevin Knight, and Daniel Marcu. 2004. Text simplification for information-seeking applications. In *Proceed- ings of Ontologies, Dabases, and Applications of Semantics (ODBASE) International Conference, volume 3290 of Lecture Notes in Computer Science*. Springer, Berlin, Heidelberg, pages 735–747.

John Carroll, Guido Minnen, Darren Pearce, Yvonne Canning, Siobhan Devlin, and John Tait. 1999. Simplifying text for language-impaired readers. In *Proceedings of the 9th Conference of the European Chapter of the Association for Computational Linguistics (EACL)*. Association for Computational Linguistics, Bergen, Norway, pages 269–270.

R. Chandrasekar, Christine Doran, and B. Srinivas. 1996. Motivations and methods for text simplification. In *Proceedings of the 16th International Conference on Computational Linguistics (COLING)*. Stroudsburg, PA, USA, pages 1041–1044.

Kyunghyun Cho, Bart van Merrienboer, Caglar Gulcehre, Dzmitry Bahdanau, Fethi Bougares, Holger Schwenk, and Yoshua Bengio. 2014. Learning phrase representations using rnn encoder–decoder for statistical machine translation. In *Proceedings of the 2014 Conference on Empirical Methods in Natural Language Processing (EMNLP)*. Association for Computational Linguistics, Doha, Qatar, pages 1724–1734.

Will Coster and David Kauchak. 2011. Learning to simplify sentences using wikipedia. In *Proceedings of the Workshop on Monolingual Text-To-Text Generation*. Association for Computational Linguistics, Portland, Oregon, pages 1–9.

Sepp Hochreiter and Jrgen Schmidhuber. 1997. Long short-term memory. *Neural Computation* 9(8):1735–1780.

Sébastien Jean, Orhan Firat, Kyunghyun Cho, Roland Memisevic, and Yoshua Bengio. 2015. Montreal neural machine translation systems for wmt15. In *Proceedings of the Tenth Workshop on Statistical Machine Translation*. Association for Computational Linguistics, Lisbon, Portugal, pages 134–140.

David Kauchak. 2013. Improving text simplification language modeling using unsimplified text data. In *Proceedings of the 51st Annual Meeting of the Association for Computational Linguistics (ACL)*. Association for Computational Linguistics, Sofia, Bulgaria, pages 1537–1546.

Diederik Kingma and Jimmy Ba. 2015. Adam: A method for stochastic optimization. In *Proceedings of the International Conference on Learning Representations (ICLR)*, Curran Associates, Inc., San Diego, CA, USA.

Kevin Knight and Daniel Marcu. 2000. Statistics-based summarization - step one: Sentence compression. In *Proceedings of the Seventeenth National Conference on Artificial Intelligence (AAAI) and Twelfth Conference on Innovative Applications of Artificial Intelligence (IAAI)*. AAAI Press, pages 703–710.

Tsendsuren Munkhdalai and Hong Yu. 2017. Neural semantic encoders. In *Proceedings of the 15th Conference of the European Chapter of the Association for Computational Linguistics (EACL)*. Association for Computational Linguistics, Valencia, Spain, pages 397–407.

Shashi Narayan and Claire Gardent. 2014. Hybrid simplification using deep semantics and machine translation. In *Proceedings of the 52nd Annual Meeting of the Association for Computational Linguistics (ACL)*. Association for Computational Linguistics, Baltimore, Maryland, pages 435–445.

Sergiu Nisioi, Sanja Štajner, Simone Paolo Ponzetto, and Liviu P. Dinu. 2017. Exploring neural text simplification models. In *Proceedings of the 55th Annual Meeting of the Association for Computational Linguistics (ACL)*. Association for Computational Linguistics, Vancouver, Canada, pages 85–91.

Kishore Papineni, Salim Roukos, Todd Ward, and Wei-Jing Zhu. 2002. Bleu: a method for automatic evaluation of machine translation. In *Proceedings of 40th Annual Meeting of the Association for Computational Linguistics (ACL)*. Association for Computational Linguistics, Philadelphia, Pennsylvania, USA, pages 311–318.

Jeffrey Pennington, Richard Socher, and Christopher Manning. 2014. Glove: Global vectors for word representation. In *Proceedings of the 2014 Conference on Empirical Methods in Natural Language Processing (EMNLP)*. Association for Computational Linguistics, Doha, Qatar, pages 1532–1543.

Mike Schuster and Kuldip K Paliwal. 1997. Bidirectional recurrent neural networks. *IEEE Transactions on Signal Processing* 45(11):2673–2681.

Advaith Siddharthan. 2003. Syntactic simplification and text cohesion. Ph.D. Thesis, University of Cambridge, University of Cambridge.

Nitish Srivastava, Geoffrey Hinton, Alex Krizhevsky, Ilya Sutskever, and Ruslan Salakhutdinov. 2014. Dropout: A simple way to prevent neural networks from overfitting. *Journal of Machine Learning Research* 15:1929–1958.

Ilya Sutskever, Oriol Vinyals, and Quoc V Le. 2014. Sequence to sequence learning with neural networks. In Z. Ghahramani, M. Welling, C. Cortes, N. D. Lawrence, and K. Q. Weinberger, editors, *Advances in Neural Information Processing Systems 27 (NIPS)*, Curran Associates, Inc., pages 3104–3112.

Sanja Štajner, Hannah Bechara, and Horacio Saggion. 2015. A deeper exploration of the standard pb-smt approach to text simplification and its evaluation. In *Proceedings of the 53rd Annual Meeting of the Association for Computational Linguistics (ACL) and the 7th International Joint Conference on Natural Language Processing (IJCNLP)*. Association for Computational Linguistics, Beijing, China, pages 823–828.

Willian Massami Watanabe, Arnaldo Candido Junior, Vinícius Rodriguez Uzêda, Renata Pontin de Mattos Fortes, Thiago Alexandre Salgueiro Pardo, and Sandra Maria Aluísio. 2009. Facilita: Reading assistance for low-literacy readers. In *Proceedings of the 27th ACM International Conference on Design of Communication (SIGDOC)*. ACM, New York, NY, USA, pages 29–36.

Kristian Woodsend and Mirella Lapata. 2011. Learning to simplify sentences with quasi-synchronous grammar and integer programming. In *Proceedings of the 2011 Conference on Empirical Methods in Natural Language Processing (EMNLP)*. Association for Computational Linguistics, Edinburgh, Scotland, UK., pages 409–420.

Sander Wubben, Antal van den Bosch, and Emiel Krahmer. 2012. Sentence simplification by monolingual machine translation. In *Proceedings of the 50th Annual Meeting of the Association for Computational Linguistics (ACL)*. Association for Computational Linguistics, Jeju Island, Korea, pages 1015–1024.

Wei Xu, Chris Callison-Burch, and Courtney Napoles. 2015. Problems in current text simplification research: New data can help. *Transactions of the Association for Computational Linguistics (TACL)* 3:283–297.

Wei Xu, Courtney Napoles, Ellie Pavlick, Quanze Chen, and Chris Callison-Burch. 2016. Optimizing statistical machine translation for text simplification. *Transactions of the Association for Computational Linguistics (TACL)* 4:401–415.

Wojciech Zaremba, Ilya Sutskever, and Oriol Vinyals. 2014. Recurrent neural network regularization. *arXiv preprint arXiv:1409.2329* .

Xingxing Zhang and Mirella Lapata. 2017. Sentence simplification with deep reinforcement learning. In *Proceedings of the 2017 Conference on Empirical Methods in Natural Language Processing (EMNLP)*. Association for Computational Linguistics, Copenhagen, Denmark, pages 595–605.

Zhemin Zhu, Delphine Bernhard, and Iryna Gurevych. 2010. A monolingual tree-based translation model for sentence simplification. In *Proceedings of the 23rd International Conference on Computational Linguistics (COLING)*. Coling 2010 Organizing Committee, Beijing, China, pages 1353–1361.

A Corpus of Non-Native Written English Annotated for Metaphor

Beata Beigman Klebanov, Chee Wee Leong, and Michael Flor
Educational Testing Service
660 Rosedale Road
Princeton, NJ, USA
`bbeigmanklebanov,cleong,mflor@ets.org`

Abstract

We present a corpus of 240 argumentative essays written by non-native speakers of English annotated for metaphor. The corpus is made publicly available. We provide benchmark performance of state-of-the-art systems on this new corpus, and explore the relationship between writing proficiency and metaphor use.

1 Introduction

With the ubiquity of metaphor across genres of written and spoken communication, the ability of NLP systems to deal with metaphor effectively is an actively researched topic (Veale et al., 2016). Most current work in the supervised machine learning paradigm uses data from the British National Corpus (**BNC**). Beigman Klebanov et al. (2015) reported an evaluation of a metaphor detection system on students' writing; however, their corpus was not released for public use. Our contributions are as follows: (1) We release metaphor annotations of 240 argumentative essays written by non-native speakers of English. This is the first publicly available metaphor annotated data in this genre we are aware of. (2) We evaluate state-of-art (**SoA**) feature sets on the new data. (3) We show that use of argumentation-relevant metaphor is a significant predictor of a holistic score of essay quality, above and beyond essay length.

2 Related Work

Research in automated assessment of students' writing, both native and non-native, is increasingly moving beyond traditional models that emphasize English conventions, sophistication of vocabulary, and organization (Attali and Burstein, 2006). Assessing aspects of content is a rapidly growing research topic, including evaluation of arguments, of the writer's use of information from source materials, of the coherence of the essay, among others

(Ghosh et al., 2016; Persing and Ng, 2015; Stab and Gurevych, 2014; Song et al., 2014; Somasundaran et al., 2014; Gurevich and Deane, 2007). Use of metaphor is another aspect of language use that goes beyond grammar and mechanics; recent research suggests that use of metaphor differs with proficiency (Beigman Klebanov et al., 2013), including in non-native writing (Littlemore et al., 2013). On top of serving as a new dataset for metaphor detection experiments, our corpus supports investigation of the relationship between metaphor use and English proficiency.

Most of the recent work on supervised metaphor identification in running text has been done on the VU Amsterdam Metaphor Corpus (**VUA**) (Steen et al., 2010), a large-scale resource containing excerpts from the BNC in four genres (news, academic, fiction, and conversation) annotated for metaphor at the word level (Beigman Klebanov et al., 2016; Haagsma and Bjerva, 2016; Rai et al., 2016; Do Dinh and Gurevych, 2016; Dunn, 2014). Recently, researchers also reported experiments on a corpus of proverbs (Özbal et al., 2016), a corpus of posts to an online breast cancer support group (Jang et al., 2016, 2015), and on argumentative essays (Beigman Klebanov et al., 2015); in these studies, feature sets originally developed for the VUA corpus served as baselines. We follow the same methodology.

3 Metaphor Annotation

3.1 Data

The data was sampled from the publicly available ETS Corpus of Non-Native Written English.[1] The data for annotation was sampled using $8 \times 3 \times 2$ design, namely, 5 essays were sampled for each of the eight prompt questions, for three native languages of the writer (Japanese, Italian, Arabic),

---

[1] https://catalog.ldc.upenn.edu/LDC2014T06

Proceedings of NAACL-HLT 2018, pages 86–91
New Orleans, Louisiana, June 1 - 6, 2018. ©2018 Association for Computational Linguistics

and for two proficiency levels – medium and high. We decided not to include data from low English proficiency writers, as the writing is often barely coherent and the authors' meaning is sometimes difficult to determine. For the experiments reported below, the data was partitioned into 75% training and 25% testing. Data partitions and feature values will be released for public use.[2]

3.2 Annotation

The annotation protocol used in this study was taken from Beigman Klebanov et al. (2013). The protocol was developed for analyzing argumentative writing, and emphasized the identification of argumentation-relevant metaphors. Argumentation-relevant metaphors are, briefly, those that help the author advance her argument. For example, if you are arguing against some action because it would *drain* resources, *drain* is a metaphor that helps you advance your argument, because it presents the expenditure in a very negative way, suggesting that resources would disappear very quickly and without control. Beigman Klebanov et al. (2013) reported inter-annotator agreement of κ = .56-.58 on binary classification of all content words in an essay into metaphor or non-metaphor.

All 240 essays in our corpus were annotated by two annotators: an annotator with a BA in English and Spanish and experience as an English-as-a-second-language (TESOL) instructor who was hired for this project (annotator A) and the lead author of this paper (annotator B). The annotation procedure was as follows. First, 3 out of 30 essays for each prompt were chosen for training and calibration; the two annotators performed an annotation on the 3 essays, and discussed disagreements. Then, each annotator independently annotated the remaining 27 essays. Inter-annotator agreement was calculated for each of the 27 essays; all essays with $\kappa < 0.5$ were selected, and annotator A was asked to review his annotations of these essays again. Once the essays were returned from annotator A's review, agreement was measured again. If the overall agreement for the set of 27 was below $\kappa = 0.55$, essays that had $\kappa < 0.5$ were selected, and annotator B reviewed her own annotations of those essays. Once these annotations were returned, the final κ for the set of 27 essays was calculated. Average inter-annotator agreement for

the first annotation pass (before reviews of their own work by A and B) was $\kappa = 0.56$. After reviews by one or both the annotators, the average agreement was $\kappa = 0.62$. For the experiments, we use the union of the two annotations: everything marked as metaphor by at least one annotator is labeled as a metaphor, consistently with the practice in prior work (Beigman Klebanov et al., 2013).

To illustrate the annotation, consider an excerpt from a response to the prompt "It is better to have broad knowledge of many academic subjects than to specialize in one specific subject"; metaphors are italicized:

> I ultimately agree with the fact that it is better to be specialized on a specific subject than to *spread* energy on different subjects. However I say ultimately, because being and staying *focused* on one subject means always to *discard* other subjects. I found the *focus* necessary and very important at a certain *late stage* of the personal working career or academic career. The reason behind this you *build up* some *"spikes* of knowledge" on a *broad* knowledge *platform*. These *sharp spikes* of knowledge will allow you to promote yourself and to *pull* with you the society *forward*.

This excerpt is rich in metaphor, painting knowledge as a tall, spiky, yet sturdy structure one builds on a broad solid platform, to serve as a grip when pulling (others) up; a metaphor of academic subjects as objects that can be neatly isolated from one another, examined in detail, and accepted to removed from possession; a life-as-a-journey element that breaks events in life into "stages". All these are working (not necessarily most elegantly) to support the notion that specialization is feasible at an appropriate time in one's life, and it would make you stand out (in the skyline, so-to-speak).

It is worth pointing out some differences between this annotation and an annotation that would have resulted from the application of the MIPVU protocol used in the VUA corpus.[3] The MIPVU protocol requires an annotator to establish the contextual meaning of a lexical item and then consider whether there exists another meaning (attested in a contemporary dictionary) that is more "basic",

---

[3]MIPVU is an extension of MIP (Pragglejaz, 2007) – Metaphor Identification Procedure.

which is defined as (i) more concrete; (ii) related to bodily action; (iii) more precise (as opposed to vague). Additional words in the excerpt shown above might have been marked as metaphors by the MIPVU protocol – such as *found* and *behind*, since their contextual senses are less concrete than the "see where something is by searching for it"[4] and "at the back of something", respectively – but these do not seem to contribute as directly to the content of the author's argument. It is debatable whether *discard* would be considered a metaphor by MIPVU, its one dictionary sense being "to get rid of something that you no longer want or need," which might or might not be considered the contextual sense depending on whether "something" in the definition is interpreted as a concrete object with shape and size or possibly an abstract entity with ill-defined boundaries. The protocol used here does not require recourse to dictionary definitions, leaving the senses to the annotator's intuition. On average, 3% (0.03) of all words in an essay are marked as metaphor according to this protocol; the standard deviation is 0.02; min = 0; max = 0.1, in the training partition.

4 State-of-art feature sets on new data

The task to be performed on the annotated data is to classify all content words (**allPOS**: verbs, nouns, adjectives, and adverbs) or just the verbs (**verbs**) in an essay into those that are being used metaphorically or those that are not. The verbs *have*, *be*, and *do* are excluded from both allPOS and verbs data. Table 1 summarizes the data.

Data	Training			Testing	
	#T	#I	%M	#T	#I
all-POS	180	26,737	7%	60	9,017
verbs	180	7,016	14%	60	2,301

Table 1: Summary of the data. #T = # of texts; #I = # of instances; %M = proportion of metaphors.

We evaluated the performance of two feature sets. The set **v-16** comes from Beigman Klebanov et al. (2016), addressing metaphoricity of verbs. The feature set **all-15** comes from Beigman Klebanov et al. (2015) and addresses all content words (all-POS). We also ran the v-16 feature set on all-POS data – lemma unigram features are calculated for all words, WordNet lexicographic categories

Feature Set	Features
all-15	unigrams (all POS), part of speech (all POS), topics (all POS), concreteness (all POS), difference in concreteness (v, adj)
v-16	lemma unigrams (v), WordNet lexicographic categories (v), difference in concreteness (v)
all-16	lemma unigrams (all POS), WordNet lexicographic categories (v), difference in concreteness (v, adj)

Table 2: Details of the VUA SoA feature sets

are used only for verbs,[5] and the difference in concreteness feature is calculated for verbs (verb vs its direct object) and for adjectives (adjective vs its head noun). We found that this feature set is competitive with all-15; we therefore include it in the benchmark, as **all-16**. Table 2 summarizes the three feature sets.

The metaphor detection systems use SoA feature sets with Logistic Regression as the classifier. The systems are evaluated for precision, recall, and F-score for the class "metaphor". The evaluations were performed with scikit-learn (Pedregosa et al., 2011) using the SKLL toolkit[6] that makes it easy to run batch scikit-learn experiments. Table 3 shows the results. Since the data is imbalanced, we applied re-weighting using grid-search optimization, parametrized as in Beigman Klebanov et al. (2015); we also report results with no re-weighting.

Sys	Optimized Re-weighting			No Re-weighting		
	P	**R**	**F**	**P**	**R**	**F**
all-15	.52	.52	.52	.68	.40	.50
all-16	.49	.58	.53	.69	.39	.50
v-16	.50	.64	.56	.69	.39	.50

Table 3: Performance of Logistic Regression with SoA feature sets on essay data.

We note that the performance of the SoA feature sets on the new data is somewhat below the published results for the VUA data. In particular, the v-16 system posted an F-score of 0.60 when trained and tested on verbs-only VUA data (Beigman Klebanov et al., 2016). Improvement of metaphor detection performance is clearly an important avenue for future work.

---

[4]Sense definitions are quoted from the MacMillan dictionary, used in MIPVU.

[5]We also expanded the WordNet feature set to use the lexicographic categories for verbs and for nouns, but the addition of nominal categories degraded performance; these results are not reported.

[6]http://github.com/ EducationalTestingService/skll

5 Metaphor use and writing proficiency

The main motivation of the study and the annotation campaign is the potential for creating features based on metaphor use for assessing the English language skills of developing writers, under the assumption that argumentation-relevant use of metaphor is a fairly advanced skill that requires solid command of vocabulary and a certain amount of cultural knowledge, among other things. In this section, we consider the relationship between holistic scores of essay quality and use of metaphor, in argumentative essays. Specifically we ask the following research questions: (1) Is there a relationship between essay score and metaphor use? (2) Is this relationship the same for the two definitions of metaphor – argumentation-relevant metaphor and the more traditional MIPVU definition? (3) Does the relationship depend on the specifics of the task set to the writer?

5.1 Data

We use six sets from three testing programs. **MGrF** and **MGrS** – Mixed Graduate Free and Source-based, respectively – come from a test of English administered to domestic and international applicants to graduate schools in the U.S. **IColF** and **IColS** – International College Free and Source-based – come from a test of English mainly administered to international applicants to U.S. colleges and universities. **DTLF** and **DTLS** – Domestic Teacher Licensure Free and Source-based – come from a test of English administered domestically to those wishing to obtain teaching certification in the U.S. The datasets vary in population (domestic vs international, early stages of higher education vs advanced) and in the tasks – for each test, one of the tasks is the standard defend-your-position-on-an-issue task (F), while the other (S) requires test-takers to use source texts to summarize, criticize, or draw on arguments presented therein. Table 4 summarizes the data.

5.2 Method

We quantify the extent of metaphor use in an essay as the logarithm of metaphor frequency per 1,000 words. Given the tendency of essay length to be a strong predictor of proficiency scores, our evaluation metric is partial correlation with essay score controlling for length.

For metaphor detection, we train all-16 model with no re-weighting.[7] We augment the 240-essay corpus described here with an additional set of 141 essays annotated using the same protocol on proprietary data from the same program as MGrF. Performance for a system trained on this combined set of essays is shown as Arg in Table 4; a system that uses the same features and the same training regime on VUA data is shown as VUA in Table 4.

5.3 Results

Dataset	# Essays	Score Scale	Arg	VUA
MGrF$^+$	40,000	1-6	.166	.020
MGrS	40,000	1-6	.060	.006
IColF$^+$	40,000	1-5	.159	.070
IColS	40,000	1-5	.067	.052
DTLF	10,000	1-6	.121	.029
DTLS	10,000	1-6	.092	.019

Table 4: Partial correlation controlling for length between essay score and metaphor use, for a system trained on essays (Arg) vs VUA data. The underlined figures are not statistically significant ($p > 0.01$). Plus signs are explained in the text.

First, we observe that Arg shows statistically significant partial correlations for all datasets; namely, use of argumentation-relevant metaphor provides information about essay score above and beyond essay length.

Second, Arg outperforms VUA. In some cases, the difference could be attributed to data being in-domain; the sets marked with a plus in Table 4 are taken from the same testing programs as the training data for Arg, although the specific prompts are different. However, Arg does better across the board, including data completely unrelated to the annotation campaign. It is likely that the protocol that emphasized specifically the need to pay attention to the role played by the metaphor in the author's argument is at least partially responsible for the higher performance indicators.

Next, we observe better performance on F sets, those with a very general, single-sentence prompt (see example in section 3.2) than on S datasets with extensive prompts that directed test-takers to criticize, summarize, or draw upon arguments presented in specific textual sources. Again, this

---

[7]Precision-oriented detection models aggregated through a logarithmic or square-root functions are common in the automated essay scoring literature (Gamon et al., 2013; Chen et al., 2017; Attali and Burstein, 2006).

could be due to the short-prompt-based arguments being more in line with the annotated data; however, since there is a similar tendency for the VUA-trained system, it could also be a more general issue of the extent to which the author controls the vocabulary in her essay. With extensive prompts that contain information that needs to be reflected in the essay, a substantial part of the vocabulary is forced by the prompt and not drawn from the author's more creative faculties and knowledge.

6 Conclusion

We present a corpus of argumentative essays written by non-native speakers of English annotated for metaphor. The corpus is made publicly available; this is the first publicly available metaphor annotated data in this genre we are aware of. We provide benchmark performance on this new corpus. We also show that use of argumentation-relevant metaphor provides information about English proficiency above and beyond essay length, especially in the standard defend-a-position-on-an-issue essays where authors have fuller control of their vocabulary.

References

Yigal Attali and Jill Burstein. 2006. Automated Essay Scoring With e-rater®V.2. *Journal of Technology, Learning, and Assessment* 4(3). https://www.learntechlib.org/p/103244/.

Beata Beigman Klebanov, Chee Wee Leong, and Michael Flor. 2013. Argumentation-relevant metaphors in test-taker essays. In *Proceedings of the First Workshop on Metaphor in NLP*. Association for Computational Linguistics, Atlanta, Georgia, pages 11–20. http://www.aclweb.org/anthology/W13-0902.

Beata Beigman Klebanov, Chee Wee Leong, and Michael Flor. 2015. Supervised word-level metaphor detection: Experiments with concreteness and reweighting of examples. In *Proceedings of the Third Workshop on Metaphor in NLP*. Association for Computational Linguistics, Denver, Colorado, pages 11–20. http://www.aclweb.org/anthology/W15-1402.

Beata Beigman Klebanov, Chee Wee Leong, E. Dario Gutierrez, Ekaterina Shutova, and Michael Flor. 2016. Semantic classifications for detection of verb metaphors. In *Proceedings of the 54th Annual Meeting of the Association for Computational Linguistics (Volume 2: Short Papers)*. Association for Computational Linguistics, Berlin, Germany, pages 101–106. http://anthology.aclweb.org/P16-2017.

Jing Chen, Mo Zhang, and Isaac I. Bejar. 2017. An investigation of the e-rater automated scoring engine's grammar, usage, mechanics, and style microfeatures and their aggregation model. *ETS Research Report Series* https://doi.org/10.1002/ets2.12131.

Erik-Lân Do Dinh and Iryna Gurevych. 2016. Token-level metaphor detection using neural networks. In *Proceedings of the Fourth Workshop on Metaphor in NLP*. Association for Computational Linguistics, San Diego, California, pages 28–33. http://www.aclweb.org/anthology/W16-1104.

Jonathan Dunn. 2014. Multi-dimensional abstractness in cross-domain mappings. In *Proceedings of the Second Workshop on Metaphor in NLP*. Association for Computational Linguistics, Baltimore, MD, pages 27–32. http://www.aclweb.org/anthology/W14-2304.

Michael Gamon, Martin Chodorow, Claudia Leacock, and Joel Tetreault. 2013. Grammatical Error Detection in Automatic Essay Scoring and Feedback. In Mark Shermis and Jill Burstein, editors, *Handbook for Automated Essay Evaluation*, New York: Taylor and Francis.

Debanjan Ghosh, Aquila Khanam, Yubo Han, and Smaranda Muresan. 2016. Coarse-grained argumentation features for scoring persuasive essays. In *Proceedings of the 54th Annual Meeting of the Association for Computational Linguistics (Volume 2: Short Papers)*. Association for Computational Linguistics, Berlin, Germany, pages 549–554. http://anthology.aclweb.org/P16-2089.

Olga Gurevich and Paul Deane. 2007. Document similarity measures to distinguish native vs. non-native essay writers. In *Human Language Technologies 2007: The Conference of the North American Chapter of the Association for Computational Linguistics; Companion Volume, Short Papers*. Association for Computational Linguistics, Rochester, New York, pages 49–52. http://www.aclweb.org/anthology/N/N07/N07-2013.

Hessel Haagsma and Johannes Bjerva. 2016. Detecting novel metaphor using selectional preference information. In *Proceedings of the Fourth Workshop on Metaphor in NLP*. Association for Computational Linguistics, San Diego, California, pages 10–17. http://www.aclweb.org/anthology/W16-1102.

Hyeju Jang, Yohan Jo, Qinlan Shen, Michael Miller, Seungwhan Moon, and Carolyn Rose. 2016. Metaphor detection with topic transition, emotion and cognition in context. In *Proceedings of the 54th Annual Meeting of the Association for Computational Linguistics (Volume 1: Long Papers)*. Association for Computational Linguistics, Berlin, Germany, pages 216–225. http://www.aclweb.org/anthology/P16-1021.

Hyeju Jang, Seungwhan Moon, Yohan Jo, and Carolyn Rose. 2015. Metaphor detection in discourse. In *Proceedings of the 16th Annual Meeting of the Special Interest Group on Discourse and Dialogue*. Association for Computational Linguistics, Prague, Czech Republic, pages 384–392. `http://aclweb.org/anthology/W15-4650`.

Jeannette Littlemore, Tina Krennmayr, James Turner, and Sarah Turner. 2013. An investigation into metaphor use at different levels of second language writing. *Applied Linguistics* `https://doi.org/10.1093/applin/amt004`.

Gözde Özbal, Carlo Strapparava, Serra Sinem Tekiroglu, and Daniele Pighin. 2016. Learning to identify metaphors from a corpus of proverbs. In *Proceedings of the 2016 Conference on Empirical Methods in Natural Language Processing*. Association for Computational Linguistics, Austin, Texas, pages 2060–2065. `https://aclweb.org/anthology/D16-1220`.

F. Pedregosa, G. Varoquaux, A. Gramfort, V. Michel, B. Thirion, O. Grisel, M. Blondel, P. Prettenhofer, R. Weiss, V. Dubourg, J. Vanderplas, A. Passos, D. Cournapeau, M. Brucher, M. Perrot, and E. Duchesnay. 2011. Scikit-learn: Machine Learning in Python. *Journal of Machine Learning Research* 12:2825–2830.

Isaac Persing and Vincent Ng. 2015. Modeling argument strength in student essays. In *Proceedings of the 53rd Annual Meeting of the Association for Computational Linguistics and the 7th International Joint Conference on Natural Language Processing (Volume 1: Long Papers)*. Association for Computational Linguistics, Beijing, China, pages 543–552. `http://www.aclweb.org/anthology/P15-1053`.

Group Pragglejaz. 2007. MIP: A Method for Identifying Metaphorically Used Words in Discourse. *Metaphor and Symbol* 22(1):1–39. `https://www.tandfonline.com/doi/abs/10.1080/10926480709336752`.

Sunny Rai, Shampa Chakraverty, and Devendra K. Tayal. 2016. Supervised metaphor detection using conditional random fields. In *Proceedings of the Fourth Workshop on Metaphor in NLP*. Association for Computational Linguistics, San Diego, California, pages 18–27. `http://www.aclweb.org/anthology/W16-1103`.

Swapna Somasundaran, Jill Burstein, and Martin Chodorow. 2014. Lexical chaining for measuring discourse coherence quality in test-taker essays. In *Proceedings of COLING*. pages 950–961. `http://aclweb.org/anthology/C/C14/C14-1090.pdf`.

Yi Song, Michael Heilman, Beata Beigman Klebanov, and Paul Deane. 2014. Applying argumentation schemes for essay scoring. In *Proceedings of the First Workshop on Argumentation Mining*. Association for Computational Linguistics, Baltimore, Maryland, pages 69–78. `http://www.aclweb.org/anthology/W14-2110`.

Christian Stab and Iryna Gurevych. 2014. Annotating argument components and relations in persuasive essays. In Junichi Tsujii and Jan Hajic, editors, *Proceedings of the 25th International Conference on Computational Linguistics (COLING 2014)*. Dublin City University and Association for Computational Linguistics, pages 1501–1510. `http://www.aclweb.org/anthology/C14-1142`.

Gerard Steen, Aletta Dorst, Berenike Herrmann, Anna Kaal, Tina Krennmayr, and Trijntje Pasma. 2010. *A Method for Linguistic Metaphor Identification*. Amsterdam: John Benjamins.

Tony Veale, Ekaterina Shutova, and Beata Beigman Klebanov. 2016. Metaphor: A computational perspective. *Synthesis Lectures on Human Language Technologies* 9(1):1–160. `https://www.morganclaypool.com/doi/abs/10.2200/S00694ED1V01Y201601HLT031`.

A Simple and Effective Approach to the Story Cloze Test

Siddarth Srinivasan, Richa Arora, Mark Riedl
Georgia Institute of Technology
{sidsrini, richa.arora, riedl}@gatech.edu

Abstract

In the Story Cloze Test, a system is presented with a 4-sentence prompt to a story, and must determine which one of two potential endings is the 'right' ending to the story. Previous work has shown that ignoring the training set and training a model on the validation set can achieve high accuracy on this task due to stylistic differences between the story endings in the training set and validation and test sets. Following this approach, we present a simpler fully-neural approach to the Story Cloze Test using skip-thought embeddings of the stories in a feed-forward network that achieves close to state-of-the-art performance on this task without any feature engineering. We also find that considering just the last sentence of the prompt instead of the whole prompt yields higher accuracy with our approach.

1 Introduction

Mostafazadeh et al. (2016) introduced the *Story Cloze Test*: given a four-sentence story prompt (or 'context'), the task is to pick the 'right' common-sense ending from two options. The Cloze Test is intended to be a general framework for evaluating story understanding, since it ostensibly requires combining semantic understanding and common-sense knowledge of our world. The task is accompanied by the Rochester story (ROCstory) corpus. The training set consists of crowdsourced five-sentence stories designed to capture common events in daily life. The validation and testing sets consist of four-sentence prompts and labeled 'right' and 'wrong' story endings. Table 1 shows such a sample story from the Rochester corpus validation set with a labeled right and wrong ending.

Many previous approaches to the Cloze Test have ignored the training set entirely and trained on the validation set since the former lacks 'negative' examples; although this greatly reduces the available training data, it circumvents the issue of obtaining negative examples during training.

Story Context
Bob loved to watch movies.
He was looking forward to a three day weekend coming up.
He made a list of his favorite movies and invited some friends over.
He spent the weekend with his friends watching all his favorite movies.
Right Ending: Bob had a great time.
Wrong Ending: Bob stopped talking to those friends.

Table 1: A sample story from the ROCStory Validation Set

Our contribution to this task is two-fold. First, we achieve near state-of-the-art performance (within 1.1%) but with a much simpler, fully-neural approach. Where previous approaches rely on feature engineering or involved neural network architectures, we achieve high accuracy with a fully neural approach involving only a single feed-forward network and pre-trained skip-thought embeddings (Kiros et al., 2015). Second, we find that considering only the last sentence of the context outperforms models that consider the full context. Previous approaches focused on the accuracy achieved by either considering the whole context or ignoring the whole context of the story. In sum, our approach differs from previous efforts in the joint use of three strategies: (1) using skip-thought embeddings (Kiros et al., 2015) for sentences in the story in a feed-forward neural network, (2) training the model on the provided validation set, and (3) considering the two endings with only the last sentence in the prompt.

This paper is structured as follows: we will discuss previous approaches to the problem and how they compare to our approach, describe our model and the experiments we ran in detail, and finally discuss reasons for our model's superior performance and why ignoring the first three sentences of the story produces better accuracy.

Proceedings of NAACL-HLT 2018, pages 92–96
New Orleans, Louisiana, June 1 - 6, 2018. ©2018 Association for Computational Linguistics

2 Related Work

Mostafazadeh et al. (2016) presented the original Story Cloze Test, and showed that while humans could achieve 100% accuracy on the task, a deep structured semantic model (Huang et al., 2013) was the best performing artificial baseline, with a test-set accuracy of 58.5%. While they do consider using skip-thought embeddings for this task, they do so by choosing the ending whose embedding was closer to the average skip-thought embedding of the context. This only achieves a test-set accuracy of 55.2%. On the other hand, we train a feed-forward network using skip-thought embeddings.

The Story Cloze Test was the shared task at LS-DSem 2017, and Mostafazadeh et al. (2017) summarize the approaches by various teams on this task. The best-performing system by Schwartz et al. (2017b) achieved a test-set accuracy of 75.2%. Like us, they train their model on the validation set, but their approach relies more heavily on feature engineering. They find that they could achieve 72.4% accuracy using just the stylistic features of the endings, suggesting that many of the 'right' endings on this task could be identified independent of the story context. Upon further investigation, Schwartz et al. (2017a) find differences not only between the 'right' and 'wrong' endings in the validation set, but also between these and the 'right' endings from the training set, providing some explanation for why models trained on the validation set outperform models trained on the training set - their data distributions are somewhat different.

Further work by Cai et al. (2017) established a neural baseline for models trained on the validation set, with a test-set accuracy of 74.7%. They were also able to achieve a marginally better accuracy of 72.5% (compared to Schwartz et al. (2017b)) when using just the sentence endings and ignoring the context; and this approach did not require any feature engineering. They showed that a human can distinguish 'right' from 'wrong' endings *without* the context with 78% accuracy, further backing the claim that the importance of context in determining the right ending is more limited than desirable on this task. Their approach involves training a hierarchical bidirectional LSTM with attention to first encode sentences and then stories, with a hinge-loss objective function.

Roemmele et al. (2017) use skip-thought embeddings for this task, but they encode the entire context using a GRU, with a binary classifier to determine if an ending was right or wrong. They train their model on the provided training set, sampling negative examples from the training set itself. Their best model achieves 67.2% accuracy on this task.

Currently, the comprehensive approach taken by Chaturvedi et al. (2017), where they model event sequence, sentiment trajectory, and topical consistency for a hidden coherence model, achieves the state-of-the-art performance on this task, with a test-set accuracy of 77.6%.

3 Approach

We trained several models on both the training set and the validation set of the ROCStory corpus. When training a model on the training set, we obtain 'negative' examples (i.e. wrong endings) by randomly choosing a sentence from another story in the corpus. In this section, we describe the choice of sentence embeddings, the architecture of the models we trained, and our experimental setup.

3.1 Embeddings

Key to our approach is the use of skip-thought embeddings (Kiros et al., 2015) in our feed-forward network (denoted **skip** in Table 2). These are 4800-dimensional embeddings of sentences trained on the task of predicting their context using the BookCorpus dataset (a large dataset of books). We use a pre-trained skip-thought encoder[1] to obtain the embeddings for all sentences in the training set, validation set, and test set.

To isolate the increase in accuracy from using skip-thought vectors, we also experiment with learning sentence embeddings directly, for this task. Unlike the skip-thought encoder that directly gives sentence embeddings, we use a bidirectional LSTM that takes in GloVe embeddings (Pennington et al., 2014) of each word in the sentence and returns a 4800 dimensional embedding of the sentence (denoted **GloVe** in Table 2) formed by concatenating the outputs of the forward and backward LSTMs. We use the GloVe model pretrained on Wikipedia 2014 and Gigaword 5 data[2].

---

[1] https://github.com/ryankiros/skip-thoughts
[2] https://nlp.stanford.edu/projects/glove/

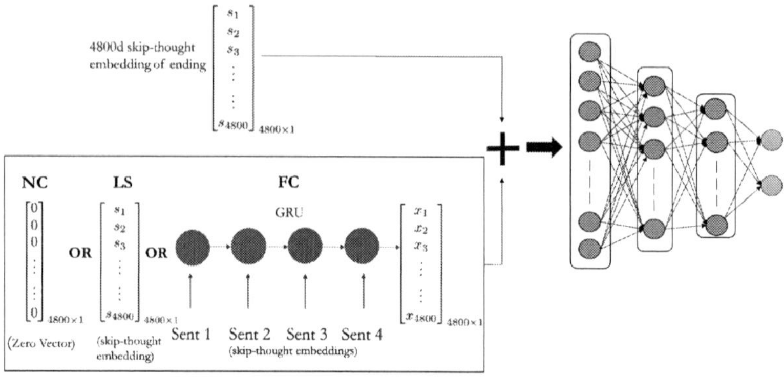

Figure 1: Model Architecture

3.2 Models

Common to all our models is a single feed-forward neural network with a softmax-layer at the end that acts as a binary classifier. This neural network takes in a 4800-dimensional input (the same dimensionality as the skip-thought embeddings) and returns the probability of the endings being 'right' and 'wrong'. During inference time, we make a forward pass with each of the two possible endings, and select the ending that has a higher probability of being the 'right' ending. We use two layer and three layer fully connected networks with Rectified Linear (ReLU) non-linearities (refer to Appendix A for model-specific architecture). We then experiment with different inputs to the neural network, as described below.

No Context (NC) This model attempts to identify the 'right' ending of a story by ignoring the story context and looking only at examples of right and wrong endings. As such, the input to the neural network is just the skip-thought embedding of the story ending, with 0/1 label indicating whether it was the 'wrong' or 'right' ending.

Last Sentence (LS) In this model, the input to the neural network is the sum of the skip-thought embedding of the last sentence of the prompt (i.e., fourth sentence in the story) and the skip-thought embedding of the ending. Essentially, we are attempting to identify the right ending based on only the ending and the preceding sentence in the story.

Full Context (FC) Here, we use a Gated Recurrent Unit (GRU) to encode the entire story prompt into a 4800-dimensional vector, add it to the skip-thought embedding of the story ending, and pass it as input to the neural network. The input to the

GRU is the skip-thought embedding of each sentence, and this model attempts to identify the right ending by considering the entire story prompt.

4 Experiments

4.1 Dataset

For all our experiments, we use the ROCStory corpus (Mostafazadeh et al., 2016). The corpus consists of a training set of 98,161 five-sentence stories, a validation set consisting of 1,871 four-sentence stories, and a test set of 1,871 four-sentence stories, with the validation and test sets providing labeled 'right' and 'wrong' story endings for each story. (Mostafazadeh et al., 2016) crowdsourced the collection of stories on Amazon Mechanical Turk; workers were asked to compose five-sentence stories about common daily situations with a clear beginning and end. To create the validation and testing sets, endings were removed from stories and an additional group of workers on Mechanical Turk were asked to provide a 'right' ending or a 'wrong' ending.

Although models trained on the validation set score higher than those trained on the training set as previously discussed, we provide the results for the same model trained on the validation set (denoted **val**) as well as the training set (denoted **trn**) in Table 2 for comparison.

4.2 Experimental Method

When training on the training set, we tuned hyper-parameters using the validation set. When training on the validation set, we hold out 10% of the validation set, and tune hyper-parameters to find a configuration that maximizes the accuracy on the

94

model	val	test
trn-NC-skip	60.3%	60.8%
val-NC-skip	73.9%	72.6%
trn-FC-skip	62.4%	62.6%
val-FC-skip	73.8%	71.6%
trn-LS-skip	62.8%	62.7%
val-LS-skip	**77.2%**	**76.5%**
val-LS-GloVe	69.7%	63.0%
Chaturvedi et al. (2017)	-	<u>77.6%</u>
Schwartz et al. (2017b)	-	75.2%
Cai et al. (2017)	-	74.7%

Table 2: Accuracies for various models on the Story Cloze Test

held out data. We use cross-entropy loss and SGD with learning rate of 0.01.

During training, we save the model every 3000 iterations, and calculate the validation accuracy. We train each model five times (except the FC models, which we train once due to time considerations), and report the average test set accuracy of the model. We use the model with the highest validation accuracy in each round to calculate the test set accuracy for that round. We present our results in Table 2.

4.3 Results and Discussion

The 3-layer feed-forward neural network trained on the validation set by summing the skip-thought embeddings of the last sentence (LS) of the story prompt and the ending gives the best accuracy (76.5%). This approach is far simpler than previous approaches in the literature; it requires no feature engineering, nor intricate neural network architecture, and achieves close to state-of-the-art accuracy. Comparing 'val-LS-skip' to 'val-LS-GloVe' (i.e., using skip-thought embeddings for sentences vs. GloVe word embeddings), we confirm that the success of this approach lies in the sizable boost to accuracy from the use of pre-trained skip-thought embeddings.

This is perhaps unsurprising given the success of skip-thought embeddings in story-related tasks (Agrawal et al. (2016), Roemmele et al. (2017)), since the model was trained on a large corpus of fiction. While the BookCorpus and ROCStories draw from different distributions, it is possible that skip-thought vectors implicitly encode a general notion of typical story continuation. In the absence of such a large dataset to learn such asso-

ciations from, the LSTM with GloVe embedding inputs is unable to encode the necessary information to do well on this task.

We note that the model trained using only the last sentence (LS) of the story context has higher accuracy compared to the model that uses a GRU to encode the full context (FC), and even the Cai et al. (2017) model which encodes the entire context. It is unclear from our experiments why this might be. One hypothesis is that as stories near conclusion, the space of possible continuations contracts. In the absence of further context, a default prior is assumed - as implicitly encoded in skip-thought vectors trained on BookCorpus - that is often correct. Providing more context may conflict with the default prior, introducing uncertainty. Another hypothesis is that the Mechanical Turk workers creating the validation and test data sets focused more on the fourth sentence when writing their 'right' and 'wrong' endings, so once again, adding context introduces error.

Finally, we observe that the Story Cloze Test is an easier task than identifying whether a given ending is coherent or not, since the former involves a forced choice between two endings. During test time, the model does not need to classify whether a given ending is 'right' or 'wrong', as it learns to do during train time; instead, it simply needs to correctly predict which ending is *less* wrong.

5 Conclusion

We have shown a simple yet effective neural model that achieves high accuracy on the Cloze Test, which is within 1.1% of the state-of-the-art approach that relies on feature engineering. Additionally, we make a minor improvement on Cai et al. (2017)'s 'ending-only' baseline accuracy of 72.5% with our val-NC-skip model.

Finally, we also showed that, for the models tested here, using the full context actually performs *worse* than using just the last sentence of the context. Future investigation will be needed to determine whether this is a property inherent to human storytelling or a form of bias introduced during data collection.

References

Harsh Agrawal, Arjun Chandrasekaran, Dhruv Batra, Devi Parikh, and Mohit Bansal. 2016. Sort story: Sorting jumbled images and captions into stories. In *EMNLP*.

Zheng Cai, Lifu Tu, and Kevin Gimpel. 2017. Pay attention to the ending: Strong neural baselines for the roc story cloze task. In *ACL*.

Snigdha Chaturvedi, Haoruo Peng, and Dan Roth. 2017. Story comprehension for predicting what happens next. In *EMNLP*.

Po-Sen Huang, Xiaodong He, Jianfeng Gao, Li Deng, Alex Acero, and Larry Heck. 2013. Learning deep structured semantic models for web search using clickthrough data. In *Proceedings of the 22nd ACM international conference on Conference on information & knowledge management*, pages 2333–2338. ACM.

Ryan Kiros, Yukun Zhu, Ruslan R Salakhutdinov, Richard Zemel, Raquel Urtasun, Antonio Torralba, and Sanja Fidler. 2015. Skip-thought vectors. In *Advances in neural information processing systems*, pages 3294–3302.

Nasrin Mostafazadeh, Nathanael Chambers, Xiaodong He, Devi Parikh, Dhruv Batra, Lucy Vanderwende, Pushmeet Kohli, and James Allen. 2016. A corpus and cloze evaluation for deeper understanding of commonsense stories. In *Proceedings of NAACL-HLT*, pages 839–849.

Nasrin Mostafazadeh, Michael Roth, Annie Louis, Nathanael Chambers, and James F Allen. 2017. Lsdsem 2017 shared task: The story cloze test. *LSDSem 2017*, pages 46–51.

Jeffrey Pennington, Richard Socher, and Christopher D. Manning. 2014. Glove: Global vectors for word representation. In *Empirical Methods in Natural Language Processing (EMNLP)*, pages 1532–1543.

Melissa Roemmele, Sosuke Kobayashi, Naoya Inoue, and Andrew M Gordon. 2017. An rnn-based binary classifier for the story cloze test. *LSDSem 2017*, pages 74–80.

Roy Schwartz, Maarten Sap, Ioannis Konstas, Leila Zilles, Yejin Choi, and Noah A. Smith. 2017a. The effect of different writing tasks on linguistic style: A case study of the roc story cloze task. In *CoNLL*.

Roy Schwartz, Maarten Sap, Ioannis Konstas, Leila Zilles, Yejin Choi, and Noah A Smith. 2017b. Story cloze task: Uw nlp system. *LSDSem 2017*, pages 52–55.

An Annotated Corpus for Machine Reading of Instructions in Wet Lab Protocols

Chaitanya Kulkarni, Wei Xu, Alan Ritter, Raghu Machiraju
Department of Computer Science and Engineering
Ohio State University
`{kulkarni.132,xu.1265,ritter.1492,machiraju.1}@osu.edu`

Abstract

We describe an effort to annotate a corpus of natural language instructions consisting of 622 wet lab protocols to facilitate automatic or semi-automatic conversion of protocols into a machine-readable format and benefit biological research. Experimental results demonstrate the utility of our corpus for developing machine learning approaches to shallow semantic parsing of instructional texts. We make our annotated Wet Lab Protocol Corpus available to the research community.[1]

1 Introduction

As the complexity of biological experiments increases, there is a growing need to automate wet laboratory procedures to avoid mistakes due to human error and also to enhance the reproducibility of experimental biological research (King et al., 2009). Several efforts are currently underway to define machine-readable formats for writing wet lab protocols (Ananthanarayanan and Thies, 2010; Soldatova et al., 2014; Vasilev et al., 2011). The vast majority of today's protocols, however, are written in natural language with jargon and colloquial language constructs that emerge as a byproduct of ad-hoc protocol documentation. This motivates the need for machine reading systems that can interpret the meaning of these natural language instructions, to enhance reproducibility via semantic protocols (e.g. the Aquarium project) and enable robotic automation (Bates et al., 2016) by mapping natural language instructions to executable actions.

In this study we take a first step towards this goal by annotating a database of wet lab protocols with semantic actions and their arguments; and conducting initial experiments to demonstrate its utility for machine learning approaches to shallow semantic parsing of natural language instructions.

---

[1]The dataset is available on the authors' websites.

Isolation of temperate phages by plaque agar overlay

1. Melt soft agar overlay tubes in boiling water and place in the 47C water bath.
2. Remove one tube of soft agar from the water bath.
3. Add 1.0 mL host culture and either 1.0 or 0.1 mL viral concentrate.
4. Mix the contents of the tube well by rolling back and forth between two hands, and immediately empty the tube contents onto an agar plate.
5. Sit RT for 5 min.
6. Gently spread the top agar over the agar surface by sliding the plate on the bench surface using a circular motion.
7. Harden the top agar by not disturbing the plates for 30 min.
8. Incubate the plates (top agar side down) overnight to 48 h.
9. Temperate phage plaques will appear as turbid or cloudy plaques, whereas purely lytic phage will appear as sharply defined, clear plaques.

Figure 1: An example wet lab protocol. The first seven steps are imperative sentences, and the last sentence describes the end results and their subsequent utilization.

To the best of our knowledge, this is the first annotated corpus of natural language instructions in the biomedical domain that is large enough to enable machine learning approaches.

There have been many recent data collection and annotation efforts that have initiated natural language processing research in new directions, for example political framing (Card et al., 2015), question answering (Rajpurkar et al., 2016) and cooking recipes (Jermsurawong and Habash, 2015). Although mapping natural language instructions to machine readable representations is an important direction with many practical applications, we believe current research in this area is hampered by the lack of available annotated corpora. Our annotated corpus of wet lab protocols could enable further research on interpreting natural language instructions, with practical applications in biology and life sciences.

Prior work has explored the problem of learning to map natural language instructions to actions, often learning through indirect supervision

Proceedings of NAACL-HLT 2018, pages 97–106
New Orleans, Louisiana, June 1 - 6, 2018. ©2018 Association for Computational Linguistics

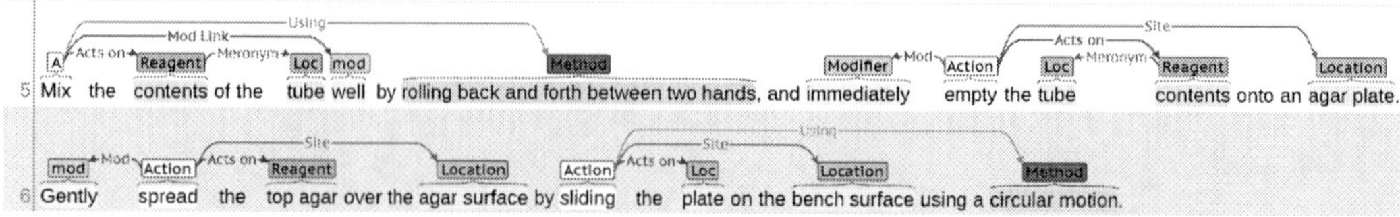

Figure 2: Example sentences (#5 and #6) from the lab protocol in Figure 1 as shown in the BRAT annotation interface.

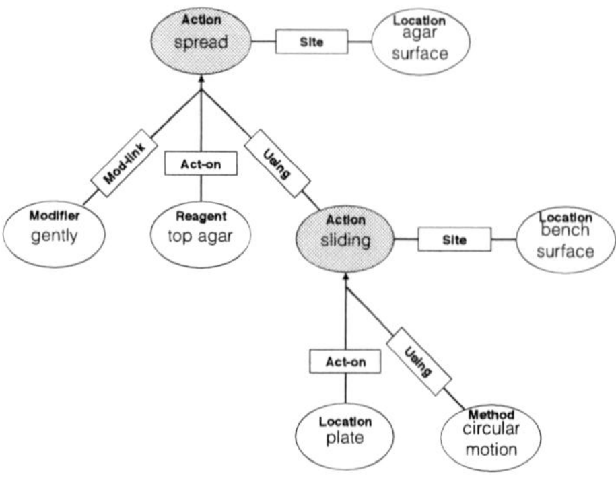

Figure 3: An action graph can be directly derived from annotations as seen in Figure 2 (example sentence #6) .

to address the lack of labeled data in instructional domains. This is done, for example, by interacting with the environment (Branavan et al., 2009, 2010) or observing weakly aligned sequences of instructions and corresponding actions (Chen and Mooney, 2011; Artzi and Zettlemoyer, 2013). In contrast, we present the first steps towards a pragmatic approach based on linguistic annotation (Figure 3). We describe our effort to exhaustively annotate wet lab protocols with actions corresponding to lab procedures and their attributes including materials, instruments and devices used to perform specific actions. As we demonstrate in §6, our corpus can be used to train machine learning models which are capable of automatically annotating lab-protocols with action predicates and their arguments (Gildea and Jurafsky, 2002; Das et al., 2014); this could provide a useful linguistic representation for robotic automation (Bollini et al., 2013) and other downstream applications.

2 Wet Lab Protocols

Wet laboratories are laboratories for conducting biology and chemistry experiments which involve chemicals, drugs, or other materials in liquid solutions or volatile phases. Figure 1 shows one representative wet lab protocol. Research groups around the world curate their own repos-

itories of protocols, each adapted from a canonical source and typically published in the Materials and Method section at the end of a scientific article in biology and chemistry fields. Only recently has there been an effort to gather collections of these protocols and make them easily available. Leveraging an openly accessible repository of protocols curated on the *https://www.protocols.io* platform, we annotated hundreds of academic and commercial protocols maintained by many of the leading bio-science laboratory groups, including Verve Net, Innovative Genomics Institute and New England Biolabs. The protocols cover a large spectrum of experimental biology, including neurology, epigenetics, metabolomics, cancer and stem cell biology, etc (Table 1). Wet lab protocols consist of a sequence of steps, mostly composed of imperative statements meant to describe an action. They also can contain declarative sentences describing the results of a previous action, in addition to general guidelines or warnings about the materials being used.

3 Annotation Scheme

In developing our annotation guidelines we had three primary goals: (1) We aim to produce a semantic representation that is well motivated from a biomedical and linguistic perspective; (2) The guidelines should be easily understood by annotators with or without biology background, as evaluated in Table 3; (3) The resulting corpus should be useful for training machine learning models to automatically extract experimental actions for downstream applications, as evaluated in §6.

We utilized the EXACT2 framework (Soldatova et al., 2014) as a basis for our annotation scheme. We borrowed and renamed 9 object-based entities from EXACT2, in addition, we created 5 measure-based (NUMERICAL, GENERIC-MEASURE, SIZE, pH, MEASURE-TYPE) and 3 other (MENTION, MODIFIER, SEAL) entity types. EXACT2 connects the entities directly to the action without

Protocol Category	Count	avg #Sentences	avg #Words	avg #Entities	avg #Relations	avg #Actions
molecular biology	186	27.42	338.06	85.25	84.20	35.77
microbiology	105	22.07	328.94	74.46	71.71	27.89
cell biology	94	19.23	236.74	61.09	60.95	23.93
Plant biology	48	17.17	219.96	44.67	43.85	20.44
Immunology	79	25.92	339.58	83.17	78.24	32.68
chemical biology	110	14.37	188.30	46.40	47.45	19.01

Table 1: Statistics of our Wet Lab Protocol Corpus by protocol category.

	Total	per Protocol	per Sentence
# of sentences	13679	21.99	–
# of words	177770	285.80	12.99
# of entities	43236	69.51	3.16
# of relations	42425	68.21	3.10
# of actions	17485	28.11	1.28

Table 2: Statistics of the Wet Lab Protocol Corpus.

Annotators	Entities+Actions	Relations
Biologist-Linguist	0.7600	0.6084
Biologist-Other	0.7621	0.6619
Linguist-Other	0.7574	0.6753
all 4 coders	0.7599	0.6625

Table 3: Inter-annotator agreement (Krippendorff's α) between annotators with biology, linguistics and other backgrounds.

describing the type of relations, whereas we defined and annotated 12 types of relations between actions and entities, or pairs of entities (see Appendix for a full description).

For each protocol, the annotators were requested to identify and mark every span of text that corresponds to one of 17 types of entities or an action (see examples in Figure 2). Intersection or overlap of text spans, and the subdivision of words between two spans were not allowed. The annotation guideline was designed to keep the span short for entities, with the average length being 1.6 words. For example, CONCENTRATION tags are often very short: *60% 10x, 10M, 1 g/ml*. The METHOD tag has the longest average span of 2.232 words with examples such as *rolling back and forth between two hands*. The methods in wet lab protocols tend to be descriptive, which pose distinct challenges from existing named entity extraction research in the medical (Kim et al., 2003) and other domains. After all entities were labelled, the annotators connected pairs of spans within each sentence by using one of 12 directed links to capture various relationships between spans tagged in the protocol text. While most protocols are written in scientific language, we also observe some non-standard usage, for example using *RT* to refer to *room temperature*, which is tagged as TEMPERATURE.

4   Annotation Process

Our final corpus consists of 622 protocols annotated by a team of 10 annotators. Corpus statistics are provided in Table 1 and 2. In the first phase of annotation, we worked with a subset of 4 annotators including one linguist and one biologist to develop the annotation guideline for 6 iterations. For each iteration, we asked all 4 annotators to annotate the same 10 protocols and measured their inter-annotator agreement, which in turn helped in determining the validity of the refined guidelines. The average time to annotate a single protocol of 40 sentences was approximately 33 minutes, across all annotators.

4.1   Inter-Annotator Agreement

We used Krippendorff's α for nominal data (Krippendorff, 2004) to measure the inter-rater agreement for entities, actions and relations. For entities, we measured agreement at the word-level by tagging each word in a span with the span's label. To evaluate inter-rater agreement for relations between annotated spans, we consider every pair of spans within a step and then test for matches between annotators (partial entity matches are allowed). We then compute Krippendorff's α over relations between matching pairs of spans. Inter-rater agreement for entities, actions and relations is presented in Figure 3.

5   Methods

To demonstrate the utility of our annotated corpus, we explore two machine learning approaches for extracting actions and entities: a maximum entropy model and a neural network tagging model. We also present experiments for relation classification. We use the standard precision, recall and F_1 metrics to evaluate and compare the performance.

5.1 Maximum Entropy (MaxEnt) Tagger

In the maximum entropy model for action and entity extraction (Borthwick and Grishman, 1999), we used three types of features based on the current word and context words within a window of size 2:

- **Parts of speech features** which were generated by the GENIA POS Tagger (Tsuruoka and Tsujii, 2005), which is specifically tuned for biomedical texts;

- **Lexical features** which include unigrams, bigrams as well as their lemmas and synonyms from WordNet (Miller, 1995) are used;

- **Dependency parse features** which include dependent and governor words as well as the dependency type to capture syntactic information related to actions, entities and their contexts. We used the Stanford dependency parser (Chen and Manning, 2014).

5.2 Neural Sequence Tagger

We utilized the state-of-the-art Bidirectional LSTM with a Conditional Random Fields (CRF) layer (Ma and Hovy, 2016; Lample et al., 2016; Plank et al., 2016), initialized with 200-dimentional word vectors pretrained on 5.5 billion words from PubMed and PMC biomedical texts (Moen and Ananiadou, 2013). Words unseen in the pretrained vocabulary were randomly initialized using a uniform distribution in the range (-0.01, 0.01). We used Adadelta (Zeiler, 2012) optimization with a mini-batch of 16 sentences and trained each network with 5 different random seeds, in order to avoid any outlier results due to randomness in the model initialization.

5.3 Relation Classification

To demonstrate the utility of the relation annotations, we also experimented with a maximum entropy model for relation classification using features shown to be effective in prior work (Li and Ji, 2014; GuoDong et al., 2005; Kambhatla, 2004). The features are divided into five groups:

- **Word features** which include the words contained in both arguments, all words in between, and context words surrounding the arguments;

- **Entity type features** which include action and entity types associated with both arguments;

Entity/Action (freq. in test set)	MaxEnt	BiLSTM	BiLSTM + CRF
Action (3519)	83.87	85.95	86.89
Amount (886)	68.25	81.59	82.34
Conc. (273)	56.84	65.36	76.36
Device (408)	49.14	58.73	64.02
Gen.-Measure (91)	05.88	06.45	25.68
Location (1007)	61.07	69.57	73.53
Meas.-Type (50)	15.38	18.75	21.62
Mention (37)	43.37	52.31	57.97
Method (177)	37.97	30.60	38.21
Modifier (720)	50.86	56.90	59.34
Numerical (129)	39.70	47.84	49.80
Reagent (2486)	60.54	71.34	74.55
Seal (43)	49.52	54.05	66.67
Size (69)	19.35	24.82	26.92
Speed (200)	74.88	85.31	91.00
Temperature (469)	80.69	86.68	91.90
Time (708)	83.68	92.69	93.94
pH (21)	41.86	53.66	70.00
Macro-avg F1	49.23	58.81	64.44
Micro-avg F1	68.03	74.99	78.03

Table 4: F1 scores for segmenting and classifying entities and action triggers compared across the various models.

MaxEnt Model	Relations		
Features	P	R	F1
Words	66.16	46.84	54.85
+ Entity Type	78.93	72.75	75.72
+ Overlap	80.81	74.73	77.65
+ Base Phrase Chunking	81.04	76.52	78.71
+ Dependency Tree	80.98	77.04	78.96

Table 5: Precision, Recall and F1 (micro-average) of the maximum entropy model for relation classification, as each feature is added.

- **Overlapping features** which are the number of words, as well as actions or entities, in between the candidate entity pair;

- **Chunk features** which are the chunk tags of both arguments predicted by the GENIA tagger;

- **Dependency features** which are context words related to the arguments in the dependency tree according to the Stanford Dependency Parser.

Also included are features indicating whether the two spans are in the same noun phrase, prepositional phrase, or verb phrase.

6 Results

The full annotated dataset of 622 protocols are randomly split into training, dev and test sets using a 6:2:2 ratio. The training set contains 374 protocols of 8207 sentences, development set contains

MaxEnt Model	Actions			Entities		
Features	P	R	F1	P	R	F1
POS	74.83	79.94	77.30*	26.66	27.93	28.77
uni/bigram	76.29	69.59	72.79	43.75	32.93	37.58
POS, uni/bigram	79.77	85.51	82.54	49.83	54.51	52.07
POS, uni/bigram, lem./syn.	80.10	85.56	82.74	49.79	54.54	52.06
POS, uni/bigram, lem./syn., dep.	**81.65**	**86.22**	**83.87**	**57.04**	**63.03**	**59.90***

Table 6: Performance of maximum entropy model with various features.*The POS features are especially useful for recognizing actions; dependency based features are more helpful for entities than actions.

POS tag (freq.)	Top 3 examples
VB (9345)	Add(1404), Incubate(638), Remove(396)
VBG (755)	adding(112), inverting(89), pipetting(34)
VBN (727)	added(43), stored(38), incubated(38)
VBP (512)	Do(80), mix(38), pour(33)
VBD (147)	resuspend(25), put(20), kept(8)
VBZ (44)	remains(5), covers(4), washes(3)
NN (4248)	Centrifuge(324), Transfer(301), Place(215)
NNP (1551)	Mix(335), Wash(277), Vortex(114)
NNS (80)	washes(9), to(7), dilutions(4)
JJ (576)	dry(66), Apply(26), decant(23)
OTHER (1080)	not(111), off(110), up(105)

Table 7: Frequency of different part-of-speech (POS) tags for action words. Majority of the action words either fall under the verb POS tags (VBs 60.48%) or nouns (NNs 30.84%). The GENIA POS tagger is under-identifying verbs in the wet lab protocols, tagging some as adjectives (JJ).

123 protocols of 2736 sentences, and test set contains 125 protocols of 2736 sentences. We use the evaluation script from the CoNLL-03 shared task (Tjong Kim Sang and De Meulder, 2003), which requires exact matches of label spans and does not reward partial matches. During the data preprocessing, all digits were replaced by '0'.

6.1 Entity Identification and Classification

Table 4 shows the performance of various methods for entity tagging. We found that the BiLSTM-CRF model consistently outperforms other methods, achieving an overall F1 score of 86.89 at identifying action triggers and 72.61 at identifying and classifying entities.

Table 6 shows the system performance of the MaxEnt tagger using various features. Dependency based features have the highest impact on the detection of entities, as illustrated by the absolute drop of 7.84% in F-score when removed. Parts of speech features alone are the most effective in capturing action words. This is largely due to action words appearing as verbs or nouns in the majority of the sentences as shown in Table 7. We also notice that the GENIA POS tagger, which is trained on Wall Street Journal and biomedical abstracts in the GENIA and PennBioIE corpora, under-identifies verbs in wet lab protocols. We suspect this is due to fewer imperative sentences in the training data. We leave further investigation for future work, and hope the release of our dataset can help draw more attention to NLP research on instructional languages.

6.2 Relation Classification

Finally, precision and recall at relation extraction are presented in Table 5. We used gold action and entity segments for the purposes of this particular evaluation. We obtained the best performance when using all feature sets.

7 Conclusions

In this paper, we described our effort to annotate wet lab protocols with actions and their semantic arguments. We presented an annotation scheme that is both biologically and linguistically motivated and demonstrated that non-experts can effectively annotate lab protocols. Additionally, we empirically demonstrated the utility of our corpus for developing machine learning approaches to shallow semantic parsing of instructions. Our annotated corpus of protocols is available for use by the research community.

Acknowledgement

We would like to thank the annotators: Bethany Toma, Esko Kautto, Sanaya Shroff, Alex Jacobs, Berkay Kaplan, Colins Sullivan, Junfa Zhu, Neena Baliga and Vardaan Gangal. We would like to thank Marie-Catherine de Marneffe and anonymous reviewers for their feedback.

References

Vaishnavi Ananthanarayanan and William Thies. 2010. Biocoder: A programming language for standardizing and automating biology protocols. In *Journal of Biological Engineering*.

Yoav Artzi and Luke Zettlemoyer. 2013. Weakly supervised learning of semantic parsers for mapping instructions to actions. In *Transactions of the Association for Computational Linguistics (TACL)*.

Maxwell Bates, Aaron J Berliner, Joe Lachoff, Paul R Jaschke, and Eli S Groban. 2016. Wet lab accelerator: a web-based application democratizing laboratory automation for synthetic biology. In *ACS synthetic biology*.

Mario Bollini, Stefanie Tellex, Tyler Thompson, Nicholas Roy, and Daniela Rus. 2013. Interpreting and executing recipes with a cooking robot. In *Proceedings of International Symposium on Experimental Robotics (ISER)*.

Andrew Borthwick and Ralph Grishman. 1999. A maximum entropy approach to named entity recognition. *Ph. D. Thesis, Dept. of Computer Science, New York University*.

Satchuthananthavale RK Branavan, Harr Chen, Luke S Zettlemoyer, and Regina Barzilay. 2009. Reinforcement learning for mapping instructions to actions. In *Proceedings of the Annual Meeting of the Association for Computational Linguistics (ACL)*.

SRK Branavan, Luke S Zettlemoyer, and Regina Barzilay. 2010. Reading between the lines: Learning to map high-level instructions to commands. In *Proceedings of the 48th Annual Meeting of the Association for Computational Linguistics (ACL)*.

Dallas Card, Amber E Boydstun, Justin H Gross, Philip Resnik, and Noah A Smith. 2015. The media frames corpus: Annotations of frames across issues. In *Proceedings of the 53rd Annual Meeting of the Association for Computational Linguistics and the 7th International Joint Conference on Natural Language Processing (ACL-IJCNLP)*.

Danqi Chen and Christopher Manning. 2014. A fast and accurate dependency parser using neural networks. In *Proceedings of the 2014 conference on empirical methods in natural language processing (EMNLP)*.

David L Chen and Raymond J Mooney. 2011. Learning to interpret natural language navigation instructions from observations. In *Proceedings of the 25th AAAI Conference on Artificial Intelligence (AAAI)*.

Dipanjan Das, Desai Chen, André FT Martins, Nathan Schneider, and Noah A Smith. 2014. Frame-semantic parsing. *Computational Linguistics*, 40(1):9–56.

Daniel Gildea and Daniel Jurafsky. 2002. Automatic labeling of semantic roles. *Computational Linguistics*, 28(3):245–288.

Zhou GuoDong, Su Jian, Zhang Jie, and Zhang Min. 2005. Exploring various knowledge in relation extraction. In *Proceedings of the 43rd Annual Meeting on Association for Computational Linguistics (ACL)*.

Jermsak Jermsurawong and Nizar Habash. 2015. Predicting the structure of cooking recipes. In *Proceedings of the 2015 Conference on Empirical Methods in Natural Language Processing (EMNLP)*.

Nanda Kambhatla. 2004. Combining lexical, syntactic, and semantic features with maximum entropy models for extracting relations. In *Proceedings of the ACL 2004 on Interactive Poster and Demonstration Sessions*.

J-D Kim, Tomoko Ohta, Yuka Tateisi, and Junichi Tsujii. 2003. GENIA corpus - a semantically annotated corpus for bio-textmining. *Bioinformatics*, 19:i180–i182.

Ross D King, Jem Rowland, Stephen G Oliver, Michael Young, Wayne Aubrey, Emma Byrne, Maria Liakata, Magdalena Markham, Pinar Pir, Larisa N Soldatova, Andrew Sparkes, Kenneth E Whelan, and Amanda Clare. 2009. The automation of science. *Science*, 324(5923):85–89.

Klaus Krippendorff. 2004. *Content analysis: An introduction to its methodology*. SAGE Publications.

Guillaume Lample, Miguel Ballesteros, Sandeep Subramanian, Kazuya Kawakami, and Chris Dyer. 2016. Neural architectures for named entity recognition. In *Proceedings of the 2016 Conference of the North American Chapter of the Association for Computational Linguistics: Human Language Technologies (NAACL-HLT)*.

Qi Li and Heng Ji. 2014. Incremental joint extraction of entity mentions and relations. In *Proceedings of the 52nd Annual Meeting of the Association for Computational Linguistics (ACL)*.

Xuezhe Ma and Eduard Hovy. 2016. End-to-end sequence labeling via bi-directional lstm-cnns-crf. In *Proceedings of the 54th Annual Meeting of the Association for Computational Linguistics (ACL)*.

George A Miller. 1995. WordNet: a lexical database for english. *Communications of the ACM*, 38(11):39–41.

SPFGH Moen and Tapio Salakoski2 Sophia Ananiadou. 2013. Distributional semantics resources for biomedical text processing. In *Proceedings of the 5th International Symposium on Languages in Biology and Medicine (LBM2013)*.

Barbara Plank, Anders Søgaard, and Yoav Goldberg. 2016. Multilingual part-of-speech tagging with bidirectional long short-term memory models and auxiliary loss. In *The 54th Annual Meeting of the Association for Computational Linguistics (ACL)*.

Pranav Rajpurkar, Jian Zhang, Konstantin Lopyrev, and Percy Liang. 2016. SQuAD: 100,000+ questions for machine comprehension of text. *Proceedings of the 2016 Conference on Empirical Methods in Natural Language Processing (EMNLP)*.

Larisa N Soldatova, Daniel Nadis, Ross D King, Piyali S Basu, Emma Haddi, Véronique Baumlé, Nigel J Saunders, Wolfgang Marwan, and Brian B Rudkin. 2014. EXACT2: the semantics of biomedical protocols. *BMC bioinformatics*.

Erik F Tjong Kim Sang and Fien De Meulder. 2003. Introduction to the conll-2003 shared task: Language-independent named entity recognition. In *Proceedings of the seventh conference on Natural language learning (CoNLL)*.

Yoshimasa Tsuruoka and Jun'ichi Tsujii. 2005. Bidirectional inference with the easiest-first strategy for tagging sequence data. In *Proceedings of the conference on human language technology and empirical methods in natural language processing (HLT-EMNLP)*.

Viktor Vasilev, Chenkai Liu, Traci Haddock, Swapnil Bhatia, Aaron Adler, Fusun Yaman, Jacob Beal, Jonathan Babb, Ron Weiss, Douglas Densmore, et al. 2011. A software stack for specification and robotic execution of protocols for synthetic biological engineering. In *3rd International Workshop on Bio-Design Automation (IWBDA)*.

Matthew D. Zeiler. 2012. ADADELTA: an adaptive learning rate method. *arXiv:1212.5701*.

A Annotation Guidelines

The wet lab protocol dataset annotation guidelines were designed primarily to provide a simple description of the various actions and their arguments in protocols so that it could be more accessible and be effectively used by non-biologists who may want to use this dataset for various natural language processing tasks such as action trigger detection or relation extraction. In the following sub-sections we summarize the guidelines that were used in annotating the 622 protocols as we explore the actions, entities and relations that were chosen to be labelled in this dataset.

A.1 Actions

Under a broad categorization, Action is a process of doing something, typically to achieve an aim. In the context of wet lab protocols, action mentions in a sentence or a step are deliberate but short descriptions of a task tying together various entities in a meaningful way. Some examples of action words, (categorized using GENIA POS tagger), are present in Table 7 along with their frequencies.

A.2 Entities

We broadly classify entities commonly seen in protocols under 17 tags. Each of the entity tags were designed to encourage short span length, with the average number of words per entity tag being 1.6. For example, `Concentration` tags are often very short: *60% 10x, 10M, 1 g/ml*, while the `Method` tag has the longest average span of 2.232 words with examples such as *rolling back and forth between two hands* (as seen in Figure 4). The methods in wet lab protocols tend to be descriptive, which pose distinct challenges from existing named entity extraction research in the medical and other domains.

A.2.1 Object Based Entities

Reagent: A substance or mixture for use in any kind of reaction in preparing a product because of its chemical or biological activity.

Location: Containers for reagents or other physical entities. They lack any operation capabilities other than acting as a container. These could be laboratory glassware or plastic tubing meant to hold chemicals or biological substances.

Device: A machine capable of acting as a container as well as performing a specific task on the objects that it holds. A device and a location are

Tag	Examples	Freq. of Tags	Avg-Word
Action	Add, Incubate, Pipette off, etc	17485	1.094
Reagent	mtDNA Adenylation Mix, Para..	13703	1.665
Location	microcentrifuge tube, PCR Plate, Petri dish, etc	5402	1.553
Amount	1 mL, 100 µl, 1.5 ml, etc	4801	1.694
Modifier	gently, at least, appropriate, proportionally, etc	4307	1.244
Time	5min, overnight, until late aft..	3590	1.962
Device	pipette, microfuge, Sorvall SS34 rotor, etc	2417	1.691
Temperature	25°C, 56 degree Celsius, room..	2369	1.436
Concentration	1X, 70%, 50 mM, 1 x 108 cells/ mL, etc	1782	1.763
Method	dialysis, transmission electron microscopy, etc	1024	2.232
Speed	14,000xg, 10,000 rpm, 44,000 ..	961	1.999
Numerical	10, 20, once, two, several, etc	743	1.167
Generic-Measure	30-kD, 100 V, 595nm, 6 V cm-..	626	2.080
Size	12 x 75 mm, 150 mm, 25mm diameter, etc	516	1.812
Measure-Type	concentration, purity and yiel..	336	1.518
Seal	dialysis cap, aluminum foil, adhesive PCR plate seal, etc	302	1.672
Mention	it, them, they, etc	225	1.098
pH	pH 7.8, neutral pH, 7.2 ± 0.2 pH, etc	132	2.023

Figure 4: Examples, Frequency and Avg-Word for actions and entities.

similar in all aspects except that a device performs a specific set of operations on its contents, usually illustrated in the sentence itself, or sometimes implied.

Seal: Any kind of lid or enclosure for the location or device. It could be a cap, or a membrane that actively participates in the protocol action, and hence is essential to capture this type of entity.

A.2.2 Measure Based Entities

Amount: The amount of any reagent being used in a given step, in terms of weight or volume.

Concentration: Measure of the relative proportions of two or more quantities in a mixture. Usually in terms of their percentages by weight or volume.

Time: Duration of a specific action described in a single step or steps, typically in secs, min, days, or weeks.

Temperature: Any temperature mentioned in degree Celsius, Fahrenheit, or Kelvin.

Method: A word or phrase used to concisely define the procedure to be performed in association with the chosen action verb. Its usually a noun, but could also be a passive verb.

Speed: Typically a measure that represents rotation per min for centrifuges.

Numerical: A generic tag for a number that

Label	Syntax/Rules	Example
Acts-on	Action $\Rightarrow$ Reagent | Location | Mention | Device | Seal	
Creates	Action $\Rightarrow$ Reagent | Mention	
Site	Action $\Rightarrow$ Location | Device | Mention | Reagent	
Using	Action $\Rightarrow$ Method | Action | Seal | Device | Mention | Reagent | Location	
Setting	Action | Device | Modifier $\Rightarrow$ Method | Action | Seal | Device | Mention | Reagent | Location	
Count	Action $\Rightarrow$ Numerical	
Measure-Type-Link	Action $\Rightarrow$ Measure-Type	
Coreference	Mention $\Rightarrow$ [Every other entity]	
Mod-Link	[Every Entity or Action] $\Rightarrow$ Modifier	
Measure	Reagent | Location | Device | Mention | Seal $\Rightarrow$ Amount | Numerical | Size | Concentration | Generic-Measure | pH	
Meronym	Reagent | Location | Device | Mention | Seal $\Rightarrow$ Reagent | Location | Device | Mention | Seal	
Or	[All Entities or Action] $\Rightarrow$ [All Entities or Action]	
Of-Type	Generic-Measure | Numerical $\Rightarrow$ Measure-Type	

Table 8: Relations along with their rules and examples

doesn't fit time, temp, etc and which isn't accompanied by its unit of measure.

Generic-Measure: Any measures that don't fit the list of defined measures in this list.

Size A measure of the dimension of an object. For example: length, area or thickness.

Measure-Type: A generic tag to mark the type of measurement associated with a number.

pH: measure of acidity or alkalinity of a solution.

A.2.3 Parts of Speech based Entities

Modifier: A word or a phrase that acts as an additional description of the entity it is modifying. For example, *quickly mix* vs *slowly mix* are clearly two different actions, informed by their modifiers "quickly" or "slowly" respectively.

Mention: Words that can refer to an object mentioned earlier in the sentence.

A.3 Relations

A.3.1 Action Relations (Action - Entity)

Acts-On: Links the reagent, or location that the action acts on, typically linking the direct objects in the sentence to the action.

Creates: This relation marks the physical entity that the action creates.

Site: A link that associates a Location or Device to an action. It indicates that the Device or Location is the site where the action is performed. It is also used as a way to indicate which entity will finally hold/contain the result of the action.

Using: Any entity that the action verb makes use of is linked with this relation.

Setting: Any measure type entity that is being used to set a device is linked to the action that is attempting to use that numerical.

Count: A Numerical entity that represents the number of times the action should take place.

Measure Type Link: Associates an action to a Measure Type entity that the Action is instructing to measure.

A.3.2 Binary Relations (Entity - Entity)

Coreference: A link that associates two phrases when those two phrases refer to the same entity.

Mod Link: A Modifier entity is linked to any entity that it is attempting to modify using this relation.

Settings: Links devices to their settings directly, only if there is no Action associated with those settings.

Measure: A link that associates the various numerical measures to the entity its trying to measure directly.

Meronym: Links reagents, locations or devices with materials contained in the reagent, location or device.

Or: Allows chaining multiple entities where either of them can be used for a given link.

Of-Type: used to specify the Measure-Type of a Generic-Measure or a Numerical, if the sentence contains this information.

Annotation Artifacts in Natural Language Inference Data

Suchin Gururangan[★][◇]   Swabha Swayamdipta[★][♡]
Omer Levy[♣]   Roy Schwartz[♣♠]   Samuel R. Bowman [†]   Noah A. Smith[♣]

[◇] Department of Linguistics, University of Washington, Seattle, WA, USA
[♡] Language Technologies Institute, Carnegie Mellon University, Pittsburgh, PA, USA
[♣] Paul G. Allen School of Computer Science & Engineering, University of Washington, Seattle, WA, USA
[♠] Allen Institute for Artificial Intelligence, Seattle, WA, USA
[†] Center for Data Science and Department of Linguistics, New York University, New York, NY, USA
{sg01,swabha,omerlevy,roysch,nasmith}@cs.washington.edu bowman@nyu.edu

Abstract

Large-scale datasets for natural language inference are created by presenting crowd workers with a sentence (premise), and asking them to generate three new sentences (hypotheses) that it entails, contradicts, or is logically neutral with respect to. We show that, in a significant portion of such data, this protocol leaves clues that make it possible to identify the label by looking only at the hypothesis, without observing the premise. Specifically, we show that a simple text categorization model can correctly classify the hypothesis alone in about 67% of SNLI (Bowman et al., 2015) and 53% of MultiNLI (Williams et al., 2018). Our analysis reveals that specific linguistic phenomena such as negation and vagueness are highly correlated with certain inference classes. Our findings suggest that the success of natural language inference models to date has been overestimated, and that the task remains a hard open problem.

1 Introduction

Natural language inference (NLI; also known as recognizing textual entailment, or RTE) is a widely-studied task in natural language processing, to which many complex semantic tasks, such as question answering and text summarization, can be reduced (Dagan et al., 2006). Given a pair of sentences, a premise p and a hypothesis h, the goal is to determine whether or not p semantically entails h.

The problem of acquiring large amounts of labeled inference data was addressed by Bowman et al. (2015), who devised a method for crowdsourcing high-agreement entailment annotations en masse, creating the SNLI and later the genre-diverse MultiNLI (Williams et al., 2018) datasets. In this process, crowd workers are presented with

a premise p drawn from some corpus (e.g., image captions), and are required to generate three new sentences (hypotheses) based on p, according to one of the following criteria:

Entailment	h is definitely true given p
Neutral	h might be true given p
Contradiction	h is definitely **not** true given p

In this paper, we observe that hypotheses generated by this crowdsourcing process contain artifacts that can help a classifier detect the correct class *without* ever observing the premise (Section 2).

A closer look suggests that the observed artifacts are a product of specific annotation strategies and heuristics that crowd workers adopt. We find, for example, that entailed hypotheses tend to contain gender-neutral references to people, purpose clauses are a sign of neutral hypotheses, and negation is correlated with contradiction (Section 3). Table 1 shows a single set of instances from SNLI that demonstrates all three phenomena.

We re-evaluate high-performing NLI models on the subset of examples on which our hypothesis-only classifier failed, which we consider to be "hard" (Section 4). Our results show that the performance of these models on the "hard" subset is dramatically lower than their performance on the rest of the instances. This suggests that, despite recently reported progress, natural language inference remains an open problem.

2 Annotation Artifacts are Common

We conjecture that the framing of the annotation task has a significant effect on the language generation choices that crowd workers make when authoring hypotheses, producing certain patterns in the data. We call these patterns *annotation artifacts*.

[★] These authors contributed equally to this work.

107

Proceedings of NAACL-HLT 2018, pages 107–112
New Orleans, Louisiana, June 1 - 6, 2018. ©2018 Association for Computational Linguistics

Premise	A woman selling bamboo sticks talking to two men on a loading dock.
Entailment	There are **at least** three **people** on a loading dock.
Neutral	A woman is selling bamboo sticks **to help provide for her family.**
Contradiction	A woman is **not** taking money for any of her sticks.

Table 1: An instance from SNLI that illustrates the artifacts that arise from the annotation protocol. A common strategy for generating entailed hypotheses is to remove gender or number information. Neutral hypotheses are often constructed by adding a purpose clause. Negations are often introduced to generate contradictions.

Model	SNLI	MultiNLI	
		Matched	Mismatched
majority class	34.3	35.4	35.2
fastText	**67.0**	**53.9**	**52.3**

Table 2: Performance of a premise-oblivious text classifier on NLI. The MultiNLI benchmark contains two test sets: matched (in-domain examples) and mismatched (out-of-domain examples). A majority baseline is presented for reference.

To determine the degree to which such artifacts exist, we train a model to predict the label of a given hypothesis *without seeing the premise*. Specifically, we use fastText (Joulin et al., 2017), an off-the-shelf text classifier that models text as a bag of words and bigrams, to predict the entailment label of the hypothesis.[1] This classifier is completely oblivious to the premise.

Table 2 shows that a significant portion of each test set can be correctly classified without looking at the premise, well beyond the most-frequent-class baseline.[2]

Our finding demonstrates that it is possible to perform well on these datasets without modeling natural language inference.

3 Characteristics of Annotation Artifacts

In the previous section we showed that more than half (MultiNLI) or even two thirds (SNLI) of the data can be classified correctly using annotation artifacts. A possible explanation for the formation and relative consistency of these artifacts is that

crowd workers adopt heuristics in order to generate hypotheses quickly and efficiently. We identify some of these heuristics by conducting a shallow statistical analysis of the data, focusing on lexical choice (Section 3.1) and sentence length (Section 3.2).

3.1 Lexical Choice

To see whether the use of certain words is indicative of the inference class, we compute the pointwise mutual information (PMI) between each word and class in the training set:

$$\mathrm{PMI}(word, class) = \log \frac{p(word, class)}{p(word, \cdot)p(\cdot, class)}$$

We apply add-100 smoothing to the raw statistics; the aggressive smoothing emphasizes word-class correlations that are highly discriminative. Table 4 shows the top words affiliated with each class by PMI, along with the proportion of training sentences in each class containing each word.

Below, we elaborate on the most discriminating words for each NLI class, and suggest possible annotation heuristics that gave rise to these particular artifacts. However, it is important to note that even the most discriminative words are not very frequent, indicating that the annotation artifacts are diverse, and that crowd workers tend to adopt multiple heuristics for generating new text.

Entailment. Entailed hypotheses have generic words such as *animal*, *instrument*, and *outdoors*, which were probably chosen to generalize over more specific premise words such as *dog*, *guitar*, and *beach*. Other heuristics seem to replace exact numbers with approximates (*some*, *at least*, *various*), and to remove explicit gender (*human* and *person* appear lower down the list). Some artifacts are specific to the domain, such as *outdoors* and *outside*, which are typical of the personal photo descriptions on which SNLI was built.

---

[1] For MultiNLI, we additionally enabled two hyperparameters: character 4-grams, and filtering words that appeared less than 10 times in the training data.

[2] Experiments with two other text classifiers, a logistic regression classifier with word and character n-gram features and a premise-oblivious version of the decomposable attention model (Parikh et al., 2016), yielded similar results.

Premise	Two dogs are running through a field.
Entailment	There are **animals outdoors.**
Neutral	Some puppies are running **to catch a stick.**
Contradiction	The pets are **sitting on a couch.**

Table 3: The example provided in the annotation guidelines for SNLI. Some of the observed artifacts (bold) can be potentially traced back to phenomena in this specific example.

	Entailment		Neutral		Contradiction	
SNLI	outdoors	2.8%	tall	0.7%	nobody	0.1%
	least	0.2%	first	0.6%	sleeping	3.2%
	instrument	0.5%	competition	0.7%	no	1.2%
	outside	8.0%	sad	0.5%	tv	0.4%
	animal	0.7%	favorite	0.4%	cat	1.3%
MNLI	some	1.6%	also	1.4%	never	5.0%
	yes	0.1%	because	4.1%	no	7.6%
	something	0.9%	popular	0.7%	nothing	1.4%
	sometimes	0.2%	many	2.2%	any	4.1%
	various	0.1%	most	1.8%	none	0.1%

Table 4: Top 5 words by $PMI(word, class)$, along with the proportion of *class* training samples containing *word*. MultiNLI is abbreviated to MNLI.

Interestingly, the example from the SNLI annotation guidelines (Table 3) contains both *animals* and *outdoors*, and also removes the number. This example likely primed the annotators, inducing the specific heuristics of replacing *dog* with *animal* and mentions of scenery with *outdoors*.

Neutral. Modifiers (*tall, sad, popular*) and superlatives (*first, favorite, most*) are affiliated with the neutral class. These modifiers are perhaps a product of a simple strategy for introducing information that is not obviously entailed by the premise, yet plausible. Another formulation of neutral hypotheses seems to be through cause and purpose clauses, which increase the prevalence of discourse markers such as *because*. Once again, we observe that the example from the SNLI annotation guidelines does just that, by adding the purpose clause *to catch a stick* (Table 3).

Contradiction. Negation words such as *nobody, no, never* and *nothing* are strong indicators of contradiction.[3] Other (non-negative) words appear to be part of heuristics for contradicting whatever information is displayed in the premise; *sleeping* contradicts any activity, and *naked* (further down the list) contradicts any description of clothing.

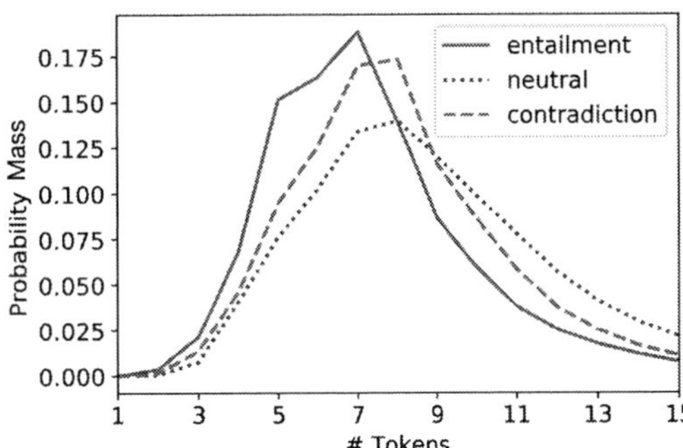

Figure 1: The probability mass function of the hypothesis length in SNLI, by class.

The high frequency of *cat* probably stems from the many dog images in the original dataset.

3.2 Sentence Length

We observe that the number of tokens in generated hypotheses is not distributed equally among the different inference classes. Figure 1 shows that, in SNLI, neutral hypotheses tend to be long, while entailed ones are generally shorter. The median length of a neutral hypothesis is 9, whereas 60% of entailments have 7 tokens or less. We also observe that half of hypotheses with at least 12 tokens are neutral, while a similar portion of hypotheses of length 5 and under are entailments, making hypothesis length an effective feature. Length is also a discriminatory feature in MultiNLI, but is less significant, possibly due to the introduction of diverse genres.

The bias in sentence length may suggest that crowd workers created many entailed hypotheses by simply removing words from the premise. Indeed, when representing each sentence as a bag of words, 8.8% of entailed hypotheses in SNLI are fully contained within their premise, while only 0.2% of neutrals and contradictions exhibit the same property. MultiNLI showed similar trends.

---

[3] Similar findings were observed in the ROC story cloze annotation (Schwartz et al., 2017).

Model	SNLI			MultiNLI Matched			MultiNLI Mismatched		
	Full	*Hard*	*Easy*	*Full*	*Hard*	*Easy*	*Full*	*Hard*	*Easy*
DAM	84.7	69.4	92.4	72.0	55.8	85.3	72.1	56.2	85.7
ESIM	85.8	71.3	92.6	74.1	59.3	86.2	73.1	58.9	85.2
DIIN	86.5	72.7	93.4	77.0	64.1	87.6	76.5	64.4	86.8

Table 5: Performance of high-performing NLI models on the full, *Hard*, and *Easy* NLI test sets.

4 Re-evaluating NLI Models

In Section 2, we showed that a model with no access to the premise can correctly classify many examples in both SNLI and MultiNLI, performing well above the most-frequent-class baseline. This raises an important question about state-of-the-art NLI models: to what extent are they "gaming" the task by learning to detect annotation artifacts?

To answer this question, we partition each NLI test set into two subsets: examples that the premise-oblivious model classified accurately are labeled *Easy*, and those it could not are *Hard*.

We then train an NLI model on the original training sets (from either SNLI or MultiNLI),[4] and evaluate on the full test set, the *Hard* test set, and the *Easy* test set. We ran this experiment on three high-performing NLI models: the Decomposable Attention Model (DAM; Parikh et al., 2016),[5] the Enhanced Sequential Inference Model (ESIM; Chen et al., 2017),[6] and the Densely Interactive Inference Network (DIIN; Gong et al., 2018).[7] All models were retrained out of the box.

Table 5 shows the performance of each model on the different splits. While the models correctly classify some *Hard* examples, the bulk of their success is attributed to the *Easy* examples. This result implies that the ability of NLI models to recognize textual entailment is lower than previously perceived, and that such models rely heavily on annotation artifacts in the hypothesis to make their predictions.

A natural question to ask is whether it is possible to select a set of NLI training and test samples which do not contain easy-to-exploit artifacts. One solution might be to filter *Easy* examples from the training set, retaining only *Hard* examples. However, initial experiments suggest that it might

not be as straightforward to eliminate annotation artifacts once the dataset has been collected.

First, after removing the *Easy* examples, *Hard* examples might not necessarily be artifact-free. For instance, removing all contradicting samples containing the word "no" (a strong indicator for contradiction, see Section 3), leaves the *Hard* dataset with this word mostly appearing in the neutral and entailing classes, thus creating a new artifact. Secondly, *Easy* examples contain important inference phenomena (e.g. the word "animal" is indeed a hypernym of "dog"), and removing these examples may hinder the model from learning such phenomena. Importantly, artifacts do not render any particular example *incorrect*; they are a problem with the sample distribution, which is skewed toward certain kinds of entailment, contradiction, and neutral hypotheses. Therefore, a better solution might not eliminate the artifacts altogether, but rather balance them across labels. Future strategies for reducing annotation artifacts might involve experimenting with the prompts or training given to crowd workers, e.g., to encourage a wide range of strategies, or incorporating baseline or adversarial systems that flag examples that appear to use over-represented heuristics. We defer research on hard-to-exploit NLI datasets to future work.

5 Discussion

We reflect on our results and relate them to other work that also analyzes annotation artifacts in NLP datasets, drawing three main conclusions.

Many datasets contain annotation artifacts. Lai and Hockenmaier (2014) demonstrated that lexical features such as the presence of negation, word overlap, and hypernym relations are highly predictive of entailment classes in the SICK dataset (Marelli et al., 2014). Chen et al. (2016) revealed problems with the CNN/DailyMail dataset (Hermann et al., 2015) which resulted from apply-

---

[4]The MultiNLI models were trained on MultiNLI data alone (as opposed to a blend of MultiNLI and SNLI data).
[5]github.com/allenai/allennlp
[6]github.com/nyu-mll/multiNLI
[7]goo.gl/kCeZXm

ing automatic tools for annotation. Levy and Dagan (2016) showed that a relation inference benchmark (Zeichner et al., 2012) is severely biased towards distributional methods, since it was created using DIRT (Lin and Pantel, 2001). Schwartz et al. (2017) and Cai et al. (2017) showed that certain biases are prevalent in the ROC stories cloze task (Mostafazadeh et al., 2016), which allow models trained on the endings alone, and not the story prefix, to yield state-of-the-art results. Rudinger et al. (2017) revealed that elicited hypotheses in SNLI contain evidence of various gender, racial, religious, and aged-based stereotypes. In parallel to this work, Poliak et al. (2018) uncovered similar annotation biases across multiple NLI datasets. Indeed, annotation artifacts are not unique to the NLI datasets, and the danger of such biases should be carefully considered when annotating new datasets.

Supervised models leverage annotation artifacts. Levy et al. (2015) demonstrated that supervised lexical inference models rely heavily on artifacts in the datasets, particularly the tendency of some words to serve as prototypical hypernyms. Agrawal et al. (2016); Jabri et al. (2016); Goyal et al. (2017) all showed that state-of-the-art visual question answering (Antol et al., 2015) systems leverage annotation biases in the dataset. Cirik et al. (2018) find that complex models for referring expression recognition achieve high performance without any text input. In parallel to this work, Dasgupta et al. (2018) found that the InferSent model (Conneau et al., 2017) relies on word-level heuristics to achieve state-of-the-art performance on SNLI. These findings coincide with ours, and strongly suggest that supervised models will exploit shortcuts in the data for gaming the benchmark, if such exist.

Annotation artifacts inflate model performance. This is a corollary of the above, since large portions of the test set can be solved by relying on annotation artifacts alone. A similar finding by Jia and Liang (2017) showed that the performance of top question-answering models trained on SQuAD (Rajpurkar et al., 2016) drops drastically by introducing simple adversarial sentences in the evidence. We release the *Hard* SNLI and MultiNLI test sets,[8] and encourage the community

---

[8]SNLI: `goo.gl/5rQKb5`, MultiNLI matched: `goo.gl/abdSbi`, MultiNLI mismatched: `goo.gl/Cu9Gp6`

to use them for evaluating NLI models (in addition to the original benchmarks). We also encourage the development of additional challenging benchmarks that expose the true performance levels of state-of-the-art NLI models.

Acknowledgments

This research was supported in part by the DARPA CwC program through ARO (W911NF-15-1-0543) and a hardware gift from NVIDIA Corporation. SB acknowledges gift support from Google and Tencent Holdings and support from Samsung Research.

References

Aishwarya Agrawal, Dhruv Batra, and Devi Parikh. 2016. Analyzing the behavior of visual question answering models. In *Proc. of EMNLP.* `https://aclweb.org/anthology/D16-1203`.

Stanislaw Antol, Aishwarya Agrawal, Jiasen Lu, Margaret Mitchell, Dhruv Batra, C Lawrence Zitnick, and Devi Parikh. 2015. VQA: Visual question answering. In *Proc. of ICCV.* `https://arxiv.org/abs/1506.00278`.

Samuel R. Bowman, Gabor Angeli, Christopher Potts, and Christopher D. Manning. 2015. A large annotated corpus for learning natural language inference. In *Proc. of EMNLP.* `https://doi.org/10.18653/v1/D15-1075`.

Zheng Cai, Lifu Tu, and Kevin Gimpel. 2017. Pay attention to the ending:strong neural baselines for the ROC Story Cloze task. In *Proc. of ACL.* `https://doi.org/10.18653/v1/P17-2097`.

Danqi Chen, Jason Bolton, and Christopher D. Manning. 2016. A thorough examination of the CNN/Daily Mail reading comprehension task. In *Proc. of ACL.* `https://doi.org/10.18653/v1/P16-1223`.

Qian Chen, Xiaodan Zhu, Zhen-Hua Ling, and Diana Inkpen. 2017. Natural language inference with external knowledge. arXiv:1711.04289. `https://arxiv.org/abs/1711.04289`.

Volkan Cirik, Louis-Philippe Morency, and Taylor Berg-Kirkpatrick. 2018. Visual referring expression recognition: What do our systems actually learn? In *Proc. of NAACL.*

Alexis Conneau, Douwe Kiela, Holger Schwenk, Loic Barrault, and Antoine Bordes. 2017. Supervised learning of universal sentence representations from natural language inference data. In *Proc. of EMNLP.* `https://doi.org/10.18653/v1/D17-1070`.

Ido Dagan, Oren Glickman, and Bernardo Magnini. 2006. The PASCAL recognising textual entailment challenge. *Machine Learning Challenges* pages 177–190. https://doi.org/10.1007/11736790_9.

Ishita Dasgupta, Demi Guo, Andreas Stuhlmüller, Samuel J Gershman, and Noah D Goodman. 2018. Evaluating compositionality in sentence embeddings. https://arxiv.org/abs/1802.04302.

Yichen Gong, Heng Luo, and Jian Zhang. 2018. Natural language inference over interaction space. In *Proc. of ICLR.* https://arxiv.org/abs/1709.04348.

Yash Goyal, Tejas Khot, Douglas Summers-Stay, Dhruv Batra, and Devi Parikh. 2017. Making the V in VQA matter: Elevating the role of image understanding in visual question answering. In *Proc. of CVPR.* https://arxiv.org/abs/1612.00837.

Karl Moritz Hermann, Tomáš Kočiský, Edward Grefenstette, Lasse Espeholt, Will Kay, Mustafa Suleyman, and Phil Blunsom. 2015. Teaching machines to read and comprehend. In *Proc. of NIPS.* http://dl.acm.org/citation.cfm?id=2969239.2969428.

Allan Jabri, Armand Joulin, and Laurens van der Maaten. 2016. Revisiting visual question answering baselines. In *Proc. of ECCV.* https://doi.org/10.1007/978-3-319-46484-8_44.

Robin Jia and Percy Liang. 2017. Adversarial examples for evaluating reading comprehension systems. In *Proc. of EMNLP.* https://www.aclweb.org/anthology/D17-1215.

Armand Joulin, Edouard Grave, Piotr Bojanowski, and Tomas Mikolov. 2017. Bag of tricks for efficient text classification. In *Proc. of EACL.* https://doi.org/10.18653/v1/E17-2068.

Alice Lai and Julia Hockenmaier. 2014. Illinois-LH: A denotational and distributional approach to semantics. In *Proc. of SemEval.* https://doi.org/10.3115/v1/S14-2055.

Omer Levy and Ido Dagan. 2016. Annotating relation inference in context via question answering. In *Proc. of ACL.* https://doi.org/10.18653/v1/P16-2041.

Omer Levy, Steffen Remus, Chris Biemann, and Ido Dagan. 2015. Do supervised distributional methods really learn lexical inference relations? In *Proc. of NAACL.* https://doi.org/10.3115/v1/N15-1098.

Dekang Lin and Patrick Pantel. 2001. Discovery of inference rules for question-answering. *Natural Language Engineering* 7(4):343–360. https://doi.org/10.1017/S1351324901002765.

Marco Marelli, Stefano Menini, Marco Baroni, Luisa Bentivogli, Raffaella Bernardi, and Roberto Zamparelli. 2014. A SICK cure for the evaluation of compositional distributional semantic models. In *Proc. of LREC.* pages 216–223. https://doi.org/10.3115/v1/S14-2001.

Nasrin Mostafazadeh, Nathanael Chambers, Xiaodong He, Devi Parikh, Dhruv Batra, Lucy Vanderwende, Pushmeet Kohli, and James Allen. 2016. A corpus and Cloze evaluation for deeper understanding of commonsense stories. In *Proc. of NAACL.* https://doi.org/10.18653/v1/N16-1098.

Ankur Parikh, Oscar Täckström, Dipanjan Das, and Jakob Uszkoreit. 2016. A decomposable attention model for natural language inference. In *Proc. of EMNLP.* https://doi.org/10.18653/v1/D16-1244.

Adam Poliak, Jason Naradowsky, Aparajita Haldar, Rachel Rudinger, and Benjamin Van Durme. 2018. Hypothesis only baselines for natural language inference. In *Proc of *SEM.*

Pranav Rajpurkar, Jian Zhang, Konstantin Lopyrev, and Percy Liang. 2016. SQuAD: 100,000+ questions for machine comprehension of text. In *Proc. of EMNLP.* https://doi.org/10.18653/v1/D16-1264.

Rachel Rudinger, Chandler May, and Benjamin Van Durme. 2017. Social bias in elicited natural language inferences. In *Proc. of EthNLP.* http://www.aclweb.org/anthology/W17-1609.

Roy Schwartz, Maarten Sap, Ioannis Konstas, Li Zilles, Yejin Choi, and Noah A. Smith. 2017. The effect of different writing tasks on linguistic style: A case study of the ROC Story Cloze task. In *Proc. of CoNLL.* https://doi.org/10.18653/v1/K17-1004.

Adina Williams, Nikita Nangia, and Samuel R. Bowman. 2018. A broad-coverage challenge corpus for sentence understanding through inference. In *Proc. of NAACL.*

Naomi Zeichner, Jonathan Berant, and Ido Dagan. 2012. Crowdsourcing inference-rule evaluation. In *Proc. of ACL.* http://www.aclweb.org/anthology/P12-2031.

Humor recognition using deep learning

Peng-Yu Chen
National Tsing Hua University
Hsinchu, Taiwan
pengyu@nlplab.cc

Von-Wun Soo
National Tsing Hua University
Hsinchu, Taiwan
soo@cs.nthu.edu.tw

Abstract

Humor is an essential but most fascinating element in personal communication. How to build computational models to discover the structures of humor, recognize humor and even generate humor remains a challenge and there have been yet few attempts on it. In this paper, we construct and collect four datasets with distinct joke types in both English and Chinese and conduct learning experiments on humor recognition. We implement a Convolutional Neural Network (CNN) with extensive filter size, number and Highway Networks to increase the depth of networks. Results show that our model outperforms in recognition of different types of humor with benchmarks collected in both English and Chinese languages on accuracy, precision, and recall in comparison to previous works.

1   Introduction

Humor, a highly intelligent communicative activity, provokes laughter or provides amusement. The role that humor plays in life can be viewed as a sociological phenomenon and function. Proper use of it can help eliminate embarrassment, establish social relationships, create positive affection in human social interactions. If computers can understand humor to some extent, it would facilitate predicting human's intention in human conversation, and thereby enhance the proficiency of many machine-human interaction systems.

However, to automate the humor recognition is also a very challenging research topic in natural language understanding. The extent to which a person may sense humor depends on his/her personal background. For example, young children may favor cartoons while the grownups may feel the humor in cartoons boring. Also, many types of humor require substantial such external knowledge as irony, wordplay, metaphor and sarcasm.

These factors make the task of automated humor recognition difficult.

Recently, with the advance of deep learning that allows end-to-end training with big data without human intervention of feature selection, humor recognition becomes promising. In this work, we propose a convolutional neural network (CNN) with augmentation of both the filter sizes and filter numbers. We use the architecture called highway network to implement a much more proficient model for humor recognition. The performance on many benchmarks shows a significant improvement in detecting different humor context genre.

2   Related Work

The task of automatic humor recognition refers to deciding whether a given sentence expresses a certain degree of humor. In early studies, most of them are formulated as a binary classification, based on selection on linguistic features. Purandare and Litman analyzed humorous spoken conversations from a classic comedy television show. They used standard supervised learning classifiers to identify humorous speech (Purandare and Litman, 2006). Taylor and Marlack focused on a specific type of humor, wordplays. Their algorithm of the study was based on the extraction of structural patterns and peculiar structure of jokes (Taylor and Mazlack, 2004). Later, Yang et al. (2015) formulated a classifier to distinguish between humorous and non-humorous instances, and also created computational models to discover the latent semantic structure behind humor from four perspectives: incongruity, ambiguity, interpersonal effect and phonetic style.

Recently, with the rise of artificial neural networks, many studies utilize the methods for humor recognition. Luke and Alfredo applied recurrent neural network (RNN) to humor detec-

113

Proceedings of NAACL-HLT 2018, pages 113–117
New Orleans, Louisiana, June 1 - 6, 2018. ©2018 Association for Computational Linguistics

tion from reviews in Yelp dataset. In addition, they also applied convolutional neural networks (CNNs) to train a model and the work shows that the model trained with CNNs has more accurate humor recognition (de Oliveira and Rodrigo, 2015). In other research (Bertero and Fung, 2016), CNNs were found to be a better sentence encoder for humor recognition as well. In a recent work, Chen and Lee predicted audience's laughter also using convolutional neural network. Their work gets higher detection accuracy and is able to learn essential feature automatically (Chen and Lee, 2017). However, there are still some limitations: (a) they focused on only a specific humor type in TED data, that is puns. (b) the datasets in most studies are English corpus. (c) the evaluations are isolated from other research.

In our work, we build the humor recognizer by using CNNs with extensive filter size and number, and the result shows higher accuracy from previous CNNs models. We conducted experiments on two different dataset, which were used in the previous studies. One is Pun of the Day (Yang et al., 2015), and the other is 16000 One-Liners (Mihalcea and Strapparava, 2005). In addition, we constructed a Chinese dataset to evaluate the generality of the method performance on humor recognition against different languages.

3 Data

To fairly evaluate the performance on humor recognition, we need the dataset to consist of both humorous (positive) and non-humorous (negative) samples. The datasets we use to construct humor recognition experiments includes four parts: Pun of the Day (Yang et al., 2015), 16000 One-Liners (Mihalcea and Strapparava, 2005), Short Jokes dataset and PTT jokes. The four datasets have different joke types, sentence lengths, data sizes and languages that allow us to conduct more comprehensive and comparative experiments. We would like to thank Yang and Mihalcea for their kindly provision of two former datasets. And we depict how we collect the latter two datasets in the following subsections. Table 1 shows the statistics of four datasets.

3.1 16000 One-Liners

16000 One-Liners dataset collected humorous samples from daily joke websites while using formal writing resources (e.g., news titles) to obtain

Dataset	#Pos	#Neg	Type	Lang
16000 One-Liners	16000	16002	One-liner	EN
Pun of the Day	2423	2403	Pun	EN
Short Jokes	231657	231657	All	EN
PTT Jokes	1425	2551	Political	CH

Table 1: Statistics of four datasets

non-humorous samples. A one-liner is a joke that usually has very few words in a single sentence with comic effects and interesting linguistic structure. While longer jokes can have a relatively complex linguistic structure, a one-liner must produce the humorous effect with very few words.

3.2 Pun of the Day

Pun of the Day dataset was constructed from the Pun of the Day website. The pun, also called paronomasia, is a form of wordplay that exploits multiple meanings of a term, or of similar-sounding words, for an intended humorous or rhetorical effect. The negative samples of this dataset are sampled from news website.

3.3 Short Jokes Dataset

Short Jokes dataset, which collected the most amount of jokes among four datasets, are from an open database on a Kaggle project[1]. It contains 231,657 short jokes with no restriction on joke types scraped from various joke websites and length ranging from 10 to 200 characters. We use it as our positive samples. For the negative samples, we choose WMT16[2] English news crawl as our non-humorous data resource. However, simply treating sentences from the resource as negative samples could result in deceptively high performance of classification due to the domain differences between positive and negative data. So we try to minimize such domain differences by selecting negative samples whose words all appear in the positive samples and whose average text length being close to the humorous ones.

3.4 PTT Jokes

PTT Bulletin Board System (PTT, Chinese: 批踢踢, telnet://ptt.cc) is the largest terminal-based bulletin board system (BBS) in Taiwan. It has more than 1.5 million registered users and over 20,000 boards covering a multitude of topics. Every day more than 20,000 articles and 500,000 comments are posted. Additionally, there is a

---

[1]https://www.kaggle.com/abhinavmoudgil95/short-jokes
[2]http://www.statmt.org/wmt16/translation-task.html

board called joke that we could acquire large amount of Chinese humor samples. Thus, we use some political-related words to extract political jokes from PTT and treat them as the positive samples. For the negative samples, we use Yahoo News in politics and select the samples by the same method we use in Short Jokes dataset to prevent from the problem of domain difference.

4 Method

In this section, we describe how we design our model for humor recognition.

4.1 CNN

Convolutional neural network (CNN) is a neural network architecture designed to extract local features in high dimensional data such as image or speech signal. When it comes to natural language processing (NLP), CNN also shows successes in several text categorization tasks (Johnson and Zhang, 2015). The input of most NLP tasks, such as a sentence or a document could be represented as a 2D structure with word embedding (Mikolov et al., 2013). In the input 2D matrix, each row is a vector of a word, a word segment or even a character that depends on the embedding methods. And typically we make the window width of the filters the same as the embedding dimension. Thus, the filter size varies according to a sliding window size we decide.

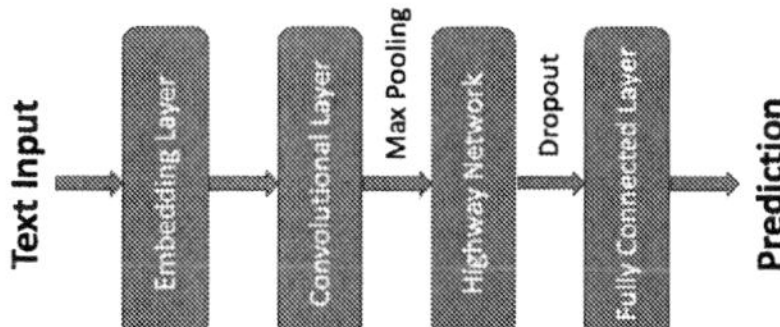

Figure 1: Network Architecture

4.2 Model Setting

In this paper, our CNN model's setup follows the Kim (2014) for the task of text classification. Figure 1 depicts the model's details. We firstly convert tokenized input sentence (length L) with word vector (dimension d) to a 2D matrix (L x d) by utilization of the GloVe embedding vectors (Pennington et al., 2014) which trained on 6B tokens and 400K vocabulary words of Wikipedia 2014 + Gigaword 5 as our embedding layer. Next, according to the average sentence length in the dataset, we tried different filter sizes with a range from 3 to 20. For each filter size, 100-200 filters are applied to the model. After convolutional layer, we exploit max pooling and then flatten the output. Assume we totally have n filters, eventually it will lead to a flatten 1D vector with dimension n at the prediction output.

4.3 Highway Layer

To improve the performance we usually can connect the flattened output with a fully connected layer and predict labels. In this paper, we would like to evaluate the performance improvement as we increase the network depth. However, the training of deeper networks becomes more difficult with increasing depth. So we use the concept of highway network (Srivastava et al., 2015) to help improve our model. The highway network allows shortcut connections with gate functions. These gates are data-dependent with parameters. It allows information unimpeded to flow through several layers in information highways. The architecture is characterized by the gate units that learn to regulate the flow of information through a network. With this architecture, we could train much deeper nets. In the end, we also use dropout and connect the results to the output layer.

5 Experiment

In this section, we describe how we formulate humor recognition as a text classification problem and conduct experiments on four datasets which we mentioned in Section 3. We validate the performance of different network structure with 10 fold cross validation and compare with the performance of previous work.

Table 2 shows the experiments on both 16000 One-Liners and Pun of the Day. We set the baseline on the previous works of Yang et al. (2015) by Random Forest with Word2Vec + Human Centric Feature (Word2Vec + HCF) and Chen and Lee (2017) by Convolutional Neural Networks. We choose a dropout rate at 0.5 and test our model's performance with two factors F and HN. F means the increase of filter size and number as we mentioned in section 4. Otherwise, the window sizes would be (5, 6, 7) and filter number is 100 that is the same with Chen and Lee (2017)'s. HN indicates that we use the highway layers to train deep networks and we set the HN layers = 3 because it has better stability and accuracy in training step. We could observe that when we use both F and

	16000 One-Liners				Pun of the Day			
	Accuracy	Precision	Recall	F1	Accuracy	Precision	Recall	F1
Previous Work								
Word2Vec+HCF	0.854	0.834	0.888	0.859	0.797	0.776	0.836	0.705
CNN					0.861	0.857	0.864	0.864
Our Methods								
CNN	0.877	**0.899**	0.856	0.877	0.867	0.880	0.859	0.869
CNN+F	0.892	0.896	0.928	0.898	0.892	0.886	0.907	0.896
CNN+HN	0.885	0.877	0.902	0.889	0.892	**0.889**	0.903	0.896
CNN+F+HN	**0.897**	0.872	**0.936**	**0.903**	**0.894**	0.866	**0.940**	**0.901**

Table 2: Comparison of Different Methods of Humor Recognition

HN our model gives the best performance on both accuracy and F1-Score and this conclusion is consistent across two datasets. The results show that our model helps increase F1-Score from 0.859 to 0.903 on 16000 One-Liners and from 0.705, 0.864 to 0.901 on Pun of the Day compared to previous work

Dataset	Accuracy	Precision	Recall	F1
Short Jokes	0.906	0.902	0.946	0.924
PTT Jokes	0.957	0.927	0.959	0.943

Table 3: Result of Short Jokes and PTT Jokes datasets

Table 3 presents the result of Short Jokes and PTT Jokes datasets. As we can see, for the datasets was construed, it achieve 0.924 on Short Jokes and 0.943 on PTT Jokes in terms of F1 score respectively. It shows that the deep learning model can, to some extent learn the humorous meaning and structure embedded in the text automatically without human selection of features.

6 Discussion

In this section, we show a sample in each category (true positive, false positive, true negative and false negative) to get a sense of what kinds of sentences are predicted correctly and incorrectly. The sentences are shown in the table 4.

	Sentence
TP	when he gave his wife a necklace he got a chain reaction
TN	the barking of a dog does not disturb the man on a camel
FP	rats know the way of rats
FN	it's a fact taller people sleep longer in bed

Table 4: Example Sentences

The TP sentence "when he gave his wife a necklace he got a chain reaction" shows that our model seems to be able to catch not only the literal meaning between the "necklace" and "got a chain reaction". Besides, the TN sentence "the barking of a dog does not disturb the man on a camel" means that if you're lucky enough to own your own camel, a little thing like a barking dog won't bother you. The example is a proverb but not a joke and our model correctly recognizes it as a non-humor one. Model misclassifies certain instances such as the FP sentence "rats know the way of rats" is actually derived from a Chinese proverb and the model predict it as humor. In addition, the FN sentence "it's a fact taller people sleep longer in bed" is obviously a joke but it is not considered as a humor by the model. To deal with more subtle humor/non-humor, the model has room to be improved.

7 Conclusion

In this study, we have extended the techniques of automatic humor recognition to different types of humor as well as different languages in both English and Chinese. We proposed a deep learning CNN architecture with high way networks that can learn to distinguish between humorous and non-humorous texts based on a large scale of balanced positive and negative dataset. The performance of the CNN model outperforms the previous work. It's worth mentioning that the recognition accuracy on PTT, political jokes in Chinese, and the short jokes dataset with various types of jokes in English are both as high as above 90%. The novel deep learning model relieves the required human intervention of selection linguistic features for humor recognition task. In future work, we would conduct more rigorous comparative evaluation with human humor recognition and look into how the humorous texts can be generated using deep learning models as well.

References

Dario Bertero and Pascale Fung. 2016. A long short-term memory framework for predicting humor in dialogues. In *NAACL HLT 2016, The 2016 Conference of the North American Chapter of the Association for Computational Linguistics: Human Language Technologies, San Diego California, USA, June 12-17, 2016*, pages 130–135.

Lei Chen and Chong MIn Lee. 2017. Predicting Audience's Laughter Using Convolutional Neural Network. *ArXiv e-prints:1702.02584*.

Rie Johnson and Tong Zhang. 2015. Effective use of word order for text categorization with convolutional neural networks. In *NAACL HLT 2015, The 2015 Conference of the North American Chapter of the Association for Computational Linguistics: Human Language Technologies, Denver, Colorado, USA, May 31 - June 5, 2015*, pages 103–112.

Yoon Kim. 2014. Convolutional neural networks for sentence classification. In *Proceedings of the 2014 Conference on Empirical Methods in Natural Language Processing, EMNLP 2014, October 25-29, 2014, Doha, Qatar, A meeting of SIGDAT, a Special Interest Group of the ACL*, pages 1746–1751.

Rada Mihalcea and Carlo Strapparava. 2005. Making computers laugh: Investigations in automatic humor recognition. In *HLT/EMNLP 2005, Human Language Technology Conference and Conference on Empirical Methods in Natural Language Processing, Proceedings of the Conference, 6-8 October 2005, Vancouver, British Columbia, Canada*, pages 531–538.

Tomas Mikolov, Ilya Sutskever, Kai Chen, Greg S Corrado, and Jeff Dean. 2013. Distributed representations of words and phrases and their compositionality. In C. J. C. Burges, L. Bottou, M. Welling, Z. Ghahramani, and K. Q. Weinberger, editors, *Advances in Neural Information Processing Systems 26*, pages 3111–3119. Curran Associates, Inc.

Luke de Oliveira and Alfredo Lainez Rodrigo. 2015. Humor detection in yelp reviews.

Jeffrey Pennington, Richard Socher, and Christopher D. Manning. 2014. Glove: Global vectors for word representation. In *Empirical Methods in Natural Language Processing (EMNLP)*, pages 1532–1543.

Amruta Purandare and Diane J. Litman. 2006. Humor: Prosody analysis and automatic recognition for f*r*i*e*n*d*s*. In *EMNLP 2007, Proceedings of the 2006 Conference on Empirical Methods in Natural Language Processing, 22-23 July 2006, Sydney, Australia*, pages 208–215.

Rupesh Kumar Srivastava, Klaus Greff, and Jürgen Schmidhuber. 2015. Training very deep networks. In *Advances in Neural Information Processing Systems 28: Annual Conference on Neural Information Processing Systems 2015, December 7-12, 2015, Montreal, Quebec, Canada*, pages 2377–2385.

Julia M. Taylor and Lawrence J. Mazlack. 2004. Computationally recognizing wordplay in jokes. In *In Proceedings of CogSci 2004*.

Diyi Yang, Alon Lavie, Chris Dyer, and Eduard H. Hovy. 2015. Humor recognition and humor anchor extraction. In *Proceedings of the 2015 Conference on Empirical Methods in Natural Language Processing, EMNLP 2015, Lisbon, Portugal, September 17-21, 2015*, pages 2367–2376.

Leveraging Intra-User and Inter-User Representation Learning for Automated Hate Speech Detection

Jing Qian, Mai ElSherief, Elizabeth M. Belding, William Yang Wang
Department of Computer Science
University of California, Santa Barbara
Santa Barbara, CA 93106 USA
{jing_qian, mayelsherif, ebelding, william}@cs.ucsb.edu

Abstract

Hate speech detection is a critical, yet challenging problem in Natural Language Processing (NLP). Despite the existence of numerous studies dedicated to the development of NLP hate speech detection approaches, the accuracy is still poor. The central problem is that social media posts are short and noisy, and most existing hate speech detection solutions take each post as an isolated input instance, which is likely to yield high false positive and negative rates. In this paper, we radically improve automated hate speech detection by presenting a novel model that leverages intra-user and inter-user representation learning for robust hate speech detection on Twitter. In addition to the target Tweet, we collect and analyze the user's historical posts to model intra-user Tweet representations. To suppress the noise in a single Tweet, we also model the similar Tweets posted by all other users with reinforced inter-user representation learning techniques. Experimentally, we show that leveraging these two representations can significantly improve the f-score of a strong bidirectional LSTM baseline model by 10.1%.

1 Introduction

The rapid rise in user-generated web content has not only yielded a vast increase in information accessibility, but has also given individuals an easy platform on which to share their beliefs and to publicly communicate with others. Unfortunately, this has also led to nefarious uses of online spaces, for instance for the propagation of hate speech.

An extensive body of work has focused on the development of automatic hate speech classifiers. A recent survey outlined eight categories of features used in hate speech detection (Schmidt and Wiegand, 2017): simple surface (Warner and Hirschberg, 2012; Waseem and Hovy, 2016), word generalization (Warner and

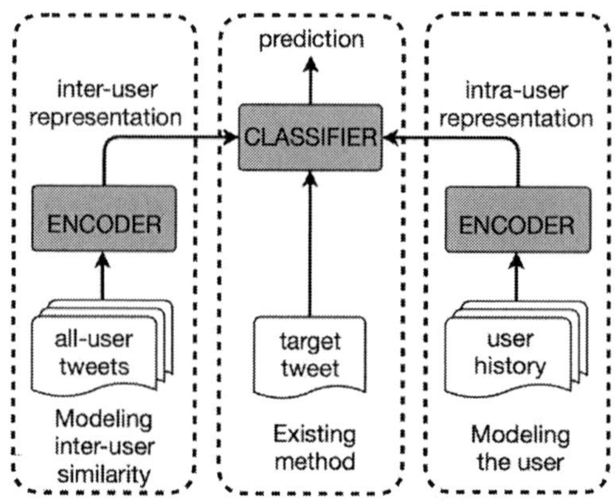

Figure 1: Our hate speech classifier. In contrast to existing methods that focus on a single target Tweet as input (center), we incorporate intra-user (right) and inter-user (left) representations to enhance performance.

Hirschberg, 2012; Zhong et al., 2016), sentiment analysis (Van Hee et al., 2015), lexical resources and linguistic features (Burnap and Williams, 2016), knowledge-based features (Dinakar et al., 2012), meta-information (Waseem and Hovy, 2016), and multi-modal information (Zhong et al., 2016). Closely related to our work is research that leverages user attributes in the classification process such as history of participation in hate speech and usage of profanity (Xiang et al., 2012; Dadvar et al., 2013). Both Xiang et al. (2012) and Dadvar et al. (2013) collect user history to enhance detection accuracy. The former requires the user history to be labeled instances. However, labeling user history requires significant human effort. The latter models the user with manually selected features. In contrast, our approach leverages unlabeled user history to automatically model the user.

In this paper, we focus on augmenting hate speech classification models by first performing

Proceedings of NAACL-HLT 2018, pages 118–123
New Orleans, Louisiana, June 1 - 6, 2018. ©2018 Association for Computational Linguistics

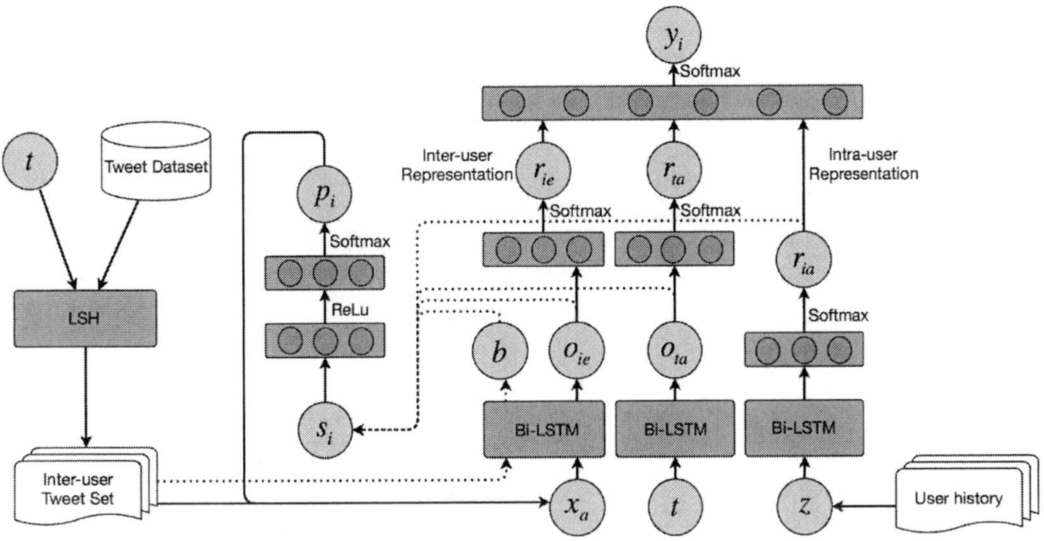

Figure 2: The overview of our proposed model. t is the input target Tweet, z denotes intra-user Tweets, and x_a is the selected inter-user Tweet. r_{ie} is the inter-user representation, r_{ia} is the intra-user representation, and r_{ta} is the representation of the target Tweet. These three branches respectively correspond to the three branches illustrated in Figure 1. y_i is the prediction at the time step i and s_i is the state input for the agent at the time step i. The computing process is detailed in Section 2.3

representation learning to model user history without supervision. The hypothesis is that, by analyzing a corpus of the user's past Tweets, our system will better understand the language and behavior of the user, leading to better hate speech detection accuracy. Another issue is that using a single Tweet as input is often noisy for any machine learning classifier. For example, the Tweet *"I'm not sexist but I can not stand women commentators"* is actually an instance of hate speech, even though the first half is misleading. To minimize noise, we also consider semantically similar Tweets posted by other users. To do so, we propose a reinforced bidirectional long short-term memory network (LSTM) (Hochreiter and Schmidhuber, 1997) to interactively leverage the similar Tweets from a large Twitter dataset to enhance the performance of the hate speech classifier. An overview of our approach is shown in Figure 1. The main contributions of our work are:

- We provide a novel perspective on hate speech detection by modeling intra-user Tweet representations.

- To improve robustness, we leverage similar Tweets from a large unlabeled corpus with reinforced inter-user representations.

- We integrate target Tweets, intra-user and inter-user representations in a unified framework, outperforming strong baselines.

2 Approach

Figure 2 illustrates the architecture of our model. It includes three branches, whose details will be described in the following subsections.

2.1 Bidirectional LSTM

Given a target Tweet, the baseline approach is to feed the embeddings of the Tweet into a bidirectional LSTM network (Hochreiter and Schmidhuber, 1997; Zhou et al., 2016; Liu et al., 2016) to obtain the prediction. This is shown in the middle branch in Figure 1. However, this method is likely to fail when the target tweet is noisy or the critical words for making predictions are out of vocabulary.

2.2 Intra-User Representation

The baseline approach does not fully utilize available information, such as the user's historical Tweets. In our approach, we collect the user's historical posts through the Twitter API. For a target Tweet t, suppose we collect m Tweets posted by this user: $Z_t = \{z_1, z_2, ..., z_m\}$. These intra-user Tweets are fed into a pre-trained model to obtain an intra-user representation. The pre-trained model has the same structure as the baseline model. This is shown in the right branch in Figures 1 and 2. The intra-user representation is then combined with the baseline branch for the final prediction. The computation process is:

$$o_{ta}(t) = f_{ta}(t, \mathbf{0}) \tag{1}$$

$$r_{ta}(t) = l_{ta}(\sigma(o_{ta}(t))) \tag{2}$$

$$o_{ia}(z_j) = f_{ia}(z_j, \mathbf{0}) \tag{3}$$

$$r_{ia}(t) = \sigma(\sum_{j=1}^{m} l_{ia}(\sigma(o_{ia}(z_j)))) \tag{4}$$

where f_{ta} is the bi-LSTM of the baseline branch; o_{ta} is the output of the bi-LSTM; and l_{ta}, l_{ia} are linear functions. Similarly, f_{ia} is the bi-LSTM of the intra-user branch and o_{ia} is the output. r_{ta} is the output prediction of the baseline branch. r_{ia} is the intra-user representation, and σ is the non-linear activation function.

2.3 Inter-User Representation

In addition to the user history, the Tweets that are semantically similar to the target Tweet can also be utilized to suppress noise in the target Tweet. We collect similar Tweets from large unlabeled Tweet set U by Locality Sensitive Hashing (LSH) (Indyk and Motwani, 1998; Gionis et al., 1999). Since the space of all Tweets is enormous, we use LSH to efficiently reduce the search space. For each target Tweet t, we use LSH to collect n nearest neighbors of t in U: $x_1, x_2, ..., x_n$. These n Tweets form the inter-user Tweet set for t: $X_t = \{x_1, x_2, ..., x_n\}$.

Due to the size of this set, a policy gradient-based deep reinforcement learning agent is trained to interactively fetch inter-user Tweets from X_t. The policy network consists of two layers as shown in the middle part of Figure 2 and the policy network is trained by the REINFORCE algorithm (Williams, 1992). At each time step i, the action of the agent is to select one Tweet x_a from X_t. x_a is then fed into a bi-LSTM followed by a linear layer. The result is combined with the intra-user representation and the baseline prediction (the right and the middle branch in Figures 1 and 2) to get the prediction at time step i. At each time step, the bi-LSTM layer that encodes the selected inter-user is initialized with the output hidden state of the last time step. The number of time steps for each target Tweet is set to be a fixed number T so that

---

Algorithm 1 Training Algorithm
___
1: **for** t in training set **do**
2:     collect X_t and Z_t;
3:     compute intra-user representation $r_{ia}(t)$;
4: **end for**
5: initialize parameters θ_p of the policy network;
6: initialize parameters θ_e of the other nets;
7: **for** $epoch = 1, E$ **do**
8:     **for** t in training set **do**
9:         compute $o_{ta}(t), r_{ta}(t)$;
10:        compute the raw prediction $y'(t)$;
11:        compute $b(X_t)$;
12:        $x_a = t$;
13:        compute $o_{ie}(t)$;
14:        initialize the state $s(t)_0$;
15:        **for** $i = 1, T$ **do**
16:           agent select action by $\epsilon - greedy$;
17:           update x_a;
18:           compute $o_{ie}(t), r_{ie}(t)$;
19:           compute $y(t)_i$ and $s(t)_i$;
20:           compute the reward $v_i(t)$;
21:        **end for**
22:        apply REINFORCE to update θ_p;
23:        update θ_e on the loss $\mathcal{L}(\theta_e) = e(y(t)_T, y^*)$;
24:     **end for**
25: **end for**
___

the agent will terminate after T fetches. The final prediction occurs at the last time step. The computation is shown by the following equations.

$$o_{ie}(x_a)_i, h_{ie}(x_a)_i = f_{ie}(x_a, h_{ie}(x_b)_{i-1}) \tag{5}$$

$$r_{ie}(x_a)_i = l_{ie}(\sigma(o_{ie}(x_a)_i)) \tag{6}$$

$$y'(t) = \sigma(l_c(r_{ta}(t) \oplus r_{ia}(t))) \tag{7}$$

$$y(t)_i = \sigma(l_c(r_{ie}(t) \oplus r_{ta}(t) \oplus r_{ia}(t))) \tag{8}$$

where x_b is the selected inter-user Tweet at time step $i - 1$. f_{ie} is the bi-LSTM of the inter-user branch. o_{ie} and h_{ie} are the output and the hidden state. l_c is a linear function. r_{ie} is the inter-user representation. y' is the prediction made without the inter-user branch and y is the prediction made with the inter-user branch. The symbol $\oplus$ means concatenation. The subscript i denotes time step i.

The state at each time step for the agent is the concatenation of encoded inter-user Tweets, the output of the Bi-LSTM in the inter-user branch and the baseline branch, together with the intra-user representation in the intra-user branch (the dotted arrows in Figure 2). Each inter-user Tweet x_j in X_t is encoded by the bi-LSTM of the inter-user branch (the dotted arrow through the Bi-LSTM of the inter-user branch).

$$b(x_j) = f_{ie}(x_j, \mathbf{0}) \tag{9}$$

$$s(t)_i[j] = o_{ie}(x_a)_i \oplus b(x_j) \oplus o_{ta}(t) \oplus r_{ia}(t) \tag{10}$$

b is the output of the bi-LSTM of the inter-user branch. In order to differentiate with o_{ie} mentioned above, we use b. $s(t)_i[j]$ is the jth row of the state at time step i.

By using reinforcement learning, the state for the agent is updated after each fetch of the inter-user Tweet. Thus, the agent can interactively make selections and update the inter-user representations step by step. The reward v_i for the agent at time step i is based on the original prediction without the agent and the prediction at the last time step with the agent. The computation is shown as:

$$q(t)_i = e(y'(t), y^*) - e(y(t)_T, y^*) \qquad (11)$$

$$v(t)_i = \begin{cases} \alpha * q(t)_i & \text{if } y'(t)! = y^* \\ q(t)_i & \text{else if } y(t)_T! = y^* \\ 0 & \text{otherwise} \end{cases} \qquad (12)$$

where e is the loss function; $q(t)$ is the basic reward; and $v(t)_i$ is the modified reward at time step i. α is a positive number used to amplify the reward when the original classification is incorrect. The intuition of this reward is to train the agent to be able to correct the misclassified Tweets. When the original prediction and the last prediction are both correct, the reward is set to 0 to make the agent focus on the misclassified instances.

The complete training process is shown in Algorithm 1. Before the training, the intra-user Tweets and inter-user Tweets are collected for each target Tweet. Then intra-user representations are computed, followed by the computation for initializing the environment and state for the agent. Next, the agent's actions, state updates, prediction, and reward are computed. Finally, the parameters are updated.

3 Experiments

3.1 Experimental Settings

Dataset: We use the dataset published by Waseem and Hovy (2016). This dataset contains 16,907 Tweets. The original dataset only contains the Tweet ID and the label for each Tweet. We expand the dataset with user ID and Tweet text. After deleting the Tweets that are no longer accessible, the dataset we use contains 15,781 Tweets from 1,808 users. The published dataset has three labels: racism, sexism and none. Since we consider a binary classification setting, we union the first two sets. In the final dataset, 67% are labeled as non-hate speech, and 33% are labeled as hate speech. 1000 Tweets are randomly selected for

Method	Prec.	Rec.	F1
SVM	**.793**	.656	.718
Logistic Regression	.782	.611	.686
Bi-LSTM + attention	.760	.665	.710
CNN-static	.701	.707	.703
CNN-non-static	.743	.699	.720
N-gram	.729	**.777**	.739
Bi-LSTM	.672	.737	.703
+ Intra. Rep.	.772	.749	.760
+ Intra.+ Randomized Inter. Rep.	.773	.764	.768
+ Intra.+ Reinforced Inter. Rep.	.775	.773	**.774**

Table 1: Experimental results. Prec.: precision. Rec.: recall. F1: F measure. Bi-LSTM: the baseline bidirectional LSTM model. Bi-LSTM + attention: an attentional bidirectional LSTM model. The experimental settings of the last three rows are illustrated in Section 3.1. + Intra. Rep.: the model consists of the target Tweet branch and the intra-user branch. + Intra. + Randomized Inter. Rep. incorporates randomly selected inter-user Tweets while + Intra. + Reinforced Inter. Rep. further incorporates the reinforced inter-user branch. The best results are in bold.

testing and the remaining 14,781 Tweets are for training.

Baseline: The baseline model is a bi-LSTM model. The input for the model is the word embeddings of the target Tweet. The word embedding is of size 200. The hidden size of the LSTM is 64. The optimizer is Adam and we use mini-batches of size 25. The word embedding model is pre-trained on a Tweet corpus containing 3,433,513 Tweets.

Intra-user Representation Learning: Based on the target Tweet, we collect at most 400 Tweets posted by the same user, with the target Tweet removed. The baseline branch and the intra-user branch are combined via a linear layer.

Combining with Inter-user Representation: The inter-user Tweet set is collected from the dataset via Locality Sensitive Hashing (LSH). In our experiments, we use a set size of either 50, 100 or 200 Tweets. At each time step, one Tweet is selected from the inter-user Tweet set by the policy agent. We also experimented with a second setting, in which we replace the agent by random selection. At each time step, an inter-user Tweet is randomly selected from X and fed into the inter-user branch.

3.2 Results

We compare the above settings with six classification models: Supported Vector Machine (SVM) (Suykens and Vandewalle, 1999), Logistic Regression, attentional BI-LSTM, two CNN models by Kim (2014), and a N-gram model (Waseem and Hovy, 2016). We evaluate these models on three metrics: precision, recall and F1 score. The results are shown in Table 1. We report results for $|U| = 100$ in Table 1, as results with sizes 50 and 200 are similar. We find that leveraging the intra-user information helps reduce false positives. The performance is further improved when integrating our model with inter-user similarity learning. Our results show that selection by the policy gradient agent is slightly better than random selection, and we hypothesize the effect would be more salient when working with a larger unlabeled dataset. The McNemar's test shows that our model gives significantly better (at $p < 0.01$) predictions than the baseline bi-LSTM and attentional bi-LSTM.

3.3 Error Analysis

There are two types of hate speech that are misclassified. The first type contains rare words and abbreviations, e.g. *FK YOU KAT AND ANDRE! #mkr*. Such intentional misspellings or abbreviations are highly varied, making it difficult for the model to learn the correct meaning. The second type of hate speech is satire or metaphor, e.g. *Congratulations Kat. Reckon you may have the whole viewer population against you now #mkr*. Satire and metaphors are extremely difficult to recognize. In the above two cases, both the baseline branch and the inter-user branch can be unreliable.

4 Conclusion

In this work, we propose a novel method for hate speech detection. We use bi-LSTM as the baseline method. However, our framework can easily augment other baseline methods by incorporating intra-user and reinforced inter-user representations. In addition to detecting potential hate speech, our method can be applied to help detect suspicious social media accounts. Considering the relationship between online hate speech and real-life hate actions, our solution has the potential to help analyze real-life extremists and hate groups. Furthermore, intra-user and inter-user representation learning can be generalized to other text classification tasks, where either user history or a large collection of unlabeled data are available.

Acknowledgments

The first author is supported by the Chancellor's Fellowship. We gratefully acknowledge the support of NVIDIA Corporation with the donation of one Titan X Pascal GPU used for this research.

References

Pete Burnap and Matthew L Williams. 2016. Us and Them: Identifying Cyber Hate on Twitter across Multiple Protected Characteristics. *EPJ Data Science* 5(1):11.

Maral Dadvar, Dolf Trieschnigg, Roeland Ordelman, and Franciska de Jong. 2013. Improving cyberbullying detection with user context. In *ECIR*. Springer, pages 693–696.

Karthik Dinakar, Birago Jones, Catherine Havasi, Henry Lieberman, and Rosalind Picard. 2012. Common Sense Reasoning for Detection, Prevention, and Mitigation of Cyberbullying. *ACM Transactions on Interactive Intelligent Systems (TiiS)* 2(3):18.

Aristides Gionis, Piotr Indyk, Rajeev Motwani, et al. 1999. Similarity search in high dimensions via hashing. In *VLDB*. volume 99, pages 518–529.

Sepp Hochreiter and Jürgen Schmidhuber. 1997. Long short-term memory. *Neural computation* 9(8):1735–1780.

Piotr Indyk and Rajeev Motwani. 1998. Approximate nearest neighbors: towards removing the curse of dimensionality. In *Proceedings of the 13th Annual ACM Symposium on Theory of Computing*. ACM, pages 604–613.

Yoon Kim. 2014. Convolutional neural networks for sentence classification. *arXiv preprint arXiv:1408.5882* .

Yang Liu, Chengjie Sun, Lei Lin, and Xiaolong Wang. 2016. Learning natural language inference using bidirectional lstm model and inner-attention. *arXiv preprint arXiv:1605.09090* .

Anna Schmidt and Michael Wiegand. 2017. A Survey on Hate Speech Detection using Natural Language Processing. In *SocialNLP'17: Proceedings of the 5th International Workshop on Natural Language Processing for Social Media*. pages 1–10.

Johan AK Suykens and Joos Vandewalle. 1999. Least squares support vector machine classifiers. *Neural processing letters* 9(3):293–300.

Cynthia Van Hee, Els Lefever, Ben Verhoeven, Julie Mennes, Bart Desmet, Guy De Pauw, Walter Daelemans, and Véronique Hoste. 2015. Detection and Fine-grained Classification of Cyberbullying Events. In *RANLP'15: International Conference Recent Advances in Natural Language Processing*. pages 672–680.

William Warner and Julia Hirschberg. 2012. Detecting Hate Speech on the World Wide Web. In *ACL'12: Proceedings of the 2nd Workshop on Language in*

Social Media. Association for Computational Linguistics, pages 19–26.

Zeerak Waseem and Dirk Hovy. 2016. Hateful Symbols or Hateful People? Predictive Features for Hate Speech Detection on Twitter. In *NAACL Student Research Workshop*. pages 88–93.

Ronald J Williams. 1992. Simple statistical gradient-following algorithms for connectionist reinforcement learning. *Machine learning* 8(3-4):229–256.

Guang Xiang, Bin Fan, Ling Wang, Jason Hong, and Carolyn Rose. 2012. Detecting Offensive Tweets via Topical Feature Discovery over a Large Scale Twitter Corpus. In *CIKM'12: Proceedings of the 21st ACM International Conference on Information and Knowledge Management*. ACM, pages 1980–1984.

Haoti Zhong, Hao Li, Anna Cinzia Squicciarini, Sarah Michele Rajtmajer, Christopher Griffin, David J Miller, and Cornelia Caragea. 2016. Content-Driven Detection of Cyberbullying on the Instagram Social Network. In *IJCAI'16: Proceedings of the 25th International Joint Conference on Artificial Intelligence*. pages 3952–3958.

Peng Zhou, Wei Shi, Jun Tian, Zhenyu Qi, Bingchen Li, Hongwei Hao, and Bo Xu. 2016. Attention-based bidirectional long short-term memory networks for relation classification. In *Proceedings of the 54th Annual Meeting of the Association for Computational Linguistics (Short Papers)*. volume 2, pages 207–212.

Reference-less Measure of Faithfulness for Grammatical Error Correction

Leshem Choshen[1] and Omri Abend[2]
[1] School of Computer Science and Engineering, [2] Department of Cognitive Sciences
The Hebrew University of Jerusalem
`leshem.choshen@mail.huji.ac.il`, `oabend@cs.huji.ac.il`

Abstract

We propose USIM, a semantic measure for Grammatical Error Correction (GEC) that measures the semantic faithfulness of the output to the source, thereby complementing existing reference-less measures (RLMs) for measuring the output's grammaticality. USIM operates by comparing the semantic symbolic structure of the source and the correction, without relying on manually-curated references. Our experiments establish the validity of USIM, by showing that (1) semantic annotation can be consistently applied to ungrammatical text; (2) valid corrections obtain a high USIM similarity score to the source; and (3) invalid corrections obtain a lower score.[1]

1 Introduction

Evaluation in Monolingual Translation, and particularly in Grammatical Error Correction (GEC) is a challenging research field, much due to the difficulty in integrating different types of rewriting operations into a single measure, and the vast number of valid outputs (Tetreault and Chodorow, 2008; Madnani et al., 2011; Chodorow et al., 2012; Bryant and Ng, 2015). These difficulties have recently motivated a number of proposals for new, improved reference-based measures (RBMs) (Dahlmeier and Ng, 2012; Felice and Briscoe, 2015; Napoles et al., 2015).

Nevertheless, the size and heterogeneity of the space of valid outputs per sentence often prohibits obtaining a reference set that covers this space well, thereby limiting the applicability of RBMs (Bryant and Ng, 2015). To address this we propose a semantic RLM, USIM, that operates by measuring the graph distance between the semantic representations of the source and the output. Reliable RLMs are appealing both in not relying on references, which are costly to collect, and in avoiding the biases incurred by selecting references that necessarily cannot exhaust the vast space of valid corrections.

Our proposal complements the RLM proposed by Napoles et al. (2016), which uses grammatical error detection techniques to assess the grammaticality of the output, and the work of Asano et al. (2017), who advocate the use of RLMs for fluency, grammaticality and meaning preservation, but state that a meaning preservation measure for GEC is currently lacking. A similar decomposition of output quality to its adequacy (similar to faithfulness) and fluency (related to grammaticality), has been used in machine translation (MT) evaluation (e.g., Banchs et al., 2015).

As a test case, we use the UCCA semantic scheme (Abend and Rappoport, 2013), motivated by its recent use in semantic evaluation of MT (Birch et al., 2016) and text simplification (Sulem et al., 2018) systems. Nevertheless, USIM can be easily adapted to other semantic schemes, such as AMR (Banarescu et al., 2013). USIM is conceptually related to RLMs developed for MT (Reeder, 2006; Albrecht and Hwa, 2007; Specia et al., 2009, 2010). Notably, XMEANT (Lo et al., 2014) compares the source to the output in terms of their semantic role labeling structures. Our use of UCCA is motivated by its wider coverage of predicate types, as opposed to MEANT's focus on verbal predicates, and UCCA's preservation of structure across translations (Sulem et al., 2015). See (Birch et al., 2016) for further discussion.

We conduct experiments to confirm USIM's validity. Specifically, we show that (1) UCCA can be consistently and automatically applied to learner language (LL) (§4.2), (2) USIM is not prone to unduly penalize valid corrections (§4.2), and (3) USIM assigns a lower score to corrections of poor quality (§4.5). Our experiments also indicate that UCCA parsing technology is already sufficiently mature for an automatic variant of USIM to provide reliable results (§4.3).

2 Background

LL Annotation. While most linguistic theories propose that each learner makes consistent use of syntax (Huebner, 1985; Tarone, 1983), this use may not conform to the syntax of the learned language, or of any other known language. This entails difficulties in defining syntactic annotation for LL, as the annotated syntax differs between learners.

---

[1]Our code is available in `https://github.com/borgr/USim`.

124

Proceedings of NAACL-HLT 2018, pages 124–129
New Orleans, Louisiana, June 1 - 6, 2018. ©2018 Association for Computational Linguistics

Syntactic schemes for LL annotate syntactically erroneous sentences in different ways. Berzak et al. (2016) and Ragheb and Dickinson (2012) annotate according to the syntax used by the learner, even if this use is not grammatical. Such annotation may be unreliable for measuring faithfulness, as GEC systems aim to alter these erroneous syntactic structures. Nagata and Sakaguchi (2016) take the opposite approach, and remain faithful to the syntax intended by the learner. This has also been the tradition in works on parser robustness (Bigert et al., 2005; Foster, 2004). However, such approach is prone to inconsistencies due to the variety of different syntactic structures that can be used to express a similar meaning.

In this paper, we use semantic annotation to structurally represent LL. Semantic structures are faithful to the intended meaning, and not to the formal realization, and thus face fewer conflicts where the syntactic structure used diverges from the one intended. We are not aware of any previous attempts to semantically annotate LL text.

The UCCA Scheme. UCCA is a semantic annotation scheme that builds on typological and cognitive linguistic theories. The scheme's aims are to provide a coarse-grained, cross-linguistically applicable representation. Importantly, UCCA's categories directly reflect semantic, rather than distributional distinctions. For instance, UCCA is not sensitive to POS distinctions: a Scene's main relation can be a verb but also an adjective ("He is **thin**") or a noun ("John's **decision**"). Indeed, Sulem et al. (2015) have found that UCCA structures are preserved remarkably well across English-French translations.

UCCA structures are directed acyclic graphs, where the words correspond to (a subset of) their leaves. The nodes of the graphs, called *units*, are either leaves or several elements jointly viewed as a single entity according to some semantic or cognitive consideration. The edges bear one or more categories, indicating the role of the sub-unit in the relation that the parent represents.

UCCA views the text as a collection of *Scenes* and relations between them. A Scene describes a movement, an action or a state which is persistent in time. Every Scene contains one main relation, zero or more *Participants*, interpreted in a broad sense to include locations, destinations and complement clauses, and *Adverbials*, such as manner or aspectual modifiers.

3 Semantic Faithfulness Measures

We start by defining a simplified measure, used for inter-annotator agreement (IAA). The measure compares two UCCA annotations over the same set of tokens. We then proceed to define USIM, which compares two UCCA structures over alignable but different sets of tokens.

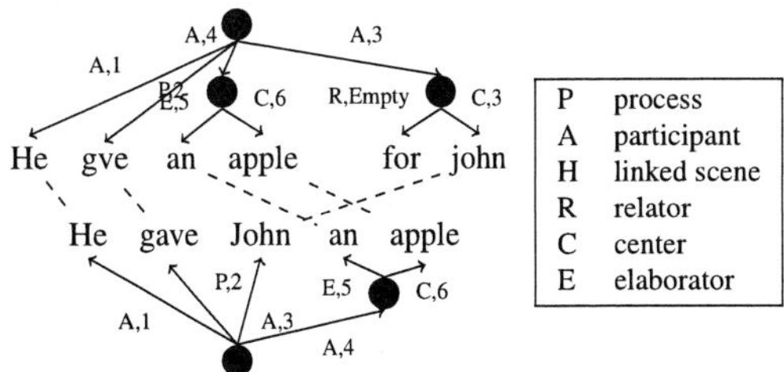

Figure 1: UCCA structures of a learner language (top) and correction (bottom) including word alignments (dashed). On the edges are labels and numbers aligned to (top) or indexes (bottom). Precision is $\frac{7}{9}$ Recall is $\frac{7}{7}$.

IAA Measure. We define a similarity measure over UCCA annotations G_1 and G_2 that share their set of leaves (tokens) W. For a node v in G_1 or G_2, define its yield $yield(v) \subseteq W$ as its set of leaf descendants. Define a pair of edges $(v_1, u_1) \in G_1$ and $(v_2, u_2) \in G_2$ to be matching if $yield(u_1) = yield(u_2)$ and they have the same label. Labeled precision and recall are defined by dividing the number of matching edges in G_1 and G_2 by $|E_1|$ and $|E_2|$ respectively. *DAG F-score* is their harmonic mean. The measure collapses to the common parsing F-score if G_1, G_2 are trees.

The USIM Measure. Computing a faithfulness measure is slightly more involved, as the source sentence graph G_s and its correction G_c do not share the same set of leaves. We assume a (possibly partial, possibly many-to-1) alignment between G_s and G_c, $A \subset V_s \times V_c$.

An edge $(v_1, v_2) \in E_c$ is said to match an edge $(u_1, u_2) \in E_s$ if they have the same label and $(v_2, u_2) \in A$. Recall (Precision) is defined as the ratio of edges in E_s (E_c) that have a match in E_c (E_s) respectively, and F-score is their harmonic mean. We note that this measure collapses to the *DAG F-score* if A includes all pairs of nodes in E_s and E_c that have the same yield. See Figure 1.

In order to define the alignment between V_s and V_c, we begin by aligning the leaves (tokens) in V_s and V_c. Alignment is cast as a weighted bipartite graph matching problem. Edge weights are assigned to be the edit distances between the tokens. We note that aligning words in GEC (and other monolingual translation tasks) is much simpler than in MT, as most of the words are unchanged, deleted fully, added, or changed slightly. Denote the resulting leaf alignment with $A_l \subset Leaves_s \times Leaves_c$. We extend A_l to define the node alignment A, aligning each non-leaf $v \in V_s$ to the node $u \in V_c$ that maximizes

$$w(v, u) = \frac{|A_l \cap (yield(u) \times yield(v))|}{|yield(u)|}.$$

We exclude from A zero-weighted pairs. USIM is defined to be the F-score resulting from A. As the alignment may differ when aligning nodes from V_c to V_s

and the other way around, we report USim in both directions.

USim is somewhat more relaxed than *DAG F-score*, as, unlike DAG *F*-score, it also aligns nodes whose yields are not in perfect alignment with one another. This relaxation is necessary, given that corrections often add or remove nodes, thus eliminating the possibility of a perfect alignment. In order to obtain comparable IAA scores, we report IAA using USim as well.

For completeness, we replicate the protocol used by Sulem et al. (2015) for comparing the UCCA annotations of standard English-French translations, which we call Distributional Similarity (DistSim). For a given UCCA label l, $c_i(l)$ is the number of l-labeled UCCA edges in the i-th source sentence, and $d_i(l)$ is the number of l-labeled UCCA edges in its corresponding correction. We define DistSim(l) between these sentences to be $\frac{1}{N}\sum_{i=1}^{N} |c_i(l) - d_i(l)|$, where N is the total number of sentence pairs.

4 Experiments

We conduct four types of experiments to validate USim, showing that: (1) semantic annotation can be consistently applied to LL through inter-annotator agreement (IAA) experiments; (2) a valid corrector scores high on USim; (3) an automatic UCCA parser can reliably replace human annotation for USim; (4) USim is sensitive to changes in meaning.

4.1 Experimental Setup.

We train two UCCA annotators, the first author and a paid in-house annotator by annotating both LL and standard English passages, until a high enough agreement is reached (6 training hours). Training passages are excluded from the evaluation. We use UCCA's annotation guidelines[2] without any adaptations.

We experiment on 7 essays and their corrections, each comprising about 500 tokens (see supplementary material 1). In order to measure IAA, we assigned 4 of these essays to both annotators. In order to measure the faithfulness score for a valid correction, we annotate both the source and the manually corrected versions of 6 essays, 3 of which were annotated by both annotators.

4.2 The Faithfulness of Valid Corrections.

We obtain an IAA *DAG F-score* of 0.845 (Precision 0.834, Recall 0.857), which is comparable to the IAA reported for English Wikipedia texts by Abend and Rappoport (2013). As another point of comparison, we doubly annotate 3 corrected NUCLE (Dahlmeier et al., 2013) passages, obtaining a similar IAA. These results suggest that UCCA annotating LL does not degrade IAA: it can be applied as consistently to LL as to standard English.

Table 1 (left-hand side) presents the USim scores obtained by comparing the NUCLE references and the

[2]http://www.cs.huji.ac.il/~oabend/ucca.html

	USim			DistSim	
	s→r	r→s	Avg	A+D	Scene
Different	0.85	0.83	0.84	0.96	0.93
Same	0.92	0.91	0.92	0.97	0.96
IAA	0.85	0.81	0.83	-	-
SAR15	-	-	-	0.95	0.96

Table 1: The faithfulness of valid corrections. The left-hand side presents USim, where s→r is the setting where alignment is computed from the source to the reference, r→s is the other way around, and Avg is their average. The right-hand side presents DistSim for the UCCA categories Participants and Adverbials together (A+D), and for Scenes (Scene). Rows indicate whether the same annotator annotated the source and reference or not. For comparison, the IAA row is the IAA computed using USim. Results show that the valid corrector's faithfulness is comparable with IAA. SAR15 are reported by Sulem et al. on English-French translations; similarity is comparable to ours.

source, or equivalently the score of a valid correction. To control for differences between the annotators, we explore both a setting where both sides are annotated by the same annotator, and a setting where they are annotated by different ones. As an upper bound on the score of a valid corrector (using different annotators), we also report the USim IAA on source sentences.

Our results indicate that a valid correction obtains a score comparable to the IAA, which indicates that USim is indeed insensitive to the surface divergence between a source sentence and its valid corrections. Finally, we compute the DistSim measure between the source and reference sentences (Table 1, right-hand side), obtaining similar results to those obtained by Sulem et al. (2015). It suggests that on a coarse grained level, UCCA structures are as robust to grammatical error corrections as they are to translation from English to French, which was shown to be very robust, specifically more robust than syntactic representation (Sulem et al., 2015).

4.3 Automatic USim.

We experiment with an automatic variant of USim, where UCCA structures are parsed automatically. We use the TUPA parser (Hershcovich et al., 2017) to generate UCCA structures, instead of the human annotators. Otherwise the setup is as above. TUPA is used with its biLSTM model, trained on the UCCA English Wikipedia corpus.

We obtain a USim score of 0.7 between the parses of the reference correction and the source, which is comparable to the parser's reported performance (0.73 in-domain, 0.68 out-of-domain), despite not performing any domain adaptation to LL. That is, the UCCA parses of the source and the correction are roughly as similar to each other as they are to their gold standard parse. This supports the hypothesis that semantic parsing technology is sufficiently mature to be applicable to USIM. Results also suggest an improvement in parsing performance may further improve these scores.

4.4 Sensitivity to Error Types

To provide another perspective on automated USIM's behaviour, we examined the measure's sensitivity to different error types, using MAEGE (Choshen and Abend, 2018a). For each NUCLE sentence and set of edits (replacements of sub-strings that contain an error by corrected ones. Such edit for the example in fig. 1 might be $"gva" \rightarrow "gave"$, with type $spelling$), we sample an order in which edits are applied. We select the source randomly to be one of the resulting sentences. We then compare the difference in USIM before and after applying each edit, and average these differences by the applied edit type. We denote the average difference in USIM due to correction of errors of type t with Δ_t. The hypothesis is that Δ_t should be close to 0 for all t, as edits are manual and are thus assumed to be faithful. We focus on edit types with high $|\Delta_t|$ to better understand where USIM fails. See table 2 in the supplementary material for complete results.

We find that among the 5 most penalized error types by USIM are "unclear meaning" and corrections of type "other", that fit no specific type; these corrections may actually change the meaning of the original sentence. In the most penalized and most rewarded changes we see "Dangling Modifier", "Pronoun Reference" and "Word Tone" errors, the first usually changes a word into a more complex structure and the latter two the opposite. Such changes alter the lower levels of the UCCA structure (near the leaves); a similarity measure that focuses on the top of the DAG, or one that performs a better lexical semantic abstraction, may address this sensitivity. Corrections of incorrect word order are also highly rewarded (high Δ_t), probably due to parser performance (the UCCA structures themselves are not affected by word order). Training the parser with LL annotated data may address this sensitivity.

Among the most rewarded changes we also see errors of replacing rare or misconstructed words with proper English words (Acronym and Mechanical errors). We assume this is due to parser performance, as TUPA only extracts features over complete words, and has no character-level encoding at this point. Thus, all misconstructed words fall into an out-of-vocabulary category and can only be labeled by the context.

Lastly, adding a missing verb is shown to be highly rewarded. Under the UCCA guidelines, a missing verb should be annotated as an implicit unit, but as TUPA does not generate implicit units, it is not surprising that when corrections transforms an implicit unit into an explicit word, the parser's output changes (and hence USIM). Future improvements to TUPA may address this.

4.5 Sensitivity to Unfaithfulness.

We have shown that UCCA is insensitive to differences between a source sentence and its valid correction. We now present an evaluation of the sensitivity of USIM to proposed corrections that diverge semantically from the source. A semantic measure is, by its definition, sensitive to variation in the semantic dimensions which it encodes. In UCCA's case, these distinctions focus on predicate-argument structures, the inter-relations between them, and the semantic heads of complex arguments. These distinctions are widely regarded as fundamental in the NLP and linguistic literature.

In order to empirically validate this claim, we present an experiment which shows that corrections of a fairly low quality indeed receive a much lower USIM faithfulness score. Current state-of-the-art systems rarely alter the source sentences enough to yield semantically unfaithful outputs (Choshen and Abend, 2018b). Consequently, their human rankings are not determined by their semantic faithfulness, rendering them unuseful for validating USIM. We instead experiment with 5 partially trained correctors, trained and evaluated on the JFLEG corpus (Napoles et al., 2017) by Sakaguchi et al. (2017).

USIM is computed automatically for each system's output on 754 source sentences. Low faithfulness results are expected, as these outputs include major changes, sometimes deleting full phrases from the output or changing every other word. Indeed, automatic USIM obtains scores of 0.32-0.39 for 4 of the systems, and 0.19 for the system that obtains the lowest GLEU (Napoles et al., 2015) score. For completeness, we run USIM on the 4 references provided by JFLEG for each source and obtain scores of 0.72-0.78, suggesting the domain change is not the reason for the low USIM score.

Taken together, these results indicate that USIM, even in its automatic variant, is sensitive to semantic changes. Consider the example:

Source	the good student must know how to understand and work hard to get the iede.
Reference	A good student must be able to understand and work hard to get the idea.
Corrector	The good student must know how to understand and work hard to get on.

USIM assigns the reference 0.71 and only 0.33 to the corrector. Moreover, although the reference makes more word changes than the proposed correction, it still obtains a higher USIM score.

5 Conclusion

We propose a measure of semantic faithfulness of a correction to the source, thereby avoiding the pitfalls of reference-based evaluation. We believe that using RLMs in conjunction with RBMs in the training and development of GEC systems will better address the challenge of over-conservatism, and the high costs of acquiring many references.

Future work will conduct user studies to assess the relative importance of different evaluation criteria. Specifically, we will explore to what extent users are tolerant to invalid changes to the sentence's structure, i.e., violation of conservatism, relative to their tolerance to invalid changes to the sentence's meaning, i.e., violation of faithfulness. A better understanding of how these interact may lead to improved semantic evaluation that will alleviate the need for a high number of references.

Acknowledgments

This work was partially supported by the Israel Science Foundation (grant No. 929/17), as well as by the HUJI Cyber Security Research Center in conjunction with the Israel National Cyber Bureau in the Prime Minister's Office. We thank Joel Tetreault and Courtney Napoles for helpful feedback and help with obtaining the partially trained GEC system outputs.

References

Omri Abend and Ari Rappoport. 2013. Universal conceptual cognitive annotation (ucca). In *ACL (1)*, pages 228–238.

Joshua Albrecht and Rebecca Hwa. 2007. A re-examination of machine learning approaches for sentence-level mt evaluation. In *Proc. of ACL*, volume 45, pages 880–887.

Hiroki Asano, Tomoya Mizumoto, and Kentaro Inui. 2017. Reference-based metrics can be replaced with reference-less metrics in evaluating grammatical error correction systems. In *Proceedings of the Eighth International Joint Conference on Natural Language Processing (Volume 2: Short Papers)*, volume 2, pages 343–348.

Laura Banarescu, Claire Bonial, Shu Cai, Madalina Georgescu, Kira Griffitt, Ulf Hermjakob, Kevin Knight, Philipp Koehn, Martha Palmer, and Nathan Schneider. 2013. Abstract meaning representation for sembanking. In *Proceedings of the 7th Linguistic Annotation Workshop and Interoperability with Discourse*, pages 178–186, Sofia, Bulgaria. Association for Computational Linguistics.

Rafael E Banchs, Luis F D'Haro, and Haizhou Li. 2015. Adequacy-fluency metrics: Evaluating mt in the continuous space model framework. *IEEE Transactions on Audio, Speech, and Language Processing*, 23(3):472–482.

Yevgeni Berzak, Jessica Kenney, Carolyn Spadine, Jing Xian Wang, Lucia Lam, Keiko Sophie Mori, Sebastian Garza, and Boris Katz. 2016. Universal dependencies for learner english. In *Proceedings of the 54th Annual Meeting of the Association for Computational Linguistics (Volume 1: Long Papers)*, pages 737–746. Association for Computational Linguistics.

Johnny Bigert, Jonas Sjöbergh, Ola Knutsson, and Magnus Sahlgren. 2005. Unsupervised evaluation of parser robustness. In *CICLing*, pages 142–154. Springer.

Alexandra Birch, Omri Abend, Ondřej Bojar, and Barry Haddow. 2016. Hume: Human ucca-based evaluation of machine translation. In *Proceedings of the 2016 Conference on Empirical Methods in Natural Language Processing*, pages 1264–1274.

Christopher Bryant and Hwee Tou Ng. 2015. How far are we from fully automatic high quality grammatical error correction? In *ACL (1)*, pages 697–707.

Martin Chodorow, Markus Dickinson, Ross Israel, and Joel R Tetreault. 2012. Problems in evaluating grammatical error detection systems. In *COLING*, pages 611–628. Citeseer.

Leshem Choshen and Omri Abend. 2018a. Automatic metric validation for grammatical error correction. In *Proceedings of the 56th Annual Meeting of the Association for Computational Linguistics (Volume 1: Long Papers)*.

Leshem Choshen and Omri Abend. 2018b. Inherent biases in reference-based evaluation for grammatical error correction and text simplification. In *Proceedings of the 56th Annual Meeting of the Association for Computational Linguistics (Volume 1: Long Papers)*.

Daniel Dahlmeier and Hwee Tou Ng. 2012. Better evaluation for grammatical error correction. In *Proceedings of the 2012 Conference of the North American Chapter of the Association for Computational Linguistics: Human Language Technologies*, pages 568–572. Association for Computational Linguistics.

Daniel Dahlmeier, Hwee Tou Ng, and Siew Mei Wu. 2013. Building a large annotated corpus of learner english: The nus corpus of learner english. In *Proceedings of the Eighth Workshop on Innovative Use of NLP for Building Educational Applications*, pages 22–31.

Mariano Felice and Ted Briscoe. 2015. Towards a standard evaluation method for grammatical error detection and correction. In *HLT-NAACL*, pages 578–587.

Jennifer Foster. 2004. Parsing ungrammatical input: an evaluation procedure. In *LREC*. Citeseer.

Daniel Hershcovich, Omri Abend, and Ari Rappoport. 2017. A transition-based directed acyclic graph parser for ucca. In *Proceedings of the 55th Annual Meeting of the Association for Computational Linguistics (Volume 1: Long Papers)*, volume 1, pages 1127–1138.

Thorn Huebner. 1985. System and variability in interlanguage syntax. *Language Learning*, 35(2):141–163.

Chi-kiu Lo, Meriem Beloucif, Markus Saers, and Dekai Wu. 2014. Xmeant: Better semantic mt evaluation without reference translations. In *Proceedings of the 52nd Annual Meeting of the Association for Computational Linguistics (Volume 2: Short Papers)*, pages 765–771, Baltimore, Maryland. Association for Computational Linguistics.

Nitin Madnani, Joel Tetreault, Martin Chodorow, and Alla Rozovskaya. 2011. They can help: Using crowdsourcing to improve the evaluation of grammatical error detection systems. In *Proceedings of the 49th Annual Meeting of the Association for Computational Linguistics: Human Language Technologies: short papers-Volume 2*, pages 508–513. Association for Computational Linguistics.

Ryo Nagata and Keisuke Sakaguchi. 2016. Phrase structure annotation and parsing for learner english. In *Proc. of ACL*, pages 1837–1847.

Courtney Napoles, Keisuke Sakaguchi, Matt Post, and Joel Tetreault. 2015. Ground truth for grammatical error correction metrics. In *Proceedings of the 53rd Annual Meeting of the Association for Computational Linguistics and the 7th International Joint Conference on Natural Language Processing*, volume 2, pages 588–593.

Courtney Napoles, Keisuke Sakaguchi, and Joel Tetreault. 2016. There's no comparison: Reference-less evaluation metrics in grammatical error correction. In *Proceedings of the 2016 Conference on Empirical Methods in Natural Language Processing*, pages 2109–2115. Association for Computational Linguistics.

Courtney Napoles, Keisuke Sakaguchi, and Joel Tetreault. 2017. Jfleg: A fluency corpus and benchmark for grammatical error correction. *arXiv preprint arXiv:1702.04066*.

Marwa Ragheb and Markus Dickinson. 2012. Defining syntax for learner language annotation. In *COLING (Posters)*, pages 965–974.

Florence Reeder. 2006. Measuring mt adequacy using latent semantic analysis. In *Proceedings of the 7th Conference of the Association for Machine Translation of the Americas. Cambridge, Massachusetts*, pages 176–184.

Keisuke Sakaguchi, Matt Post, and Benjamin Van Durme. 2017. Grammatical error correction with neural reinforcement learning. *arXiv preprint arXiv:1707.00299*.

Lucia Specia, Dhwaj Raj, and Marco Turchi. 2010. Machine translation evaluation versus quality estimation. *Machine translation*, 24(1):39–50.

Lucia Specia, Marco Turchi, Nicola Cancedda, Marc Dymetman, and Nello Cristianini. 2009. Estimating the sentence-level quality of machine translation systems. In *13th Conference of the European Association for Machine Translation*, pages 28–37.

Elior Sulem, Omri Abend, and Ari Rappoport. 2015. Conceptual annotations preserve structure across translations: A french-english case study. *Proceedings of S2MT 2015*, page 11.

Elior Sulem, Omri Abend, and Ari Rappoport. 2018. Semantic structural annotation for text simplification. In *Proc. of NAACL*. To appear.

Elaine Tarone. 1983. On the variability of interlanguage systems. *Applied linguistics*, 4(2):142–164.

Joel R Tetreault and Martin Chodorow. 2008. Native judgments of non-native usage: Experiments in preposition error detection. In *Proceedings of the Workshop on Human Judgements in Computational Linguistics*, pages 24–32. Association for Computational Linguistics.

Training Structured Prediction Energy Networks
with Indirect Supervision

Amirmohammad Rooshenas, Aishwarya Kamath, Andrew McCallum
College of Information and Computer Sciences
University of Massachusetts Amherst
{pedram,akamath,mccallum}@cs.umass.edu

Abstract

This paper introduces rank-based training of structured prediction energy networks (SPENs). Our method samples from output structures using gradient descent and minimizes the ranking violation of the sampled structures with respect to a scalar scoring function defined using domain knowledge. We have successfully trained SPEN for citation field extraction without any labeled data instances, where the only source of supervision is a simple human-written scoring function. Such scoring functions are often easy to provide; the SPEN then furnishes an efficient structured prediction inference procedure.

1 Introduction

Structured prediction, or the task of predicting multiple inter-dependent variables, is important in many domains, including computer vision, computational biology and natural language processing. For example, in sequence labelling, image segmentation, and parsing we are given input variables $\mathbf{x}$, and must predict output variables $\mathbf{y}$, where the number of possible $\mathbf{y}$ values are typically exponential in the number of variables that comprise it. Not only does this sometimes give rise to computational difficulties, it also leads to statistical parameter estimation issues, where learning precise models requires large amounts of labeled training data.

In some cases, unsupervised learning from plentiful unlabeled data may provide helpful outputs (Daumé III, 2009; Ammar et al., 2014). But usually some form of more direct supervision is required to create a model truly useful to the task at hand. In the absence of abundant labeled data we may consider alternative forms of supervision. For example, rather than providing labeled data instances, humans may more easily inject their domain knowledge by providing "labels on features," or "expectations" about correct outputs, as in generalized expectation criteria (Mann and McCallum, 2010), or by providing constraints, as in posterior regularization (Ganchev et al., 2010) or constraint driven learning (Chang et al., 2007). A major weakness of these methods, however, is that at training time inference must be done in the factor graph encompassing the *union* of the model's factor graph and the expectation dependencies—often leading to prohibitively expensive inference. Moreover, these methods cannot learn from non-decomposable domain knowledge, where the domain knowledge is not in a form of a set of labeled features or constraints.

An easy way for humans to express domain knowledge is by writing a simple scalar scoring function that indicates preferences among choices for $\mathbf{y}$ given $\mathbf{x}$. These human-coded functions may, for example, be based on arbitrary rule systems (or even Turing-complete programs) of the sort written by humans to solve problems before machine learning became so wide-spread.

In general, the human written domain knowledge functions are not expected to be perfect—most likely only examining a subset of features and not covering all cases. Thus we are now faced with two challenges: (1) the domain knowledge functions have limited generalization; (2) the domain knowledge functions provide a ranking, but do not provide an inference (search) procedure.

This paper presents a new training method for structured prediction energy networks (SPENs) (Belanger and McCallum, 2016; Belanger et al., 2017) that aims to address both these challenges, yielding efficient inference for structured prediction, trained from human-coded domain knowledge plus unlabeled data, but not requiring any labeled data instances. In SPENs, the factor graph that typically represents

130

Proceedings of NAACL-HLT 2018, pages 130–135
New Orleans, Louisiana, June 1 - 6, 2018. ©2018 Association for Computational Linguistics

output variable dependencies is replaced with a deep neural network that takes $\mathbf{y}$ and $\mathbf{x}$ as input and outputs a scalar energy score, but is able to learn much richer correlations than are typically captured in factor graphs. Inference in SPENs is performed by gradient descent in the energy, back-propagated to cause steps in a relaxed $\mathbf{y}$ space. Whereas previous training procedures for SPENs used labeled data, here we train SPENs from only unlabeled data plus human-coded domain knowledge in the form of a scoring function. We do so by building on SampleRank (Rohanimanesh et al., 2011; Singh et al., 2010), which enforces that the rank of two sampled $\mathbf{y}$s according to the trained factor graph is consistent with their rank according to distance to the labeled, true $\mathbf{y}$. In our training method, pairs of $\mathbf{y}$'s are obtained from successive steps of training-time gradient-descent inference on $\mathbf{y}$; when their rank is not consistent with that of the domain knowledge function, we accordingly update the energy network parameters.

We demonstrate our method on a citation field extraction task, for which we learn a neural network (1) that generalizes beyond the original domain knowledge function, and (2) that provides efficient test-time inference by gradient descent.

2 Structured Prediction Energy Networks

In general, SPEN parameterizes an energy function $E_{\mathbf{w}}(\mathbf{y}, \mathbf{x})$ using deep neural networks over output variables $\mathbf{y}$ as well as input variables $\mathbf{x}$, where $\mathbf{w}$ denotes the neural network's parameters. Belanger and McCallum (2016) separate the energy function into global and local terms. The role of the local terms is to capture the dependency among input $\mathbf{x}$ and each individual output variable y_i, while the global term aims to capture long-range dependencies among output variables.

Prediction in SPENs requires finding $\hat{\mathbf{y}} = \operatorname{argmin}_{\mathbf{y} \in \mathcal{Y}} E_{\mathbf{w}}(\mathbf{y}, \mathbf{x})$ for the given input $\mathbf{x}$. This inference problem is solved using gradient descent. However, the energy surface is non-convex, which prevents gradient descent inference from finding the exact structure $\mathbf{y}_{min}$ that globally minimizes the energy function. One approach to address this problem is to parameterize the energy function such that the SPEN is convex in the output variables $\mathbf{y}$ (Amos et al., 2017), but this limits the representational power of SPENs. Al-

though gradient descent inference does not guarantee an exact solution, it has successfully been used in several domains such as multi-label classification (Belanger and McCallum, 2016), image-segmentation (Gygli et al., 2017), and semantic role labeling (Belanger et al., 2017).

3 Rank-Based Training of SPENs

Different methods have been introduced for training SPENs: margin-based training (Belanger and McCallum, 2016), end-to-end learning (Belanger et al., 2017), and value matching (Gygli et al., 2017). Margin-based training enforces the energy of the ground truth structure to be lower than the energy of every incorrect structure by a margin, which is calculated as the Hamming loss between the two structures. End-to-end learning unrolls the energy minimization into a differentiable computation graph to output the predicted structure. It then trains the model by directly minimizing the loss between the predicted and ground-truth structures. Finally, the value matching approach trains SPENs such that the energy value matches the value of a given target function, such as the L_2 distance between the ground-truth and predicted structures.

All of these methods strongly depend on the existence of the ground truth values either as labeled data or as the value of a function applied to it. While dependence of the margin-based and end-to-end learning approaches on the labeled data is explicit, this dependency in the case of value-matching may not be obvious. In the absence of labeled data, we have to use the model's predictions instead, for training. These predictions are often incorrect, especially at early stages of training. As a result, value-matching training is constrained to match the score of these predictions with the value of the energy function defined by SPEN. This requires matching several incorrect structures for a given input, which hinders gradient descent inference from finding the exact solution by introducing many local optima. To address this problem, we use a ranking objective similar to SampleRank (Rohanimanesh et al., 2011) such that it preserves the optimum points of the score function.

In general, if SPEN ranks every pair of output structures identical to the score function, the optimum points of the score function match those of SPEN. However, forcing the ranking constraint for every pair of output structures is not tractable, so we need to approximate it by sampling some candidate pairs. Given a score function $V(\mathbf{y}, \mathbf{x})$, we are able to rank every two consecutive candidate structures based on their score values. Consider two candidate output structures $\mathbf{y}_1$ and $\mathbf{y}_2$ for the given input $\mathbf{x}$. We define $\mathbf{y}_h$ and $\mathbf{y}_l$ based on the score function as the following:

$$\mathbf{y}_h = \underset{\mathbf{y} \in \{\mathbf{y}_1, \mathbf{y}_2\}}{\mathrm{argmax}}\ V(\mathbf{y}, \mathbf{x}),$$

$$\mathbf{y}_l = \underset{\mathbf{y} \in \{\mathbf{y}_1, \mathbf{y}_2\}}{\mathrm{argmin}}\ V(\mathbf{y}, \mathbf{x}). \tag{1}$$

We expect that these two structures have the same ranking with respect to $E_{\mathbf{w}}(., \mathbf{x})$, which can be described as: $\alpha(V(\mathbf{y}_h, \mathbf{x}) - V(\mathbf{y}_l, \mathbf{x})) < E_{\mathbf{w}}(\mathbf{y}_h, \mathbf{x}) - E_{\mathbf{w}}(\mathbf{y}_l, \mathbf{x})$, where α is a tunable positive scalar. Therefore, the rank-based objective minimizes the constraint violations:

$$\min_{\mathbf{w}} \sum_{\mathbf{x} \in \mathcal{D}} [\alpha(V(\mathbf{y}_h, \mathbf{x}) - V(\mathbf{y}_l, \mathbf{x})) -$$
$$E_{\mathbf{w}}(\mathbf{y}_h, \mathbf{x}) + E_{\mathbf{w}}(\mathbf{y}_l, \mathbf{x})]_+ \tag{2}$$

$[.]_+$ is $max(., 0)$. Figure 1 shows a ranking violation for two structures $\mathbf{y}_1$ and $\mathbf{y}_2$ for a given $\mathbf{x}$. The arrows indicate the direction of update over the energy surface. Note that we ignore the dependence of $\mathbf{y}$ on $\mathbf{w}$, which introduces approximation in the gradient of Eq. 2. For the supervised setting, Belanger et al. (2017) address this problem by unrolling the inference steps as an inference network and back-propagating through the inference network. We leave exploring similar approaches for rank-based training for future work. To compute Eq. 2, we need to find configurations $\mathbf{y}_i$ and $\mathbf{y}_j$ such that both are candidate solutions for $\mathrm{argmin}_{\mathbf{y} \in \mathcal{Y}} E_{\mathbf{w}}(\mathbf{y}, \mathbf{x})$. If not, the number of required samples would be exponential in $|\mathcal{Y}|$. Since at test time we use gradient descent inference, a similar method is used for generating candidate structures: the trajectory of points in the inference mechanism is used as the set of possible candidates. The idea of deterministic sampling from SPEN energy surface was first introduced by David Belanger (2017). We define the inference trajectory, $\mathcal{T}(\mathbf{x})$, as a sequence of output structures generated using projected gradient descent inference in order to find the minimum solution of $E_{\mathbf{w}}(., \mathbf{x})$.

Given a random initial structure $\mathbf{y}_0$, we define the inference trajectory as: $\mathcal{T}(\mathbf{x}) =$

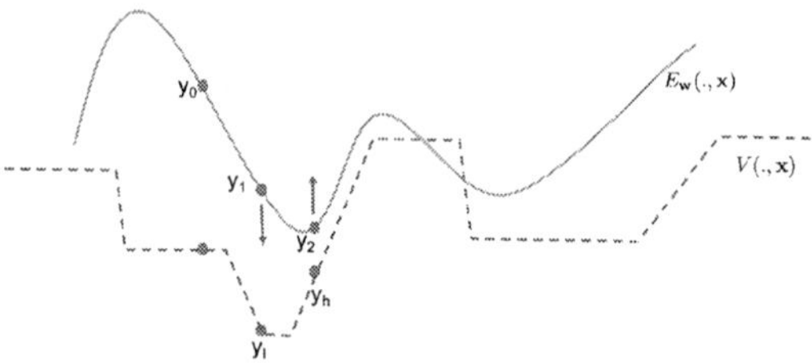

Figure 1: Schematic machinery of rank-based training. The dashed line is the surface of score function $V(., \mathbf{x})$ and the solid line is the surface of SPEN $E(., \mathbf{x})$, both conditioned on input $\mathbf{x}$. Here, $\mathbf{y}_2$ and $\mathbf{y}_3$ violate the ranking constraint, and the arrows show the direction of updates on the energy surface.

$\{\mathbf{y}_1, \cdots, \mathbf{y}_m\}$, where $\mathbf{y}_{t+1} = \mathcal{P}_{\mathbf{y} \in \Delta_L}(\mathbf{y}_t - \eta \frac{\partial}{\partial \mathbf{y}} E_{\mathbf{w}}(\mathbf{y}_t, \mathbf{x}))$. $\mathcal{P}_{\mathbf{y} \in \Delta_L}$ projects the values of $\mathbf{y}$ onto the probability simplex Δ_L over L values that each variable y can take. For each input $\mathbf{x}$ in the training data, we find the first consecutive structures $\mathbf{y}_i$, $\mathbf{y}_{i+1} \in \mathcal{T}(\mathbf{x})$ that violate the ranking constraint, then use Eq. 2 to reduce the number of violations. Algorithm 1 describes the complete training algorithm.

Algorithm 1 Rank-based training of SPEN

$\mathcal{D} \leftarrow$ unlabeled mini-batch of training data
$V(., .) \leftarrow$ scoring function
$E_{\mathbf{w}}(., .) \leftarrow$ input SPEN
for each $\mathbf{x}$ in $\mathcal{D}$ **do**
    $\mathcal{T}(\mathbf{x}) \leftarrow$ samples using GD inference in $E_{\mathbf{w}}(., \mathbf{x})$.
    $\xi \leftarrow \emptyset$.
    for each pair $(\mathbf{y}_i, \mathbf{y}_{i+1})$ in $\mathcal{T}(\mathbf{x})$ **do**
        Construct $\mathbf{y}_h$ and $\mathbf{y}_l$ using Eq.1
        if $\alpha(V(\mathbf{y}_h, \mathbf{x}) - V(\mathbf{y}_l, \mathbf{x})) > E_{\mathbf{w}}(\mathbf{y}_h, \mathbf{x}) - E_{\mathbf{w}}(\mathbf{y}_l, \mathbf{x})$ **then**
            $\xi \leftarrow \xi \cup (\mathbf{x}, \mathbf{y}_h, \mathbf{y}_l)$.
        end if
    end for
    Optimize Eq.2 using ξ.
end for

---

4 Citation Field Extraction

To show the success of rank-based learning with indirect supervision, we conduct experiments on citation field extraction as an instance of structured prediction problems. The goal of citation field extraction is to segment citation text into its constituent parts such as Author, Title, Journal, Page, and Date. We used the Cora citation dataset (Seymore et al., 1999), which includes 100 labeled examples as the test set and another 100 labeled examples for the validation set. Our training data consists of 300 training examples from the Cora citation data set for which we dismiss the labels, as well as another 700 unlabeled citations acquired across the web, which adds up to 1000 unlabeled data points. Each token can be labeled with one of 13 possible tags. We use fixed-length input data by padding all citation text to the maximum citation length in the dataset, which is 118 tokens. We report token-level accuracy measured on non-pad tokens.

We provide the learning algorithm with a human written score function that takes the citation text and predicted tags as input. The score function then checks for violations of its rules and penalizes the predicted tags accordingly. Figure 2 shows examples of rules in the score function. Our complete score function consists of around 50 rules.

We used two 2-layer neural networks with 1000 and 500 hidden nodes to parameterize the local and global energy functions of SPEN. We examine different α (Eq. 2) values of 0.1, 1.0, 2.0, 5.0, and 10.0, and setting α value to 2.0 has the best performance on the validation set. We use gradient descent inference with ten gradient descent steps and $\eta = 0.1$ for both training and test.

We include the results of generalized expectation (GE) from Mann and McCallum (2010) that use the same dataset and setting. Our results show that R-SPEN achieves significantly better token-level accuracy as compared to GE.

We also compare R-SPEN with different inference algorithms that search using the score function to find the best configuration with maximum score. The results of these are listed in Table 1. Greedy search first randomly initializes the output tags and then iteratively replaces each assigned tag with a tag that results in the maximum score until the end of the citation is reached. This process is repeated until convergence, measured by no tag changing in an iteration. To avoid the effects of random initialization, this is repeated with varied number of random restarts, as reported in Table 1, where the best configuration is used in the scores reported. For the baseline that implements beam search, each citation is labeled by employing a beam search on the space of all tags for each token and their subsequent configurations, while keeping track of the best k configurations from one token to the next. This search is further augmented by restarting the search from the best k found after one complete search, for a total of 10 times and 10 random restarts.

```
score <- Contains the score of each example
first_seen <- Contains the index of
          the first appearance of each tag
j <- Index of the current token
i <- Index of the current example

# Parantheses have the same tag of what comes inside
if j > 0 and last_token == '(' or current_token == ')':
   if tags[j] != tags[j-1]:
     score[i] -= 1

# Period takes that tag of its predecessor
if j > 0 and current_token == '.':
   if j > 0 and tags[j] != tags[j-1]:
     score[i] -= 1

# Only one of the booktitle, journal,
#     or techinical report can appear
if first_seen[booktitle_tag] >= 0 :
   if first_seen[journal_tag] >= 0
       or first_seen[technical_report_tag] >= 0:
     score[i] -= 1

if first_seen[journal_tag] >= 0:
   if first_seen[booktitle_tag] >= 0
       or first_seen[technical_report_tag] >= 0:
     score[i] -= 1

if first_seen[techincal_report_tag] >= 0:
   if first_seen[booktitle_tag] >= 0
       or first_seen[journal_tag] >= 0:
     score[i] -= 1
```

Figure 2: Examples of rules in the score function. The first two rules constrain the relation of token and tags, while the last rule targets the relationship between tags.

Consulting Table 1, we can confirm that both greedy search and beam search find much better output structures in term of score values as compared to R-SPEN; however, they achieve poor accuracy because the domain knowledge function does not comprehensively provide rules regarding all possible output structures. We report the average score values of the R-SPEN predictions on test data as a function of training iterations in Figure 3. Within 1000 iterations, R-SPEN is able to achieve a test set accuracy of 38%, outperforming all baselines, while the average score is -18.0. R-SPEN generalizes beyond the domain knowledge function because it successfully captures the correlation among output variables through rank-based training on unlabeled data, so its predictions may have lower score values but are more accurate.

The test time inference of R-SPEN is much faster than search algorithms because SPEN provides efficient approximate inference.

5 Related Work

Generalized Expectation (GE) (Mann and McCallum, 2010), Posterior Regularization (Ganchev et al., 2010) and Constraint Driven Learning (Chang et al., 2007) are among well-known approaches to learn from domain knowledge decomposed over a set of constraints or labeled features. However, these methods cannot learn from black box domain knowledge based score functions. Score functions of this type are abundant in

Table 1: Comparison of R-SPEN with GE and different search algorithms in terms of token-level accuracy, test set average score, and time taken for inference during test time.

Method	Acc.	Avg. Score	Time (s)
GE	37.3%	N/A	—
Greedy Search			
10 restarts	22.6%	-4.92	700
100 restarts	26.0%	-3.26	6997
1000 restarts	26.1%	-2.51	69272
Beam Search			
k=2	30.0%	-1.87	4953
k=5	30.4%	-1.80	12217
k=10	31.0%	-1.44	22898
R-SPEN	47.1%	-20.33	<1

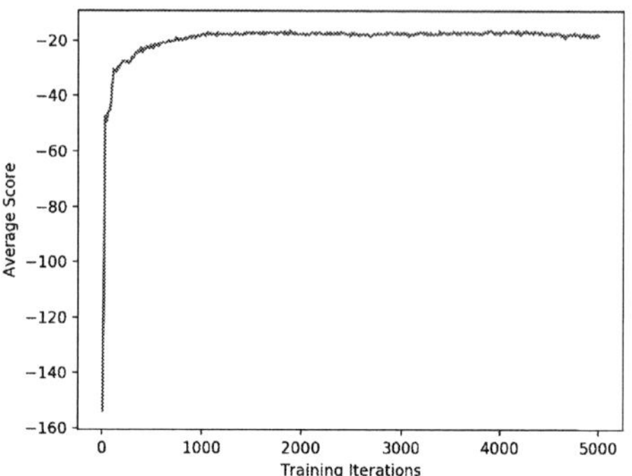

Figure 3: Average test set score values during training of R-SPEN.

various fields, for example, when the score is the result of evaluating a non-differentiable function over output structures.

Stewart and Ermon (2017) train a neural network using a score function that guides the training based on physics of moving objects. They have defined a differentiable score function which provides the learning algorithm with the gradient of the score function. However, in our approach the score function could be any complex non-differentiable function.

Peng et al. (2017) and Iyyer et al. (2017) use energy-based max-margin training for learning from an implicit source of supervision. This can be viewed as a score function evaluating the predicted output structure based on some real-world domain. For example, if the output structure is the SQL query associated with a natural language question, the score function can be specified as the Jaccard similarity of the extracted cells from the table using the generated SQL query and the set of gold answers for the natural language query as in Iyyer et al (2017).

6 Conclusion and Future Work

We have introduced a method to train structured prediction energy networks with indirect supervision that is derived from domain knowledge. This domain knowledge is a scalar function that is represented in the form of certain set of rules, easily provided by humans. By using a rank-based training we are able to effectively generalize beyond the domain knowledge function in problem instances where we do not have access to labeled data, thus establishing a viable option for solving structured prediction problems in those regimes.

R-SPEN only uses unlabeled data and domain knowledge for training. We should also effectively benefit from annotated data if any is available for the task. This can be accomplished by augmenting the domain knowledge with rules that take into account the distance between predicted and ground truth labels.

In the future, we wish to explore the effectiveness of R-SPEN on various tasks using domain knowledge functions with varying degrees of complexity.

Acknowledgments

This research was funded by DARPA grant FA8750-17-C-0106. The views and conclusions contained in this document are those of the authors and should not be interpreted as necessarily representing the official policies, either expressed or implied, of DARPA or the U.S. Government.

References

Waleed Ammar, Chris Dyer, and Noah A Smith. 2014. Conditional random field autoencoders for unsupervised structured prediction. In *Advances in Neural Information Processing Systems*, pages 3311–3319.

Brandon Amos, Lei Xu, and J Zico Kolter. 2017. Input convex neural networks. In *Proceedings of the International Conference on Machine Learning*.

David Belanger. 2017. Deep energy-based models for structured prediction. *Ph.D. Dissertation*.

David Belanger and Andrew McCallum. 2016. Structured prediction energy networks. In *Proceedings of the International Conference on Machine Learning*.

David Belanger, Bishan Yang, and Andrew McCallum. 2017. End-to-end learning for structured prediction energy networks. In *Proceedings of the International Conference on Machine Learning*.

Ming-Wei Chang, Lev Ratinov, and Dan Roth. 2007. Guiding semi-supervision with constraint-driven learning. In *ACL*, pages 280–287.

Hal Daumé III. 2009. Unsupervised search-based structured prediction. In *Proceedings of the International Conference on Machine Learning*, pages 209–216.

Kuzman Ganchev, Jennifer Gillenwater, Ben Taskar, et al. 2010. Posterior regularization for structured latent variable models. *Journal of Machine Learning Research*, 11(Jul):2001–2049.

Michael Gygli, Mohammad Norouzi, and Anelia Angelova. 2017. Deep value networks learn to evaluate and iteratively refine structured outputs. In *Proceedings of the International Conference on Machine Learning*.

Mohit Iyyer, Wen-tau Yih, and Ming-Wei Chang. 2017. Search-based neural structured learning for sequential question answering. In *Proceedings of the 55th Annual Meeting of the Association for Computational Linguistics (Volume 1: Long Papers)*, volume 1, pages 1821–1831.

Gideon S Mann and Andrew McCallum. 2010. Generalized expectation criteria for semi-supervised learning with weakly labeled data. *Journal of machine learning research*, 11(Feb):955–984.

Haoruo Peng, Ming-Wei Chang, and Wen-tau Yih. 2017. Maximum margin reward networks for learning from explicit and implicit supervision. In *Proceedings of the 2017 Conference on Empirical Methods in Natural Language Processing*, pages 2368–2378.

Khashayar Rohanimanesh, Kedar Bellare, Aron Culotta, Andrew McCallum, and Michael L Wick. 2011. Samplerank: Training factor graphs with atomic gradients. In *Proceedings of the International Conference on Machine Learning*, pages 777–784.

Kristie Seymore, Andrew McCallum, and Roni Rosenfeld. 1999. Learning hidden markov model structure for information extraction. In *AAAI-99 workshop on machine learning for information extraction*, pages 37–42.

Sameer Singh, Limin Yao, Sebastian Riedel, and Andrew McCallum. 2010. Constraint-driven rank-based learning for information extraction. In *Human Language Technologies: The 2010 Annual Conference of the North American Chapter of the Association for Computational Linguistics*, pages 729–732. Association for Computational Linguistics.

Russell Stewart and Stefano Ermon. 2017. Label-free supervision of neural networks with physics and domain knowledge. In *AAAI*, pages 2576–2582.

Sí o no, ¿què penses?
Catalonian Independence and Linguistic Identity on Social Media

Ian Stewart[*] and Yuval Pinter[*] and Jacob Eisenstein
School of Interactive Computing
Georgia Institute of Technology
Atlanta, GA, USA
{istewart6, uvp, jacobe}@gatech.edu

Abstract

Political identity is often manifested in language variation, but the relationship between the two is still relatively unexplored from a quantitative perspective. This study examines the use of Catalan, a language local to the semi-autonomous region of Catalonia in Spain, on Twitter in discourse related to the 2017 independence referendum. We corroborate prior findings that pro-independence tweets are more likely to include the local language than anti-independence tweets. We also find that Catalan is used more often in referendum-related discourse than in other contexts, contrary to prior findings on language variation. This suggests a strong role for the Catalan language in the expression of Catalonian political identity.

1 Introduction

Social identity is often constructed through language use, and variation in language therefore reflects social differences within the population (Labov, 1963). In a multilingual setting, an individual's preference to use a local language rather than the national one may reflect their political stance, as the local language can have strong ties to cultural and political identity (Moreno et al., 1998; Crameri, 2017). The role of linguistic identity is enhanced in extreme situations such as referenda, where the voting decision may be driven by identification with a local culture or language (Schmid, 2001).

In October 2017, the semi-autonomous region of Catalonia held a referendum on independence from Spain, where 92% of respondents voted for independence (Fotheringham, 2017). To determine the role of the local language Catalan in

this setting, we apply the methodology used by Shoemark et al. (2017) in the context of the 2014 Scottish independence referendum to a dataset of tweets related to the Catalonian referendum. We use the phenomenon of *code-switching* between Catalan and Spanish to pursue the following research questions in order to understand the choice of language in the context of the referendum:

1. Is a speaker's stance on independence strongly associated with the rate at which they use Catalan?

2. Does Catalan usage vary depending on whether the discussion topic is related to the referendum, and on the intended audience?

For the first question, our findings are similar to those in the Scottish case: pro-independence tweets are more likely to be written in Catalan than anti-independence tweets, and pro-independence Twitter users are more likely to use Catalan than anti-independence Twitter users (Section 4). With respect to the second question, we find that Twitter users are more likely to use Catalan in referendum-related tweets, and that they are more likely to use Catalan in tweets with a broader audience (Section 5).[1]

2 Related work

Code-switching, the alternation between languages within conversation (Poplack, 1980), has been shown to be the product of grammatical factors, such as syntax (Pfaff, 1979), and social factors, such as intended audience (Gumperz,

---

[*]Equal contributions.

[1]Code for collecting data and rerunning the experiments is available at `https://github.com/ianbstewart/catalan`.

Proceedings of NAACL-HLT 2018, pages 136–141
New Orleans, Louisiana, June 1 - 6, 2018. ©2018 Association for Computational Linguistics

Neutral	#1O (748), #1Oct (1351), #1Oct2017 (171), #1Oct2017votarem (28), #CatalanRef2017 (46), #CatalanReferendum (3244), #CatalanReferendum2017 (72), #JoVoto (54), #Ref1oct (90), #Referéndum (640), #Referendum1deoctubre (146), #ReferendumCAT (457), #Referendum-Catalan (298), #Votarem (954)
Pro-independence	#1ONoTincPor (18), #1octL6 (184), #CataloniaIsNotSpain (10), #CATvotaSí (3), #CataluñaLibre (27), #FreePiolin (293), #Freedom4Catalonia (2), #IndependenciaCataluña (9), #LetCatalansVote (3), #Marxem (102), #RepúblicaCatalana (212), #Spainispain (8), #SpanishDictatorship (9), #SpanishRepression (3), #TotsSomCatalunya (261)
Anti-independence	#CataluñaEsEspaña (69), #DontDUIt (12), #EspanaNoSeRompe (29), #EspañaUnida (4), #OrgullososDeSerEspañoles (55), #PorLaUnidadDeEspaña (2), #ProuPuigdemont (187)

Table 1: Hashtags related to the Catalonian referendum, their stances (neutral/pro/anti) and their frequencies in the CT dataset.

1977). While many studies have examined code-switching in the spoken context (Auer, 2013), social media platforms such as Twitter provide an opportunity to study code-switching in online discussions (Androutsopoulos, 2015). In the online context, choice of language may reflect the writer's intended audience (Kim et al., 2014) or identity (Christiansen, 2015; Lavendar, 2017), and the explicit social signals in online discussions such as @-replies can be leveraged to test claims about code-switching at a large scale (Nguyen et al., 2015).

A relatively unexplored area of code-switching behavior is politically-motivated code-switching, which we assume has a different set of constraints compared to everyday code-switching. With respect to political separatism, Shoemark et al. (2017) studied the use of Scots, a language local to Scotland, in the context of the 2014 Scotland independence referendum. They found that Twitter users who openly supported Scottish independence were more likely to incorporate words from Scots in their tweets. They also found that Twitter users who tweeted about the referendum were less likely to use Scots in referendum-related tweets than in non-referendum tweets.

This study considers the similar scenario which took place in 2017 vis-à-vis the semi-autonomous region of Catalonia. Our main methodological divergence from Shoemark et al. (2017) relates to the linguistic phenomenon at hand: while Scots is mainly manifested as interleaving individual words within English text (code-mixing), Catalan is a distinct language which, when used, usually replaces Spanish altogether for the entire tweet (code-switching).

3 Data

The initial set of tweets for this study, $\mathcal{T}$, was drawn from a 1% Twitter sample mined between January 1 and October 31, 2017, covering nearly a year of activity before the referendum, as well as its immediate aftermath.[2]

The first step in building this dataset was to manually develop a seed set of hashtags related to the referendum. Through browsing referendum content on Twitter, the following seed hashtags were selected: *#CataluñaLibre, #IndependenciaCataluña, #CataluñaEsEspaña, #EspañaUnida,* and *#CatalanReferendum.* All tweets containing at least one of these hashtags were extracted from $\mathcal{T}$, and the top 1,000 hashtags appearing in the resulting dataset were manually inspected for relevance to the referendum. From these co-occurring hashtags, we selected a set of 46 hashtags and divided it into pro-independence, anti-independence, and neutral hashtags, based on translations of associated tweet content.[3] After including ASCII-equivalent variants of special characters, as well as lowercased variants, our final hashtag set comprises 111 unique strings.

Next, all tweets containing any referendum hashtag were extracted from $\mathcal{T}$, yielding 190,061 tweets. After removing retweets and tweets from users whose tweets frequently contained URLs (i.e., likely bots), our final "Catalonian Independence Tweets" (CT) dataset is made up of 11,670 tweets from 10,498 users (cf. the Scottish referendum set IT with 59,664 tweets and 18,589 users in Shoemark et al. (2017)). 36 referendum-related hashtags appear in the filtered dataset. They are shown with their frequencies (including variants) in Table 1 (cf. the 47 hashtags and similar frequency distribution in Table 1 of Shoemark et al. (2017)).

To address the control condition, all authors of

---

[2]A preliminary check of our data revealed that the earliest referendum discussions began in January, 2017.

[3]Authors have a reading knowledge of Spanish. For edge cases we consulted news articles relating to the hashtag.

tweets in the CT dataset were collected to form a set $\mathcal{U}$, and all other tweets in $\mathcal{T}$ written by these users were extracted into a control dataset (XT) of 45,222 tweets (cf. the 693,815 control tweets in Table 6 of Shoemark et al. (2017)).

The CT dataset is very balanced with respect to the number of tweets per user: only four users contribute over ten tweets (max = 14) and only 16 have more than five. The XT dataset also has only a few "power" users, such that nine users have over 1,000 tweets (max = 3,581) and a total of 173 have over 100 tweets. Since the results are macro-averaged over all users, these few power users should not significantly distort the findings.

Language Identification. This study compares variation between two distinct languages, Catalan and Spanish. We used the *langid* language classification package (Lui and Baldwin, 2012), based on character n-gram frequencies, to identify the language of all tweets in CT and XT. Tweets that were not classified as either Spanish or Catalan with at least 90% confidence were discarded. This threshold was chosen by manual inspection of the *langid* output. In the referendum dataset CT (control set XT), *langid* confidently labeled 4,014 (56,892) tweets as Spanish and 2,366 (10,178) as Catalan. To address the possibility of code-mixing within tweets, the first two authors manually annotated a sample of 100 tweets, of which half were confidently labeled as Spanish, and the other half as Catalan. They found only two examples of potential code-mixing, both of Catalan words in Spanish text.

4 Catalan Usage and Political Stance

The first research question concerns political stance: do pro-independence users tweet in Catalan at a higher rate than anti-independence users?

We analyze the relationship between language use and stance on independence under two conditions, comparing the use of Catalan among pro-independence users vs. anti-independence users in (1) opinionated referendum-related tweets (tweets with Pro/Anti hashtags); and (2) all tweets. These conditions address the possibilities that the language distinction is relevant for pro/anti-independence Twitter users in political discourse and outside of political discourse, respectively.

Method. The first step is to divide the Twitter users in $\mathcal{U}$ into pro-independence (*PRO*) and anti-

	Tweets with Pro/Anti hashtags		All tweets	
Group	*PRO*	*ANTI*	*PRO*	*ANTI*
# Users	713	242	1,011	312
# Tweets	858	288	44,229	22,841

Table 2: Tweet and user counts for the stance study.

	Tweets with Pro/Anti hashtags	All tweets
$\hat{p}_{pro}$	0.3136	0.2772
$\hat{p}_{anti}$	0.0613	0.0586
d	0.2523	0.2186
p-value	$< 10^{-5}$	$< 10^{-5}$

Table 3: Results of the stance study. $d = \hat{p}_{pro} - \hat{p}_{anti}$.

independence (*ANTI*) groups. First, the proportion of tweets from each user that include a pro-independence hashtag is computed as $\frac{N_{pro}^{(u)}}{N_{pro}^{(u)}+N_{anti}^{(u)}}$, where $N_{pro}^{(u)}$ ($N_{anti}^{(u)}$) is the count of tweets from user u that contain a pro- (anti-) independence hashtag. The *PRO* user set ($\mathcal{U}_{pro}$) includes all users whose pro-independence proportion was above or equal to 75%, and the *ANTI* user set ($\mathcal{U}_{anti}$) includes all users whose pro-independence proportion was below or equal to 25%. The counts of users and tweets identified as either Spanish or Catalan are presented in Table 2.

To measure Catalan usage, let $n_{CA}^{(u)}$ and $n_{ES}^{(u)}$ denote the counts of Catalan and Spanish tweets user u posted, respectively. We quantify Catalan usage using the proportion $\hat{p}^{(u)} = \frac{n_{CA}^{(u)}}{n_{CA}^{(u)}+n_{ES}^{(u)}}$, computing the macro-average over each group $\mathcal{U}_G$'s members to produce $\hat{p}_G = \frac{1}{|\mathcal{U}_G|} \sum_{u \in \mathcal{U}_G} \hat{p}^{(u)}$. The test statistic is then the difference in Catalan usage between the pro- and anti-independence groups, $d = \hat{p}_{pro} - \hat{p}_{anti}$.

To determine significance, the users are randomly shuffled between the two groups to recompute d over 100,000 iterations. The p-value is the proportion of permutations in which the randomized test statistic was greater than or equal to the original test statistic from the unpermuted data.

Results. Catalan is used more often among the pro-independence users compared to the anti-independence users, across both the hashtag-only and all-tweet conditions. Table 3 shows that the proportion of tweets in Catalan for pro-independence users ($\hat{p}_{pro}$) is significantly higher than the proportion for anti-independence users

($\hat{p}_{anti}$). This is consistent with Shoemark et al. (2017), who found more Scots usage among pro-independence users ($d = 0.00555$ for pro/anti tweets, $d = 0.00709$ for all tweets). The relative differences between the groups are large: in the all-tweet condition, $\hat{p}_{pro}$ is five times greater than $\hat{p}_{anti}$, whereas Shoemark et al. found a twofold difference ($\hat{p}_{pro} = 0.01443$ versus $\hat{p}_{anti} = 0.00734$ for all-tweet condition). All raw proportions are two orders of magnitude greater than those in the Scottish study, a result of the denser language variable used in this study (full-tweet code-switching vs. intermittent code-mixing).

5 Catalan Usage, Topic, and Audience

One way to explain the variability in Catalan usage is through *topic-induced variation*, which proposes that people adapt their language style in response to a shift in topic (Rickford and McNair-Knox, 1994). This leads to our second research question: is Catalan more likely to be used in discussions of the referendum than in other topics? This analysis is conducted under three conditions. The first two conditions compare Catalan usage in referendum-hashtag tweets (pro, anti, and neutral) against (1) all tweets; and (2) tweets that contain a non-referendum hashtag. This second condition is meant to control for the general role of hashtags in reaching a wider audience (Pavalanathan and Eisenstein, 2015), and its results motivate the third analysis, comparing (3) @-reply tweets with hashtag tweets.

5.1 Referendum Hashtags

Method. We extract all users in $\mathcal{U}$ who have posted at least one referendum-related tweet and at least one tweet unrelated to the referendum into a new set, $\mathcal{U}_R$. Tweet and user counts for all conditions are provided in Table 4. The small numbers are a result of the condition require-ment and the language constraint (tweets must be identified as Spanish or Catalan with 90% con-fidence). For a user u, we denote the propor-tion of u's referendum-related tweets written in Catalan by $\hat{p}_C^{(u)}$, and the proportion of u's control tweets written in Catalan by $\hat{p}_X^{(u)}$. We are inter-ested in the difference between these two propor-tions $d^{(u)} = \hat{p}_C^{(u)} - \hat{p}_X^{(u)}$ and its average across all users $\bar{d}_{\mathcal{U}_R} = \frac{1}{|\mathcal{U}_R|} \sum_{u \in \mathcal{U}_R} d^{(u)}$. Under the null hy-pothesis that Catalan usage is unrelated to topic, $\bar{d}_{\mathcal{U}_R}$ would be equal to 0, which we test for signif-

Treatment set Control set	Ref. hash All tweets	Ref. hash All hash	Replies All hash
Users	772	548	654
Treatment tweets	887	656	6225
Control tweets	31,151	13,954	10,319

Table 4: Tweet and user counts for each condition in the topic/audience study. 'hash' stands for 'tweets with hashtags'.

Treatment set Control set	Ref. hash All tweets	Ref. hash All hash	Replies All hash
$\bar{d}_{\mathcal{U}_R}$	0.033	0.018	-0.031
Standard error	0.011	0.011	0.011
t-statistic	3.02	1.59	-2.79
p-value	0.002	0.111	0.005

Table 5: Results of the topic/audience study. $\bar{d}_{\mathcal{U}_R}$ is the difference in rate of Catalan use between treatment settings and control settings, averaged across users.

icance using a one-sample t-test.

Results. Our results, presented in the middle columns of Table 5, show that users tweet in Catalan at a significantly higher rate in referen-dum tweets than in all control tweets (first re-sults column), but no significant difference was observed in the control condition where tweets include at least one hashtag (second results col-umn). The lack of a significant difference between referendum-related hashtags and other hashtags suggests that the topic being discussed is not as central in choosing one's language, compared with the audience being targeted.

Our second result is the opposite of the prior finding that there were significantly *fewer* Scots words in referendum-related tweets than in con-trol tweets (cf. Table 7 in Shoemark et al. (2017); $\bar{d}_u = -0.0015$ for all controls). This suggests that Catalan may serve a different function than Scots in terms of political identity expression. Rather than suppressing their use of Catalan in broadcast tweets, users increase their Catalan use, perhaps to signal their Catalonian identity to a broader au-dience. This is supported by literature highlight-ing the integral role Catalan plays in the Catalo-nian national narrative (Crameri, 2017), as well as the relatively high proportion of Catalan speakers in Catalonia: 80.4% of the population has speak-ing knowledge of Catalan (Government of Cat-alonia, 2013), versus 30% population of Scotland with speaking knowledge of Scots (Scots Lan-guage Centre, 2011). There are also systemic differences between the political settings of the two cases: the Catalonian referendum had much larger support for separation among those who voted (92% in Catalonia vs. 45% in Scotland) (Fotheringham, 2017; Jeavens, 2014). These factors suggest a different public perception of national identity in the two regions within the context of the referenda, resulting in different motivations behind language choice.

5.2 Reply Tweets

Earlier work has highlighted the role of hashtags and @-replies as affordances for selecting large and small audiences, and their interaction with the use of non-standard vocabulary (Pavalanathan and Eisenstein, 2015). To test the role of audience size in Catalan use, we compare the proportion of Catalan in @-reply tweets against hashtag tweets.

Method. In this analysis, we take the treatment set to be all tweets made by users in $\mathcal{U}_R$ which contain an @-reply but not a hashtag (narrow audience), and control against all tweets which contain a hashtag but not an @-reply (wide audience).

Results. The results in the rightmost column of Table 5 demonstrate a significant tendency toward less Catalan use in @-replies than in hashtag tweets. This trend supports the hypothesis that Catalan is intended for a wider audience.

This effect may also be explained by a subset of reply tweets in political discourse being targeted at national figures, possibly seeking to direct the message at the target's followers rather than to engage in discussion with the target. For example, one of the reply-tweets addresses a Spanish politician ("user1") in a conversation about a recent court case: *"@user1 @user2 What justice are you talking about? What can a JUDGE like this impart?"*[4]. The same writer uses Catalan in a more broadcast-oriented message: *"Enough [being] dumb! We'll get to work and do not divert us from our way. First independence, then what is needed! My part; #CatalonianRepublic"*[5]. This provides a new perspective on the earlier finding by Pavalanathan and Eisenstein (2015): by replying to tweets from well-known individuals, it may

be possible to reach a large audience, similar to the use of popular hashtags.

6 Conclusion

This study demonstrates the association of code-switching with political stance, topic and audience, in the context of a political referendum. We corroborate prior work by showing that the use of a minority language is associated with pro-independence political sentiment, and we also provide a result in contrast to prior work, that the use of a minority language is associated with a broader intended audience. This study extends the setting of code-switching from everyday conversation into specifically political conversation, which is subject to different expectations and constraints.

This study does not use geographic signals, because the sparsity of geotagged tweets prevented us from restricting the scope to data generated in Catalonia proper. Another potential limitation is that assumption that political hashtags are robust signals for political stance. Other work has shown that political hashtags can be co-opted by opposing parties (Stewart et al., 2017).

Our findings extend prior work on political use of Scots words on the inter-speaker level and Scots-English code-mixing on the intra-speaker level to examining language choice and code-switching, respectively. Further work is required to reconcile our results with prior work on topic differences and audience size (Pavalanathan and Eisenstein, 2015). Future work may also compare the Catalonian situation with multilingual societies in which a minority language is discouraged (Karrebæk, 2013), or in which the languages are more equally distributed (Blommaert, 2011).

Acknowledgments

We thank Sandeep Soni, Umashanthi Pavalanathan, our anonymous reviewers, and members of Georgia Tech's Computational Social Science class for their feedback. This research was supported by NSF award IIS-1452443 and NIH award R01-GM112697-03.

References

---

[4] @user1 @user2 De que justícia hablas? De la que pueda impartir un JUEZ como este?

[5] Prou rucades! Anem per feina i no ens desviem del camí. El primer la independència, després el que calgui! El meu parti; #republicacatalana

Jannis Androutsopoulos. 2015. Networked multilingualism: Some language practices on Facebook and their implications. *International Journal of Bilingualism* 19(2):185–205.

Peter Auer. 2013. *Code-switching in conversation: Language, interaction and identity*. Routledge, London, UK.

Jan Blommaert. 2011. The long language-ideological debate in Belgium. *Journal of Multicultural Discourses* 6(3):241–256.

M. Sidury Christiansen. 2015. 'A ondi queras': Ranchero identity construction by U.S. born Mexicans on Facebook. *Journal of Sociolinguistics* 19(5):688–702.

Kathryn Crameri. 2017. *Language, the novelist and national identity in post-Franco Catalonia*. Routledge, Oxford, UK.

Alasdair Fotheringham. 2017. Catalan independence referendum: Region votes overwhelmingly for secession from Spain. *Independent* Accessed on 30 Oct 2017. `https://www.independent.co.uk/news/world/europe/catalan-independence-referendum\-catalonia-vote-secession-spain\-violence-police-a7977676.html`.

Government of Catalonia. 2013. Language Use of the Population of Catalonia. Technical report. Accessed on 30 Oct 2017. `http://llengua.gencat.cat/web/.content/documents/publicacions/altres/arxius/EULP2013_angles.pdf`.

John J Gumperz. 1977. The sociolinguistic significance of conversational code-switching. *RELC Journal* 8(2):1–34.

Christine Jeavens. 2014. In maps: How close was the Scottish referendum vote? *BBC News* Accessed on 30 Oct 2017. `http://www.bbc.co.uk/news/uk-scotland-scotland-politics\-29255449`.

Martha Sif Karrebæk. 2013. 'Don't speak like that to her!': Linguistic minority children's socialization into an ideology of monolingualism. *Journal of Sociolinguistics* 17(3):355–375.

Suin Kim, Ingmar Weber, Li Wei, and Alice Oh. 2014. Sociolinguistic Analysis of Twitter in Multilingual Societies. In *Proceedings of the 25th ACM Conference on Hypertext and Social Media*. pages 243–248.

William Labov. 1963. The Social Motivation of a Sound Change. *Word* 19(3):273–309.

Jordan Lavendar. 2017. Comparing the pragmatic function of code switching in oral conversation and in Twitter in bilingual speech from Valencia, Spain. *Catalan Review* 31:15–39.

Marco Lui and Timothy Baldwin. 2012. langid. py: An off-the-shelf language identification tool. In *Proceedings of the Association for Computational Linguistics*. pages 25–30.

Luis Moreno, Ana Arriba, and Araceli Serrano. 1998. Multiple identities in decentralized Spain: The case of Catalonia. *Regional & Federal Studies* 8(3):65–88.

Dong Nguyen, Dolf Trieschnigg, and Leonie Cornips. 2015. Audience and the Use of Minority Languages on Twitter. In *Proceedings of the International Conference on Web and Social Media*. pages 666–669.

Umashanthi Pavalanathan and Jacob Eisenstein. 2015. Audience-Modulated Variation in Online Social Media. *American Speech* 90(2):187–213.

Carol W Pfaff. 1979. Constraints on language mixing: intrasentential code-switching and borrowing in spanish/english. *Language* pages 291–318.

Shana Poplack. 1980. Sometimes I'll start a sentence in Spanish y termino en español: toward a typology of code-switching. *Linguistics* 18(7-8):581–618.

John R Rickford and Faye McNair-Knox. 1994. Addressee-and topic-influenced style shift: A quantitative sociolinguistic study. In *Sociolinguistic perspectives on register*, Oxford: Oxford University Press, pages 235–276.

Carol L Schmid. 2001. *The politics of language: Conflict, identity and cultural pluralism in comparative perspective*. Oxford University Press, New York, New York.

Scots Language Centre. 2011. Brief Analysis of the 2011 Census Results. Technical report. Accessed on 30 Oct 2017. `http://media.scotslanguage.com/library/document/SLC%20Analysis%20of%20Census%202011%20for%20Scots.pdf`.

Phillippa Shoemark, Debnil Sur, Luke Shrimpton, Iain Murray, and Sharon Goldwater. 2017. Aye or naw, whit dae ye hink? Scottish independence and linguistic identity on social media. In *Proceedings of the European Association of Computational Linguistics*. pages 1239–1248.

Leo Stewart, Ahmer Arif, A Conrad Nied, Emma S Spiro, and Kate Starbird. 2017. Drawing the lines of contention: Networked frame contests within# blacklivesmatter discourse. In *Proceedings of the Association for Computing Machinery on Human-Computer Interaction*.

A Transition-based Algorithm for Unrestricted AMR Parsing

David Vilares
Universidade da Coruña
FASTPARSE Lab, LyS Group
Departamento de Computación
Campus de A Elviña s/n, 15071
A Coruña, Spain
david.vilares@udc.es

Carlos Gómez-Rodríguez
Universidade da Coruña
FASTPARSE Lab, LyS Group
Departamento de Computación
Campus de A Elviña s/n, 15071
A Coruña, Spain
carlos.gomez@udc.es

Abstract

Non-projective parsing can be useful to handle cycles and reentrancy in AMR graphs. We explore this idea and introduce a greedy left-to-right non-projective transition-based parser. At each parsing configuration, an oracle decides whether to create a concept or whether to connect a pair of existing concepts. The algorithm handles reentrancy and arbitrary cycles natively, i.e. within the transition system itself. The model is evaluated on the LDC2015E86 corpus, obtaining results close to the state of the art, including a Smatch of 64%, and showing good behavior on reentrant edges.

1 Introduction

Abstract Meaning Representation (AMR) is a semantic representation language to map the meaning of English sentences into directed, cycled, labeled graphs (Banarescu et al., 2013). Graph vertices are concepts inferred from words. The concepts can be represented by the words themselves (e.g. `dog`), PropBank framesets (Palmer et al., 2005) (e.g. `eat-01`), or keywords (like named entities or quantities). The edges denote relations between pairs of concepts (e.g. `eat-01 :ARG0 dog`). AMR parsing integrates tasks that have usually been addressed separately in natural language processing (NLP), such as named entity recognition (Nadeau and Sekine, 2007), semantic role labeling (Palmer et al., 2010) or co-reference resolution (Ng and Cardie, 2002; Lee et al., 2017). Figure 1 shows an example of an AMR graph.

Several transition-based dependency parsing algorithms have been extended to generate AMR. Wang et al. (2015) describe a two-stage model, where they first obtain the dependency parse of a sentence and then transform it into a graph. Damonte et al. (2017) propose a variant of the ARC-EAGER algorithm to identify labeled edges between concepts. These concepts are identified

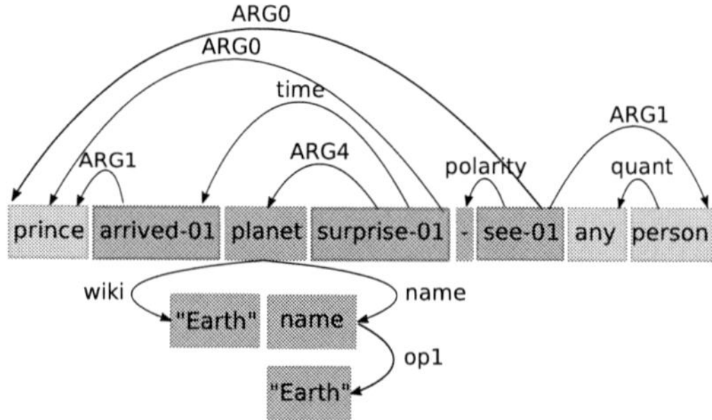

Figure 1: AMR graph for 'When the prince arrived on the Earth, he was surprised not to see any people'. Words can refer to concepts by themselves (green), be mapped to PropBank framesets (red) or be broken down into multiple-term/non-literal concepts (blue). `Prince` plays different semantic roles.

using a lookup table and a set of rules. A restricted subset of reentrant edges are supported by an additional classifier. A similar configuration is used in (Gildea et al., 2018; Peng et al., 2018), but relying on a cache data structure to handle reentrancy, cycles and restricted non-projectivity. A feed-forward network and additional hooks are used to build the concepts. Ballesteros and Al-Onaizan (2017) use a modified ARC-STANDARD algorithm, where the oracle is trained using stack-LSTMs (Dyer et al., 2015). Reentrancy is handled through SWAP (Nivre, 2009) and they define additional transitions intended to detect concepts, entities and polarity nodes.

This paper explores unrestricted non-projective AMR parsing and introduces AMR-COVINGTON, inspired by Covington (2001). It handles arbitrary non-projectivity, cycles and reentrancy in a natural way, as there is no need for specific transitions, but just the removal of restrictions from the original algorithm. The algorithm has full coverage and keeps transitions simple, which is a matter of concern in recent studies (Peng et al., 2018).

Proceedings of NAACL-HLT 2018, pages 142–149
New Orleans, Louisiana, June 1 - 6, 2018. ©2018 Association for Computational Linguistics

2   Preliminaries and Notation

Notation   We use `typewriter` font for concepts and their indexes (e.g. `dog` or `1`), regular font for raw words (e.g. dog or 1), and a bold style font for vectors and matrices (e.g. $\mathbf{v}$, $\mathbf{W}$). Covington (2001) describes a fundamental algorithm for unrestricted non-projective dependency parsing. The algorithm can be implemented as a left-to-right transition system (Nivre, 2008). The key idea is intuitive. Given a word to be processed at a particular state, the word is compared against the words that have previously been processed, deciding to establish or not a syntactic dependency arc from/to each of them. The process continues until all previous words are checked or until the algorithm decides no more connections with previous words need to be built, then the next word is processed. The runtime is $\mathcal{O}(n^2)$ in the worst scenario. To guarantee the single-head and acyclicity conditions that are required in dependency parsing, explicit tests are added to the algorithm to check for transitions that would break the constraints. These are then disallowed, making the implementation less straightforward.

3   The AMR-Covington algorithm

The acyclicity and single-head constraints are not needed in AMR, as arbitrary graphs are allowed. Cycles and reentrancy are used to model semantic relations between concepts (as shown in Figure 1) and to identify co-references. By removing the constraints from the Covington transition system, we achieve a natural way to deal with them.[1]

Also, AMR parsing requires words to be transformed into concepts. Dependency parsing operates on a constant-length sequence. But in AMR, words can be removed, generate a single concept, or generate several concepts. In this paper, additional lookup tables and transitions are defined to create concepts when needed, following the current trend (Damonte et al., 2017; Ballesteros and Al-Onaizan, 2017; Gildea et al., 2018).

3.1   Formalization

Let $G=(V,E)$ be an edge-labeled directed graph where: $V=\{0,1,2,\ldots,M\}$ is the set of concepts and $E = V \times E \times V$ is the set of labeled edges, we will denote a connection between a head concept

---

[1] This is roughly equivalent to going back to the naive parser called ESH in (Covington, 2001), which has not seen practical use in parsing due to the lack of these constraints.

`i` $\in V$ and a dependent concept `j` $\in V$ as `i` $\overset{l}{\rightarrow}$ `j`, where l is the semantic label connecting them.

The parser will process sentences from left to right. Each decision leads to a new parsing configuration, which can be abstracted as a 4-tuple $(\lambda_1, \lambda_2, \beta, E)$ where:

- β is a buffer that contains unprocessed words. They await to be transformed to a concept, a part of a larger concept, or to be removed. In $b|\beta$, b represents the head of β, and it optionally can be a concept. In that case, it will be denoted as `b`.

- λ_1 is a list of previously created concepts that are waiting to determine its semantic relation with respect to `b`. Elements in λ_1 are concepts. In $\lambda_1|$`i`, `i` denotes its last element.

- λ_2 is a list that contains previously created concepts for which the relation with `b` has already been determined. Elements in λ_2 are concepts. In `j`$|\lambda_2$, `j` denotes the head of λ_2.

- E is the set of the created edges.

Given an input sentence, the parser starts at an initial configuration $c_s = ([0], [], 1|\beta, \{\})$ and will apply valid transitions until a final configuration c_f is reached, such that $c_f = (\lambda_1, \lambda_2, [], E)$. The set of transitions is formally defined in Table 1:

- LEFT-ARC$_l$: Creates an edge `b` $\overset{l}{\rightarrow}$ `i`. `i` is moved to λ_2.

- RIGHT-ARC$_l$: Creates an edge `i` $\overset{l}{\rightarrow}$ `b`. `i` is moved to λ_2.

- SHIFT: Pops `b` from β. λ_1, λ_2 and `b` are appended.

- NO ARC: It is applied when the algorithm determines that there is no semantic relationship between `i` and `b`, but there is a relationship between some other node in λ_1 and `b`.

- CONFIRM: Pops b from β and puts the concept `b` in its place. This transition is called to handle words that only need to generate one (more) concept.

- BREAKDOWN$_\alpha$: Creates a concept `b` from b, and places it on top of β, but b is not popped, and the new buffer state is `b`$|b|\beta$. It is used to handle a word that is going to be mapped

Transitions	Step t	Step $t+1$
LEFT-ARC$_l$	$(\lambda_1\|\texttt{i}, \lambda_2, \texttt{b}\|\beta, E)$	$(\lambda_1, \texttt{i}\|\lambda_2, \texttt{b}\|\beta, E \cup \{\texttt{b} \xrightarrow{l} \texttt{i}\})$
RIGHT-ARC$_l$	$(\lambda_1\|\texttt{i}, \lambda_2, \texttt{b}\|\beta, E)$	$(\lambda_1, \texttt{i}\|\lambda_2, \texttt{b}\|\beta, E \cup \{\texttt{i} \xrightarrow{l} \texttt{b}\})$
MULTIPLE-ARC$_{l_1,l_2}$	$(\lambda_1\|\texttt{i}, \lambda_2, \texttt{b}\|\beta, E)$	$(\lambda_1, \texttt{i}\|\lambda_2, \texttt{b}\|\beta, E \cup \{\texttt{b} \xrightarrow{l} \texttt{i}\} \cup \{\texttt{i} \xrightarrow{l_2} \texttt{b}\})$
SHIFT	$(\lambda_1, \lambda_2, \texttt{b}\|\beta, E)$	$(\lambda_1 \cdot \lambda_2\|\texttt{b}, [], \beta, E)$
NO-ARC	$(\lambda_1\|\texttt{i}, \lambda_2, \beta, E)$	$(\lambda_1, \texttt{i}\|\lambda_2, \beta, E)$
CONFIRM	$(\lambda_1, \lambda_2, b\|\beta, E)$	$(\lambda_1, \lambda_2, \texttt{b}\|\beta, E)$
BREAKDOWN$_\alpha$	$(\lambda_1, \lambda_2, b\|\beta, E)$	$(\lambda_1, \lambda_2, \texttt{b}\|b\|\beta, E)$
REDUCE	$(\lambda_1, \lambda_2, b\|\beta, E)$	$(\lambda_1, \lambda_2, \beta, E)$

Table 1: Transitions for AMR-COVINGTON

to multiple concepts. To guarantee termination, BREAKDOWN is parametrized with a constant α, banning generation of more than α consecutive concepts by using this operation. Otherwise, concepts could be generated indefinitely without emptying β.

- REDUCE: Pops b from β. It is used to remove words that do not add any meaning to the sentence and are not part of the AMR graph.

LEFT and RIGHT-ARC handle cycles and reentrancy with the exception of cycles of length 2 (which only involve i and b). To assure full coverage, we include an additional transition: MULTIPLE-ARC$_{(l_1,l_2)}$ that creates two edges b $\xrightarrow{l_1}$ i and i $\xrightarrow{l_2}$ b. i is moved to λ_2. MULTIPLE-ARCs are marginal and will not be learned in practice. AMR-COVINGTON can be implemented without MULTIPLE-ARC, by keeping i in λ_1 after creating an arc and using NO-ARC when the parser has finished creating connections between i and b, at a cost to efficiency as transition sequences would be longer. Multiple edges in the same direction between i and b are handled by representing them as a single edge that merges the labels.

Example Table 2 illustrates a valid transition sequence to obtain the AMR graph of Figure 1.

3.2 Training the classifiers

The algorithm relies on three classifiers: (1) a transition classifier, T_c, that learns the set of transitions introduced in §3.1, (2) a relation classifier, R_c, to predict the label(s) of an edge when the selected action is a LEFT-ARC, RIGHT-ARC or MULTIPLE-ARC and (3) a hybrid process (a concept classifier, C_c, and a rule-based system) that determines which concept to create when the selected action is a CONFIRM or BREAKDOWN.

Preprocessing Sentences are tokenized and aligned with the concepts using JAMR (Flanigan et al., 2014). For lemmatization, tagging and dependency parsing we used UDpipe (Straka et al., 2016) and its English pre-trained model (Zeman et al., 2017). Named Entity Recognition is handled by Stanford CoreNLP (Manning et al., 2014).

Architecture We use feed-forward neural networks to train the tree classifiers. The transition classifier uses 2 hidden layers (400 and 200 input neurons) and the relation and concept classifiers use 1 hidden layer (200 neurons). The activation function in hidden layers is a $relu(x){=}max(0,x)$ and their output is computed as $relu(W_i \cdot \mathbf{x}_i + b_i)$ where W_i and b_i are the weights and bias tensors to be learned and $\mathbf{x}_i$ the input at the ith hidden layer. The output layer uses a $softmax$ function, computed as $P(y = s|\mathbf{x}) = \frac{e^{\mathbf{x}^\mathbf{T}\theta_s}}{\sum_{s'=1}^{S} e^{\mathbf{x}^\mathbf{T}\theta_{s'}}}$. All classifiers are trained in mini-batches (size=32), using Adam (Kingma and Ba, 2015) (learning rate set to $3e^{-4}$), early stopping (no patience) and dropout (Srivastava et al., 2014) (40%). The classifiers are fed with features extracted from the preprocessed texts. Depending on the classifier, we are using different features. These are summarized in Appendix A (Table 5), which also describes (B) other design decisions that are not shown here due to space reasons.

3.3 Running the system

At each parsing configuration, we first try to find a multiword concept or entity that matches the head elements of β, to reduce the number of BREAKDOWNs, which turned out to be a difficult transition to learn (see §4.1). This is done by looking at a lookup table of multiword concepts[2] seen in

---

[2] The most frequent subgraph.

λ_1	λ_2	β	Action (times)
		w, t, p	REDUCE$\times 2_1$
		p, a, o	CONFIRM$_2$
		p, a, o	SHIFT$_3$
p		a, o, t	CONFIRM$_4$
p		a, o, t	LEFT-ARC$_5$
	p	a, o, t	SHIFT$_6$
p, a		o, t, E	REDUCE$\times 2_7$
p, a		E, h, w	BREAKDOWN$_8$
p, a		'E', E, h	SHIFT$_9$
p, a, 'E'		E, h, w	BREAKDOWN$_{10}$
p, a, 'E'		'E', h, w	SHIFT$_{11}$
a, 'E', 'E'		E, h, w	BREAKDOWN$_{12}$
a, 'E', 'E'		n, h, w	LEFT-ARC$_{12}$
a, 'E'	'E'	n, h, w	SHIFT$_{13}$
'E', 'E', n		E, h, w	CONFIRM$_{14}$
'E', 'E', n		p2, h, w	LEFT-ARC$_{15}$
a, 'E', 'E'	n,	p2, h, w	NO-ARC$_{16}$
p, a, 'E'	'E', n,	p2, h, w	LEFT-ARC$_{17}$
p, a	'E', 'E', n,	p2, h, w	SHIFT$_{18}$
'E', n, p2		h, w, s	REDUCE$\times 2_{19}$
'E', n, p2		s, n, t	CONFIRM$_{20}$
'E', n, p2		s, n, t	LEFT-ARC$_{21}$
'E', 'E', n	p2	s, n, t	NO-ARC$\times 3_{22}$
p, a	'E', 'E', n	s, n, t	LEFT-ARC$\times 2_{23}$
	p, a, 'E'	s, n, t	SHIFT$_{24}$
n, p2, s		n, t, s2	CONFIRM$_{25}$
n, p2, s		−, t, s2	SHIFT$_{26}$
p2, s, −		t, s2, a2	REDUCE$_{27}$
p2, s, −		s2, a2, p3	CONFIRM$_{28}$
p2, s, −		s2, a2, p3	LEFT-ARC$_{29}$
n, p2, s	−	s2, a2, p3	NO-ARC $\times 5_{30}$
p	a, 'E', 'E'	s2, a2, p3	LEFT-ARC$_{31}$
	p, a, 'E'	s2, a2, p3	SHIFT$_{32}$
s, −, s2		a2, p3	CONFIRM$_{33}$
s, −, s2		a2, p3	SHIFT$_{34}$
−, s2, a2		p3	CONFIRM$_{35}$
−, s2, a2		p3	LEFT-ARC$_{36}$
s, −, s2	a2	p3	RIGHT-ARC$_{37}$
s2, a2, p3			SHIFT$_{38}$

Table 2: Sequence of gold transitions to obtain the AMR graph for the sentence 'When the prince arrived on the Earth, he was surprised not to see any people', introduced in Figure 1. For brevity, we represent words (and concepts) by their first character (plus an index if it is duplicated) and we only show the top three words for λ_1, λ_2 and β. Steps from 20 to 23(2) and from 28 to 31 manage the reentrant edges for `prince` (p) from `surprise-01` (s) and `see-01` (s2).

the training set and a set of rules, as introduced in (Damonte et al., 2017; Gildea et al., 2018).

We then invoke T_c and call the corresponding subprocess when an additional concept or edge-label identification task is needed.

Concept identification If the word at the top of β occurred more than 4 times in the training set, we call a supervised classifier to predict the concept. Otherwise, we first look for a word-to-concept mapping in a lookup table. If not found, if it is a verb, we generate the concept `lemma-01`, and otherwise `lemma`.

Edge label identification The classifier is invoked every time an edge is created. We use the list of valid ARGs allowed in propbank framesets by Damonte et al. (2017). Also, if p and o are a propbank and a non-propbank concept, we restore inverted edges of the form o $\xrightarrow{\text{1-of}}$ p as o $\xrightarrow{1}$ p.

4 Methods and Experiments

Corpus We use the LDC2015E86 corpus and its official splits: 16 833 graphs for training, 1 368 for development and 1 371 for testing. The final model is only trained on the training split.

Metrics We use Smatch (Cai and Knight, 2013) and the metrics from Damonte et al. (2017).[3]

Sources The code and the pretrained model used in this paper can be found at `https://github.com/aghie/tb-amr`.

4.1 Results and discussion

Table 3 shows accuracy of T_c on the development set. CONFIRM and REDUCE are the easiest transitions, as local information such as POS-tags and words are discriminative to distinguish between content and function words. BREAKDOWN is the hardest action.[4] In early stages of this work, we observed that this transition could learn to correctly generate multiple-term concepts for named-entities that are not sparse (e.g. countries or people), but failed with sparse entities (e.g. dates or percent quantities). Low performance on identifying them negatively affects the edge metrics, which require both concepts of an edge to be correct. Because of this and to identify them properly, we use the mentioned complementary rules to handle named entities. RIGHT-ARCs are harder than LEFT-ARCs, although the reason for this issue remains as an open question for us. The performance for NO-ARCs is high, but it would be interesting to achieve a higher recall at a cost of a lower precision, as predicting NO-ARCs makes the transition sequence longer, but could help identify more distant reentrancy. The accuracy of T_c is ∼86%. The accuracy of R_c is ∼79%. We do

---

[3] It is worth noting that the calculation of Smatch and metrics derived from it suffers from a random component, as they involve finding an alignment between predicted and gold graphs with an approximate algorithm that can produce a suboptimal solution. Thus, as in previous work, reported Smatch scores may slightly underestimate the real score.

[4] This transition was trained/evaluated for non named-entity words that generated multiple nodes, e.g. father, that maps to `have-rel-role-91 :ARG2 father`.

Action	Prec.	Rec.	F-score
LEFT-ARC	81.62	87.73	84.57
RIGHT-ARC	75.53	78.71	77.08
MULTIPLE-ARC	00.00	00.00	00.00
SHIFT	80.44	81.11	80.77
NO-ARC	89.71	86.71	88.18
CONFIRM	84.91	96.11	90.16
REDUCE	96.77	91.53	94.08
BREAKDOWN	85.09	50.23	63.17

Table 3: T_c scores on the development set.

Metric	F	W	F'	D	P	Ours
Smatch	58	63	67	64	64	64
Unlabeled	61	69	69	69	-	68
No-WSD	58	64	68	65	-	65
NER	75	75	79	83	-	83
Wiki	0	0	75	64	-	70
Negations	16	18	45	48	-	47
Concepts	79	80	83	83	-	83
Reentrancy	38	41	42	41	-	44
SRL	55	60	60	56	-	57

Table 4: F-score comparison with F (Flanigan et al., 2014), W (Wang et al., 2015), F' (Flanigan et al., 2016), D (Damonte et al., 2017), P (Peng et al., 2018). D, P and our system are left-to-right transition-based.

not show the detailed results since the number of classes is too high. C_c was trained on concepts occurring more than 1 time in the training set, obtaining an accuracy of ~83%. The accuracy on the development set with all concepts was ~77%.

Table 4 compares the performance of our systems with state-of-the-art models on the test set. AMR-COVINGTON obtains state-of-the-art results for all the standard metrics. It outperforms the rest of the models when handling reentrant edges. It is worth noting that D requires an additional classifier to handle a restricted set of reentrancy and P uses up to five classifiers to build the graph.

Discussion In contrast to related work that relies on *ad-hoc* procedures, the proposed algorithm handles cycles and reentrant edges natively. This is done by just removing the original constraints of the arc transitions in the original Covington (2001) algorithm. The main drawback of the algorithm is its computational complexity. The transition system is expected to run in $\mathcal{O}(n^2)$, as the original Covington parser. There are also collateral issues that impact the real speed of the system, such as predicting the concepts in a supervised

way, given the large number of output classes (discarding the less frequent concepts the classifier needs to discriminate among more than 7 000 concepts). In line with previous discussions (Damonte et al., 2017), it seems that using a supervised feedforward network to predict the concepts does not lead to a better overall concept identification with respect of the use of simple lookup tables that pick up the most common node/subgraph. Currently, every node is kept in λ, and it is available to be part of new edges. We wonder if only storing in λ the head node for words that generate multiple-node subgraphs (e.g. for the word father that maps to `have-rel-role-91 :ARG2 father`, keeping in λ only the concept `have-rel-role-91`) could be beneficial for AMR-COVINGTON.

As a side note, current AMR evaluation involves elements such as neural network initialization, hooks and the (sub-optimal) alignments of evaluation metrics (e.g. Smatch) that introduce random effects that were difficult to quantify for us.

5 Conclusion

We introduce AMR-COVINGTON, a non-projective transition-based parser for unrestricted AMR. The set of transitions handles reentrancy natively. Experiments on the LDC2015E86 corpus show that our approach obtains results close to the state of the art and a good behavior on re-entrant edges.

As future work, AMR-COVINGTON produces sequences of NO-ARCs which could be shortened by using non-local transitions (Qi and Manning, 2017; Fernández-González and Gómez-Rodríguez, 2017). Sequential models have shown that fewer hooks and lookup tables are needed to deal with the high sparsity of AMR (Ballesteros and Al-Onaizan, 2017). Similarly, BIST-COVINGTON (Vilares and Gómez-Rodríguez, 2017) could be adapted for this task.

Acknowledgments

This work is funded from the European Research Council (ERC), under the European Union's Horizon 2020 research and innovation programme (FASTPARSE, grant agreement No 714150), from the TELEPARES-UDC project (FFI2014-51978-C2-2-R) and the ANSWER-ASAP project (TIN2017-85160-C2-1-R) from MINECO, and from Xunta de Galicia (ED431B 2017/01). We gratefully acknowledge NVIDIA Corporation for the donation of a GTX Titan X GPU.

References

Miguel Ballesteros and Yaser Al-Onaizan. 2017. AMR Parsing using Stack-LSTMs. In *Proceedings of the 2017 Conference on Empirical Methods in Natural Language Processing*, pages 1280–1286, Copenhagen, Denmark. Association for Computational Linguistics.

Laura Banarescu, Claire Bonial, Shu Cai, Madalina Georgescu, Kira Griffitt, Ulf Hermjakob, Kevin Knight, Philipp Koehn, Martha Palmer, and Nathan Schneider. 2013. Abstract meaning representation for sembanking. In *Proceedings of the 7th Linguistic Annotation Workshop and Interoperability with Discourse*, pages 178–186.

Shu Cai and Kevin Knight. 2013. Smatch: an Evaluation Metric for Semantic Feature Structures. In *ACL (2)*, pages 748–752.

Michael A Covington. 2001. A fundamental algorithm for dependency parsing. In *Proceedings of the 39th annual ACM southeast conference*, pages 95–102.

Marco Damonte, Shay B. Cohen, and Giorgio Satta. 2017. An Incremental Parser for Abstract Meaning Representation. In *Proceedings of the 15th Conference of the European Chapter of the Association for Computational Linguistics: Volume 1, Long Papers*, pages 536–546, Valencia, Spain. Association for Computational Linguistics.

Chris Dyer, Miguel Ballesteros, Wang Ling, Austin Matthews, and Noah A. Smith. 2015. Transition-Based Dependency Parsing with Stack Long Short-Term Memory. In *Proceedings of the 53rd Annual Meeting of the Association for Computational Linguistics and the 7th International Joint Conference on Natural Language Processing (Volume 1: Long Papers)*, pages 334–343, Beijing, China. Association for Computational Linguistics.

D. Fernández-González and C. Gómez-Rodríguez. 2017. Non-Projective Dependency Parsing with Non-Local Transitions. *ArXiv e-prints*.

Jeffrey Flanigan, Chris Dyer, Noah A Smith, and Jaime Carbonell. 2016. CMU at SemEval-2016 task 8: Graph-based AMR Parsing with Infinite Ramp Loss. In *Proceedings of the 10th International Workshop on Semantic Evaluation (SemEval-2016)*, pages 1202–1206.

Jeffrey Flanigan, Sam Thomson, Jaime Carbonell, Chris Dyer, and Noah A. Smith. 2014. A Discriminative Graph-Based Parser for the Abstract Meaning Representation. In *Proceedings of the 52nd Annual Meeting of the Association for Computational Linguistics (Volume 1: Long Papers)*, pages 1426–1436, Baltimore, Maryland. Association for Computational Linguistics.

Daniel Gildea, Giorgio Satta, and Xiaochang Peng. 2018. Cache Transition Systems for Graph Parsing. *Computational Linguistics*, in press.

Diederik Kingma and Jimmy Ba. 2015. Adam: A method for stochastic optimization. In *Proceedings of the 3rd International Conference for Learning Representations*, San Diego, USA.

Heeyoung Lee, Mihai Surdeanu, and Dan Jurafsky. 2017. A scaffolding approach to coreference resolution integrating statistical and rule-based models. *Natural Language Engineering*, pages 1–30.

Christopher D. Manning, Mihai Surdeanu, John Bauer, Jenny Finkel, Steven J. Bethard, and David Mc-Closky. 2014. The Stanford CoreNLP natural language processing toolkit. In *Association for Computational Linguistics (ACL) System Demonstrations*, pages 55–60.

David Nadeau and Satoshi Sekine. 2007. A survey of named entity recognition and classification. *Lingvisticae Investigationes*, 30(1):3–26.

Vincent Ng and Claire Cardie. 2002. Improving machine learning approaches to coreference resolution. In *Proceedings of the 40th annual meeting on association for computational linguistics*, pages 104–111. Association for Computational Linguistics.

Joakim Nivre. 2008. Algorithms for deterministic incremental dependency parsing. *Computational Linguistics*, 34(4):513–553.

Joakim Nivre. 2009. Non-projective dependency parsing in expected linear time. In *Proceedings of the Joint Conference of the 47th Annual Meeting of the ACL and the 4th International Joint Conference on Natural Language Processing of the AFNLP: Volume 1-Volume 1*, pages 351–359. Association for Computational Linguistics.

Martha Palmer, Daniel Gildea, and Paul Kingsbury. 2005. The proposition bank: An annotated corpus of semantic roles. *Computational linguistics*, 31(1):71–106.

Martha Palmer, Daniel Gildea, and Nianwen Xue. 2010. Semantic role labeling. *Synthesis Lectures on Human Language Technologies*, 3(1):1–103.

Xiaochang Peng, Daniel Gildea, and Giorgio Satta. 2018. AMR parsing with cache transition systems. In *Proceedings of the National Conference on Artificial Intelligence (AAAI-18)*. In press.

Peng Qi and Christopher D. Manning. 2017. Arc-swift: A Novel Transition System for Dependency Parsing. In *Proceedings of the 55th Annual Meeting of the Association for Computational Linguistics (Volume 2: Short Papers)*, pages 110–117, Vancouver, Canada. Association for Computational Linguistics.

Nitish Srivastava, Geoffrey E Hinton, Alex Krizhevsky, Ilya Sutskever, and Ruslan Salakhutdinov. 2014. Dropout: a simple way to prevent neural networks from overfitting. *Journal of machine learning research*, 15(1):1929–1958.

Milan Straka, Jan Hajic, and Jana Straková. 2016. UD-Pipe: Trainable Pipeline for Processing CoNLL-U Files Performing Tokenization, Morphological Analysis, POS Tagging and Parsing. In *LREC*.

David Vilares and Carlos Gómez-Rodríguez. 2017. A non-projective greedy dependency parser with bidirectional lstms. *Proceedings of the CoNLL 2017 Shared Task: Multilingual Parsing from Raw Text to Universal Dependencies*, pages 152–162.

Chuan Wang, Nianwen Xue, and Sameer Pradhan. 2015. A transition-based algorithm for AMR parsing. In *Proceedings of the 2015 Conference of the North American Chapter of the Association for Computational Linguistics: Human Language Technologies*, pages 366–375.

Daniel Zeman, Martin Popel, Milan Straka, Jan Hajic, Joakim Nivre, Filip Ginter, Juhani Luotolahti, Sampo Pyysalo, Slav Petrov, Martin Potthast, et al. 2017. CoNLL 2017 shared task: multilingual parsing from raw text to universal dependencies. *Proceedings of the CoNLL 2017 Shared Task: Multilingual Parsing from Raw Text to Universal Dependencies*, pages 1–19.

A Supplemental Material

Table 5 indicates the features used to train the different classifiers. Concept features are randomized by $\epsilon = 2e^{-3}$ to an special index that refers to an `unknown concept` during the training phase. This helps learn a generic embedding for unseen concepts in the test phase. Also, concepts that occur only one time in the training set are not considered as output classes by C_c.

Internal and external (from GloVe) word embedding sizes are set to 100. The size of the concept embedding is set to 50. The rest of the embeddings size are set to 20. The weights are initialized to zero.

B Additional design decisions

We try to list more in detail the main hooks and design decisions followed in this work to mitigate the high sparsity in Abstract Meaning Representation which, at least in our experience, was a struggling issue. These decisions mainly affect the mapping from words to multiple-concept subgraphs.

- We identify named entities and nationalities, and update the training configurations to generate the corresponding subgraph by applying a set of hooks.[5] The intermediate training config-

---

Features	T_c	R_c	C_c
From $\beta_0, \beta_1, \lambda_{1_0}, \lambda_{1_1}$			
POS	✓	✓	✓
W	✓	✓	✓
EW	✓	✓	✓
C	✓	✓	✓
ENTITY	✓	✓	✓
LM_h	✓	✓	
LM_c	✓	✓	
LM_{cc}	✓	✓	
RM_h	✓	✓	
RM_c	✓	✓	
RM_{cc}	✓	✓	
NH, NC	✓	✓	
DEPTH	✓	✓	✓
NPUNKT	✓	✓	
HL	✓	✓	
CT	✓	✓	
G			✓
Labels from the predicted dependency tree			
$D(b_j, i_k) \, \forall j, k \; j \in [0, 1] \; \wedge \; k \in [0, 1, 2, 3]$	✓	✓	✓

Table 5: Set of proposed features for each classifier. POS, W, C, ENTITY are part-of-speech tag, word, concept and entity embeddings. EW are pre-trained external word embeddings, fine-tuned during the training phase (http://nlp.stanford.edu/data/glove.6B.zip, 100 dimensions). LM and RM are the leftmost and the rightmost function; and h, c, cc represent head, child and grand-child concepts of a concept; so, for example, LM_c stands for the leftmost child of the concept. NH and NC are the number of heads and children of a concept. NPUNKT indicates the number of '.', ';', ':', '?', '!' that have already been processed. HL denotes the labels of the last assigned head. CT indicates the type of concept (constant, propbank frameset, other). G indicates if a concept was generated using a CONFIRM or BREAKDOWN. D denotes the dependency label existing in the dependency tree between the word at the jth position in β and the kth last in λ_1 and vice versa. The word that generated a concept is still accessible after creating the concept.

urations are not fed as samples to the classifier. On early experiments it was observed that the BREAKDOWN transition could acceptably learn non-sparse named entities (e.g. countries and nationalities), but failed on the sparse ones (e.g. dates or money amounts). By processing the named entities with hooks instead, the aim was to make the parser familiar with the parsing configurations that are obtained after applying the hooks.

- Additionally, named-entity subgraphs and subgraphs coming from phrases (involving two or more terms) from the training set are saved into a lookup table. The latter ones had little impact.

---

[5]The hooks are based on the text file resources for countries, cities, etc, released by Damonte et al. (2017) and an analysis of how named entities are generated in the training/development set.

- We store in a lookup table some single-word expressions that generated multiple-concept subgraphs in the training set, based on simple heuristics. We store words that denote a negative expression (e.g. undecided that maps to `decide-01 :polarity -`). We store words that always generated the same subgraph and occurred more than 5 times. We also store capitalized single words that were not previously identified as named entities.

- We use the verbalization list from Wang et al. (2015) (another lookup table).

- When predicting a CONFIRM or BREAKDOWN for an uncommon word, we check if that word was mapped to a concept in the training set. If not, we generate the concept `lemma-01` if it is a verb, otherwise `lemma`.

- Dates formatted as YYMMDD or YYYYMMDD are identified using a simple criterion (sequence of 6 or 8 digits) and transformed into YYYY-MM-DD on the test phase, as they were consistently misclassified as integer numbers in the development set.

- We apply a set of hooks similar to (Damonte et al., 2017) to determine if the predicted label is valid for that edge.

- We forbid to generate the same concept twice consecutively. Also, we set $\alpha = 4$ for BREAKDOWN$_\alpha$.

- If a node is created, but it is not attached to any head node, we post-process it and connect to the root node.

- We assume multi-sentence graphs should contain sentence punctuation symbols. If we predict a multi-sentence graph, but there is no punctuation symbol that splits sentences, we post-process the graph and transform the root node into an AND node.

Analogies in Complex Verb Meaning Shifts:
The Effect of Affect in Semantic Similarity Models

Maximilian Köper   **Sabine Schulte im Walde**

Institut für Maschinelle Sprachverarbeitung

Universität Stuttgart, Germany

{maximilian.koeper,schulte}@ims.uni-stuttgart.de

Abstract

We present a computational model to detect and distinguish analogies in meaning shifts between German base and complex verbs. In contrast to previous corpus-based studies, a novel dataset demonstrates that "regular" shifts represent the smallest class. Classification experiments relying on a standard similarity model successfully distinguish between four types of shifts, with verb classes boosting the performance, and affective features for abstractness, emotion and sentiment representing the most salient indicators.

1 Introduction

German particle verbs are complex verb structures such as *anstrahlen* 'to beam/smile at' that combine a prefix particle (*an*) with a base verb (*strahlen* 'to beam'). They are highly ambiguous, and they often trigger meaning shifts of the base verbs (Springorum et al., 2013; Köper and Schulte im Walde, 2016). More specifically, Springorum et al. (2013) presented a manual corpus exploration suggesting regular mechanisms in meaning shifts from base verbs (BVs) to particle verbs (PVs) that apply across a semantically coherent set of BVs. For example, the two sound BVs *brummen 'to hum'* and *donnern 'to rumble'* both describe a displeasing loud noise. Combining them with the particle *auf*, the PVs *aufbrummen* and *aufdonnern* are near-synonyms in one of their senses, roughly meaning *'to forcefully assign a task'*. In a similar vein, Morgan (1997) used schematic diagrams to illustrate meaning shifts of English complex verbs with the particle *out*.

The goal of this work is to provide a computational model of meaning shifts for German particle verbs. We define our task from the perspective of an analogy, comparing a BV pair with a PV pair, cf. Figure 1. A BV–PV model of regular meaning shifts expects (i) semantic coherence

sim(BV₁,BV₂) between the two BVs (i.e., overlap in a selected set of semantically salient features), (ii) strong semantic similarity *sim(PV₁,PV₂)* between the PVs, and (iii) low semantic similarity *sim(BVᵢ,PVᵢ)* between the corresponding BV–PV pairs, where the shifts take place.

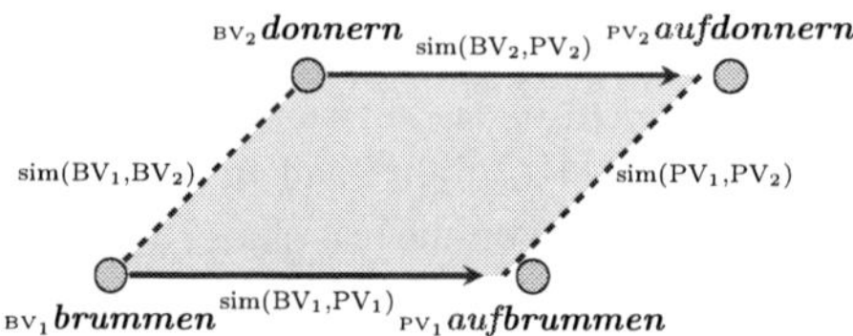

Figure 1: Analogy model applied to BV–PV shifts.

In a similar vein, a rich tradition on computational work on analogies focuses on finding a relational analogy in multiple choices as required by the SAT Scholastic Aptitude Test (Turney, 2006, 2012; Speer et al., 2017). While the SAT questions provide a limited set of possible answers, more recent attention has been spent on open vocabulary tasks of the form *A:B::C:?* (Mikolov et al., 2013; Levy and Goldberg, 2014).

The contribution of our analogy model is two-fold: (i) it makes a step forward from hand-selected manual datasets of meaning shifts to larger-scale automatic classification; and (ii) it aims to deepen the linguistic insights into complex verb meaning shifts. While we focus on German particle verbs, we expect our explorations to be applicable also to other types of meaning shifts or languages. Most importantly, we show that (a) there are variants of (ir)regular meaning shifts that go beyond what was found in corpus-based explorations; (b) generalisation via classification boosts the strengths of salient verb features; and (c) affective features (i.e., abstractness, emotion and sentiment) play the predominant role in similarity models of meaning shifts.

150

Proceedings of NAACL-HLT 2018, pages 150–156

New Orleans, Louisiana, June 1 - 6, 2018. ©2018 Association for Computational Linguistics

2 A Collection of BV–PV Analogies

As to our knowledge, no datasets of human-annotated complex verb meaning shifts are available, apart from small-scale case studies (Springorum et al., 2013). We therefore collected human judgements for analogy combinations of BV–PV pairs of the form

$$BV_1 : PV_1 :: BV_2 : PV_2$$

such as *klappern:abklappern::klopfen:abklopfen*. We aimed for ≈200 analogies per particle type, focusing on the four highly frequent particle types *ab, an, auf, aus*. The target selection was restricted to PV_1/PV_2 combinations with identical particles, and where the two PVs were deemed (near-)synonyms according to the German standard dictionary DUDEN[1] or the German Wiktionary[2], as we were interested in BV–PV analogies with semantically highly similar PVs.

In total, we collected 794 analogy questions.[3] The BV–PV pairs were distributed over four lists according to the four particle types, and annotated by five German native speakers with a background in linguistics. To avoid a sense-specific bias, we provided no contextual information and therefore conducted the annotation on the type level. The annotators were asked to classify the analogies into four categories to distinguish between meaning shifts in no/one/both BV–PV pairs:

1. **COMP**: no BV–PV pair has a meaning shift, i.e., both PVs are compositional regarding their BVs, and therefore all four verbs are (near-)synonyms; example: *(ab)feilen::(ab)schleifen* 'to grind (off)'

2. **ASYMCOMP**: only one of the BV–PV pairs undergoes a meaning shift; in this case, the annotators also indicated that pair; example: *(auf)wühlen::(auf)graben* lit. 'to churn::dig (up)', where *aufwühlen* includes a strong emotion component

3. **SHIFTDIFF**: both BV–PV pairs show a meaning shift, but the BVs are not semantically similar; example: *(aus)baden::(aus)bügeln* 'to pay for an error' with *baden* 'to take a bath' and *bügeln* 'to iron'

4. **SHIFTREG**: both BV–PV pairs undergo a meaning shift, and the BVs are semantically similar; example: *(an)graben::(an)baggern* 'to hit on so.' with both *graben* and *baggern* 'to dig'

For practical reasons, we merged the left/right asymmetric cases ASYMCOMP such that the annotated meaning shift was always on the left-hand side (by swapping the asymmetric-right pairs), since these cases represent instances of the same phenomenon, i.e., where just one of the pairs underwent a meaning shift.

Despite a distinction into four categories per instance, we obtained a moderate Fleiss' κ agreement of 0.43 as the mean across the four particles:

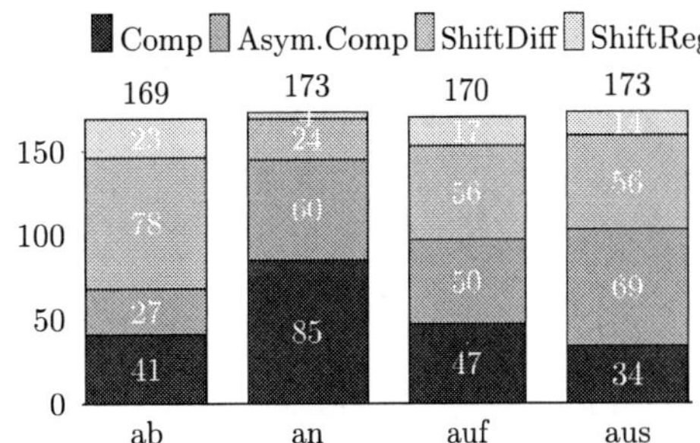

Figure 2: Number of majority class instances for four meaning shift categories by particle type.

We transformed the annotations to actual class assignments by removing all instances from the dataset without a category majority, i.e., we only included BV–PV analogy pairs where at least 3 out of 5 annotators agreed on the shift category. We assigned the majority decision as class label. The final collection still contains 685 analogy pairs.

The distribution across the four particles and the four categories is illustrated in Figure 2, examples are listed in Table 1. While meaning shifts have been observed across all four particle types, the analogical case SHIFTREG mentioned in previous corpus explorations represents the smallest class overall (8.5%). For the particle *an*, the cases with two meaning shifts (SHIFTDIFF+SHIFTREG) are especially rare (16.2%).

A manual inspection revealed that etymology and semantic change often led to opaque PVs annotated as SHIFTDIFF; an example is *abkupfern* 'to plagiarise'. The origin of this meaning is based on the 18th century engravers who etched replicas of text and images into copper (*Kupfer*) plates.

---

[1] www.duden.de/suchen/dudenonline/
[2] https://www.wiktionary.org/
[3] The dataset is publicly available at www.ims.uni-stuttgart.de/data/pv-meaning-shift.

COMP	ASYMCOMP	SHIFTDIFF	SHIFTREG
abfeilen::abschleifen	abbauen::abmontieren	abschreiben::abkupfern	abstottern::abrattern
abkuppeln::abhängen	abchecken::abprüfen	abschweifen::abdriften	abrauschen::abzischen
aneignen::anlernen	anfeuern::anbrennen	ankreiden::anlasten	anheizen::anfeuern
anbrüllen::anschreien	anhängen::anheften	anfechten::angreifen	anwerfen::anschmeißen
auftupfen::auftropfen	aufdrehen::aufzwirbeln	auftreiben::aufspüren	aufwirbeln::aufrühren
auffuttern::aufessen	aufmotzen::aufstylen	aufkreuzen::auftauchen	aufbrummen::aufdonnern
aufritzen::aufschlitzen	aufwühlen::aufgraben	auferlegen::aufbrummen	aufkeimen::aufblühen
ausrupfen::ausjäten	ausposaunen::ausplaudern	ausfeilen::ausbrüten	ausweinen::ausheulen
ausschnaufen::ausatmen	aussaugen::auspumpen	ausstechen::ausbremsen	auskochen::ausbrüten

Table 1: Example of BV–PV analogies across the four meaning shift categories.

3 Representations of BV–PV Analogies

The parallelogram in Figure 1 illustrates the (dis-) similarities between BVs and PVs that come into play when distinguishing between the four types of (non-)shifts in our dataset: COMP requires all four sides in the parallelogram to provide strong similarites; SHIFTREG requires the BV_i–BV_j and the PV_i–PV_j sides to provide strong similarities, and both BV_i–PV_i sides to provide strong dissimilarities; etc. An obvious option to address the classification of the BV–PV analogies is thus by relying on standard cosine scores, when representing the verbs in a distributional semantic model (DSM). The following paragraphs describe such a basic cosine-similarity model that we used as a baseline, as well as alternative features which we added as potentially salient regarding our task.

3.1 Basic Distributional Similarity Model

We created a basic DSM to represent all BVs and all PVs by using a corpus-derived 300-dimensional vector representation. As corpus resource we relied on *DECOW14AX*, a German web corpus containing 12 billion tokens (Schäfer and Bildhauer, 2012; Schäfer, 2015). The verb vectors were obtained by looking at all context words within a symmetrical window of size 3. We applied positive pointwise mutual information (PPMI) feature weighting together with singular value decomposition (SVD). Measuring the cosine similarities between the BVs and PVs as suggested by Figure 1 then represents our basic distributional similarity model containing four cosine values.

Figure 3 looks into cosine values across combinations of meaning shift categories. Figure 3 (a) shows box plots for BV-PV pairs in the two compositional categories vs. the meaning-shifted categories. It illustrates that BV-PV combinations with a meaning shift indeed have lower cosine values between BVs and PVs than BV-PV combinations without meaning shifts. The similarity between BVs is expected to be higher for the regularly shifted cases, where the base verbs have something in common, in contrast to the irregular cases. This is also confirmed, cf. Figure 3 (b).

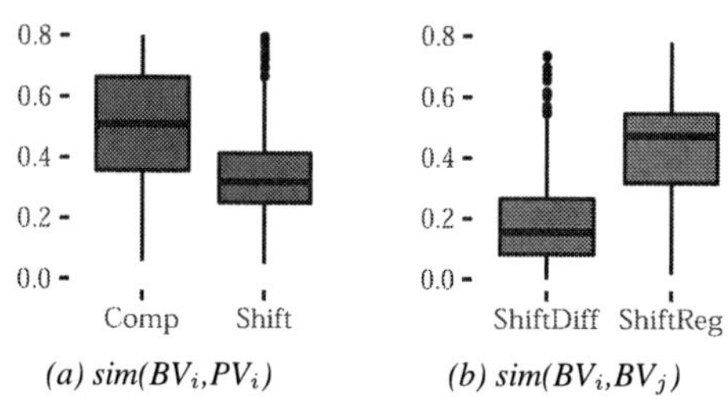

(a) $sim(BV_i, PV_i)$ (b) $sim(BV_i, BV_j)$

Figure 3: Cosine distributions across categories.

3.2 Generalisation Models

Classes and clusters are powerful techniques to generalise over unseen or infrequent events. We therefore extended the basic similarity model by adding class label features for the four involved verbs. We compared three different classifications. (1) We used the 15 verb classes from *GermaNet* (Hamp and Feldweg, 1997; Kunze, 2000). For particle verbs not covered by *GermaNet*, we used the existing verbs as a seed set and applied a nearest-prototype (centroid) classifier to all other BVs and PVs, with a centroid for each of the 15 classes. Thus we were able to assign class labels to all verbs in our dataset. (2) For three out of our four particle types (*ab, an, auf*), we found existing manual semantic classifications with 9, 8 and 11 classes, respectively (Lechler and Roßdeutscher, 2009; Kliche, 2011; Springorum, 2011). To obtain class labels for all verbs, we applied the same nearest-centroid technique as for the *GermaNet* classes. (3) We compared the two resource-based methods with an unsupervised k-Means clustering based on the verbs' vector representations. Unlike the other methods, k-Means learns the centroids without manually defined seed assignments. We set the number of clusters to $k = 10$, as this granularity was similar to the manual classifications.

3.3 Affect Models

A BV–PV meaning shift often involves a change in emotion and/or sentiment. For example, while the BV *servieren* 'to serve' is perceived as rather neutral or slightly positive, the PV *abservieren* 'to dump sb.' has a clearly negative meaning and correlates with the emotion *sadness*. On the other hand, the BV *motzen* 'to grumble' is associated with a negative sentiment and the emotion *anger*, while its PV *aufmotzen* 'to shine up, soup up' indicates a positive change.

In a slightly different vein, non-literal word usage often correlates with the degree of abstractness of the word's contexts (Turney et al., 2011; Tsvetkov et al., 2014; Köper and Schulte im Walde, 2016). For example, the PV *abschminken* with the BV *schminken* 'to put on make-up' has a literal, very concrete meaning ('to remove make-up') and also a shifted, very abstract non-literal meaning ('to forget about something').

We enriched the basic similarity model by integrating affective information from human-created lexicons. Since affective datasets are typically small-scale and mostly exist for English, we applied a cross-lingual approach (Smith et al., 2017) to learn a linear transformation that aligns monolingual vectors from two languages in a single vector space. We took off-the-shelf word representations[4] for German and English that live in the same semantic space, learned a regression model based on the English data, and applied it to the German data by relying on findings from Köper and Schulte im Walde (2017), who showed that a feed-forward neural network obtained a high correlation with human-annotated ratings.

The procedure was applied to a range of affective norm datasets in isolation: The *NRC Hashtag Emotion Lexicon* (Mohammad and Kiritchenko, 2015) contains emotional ratings for $17k$ words; we used *anger, disgust, fear, joy*, and *sadness*.

Warriner et al. (2013) collected $14k$ ratings for *valence* and *arousal*. For *concreteness*, we relied on the $40k$ ratings from Brysbaert et al. (2014). Finally, we used the $10k$ ratings for *happiness* from Dodds et al. (2011). In total, we obtained nine affective values for 2.2 million words.[5]

We added the affective features to our basic similarity model by first looking up the 9-dimensional affect vectors for all four verbs involved in an analogy, and then calculating for each of the four similarities in the analogy parallelogram (Figure 1) the element-wise differences between the nine affective dimensions of the respective two verbs, resulting in $4 \times 9 = 36$ extra vector dimensions.

In addition to looking at the verbs' affective values we also looked at the affect of the respective context words: For each verb we created a second 9-dimensional vector with average affective values across the 500 most associated context words, according to PPMI. With respect to the four verbs in the analogy, this resulted in another $4 \times 9 = 36$ extra vector dimensions.

We further added affect information restricted to the common context words of the involved verbs (red and blue intersections in Figure 4): For each intersection of the two BVs and the two PVs as well as the two BV–PV combinations, we learned another 9-dimensional emotional centroid, now only based on the shared context words, and provided the element-wise differences between the two centroids as a feature.

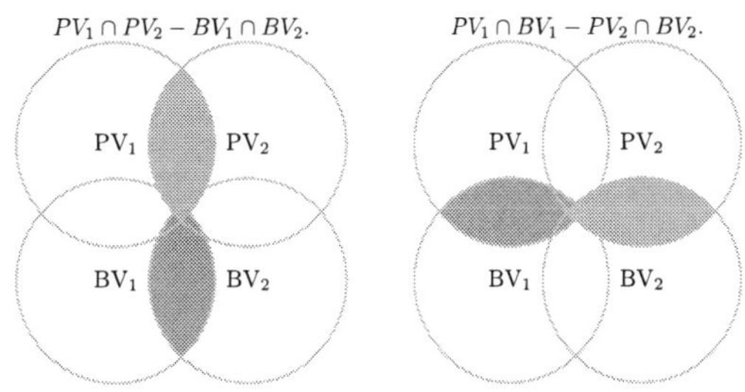

Figure 4: Venn diagrams with intersections.

4 Experiments on BV–PV Analogies

Two classification scenarios were implemented: a four-class distinction between our four shift categories (*4-Classes*), and a binary distinction between cases where both BV–PV pairs include a

---

[4] https://github.com/Babylonpartners/fastText_multilingual

[5] These ratings are also available at www.ims.uni-stuttgart.de/data/pv-meaning-shift.

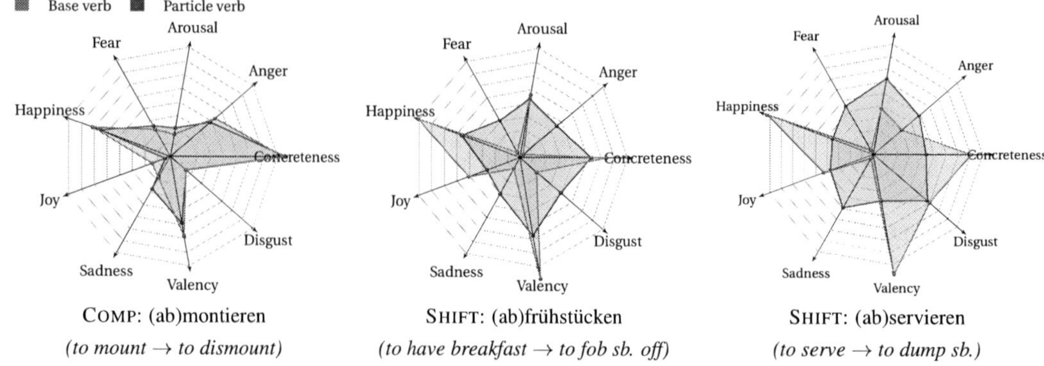

Figure 5: Changes in affect and emotion for one compositional and two shifted BV–PV pairs. The affect/emotion values are based on the top associated context words according to PPMI.

meaning shift vs. BV–PV pairs including cases of compositionality (*Shift-vs-Comp*).

We applied a supervised classification setting based on support vector machines (SVMs) with an RBF kernel (Chang and Lin, 2011), using 10-fold cross-validation. Next to the similarity, generalisation and affect features, we provided the particle type as a feature in all settings. Table 2 reports the results across feature sets. As evaluation metric we report accuracy and a macro-average (equally-weighted) f-score (F_1) over all classes.

	4-Classes		Shift-vs-Comp	
	Acc	F_1	Acc	F_1
Majority baseline	31.24	.12	60.29	.38
Basic Sim	40.73	.32	65.10	.60
Sim+GermaNet	43.36	.34	67.15	.59
Sim+ManClass	45.55	.36	69.05	.62
Sim+k-Means	52.99	.37	70.51	.66
Affect (full)	57.08	.44	76.49	.74
Affect only verbs	47.73	.37	69.05	.65
Affect only context	**58.39**	**.45**	**78.54**	**.77**
Combination	56.20	.44	77.08	.75

Table 2: Results for 4- and 2-class distinctions, reporting accuracy and macro-F_1.

All models perform significantly[6] better than the majority baseline. In addition, the full and the context-only affective models perform significantly better than the similarity models with and without generalisation, even though the unsupervised k-Means clustering improves the basic similarity model significantly (*Sim+k-Means*). Finally, the context-only affective model outperforms the verb-only affective model. Interestingly, a combination of all features (*Combination*) does not perform better than the context-only affective model

---

[6]Significance relies on χ^2 with $p < 0.001$.

in isolation.

A leave-one-out classification using the best classifier *Affect only context* as starting point revealed that most performance (accuracy) is lost when removing the emotion *fear* (-2.77), followed by the emotion *joy* (-1.46) and *arousal* (-0.88). In contrast, features related to *disgust* showed no impact on the overall performance.

Figure 5 illustrates that we can spot changes in affect and emotion even on the verb level: For three BV–PV verb pairs with particle *ab*, it plots the nine affective and emotion ratings for both verbs, after rescaling to an interval of $[0, 10]$. In the compositional case (a) the PV is highly similar to the BV in all dimensions, creating roughly the same shape as the BV. In the shift cases (b) and (c), the PVs are less concrete and evoke less *happiness* and *joy* than the BVs, while they evoke more *fear*, *anger* and *sadness* in comparison to their BVs.

5 Conclusion

This paper presented a computational model of meaning shifts for German particle verbs. Relying on a novel dataset, we found that shifts were observed across all our four particle types, but the analogical case mentioned in previous corpus explorations only represented the smallest class overall (8.5%). SVM models successfully distinguished between shift categories, with verb classes boosting standard cosine similarity performance, and affective context features representing the most salient indicators.

Acknowledgments

The research was supported by the DFG Collaborative Research Centre SFB 732.

References

Marc Brysbaert, Amy Beth Warriner, and Victor Kuperman. 2014. Concreteness Ratings for 40 Thousand generally known English Word Lemmas. *Behavior Research Methods* 64:904–911.

Chih-Chung Chang and Chih-Jen Lin. 2011. LIBSVM: A Library for Support Vector Machines. *ACM Transactions on Intelligent Systems and Technology* 2:1–27. Software available at http://www.csie.ntu.edu.tw/~cjlin/libsvm.

Peter Sheridan Dodds, Kameron D. Harris, Isabel M. Kloumann, Catherine A. Bliss, and C. M. Danforth. 2011. Temporal Patterns of Happiness and Information in a Global Social Network: Hedonometrics and Twitter. *PLOS ONE* 6(12):1–26.

Birgit Hamp and Helmut Feldweg. 1997. GermaNet – A Lexical-Semantic Net for German. In *Proceedings of the ACL Workshop on Automatic Information Extraction and Building Lexical Semantic Resources for NLP Applications*. Madrid, Spain, pages 9–15.

Fritz Kliche. 2011. Semantic Variants of German Particle Verbs with "ab". *Leuvense Bijdragen* 97:3–27.

Maximilian Köper and Sabine Schulte im Walde. 2016. Distinguishing Literal and Non-Literal Usage of German Particle Verbs. In *Proceedings of the Conference of the North American Chapter of the Association for Computational Linguistics: Human Language Technologies*. San Diego, California, USA, pages 353–362.

Maximilian Köper and Sabine Schulte im Walde. 2017. Improving Verb Metaphor Detection by Propagating Abstractness to Words, Phrases and Individual Senses. In *Proceedings of the 1st Workshop on Sense, Concept and Entity Representations and their Applications*. Valencia, Spain, pages 24–30.

Claudia Kunze. 2000. Extension and Use of GermaNet, a Lexical-Semantic Database. In *Proceedings of the 2nd International Conference on Language Resources and Evaluation*. Athens, Greece, pages 999–1002.

Andrea Lechler and Antje Roßdeutscher. 2009. German Particle Verbs with *auf*. Reconstructing their Composition in a DRT-based Framework. *Linguistische Berichte* 220:439–478.

Omer Levy and Yoav Goldberg. 2014. Linguistic Regularities in Sparse and Explicit Word Representations. In *Proceedings of the 18th Conference on Computational Natural Language Learning*. Maryland, USA, June, pages 171–180.

Tomas Mikolov, Wen tau Yih, and Geoffrey Zweig. 2013. Linguistic Regularities in Continuous Space Word Representations. In *Proceedings of the Conference of the North American Chapter of the Association for Computational Linguistics: Human Language Technologies*. Atlanta, GA, USA, pages 746–751.

Saif M. Mohammad and Svetlana Kiritchenko. 2015. Using Hashtags to Capture Fine Emotion Categories from Tweets. *Computational Intelligence* 31(2):301–326.

Pamela S. Morgan. 1997. Figuring out *figure out*: Metaphor and the Semantics of English Verb-Particle Constructions. *Cognitive Linguistics* 8(4):327–357.

Roland Schäfer. 2015. Processing and Querying Large Web Corpora with the COW14 Architecture. In Piotr Bański, Hanno Biber, Evelyn Breiteneder, Marc Kupietz, Harald Lüngen, and Andreas Witt, editors, *Proceedings of the 3rd Workshop on Challenges in the Management of Large Corpora*. pages 28 – 34.

Roland Schäfer and Felix Bildhauer. 2012. Building Large Corpora from the Web Using a New Efficient Tool Chain. In *Proceedings of the 8th International Conference on Language Resources and Evaluation*. Istanbul, Turkey, pages 486–493.

Samuel L. Smith, David H. P. Turban, Steven Hamblin, and Nils Y. Hammerla. 2017. Offline Bilingual Word Vectors, Orthogonal Transformations and the Inverted Softmax. In *Proceedings of 5th International Conference on Learning Representations*. Toulon, France.

Robert Speer, Joshua Chin, and Catherine Havasi. 2017. ConceptNet 5.5: An Open Multilingual Graph of General Knowledge. In *Proceedings of the 31st AAAI Conference on Artificial Intelligence*. San Francisco, California, USA.

Sylvia Springorum. 2011. DRT-based Analysis of the German Verb Particle "an". *Leuvense Bijdragen* 97:80–105.

Sylvia Springorum, Jason Utt, and Sabine Schulte im Walde. 2013. Regular Meaning Shifts in German Particle Verbs: A Case Study. In *Proceedings of the 10th International Conference on Computational Semantics*. Potsdam, Germany, pages 228–239.

Yulia Tsvetkov, Leonid Boytsov, Anatole Gershman, Eric Nyberg, and Chris Dyer. 2014. Metaphor Detection with Cross-Lingual Model Transfer. In *Proceedings of the 52nd Annual Meeting of the Association for Computational Linguistics*. Baltimore, Maryland, pages 248–258.

Peter D. Turney. 2006. Similarity of Semantic Relations. *Computational Linguistics* 32(3):379–416.

Peter D. Turney. 2012. Domain and Functions: A Dual-Space Model of Semantic Relations and Compositions. *Journal of Artificial Intelligence Research* 44:533–585.

Peter D. Turney, Yair Neuman, Dan Assaf, and Yohai Cohen. 2011. Literal and Metaphorical Sense Identification through Concrete and Abstract Context. In *Proceedings of the Conference on Empirical Methods in Natural Language Processing*. Edinburgh, UK, pages 680–690.

Amy Beth Warriner, Victor Kuperman, and Marc Brysbaert. 2013. Norms of Valence, Arousal, and Dominance for 13,915 English Lemmas. *Behavior Research Methods* 45(4):1191–1207.

Character-based Neural Networks for Sentence Pair Modeling

Wuwei Lan and **Wei Xu**
Department of Computer Science and Engineering
Ohio State University
{lan.105, xu.1265}@osu.edu

Abstract

Sentence pair modeling is critical for many NLP tasks, such as paraphrase identification, semantic textual similarity, and natural language inference. Most state-of-the-art neural models for these tasks rely on pretrained word embedding and compose sentence-level semantics in varied ways; however, few works have attempted to verify whether we really need pretrained embeddings in these tasks. In this paper, we study how effective subword-level (character and character n-gram) representations are in sentence pair modeling. Though it is well-known that subword models are effective in tasks with single sentence input, including language modeling and machine translation, they have not been systematically studied in sentence pair modeling tasks where the semantic and string similarities between texts matter. Our experiments show that subword models without any pretrained word embedding can achieve new state-of-the-art results on two social media datasets and competitive results on news data for paraphrase identification.

1   Introduction

Recently, there have been various neural network models proposed for sentence pair modeling tasks, including semantic similarity (Agirre et al., 2015), paraphrase identification (Dolan et al., 2004; Xu et al., 2015), natural language inference (Bowman et al., 2015), etc. Most, if not all, of these state-of-the-art neural models (Yin et al., 2016; Parikh et al., 2016; He and Lin, 2016; Tomar et al., 2017; Shen et al., 2017) have achieved the best performances for these tasks by using pretrained word embeddings, but results without pretraining are less frequently reported or noted. In fact, we will show that, even with fixed randomized word vectors, the pairwise word interaction model (He and Lin, 2016) based on contextual word vector

similarities can still achieve strong performance by capturing identical words and similar surface context features. Moreover, pretrained word embeddings generally have poor coverage in social media domain where out-of-vocabulary rate often reaches over 20% (Baldwin et al., 2013).

We investigated the effectiveness of subword units, such as characters and character n-grams, in place of words for vector representations in sentence pair modeling. Though it is well-known that subword representations are effective to model out-of-vocabulary words in many NLP tasks with a single sentence input, such as machine translation (Luong et al., 2015; Costa-jussà and Fonollosa, 2016), language modeling (Ling et al., 2015; Vania and Lopez, 2017), and sequence labeling (dos Santos and Guimarães, 2015; Plank et al., 2016), they are not systematically studied in the tasks that concern pairs of sentences. Unlike in modeling individual sentences, subword representations have impacts not only on the out-of-vocabulary words but also more directly on the relation between two sentences, which is calculated based on vector similarities in many sentence pair modeling approaches (more details in Section 2.1). For example, while subwords may capture useful string similarities between a pair of sentences (e.g. spelling or morphological variations: *sister* and *sista*, *teach* and *teaches*), they could introduce errors (e.g. similarly spelled words with completely different meanings: *ware* and *war*).

To better understand the role of subword embedding in sentence pair modeling, we performed experimental comparisons that vary (1) the type of subword unit, (2) the composition function, and (3) the datasets of different characteristics. We also presented experiments with language modeling as an auxiliary multi-task learning objective, showing consistent improvements. Taken together, subword and language modeling establish

157

Proceedings of NAACL-HLT 2018, pages 157–163
New Orleans, Louisiana, June 1 - 6, 2018. ©2018 Association for Computational Linguistics

new state-of-the-art results in two social media datasets and competitive results in a news dataset for paraphrase identification without using any pretrained word embeddings.

2 Sentence Pair Modeling with Subwords

The current neural networks for sentence pair modeling (Yin et al., 2016; Parikh et al., 2016; He and Lin, 2016; Liu et al., 2016; Tomar et al., 2017; Wang et al., 2017; Shen et al., 2017, etc) follow a more or less similar design with three main components: (a) contextualized word vectors generated via Bi-LSTM, CNN, or attention, as inputs; (b) soft or hard word alignment and interactions across sentences; (c) and the output classification layer. Different models vary in implementation details, and most importantly, to capture the same essential intuition in the word alignment (also encoded with contextual information) – the semantic relation between two sentences depends largely on the relations of aligned chunks (Agirre et al., 2016). In this paper, we used pairwise word interaction model (He and Lin, 2016) as a representative example and staring point, which reported robust performance across multiple sentence pair modeling tasks and the best results by neural models on social media data (Lan et al., 2017).

2.1 Pairwise Word Interaction (PWI) Model

Let $w^a = (w_1^a, ..., w_m^a)$ and $w^b = (w_1^a, ..., w_n^b)$ be the input sentence pair consisting of m and n tokens, respectively. Each word vector $w_i \in \mathbb{R}^d$ is initialized with pretrained d-dimensional word embedding (Pennington et al., 2014; Wieting et al., 2015, 2016), then encoded with word context and sequence order through bidirectional LSTMs:

$$\overrightarrow{h}_i = LSTM^f(w_i, \overrightarrow{h}_{i-1}) \tag{1}$$

$$\overleftarrow{h}_i = LSTM^b(w_i, \overleftarrow{h}_{i+1}) \tag{2}$$

$$\overleftrightarrow{h}_i = [\overrightarrow{h}_i, \overleftarrow{h}_i] \tag{3}$$

$$h_i^+ = \overrightarrow{h}_i + \overleftarrow{h}_i \tag{4}$$

where $\overrightarrow{h}_i$ represents forward hidden state, $\overleftarrow{h}_i$ represents backward hidden state, and $\overleftrightarrow{h}_i$ and h_i^+ are the concatenation and summation of two directional hidden states.

For all word pairs (w_i^a, w_j^b) across sentences, the model directly calculates word pair interactions using cosine similarity, Euclidean distance, and dot product over the outputs of the encoding layer:

$$D(\overrightarrow{h}_i, \overrightarrow{h}_j) = [cos(\overrightarrow{h}_i, \overrightarrow{h}_j), \tag{5}$$
$$L2Euclid(\overrightarrow{h}_i, \overrightarrow{h}_j),$$
$$DotProduct(\overrightarrow{h}_i, \overrightarrow{h}_j)].$$

The above equation can also apply to other states $\overleftarrow{h}$, $\overleftrightarrow{h}$ and h^+, resulting in a tensor $\mathbf{D}^{13 \times m \times n}$ after padding one extra bias term. A "hard" attention is applied to the interaction tensor to further enforce the word alignment, by sorting the interaction values and selecting top ranked word pairs. A 19-layer-deep CNN is followed to aggregate the word interaction features and the softmax layer to predicate classification probabilities.

2.2 Embedding Subwords in PWI Model

Our subword models only involve modification of the input representation layer in the pairwise interaciton model. Let $c_1, ..., c_k$ be the subword (character unigram, bigram and trigram) sequence of a word w. The subword embedding matrix is $\mathbf{C} \in \mathbb{R}^{d' * k}$, where each subword is encoded into the d'-dimension vector. The same subwords will share the same embeddings. We considered two different composition functions to assemble subword embeddings into word embedding:

Char C2W (Ling et al., 2015) applies Bi-LSTM to subword sequence $c_1, ..., c_k$, then the last hidden state $\overrightarrow{h}_k^{char}$ in forward direction and the first hidden state $\overleftarrow{h}_0^{char}$ of the backward direction are linearly combined into word-level embedding w:

$$w = \mathbf{W}_f \cdot \overrightarrow{h}_k^{char} + \mathbf{W}_b \cdot \overleftarrow{h}_0^{char} + b \tag{6}$$

where $\mathbf{W}_f$, $\mathbf{W}_b$ and b are parameters.

Char CNN (Kim et al., 2016) applies a convolution operation between subword sequence matrix $\mathbf{C}$ and a filter $\mathbf{F} \in \mathbb{R}^{d' \times l}$ of width l to obtain a feature map $\mathbf{f} \in \mathbb{R}^{k-l+1}$:

$$\mathbf{f}_j = tanh(\langle \mathbf{C}[*, j : j + l - 1], \mathbf{F} \rangle + b) \tag{7}$$

where $\langle A, B \rangle = Tr(AB^T)$ is the Frobenius inner product, b is a bias and $\mathbf{f}_j$ is the jth element of $\mathbf{f}$. We then take the max-over-time operation to select the most important element:

$$y_{\mathbf{f}} = \max_j \mathbf{f}_j. \tag{8}$$

Dataset	Training Size	Test Size	# INV	# OOV	OOV Ratio	Source
PIT-2015	11530	838	7771	1238	13.7%	Twitter trends
Twitter-URL	42200	9324	24905	11440	31.5%	Twitter/news
MSRP	4076	1725	16226	1614	9.0%	news

Table 1: Statistics of three benchmark datasets for paraphrase identification. The training and testing sizes are in numbers of sentence pairs. The number of unique in-vocabulary (INV) and out-of-vocabulary (OOV) words are calculated based on the publicly available GloVe embeddings (details in Section 3.2).

After applying q filters with varied lengths, we can get the array $w = [y_1, ..., y_q]$, which is followed by a one-layer highway network to generate final word embedding.

2.3 Auxiliary Language Modeling (LM)

We adapted a multi-task structure, originally proposed by (Rei, 2017) for sequential tagging, to further improve the subword representations in sentence pair modeling. In addition to training the model for sentence pair tasks, we used a secondary language modeling objective that predicts the next word and previous word using softmax over the hidden states of Bi-LSTM as follows:

$$\overrightarrow{E}_{LM} = -\sum_{t=1}^{T-1}(\log(P(w_{t+1}|\overrightarrow{m_t}))) \tag{9}$$

$$\overleftarrow{E}_{LM} = -\sum_{t=2}^{T}(\log(P(w_{t-1}|\overleftarrow{m_t}))) \tag{10}$$

where $\overrightarrow{m_t} = tanh(\overrightarrow{W}_{hm}\overrightarrow{h}_t)$ and $\overleftarrow{m_t} = tanh(\overleftarrow{W}_{hm}\overleftarrow{h}_t)$. The Bi-LSTM here is separate from the one in PWI model. The language modeling objective can be combined into sentence pair modeling through a joint objective function:

$$E_{joint} = E + \gamma(\overrightarrow{E}_{LM} + \overleftarrow{E}_{LM}), \tag{11}$$

which balances subword-based sentence pair modeling objective E and language modeling with a weighting coefficient γ.

3 Experiments

3.1 Datasets

We performed experiments on three benchmark datasets for paraphrase identification; each contained pairs of naturally occurring sentences manually labeled as paraphrases and non-paraphrases for binary classification: **Twitter URL** (Lan et al., 2017) was collected from tweets sharing the same URL with major news outlets such as @CNN. This dataset keeps a balance between formal and informal language. **PIT-2015** (Xu et al., 2014,

2015) comes from the Task 1 of Semeval 2015 and was collected from tweets under the same trending topic, which contains varied topics and language styles. **MSRP** (Dolan and Brockett, 2005) was derived from clustered news articles reporting the same event in formal language. Table 1 shows vital statistics for all three datasets.

3.2 Settings

To compare models fairly without implementation variations, we reimplemented all models into a single PyTorch framework.[1] We followed the setups in (He and Lin, 2016) and (Lan et al., 2017) for the pairwise word interaction model, and used the 200-dimensional GloVe word vectors (Pennington et al., 2014), trained on 27 billion words from Twitter (vocabulary size of 1.2 milion words) for social media datasets, and 300-dimensional GloVe vectors, trained on 840 billion words (vocabulary size of 2.2 milion words) from Common Crawl for the MSRP dataset. For cases without pretraining, the word/subword vectors were initialized with random samples drawn uniformly from the range [0.05, 0.05]. We used the same hyperparameters in the C2W (Ling et al., 2015) and CNN-based (Kim et al., 2016) compositions for subword models, except that the composed word embeddings were set to 200- or 300- dimensions as the pretrained word embeddings to make experiment results more comparable. For each experiment, we reported results with 20 epochs.

3.3 Results

Table 2 shows the experiment results on three datasets. We reported maximum F1 scores of any point on the precision-recall curve (Lipton et al., 2014) following previous work.

Word Models The word-level pairwise interaction models, even without pretraining (randomzied) or fine-tuning (fixed), showed strong performance across all three datasets. This reflects

---

[1]The code and data can be obtained from the first and second author's websites.

Model	Model Variations	pre-train	#parameters	Twitter URL	PIT-2015	MSRP
Word Models	Logistic Regression	–	–	0.683	0.645	0.829
	(Lan et al., 2017)	Yes	9.5M	0.749	<u>0.667</u>	0.834
	pretrained, fixed	Yes	2.2M	0.753	0.632	0.834
	pretrained, updated	Yes	9.5M	0.756	0.656	0.832
	randomized, fixed	–	2.2M	0.728	0.456	0.821
	randomized, updated	–	9.5M	0.735	0.625	0.834
Subword Models	C2W, unigram	–	2.6M	0.742	0.534	0.816
	C2W, bigram	–	2.7M	0.742	0.563	0.825
	C2W, trigram	–	3.1M	0.729	0.576	0.824
	CNN, unigram	–	6.5M	0.756	0.589	0.820
	CNN, bigram	–	6.5M	0.760	0.646	0.814
	CNN, trigram	–	6.7M	0.753	<u>0.667</u>	0.818
Subword+LM	LM, C2W, unigram	–	3.5M	0.760	**0.691**	0.831
	LM, C2W, bigram	–	3.6M	**0.768**	0.651	0.830
	LM, C2W, trigram	–	4.0M	<u>0.765</u>	0.659	0.831
	LM, CNN, unigram	–	7.4M	0.754	0.665	**0.840**
	LM, CNN, bigram	–	7.4M	0.761	<u>0.667</u>	<u>0.835</u>
	LM, CNN, trigram	–	7.6M	0.759	<u>0.667</u>	0.831

Table 2: Results in F1 scores on Twitter-URL, PIT-2015 and MSRP datasets. The best performance figure in each dataset is denoted in **bold** typeface and the second best is denoted by an <u>underline</u>. Without using any pretrained word embeddings, the Subword+LM models achieve better or competitive performance compared to word models.

the effective design of the BiLSTM and word interaction layers, as well as the unique character of sentence pair modeling, where n-gram overlapping positively signifies the extent of semantic similarity. As a reference, a logistic regression baseline with simple n-gram (also in stemmed form) overlapping features can also achieve good performance on PIT-2015 and MSRP datasets. With that being said, pretraining and fine-tuning word vectors are mostly crucial for pushing out the last bit of performance from word-level models.

Subword Models (+LMs) Without using any pretrained word embeddings, subword-based pairwise word interaction models can achieve very competitive results on social media datasets compared with the best word-based models (pretrained, fixed). For MSRP with only 9% of OOV words (Table 1), the subword models do not show advantages. Once the subword mod-

els are trained with multi-task language modeling (Subword+LM), the performance on all datasets are further improved, outperforming the best previously reported results by neural models (Lan et al., 2017). A qualitative analysis reveals that subwords are crucial for out-of-vocabulary words while language modeling ensures more semantic and syntactic compatibility (Table 3).

3.4 Combining Word and Subword Representations

In addition, we experimented with combining the pretrained word embeddings and subword models with various strategies: concatenation, weighted average, adaptive models (Miyamoto and Cho, 2016) and attention models (Rei et al., 2016). The weighted average outperformed all others but only showed slight improvement over word-based models in social media datasets; other combination strategies could even lower the performance. The best performance was 0.763 F1 in Twitter-URL and 0.671 in PIT-2015 with a weighted average: $0.75 \times$ word embedding $+ 0.25 \times$ subword embedding.

4 Model Ablations

In the original PWI model, He and Lin (2016) performed pattern recognition of complex semantic relationships by applying a 19-layer deep convolutional neural network (CNN) on the word pair interaction tensor (Eq. 5). However, the SemEval task on Interpretable Semantic Textual Similarity

Model	INV Words		OOV Words	
	any	walking	#airport	brexit
Word	anything	walk	salomon	bollocks
	anyone	running	363	misogynistic
	other	dead	#trumpdchotel	patriarchy
	there	around	hillarys	sexist
Subword	analogy	waffling	@atlairport	grexit
	nay	slagging	#dojreport	bret
	away	scaling	#macbookpro	juliet
	andy	#hacking	#guangzhou	#brexit
Subword + LM	any1	warming	airport	#brexit
	many	wagging	#airports	brit
	ang	waging	rapport	ofbrexit
	nanny	waiting	#statecapturereport	drought-hit

Table 3: Nearest neighbors of word vectors under cosine similarity in Twitter-URL dataset.

	Model Variations	CNN[19]	#parameters	#hours/epoch	Twitter URL	PIT-2015	MSRP
Word Models	Logistic Regression	–	–	–	0.683	0.645	0.829
	pretrained, fixed	Yes	2.2M	4.5h	0.753	0.632	<u>0.834</u>
		–	1.4M	3.2h	0.741	0.602	0.827
Subword Models	C2W, unigram	Yes	2.6M	5.8h	0.742	0.534	0.816
		–	1.4M	4.6h	0.741	0.655	0.808
	CNN, unigram	Yes	6.5M	5.4h	0.756	0.589	0.820
		–	5.3M	4.2h	<u>0.759</u>	0.659	0.809
Subword+LM	LM, C2W, unigram	Yes	3.5M	6.5h	**0.760**	**0.691**	0.831
		–	2.3M	5.3h	0.746	0.625	0.811
	LM, CNN, unigram	Yes	7.4M	5.8h	0.754	<u>0.665</u>	**0.840**
		–	6.2M	4.6h	0.758	0.659	0.809

Table 4: Comparison of F1 scores between the original PWI model with 19-layer CNN for aggregation and the simplified model without 19-layer CNN on Twitter-URL, PIT-2015 and MSRP datasets. The number of parameters and training time per epoch shown are based on the Twitter URL dataset and a single NVIDIA Pascal P100 GPU.

(Agirre et al., 2016) in part demonstrated that the semantic relationship between two sentences depends largely on the relations of aligned words or chunks. Since the interaction tensor in the PWI model already encodes word alignment information in the form of vector similarities, a natural question is whether a 19-layer CNN is necessary.

Table 4 shows the results of our systems with and without the 19-layer CNN for aggregating the pairwise word interactions before the final softmax layer. While in most cases the 19-layer CNN helps to achieve better or comparable performance, it comes at the expense of ∼25% increase of training time. An exception is the character-based PWI without language model, which performs well on the PIT-2015 dataset without the 19-layer CNN and comparably to logistic regression with string overlap features (Eyecioglu and Keller, 2015). A closer look into the datasets reveals that PIT-2015 has a similar level of unigram overlap as the Twitter URL corpus (Table 5),[2] but lower character bigram overlap (indicative of spelling variations) and lower word bigram overlap (indicative of word reordering) between the pairs of sentences that are labeled as paraphrase.

The 19-layer CNN appears to be crucial for the MSRP dataset, which has the smallest training size and is skewed toward very high word overlap.[2] For the two social media datasets, our subword models have improved performance compared to pretrained word models regardless of having or not having the 19-layer CNN.

5 Conclusion

We presented a focused study on the effectiveness of subword models in sentence pair modeling and showed competitive results without using pretrained word embeddings. We also showed that subword models can benefit from multi-task learning with simple language modeling, and established new start-of-the-art results for paraphrase identification on two Twitter datasets, where out-of-vocabulary words and spelling variations are profound. The results shed light on future work on language-independent paraphrase identification and multilingual paraphrase acquisition where pretrained word embeddings on large corpora are not readily available in many languages.

Acknowledgments

We thank John Wieting and Mikhail Belkin for valuable discussions, and Ohio Supercomputer Center (Center, 2012) for computing resources. Funding was provided by the U.S. Army Research Office (ARO) and Defense Advanced Research Projects Agency (DARPA) under Contract Number W911NF-17-C-0095. The content of the information in this document does not necessarily reflect the position or the policy of the Government, and no official endorsement should be inferred. The U.S. Government is authorized to reproduce and distribute reprints for government purposes notwithstanding any copyright notation here on.

	Twitter URL	PIT-2015	MSRP
#char unigrams in shorter sentence (all)	67.5	36.2	109.0
#char unigrams in longer sentence (all)	97.7	50.5	128.5
#char unigrams of the union (all)	101.1	53.0	130.0
#char unigrams of the intersection (all)	64.1	33.7	107.4
char unigram overlap (all)	63.4%	63.5%	82.6%
char unigram overlap (paraphrase-only)	68.8%	67.0%	84.7%
char bigram overlap (all)	30.8%	33.6%	67.4%
char bigram overlap (paraphrase-only)	48.2%	42.4%	71.6%
word unigram overlap (all)	13.3%	21.7%	54.8%
word unigram overlap (paraphrase-only)	32.0%	30.2%	59.1%
word bigram overlap (all)	5.3%	8.4%	33.2%
word bigram overlap (paraphrase-only)	17.9%	12.3%	36.8%

Table 5: Character and word overlap comparison.

---

[2] See more discussions in (Lan et al., 2017).

References

Eneko Agirre, Carmen Banea, Claire Cardie, Daniel Cer, Mona Diab, Aitor Gonzalez-Agirre, Weiwei Guo, Inigo Lopez-Gazpio, Montse Maritxalar, Rada Mihalcea, German Rigau, Larraitz Uria, and Janyce Wiebe. 2015. SemEval-2015 task 2: Semantic textual similarity, English, Spanish and pilot on interpretability. In *Proceedings of the 9th International Workshop on Semantic Evaluation (SemEval).*

Eneko Agirre, Aitor Gonzalez-Agirre, Inigo Lopez-Gazpio, Montse Maritxalar, German Rigau, and Larraitz Uria. 2016. SemEval-2016 task 2: Interpretable semantic textual similarity. In *Proceedings of the 10th International Workshop on Semantic Evaluation (SemEval).*

Timothy Baldwin, Paul Cook, Marco Lui, Andrew MacKinlay, and Li Wang. 2013. How noisy social media text, how diffrnt social media sources? In *Proceedings of the Sixth International Joint Conference on Natural Language Processing (IJCNLP).*

Samuel R. Bowman, Gabor Angeli, Christopher Potts, and Christopher D. Manning. 2015. A large annotated corpus for learning natural language inference. In *Proceedings of the 2015 Conference on Empirical Methods in Natural Language Processing (EMNLP).*

Ohio Supercomputer Center. 2012. Oakley supercomputer. http://osc.edu/ark:/19495/hpc0cvqn.

Marta R. Costa-jussà and José A. R. Fonollosa. 2016. Character-based neural machine translation. In *Proceedings of the 54th Annual Meeting of the Association for Computational Linguistics (ACL).*

Bill Dolan, Chris Quirk, and Chris Brockett. 2004. Unsupervised construction of large paraphrase corpora: Exploiting massively parallel news sources. In *Proceedings of the 20th International Conference on Computational Linguistics (COLING).*

William B Dolan and Chris Brockett. 2005. Automatically constructing a corpus of sentential paraphrases. In *Proceedings of the Third International Workshop on Paraphrasing (IWP).*

Cicero dos Santos and Victor Guimarães. 2015. Boosting named entity recognition with neural character embeddings. In *Proceedings of the Fifth Named Entity Workshop.*

Asli Eyecioglu and Bill Keller. 2015. ASOBEK: Twitter paraphrase identification with simple overlap features and SVMs. In *Proceedings of the 9th International Workshop on Semantic Evaluation (SemEval).*

Hua He and Jimmy Lin. 2016. Pairwise word interaction modeling with deep neural networks for semantic similarity measurement. In *Proceedings of the 2016 Conference of the North American Chapter of the Association for Computational Linguistics: Human Language Technologies (NAACL-HLT).*

Yoon Kim, Yacine Jernite, David Sontag, and Alexander M Rush. 2016. Character-aware neural language models. In *Proceedings of the Thirtieth AAAI Conference on Artificial Intelligence (AAAI).*

Wuwei Lan, Siyu Qiu, Hua He, and Wei Xu. 2017. A continuously growing dataset of sentential paraphrases. In *Proceedings of The 2017 Conference on Empirical Methods on Natural Language Processing (EMNLP).*

Wang Ling, Tiago Luís, Luís Marujo, Rámon Fernandez Astudillo, Silvio Amir, Chris Dyer, Alan W Black, and Isabel Trancoso. 2015. Finding function in form: Compositional character models for open vocabulary word representation. In *Proceedings of the 2015 Conference on Empirical Methods in Natural Language Processing (EMNLP).*

Zachary C. Lipton, Charles Elkan, and Balakrishnan Naryanaswamy. 2014. Optimal thresholding of classifiers to maximize F1 measure. In *Proceedings of the 2014th European Conference on Machine Learning & Principles and Practice of Knowledge Discovery in Databases (ECML-PKDD).*

Pengfei Liu, Xipeng Qiu, Yaqian Zhou, Jifan Chen, and Xuanjing Huang. 2016. Modelling interaction of sentence pair with coupled-LSTMs. In *Proceedings of the 2016 Conference on Empirical Methods in Natural Language Processing (EMNLP).*

Thang Luong, Ilya Sutskever, Quoc Le, Oriol Vinyals, and Wojciech Zaremba. 2015. Addressing the rare word problem in neural machine translation. In *Proceedings of the 53rd Annual Meeting of the Association for Computational Linguistics and the 7th International Joint Conference on Natural Language Processing (ACL-IJCNLP).*

Yasumasa Miyamoto and Kyunghyun Cho. 2016. Gated word-character recurrent language model. In *Proceedings of the 2016 Conference on Empirical Methods in Natural Language Processing (EMNLP).*

Ankur Parikh, Oscar Täckström, Dipanjan Das, and Jakob Uszkoreit. 2016. A decomposable attention model for natural language inference. In *Proceedings of the 2016 Conference on Empirical Methods in Natural Language Processing (EMNLP).*

Jeffrey Pennington, Richard Socher, and Christopher D. Manning. 2014. GloVe: Global vectors for word representation. In *Proceedings of the 2014 Conference on Empirical Methods in Natural Language Processing (EMNLP).*

Barbara Plank, Anders Søgaard, and Yoav Goldberg. 2016. Multilingual part-of-speech tagging with bidirectional long short-term memory models and auxiliary loss. In *Proceedings of the 54th Annual Meeting of the Association for Computational Linguistics.*

Marek Rei. 2017. Semi-supervised multitask learning for sequence labeling. In *Proceedings of the 55th Annual Meeting of the Association for Computational Linguistics (ACL)*.

Marek Rei, Gamal Crichton, and Sampo Pyysalo. 2016. Attending to characters in neural sequence labeling models. In *Proceedings of the 26th International Conference on Computational Linguistics: Technical Papers (COLING)*.

Gehui Shen, Yunlun Yang, and Zhi-Hong Deng. 2017. Inter-weighted alignment network for sentence pair modeling. In *Proceedings of the 2017 Conference on Empirical Methods in Natural Language Processing (EMNLP)*.

Gaurav Singh Tomar, Thyago Duque, Oscar Täckström, Jakob Uszkoreit, and Dipanjan Das. 2017. Neural paraphrase identification of questions with noisy pretraining. In *Proceedings of the First Workshop on Subword and Character Level Models in NLP (SCLeM)*.

Clara Vania and Adam Lopez. 2017. From characters to words to in between: Do we capture morphology? In *Proceedings of the 55th Annual Meeting of the Association for Computational Linguistics (ACL)*.

Zhiguo Wang, Wael Hamza, and Radu Florian. 2017. Bilateral multi-perspective matching for natural language sentences. In *Proceedings of the Twenty-Sixth International Joint Conference on Artificial Intelligence (IJCAI)*.

John Wieting, Mohit Bansal, Kevin Gimpel, and Karen Livescu. 2015. From paraphrase database to compositional paraphrase model and back. *Transactions of the Association for Computational Linguistics (TACL)* 3:345–358.

John Wieting, Mohit Bansal, Kevin Gimpel, and Karen Livescu. 2016. Towards universal paraphrastic sentence embeddings. In *Proceedings of the 4th International Conference on Learning Representations (ICLR)*.

Wei Xu, Chris Callison-Burch, and William B. Dolan. 2015. SemEval-2015 task 1: Paraphrase and semantic similarity in Twitter. In *Proceedings of the 9th International Workshop on Semantic Evaluation (SemEval)*.

Wei Xu, Alan Ritter, Chris Callison-Burch, William B. Dolan, and Yangfeng Ji. 2014. Extracting lexically divergent paraphrases from Twitter. *Transactions of the Association for Computational Linguistics (TACL)* 2(1).

Wenpeng Yin, Hinrich Schütze, Bing Xiang, and Bowen Zhou. 2016. ABCNN: Attention-based convolutional neural network for modeling sentence pairs. *Transactions of the Association for Computational Linguistics (TACL)* 4:259–272.

Determining Event Durations: Models and Error Analysis

Alakananda Vempala, Eduardo Blanco and Alexis Palmer
University Of North Texas
`alakanandavempala@my.unt.edu, eduardo.blanco@unt.edu`
`alexis.palmer@unt.edu`

Abstract

This paper presents models to predict event durations. We introduce aspectual features that capture deeper linguistic information than previous work, and experiment with neural networks. Our analysis shows that tense, aspect and temporal structure of the clause provide useful clues, and that an LSTM ensemble captures relevant context around the event.

1 Introduction

Robust textual understanding requires identifying events and temporal relations between them. Beyond event participants, a crucial piece of information regarding events is their duration, an attribute rarely mentioned explicitly. For example, *taking a shower* lasts a few minutes (not days), and a *vacation* lasts a few days (not years). Core tasks such as temporal understanding and reasoning, as well as applications such as temporal question answering (Llorens et al., 2015) would benefit from knowing the expected duration of events.

Consider a system that extracts temporal relations such as IS_INCLUDED (Cassidy et al., 2014, among others). When deciding whether a relation holds between an event and a temporal expression, such a system would benefit from knowing the duration of the event at hand. For example, argument *y* of IS_INCLUDED(*built a house*, *y*) must be a temporal span ranging from a few weeks to a year—the expected duration of *built a house*. Thus relation candidates such as IS_INCLUDED(*built a house, 4/5/2016*) could be discarded right away.

Similarly, event durations combined with event ordering and temporal anchoring would help to determine the time of subsequent events. For example, if John Doe started *his drive to work* at 8:00am, it is reasonable to expect him to start working by 9:00am because commuting took him (most likely) between a few minutes to an hour.

In this paper, we classify events based on their expected duration. Specifically, we differentiate between events whose duration is less than a day, and events whose duration is a day or more. The main contributions are: (a) linguistically motivated features that yield better results than previous work, (b) an LSTM ensemble that obtains the best results to date, and (c) error analysis shedding light on the benefits of our models.

2 Related Work

TimeBank (Pustejovsky et al., 2006) is the corpus of reference for temporal information. The annotations follow TimeML (Pustejovsky et al., 2010) and include events, temporal expressions (e.g., *last Friday*), temporal signals (e.g., *when*, *during*), and links encoding relations. TimeBank does not annotate the expected duration of events.

Annotating and learning event durations was pioneered by Pan et al. (2011), who annotated the events in TimeBank with their expected durations. Gusev et al. (2011) use query patterns in an unsupervised approach to predict the duration of events. The work presented here builds upon these previous works: we introduce additional features and an LSTM ensemble that obtains the best results to date. The new features are inspired by previous work on assigning situation entity (SE) type labels to clauses (Friedrich et al., 2016). SE types are a linguistic categorization of semantic clause type, whereby each clause is labeled according to the type of situation it introduces to a discourse (STATE, EVENT, GENERIC, and GENERALIZING SENTENCE (also known as habituals)).

Other related works include efforts modeling event durations in social media (Williams and Katz, 2012), and temporal anchoring of, among others, durative events (Reimers et al., 2016).

Proceedings of NAACL-HLT 2018, pages 164–168
New Orleans, Louisiana, June 1 - 6, 2018. ©2018 Association for Computational Linguistics

	#	Description
Pan et al.	1-3	event token, lemma and POS tag
	4-9	head word, lemma and POS tags of the syntactic subject and object of the event
	10-18	three closest hypernyms of the event, subject and object
Gusev et al.	19-20	named entity types of the syntactic subject and object of the event
	21	flag indicating if the event is a reporting verb
	22-25	flags indicating presence of *dobj, iobj, pobj* and *advmod* syntactic dependencies of the verb
Aspectual features inspired by situation entities (Friedrich et al.)	26	event tense: past, present or future, and simple, perfect or continuous form
	27	whether the event is in active or passive voice
	28	type of determiner present in the subject
	29	noun type of the subject
	30	subject person
	31	whether the subject is a bare plural
	32-40	synset id of the two closest hypernyms in WordNet of the event, subject and object
	41-43	lexical filename of the event, subject and object in WordNet
	44-46	depth of the event, subject and object in the WordNet taxonomy
	47	countability from WebCelex of the subject and object
	48	number of modifiers in the sentence
	49	adverbial degree of the sentence
	50	whether the sentence contains an adverb
	51-700	flags indicating the Brown clusters present in the sentence

Table 1: Feature set to predict the expected duration of events with SVM. Features 1–25 were previously proposed for the same task. Features 26–700 are inspired by previous work assigning situation entity types to clauses (2016).

3 Corpus

We use the corpus by Pan et al. (2011), who annotated the events in TimeBank (Pustejovsky et al., 2003) with their expected durations by specifying upper and lower bounds. The authors clustered these bounds into two labels: less than a day (<day) and a day or longer (≥day), and the corpus contains 2,354 events (<day: 958, ≥day: 1,396). The same event predicate may have different durations depending on context as exemplified below:

- *I want to be absolutely clear, to the extent there is any implication that Mrs. Currie believes that the President or anyone else tried to influence her recollection, that is absolutely false and a mischaracterization of the facts.* Duration of *want*: <day.
- *Nationalists want to move towards Irish unity and see this process as a bridge in that direction.* Duration of *want*: ≥day.

4 Experiments and Results

We experiment with traditional SVM and neural networks. Our rationale behind SVM is to (a) incorporate deeper linguistic features than previous work, and (b) establish a solid baseline. We experiment with neural networks to evaluate the ability of word embeddings and recurrent neural networks to capture the context required to determine event durations. Regarding SVM, we use scikit-learn (Pedregosa et al., 2011). Regarding neural networks, we use Keras (Chollet et al., 2015) with TensorFlow backend (Abadi et al., 2015). All networks use GloVe embeddings with 300 dimensions (Pennington et al., 2014) and the Adam optimizer (Kingma and Ba, 2014). We use grid search and 5-fold cross-validation to tune hyperparameters (C and γ for SVM, and batch size, dropout rate, etc. for neural networks).

4.1 Support Vector Machine

Table 1 describes the full feature set. We use spaCy[1] to tokenize the input text and extract lemmas, part-of-speech tags, named entities, and dependencies. The features by Pan et al. (2011) and Gusev et al. (2011) capture primarily lexical information, relying on tendencies of particular words to denote events of certain durations. These tendencies are, however, subject to contextual influence. Duration is one component of the internal temporal structure of events, and as such it is an important factor for distinguishing between various aspectual categories (Vendler, 1957; Smith, 1991). It thus stands to reason that other features which capture aspectual distinctions may also correlate with event duration and be useful for classifying the duration of events in texts. In order to explore this intuition, we adapt features from a system designed to assign situation entity types to clauses (Friedrich et al., 2016). Diagnostic criteria for situation entity types include lexical aspect (stative vs. dynamic) of the main verb, genericity of the clause's subject, and whether the clause

---

[1] https://github.com/explosion/spaCy

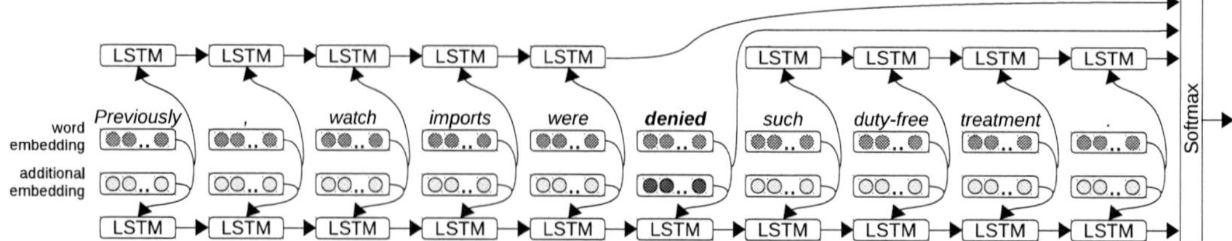

Figure 1: Neural network architecture to predict event durations. The output layer combines (a) the embedding of the verb at hand and (b) the output of three LSTMs: one for the whole sentence (bottom), one for the tokens before the event (top left), and one for the tokens after the event (top right).

is episodic, habitual, or static. It is primarily these criteria which features 26-50 aim to capture. For example, bare plural subjects with a simple present tense verb (e.g., *Bats eat mosquitos*) are a hallmark of GENERIC clauses. Although situation entity types do not directly map onto the duration labels ($<$day or $\geq$day), the criteria which contribute to determining them clearly influence aspectual interpretation, thus influencing understanding of the duration of events. Regarding Brown clusters, we use freely available clusters trained on news data by Turian et al. (2010) using the implementation by Liang (2005). We include one feature per cluster and set it to true if any word in the sentence belongs to the cluster.

4.2 Feed-Forward Neural Network

The first neural network we experiment with is a one-hidden-layer feed-forward neural network that takes as input the event embedding. The tuning process revealed that the size of the hidden layer is not important, thus we report results using a hidden layer with 5 neurons. Intuitively, this vanilla network evaluates whether pretrained word embeddings can predict the duration of events.

4.3 LSTM Ensemble

The LSTM ensemble is an improvement of the vanilla feed-forward neural network. It combines the event embedding with three LSTMs (Hochreiter and Schmidhuber, 1997) capturing different context around the event (Figure 1). The first LSTM (200 units, bottom in Figure 1) take as inputs the full sentence, and each token is represented by two embeddings: the word embedding (blue in Figure 1) and an additional embedding indicating whether the token is the event of interest or not (light and dark grey). The other two LSTMs (200 units each, top in Figure 1) take as input the sequence of tokens before and after the event at

		P	R	F1
Pan et al.	$<$day	.76	.57	.65
	$\geq$ day	.70	.85	.77
	Avg.	.73	.72	.71
Pan et al. + Gusev et al.	$<$day	.73	.52	.61
	$\geq$ day	.68	.84	.75
	Avg.	.70	.69	.68
Pan et al. + Gusev et al. + Situation Entities	$<$day	.82	.63	.71
	$\geq$ day	.74	.89	.81
	Avg.	.78	.77	*.76
Feed-forward neural network	$<$day	.87	.63	.73
	$\geq$day	.77	.93	.84
	Avg.	.81	.80	*.80
LSTM ensemble	$<$day	.97	.62	.76
	$\geq$day	.78	.99	.87
	Avg.	.86	.83	*.82

Table 2: Results obtained using SVM and several feature combinations (top), and neural networks (bottom). We indicate statistical significance with respect to Pan et al. (2011) with *. Avg. stands for weighted average.

hand, respectively, and each token is represented by the corresponding word embedding. Word embeddings remain fixed, but the additional embeddings are initialized randomly and tuned during training along with all other network parameters.

4.4 Results

Table 2 presents results obtained with the test set (WSJ data with 156 event instances). We used the same train and test splits as Pan et al. (2011) and Gusev et al. (2011), but reimplemented their systems and obtained better results than those reported by the authors. We believe this is due to the fact that spaCy (and the state-of-the-art in general) is more robust than older tools. Regarding SVM, the feature sets previously proposed obtain moderate results (F1: 0.71 and 0.68). These previous features clearly benefit from the new aspectual features (F1: 0.76), showing that the latter features capture contextual information useful to determine event durations. The feed-forward neural network outperforms the SVM (F1: 0.80) although it doesn't have access to the context surrounding the event at hand. This shows that embeddings alone are effective at predicting event durations. Finally, despite the relatively small dataset, the LSTM ensemble complements the pretrained verb embedding with distributional representations of the context around it (the full sentence, and the words before and after the event), yielding an 0.82 F1.

5 Error Analysis

In this section, we provide insights into why the additional aspectual features and neural networks are useful to predict event durations.

Aspectual features yield 7% improvement in overall F1 (0.71 vs. 0.76). Here are some examples that benefit from these features:

- *The company said 80% of its auction business is usually conducted in the second and fourth quarters.* The *adverbial degree* feature (feature 49) characterizes that *conducted* is a habitual event and made the SVM correctly classify this event into ≥day.
- *Nationalists want to move towards Irish unity and see this process as a bridge in that direction.* The subject of *want* is the bare plural *Nationalists* (feature 31), which in turn indicates that the event duration is ≥day.
- *Sotheby's Holdings Inc., the parent of the auction house Sotheby's, said its net loss for the seasonally slow third quarter narrowed from a year earlier on a leap in operating revenue.* The event *narrowed* belongs to the WordNet lexical filename *verb.change* and its object (*loss*) belongs to *noun.possession*. These semantic classes (features 41–43) made the classifier correctly predict ≥day. Another important lexical filename is *verb.possession*, all events belonging to this filename are annotated ≥day.

Neural Networks outperform any feature combination despite not having explicit access to any information beyond the sentence to which the event belongs and pretrained word embeddings. Word embeddings alone are surprisingly effective for this task (feed-forward neural network F1: 0.80), and benefit especially when the event at hand has not been seen in training. Similar to the Word-

Net lexical filenames, embeddings cluster together events with similar durations. The benefit of embeddings is, however, that they are pretrained on massive amounts of data and virtually account for any event (all the events annotated in the corpus we work with have a GloVe embedding). Here is an example of an unseen event in training that the embeddings predict correctly:

- *Revenue totaled $1.01 billion, a 43% increase from $704.4 million, reflecting the company's acquisition of Emery earlier this year.* The feed-forward neural network and embeddings learnt that mathematical expressions last less than a day (<day).

Although the difference in F1 is small (0.82 vs. 0.80), the LSTM ensemble successfully captures context required to predict event durations. Here are two examples that benefit:

- *The Portland, Ore., thrift said the restructuring should help it meet new capital standards from the Financial Institution Reform, Recovery and Enforcement Act.* The fact that *restructuring* appears nearby and has duration ≥day helps the LSTM ensemble predict that *meet* also has duration ≥day in this context, despite most meetings lasting less than a day. Also, the LSTM ensemble has access only to the nearby events but not to their duration.
- *In over-the-counter trading yesterday, Benjamin Franklin rose 25 cents to $4.25* (duration: <day). The LSTM ensemble is very successful when temporal cues surrounding the event at hand are present (e.g., *yesterday*).

6 Conclusions

In this paper, we classify events into those whose duration is shorter than a day (<day) or a day or longer (≥day). We have presented aspectual features that account for deeper linguistic information than previous work, and showed that they complement basic features used previously. We have also experimented with neural networks, and showed that (a) pretrained word embeddings successfully solve this task, and (b) an LSTM ensemble captures relevant context around the event despite that the corpus we work with is relatively small. We believe that determining the duration of events has the potential to help temporal reasoning in general. For example, somebody can participate in two events taking place at different locations only if they do not overlap temporally.

References

Martín Abadi, Ashish Agarwal, Paul Barham, Eugene Brevdo, Zhifeng Chen, Craig Citro, Greg S. Corrado, Andy Davis, Jeffrey Dean, Matthieu Devin, Sanjay Ghemawat, Ian Goodfellow, Andrew Harp, Geoffrey Irving, Michael Isard, Yangqing Jia, Rafal Jozefowicz, Lukasz Kaiser, Manjunath Kudlur, Josh Levenberg, Dan Mané, Rajat Monga, Sherry Moore, Derek Murray, Chris Olah, Mike Schuster, Jonathon Shlens, Benoit Steiner, Ilya Sutskever, Kunal Talwar, Paul Tucker, Vincent Vanhoucke, Vijay Vasudevan, Fernanda Viégas, Oriol Vinyals, Pete Warden, Martin Wattenberg, Martin Wicke, Yuan Yu, and Xiaoqiang Zheng. 2015. TensorFlow: Large-scale machine learning on heterogeneous systems. Software available from tensorflow.org.

Taylor Cassidy, Bill McDowell, Nathanael Chambers, and Steven Bethard. 2014. An annotation framework for dense event ordering. In *Proceedings of the 52nd Annual Meeting of the Association for Computational Linguistics (Volume 2: Short Papers)*, pages 501–506, Baltimore, Maryland. Association for Computational Linguistics.

François Chollet et al. 2015. Keras. `https://github.com/fchollet/keras`.

Annemarie Friedrich, Alexis Palmer, and Manfred Pinkal. 2016. Situation entity types: automatic classification of clause-level aspect. In *Proceedings of the 54th Annual Meeting of the Association for Computational Linguistics (Volume 1: Long Papers)*, pages 1757–1768, Berlin, Germany. Association for Computational Linguistics.

Andrey Gusev, Nathanael Chambers, Pranav Khaitan, Divye Khilnani, Steven Bethard, and Dan Jurafsky. 2011. Using query patterns to learn the duration of events. In *Proceedings of the Ninth International Conference on Computational Semantics*, IWCS '11, pages 145–154, Stroudsburg, PA, USA. Association for Computational Linguistics.

Sepp Hochreiter and Jürgen Schmidhuber. 1997. Long short-term memory. *Neural Comput.*, 9(8):1735–1780.

Diederik P. Kingma and Jimmy Ba. 2014. Adam: A method for stochastic optimization. *CoRR*, abs/1412.6980.

Percy Liang. 2005. *Semi-supervised learning for natural language*. Ph.D. thesis, Massachusetts Institute of Technology.

Hector Llorens, Nathanael Chambers, Naushad UzZaman, Nasrin Mostafazadeh, James Allen, and James Pustejovsky. 2015. Semeval-2015 task 5: Qa tempeval - evaluating temporal information understanding with question answering. In *Proceedings of the 9th International Workshop on Semantic Evaluation (SemEval 2015)*, pages 792–800, Denver, Colorado. Association for Computational Linguistics.

Feng Pan, Rutu Mulkar-Mehta, and Jerry R Hobbs. 2011. Annotating and learning event durations in text. *Computational Linguistics*, 37(4):727–752.

F. Pedregosa, G. Varoquaux, A. Gramfort, V. Michel, B. Thirion, O. Grisel, M. Blondel, P. Prettenhofer, R. Weiss, V. Dubourg, J. Vanderplas, A. Passos, D. Cournapeau, M. Brucher, M. Perrot, and E. Duchesnay. 2011. Scikit-learn: Machine learning in Python. *Journal of Machine Learning Research*, 12:2825–2830.

Jeffrey Pennington, Richard Socher, and Christopher D. Manning. 2014. Glove: Global vectors for word representation. In *Empirical Methods in Natural Language Processing (EMNLP)*, pages 1532–1543.

J. Pustejovsky, P. Hanks, R. Sauri, A. See, R. Gaizauskas, A. Setzer, D. Radev, B. Sundheim, D. Day, L. Ferro, and M. Lazo. 2003. The TIMEBANK corpus. In *Proceedings of Corpus Linguistics 2003*, pages 647–656, Lancaster.

James Pustejovsky, Kiyong Lee, Harry Bunt, and Laurent Romary. 2010. Iso-timeml: An international standard for semantic annotation. In *Proceedings of the Seventh International Conference on Language Resources and Evaluation (LREC'10)*, Valletta, Malta. European Language Resources Association (ELRA).

James Pustejovsky, Mark Verhagen, Roser Saurí, Jessica Littman, Robert Gaizauskas, Graham Katz, Inderjeet Mani, Robert Knippen, and Andrea Setzer. 2006. Timebank 1.2. Linguistic Data Consortium.

Nils Reimers, Nazanin Dehghani, and Iryna Gurevych. 2016. Temporal anchoring of events for the timebank corpus. In *Proceedings of the 54th Annual Meeting of the Association for Computational Linguistics (Volume 1: Long Papers)*, pages 2195–2204, Berlin, Germany. Association for Computational Linguistics.

Carlota S Smith. 1991. *The parameter of Aspect, vol. 43 of Studies in Linguistics and Philosophy*. Kluwer, Dordrecht.

Joseph Turian, Lev Ratinov, and Yoshua Bengio. 2010. Word representations: a simple and general method for semi-supervised learning. In *Proceedings of the 48th annual meeting of the association for computational linguistics*, pages 384–394. Association for Computational Linguistics.

Zeno Vendler. 1957. Verbs and times. *The philosophical review*, pages 143–160.

Jennifer Williams and Graham Katz. 2012. Extracting and modeling durations for habits and events from twitter. In *Proceedings of the 50th Annual Meeting of the Association for Computational Linguistics (Volume 2: Short Papers)*, pages 223–227, Jeju Island, Korea. Association for Computational Linguistics.

Diachronic Usage Relatedness (DURel):
A Framework for the Annotation of Lexical Semantic Change

*Dominik Schlechtweg, *Sabine Schulte im Walde, †Stefanie Eckmann

*Institute for Natural Language Processing, University of Stuttgart, Germany

†Historical and Indo-European Linguistics, LMU Munich, Germany

dominik.schlechtweg@ims.uni-stuttgart.de, schulte@ims.uni-stuttgart.de,

stefanie.eckmann@campus.lmu.de

Abstract

We propose a framework that extends synchronic polysemy annotation to diachronic changes in lexical meaning, to counteract the lack of resources for evaluating computational models of lexical semantic change. Our framework exploits an intuitive notion of semantic relatedness, and distinguishes between innovative and reductive meaning changes with high inter-annotator agreement. The resulting test set for German comprises ratings from five annotators for the relatedness of 1,320 use pairs across 22 target words.

1 Introduction

We see an increasing interest in the automatic detection of semantic change in computational linguistics (Hamilton et al., 2016; Frermann and Lapata, 2016; Schlechtweg et al., 2017, i.a.), motivated by expected performance improvements of practical NLP applications, or theoretical interest in language or cultural change. However, a major obstacle in the computational modeling of semantic change is evaluation (Lau et al., 2012; Cook et al., 2014; Frermann and Lapata, 2016; Dubossarsky et al., 2017). Most importantly, there is no reliable test set of semantic change for any language that goes beyond a small set of hand-selected targets. We counteract this lack of resources by extending a framework of synchronic polysemy annotation to the annotation of Diachronic Usage Relatedness (DURel). DURel has a strong theoretical basis and at the same time makes use of established synchronic procedures that rely on the intuitive notion of semantic relatedness. The annotations distinguish between innovative and reductive meaning change with high inter-annotator agreement. DURel is language-independent and thus applicable across languages;

this paper introduces the first test set of lexical semantic change for German.

2 Related Work

A large number of studies has been performed on synchronic word sense annotation (see Ide and Pustejovsky, 2017 for an overview). Within this set, our paper is most related to work focusing on graded polysemy annotation. Most prominently, Soares da Silva (1992) is interested in the question of whether the theoretical distinction between polysemy and homonymy can be experimentally verified; Brown (2008) wants to know how fine-grained word senses are, and Erk et al. (2009, 2013) examine whether we should adopt a graded notion of word meaning.

In contrast, there is little work on annotation with a focus on semantic change, despite the growing interest and modeling efforts in the field of semantic change detection. Lau et al. (2012) and Cook et al. (2014) aim at verifying the semantic developments of their targets by a quasi-annotation procedure of dictionary entries, however without reporting inter-annotator agreement or other measures of reliability. Gulordava and Baroni (2011) ask annotators for their intuitions about changes but without direct relation to language data. Bamman and Crane (2011) exploit aligned translated texts as source of word senses and conduct a very limited annotation study on Latin texts from different time periods. Schlechtweg et al. (2017) propose a small-scale annotation of metaphoric change, but altogether there is no standard test set across languages that goes beyond a few hand-selected examples.

3 Lexical Semantic Change

It is well-known that lexical semantic change and polysemy are tightly connected. For example, Blank (1997) develops an elaborate theory where polysemy is the synchronic, observable result of

Proceedings of NAACL-HLT 2018, pages 169–174

New Orleans, Louisiana, June 1 - 6, 2018. ©2018 Association for Computational Linguistics

lexical semantic change. He distinguishes two main types of lexical semantic change:

- **innovative meaning change**: emergence of a full-fledged additional meaning of a word; old and new meaning are related by polysemy

- **reductive meaning change**: loss of a full-fledged meaning of a word

An example of innovative meaning change is the emergence of polysemy in the German word *Donnerwetter* around 1800 (Paul, 2002). Before ≈1800 *Donnerwetter* was only used in the meaning of 'thunderstorm'. After 1800 we still observe this meaning, and in addition we find a new, clearly distinguished meaning as a swear word 'Man alive!'. An example of reductive meaning change is the German word *Zufall*. It had two meanings ≈1850, 'seizure' and 'coincidence' (Osman, 1971). After 1850, the word occurs less and less often in the former meaning, until it is exclusively used in the meaning of 'coincidence'. *Zufall* lost the meaning 'seizure'.

3.1 Semantic Proximity

Based on Prototype Theory (Rosch and Mervis, 1975), Blank develops criteria to decide whether word uses are related by polysemy. He defines a continuum of *semantic proximity* with polysemy located between identity and homonymy, as depicted in Table 1.

> Identity
> Context Variance
> Polysemy
> Homonymy

Table 1: Continuum of semantic proximity (cf. Blank, 1997, p. 418).

While it is difficult to directly apply these criteria to practical annotation tasks, we exploit the scale of semantic proximity indirectly, as previously done by synchronic research on polysemy applying similar scales (Soares da Silva, 1992; Brown, 2008; Erk et al., 2013). Especially Erk et al.'s in-depth study validates an annotation framework relying on a scale of semantic proximity, revealing high inter-annotator agreement and strong correlation with traditional single-sense annotation as well as annotation of multiple lexical paraphrases. For our study, we decided to adopt

a relatedness scale similar to Brown's, shown in Table 2.

> 4: Identical
> 3: Closely Related
> 2: Distantly Related
> 1: Unrelated
>
> 0: Cannot decide

Table 2: Our 4-point scale of relatedness derived from Brown (2008).

3.2 Diachronic Usage Relatedness (DURel)

We frame our interest in lexical semantic change as judging the strength of semantic relatedness across use pairs of a target word w within a specific time period t_i. A high mean proximity value indicates meaning identity or context variance, while a low value indicates polysemy or homonymy, cf. Table 1. This strategy is applied independently to two time periods t_1 and t_2, as illustrated in Figure 1. Innovative vs. reductive meaning change can then be measured by decrease vs. increase in the mean relatedness value of w from t_1 to t_2. To see why this is justified, consider the different semantic constellations of w's use pairs in t_1 and t_2 in Figure 1. If w is monosemous in t_1 and undergoes innovative meaning change between the two time periods, we expect to find use pairs in the later period t_2 combining the old and new meaning which are less related (score: 2) than the use pairs from the earlier period t_1 (score: 3). According to this rationale, the mean relatedness values across w's use pairs should be lower in t_2 than in t_1. The reverse applies to reductive meaning change.

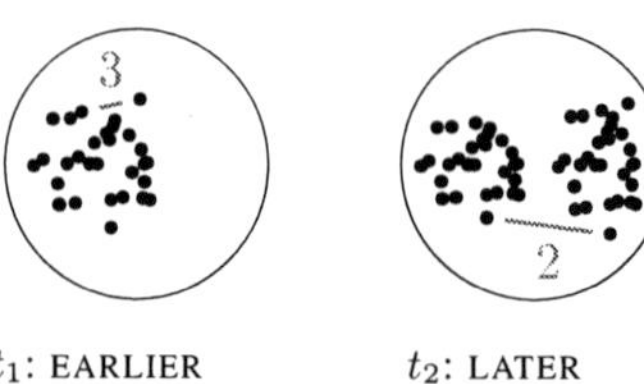

Figure 1: Two-dimensional use spaces (Tuggy, 1993; Zlatev, 2003) in two time periods with a target word w undergoing innovative meaning change. Dots represent uses of w. Spatial proximity of two uses means high relatedness.

There are a number of other, more complex semantic constellations. For example, if w not only gains a new meaning, but rapidly loses the old meaning, we cannot necessarily expect the mean relatedness of w's use pairs to be higher in the later than in the earlier time period. In order to cover such cases, we will not only measure the mean relatedness within the EARLIER and the LATER groups of use pairs but also in a mixed COMPARE group where each pair consists of a use from the EARLIER and a use from the LATER group. By this, old and new meaning are directly compared, and we do not have to rely on the assumption that the old meaning is still present.

By applying the above-described procedure to all target words and sorting them according to their mean relatedness scores, we obtain a ranked list for each of the three groups EARLIER, LATER and COMPARE. We then exploit two measures of change: (i) ΔLATER measures changes in the degree of mean relatedness of words, and is derived by subtracting a target w's mean in EARLIER from its mean in LATER: $\Delta\text{LATER}(w) = Mean_l(w) - Mean_e(w)$. Positive vs. negative values on this measure indicate innovative vs. reductive meaning change. (ii) COMPARE directly measures the relatedness *between* the EARLIER and the LATER group and thus corresponds to w's mean in the COMPARE group: $\text{COMPARE}(w) = Mean_c(w)$. High vs. low values on COMPARE indicate weak vs. strong change, where the change includes both innovative and reductive meaning changes.

4 Annotation Study

Five native speakers of German were asked to rate 1,320 use pairs on our 4-point scale of relatedness in Table 2. All annotators were students of linguistics. We explicitly chose two annotators with a background in historical linguistics in order to see whether knowledge about historical linguistics has an effect on the annotation. Annotators were not told that the study is related to semantic change.[1]

Target Words. The target words were selected by manually checking a corpus for innovative and reductive meaning changes, based on cases of metaphoric, metonymic change and narrowing (innovative) as reported by Paul (2002), and cases of reduction due to homonymy (reductive) as re-

---

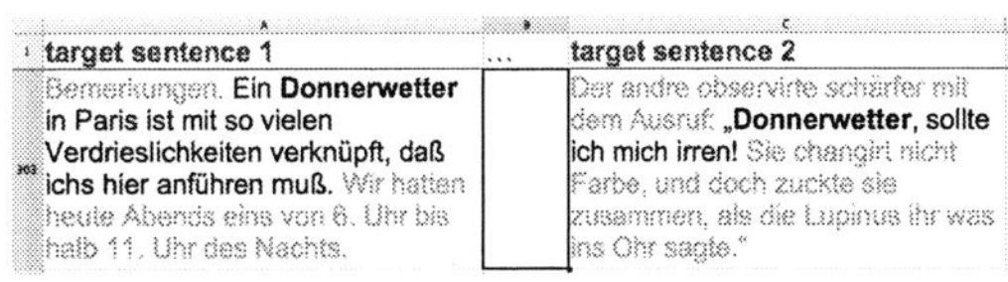

Figure 2: Use pair from annotation table (English adaption).

ported by Osman (1971). The corpus we used is DTA (Deutsches Textarchiv, 2017), a freely available diachronic corpus of German. By focusing on a late time period (19th century), we tried to reduce problems coming with historical language data as much as possible. We still normalized special characters to modern orthography.

We included only those words as targets for which we found the change suggested by the literature reflected in the corpus, either weakly or strongly, because an annotation relying on a random selection of words suggested to undergo change is likely to produce a set with very similar and rather low values representing small effects. We thus guaranteed to include both: words for which we expected weak effects as well as words for which we expected strong effects. We ended up with 19 cases of innovation and 9 cases of reduction. Three words, *Anstalt*, *Anstellung* and *Vorwort* represent especially interesting cases and were selected more than once for the test set since they undergo both innovative *and* reductive change between the investigated time periods.

Sampling. For each target word we randomly sampled 20 use pairs from DTA (searching for the respective lemma and POS) for each of the groups EARLIER (1750-1800), LATER (1850-1900) and COMPARE, yielding 60 use pairs per word and 1,320 use pairs for 22 target words in total.

A use of a word is defined as the sentence the word occurs in. The annotators were provided these sentences as well as the preceding and the following sentence in the corpus, cf. Figure 2. We double-checked that each use of a word was only sampled once within each group. If the total number of uses in the group was less than needed, uses were allowed twice across pairs. Before presenting the use pairs to the annotators in a spreadsheet, uses within pairs were randomized, and pairs from all groups were mixed and randomly ordered.

---

[1]The guidelines (adapted from the synchronic study by Erk et al., 2013) and the experiment data are publicly available at `www.ims.uni-stuttgart.de/data/durel/`.

5   Results

Agreement.   In line with Erk et al. (2013) we measure inter-annotator agreement as the average over pairwise Spearman's ρ correlations (omitting 0-judgments), cf. Table 3. The bottom line provides the agreement of each annotator's judgments against the average judgment score across the other annotators. The range of correlation coefficients is between 0.57 and 0.68, with an average correlation of 0.66. All the pairs are highly significantly correlated ($p < 0.01$).

	1	2	3	4	5
1		0.59	0.63	0.67	0.66
2			0.57	0.64	0.65
3				0.64	0.62
4					0.68
avg	0.71	0.68	0.68	0.75	0.74

Table 3: Correlation matrix for pairwise correlation agreement; *avg* refers to agreement of the annotator in the column against the average across the other annotators.

The annotators with historical background are annotators 4 and 5, who show the highest pairwise agreement and also the highest agreement with the average of the other annotators. This indicates that historical knowledge makes a positive difference when annotating DURel. Yet, the agreements of the non-expert annotators only deviate slightly.

Overall, our correlations are comparable and even moderately higher than the ones found in Erk et al. (2013), who report average correlation scores between 0.55 and 0.62. This difference is remarkable, given that annotators had to judge historical data. Note, however, that the studies are not exactly comparable, as Erk et al. used a more fine-grained 5-point scale, and we presumably excluded a larger number of 0-judgments.

Qualitative Analysis.   Figure 3 shows the target words ranked according to their values on ΔLATER. We can clearly identify three groups: words with values >0, <0, and a majority with values ≈ 0 difference in mean between the earlier and the later time period. The three topmost words have previously been classified as reductive, the three lowermost words as innovative meaning changes.

Figure 4 compares the distributions across re-

latedness scores for our two example words *Zufall* and *Donnerwetter* from above. In EARLIER, *Zufall*'s ratings (i.e., the number of times a specific rating 0–4 was provided) vary much more than in LATER where it has a high number of 4-judgments. The contrary is the case for *Donnerwetter*. In addition, we find a clear difference between the two words in the COMPARE group, because *Donnerwetter* is used in a variety of new figurative ways in LATER, while *Zufall*, besides losing the meaning 'seizure', retains the prevalent meaning 'coincidence' in both time periods.

Upon closer inspection, the words deviating most from our predictions show either that the change is already present before 1800 (e.g., *Steckenpferd*, 'toy > toy; hobby'), that the new meaning has a very low prevalence (e.g., *Museum*, 'study room; arts collection > arts collection'), or that there are additional, previously not identified uses in the later time period (e.g., *Feine*, 'fineness; grandeur > grandeur'). The mean value for reduction is 0.39, while it is -0.18 for innovation.

Overall, these findings confirm our predictions and validate ΔLATER as a measure of lexical semantic change. The case of *Presse*, 'printing press > printing press; print product/producer', however, shows its shortcomings: ΔLATER wrongly predicts no change for *Presse*, although it is clearly present, because the new meaning has a very high prevalence. ΔLATER cannot capture such cases, while COMPARE can: it predicts strong change for *Presse*.

Since COMPARE measures the degree of change rather than distinguishing between types of change, the highest values in its ranked list refer to cases with values≈ 0 in ΔLATER, and the lowest values refer to cases with extreme values of ΔLATER. A special case is *Feder* 'bird feather > bird feather; steel clip', which reveals the need for normalization of the COMPARE-measure: the word is highly polysemous and has approximately the same distribution in every group, because the new meaning 'steel clip' has a very low prevalence. For ΔLATER this correctly leads to a 0-prediction. In contrast, COMPARE predicts strong change, because due to polysemy there is a high probability to sample distantly related use pairs in the COMPARE group.

Discussion.   While our measures enable us to predict various semantic change constellations, we also demonstrated that they collapse in cer-

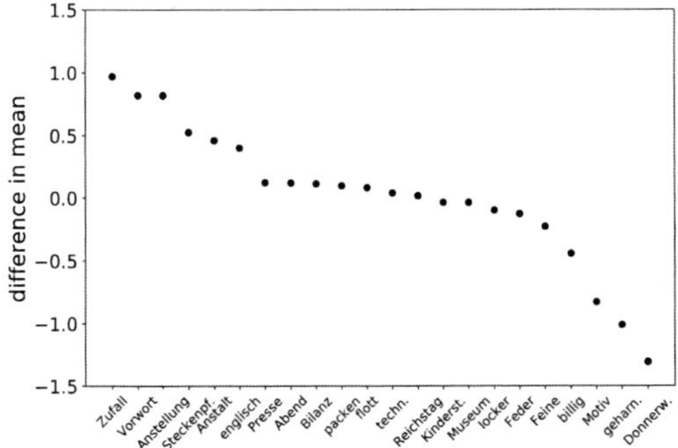

Figure 3: ΔLATER: Rank of target words according to increase in mean usage relatedness from EARLIER to LATER.

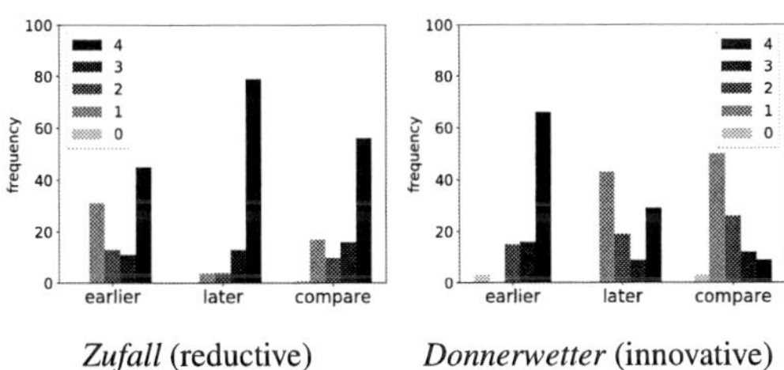

Zufall (reductive)   *Donnerwetter* (innovative)

Figure 4: Plots of judgment freq. for target words per group.

tain semantic constellations: ΔLATER is accurate when used for simple semantic constellations (i.e., only one reductive or innovative meaning change), where the old meaning roughly maintains its prevalence, thus making ΔLATER be prone to corpus effects such as changes in text genre. For an optimal application of this measure we therefore recommend (i) to choose directly adjacent and short time periods for annotation, as the number of changes increases with the length of the time period, and (ii) to use a well-balanced corpus for the annotation, ideally across all periods.

Unlike ΔLATER, COMPARE has the advantage to capture multiple changes over time, but it confuses polysemy and meaning change. In future work, we aim to solve this issue by normalizing COMPARE with a measure of polysemy: For any target word w the values from the EARLIER group determine its degree of polysemy in the earlier time period. Hence, the normalized ΔCOMPARE$(w) = Mean_c(w) - Mean_e(w)$ intuitively measures how much the values in the COMPARE group differ from what we would already expect from w's early polysemy, so it predicts no change in the case of a stable polysemous word,

and it predicts change if the word gains or loses a meaning.

6 Conclusion

This paper presented a general framework DURel for language-independent annotation of Diachronic Usage Relatedness, in order to develop test sets for lexical semantic change. In addition to a strong theoretical basis, DURel shows empirical validity in our annotation study with high inter-annotator agreement. It relies on an intuitive notion of semantic relatedness and needs no definition of word senses.

Furthermore, we proposed two measures of lexical semantic change that predict various semantic change constellations. While one measure successfully distinguishes between innovative and reductive meaning change, we also demonstrated the need to refine and normalize the measures in order to capture more variants of constellations regarding the interplay of polysemy and meaning reduction/innovation.

The annotated test set for German is publicly available and can be used to compare computational models of semantic change, and more generally to evaluate models of lexical variation in corpora across times, domains, etc. Further test sets across languages can be obtained by applying DURel to the respective language uses.

Acknowledgments

The research was supported by the DFG Collaborative Research Centre SFB 732. We thank Katrin Erk, Diana McCarthy and Susan Brown Windisch for providing their expertise, experience and data; Eleonore Brandner, Jun Chen, Fabian Bross and Diego Frassinelli for helpful discussions and comments; Delia Alf, Pavlos Musenidis, Cornelia van Scherpenberg and Jennifer Schild for help with the annotations; and the three reviewers for their constructive criticism.

References

D. Bamman and G. Crane. 2011. Measuring historical word sense variation. In *Proceedings of the 11th Annual International ACM/IEEE Joint Conference on Digital Libraries*. ACM, New York, NY, USA, pages 1–10.

A. Blank. 1997. *Prinzipien des lexikalischen Bedeutungswandels am Beispiel der romanischen Sprachen*. Niemeyer, Tübingen.

S. W. Brown. 2008. Choosing sense distinctions for WSD: Psycholinguistic evidence. In *Proceedings of the 46th Annual Meeting of the Association for Computational Linguistics on Human Language Technologies: Short Papers*. Stroudsburg, PA, USA, pages 249–252.

P. Cook, J. H. Lau, D. McCarthy, and T. Baldwin. 2014. Novel word-sense identification. In *25th International Conference on Computational Linguistics, Proceedings of the Conference: Technical Papers, August 23-29, 2014, Dublin, Ireland*. pages 1624–1635.

Deutsches Textarchiv. 2017. Grundlage für ein Referenzkorpus der neuhochdeutschen Sprache. Herausgegeben von der Berlin-Brandenburgischen Akademie der Wissenschaften. http://www.deutschestextarchiv.de/.

Haim Dubossarsky, Daphna Weinshall, and Eitan Grossman. 2017. Outta control: Laws of semantic change and inherent biases in word representation models. In *Proceedings of the 2017 Conference on Empirical Methods in Natural Language Processing*. Copenhagen, Denmark, pages 1147–1156.

K. Erk, D. McCarthy, and N. Gaylord. 2009. Investigations on word senses and word usages. In *Proceedings of the Joint Conference of the 47th Annual Meeting of the ACL and the 4th International Joint Conference on Natural Language Processing of the AFNLP: Volume 1*. Stroudsburg, PA, USA, pages 10–18.

K. Erk, D. McCarthy, and N. Gaylord. 2013. Measuring word meaning in context. *Computational Linguistics* 39(3):511–554.

L. Frermann and M. Lapata. 2016. A Bayesian model of diachronic meaning change. *Transactions of the Association for Computational Linguistics* 4:31–45.

K. Gulordava and M. Baroni. 2011. A distributional similarity approach to the detection of semantic change in the Google Books Ngram corpus. In *Proceedings of the Workshop on Geometrical Models of Natural Language Semantics*. Stroudsburg, PA, USA, pages 67–71.

W. L. Hamilton, J. Leskovec, and D. Jurafsky. 2016. Cultural shift or linguistic drift? Comparing two computational measures of semantic change. In *Proceedings of the 2016 Conference on Empirical Methods in Natural Language Processing*. Austin, Texas, pages 2116–2121.

N. Ide and J. Pustejovsky, editors. 2017. *Handbook of Linguistic Annotation*. Springer, Dordrecht.

J. H. Lau, P. Cook, D. McCarthy, D. Newman, and T. Baldwin. 2012. Word sense induction for novel sense detection. In *Proceedings of the 13th Conference of the European Chapter of the Association for Computational Linguistics*. Stroudsburg, PA, USA, pages 591–601.

N. Osman. 1971. *Kleines Lexikon untergegangener Wörter: Wortuntergang seit dem Ende des 18. Jahrhunderts*. Beck, München.

H. Paul. 2002. *Deutsches Wörterbuch: Bedeutungsgeschichte und Aufbau unseres Wortschatzes*. Niemeyer, Tübingen, 10. edition.

E. Rosch and C.B. Mervis. 1975. Family resemblances: Studies in the internal structure of categories. *Cognitive Psychology* 7:573–605.

D. Schlechtweg, S. Eckmann, E. Santus, S. Schulte im Walde, and D. Hole. 2017. German in flux: Detecting metaphoric change via word entropy. In *Proceedings of the 21st Conference on Computational Natural Language Learning*. Vancouver, Canada, pages 354–367.

A. Soares da Silva. 1992. Homonímia e polissemia: Análise sémica e teoria do campoléxico. In *Actas do XIX Congreso Internacional de Lingüística e Filoloxía Románicas*. Fundación Pedro Barrié de la Maza, La Coruña, volume 2 of *Lexicoloxía e Metalexicografía*, pages 257–287.

David Tuggy. 1993. Ambiguity, polysemy, and vagueness. *Cognitive Linguistics* 4(3):273–290.

J. Zlatev. 2003. *Polysemy or generality? Mu*, Mouton de Gruyter, volume 23 of *Cognitive Approaches to Lexical Semantics*, pages 447–494.

Directional Skip-Gram: Explicitly Distinguishing
Left and Right Context for Word Embeddings

Yan Song, Shuming Shi, Jing Li, Haisong Zhang
Tencent AI Lab
`{clksong,shumingshi,ameliajli,hansonzhang}@tencent.com`

Abstract

In this paper, we present directional skip-gram (DSG), a simple but effective enhancement of the skip-gram model by explicitly distinguishing left and right context in word prediction. In doing so, a direction vector is introduced for each word, whose embedding is thus learned by not only word co-occurrence patterns in its context, but also the directions of its contextual words. Theoretical and empirical studies on complexity illustrate that our model can be trained as efficient as the original skip-gram model, when compared to other extensions of the skip-gram model. Experimental results show that our model outperforms others on different datasets in semantic (word similarity measurement) and syntactic (part-of-speech tagging) evaluations, respectively.

1 Introduction

Word embedding and its related techniques have shown to be vital for natural language processing (NLP) (Bengio et al., 2003; Collobert and Weston, 2008; Turney and Pantel, 2010; Collobert et al., 2011; Weston et al., 2015; Song and Lee, 2017). The skip-gram (SG) model with negative sampling (Mikolov et al., 2013a,c) is a popular choice for learning word embeddings and has had large impact in the community, for its efficient training and good performance in downstream applications. Although widely used for multiple tasks, SG model relies on word co-occurrence within local context in word prediction but ignores further detailed information such as word orders, positions.

To improve original word embedding models, there are various studies leveraging external knowledge to update word embeddings with post processing (Faruqui et al., 2015; Kiela et al., 2015; Song et al., 2017) or supervised objectives (Yu and Dredze, 2014; Nguyen et al., 2016). However, these approaches are limited by reliable semantic resources, which are hard to obtain or annotate. To overcome such limitations, there are many approaches to further exploiting the characteristics of the running text, e.g., internal structure of the context. These approaches include enlarging the projection layer with consideration of word orders (Bansal et al., 2014; Ling et al., 2015a), learning context words with different weights (Ling et al., 2015b), etc. They are advantageous of learning word embeddings in an end-to-end unsupervised manner without requiring additional resources. Yet, they are also restricted in their implementation such as that they normally require a larger hidden layer or additional weights, which demand higher computation burden and could result in gradient explosion when embedding dimensions are enlarged. Another issue is that when considering word orders, they may suffer from data sparsity problem since n-gram coverage is much less than word, especially in the cold start scenario for a new domain where training data is limited.

To address the aforementioned issues, in this paper, we propose a simple, but effective adaptation of the SG model, namely, directional skip-gram (DSG), with consideration of not only the word co-occurrence patterns, but also their relative positions modeled by a special "direction" vector, which indicates whether the word to be predicted is on the left or right side of the given word. Although similarly motivated as the structured skip-gram (SSG) model (Ling et al., 2015a), DSG produces word embeddings of higher quality with lower space and time complexities. Empirical study shows that DSG can be trained efficiently (as fast as SG, while much faster than SSG). To test the effectiveness of the embeddings produced by DSG, we conduct experiments on semantic (word similarity evaluation) and syntactic (part-of-speech tagging) tasks. The results confirm the superiority of DSG to other models.

175

Proceedings of NAACL-HLT 2018, pages 175–180
New Orleans, Louisiana, June 1 - 6, 2018. ©2018 Association for Computational Linguistics

2 Approach

2.1 Skip-Gram Model

The SG model (Mikolov et al., 2013b) is a popular choice to learn word embeddings by leveraging the relations between a word and its neighboring words. In detail, the SG model is to predict the context for each given word w_t, and maximizes

$$\mathcal{L}_{SG} = \frac{1}{|V|} \sum_{t=1}^{|V|} \sum_{0 < |i| \leq c} \log f(w_{t+i}, w_t) \quad (1)$$

on a given corpus with vocabulary V, where w_{t+i} denotes the context words in a window w_{t-c}^{t+c}, with c denoting the window size. Herein $f(w_{t+i}, w_t) = p(w_{t+i} \mid w_t)$, and the probability to predict context word is estimated by

$$p(w_{t+i} \mid w_t) = \frac{exp(v'_{w_{t+i}}{}^{\top} v_{w_t})}{\sum_{w_{t+i} \in V} exp(v'_{w_{t+i}}{}^{\top} v_{w_t})} \quad (2)$$

where v_{w_t} is the embedding for w_t, and v and v' refer to input and output embeddings, respectively. The training processing of SG model is thus to maximize $\mathcal{L}_{SG}$ over a corpus iteratively. For a large vocabulary, `word2vec` uses hierarchical softmax or negative sampling (Mikolov et al., 2013b) to address the computational complexity that requires $|V| \times d$ matrix multiplications.

2.2 Structured Skip-Gram Model

The SSG model (Ling et al., 2015a) is an adaptation of SG model with consideration of words' order. The overall likelihood of SSG model shares the same form of SG model as Equation 1, however, with an adapted $f(w_{t+i}, w_t)$ where the probability of predicting w_{t+i} considers not only the word-word relations but also its relative position to w_t. In practice, each word in w_{t-c}^{t+c} is not predicted by a single predictor operating on the output embeddings $v'_{w_{t+i}}$. Instead, w_{t+i} is predicted by $2c$ predictors according to where it appears in w_t's context. As a result, every word in SSG should have $2c$ output embeddings for the $2c$ relative positions. The probability of predicting w_{t+i} in SSG is thus formulated as

$$p(w_{t+i} \mid w_t) = \frac{exp(\sum_{r=-c}^{c} v'_{r, w_{t+i}}{}^{\top} v_{w_t})}{\sum_{w_{t+i} \in V} exp(\sum_{r=-c}^{c} v'_{r, w_{t+i}}{}^{\top} v_{w_t})} \quad (3)$$

where $v_{r, w_{t+i}}$ defines the positional output embeddings for w_{t+i} at position r with respect to w_t. The embedding of w_t is thus updated with word order information implicitly recorded in $v_{r, w_{t+i}}$.

Model	Parameters	Operations
SG	$2\lvert V \rvert d$	$2c\mathcal{C}(n+1)o$
SSG	$(2c+1)\lvert V \rvert d$	$4c^2\mathcal{C}(n+1)o$
SSSG	$3\lvert V \rvert d$	$4c\mathcal{C}(n+1)o$
DSG	$3\lvert V \rvert d$	$2c\mathcal{C}(n+2)o$

Table 1: Complexities of different SG models. The column of "Parameters" and "Operations" reports space and time complexity, respectively. d: embedding dimension. $\mathcal{C}$: corpus size. o: unit operation of predicting and updating one word's embedding. n: the number of negative samples.

2.3 Directional Skip-Gram Model

The intuition behind this model is that word sequence is an important factor affecting the generation of our languages; a word should be biased associated with other words on its left or right side. For instance, *"merry"* and *"eve"* both co-occur frequently with *"Christmas"* in *"merry Christmas"* and *"Christmas eve"*, respectively. Given the context word "Christmas", it is useful to identify the word to be predicted is on the left or right for learning the embeddings of *"merry"* and *"eve"*.[1] Motivated by this, we propose a softmax function

$$g(w_{t+i}, w_t) = \frac{exp(\delta_{w_{t+i}}{}^{\top} v_{w_t})}{\sum_{w_{t+i} \in V} exp(\delta_{w_{t+i}}{}^{\top} v_{w_t})} \quad (4)$$

to measure how a context word w_{t+i} is associated with w_t in its left or right context, by introducing a new vector δ for each w_{t+i} to present its relative direction to w_t. The function g shares an updating paradigm similar to negative sampling:

$$v_{w_t}^{(new)} = v_{w_t}^{(old)} - \gamma(\sigma(v_{w_t}^{\top} \delta_{w_{t+i}}) - \mathcal{D})\delta_{w_{t+i}}$$
$$\delta_{w_{t+i}}^{(new)} = \delta_{w_{t+i}}^{(old)} - \gamma(\sigma(v_{w_t}^{\top} \delta_{w_{t+i}}) - \mathcal{D})v_{w_t}$$

where σ denotes the sigmoid function and γ the discounting learning rate. Particularly, $\mathcal{D}$ is the target label specifying the relative direction of w_{t+i} given w_t, defined as

$$\mathcal{D} = \begin{cases} 1 & i < 0 \\ 0 & i > 0 \end{cases}$$

according on the relative position of w_{t+i} respect to w_t. The final model is defined as Equation 1 with $f(w_{t+i}, w_t) = p(w_{t+i} \mid w_t) + g(w_{t+i}, w_t)$.

---

[1] Although SSG can also model this case because "merry" and "eve" are normally associated with "Christmas" at fixed positions, the intention of this example is to illustrate that word sequence can be effectively modeled by distinguishing left and right context.

Dimension	200
Window size	5
Frequency cut-off	5
Negative samples	5
Starting learning rate	0.025
Iteration	5

Table 2: Model settings for training embeddings.

2.4 Complexity Analysis

To qualitatively analyze the efficiency of our proposed model, we draw Table 1, which compares the complexity of the aforementioned SG models. The *Parameters* column reports parameter size, which refers to the space complexity. The *Operations* column reports the number of operations in computation, referring to the time complexity. Note that the above complexity analysis is based on negative sampling. If using hierarchical softmax, one can replace $n + 1$ into h, which represents the average depth of the hierarchical tree.

Compared to SG model, the SSG model demands obviously higher complexity in terms of both space and time when context gets larger, while every word in the DSG model only requires one extra operation in addition to the original SG model. Thus, if one enlarges the context, the DSG model could have similar speed of SG model.

To fairly compare the efficiency of our model and SSG, we additionally propose a simplified SSG (SSSG) model that only models left and right context for a given word. Instead of having $2c$ output embeddings in SSG, each word in SSSG has only two output embeddings representing left and right context. This is an approximation of our model within the SSG framework. On the output side, SSSG has two "word" vectors respectively for left and right context, while DSG has one "word" vector and one "direction" vector. As a result, the direction vector of DSG can be used to explicitly predict whether the context is on the left or right in word prediction, while SSSG doesn't.

3 Experiments

We use intrinsic and extrinsic evaluations to evaluate the effectiveness of different embeddings. To test and verify our analysis in §2.4, the efficiencies of aforementioned SG models are investigated based on their training speed. The setups for all experiments are illustrated as follows.

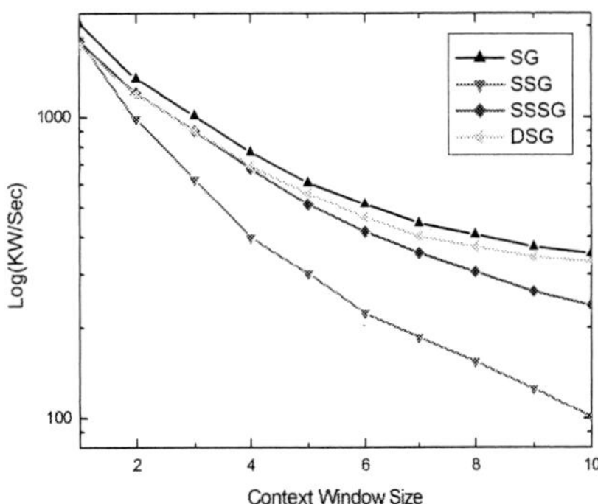

Figure 1: Comparisons of training speed in logarithm against different context window size. KW/Sec refers to thousand words per second.

Dataset. The embeddings were trained on the latest dump of Wikipedia articles[2], which contains approximately 2 billion word tokens.

Comparison. Since the focus of this paper is to enhance the SG model, we mainly consider the SG model (Mikolov et al., 2013b), SSG model (Ling et al., 2015a) and its simplified version SSSG model, as baselines for comparison.

Settings. Different models share the same hyperparameters in training word embeddings, which are presented in Table 2.

3.1 Training Speed

Figure 1 illustrates the training speed of different SG models, i.e., SG, SSG, SSSG, and DSG, given various size of context window.[3] Compared to the original SG model, SSG model shows a relatively large drop of speed when enlarging the context window, while there is much less drop observed for the DSG model. Overall, the curves of four models roughly comply with the qualitative analysis in Table 1. When starting with only one context word, the SSG, SSSG, and DSG model share similar training speed since their time complexities are not affected by the limited context window size under this circumstance. When enlarging the context window, the speed gap between the SSG and SG model is getting larger while the gap between DSG and SG becomes smaller.[4]

---

[2]https://dumps.wikimedia.org/enwiki/latest/

[3]The numbers on the curves are obtained when running on an Intel Xeon CPU E5-2680 v4 with 12 threads.

[4]Note that the derivations in Table 1 represents the upper bound of the complexities, where every two words co-occur in a context window, which hardly happens in real scenarios. As a result, the observed gaps are slightly smaller from what are presented in Table 1.

	MEN-3k	SimLex-999	WS-353
CBOW	70.96	34.32	69.25
CWin	**74.28**	36.06	72.21
SG	71.90	34.35	70.11
SSG	71.26	31.80	69.46
SSSG	72.07	33.62	70.90
DSG	73.76	**36.10**	**72.60**

Table 3: Word similarity results ($\rho \times 100$) from embeddings trained on the large corpus.

	MEN-3k	SimLex-999	WS-353
CBOW	58.23	26.67	64.40
CWin	59.68	25.19	62.82
SG	60.19	27.14	65.23
SSG	55.42	24.00	61.95
SSSG	62.70	26.55	66.10
DSG	**63.18**	**27.51**	**66.71**

Table 4: Word similarity results ($\rho \times 100$) from embeddings trained on the small corpus.

3.2 Word Similarity Evaluation

As a conventional intrinsic evaluation, word similarity test is performed on the MEN-3k (Bruni et al., 2012), SimLex-999 (Hill et al., 2015) and WordSim-353 (Finkelstein et al., 2002) datasets for quantitative comparisons among different embeddings. The Spearman's rank correlation (ρ) (Zar, 1998) is adopted to measure how close the similarity scores to human judgments on the three datasets. Besides SG, SSG and SSSG, we also include CBOW and CWin[5] as reference baselines in this word similarity evaluation.

Table 3 reports word similarity results when the embeddings are trained on the entire Wiki corpus. Besides, we created a small corpus by sampling 0.1% Wiki data to simulate the cold-start scenario that limited data is used to train word embeddings. The word similarity performance of all models on this small corpus is reported in Table 4. Overall, the results of all models are worse when trained on the small dataset, especially the models taking structure information of context into account, such as CWin and SSG. The reason may be largely due to that modeling order dependence is sensitive to data sparsity, hence CWin model fails to generate meaningful representations for low-frequency words, which are prevalent on small corpus. This observation indicates that data sparsity problem is critical in learning word embeddings. Nevertheless, DSG yields robust results on different scale of training data, which suggests that our model provides an effective solution to learn embeddings with exploiting the structure in context, while not severely suffered from the data sparsity problem. Particularly among all SG models, DSG produces the best performance when trained on either the large or the small corpus. This fact further proves the effectiveness of distinguishing left and right context for SG embeddings.

3.3 Part-of-Speech Tagging

Besides the intrinsic evaluation to test the embeddings semantically, we also evaluate different embeddings syntactically with an extrinsic evaluation: part-of-speech (POS) tagging. Following Ling et al. (2015a), this task is performed in both news and social media data. For news data, we use Wall Street Journal (WSJ) proportion from the Penn Treebank (Marcus et al., 1993) and follow the standard split of 38,219/5,527/5,462 sentences for training, development, and test, respectively. The social media data is based on ARK dataset (Gimpel et al., 2011), which contains manual POS annotations on English tweets. The standard split of ARK contains 1,000/327/500 tweets as training/development/test set, respectively.

POS prediction is conducted by a bidirectional LSTM-CRF (Huang et al., 2015; Lample et al., 2016) taking the produced embeddings as input. LSTM state size is setting to 200. For WSJ, we use the aforementioned embeddings trained from the Wiki corpus. For ARK, we prepare a Twitter corpus (TWT) to build embeddings. This data contains 100 million tweets collected through Twitter streaming API[6], followed by preprocessing using the toolkit described in Owoputi et al. (2013). The TWT embeddings are trained under the same procedure as the Wiki embeddings. Similar to word similarity task, we use CBOW, SG, CWin, SSG and SSSG as baselines in this task.

Results are reported in Table 5. We observe that the DSG embeddings can best indicate POS tags in comparison. It suggests that by exploring word context in left and right directions, DSG model can effectively capture syntactic information, which is

---

[5]Continuous window model, the counterpart of SSG proposed in Ling et al. (2015a).

[6]https://developer.twitter.com/en/docs/tweets/filter-realtime/overview

	WSJ		ARK	
	Dev	Test	Dev	Test
CBOW	96.86	97.01	89.36	88.36
CWin	96.98	97.25	90.03	89.94
SG	96.95	97.12	89.26	88.77
SSG	97.08	97.31	90.05	90.15
SSSG	97.01	97.19	89.83	89.78
DSG	**97.16**	**97.37**	**90.12**	**90.43**

Table 5: POS tagging results (accuracy) on WSJ and ARK datasets.

useful in predicting POS tags. Although embeddings trained on TWT could be affected by the noisiness and informal nature of tweets, POS taggers with DSG embeddings achieve the best accuracy on ARK data. This observation indicates that, when learning word embeddings with context structures on noisy data, DSG has its superiority to other models such as SSG and SSSG.

4 Conclusions

This paper presents DSG, a simple yet effective extension to the SG model for learning word embeddings. Given an input word, our model jointly predicts its context words as well as their direction to the given word. It is analyzed and experimented that our model can be trained as fast as the original SG model. Experiments on word similarity evaluation and POS tagging demonstrate that DSG produces better semantic and syntactic representations when it is compared with competitive baselines. More importantly, it is also proved that DSG can effectively predict word similarities when trained on small dataset and is therefore less sensitive to data sparsity than existing methods.

Acknowledgements

We thank the three anonymous reviewers for their insightful comments on this work.

References

Mohit Bansal, Kevin Gimpel, and Karen Livescu. 2014. Tailoring Continuous Word Representations for Dependency Parsing. In *Proceedings of the 52nd Annual Meeting of the Association for Computational Linguistics (Volume 2: Short Papers)*. Baltimore, Maryland, pages 809–815.

Yoshua Bengio, Réjean Ducharme, Pascal Vincent, and Christian Janvin. 2003. A Neural Probabilistic Language Model. *Journal of Machine Learning Research* 3:1137–1155.

Elia Bruni, Gemma Boleda, Marco Baroni, and Nam Khanh Tran. 2012. Distributional Semantics in Technicolor. In *Proceedings of the 50th Annual Meeting of the Association for Computational Linguistics (Volume 1: Long Papers)*. Jeju Island, Korea, pages 136–145.

Ronan Collobert and Jason Weston. 2008. A Unified Architecture for Natural Language Processing: Deep Neural Networks with Multitask Learning. In *Proceedings of the 25th International Conference on Machine Learning*. ACM, New York, NY, USA, ICML '08, pages 160–167.

Ronan Collobert, Jason Weston, Léon Bottou, Michael Karlen, Koray Kavukcuoglu, and Pavel Kuksa. 2011. Natural Language Processing (Almost) from Scratch. *Journal of Machine Learning Research* 12:2493–2537.

Manaal Faruqui, Jesse Dodge, Sujay Kumar Jauhar, Chris Dyer, Eduard Hovy, and Noah A. Smith. 2015. Retrofitting Word Vectors to Semantic Lexicons. In *Proceedings of the 2015 Conference of the North American Chapter of the Association for Computational Linguistics: Human Language Technologies*. Denver, Colorado, pages 1606–1615.

Lev Finkelstein, Evgeniy Gabrilovich, Yossi Matias, Ehud Rivlin, Zach Solan, Gadi Wolfman, and Eytan Ruppin. 2002. Placing Search in Context: the Concept Revisited. *ACM Transaction on Information Systems* 20(1):116–131.

Kevin Gimpel, Nathan Schneider, Brendan O'Connor, Dipanjan Das, Daniel Mills, Jacob Eisenstein, Michael Heilman, Dani Yogatama, Jeffrey Flanigan, and Noah A. Smith. 2011. Part-of-Speech Tagging for Twitter: Annotation, Features, and Experiments. In *Proceedings of the 49th Annual Meeting of the Association for Computational Linguistics: Human Language Technologies*. Portland, Oregon, USA, pages 42–47.

Felix Hill, Roi Reichart, and Anna Korhonen. 2015. Simlex-999: Evaluating Semantic Models with Genuine Similarity Estimation. *Computational Linguistics* 41(4):665–695.

Zhiheng Huang, Wei Xu, and Kai Yu. 2015. Bidirectional LSTM-CRF Models for Sequence Tagging. *arXiv preprint* abs/1508.01991.

Douwe Kiela, Felix Hill, and Stephen Clark. 2015. Specializing word embeddings for similarity or relatedness. In *Proceedings of the 2015 Conference on Empirical Methods in Natural Language Processing*. Association for Computational Linguistics, Lisbon, Portugal, pages 2044–2048.

Guillaume Lample, Miguel Ballesteros, Sandeep Subramanian, Kazuya Kawakami, and Chris Dyer. 2016. Neural Architectures for Named Entity Recognition.

In *Proceedings of the 2016 Conference of the North American Chapter of the Association for Computational Linguistics: Human Language Technologies*. San Diego, California, pages 260–270.

Wang Ling, Chris Dyer, Alan W Black, and Isabel Trancoso. 2015a. Two/Too Simple Adaptations of Word2Vec for Syntax Problems. In *Proceedings of the 2015 Conference of the North American Chapter of the Association for Computational Linguistics: Human Language Technologies*. Association for Computational Linguistics, Denver, Colorado, pages 1299–1304.

Wang Ling, Yulia Tsvetkov, Silvio Amir, Ramon Fermandez, Chris Dyer, Alan W Black, Isabel Trancoso, and Chu-Cheng Lin. 2015b. Not All Contexts Are Created Equal: Better Word Representations with Variable Attention. In *Proceedings of the 2015 Conference on Empirical Methods in Natural Language Processing*. Lisbon, Portugal, pages 1367–1372.

Mitch Marcus, Mary Ann Marcinkiewicz, and Beatrice Santorini. 1993. Building a large annotated corpus of English: the Penn Treebank. *Computational Linguistics* 19(2):313–330.

Tomas Mikolov, Kai Chen, Greg Corrado, and Jeffrey Dean. 2013a. Efficient Estimation of Word Representations in Vector Space. *arXiv preprint* abs/1301.3781.

Tomas Mikolov, Ilya Sutskever, Kai Chen, Greg S Corrado, and Jeff Dean. 2013b. Distributed Representations of Words and Phrases and their Compositionality. In C.J.C. Burges, L. Bottou, M. Welling, Z. Ghahramani, and K.Q. Weinberger, editors, *Advances in Neural Information Processing Systems 26*, pages 3111–3119.

Tomas Mikolov, Wen-tau Yih, and Geoffrey Zweig. 2013c. Linguistic Regularities in Continuous Space Word Representations. In *Proceedings of the 2013 Conference of the North American Chapter of the Association for Computational Linguistics: Human Language Technologies*. Association for Computational Linguistics, Atlanta, Georgia, pages 746–751.

Kim Anh Nguyen, Sabine Schulte im Walde, and Ngoc Thang Vu. 2016. Integrating distributional lexical contrast into word embeddings for antonym-synonym distinction. In *Proceedings of the 54th Annual Meeting of the Association for Computational Linguistics (Volume 2: Short Papers)*. Berlin, Germany, pages 454–459.

Olutobi Owoputi, Brendan O'Connor, Chris Dyer, Kevin Gimpel, Nathan Schneider, and Noah A. Smith. 2013. Improved Part-of-Speech Tagging for Online Conversational Text with Word Clusters. In *Proceedings of the 2013 Conference of the North American Chapter of the Association for Computational Linguistics: Human Language Technologies*. Atlanta, Georgia, pages 380–390.

Yan Song and Chia-Jung Lee. 2017. Learning user embeddings from emails. In *Proceedings of the 15th Conference of the European Chapter of the Association for Computational Linguistics*. Valencia, Spain, pages 733–738.

Yan Song, Chia-Jung Lee, and Fei Xia. 2017. Learning word representations with regularization from prior knowledge. In *Proceedings of the 21st Conference on Computational Natural Language Learning (CoNLL 2017)*. Vancouver, Canada, pages 143–152.

Peter D. Turney and Patrick Pantel. 2010. From Frequency to Meaning: Vector Space Models of Semantics. *Journal of Artificial Intelligence Research* 37(1):141–188.

Jason Weston, Antoine Bordes, Sumit Chopra, and Tomas Mikolov. 2015. Towards AI-Complete Question Answering: A Set of Prerequisite Toy Tasks. *arXiv pre-print* abs/1502.05698.

Mo Yu and Mark Dredze. 2014. Improving lexical embeddings with semantic knowledge. In *Proceedings of the 52nd Annual Meeting of the Association for Computational Linguistics (Volume 2: Short Papers)*. Baltimore, Maryland, pages 545–550.

Jerrold H Zar. 1998. Spearman rank correlation. *Encyclopedia of Biostatistics* .

Discriminating between Lexico-Semantic Relations
with the Specialization Tensor Model

Goran Glavaš
Data and Web Science Group
University of Mannheim
B6, 29, DE-68161 Mannheim
goran@informatik.uni-mannheim.de

Ivan Vulić
Language Technology Lab
University of Cambridge
9 West Road, Cambridge CB3 9DA
iv250@cam.ac.uk

Abstract

We present a simple and effective feed-forward neural architecture for discriminating between lexico-semantic relations (synonymy, antonymy, hypernymy, and meronymy). Our Specialization Tensor Model (STM) simultaneously produces multiple different specializations of input distributional word vectors, tailored for predicting lexico-semantic relations for word pairs. STM outperforms more complex state-of-the-art architectures on two benchmark datasets and exhibits stable performance across languages. We also show that, if coupled with a lingual distributional space, the proposed model can transfer the prediction of lexico-semantic relations to a resource-lean target language without any training data.

1 Introduction

Distributional vector spaces (i.e., word embeddings) (Mikolov et al., 2013; Pennington et al., 2014; Bojanowski et al., 2017) are ubiquitous in modern natural language processing (NLP). While such vector spaces capture general semantic relatedness, their well-known limitation is the inability to indicate the exact nature of the semantic relation that holds between words. Yet, the ability to recognize the exact semantic relation between words is crucial for many NLP applications: taxonomy induction (Fu et al., 2014; Ristoski et al., 2017), natural language inference (Tatu and Moldovan, 2005; Chen et al., 2017), text simplification (Glavaš and Štajner, 2015), and paraphrase generation (Madnani and Dorr, 2010), to name a few.

This is why numerous methods have been proposed that either (1) specialize distributional vectors to better reflect a particular relation (most commonly synonymy) (Faruqui et al., 2015; Kiela et al., 2015; Mrkšić et al., 2017; Vulić et al., 2017) or (2) train supervised relation classifiers using lexico-semantic relations (i.e., labeled word pairs)

from external resources such as WordNet (Fellbaum, 1998) as training data (Baroni et al., 2012; Roller et al., 2014; Shwartz et al., 2016; Glavaš and Ponzetto, 2017).

Contributions. We present the Specialization Tensor Model (STM), a simple and effective feed-forward neural model for discriminating between (arguably) most prominent lexico-semantic relations – *synonymy*, *antonymy*, *hypernymy*, and *meronymy*. The STM architecture is based on the hypothesis that different specializations of input distributional vectors are needed for predicting different lexico-semantic relations. Our results show that, despite its simplicity, STM outperforms more complex models on the benchmarking CogALex-V dataset (Santus et al., 2016). Further, it exhibits stable performance across languages. Finally, we show that, when coupled with a method for inducing a multilingual distributional space (Artetxe et al., 2017; Smith et al., 2017, *inter alia*), STM can predict lexico-semantic relations also for languages with no training data available from external linguistic resources. While in this work we use STM to discriminate between four prominent lexico-semantic relations, it can, at least conceptually, be trained to predict over an arbitrary set of lexico-semantic relations, provided the availability of respective training data.

2 Related Work

Specializing distributional vectors. Given a pair of words, we cannot reliably determine the nature of the lexico-semantic association between them (if any), purely based on their distributional word vectors (Mikolov et al., 2013; Pennington et al., 2014, *inter alia*). It is a well-known property of distributional methods to conflate different types of semantic associations between words. This is why methods for specializing word embeddings for par-

Proceedings of NAACL-HLT 2018, pages 181–187
New Orleans, Louisiana, June 1 - 6, 2018. ©2018 Association for Computational Linguistics

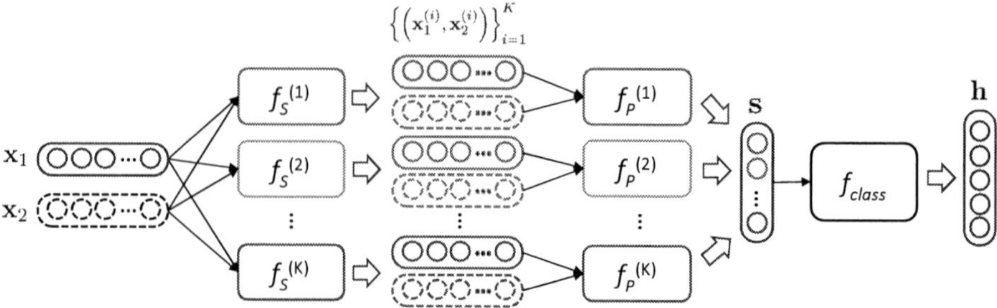

Figure 1: Architecture of the Specialization Tensor Model (STM).

ticular relations use external linguistic constraints (e.g., from WordNet) to either (1) modify the original objective of general embedding algorithms and directly train relation-specific embeddings from corpora (Yu and Dredze, 2014; Kiela et al., 2015) or (2) post-process the pre-trained distributional space by moving closer together (or further apart) words that stand in a particular relation (Wieting et al., 2015; Mrkšić et al., 2017; Vulić and Mrkšić, 2018). While these methods specialize the distributional space to better reflect properties of a particular relation, e.g., synonymy (Wieting et al., 2015; Mrkšić et al., 2017) or hypernymy (Vendrov et al., 2016; Vulić and Mrkšić, 2018), they are not able to discriminate between multiple lexico-semantic relations at the same time, i.e., the embedding space gets post-specialized for one particular relation.

Classifying lexico-semantic relations. Supervised relation classifiers learn to either identify one particular relation of interest (Baroni et al., 2012; Roller et al., 2014; Shwartz et al., 2016; Glavaš and Ponzetto, 2017) or to discriminate between multiple relations (Attia et al., 2016; Shwartz and Dagan, 2016), using labeled word pairs from external resources like WordNet. The LexNet model (Shwartz and Dagan, 2016) combines distributional vectors with recurrent encodings of syntactic paths taken from word co-occurrences in text corpora. While adding the syntactic information boosts performance, it limits the model's portability to other languages. Attia et al. (2016) train a convolutional model in a multi-task setting, coupling multi-class relation classification with binary classification of word relatedness. Unlike LexNet, this model requires only distributional vectors as input. Our specialization tensor model also requires only distributional vectors as input, but compared to the model of Attia et al. (2016), it has a simpler and more intuitive feed-forward architecture.

Glavaš and Ponzetto (2017) recently showed that asymmetric specialization of distributional vectors helps to detect asymmetric relations (hypernymy, meronymy). Following these findings, we hypothesize that detection of different relations requires different specializations of distributional vectors, so we design STM accordingly.

3   Specialization Tensor Model

The high-level architecture of the Specialization Tensor Model is depicted in Figure 1. The input to the model is a pair of unspecialized distributional word vectors $(\mathbf{x}_1, \mathbf{x}_2)$. Both input vectors are first transformed in K different ways with functions $f_S^{(1)}, \ldots, f_S^{(K)}$. Each pair of corresponding specializations $f_S^{(i)}(\mathbf{x}_1)$ and $f_S^{(i)}(\mathbf{x}_2)$ is then forwarded to the respective scoring function $f_P^{(i)}$. Finally, we feed the K scores obtained from K pairs of differently specialized distributional vectors as features to the multi-class relation classifier f_{class}.

3.1   Specialization Tensor

STM assumes that different word vector specializations emphasize different subsets of semantic properties of words that are more informative for predicting some lexico-semantic relations than others. In other words, we assume that a particular specialization function $f_S^{(i)}$ can be trained to transform the input vectors $\mathbf{x}_1$ and $\mathbf{x}_2$ into vectors that encode properties suitable for predicting a particular relation, e.g., *hypernymy*. We set the specialization function $f_S^{(i)} : \mathbb{R}^m \to \mathbb{R}^n$ to be a non-linear feed-forward network with a single hidden layer: it transforms the input vector $\mathbf{x} \in \mathbb{R}^m$ into a specialized vector $\mathbf{x}^{(i)} \in \mathbb{R}^n$:[1]

$$f_S^{(i)}(\mathbf{x}) = \tanh\left(\mathbf{W}_S^{(i)}\mathbf{x} + \mathbf{b}_S^{(i)}\right)$$

---

[1] We have also experimented with more hidden layers but $f_S^{(i)}$ with a single hidden layer yielded best performance.

with $\mathbf{W}_S^{(i)} \in \mathbb{R}^{n \times m}$ and $\mathbf{b}_S^{(i)} \in \mathbb{R}^n$ parameterizing the specialization function. Transformation matrices $\mathbf{W}_S^{(i)}$ of different specialization functions $f_S^{(i)}$ can be seen as slices of a specialization tensor $\mathbf{W}_S^{[1..\mathbf{K}]}$ (hence the model name), coupled with the specialization bias matrix $\mathbf{B}_S = \mathbf{b}_S^{[1..\mathbf{K}]}$. The number of specialization functions K (i.e., the number of slices of the specialization tensor) is the hyperparameter of the model.

3.2 Bilinear Product Scores

Following the assumption that specialization tensor slices generate relation-specific representations, we assume that an interaction between the corresponding specialized vectors $\mathbf{x}_1^{(i)} = f_S^{(i)}(\mathbf{x}_1)$ and $\mathbf{x}_2^{(i)} = f_S^{(i)}(\mathbf{x}_2)$, produced by the i-th specialization tensor slice, generates an informative score (i.e., a feature) for classifying the lexico-semantic relation for a word pair. We produce a single feature for each pair of specialized vectors $(\mathbf{x}_1^{(i)}, \mathbf{x}_2^{(i)})$ by non-linearly squashing their bilinear product:

$$f_P^{(i)}\left(\mathbf{x}_1^{(i)}, \mathbf{x}_2^{(i)}\right) = \tanh\left(\mathbf{x}_1^{(i)^T} \mathbf{W}_P^{(i)} \mathbf{x}_2^{(i)} + b_P^{(i)}\right)$$

with the bilinear product matrices $\mathbf{W}_P^{(i)} \in \mathbb{R}^{n \times n}$ and bias terms $b_P^{(i)} \in \mathbb{R}$ being trainable model parameters. Bilinear product matrices $\mathbf{W}_P^{(i)}$ may be seen as slices of the bilinear product tensor, $\mathbf{W}_P^{[1..\mathbf{K}]}$, coupled with the bias vector $\mathbf{b}_P = [b_P^{(1)}, \ldots, b_P^{(K)}]^T$. The final K-dimensional feature vector is then simply the concatenation of bilinear product scores, that is, $\mathbf{s} = [f_P^{(1)}, \ldots, f_P^{(K)}]^T$.

3.3 Classification Objective

As the final step, we feed the feature vector $\mathbf{s}$ to the relation classifier f_{class}, a feed-forward network with a single hidden layer:

$$f_{class}(\mathbf{s}) = \tanh\left(\mathbf{W}_{cl}\mathbf{s} + \mathbf{b}_{cl}\right)$$

with parameters $\mathbf{W}_{cl} \in \mathbb{R}^{C \times K}$ and $\mathbf{b}_{cl} \in \mathbb{R}^C$, where C is the number of lexico-semantic relations between which we are discriminating. We obtain the final prediction vector $\mathbf{h}$ by applying the softmax function on the output of the relation classification component: $\mathbf{h} = softmax\left(f_{class}(\mathbf{s})\right)$.

STM is parametrized by (1) the specialization tensor and bias matrix, (2) product tensor and bias vector, and (3) classifier parameters, i.e.,

$\Omega = \{\mathbf{W}_S^{[1:\mathbf{K}]}, \mathbf{B}_S, \mathbf{W}_P^{[1:\mathbf{K}]}, \mathbf{b}_P, \mathbf{W}_{cl}, \mathbf{b}_{cl}\}$. Assume the training set of N triples, each consisting of distributional vectors of two words and one-hot encoding of the relation that holds between these words, $\{(\mathbf{x}_{1_k}, \mathbf{x}_{2_k}, \mathbf{y}_k)\}_{k=1}^N$. We optimize STM's parameters by minimizing the regularized cross-entropy loss (i.e., negative log-likelihood):

$$J(\Omega) = \lambda\|\Omega\|_2 - \sum_{k=1}^N \sum_{j=1}^C y_k^j \ln(h_k^j)$$

where h_k^j is the probability that the j-th relation holds in the k-th training example (as predicted by the model), and λ is the regularization factor.

4 Evaluation

We first describe the evaluation setup (datasets, baselines, and model optimization) and then show STM's performance on a benchmarking relation classification dataset (Santus et al., 2016). Finally, we report how STM performs for different languages and in the language transfer setting.

4.1 Experimental Setup

Datasets. We use the CogALex-V dataset from the shared task on corpus-based identification of semantic relations (Santus et al., 2016). Its train and test portions contain 3,054 and 4,260 word pairs, respectively, covering four relations (synonymy: 5.4%; antonymy: 8.8%; hypernymy: 8.6%; and meronymy: 6.1%) and randomly paired words (71.1%). CogALex-V is severely skewed in favor of random word pairs and its training portion is very limited in size. Nonetheless to the best of our knowledge, it is the only publicly available dataset for multi-class classification of lexico-semantic relations on which other models have been comparatively evaluated (Attia et al., 2016; Shwartz and Dagan, 2016).

Besides the skewed class distribution and the limited size, CogALex-V also suffers from lexical repetitiveness.[2] We have thus created an additional larger and more balanced dataset by randomly sampling triples from WordNet (Fellbaum, 1998). This dataset, termed WN-LS, contains 10,000 word pairs (approximately 2,000 pairs for each of the four lexico-semantic relations and 2,000

---

[2] A single word can be present in up to ten pairs (although there is no lexical overlap between the train and test data).

randomly created pairs), split by 8:2 train-to-test ratio. To support the multilingual analysis, we semi-automatically translated the whole English (EN) WN-LS dataset into German (DE) and Spanish (ES).[3] We additionally translated the test portion of WN-LS to Croatian (HR), as an example of a resource-lean language.[4]

Baselines. We compare STM against two baseline models. The first baseline (CONCAT) feeds the concatenation of the distributional embeddings to a feed-forward classifier with a single hidden layer:

$$\mathbf{h}(\mathbf{x}_1, \mathbf{x}_2) = softmax\left(\tanh\left(\mathbf{W}_{cl}[\mathbf{x}_1; \mathbf{x}_2] + \mathbf{b}_{cl}\right)\right).$$

The second baseline, named BILIN-TENS is an STM reduction in which we directly forward the input vectors into the bilinear product tensor $\mathbf{W}_P^{[1..K]}$, without being specialized. It can be seen as STM with tensor specialization slices $\mathbf{W}_S^{(i)}$ fixed to identity matrices and biases $\mathbf{b}_S^{(i)}$ to zero vectors. Comparing STM with BILIN-TENS directly quantifies the effect the specialization tensor has on relation classification performance.

Optimization. We learn the STM's parameters using the Adam algorithm (Kingma and Ba, 2015), with initial learning rate set to 0.0001. We train in mini-batches of size $N_b = 50$ and apply dropout with the retaining probability of 0.5 to all model layers. In all experiments, we find the optimal hyperparameters (the number of specialization tensor slices K, the size of the specialized vectors n, and the regularization factor λ) via grid search within the 5-fold cross-validation on the training set.

4.2 Results and Discussion

Evaluation on CogALex-V. We show performance (F_1 score for all relations and micro-averaged F_1) on the CogALex-V dataset in Table 1.[5] For a more direct comparison with the best-performing shared task models, LexNet (Shwartz et al., 2016) and the model of Attia et al. (2016), we used 300-dimensional GloVe (Pennington et al., 2014) distributional vectors as input.

Although not by a wide margin, STM outperforms both best-performing models from the

Model	SYN	ANT	HYP	MER	All
Attia et al. (2016)	20.4	44.8	49.1	49.7	42.3
LexNet (2016)	**29.7**	42.5	**52.6**	49.3	44.5
CONCAT	10.9	28.5	34.8	32.9	27.4
BILIN-TENS	15.7	40.3	47.9	43.3	38.9
STM	22.1	**50.4**	49.8	**50.4**	**45.3**

Table 1: Performance on the CogALex-V dataset.

Model	Lang.	SYN	ANT	HYP	MER	All
LexNet	EN	57.6	77.8	**65.9**	**83.3**	70.9
STM	EN	**58.6**	**86.6**	63.5	79.5	**72.5**
STM	DE	48.0	79.6	55.9	78.6	66.0
STM	ES	52.3	80.5	62.6	78.8	68.6

Table 2: STM performance for three languages on (respective translations of) the WN-LS dataset.

CogaLex-V shared task (Attia et al., 2016; Shwartz et al., 2016), which is encouraging, given that STM is simpler than both of these neural architectures. STM outscores the model of Attia et al. (2016), which uses the same input signal (i.e., only distributional vectors) across the board. Overall, STM also slightly outperforms LexNet (Shwartz and Dagan, 2016), despite the fact that LexNet additionally employs rich syntactic signal. STM's 6-point edge over BILIN-TENS demonstrates the effectiveness of multiple vector specializations, since this performance gain can only be credited to the specialization tensor $\mathbf{W}_S^{[1..K]}$. *Antonymy* is the relation for which STM yields largest gain with respect to other models.

Multilingual comparison. Table 2 displays classification performance for English, German, and Spanish on respective variants of the WN-LS dataset. On the EN WN-LS version we compare STM's performance against the LexNet model (Shwartz and Dagan, 2016). To allow for a more transparent comparison of STM's performance across languages, we employed 300-dimensional English, German, and Spanish `fastText` embeddings (Bojanowski et al., 2017), pre-trained on Wikipedia.[6] STM slightly outperforms the more complex LexNet model (Shwartz and Dagan, 2016) on the WN-LS dataset as well. We believe STM's (not drastically) lower scores for German and Spanish are due to (1) distributional

---

[3]We first translated the dataset automatically with Google Translate and then manually fixed the translation errors.

[4]We make WN-LS dataset publicly available, together with the implementation of the specialization tensor model, at `https://github.com/codogogo/stm`.

[5]Optimal STM config.: $K = 5$, $n = 300$, and $\lambda = 0.001$.

[6]`https://github.com/facebookresearch/fastText/blob/master/pretrained-vectors.md`

Train	Test	SYN	ANT	HYP	MER	All
EN	DE	39.1	66.8	49.3	67.6	**55.1**
EN	ES	41.7	73.0	52.6	69.0	**58.6**
EN	HR	30.5	64.7	49.1	60.5	**51.5**
DE	EN	34.0	68.6	47.2	62.4	54.2
DE	ES	39.1	61.9	44.4	60.5	50.6
DE	HR	30.3	59.8	37.7	51.7	45.2
ES	EN	47.9	74.9	46.4	68.2	**59.9**
ES	DE	37.8	66.7	47.9	62.7	53.3
ES	HR	36.1	62.2	44.6	61.5	51.4

Table 3: Zero-shot cross-lingual transfer. Best performance for each test set is shown in bold.

Train	Test	SYN	ANT	HYP	MER	All
EN+ES	HR	31.7	59.8	**52.3**	**68.3**	**54.4**
EN+DE	HR	29.0	61.7	46.5	65.3	51.5
DE+ES	HR	**36.6**	61.4	47.5	65.7	53.1
EN+ES+DE	HR	36.5	**64.6**	51.2	64.7	54.1

Table 4: Language transfer results on the HR WN-LS. Training on combinations of EN, ES, and DE data.

vectors built from smaller corpora (ES and DE Wikipedia being smaller than EN Wikipedia) and (2) language-specific phenomena (e.g., a large number of compounds in German).

Zero-shot language transfer. Finally, we investigate whether a pre-trained STM model can be leveraged to predict lexico-semantic relations for a new language, from which it has observed no training instances. We are particularly interested in such zero-shot language transfer for resource-lean languages, for which resources like WordNet do not exist. To enable transfer experiments, we needed to induce a shared bilingual (or multilingual) vector space. In all experiments, we induced the shared distributional spaces using the mapping approach and translation matrices from Smith et al. (2017).

In the first set of transfer experiments, we trained STM on the WN-LS train portion in one language (EN, ES, or DE) and evaluated it on the test WN-LS portions of all other languages, including Croatian as a resource-lean language. We show the results of these experiments in Table 3. Performance drops, compared to respective monolingual settings (i.e., performance of models trained on the WN-LS train set of the same language, see Table 2), range between 10% (EN→ES compared to monolingual ES results) and 18% (DE→EN performance compared to monolingual EN performance). These drops in zero-shot language transfer are due to imperfect bilingual embedding spaces. In fact, language transfer results seem to be very correlated with the quality of corresponding embedding translation matrices (highest for transfers between EN and ES and lowest for DE→HR transfer).[7] It is encouraging that we can build a reasonable relation classifier even for a resource-lean language, without a single training instance for that language.

Finally, we examine whether we can improve prediction performance for a resource-lean language (i.e., Croatian) by combining the training data from multiple resource-rich languages (i.e., English, German, and Spanish). We show the results for this experiment in Table 4. By combining training data from different resource-rich languages, we further improve prediction performance for a resource-lean language. Compared to the EN→HR transfer, we observe 3% overall performance gain when training on merged (EN+ES and EN+ES+DE) datasets. ES and DE training instances are, however, merely translations of the original EN instances, i.e., there is no additional external knowledge being introduced. We thus believe that the observed gains are due to additional regularization provided by the multilingual training provides, which allows us to learn a model that better generalizes across languages.

5 Conclusion

We have presented a novel neural architecture for predicting lexico-semantic relations between words. The proposed tensor-based specialization model specializes distributional vectors in multiple ways and then uses these specializations to compute features for relation classification. We have demonstrated that our model outperforms more complex and resource-heavier models on two benchmarking datasets. We have further shown that our model is by design portable across languages and that it supports zero-shot knowledge transfer to resource-lean languages. As future work, we plan to experiment with more advanced neural architectures and finer-grained relations. We also intend to port the model to more languages.

Acknowledgments

Ivan Vulić is supported by the ERC Consolidator Grant LEXICAL (no. 648909).

---

[7]For example, Smith et al. (2017) report P@1 bilingual lexicon extraction performance of 73% for ES-EN, 61% for DE-EN, and 55% for HR-EN.

References

Mikel Artetxe, Gorka Labaka, and Eneko Agirre. 2017. Learning bilingual word embeddings with (almost) no bilingual data. In *Proceedings of the Annual Meeting of the Association for Computational Linguistics (ACL)*, pages 451–462.

Mohammed Attia, Suraj Maharjan, Younes Samih, Laura Kallmeyer, and Thamar Solorio. 2016. CogALex-V shared task: GHHH-detecting semantic relations via word embeddings. In *Proceedings of the 5th Workshop on Cognitive Aspects of the Lexicon (CogALex-V)*, pages 86–91.

Marco Baroni, Raffaella Bernardi, Ngoc-Quynh Do, and Chung-chieh Shan. 2012. Entailment above the word level in distributional semantics. In *Proceedings of the Conference of the European Chapter of the Association for Computational Linguistics (EACL)*, pages 23–32.

Piotr Bojanowski, Edouard Grave, Armand Joulin, and Tomas Mikolov. 2017. Enriching word vectors with subword information. *Transactions of the Association for Computational Linguistics (TACL)*, 5:135–146.

Qian Chen, Xiaodan Zhu, Zhen-Hua Ling, and Diana Inkpen. 2017. Natural language inference with external knowledge. *arXiv preprint arXiv:1711.04289*.

Manaal Faruqui, Jesse Dodge, Sujay Kumar Jauhar, Chris Dyer, Eduard Hovy, and Noah A. Smith. 2015. Retrofitting word vectors to semantic lexicons. In *Proceedings of the Conference of the North American Chapter of the Association for Computational Linguistics: Human Language Technologies (NAACL-HLT)*, pages 1606–1615.

Christiane Fellbaum, editor. 1998. *WordNet: An Electronic Lexical Database*. MIT Press.

Ruiji Fu, Jiang Guo, Bing Qin, Wanxiang Che, Haifeng Wang, and Ting Liu. 2014. Learning semantic hierarchies via word embeddings. In *Proceedings of the Annual Meeting of the Association for Computational Linguistics (ACL)*, pages 1199–1209.

Goran Glavaš and Sanja Štajner. 2015. Simplifying lexical simplification: Do we need simplified corpora? In *Proceedings of the Annual Meeting of the Association for Computational Linguistics*, pages 63–68.

Goran Glavaš and Simone Paolo Ponzetto. 2017. Dual tensor model for detecting asymmetric lexico-semantic relations. In *Proceedings of the Conference on Empirical Methods in Natural Language Processing (EMNLP)*, pages 1757–1767.

Douwe Kiela, Felix Hill, and Stephen Clark. 2015. Specializing word embeddings for similarity or relatedness. In *Proceedings of the Conference on Empirical Methods in Natural Language Processing (EMNLP)*, pages 2044–2048.

Diederik P. Kingma and Jimmy Ba. 2015. Adam: A method for stochastic optimization. In *Proceedings of the International Conference on Learning Representations (ICLR)*.

Nitin Madnani and Bonnie J Dorr. 2010. Generating phrasal and sentential paraphrases: A survey of data-driven methods. *Computational Linguistics*, 36(3):341–387.

Tomas Mikolov, Ilya Sutskever, Kai Chen, Greg S Corrado, and Jeff Dean. 2013. Distributed representations of words and phrases and their compositionality. In *Proceedings of the Conference on Neural Information Processing Systems (NIPS)*, pages 3111–3119.

Nikola Mrkšić, Ivan Vulić, Diarmuid O'Seaghdha, Ira Leviant, Roi Reichart, Milica Gašić, Anna Korhonen, and Steve Young. 2017. Semantic specialization of distributional word vector spaces using monolingual and cross-lingual constraints. *Transactions of the Association for Computational Linguistics (TACL)*, 5:309–324.

Jeffrey Pennington, Richard Socher, and Christopher D Manning. 2014. Glove: Global vectors for word representation. In *Proceedings of the Conference on Empirical Methods in Natural Language Processing (EMNLP)*, pages 1532–1543.

Petar Ristoski, Stefano Faralli, Simone Paolo Ponzetto, and Heiko Paulheim. 2017. Large-scale taxonomy induction using entity and word embeddings. In *Proceedings of the International Conference on Web Intelligence*, pages 81–87.

Stephen Roller, Katrin Erk, and Gemma Boleda. 2014. Inclusive yet selective: Supervised distributional hypernymy detection. In *Proceedings of the International Conference on Computational Linguistics (COLING)*, pages 1025–1036.

Enrico Santus, Anna Gladkova, Stefan Evert, and Alessandro Lenci. 2016. The CogALex-V shared task on the corpus-based identification of semantic relations. In *Proceedings of the 5th Workshop on Cognitive Aspects of the Lexicon (CogALex-V)*, pages 69–79.

Vered Shwartz and Ido Dagan. 2016. CogALex-V Shared Task: LexNET-integrated path-based and distributional method for the identification of semantic relations. In *Proceedings of the 5th Workshop on Cognitive Aspects of the Lexicon (CogALex-V)*, pages 80–85.

Vered Shwartz, Yoav Goldberg, and Ido Dagan. 2016. Improving hypernymy detection with an integrated path-based and distributional method. In *Proceedings of the Annual Meeting of the Association for Computational Linguistics (ACL)*, pages 2389–2398.

Samuel L. Smith, David H.P. Turban, Steven Hamblin, and Nils Y. Hammerla. 2017. Offline bilingual word vectors, orthogonal transformations and the inverted softmax. In *Proceedings of the International Conference on Learning Representations (ICLR)*.

Marta Tatu and Dan Moldovan. 2005. A semantic approach to recognizing textual entailment. In *Proceedings of the Conference on Empirical Methods in Natural Language Processing (EMNLP)*, pages 371–378.

Ivan Vendrov, Ryan Kiros, Sanja Fidler, and Raquel Urtasun. 2016. Order-embeddings of images and language. In *Proceedings of the International Conference on Learning Representations (ICLR)*.

Ivan Vulić and Nikola Mrkšić. 2018. Specialising word vectors for lexical entailment. In *Proceedings of the Conference of the North American Chapter of the Association for Computational Linguistics: Human Language Technologies (NAACL-HLT)*.

Ivan Vulić, Nikola Mrkšić, Roi Reichart, Diarmuid Ó Séaghdha, Steve Young, and Anna Korhonen. 2017. Morph-fitting: Fine-tuning word vector spaces with simple language-specific rules. In *Proceedings of the Annual Meeting of the Association for Computational Linguistics (ACL)*, pages 56–68.

John Wieting, Mohit Bansal, Kevin Gimpel, and Karen Livescu. 2015. From paraphrase database to compositional paraphrase model and back. *Transactions of the Association for Computational Linguistics (TACL)*, 3:345–358.

Mo Yu and Mark Dredze. 2014. Improving lexical embeddings with semantic knowledge. In *Proceedings of the Annual Meeting of the Association for Computational Linguistics (ACL)*, pages 545–550.

Evaluating bilingual word embeddings on the long tail

Fabienne Braune[1,2], Viktor Hangya[1], Tobias Eder[1], Alexander Fraser[1]
[1]Center for Information and Language Processing
LMU Munich, Germany
[2]Volkswagen Data Lab Munich, Germany
`fabienne.braune@volkswagen.de`
`{hangyav, fraser}@cis.uni-muenchen.de`
`tobias.eder@germanistik.uni-muenchen.de`

Abstract

Bilingual word embeddings are useful for bilingual lexicon induction, the task of mining translations of given words. Many studies have shown that bilingual word embeddings perform well for bilingual lexicon induction but they focused on frequent words in general domains. For many applications, bilingual lexicon induction of rare and domain-specific words is of critical importance. Therefore, we design a new task to evaluate bilingual word embeddings on rare words in different domains. We show that state-of-the-art approaches fail on this task and present simple new techniques to improve bilingual word embeddings for mining rare words. We release new gold standard datasets and code to stimulate research on this task.

1 Introduction

Bilingual lexicon induction (BLI) is the task of generating accurate translations for each word in a list of source language words. Being able to perform BLI without parallel data is critical in many low resource scenarios. Bilingual word embeddings (BWEs) represent words from two different languages in the same vector space. BWEs have been shown to be very effective for BLI given a *small* seed lexicon (around 5000 word-pairs) as the only bilingual signal. Until now, BWEs have been evaluated on frequent words from parliament proceedings or Wikipedia articles and reached good accuracies on these datasets. However, evaluations on rare and domain-specific words have not yet been provided even though such evaluation scenarios are critical for applications like machine translation (e.g., mining of translations for OOV (out-of-vocabulary) items) or bilingual terminology mining. In this paper, we design a novel evaluation scenario for BWEs: given (i) large amounts of monolingual data and

(ii) a seed lexicon of frequent word-pairs, the goal is to create BWEs that enable accurate mining of rare words. As gold standard data, we release manually annotated pairs of rare words and their translations from three domains: (i) web crawls (ii) news commentaries (iii) medical texts. We show that state-of-the-art BWEs perform poorly on these data sets. We present simple techniques to build and combine BWEs that yield strong performance improvements. We study using fast-text to build BWEs, using ensembles of BWEs, and dealing with orthographic distance in BWEs, all of which improve results for the new task of rare word translation mining. A secondary contribution is improvements over state-of-the-art approaches on frequent words (which have been already extensively studied in previous work). We make our datasets and code publicly available[1].

2 Bilingual Induction of Rare Words

We briefly present how BLI is performed using BWEs and then introduce our new datasets.

Bilingual Lexicon Induction. The goal is to generate translations t in target language V_t of provided words s from source language V_s. Given a BWE representing V_s and V_t, an n-best list of translations for each word $s \in V_s$ can be induced by taking the top n words $t_i \in V_t$ whose representation $\vec{x_{t_i}}$ in the BWE is closest to the representation $\vec{x_s}$ according to cosine distance.

Datasets. To create BWEs we use *post-hoc mapping* which requires only monolingual texts and a small seed lexicon (see §3). Our training set consists of two large monolingual corpora:

- GENERAL: 4,400,309 English and German sentences from parliament proceedings, news

---

[1]`https://github.com/braunefe/BWEeval`

Proceedings of NAACL-HLT 2018, pages 188–193
New Orleans, Louisiana, June 1 - 6, 2018. ©2018 Association for Computational Linguistics

commentaries and web crawls taken from the WMT 2016 shared task (Bojar et al., 2016).

- MEDICAL: 3,108,183 English and German sentences from titles of medical Wikipedia articles, medical term-pairs, patents, documents from the European Medicines Agency.[2]

Seed Lexicons. Throughout the paper, we work with two lexicons. For each lexicon, we take the most common words and translate these by taking the top-ranked translation from a probabilistic dictionary.[3] BWEs trained using this data are evaluated on our gold standards containing pairs of rare words (we will also report results on frequent words, as in previous work, see below).

- GENLEX: 4955 most frequent words from GENERAL
- MEDLEX: 6079 most frequent words from MEDICAL

Gold Standards for Rare Words. We created gold standard data for rare words by randomly sampling words occurring between 3 and 5 times[4] in GENERAL and MEDICAL. For GENERAL we sample rare words from news commentaries and web crawls separately, so we have two rare word data sets here. For each (English) sampled word, a German native speaker generated a German translation. We indicate the division into validation and test sets:

- CRAWLRARE: 1000 rare words from web crawls of GENERAL (250 validation, 750 test)
- NEWSRARE: 1144 rare words from news commentaries of GENERAL (369 validation, 775 test)
- MEDRARE: 2109 rare words from MEDICAL (1000 validation, 1109 test)

As English-German BLI of frequent words has not been studied before, following previous work, we annotated 2000 frequent English words taken from each of the General and Medical corpora with their German translations using the same probabilistic dictionary as was used to generate the Lexicon sets. These two silver standard datasets will also be released with the paper:

- GENFREQ: 2000 frequent words from GENERAL (1000 validation, 1000 test)
- MEDFREQ: 2000 frequent words from MEDICAL (1000 validation, 1000 test)

3 Bilingual Word Embedding Creation

To create bilingual word embeddings, we use *post-hoc mapping* (PHM), a method that projects monolingual words embeddings (MWEs) into a shared space using a linear transformation trained with a small seed lexicon (Mikolov et al., 2013b; Faruqui and Dyer, 2014; Xing et al., 2015; Lazaridou et al., 2015; Vulić and Korhonen, 2016). Among methods to generate BWEs, PHM uses a very cheap bilingual signal.[5]

Given MWEs in two languages V_s and V_t, the goal of post-hoc mapping is to find a matrix $\mathbf{W} \in \mathbb{R}^{d_1 \times d_2}$ that maps each representation $\vec{x_s} \in \mathbb{R}^{d_1}$ of a source word $s \in V_s$ to the representation $\vec{y_t} \in \mathbb{R}^{d_2}$ of its translation $t \in V_t$. Typically, $\mathbf{W}$ is learned using a seed lexicon $L = \{(\vec{x_1}, \vec{y_1}), \ldots, (\vec{x_n}, \vec{y_n})\}$, where each pair $(\vec{x_i}, \vec{y_i}) \in V_s \times V_t$ are mutual translations. A common objective for cross-lingual mapping is ridge regression (Mikolov et al., 2013b) (RIDGE), where $\mathbf{W}$ is estimated by:

$$\mathbf{W}^* = \underset{\mathbf{W} \in \mathbb{R}^{d_1 \times d_2}}{\arg\min} \ \| \mathbf{XW} - \mathbf{Y} \| + \lambda \| \mathbf{W} \| \quad (1)$$

where $\mathbf{X}$ and $\mathbf{Y}$ are stacked vectors of $\vec{x_i}$ and $\vec{y_i}$ respectively. Lazaridou et al. (2015) use a max-margin ranking loss (MAX-MARG) to estimate $\mathbf{W}$. For each $(\vec{x_i}, \vec{y_i}) \in L$, a candidate $\vec{y_i^*} = \mathbf{W} \cdot \vec{x_i}$ is computed. The ranking loss is:

$$\sum_{j \neq i}^{k} \max\{0, \gamma + sim(\vec{y_i^*}, \vec{y_i}) - sim(\vec{y_i^*}, \vec{y_j})\} \quad (2)$$

where $\vec{y_j}$ is a randomly selected negative example, i.e., it is not a translation of $\vec{x_i}$, k is the number of negative examples and $sim(\vec{x}, \vec{y})$ computes cosine similarity between $\vec{x}$ and $\vec{y}$. Hyperparameters γ and k are tuned on held-out validation data.[6]

---

[2]This is taken from the in-domain part of: `https://ufal.mff.cuni.cz/ufal_medical_corpus`.

[3]This word-level dictionary is taken from a standard phrase-based SMT system trained on WMT 2017 data.

[4]Words with frequencies 1 and 2 are very often tokenization errors or borrowings from other languages, therefore we start at frequency 3. We did not consider tokenization errors as rare words and removed those from our data.

[5]Gouws and Søgaard (2015) and Duong et al. (2016) also leverage seed lexicons. However, in order to generate high quality BWEs, these approaches leverage much larger bilingual dictionaries.

[6]Ideally, the sum in Equation 2 should be computed over the complete target vocabulary (i.e., $k = | V_t |$). Since this is not feasible in practice, Lazaridou et al. (2015) treat k as another hyperparameter tuned together with γ.

Domain	mapping	w2v skip	w2v cbow
genFreq	ridge	27.1 (43.7)	24.0 (41.4)
	max-marg	**32.1 (47.7)**	22.8 (40.0)
medFreq	ridge	14.9 (24.0)	**18.1 (30.1)**
	max-marg	16.0 (27.2)	16.8 (27.2)

Table 1: Bilingual lexicon induction of **frequent** word-pairs on **general and medical domain** data. We report top-1 and (top-5 in brackets) percentage accuracy. In this paper, bolding indicates a best result so far for a particular dataset.

3.1 Testing Previous Work

We reimplement Mikolov et al. (2013b) as well as Lazaridou et al. (2015). To replicate their setup on English-German texts we first evaluate these on two standard tasks, mining frequent words from GENERAL and MEDICAL. We follow the approach of (Heyman et al., 2017) and use English as the source language. First, we train 300 dimensional MWEs on the monolingual data using W2V[7] with default parameters except that we lowered the minimum word frequency threshold to 3 (Mikolov et al., 2013a). To generate BWEs, we use MEDICAL and MEDLEX for MEDRARE and MEDFREQ, while we use GENERAL and GENLEX for the rest of the test sets. We report results with the combination of skip-gram (W2V SKIP) or cbow (W2V CBOW) and RIDGE or MAX-MARG. As in previous work, we use top-1 (translation is the closest neighbor) and top-5 (translation is one of 5 closest neighbors) accuracies. The results in Table 1 show that the best performing setups are W2V SKIP with MAX-MARG for GENFREQ and W2V CBOW with RIDGE for MEDFREQ. Accuracies are comparable to previous work (which was on different language pairs). The poor performance on MEDFREQ is consistent with Heyman et al. (2017), who introduced the task of mining frequent medical terms.

4 Applying BWEs for Mining Rare Word-Pairs

We use the exact same BWEs training setup as above (§3) and perform BLI on our new test sets of rare words. The results in Table 2 show that on **low frequency** word-pairs BWEs perform very poorly. Compared to standard evaluation scenarios (see Table 1) a massive performance decrease is observed. Low accuracy is clearly caused by the inability of context-based models (W2V) to build accurate embedding vectors for words occurring

---

Domain	mapping	w2v skip	w2v cbow
crawlRare	ridge	**2.3** (3.2)	2.0 (2.4)
	max-marg	2.1 **(3.3)**	1.7 (2.3)
newsRare	ridge	4.6 (9.4)	1.9 (4.9)
	max-marg	**5.5 (11.0)**	2.3 (4.8)
medRare	ridge	0.1 (0.2)	0.1 (0.1)
	max-marg	**0.1 (0.4)**	0.1 (0.1)

Table 2: Bilingual lexicon induction of **low frequency** word-pairs in different domains.

Domain	mapping	FTT skip	FTT cbow
crawlRare	ridge	10.1 (14.7)	4.7 (6.7)
	max-marg	**11.5 (15.9)**	7.3 (12.1)
newsRare	ridge	23.2 (37.7)	6.8 (13.5)
	max-marg	**25.3 (39.5)**	15.1 (24.1)
medRare	ridge	12.2 (19.0)	8.2 (14.2)
	max-marg	**12.5 (20.0)**	8.8 (15.3)
genFreq	ridge	33.8 (51.4)	16.2 (32.1)
	max-marg	**38.7 (56.5)**	28.3 (45.3)
medFreq	ridge	17.8 (33.6)	14.9 (26.7)
	max-marg	**29.3 (42.7)**	19.9 (33.2)

Table 3: Bilingual lexicon induction using MWEs trained with FASTTEXT (FTT).

in very few contexts only. Through post-hoc mapping, these (poor) embeddings get projected randomly into the bilingual space which results in very poor performance on BLI especially for the medical domain.

4.1 Using Subword Models

A first way to create BWEs that are better adapted to rare words is to generate MWEs that provide better vector representations for the words. One simple idea is to try to add subword information. We show empirically this helps BLI of rare words, which has not been shown before, to our knowledge. FASTTEXT (Bojanowski et al., 2017) extends W2V by adding subword information $s(w, c)$ to the context-based objective as follows:

$$s(w, c) = \sum_{g \in G_w} z_g^\top v_c \qquad (3)$$

where $G_w \subset \{1, ..., G\}$ is a set of character n-gram indices corresponding to the n-grams that appear in the word w, z_g is the vector representation of the n-gram and v_c is the vector of the context words. Subword information helps for rare words (by using n-gram information shared between words) and generates more accurate MWEs especially for morphologically rich languages like German. We create 300 dimensional MWEs using FASTTEXT skip-gram and cbow models with default parameters and with the same exception as before, i.e., we lowered the minimum word

Domain	mapping	ensemble	ensemble + edit	edit only	% orth. close
crawlRare	ridge	10.3 (14.6)	19.5 (22.1)	19.0 (21.7)	60.3
	max-marg	13.2 (17.6)	**19.5 (22.3)**		
newsRare	ridge	24.3 (39.9)	32.0 (42.8)	21.8 (29.5)	39.8
	max-marg	27.2 (40.0)	**32.8 (43.5)**		
medRare	ridge	15.1 (20.6)	25.5 (26.8)	26.0 (28.2)	76.7
	max-marg	12.5 (21.2)	**26.3 (28.2)**		
genFreq	ridge	42.9 (60.7)	44.8 (62.0)	16.0 (27.1)	26.5
	max-marg	45.4 (63.2)	**47.2 (63.6)**		
medFreq	ridge	31.6 (37.0)	35.5 (44.2)	20.7 (32.9)	55.7
	max-marg	37.7 (46.7)	**38.6 (47.4)**		

Table 4: Bilingual lexicon induction of **low-frequency** and **frequent** word-pairs in different domains. *Ensemble* denotes the results for ensembling all BWE models, *ensemble + edit* shows results by adding orthographic similarity, *edit only* denotes the results obtained by using only orthographic distance (all other weights set to 0) and *% orth. close* shows the percentage of orthographically similar gold standard word pairs (whose normalized Levenshtein distance is at most 0.3).

No.	source	model1	model2	corpus	glossary
		w2v skip	FTT skip		
1.	snowstorms	skinhead	**schneestürme**	crawlRare	skinhead
2.	fire-extinguishers	goldzertifikate	**feuerlöschern**	crawlRare	gold certificates
3.	tissue-specificity	basismilieu	**gewebespezifizität**	medRare	base environment
4.	university	**universität**	harvard-universität	crawlRare	Harvard University
5.	cabin	**kabine**	flugzeugkabine	newsRare	airplane cabin
		FTT skip	ensemble		
6.	rubbish	mülltonnen	**müll**	newsRare	trashcan
7.	bathtub	badezimmer	**badewanne**	newsRare	bathroom
8.	parenthood	vaterschaft	**elternschaft**	newsRare	fatherhood
9.	cognitively	neurokognitiven	**kognitiv**	medRare	neuro cognitive
10.	nanojoules	**nanojoule**	mikrotröpfchen	medRare	microdroplet
		ensemble	ensemble + edit		
11.	sleddogs	pferdeschlittenfahrten	**schlittenhunde**	crawlRare	sled rides
12.	gnome-applets	gtkhtml	**gnome-anwendungen**	crawlRare	layout engine used by Gnome
13.	glutenins	getreideproteinen	**glutenine**	medRare	grain proteins
14.	esterify	verestern	esteröl	medRare	ester oil

Table 5: Examples comparing the predictions of the indicated models using ridge for the mapping where *model1* and *model2* shows the induced words for the given source. Bolding indicates the correct prediction and we give glosses for the incorrect predictions.

frequency value to 3. We perform PHM using RIDGE and MAX-MARGIN. The results in Table 3 show that this procedure yields impressive performance improvements. After evaluation[8] we manually looked at the prediction of our models. We present examples in table 5. Examples 1–3 shows that the model improves non-trivial cases as well where the meanings of the incorrect predictions induced by W2V are not close to that of the input. We also show counterexamples 4 and 5 where subword elements cause errors by inducing hyponymies of the correct words. Generating BWEs with MAX-MARGIN on these improved MWEs is particularly effective. By analyzing word similarities we saw that in BWEs acquired with RIDGE rare English words are often mapped near to noise.

Because MAX-MARGIN uses negative noisy word pairs as training examples this phenomenon is not as strongly present there.

4.2 Model Ensembling

Although BWEs obtained with FASTTEXT and MAX-MARGIN clearly outperform other methods on rare words, a combination of BWEs obtained with different models can further improve performance by integrating several sources of information. We ensemble BWEs obtained using different MWEs as follows: we generate n-best lists ($n = 100$) of translation candidates using each model. For each pair (s, t) of candidate translations, we compute an ensemble weight given by a weighted sum of similarity scores $Sim_i(s, t)$ ob-

---

[8]We added these examples to the camera-ready paper after the results were finalized.

tained on each BWE:

$$\sum_{i=1}^{M} \gamma_i Sim_i(s,t) \qquad (4)$$

$Sim_i(s,t)$ is computed using cosine similarity. When a candidate pair (s,t) is not in the n-best list generated by a model i then $Sim_i(s,t)$ is set to 0. The weights γ_i for each test set are tuned on validation sets separately (presented in §2) using grid search. The results (Table 4) show that ensembling yields significant gains over subword models alone for all data sets. We again looked for examples after evaluation (Table 5) where ensembling helped compared with the previous best setup (examples 6–9) and saw that the method again improves upon hard cases where the incorrect predictions are very close, in terms of meaning, to the gold annotation. Row 10 shows a counterexample. We note that this idea could be used in a supervised neural network for BLI as well, where information from multiple models could be integrated by concatenating embeddings from them for a given word.

4.3 Adding Orthographic Distance

While subword information captures orthographic properties of words to a certain extent, it cannot precisely represent the orthographic distance of each word pairs in a predefined number of dimensions, especially not that of source and target word pairs when performining post-hoc mapping (MWEs are trained separately thus there is no such cross-lingual information). Thus, it is beneficial to strengthen BWEs by integrating a similarity measure between word strings directly. The BWEs ensemble in Equation 4 can easily be augmented with a weighted term $\gamma_{M+1} OSim(s,t)$ that measures the orthographic similarity (which we define as one minus the normalized Levenshtein distance) between the surface-forms of words s and t. We generate n-best lists of candidate translations using different BWE models as in §4.2. In addition, we generate a list containing the n closest target words according to $OSim(s,t)$ and ensemble all lists together. Results are shown in Table 4. To measure the impact of orthographic information alone, we also report results obtained when using this information only (all other ensemble weights set to 0). For **low frequency** wordpairs, orthographic information leads to massive performance gains. We analyzed the gold standard word pairs in our datasets from the perspective of orthographic similarity. For CRAWLRARE and MEDRARE the ratios of similar words are high which explains the large improvements obtained by adding this measure. Even though the ratio is not high for NEWSRARE and the two frequent datasets, orthographic information still improves performance which shows the advantage of using the technique in all cases. Table 5 shows nontrivial examples (11–13) where orthographic distance improves performance. Example 11 shows the advantage of combining the vector representation with orthographic distance, i.e., our model could find translations of *sleddogs* that have similar meaning, while in examples 12 and 13 orthographic distance helped to pick the correct translation which is the closest in terms of edit distance. On the other hand, in example 14 orthographic distance caused an error because the incorrect prediction is too close to the source word in orthographic distance.

5 Conclusion

We evaluated BWEs on the novel task of rare term mining in different domains. Our experiments show that previous approaches to bilingual lexicon induction fail when mining rare words. We have studied techniques for decreasing the impact of these problems. By ensembling different BWEs and combining those with orthographic cues, we have reached state-of-the-art results. By making our code and datasets publicly available, we hope to encourage other researchers to further enhance BWEs to perform well on this important task. In the future, we would like to work on BLI of multiword translations and compound words.

Acknowledgments

We would like to thank Helmut Schmid and the anonymous reviewers for their valuable input. This project has received funding from the European Unions Horizon 2020 research and innovation programme under grant agreement № 644402 (HimL). This project has received funding from the European Research Council (ERC) under the European Union's Horizon 2020 research and innovation programme (grant agreement № 640550).

References

Piotr Bojanowski, Edouard Grave, Armand Joulin, and Tomas Mikolov. 2017. Enriching word vectors with subword information. *TACL* .

Ondřej Bojar, Rajen Chatterjee, Christian Federmann, Yvette Graham, Barry Haddow, Matthias Huck, Antonio Jimeno Yepes, Philipp Koehn, Varvara Logacheva, Christof Monz, Matteo Negri, Aurelie Neveol, Mariana Neves, Martin Popel, Matt Post, Raphael Rubino, Carolina Scarton, Lucia Specia, Marco Turchi, Karin Verspoor, and Marcos Zampieri. 2016. Findings of the 2016 conference on machine translation. In *Proceedings of the First Conference on Machine Translation*. Association for Computational Linguistics, Berlin, Germany, pages 131–198.

Long Duong, Hiroshi Kanayama, Tengfei Ma, Steven Bird, and Trevor Cohn. 2016. Learning crosslingual word embeddings without bilingual corpora. In *Proc. EMNLP*.

Manaal Faruqui and Chris Dyer. 2014. Improving vector space word representations using multilingual correlation. In *Proc. EACL*.

Stephan Gouws and Anders Søgaard. 2015. Simple task-specific bilingual word embeddings. In *Proc. NAACL*.

Geert Heyman, Ivan Vulić, and Marie-Francine Moens. 2017. Bilingual lexicon induction by learning to combine word-level and character-level representations. In *Proc. EACL*.

Angeliki Lazaridou, Georgiana Dinu, and Marco Baroni. 2015. Hubness and pollution: Delving into cross-space mapping for zero-shot learning. In *Proc. ACL*.

Tomas Mikolov, Kai Chen, Greg Corrado, and Jeffrey Dean. 2013a. Efficient estimation of word representations in vector space. In *ICLR*.

Tomas Mikolov, Quoc V Le, and Ilya Sutskever. 2013b. Exploiting similarities among languages for machine translation. *CoRR* abs/1309.4168.

Tomas Mikolov, Ilya Sutskever, Kai Chen, Greg S Corrado, and Jeff Dean. 2013c. Distributed representations of words and phrases and their compositionality. In C. J. C. Burges, L. Bottou, M. Welling, Z. Ghahramani, and K. Q. Weinberger, editors, *Advances in Neural Information Processing Systems 26*. Curran Associates, Inc., pages 3111–3119.

Ivan Vulić and Anna Korhonen. 2016. On the role of seed lexicons in learning bilingual word embeddings. In *Proc. ACL*.

Chao Xing, Dong Wang, Chao Liu, and Yiye Lin. 2015. Normalized word embedding and orthogonal transform for bilingual word translation. In *Proc. NAACL*.

Frustratingly Easy Meta-Embedding – Computing Meta-Embeddings by Averaging Source Word Embeddings

Joshua N Coates
Department of Computer Science
University of Liverpool
`j.n.coates@liverpool.ac.uk`

Danushka Bollegala
Department of Computer Science
University of Liverpool
`danushka@liverpool.ac.uk`

Abstract

Creating accurate meta-embeddings from pre-trained source embeddings has received attention lately. Methods based on global and locally-linear transformation and concatenation have shown to produce accurate meta-embeddings. In this paper, we show that the arithmetic mean of two distinct word embedding sets yields a performant meta-embedding that is comparable or better than more complex meta-embedding learning methods. The result seems counter-intuitive given that vector spaces in different source embeddings are not comparable and cannot be simply averaged. We give insight into why averaging can still produce accurate meta-embedding despite the incomparability of the source vector spaces.

1 Introduction

Distributed vector representations of words, henceforth referred to as word embeddings, have been shown to exhibit strong performance on a variety of NLP tasks (Turian et al., 2010; Zou et al., 2013). Methods for producing word embedding sets exploit the distributional hypothesis to infer semantic similarity between words within large bodies of text, in the process they have been found to additionally capture more complex linguistic regularities, such as analogical relationships (Mikolov et al., 2013c). A variety of methods now exist for the production of word embeddings (Collobert and Weston, 2008; Mnih and Hinton, 2009; Huang et al., 2012; Pennington et al., 2014; Mikolov et al., 2013a). Comparative work has illustrated a variation in performance between methods across evaluative tasks (Chen et al., 2013; Yin and Schütze, 2016).

Methods of "meta-embedding", as first proposed by Yin and Schütze (2016), aim to conduct a complementary combination of information from an ensemble of distinct word embedding sets, each trained using different methods, and resources, to yield an embedding set with improved overall quality.

Several such methods have been proposed. 1TON (Yin and Schütze, 2016), takes an ensemble of K pre-trained word embedding sets, and employs a linear neural network to learn a set of meta-embeddings along with K global projection matrices, such that through projection, for every word in the meta-embedding set, we can recover its corresponding vector within each source word embedding set. 1TON+ (Yin and Schütze, 2016), extends this method by predicting embeddings for words not present within the intersection of the source word embedding sets. An unsupervised locally linear meta-embedding approach has since been taken (Bollegala et al., 2017), for each source embedding set, for each word; a representation as a linear combination of its nearest neighbours is learnt. The local reconstructions within each source embedding set are then projected to a common meta-embedding space.

The simplest approach considered to date, has been to concatenate the word embeddings across the source sets (Yin and Schütze, 2016). Despite its simplicity, concatenation has been used to provide a good baseline of performance for meta-embedding.

A method which has not yet been proposed is to conduct a direct averaging of embeddings. The validity of this approach may perhaps not seem obvious, owing to the fact that no correspondence exists between the dimensions of separately trained word embedding sets. In this paper we first provide some analysis and justification that, despite this dimensional disparity, averaging can provide an approximation of the performance of concatenation without increasing the dimension of the embeddings. We give empirical results demonstrating the quality of average meta-embeddings. We

194

Proceedings of NAACL-HLT 2018, pages 194–198
New Orleans, Louisiana, June 1 - 6, 2018. ©2018 Association for Computational Linguistics

make a point of comparison to concatenation since it is the most comparable in terms of simplicity, whilst also providing a good baseline of performance on evaluative tasks. Our aim is to highlight the validity of averaging across distinct word embedding sets, such that it may be considered as a tool in future meta-embedding endeavours.

2 Analysis

To evaluate semantic similarity between word embeddings we consider the Euclidean distance measure. For ℓ_2 normalised word embeddings, Euclidean distance is a monotonically decreasing function of the cosine similarity, which is a popular choice in NLP tasks that use word embeddings such as semantic similarity prediction and analogy detection (Levy et al., 2015; Levy and Goldberg, 2014). We defer the analysis of other types of distance measures to future work. By evaluating the relationship between the Euclidean distances of pairs of words in the source embedding sets and their corresponding Euclidean distances in the meta-embedding space we can obtain a view as to how the meta-embedding procedure is combining semantic information. We begin by examining concatenation through this lens, before moving on to averaging.

2.1 Concatenation

We can express concatenation by first zero-padding our source embeddings, before combining them through addition.

Without loss of generality, we consider both concatenation and averaging over only two source word embedding sets for ease of exposition. Let $\mathcal{S}_1$ and $\mathcal{S}_2$ be unique embedding sets of real-valued continuous embeddings. We make no assumption that $\mathcal{S}_1$ and $\mathcal{S}_2$ were trained using the same method or resources. Consider two semantically similar words u and v such that $u, v \in \mathcal{S}_1 \cap \mathcal{S}_2$. Let $u_{\mathcal{S}_1}$ and $v_{\mathcal{S}_1}$, and $u_{\mathcal{S}_2}$ and $v_{\mathcal{S}_2}$ denote the specific word embeddings of u and v within the embeddings $\mathcal{S}_1$, and $\mathcal{S}_2$ respectively.

Let the dimensions of embeddings $\mathcal{S}_1$, and $\mathcal{S}_2$ be denoted $d_{\mathcal{S}_1}$, and $d_{\mathcal{S}_2}$ respectively. We zero-pad embeddings from $\mathcal{S}_1$ by front-loading $d_{\mathcal{S}_2}$ zero entries to each word embedding vector. In contrast, we zero-pad embeddings from $\mathcal{S}_2$ by adding $d_{\mathcal{S}_1}$ zero entries to the end of each embedding vector. The resulting embeddings from $\mathcal{S}_1$ and $\mathcal{S}_2$ now share a common dimension of $d_{\mathcal{S}_1} + d_{\mathcal{S}_2}$. Denote

the resulting embeddings of any word $u \in \mathcal{S}_1 \cap \mathcal{S}_2$, as $u_{\mathcal{S}_1}^{zero}$ and $u_{\mathcal{S}_2}^{zero}$ respectively. Now, combining our source embeddings through addition we obtain equivalency to concatenation.

$$u_{\mathcal{S}_1}^{zero} + u_{\mathcal{S}_2}^{zero} = \begin{bmatrix} u_{\mathcal{S}_2(1)} \\ u_{\mathcal{S}_2(2)} \\ \vdots \\ u_{\mathcal{S}_2(d_{\mathcal{S}_2})} \\ u_{\mathcal{S}_1(1)} \\ u_{\mathcal{S}_1(2)} \\ \vdots \\ u_{\mathcal{S}_1(d_{\mathcal{S}_1})} \end{bmatrix} = \begin{bmatrix} u_{\mathcal{S}_2} \\ u_{\mathcal{S}_1} \end{bmatrix} \quad (1)$$

Note that the zero-padded vectors are orthogonal.

Let the Euclidean distance between these words in each embedding be denoted by $E_{\mathcal{S}_1}$ and $E_{\mathcal{S}_2}$. Note that for any vector $u \in \mathbb{R}^n$ the addition of zero-valued dimensions does not affect the value of its ℓ_2-norm. So we have

$$E_{\mathcal{S}_1} = ||u_{\mathcal{S}_1} - v_{\mathcal{S}_1}||_2 = ||u_{\mathcal{S}_1}^{zero} - v_{\mathcal{S}_1}^{zero}||_2 \quad (2)$$

$$E_{\mathcal{S}_2} = ||u_{\mathcal{S}_2} - v_{\mathcal{S}_2}||_2 = ||u_{\mathcal{S}_2}^{zero} - v_{\mathcal{S}_2}^{zero}||_2 \quad (3)$$

Consider the Euclidean distance between u and v after concatenation.

$$\begin{aligned} E_{CONC} \\ = \left|\left|\begin{bmatrix} u_{\mathcal{S}_2} \\ u_{\mathcal{S}_1} \end{bmatrix} - \begin{bmatrix} v_{\mathcal{S}_2} \\ v_{\mathcal{S}_1} \end{bmatrix}\right|\right|_2 \\ = ||(u_{\mathcal{S}_1}^{zero} + u_{\mathcal{S}_2}^{zero}) - (v_{\mathcal{S}_1}^{zero} + v_{\mathcal{S}_2}^{zero})||_2 \\ = ||(u_{\mathcal{S}_1}^{zero} - v_{\mathcal{S}_1}^{zero}) - (v_{\mathcal{S}_2}^{zero} - u_{\mathcal{S}_2}^{zero})||_2 \\ = \sqrt{(E_{\mathcal{S}_1})^2 + (E_{\mathcal{S}_2})^2 - 2 E_{\mathcal{S}_1} E_{\mathcal{S}_2} cos(\theta)} \\ = \sqrt{(E_{\mathcal{S}_1})^2 + (E_{\mathcal{S}_2})^2 - 2 E_{\mathcal{S}_1} E_{\mathcal{S}_2} (0)} \\ = \sqrt{(E_{\mathcal{S}_1})^2 + (E_{\mathcal{S}_2})^2} \end{aligned}$$

For any two words belonging to the resultant embedding obtained by concatenation, the distance between these words in the resultant space is the root of the sum of squares of Euclidean distances between these words in $\mathcal{S}_1$ and $\mathcal{S}_2$.

2.2 Average word embeddings

Here we now make the assumption that $\mathcal{S}_1$ and $\mathcal{S}_2$ have common dimension d.[1]

---

[1]Without loss of generality, source embeddings with different dimensionality can be appropriately padded to have the same dimensionality.

Despite there being no obvious correspondence between dimensions of $\mathcal{S}_1$ and $\mathcal{S}_2$ we can show that the average embedding set retains semantic information through preservation of the relative distances between words.

Consider the positioning of words u, and v after performing a word-wise average between the source embedding sets. The Euclidean distance between u and v in the resultant meta-embedding is given by

$$
\begin{aligned}
E_{AVG} &= \left\| \frac{(u_{\mathcal{S}_1} + u_{\mathcal{S}_2})}{2} - \frac{(v_{\mathcal{S}_1} + v_{\mathcal{S}_2})}{2} \right\|_2 \\
&= \frac{1}{2} \|(u_{\mathcal{S}_1} - v_{\mathcal{S}_1}) - (v_{\mathcal{S}_2} - u_{\mathcal{S}_2})\|_2 \\
&\propto \sqrt{(E_{\mathcal{S}_1})^2 + (E_{\mathcal{S}_2})^2 - 2E_{\mathcal{S}_1} E_{\mathcal{S}_2} \cos(\theta)}
\end{aligned}
$$

Now in this case, unlike concatenation, we have not designed our source embedding sets such that they are orthogonal to each other, and so it seems we are left with a term dependant on the angle between $(u_{\mathcal{S}_1} - v_{\mathcal{S}_1})$ and $(v_{\mathcal{S}_2} - u_{\mathcal{S}_2})$. However, Cai et al. (2013) showed that, if $\mathcal{X}$ is a set of random points $\in \mathbb{R}^n$ with cardinality $|\mathcal{X}|$, then the limiting distribution of angles, as $|\mathcal{X}| \to \infty$, between pairs of elements from $\mathcal{X}$, is Gaussian with mean $\pi/2$. In addition, Cai et al. (2013) showed that the variance of this distribution shrinks as the dimensionality increases.

Word embedding sets typically contain in the order of ten thousand or more points, and are typically of relatively high dimension. Moreover, assuming the difference vector between any two words in an embedding set is sufficiently random, we may approximate the limiting Gaussian distribution described by Cai et al. (2013). In such a case the expectation would then be that the vectors $(u_{\mathcal{S}_1} - v_{\mathcal{S}_1})$ and $(v_{\mathcal{S}_2} - u_{\mathcal{S}_2})$ are orthogonal, leading to the following result.

$$
\mathbb{E}[E_{AVG}] = \frac{1}{2}\sqrt{(E_{\mathcal{S}_1})^2 + (E_{\mathcal{S}_2})^2} \propto E_{CONC} \tag{4}
$$

To summarise, if word embeddings can be shown to be approximately orthogonal, then averaging will approximate the same information as concatenation, without increasing the dimensionality of the embeddings.

3   Experiments

We first empirically test our theory that word embeddings are sufficiently random and high dimensional, such that they are approximately all orthogonal to each other. We then present an empirical evaluation of the performance of the meta-embeddings produced through averaging, and compare against concatenation.

3.1   Datasets

We use the following pre-trained embedding sets that have been used in prior work on meta-embedding learning (Yin and Schütze, 2016; Bollegala et al., 2017) for experimentation.

- **GloVe** (Pennington et al., 2014). 1,917,494 word embeddings of dimension 300.

- **CBOW** (Mikolov et al., 2013b). Phrase embeddings discarded, leaving 929,922 word embeddings of dimension 300.

- **HLBL** (Turian et al., 2010). 246,122 hierarchical log-bilinear (Mnih and Hinton, 2009) word embeddings of dimension 100.

Note that the purpose of this experiment is not to compare against previously proposed meta-embedding learning methods, but to empirically verify averaging as a meta-embedding method and validate the assumptions behind the theoretical analysis. By using three pre-trained word embeddings with different dimensionalities and empirical accuracies, we can evaluate the averaging-based meta-embeddings in a robust manner.

We pad HLBL embeddings to the rear with 200 zero-entries to bring their dimension up to 300. For GloVe, we ℓ_2 normalise each dimension of the embedding across the vocabulary, as recommended by the authors. Every individual word embedding from each embedding set is then ℓ_2-normalised. The proposed averaging operation, as well as concatenation, operate only on the intersection of these embeddings. The intersectional vocabularies GloVe $\cap$ CBOW, GloVe $\cap$ HLBL, and CBOW $\cap$ HLBL contain 154,076; 90,254; and 140,479 word embeddings respectively.

3.2   Empirical distribution analysis

We conduct an empirical analysis of the distribution of the angle $\sphericalangle[(u_{\mathcal{S}_1} - v_{\mathcal{S}_1}), (v_{\mathcal{S}_2} - u_{\mathcal{S}_2})]$ for each pair of datasets. Table 1 shows the mean and variance of these distributions, obtained

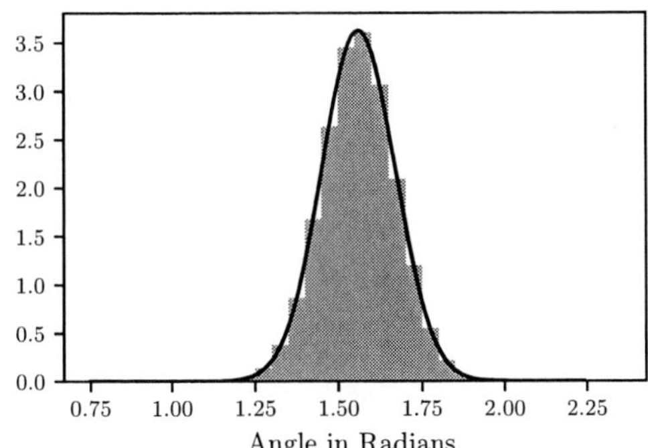

Figure 1: Distribution of angles between embeddings within GloVe ∩ CBOW.

from samples of 200,000 random pairs of words from each intersectional vocabulary. We find that the angles are approximately normally distributed around $\pi/2$.

Embeddings	μ	σ^2
GloVe & CBOW	1.5609	0.0121
GloVe & HLBL	1.5709	0.0129
CBOW & HLBL	1.5740	0.0126

Table 1: Observed distribution parameters.

Figure 1 shows a normalised histogram of the results for GloVe ∩ CBOW, along with a normal distribution characterised by the sample mean and variance. GloVe ∩ HLBL, and CBOW ∩ HLBL plots are not shown due to space limitations, but are similarly normally distributed. This result shows that the pre-trained word embeddings approximately satisfy the predictions made by Cai et al. (2013), thereby empirically justifying the assumption made in the derivation of (4).

3.3 Evaluation Tasks

3.3.1 Semantic Similarity

We measure the similarity between words by calculating the cosine similarity between their embeddings; we then calculate Spearman correlation against human similarity scores. The following datasets are used: **RG** (Rubenstein and Goodenough, 1965), **MC** (Miller and Charles, 1991), **WS** (Finkelstein et al., 2001), **RW** (Luong et al., 2013), and **SL** (Hill et al., 2015).

3.3.2 Word Analogy

Using the Google dataset **GL** (Mikolov et al., 2013b) (19544 analogy questions), we solve questions of the form *a is to b as c is to what?*, using

Embeddings	RG	MC	WS	RW	SL	GL
sources						
HLBL 100	35.3	49.3	35.7	19.1	22.1	15.0
CBOW 300	76.0	82.2	69.8	53.4	44.2	67.1
GloVe 300	82.9	87.0	75.4	48.7	45.3	68.7
AVG						
CBOW+HLBL 300	69.2	81.0	60.1	48.7	37.3	49.4
GloVe+CBOW 300	82.2	87.0	74.5	52.9	**46.5**	73.8
GloVe+HLBL 300	73.7	74.1	64.2	44.6	38.8	49.5
CONC						
CBOW+HLBL 400	68.7	80.2	62.9	49.1	39.6	53.2
GloVe+CBOW 600	**83.0**	**88.8**	**76.4**	**54.8**	46.3	**75.5**
GloVe+HLBL 400	73.7	80.1	65.5	46.4	40.0	53.8

Table 2: Results on word similarity, and analogical tasks. Best performances bolded per task. Dimensionality of the meta embedding is shown next to the source embedding names.

the CosAdd method (Mikolov et al., 2013c) shown in (5). Specifically, we determine a fourth word d such that the similarity between $(b - a + c)$ and d is maximised.

$$\mathrm{CosAdd}(a : b, c : d) = \cos(b - a + c, d) \quad (5)$$

3.4 Discussion of results

Table 2 shows task performance for each source embedding set, and for both methods on every pair of datasets. In our experiments concatenation obtains better overall performance. However, averaging offers improvements over the source embedding sets for semantic similarity task **SL** and word analogy task **GL**, on the combination of CBOW and GloVe. HLBL has a negative effect on CBOW and GloVe, but the performance of averaging is close to that of concatenation. An advantage of averaging when compared against concatenation, is that the dimensionality of the produced meta-embedding is not increased beyond the maximum dimension present within the source embeddings, resulting in a meta-embedding which is easier to process and store.

4 Conclusion

We have presented an argument for averaging as a valid meta-embedding technique, and found experimental performance to be close to, or in some cases better than that of concatenation, with the additional benefit of reduced dimensionality. We propose that when conducting meta-embedding, both concatenation and averaging should be considered as methods of combining embedding spaces, and their individual advantages considered.

References

Danushka Bollegala, Kohei Hayashi, and Ken-ichi Kawarabayashi. 2017. Think globally, embed locally—locally linear meta-embedding of words. *arXiv preprint arXiv:1709.06671* .

Tony Cai, Jianqing Fan, and Tiefeng Jiang. 2013. Distributions of angles in random packing on spheres. *The Journal of Machine Learning Research* 14(1):1837–1864.

Yanqing Chen, Bryan Perozzi, Rami Al-Rfou, and Steven Skiena. 2013. The expressive power of word embeddings. *arXiv preprint arXiv:1301.3226* .

Ronan Collobert and Jason Weston. 2008. A unified architecture for natural language processing: Deep neural networks with multitask learning. In *Proceedings of the 25th international conference on Machine learning*. ACM, pages 160–167.

Lev Finkelstein, Evgeniy Gabrilovich, Yossi Matias, Ehud Rivlin, Zach Solan, Gadi Wolfman, and Eytan Ruppin. 2001. Placing search in context: The concept revisited. In *Proceedings of the 10th international conference on World Wide Web*. ACM, pages 406–414.

Felix Hill, Roi Reichart, and Anna Korhonen. 2015. Simlex-999: Evaluating semantic models with (genuine) similarity estimation. *Computational Linguistics* 41(4):665–695.

Eric H Huang, Richard Socher, Christopher D Manning, and Andrew Y Ng. 2012. Improving word representations via global context and multiple word prototypes. In *Proceedings of the 50th Annual Meeting of the Association for Computational Linguistics: Long Papers-Volume 1*. Association for Computational Linguistics, pages 873–882.

Omer Levy and Yoav Goldberg. 2014. Linguistic regularities in sparse and explicit word representations. In *CoNLL*.

Omer Levy, Yoav Goldberg, and Ido Dagan. 2015. Improving distributional similarity with lessons learned from word embeddings. *Transactions of Association for Computational Linguistics* 3:211–225.

Thang Luong, Richard Socher, and Christopher D Manning. 2013. Better word representations with recursive neural networks for morphology. In *CoNLL*. pages 104–113.

Tomas Mikolov, Kai Chen, Greg Corrado, and Jeffrey Dean. 2013a. Efficient estimation of word representations in vector space. *arXiv preprint arXiv:1301.3781* .

Tomas Mikolov, Ilya Sutskever, Kai Chen, Greg S Corrado, and Jeff Dean. 2013b. Distributed representations of words and phrases and their compositionality. In *Advances in neural information processing systems*. pages 3111–3119.

Tomas Mikolov, Wen-tau Yih, and Geoffrey Zweig. 2013c. Linguistic regularities in continuous space word representations. In *Hlt-naacl*. volume 13, pages 746–751.

George A Miller and Walter G Charles. 1991. Contextual correlates of semantic similarity. *Language and cognitive processes* 6(1):1–28.

Andriy Mnih and Geoffrey E Hinton. 2009. A scalable hierarchical distributed language model. In *Advances in neural information processing systems*. pages 1081–1088.

Jeffrey Pennington, Richard Socher, and Christopher D Manning. 2014. Glove: Global vectors for word representation. In *EMNLP*. volume 14, pages 1532–1543.

Herbert Rubenstein and John B Goodenough. 1965. Contextual correlates of synonymy. *Communications of the ACM* 8(10):627–633.

Joseph Turian, Lev Ratinov, and Yoshua Bengio. 2010. Word representations: a simple and general method for semi-supervised learning. In *Proceedings of the 48th annual meeting of the association for computational linguistics*. Association for Computational Linguistics, pages 384–394.

Wenpeng Yin and Hinrich Schütze. 2016. Learning word meta-embeddings. In *Proceedings of the 54th Annual Meeting of the Association for Computational Linguistics (Volume 1: Long Papers)*. Association for Computational Linguistics, Berlin, Germany, pages 1351–1360.

Will Y Zou, Richard Socher, Daniel M Cer, and Christopher D Manning. 2013. Bilingual word embeddings for phrase-based machine translation. In *EMNLP*. pages 1393–1398.

Introducing two Vietnamese Datasets for Evaluating Semantic Models of (Dis-)Similarity and Relatedness

Kim Anh Nguyen and **Sabine Schulte im Walde** and **Ngoc Thang Vu**
Institut für Maschinelle Sprachverarbeitung
Universität Stuttgart
Pfaffenwaldring 5B, 70569 Stuttgart, Germany
{nguyenkh, schulte, thangvu}@ims.uni-stuttgart.de

Abstract

We present two novel datasets for the low-resource language Vietnamese to assess models of semantic similarity: *ViCon* comprises pairs of synonyms and antonyms across word classes, thus offering data to distinguish between similarity and dissimilarity. *ViSim-400* provides degrees of similarity across five semantic relations, as rated by human judges. The two datasets are verified through standard co-occurrence and neural network models, showing results comparable to the respective English datasets.

1 Introduction

Computational models that distinguish between semantic similarity and semantic relatedness (Budanitsky and Hirst, 2006) are important for many NLP applications, such as the automatic generation of dictionaries, thesauri, and ontologies (Biemann, 2005; Cimiano et al., 2005; Li et al., 2006), and machine translation (He et al., 2008; Marton et al., 2009). In order to evaluate these models, gold standard resources with word pairs have to be collected (typically across semantic relations such as synonymy, hypernymy, antonymy, co-hyponymy, meronomy, etc.) and annotated for their degree of similarity via human judgements.

The most prominent examples of gold standard similarity resources for English are the Rubenstein & Goodenough (RG) dataset (Rubenstein and Goodenough, 1965), the TOEFL test questions (Landauer and Dumais, 1997), WordSim-353 (Finkelstein et al., 2001), MEN (Bruni et al., 2012), SimLex-999 (Hill et al., 2015), and the lexical contrast datasets by (Nguyen et al., 2016a, 2017). For other languages, resource examples are the translation of the RG dataset to German (Gurevych, 2005), the German dataset of paradigmatic relations (Scheible and Schulte im Walde,

2014), and the translation of WordSim-353 and SimLex-999 to German, Italian and Russian (Leviant and Reichart, 2015). However, for low-resource languages there is still a lack of such datasets, which we aim to fill for Vietnamese, a language without morphological marking such as case, gender, number, and tense, thus differing strongly from Western European languages.

We introduce two novel datasets for Vietnamese: a dataset of lexical contrast pairs **ViCon** to distinguish between similarity (synonymy) and dissimilarity (antonymy), and a dataset of semantic relation pairs **ViSim-400** to reflect the continuum between similarity and relatedness. The two datasets are publicly available.[1] Moreover, we verify our novel datasets through standard and neural co-occurrence models, in order to show that we obtain a similar behaviour as for the corresponding English datasets *SimLex-999* (Hill et al., 2015), and the lexical contrast dataset (henceforth *LexCon*), cf. Nguyen et al. (2016a).

2 Related Work

Over the years a number of datasets have been collected for studying and evaluating semantic similarity and semantic relatedness. For English, Rubenstein and Goodenough (1965) presented a small dataset (RG) of 65 noun pairs. For each pair, the degree of similarity in meaning was provided by 15 raters. The RG dataset is assumed to reflect similarity rather than relatedness. Finkelstein et al. (2001) created a set of 353 English noun-noun pairs (WordSim-353)[2], where each pair was rated by 16 subjects according to the degree of semantic relatedness on a scale from 0 to 10. Bruni et al. (2012) introduced a large test collec-

---

[1] www.ims.uni-stuttgart.de/data/vnese_sem_datasets
[2] www.cs.technion.ac.il/~gabr/resources/data/wordsim353

Proceedings of NAACL-HLT 2018, pages 199–205
New Orleans, Louisiana, June 1 - 6, 2018. ©2018 Association for Computational Linguistics

tion called MEN[3]. Similar to WordSim-353, the authors refer to both similarity and relatedness when describing the MEN dataset, although the annotators were asked to rate the pairs according to relatedness. Unlikely the construction of the RG and WordSim-353 datasets, each pair in the MEN dataset was only evaluated by one rater who ranked it for relatedness relative to 50 other pairs in the dataset. Recently, Hill et al. (2015) presented SimLex-999, a gold standard resource for the evaluation of semantic representations containing similarity ratings of word pairs across different part-of-speech categories and concreteness levels. The construction of SimLex-999 was motivated by two factors, (i) to consistently quantify similarity, as distinct from association, and apply it to various concept types, based on minimal intuitive instructions, and (ii) to have room for the improvement of state-of-the-art models which had reached or surpassed the human agreement ceiling on WordSim-353 and MEN, the most popular existing gold standards, as well as on RG. Scheible and Schulte im Walde (2014) presented a collection of semantically related word pairs for German and English,[4] which was compiled via Amazon Mechanical Turk (AMT)[5] human judgement experiments and comprises (i) a selection of targets across word classes balanced for semantic category, polysemy, and corpus frequency, (ii) a set of human-generated semantically related word pairs (synonyms, antonyms, hypernyms) based on the target units, and (iii) a subset of the generated word pairs rated for their relation strength, including positive and negative relation evidence.

For other languages, only a few gold standard sets with scored word pairs exist. Among others, Gurevych (2005) replicated Rubenstein and Goodenough's experiments after translating the original 65 word pairs into German. In later work, Gurevych (2006) used the same experimental setup to increase the number of word pairs to 350. Leviant and Reichart (2015) translated two prominent evaluation sets, WordSim-353 (association) and SimLex-999 (similarity) from English to Italian, German and Russian, and collected the scores for each dataset from the respective native speakers via crowdflower[6].

---

[3]clic.cimec.unitn.it/~elia.bruni/MEN
[4]www.ims.uni-stuttgart.de/data/sem-rel-database/
[5]www.mturk.com
[6]www.crowdflower.com/

3 Dataset Design

3.1 Criteria

Semantic similarity is a narrower concept than *semantic relatedness* and holds between lexical terms with similar meanings. Strong similarity is typically observed for the lexical relations of synonymy and co-hyponymy. For example, in Vietnamese "đội" (*team*) and "nhóm" (*group*) represents a synonym pair; "ô_tô" (*car*) and "xe_đạp" (*bike*) is a co-hyponymy pair. More specifically, words in the pair "ô_tô" (*car*) and "xe_đạp" (*bike*) share several features such as physical (e.g. bánh_xe / *wheels*) and functional (e.g. vận_tải / *transport*), so that the two Vietnamese words are interchangeable regarding the kinds of transportation. The concept of semantic relatedness is broader and holds for relations such as meronymy, antonymy, functional association, and other "non-classical relations" (Morris and Hirst, 2004). For example, "ô_tô" (*car*) and "xăng_dầu" (*petrol*) represent a meronym pair. In contrast to similarity, this meronym pair expresses a clearly functional relationship; the words are strongly associated with each other but not similar.

Empirical studies have shown that the predictions of distributional models as well as humans are strongly related to the part-of-speech (POS) category of the learned concepts. Among others, Gentner (2006) showed that verb concepts are harder to learn by children than noun concepts.

Distinguishing antonymy from synonymy is one of the most difficult challenges. While antonymy represents words which are strongly associated but highly dissimilar to each other, synonymy refers to words that are highly similar in meaning. However, antonyms and synonyms often occur in similar context, as they are interchangeable in their substitution.

3.2 Resource for Concept Choice: Vietnamese Computational Lexicon

The Vietnamese Computational Lexicon (VCL)[7] (Nguyen et al., 2006) is a common linguistic database which is freely and easily exploitable for automatic processing of the Vietnamese language. VCL contains 35,000 words corresponding to 41,700 concepts, accompanied by morphological, syntactic and semantic information. The morphological information consists of 8 morphemes

---

[7]https://vlsp.hpda.vn/demo/?page=vcl

including simple word, compound word, reduplicative word, multi-word expression, loan word, abbreviation, bound morpheme, and symbol. For example, "bàn" (*table*) is a simple word with definition "đồ thường làm bằng gỗ, có mặt phẳng và chân đỡ . . . " (*pieces of wood, flat and supported by one or more legs . . .*). The syntactic information describes part-of-speech, collocations, and subcategorisation frames. The semantic information includes two types of constraints: logical and semantic. The logical constraint provides category meaning, synonyms and antonyms. The semantic constraint provides argument information and semantic roles. For example, "yêu" (*love*) is a verb with category meaning *"emotion"* and antonym "ghét" (*hate*).

VCL is the largest linguistic database of its kind for Vietnamese, and it encodes various types of morphological, syntactic and semantic information, so it presents a suitable starting point for the choice of lexical units for our purpose.

3.3 Choice of Concepts

3.3.1 Concepts in ViCon

The choice of related pairs in this dataset was drawn from VCL in the following way. We extracted all antonym and synonym pairs according to the three part-of-speech categories: noun, verb and adjective. We then randomly selected 600 adjective pairs (300 antonymous pairs and 300 synonymous pairs), 400 noun pairs (200 antonymous pairs and 200 synonymous pairs), and 400 verb pairs (200 antonymous pairs and 200 synonymous pairs). In each part-of-speech category, we balanced for the size of morphological classes in VCL, for both antonymous and synonymous pairs.

3.3.2 Concepts in ViSim-400

The choice of related pairs in this dataset was drawn from both the VLC and the *Vietnamese WordNet*[8] (VWN), cf. Nguyen et al. (2016b). We extracted all pairs of the three part-of-speech categories: noun, verb and adjective, according to five semantic relations: synonymy, antonymy, hypernymy, co-hoponymy and meronymy. We then sampled 400 pairs for the ViSim-400 dataset, accounting for 200 noun pairs, 150 verb pairs and 50 adjective pairs. Regarding noun pairs, we balanced the size of pairs in terms of six relations: the five extracted relations from VCL and VWN,

and an "unrelated" relation. For verb pairs, we balanced the number of pairs according to five relations: synonymy, antonymy, hypernymy, co-hyponymy, and unrelated. For adjective pairs, we balanced the size of pairs for three relations: synonymy, antonymy, and unrelated. In order to select the unrelated pairs for each part-of-speech category, we paired the unrelated words from the selected related pairs at random. From these random pairs, we excluded those pairs that appeared in VCL and VWN. Furthermore, we also balanced the number of selected pairs according to the sizes of the morphological classes and the lexical categories.

3.4 Annotation of ViSim-400

For rating ViSim-400, 200 raters who were native Vietnamese speakers were paid to rate the degrees of similarity for all 400 pairs. Each rater was asked to rate 30 pairs on a 0–6 scale; and each pair was rated by 15 raters. Unlike other datasets which performed the annotation via Amazon Mechanical Turk, each rater for ViSim-400 conducted the annotation via a survey which detailed the exact annotation guidelines.

The structure of the questionnaire was motivated by the SimLex-999 dataset: we outlined the notion of similarity via the well-understood idea of the six relations included in the ViSim-400 dataset. Immediately after the guidelines of the questionnaire, a checkpoint question was posed to the participants to test whether the person understood the guidelines: the participant was asked to pick the most similar word pair from three given word pairs, such as kiêu_căng/kiêu_ngao (*arrogant/cocky*) vs. trầm/bổng (*high/low*) vs. cổ_điển/biếng (*classical/lazy*). The annotators then labeled the kind of relation and scored the degree of similarity for each word pair in the survey.

3.5 Agreement in ViSim-400

We analysed the ratings of the ViSim-400 annotators with two different inter-annotator agreement (IAA) measures, Krippendorff's alpha coefficient (Krippendorff, 2004), and the average standard deviation (STD) of all pairs across word classes. The first IAA measure, IAA-pairwise, computes the average pairwise Spearman's ρ correlation between any two raters. This IAA measure has been a common choice in previous data collections in distributional semantics (Padó et al., 2007; Reisinger and Mooney, 2010; Hill et al., 2015).

---

[8]http://viet.wordnet.vn/wnms/

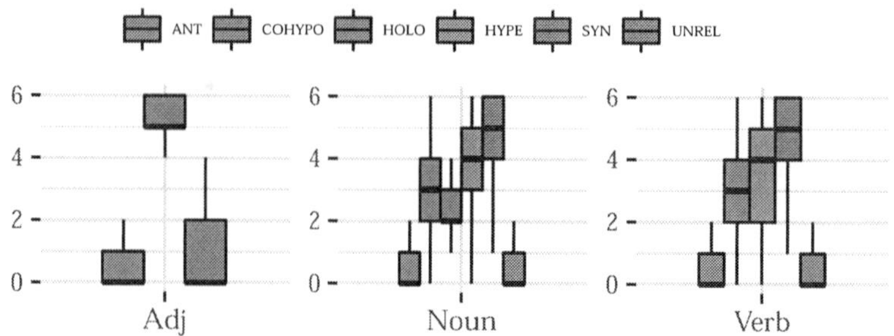

Figure 1: Distribution of scored pairs in ViSim-400 across parts-of-speech and semantic relations.

	All	**Noun**	**Verb**	**Adjective**
IAA-Mean ρ	0.86	0.86	0.86	0.78
IAA-Pairwise ρ	0.79	0.76	0.78	0.75
Krippendorff's α	0.78	0.76	0.78	0.86
STD	0.87	0.87	0.90	0.82

Table 1: Inter-annotator agreements measured by Spearman's ρ, Krippendorff's α, and the average standard deviation (STD) of all pairs across word classes.

The second IAA measure, IAA-mean, compares the average correlation of the human raters with the average of all other raters. This measure would smooth individual annotator effects, and serve as a more appropriate *"upper bound"* for the performance of automatic systems than IAA-pairwise (Vulić et al., 2017). Finally, Krippendorff's α coefficient reflects the disagreement of annotators rather than their agreement, in addition to correcting for agreement by chance.

Table 1 shows the inter-annotator agreement values, Krippendorff's α coefficient, and the response consistency measured by STD over all pairs and different word classes in ViSim-400. The overall IAA-pairwise of ViSim-400 is $\rho = 0.79$, comparing favourably with the agreement on the SimLex-999 dataset ($\rho = 0.67$ using the same IAA-pairwise measure). Regarding IAA-mean, ViSim-400 also achieves an overall agreement of $\rho = 0.86$, which is similar to the agreement in Vulić et al. (2017), $\rho = 0.86$. For Krippendorff's α coefficient, the value achieves $\alpha = 0.78$, also reflecting the reliability of the annotated dataset.

Furthermore, the box plots in Figure 1 present the distributions of all rated pairs in terms of the fine-grained semantic relations across word classes. They reveal that –across word classes– synonym pairs are clearly rated as the most similar words, and antonym as well as unrelated pairs are clearly rated as the most dissimilar words. Hypernymy, co-hyponymy and holonymy are in between, but rather similar than dissimilar.

4 Verification of Datasets

In this section, we verify our novel datasets ViCon and ViSim-400 through standard and neural co-occurrence models, in order to show that we obtain a similar behaviour as for the corresponding English datasets.

4.1 Verification of ViSim-400

We adopt a comparison of neural models on SimLex-999 as suggested by Nguyen et al. (2016a). They applied three models, a Skip-gram model with negative sampling SGNS (Mikolov et al., 2013), the dLCE model (Nguyen et al., 2016a), and the mLCM model (Pham et al., 2015). Both the dLCE and the mLCM models integrated lexical contrast information into the basic Skip-gram model to train word embeddings for distinguishing antonyms from synonyms, and for reflecting degrees of similarity.

The three models were trained with 300 dimensions, a window size of 5 words, and 10 negative samples. Regarding the corpora, we relied on Vietnamese corpora with a total of $\approx$145 million tokens, including the *Vietnamese Wikipedia*,[9] *VNESEcorpus* and *VNTQcorpus*,[10] and the *Leipzig Corpora Collection for Vietnamese*[11] (Goldhahn et al., 2012). For word segmentation and POS tagging, we used the open-source toolkit *UETnlp*[12] (Nguyen and Le, 2016). The antonym and synonym pairs to train the

---

[9] https://dumps.wikimedia.org/viwiki/latest/
[10] http://viet.jnlp.org/download-du-lieu-tu-vung-corpus
[11] http://wortschatz.uni-leipzig.de/en/download
[12] https://github.com/phongnt570/UETnlp

dLCE and mLCM models were extracted from VWN consisting of 49,458 antonymous pairs and 338,714 synonymous pairs. All pairs which appeared in ViSim-400 were excluded from this set.

Table 2 shows Spearman's correlations ρ, comparing the scores of the three models with the human judgements for ViSim-400. As also reported for English, the dLCE model produces the best performance, SGNS the worst.

	SGNS	mLCM	dLCE
ViSim-400	0.37	0.60	**0.62**
SimLex-999	0.38	0.51	**0.59**

Table 2: Spearman's correlation ρ on ViSim-400 in comparison to SimLex-999, cf. Nguyen et al. (2016a).

In a second experiment, we computed the cosine similarities between all word pairs, and used the area under curve (AUC) to distinguish between antonyms and synonyms. Table 3 presents the AUC results of the three models. Again, the models show a similar behaviour in comparison to SimLex-999, where also the dLCE model outperforms the two other models, and the SGNS model is by far the worst.

	Model	Noun	Verb	Adj
	SGNS	0.66	0.63	0.70
ViSim-400	mLCM	0.81	0.92	0.96
	dLCE	**0.92**	**0.95**	**0.98**
	SGNS	0.66	0.65	0.64
SimLex-999	mLCM	0.69	0.71	0.85
	dLCE	**0.72**	**0.81**	**0.90**

Table 3: AUC scores for distinguishing antonyms from synonyms in ViSim-400.

4.2 Verification of ViCon

In order to verify ViCon, we applied three co-occurrence models to rank antonymous and synonymous word pairs according to their cosine similarities: two standard co-occurrence models based on positive point-wise mutual information (PPMI) and positive local mutual information (PLMI) (Evert, 2005) as well as an improved feature value representation **weight**^{SA} as suggested by Nguyen et al. (2016a). For building the vector space co-occurrence models, we relied on the same Vietnamese corpora as in the previous section. For inducing the word vector representations via **weight**^{SA}, we made use of the antonymous and synonymous pairs in VWN, as in the previous section, and then removed all pairs which appeared in ViCon. Optionally, we applied singular value decomposition (SVD) to reduce the dimensionalities of the word vector representations.

As in Nguyen et al. (2016a), we computed the cosine similarities between all word pairs, and then sorted the pairs according to their cosine scores. Average Precision (AP) evaluated the three vector space models. Table 4 presents the results of the three vector space models with and without SVD. As for English, the results on the Vietnamese dataset demonstrate significant improvements (χ^2,* $p < .001$) of **weight**^{SA} over PPMI and PLMI, both with and without SVD, and across word classes.

	Metric	ADJ		NOUN		VERB	
		SYN	ANT	SYN	ANT	SYN	ANT
	PPMI	0.70	0.38	0.68	0.39	0.69	0.38
	PLMI	0.59	0.44	0.61	0.42	0.63	0.41
ViCon	weight^{SA}	**0.93***	**0.31***	**0.94***	**0.31**	**0.96**	**0.31**
	PPMI + SVD	0.76	0.36	0.66	0.40	0.81	0.34
	PLMI + SVD	0.49	0.51	0.55	0.46	0.51	0.49
	weight^{SA} + SVD	**0.91***	**0.32***	**0.81***	**0.34***	**0.92***	**0.32***
	PLMI	0.56	0.46	0.60	0.42	0.62	0.42
LexCon	weight^{SA}	**0.75**	**0.36**	**0.66**	**0.40**	**0.71**	**0.38**
	PLMI + SVD	0.55	0.46	0.55	0.46	0.58	0.44
	weight^{SA} + SVD	**0.76***	**0.36***	**0.66**	**0.40**	**0.70***	**0.38***

Table 4: AP evaluation of co-occurrence models on ViCon in comparison to LexCon (Nguyen et al., 2016a).

5 Conclusion

This paper introduced two novel datasets for the low-resource language Vietnamese to assess models of semantic similarity: *ViCon* comprises synonym and antonym pairs across the word classes of nouns, verbs, and adjectives. It offers data to distinguish between similarity and dissimilarity. *ViSim-400* contains 400 word pairs across the three word classes and five semantic relations. Each pair was rated by human judges for its degree of similarity, to reflect the continuum between similarity and relatedness. The two datasets were verified through standard co-occurrence and neural network models, showing results comparable to the respective English datasets.

Acknowledgments

The research was supported by the Ministry of Education and Training of the Socialist Republic of Vietnam (Scholarship 977/QD-BGDDT; Kim-Anh Nguyen), and the DFG Collaborative Research Centre SFB 732 (Kim-Anh Nguyen, Sabine Schulte im Walde, Ngoc Thang Vu).

References

Chris Biemann. 2005. Ontology learning from text: A survey of methods. *LDV Forum* 20(2):75–93.

Elia Bruni, Gemma Boleda, Marco Baroni, and Nam-Khanh Tran. 2012. Distributional semantics in technicolor. In *Proceedings of the 50th Annual Meeting of the Association for Computational Linguistics*. Jeju Island, Korea, pages 136–145.

Alexander Budanitsky and Graeme Hirst. 2006. Evaluating WordNet-based measures of lexical semantic relatedness. *Computational Linguistics* 32(1):13–47.

Philipp Cimiano, Andreas Hotho, and Steffen Staab. 2005. Learning concept hierarchies from text corpora using formal concept analysis. *Journal of Artificial Intelligence Research* 24(1):305–339.

Stefan Evert. 2005. *The Statistics of Word Cooccurrences*. Ph.D. thesis, University of Stuttgart.

Lev Finkelstein, Evgeniy Gabrilovich, Yossi Matias, Ehud Rivlin, Zach Solan, Gadi Wolfman, and Eytan Ruppin. 2001. Placing search in context: The concept revisited. In *Proceedings of the 10th International Conference on World Wide Web*. Hong Kong, Hong Kong, pages 406–414.

Dedre Gentner. 2006. Why verbs are hard to learn. In Kathryn A. Hirsh-Pasek and Roberta M. Golinkoff, editors, *Action meets word: How Children Learn Verbs*, Oxford University Press, pages 544–564.

Dirk Goldhahn, Thomas Eckart, and Uwe Quasthoff. 2012. Building large monolingual dictionaries at the Leipzig corpora collection: From 100 to 200 languages. In *Proceedings of the 8th International Conference on Language Resources and Evaluation*. pages 759–765.

Iryna Gurevych. 2005. Using the structure of a conceptual network in computing semantic relatedness. In *Proceedings of the 2nd International Joint Conference on Natural Language Processing*. Jeju Island, Republic of Korea, pages 767–778.

Iryna Gurevych. 2006. Thinking beyond the nouns: Computing semantic relatedness across parts of speech. In *Proceedings of Sprachdokumentation & Sprachbeschreibung, 28. Jahrestagung der Deutschen Gesellschaft für Sprachwissenschaft*. Bielefeld, Germany, page 226.

Xiaodong He, Mei Yang, Jianfeng Gao, Patrick Nguyen, and Robert Moore. 2008. Indirect-HMM-based hypothesis alignment for combining outputs from machine translation systems. In *Proceedings of the Conference on Empirical Methods in Natural Language Processing*. Honolulu, Hawaii, pages 98–107.

Felix Hill, Roi Reichart, and Anna Korhonen. 2015. Simlex-999: Evaluating semantic models with genuine similarity estimation. *Computational Linguistic* 41(4):665–695.

Klaus Krippendorff. 2004. *Content Analysis: An Introduction to its Methodology*. Sage Publications.

Thomas K. Landauer and Susan T. Dumais. 1997. A solution to Plato's problem: The latent semantic analysis theory of acquisition, induction and representation of knowledge. *Psychological Review* 104(2):211–240.

Ira Leviant and Roi Reichart. 2015. Judgment language matters: Multilingual vector space models for judgment language aware lexical semantics. *CoRR* abs/1508.00106.

Mu Li, Yang Zhang, Muhua Zhu, and Ming Zhou. 2006. Exploring distributional similarity-based models for query spelling correction. In *Proceedings of the 44th Annual Meeting of the Association for Computational Linguistics*. Sydney, Australia, pages 1025–1032.

Yuval Marton, Chris Callison-Burch, and Philip Resnik. 2009. Improved statistical machine translation using monolingually-derived paraphrases. In *Proceedings of the 2009 Conference on Empirical Methods in Natural Language Processing*. Singapore, pages 381–390.

Tomas Mikolov, Ilya Sutskever, Kai Chen, Greg Corrado, and Jeffrey Dean. 2013. Distributed representations of words and phrases and their compositionality. In *Proceedings of the 26th International Conference on Neural Information Processing Systems*. Lake Tahoe, Nevada, pages 3111–3119.

Jane Morris and Graeme Hirst. 2004. Non-classical lexical semantic relations. In *Proceedings of the HLT-NAACL Workshop on Computational Lexical Semantics*. Boston, Massachusetts, pages 46–51.

Kim Anh Nguyen, Sabine Schulte im Walde, and Ngoc Thang Vu. 2017. Distinguishing antonyms and synonyms in a pattern-based neural network. In *Proceedings of the 15th Conference of the European Chapter of the Association for Computational Linguistics*. Valencia, Spain, pages 76–85.

Kim-Anh Nguyen, Sabine Schulte im Walde, and Thang Vu. 2016a. Integrating distributional lexical contrast into word embeddings for antonym-synonym distinction. In *Proceedings of the 54th Annual Meeting of the Association for Computational Linguistics*. Berlin, Germany, pages 454–459.

Phuong-Thai Nguyen, Van-Lam Pham, Hoang-An Nguyen, Huy-Hien Vu, Ngoc-Anh Tran, and Thi-Thu-Ha Truong. 2016b. A two-phase approach for building a Vietnamese WordNet. In *Proceedings of the 8th Global WordNet Conference*. Bucharest, Romania, pages 259–264.

Thi Minh Huyen Nguyen, Laurent Romary, Mathias Rossignol, and Xuan Luong Vu. 2006. A lexicon for Vietnamese language processing. *Language Resources and Evaluation* 40(3-4):291–309.

Tuan-Phong Nguyen and Anh-Cuong Le. 2016. A hybrid approach to Vietnamese word segmentation. In *Proceedings of the International Conference on Computing Communication Technologies, Research, Innovation, and Vision for the Future*. Hanoi, Vietnam, pages 114–119.

Sebastian Padó, Ulrike Padó, and Katrin Erk. 2007. Flexible, corpus-based modelling of human plausibility judgements. In *Proceedings of the joint Conference on Empirical Methods in Natural Language Processing and Computational Natural Language Learning*. Prague, Czech Republic.

Nghia The Pham, Angeliki Lazaridou, and Marco Baroni. 2015. A multitask objective to inject lexical contrast into distributional semantics. In *Proceedings of the 53rd Annual Meeting of the Association for Computational Linguistics and the 7th International Joint Conference on Natural Language Processing*. Beijing, China, pages 21–26.

Joseph Reisinger and Raymond Mooney. 2010. A mixture model with sharing for lexical semantics. In *Proceedings of the 2010 Conference on Empirical Methods in Natural Language Processing*. Cambridge, Massachusetts, pages 1173–1182.

Herbert Rubenstein and John B. Goodenough. 1965. Contextual correlates of synonymy. *Communications of the ACM* 8(10):627–633.

Silke Scheible and Sabine Schulte im Walde. 2014. A database of paradigmatic semantic relation pairs for German nouns, verbs and adjectives. In *Proceedings of the COLING Workshop Lexical and Grammatical Resources for Language Processing*. Dublin, Ireland, pages 111–119.

Ivan Vulić, Daniela Gerz, Douwe Kiela, Felix Hill, and Anna Korhonen. 2017. Hyperlex: A large-scale evaluation of graded lexical entailment. *Computational Linguistics* 43(4):781–835.

Lexical Substitution for Evaluating
Compositional Distributional Models

Maja Buljan[*]   **Sebastian Padó**[*]   **Jan Šnajder**[†]

[*] Institut für Maschinelle Sprachverarbeitung, University of Stuttgart
{maja.buljan,pado}@ims.uni-stuttgart.de

[†] TakeLab, Faculty of Electrical Engineering and Computing, University of Zagreb
jan.snajder@fer.hr

Abstract

Compositional Distributional Semantic Models (CDSMs) model the meaning of phrases and sentences in vector space. They have been predominantly evaluated on limited, artificial tasks such as semantic sentence similarity on hand-constructed datasets. This paper argues for lexical substitution as a means to evaluate CDSMs. Lexical substitution is a more natural task, enables us to evaluate meaning composition at the level of individual words, and provides a common ground to compare CDSMs with dedicated lexical substitution models. We create a lexical substitution dataset for CDSM evaluation from an English-language corpus with manual "all-words" lexical substitution annotation. Our experiments indicate that the Practical Lexical Function CDSM outperforms simple component-wise CDSMs and performs on par with the context2vec lexical substitution model using the same context.

1   Introduction

Compositional Distributional Semantics Models (CDSMs) compute phrase meaning in semantic space as a function of the meanings of the phrase constituents (Baroni et al., 2014). The most basic CDSMs represent words as vectors and compose phrase vectors by component-wise operations of the constituent vectors (Mitchell and Lapata, 2008). More complex models represent predicates with matrices and tensors (Baroni and Zamparelli, 2010; Grefenstette, 2013; Paperno et al., 2014).

Given the large number of different CDSMs proposed in the literature (Erk, 2012), meaningful evaluation becomes crucial. The dominant evaluation method, adopted by the majority of CDSM studies, is pairwise phrase similarity (Mitchell and Lapata, 2008; Guevara, 2010; Grefenstette et al., 2012; Grefenstette, 2013; Paperno et al., 2014). Only a

handful of studies pursued other evaluation tasks, such as textual entailment (Marelli et al., 2014a,b) or sentiment analysis (Socher et al., 2013).

Arguably, phrase similarity evaluation has three major problems. First, the task is affected by the general limitations of rating scales, such as inconsistencies in annotations, scale region bias, and fixed granularity (Schuman and Presser, 1996). Phrase similarity datasets used for CDSM evaluation demonstrate slight to fair inter-annotator agreement, as well as overlap between groups of items rated as *low* and *high* in similarity (Mitchell and Lapata, 2008).

Secondly, phrase similarity is a task that is rather difficult to put down precisely, especially for long phrases. Generally, phrases can be (dis)similar in any number of ways. Annotators commonly agree that some sentence pairs are semantically highly similar (*private company files annual account* and *private company registers annual account*, Pickering and Frisson 2001), and others are semantically unrelated (*man waves hand* vs. *employee leaves company*). In contrast, their assessments become less confident for cases like *delegate buys land* and *agent sells property* (Kartsaklis et al., 2013), where there is a semantic relation other than synonymy. Similarity is also arguably not a useful measure when sentences are semantically deviant, as it is often the case in the datasets: how similar are *private company files annual account* and *private company smooths annual account*?

The third problem is that the most widely used phrase similarity datasets are constructed in a balanced fashion along psycholinguistic principles. For instance, the adjective-noun-verb-adjective-noun ("ANVAN") dataset (Pickering and Frisson, 2001; Kartsaklis et al., 2013), from which the examples above are drawn, was constructed from a set of particularly ambiguous verbs paired with strongly disambiguating contexts. Such setups often do not

Proceedings of NAACL-HLT 2018, pages 206–211
New Orleans, Louisiana, June 1 - 6, 2018. ©2018 Association for Computational Linguistics

correlate well with usefulness on more natural data. In a previous study on lexical substitution, Kremer et al. (2014) found that the advantage of machine learning-based models over simple baselines was much harder to show on a real-world corpus than on the previously used manually constructed benchmark dataset (McCarthy and Navigli, 2009).

In this paper, we pursue the idea that lexical substitution (McCarthy and Navigli, 2009) is a more suitable evaluation task for CDSMs. Lexical substitution is the task of finding meaning-preserving substitutes for a target word in context: e.g., the word *submits* is a legitimate substitute for *files* in *private company files annual account*, but not in *office clerk files old papers*. Lexical substitution provides a frame for comparing synonyms in context, and disambiguating the context-appropriate sense of polysemous words. Since this is a problem CDSMs can account for, lexical substitution seems a suitable task for testing and comparing different CDSMs. Additionally, lexical substitution is a more natural task than similarity ratings, it makes it possible to evaluate meaning composition at the level of individual words, and provides a common ground to compare CDSMs with dedicated lexical substitution models.

2 The ANVAN-LS Dataset

To perform more realistic evaluations for CDSMs, we would like to test them on a sample of actual human utterances rather than hand-selected examples. That being said, for the evaluation to be useful, the structures on which we evaluate should be relatively uniform and limited, at least initially while moving from artificial to natural datasets. We thus construct a dataset[1] for English that strikes a balance between these factors: we maintain the adjective-noun-verb-adjective-noun (ANVAN) format, but our phrases are based on corpus sentences, and some or all words in the ANVAN can form the targets of lexical substitution ranking tasks.

Sampling ANVAN Queries. The starting point of our corpus construction is the English CoInCo corpus (Kremer et al., 2014), which consists of roughly 2,500 sentences taken from the *news* and *fiction* section of the MASC corpus and provides manually annotated lexical substitutes for all content words (nouns, adjectives, verbs, and adverbs).

We extracted all clauses from CoInCo that met the following requirements: (1) the dependency structure of the clause includes an ANVAN structure; (2) at least one constituent word of the AN-VAN sub-clause has at least two human-provided single-word substitutes that exceeded a minimal frequency threshold (more than 5 occurrences in a large corpus, cf. Section 3); (3) the POS tags were correct. This resulted in 165 ANVAN phrases, which contained an average of 4.4 (out of 5) target words with substitutes, for a total of 732 target words for lexical substitution.

An issue that required additional consideration was the adjective positions of the ANVANs. In the CoInCo, we found a substantial number of noun-noun compounds whose modifiers were tagged as adjectives. Conversely, many adjective modifiers in the corpus were substituted with nouns by human annotators. To account for this variability, we extended the ANVAN schema conservatively by allowing nouns to fill the A position if it was observed in the large corpus robustly as a modifier (i.e., as part of at least 100 N-N bigram types, each of which occurred at least 300 times).

Building Lexical Substitution Tasks. For each of the 732 target words, we constructed a lexical substitution query by pairing the target with two correct substitutes and two confounders (see Table 1). Since substitutes provided by more annotators in CoInCo tend to be more reliable, we picked the two most frequently given substitutes for each target. In the case of ties, we chose the lemma with the highest corpus frequency.

To acquire challenging confounders, we retrieved the 20 most similar lemmas with the same part of speech for each target (according to the unigram space; cf. Section 3) and then eliminated all annotator-provided substitutes for this target. From the remainder, we chose the two most closely matched by corpus frequency to the frequencies of the two chosen annotator-provided substitutes. Given the relatively high number of human substitutes in CoInCo, this results in highly similar, but contextually inappropriate confounders. Finally, the acquired confounders were manually checked to make sure that the automatic selection process did not yield a context-appropriate substitute or a semantically unrelated term. In such cases, the next best candidate (by lemma similarity and frequency) was chosen.

---

[1] The corpus is freely available at `http://www.ims.uni-stuttgart.de/forschung/ressourcen/korpora/ANVAN-LS.html`

target	construction	**arm**	build	large	airfield
substitute₁	construction	*branch*	build	large	airfield
substitute₂	construction	*part*	build	large	airfield
confounder₁	construction	*back*	build	large	airfield
confounder₂	construction	*hand*	build	large	airfield

Table 1: ANVAN-LS lexical substitution example

3 Experimental Setup

Task and Evaluation. We evaluate models on
ANVAN-LS in the form of a ranking task for each
query: models are supposed to rank the correct substitutes for each target higher than its confounders.
Our evaluation measure is the mean average precision (MAP) of all queries. In our case,

$$\text{MAP} = \frac{1}{N} \sum_{i=1}^{N} \sum_{k=1}^{4} P_{l_i}(k) \Delta r_{l_i}(k)$$

where k is the rank in the 4-item list l of substitution candidates, $P_l(k)$ is the precision at cut-off
point k in list l, the $\Delta r_l(k)$ is the change in recall
from items $k-1$ to k in l, and N is the total number
of ANVAN queries. We calculate MAP both over-
all, and by target positions in ANVAN, to obtain
more detailed insights into performance depending
on part of speech and word position.

Corpus and Semantic Space. Following Baroni
and Zamparelli (2010) and Paperno et al. (2014),
we use a concatenation of the ukWaC, BNC, and
English Wikipedia corpora (around 2.8G words).
We build a square co-occurrence matrix, using
the complete vocabulary of our ANVAN sentence
dataset, and a set of the most frequent content
words in our corpus, for a total of 30K words. In
addition, we built two co-occurrence matrices of
bigrams, composed of all predicates (adjectives and
verbs) in our vocabulary and their most frequent
noun co-occurrents, as observed in the corpus, with
a threshold of 300. The bigrams were observed in
co-occurrence with the aforementioned 30K vocabulary and most frequent corpus terms, resulting in
a 650K-by-30K matrix for A-N and N-N bigrams
and a 620K-by-30K matrix for V-N bigrams.

For all three matrices, the 3-word-window co-
occurrence counts were transformed with PPMI
and reduced to 300 dimensions with SVD. All models were built with DISSECT (Dinu et al., 2013).

CDSMs. We consider two component-wise
CDSMs: the simple additive and multiplicative
models (Mitchell and Lapata, 2008), defined as

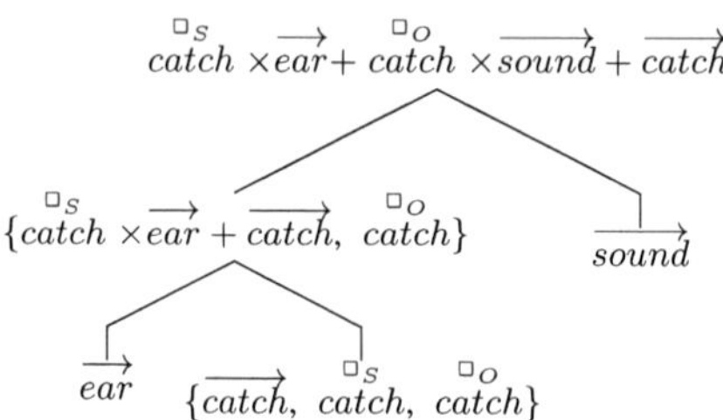

Figure 1: Example for Practical Lexical Function
model composition for *ear catch sound*

$\mathbf{p} = \mathbf{u} \oplus \mathbf{v}$, where $\oplus$ is either component-wise addition or multiplication. We also work with two
variants of the Practical Lexical Function model
(PLF), which are derived from the Lexical Function Model (LF, Baroni and Zamparelli (2010)),
which represents predicates (verbs and adjectives
in our case) as matrices to be multiplied with vector
representations of their nominal arguments. More
specifically, when applied to an ANVAN sentence
(such as *pointed ear catch sharp sound*), the PLF
model incorporates vector representations for each
of the five constituent words, along with an adjective matrix for *pointed* and *sharp*, as well as
verb$_{\text{subject}}$ and verb$_{\text{object}}$ matrices for the verb and
its subject and object arguments. An example of
composition for a verb with its subject and object
arguments is given in Figure 1.

Formally, the standard PLF (PLF$_{\text{Paperno}}$) defines
the composition for ANVAN-style sentences as:
$V_S^{\square} \cdot \vec{S} + V_O^{\square} \cdot \vec{O} + \vec{V}$, where $\vec{S}$ and $\vec{O}$ are the
composed A-N bigrams, $A^{\square} \cdot \vec{N}$. The required
matrices are learned with ridge regression from
unigram and bigram vectors.

Gupta et al. (2015) pointed out that the standard
PLF "overcounts" the predicate by adding it explicitly, and proposed a rectified variant which simply
leaves out the function word vector $\vec{V}$. We also
experiment with this model, PLF$_{\text{Gupta}}$.

All CDSMs rank the four candidates for each
target (cf. Table 1) by comparing the vector for the
original sentence against four sentences in which
the target is replaced by the two correct and two
incorrect substitutes. We use the raw dot product
as similarity measure, following Roller and Erk
(2016), to boost frequent candidates.

Lexical Substitution Model. As competitor, we
consider a dedicated lexical substitution model,
namely context2vec (Melamud et al., 2016). Since
it has demonstrated state-of-the-art performance on
lexical substitution and word sense disambiguation

tasks, it is a suitable competitor model for CDSMs on a similar problem. Context2vec uses word embeddings to compute a set of viable substitutes given a context, using a bidirectional LSTM recurrent neural network to build a sentential context representation. We work with two instantiations: first, using only ANVAN as context ($C2V_{ANVAN}$), and second, using the full CoInCo sentence from which the ANVAN was extracted ($C2V_{Sent}$). The first model is directly comparable to the CDSMs in that it uses the same context information, while the second one enables us to gauge to what extent the models can benefit from a richer context. We let context2vec generate 1000 substitutions for each target word. If any substitution candidates were not included in this list, the missing items were defined to be tied at the last position, and the AP was defined as the MAP of all permutations of the missing items with respect to their ranking.

Baselines. Two baselines are defined to compare our models against. The first is the random baseline (Random): the MAP of all possible rankings of two relevant and two irrelevant items, equal to 0.680. The second baseline (LemmaSim) ranks the lemma-level similarities of the target word and its substitutes candidates without context.

4 Results

Table 2 lists the performance of our experiments on ANVAN-LS, first evaluated for each target word position (top rows) and then averaged across all target positions (bottom row). The rightmost column shows the average performance of all tested models. Even though there is some variance in the numbers between subject-position targets and object-position targets, we see consistent patterns by part of speech: adjectives are easiest to substitute, followed by nouns, while verbs are substantially more difficult. The difficulty with verbs corresponds to the findings of Medić et al. (2017) for Croatian, who proposed a correlation between the syntactic valence of words and their difficulty (but see below).

The worst model by far is LemmaSim. This is surprising, given that Kremer et al. (2014) found lemma-level similarity to be very competitive. Further analysis showed that its bad performance is due to our choice of confounders as highly similar lemmas (cf. Section 2). An example where high similarity indicates syntagmatic rather than paradigmatic relatedness is *ohio democrat embark over-*

*land **trip**/*itinerary/*sightseeing/journey/travel*,[2] where the two confounders can form noun compounds with the target, like *sightseeing trip*. The simple Add and Mult models also perform worse than random, in contrast to many other studies, underscoring the difficulty of performing well on our dataset. They do relatively well for adjectives, but worse on nouns, and Add struggles with verbs.

The $PLF_{Paperno}$ model performs at baseline level overall, but shows particularly clear differences among parts of speech. It does very well for all adjectives and nouns, but very poorly on verbs, where it is in fact the worst model overall, both measured absolutely, and relatively to the overall performance of the model. An analysis showed that this is indeed, as Gupta et al. (2015) claim, due to the overpowering effect of the predicate vector which is added in the final step of the composition and thus tends to dominate the composed phrase. Consequently, $PLF_{Paperno}$ essentially falls back to verb lemma similarity (cf. the example *russian team **win**/earn/*clinch/get/*succeed gold medal*).

PLF_{Gupta} performs comparable to $PLF_{Paperno}$ in all positions, but demonstrates a significant improvement on verbs, for example *russian team **win**/earn/get/*clinch/*succeed gold medal*. The PLF_{Gupta} model also outperforms the baselines, overall and for all individual positions, it emerges as the best performing CDSM.

Finally, the two context2vec models beat the baseline both on all positions and overall. Interestingly, $C2V_{ANVAN}$, which uses the same information provided to the CDSMs, performs roughly on par with PLF_{Gupta}, the best-scoring CDSM. Evidently, Context2Vec (as a lexical substitution model) and PLF (as a CDSM) perform comparably – it is not the case that one of the two model families shows a clear advantage over the other, given the same context. $C2V_{Sent}$, which has access to richer context, shows another substantial improvement. An interesting difference between PLF and Context2Vec is that the lexical substitution models – which do not take syntactic structure into account – show less variance among positions than the PLF, which does take syntactic structure into account.

In their analysis of CDSM performance on a Croatian language ANVAN dataset, Medić et al. (2017) found a superior performance of simple

---

[2]The substitute candidates are ordered by decreasing similarity, and the confounders marked with asterisks.

	Baselines		CDSMs				Lexical substitution		All
Position	Random	LemmaSim	Add	Mult	PLF$_{Paperno}$	PLF$_{Gupta}$	C2V$_{ANVAN}$	C2V$_{Sent}$	Average
ANVAN	.680	.680	.716	.715	.730	.727	.694	.707	.706
A**N**VAN	.680	.575	.652	.633	.695	.688	.708	.744	.672
AN**V**AN	.680	.537	.618	.670	.536	.680	.697	.723	.643
ANV**A**N	.680	.625	.668	.668	.721	.715	.690	.710	.685
ANVA**N**	.680	.580	.633	.666	.725	.723	.723	.772	.688
Average	.680	.599	.656	.669	.681	.706	.702	.731	.678

Table 2: Evaluation results on ANVAN-LS (mean average precision)

CDSMs (such as addition) for nouns while the PLF performed better on verbs. They attributed this to the role of valence, arguing that the functional role of the verbs, and the disambiguation potential of its argument positions, is better captured by the PLF. In contrast, the variance in performance between word positions that we find for the different models on the ANVAN-LS dataset indicates that the difficulty of substituting verbs might not be due to the intrinsic factor of valence, but due to remaining shortcomings in all CDSM models to properly model predicate-argument combination.

5 Conclusion

This paper presented the case for using lexical substitution as a better evaluation setup for compositional distributional semantic models (CDSMs). We created a new corpus, ANVAN-LS, on the basis of a corpus with manually annotated lexical substitution, and evaluated a battery of models. Our evaluation on this corpus (1) uses a corpus-based, rather than manually constructed, dataset, and should be more indicative for the performance of models on "real-world data" than previous ANVAN-based evaluations; (2) is challenging, with a high baseline, which simple CDSMs like component-wise addition and multiplication were indeed not able to beat; (3) enables a detailed evaluation at a per-position level; (4) makes it possible, to our knowledge for the first time, to compare CDSMs with dedicated lexical substitution models on par, and shows that the two model families perform comparably when using the same context, but differ in their performance by position.

The last result in particular opens up a new line of research, namely an investigation of similarities and differences between the two model families. The improvement we observe for C2V$_{Sent}$ over C2V$_{ANVAN}$ in particular calls for a move from ANVAN-style sentences to more complex and varied sentence structures. It remains to be researched how capable CDSMs are to model meaning modulation that extends beyond the immediate predicate-argument structure (Kremer et al., 2014).

Acknowledgments. We acknowledge partial funding by Deutsche Forschungsgemeinschaft through SFB 732 (project D10) and by the Croatian Science Foundation under the project UIP-2014-09-7312. We would also like to thank Domagoj Alagić for his support.

References

Marco Baroni, Raffaela Bernardi, and Roberto Zamparelli. 2014. Frege in space: A program of compositional distributional semantics. *LiLT (Linguistic Issues in Language Technology)* 9.

Marco Baroni and Roberto Zamparelli. 2010. Nouns are vectors, adjectives are matrices: Representing adjective-noun constructions in semantic space. In *Proceedings of EMNLP*. Cambridge, MA, pages 1183–1193.

Georgiana Dinu, Nghia The Pham, and Marco Baroni. 2013. DISSECT – distributional semantics composition toolkit. In *Proceedings of ACL*. Sofia, Bulgaria, pages 31–36.

Katrin Erk. 2012. Vector Space Models of Word Meaning and Phrase Meaning: A Survey. *Language and Linguistics Compass* 6(10):635–653.

Edward Grefenstette. 2013. Category-theoretic quantitative compositional distributional models of natural language semantics. *arXiv preprint arXiv:1311.1539* .

Edward Grefenstette, Georgiana Dinu, Yao-Zhong Zhang, Mehrnoosh Sadrzadeh, and Marco Baroni. 2012. Multi-step regression learning for compositional distributional semantics. In *Proceedings of IWCS 2012*. Potsdam, Germany.

Emiliano Guevara. 2010. A regression model of adjective-noun compositionality in distributional semantics. In *Proceedings of the 2010 Workshop on GEometrical Models of Natural Language Semantics*. Uppsala, Sweden, pages 33–37.

Abhijeet Gupta, Jason Utt, and Sebastian Padó. 2015. Dissecting the practical lexical function model for compositional distributional semantics. In *Proceedings of STARSEM*. Denver, Colorado, pages 153–158.

Dimitri Kartsaklis, Mehrnoosh Sadrzadeh, and Stephen Pulman. 2013. Separating disambiguation from composition in distributional semantics. In *Proceedings of CoNLL*. Sofia, Bulgaria, pages 114–123.

Gerhard Kremer, Katrin Erk, Sebastian Padó, and Stefan Thater. 2014. What substitutes tell us-analysis of an "all-words" lexical substitution corpus. In *Proceedings of EACL*. Gothenburg, Sweden, pages 540–549.

Marco Marelli, Luisa Bentivogli, Marco Baroni, Raffaella Bernardi, Stefano Menini, and Roberto Zamparelli. 2014a. SemEval-2014 Task 1: Evaluation of compositional distributional semantic models on full sentences through semantic relatedness and textual entailment. In *Proceedings of SemEval*. Dublin, Ireland, pages 1–8.

Marco Marelli, Stefano Menini, Marco Baroni, Luisa Bentivogli, Raffaella Bernardi, and Roberto Zamparelli. 2014b. A SICK cure for the evaluation of compositional distributional semantic models. In *Proceedings of LREC*. Reykjavík, Iceland, pages 216–223.

Diana McCarthy and Roberto Navigli. 2009. The English lexical substitution task. *Language Resources and Evaluation* 43(2):139–159.

Zoran Medić, Jan Šnajder, and Sebastian Padó. 2017. Does free word order hurt? Assessing the Practical Lexical Function model for Croatian. In *Proceedings of STARSEM*. Vancouver, BC, pages 115–120.

Oren Melamud, Jacob Goldberger, and Ido Dagan. 2016. context2vec: Learning generic context embedding with bidirectional LSTM. In *Proceedings of CONLL*. Berlin, Germany, pages 51–61.

Jeff Mitchell and Mirella Lapata. 2008. Vector-based models of semantic composition. In *Proceedings of ACL*. Columbus, OH, pages 236–244.

Denis Paperno, Nghia The Pham, and Marco Baroni. 2014. A practical and linguistically-motivated approach to compositional distributional semantics. In *Proceedings of ACL*. Baltimore, MD, pages 90–99.

Martin Pickering and Steven Frisson. 2001. Processing ambiguous verbs: Evidence from eye movements. *Journal of Experimental Psychology: Learning, Memory, and Cognition* 27(2).

Stephen Roller and Katrin Erk. 2016. Pic a different word: A simple model for lexical substitution in context. In *Proceedings of NAACL/HLT*. San Diego, CA, pages 1121–1126.

Howard Schuman and Stanley Presser. 1996. *Questions and answers in attitude surveys: Experiments on question form, wording, and context*. Sage.

Richard Socher, Alex Perelygin, Jean Wu, Jason Chuang, Christopher D Manning, Andrew Ng, and Christopher Potts. 2013. Recursive deep models for semantic compositionality over a sentiment treebank. In *Proceedings of EMNLP*. Seattle, WA, pages 1631–1642.

Mittens: An Extension of GloVe for Learning Domain-Specialized Representations

Nicholas Dingwall
Roam Analytics
nick@roamanalytics.com

Christopher Potts
Stanford University and Roam Analytics
cgpotts@stanford.edu

Abstract

We present a simple extension of the GloVe representation learning model that begins with general-purpose representations and updates them based on data from a specialized domain. We show that the resulting representations can lead to faster learning and better results on a variety of tasks.

1 Introduction

Many NLP tasks have benefitted from the public availability of general-purpose vector representations of words trained on enormous datasets, such as those released by the GloVe (Pennington et al., 2014) and fastText (Bojanowski et al., 2016) teams. These representations, when used as model inputs, have been shown to lead to faster learning and better results in a wide variety of settings (Erhan et al., 2009, 2010; Cases et al., 2017).

However, many domains require more specialized representations but lack sufficient data to train them from scratch. We address this problem with a simple extension of the GloVe model (Pennington et al., 2014) that synthesizes general-purpose representations with specialized data sets. The guiding idea comes from the retrofitting work of Faruqui et al. (2015), which updates a space of existing representations with new information from a knowledge graph while also staying faithful to the original space (see also Yu and Dredze 2014; Mrkšić et al. 2016; Pilehvar and Collier 2016). We show that the GloVe objective is amenable to a similar retrofitting extension. We call the resulting model 'Mittens', evoking the idea that it is 'GloVe with a warm start' or a 'warmer GloVe'.

Our hypothesis is that Mittens representations synthesize the specialized data and the general-purpose pretrained representations in a way that gives us the best of both. To test this, we conducted a diverse set of experiments. In the first, we learn GloVe and Mittens representations on IMDB movie reviews and test them on separate IMDB reviews using simple classifiers. In the second, we learn our representations from clinical text and apply them to a sequence labeling task using recurrent neural networks, and to edge detection using simple classifiers. These experiments support our hypothesis about Mittens representations and help identify where they are most useful.

2 Mittens

This section defines the Mittens objective. We first vectorize GloVe to help reveal why it can be extended into a retrofitting model.

2.1 Vectorizing GloVe

For a word i from vocabulary V occurring in the context of word j, GloVe learns representations w_i and $\widetilde{w}_j$ whose inner product approximates the logarithm of the probability of the words' co-occurrence. Bias terms b_i and $\tilde{b}_j$ absorb the overall occurrences of i and j. A weighting function f is applied to emphasize word pairs that occur frequently and reduce the impact of noisy, low frequency pairs. This results in the objective

$$J = \sum_{i,j=1}^{V} f\left(X_{ij}\right) \left(w_i^\top \widetilde{w}_j + b_i + \tilde{b}_j - \log X_{ij}\right)^2$$

where X_{ij} is the co-occurrence of i and j. Since $\log X_{ij}$ is only defined for $X_{ij} > 0$, the sum excludes zero-count word pairs. As a result, existing implementations of GloVe use an inner loop to compute this cost and associated derivatives.

However, since $f(0) = 0$, the second bracket is irrelevant whenever $X_{ij} = 0$, and so replacing $\log X_{ij}$ with

$$g(X_{ij}) = \begin{cases} k, & \text{for } X_{ij} = 0 \\ \log(X_{ij}), & \text{otherwise} \end{cases}$$

Proceedings of NAACL-HLT 2018, pages 212–217
New Orleans, Louisiana, June 1 - 6, 2018. ©2018 Association for Computational Linguistics

| | | Vocabulary size | | | | |
| Implementation | | CPU | | | GPU | |
	5K	10K	20K	5K	10K	20K
Non-vectorized TensorFlow	14.02	63.80	252.65	13.56	55.51	226.41
Vectorized Numpy	1.48	7.35	50.03	–	–	–
Vectorized TensorFlow	1.19	5.00	28.69	0.27	0.95	3.68
Official GloVe (in C)	0.66	1.24	3.50	–	–	–

Table 1: Speed comparisons. The values are seconds per iteration, averaged over 10 iterations each on 5 simulated corpora that produced count matrices with about 10% non-zero cells. Only the training step for each model is timed. The CPU experiments were done on a machine with a 3.1 GHz Intel Core i7 chip and 16 GB of memory, and the GPU experiments were done on machine with a 16 GB NVIDIA Tesla V100 GPU and 61 GB of memory. Dashes mark tests that aren't applicable because the implementation doesn't perform GPU computations.

(for any k) does not affect the objective and reveals that the cost function can be readily vectorized as

$$J = f(X)M^\top M$$

where $M = W^\top \widetilde{W} + b1^\top + 1\tilde{b}^\top - g(X)$. W and $\widetilde{W}$ are matrices whose columns comprise the word and context embedding vectors, and g is applied elementwise. Because $f(X_{ij})$ is a factor of all terms of the derivatives, the gradients are identical to the original GloVe implementation too.

To assess the practical value of vectorizing GloVe, we implemented the model[1] in pure Python/Numpy (van der Walt et al., 2011) and in TensorFlow (Abadi et al., 2015), and we compared these implementations to a non-vectorized Tensor-Flow implementation and to the official GloVe C implementation (Pennington et al., 2014).[2] The results of these tests are in tab. 1. Though the C implementation is the fastest (and scales to massive vocabularies), our vectorized TensorFlow implementation is a strong second-place finisher, especially where GPU computations are possible.

2.2 The Mittens Objective Function

This vectorized implementation makes it apparent that we can extend GloVe into a retrofitting model by adding a term to the objective that penalizes the squared euclidean distance from the learned embedding $\widehat{w}_i = w_i + \widetilde{w}_i$ to an existing one, r_i:

$$J_{\text{Mittens}} = J + \mu \sum_{i \in R} \|\widehat{w}_i - r_i\|^2.$$

Here, R contains the subset of words in the new vocabulary for which prior embeddings are available (i.e., $R = V \cap V'$ where V' is the vocabulary used to generate the prior embeddings), and μ is a non-negative real-valued weight. When $\mu = 0$ or R is empty (i.e., there is no original embedding), the objective reduces to GloVe's.

As in retrofitting, this objective encodes two opposing pressures: the GloVe objective (left term), which favors changing representations, and the distance measure (right term), which favors remaining true to the original inputs. We can control this trade off by decreasing or increasing μ.

In our experiments, we always begin with 50-dimensional 'Wikipedia 2014 + Gigaword 5' GloVe representations[3] – henceforth 'External GloVe' – but the model is compatible with any kind of "warm start".

2.3 Notes on Mittens Representations

GloVe's objective is that the log probability of words i and j co-occurring be proportional to the dot product of their learned vectors. One might worry that Mittens distorts this, thereby diminishing the effectiveness of GloVe. To assess this, we simulated 500-dimensional square count matrices and original embeddings for 50% of the words. Then we ran Mittens with a range of values of μ. The results for five trials are summarized in fig. 1: for reasonable values of μ, the desired correlation remains high (fig. 1a), even as vectors with initial embeddings stay close to those inputs, as desired (fig. 1b).

---

[1] https://github.com/roamanalytics/mittens

[2] We also considered a non-vectorized Numpy implementation, but it was too slow to be included in our tests (a single iteration with a 5K vocabulary took 2 hrs 38 mins).

[3] http://nlp.stanford.edu/data/glove.6B.zip

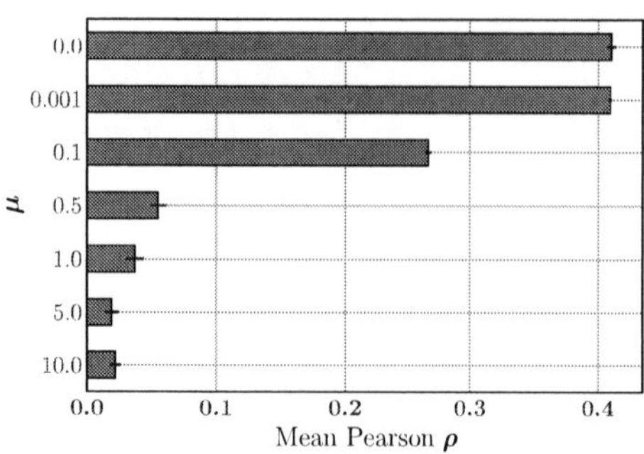

(a) Correlations between the dot product of pairs of learned vectors and their log probabilities.

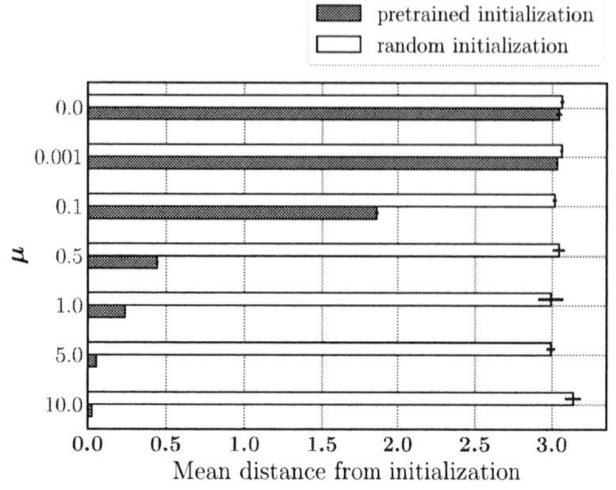

(b) Distances between initial and learned embeddings, for words with and without pretrained initializations. As μ gets larger, the pressure to stay close to the original increases.

Figure 1: Simulations assessing Mittens' faithfulness to the original GloVe objective and to its input embeddings. $\mu = 0$ is regular GloVe.

3 Sentiment Experiments

For our sentiment experiments, we train our representations on the unlabeled part of the IMDB review dataset released by Maas et al. (2011). This simulates a common use-case: Mittens should enable us to achieve specialized representations for these reviews while benefiting from the large datasets used to train External GloVe.

3.1 Word Representations

All our representations begin from a common count matrix obtained by tokenizing the unlabeled movie reviews in a way that splits out punctuation, downcases words unless they are written in all uppercase, and preserves emoticons and other common social media mark-up. We say word i co-occurs with word j if i is within 10 words to

Representations	Accuracy	95% CI
Random	62.00	$[61.28, 62.53]$
External GloVe	72.19	–
IMDB GloVE	76.38	$[75.76, 76.72]$
Mittens	**77.39**	$[77.23, 77.50]$

Table 2: IMDB test-set classification results. A difference of 1% corresponds to 250 examples. For all but 'External GloVE', we report means (with bootstrapped confidence intervals) over five runs of creating the embeddings and cross-validating the classifier's hyperparameters, mainly to help verify that the differences do not derive from variation in the representation learning phase.

the left or right of j, with the counts weighted by $1/d$ where d is the distance in words from j. Only words with at least 300 tokens are included in the matrix, yielding a vocabulary of 3,133 words.

For regular GloVe representations derived from the IMDB data – 'IMDB GloVE' – we train 50-dimensional representations and use the default parameters from Pennington et al. 2014: $\alpha = 0.75$, $x_{\max} = 100$, and a learning rate of 0.05. We optimize with AdaGrad (Duchi et al., 2011), also as in the original paper, training for 50K epochs.

For Mittens, we begin with External GloVe. The few words in the IMDB vocabulary that are not in this GloVe vocabulary receive random initializations with a standard deviation that matches that of the GloVe representations. Informed by our simulations, we train representations with the Mittens weight $\mu = 0.1$. The GloVe hyperparameters and optimization settings are as above. Extending the correlation analysis of fig. 1a to these real examples, we find that the GloVe representations generally have Pearson's $\rho \approx 0.37$, Mittens $\rho \approx 0.47$. We speculate that the improved correlation is due to the low-variance external GloVe embedding smoothing out noise from our co-occurrence matrix.

3.2 IMDB Sentiment Classification

The labeled part of the IMDB sentiment dataset defines a positive/negative classification problem with 25K labeled reviews for training and 25K for testing. We represent each review by the element-wise sum of the representation of each word in the review, and train a random forest model (Ho, 1995; Breiman, 2001) on these representations.

1. No/O eye/R pain/R or/O eye/R discharge/R ./O
2. Asymptomatic/D bacteriuria/D ,/O could/O be/O neurogenic/C bladder/C disorder/C ./O
3. Small/C embolism/C in/C either/C lung/C cannot/O be/O excluded/O ./O

(a) Short disease diagnosis labeled examples. 'O': 'Other'; 'D': 'Positive Diagnosis'; 'C': 'Concern'; 'R': 'Ruled Out'.

Table 3: Disease diagnosis examples.

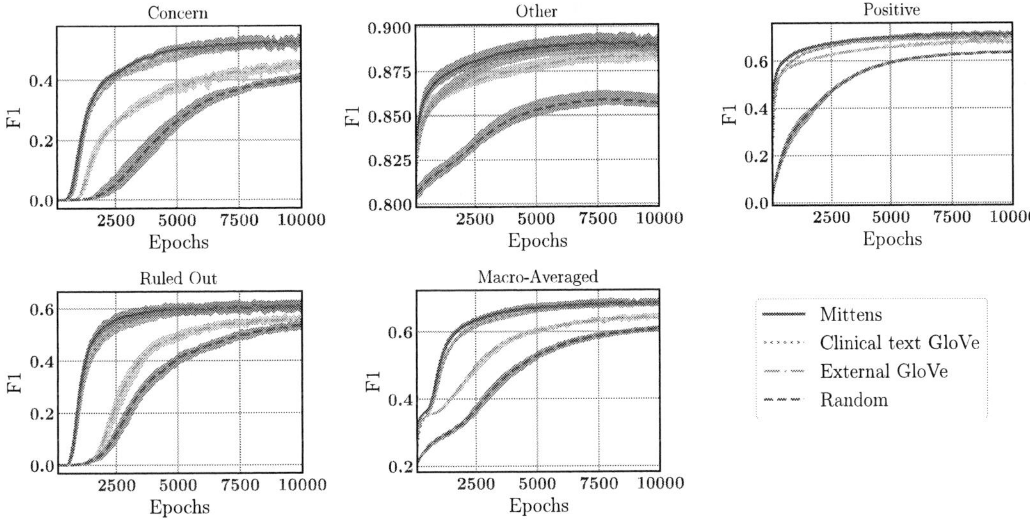

Figure 2: Disease diagnosis test-set accuracy as a function of training epoch, with bootstrapped confidence intervals. Mitten learns fastest for all categories.

The rationale behind this experimental set-up is that it fairly directly evaluates the vectors themselves; whereas the neural networks we evaluate next can update the representations, this model relies heavily on their initial values.

Via cross-validation on the training data, we optimize the number of trees, the number of features at each split, and the maximum depth of each tree. To help factor out variation in the representation learning step (Reimers and Gurevych, 2017), we report the average accuracies over five separate complete experimental runs.

Our results are given in tab. 2. Mittens outperforms External GloVe and IMDB GloVe, indicating that it effectively combines complementary information from both.

4   Clinical Text Experiments

Our clinical text experiments begin with 100K clinical notes (transcriptions of the reports healthcare providers create summarizing their interactions with patients during appointments) from Real Health Data.[4] These notes are divided into informal segments that loosely follow the 'SOAP' convention for such reporting (Subjective, Objective, Assessment, Plan). The sample has 1.3 million such segments, and these segments provide our notion of 'document'.

4.1   Word Representations

The count matrix is created from the clinical text using the specifications described in sec. 3.1, but with the count threshold set to 500 to speed up optimization. The final matrix has a 6,519-word vocabulary. We train Mittens and GloVe as in sec. 3.1. The correlations in the sense of fig. 1a are $\rho \approx 0.51$ for both GloVe and Mittens.

4.2   Disease Diagnosis Sequence Modeling

Here we use a recurrent neural network (RNN) to evaluate our representations. We sampled 3,206 sentences from clinical texts (disjoint from the data used to learn word representations) containing disease mentions, and labeled these mentions as 'Positive diagnosis', 'Concern', 'Ruled Out', or

---

[4] http://www.realhealthdata.com

215

Subgraph	Nodes	Edges
disorder	$72,551$	$408,411$
procedure	$53,616$	$264,000$
finding	$35,544$	$76,563$
organism	$33,721$	$41,090$
substance	$26,207$	$46,333$

(a) Subgraph sizes.

Representations	disorder	procedure	finding	organism	substance
Random	56.05	55.97	75.14	68.15	64.72
External GloVe	**69.31**	65.89	*80.72*	74.12	**77.58**
Clinical text GloVe	66.19	64.96	79.18	73.42	73.37
Mittens	67.59	**66.59**	**80.74**	**74.53**	76.51

(b) Mean macro-F1 by subgraph (averages from 10 random train/test splits). Italics mark systems for which $p \geq 0.05$ in a comparison with the top system numerically, according to a Wilcoxon signed-rank test.

Table 4: SNOMED subgraphs and results. For the 'disorder' graph (the largest), a difference of 0.1% corresponds to 408 examples. For the 'substance' graph (the smallest), it corresponds to 46 examples.

'Other'. Tab. 3a provides some examples. We treat this as a sequence labeling problem, using 'Other' for all unlabeled tokens. Our RNN has a single 50-dimensional hidden layer with LSTM cells (Hochreiter and Schmidhuber, 1997), and the inputs are updated during training.

Fig. 2 summarizes the results of these experiments based on 10 random train/test with 30% of the sentences allocated for testing. Since the inputs can be updated, we expect all the initialization schemes to converge to approximately the same performance eventually (though this seems not to be the case in practical terms for Random or External GloVE). However, Mittens learns fastest for all categories, reinforcing the notion that Mittens is a sensible default choice to leverage both domain-specific and large-scale data.

4.3 SNOMED CT edge prediction

Finally, we wished to see if Mittens representations would generalize beyond the specific dataset they were trained on. SNOMED CT is a public, widely-used graph of healthcare concepts and their relationships (Spackman et al., 1997). It contains 327K nodes, classified into 169 semantic types, and 3.8M edges. Our clinical notes are more colloquial than SNOMED's node names and cover only some of its semantic spaces, but the Mittens representations should still be useful here.

For our experiments, we chose the five largest semantic types; tab. 4a lists these subgraphs along with their sizes. Our task is edge prediction: given a pair of nodes in a subgraph, the models predict whether there should be an edge between them. We sample 50% of the non-existent edges to create a balanced problem. Each node is represented by the sum of the vectors for the words in its primary name, and the classifier is trained on the concatenation of these two node representations. To

help assess whether the input representations truly generalize to new cases, we ensure that the sets of nodes seen in training and testing are disjoint (which entails that the edge sets are disjoint as well), and we train on just 50% of the nodes. We report the results of ten random train/test splits.

The large scale of these problems prohibits the large hyperparameter search described in sec. 3.2, so we used the best settings from those experiments (500 trees per forest, square root of the total features at each split, no depth restrictions).

Our results are summarized in tab. 4b. Though the differences are small numerically, they are meaningful because of the large size of the graphs (tab. 4a). Overall, these results suggest that Mittens is at its best where there is a highly-specialized dataset for learning representations, but that it is a safe choice even when seeking to transfer the representations to a new domain.

5 Conclusion

We introduced a simple retrofitting-like extension to the original GloVe model and showed that the resulting representations were effective in a number of tasks and models, provided a substantial (unsupervised) dataset in the same domain is available to tune the representations. The most natural next step would be to study similar extensions of other representation-learning models.

6 Acknowledgements

We thank Real Health Data for providing our clinical texts, Ben Bernstein, Andrew Maas, Devini Senaratna, and Kevin Reschke for valuable comments and discussion, and Grady Simon for making his Tensorflow implementation of GloVe available (Simon, 2017).

References

Martín Abadi, Ashish Agarwal, Paul Barham, Eugene Brevdo, Zhifeng Chen, Craig Citro, Greg S. Corrado, Andy Davis, Jeffrey Dean, Matthieu Devin, Sanjay Ghemawat, Ian Goodfellow, Andrew Harp, Geoffrey Irving, Michael Isard, Yangqing Jia Jozefowicz, Rafal, Lukasz Kaiser, Manjunath Kudlur, Josh Levenberg, Dandelion Mané, Rajat Monga, Sherry Moore, Derek Murray, Chris Olah, Mike Schuster, Jonathon Shlens, Benoit Steiner, Ilya Sutskever, Kunal Talwar, Paul Tucker, Vincent Vanhoucke, Vijay Vasudevan, Fernanda Viégas, Oriol Vinyals, Pete Warden, Martin Wattenberg, Martin Wicke, Yuan Yu, and Zheng Xiaoqiang. 2015. TensorFlow: Large-scale machine learning on heterogeneous systems.

Piotr Bojanowski, Edouard Grave, Armand Joulin, and Tomas Mikolov. 2016. Enriching word vectors with subword information. ArXiv:1607.04606.

Leo Breiman. 2001. Random forests. *Machine learning*, 45(1):5–32.

Ignacio Cases, Minh-Thang Luong, and Christopher Potts. 2017. On the effective use of pretraining for natural language inference. ArXiv:1710.02076.

John Duchi, Elad Hazan, and Yoram Singer. 2011. Adaptive subgradient methods for online learning and stochastic optimization. *Journal of Machine Learning Research*, pages 2121–2159.

Dumitru Erhan, Yoshua Bengio, Aaron Courville, Pierre-Antoine Manzagol, Pascal Vincent, and Samy Bengio. 2010. Why does unsupervised pre-training help deep learning? *The Journal of Machine Learning Research*, 11:625–660.

Dumitru Erhan, Pierre-Antoine Manzagol, Yoshua Bengio, Samy Bengio, and Pascal Vincent. 2009. The difficulty of training deep architectures and the effect of unsupervised pre-training. In *International Conference on Artificial Intelligence and Statistics*, pages 153–160.

Manaal Faruqui, Jesse Dodge, Sujay Kumar Jauhar, Chris Dyer, Eduard Hovy, and Noah A. Smith. 2015. Retrofitting word vectors to semantic lexicons. In *Proceedings of the 2015 Conference of the North American Chapter of the Association for Computational Linguistics: Human Language Technologies*, pages 1606–1615, Stroudsburg, PA. Association for Computational Linguistics.

Tin Kam Ho. 1995. Random decision forests. In *Proceedings of the Third International Conference on Document Analysis and Recognition*, volume 1, pages 278–282. IEEE.

Sepp Hochreiter and Jürgen Schmidhuber. 1997. Long short-term memory. *Neural Computation*, 9(8):1735–1780.

Andrew L. Maas, Raymond E. Daly, Peter T. Pham, Dan Huang, Andrew Y. Ng, and Christopher Potts. 2011. Learning word vectors for sentiment analysis. In *Proceedings of the 49th Annual Meeting of the Association for Computational Linguistics*, pages 142–150, Portland, Oregon. Association for Computational Linguistics.

Nikola Mrkšić, Diarmuid Ó Séaghdha, Blaise Thomson, Milica Gašić, Lina M. Rojas-Barahona, Pei-Hao Su, David Vandyke, Tsung-Hsien Wen, and Steve Young. 2016. Counter-fitting word vectors to linguistic constraints. In *Proceedings of the 2016 Conference of the North American Chapter of the Association for Computational Linguistics: Human Language Technologies*, pages 142–148. Association for Computational Linguistics.

Jeffrey Pennington, Richard Socher, and Christopher D. Manning. 2014. GloVe: Global vectors for word representation. In *Proceedings of the 2014 Conference on Empirical Methods in Natural Language Processing (EMNLP)*, pages 1532–1543, Doha, Qatar. Association for Computational Linguistics.

Mohammad Taher Pilehvar and Nigel Collier. 2016. Improved semantic representation for domain-specific entities. In *Proceedings of the 15th Workshop on Biomedical Natural Language Processing*, pages 12–16. Association for Computational Linguistics.

Nils Reimers and Iryna Gurevych. 2017. Reporting score distributions makes a difference: Performance study of LSTM-networks for sequence tagging. *arXiv:1707.09861*.

Grady Simon. 2017. An implementation of GloVe in TensorFlow.

Kent A Spackman, Keith E Campbell, and Roger A Côté. 1997. SNOMED RT: A reference terminology for health care. In *Proceedings of the AMIA Annual Fall Symposium*, page 640. American Medical Informatics Association.

Stéfan van der Walt, S. Chris Colbert, and Gaël Varoquaux. 2011. The NumPy array: A structure for efficient numerical computation. *Computing in Science and Engineering*, 13:22–30.

Mo Yu and Mark Dredze. 2014. Improving lexical embeddings with semantic knowledge. In *Proceedings of the 52nd Annual Meeting of the Association for Computational Linguistics (Volume 2: Short Papers)*, pages 545–550. Association for Computational Linguistics.

Olive Oil is Made *of* Olives, Baby Oil is Made *for* Babies: Interpreting Noun Compounds using Paraphrases in a Neural Model

Vered Shwartz[*]
Computer Science Department
Bar-Ilan University
Ramat-Gan, Israel
`vered1986@gmail.com`

Chris Waterson
Google Inc.
1600 Amphitheatre Parkway
Mountain View, California 94043
`waterson@google.com`

Abstract

Automatic interpretation of the relation between the constituents of a noun compound, e.g. *olive oil* (source) and *baby oil* (purpose) is an important task for many NLP applications. Recent approaches are typically based on either noun-compound representations or paraphrases. While the former has initially shown promising results, recent work suggests that the success stems from memorizing single prototypical words for each relation. We explore a neural paraphrasing approach that demonstrates superior performance when such memorization is not possible.

1 Introduction

Automatic classification of a noun-compound (NC) to the implicit semantic relation that holds between its constituent words is beneficial for applications that require text understanding. For instance, a personal assistant asked "do I have a *morning meeting* tomorrow?" should search the calendar for meetings occurring in the morning, while for *group meeting* it should look for meetings with specific participants. The NC classification task is a challenging one, as the meaning of an NC is often not easily derivable from the meaning of its constituent words (Spärck Jones, 1983).

Previous work on the task falls into two main approaches. The first maps NCs to paraphrases that express the relation between the constituent words (e.g. Nakov and Hearst, 2006; Nulty and Costello, 2013), such as mapping *coffee cup* and *garbage dump* to the pattern $[w_1]$ CONTAINS $[w_2]$. The second approach computes a representation for NCs from the distributional representation of their individual constituents. While this approach

yielded promising results, recently, Dima (2016) showed that similar performance is achieved by representing the NC as a concatenation of its constituent embeddings, and attributed it to the *lexical memorization* phenomenon (Levy et al., 2015).

In this paper we apply lessons learned from the parallel task of semantic relation classification. We adapt HypeNET (Shwartz et al., 2016) to the NC classification task, using their path embeddings to represent paraphrases and combining with distributional information. We experiment with various evaluation settings, including settings that make lexical memorization impossible. In these settings, the integrated method performs better than the baselines. Even so, the performance is mediocre for all methods, suggesting that the task is difficult and warrants further investigation.[1]

2 Background

Various tasks have been suggested to address noun-compound interpretation. NC paraphrasing extracts texts explicitly describing the implicit relation between the constituents, for example *student protest* is a protest LED BY, BE SPONSORED BY, or BE ORGANIZED BY students (e.g. Nakov and Hearst, 2006; Kim and Nakov, 2011; Hendrickx et al., 2013; Nulty and Costello, 2013). Compositionality prediction determines to what extent the meaning of the NC can be expressed in terms of the meaning of its constituents, e.g. *spelling bee* is non-compositional, as it is not related to *bee* (e.g. Reddy et al., 2011). In this paper we focus on the NC classification task, which is defined as follows: given a pre-defined set of relations, classify $nc = w_1 w_2$ to the relation that holds between w_1 and w_2. We review the various

---

[*]Work done during an internship at Google.

[1]The code is available at `https://github.com/tensorflow/models/tree/master/research/lexnet_nc`.

Proceedings of NAACL-HLT 2018, pages 218–224
New Orleans, Louisiana, June 1 - 6, 2018. ©2018 Association for Computational Linguistics

features used in the literature for classification.[2]

2.1 Compositional Representations

In this approach, classification is based on a vector representing the NC (w_1 w_2), which is obtained by applying a function to its constituents' distributional representations: $\vec{v}_{w_1}, \vec{v}_{w_2} \in \mathcal{R}^n$. Various functions have been proposed in the literature.

Mitchell and Lapata (2010) proposed 3 simple combinations of $\vec{v}_{w_1}$ and $\vec{v}_{w_2}$ (additive, multiplicative, dilation). Others suggested to represent compositions by applying linear functions, encoded as matrices, over word vectors. Baroni and Zamparelli (2010) focused on adjective-noun compositions (AN) and represented adjectives as matrices, nouns as vectors, and ANs as their multiplication. Matrices were learned with the objective of minimizing the distance between the learned vector and the observed vector (computed from corpus occurrences) of each AN. The full-additive model (Zanzotto et al., 2010; Dinu et al., 2013) is a similar approach that works on any two-word composition, multiplying each word by a square matrix: $nc = A \cdot \vec{v}_{w_1} + B \cdot \vec{v}_{w_2}$.

Socher et al. (2012) suggested a non-linear composition model. A recursive neural network operates bottom-up on the output of a constituency parser to represent variable-length phrases. Each constituent is represented by a vector that captures its meaning and a matrix that captures how it modifies the meaning of constituents that it combines with. For a binary NC, $nc = g(W \cdot [\vec{v}_{w_1}; \vec{v}_{w_2}])$, where $W \in \mathcal{R}^{2n \times n}$ and g is a non-linear function.

These representations were used as features in NC classification, often achieving promising results (e.g. Van de Cruys et al., 2013; Dima and Hinrichs, 2015). However, Dima (2016) recently showed that similar performance is achieved by representing the NC as a concatenation of its constituent embeddings, and argued that it stems from memorizing prototypical words for each relation. For example, classifying any NC with the head *oil* to the SOURCE relation, regardless of the modifier.

2.2 Paraphrasing

In this approach, the paraphrases of an NC, i.e. the patterns connecting the joint occurrences of the constituents in a corpus, are treated as features. For example, both *paper cup* and *steel knife*

may share the feature MADE OF. Séaghdha and Copestake (2013) leveraged this "relational similarity" in a kernel-based classification approach. They combined the relational information with the complementary lexical features of each constituent separately. Two NCs labeled to the same relation may consist of similar constituents (*paper-steel*, *cup-knife*) and may also appear with similar paraphrases. Combining the two information sources has shown to be beneficial, but it was also noted that the relational information suffered from data sparsity: many NCs had very few paraphrases, and paraphrase similarity was based on ngram overlap.

Recently, Surtani and Paul (2015) suggested to represent NCs in a vector space model (VSM) using paraphrases as features. These vectors were used to classify new NCs based on the nearest neighbor in the VSM. However, the model was only tested on a small dataset and performed similarly to previous methods.

3 Model

We similarly investigate the use of paraphrasing for NC relation classification. To generate a signal for the joint occurrences of w_1 and w_2, we follow the approach used by HypeNET (Shwartz et al., 2016). For an $w_1 w_2$ in the dataset, we collect all the dependency paths that connect w_1 and w_2 in the corpus, and learn path embeddings as detailed in Section 3.2. Section 3.1 describes the classification models with which we experimented.

3.1 Classification Models

Figure 1 provides an overview of the models: path-based, integrated, and integrated-NC, each which incrementally adds new features not present in the previous model. In the following sections, $\vec{x}$ denotes the input vector representing the NC. The network classifies NC to the highest scoring relation: $r = \text{argmax}_i \, \text{softmax}(\vec{o})_i$, where $\vec{o}$ is the output layer. All networks contain a single hidden layer whose dimension is $\frac{|x|}{2}$. k is the number of relations in the dataset. See Appendix A for additional technical details.

Path-based. Classifies the NC based only on the paths connecting the joint occurrences of w_1 and w_2 in the corpus, denoted $P(w_1, w_2)$. We define the feature vector as the average of its path embeddings, where the path embedding $\vec{p}$ of a path p is

---

[2] Leaving out features derived from lexical resources (e.g. Nastase and Szpakowicz, 2003; Tratz and Hovy, 2010).

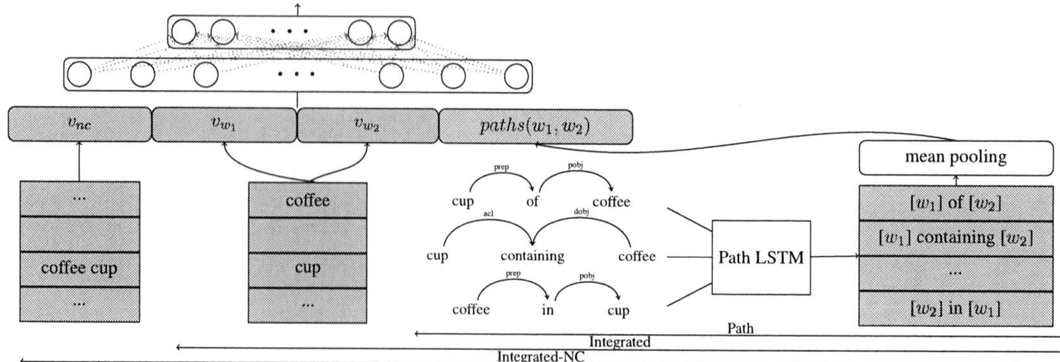

Figure 1: An illustration of the classification models for the NC *coffee cup*. The model consists of two parts: (1) the distributional representations of the NC (left, orange) and each word (middle, green). (2) the corpus occurrences of *coffee* and *cup*, in the form of dependency path embeddings (right, purple).

weighted by its frequency $f_{p,(w_1,w_2)}$:

$$\vec{x} = \vec{v}_{P(w_1,w_2)} = \frac{\sum_{p \in P(w_1,w_2)} f_{p,(w_1,w_2)} \cdot \vec{p}}{\sum_{p \in P(w_1,w_2)} f_{p,(w_1,w_2)}}$$

Integrated. We concatenate w_1 and w_2's word embeddings to the path vector, to add distributional information: $x = [\vec{v}_{w_1}, \vec{v}_{w_2}, \vec{v}_{P(w_1,w_2)}]$. Potentially, this allows the network to utilize the contextual properties of each individual constituent, e.g. assigning high probability to SUBSTANCE-MATERIAL-INGREDIENT for edible w_1s (e.g. *vanilla pudding, apple cake*).

Integrated-NC. We add the NC's *observed* vector $\vec{v}_{nc}$ as additional distributional input, providing the contexts in which $w_1 w_2$ occur as an NC: $\vec{v}_{nc} = [\vec{v}_{w_1}, \vec{v}_{w_2}, \vec{v}_{nc}, \vec{v}_{P(w_1,w_2)}]$. Like Dima (2016), we learn NC vectors using the GloVe algorithm (Pennington et al., 2014), by replacing each NC occurrence in the corpus with a single token.

This information can potentially help clustering NCs that appear in similar contexts despite having low pairwise similarity scores between their constituents. For example, *gun violence* and *abortion rights* belong to the TOPIC relation and may appear in similar news-related contexts, while *(gun, abortion)* and *(violence, rights)* are dissimilar.

3.2 Path Embeddings

Following HypeNET, for a path p composed of edges $e_1, ..., e_k$, we represent each edge by the concatenation of its lemma, part-of-speech tag, dependency label and direction vectors: $\vec{v_e} = [\vec{v_l}, \vec{v_{pos}}, \vec{v_{dep}}, \vec{v_{dir}}]$. The edge vectors $\vec{v_{e_1}}, ..., \vec{v_{e_k}}$ are encoded using an LSTM (Hochreiter and Schmidhuber, 1997), and the last output vector $\vec{p}$ is used as the path embedding.

We use the NC labels as distant supervision. While HypeNET predicts a word pair's label from the frequency-weighted average of the path vectors, we differ from it slightly and compute the label from the frequency-weighted average of the predictions obtained from each path separately:

$$\vec{o} = \frac{\sum_{p \in P(w_1,w_2)} f_{p,(w_1,w_2)} \cdot \text{softmax}(\vec{p})}{\sum_{p \in P(w_1,w_2)} f_{p,(w_1,w_2)}}$$

$$r = \text{argmax}_i \vec{o}_i$$

We conjecture that label distribution averaging allows for more efficient training of path embeddings when a single NC contains multiple paths.

4 Evaluation

4.1 Dataset

We follow Dima (2016) and evaluate on the Tratz (2011) dataset, with 19,158 instances and two levels of labels: fine-grained (`Tratz-fine`, 37 relations) and coarse-grained (`Tratz-coarse`, 12 relations). We report results on both versions. See Tratz (2011) for the list of relations.

Dataset Splits Dima (2016) showed that a classifier based only on v_{w_1} and v_{w_2} performs on par with compound representations, and that the success comes from lexical memorization (Levy et al., 2015): memorizing the majority label of single words in particular slots of the compound (e.g. TOPIC for *travel guide, fishing guide*, etc.). This memorization paints a skewed picture of the state-of-the-art performance on this difficult task.

To better test this hypothesis, we evaluate on 4 different splits of the datasets to train, test, and validation sets: (1) **random**, in a 75:20:5 ratio, (2) **lexical-full**, in which the train, test, and validation

220

Dataset	Split	Best Freq	Dist	Dist-NC	Best Comp	Path	Int	Int-NC
Tratz-fine	Rand	0.319	0.692	0.673	**0.725**	0.538	0.714	0.692
	Lex_{head}	0.222	0.458	0.449	0.450	0.448	**0.510**	0.478
	Lex_{mod}	0.292	0.574	0.559	0.607	0.472	**0.613**	0.600
	Lex_{full}	0.066	0.363	0.360	0.334	0.423	0.421	**0.429**
Tratz-coarse	Rand	0.256	0.734	0.718	**0.775**	0.586	0.736	0.712
	Lex_{head}	0.225	0.501	0.497	0.538	0.518	**0.558**	0.548
	Lex_{mod}	0.282	0.630	0.600	0.645	0.548	**0.646**	0.632
	Lex_{full}	0.136	0.406	0.409	0.372	0.472	0.475	**0.478**

Table 1: All methods' performance (F_1) on the various splits: **best freq**: best performing frequency baseline (head / modifier),[3] **best comp**: best model from Dima (2016).

Dataset	Split	Train	Validation	Test
TRATZ-FINE	Lex_{full}	4,730	1,614	869
	Lex_{head}	9,185	5,819	4,154
	Lex_{mod}	9,783	5,400	3,975
	Rand	14,369	958	3,831
TRATZ-COARSE	Lex_{full}	4,746	1,619	779
	Lex_{head}	9,214	5,613	3,964
	Lex_{mod}	9,732	5,402	3,657
	Rand	14,093	940	3,758

Table 2: Number of instances in each dataset split.

sets each consists of a distinct vocabulary. The split was suggested by Levy et al. (2015), and it randomly assigns words to distinct sets, such that for example, including *travel guide* in the train set promises that *fishing guide* would not be included in the test set, and the models do not benefit from memorizing that the head *guide* is always annotated as TOPIC. Given that the split discards many NCs, we experimented with two additional splits: (3) **lexical-mod** split, in which the w_1 words are unique in each set, and (4) **lexical-head** split, in which the w_2 words are unique in each set. Table 2 displays the sizes of each split.

4.2 Baselines

Frequency Baselines. *mod freq* classifies $w_1 w_2$ to the most common relation in the train set for NCs with the same modifier ($w_1 w_2'$), while *head freq* considers NCs with the same head ($w_1' w_2$).[4]

Distributional Baselines. Ablation of the path-based component from our models: **Dist** uses only w_1 and w_2's word embeddings: $\vec{x} = [\vec{v}_{w_1}, \vec{v}_{w_2}]$, while **Dist-NC** includes also the NC embedding: $\vec{x} = [\vec{v}_{w_1}, \vec{v}_{w_2}, \vec{v}_{nc}]$. The network architecture is defined similarly to our models (Section 3.1).

Compositional Baselines. We re-train Dima's (2016) models, various combinations of NC representations (Zanzotto et al., 2010; Socher et al.,

2012) and single word embeddings in a fully connected network.[5]

4.3 Results

Table 1 shows the performance of various methods on the datasets. Dima's (2016) compositional models perform best among the baselines, and on the random split, better than all the methods. On the lexical splits, however, the baselines exhibit a dramatic drop in performance, and are outperformed by our methods. The gap is larger in the lexical-full split. Finally, there is usually no gain from the added NC vector in Dist-NC and Integrated-NC.

5 Analysis

Path Embeddings. To focus on the changes from previous work, we analyze the performance of the path-based model on the Tratz-fine random split. This dataset contains 37 relations and the model performance varies across them. Some relations, such as MEASURE and PER-SONAL_TITLE yield reasonable performance (F_1 score of 0.87 and 0.68). Table 3 focuses on these relations and illustrates the indicative paths that the model has learned for each relation. We compute these by performing the analysis in Shwartz et al. (2016), where each path is fed into the path-based model, and is assigned to its best-scoring relation. For each relation, we consider paths with a score ≥ 0.8.

Other relations achieve very low F_1 scores, indicating that the model is unable to learn them at all. Interestingly, the four relations with the lowest performance in our model[6] are also those with the highest error rate in Dima (2016), very

---

[3]In practice, in lexical-full this is a random baseline, in lexical-head it is the modifier frequency baseline, and in lexical-mod it is the head frequency baseline.

[4]Unseen heads/modifiers are assigned a random relation.

[5]We only include the compositional models, and omit the "basic" setting which is similar to our Dist model. For the full details of the compositional models, see Dima (2016).

[6]LEXICALIZED, TOPIC_OF_COGNITION&EMOTION, WHOLE+ATTRIBUTE&FEAT, PARTIAL_ATTR_TRANSFER

Relation	Path	Examples
MEASURE	$[w_2]$ varies by $[w_1]$ 2,560 $[w_1]$ portion of $[w_2]$	*state limit, age limit* *acre estate*
PERSONAL TITLE	$[w_2]$ Anderson $[w_1]$ $[w_2]$ Sheridan $[w_1]$	*Mrs. Brown* *Gen. Johnson*
CREATE-PROVIDE-GENERATE-SELL	$[w_2]$ produce $[w_1]$ $[w_2]$ selling $[w_1]$ $[w_2]$ manufacture $[w_1]$	*food producer, drug group* *phone company, merchandise store* *engine plant, sugar company*
TIME-OF1	$[w_2]$ begin $[w_1]$ $[w_2]$ held Saturday $[w_1]$	*morning program* *afternoon meeting, morning session*
SUBSTANCE-MATERIAL-INGREDIENT	$[w_2]$ made of wood and $[w_1]$ $[w_2]$ material includes type of $[w_1]$	*marble table, vinyl siding* *steel pipe*

Table 3: Indicative paths for selected relations, along with NC examples.

Test NC		Most Similar NC	
NC	Label	NC	Label
majority party	EQUATIVE	*minority party*	WHOLE+PART_OR_MEMBER_OF
enforcement director	OBJECTIVE	*enforcement chief*	PERFORM&ENGAGE_IN
fire investigator	OBJECTIVE	*fire marshal*	ORGANIZE&SUPERVISE&AUTHORITY
stabilization plan	OBJECTIVE	*stabilization program*	PERFORM&ENGAGE_IN
investor sentiment	EXPERIENCER-OF-EXPERIENCE	*market sentiment*	TOPIC_OF_COGNITION&EMOTION
alliance member	WHOLE+PART_OR_MEMBER_OF	*alliance leader*	OBJECTIVE

Table 4: Example of NCs from the `Tratz-fine` random split test set, along with the most similar NC in the embeddings, where the two NCs have different labels.

likely since they express complex relations. For example, the LEXICALIZED relation contains non-compositional NCs (*soap opera*) or lexical items whose meanings departed from the combination of the constituent meanings. It is expected that there are no paths that indicate lexicalization. In PAR-TIAL_ATTRIBUTE_TRANSFER (*bullet train*), w_1 transfers an attribute to w_2 (e.g. *bullet* transfers speed to *train*). These relations are not expected to be expressed in text, unless the text aims to explain them (e.g. *train as fast as a bullet*).

Looking closer at the model confusions shows that it often defaulted to general relations like OB-JECTIVE (*recovery plan*) or RELATIONAL-NOUN-COMPLEMENT (*eye shape*). The latter is described as "indicating the complement of a relational noun (e.g., son of, price of)", and the indicative paths for this relation indeed contain many variants of "$[w_2]$ of $[w_1]$", which potentially can occur with NCs in other relations. The model also confused between relations with subtle differences, such as the different topic relations. Given that these relations were conflated to a single relation in the inter-annotator agreement computation in Tratz and Hovy (2010), we can conjecture that even humans find it difficult to distinguish between them.

NC Embeddings. To understand why the NC embeddings did not contribute to the classification, we looked into the embeddings of the

`Tratz-fine` test NCs; 3091/3831 (81%) of them had embeddings. For each NC, we looked for the 10 most similar NC vectors (in terms of cosine similarity), and compared their labels. We have found that only 27.61% of the NCs were mostly similar to NCs with the same label. The problem seems to be inconsistency of annotations rather than low embeddings quality. Table 4 displays some examples of NCs from the test set, along with their most similar NC in the embeddings, where the two NCs have different labels.

6 Conclusion

We used an existing neural dependency path representation to represent noun-compound para-phrases, and along with distributional information applied it to the NC classification task. Following previous work, that suggested that distributional methods succeed due to lexical memorization, we show that when lexical memorization is not possible, the performance of all methods is much worse. Adding the path-based component helps mitigate this issue and increase performance.

Acknowledgments

We would like to thank Marius Pasca, Susanne Riehemann, Colin Evans, Octavian Ganea, and Xiang Li for the fruitful conversations, and Corina Dima for her help in running the compositional baselines.

References

Martín Abadi, Ashish Agarwal, Paul Barham, Eugene Brevdo, Zhifeng Chen, Craig Citro, Greg S Corrado, Andy Davis, Jeffrey Dean, Matthieu Devin, et al. 2016. Tensorflow: Large-scale machine learning on heterogeneous distributed systems. *arXiv preprint arXiv:1603.04467* .

Marco Baroni and Roberto Zamparelli. 2010. Nouns are vectors, adjectives are matrices: Representing adjective-noun constructions in semantic space. In *Proceedings of the 2010 Conference on Empirical Methods in Natural Language Processing*. Association for Computational Linguistics, pages 1183–1193.

Corina Dima. 2016. *Proceedings of the 1st Workshop on Representation Learning for NLP*, Association for Computational Linguistics, chapter On the Compositionality and Semantic Interpretation of English Noun Compounds, pages 27–39. https://doi.org/10.18653/v1/W16-1604.

Corina Dima and Erhard Hinrichs. 2015. Automatic noun compound interpretation using deep neural networks and word embeddings. *IWCS 2015* page 173.

Georgiana Dinu, Nghia The Pham, and Marco Baroni. 2013. General estimation and evaluation of compositional distributional semantic models. In *Proceedings of the Workshop on Continuous Vector Space Models and their Compositionality*. Association for Computational Linguistics, Sofia, Bulgaria, pages 50–58. http://www.aclweb.org/anthology/W13-3206.

Iris Hendrickx, Zornitsa Kozareva, Preslav Nakov, Diarmuid Ó Séaghdha, Stan Szpakowicz, and Tony Veale. 2013. Semeval-2013 task 4: Free paraphrases of noun compounds. In *Second Joint Conference on Lexical and Computational Semantics (*SEM), Volume 2: Proceedings of the Seventh International Workshop on Semantic Evaluation (SemEval 2013)*. Association for Computational Linguistics, pages 138–143. http://aclweb.org/anthology/S13-2025.

Sepp Hochreiter and Jürgen Schmidhuber. 1997. Long short-term memory. *Neural computation* 9(8):1735–1780.

Nam Su Kim and Preslav Nakov. 2011. Large-scale noun compound interpretation using bootstrapping and the web as a corpus. In *Proceedings of the 2011 Conference on Empirical Methods in Natural Language Processing*. Association for Computational Linguistics, pages 648–658. http://aclweb.org/anthology/D11-1060.

Diederik Kingma and Jimmy Ba. 2014. Adam: A method for stochastic optimization. *arXiv preprint arXiv:1412.6980* .

Omer Levy, Steffen Remus, Chris Biemann, and Ido Dagan. 2015. Do supervised distributional methods really learn lexical inference relations? In *Proceedings of the 2015 Conference of the North American Chapter of the Association for Computational Linguistics: Human Language Technologies*. Association for Computational Linguistics, Denver, Colorado, pages 970–976. http://www.aclweb.org/anthology/N15-1098.

Jeff Mitchell and Mirella Lapata. 2010. Composition in distributional models of semantics. *Cognitive science* 34(8):1388–1429.

Preslav Nakov and Marti Hearst. 2006. Using verbs to characterize noun-noun relations. In *International Conference on Artificial Intelligence: Methodology, Systems, and Applications*. Springer, pages 233–244.

Vivi Nastase and Stan Szpakowicz. 2003. Exploring noun-modifier semantic relations. In *Fifth international workshop on computational semantics (IWCS-5)*. pages 285–301.

Paul Nulty and Fintan Costello. 2013. General and specific paraphrases of semantic relations between nouns. *Natural Language Engineering* 19(03):357–384.

Jeffrey Pennington, Richard Socher, and Christopher Manning. 2014. Glove: Global vectors for word representation. In *Proceedings of the 2014 Conference on Empirical Methods in Natural Language Processing (EMNLP)*. Association for Computational Linguistics, Doha, Qatar, pages 1532–1543. http://www.aclweb.org/anthology/D14-1162.

Siva Reddy, Diana McCarthy, and Suresh Manandhar. 2011. An empirical study on compositionality in compound nouns. In *Proceedings of 5th International Joint Conference on Natural Language Processing*. Asian Federation of Natural Language Processing, Chiang Mai, Thailand, pages 210–218. http://www.aclweb.org/anthology/I11-1024.

Diarmuid O Séaghdha and Ann Copestake. 2013. Interpreting compound nouns with kernel methods. *Natural Language Engineering* 19(3):331–356.

Vered Shwartz, Yoav Goldberg, and Ido Dagan. 2016. Improving hypernymy detection with an integrated path-based and distributional method. In *Proceedings of the 54th Annual Meeting of the Association for Computational Linguistics (Volume 1: Long Papers)*. Association for Computational Linguistics, Berlin, Germany, pages 2389–2398. http://www.aclweb.org/anthology/P16-1226.

Richard Socher, Brody Huval, D. Christopher Manning, and Y. Andrew Ng. 2012. Semantic compositionality through recursive matrix-vector spaces. In *Proceedings of the 2012 Joint Conference on Empirical Methods in Natural Language Processing and*

Computational Natural Language Learning. Association for Computational Linguistics, pages 1201–1211. http://aclweb.org/anthology/D12-1110.

Karen Spärck Jones. 1983. Compound noun interpretation problems. Technical report, University of Cambridge, Computer Laboratory.

Nitesh Surtani and Soma Paul. 2015. A vsm-based statistical model for the semantic relation interpretation of noun-modifier pairs. In *RANLP*. pages 636–645.

Stephen Tratz. 2011. *Semantically-enriched parsing for natural language understanding*. University of Southern California.

Stephen Tratz and Eduard Hovy. 2010. A taxonomy, dataset, and classifier for automatic noun compound interpretation. In *Proceedings of the 48th Annual Meeting of the Association for Computational Linguistics*. Association for Computational Linguistics, Uppsala, Sweden, pages 678–687. http://www.aclweb.org/anthology/P10-1070.

Tim Van de Cruys, Stergos Afantenos, and Philippe Muller. 2013. Melodi: A supervised distributional approach for free paraphrasing of noun compounds. In *Second Joint Conference on Lexical and Computational Semantics (*SEM), Volume 2: Proceedings of the Seventh International Workshop on Semantic Evaluation (SemEval 2013)*. Association for Computational Linguistics, Atlanta, Georgia, USA, pages 144–147. http://www.aclweb.org/anthology/S13-2026.

Fabio Massimo Zanzotto, Ioannis Korkontzelos, Francesca Fallucchi, and Suresh Manandhar. 2010. Estimating linear models for compositional distributional semantics. In *Proceedings of the 23rd International Conference on Computational Linguistics*. Association for Computational Linguistics, pages 1263–1271.

A Technical Details

To extract paths, we use a concatenation of English Wikipedia and the Gigaword corpus.[7] We consider sentences with up to 32 words and dependency paths with up to 8 edges, including satellites, and keep only 1,000 paths for each noun-compound. We compute the path embeddings in advance for all the paths connecting NCs in the dataset (§3.2), and then treat them as fixed embeddings during classification (§3.1).

We use TensorFlow (Abadi et al., 2016) to train the models, fixing the values of the hyperparameters after performing preliminary experiments on the validation set. We set the mini-batch size to 10, use Adam optimizer (Kingma and Ba, 2014) with the default learning rate, and apply word dropout with probability 0.1. We train up to 30 epochs with early stopping, stopping the training when the F_1 score on the validation set drops 8 points below the best performing score.

We initialize the distributional embeddings with the 300-dimensional pre-trained GloVe embeddings (Pennington et al., 2014) and the lemma embeddings (for the path-based component) with the 50-dimensional ones. Unlike HypeNET, we do not update the embeddings during training. The lemma, POS, and direction embeddings are initialized randomly and updated during training. NC embeddings are learned using a concatenation of Wikipedia and Gigaword. Similarly to the original GloVe implementation, we only keep the most frequent 400,000 vocabulary terms, which means that roughly 20% of the noun-compounds do not have vectors and are initialized randomly in the model.

---

[7]https://catalog.ldc.upenn.edu/ldc2003t05

Semantic Pleonasm Detection

Omid Kashefi **Andrew T. Lucas** **Rebecca Hwa**
School of Computing and Information
University of Pittsburgh
Pittsburgh, PA, 15260
`{kashefi, andrew.lucas, hwa}@cs.pitt.edu`

Abstract

Pleonasms are words that are redundant. To aid the development of systems that detect pleonasms in text, we introduce an annotated corpus of semantic pleonasms. We validate the integrity of the corpus with inter-annotator agreement analyses. We also compare it against alternative resources in terms of their effects on several automatic redundancy detection methods.

1 Introduction

Pleonasm is the use of extraneous words in an expression such that removing them would not significantly alter the meaning of the expression (Merriam-Webster, 1983; Quinn, 1993; Lehmann, 2005). Although pleonastic phrases may serve literary functions (e.g., to add emphasis) (Miller, 1951; Chernov, 1979), most modern writing style guides caution against them in favor of concise writing (Hart et al., 1905; Williams, 2003; Turabian, 2013; Gowers, 2014; Strunk, 1920).

An automatic pleonasm detector would be beneficial for natural language processing (NLP) applications that support student writing, such as grammar error correction (GEC) (Han et al., 2006; Rozovskaya and Roth, 2010; Tetreault et al., 2010; Dahlmeier and Ng, 2011), automatic essay grading (Larkey, 1998; Landauer, 2003; Ong et al., 2014), and intelligent writing tutors (Merrill et al., 1992; Aleven et al., 2009; Atkinson, 2016). Pleonastic phrases may also negatively impact NLP applications in general because they introduce an unnecessary complexity to the language. Their removal might facilitate NLP tasks such as parsing, summarization, and machine translation. However, automated pleonasm detection is a challenging problem, in parts because there is no appropriate resources to support the development of such systems. While

some GEC corpora do annotate some words or phrases as "redundant" or "unnecessary," they are typically a manifestation of grammar errors (e.g., *we still have room to improve* **for** *our current welfare system*) rather than a stylistic redundancy (e.g., *we aim to* **better** *improve our welfare system*).

This paper presents a new Semantic Pleonasm Corpus (SPC), a collection of three thousand sentences. Each sentence features a pair of potentially semantically related words (chosen by a heuristic); human annotators determine whether either (or both) of the words is redundant. The corpus offers two improvements over current resources. First, the corpus filters for grammatical sentences so that the question of redundancy is separated from grammaticality. Second, the corpus is filtered for a balanced set of positive and negative examples (i.e., no redundancy). The negative examples may make useful benchmark data – because they all contain a pair of words that are deemed to be semantically related, a successful system cannot rely on simple heuristics, such as semantic distances, for discrimination. We evaluate the corpus in terms of inter-annotator agreement, and in terms of its usefulness for developing automatic pleonasm detectors.

2 Semantic Pleonasm

Although pleonasm is generally a semantic and rhetorical concept, it could have different aspects and be formed in different layers of language, including morphemic (e.g., "**irregardless**" (Berube, 1985)) and syntactic layers (e.g., "*the* **most unkindest** *cut of all*"). Detecting and correcting morphemic and syntactic pleonasms are more in the scope of GEC research, especially when they cause errors. Semantic pleonasm, on the other hand, is "a question of style or taste, not gram-

Proceedings of NAACL-HLT 2018, pages 225–230
New Orleans, Louisiana, June 1 - 6, 2018. ©2018 Association for Computational Linguistics

mar" (Evans and Evans, 1957). It occurs when the meaning of a word (or phrase) is already implied by other words in the sentence. For example, the following is a grammatical sentence that has a redundant word: *I received a* **free** *gift*. While writers might intentionally include the redundant word for emphasis, the overuse of pleonasm may weaken the expression, making it "boring rather than striking the hearer." (Fowler, 1994).

3 A Semantic Pleonasm Corpus

Semantic pleonasm is a complex linguistic phenomenon; to develop a useful corpus for it, we need to make some design decisions in terms of a trading off between the breadth and depth of our coverage.

3.1 Data Source

We want to start from a source that is likely to contain semantic redundancies. Because good writers are trained to guard against redundant phrasings, professionally written text from Project Gutenberg or the Wall Street Journal would not be appropriate. Because we want to separate the issues of grammaticality from redundancy, learner corpora would also not be appropriate. A data source that seems promising is amateur product reviews. The writers tend to produce more emotional prose that are at times exasperated or gushing; the writing is more off-the-cuff and casual, and may contain more redundancy. Ultimately, we chose to work with restaurant reviews from Round Seven of the Yelp Dataset Challenge[1] because it is widely distributed.

3.2 Filtering

Although redundant words and phrases occur frequently enough that exhortations to excise them is a constant refrain in writing guides, most sentences still skew toward not containing pleonasms. Annotating all sentences would dilute the impact of the positive examples, further complicate the annotation scheme, and increase the cost of the corpus creation. Thus, we opt to construct a balanced corpus of positive and negative examples for a specific kind of redundancy in a specific configuration. In particular, we extract all sentences that contained a pair of adjacent words that are likely to be semantically similar. We restrict our attention to adjacent word pairs to increase the chance

of finding redundancy, since semantically related words that are farther apart are more likely to have different syntactic and semantic roles. To determine semantic similarity, we use the TextBlob Python interface[2], which, for a given word, provides access to WordNet synsets (Miller, 1995) corresponding to each of the word's senses. We compare each pair of adjacent words in the dataset to see whether they share any synsets. Since WordNet serves as a coarse filter, we need to further improve recall. We select any sentences that contains a pair of adjacent words such that one of the words has a synset that is *similar to* a synset of the other word. TextBlob provides this "similar to" functionality, which finds synsets that are close to a given synset in WordNet's taxonomy tree. (note, however, that these words may not be used in those senses in the sentence). Applying these filtering rules, we are able to eliminate a large percentage of sentences that do not contain semantic redundancy; the method also help us identify a pair of words in each sentence that is likely to have a redundancy. In the second step of filtering, we manually removed sentences that contained obvious grammatical mistakes.

3.3 Annotation

We set up a Amazon Mechanical Turk service to determine whether the potentially redundant word pairs are actually redundant. Because we want to build a balanced corpus, we first perform a quick internal first pass, marking each sentence as either "possibly containing redundancy" or "probably not containing redundancy" so that we can distribute the instances to the Turkers with equal probability (they do not see our internal annotations). The Turkers are given six sentences at a time, each containing a highlighted pair of words. The workers have to decide whether to delete the first word, the second word, both, or neither. Then, they indicate their confidence: "Certain," "Somewhat certain," or "Uncertain." Lastly, they are given the opportunity to provide additional explanations. Each sentence has been reviewed by three different workers. For about ninety percent of the sentences, three annotations proved sufficient to achieve a consensus. We collect a fourth annotation for the remaining sentences, and are then able to declare a consensus.

---

[1] `https://www.yelp.com/dataset/challenge`

[2] `http://textblob.readthedocs.io/en/dev/`

Consensus Level	Fleiss's Kappa
Word Level	0.384
Sentence Level	0.482

Table 1: Inter-Annotator Agreement

One		Both	Neither	Total
First	Second			
955	765	16	1,283	3,019
32%	25%	1%	42%	100%
57%				

Table 2: Statistics of the Semantic Pleonasm Corpus

A Few Examples

- Sentence: *Freshly squeezed and no additives, just* **plain pure** *fruit pulp.*
  Consensus: <u>plain</u> is redundant.

- Sentence: *It is clear that I will never have another* **prime first** *experience like the one I had at Chompies.*
  Consensus: <u>neither word</u> is redundant.

- Sentence: *The dressing is absolutely* **incredibly fabulously** *flavorful!*
  Consensus: <u>both words</u> are redundant.

3.4 Inter-Annotator Agreement

Because our corpus is annotated by many Turkers, with some labeling only a handful of sentences while others contributed hundreds, the typical pair-wise inter-annotated agreement is not appropriate. Instead, we compute Fleiss's Kappa (Fleiss, 1971), which measures the degree of agreement in classification over what would be expected by chance for more than two annotator.

We analyze agreements at two levels of granularity: *word level* indicates the consensus on whether the first, second, both, or neither of the candidates is pleonastic; *sentence level* indicates the consensus on whether a sentence has a pleonastic construction.

Table 1 shows that annotators are more likely to agree whether a sentence contains a pleonasm than exactly which words should be considered redundant. In many cases, a majority consensus is achieved with one annotator disagreeing with the others. The result suggests that when there is a single word redundancy, removing either of the synonyms could be appropriate.

3.5 Properties

The final dataset consists of 3,019 sentences. Their final labels are based on a majority consensus: 1,283 sentences are marked as not having a redundant word; 1,720 sentences are marked as containing a single word redundancy; and for 16 sentences, both words are marked as redundant. Table 2. shows the statistics of annotators consensus. The corpus, including all annotations and the final consensus, is available in JSON format from `http://pleonasm.cs.pitt.edu`

4 Automatic Pleonasm Detection

Given our design choices, the current SPC is not a large corpus; we posit that it can nonetheless serve as a valuable resource for developing systems to detect semantic pleonasm. For example, the earlier work of Xue and Hwa (2014) might have benefited from this resource. They wanted to detect the word in a sentence that contributes the least to the meaning of the sentence; however, their experiments were hampered by a mismatch between their intended domain and the corpus they evaluated on – while their model estimated a word's semantic redundancy, their experiments were performed on NUCLE (Dahlmeier et al., 2013), a learner corpus that focused more on grammatical errors. Moreover, since their detector always returned the word with the lowest meaning contribution score, they only evaluated their model on sentences known to contain an unnecessary word; without appropriate negative examples, it is not clear how to apply their system to sentences with no redundancy. These are two use-case scenarios that the SPC may address. To verify our claim, we will first compare the performances of several word redundancy metrics, including a replication of the metric of Xue and Hwa, on our corpus with their performances on NUCLE. We will then show that the SPC can train a classifier that predicts whether a sentence contains semantic pleonasm.

4.1 Pleonastic Word Detection

This experiment focuses on the positive examples – the methods under evaluation are all metrics for detecting the most redundant word from sentences known to contain one. We compare the performances of different word detectors under SPC and

NUCLE. Note that our experimental goal is not to obtain a method that reports a high accuracy on SPC (we do not want a corpus that overfits to some particular method). Rather, it is to demonstrate that the human-annotated SPC captures aspects of semantic redundancy that are not available in other resources.

In order to shed lights on the differences between SPC and NUCLE, we compare them using detectors that are formulated from different strategies. First, we have replicated the metric proposed by Xue and Hwa, which consists of two main components: a language model and a word meaning contribution model that is derived from word alignments from machine translation[3]. This method is the most focused on lexical semantic, so we expect it to be better at detecting redundant words on the SPC. Next, we have implemented three simple metrics: SIM computes the semantic similarity between a full sentence and that sentence with the target word removed[4]; GEN estimates the degree to which a word is general (therefore more likely to be redundant) by its number of synonyms; and SMP estimates the simplicity of a word based on an implementation of the Flesch-Kincaid readability score (Kincaid et al., 1975). Of these, only SIM directly models semantics; we expect it to be better at detecting redundant words on the SPC than the two other, more general, metrics. Finally, as a point of contrast, we consider a GEC system using *languagetools*[5] (Naber, 2003); we expect the GEC system to be better at detecting grammar error related redundancy found on NUCLE than cases of semantic redundancy found in the SPC.

To conduct the experiment, we selected 1,140 NUCLE sentences that contain one local redundancy ($RLOC$) error; for SPC, 1,720 sentences with one semantic pleonasm are used. Table 3 shows the accuracy of each method under both corpora. Our implementation of Xue and Hwa's model replicates their reported outcome with NUCLE, and, as expected, their method is more successful on the SPC. All three simple metrics are more successful at picking out redundant word on the SPC than NUCLE, with SIM showing a bigger

---

³In our re-implementation, the language model is trained on a portion of English Gigaword (Graff et al., 2003) using KenLM (Heafield, 2011); the word alignments are derived from Bing's English-French Translator

⁴using *sense2vec* word-embeddings (Trask et al., 2015)

⁵https://languagetool.org/

Method	NUCLE	SPC
Xue&Hwa	22.8%	31.7%
SIM	11.1%	16.6%
GEN	9.6%	13.3%
SMP	16.1%	20.6%
SIM + SMP + GEN	18.2%	27.6%
ALL	31.1%	39.4%
GEC	11.9%	4.7%

Table 3: The accuracy of detecting the redundant word in sentences with different methods under two corpora: NUCLE and SPC. *ALL* is a composite metric from the other four: $Xue\&Hwa + SIM + SMP + GEN$.

difference than the other two. Comparing the four methods' between corpora differences, we see that the method of Xue&Hwa has the most to gain, perhaps because it has the strongest domain mismatch. Yet, a combination of all four metrics results in an improved accuracy of 39.4%, suggesting that the four strategies capture different aspect of semantic redundancy. That this highest achieving accuracy is still quite low suggests that there is ample room for improvement in terms of word detector development. In contrast, the GEC method performed much better on NUCLE (11.9%) than on the SPC (4.7%). Taken as a whole, these results suggest that the SPC, while small, is a better fit for the task of detecting semantic redundancy than NUCLE.

4.2 Sentential Pleonasm Detection

All the methods shown in the previous experiment are metrics that assign a redundancy score to each word within a sentence; they still have to be incorporated into an outer classifier to determine whether the sentence indeed contains a pleonasm. A corpus of naturally occurring text is unsuitable for training the classifier because the distribution is heavily skewed toward the *no redundancy* case. Random down-sampling is also not ideal because some might be too obvious (e.g., very short sentences). SPC addresses this problem by filtering for challenging negative cases: sentences that contain a pair of words that are heuristically deemed to be semantically related, but are not judged to

Feature	Description
UG	the one-hot representation (Harris and Harris, 2010) of unigrams of the sentence
TG	the one-hot representation of trigrams of the sentence
TFIDF	the one-hot representation of smoothed TFIDF tuples of trigrams of the sentence
WSTAT	[max(ALL), avg(ALL), min(ALL), Len(s), LM(s)]

Table 4: Features for sentential level pleonasm detection. ALL represents the collection of word-level metrics: $Xue\&Hwa$, SIM, GEN, and SMP; Len(s) is the number of words in sentence s; LM(s) is the trigram probability for sentence s.

Baseline	SPC	
	MaxEnt	Naive Bayes
UG	79.2	88.4
TG	79.9	88.8
TFIDF	83.0	90.5
WSTAT	63.1	53.2
WSTAT+UG	82.3	89.2
WSTAT+TG	83.7	89.3
WSTAT+TFIDF	84.5	92.2

Table 5: The accuracy of a binary classifier using different feature set to predict whether a sentence contains a pleonastic construction.

be redundant by human annotators. In this experiment, we use SPC to train a binary classifier; our feature set is summarized in Table 4.

To train the classifiers, we performed 5-fold cross-validation on the full SPC corpus. We experimented with both a Maximum Entropy and a Binomial Naive Bayes binary classifier. We considered the number of features from χ^2 test, regularization coefficient, the choice of penalty function and solver as hyperparameters and optimized them using the Particle Swarm algorithm (Clerc and Kennedy, 2002) in the Optunity[6] optimizer package.

Table 5 presents the results. We observe that

[6]`https://github.com/claesenm/optunity`

the three features that directly encode the words of the sentence are more relevant (UG, TG, $TFIDF$) than the group of statistics over the word redundancy metrics ($WSTAT$). For our corpus size, Naive Bayes seems to converge faster to the minimum error rate than MaxEnt (Ng and Jordan, 2002). In combination, $WSTAT + TFIDF$ gave the highest accuracy, at around 92%. This result also reinforces our inter-annotator agreement rate, suggesting that determining whether a sentence contains a semantic pleonasm is easier than deciding which word is pleonastic.

5 Conclusion

We have introduced a semantic pleonasm corpus in which each sentence contains a word pair that is potentially semantically related. These sentences are reviewed by human annotators, who determine whether any of the words are redundant. Our corpus offers two main contributions. First, as a corpus that focuses on semantic similarity, it provides a more appropriate resource for systems that aim to detect stylistic redundancy rather than grammatical errors. Second, as a balanced corpus of positive and near-miss negative examples, it allows systems to evaluate their ability to detect "no redundancy."

Acknowledgments

We would like to thank the anonymous reviewers for their helpful comments. This material is based upon work supported by the National Science Foundation under Grant Number #1735752.

References

Vincent Aleven, Bruce M Mclaren, Jonathan Sewall, and Kenneth R Koedinger. 2009. Example-Tracing Tutors: A New Paradigm for Intelligent Tutoring Systems. *International Journal of Artificial Intelligence in Education* 19(2):105–154.

Robert Kenneth Atkinson. 2016. *Intelligent tutoring systems: Structure, applications and challenges.* Nova Science Publishers, Inc.

Margery Berube. 1985. *The American Heritage Dictionary: Second College Edition.* Houghton Mifflin.

Ghelly V Chernov. 1979. Semantic Aspects of Psycholinguistic Research in Simultaneous Interpretation. *Language and Speech* 22(3):277–295.

Maurice Clerc and James Kennedy. 2002. The particle swarm-explosion, stability, and convergence in a multidimensional complex space. *IEEE Transactions on Evolutionary Computation* 6(1):58–73.

Daniel Dahlmeier and Hwee Tou Ng. 2011. Grammatical Error Correction with Alternating Structure Optimization. In *Proceedings of the 49th Annual Meeting of the ACL-HLT*. pages 915–923.

Daniel Dahlmeier, Hwee Tou Ng, and Siew Mei Wu. 2013. Building a Large Annotated Corpus of Learner English: The NUS Corpus of Learner English. In *Proceedings of the Eighth Workshop on Innovative Use of NLP for Building Educational Applications*. pages 22–31.

Bergen Evans and Cor Nelia Evans. 1957. *A Dictionary of Contemporary American Usage*. Random House, Inc.

Joseph L Fleiss. 1971. Measuring Nominal Scale Agreement Among Many Raters. *Psychological Bulletin* 76(5):378.

Henry Watson Fowler. 1994. *A Dictionary of Modern English Usage*. Wordsworth Editions.

Ernest Gowers. 2014. *Plain Words*. Penguin UK.

David Graff, Junbo Kong, Ke Chen, and Kazuaki Maeda. 2003. English Gigaword. *Linguistic Data Consortium, Philadelphia* 4:1.

Na-Rae Han, Martin Chodorow, and Claudia Leacock. 2006. Detecting errors in English article usage by non-native speakers. *Natural Language Engineering* 12(02):115–129.

David Harris and Sarah Harris. 2010. *Digital Design and Computer Architecture*. Morgan Kaufmann.

Horace Hart, James Augustus Henry Murray, and Henry Bradley. 1905. *Rules for Compositors and Readers at the University Press, Oxford*.

Kenneth Heafield. 2011. Kenlm: Faster and smaller language model queries. In *Proceedings of the Sixth Workshop on Statistical Machine Translation*. pages 187–197.

J Peter Kincaid, Robert P Fishburne Jr, Richard L Rogers, and Brad S Chissom. 1975. Derivation Of New Readability Formulas (Automated Readability Index, Fog Count And Flesch Reading Ease Formula) For Navy Enlisted Personnel.

Thomas K Landauer. 2003. Automatic Essay Assessment. *Assessment in Education: Principles, Policy & Practice* 10(3):295–308.

Leah S Larkey. 1998. Automatic Essay Grading Using Text Categorization Techniques. In *Proceedings of the 21st Annual International ACM SIGIR Conference on Research and Development in Information Retrieval*. ACM, pages 90–95.

Christian Lehmann. 2005. Pleonasm and Hypercharacterisation. *Yearbook of Morphology 2005* pages 119–154.

Inc Merriam-Webster. 1983. *Webster's Ninth New Collegiate Dictionary*. Merriam-Webster.

Douglas C Merrill, Brian J Reiser, Michael Ranney, and J Gregory Trafton. 1992. Effective Tutoring Techniques: A Comparison of Human Tutors and Intelligent Tutoring Systems. *The Journal of the Learning Sciences* 2(3):277–305.

George A Miller. 1995. WordNet: A Lexical Database for English. *Communications of the ACM* 38(11):39–41.

George Armitage Miller. 1951. *Language and Communication*. McGraw-Hill.

Daniel Naber. 2003. *A Rule-Based Style and Grammar Checker*. B.S. Thesis, Bielefeld University.

Andrew Y Ng and Michael I Jordan. 2002. On Discriminative vs. Generative Classifiers: A comparison of logistic regression and Naive Bayes. In *Advances in Neural Information Processing Systems*. pages 841–848.

Nathan Ong, Diane Litman, and Alexandra Brusilovsky. 2014. Ontology-Based Argument Mining and Automatic Essay Scoring. In *Proceedings of the First Workshop on Argumentation Mining*. pages 24–28.

Arthur Quinn. 1993. *Figures of Speech: 60 Ways to Turn a Phrase*. Psychology Press.

Alla Rozovskaya and Dan Roth. 2010. Generating Confusion Sets for Context-Sensitive Error Correction. In *Proceedings of the EMNLP*. pages 961–970.

William Strunk. 1920. *The Elements of Style*. New York: Harcourt, Brace and Howe.

Joel Tetreault, Jennifer Foster, and Martin Chodorow. 2010. Using Parse Features for Preposition Selection and Error Detection. In *Proceedings of the ACL Short Papers*. pages 353–358.

Andrew Trask, Phil Michalak, and John Liu. 2015. sense2vec - A Fast and Accurate Method for Word Sense Disambiguation In Neural Word Embeddings. *arXiv preprint arXiv:1511.06388* .

Kate L Turabian. 2013. *A Manual for Writers of Research Papers, Theses, and Dissertations: Chicago Style for Students and Researchers*. University of Chicago Press.

Joseph M Williams. 2003. *Style*. Longman.

Huichao Xue and Rebecca Hwa. 2014. Redundancy Detection in ESL Writings. In *EACL*. pages 683–691.

Similarity Measures for the Detection of Clinical Conditions with Verbal Fluency Tasks

Felipe S. F. Paula[1], Rodrigo Wilkens[2], Marco A. P. Idiart[3], Aline Villavicencio[1,4]
[1] Institute of Informatics, Federal University of Rio Grande do Sul (Brazil)
[2] CENTAL, Université catholique de Louvain (Belgium)
[3] Institute of Physics, Federal University of Rio Grande do Sul (Brazil)
[4] School of Computer Science and Electronic Engineering, University of Essex (UK)
`felipesfpaula@gmail.com, rodrigo.wilkens@uclouvain.be,`
`marco.idiart@gmail.com, avillavicencio@inf.ufrgs.br`

Abstract

Semantic Verbal Fluency tests have been used in the detection of certain clinical conditions, like Dementia. In particular, given a sequence of semantically related words, a large number of switches from one semantic class to another has been linked to clinical conditions. In this work, we investigate three similarity measures for automatically identify switches in semantic chains: semantic similarity from a manually constructed resource, and word association strength and semantic relatedness, both calculated from corpora. This information is used for building classifiers to distinguish healthy controls from clinical cases with early stages of Alzheimer's Disease and Mild Cognitive Deficits. The overall results indicate that for clinical conditions the classifiers that use these similarity measures outperform those that use a gold standard taxonomy.

1 Introduction

In the diagnosis of clinical conditions, language production along with socio-educational and cognitive factors have been regarded as providing important clues about the health of the semantic memory and of the mental lexicon (Troyer et al., 1998). Some neuropsychiatric protocols for the assessment of clinical conditions like Alzheimer's Disease (AD) and Mild Cognitive Deficits (MCD) often adopt Semantic Verbal Fluency (SVF) (Zhao et al., 2013), since linguistic impairments in such conditions are most likely located at the semantic level (Taler and Phillips, 2008). In these tests participants are asked to produce words related to a given theme (e.g. animals or supermarket items) in a short period of time (e.g. one minute) avoiding repetitions. The answers tend to contain subgroups (Bousfield and Sedgewick, 1944), referred to as clusters and their borders as switches. For instance, a sequence like *dog, mouse, cat, horse, pig*, and *cow* could be divided into two clusters with a switch: pets (dog, mouse, and cat) and farm animals (horse and pig). Clues like the size of semantic clusters and the number of switches (Troyer et al., 1998) have been correlated with clinical

conditions (Murphy et al., 2006; Pekkala et al., 2008; Price et al., 2012; Bertola et al., 2014b), and, in some cases, data derived from SVF tests have indicated dementia five years before its onset (Raoux et al., 2008).

The analysis of clusters and switches requires manual annotation by specialists, based on preexisting manually constructed taxonomies, in a process that can be very time consuming and prone to coverage limitations. In this paper we investigate three similarity measures for detecting switches in word sequences: semantic similarity using a manually constructed resource, as well as word association strength and semantic relatedness both calculated from corpora. We then apply this information to distinguish different clinical groups using classifiers in a fully automated way. This paper is structured as follows: in §2, we review the detection of neuropsychiatric diseases with SVF tests. In §3 we discuss the data and the switch detection strategies. In §4 reports results. We finish with conclusions and future work.

2 Related Works

The cluster and switch dynamic is a classic source of information for separating clinical groups in SVF tests, due to their deep connections to executive functions and semantic memory (Troyer et al., 1998). Clinical detection approaches are widely based on SVF tests and analyze word productivity (Murphy et al., 2006), word repetitions (Raoux et al., 2008; Pekkala et al., 2008; Henry and Phillips, 2006), and number of clusters and switches (Gocer March and Pattison, 2006; Price et al., 2012).

Computational approaches for prediction of switches in SVFs have used information about semantic relatedness from distributional semantic models (Linz et al., 2017). Prediction of semantic clusters has been done with clustering algorithms using LSA similarity between pairs of words. These clusters were then used to detect bipolarity and schizophrenia (Rosenstein et al., 2015).

SVF tests have also been computationally modeled in terms of graphs with nodes corresponding to words and edges to the temporal connections between them. Topological measures, such as, the number of nodes and edges, shortest path, diameter, and density were

231

Proceedings of NAACL-HLT 2018, pages 231–235
New Orleans, Louisiana, June 1 - 6, 2018. ©2018 Association for Computational Linguistics

used to distinguish the control from clinical groups diagnosed with schizophrenia and manic depression disorder (Mota et al., 2012), AD and MCD (Bertola et al., 2014b).

In this work we use similarity measures based on the **association strength** between two words, their **semantic similarity** and their **semantic relatedness** for detecting switches in SVFs involving AD and MCD groups.[1]

3 Methods

3.1 SVF Dataset

The SVF dataset (Bertola et al., 2014a) contains the responses of 100 participants (mean age of 75.78, $sd = 7.13$) of both genders and of similar levels of education. The participants are classified into four groups of 25 individuals. One is a control group with normal cognitive performance, and three are groups with clinical conditions according to assessment guidelines (de Paula et al., 2013; McKhann et al., 1984; Winblad et al., 2004): Amnestic Mild Cognitive Deficit (aMCD), Multi-domain Mild Cognitive Deficit (mMCD) and Alzheimer's Disease (AD). Since the groups are homogeneous, there is no significant differences between members of the same group. Additionally, we also considered a fifth group, the Cognitively Impaired (CI) group, that includes randomly selected participants from the three clinical groups. The responses of each participant are annotated following the guidelines adopted by Troyer et al. (1998); Bertola et al. (2014b).

3.2 Switch identification

In this paper we explore different types of similarity for detecting switches in SVF. An SVF can be divided in semantic chains, which we define as sequences of consecutive words whose similarity falls above a certain threshold (Morris and Hirst, 1991; Pakhomov and Hemmy, 2014). Different semantic chains are separated by switches[2]. Switches form the basis for training classifiers to distinguish control from clinical cases in the SVF dataset (Bertola et al., 2014a). We use Random Forest classifiers (Breiman, 2001) trained with the following features: the number of switches, n; the largest chain size, $c_{max} = \max(c_a)$; the average chain length, $\bar{c} = \frac{1}{n+1} \sum_{a=1}^{n+1} c_a$; the fraction of occurrence of the smallest chain, $f_{min} = \#(c_{min})/(n+1)$, where $\#(c)$ indicates the number of chains of size c in the SVF test of a participant.

Results are reported in terms of average area under the receiver operator characteristic curve (AUC) from 10 times 10-fold-cross validation.[3]

To determine the effectiveness of different types of similarity measures for switch identification we examine semantic similarity from a manually constructed resource, as well as two measures derived from corpora: word association strength, and semantic relatedness. Semantic similarity is determined from the shortest path that connects two words according to the WordNet (Fellbaum, 1998; Perkins, 2010) hypernym taxonomy. The association strength is calculated using the positive value of the Pointwise Mutual Information (PMI) (Church and Hanks, 1990), and the semantic relatedness using the cosine similarity between two GloVe word embeddings (Pennington et al., 2014).'

WordNet provides a high quality manual resource but is not available for all languages. In this work we translated the SVF responses from Brazilian Portuguese to English.[4] Similarity using association strength and semantic relatedness can be constructed from raw corpora, which makes them an attractive alternative for low-resourced languages like Portuguese. In this work we used a corpus built from the Portuguese Wikipedia[5], which was lemmatized and had high frequency function words removed. After preprocessing, the corpus contained more than 118 million tokens, and 44,000 types. PMI for word pairs was calculated using a sliding window of size 7 over the corpus. GloVe[6] word embeddings were constructed using default parameters, with the exception of the window size and vector dimension which were set to 7 and 300, respectively.

Formally the switch is a binary function $\psi(x_i)$ that operates on the sequence of N words $(w_1, w_2, \cdots, w_N)$ produced by a subject in the SVF test. There is a switch between consecutive words w_i and w_{i+1} when their similarity $x_i = s(w_i, w_{i+1})$ falls below a threshold, in which case $\psi(x_i) = 1$, otherwise $\psi(x_i) = 0$. In this paper we explore three heuristics for the switch function:

Detection based on the global mean. The threshold is given by the average similarity of the list.

$$\psi_{global}(x_i) = H\left(\frac{1}{N-1}\sum_{j=1}^{N-1} x_j - x_i\right)$$

where $H(x) = 1$ if $x \geq 0$ and $H(x) = 0$ otherwise.

Detection based in the local mean. The threshold is given by the average similarity of the last k pairs of words.

$$\psi_k(x_i) = H\left(\frac{1}{k}\sum_{j=1}^{k} x_{i-j} - x_i\right)$$

---

[1]Although lexical and distributional characteristics of SVFs, like the total number of words and their frequencies, may be effective indicators of clinical conditions, in this paper we focus on switch information and how it can be approximated.

[2]For simplicity sake we consider that a chain may have a single word in which case it has length one.

[3]The models were trained with the Caret Package: `topepo.github.io/caret`

[4]Given the limitations in WordNet coverage, animals that were not found were replaced by similar animals found in WordNet and with the same frequency profile.

[5]Wikipedia dump corpus from June of 2015

[6]`nlp.stanford.edu/projects/glove/`

Hibrid detection. We combine the local and global approach in a voting system where a switch is considered if it receives at least v votes from previously switch criteria. Here we consider a combination of global with locals $k = 2$ and 3:

$$\psi_{vot_v}(x_i) = H(\psi_{global}(x_i) + \psi_2(x_i) + \psi_3(x_i) - v)$$

where v can be 1, 2 (majority voting), and 3 (total agreement).

4   Results

Evaluation is carried out at two levels of granularity: a rough-grained classification for the detection of a clinical condition in general (control vs. CI group), and a fine-grained classification for one of the three conditions (aMCD, mMCD and AD groups). Table 3.2 displays the average AUC per heuristic for the different sources, with the highest scores shown in bold along with other scores that are not statistically different, considering p-values adjusted with the Benjamini-Hochberg procedure (Benjamini and Hochberg, 1995). The last line of each subtable shows the scores obtained by training the classifiers with the gold standard manual annotation with the taxonomy used by Troyer et al. (1998) (GS in the tables).

Overall, in terms of the type of similarity both the semantic similarity (WordNet) and word association strength (PMI) were significantly better than the gold standard manual annotation for the rough-grained classification and for two of the three clinical cases (mMCD was the exception). This indicates the complementary nature of these additional types of similarity beyond what the smaller and possibly stricter GS taxonomy can offer. Examining the specific groups, the lower scores for aMCD and mMCD also seem to reflect the potential progression of these condition from the control to the more severe impairments of the AD group (aMCD < mMCD < AD).

Among the different measures, the strict total agreement voting (ψ_{vot_3}) provides the best results with association strength for the rough-grained classification (Table3.2(a)), and for the fine-grained classifications of the mMCD (Table3.2(c)) and AD groups (Table3.2(d)). These results suggest that a more conservative identification of switches leading to larger chains provides a better approximation for these three groups.

For the two intermediate clinical groups, aMCD and mMCD, the use of local average information from a small window including only the previous word (ψ_1) also produces good results. However, there is no consensus regarding the source of switch identification, as for aMCD both semantic similarity and association strength were effective, and for mMCD it was semantic relatedness that provided a better characterization of the groups.

Finally, for the AD group various combinations of measures and sources of semantic information lead to effective distinction from the control group, with

the best results using the strict total agreement voting. These results are indicative of AD as the clinical group with strongest cognitive impairment in relation to the control.

For a qualitative assessment of the results, we also examine the vocabulary overlap among the groups, using the Jaccard index as shown in Table 4, which presents the average Jaccard index between subjects across all groups. It shows a higher agreement among the control than among the other groups. This is compatible with the discussion by Brandt and Manning (2009) who identified a more systematic strategy for vocabulary exploration in the control than in 'the clinical groups.

Given that the switches derived by our best models were more effective for the detection of the clinical conditions than the gold standard, we explored the idea that maybe the human annotation could be further improved. To test that, we asked subjects to re-annotate 594 pairs of words for which there was disagreement between the gold standard and the predicted switches. Each pair was annotated by an average of 8.1 annotators ($sd = 2.28$) using four context words. When compared with the gold standard, the new annotation resulted in a change of judgment for 12.7% of the word pairs, with higher agreement with the switches predicted by our heuristics. For instance, for $\psi_{vot3}(x_i)$ it increased agreement in 11% for WordNet similarity, 15% for GloVe relatedness, and 16% for PMI word association strength.

These results confirm the effectiveness of semantic similarity and association strength as indicators of clinical conditions. Moreover, the results suggest that these measures also capture the progression of these conditions and changes in strategies adopted for vocabulary production (Brandt and Manning, 2009), since aMCD can progress to mMCD, which may evolves to others, such as AD and Parkinson disease.

5   Conclusions and Future Work

In this paper we examined the use of three similarity measures (association strength, semantic similarity, and semantic relatedness) for detection of switches in SVF tests, and their effectiveness in detecting clinical conditions. Random forest classifiers trained using the predicted switches were able to successfully identify clinical conditions, and in a fine-grained evaluation were particularly effective for distinguishing the control from clinical group. Our results also outperformed the graph-based approach used by Bertola et al. (2014b) over the same dataset.

Future work includes investigation of the accuracy of these methods for different clinical conditions, and languages. However, the results obtained here show the potential of the method as a tool to help health professionals in diagnosing clinical groups.

	(a) CI			(b) aMCD		
	WordNet	Glove	PMI	WordNet	Glove	PMI
ψ_{global}	0.64 (0.22)	0.66 (0.19)	0.66 (0.19)	0.44 (0.26)	0.56 (0.28)	**0.66 (0.28)**
ψ_1	0.65 (0.21)	0.71 (0.17)	0.68 (0.20)	**0.68 (0.25)**	0.50 (0.29)	**0.65 (0.27)**
ψ_2	0.66 (0.22)	0.66 (0.19)	0.70 (0.18)	0.50 (0.30)	0.60 (0.27)	**0.65 (0.27)**
ψ_3	**0.75 (0.19)**	0.68 (0.18)	0.66 (0.20)	0.59 (0.27)	0.58 (0.30)	0.57 (0.29)
ψ_{vot1}	**0.74 (0.17)**	0.71 (0.18)	0.62 (0.20)	**0.63 (0.27)**	**0.62 (0.27)**	0.46 (0.28)
ψ_{vot2}	**0.72 (0.19)**	0.55 (0.21)	0.69 (0.20)	**0.64 (0.28)**	0.45 (0.28)	**0.63 (0.26)**
ψ_{vot3}	**0.72 (0.18)**	0.62 (0.18)	**0.76 (0.14)**	0.61 (0.28)	0.40 (0.28)	0.54 (0.29)
GS	0.68 (0.17)			0.58 (0.27)		

	(c) mMCD			(d) AD		
	WordNet	Glove	PMI	WordNet	Glove	PMI
ψ_{global}	0.60 (0.27)	0.55 (0.27)	0.54 (0.30)	0.87 (0.17)	0.78 (0.24)	0.80 (0.23)
ψ_1	0.56 (0.30)	**0.75 (0.26)**	0.66 (0.28)	0.71 (0.25)	0.81 (0.21)	0.76 (0.22)
ψ_2	0.65 (0.28)	**0.70 (0.25)**	0.65 (0.27)	0.81 (0.21)	0.83 (0.19)	0.77 (0.25)
ψ_3	**0.71 (0.25)**	0.51 (0.27)	**0.68 (0.28)**	**0.91 (0.15)**	0.85 (0.24)	0.82 (0.20)
ψ_{vot1}	**0.70 (0.26)**	0.60 (0.30)	0.56 (0.28)	0.87 (0.22)	0.86 (0.20)	0.78 (0.23)
ψ_{vot2}	**0.70 (0.26)**	0.46 (0.26)	0.64 (0.24)	0.89 (0.16)	0.77 (0.22)	0.77 (0.21)
ψ_{vot3}	0.67 (0.24)	0.59 (0.25)	**0.73 (0.21)**	0.87 (0.18)	0.84 (0.21)	**0.93 (0.13)**
GS	0.67 (0.24)			0.82 (0.22)		

Table 1: Average scores and standard deviation for random forest classifiers trained to distinguish control from clinical groups. Switch detection with different sources of similarity (WordNet, GloVe and PMI) as well as gold standard taxonomy (GS). Control vs. Cognitive Impairment (CI), Control vs. Amnestic Mild Cognitive Deficit (aMCD), Control vs. Multi-domain Mild Cognitive Deficit (mMCD) and Control vs. Alzheimer's Disease (AD)

	CTRL	aMCD	mMCD	AD
CTRL	**0.27**	0.21	0.20	0.20
aMCD		0.22	0.19	0.19
mMCD			0.23	0.20
AD				0.24

Table 2: Jaccard index for vocabulary agreement between groups

Acknowledgments

We would like to thank Laiss Bertola for sharing the dataset. This research was partly supported by CNPq (projects 312114/2015-0, 423843/2016-8, and 133629/2018-0) and BEWARE (project 1610378).

References

Yoav Benjamini and Yosef Hochberg. 1995. Controlling the false discovery rate: a practical and powerful approach to multiple testing. *Journal of the royal statistical society. Series B (Methodological)* pages 289–300.

Laiss Bertola, Maria Luiza Cunha Lima, Marco A. Romano-Silva, Edgar N. de Moraes, Breno Satler Diniz, and Leandro F. Malloy-Diniz. 2014a. Impaired generation of new subcategories and switching in a semantic verbal fluency test in older adults with mild cognitive impairment. *Frontiers in Aging Neuroscience* 6. https://doi.org/10.3389/fnagi.2014.00141.

Laiss Bertola, Natalia B. Mota, Mauro Copelli, Thiago Rivero, Breno Satler Diniz, Marco A. Romano-Silva, Sidarta Ribeiro, and Leandro F. Malloy-Diniz. 2014b. Graph analysis of verbal fluency test discriminate between patients with alzheimer's disease, mild cognitive impairment and normal elderly controls. *Frontiers in Aging Neuroscience* 6. https://doi.org/10.3389/fnagi.2014.00185.

W. A. Bousfield and C. H. W. Sedgewick. 1944. An analysis of sequences of restricted associative responses. *The Journal of General Psychology* 30(2):149–165. https://doi.org/10.1080/00221309.1944.10544467.

Jason Brandt and Kevin J Manning. 2009. Patterns of word-list generation in mild cognitive impairment and alzheimer's disease. *The Clinical Neuropsychologist* 23(5):870–879.

Leo Breiman. 2001. Random forests. *Machine learning* 45(1):5–32.

Kenneth Ward Church and Patrick Hanks. 1990. Word association norms, mutual information, and lexicography. *Comput. Linguist.* 16(1):22–29. http://dl.acm.org/citation.cfm?id=89086.89095.

Jonas Jardim de Paula, Laiss Bertola, Rafaela Teixeira Ávila, Lafaiete Moreira, Gabriel Coutinho, Edgar Nunes de Moraes, Maria Aparecida Camargos Bicalho, Rodrigo Nicolato, Breno Satler

Diniz, and Leandro Fernandes Malloy-Diniz. 2013. Clinical applicability and cutoff values for an unstructured neuropsychological assessment protocol for older adults with low formal education. *PLoS ONE* 8(9):e73167. https://doi.org/10.1371/journal.pone.0073167.

Christiane Fellbaum. 1998. *WordNet*. Wiley Online Library.

Evrim Gocer March and Philippa Pattison. 2006. Semantic verbal fluency in alzheimer's disease: approaches beyond the traditional scoring system. *Journal of Clinical and Experimental Neuropsychology* 28(4):549–566.

Julie D Henry and Louise H Phillips. 2006. Covariates of production and perseveration on tests of phonemic, semantic and alternating fluency in normal aging. *Aging, Neuropsychology, and Cognition* 13(3-4):529–551.

Nicklas Linz, Johannes Tröger, Jan Alexandersson, and Alexandra König. 2017. Using neural word embeddings in the analysis of the clinical semantic verbal fluency task. In *IWCS 2017–12th International Conference on Computational Semantics–Short papers*.

Guy McKhann, David Drachman, Marshall Folstein, Robert Katzman, Donald Price, and Emanuel M. Stadlan. 1984. Clinical diagnosis of Alzheimer's disease: report of the NINCDS-ADRDA Work Group under the auspices of Department of Health and Human Services Task Force on Alzheimer's Disease. *Neurology* 34(7):939–944.

Jane Morris and Graeme Hirst. 1991. Lexical cohesion computed by thesaural relations as an indicator of the structure of text. *Computational linguistics* 17(1):21–48.

Natalia B Mota, Nivaldo AP Vasconcelos, Nathalia Lemos, Ana C Pieretti, Osame Kinouchi, Guillermo A Cecchi, Mauro Copelli, and Sidarta Ribeiro. 2012. Speech graphs provide a quantitative measure of thought disorder in psychosis. *PloS one* 7(4):e34928.

Kelly J Murphy, Jill B Rich, and Angela K Troyer. 2006. Verbal fluency patterns in amnestic mild cognitive impairment are characteristic of alzheimer's type dementia. *Journal of the International Neuropsychological Society* 12(4):570–574.

Serguei VS Pakhomov and Laura S Hemmy. 2014. A computational linguistic measure of clustering behavior on semantic verbal fluency task predicts risk of future dementia in the nun study. *Cortex* 55:97–106.

Seija Pekkala, Martin L. Albert, Avron Spiro III, and TIMO Erkinjuntti. 2008. Perseveration in alzheimer's disease. *Dementia and geriatric cognitive disorders* 25(2):109–114.

Jeffrey Pennington, Richard Socher, and Christopher Manning. 2014. Glove: Global vectors for word representation. In *Proceedings of the 2014 Conference on Empirical Methods in Natural Language Processing (EMNLP)*. Association for Computational Linguistics (ACL). https://doi.org/10.3115/v1/d14-1162.

Jacob Perkins. 2010. *Python text processing with NLTK 2.0 cookbook*. Packt Publishing Ltd.

Sarah E Price, Glynda J Kinsella, Ben Ong, Elsdon Storey, Elizabeth Mullaly, Margaret Phillips, Lanki Pangnadasa-Fox, and Diana Perre. 2012. Semantic verbal fluency strategies in amnestic mild cognitive impairment. *Neuropsychology* 26(4):490.

Nadine Raoux, Hélène Amieva, Mélanie Le Goff, Sophie Auriacombe, Laure Carcaillon, Luc Letenneur, and Jean-François Dartigues. 2008. Clustering and switching processes in semantic verbal fluency in the course of alzheimer's disease subjects: Results from the paquid longitudinal study. *Cortex* 44(9):1188–1196.

Mark Rosenstein, Peter Foltz, Anja Vaskinn, and Brita Elvevåg. 2015. Practical issues in developing semantic frameworks for the analysis of verbal fluency data: A norwegian data case study. In *Proceedings of the 2nd Workshop on Computational Linguistics and Clinical Psychology: From Linguistic Signal to Clinical Reality*. Association for Computational Linguistics, Denver, Colorado, pages 124–133. http://www.aclweb.org/anthology/W15-1215.

Vanessa Taler and Natalie A Phillips. 2008. Language performance in alzheimer's disease and mild cognitive impairment: a comparative review. *Journal of clinical and experimental neuropsychology* 30(5):501–556.

Angela K Troyer, Morris Moscovitch, Gordon Winocur, Michael P Alexander, and Don Stuss. 1998. Clustering and switching on verbal fluency: the effects of focal frontal- and temporal-lobe lesions. *Neuropsychologia* 36(6):499–504. https://doi.org/10.1016/s0028-3932(97)00152-8.

Berndt Winblad, Katie Palmer, Miia Kivipelto, V Jelic, Laura Fratiglioni, L-O Wahlund, A Nordberg, L Bäckman, Michael Albert, O Almkvist, et al. 2004. Mild cognitive impairment–beyond controversies, towards a consensus: report of the international working group on mild cognitive impairment. *Journal of internal medicine* 256(3):240–246.

Qianhua Zhao, Qihao Guo, and Zhen Hong. 2013. Clustering and switching during a semantic verbal fluency test contribute to differential diagnosis of cognitive impairment. *Neuroscience Bulletin* 29(1):75–82. https://doi.org/10.1007/s12264-013-1301-7.

Sluice resolution
without hand-crafted features over brittle syntax trees

Ola Rønning
University of Copenhagen
ronning@protonmail.com

Daniel Hardt
Copenhagen Business School
dh.digi@cbs.dk

Anders Søgaard
University of Copenhagen
soegaard@di.ku.dk

Abstract

Sluice resolution in English is the problem of finding antecedents of *wh*-fronted ellipses. Previous work has relied on hand-crafted features over syntax trees that scale poorly to other languages and domains; in particular, to dialogue, which is one of the most interesting applications of sluice resolution. Syntactic information is arguably important for sluice resolution, but we show that multi-task learning with partial parsing as auxiliary tasks effectively closes the gap and buys us an additional 9% error reduction over previous work. Since we are not directly relying on features from partial parsers, our system is more robust to domain shifts, giving a 26% error reduction on embedded sluices in dialogue.

1 Introduction

Sluices, also known as *wh*-fronted ellipses, are questions where the specification of what is asked for (beyond the *wh*-word), is elided (and thus needs to be retrieved from context). Below we distinguish two types of sluices: (i) embedded sluices, and (ii) root sluices. Embedded sluices occur in both single-authored texts and dialogue, while root sluices are particularly frequent in dialogue.

(1) If [this is not practical], explain *why*.

(2) A: [Jennifer is looking for you/~~me~~].
    B: Why?

Example 1 is an embedded sluice. In it, *why* is the remnant of the embedded question, which we understand to mean '*why* this is not practical'.

Example 2 is a root sluice. Again, *why* is the remnant of the question; however, the *wh*-word is not embedded in a larger structure. In both cases, we consider the antecedent of a *wh*-fronted ellipsis to be the content in the prior discourse that most intuitively provides the elided material, i.e., *[this is not practical]* in Example 1, and *[Jennifer is looking for ~~you~~/me]* in Example 2.[1]

Contributions This paper presents a more robust, neural model for sluice resolution in English based on multi-task learning. Our model significantly outperforms the only previous work on sluice resolution on available newswire corpora, but also has a number of advantages over this work. In particular, our model (a) does not require full syntactic parsing as a pre-processing step, (b) does not require manual feature engineering, and (c) is more robust when evaluated on speech corpora, because it is not dependent on full syntactic parsers (a). The lack of dependence on full syntactic parsers should also make it easier to transfer our model to new languages. In addition to the implementation of our architecture, which we make publicly available, we also make a new benchmark available for sluice resolution in English dialogue.

2 Related Work

Anand and McCloskey (2015) introduced the problem of sluice resolution and presented the newswire corpus which we use in our experiments below.

Anand and Hardt (2016) presented the first, and to the best of our knowledge only previous, sluice resolution system. They learn a linear combination of fifteen features across five feature groups, through a simple hill climbing procedure. Each

---

[1] In this work, we set aside cases where the discourse context does not provide an explicit antecedent.

Proceedings of NAACL-HLT 2018, pages 236–241
New Orleans, Louisiana, June 1 - 6, 2018. ©2018 Association for Computational Linguistics

feature is a score that represents a linguistic property defined over syntax trees. One feature group is *distance*, for example, which consists of various features encoding tree distances between candidate antecedents and the sluice. Candidates are restricted to be subtrees decorated with sentence labels. Note that this means that the model will ignore many candidates in domains where the syntactic parser is unable to identify full sentence subtrees. The other feature groups include: ii) *containment* of the sluice inside the candidate, iii) *discourse* structure encoding the discourse role of the candidate, iv) *content*, i.e., the semantic overlap between the candidate and the sluice, and v) *correlate*, i.e., semantic properties of the candidate, which may be predictive of sluice type (temporal, reason, degree, etc.). The linear model ranks all candidates and resolves a sluice by choosing the highest ranking candidate. Anand and Hardt (2016) use a slightly different metric than we do, because they rank syntactic subtrees that are potential antecedents, rather than labeling individual words in sequence. See §4. This paper is, to the best of our knowledge, the first to consider sluice resolution in dialogue, but Baird et al. (2018) consider sluice type classification in dialogue data.

Our work builds on recent progress in multi-task training of neural networks. Multi-task training of neural networks goes back to Caruana (1993), but was popularized by Collobert et al. (2011) and Søgaard and Goldberg (2016). The most common approach to multi-task training is to share all hidden parameters between different networks trained in parallel on different, but related datasets. The only requirement to the datasets is that they are defined in the same input space, and that there is a shared optimal hypothesis class for the shared parameters (Baxter, 2000), i.e., that there is a representation that is optimal for all the related tasks in question. Obvious extensions to this approach include sharing only parameters in specific layers (Søgaard and Goldberg, 2016; Misra et al., 2016), subspaces (Bousmalis et al., 2016), or doing only soft sharing (Duong et al., 2015), i.e., penalizing the ℓ_p distance between the models.

In addition to a single-task recurrent neural network baseline, we use the approach in Søgaard and Goldberg (2016) where only initial layers are shared, as our baseline. Our approach to sluice resolution is largely inspired by the network architecture in Hashimoto et al. (2016).

3   Our approach

Our approach is an extension of previous work on multi-task learning, largely inspired by Hashimoto et al. (2016). We construct a neural architecture based on recurrent neural networks (Hochreiter and Schmidhuber, 1997), which differ only from the architectures discussed above in using label embeddings that are also passed on to subsequent layers, skip connections from the embedding layer, and regularization. The stacking on label embeddings from auxiliary tasks makes our approach similar to stacked learning (Wolpert, 1992) and progressive neural networks (Rusu et al., 2016).

Unlike Hashimoto et al. (2016), we do not optimize for a joint optimum, only for sluice resolution performance. The architecture that performs best on development data has two interesting properties: (a) It was also the architecture that converged the fastest. (b) It induces a linguistically motivated ordering of the auxiliary tasks in terms of abstractness. The architecture learns part of speech (POS) tagging at the initial layer; then syntactic chunking, then combinatory categorial grammar (CCG) supertags, before learning sluice resolution at the outer layer. See Figure 1 for a diagram of our architecture. We train our architecture by sampling from all our tasks with equal probability. The instance loss is computed at the appropriate level of the network, and backpropagation will only affect the previous levels. All our neural networks use 50 dimensional pre-trained GloVe embeddings, trained by (Pennington et al., 2014) on Wikipedia and Gigaword 5. The word embeddings are *not* updated during training. Similarly, all our networks were trained for 30 epochs. They all use ZoneOut (Krueger et al., 2016) regularization with Z-state 0 and Z-cell 0.2 (except the single-task baseline, which used Z-cell 0.0), batches of 10 examples and are optimized using the Adam optimizer (Kingma and Ba, 2014) with initial learning rate 0.001 (except the single-task baseline, which used a learning rate of 0.01). All LSTMs contain 64 hidden units. All additional hyper-parameters were tuned manually.

4   Experiments

Corpora   We evaluate our models on two datasets, the newswire corpus introduced in Anand

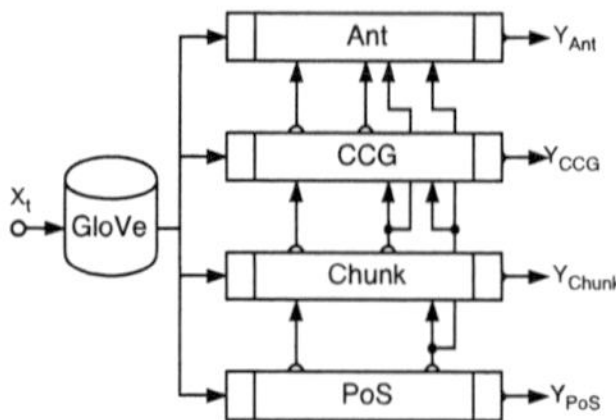

Figure 1: Our architecture. *Ant* is for sluice antecedent tagging.

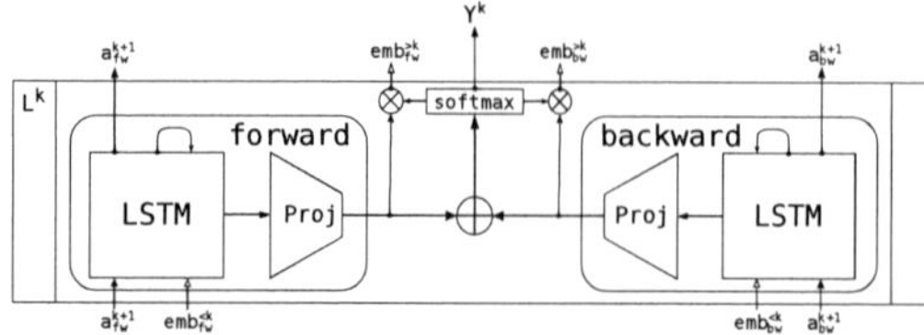

Figure 2: Graphical representation of layer L^k in our architecture. L^k solves task k. Input to L^k: Word w_t embedded into $\mathbb{R}^n$, activation a_t^{k-1}, and label embeddings $emb_t^{<k}$. L^k outputs: estimated label $\hat{y}_t^k$, embedding of $\hat{y}_t^k$ in $\mathbb{R}^H$ and LSTM activations a_t^k.

and McCloskey (2015) (ESC) and a novel corpus of annotated sluices, which is a small subset of the English part of the OpenSubtitles corpus (Tiedemann, 2009). All models are trained on ESC and evaluated on both datasets.

ESC consist of 3103 annotated examples of embedded sluices in written language. The sluices were collected in the New York Times section of English Gigaword. The annotations provide us with the antecedent, a paraphrasing without *wh*-ellipsis, and automatically obtained syntactic trees. We follow Anand and Hardt (2016) in treating the first annotator in each example as the gold-standard.

To measure the sensitivity of our systems to domain shifts, we annotate a total of 2000 examples from the OpenSubtitles corpus. 1000 examples are root sluices, and 1000 are embedded sluices. Each example is annotated by two annotators. Inter-annotator scores were 0.77 for embedded sluices, and 0.83 for root sluices.

Auxiliary Tasks   We use four auxiliary tasks in our experiments below:

POS tagging is the task of determining the syntactic category (part of speech) of a word

in context. Our data is from the Wall Street Journal section of the English Penn Treebank, using the splits in the CONLL 2007 shared task (Nivre et al., 2007).

Chunk-ing is a partial parsing task in which we need to identify the boundary of the main phrases in a sentence. Our data is from the 2000 CoNLL shared task (Tjong Kim Sang and Buchholz, 2000).

Com Sentence compression is the task of sentence parts that can be dropped without loosing coherence nor salient information. We use the dataset also used in (Knight and Marcu, 2000).

CCG super-tagging is another form of partial parsing, using a more fine-grained tagset. We use the CCGBank with standard splits.[2]

The Søgaard and Goldberg (2016) model uses sentence compression at the lowest layer, then chunking, and finally antecedent tagging at the highest.

We observed a detrimental effect when including compression in the same stack as the other auxiliaries for the model presented here. This effect vanished when compression is placed in a separate stack.

Evaluation metrics   We evaluate predicted antecedents using (token-level) F1 scores. This metric is motivated by the observation that annotated spans vary in length, and that annotators often disagree about the exact bracketing; it differs from the one used in Anand and Hardt (2016), however, and we stress that our results are therefore not directly comparable to those reported in their paper. Moreover, Anand and Hardt (2016) used cross-validation; we compare systems and baselines on a fixed split.

Baselines   In addition to comparing to Anand and Hardt (2016), the only previous work on sluice resolution, we compare our performance to two baseline neural network architectures: a single-task architecture and a multi-task architecture similar to Søgaard and Goldberg (2016).

Our first baseline is a single-task, two-layered long-short-term memory (LSTM) network, with

---

[2] `http://groups.inf.ed.ac.uk/ccg/ccgbank.html`

	Newswire	Dialogue	
Model	Embedded	Embedded	Root
Anand and Hardt (2016)	0.67	0.23	0.06
Single-task baseline	0.54	0.41	**0.28**
Søgaard and Goldberg (2016)	0.64	0.41	0.20
This work	**0.70**	**0.51**	0.17

Table 1: F1 scores on embedded sluices from ESC (Newswire) and embedded and root sluices from OpenSubtitles (Dialogue).

a projection layer and a softmax layer. Our second baseline is a cascading, three-layered LSTM, as described by (Klerke et al., 2016). See §3 for hyper-parameters.

Replicability We make our corpus splits, our annotations, our final models, and our source code available at `https://github.com/OlaRonning/sluice_antecedent_selection`.

5 Results

Scores are listed in Table 1. We first observe that using multi-task learning closes the gap between our neural network baselines and previous work, providing a new state-of-the-art for sluice resolution. We also note that our model converges on the validation set after only 5 epochs, as compared to 20-25 epochs for our neural baseline architectures.

Moving from newswire to dialogue, the gap between our system and previous work widens. This indicates that our architecture is much more robust to domain shifts than previous work. Our neural baselines also do better than previous work when doing evaluation in a cross-domain setup.

All systems perform significantly worse on out-of-domain data than on newswire. In particular, we see all models struggle with root sluices. Here, interestingly, our single-task baseline actually performs best of all systems, with a token-level F1 score of 0.28.

6 Error analysis

Previous work is sensitive to parse quality Our most important observation in our error analysis is that the system by Anand and Hardt (2016) is very sensitive to the quality of the syntactic parse trees. If we consider only test examples where the antecedent forms a syntactic constituent, ac-

cording to the error prone parse tree, Anand and Hardt (2016) achieve a token-level F1 score of 0.81. Antecedents need not, but are generally expected to be syntactic constituents, so the lower performance on the rest of the examples (token-level F1 0.53) is likely due to errors introduced by the syntactic parser.

Long distance sluice resolution is hard Both previous work and all our neural systems perform relatively well on examples where the distance between sluice and antecedent is short, e.g., one or two sentences, but none of the systems are good at resolving sluices with three or more sentences between sluice and antecedent. These cases are very rare, about one percent, in ESC, and we leave long distance sluice resolution as an open research problem for now.

Dialogue is harder - root sluices, in particular We also note that some errors in the dialogue corpus derive from examples where the sluices do not have *any* antecedents in the dialog. Here, instead, physical interactions trigger *wh*-fronted ellipses; see Example 3, for example:

(3) *A enters room*
     B: What ~~do you want~~ ?

In order to resolve such examples, we would need to use multi-modal input and learn from both visual and auditory cues.

7 Conclusion

We have presented a neural architecture for English sluice resolution and shown that it outperforms previous work on sluice resolution. Our approach also has several advantages over previous work; most importantly, not relying on hand-crafted features over full syntactic trees. Instead we use multi-task learning to induce syntactic information in a way that does not require access to syntactic information at test time. Not conditioning on features defined over brittle syntax trees also makes our approach less vulnerable to domain shifts. In order to show this, we annotate a new benchmark dataset for sluice resolution in English spoken language. On spoken language data, the gap between our architecture and previous work widens significantly. That said, sluice resolution in spoken language is much harder than sluice resolution in newswire for models trained on newswire; and all the models in our experiments found it particularly hard to resolve root sluices as opposed to embedded ones. Our error analysis also indicates that long distance sluice resolution remains an open problem.

Acknowledgments

We would like to thank Anissa Hamza for her assistance with annotating, and Austin Baird for help with the AntRank system. Thanks also to Pranav Anand and Jim McCloskey for help with the sluicing newswire data. Anders Søgaard was supported by the European Research Council and the Innovation Fund Denmark. Daniel Hardt was supported by the U.S. National Science Foundation, grant 1451819.

References

Pranav Anand and Daniel Hardt. 2016. Antecedent selection for sluicing: Structure and content. In *EMNLP*. pages 1234–1243.

Pranav Anand and Jim McCloskey. 2015. Annotating the implicit content of sluices. In *Proceedings of The 9th Linguistic Annotation Workshop*. Association for Computational Linguistics, Denver, Colorado, USA, pages 178–187. http://www.aclweb.org/anthology/W15-1621.

Austin Baird, Anissa Hamza, and Daniel Hardt. 2018. Classifying Sluice Occurrences in Dialogue. In *LREC*.

Jonathan Baxter. 2000. A model of inductive bias learning. *Journal of Artificial Intelligence Research* 12:149–198.

Konstantinos Bousmalis, George Trigeorgis, Nathan Silberman, Dilip Krishnan, and Dumitru Erhan. 2016. Domain Separation Networks. In *Proceedings of NIPS*.

Rich Caruana. 1993. Multitask learning: a knowledge-based source of inductive bias. In *ICML*.

Ronan Collobert, Jason Weston, Léon Bottou, Michael Karlen, Koray Kavukcuoglu, and Pavel Kuksa. 2011. Natural language processing (almost) from scratch. *The Journal of Machine Learning Research* 12:2493–2537.

Long Duong, Trevor Cohn, Steven Bird, and Paul Cook. 2015. Low Resource Dependency Parsing: Cross-lingual Parameter Sharing in a Neural Network Parser. In *Proceedings of ACL*.

Kazuma Hashimoto, Caiming Xiong, Yoshimasa Tsuruoka, and Richard Socher. 2016. A joint many-task model: Growing a neural network for multiple nlp tasks. *arXiv preprint arXiv:1611.01587* .

Sepp Hochreiter and Jürgen Schmidhuber. 1997. Long short-term memory. *Neural computation* 9(8):1735–1780.

Diederik Kingma and Jimmy Ba. 2014. Adam: A method for stochastic optimization. *arXiv preprint arXiv:1412.6980* .

Sigrid Klerke, Yoav Goldberg, and Anders Søgaard. 2016. Improving sentence compression by learning to predict gaze. *arXiv preprint arXiv:1604.03357* .

Kevin Knight and Daniel Marcu. 2000. Statistics-based summarization-step one: Sentence compression. *AAAI/IAAI* 2000:703–710.

David Krueger, Tegan Maharaj, János Kramár, Mohammad Pezeshki, Nicolas Ballas, Nan Rosemary Ke, Anirudh Goyal, Yoshua Bengio, Hugo Larochelle, Aaron Courville, et al. 2016. Zoneout: Regularizing rnns by randomly preserving hidden activations. *arXiv preprint arXiv:1606.01305* .

Ishan Misra, Abhinav Shrivastava, Abhinav Gupta, and Martial Hebert. 2016. Cross-Stitch Networks for Multi-Task Learning. In *Proceedings of CVPR*.

Joakim Nivre, Johan Hall, Sandra Kübler, Ryan McDonald, Jens Nilsson, Sebastian Riedel, and Deniz Yuret. 2007. The conll 2007 shared task on dependency parsing. In *Proceedings of the 2007 Joint Conference on Empirical Methods in Natural Language Processing and Computational Natural Language Learning (EMNLP-CoNLL)*.

Jeffrey Pennington, Richard Socher, and Christopher D. Manning. 2014. Glove: Global vectors for word representation. In *Empirical Methods in Natural Language Processing (EMNLP)*. pages 1532–1543.

Andrei A Rusu, Neil C Rabinowitz, Guillaume Desjardins, Hubert Soyer, James Kirkpatrick, Koray Kavukcuoglu, Razvan Pascanu, and Raia Hadsell. 2016. Progressive neural networks. *arXiv preprint arXiv:1606.04671* .

Anders Søgaard and Yoav Goldberg. 2016. Deep multitask learning with low level tasks superviser at lower layers. In *ACL*.

Jörg Tiedemann. 2009. News from OPUS - A collection of multilingual parallel corpora with tools and interfaces. In N. Nicolov, K. Bontcheva, G. Angelova, and R. Mitkov, editors, *Recent Advances in Natural Language Processing*, John Benjamins, Amsterdam/Philadelphia, Borovets, Bulgaria, volume V, pages 237–248.

Erik F Tjong Kim Sang and Sabine Buchholz. 2000. Introduction to the conll-2000 shared task: Chunking. In *Proceedings of the 2nd workshop on Learning language in logic and the 4th conference on Computational natural language learning-Volume 7*. Association for Computational Linguistics, pages 127–132.

David Wolpert. 1992. Stacked generalization. *Neural Networks* 5:241–259.

The word analogy testing caveat

Natalie Schluter
Department of Computer Science
IT University of Copenhagen
Copenhagen, Denmark
natschluter@itu.dk

Abstract

There are some important problems in the evaluation of word embeddings using standard word analogy tests. In particular, in virtue of the assumptions made by systems generating the embeddings, these remain tests over randomness. We show that even supposing there were such word analogy regularities that should be detected in the word embeddings obtained via unsupervised means, standard word analogy test implementation practices provide distorted or contrived results. We raise concerns regarding the use of Principal Component Analysis to 2 or 3 dimensions as a provision of visual evidence for the existence of word analogy relations in embeddings. Finally, we propose some solutions to these problems.

1 Introduction

Continuous dense representations of words, or *word embeddings*, are d-dimensional vectors obtained from raw unannotated text. As weight vectors, they provide, given some model, predictions of either (1) some context of a word, or (2) a word given its context. The word embeddings are meant to reflect distributional structure as a proxy to semantics and syntax à la Harris (Harris, 1954). A natural and desirable effect of such context driven learning of word embeddings is distributional similarity, whereby words that are similar to each other will tend to group together in the target hyperspace. Thus *Frenchman*, *Spaniard*, and *Dane* should group together, as should *loves*, *likes*, and *admires*, or *French*, *Spanish* and *Danish*, as respectively "a set of words for humans from specific countries", "a set of present tense transitive verbs denoting fondness", and "a set of languages".

By employing a transfer learning approach with the use of word embeddings in the place of one-hot word feature vectors, word embeddings obtained in this way have been shown to both simplify and improve the performance of systems across a wide range of NLP tasks. Moreover, word embeddings trained this way and used as initial word representations are now commonly understood to improve the learning process in neural network based systems across the same array of NLP tasks.

There has been some progress in understanding why these representations work so well and a number of simple tasks developed to evaluate them independently such as (1) word similarity tests, (2) synonym selection tests, and (3) word analogy tests, in addition to a variety of possible downstream system tests. That the distributional representations of words should reflect semantic similarity (i.e., as tested by (1) and (2)) is inherent in the definition of the word embedding learning task. However that similar *relations* between words should be described by word embeddings obtained this way is not straightforward. There are also standard engineering practices in analogy evaluations that would prevent accurate analogy testing even if it were applicable.

In this paper, we hope to survey some main problems concerning the word analogy test as it is currently being calculated, in three separate directions:

1. **Theoretical assumption misalignment:** A purely distributional hypothesis misaligns with testing for analogy relations.

2. **Poor conventional engineering choices:**

   (a) Word embeddings are normalised and therefore distorted before testing.

   (b) Premise vectors are excluded before prediction.

3. **Problematic visual evidence:** Visualisations

Proceedings of NAACL-HLT 2018, pages 242–246
New Orleans, Louisiana, June 1 - 6, 2018. ©2018 Association for Computational Linguistics

based on the output of Principal Component Analysis (PCA) are misleading.

2   The word analogy tests and associated benchmarking data

The **word analogy assumption**, introduced by Mikolov et al. (2013b), elaborated with more precision by Levy and Goldberg (2014) and adapted partially from Jurgens et al. (2012) goes as follows. Suppose we have representations for two pairs of words

$$(\mathbf{a_1}, \mathbf{b_1}), (\mathbf{a_2}, \mathbf{b_2}) \tag{1}$$

having an analogous syntactic or semantic relation: $\mathbf{a_1}$ is to $\mathbf{b_1}$ what $\mathbf{a_2}$ is to $\mathbf{b_2}$. By the word analogy assumption, this analogous relation should be represented in terms of some optimal vector $\mathbf{r}$:

$$\mathbf{r} \approx \mathbf{a_1} - \mathbf{b_1} \approx \mathbf{a_2} - \mathbf{b_2} \tag{2}$$

The typical example used is

$$\mathbf{r} \approx king - man \approx queen - woman$$

and r approximately represents something like "is a royal version of". This can be rewritten as

$$king - man + woman \approx queen. \tag{3}$$

From this latter equation, the first standard word analogy test arises.

The prediction test and its dataset.   In the prediction test, for the pairs of words in (1), evaluation proceeds by using the word analogy assumption

$$\mathbf{a_1} - \mathbf{b_1} + \mathbf{b_2} \approx \mathbf{a_2} \tag{4}$$

by means of showing that the left side of this equation (consisting of **premise vectors**) predicts–that is, it is closer to–the word represented by $\mathbf{a_2}$ (the **gold vector**) than to any other word in the vocabulary, according to some distance metric, which is generally accepted to be cosine similarity. The micro-averaged accuracy is then reported.

The test data for the prediction test consists of the MSR and GOOGLE datasets. The MSR dataset has 8000 analogy questions of morpho-syntactic nature and concerning adjectives, nouns and verbs.[1]   The GOOGLE dataset consists of 19,544 analogy questions, across 14 relation types, half of which are semantic relations and half morpho-syntactic.

The ranking test and its dataset.   In the ranking test, a list of word pairs is given that hold the same relation, but to differing degrees. The task is to rank these pairs by order of strength of the relation. Using the prediction test, this task requires the system to calculate the prediction for each pair of words $(\mathbf{a}, \mathbf{b})$ with respect the rest of the pairs on the list, and average these scores for $(\mathbf{a}, \mathbf{b})$. Pairs are ranked according to this average. The larger the average, the more typical a pair is predicted to be of the relation in question. Rankings are compared with a gold ranking by computing the Spearman's correlation rank coefficient.

The SEMEVAL 2012 Task 2 dataset is the standard word analogy ranking test test. It contains lists of pairs for 79 semantic relations.[2]

Implementation considerations.   In our testing, out-of-vocabulary words were given the the component-wise average word embedding. It is important to note that in *all* test suites (also for those developed within embedding learning systems), we have found two conventional engineering choices: (1) normalisation of all word embeddings before testing, and (2) exclusion of the possibility to predict any premise vectors. We discuss these and other issues in the following section.

3   Problems with word analogy tests and empirical results

We identify three types of causes for concern when applying analogy testing, having to do with (1) a misalignment of assumptions in generating and testing word embeddings, (2) conventional engineering choices, and (3) problematic visual evidence derived from PCA for data projection to two dimensions.

For reasons of reproducibility, we downloaded and directly used all dimensionalities of GloVe pretrained word embeddings generated over a 2014 Wikpedia dump and the Gigaword corpus, combined for a 6 billion token corpus (Pennington et al., 2014).[3]   In the tests, embeddings for unknown words are replaced by the mean vectors. All tests are made using a version of a freely available embedding benchmarking software that we have extended for the purposes of this paper.[4]

---

[1] http://research.microsoft.com/en-us/um/people/gzweig/Pubs/myz_naacl13_test_set.tgz

[2] https://sites.google.com/site/semeval2012task2/

[3] Available at http://nlp.stanford.edu/projects/glove/

[4] https://github.com/natschluter/

3.1 Misalignment of assumptions

To date, methods for generating monolingual word embeddings purely from raw text, which make no use of hand-crafted or other lexical resources, nor any system of enrichment of the text, like parsers, POS-taggers or otherwise, have been based only on the distributional hypothesis: that words can be described sufficiently in terms of their distribution in language. Systems generating word embeddings in this manner use their generated representations to predict word contexts, or vice versa. So it is plausible that words that share much contextual information, and therefore much distributional information, will share similar representations and naturally group together in their hyperspace.

Supposing that such a word embedding generation system groups together words for humans from specific countries, like *Frenchman*, *Spaniard*, and *Dane*. We assume the same for the words *French*, *Spanish*, and *Danish*. While the system has probably successfully represented the distributional character of the words by grouping each set together, there is no reason why within each individual group, *Danish* and *Dane*'s relative positions should be similar to that of both pairs (*Spanish*, *Spain*) and (*French*, *Frenchman*). The assumption of distributional similarity does not align with the word analogy assumption.

In the extreme, we could theoretically have the pair (*Danish*, *Dane*)'s relative position most similar to that of the shuffled pairs (*French*, *Spaniard*) and (*Spanish*, *Frenchman*) and maintain identical word similarity scores on average. Indeed, one could shuffle the vector representations of all the words considered to be synonymous from the similarity benchmarking dataset; this would maintain precisely the same similarity score, using a cosine similarity metric.[5] Let $\pi : V \to V$ be a permutation of word vectors such that similar word remain close in the space. In particular, let's suppose that π shuffles the vectors of all nationalities, like *Dane* and *Frenchman*, but maintains the same language vectors like *Danish* and *French*. The average of similarities remains the same, as all terms appear-

ing in the sum in (5) also appear in (6):

$$\frac{1}{n(n-1)/2} \sum_{\substack{i<j \\ i,j \in [n]}} \cos(\mathbf{a_i}, \mathbf{a_j}) \qquad (5)$$

$$= \frac{1}{n(n-1)/2} \sum_{\substack{i<j \\ i,j \in [n]}} \cos(\pi(\mathbf{a_i}), \pi(\mathbf{a_j})) \qquad (6)$$

However, the word analogy assumption is now most certainly broken: suppose that π permutes only two vectors, $\mathbf{a_2}$ and $\mathbf{a_3}$ and leaves all other vectors as is:

$$\mathbf{a_1} - \mathbf{b_1} + \mathbf{b_2} = \pi(\mathbf{a_2}) = \mathbf{a_3} \neq \mathbf{a_2}.$$

3.2 Conventional engineering choices

There are two conventional practices in evaluating word embeddings that we aim to show are problematic: normalisation and the exclusion of premise vectors in prediction.

Distortion by normalisation. It is common practice to normalise word embeddings before they are used, and in the case of word analogies, before they are tested. Unfortunately, this practice distorts the original spread of the word embeddings, which greatly effects testing for word analogies. In Table 1 we list the mean and variance of the norms of GloVe word vectors. We notice that on average the norm of the vectors is far from length 1, and the variance is so small that a large majority of vectors have length larger than 1. The word embedding learner was originally free to and would generally make use of a much larger portion of the hyperspace to discriminate based on word distribution.

d	mean	variance
50	4.475	0.744
100	3.977	0.847
300	4.966	1.471

Table 1: Spread of norms of GloVe word vectors across dimensions d.

We observe in Table 2 that scores change (and in fact drop) significantly when vectors are not normalised, for the GOOGLE and MSR tests. This suggests additionally that much of the success in analogy testing was misleading, resulting generally from collapsing the vocabulary of vectors onto

---

[5] This also works for a euclidean distance similarity metric.

the unit hypersphere. Any possible use of meaningful collinearity by the word-embedding model is lost after normalisation.

Exclusion of premise vectors from predictions. Another conventional practice in evaluating word embeddings by word analogy is the exclusion of premise vectors from the possibility of being predicted. As we can see in the results in Table 2, between 15-60% of the time, the system predicts a premise vector on the GOOGLE analogy data, for example. Upon closer analysis, we find that 99% of these latter prediction mis-hits are with the premise in the gold vector's own word pair; this means that words a_1, b_1 in word pairs are often so close together that they cancel each other out: $a_1 - b_1 \approx 0$. If the data truly scored high on the word analogy test, it would not need to exclude premise vectors from the possibility of prediction.

3.3 PCA to two dimensions from dimension d can be misleading

Results of the word analogy test are often accompanied by a visualisation of projected word vectors to the two dimensional plane using Principal Component Analysis (PCA) ((Mikolov et al., 2013a; Sun et al., 2015) for example). Though these are generally not claimed to be part of the evaluation, the visualisations are included to convince the reader of the quality of the word embeddings with respect to word analogies–the line connecting a_1 and b_1 being approximately parallel to the line through a_2 and b_2 whenever word analogy recovery is optimal (as in Equation (2)).

PCA is an unsupervised approach for finding the "core" features from the data, supposing a normal distribution feature-wise. For two dimensions, the objective is to find the two directions e_1, e_2 along which the data has the highest variability, and model the instances $x_k, k \in [N]$ by the respective distances a_{k1}, a_{k2} between the point x_k and lines through the mean vector, $\mathbf{m} = \frac{1}{n} \sum_{k=1}^{n} \mathbf{x_k}$ in the respective directions e_1 and e_2.

There are two main problems with this sort of evidence. Firstly, even if word analogies as described by Equation (4) existed in the data, it would only be a matter of chance that applying PCA to the entire dataset would recover even slightly these parallel (analogous) word relations visually. That is, there is no reason to believe that the line through the words in a pair is not almost perpendicular to the surface they are mapped to.

Secondly, if one is tempted to apply PCA only to the set of vectors corresponding to the two word groups in question, it is rather straightforward to produce the desired visualisation, so long as the two groups are clustered together. PCA should derive a surface that cuts through these two groups. So unless there is absolutely no clustering of similarly behaving words, PCA will give the evidence of word analogies one desires.

d			GOOGLE	MSR	SEMEVAL
50			46.24	35.56	13.99
	H		30.43	20.36	13.99
	D		20.58	10.01	14.76
	H,D		17.96	6.9	14.76
100			63.19	55.09	16.53
	H		33.47	24.87	16.53
	D		49.92	35.58	17.12
	H,D		34.44	18.06	17.12
300			71.85	61.64	17.0
	H		19.42	11.85	17.0
	D		65.32	51.58	16.91
	H,D		25.94	12.84	16.91

Table 2: Results of the word analogy tests, also without distortion through normalisation (D), without removing premise vectors from the set of possible gold vectors (H), and without either (H,D).

4 Concluding remarks

We have shown that there are serious problems with the appropriateness and informativeness of word analogy tests in current distributional word embedding evaluation. The first problem that should be addressed is the appropriateness. If word analogies are considered important enough, then word embedding generation systems should start to reflect this assumption. Until then, word analogies, as they are defined here, happen by rather chance. Once this assumption is built into systems, we still should put into question various details of the tests. Is a one-hit accuracy sufficiently informing on success in word analogy, or do we need a softer measure from for example the ranking world? These questions remain open for future work.

References

Zellig Harris. 1954. Distributional structure. *Word* 10:146–162.

David Jurgens, Saif Mohammad, Peter D. Turney, and Keith J. Holyoak. 2012. Semeval-2012 task 2: Measuring degrees of relational similarity. In *Proceedings of the 6th International Workshop on Semantic Evaluation, SemEval@NAACL-HLT 2012*. Montréal, Canada, pages 356–364.

Omer Levy and Yoav Goldberg. 2014. Linguistic regularities in sparse and explicit word representations. In *Proc of Coling*. pages 171–180.

Tomas Mikolov, Ilya Sutskever, Kai Chen, Greg S Corrado, and Jeff Dean. 2013a. Distributed representations of words and phrases and their compositionality. In *Advances in Neural Information Processing Systems 26*, pages 3111–3119.

Tomas Mikolov, Yih Wen-tau, and Geoffrey Zweig. 2013b. Linguistic regularities in continuous space word representations. In *Proc of NAACL-HLT*. Atlanta, Georgia, pages 746–751.

Jeffrey Pennington, Richard Socher, and Christopher Manning. 2014. Glove: Global vectors for word representation. In *Proceedings of the 2014 Conference on Empirical Methods in Natural Language Processing (EMNLP)*. Doha, Qatar.

Fei Sun, Jiafeng Guo, Yanyan Lan, Jun Xu, and Xueqi Cheng. 2015. Learning word representations by jointly modeling syntagmatic and paradigmatic relations. In *Proceedings of the 53rd Annual Meeting of the Association for Computational Linguistics and the 7th International Joint Conference on Natural Language Processing*. Beijing, China, pages 136–145.

Transition-based Chinese AMR Parsing

Chuan Wang[1] **Bin Li**[2] **Nianwen Xue**[1]
[1]Michtom School of Computer Science
Brandeis University
{cwang24;xuen}@brandeis.edu
[2]School of Chinese Language and Literature
Nanjing Normal University
libin.njnu@gmail.com

Abstract

This paper presents the first AMR parser built on the Chinese AMR bank. By applying a transition-based AMR parsing framework to Chinese, we first investigate how well the transitions first designed for English AMR parsing generalize to Chinese and provide a comparative analysis between the transitions for English and Chinese. We then perform a detailed error analysis to identify the major challenges in Chinese AMR parsing that we hope will inform future research in this area.

1 Introduction

Abstract Meaning Representation (AMR) (Banarescu et al., 2013) is a semantic representation where the meaning of a sentence is encoded as a rooted, directed and acyclic graph. AMR parsing has received a significant amount of attention in the NLP research community. Since the release of the AMR bank a number of AMR parsers have been developed in recent years (Flanigan et al., 2014; Wang et al., 2015b; Artzi et al., 2015; Pust et al., 2015; Peng et al., 2015; Zhou et al., 2016; Goodman et al., 2016). The initial benefit of AMR parsing has also been demonstrated in various downstream applications such as Information Extraction (Pan et al., 2015; Huang et al., 2016), Machine Comprehension (Sachan and Xing, 2016), and Natural Language Generation (Flanigan et al., 2016; Butler, 2016).

In this paper, we present the first AMR parser built using the Chinese AMR Bank (Li et al., 2016). We adopt the transition-based parsing framework first proposed for English (Wang et al., 2015b, 2016), where AMR parsing is modeled as a dependency tree to AMR graph transformation using a set of linguistically motivated actions. We briefly describe the Chinese AMR Bank in Section 2, present the transition-based Chinese AMR

parsing model in Section 3, report and analyze experimental results in Section 4, and conclude our paper in Section 5.

2 The Chinese AMR Bank

In our experiment, we use a pre-release version of the Chinese AMR Bank (Li et al., 2016)[1] consisting of 10,149 sentences extracted from the Chinese Treebank (CTB) 8.0 (Xue et al., 2005) [2], which mainly consists of Chinese texts of web logs and discussion forums. The average sentence length is 22.43 words.

Similar to English, the Chinese AMRs are also represented as rooted, directed and acyclic graphs that share the *abstract* concepts and relations used in the English AMR Bank. The sense-disambiguated predicates are drawn from the frame files developed for the Chinese Propbank(Xue and Palmer, 2009), just as the sense-disambiguated predicates in the AMR Bank are drawn from the Propbank (Palmer et al., 2005). About 47% of the 10,149 sentences have reentrancies, meaning that they have a graph structure that cannot be represented with a tree representation.

3 Transition-based AMR Parsing

In a transition-based AMR parsing framework an input sentence is first parsed into a dependency tree and then transformed into an AMR graph via a series of transitions formulated as "actions". The full set of actions are summarized in Table 1, and we refer the reader to (Wang et al., 2015b,a) for details regarding the training procedure and decoding algorithm. Note that NEXT-EDGE-l_r and NEXT-NODE-l_c are action to label the current node

---

[1]http://www.cs.brandeis.edu/~clp/camr/camr.html.
[2]Available at https://catalog.ldc.upenn.edu/LDC2013T21.

Proceedings of NAACL-HLT 2018, pages 247–252
New Orleans, Louisiana, June 1 - 6, 2018. ©2018 Association for Computational Linguistics

or current edge, where the candidate label is defined as a parameter to the action. The INFER-l_c (ifr) is devised to predict *abstract concepts* that are not aligned to any specific word in a sentence. The rest of the actions are responsible for transforming the structure of the partial graph.

4   Experiments

In this section, we present experiments designed to probe the behavior of our Chinese AMR parser, and where appropriate, compare it to its English counterpart. We also devise several ablation tests to further investigate the errors produced by our Chinese AMR parser to gain insight that can be used to guide future research.

4.1   Experiment Settings

We use the 10,149 sentences from the Chinese AMR Bank and split the data according to their original CTB8.0 document IDs, where articles 5061-5558 are used as the training set, articles 5000-5030 are used as the development set and articles 5031-5060 are used as the test set. The train/development/test ratio in this dataset is 7608/1264/1277. As the data are drawn from the Chinese Treebank where words are manually segmented, we will simply use the gold segmentation in our experiments. We then process the whole Chinese dataset using the Stanford CoreNLP (Manning et al., 2014) toolkit to get the POS and Named Entity tags. To get the dependency parse for the Chinese data, we use the transition-based constituent parser in (Wang and Xue, 2014) to first parse the Chinese sentences into constituent trees, which are then transformed into dependency trees using the converter in the Stanford CoreNLP toolkit. Note that this Chinese constituent parser also uses the Chinese Treebank 8.0 to train its model. To avoid training on the parser on AMR test set, we train the constituent parser using a 10-fold cross-validation with each fold parsed using a model trained on the other 9 folds. In order to compare results between Chinese and English, we also train an English AMR parsing model on the LDC2015E86 dataset used in SemEval 2016 Task 8 with the standard split 16833/1368/1371 and the English AMR parser, CAMR, is utilized to train the English model. All the AMR parsing results are evaluated by the

Smatch toolkit (Cai and Knight, 2013)[3].

4.2   Action Distribution

Before we train the parser, we first perform a quantitative comparison of the actions that are invoked in English and Chinese AMR parsing. We run the *oracle* function separately on the training data of both languages and record the distribution of the actions invoked, as shown in Figure 1. Note that without any modification of the action set designed for English, the "pseudo-gold" graphs generated by the *oracle* function have reached F1-score of 0.99 when evaluated against gold Chinese AMR graphs, and this indicates that the action set is readily generalizable to Chinese. The histograms in Figure 1 shows the distribution of action types for both English and Chinese. We leave out the NEXT-EDGE-l_r and NEXT-NODE-l_c actions in the histogram as they do not trigger structural transformations like other actions, and thus are not our point of interest.

In Figure 1 we can see that there is a large difference in action distribution between Chinese and English. First of all, there are a lot fewer DELETE-NODE actions applied in the dependency-to-AMR transformation process for Chinese, which indicates that in Chinese data there is a smaller percentage of "stop words" that do not encode semantic information. Also, in the Chinese data, more INFER-l_c actions are invoked than in English, implying that Chinese AMRs use more abstract concepts that don't align to any word token.

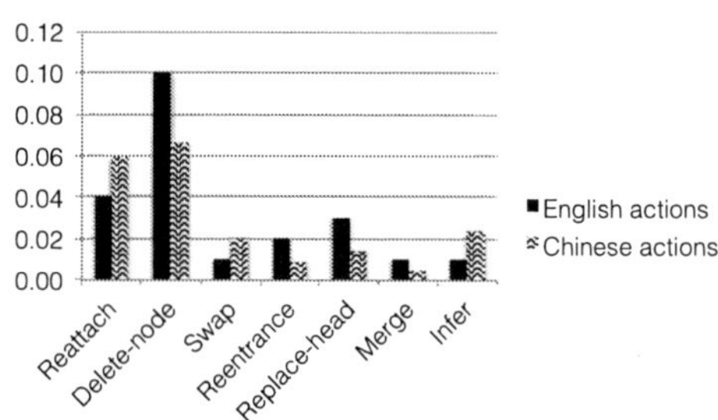

Figure 1: Action distribution on English and Chinese

To further investigate the different linguistic patterns associated with each action in the two languages, for each action type t, we randomly sample 100 sentences in which action t is invoked for both English and Chinese. We then conduct

<hr>

[3]http://alt.qcri.org/semeval2016/task8/data/uploads/smatch-v2.0.2.tar.gz

Action	Description
NEXT-EDGE-l_r (ned)	Assign the current edge with edge label l_r and go to next edge.
SWAP-l_r (sw)	Swap the current edge, make the current dependent as the new head, and assign edge label l_r to the swapped edge.
REATTACH$_k$-l_r (reat)	Reattach current dependent to node k and assign label l_r to new edge.
REPLACE-HEAD (rph)	Replace current head node with current dependent node.
REENTRANCE$_k$-l_r (reen)	Add another head node k to current dependent and assign label l_r to edge between k and current dependent.
MERGE (mrg)	Merge two nodes connected by the edge into one node.
NEXT-NODE-l_c (nnd)	Assign the current node with concept label l_c and go to next node.
DELETE-NODE (dnd)	Delete the current node and all edges associated with current node.
INFER-l_c (ifr)	Insert concept with label l_c between current node and its parent.

Table 1: Action set in Chinese AMR Parsing, where k,l_r,l_c are parameters of the action.

a detailed analysis of the sampled data. We find that MERGE is mostly responsible for combining spans of words to form a named entity in English parsing. However, in Chinese AMR parsing, in addition to forming named entity concepts, MERGE also handles a large portion of split verb constructions. A "split verb" is a linguistic phenomenon in Chinese in which the characters in a multi-character verb are split into two discontinuous parts by other lexical items. For example, in (1), the sentence has a split verb "帮 /help ⋯ 忙/business" that are merged by the MERGE action to form the AMR concept "帮忙-01", as shown in Figure 2.

In the cases of SWAP and REPLACE-HEAD, we notice that the linguistic patterns associated with the two actions are mostly consistent across the two languages. For example, as we already mentioned, the SWAP action is used to handle the structural divergence between the dependency tree and AMR graph of coordination constructions. This holds for both English and Chinese. Similarly, the REPLACE-HEAD action is designed to resolve the structural divergence between the dependency tree and AMR graph of propositional phrases. Based on our analysis of sampled data, the REPLACE-HEAD action resolves the same dependency-AMR divergence in Chinese AMR parsing.

(1) 他^1 帮^2　了^3　我^4 很^5 大^6 的^7 忙^8。
He　helped PAST me　very big DE business
"He helped me a lot."

Being able to identify the linguistic environment for each action helps us understand what the parser actually does when actions are applied. More importantly, making the relation between the

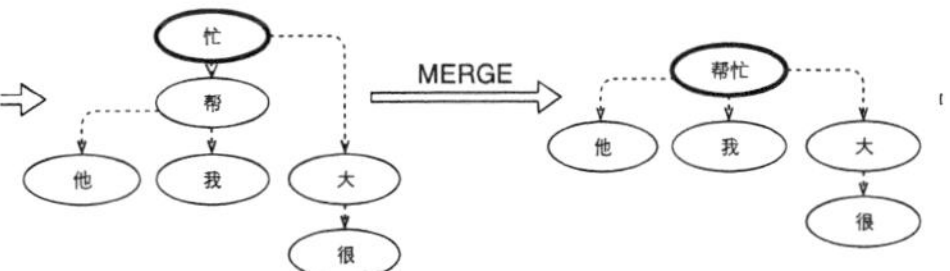

Figure 2: AMR for Example (1)

linguistic structure and the parser actions transparent is crucial to our ability to devise effective features for the parsing model which directly impacts the performance of the parser. For example, knowing that the MERGE action is responsible for producing concepts from split verb constructions helps us understand the need to design character-level features in addition to features targeting named entities.

4.3 Main results for Chinese AMR Parsing

Using the configuration in Section 4.1, we train our Chinese AMR parser with 5 iterations and report results on both the development and test set.

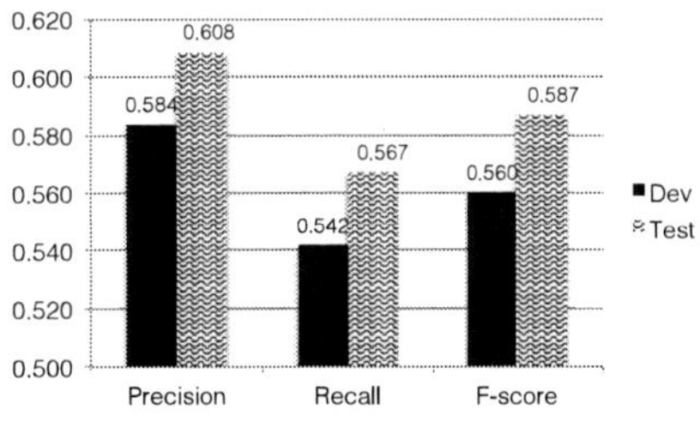

Figure 3: Parsing performance on the development and test set

Figure 3 presents the parsing performance on the development and test set in terms of the

Smatch score. Compared with the state of the art in English AMR parsing, which is in the high 60 percentage points (May, 2016), this initial parsing performance here is very strong, considering the model is trained on a smaller training set. The Chinese AMR parsing model also does not benefit from the more extensive feature engineering that has been done for English AMR parsing. For example, the English AMR parser, CAMR, uses semantic roles and coreference features that are not available to the Chinese AMR parser. The other important factor is that most of the Chinese linguistic analyzers (dependency parsers, named entity taggers, etc.) have a lower accuracy than their English counterparts, and when used as preprocessors for the AMR parser, could further disadvantage the Chinese AMR parsing model.

4.4 Fine-grained Error Analysis

So far, all of our experiments are evaluated using the Smatch score, where only precision, recall and F-score are reported based on the overall performance of the parser. To gain more insights, we further break down the Smatch score and report the performance for each component using the evaluation tool from Damonte et al. (2017). The evaluation tool examines different aspects of the AMR parsing result through different ablation tests that we summarize as follows. The detailed description of the ablation test can be found in Damonte et al. (2017).

- **Unlabeled**. Smatch score obtained by ignoring the edge labels (relation).

- **No WSD**. Smatch score without the word sense disambiguation.

- **NP (Noun Phrase)-only**. Only evaluating the noun phrases.

- **Reentrancy**. Only evaluating reentrancy edges.

- **Concepts**. Evaluating the node labels (concept).

- **Named Ent**. Named entity evaluation.

- **Negation**. Evaluation on negation detection.

- **SRL**. Semantic Role Labeling, which only evaluates triples in AMR that have relations starting with *:ARG*.

Note that we simply ignore the wikification evaluation as Chinese AMRs do not have wikification annotation at the current stage.

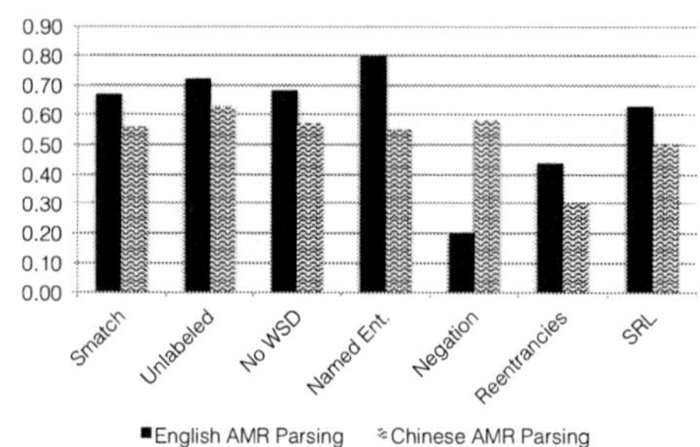

Figure 4: Fine-grained AMR parsing evaluation on dev

Figure 4 shows the performance breakdown on the Chinese and English development sets, where we can see that the overall performance gap between English and Chinese is around 0.11 Smatch score and there is a similar gap for **Unlabeled**, **No WSD** and **SRL** evaluations. However, the largest performance comes from **Named Ent.**, where the F-score for Chinese is 0.55 which is 0.25 lower than English. This indicates that named entity is one of the bottlenecks in Chinese AMR parsing. This indicates that improving named entity recognition, either as a preprocessing step or as an integral part of the parsing model, is crucial to Chinese AMR parsing.

5 Conclusion

We present the first Chinese AMR parser trained on the Chinese AMR Bank. We show that a transition-based AMR parsing framework first proposed for English is general enough to handle the linguistic phenomena in Chinese and has produced a strong baseline that future research can build on. In addition, we perform a detailed comparative analysis of the transition distributions for English and Chinese as well as errors in Chinese AMR parsing that we hope will inform future Chinese AMR parsing research.

Acknowledgements

We want to thank the anonymous reviewers for their suggestions. We also want to thank Yuan Wen, Lijun Bu and Li Song on their contributions to the creation of the Chinese AMR corpus. The second author would also like to acknowledge support by the National Science Foundation of China (61772278, 61472191).

References

Yoav Artzi, Kenton Lee, and Luke Zettlemoyer. 2015. Broad-coverage CCG semantic parsing with AMR. In *Proceedings of the 2015 Conference on Empirical Methods in Natural Language Processing*, pages 1699–1710, Lisbon, Portugal. Association for Computational Linguistics.

Laura Banarescu, Claire Bonial, Shu Cai, Madalina Georgescu, Kira Griffitt, Ulf Hermjakob, Kevin Knight, Philipp Koehn, Martha Palmer, and Nathan Schneider. 2013. Abstract meaning representation for sembanking. In *Proceedings of the 7th Linguistic Annotation Workshop and Interoperability with Discourse*, pages 178–186, Sofia, Bulgaria.

Alastair Butler. 2016. Deterministic natural language generation from meaning representations for machine translation. In *Proceedings of the 2nd Workshop on Semantics-Driven Machine Translation (SedMT 2016)*, pages 1–9. Association for Computational Linguistics.

Shu Cai and Kevin Knight. 2013. Smatch: an evaluation metric for semantic feature structures. In *Proceedings of the 51st Annual Meeting of the Association for Computational Linguistics (Volume 2: Short Papers)*, pages 748–752. Association for Computational Linguistics.

Marco Damonte, Shay B. Cohen, and Giorgio Satta. 2017. An incremental parser for abstract meaning representation. In *Proceedings of the 15th Conference of the European Chapter of the Association for Computational Linguistics: Volume 1, Long Papers*, pages 536–546, Valencia, Spain. Association for Computational Linguistics.

Jeffrey Flanigan, Chris Dyer, A. Noah Smith, and Jaime Carbonell. 2016. Generation from Abstract Meaning Representation using tree transducers. In *Proceedings of the 2016 Conference of the North American Chapter of the Association for Computational Linguistics: Human Language Technologies*, pages 731–739. Association for Computational Linguistics.

Jeffrey Flanigan, Sam Thomson, Jaime Carbonell, Chris Dyer, and Noah A. Smith. 2014. A Discriminative Graph-Based Parser for the Abstract Meaning Representation. In *Proceedings of the 52nd Annual Meeting of the Association for Computational Linguistics (Volume 1: Long Papers)*, pages 1426–1436, Baltimore, Maryland. Association for Computational Linguistics.

James Goodman, Andreas Vlachos, and Jason Naradowsky. 2016. Noise reduction and targeted exploration in imitation learning for abstract meaning representation parsing. In *Proceedings of the 54th Annual Meeting of the Association for Computational Linguistics (Volume 1: Long Papers)*, pages 1–11. Association for Computational Linguistics.

Lifu Huang, Taylor Cassidy, Xiaocheng Feng, Heng Ji, R. Clare Voss, Jiawei Han, and Avirup Sil. 2016. Liberal event extraction and event schema induction. In *Proceedings of the 54th Annual Meeting of the Association for Computational Linguistics (Volume 1: Long Papers)*, pages 258–268. Association for Computational Linguistics.

Bin Li, Yuan Wen, Q. U. Weiguang, Lijun Bu, and Nianwen Xue. 2016. Annotating the little prince with chinese amrs. In *Linguistic Annotation Workshop Held in Conjunction with ACL*, pages 7–15.

Christopher Manning, Mihai Surdeanu, John Bauer, Jenny Finkel, Steven Bethard, and David McClosky. 2014. The stanford corenlp natural language processing toolkit. In *Proceedings of 52nd Annual Meeting of the Association for Computational Linguistics: System Demonstrations*, pages 55–60, Baltimore, Maryland. Association for Computational Linguistics.

Jonathan May. 2016. Semeval-2016 task 8: Meaning representation parsing. *Proceedings of SemEval*, pages 1063–1073.

Martha Palmer, Daniel Gildea, and Paul Kingsbury. 2005. The proposition bank: An annotated corpus of semantic roles. *Computational Linguistics*, 31(1):71–105.

Xiaoman Pan, Taylor Cassidy, Ulf Hermjakob, Heng Ji, and Kevin Knight. 2015. Unsupervised entity linking with abstract meaning representation. In *Proceedings of the 2015 Conference of the North American Chapter of the Association for Computational Linguistics: Human Language Technologies*, pages 1130–1139.

Xiaochang Peng, Linfeng Song, and Daniel Gildea. 2015. A synchronous hyperedge replacement grammar based approach for AMR parsing. In *Proceedings of the Nineteenth Conference on Computational Natural Language Learning*.

Michael Pust, Ulf Hermjakob, Kevin Knight, Daniel Marcu, and Jonathan May. 2015. Parsing English into abstract meaning representation using syntax-based machine translation. In *Proceedings of the 2015 Conference on Empirical Methods in Natural Language Processing*, pages 1143–1154, Lisbon, Portugal. Association for Computational Linguistics.

Mrinmaya Sachan and Eric Xing. 2016. Machine comprehension using rich semantic representations. In *Proceedings of the 54th Annual Meeting of the Association for Computational Linguistics (Volume 2: Short Papers)*, pages 486–492. Association for Computational Linguistics.

Chuan Wang, Sameer Pradhan, Xiaoman Pan, Heng Ji, and Nianwen Xue. 2016. CAMR at semeval-2016 task 8: An extended transition-based AMR parser. In *Proceedings of the 10th International*

Workshop on Semantic Evaluation (SemEval-2016), pages 1173–1178, San Diego, California. Association for Computational Linguistics.

Chuan Wang, Nianwen Xue, and Sameer Pradhan. 2015a. Boosting transition-based AMR parsing with refined actions and auxiliary analyzers. In *Proceedings of the 53rd Annual Meeting of the Association for Computational Linguistics and the 7th International Joint Conference on Natural Language Processing (Short Papers)*, pages 857–862.

Chuan Wang, Nianwen Xue, and Sameer Pradhan. 2015b. A transition-based algorithm for AMR parsing. In *Proceedings of the 2015 Conference of the North American Chapter of the Association for Computational Linguistics: Human Language Technologies*, pages 366–375, Denver, Colorado. Association for Computational Linguistics.

Zhiguo Wang and Nianwen Xue. 2014. Joint pos tagging and transition-based constituent parsing in chinese with non-local features. In *Proceedings of the 52nd Annual Meeting of the Association for Computational Linguistics (Volume 1: Long Papers)*, pages 733–742, Baltimore, Maryland. Association for Computational Linguistics.

Nianwen Xue and Martha Palmer. 2009. Adding semantic roles to the chinese treebank. *Natural Language Engineering*, 15(1):143–172.

Nianwen Xue, Fei Xia, Fudong Chiou, and Martha Palmer. 2005. The penn chinese treebank: Phrase structure annotation of a large corpus. *Natural Language Engineering*, 11(2):207–238.

Junsheng Zhou, Feiyu Xu, Hans Uszkoreit, Weiguang QU, Ran Li, and Yanhui Gu. 2016. AMR Parsing with an Incremental Joint Model. In *Proceedings of the 2016 Conference on Empirical Methods in Natural Language Processing*, pages 680–689, Austin, Texas. Association for Computational Linguistics.

Knowledge-enriched Two-layered Attention Network for Sentiment Analysis

Abhishek Kumar[a], **Daisuke Kawahara**[b], **Sadao Kurohashi**[b]
[a]Indian Institute of Technology Patna, India
[b]Kyoto University, Japan
`{abhishek.ee14}@iitp.ac.in`
`{dk,kuro}@i.kyoto-u.ac.jp`

Abstract

We propose a novel two-layered attention network based on Bidirectional Long Short-Term Memory for sentiment analysis. The novel two-layered attention network takes advantage of the external knowledge bases to improve the sentiment prediction. It uses the Knowledge Graph Embedding generated using the Word-Net. We build our model by combining the two-layered attention network with the supervised model based on Support Vector Regression using a Multilayer Perceptron network for sentiment analysis. We evaluate our model on the benchmark dataset of SemEval 2017 Task 5. Experimental results show that the proposed model surpasses the top system of SemEval 2017 Task 5. The model performs significantly better by improving the state-of-the-art system at SemEval 2017 Task 5 by 1.7 and 3.7 points for sub-tracks 1 and 2 respectively.

1 Introduction

With the rise of microblogging websites, people have access and option to reach to the large crowd using as few words as possible. Microblog and news headlines are one of the common ways to dispense information online. The dynamic nature of these texts can be effectively used in the financial domain to track and predict the stock prices (Goonatilake and Herath, 2007). These can be used by an individual or an organization to make an informed prediction related to any company or stock (Si et al., 2013).

This gives rise to an interesting problem of sentiment analysis in financial domain. A study indicates that sentiment analysis of public mood derived from Twitter feeds can be used to eventually forecast movements of individual stock prices (Smailović et al., 2014). An efficient system for sentiment analysis is a core component of a company involved in financial stock market price prediction.

Social media texts are prone to word shortening, exaggeration, lack of grammar and appropriate punctuations. Moreover, the word limit constraint forces a user to limit their content and squeeze in their opinion about companies. These inconsistencies make it challenging to solve any natural language processing tasks including sentiment analysis (Khanarian and Alwarez-Melis, 2012).

Bag-of-words and named entities were used by Schumaker and Chen (2009) for predicting stock market. For predicting the explicit and implicit sentiment in the financial text, de Kauter et al. (2015) used a fine-grained sentiment annotation scheme. Kumar et al. (2017) used a classical supervised approach based on Support Vector Regression for sentiment analysis in financial domain. Oliveira et al. (2013) relied on multiple regression models. Akhtar et al. (2017) used an ensemble of four different systems for predicting the sentiment. It used a combination of Long Short-Term Memory (LSTM) (Hochreiter and Schmidhuber, 1997), Gated Recurrent Unit (GRU) (Cho et al., 2014), Convolutional Neural Network (CNN) (Kim, 2014) and Support Vector Regression (SVR) (Smola and Schölkopf, 2004). Yang et al. (2016) used a hierarchical attention network to build the document representation incrementally for document classification.

Our model focuses on interpretability and usage of knowledge bases. Knowledge bases have been recognized important for natural language understanding tasks (Minsky, 1986). Our main contribution is a two-layered attention network which utilizes background knowledge bases to build good word level representation at the primary level. The secondary attention mechanism works on top of the primary layer to build meaningful sentence representations. This provides a good intuitive working insight of the attention network.

Proceedings of NAACL-HLT 2018, pages 253–258
New Orleans, Louisiana, June 1 - 6, 2018. ©2018 Association for Computational Linguistics

2 Proposed Methodology

We propose a two-layered attention network which leverages external knowledge for sentiment analysis. It consists of a bidirectional Long Short-Term Memory (BiLSTM) (Graves et al., 2005) based word encoder, word level attention mechanism for capturing the background knowledge and a sentence level attention mechanism aimed at grasping the context and the important words. The output of the two-layered attention network is then ensembled with the output of the feature based SVR using the Multilayer perceptron based approach described in Akhtar et al. (2017). The overall ensembled system is shown in Figure 2. Each of the components is explained in the following subsections and an overview of the two-layered attention network is depicted in Figure 1.

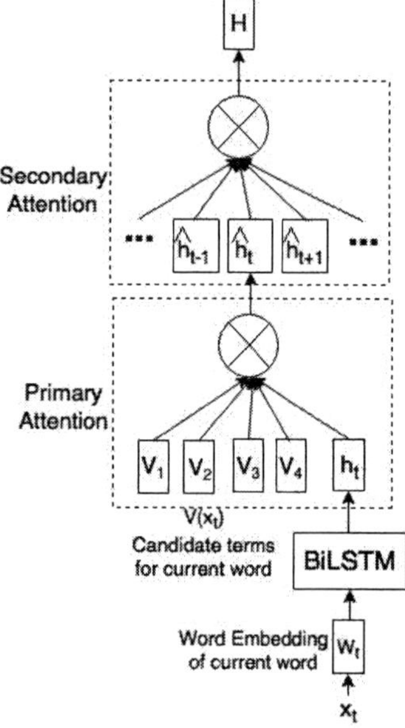

Figure 1: Two-layered attention network

2.1 Two Layered Attention Model

2.1.1 BiLSTM based word encoder

A Long-Short Term Memory (LSTM) is a special kind of Recurrent Neural Network. It handles the long-term dependencies where the current output is dependent on many prior inputs. BiLSTM, in essence, is a combination of two different LSTM - one working in forward and the other working in the backward direction. The contextual information about both past and future helps in determining the current output.

The two hidden states $\overrightarrow{h_t}$ and $\overleftarrow{h_t}$ for forward and backward LSTM are the information about past and future respectively at any time step t. Their concatenation $h_t = [\overrightarrow{h_t}, \overleftarrow{h_t}]$ provides complete information. Each word of the sentence is fed to the network in form of word embeddings which are encoded using the BiLSTM.

2.1.2 Word Level Attention

External knowledge in form of Knowledge Graph Embedding (Yang et al., 2015) or top-k similar words are captured by using the word level attention mechanism. This serves the purpose of primary attention which leverages the external knowledge to get the best representation for each word. At each time step we get $V(x_t)$ relevant terms of each input x_t with v_i being the embedding for each term. (Relevant terms and embeddings are described in next section). The primary attention mechanism assigns an attention coefficient to each of relevant term having index $i \in V(x_t)$:

$$\alpha_{ti} \propto h_t^T W_v v_i \tag{1}$$

where W_v is a parameter matrix to be learned.

$$m_t = \sum_{i \in V(x_t)} \alpha_{ti} v_i \tag{2}$$

$$\hat{h}_t = m_t + h_t \tag{3}$$

The knowledge aware vector (m_t) is calculated as Equation 2, which is concatenated with the hidden state vector to get the final vector representation for each word.

2.1.3 Sentence Level Attention

The secondary attention mechanism captures important words in a sentence with the help of context vectors. Each final vector representing the words is assigned a weight indicating its relative importance with respect to other words. The attention coefficient α_t for each final vector representation is calculated as:

$$\alpha_t \propto \hat{h}_t^T W_s u_s \tag{4}$$

$$H = \sum_t \alpha_t \hat{h}_t \tag{5}$$

where W_s is a parameter matrix and u_s is the context vector to be learned. H is finally fed to a one layer feed forward neural network.

2.2 Relevant Terms and Embeddings

External knowledge can provide explicit information for the model which the training data lacks. This helps the model to make better predictions. We relied on Knowledge Graph Embeddings based on WordNet and Distributional Thesaurus to get relevant terms and their corresponding embeddings for each word in the text.

2.2.1 Knowledge Graph Embedding

WordNet[1] is a lexical database which contains triplets in the form of (subject, relation, object). Both subject and object are synsets in WordNet. Each word in the text serves as the subject of the triplet. The relevant terms for the current word are the triplets having the current word as the subject. We then employ Knowledge Graph Embeddings to learn the representation of the triplet. A 100-dimensional dense vector representation for each subject, relation and object were learned using the DistMult approach (Yang et al., 2015) and concatenated. These served as the relevant embeddings. An example of triplet in WordNet is (*bronze_age*, *part_of*, *prehistory*).

2.2.2 Distributional Thesaurus

Distributional Thesaurus (DT) (Biemann and Riedl, 2013) is an automatically computed word list which ranks words according to their semantic similarity. We use a pre-trained DT to expand a current word. For each current word, top-4 target words are found which are the relevant terms. The relevant embeddings are obtained by using a 300-dimensional pre-trained Word2Vec (Mikolov et al., 2013) and GloVe (Pennington et al., 2014) model. An example of the DT expansion of the word 'touchpad' is *mouse, trackball, joystick* and *trackpad*.

2.3 Feature Based Model - SVR

The following hand-crafted features are extracted and used to train a Support Vector Regression (SVR).

- Tf-Idf: Term frequency-inverse document frequency (Tf-Idf) reflects the importance of each word in a document. We use Tf-Idf score as a feature value for each word.

- Lexicon Features: Sentiment lexicons are an important resource for sentiment analysis. We employ the following lexicons: Bing Liu opinion lexicon (Ding et al., 2008) and MPQA subjectivity

---

lexicon (Wilson et al., 2005), SentiWordNet (Baccianella et al., 2010) and Vader sentiment (Gilbert, 2014). From the above lexicons we extracted the agreement score (Rao and Srivastava, 2012) and the count of the number of occurrences of all positive and negative words in the text.

- Word embedding: We use the 300-dimensional pre-trained Word2Vec and GloVe embedding. The sentence embedding was obtained by concatenating the embedding for all words in the sentence.

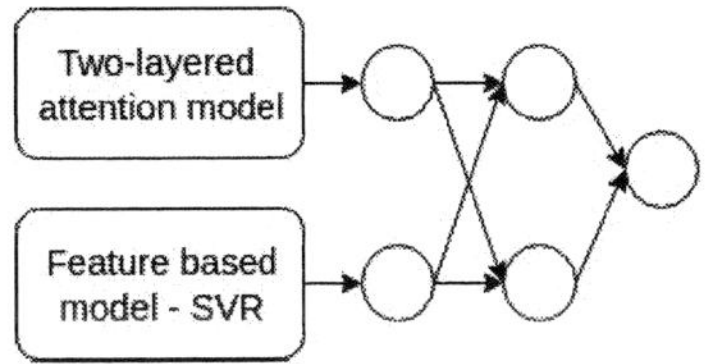

Figure 2: Multilayer perceptron based ensemble

3 Experiments

3.1 Dataset

We evaluate our proposed approach for sentiment analysis on the benchmark datasets of SemEval-2017 shared task 5. The task 'Fine-Grained Sentiment Analysis on Financial Microblogs and News' (Keith Cortis and Davis, 2017) had two sub-tracks. Track 1 - 'Microblog Messages' had 1,700 and 800 train and test instances respectively. Track 2 - 'News Statements & Headlines' had 1,142 and 491 train and test instances respectively. The task was to predict a regression score in between -1 and 1 indicating the sentiment with -1 being negative and +1 being positive.

3.2 Implementation Details

We implement our model using Tensorflow and Scikit-learn on a single GPU. We use a single layer BiLSTM with the two-layered attention mechanism followed by a one layer feed forward neural network. The number of units in each LSTM cell of the BiLSTM was 150. The batch size was 64 and the dropout was 0.3 (Srivastava et al., 2014) with the Adam (Kingma and Ba, 2014) optimizer. The length of context vector in the secondary attention network was 300. For each experiment, we report the average of five random runs. Cosine similarity is a measure of similarity. It represents the degree of agreement between the predicted and gold values. Cosine similarity was used for evaluation as per the guideline.

3.3 Results

We compare our system with the state-of-the-art systems of SemEval 2017 Task 5 and the system proposed by Akhtar et al. (2017). Table 1 shows evaluation of our various models. Team ECNU (Lan et al., 2017) and Fortia-FBK (Mansar et al., 2017) were the top systems for sub-tracks 1 and 2 respectively. Team ECNU and Fortia-FBK reported a cosine similarity of 0.777 and 0.745 for sub-tracks 1 and 2 respectively. Team ECNU employed a number of systems - Support Vector Regression, XGBoost Regressor, AdaBoost Regressor and Bagging Regressor ensembled together. Team Fortia-FBK used a Convolutional Neural Network for this task. The system proposed by Akhtar et al. utilizes an ensemble of LSTM, GRU, CNN and a SVR and reported a cosine similarity of 0.797 and 0.786 for the two sub-tracks.

Our proposed system has a cosine similarity of 0.794 and 0.782 for sub-tracks 1 and 2 respectively. The proposed system performs significantly better than top systems of SemEval 2017 Task 5 for both the tasks. Moreover, the system performs at par with the system proposed by Akhtar et al. with half the number of subsystems involved in the ensemble. This shows that our proposed system is not only robust since it performs for both the task equally well but also powerful as it involves fewer subcomponents while having the same expressive power.

The two-layered attention network alone performs better than the best system of SemEval 2017 Task for both the sub-track. It manages to achieve much higher score than any of the deep learning component utilized by the system proposed by Akhtar et al. (2017) as shown in Table 2. This shows that the two-layered attention network helps to reduce overall model complexity without compromising the performance.

	Models	Microblog	News
Layered Attention Network			
L1	Knowledge Graph Embedding	0.758	0.727
L2	Distributional Thesaurus + GloVe	0.764	0.749
L3	Distributional Thesaurus + Word2Vec	0.779	0.763
Support Vector Regression			
S1	Tf-Idf + Lexicon	0.735	0.720
S2	Tf-Idf + Lexicon + GloVe	0.755	0.753
S3	Tf-Idf + Lexicon + Word2Vec	0.743	0.740
Ensemble			
E1	L3 + S2	0.794	0.782

Table 1: Cosine similarity score of various models on test dataset.

Models	Microblog	News
Single systems		
Mansar et al. (Team Fortia-FBK)	-	0.745
Akhtar et al. - LSTM	0.727	0.720
Akhtar et al. - GRU	0.721	0.721
Akhtar et al. - CNN	0.724	0.722
L3 (proposed)	0.779	0.763
Ensembled systems		
Lan et al. (Team ECNU)	0.777	0.710
Akhtar et al.	0.797	0.786
E1 (proposed)	0.794	0.782

Table 2: Comparison with the state-of-the-art systems.

3.4 Error Analysis

We performed error analysis and observed that the proposed system faces difficulty at times. Following are the situations when the system failed and incorrectly predicted values of the opposite polarity:

• Sometimes the system fails to identify an intensifier. In the example below, 'pure' is used as an intensifier.

Text : Pure garbage stock

Actual: -0.946   **Predicted:** 0.042

• The system fails when it does not have enough real-world information. In the example below, a low share price is a good opportunity to buy for an individual but from a company's point of view, a low share price does not indicate a prosperous situation.

Text : Good opportunity to buy

Actual: -0.771   **Predicted:** 0.260

4 Conclusion

In this paper, we proposed an ensemble of a novel two-layered attention network and a classical supervised Support Vector Regression for sentiment analysis. The two-layered attention network has an intuitive working. It builds the representation hierarchically from word to sentence level utilizing the knowledge bases. The proposed system performed remarkably well on the benchmark datasets of SemEval 2017 Task 5. It outperformed the existing top systems for both the sub-tracks comfortably. Experimental results demonstrate that the system improves the state-of-the-art system of SemEval 2017 Task 5 by 1.7 and 3.7 points for sub-tracks 1 and 2 respectively. This robust system can be effectively used as a submodule in an end-to-end stock market price prediction system.

5   Acknowledgements

This work was supported by the Kyoto University Cooperative Intelligence Short-term Internship Program.

References

Md Shad Akhtar, Abhishek Kumar, Deepanway Ghosal, Asif Ekbal, and Pushpak Bhattacharyya. 2017. A multilayer perceptron based ensemble technique for fine-grained financial sentiment analysis. In *Proceedings of the 2017 Conference on Empirical Methods in Natural Language Processing*, pages 551–557.

Stefano Baccianella, Andrea Esuli, and Fabrizio Sebastiani. 2010. Sentiwordnet 3.0: An enhanced lexical resource for sentiment analysis and opinion mining. In *LREC*, volume 10, pages 2200–2204.

Chris Biemann and Martin Riedl. 2013. Text: now in 2D! A framework for lexical expansion with contextual similarity. *J. Language Modelling*, 1(1):55–95.

KyungHyun Cho, Bart van Merrienboer, Dzmitry Bahdanau, and Yoshua Bengio. 2014. On the Properties of Neural Machine Translation: Encoder-Decoder Approaches. *CoRR*, abs/1409.1259.

Xiaowen Ding, Bing Liu, and Philip S Yu. 2008. A Holistic Lexicon-Based Approach to Opinion Mining. In *Proceedings of the 2008 international conference on web search and data mining*, pages 231–240. ACM.

CJ Hutto Eric Gilbert. 2014. VADER: A Parsimonious Rule-based Model for Sentiment Analysis of Social Media Text. In *Eighth International Conference on Weblogs and Social Media (ICWSM-14). Available at (20/04/16) http://comp. social. gatech. edu/papers/icwsm14. vader. hutto. pdf.*

Rohitha Goonatilake and Susantha Herath. 2007. The Volatility of the Stock Market and News. *International Research Journal of Finance and Economics*, 3(11):53–65.

Alex Graves, Santiago Fernández, and Jürgen Schmidhuber. 2005. Bidirectional lstm networks for improved phoneme classification and recognition. In *Proceedings of the 15th International Conference on Artificial Neural Networks: Formal Models and Their Applications - Volume Part II*, ICANN'05, pages 799–804, Berlin, Heidelberg. Springer-Verlag.

Sepp Hochreiter and Jürgen Schmidhuber. 1997. Long Short-Term Memory. *Neural computation*, 9(8):1735–1780.

Marjan Van de Kauter, Diane Breesch, and Vronique Hoste. 2015. Fine-grained analysis of explicit and implicit sentiment in financial news articles. *Expert Systems with Applications*, 42(11):4999 – 5010.

Tobias Daudert Manuela Huerlimann Manel Zarrouk Keith Cortis, Andre Freitas and Brian Davis. 2017. SemEval-2017 Task 5: Fine-Grained Sentiment Analysis on Financial Microblogs and News. In *Proceedings of the 11th International Workshop on Semantic Evaluations (SemEval-2017)*, pages 519–535, Vancouver, Canada. ACL.

Michael Khanarian and David Alwarez-Melis. 2012. Sentiment classification in twitter: A comparison between domain adaptation and distant supervision. Technical report, CSAIL, MIT. Statistical NLP Final Project.

Yoon Kim. 2014. Convolutional Neural Networks for Sentence Classification. In *Proceedings of the 2014 Conference on Empirical Methods in Natural Language Processing, EMNLP 2014, October 25-29, 2014, Doha, Qatar, A meeting of SIGDAT, a Special Interest Group of the ACL*, pages 1746–1751.

Diederik P. Kingma and Jimmy Ba. 2014. Adam: A Method for Stochastic Optimization. *CoRR*, abs/1412.6980.

Abhishek Kumar, Abhishek Sethi, Md Shad Akhtar, Asif Ekbal, Chris Biemann, and Pushpak Bhattacharyya. 2017. Iitpb at semeval-2017 task 5: Sentiment prediction in financial text. In *Proceedings of the 11th International Workshop on Semantic Evaluation (SemEval-2017)*, pages 894–898.

Man Lan, Mengxiao Jiang, and Yuanbin Wu. 2017. ECNU at SemEval-2017 Task 5: An Ensemble of Regression Algorithms with Effective Features for Fine-grained Sentiment Analysis in Financial Domain. In *Proceedings of the 11th International Workshop on Semantic Evaluation (SemEval-2017)*, pages 888–893, Vancouver, Canada. ACL.

Youness Mansar, Lorenzo Gatti, Sira Ferradans, Marco Guerini, and Jacopo Staiano. 2017. Fortia-FBK at SemEval-2017 Task 5: Bullish or Bearish? Inferring Sentiment towards Brands from Financial News Headlines. In *Proceedings of the 11th International Workshop on Semantic Evaluation (SemEval-2017)*, pages 817–822, Vancouver, Canada. ACL.

Tomas Mikolov, Ilya Sutskever, Kai Chen, Greg S. Corrado, and Jeff Dean. 2013. Distributed representations of words and phrases and their compositionality. In *Advances in neural information processing systems*, pages 3111–3119, Lake Tahoe, NV, USA.

Marvin Minsky. 1986. *The Society of Mind*. Simon & Schuster, Inc., New York, NY, USA.

Nuno Oliveira, Paulo Cortez, and Nelson Areal. 2013. On the Predictability of Stock Market Behavior Using StockTwits Sentiment and Posting Volume. In *EPIA*, volume 8154 of *Lecture Notes in Computer Science*, pages 355–365. Springer.

Jeffrey Pennington, Richard Socher, and Christopher D. Manning. 2014. Glove: Global vectors for word representation. In *Empirical Methods in Natural Language Processing (EMNLP)*, pages 1532–1543.

Tushar Rao and Saket Srivastava. 2012. Analyzing stock market movements using twitter sentiment analysis. In *Proceedings of the 2012 International Conference on Advances in Social Networks Analysis and Mining (ASONAM 2012)*, pages 119–123. IEEE Computer Society.

Robert P. Schumaker and Hsinchun Chen. 2009. Textual Analysis of Stock Market Prediction Using Breaking Financial News: The AZFin Text System. *ACM Transactions on Information Systems*, 27(2).

Jianfeng Si, Arjun Mukherjee, Bing Liu, Qing Li, Huayi Li, and Xiaotie Deng. 2013. Exploiting topic based twitter sentiment for stock prediction. In *Proceedings of the 51st Annual Meeting of the Association for Computational Linguistics (Volume 2: Short Papers)*, pages 24–29, Sofia, Bulgaria. Association for Computational Linguistics.

Jasmina Smailović, Miha Grčar, Nada Lavrač, and Martin Žnidaršič. 2014. Stream-based active learning for sentiment analysis in the financial domain. *Information Sciences*, 285:181–203.

Alex J. Smola and Bernhard Schölkopf. 2004. A Tutorial on Support Vector Regression. *Statistics and Computing*, 14(3):199–222.

Nitish Srivastava, Geoffrey Hinton, Alex Krizhevsky, Ilya Sutskever, and Ruslan Salakhutdinov. 2014. Dropout: A simple way to prevent neural networks from overfitting. *Journal of Machine Learning Research*, 15:1929–1958.

Theresa Wilson, Janyce Wiebe, and Paul Hoffmann. 2005. Recognizing Contextual Polarity in Phrase-level Sentiment Analysis. In *Proceedings of the Conference on Human Language Technology and Empirical Methods in Natural Language Processing*, pages 347–354. Association for Computational Linguistics.

Bishan Yang, Wen-tau Yih, Xiaodong He, Jianfeng Gao, and Li Deng. 2015. Embedding entities and relations for learning and inference in knowledge bases. In *International Conference on Learning Representations (ICLR)*.

Zichao Yang, Diyi Yang, Chris Dyer, Xiaodong He, Alex Smola, and Eduard Hovy. 2016. Hierarchical attention networks for document classification. In *Proceedings of the 2016 Conference of the North American Chapter of the Association for Computational Linguistics: Human Language Technologies*, pages 1480–1489.

Letting Emotions Flow: Success Prediction by Modeling the Flow of Emotions in Books

Suraj Maharjan* Sudipta Kar* Manuel Montes-y-Gómez[†]
Fabio A. González[‡] Thamar Solorio*
*Department of Computer Science, University of Houston
[†]Instituto Nacional de Astrofisica Optica y Electronica, Puebla, Mexico
[‡]Systems and Computer Engineering Department, Universidad Nacional de Colombia
{smaharjan2, skar3}@uh.edu, solorio@cs.uh.edu
mmontesg@ccc.inoep.mx
fagonzalezo@unal.edu.co

Abstract

Books have the power to make us feel happiness, sadness, pain, surprise, or sorrow. An author's dexterity in the use of these emotions captivates readers and makes it difficult for them to put the book down. In this paper, we model the flow of emotions over a book using recurrent neural networks and quantify its usefulness in predicting success in books. We obtained the best weighted F1-score of 69% for predicting books' success in a multitask setting (simultaneously predicting success and genre of books).

1 Introduction

Books have the power to evoke a multitude of emotions in their readers. They can make readers laugh at a comic scene, cry at a tragic scene and even feel pity or hate for the characters. Specific patterns of emotion flow within books can compel the reader to finish the book, and possibly pursue similar books in the future. Like a musical arrangement, the right emotional rhythm can arouse readers, but even a slight variation in the composition might turn them away.

Vonnegut (1981) discussed the potential of plotting emotions in stories on the "Beginning-End" and the "Ill Fortune-Great Fortune" axes. Reagan et al. (2016) used mathematical tools like Singular Value Decomposition, agglomerative clustering, and Self Organizing Maps (Kohonen et al., 2001) to generate basic shapes of stories. They found that stories are dominated by six different shapes. They even correlated these different shapes to the success of books. Mohammad (2011) visualized emotion densities across books of different genres. He found that the progression of emotions varies with the genre. For example, there is a stronger progression into darkness in horror stories than in comedy. Likewise, Kar et al. (2018)

showed that movies having similar flow of emotions across their plot synopses were assigned similar set of tags by the viewers.

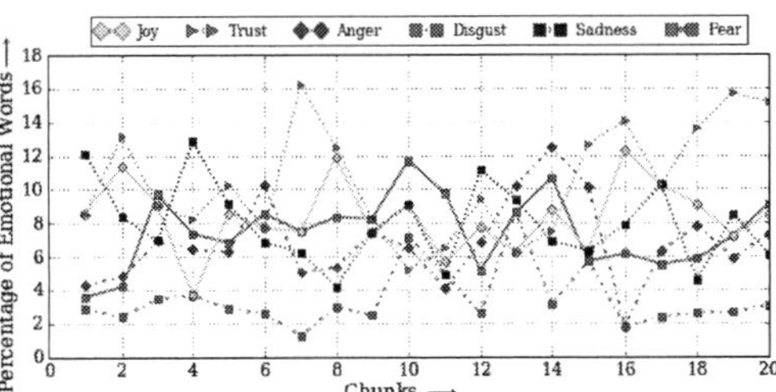

Figure 1: Flow of emotions in *Alice in Wonderland*.

As an example, in Figure 1, we draw the flow of emotions across the book: *Alice in Wonderland*. The plot shows continuous change in *trust*, *fear*, and *sadness*, which relates to the main character's getting into and out of trouble. These patterns present the emotional arcs of the story. Even though they do not reveal the actual plot, they indicate major events happening in the story.

In this paper, we hypothesize that readers enjoy emotional rhythm and thus modeling emotion flows will help predicting a book's potential success. In addition, we show that using the entire content of the book yields better results. Considering only a fragment, as done in earlier work that focuses mainly on style (Maharjan et al., 2017; Ashok et al., 2013), disregards important emotional changes. Similar to Maharjan et al. (2017), we also find that adding genre as an auxiliary task improves success prediction.

2 Methodology

We extract emotion vectors from different chunks of a book and feed them to a recurrent

---

The source code and data for this paper can be downloaded from https://github.com/sjmaharjan/emotion_flow

Proceedings of NAACL-HLT 2018, pages 259–265
New Orleans, Louisiana, June 1 - 6, 2018. ©2018 Association for Computational Linguistics

neural network (RNN) to model the sequential flow of emotions. We aggregate the encoded sequences into a single book vector using an attention mechanism. Attention models have been successfully used in various Natural Language Processing tasks (Wang et al., 2016; Yang et al., 2016; Hermann et al., 2015; Chen et al., 2016; Rush et al., 2015; Luong et al., 2015). This final vector, which is emotionally aware, is used for success prediction.

Representation of Emotions: NRC Emotion Lexicons provide ~14K words (Version 0.92) and their binary associations with eight types of elementary emotions (*anger, anticipation, joy, trust, disgust, sadness, surprise,* and *fear*) from the Hourglass of emotions model with polarity (*positive* and *negative*) (Mohammad and Turney, 2013, 2010). These lexicons have been shown to be effective in tracking emotions in literary texts (Mohammad, 2011).

Inputs: Let X be a collection of books, where each book $x \in X$ is represented by a sequence of n chunk emotion vectors, $x = (x_1, x_2, ..., x_n)$, where x_i is the aggregated emotion vector for chunk i, as shown in Figure 2. We divide the book into n different chunks based on the number of sentences. We then create an emotion vector for each sentence by counting the presence of words of the sentence in each of the ten different types of emotions of the NRC Emotion Lexicons. Thus, the sentence emotion vector has a dimension of 10. Finally, we aggregate these sentence emotion vectors into a chunk emotion vector by taking the average and standard deviation of sentence vectors in the chunk. Mathematically, the ith chunk emotion vector (x_i) is defined as follows:

$$x_i = \left[\frac{\sum_{j=1}^{N} s_{ij}}{N} ; \sqrt{\frac{\sum_{j=1}^{N} \left(s_{ij} - \bar{s}_i\right)^2}{N}} \right] \quad (1)$$

where, N is the total number of sentences, s_{ij} and $\bar{s}_i$ are the jth sentence emotion vector and the mean of the sentence emotion vectors for the ith chunk, respectively. The chunk vectors have a dimension of 20 each. The motivation behind using the standard deviation as a feature is to capture the dispersion of emotions within a chunk.

Model: We then use bidirectional Gated Recurrent Units (GRUs) (Bahdanau et al., 2014) to summa-

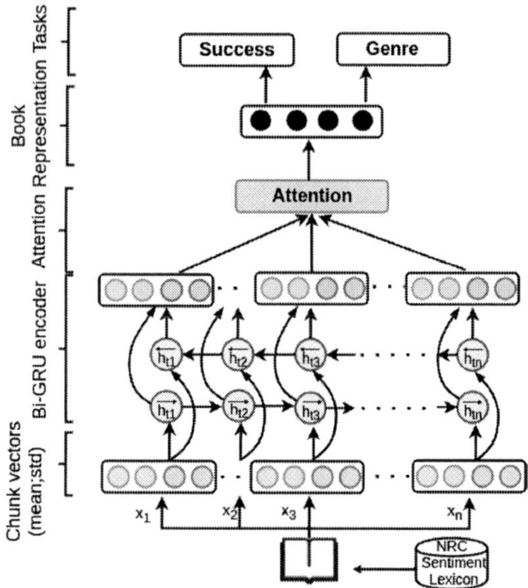

Figure 2: Multitask Emotion Flow Model.

rize the contextual emotion flow information from both directions. The forward and backward GRUs will read the sequence from x_1 to x_n, and from x_n to x_1, respectively. These operations will compute the forward hidden states $(\overrightarrow{h_1}, \ldots, \overrightarrow{h_n})$ and backward hidden states $(\overleftarrow{h_1}, \ldots, \overleftarrow{h_n})$. The annotation for each chunk x_i is obtained by concatenating its forward hidden states $\overrightarrow{h_i}$ and its backward hidden states $\overleftarrow{h_i}$, i.e. $h_i = [\overrightarrow{h_i}; \overleftarrow{h_i}]$. We then learn the relative importance of these hidden states for the classification task. We combine them by taking the weighted sum of all h_i and represent the final book vector r using the following equation:

$$r = \sum_i \alpha_i h_i \quad (2)$$

$$\alpha_i = \frac{\exp(score(h_i))}{\sum_{i'} \exp(score(h_{i'}))} \quad (3)$$

$$score(h_i) = v^T selu(W_a h_i + b_a) \quad (4)$$

where, α_i are the weights, W_a is the weight matrix, b_a is the bias, v is the weight vector, and $selu$ (Klambauer et al., 2017) is the nonlinear activation function. Finally, we apply a linear transformation that maps the book vector r to the number of classes. In case of the single task (ST) setting, where we only predict success, we apply sigmoid activation to get the final prediction probabilities and compute errors using binary cross entropy loss. Similarly, in the multitask

(MT) setting, where we predict both success and genre (Maharjan et al., 2017), we apply a softmax activation to get the final prediction probabilities for the genre prediction. Here, we add the losses from both tasks, i.e. $L_{total}=L_{suc} + L_{gen}$ (L_{suc} and L_{gen} are success and genre tasks' losses, respectively), and then train the network using backpropagation.

3 Experiments

3.1 Dataset

We experimented with the dataset introduced by Maharjan et al. (2017). The dataset consists of 1,003 books from eight different genres collected from Project Gutenberg[1]. The authors considered only those books that were at least reviewed by ten reviewers. They categorized these books into two classes, *Successful* (654 books) and *Unsuccessful* (349 books), based on the average rating for the books in Goodreads[2] website. They considered only the first 1K sentences from each book.

3.2 Baselines

We compare our proposed methods with the following baselines:

Majority Class: The majority class in training data is *success*. This baseline obtains a weighted F1-score of 0.506 for all the test instances.

SentiWordNet+SVM: Maharjan et al. (2017) used SentiWordNet (Baccianella et al., 2010) to compute the sentiment features along with counts of different Part of Speech (PoS) tags for every 50 consecutive sentences (20 chunks from 1K sentences) and used an SVM classifier.

NRC+SVM: We concatenate the chunk emotion vectors (x_i) created using the NRC lexicons and feed them to the SVM classifier. We experiment by varying the number of book chunks.

These baseline methods do not incorporate the sequential flow of emotions across the book and treat each feature independently of each other.

3.3 Experimental Setup

We experimented with the same random stratified splits of 70:30 training to test ratio as used by Maharjan et al. (2017). We use the SVM algorithm for the baselines and RNN for our proposed emotion flow method. We tuned the C hyperparameter of the SVM classifier by performing grid search on the values ($1e\{-4,...,4\}$), using three fold cross validation on the training split. For the experiments with RNNs, we first took a random stratified split of 20% from the training data as validation set. We then tuned the RNN hyperparameters by running 20 different experiments with a random selection of different values for the hyperparameters. We tuned the weight initialization (Glorot Uniform (Glorot and Bengio, 2010), LeCun Uniform (LeCun et al., 1998)), learning rate with Adam (Kingma and Ba, 2015) $\{1e-4,...,1e-1\}$, dropout rates $\{0.2,0.4,0.5\}$, attention and recurrent units $\{32, 64\}$, and batch-size $\{1, 4, 8\}$ with early stopping criteria.

4 Results

Book Content		1000 sents		All	
Methods	Chunks	ST	MT	ST	MT
Majority Class	-	0.506	0.506	0.506	0.506
SentiWordNet + SVM	20	0.582	0.610	-	-
NRC + SVM	10	0.526	0.597	0.541	0.641
NRC + SVM	20	0.537	0.590	0.577	0.604
NRC + SVM	30	0.587	0.576	0.595	0.600
NRC + SVM	50	0.611	0.586	0.597	0.636
Emotion Flow	10	0.632	0.643	0.650	0.660
Emotion Flow	20	0.612	0.639	0.640	0.668
Emotion Flow	30	0.630	0.657	0.662	0.677
Emotion Flow	50	0.656	0.666	0.674	**0.690***

Table 1: Weighted F1-scores for success classification in single task (ST) and multi task (MT) settings with varying chunk sequences when using all the book or only the first 1K sentences. $*p < 0.05$ (McNemar significance test between Emotion Flow (chunks 50, MT, All) and NRC+SVM (chunk 10, MT, All))

Table 1 presents the results. Our proposed method performs better than different baseline methods and obtains the highest weighted F1-score of 0.690. The results highlight the importance of taking into account the sequential flow of emotions across books to predict how much readers will like a book. We obtain better performance when we use an RNN to feed the sequences of emotion chunk vectors. The performance decreases with the SVM classifier, which discards this sequential information by treating each feature independently of each other. Moreover, increasing the granularity of the emotions by increasing the number of chunks seems to be helpful for success prediction. However, we see a slight decrease in performance beyond 50 chunks (weighted F1 score of 0.662 and 0.664 for 60 and 100 chunks, respectively).

The results also show that the MT setting is beneficial over the ST setting, whether we consider

---

[1] https://www.gutenberg.org/
[2] https://www.goodreads.com/

the first 1K sentences or the entire book. This finding is akin to Maharjan et al. (2017). Similar to them, we suspect the auxiliary task of genre classification is acting as a regularizer.

Considering only the first 1K sentences of books may miss out important details, especially when the only input to the model is the distribution of emotions. It is necessary to include information from later chapters and climax of the story as they gradually reveal the answers to the suspense, the events, and the emotional ups and downs in characters that build up through the course of the book. Accordingly, our results show that it is important to consider emotions from the entire book rather than from just the first 1K sentences.

5 Attention Analysis

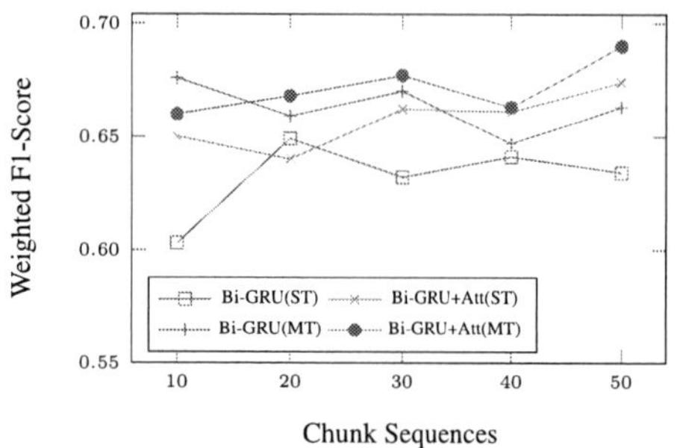

Figure 3: Comparison of the Emotion Flow with and without attention mechanism for different chunk sequences.

From Figure 3, we see that using the attention mechanism to aggregate vectors is better than just concatenating the final forward and backward hidden states to represent the book in both ST and MT settings. We also observe that the multitask approach performs better than the singe task one regardless of the number of chunks and the use of attention.

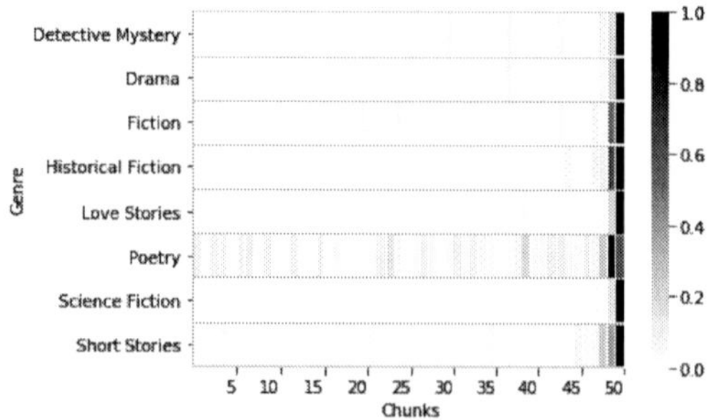

Figure 4: Attention weights visualization per genre.

Figure 4 plots the heatmap of the average attention weights for test books grouped by their genre. The model has learned that the last two to three chunks that represent the climax, are most important for predicting success. Since this is a bidirectional RNN model, hidden representations for each chunk carry information from the whole book. Thus, using only the last chunks will probably result in lower performance. Also, the weights visualization shows an interesting pattern for *Poetry*. In *Poetry*, emotions are distributed across the different regions. This may be due to sudden important events or abrupt change in emotions. For *Short stories*, initial chunks also receive some weights, suggesting the importance of the premise.

6 Emotion Analysis

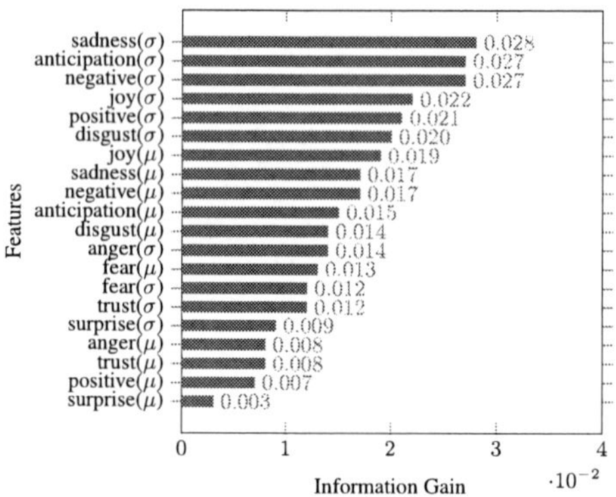

Figure 5: Feature ranking with information gain.

Climax Emotions: Since the last chunk is assigned more weights than other chunks, we used information gain to rank features of that chunk. From Figure 5, we see that features capturing the variation of different emotions are ranked higher than features capturing the average scores. This suggests that readers tend to enjoy emotional ups and downs portrayed in books, making the standard deviation features more important than the average features for the same emotions.

Table 2 shows the mean (μ) and standard deviation (σ) for different emotions extracted for all the data, and further categorized by *Successful* and *Unsuccessful* label from the last chunk. We see that authors generally end books with higher rates of positive words ($\mu = 0.888$) than negative words ($\mu = 0.599$) and the difference is significant ($p < 0.001$). Similarly the means for *anticipation*, *joy*, *trust*, and *fear* are higher than for *sadness*, *surprise*, *anger*, and *disgust*. This further vali-

Dataset	Anger		Anticipation		Disgust		Fear		Joy		Sadness		Surprise		Trust	
	μ	σ	μ	σ	μ	σ	μ	σ	μ	σ	μ	σ	μ	σ	μ	σ
Corpus	0.248	0.249	0.414	0.372	0.179	0.200	0.340	0.327	0.399	0.431	0.323	0.309	0.225	0.191	0.492	0.441
Successful	0.270	0.263	0.447	0.374	0.194	0.207	0.377	0.353	0.435	0.416	0.358	0.334	0.236	0.207	0.517	0.427
Unsuccessful	0.207	0.214	0.351	0.359	0.153	0.183	0.270	0.258	0.331	0.451	0.258	0.243	0.205	0.155	0.445	0.463

Table 2: Mean (μ) and standard deviation (σ) for eight type of emotions for the last chunk.

dates that authors prefer happy ending. Moving on to *Successful* and *Unsuccessful* categories, we see that the means for *Successful* books are higher than *Unsuccessful* books for *anger, anticipation, disgust, fear, joy,* and *sadness* (highly significant, $p < 0.001$). We observe the same pattern for *trust*, and *surprise*, although the p value is only $p < 0.02$ in this case. Moreover, the standard deviations for all emotions are significantly different across the two categories ($p < 0.001$). Thus, emotion concentration (μ) and variation (σ) for *Successful* books are higher than for *Unsuccessful* books for all emotions in the NRC lexicon.

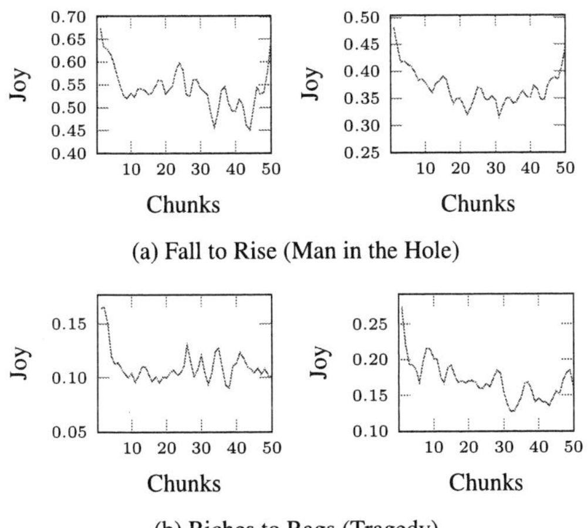

(a) Fall to Rise (Man in the Hole)

(b) Riches to Rags (Tragedy)

Figure 6: Emotion flow for four cluster centroids in the dataset. The two curves on top match the "Fall to Rise" shape and the two at the bottom match the "Tragedy" one defined in Reagan et al. (2016).

Emotion Shapes: We visualize the prominent emotion flow shapes in the dataset using K-means clustering algorithm. We took the average *joy* across 50 chunks for all books and clustered them into 100 different clusters. We then plotted the smoothed centroid of clusters having ≥ 20 books. We found two distinct shapes ("Man in the hole" (fall to rise) and "Tragedy" or "Riches to rags" (fall)). Figure 6 shows such centroid plots. The plot also shows that the "Tragedy" shapes have an overall lower value of joy than the "Man in the hole" shapes. Upon analyzing the distribu-

tion of *Successful* and *Unsuccessful* books within these shapes, we found that the "Man in the hole" shapes have a higher number of successful books whereas, the "Tragedy" shapes have the opposite.

7 Conclusions and Future Work

In this paper, we showed that modeling emotions as a flow, by capturing the emotional content at different stages, improves prediction accuracy. We learned that most of the attention weights are given to the last fragment in all genres, except for *Poetry* where other fragments seem to be relevant as well. We also showed empirically that adding an attention mechanism is better than just considering the last forward and backward hidden states from the RNN. We found two distinct emotion flow shapes and found that the clusters with "Tragedy" shape had more unsuccessful books than successful ones. In future work, we will be exploring how we can use these flows of emotions to detect important events that result in suspenseful scenes. Also, we will be applying hierarchical methods that take in the logical grouping of books (sequence of paragraphs to form a chapter and sequence of chapters to form a book) to build books' emotional representations.

Acknowledgments

We would like to thank the National Science Foundation for funding this work under award 1462141. We are also grateful to the anonymous reviewers for reviewing the paper and providing helpful comments and suggestions.

References

Vikas Ashok, Song Feng, and Yejin Choi. 2013. Success with style: Using writing style to predict the success of novels. In *Proceedings of the 2013 Conference on Empirical Methods in Natural Language Processing*. Association for Computational Linguistics, Seattle, Washington, USA, pages 1753–1764. http://www.aclweb.org/anthology/D13-1181.

Stefano Baccianella, Andrea Esuli, and Fabrizio Sebastiani. 2010. Sentiwordnet 3.0: An enhanced lexical resource for sentiment analysis and opinion mining. In *LREC*. volume 10, pages 2200–2204.

Dzmitry Bahdanau, Kyunghyun Cho, and Yoshua Bengio. 2014. Neural machine translation by jointly learning to align and translate. *CoRR* abs/1409.0473. `http://arxiv.org/abs/1409.0473`.

Danqi Chen, Jason Bolton, and Christopher D. Manning. 2016. A thorough examination of the cnn/daily mail reading comprehension task. In *Proceedings of the 54th Annual Meeting of the Association for Computational Linguistics (Volume 1: Long Papers)*. Association for Computational Linguistics, Berlin, Germany, pages 2358–2367. `http://www.aclweb.org/anthology/P16-1223`.

Xavier Glorot and Yoshua Bengio. 2010. Understanding the difficulty of training deep feedforward neural networks. In Yee Whye Teh and Mike Titterington, editors, *Proceedings of the Thirteenth International Conference on Artificial Intelligence and Statistics*. PMLR, Chia Laguna Resort, Sardinia, Italy, volume 9 of *Proceedings of Machine Learning Research*, pages 249–256. `http://proceedings.mlr.press/v9/glorot10a.html`.

Karl Moritz Hermann, Tomas Kocisky, Edward Grefenstette, Lasse Espeholt, Will Kay, Mustafa Suleyman, and Phil Blunsom. 2015. Teaching machines to read and comprehend. In C. Cortes, N. D. Lawrence, D. D. Lee, M. Sugiyama, and R. Garnett, editors, *Advances in Neural Information Processing Systems 28*, Curran Associates, Inc., pages 1693–1701. `http://papers.nips.cc/paper/5945-teaching-machines-to-read-and-comprehend.pdf`.

Sudipta Kar, Suraj Maharjan, A. Pastor López-Monroy, and Thamar Solorio. 2018. MPST: A corpus of movie plot synopses with tags. In *Proceedings of the Eleventh International Conference on Language Resources and Evaluation (LREC 2018)*. European Language Resources Association (ELRA), Paris, France.

Diederik Kingma and Jimmy Ba. 2015. Adam: a method for stochastic optimization. In *International Conference on Learning Representations*.

Günter Klambauer, Thomas Unterthiner, Andreas Mayr, and Sepp Hochreiter. 2017. Self-normalizing neural networks. *CoRR* abs/1706.02515. `http://arxiv.org/abs/1706.02515`.

T. Kohonen, M. R. Schroeder, and T. S. Huang, editors. 2001. *Self-Organizing Maps*. Springer-Verlag New York, Inc., Secaucus, NJ, USA, 3rd edition.

Yann LeCun, Léon Bottou, Genevieve B. Orr, and Klaus-Robert Müller. 1998. Efficient backprop. In *Neural Networks: Tricks of the Trade, This Book is an Outgrowth of a 1996 NIPS Workshop*.

Springer-Verlag, London, UK, UK, pages 9–50. `http://dl.acm.org/citation.cfm?id=645754.668382`.

Thang Luong, Hieu Pham, and Christopher D. Manning. 2015. Effective approaches to attention-based neural machine translation. In *Proceedings of the 2015 Conference on Empirical Methods in Natural Language Processing*. Association for Computational Linguistics, Lisbon, Portugal, pages 1412–1421. `http://aclweb.org/anthology/D15-1166`.

Suraj Maharjan, John Arevalo, Manuel Montes, Fabio A. González, and Thamar Solorio. 2017. A multi-task approach to predict likability of books. In *Proceedings of the 15th Conference of the European Chapter of the Association for Computational Linguistics: Volume 1, Long Papers*. Association for Computational Linguistics, Valencia, Spain, pages 1217–1227. `http://www.aclweb.org/anthology/E17-1114`.

Saif Mohammad. 2011. From once upon a time to happily ever after: Tracking emotions in novels and fairy tales. In *Proceedings of the 5th ACL-HLT Workshop on Language Technology for Cultural Heritage, Social Sciences, and Humanities*. Association for Computational Linguistics, Stroudsburg, PA, USA, LaTeCH '11, pages 105–114. `http://dl.acm.org/citation.cfm?id=2107636.2107650`.

Saif Mohammad and Peter Turney. 2010. Emotions evoked by common words and phrases: Using mechanical turk to create an emotion lexicon. In *Proceedings of the NAACL HLT 2010 Workshop on Computational Approaches to Analysis and Generation of Emotion in Text*. Association for Computational Linguistics, Los Angeles, CA, pages 26–34. `http://www.aclweb.org/anthology/W10-0204`.

Saif M. Mohammad and Peter D. Turney. 2013. Crowdsourcing a word–emotion association lexicon. *Computational Intelligence* 29(3):436–465. `https://doi.org/10.1111/j.1467-8640.2012.00460.x`.

Andrew J. Reagan, Lewis Mitchell, Dilan Kiley, Christopher M. Danforth, and Peter Sheridan Dodds. 2016. The emotional arcs of stories are dominated by six basic shapes. *CoRR* abs/1606.07772. `http://arxiv.org/abs/1606.07772`.

Alexander M. Rush, Sumit Chopra, and Jason Weston. 2015. A neural attention model for abstractive sentence summarization. In *Proceedings of the 2015 Conference on Empirical Methods in Natural Language Processing*. Association for Computational Linguistics, Lisbon, Portugal, pages 379–389. `http://aclweb.org/anthology/D15-1044`.

Kurt Vonnegut. 1981. Palm sunday: An autobiographical collage.

Yequan Wang, Minlie Huang, xiaoyan zhu, and Li Zhao. 2016. Attention-based lstm for aspect-level sentiment classification. In *Proceedings of the 2016 Conference on Empirical Methods in Natural Language Processing*. Association for Computational Linguistics, Austin, Texas, pages 606–615. https://aclweb.org/anthology/D16-1058.

Zichao Yang, Diyi Yang, Chris Dyer, Xiaodong He, Alex Smola, and Eduard Hovy. 2016. Hierarchical attention networks for document classification. In *Proceedings of the 2016 Conference of the North American Chapter of the Association for Computational Linguistics: Human Language Technologies*. Association for Computational Linguistics, San Diego, California, pages 1480–1489. http://www.aclweb.org/anthology/N16-1174.

Modeling Inter-Aspect Dependencies for Aspect-Based Sentiment Analysis

Devamanyu Hazarika*
School of Computing,
National University of Singapore
devamanyu@comp.nus.edu.sg

Soujanya Poria*
Artificial Intelligence Initiative,
A*STAR, Singapore
sporia@ihpc.a-star.edu.sg

Prateek Vij
Department of Computer Science
and Engineering, IIT, Guwahati
v.prateek@iitg.ernet.in

Gangeshwar Krishnamurthy
Artificial Intelligence Initiative,
A*STAR, Singapore
gangeshwark@ihpc.a-star.edu.sg

Erik Cambria
School of Computer Science and
Engineering, NTU, Singapore
cambria@ntu.edu.sg

Roger Zimmermann
School of Computing,
National University of Singapore
rogerz@comp.nus.edu.sg

Abstract

Aspect-based Sentiment Analysis is a fine-grained task of sentiment classification for multiple aspects in a sentence. Present neural-based models exploit aspect and its contextual information in the sentence but largely ignore the inter-aspect dependencies. In this paper, we incorporate this pattern by simultaneous classification of all aspects in a sentence along with temporal dependency processing of their corresponding sentence representations using recurrent networks. Results on the benchmark SemEval 2014 dataset suggest the effectiveness of our proposed approach.

1 Introduction

Aspect-based Sentiment Analysis (ABSA) is a fine-grained task of sentiment classification. Sentimentally involved sentences in reviews, debates, etc., often comprise of multiple aspects that have varied sentiment polarities. An important sub-task of ABSA is aspect or aspect-term classification which involves predicting sentiment of aspects embodied in a sentence (Young et al., 2017). Present works in the literature approach this task by analyzing associations between aspects and their contexts provided in the sentence. In this work, we argue that to classify an aspect into sentiment categories, knowledge of surrounding aspects, their sentiment orientation, and resulting inter-dependencies, is beneficial.

Inter-aspect dependencies abound in sentences with multiple aspects. Largely ignored in present

literature, these dependencies may reveal themselves in many forms, such as a) *Incomplete information*, where a certain aspect does not contain enough contextual information to convey the sentiment. In such cases, the surrounding aspects and their sentiment tone become crucial to fill the contextual gap. As an example, in the sentence *The menu is very limited - I think we counted 4 or 5 entries.*, the subsentence *I think ... entries* containing aspect *entries* does not provide the required sentiment unless considered with the aspect *menu*. Here, the negative sentiment of *menu* induces *entries* to have the same sentiment. b) *Sentiment influence in conjunctions*, in which, the sentiment of an aspect in a sentence influences the succeeding aspects due to the presence of conjunctions. In particular, for sentences containing conjunctions like *and, not only, also, but, however, though*, etc., aspects tend to share/contrast their sentiments. In the sentence *Food is usually very good, though I wonder about freshness of raw vegetables*, the aspect *raw vegetables* does not have any sentiment marker linked to it. However, the positive sentiment of *food* due to the word *good* and presence of conjunction *though* determines the sentiment of *raw vegetables* to be negative. Thus, aspects when arranged as a sequence, reveal high correlation and interplay of sentiments.

In this paper, we facilitate such phenomena by proposing a neural network where the information is shared among the aspects by means of a Long Short-Term Memory (LSTM) network (Hochreiter and Schmidhuber, 1997). In other words, we model the sequential relationship between the aspects as per their occurrence in the sentence.

---

* means authors contributed equally.

Proceedings of NAACL-HLT 2018, pages 266–270
New Orleans, Louisiana, June 1 - 6, 2018. ©2018 Association for Computational Linguistics

Specifically, our model first takes a sentence along with all of its aspect-terms and then generates the sentential representations relative to each aspect to get better aspect-oriented features (Tang et al., 2016a). This is done using an attention-based LSTM network, where the attention mechanism enables the model to focus on key parts of the sentence that modulate the sentiment of the aspects. To further guide the attention process the model incorporates aspect information at the word-level by concatenating aspect representations with each word (Wang et al., 2016). Finally, to capture the inter-aspect dependencies, the aspect-based sentential representations are ordered as a sequence and temporally modeled using another LSTM. Each timestep of this LSTM corresponds to a particular aspect. The hidden state output for each timestep is then projected to a dense layer and fed to a softmax classifier to predict the polarities of the corresponding aspect. To the best of our knowledge, use of inter-aspect dependencies in neural models is unprecedented and fills a significant gap in the literature.

In the remaining paper, Section 2 first provides a summary of existing works; Section 3 then describes the proposed approach in detail; Section 4 gives training and dataset details followed by results and a qualitative case study. Finally, Section 5 concludes the paper.

2 Related Works

Traditional methods in this field leveraged sentiment lexicons to solve this task (Rao and Ravichandran, 2009; Perez-Rosas et al., 2012) whereas present methods have transitioned to neural-based approaches. Tang et al. 2016a introduced the idea of aspect-based sentential representations which generates a custom representation of the sentence based on the aspect. This approach has been heavily adapted by modern works. Wang et al. 2016 built on this framework and introduced attention mechanism for generating these sentential features. They also incorporated aspect information into the attention module by concatenating them with the words. More recently, Ma et al. 2017 proposed a model where both context and aspect representations interact with each other's attention mechanism to generate the overall representation. Tay et al. 2017 proposed word-aspect associations using circular correlation as an improvement over Wang et al.'s work. ABSA has

also been approached from a question-answering perspective where memory networks have played a major role (Tang et al., 2016b; Li et al., 2017). Our work is different from all these works since we train all aspects of a particular sentence together and capitalize on inter-aspect dependency modeling which they ignore.

3 Proposed Approach

Let us take a sentence $S = [w^1, ..., w^n]$ having n words. Each word is represented as a low-dimensional real-valued vector of size d_{em}, called word embedding. To get the embeddings, we use the pre-trained Glove vectors (Pennington et al., 2014) having $d_{em} = 300$. We can thus represent S as a matrix of dimensions $\mathbb{R}^{d_{em} \times n}$.

The sentence S also contains m aspect-terms (or aspects), where for each $i \in [1, m]$, aspect A_i is a multi-word subsequence of S, i.e., $\exists j \in [1, n]$, such that, $A_i = [w^j, ..., w^{j+|A_i|-1}] \in \mathbb{R}^{d_{em} \times |A_i|}$. All the aspects $A_1, ..., A_m$ are enumerated as per their order of occurrence in the sentence. The goal is to determine the sentiment label for each of these m aspects belonging to S.

The proposed model comprises two distinct phases (Figure 1). The first phase involves the generation of aspect-based sentential representations $s_1, ..., s_m$, where, vector s_i is created by coupling aspect A_i with sentence S. The second phase models the inter-aspect dependencies in a sentence using an LSTM which is followed by the sentiment prediction for all the aspects.

3.1 Phase 1: Aspect-based sentential representations

Below, we describe the methodology to generate the ith aspect-based sentential representation s_i for aspect A_i and sentence S.

Given sentence S and aspect-term A_i, the model first generates the aspect representation t_i. This is done by passing A_i through an LSTM, named $LSTM_a$, having internal dimension d_a. $LSTM_a$'s final hidden state vector $h_a^{|A_i|} \in \mathbb{R}^{d_a}$ is taken to be this representation, i.e., $t_i = h_a^{|A_i|}$.

Following this, an attention-based LSTM model is used to create s_i using S and t_i (Wang et al., 2016). First, each word vector w^j in S is concatenated with aspect t_i to create a comprehensive feature vector $x_i^j = (w^j; t_i) \in \mathbb{R}^{(d_{em}+d_a)}$, where ; is the concatenation operator. We then take this new sequence representation $X_i = [x_i^1, ..., x_i^n]$ and

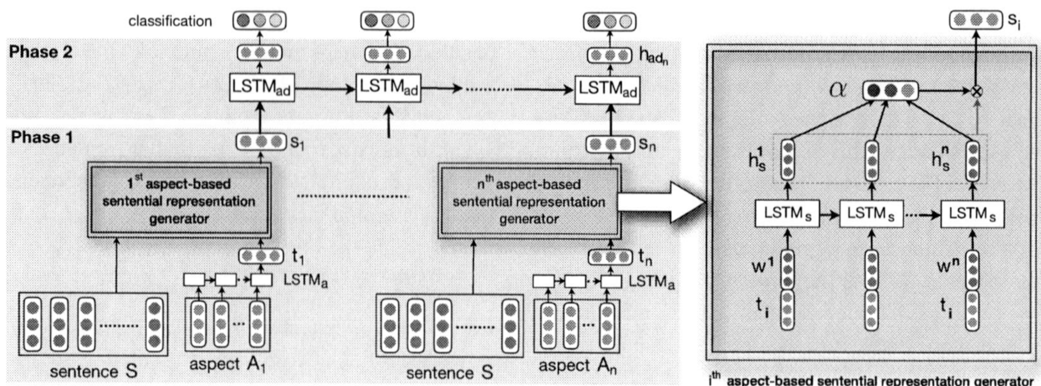

Figure 1: Overall architecture of the proposed method. The *aspect-based sentential representation generator* is described in the right end of the figure.

apply an LSTM, named $LSTM_s$ with dimension d_s, to model the long-term temporal dependencies within the sentence. The hidden state memory vectors across all n timesteps result in matrix $H_i = [h_s^1, ..., h_s^n] \in \mathbb{R}^{d_s \times n}$.

Attention: Attention mechanism is applied on H_i to get an attention vector α, which is in turn used to generate a weighted representation of H_i. We use this weighted representation to be the ith aspect's sentential representation s_i. Previous concatenations of words with the aspect-representations infuse aspect information into the attention process. This enables the attention mechanism to focus on relevant segments in the sentence with respect to the aspect. The overall attention mechanism to generate s_i is summarized as:

$$M = tanh(H_i.W_h) \qquad (1)$$
$$\alpha = softmax(M^T.W_b) \qquad (2)$$
$$s_i = H.\alpha^T \qquad (3)$$

where, $W_h \in \mathbb{R}^{n \times 1}$ and $W_b \in \mathbb{R}^{d_s \times n}$ are projection parameters to be learnt during training and d_s is the dimension of the final sentence vector, i.e., $s_i \in \mathbb{R}^{d_s}$.

The overall process described above is individually applied to all m aspects to get sentential representations $s_1, ..., s_m$.

3.2 Phase 2: Inter-aspect relationship

To capture the implicit inter-aspect dependencies, we model the sentential representations as a sequence $[s_1, ..., s_m]$, following the order of occurrence of their corresponding aspect-terms in sen-

tence S. An LSTM, named $LSTM_{ad}$ with dimension d_{ad} is then applied on this sequence and at each of the ith timestep, its hidden state is projected to another vector having dimensions equal to the number of classes to predict. Finally, softmax operation is applied on this vector to get the prediction probabilities for the sentiment of this i^{th} aspect-term for sentence S. The transitions are as follows:

$$[h_{ad_1}, ..., h_{ad_m}] = LSTM_{ad}([s_1, ..., s_m]) \qquad (4)$$
$$\hat{y}_i = softmax(W_{ad}.h_{ad_i}) \qquad (5)$$

Here, $\hat{y}_i \in \mathbb{R}^C$ is the predicted probability distribution for the ith aspect of sentence S where C is the number of sentiment classes. $W_{ad} \in \mathbb{R}^{C \times d_{ad}}$ is a parameter and $softmax(x_i) = e^{x_i} / \sum_j e^{x_j}$.

Loss Function: We use categorical cross-entropy as the loss function which is averaged over all aspects for a sentence. Thus, stochastic loss for sentence S is calculated as:

$$Loss = \frac{-1}{m} \sum_{i=1}^{m} \sum_{j=1}^{C} y_{i,j} \, log_2(\hat{y}_{i,j}) + \lambda \| \theta \|^2 \qquad (6)$$

Here, m is the number of aspects for a sentence and C is the number of sentiment categories. y_i is the one-hot vector ground truth of ith aspect of sentence S and $\hat{y}_{i,j}$ is its predicted probability of belonging to sentiment class j. λ is the L$_2$ - regularization term and θ is the parameter set, i.e., $\theta = \{W_{[h,b,ad]}, LSTM_{[t,s,ad]}\}$, where $LSTM_{[]}$ represents the internal parameters of that LSTM.

4 Experimentation

Training details: To perform experiments and subsequent hyperparameter tuning, we first split

268

the training set randomly in the ratio $9 : 1$ to get a held-out validation set. For optimization, we use the Adam optimizer (Kingma and Ba, 2014) having learning rate 0.01. Embedding dimensions are set as follows, $d_a = 100, d_s$ and $d_{ad} = 300$. To facilitate batch processing, we attach dummy aspects in sentences with lesser aspects and also provide masking schemes. For termination, we use the early-stopping procedure with a patience value of 10 that is monitored on the validation loss.

Dataset: We conduct our experiments using the dataset for SemEval 2014 Task 4 containing customer reviews on restaurants and laptops. Each review has one or more aspects with their corresponding polarities. The polarity of an aspect can be positive, negative, neutral or conflict; however, we consider the first three labels for classification. Table 1 contains the statistics for the dataset.

4.1 Results

Table 2 presents the results of our proposed model along with state-of-the-art methods. Our model significantly surpasses the performance of ATAE-LSTM (Wang et al., 2016). Given that ATAE's architecture has a strong correlation to our aspect-based sentential generator (see Figure 1), their work can be categorized as a baseline to our model. This reinforces our hypothesis that a model capable of capturing inter-aspect dependencies indeed performs better. We also compare our model to the recently proposed IAN (Ma et al., 2017). On both datasets, our model performs competitively with IAN and produces nominal improvement. Given that IAN explores the inter-dependencies of aspects with their contexts, while we try to model inter-dependencies between aspects, an interesting direction would be to explore the IAN modeled in our proposed setting (Phase 2 of Figure 1). We set this path as an option for future research.

Table 1 also presents variations of our proposed

Data		Aspect Labels			No. of reviews
		Positive	Negative	Neutral	
Rest.	Train	2148	790	628	1977
	Test	725	195	196	600
Laptop	Train	974	839	450	1462
	Test	340	125	169	411

* Rest. = Restaurant

Table 1: Labels and review statistics for the dataset SemEval 2014.

Models	Attn.	Fusion	3-way classification	
			Rest.	Laptop
LSTM	✗	-	74.3	66.5
AE-LSTM	✓	Concat	76.6	68.9
ATAE-LSTM	✓	Concat	77.2	68.7
IAN	✓	-	78.6	72.1
Our Model	✓	Hadamard	73.42	63.7
Our Model	✗	Concat	74.5	69.6
Our Model	✓	Concat	**79.0**	**72.5**

* Attn. = Attention, Rest. = Restaurant

Table 2: Accuracies for three-way classification on the Restaurant and Laptop SemEval 2014 dataset.

model. Specifically, we try out variants (a) *Without attention:* in this setting, we omit the attention mechanism while generating aspect-based sentential representation s_i (Equation 1-3). Instead, we define s_i to be h_s^n, i.e., the last hidden state vector of $LSTM_s$ with input S and A_i. However, removing attention brings degradation in the performance of our model on the Restaurant and Laptop dataset by 4% and 3%, respectively. This signifies the importance of an attention mechanism to derive the aspect-based sentential representations. (b) *With hadamard fusion:* instead of concatenation of w^j and t_i, we use the hadamard product which is the element wise multiplication of the vectors. Although this variation reduces the total parameter sizes of the network, it still does not benefit the model and gives a poorer performance to simple concatenation. Numerous other fusion methods such as tensor fusion (Zadeh et al., 2017), compact bilinear pooling (Gao et al., 2016), attention-based fusion (Poria et al., 2017; Hazarika et al., 2018), etc. are applicable, whose analyses, however, is not the focus of this paper.

4.2 Case Study

A qualitative study on the test set classifications by our model reveals its capability to learn inter-aspect dependencies (Section 1). For the sentence *I love the keyboard and the screen*, the model correctly identifies the sentiment of *screen* as positive which is hinted by positive aspect *keyboard* and conjunction *and*. In another case, for the sentence *The best thing about this laptop is the price along with some of the newer features*, aspect *features* is correctly classified as positive which is influenced by aspect *price* and positive word *best*. This shows that our model is performing well in classifying joint aspects having conjunctions. For the slightly harder case of tackling incomplete information, our model fares well in sentences having this pattern. For example, one of the sentence *Boot up slowed significantly after all windows updates were installed* has aspect *windows update* which does not have a clear sentiment orientation but is implicitly dependent on the aspect *boot up* having a negative sentiment. This was also correctly classified by our model. Moreover, the above examples were incorrectly classified by ATAE. This reaffirms our hypothesis that the ability to learn inter-aspect dependencies is a crucial factor in the task of ABSA.

5 Conclusion

In this paper, we present a way to incorporate inter-aspect dependencies in the task of Aspect-based Sentiment Analysis. Our results suggest that capturing such information indeed improves the task of prediction. Through this work, we hope that future attempts by researchers include this idea in their methods.

6 Acknowledgement

This research was supported in part by the National Natural Science Foundation of China under Grant no. 61472266 and by the National University of Singapore (Suzhou) Research Institute, 377 Lin Quan Street, Suzhou Industrial Park, Jiang Su, People's Republic of China, 215123. We would also like to thank the anonymous reviewers for their valuable feedback.

References

Yang Gao, Oscar Beijbom, Ning Zhang, and Trevor Darrell. 2016. Compact bilinear pooling. In *Proceedings of the IEEE Conference on Computer Vision and Pattern Recognition*, pages 317–326.

Devamanyu Hazarika, Sruthi Gorantla, Soujanya Poria, and Roger Zimmermann. 2018. Self-attentive feature-level fusion for multimodal emotion detection.

Sepp Hochreiter and Jürgen Schmidhuber. 1997. Long short-term memory. *Neural computation*, 9(8):1735–1780.

Diederik Kingma and Jimmy Ba. 2014. Adam: A method for stochastic optimization. *arXiv preprint arXiv:1412.6980*.

Cheng Li, Xiaoxiao Guo, and Qiaozhu Mei. 2017. Deep memory networks for attitude identification. In *Proceedings of the Tenth ACM International Conference on Web Search and Data Mining*, pages 671–680. ACM.

Dehong Ma, Sujian Li, Xiaodong Zhang, and Houfeng Wang. 2017. Interactive attention networks for aspect-level sentiment classification. *arXiv preprint arXiv:1709.00893*.

Jeffrey Pennington, Richard Socher, and Christopher Manning. 2014. Glove: Global vectors for word representation. In *Proceedings of the 2014 conference on empirical methods in natural language processing (EMNLP)*, pages 1532–1543.

Veronica Perez-Rosas, Carmen Banea, and Rada Mihalcea. 2012. Learning sentiment lexicons in spanish. In *LREC*, volume 12, page 73.

Soujanya Poria, Erik Cambria, Devamanyu Hazarika, Navonil Mazumder, Amir Zadeh, and Louis-Philippe Morency. 2017. Multi-level multiple attentions for contextual multimodal sentiment analysis. In *2017 IEEE International Conference on Data Mining (ICDM)*, pages 1033–1038. IEEE.

Delip Rao and Deepak Ravichandran. 2009. Semi-supervised polarity lexicon induction. In *Proceedings of the 12th Conference of the European Chapter of the Association for Computational Linguistics*, pages 675–682. Association for Computational Linguistics.

Duyu Tang, Bing Qin, Xiaocheng Feng, and Ting Liu. 2016a. Effective lstms for target-dependent sentiment classification. In *Proceedings of COLING 2016, the 26th International Conference on Computational Linguistics: Technical Papers*, pages 3298–3307.

Duyu Tang, Bing Qin, and Ting Liu. 2016b. Aspect level sentiment classification with deep memory network. *arXiv preprint arXiv:1605.08900*.

Yi Tay, Anh Tuan Luu, and Siu Cheung Hui. 2017. Learning to attend via word-aspect associative fusion for aspect-based sentiment analysis. *arXiv preprint arXiv:1712.05403*.

Yequan Wang, Minlie Huang, Xiaoyan Zhu, and Li Zhao. 2016. Attention-based lstm for aspect-level sentiment classification. In *EMNLP*, pages 606–615.

Tom Young, Devamanyu Hazarika, Soujanya Poria, and Erik Cambria. 2017. Recent trends in deep learning based natural language processing. *arXiv preprint arXiv:1708.02709*.

Amir Zadeh, Minghai Chen, Soujanya Poria, Erik Cambria, and Louis-Philippe Morency. 2017. Tensor fusion network for multimodal sentiment analysis. In *Proceedings of the 2017 Conference on Empirical Methods in Natural Language Processing*, pages 1103–1114.

Multi-task Learning Framework for Mining Crowd Intelligence towards Clinical Treatment

Shweta Yadav[*], **Asif Ekbal**[*], **Sriparna Saha**[*], **Pushpak Bhattacharyya**[*], and **Amit Sheth**[†]

[*]Indian Institute of Technology Patna, India

[†]Kno.e.sis Center, Wright State University, USA

[*]{shweta.pcs14,asif,sriparna,pb}@iitp.ac.in, [†]amit@knoesis.org

Abstract

In recent past, social media has emerged as an active platform in the context of health-care and medicine. In this paper, we present a study where medical user's opinions on health-related issues are analyzed to capture the medical sentiment at a blog level. The medical sentiments can be studied in various facets such as *medical condition*, *treatment*, and *medication* that characterize the overall health status of the user. Considering these facets, we treat analysis of this information as a multi-task classification problem. In this paper, we adopt a novel adversarial learning approach[1] for our multi-task learning framework to learn the sentiment's strengths expressed in a medical blog. Our evaluation shows promising results for our target tasks.

1 Introduction

"Can someone help me please????". These types of queries have swamped the web with the phenomenal rise in social media contents almost in every domain including health care. Generally, the users posts seeking for health-related information, sharing medical experiences and opinions of other users (i.e., patients, health professional or doctors). With the enormous amount of posts increasing day after day, it is difficult for the health professionals to read and answer every post. It would be helpful to have a sentiment analyzer that could study the user's sentiment associated with the post related to his/her health-status. In this paper, we make an attempt to capture *medical sentiment* (MS) by analyzing the subjectivity expressions describing a patient's medical conditions at the blog level. MS can be studied as an event that characterizes the patient's medical condition, in which the patient expresses stance

towards clinical and social situations. The notion of sentiment in medical context unlike traditional sentiment analysis (SA) is more granular which can be studied after considering various aspects (Denecke and Deng, 2015) that can directly impact the users' health conditions, such as:

(1) Changes in the medical condition (e.g., *Sentiment can be observed as a change in a patient's medical condition which can improve or worsen over a time.*)

(2) Severity of the medical condition that impacts patient life (e.g., *severe headache impacts the patient's life more than a mild headache.*)

(3) Outcome of a treatment (e.g., *there may be positive or negative impacts in a patient's treatment.*)

In the current study, the problem of medical sentiment identification is addressed by exploiting two important associated aspects as shown in Figure-1 and leveraging their synergies in a deep multi-task learning framework. In recent years, neural network models have gained their popularity for solving problems in several domains (Misra et al., 2016; Luong et al., 2015), as they facilitate an efficient way of amalgamating information from several tasks. This method of multi-task learning provides advantages in (1) minimizing the number of parameters and (2) reducing the risk of over-fitting. The aim of multi-task learning (MTL) is to efficiently enhance the system performance by integrating the other similar tasks. The primal factor of MTL is the sharing scheme in latent feature space. Most of the existing methods on multi-task classification attempt to divide the features of different tasks based on task-specific and task-invariant feature space, considering only parameters of some components that could be shared. The major drawback of this mechanism is that the common feature space often incorporates some redundant task-variant

---

[1]The reader is encouraged to contact the authors regarding the availability of data and source code

Proceedings of NAACL-HLT 2018, pages 271–277
New Orleans, Louisiana, June 1 - 6, 2018. ©2018 Association for Computational Linguistics

Task1: Medical Condition			Task2: Medication		
Medical Blog-text	**Label**	**Description**	**Medical Blog-text**	**Label**	**Description**
*"I felt an **incredible surge of unsteadiness**"*	Exist	User shares the **symptoms (negative sentiment)** of any medical problem.	"Hi been on Sertaline now for abut 4 weeks. My mood has **definitely improved**"	Effective	User shares the **positive sentiment** in the form of **usefulness of the treatment.**
*"Previously I have taken flixonase which has given no long term relief 10 days ago I went back to the doctor and was given Betnesol. This has **immediately relieved me all symptoms**"*	Recover	User shares the **recovering status (positive sentiment)** from the previous medical problems.	"Had anxiety for few months on 2mg diazapam. Nothing seems to help been in bed for two days **cant sleep waking at 3 4 5 am**"	Ineffective	The **no effect** of the **treatment** is reported in the user narration.
*"I recently started lexapro 3 days, Im absolutely lost I feel **weak and shaky** everyday and **cant eat right I dont sleep normal. Ill die young** and thecause will be cardiac arrest"*	Deteriorate	User describes its medical condition to be **worsen (negative sentiment)** over the span of medical treatment.	"Day 6 that I have taken my citalopram. Anxiety is down, but now Im starting to **feel more and more off..** Random **high chest pains** Plus feeling a **bit foggy and spacey..**"	Serious Adverse Effect	User shares the **negative opinion** towards the treatment mainly in the form of adverse drug effect.

Figure 1: Exemplar description of medical blog-text from two different medical aspects (medical condition and medication). The texts in bold indicates the sentiment word.

features, while certain common features could also lie in the task specific feature space, leading to feature redundancy.

Adversarial learning (Goodfellow et al., 2014) is the process of learning a model to correctly classify both unmodified data and adversarial data through the regularization method. It can be used to combat this issue by ensuring the mutual representation between the task that could inherently disjoint task-specific and task-invariant feature space. This helps in eliminating redundant features from the feature space.

Motivated by the success of adversarial learning in several classification tasks (Miyato et al., 2016; Ge et al., 2017), we adopt the adversarial multi-learning framework to capture the MS in various medical aspects.

Contribution: (i) a description of the medical-sentiment classification task by mining medical blogs using users sentiments towards medical condition and medication, and **(ii)** a method for analysis of medical sentiments over various aspects by exploiting the multi-task adversarial training framework which enables multiple aspects of MS tasks to be jointly trained.

2   Related Works

In the recent past, there has been a significant growth in the studies to analyze the sentiment of users in a healthcare/medical domain. The study conducted by Denecke and Deng (2015) provides the quantitative assessment of sentiment across the clinical narrative and social media sources. Towards this, they created a domain-specific corpus from MIMIC II database containing clinical doc-

uments (nurse letters, radiology reports, and discharge summaries). They also studied users self reported drug reviews on blogs (WebMD, DrugRating) to asses the possible medical sentiments. Majority of the current research in medical sentiment analysis are focused on understanding the mental health disorder, mainly depression. Several shared tasks (Losada et al., 2017; Hollingshead et al., 2017) have also been organized to study the patient health-related opinions on social media. The challenge defined in Milne et al. (2016) aims to automatically classify the user posts from an online mental health forum into four different categories (crisis/red/amber/green) according to how urgently the post needs the attention.

Shickel et al. (2016) introduced the notion of applying sentiment analysis to the mental health domain by defining new polarity classification scheme. They split the traditional 'neutral' class into both a dual polarity sentiment (both positive and negative) and a 'neither positive nor negative' sentiment class. Some of the other prominent works in the opinion mining in medical setting, includes studies by (Bobicev et al., 2012; Sokolova and Bobicev, 2011; Ali et al., 2013).

In the study conducted by (Pestian et al., 2012), authors analyzed the emotions and sentiment of suicide notes. The other study in medical sentiment analysis includes the work of Bobicev et al. (2014), where they analyzed sequences of sentiments (encouragement, gratitude, confusion, facts, and endorsement) in In Vitro Fertilization (IVF) medical forum.

In terms of methods, majority of the work utilizes machine learning technique (SVM, naive Bayes, logistic regression) by exploiting features such as

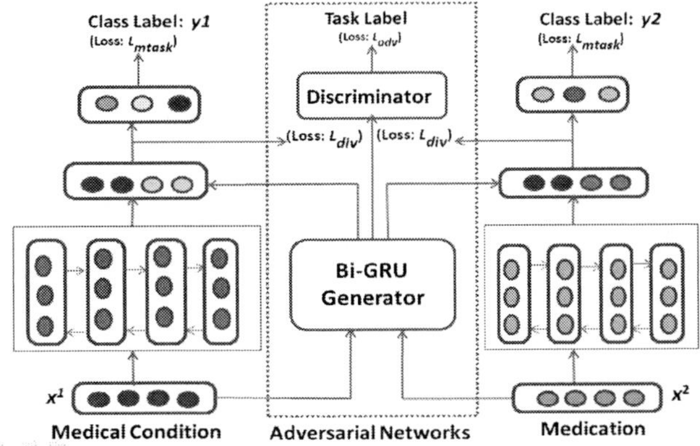

Figure 2: Architecture of proposed methodology

bigram, trigram, parts of speech. Also, there has been predominant use of general sentiment lexicon, however their analysis shows that it does not help in capturing the medical sentiment. More domain specific knowledge is also embedded using medical knowledge graph such as UMLS to identify the medical condition and treatment (Sokolova et al., 2013).

3 Overview of the proposed model

We formulate the MS analysis problem as a multi-task classification problem.

Problem Statement: Let us assume that a blog-text P consisting of k sentences i.e., $P = \{s_1, s_2 \ldots s_k\}$ and the set of tasks, $T = \{t_1, t_2\}$ be given. Let the data set of task $t \in T$ be $\mathscr{D}_t = \{(x_t^n, y_t^n) : n = 1 \ldots N_t\}$, where x_t^n denotes a blog-text P with the corresponding label y_t^n from a task t having N_t instances. The task is to predict $\bar{y}_t$ such that $\bar{y}_t = \text{argmax}_{y_t}\{p(y_t|x_t)\}$.

We clearly illustrate the two tasks related to MS identification in Figure-1.

In this section, we present an overview of the proposed model for multi-task medical sentiment classification. We use the bi-directional gated recurrent units (Bi-GRU) (Chung et al., 2014) to encode the blog-text as it is computationally cheaper than long short term memory (LSTM) (Hochreiter and Schmidhuber, 1997). The updates for Bi-GRU units can be computed by

$$h_t = BiGRU(h_{t-1}, x_t) \quad (1)$$

where, h_t and h_{t-1} are the hidden units at time t and $(t-1)$, respectively. x_t is the input at time t.

3.1 Classification of Medical Blog

Let us assume that a blog-text P having k sentences and word sequence $w = \{w_1, w_2, \ldots w_l\}$ be given. The embedding layer is used to find out the vector representation $x_i \in \mathcal{R}^{d \times V}$ from a d dimensional pre-trained word embedding of vocabulary V. Each word $w_i \in w$ will be represented by its respective word embedding x_i . The hidden units h_l learned at the last time step (l) of sequence are considered as the encoding of the medical blog, P. The representations h_l generated from the Eq 1 are fed to a fully connected softmax layer to generate the probability distribution over the given classes.

$$\bar{y} = softmax(h_l^T W + z) \quad (2)$$

Here, W and z are weight matrix and bias vector, respectively. The term $\bar{y}$ denotes the predicted probability distribution.

Loss Function: Cross entropy is used to define the loss function. Given a training dataset $\mathscr{D} = \{(x^i, y^i) : i = 1 \ldots N\}$, the network parameters are trained to minimize the cross entropy of the predicted probability distributions ($\bar{y}$) and true probability distributions (y) over the C number of classes.

$$\mathcal{L}(y, \bar{y}) = -\sum_{i=1}^{N} \sum_{j=1}^{C} y_i^j log(\bar{y}_i^j) \quad (3)$$

The above loss function can be extended for our problem in the following ways:

$$\mathcal{L}_{mtask} = \lambda_1 \mathcal{L}(y_1, \bar{y}_1) + \lambda_2 \mathcal{L}(y_2, \bar{y}_2) \quad (4)$$

where λ_1 and λ_2 are the weight factors for the task 'Medical condition' and 'Medication', respectively.

Task 1: Medical Condition					
Total blog-post	Exist	Recover	Deteriorate	Avg # of sentences	Avg # of words
5188	2396	703	2089	10	192
Task 2: Medication					
Total blog-post	Effective	Ineffective	Serious Adverse Effect	Avg # of sentences	Avg # of words
2301	462	613	1,226	9	176

Table 1: Dataset statistics for Task 1 and Task 2

Features for multi-task learning: The multi-task learning is governed by sharing the latent features over different tasks. In the proposed neural network based model, the features are the hidden states of BiGRU at the end of sequence. Motivated by the shared-private feature sharing scheme in (Liu et al., 2017), for each task we define two feature spaces; task-specific and task-invariant. Mathematically, for a given blog-text P of task t, we can compute its task-specific features $h_l^t = BiGRU(h_{l-1}^t, x_l)$ and task-invariant features $f_l^t = BiGRU(f_{l-1}^t, x_l)$. Subsequently, the final features will be the concatenation of both features.

3.2 Adversarial Training

Although the feature sharing scheme separates the features into two features spaces, but there is no guarantee that contamination will not be made. Inspired by adversarial networks, we follow the generative-discriminative strategy to avoid the contamination in features space in which a BiGRU works as generator (G) to generate task-invariant features. A discriminator model (D) is used to map the task-invariant features of a blog-text into a probability distribution. It is mainly a multi-layer perceptron classifier which classifies a blog sentence into its respective tasks. The adversarial loss is used to train the model which produces task-invariant features such that a classifier cannot reliably predict the task based on these features. Similar to (Goodfellow et al., 2014; Liu et al., 2017), we use the following adversarial loss function

$$\mathcal{L}_{adv} = \min_G \left(\max_D \left(\sum_{t=1}^T \sum_{i=1}^{N_t} d_i^t log[D(G(x^t))] \right) \right) \tag{5}$$

where d_i^t is the gold label indicating the type of the current task. Based on the recent work (Bousmalis et al., 2016; Liu et al., 2017) on shared-private latent space analysis, we introduce another divergence loss function $\mathcal{L}_{div}$ to castigate the redundant features and encourage the task-invariant and task-specific feature extractors to encode different

aspects of the inputs. The divergence loss function can be computed as $\mathcal{L}_{div} = \sum_{t=1}^T \|F^{t^T} H^t\|_F$, where F^t and H^t are two matrices, where rows are task-invariant and task-specific features of a blog-text from a task t. The $\|.\|_F$ denotes the Frobenius norm of the matrix. The final loss function $\mathcal{L} = \alpha_1 \mathcal{L}_{mtask} + \alpha_2 \mathcal{L}_{adv} + \alpha_3 \mathcal{L}_{div}$ is used as underlying loss function to train the network. Here α_1, α_2 and α_3 are the hyper-parameters of the networks.

4 Dataset and Experimental Setup

We generate a corpus[2] of $7,490$ blog-text collected on four popular groups, namely *Depression, Allergy, Asthma, and Anxiety*. Out of total blog-text, $5,188$ blogs concern about the *medical conditions* and $2,302$ are classified as *medication*. We provide the detailed dataset statistics for both the task is presented in Table-1. A team of three annotators [3] independently annotated the user posts with three classes on both the classification strategies. The Cohen's kappa approach (Cohen, 1960) was used to measure the inter-annotator agreement. We observe high agreement ratio of 0.79 (task 1) and 0.84 (task 2) for exact matching of the class w.r.t each blog post. We have performed 5-fold cross-validation experiment on both the datasets. The pre-trained embeddings (Mikolov et al., 2013) of dimension 300 were used in the experiments. The dimension of Bi-GRU hidden unit is set to 100 via grid search, on the basis of cross-validation performance. We choose the same value of 0.5 for both the weight factors λ_1 and λ_2 to impose equal importance on both the tasks. Training was performed using stochastic gradient descent over mini-batches of size 50 considering the Adadelta (Zeiler, 2012) update rule with an initial learning rate of 0.01. The min-max optimization is performed with the help of gradient reversal layer (Ganin et al., 2016). As a regularizer, we use dropout (Hinton et al., 2012) with a probability of 0.5. We train the network with 130 epochs. The optimal [4] hyper-parameter values are obtained via a grid search for α_1, α_2, and α_3 over the best cross-validation performance.

---

[2] Accepted at LREC-2018; entitled "Medical Sentiment Analysis using Social Media: Towards building a Patient Assisted System" and will be publicly available.

[3] undergraduate students with the medical knowledge

[4] $\alpha_1 = 0.88$, $\alpha_2 = 0.12$ and $\alpha_3 = 0.03$

Models	Task 1: Medical Condition			Task 2: Medication		
	Precision	Recall	F-Score	Precision	Recall	F-Score
Baseline 1: MT-LSTM	63.40	61.38	62.37	88.23	77.38	82.45
Baseline 2: ST-LSTM	63.19	62.47	62.83	85.94	77.46	81.48
Proposed Approach	66.82	63.61	65.18	85.83	81.79	83.76

Table 2: Performance comparisons of our proposed approach with baselines.

4.1 Performance Evaluation

In order to show the effectiveness of our proposed method, we chose the neural network models popular in single task and multitask setting for our specified problem of text classification.

Baseline 1: Single Task-LSTM

Baseline 2: Multi Task-LSTM (Liu et al., 2016). Table-2 reports the results of our proposed approach with baselines system. From the results, we observe that the performance on both the tasks significantly increase with the introduction of adversarial learning in multi-task framework. More specifically, compared to baseline 1, we observe the performance improvement of 2.81 and 1.31 F-score points on Task 1 & 2, respectively. In multi-task framework (Baseline 2), our system achieves the improvements of 2.35 and 2.28 F-score points on Task 1 & 2, respectively. We also analyze that mere introduction of multi-task framework sometimes may cause a drop in performance. This is because of the shared feature-space which includes both private and shared features leading to redundancy. Statistical significance test shows that the improvements over both the baselines are statistically significant as (p-value < 0.05).

4.2 Analysis

Our analysis on medical blog-text discovers that unlike traditional SA study on social media text, SA on medical text owes several unique challenges which have formed the major causes of the errors:

(1) Usually, the user present the health related information in a more elusive way which requires deeper analysis of metaphor and sarcasm. For example:

" Lol I'm just a big ball of anxiety fun.",

" My head is like air."

(2) MS is often presented implicitly which need to be inferred, for instance, from the medical concepts used in documents. Implicit MS (Exist) present in the blog are for example:

"It almost feels like im half awake and half asleep."

(3) The usage of abbreviated and short words have become ubiquitous in medical blog text. For e.g.,*"Cit" for the "Citopram".*

(4) The context scope of a sentiment changes extensively from a single phrase to multiple sentences. Moreover, adversative transitive words were widely used to link these phrases or sentences. The medical sentiment was bounded and implied by these inter and intra- sentence discourse relations. For example:

"The thoughts are of anything which is quite good. I have an anxiety disorder but I can't cope with it..."

5 Conclusion and Future Work

In this paper, we have introduced different aspects of sentiments in the context of medicine such as 'medication' and 'medical condition' instead of conventional polarity to judge user's health status. For this, we have utilized highly representative medical blog text to validate our study. We have proposed a robust sentiment-sensitive multi-task framework, settling on adversarial learning to capture the medical sentiment in the user's blog-post. We were able to obtain significant performance improvements over the state-of-the-art baseline system in all the cases. In future, we plan to address the implicit and sarcastic medical sentiments that account to the majority of the errors.

Acknowledgement

Asif Ekbal acknowledges Young Faculty Research Fellowship (YFRF), supported by Visvesvaraya PhD scheme for Electronics and IT, Ministry of Electronics and Information Technology (MeitY), Government of India, being implemented by Digital India Corporation (formerly Media Lab Asia). Amit Sheth acknowledged partial support from NMH award R01MH105384 "Modeling Social Behavior for Healthcare Utilization in Depression. All findings and opinions are of authors and not sponsors.

References

Tanveer Ali, Marina Sokolova, David Schramm, and Diana Inkpen. 2013. Opinion learning from medical forums. In *Proceedings of the International Conference Recent Advances in Natural Language Processing RANLP 2013*. pages 18–24.

Victoria Bobicev, Marina Sokolova, Yasser Jafer, and David Schramm. 2012. Learning sentiments from tweets with personal health information. In *Canadian Conference on Artificial Intelligence*. Springer, pages 37–48.

Victoria Bobicev, Marina Sokolova, and Michael Oakes. 2014. Recognition of sentiment sequences in online discussions. In *Proceedings of the Second Workshop on Natural Language Processing for Social Media (SocialNLP)*. pages 44–49.

Konstantinos Bousmalis, George Trigeorgis, Nathan Silberman, Dilip Krishnan, and Dumitru Erhan. 2016. Domain separation networks. In *Advances in Neural Information Processing Systems*. pages 343–351.

Junyoung Chung, Caglar Gulcehre, KyungHyun Cho, and Yoshua Bengio. 2014. Empirical evaluation of gated recurrent neural networks on sequence modeling. *arXiv preprint arXiv:1412.3555* .

Jacob Cohen. 1960. A coefficient of agreement for nominal scales. *Educational and psychological measurement* 20(1):37–46.

Kerstin Denecke and Yihan Deng. 2015. Sentiment analysis in medical settings: New opportunities and challenges. *Artificial intelligence in medicine* 64(1):17–27.

Yaroslav Ganin, Evgeniya Ustinova, Hana Ajakan, Pascal Germain, Hugo Larochelle, François Laviolette, Mario Marchand, and Victor Lempitsky. 2016. Domain-adversarial training of neural networks. *Journal of Machine Learning Research* 17(59):1–35.

ZongYuan Ge, Sergey Demyanov, Zetao Chen, and Rahil Garnavi. 2017. Generative openmax for multi-class open set classification. *arXiv preprint arXiv:1707.07418* .

Ian Goodfellow, Jean Pouget-Abadie, Mehdi Mirza, Bing Xu, David Warde-Farley, Sherjil Ozair, Aaron Courville, and Yoshua Bengio. 2014. Generative adversarial nets. In *Advances in neural information processing systems*. pages 2672–2680.

Geoffrey E Hinton, Nitish Srivastava, Alex Krizhevsky, Ilya Sutskever, and Ruslan R Salakhutdinov. 2012. Improving neural networks by preventing co-adaptation of feature detectors. *arXiv preprint arXiv:1207.0580* .

Sepp Hochreiter and Jürgen Schmidhuber. 1997. Long short-term memory. *Neural computation* 9(8):1735–1780.

Kristy Hollingshead, Molly E. Ireland, and Kate Loveys, editors. 2017. *Proceedings of the Fourth Workshop on Computational Linguistics and Clinical Psychology — From Linguistic Signal to Clinical Reality*. Association for Computational Linguistics, Vancouver, BC. http://www.aclweb.org/anthology/W17-31.

Pengfei Liu, Xipeng Qiu, and Xuanjing Huang. 2016. Recurrent neural network for text classification with multi-task learning. *arXiv preprint arXiv:1605.05101* .

Pengfei Liu, Xipeng Qiu, and Xuanjing Huang. 2017. Adversarial multi-task learning for text classification. In *Proceedings of the 55th Annual Meeting of the Association for Computational Linguistics (Volume 1: Long Papers)*. Association for Computational Linguistics, Vancouver, Canada, pages 1–10. http://aclweb.org/anthology/P17-1001.

David E Losada, Fabio Crestani, and Javier Parapar. 2017. Clef 2017 erisk overview: Early risk prediction on the internet: Experimental foundations .

Minh-Thang Luong, Quoc V Le, Ilya Sutskever, Oriol Vinyals, and Lukasz Kaiser. 2015. Multi-task sequence to sequence learning. *arXiv preprint arXiv:1511.06114* .

Tomas Mikolov, Kai Chen, Greg Corrado, and Jeffrey Dean. 2013. Efficient estimation of word representations in vector space. *arXiv preprint arXiv:1301.3781* .

David N Milne, Glen Pink, Ben Hachey, and Rafael A Calvo. 2016. Clpsych 2016 shared task: Triaging content in online peer-support forums. In *Proceedings of the Third Workshop on Computational Lingusitics and Clinical Psychology*. pages 118–127.

Ishan Misra, Abhinav Shrivastava, Abhinav Gupta, and Martial Hebert. 2016. Cross-stitch networks for multi-task learning. In *Proceedings of the IEEE Conference on Computer Vision and Pattern Recognition*. pages 3994–4003.

Takeru Miyato, Andrew M Dai, and Ian Goodfellow. 2016. Adversarial training methods for semi-supervised text classification. *arXiv preprint arXiv:1605.07725* .

John P Pestian, Pawel Matykiewicz, Michelle Linn-Gust, Brett South, Ozlem Uzuner, Jan Wiebe, K Bretonnel Cohen, John Hurdle, and Christopher Brew. 2012. Sentiment analysis of suicide notes: A shared task. *Biomedical informatics insights* 5:BII–S9042.

Benjamin Shickel, Martin Heesacker, Sherry Benton, Ashkan Ebadi, Paul Nickerson, and Parisa Rashidi. 2016. Self-reflective sentiment analysis. In *Proceedings of the Third Workshop on Computational Lingusitics and Clinical Psychology*. pages 23–32.

Marina Sokolova and Victoria Bobicev. 2011. Sentiments and opinions in health-related web messages. In *Proceedings of the International Conference Recent Advances in Natural Language Processing 2011*. pages 132–139.

Marina Sokolova, Stan Matwin, Yasser Jafer, and David Schramm. 2013. How joe and jane tweet about their health: Mining for personal health information on twitter. In *Proceedings of the International Conference Recent Advances in Natural Language Processing RANLP 2013*. pages 626–632.

Matthew D. Zeiler. 2012. ADADELTA: an adaptive learning rate method. *CoRR* abs/1212.5701. http://arxiv.org/abs/1212.5701.

Recurrent Entity Networks with Delayed Memory Update for Targeted Aspect-based Sentiment Analysis

Fei Liu   **Trevor Cohn**   **Timothy Baldwin**
School of Computing and Information Systems
The University of Melbourne
Victoria, Australia
`fliu3@student.unimelb.edu.au`
`t.cohn@unimelb.edu.au` `tb@ldwin.net`

Abstract

While neural networks have been shown to achieve impressive results for sentence-level sentiment analysis, targeted aspect-based sentiment analysis (TABSA) — extraction of fine-grained opinion polarity w.r.t. a pre-defined set of aspects — remains a difficult task. Motivated by recent advances in memory-augmented models for machine reading, we propose a novel architecture, utilising external "memory chains" with a delayed memory update mechanism to track entities. On a TABSA task, the proposed model demonstrates substantial improvements over state-of-the-art approaches, including those using external knowledge bases.[1]

1 Introduction

Targeted aspect-based sentiment analysis (TABSA) is the task of identifying fine-grained opinion polarity towards a specific aspect associated with a given target. The task requires classification of opinions on different entities across a range of different attributes, with the expectation that there will be no overt opinion expressed on a given entity for many attributes. This can be seen in Example (1), e.g., where opinions on the aspects SAFETY and PRICE are expressed for entity *LOC1* but not entity *LOC2*:[2]

(1) LOC1 is your best bet for secure although expensive and LOC2 is too far.

Target	Aspect	Sentiment
LOC1	SAFETY	positive
LOC1	PRICE	negative
LOC2	TRANSIT-LOCATION	negative

The earliest work on (T)ABSA relied heavily on feature engineering (Wagner et al., 2014; Kiritchenko et al., 2014), but more recent work based on deep learning has used models such as LSTMs to automatically learn aspect-specific word and sentence representations (Tang et al., 2016a).

Despite these successes, keeping track of multiple entity–aspect pairs remains a difficult task, even for an LSTM. As reported in Saeidi et al. (2016), a target-dependent biLSTM is ineffective, both in terms of aspect detection and sentiment classification, compared to a simple logistic regression model with n-gram features. Intuitively, we would expect that a model which better captures linguistic structure via the original word sequencing should perform better, which provides the motivation for this research.

More recently, successful works in (T)ABSA have explored the idea of leveraging external memory (Tang et al., 2016b; Chen et al., 2017). Their models are largely based on memory networks (Weston et al., 2015), originally developed for reasoning-focused machine reading comprehension tasks. In contrast to memory networks, where each input sentence/word occupies a memory slot and is then accessed via attention independently, recent advances in machine reading suggest that processing inputs sequentially is beneficial to overall performance (Seo et al., 2017; Henaff et al., 2017).

However, successful machine reading models may not be directly applicable to TABSA due to the key difference in the granularity of inputs between the two tasks: on the Children's Book Test corpus (CBT), for example, competitive models take as input a window of text, centred around candidate entities, with crucial information contained within that window (Hill et al., 2015; Henaff et al., 2017). In TABSA, given the fine-grained nature of the task, it is common practice for models to

---

[1]Code available at `https://github.com/liufly/delayed-memory-update-entnet`.

[2]Note that in our dataset, all entity mentions have been pre-nomalised to *LOCn*, where n is an index.

Proceedings of NAACL-HLT 2018, pages 278–283
New Orleans, Louisiana, June 1 - 6, 2018. ©2018 Association for Computational Linguistics

operate at the word- rather than chunk/sentence-level. It is not uncommon to see examples like Example (1), where the sentence starts with *LOC1*, but the negative PRICE sentiment towards the entity is not expressed until much later. Moreover, phrases such as *best bet* and *although* play the role of triggers, indicating that succeeding tokens bear aspect/sentiment signal. This key difference necessitates the ability to model the delayed activation of memory updates.

In this work, we propose a novel model architecture for TABSA, augmented with multiple "memory chains", and equipped with a delayed memory update mechanism, to keep track of numerous entities independently. We evaluate the effectiveness of the proposed model over the task of TABSA, and achieve substantial improvements over a number of baselines, including one incorporating external knowledge bases, setting a new state of the art in both sentiment classification and aspect detection.

2   Methodology

Task description. In TABSA, a sentence s typically consists of a sequence of words: $\{w_1, \ldots, w_i, \ldots, w_m\}$ where w_i denotes words interleaved with one or more targets (t), which we assume to be pre-identified as with *LOC1* and *LOC2* in Example (1). Following Saeidi et al. (2016), we frame the task as a 3-class classification problem: given a sentence s, a pre-identified set of target entities T and fixed set of aspects A, predict the sentiment polarity $y \in \{positive, negative, none\}$ over the full set of target–aspect pairs $\{(t, a) : t \in T, a \in A\}$. For example, (*LOC1*,SAFETY) has gold-standard polarity *positive*, while (*LOC1*,TRANSIT-LOCATION) has polarity *none*.

Proposed model. To this end, we design a neural network architecture, capable of tracking and updating the states of entities at the right time with external memory, making it a natural fit for the task. Specifically, our model maintains a number of "memory chains" h^j, one for each entity with the key k^j and dynamically updates the states (h^j) of them as it progresses through the sentence with the help of the delay recurrence d^j, taking previous activations into account. An illustration of our model is provided in Figure 1.

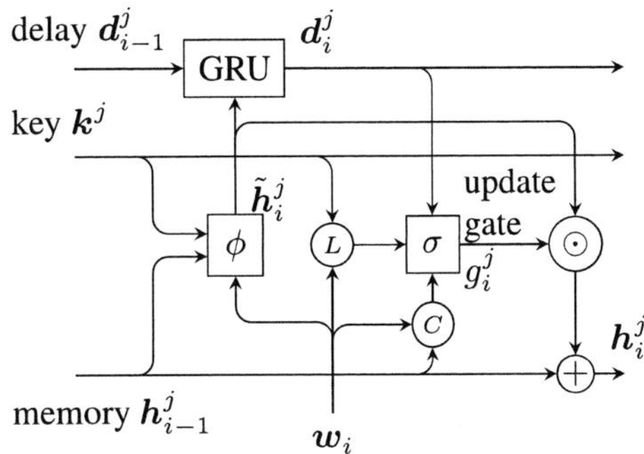

Figure 1: Illustration of our model with a single memory chain at time i. σ, ϕ and GRU represent Equations (2), (3) and (4), while circled nodes L, C, $\odot$ and $+$ depict the location, content terms, Hadamard product, and addition, resp.

Delayed memory update. Update of each memory chain is controlled by a gating mechanism, consisting of three components: the "content" term $w_i \cdot h_{i-1}^j$, the "location" term $w_i \cdot k^j$ and the "delay" term $v \cdot d_i^j$ where d_i^j carries knowledge regarding previous activation of the gate and v is a trainable parameter vector. All three terms may lead to the activation of g_i^j, but differ in how they turn the gate on. While the "location" term causes the gate to open for memory chains whose keys (k^j) match the input, the "content" term triggers the activation when the content of the entities (h_{i-1}^j) matches the input. The delay term models how and when the gate was turned on in the past with a GRU (Chung et al., 2014) and how past activations should influence the current one.

More formally, with arrows denoting processing direction, the update gate is defined as:

$$\overrightarrow{g}_i^j = \sigma(w_i \cdot \overrightarrow{h}_{i-1}^j + w_i \cdot k^j + \overrightarrow{v} \cdot \overrightarrow{d}_i^j) \quad (2)$$

where $\overrightarrow{g}_i^j$ is the update gate value for the j-th memory at time i,[3] k^j is the embedding for the j-th entity (key), $\overrightarrow{h}_{i-1}^j$ is the hidden memory representation responsible for keeping track of the state of the j-th entity (content), and σ is the sigmoid activation function. The delay recurrence $\overrightarrow{d}_i^j$ is defined as:

$$\overrightarrow{h}_i^j = \phi(\overrightarrow{U}\,\overrightarrow{h}_{i-1}^j + \overrightarrow{V}k^j + \overrightarrow{W}w_i) \quad (3)$$

$$\overrightarrow{d}_i^j = \overrightarrow{\text{GRU}}(\overrightarrow{h}_i^j, \overrightarrow{d}_{i-1}^j) \quad (4)$$

---

[3] While $\overrightarrow{g}_i^j$ could instead be a vector for finer-grained control, following Henaff et al. (2017), we use a scalar for simplicity.

where $\overrightarrow{h}{}_i^j$ is the new candidate memory vector to be incorporated into the existing memory $\overrightarrow{h}{}_{i-1}^j$ to form the new memory $\overrightarrow{h}{}_i^j$, ϕ is the parametric ReLU activation function (He et al., 2015), and $\overrightarrow{U}$, $\overrightarrow{V}$ and $\overrightarrow{W}$ are trainable weight matrices.

Once the update gate value has been computed, the j-th memory is then updated according to the intensity of $\overrightarrow{g}{}_i^j$:

$$\overrightarrow{\mathring{h}}{}_i^j = \overrightarrow{h}{}_{i-1}^j + \overrightarrow{g}{}_i^j \odot \overrightarrow{h}{}_i^j \qquad (5)$$

where $\odot$ is the Hadamard product, and $\overrightarrow{\mathring{h}}{}_i^j$ is the unnormalised memory representation for the j-th entity.

Essentially, gate $\overrightarrow{g}{}_i^j$ determines how much the j-th memory should be updated, factoring in three elements: (1) how similar the current input w_i is to the entity being tracked (k^j); (2) how related the current input w_i is to the state of the j-th entity ($\overrightarrow{h}{}_{i-1}^j$); and (3) how past activation should influence the current one. Update of the memory of an entity is only triggered when the gate is activated.

Normalisation. Following the update, the model performs a normalisation step, allowing the memory to forget: $\overrightarrow{h}{}_i^j = \overrightarrow{\mathring{h}}{}_i^j / \| \overrightarrow{\mathring{h}}{}_i^j \|$ where $\| \overrightarrow{\mathring{h}}{}_i^j \|$ denotes the Euclidean norm of $\overrightarrow{\mathring{h}}{}_i^j$. As all information stored in $\overrightarrow{h}{}_i^j$ is constrained to be of unit length, when new information $\overrightarrow{\mathring{h}}{}_i^j$ is added to the existing memory $\overrightarrow{h}{}_{i-1}^j$, the cosine distance between the original and updated memory decreases, allowing the model to forget information deemed out-of-date.

Bi-directionality. We apply the above steps both forward and backward over the sentence, enabling the model to capture sentiment terms appearing before and after its associated entity. The memory representation incorporating contexts from both directions is obtained by $h_i^j = \overrightarrow{h}{}_i^j + \overleftarrow{h}{}_i^j$, with $\overleftarrow{h}{}_i^j$ computed analogously to $\overrightarrow{h}{}_i^j$.

Final classifier. Our model predicts the sentiment polarity $\hat{y}$ to the given target t and aspect a embeddings by incorporating the states of all tracked entities in the form of a weighted sum u:

$$p^j = \mathrm{softmax}\left((k^j)^\top W_{att} \begin{bmatrix} t \\ a \end{bmatrix} \right) \qquad (6)$$

$$u = \sum_j p^j h_m^j \qquad (7)$$

where $[\,]$ denotes concatenation, m is sentence length, and W_{att} is a trainable weight matrix. Here, the values of both t and a take the embedding values of their corresponding words (i.e. t and a are drawn from the same embedding matrix as are the input words w_i). In the case of multi-word aspect expressions (e.g. TRANSIT-LOCATION), we take the mean of the embeddings of the constituent words. We then transform u to get:

$$\hat{y} = \mathrm{softmax}(R\phi(Hu + a)) \qquad (8)$$

Training is carried out based on cross entropy loss.

$$\mathcal{L} = \mathrm{CrossEntropy}(y, \hat{y}) \qquad (9)$$

Comparision with `EntNet`. While our model is largely inspired by Recurrent Entity Networks (`EntNets`: Henaff et al. (2017)), it differs in three main respects. First, we explicitly model the delay of activation of the update gates g^j with the GRU in Equations (2) and (4) as opposed to making h_i^j implicitly assume the same responsibility in `EntNets`. Admittedly, for `EntNets` on `bAbI` and `CBT`, given the coarse-grained nature and the difference in the granularity of inputs (sentences vs. words), the demand for modelling delayed memory update is less obvious. With this delayed gate activation mechanism, we essentially decouple the duty of capturing transitions of activations between steps from the task of entity state tracking. That is, h_i^j is now dedicated to keeping track of the state of the j-th entity only and released from the burden of monitoring the activation of the update gate. Second, tailoring to the task of TABSA, we incorporate not only the target t but also the aspect a when trying to determine the attention in the softmax function. Third, the proposed model is bi-directional.

3 Experiments

3.1 Experimental Setup

Dataset. To test the effectiveness of our model, we use `Sentihood`, a dataset constructed by Saeidi et al. (2016) for the purpose of detecting aspects and identifying sentiments for each target–aspect pair, consisting of $5,215$ sentences, $3,862$ of which contain a single target, and the remainder multiple targets. Each sentence is annotated with a list of tuples $\{(t, a, y)\}$ with each identifying the sentiment polarity y towards a specific aspect a of

Model	Aspect			Sentiment	
	Acc.	F_1	AUC	Acc.	AUC
LR (Saeidi et al., 2016)	—	39.3	92.4	87.5	90.5
LSTM-Final (Saeidi et al., 2016)	—	68.9	89.8	82.0	85.4
LSTM-Loc (Saeidi et al., 2016)	—	69.3	89.7	81.9	83.9
LSTM+TA+SA (Ma et al., 2018)	66.4	76.7	—	86.8	—
SenticLSTM (Ma et al., 2018)	67.4	78.2	—	89.3	—
EntNet†	66.3	69.8	89.5	87.6	89.7
Our model†	**73.5**	**78.5**	**94.4**	**91.0**	**94.8**

Table 1: Performance on Sentihood. We take the results reported in Saeidi et al. (2016) and Ma et al. (2018), resp; **Bold** = best performance; "—" = not reported; † = average performance over 5 runs.

a given target t in s. Ultimately, given a sentence s, we are interested in both detecting the mention of an aspect a for target t (a label other than *none*), and also identifying the specific sentiment y w.r.t. the target–aspect pair. A detailed description of the task is presented in Section 2.

Model configuration. We initialise our model with GloVe (300-D, trained on 42B tokens, 1.9M vocab, not updated during training: Pennington et al. (2014)) [4] and pre-process the corpus with tokenisation using NLTK (Bird et al., 2009) and case folding. Training is carried out over 800 epochs with the FTRL optimiser (McMahan et al., 2013) and a batch size of 128 and learning rate of 0.05. We use the following hyper-parameters for weight matrices in both directions: $R \in \mathbb{R}^{300 \times 3}$, H, U, V, W are all matrices of size $\mathbb{R}^{300 \times 300}$, $v \in \mathbb{R}^{300}$, and hidden size of the GRU in Equation (4) is 300. Dropout is applied to the output of ϕ in the final classifier (Equation (8)) with a rate of 0.2. Moreover, we employ the technique introduced by Gal and Ghahramani (2016) where the same dropout mask is applied to the input w_i at every step with a rate of 0.2. Lastly, to curb overfitting, we regularise the last layer (Equation (8)) with an L_2 penalty on its weights: $\lambda \|R\|$ where $\lambda = 0.001$.

We empirically set the number of memory chains to 6, with the keys of two of them set to the same embeddings as the target words *LOC1* and *LOC2*, resp., and the other 4 chains with free key embeddings which are updated during training, and therefore free to capture any entities.[5]

Consistent with Saeidi et al. (2016), we tackle the data unbalanced problem (*none* $\gg$ *positive* + *negative*) by sampling the same number of training instances within a batch randomly from each class.

Evaluation. We benchmark against baseline systems presented in the works of Saeidi et al. (2016) and Ma et al. (2018): (1) LR: a logistic regression classifier with n-gram and POS tag features; (2) LSTM-Final: a biLSTM taking the final states as representations; (3) LSTM-Loc: a biLSTM taking the states at the location where target t is mentioned as representations; (4) LSTM+TA+SA: a biLSTM equipped with complex target and sentence-level attention mechanisms; (5) SenticLSTM: an improved version of (4) incorporating the SenticNet external knowledge base (Cambria et al., 2016). We additionally implement a bi-directional EntNet with the same hyper-parameter settings and GloVe embeddings as our model (Henaff et al., 2017).

In terms of evaluation, we adopt the standard 70/10/20 train/validation/test split, and report the test performance corresponding to the model with the best validation score. Following Saeidi et al. (2016), we consider the top 4 aspects only (GENERAL, PRICE, TRANSIT-LOCATION, and SAFETY) and employ the following evaluation metrics: macro-average F_1 and AUC for aspect detection ignoring the *none* class, and accuracy and macro-average AUC for sentiment classification. Following Ma et al. (2018), we also report strict accuracy for aspect detection, as the fraction of sentences where all aspects are detected correctly.

---

[4] http://nlp.stanford.edu/data/glove.42B.300d.zip

[5] In line with the findings of Henaff et al. (2017) that tying key vectors damages model performance, we observed similar performance deterioration when using tied keys only. While we also experimented with various configurations (all tied vs. all free), this hybrid setup results in the best performance on the validation set.

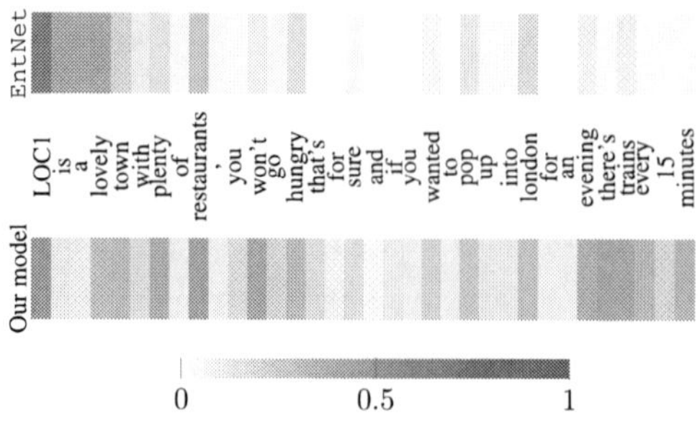

Figure 2: Example of the gate value g_t averaged across memory chains, forward and backward, in EntNet vs. our model.

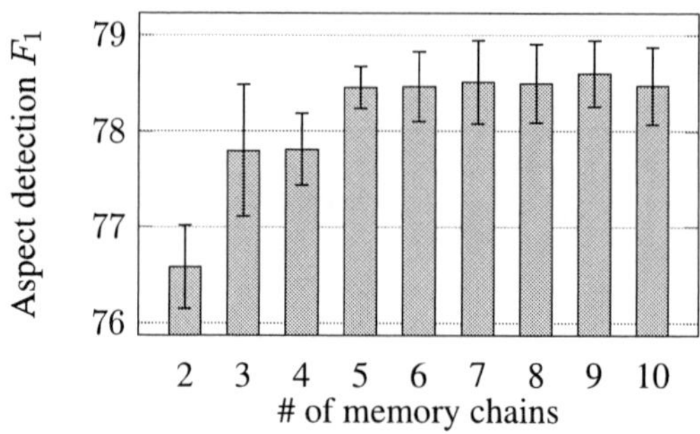

Figure 3: Sensitivity study of model performance to # of memory chains n. Note that we report average performance over 5 runs with standard deviation.

3.2 Results

The experimental results are presented in Table 1.

State-of-the-art results. Our model achieves state-of-the-art results for both aspect detection and sentiment classification. It is impressive that the proposed model, equipped only with domain-independent general-purpose GloVe embeddings, outperforms SenticLSTM, an approach heavily reliant on external knowledge bases and domain-specific embeddings.

EntNet vs. our model. We see consistent performance gains for our model in both aspect detection and sentiment classification, compared to EntNet, esp. for aspect detection, underlining the benefit of delayed update gate activation.

3.3 Discussion

To better understand what the model has learned, we visualise the average gate value g_t in Figure 2, where colour intensity indicates how much memory is updated. Observe that, while updated less by the mention of *LOC1*, our model carries out memory updates upon seeing *lovely town* and *plenty of restaurants*, key phrases associated with aspects such as GENERAL and DINNING. Perhaps even more importantly, despite the distance between *LOC1* and the final portion of the sentence, our model recognises the relevance to TRANSIT-LOCATION and keeps the update gates open to track this particular aspect, as opposed to EntNet where the last phase is overlooked. The ultimate prediction for the TRANSIT-LOCATION aspect of *LOC1* is correct with our model (*positive*), but not detected by EntNet (*none*), resulting in a false negative. More interestingly, with EntNet, once distant from a target, it can be frequently observed

that the activation rate of g_t tends to drop, a tendency not so apparent with our model.

In Figure 3, we further study the sensitivity of model performance to the number of memory chains n (2 of which are constrained to track *LOC1* and *LOC2*, the rest are unconstrained chains). Observe that, when $n < 5$, the model suffers from insufficient capacity (not enough memory chains) to capture the various aspects required by the task, with aspect detection F_1 remaining below 78. In particular, when $n = 2$ (no unconstrained chains), model performance drops substantially to a F_1 of 76.6 ± 0.4. Once $n \geq 5$, aspect detection F_1 increases to around 78, and is quite stable even with as many as $n = 10$ chains.

4 Conclusion

In this paper, we have proposed a model which is capable of dynamically tracking entities with a delayed memory update mechanism, and demonstrated the effectiveness of the method over the task of targeted aspect-based sentiment analysis.

Acknowledgments

We thank the anonymous reviewers for their valuable feedback, and gratefully acknowledge the support of Australian Government Research Training Program Scholarship and National Computational Infrastructure (NCI Australia). This work was also supported in part by the Australian Research Council.

References

Steven Bird, Ewan Klein, and Edward Loper. 2009. *Natural Language Processing with Python*. O'Reilly Media.

Erik Cambria, Soujanya Poria, Rajiv Bajpai, and Bjoern Schuller. 2016. Senticnet 4: A semantic resource for sentiment analysis based on conceptual primitives. In *Proceedings of the 26th International Conference on Computational Linguistics (COLING 2016)*. Osaka, Japan, pages 2666–2677.

Peng Chen, Zhongqian Sun, Lidong Bing, and Wei Yang. 2017. Recurrent attention network on memory for aspect sentiment analysis. In *Proceedings of the 2017 Conference on Empirical Methods in Natural Language Processing (EMNLP 2017)*. Copenhagen, Denmark, pages 452–461.

Junyoung Chung, Caglar Gulcehre, KyungHyun Cho, and Yoshua Bengio. 2014. Empirical evaluation of gated recurrent neural networks on sequence modeling. In *Proceedings of the NIPS 2014 Deep Learning and Representation Learning Workshop*. Montréal, Canada.

Yarin Gal and Zoubin Ghahramani. 2016. A theoretically grounded application of dropout in recurrent neural networks. In *Proceedings of Advances in Neural Information Processing Systems (NIPS 2016)*. Barcelona, Spain, pages 1027–1035.

Kaiming He, Xiangyu Zhang, Shaoqing Ren, and Jian Sun. 2015. Delving deep into rectifiers: Surpassing human-level performance on imagenet classification. In *Proceedings of the 2015 IEEE International Conference on Computer Vision (ICCV 2015)*. Washington, DC, USA, pages 1026–1034.

Mikael Henaff, Jason Weston, Arthur Szlam, Antoine Bordes, and Yann LeCun. 2017. Tracking the world state with recurrent entity networks. In *Proceedings of the 5th International Conference on Learning Representations (ICLR 2017)*. Toulon, France.

Felix Hill, Antoine Bordes, Sumit Chopra, and Jason Weston. 2015. The goldilocks principle: Reading children's books with explicit memory representations. In *Proceedings of the 4th International Conference on Learning Representations (ICLR 2016)*. San Juan, Puerto Rico.

Svetlana Kiritchenko, Xiaodan Zhu, Colin Cherry, and Saif Mohammad. 2014. NRC-Canada-2014: Detecting Aspects and Sentiment in Customer Reviews. In *Proceedings of the 8th International Workshop on Semantic Evaluation (SemEval 2014)*. Dublin, Ireland, pages 437–442.

Yukun Ma, Haiyun Peng, and Erik Cambria. 2018. Targeted aspect-based sentiment analysis via embedding commonsense knowledge into an attentive lstm. In *Proceedings of the 32rd AAAI Conference on Artificial Intelligence (AAAI 2018)*. New Orleans, USA.

H. Brendan McMahan, Gary Holt, David Sculley, Michael Young, Dietmar Ebner, Julian Grady, Lan Nie, Todd Phillips, Eugene Davydov, Daniel Golovin, et al. 2013. Ad click prediction: A view from the trenches. In *Proceedings of the 19th ACM SIGKDD International Conference on Knowledge Discovery and Data Mining (KDD 2013)*. Chicago, USA, pages 1222–1230.

Jeffrey Pennington, Richard Socher, and Christopher Manning. 2014. GloVe: Global vectors for word representation. In *Proceedings of the 2014 Conference on Empirical Methods in Natural Language Processing (EMNLP 2014)*. Doha, Qatar, pages 1532–1543.

Marzieh Saeidi, Guillaume Bouchard, Maria Liakata, and Sebastian Riedel. 2016. Sentihood: Targeted aspect based sentiment analysis dataset for urban neighbourhoods. In *Proceedings of the 26th International Conference on Computational Linguistics (COLING 2016)*. Osaka, Japan, pages 1546–1556.

Minjoon Seo, Sewon Min, Ali Farhadi, and Hannaneh Hajishirzi. 2017. Query-reduction networks for question answering. In *Proceedings of the 5th International Conference on Learning Representations (ICLR 2017)*. Toulon, France.

Duyu Tang, Bing Qin, Xiaocheng Feng, and Ting Liu. 2016a. Effective lstms for target-dependent sentiment classification. In *Proceedings of the 26th International Conference on Computational Linguistics (COLING 2016)*. Osaka, Japan, pages 3298–3307.

Duyu Tang, Bing Qin, and Ting Liu. 2016b. Aspect level sentiment classification with deep memory network. In *Proceedings of the 2016 Conference on Empirical Methods in Natural Language Processing (EMNLP 2016)*. Austin, USA, pages 214–224.

Joachim Wagner, Piyush Arora, Santiago Cortes, Utsab Barman, Dasha Bogdanova, Jennifer Foster, and Lamia Tounsi. 2014. DCU: Aspect-based polarity classification for SemEval task 4. In *Proceedings of the 8th International Workshop on Semantic Evaluation (SemEval 2014)*. Dublin, Ireland, pages 223–229.

Jason Weston, Sumit Chopra, and Antoine Bordes. 2015. Memory networks. In *Proceedings of the 3rd International Conference on Learning Representations (ICLR 2015)*. San Diego, USA.

Near Human-Level Performance in Grammatical Error Correction
with Hybrid Machine Translation

Roman Grundkiewicz
University of Edinburgh
10 Crichton St, Edinburgh EH8 9AB, Scotland
`rgrundki@inf.ed.ac.uk`

Marcin Junczys-Dowmunt
Microsoft
Redmond, WA 98052, USA
`marcinjd@microsoft.com`

Abstract

We combine two of the most popular approaches to automated Grammatical Error Correction (GEC): GEC based on Statistical Machine Translation (SMT) and GEC based on Neural Machine Translation (NMT). The hybrid system achieves new state-of-the-art results on the CoNLL-2014 and JFLEG benchmarks. This GEC system preserves the accuracy of SMT output and, at the same time, generates more fluent sentences as it typical for NMT. Our analysis shows that the created systems are closer to reaching human-level performance than any other GEC system reported so far.

1 Introduction

Currently, the most effective GEC systems are based on phrase-based statistical machine translation (Rozovskaya and Roth, 2016; Junczys-Dowmunt and Grundkiewicz, 2016; Chollampatt and Ng, 2017). Systems that rely on neural machine translation (Yuan and Briscoe, 2016; Xie et al., 2016; Schmaltz et al., 2017; Ji et al., 2017) are not yet able to achieve as high performance as SMT systems according to automatic evaluation metrics (see Table 1 for comparison on the CoNLL-2014 test set). However, it has been shown that the neural approach can produce more fluent output, which might be desirable by human evaluators (Napoles et al., 2017). In this work, we combine both MT flavors within a hybrid GEC system. Such a GEC system preserves the accuracy of SMT output and at the same time generates more fluent sentences achieving new state-of-the-art results on two different benchmarks: the annotation-based CoNLL-2014 and the fluency-based JFLEG benchmark. Moreover, comparison with human gold standards shows that the created systems are

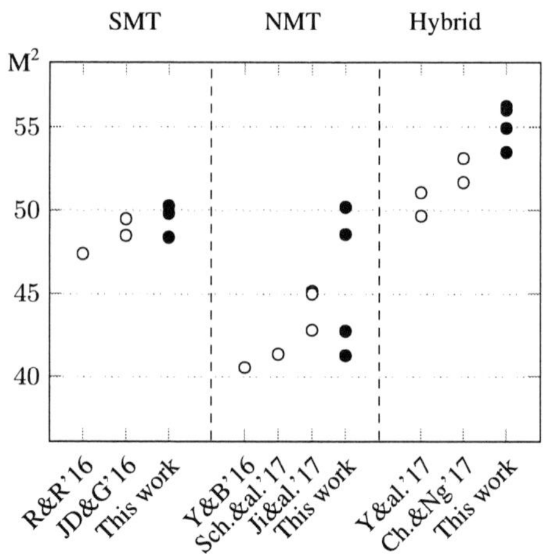

Figure 1: Comparison of SMT, NMT and hybrid GEC systems on the CoNLL-2014 test set (M²).

closer to reaching human-level performance than any other GEC system described in the literature so far.

Using consistent training data and preprocessing (§ 2), we first create strong SMT (§ 3) and NMT (§ 4) baseline systems. Then, we experiment with system combinations through pipelining and reranking (§ 5). Finally, we compare the performance with human annotations and identify issues with current state-of-the-art systems (§ 6).

2 Data and preprocessing

Our main training data is NUCLE (Dahlmeier et al., 2013). English sentences from the publicly available Lang-8 Corpora (Mizumoto et al., 2012) serve as additional training data.

We use official test sets from two CoNLL shared tasks from 2013 and 2014 (Ng et al., 2013, 2014) as development and test data, and evaluate using M² (Dahlmeier and Ng, 2012). We also report results on JFLEG (Napoles et al., 2017) with the

Proceedings of NAACL-HLT 2018, pages 284–290
New Orleans, Louisiana, June 1 - 6, 2018. ©2018 Association for Computational Linguistics

Corpus	Sentences	Tokens
NUCLE	57,151	1,162K
Lang-8 NAIST	1,943,901	25,026K
CoNLL-2013 (dev)	1,381	29K
CoNLL-2014 (test)	1,312	30K
JFLEG Dev	754	14K
JFLEG Test	747	13K

Table 1: Statistics for training and testing data sets.

System	CoNLL			JFLEG
	P	R	M^2	GLEU
SMT Dense	56.91	30.25	48.38	54.68
+ Sparse	60.28	29.40	**49.82**	55.25
+ Char. ops	60.27	30.21	**50.27**	55.79

Table 2: Results for SMT baseline systems on the CoNLL-2014 (M^2) and JFLEG Test (GLEU) sets.

GLEU metric (Napoles et al., 2015). The data set is provided with a development and test set split. All data sets are listed in Table 1.

We preprocess Lang-8 with the NLTK tokenizer (Bird and Loper, 2004) and preserve the original tokenization in NUCLE and JFLEG. Sentences are truecased with scripts from Moses (Koehn et al., 2007). For dealing with out-of-vocabulary words, we split tokens into 50k subword units using Byte Pair Encoding (BPE) by Sennrich et al. (2016b). BPE codes are extracted only from correct sentences from Lang-8 and NUCLE.

3 SMT systems

For our SMT-based systems, we follow recipes proposed by Junczys-Dowmunt and Grundkiewicz (2016), and use a phrase-based SMT system with a log-linear combination of task-specific features. We use word-level Levenshtein distance and edit operation counts as dense features (Dense), and correction patterns on words with one word left/right context on Word Classes (WC) as sparse features (Sparse). We also experiment with additional character-level dense features (Char. ops). All systems use a 5-gram Language Model (LM) and OSM (Durrani et al., 2011) both estimated from the target side of the training data, and a 5-gram LM and 9-gram WCLM trained on Common Crawl data (Buck et al., 2014).

Experiment settings Translation models are trained with Moses (Koehn et al., 2007), word-alignment models are produced with MGIZA++ (Gao and Vogel, 2008), and no reordering models are used. Language models are built using KenLM (Heafield, 2011), while word classes are trained with word2vec[1].

We tune the systems separately for M^2 and GLEU metrics. MERT (Och, 2003) is used for tuning dense features and Batch Mira (Cherry and Foster, 2012) for sparse features. For M^2 tunning

we follow the 4-fold cross-validation on NUCLE with adapted error rate recommended by Junczys-Dowmunt and Grundkiewicz (2016). Models evaluated on GLEU are optimized on JFLEG Dev using the GLEU scorer, which we added to Moses. We report results for models using feature weights averaged over 4 tuning runs.

Results Other things being equal, using the original tokenization, applying subword units, and extending edit-based features result in a similar system to Junczys-Dowmunt and Grundkiewicz (2016): 49.82 vs 49.49 M^2 (Table 2).

The phrase-based SMT systems do not deal well with orthographic errors (Napoles et al., 2017) — if a source word has not been seen in the training corpus, it is likely copied as a target word. Subword units can help to solve this problem partially. Adding features based on character-level edit counts increases the results on both test sets.

A result of 55.79 GLEU on JFLEG Test is already 2 points better than the GLEU-tuned NMT system of Sakaguchi et al. (2017) and only 1 point worse than the best reported result by Chollampatt and Ng (2017) with their M^2-tuned SMT system, even though no additional spelling correction has been used at this point. We experiment with specialized spell-checking methods in later sections.

4 NMT systems

The model architecture we choose for our NMT-based systems is an attentional encoder-decoder model with a bidirectional single-layer encoder and decoder, both using GRUs as their RNN variants (Sennrich et al., 2017). A similar architecture has been already tested for the GEC task by Sakaguchi et al. (2017), but we use different hyperparameters.

To improve the performance of our NMT models, similarly to Xie et al. (2016) and Ji et al. (2017), we combine them with an additional large-scale language model. In contrast to previous studies, which use an n-gram probabilistic LM, we build a 2-layer Recurrent Neural Network Language Model (RNN

---

[1] https://github.com/dav/word2vec

System	CoNLL			JFLEG
	P	R	M^2	GLEU
NMT	66.61	17.58	42.76	50.08
NMT + RNN-LM	61.05	**26.71**	48.56	56.04
NMT×4	**71.10**	15.42	41.29	50.30
NMT×4 + RNN-LM	60.27	30.08	**50.19**	**56.74**

Table 3: Results for NMT systems on the CoNLL-2014 (M^2) and JFLEG Test (GLEU) sets.

LM) with GRU cells which we train again on English Common Crawl data (Buck et al., 2014).

Experimental settings We train with the Marian toolkit (Junczys-Dowmunt et al., 2018) on the same data we used for the SMT baselines, i.e. NUCLE and Lang-8. The RNN hidden state size is set to 1024, embedding size to 512. Source and target vocabularies as well as subword units are the same.

Optimization is performed with Adam (Kingma and Ba, 2014) and the mini-batch size fitted into 4GB of GPU memory. We regularize the model with scaling dropout (Gal and Ghahramani, 2016) with a dropout probability of 0.2 on all RNN inputs and states. Apart from that we dropout entire source and target words with probabilities of 0.2 and 0.1 respectively. We use early stopping with a patience of 10 based on the cross-entropy cost on the CoNLL-2013 test set. Models are validated and saved every 10,000 mini-batches. As final models we choose the one with the best performance on the development set among the last ten model check-points based on the M^2 or GLEU metrics.

Size of RNN hidden state and embeddings, target vocabulary, and optimization options for the RNN LM are identical to those used for our NMT models. Decoding is done by beam search with a beam size of 12. We normalize scores for each hypothesis by sentence length.

Results A single NMT model achieves lower performance than the SMT baselines (Table 3). However, the M^2 score of 42.76 for CoNLL-2014 is already higher than the best published result of 41.53 M^2 for a strictly neural GEC system of Ji et al. (2017) that has not been enhanced by an additional language model.

Our RNN LM is integrated with NMT models through ensemble decoding (Sennrich et al., 2016a). Similarly to Ji et al. (2017), we choose the weight of the language model using grid search on the development set[2]. This strongly improves recall,

---

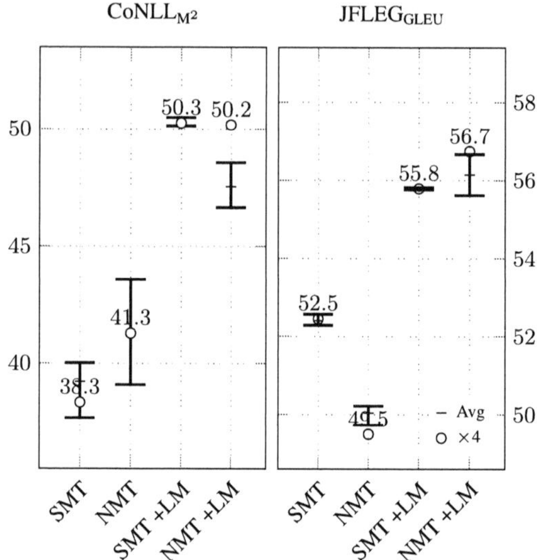

Figure 2: Contribution of a language model (LM) for SMT and NMT GEC systems.

and thus boosts the results significantly on both test sets (+5.8 M^2 and +5.96 GLEU).

An ensemble of four independently trained models[3] (NMT×4), on the other hand, increases precision at the expense of recall, which may even lead to a performance drop. Adding the RNN LM to that ensemble balances this negative effect, resulting in 50.19 M^2. These are by far the highest results reported on both benchmarks for pure neural GEC systems.

Comparison to SMT systems With model ensembling, the neural systems achieve performance similar to SMT baselines (Figure 2). A stripped-down SMT system without CCLM, quite surprisingly gives better results on JFLEG than the NMT system, and the opposite is true for CoNLL-2014. The reason for the lower performance on JFLEG might be a large amount of spelling errors, which are more efficiently corrected by the SMT system using subword units.

If both systems are enhanced by a large-scale language model, the neural system outperforms the SMT system on JFLEG and it is competitive with SMT systems on CoNLL-2014. However, it is not known if the results would preserve if the NMT model is combined with a probabilistic n-gram LM instead as it has been proposed in the previous works (Xie et al., 2016; Ji et al., 2017).

---

[2]Used weights are 0.2 and 0.25 for M^2 and GLEU evaluation, respectively.

[3]Each model is weighted equally during decoding.

System	CoNLL			JFLEG
	P	R	M^2	GLEU
Best SMT	60.27	30.21	50.27	55.79
→ Pip. NMT	60.25	34.80	52.56	57.21
→ Pip. NMT+LM	58.87	**39.23**	53.51	**58.83**
+ Res. RNN-LM	70.97	24.86	51.77	56.97
+ Res. NMT	70.40	26.69	53.03	57.21
+ Res. NMT+LM	71.40	**28.60**	**54.95**	57.53
→ Pip. NMT+LM	65.73	33.36	**55.05**	**58.83**
+ Spell SMT	70.80	30.57	56.05	60.09
→ Pip. NMT+LM	66.77	34.49	**56.25**	**61.50**

Table 4: Results for hybrid SMT-NMT systems on the CoNLL-2014 (M^2) and JFLEG Test (GLEU) sets.

5 Hybrid SMT-NMT systems

We experiment with pipelining and rescoring methods in order to combine our best SMT and NMT GEC systems[4].

SMT-NMT pipelines The output corrected by an SMT system is passed as an input to the NMT ensemble with or without RNN LM[5]. In this case the NMT system serves as an automatic post-editing system. Pipelining improves the results on both test sets by increasing recall (Table 4). As the performance of the NMT system without a RNN LM is much lower than the performance of the SMT system alone, this implies that both approaches produce complementary corrections.

Rescoring with NMT Rescoring of an n-best list obtained from one system by another is a commonly used technique in GEC, which allows to combine multiple different systems or even different approaches (Hoang et al., 2016; Yannakoudakis et al., 2017; Chollampatt and Ng, 2017; Ji et al., 2017). In our experiments, we generate a 1000 n-best list with the SMT system and add separate scores from each neural component. Scores of NMT models and the RNN LM are added in the form of probabilities in negative log space. The re-scored weights are obtained from a single run of the Batch Mira algorithm (Cherry and Foster, 2012) on the development set.

As opposed to pipelining, rescoring improves precision at the expense of recall and is more effective for the CoNLL data resulting in up to 54.95 M^2. On JFLEG, rescoring only with the RNN LM

System	CoNLL-10			JFLEG
	P	R	M^2	GLEU
Human Avg.	73.17	**68.75**	72.15	62.38
Ch&Ng'17	79.46	43.73	68.29	56.78
Ratio (%)	1.08	0.64	94.66	91.02
This work	**83.15**	46.97	72.04	61.50
Ratio (%)	1.14	0.68	**99.85**	**98.59**

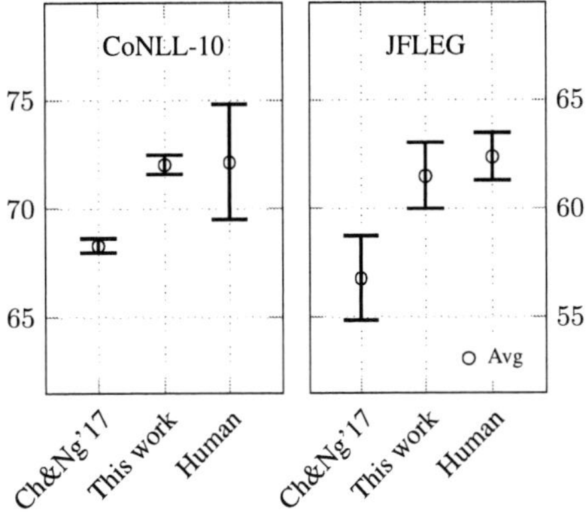

Figure 3: Comparison with human annotators. The figure presents average M^2 and GLEU scores with standard deviations.

produces similar results as rescoring with the NMT ensemble. However, the best result for rescoring is lower than for pipelining on that test set. It seems the SMT system is not able to produce as diversified corrections in an n-best list as those generated by the NMT ensemble.

Spelling correction and final results Pipelining the NMT-rescored SMT system and the NMT system leads to further improvement. We believe this can be explained by different contributions to precision and recall trade-offs for the two methods, similar to effects observed for the combination of the NMT ensemble and our RNN LM.

On top of our final hybrid system we add a spell-checking component, which is run before pipelining. We use a character-level SMT system following Chollampatt and Ng (2017) which they deploy for unknown words in their word-based SMT system. As our BPE-based SMT does not really suffer from unknown words, we run the spell-checking component on words that would have been segmented by the BPE algorithm. This last system achieves the best results reported in this paper: 56.25 M^2 on CoNLL-2014 and 61.50 GLEU on JFLEG Test.

System	Example
Source	*but now every thing is change , the life becom more dificullty .*
Best SMT	*But now **everything is changed** , the life becom more dificullty .*
Best NMT	*But now **everything is changing** , the life **becomes** more **difficult** .*
Pipeline	*But now **everything is changed** , the life **becomes** more **difficult** .*
Rescoring	*But now **everything has changed** , the life becom more dificullty .*
+ Pipeline	*But now **everything has changed** , the life **becomes** more **difficult** .*
Reference 1	*Now everything has changed , and life becomes more difficult .*
Reference 2	*Everything has changed now and life has become more difficult .*
Reference 3	*But now that everything changes , life becomes more difficult .*
Reference 4	*But now that everything is changing , life becomes more difficult .*

Table 5: System outputs for the example source sentence from the JFLEG Test set.

6 Analysis and future work

For both benchmarks our systems are close to automatic evaluation results that have been claimed to correspond to human-level performance on the CoNLL-2014 test set and on JFLEG Test.

Example outputs Table 5 shows system outputs for an example source sentence from the JFLEG Test corpus that illustrate the complementarity of the statistical and neural approaches. The SMT and NMT systems produce different corrections. Rescoring is able to generate a unique correction (*is change→has changed*), but it fails in generating some corrections from the neural system, e.g. misspellings (*becom* and *dificullty*). Pipelining, on the other hand, may not improve a local correction made by the SMT system (*is changed*). The combination of the two methods produces output, which is most similar to the references.

Comparison with human annotations Bryant and Ng (2015) created an extension of the CoNLL-2014 test set with 10 annotators in total, JFLEG already incorporates corrections from 4 annotators. Human-level results for M^2 and GLEU were calculated by averaging the scores for each annotator with regard to the remaining 9 (CoNLL) or 3 (JFLEG) annotators, respectively.

Figure 3 contains human level scores, our results, and previously best reported results by Chollampatt and Ng (2017). Our best system reaches nearly 100% of the average human score according to M^2 and nearly 99% for GLEU being much closer to that bound than previous works[6].

---

[6]During the camera-ready preparation, Chollampatt and Ng (2018) have published a GEC system based on a multi-layer convolutional encoder-decoder neural network with a character-based spell-checking module improving the previous best result to 54.79 M^2 on CoNLL-2014 and 57.47 GLEU on JFLEG Test.

Further inspection reveals, however, that the precision/recall trade-off for the automatic system indicates lower coverage compared to human corrections — lower recall is compensated with high precision[7]. Automatic systems might, for example, miss some obvious error corrections and therefore easily be distinguishable from human references. Future work would require a human evaluation effort to draw more conclusions.

Acknowledgments

This work was partially funded by Facebook. The views and conclusions contained herein are those of the authors and should not be interpreted as necessarily representing the official policies or endorsements, either expressed or implied, of Facebook.

References

Steven Bird and Edward Loper. 2004. NLTK: the natural language toolkit. In *Proceedings of the ACL 2004 on Interactive poster and demonstration sessions*. Association for Computational Linguistics, page 31.

Christopher Bryant and Hwee Tou Ng. 2015. How far are we from fully automatic high quality grammatical error correction? In *Proceedings of the 53rd Annual Meeting of the Association for Computational Linguistics and the 7th International Joint Conference on Natural Language Processing (Volume 1: Long Papers)*. Association for Computational Linguistics, Beijing, China, pages 697–707. http://www.aclweb.org/anthology/P15-1068.

Christian Buck, Kenneth Heafield, and Bas van Ooyen. 2014. N-gram counts and language models from the Common Crawl. In *Proceedings of the Language Resources and Evaluation Conference*. Reykjavík, Iceland, pages 3579–3584.

---

[7]A similar imbalance between precision and recall is visible on JFLEG when the M^2 metric is used.

Colin Cherry and George Foster. 2012. Batch tuning strategies for statistical machine translation. In *Proceedings of the 2012 Conference of the North American Chapter of the Association for Computational Linguistics: Human Language Technologies*. Association for Computational Linguistics, Stroudsburg, USA, pages 427–436.

Shamil Chollampatt and Hwee Tou Ng. 2017. Connecting the dots: towards human-level grammatical error correction. In *Proceedings of the 12th Workshop on Innovative Use of NLP for Building Educational Applications*. Association for Computational Linguistics, Copenhagen, Denmark, pages 327–333. http://www.aclweb.org/anthology/W17-5037.

Shamil Chollampatt and Hwee Tou Ng. 2018. A multilayer convolutional encoder-decoder neural network for grammatical error correction. In *Proceedings of the Thirty-Second AAAI Conference on Artificial Intelligence*.

Daniel Dahlmeier and Hwee Tou Ng. 2012. Better evaluation for grammatical error correction. In *Proceedings of the 2012 Conference of the North American Chapter of the Association for Computational Linguistics: Human Language Technologies*. Association for Computational Linguistics, pages 568–572.

Daniel Dahlmeier, Hwee Tou Ng, and Siew Mei Wu. 2013. Building a large annotated corpus of learner english: The NUS corpus of learner english. In *Proceedings of the Eighth Workshop on Innovative Use of NLP for Building Educational Applications*. pages 22–31.

Nadir Durrani, Helmut Schmid, and Alexander Fraser. 2011. A joint sequence translation model with integrated reordering. In *Proceedings of the 49th Annual Meeting of the Association for Computational Linguistics: Human Language Technologies*. Association for Computational Linguistics, Portland, Oregon, USA, pages 1045–1054. http://www.aclweb.org/anthology/P11-1105.

Yarin Gal and Zoubin Ghahramani. 2016. A theoretically grounded application of dropout in recurrent neural networks. In *Advances in neural information processing systems*. pages 1019–1027.

Qin Gao and Stephan Vogel. 2008. Parallel implementations of word alignment tool. In *Software Engineering, Testing, and Quality Assurance for Natural Language Processing*. ACL, pages 49–57.

Kenneth Heafield. 2011. KenLM: Faster and smaller language model queries. In *Proceedings of the Sixth Workshop on Statistical Machine Translation*. Association for Computational Linguistics, Stroudsburg, USA, WMT '11, pages 187–197.

Duc Tam Hoang, Shamil Chollampatt, and Hwee Tou Ng. 2016. Exploiting n-best hypotheses to improve an SMT approach to grammatical error correction. In *Proceedings of the Twenty-Fifth International Joint Conference on Artificial Intelligence*. IJCAI/AAAI Press, pages 2803–2809.

Jianshu Ji, Qinlong Wang, Kristina Toutanova, Yongen Gong, Steven Truong, and Jianfeng Gao. 2017. A nested attention neural hybrid model for grammatical error correction. In *Proceedings of the 55th Annual Meeting of the Association for Computational Linguistics*. Association for Computational Linguistics, pages 753–762.

Marcin Junczys-Dowmunt and Roman Grundkiewicz. 2016. Phrase-based machine translation is state-of-the-art for automatic grammatical error correction. In *Proceedings of the 2016 Conference on Empirical Methods in Natural Language Processing*. Association for Computational Linguistics, Austin, Texas, pages 1546–1556. https://aclweb.org/anthology/D16-1161.

Marcin Junczys-Dowmunt, Roman Grundkiewicz, Tomasz Dwojak, Hieu Hoang, Kenneth Heafield, Tom Neckermann, Frank Seide, Ulrich Germann, Alham Fikri Aji, Nikolay Bogoychev, André F. T. Martins, and Alexandra Birch. 2018. Marian: Fast neural machine translation in C++. *arXiv preprint arXiv:1804.00344* https://arxiv.org/abs/1804.00344.

Diederik Kingma and Jimmy Ba. 2014. Adam: A method for stochastic optimization. *Proceedings of the 3rd International Conference on Learning Representations (ICLR)* .

Philipp Koehn, Hieu Hoang, Alexandra Birch, Chris Callison-Burch, Marcello Federico, Nicola Bertoldi, Brooke Cowan, Wade Shen, Christine Moran, Richard Zens, Chris Dyer, Ondrej Bojar, Alexandra Constantin, and Evan Herbst. 2007. Moses: Open source toolkit for statistical machine translation. In *Annual Meeting of the Association for Computational Linguistics*. The Association for Computer Linguistics.

Tomoya Mizumoto, Yuta Hayashibe, Mamoru Komachi, Masaaki Nagata, and Yu Matsumoto. 2012. The effect of learner corpus size in grammatical error correction of ESL writings. In *Proceedings of COLING 2012*. pages 863–872.

Courtney Napoles, Keisuke Sakaguchi, Matt Post, and Joel Tetreault. 2015. Ground truth for grammatical error correction metrics. In *Proceedings of the 53rd Annual Meeting of the Association for Computational Linguistics and the 7th International Joint Conference on Natural Language Processing (Volume 2: Short Papers)*. Association for Computational Linguistics, Beijing, China, pages 588–593. http://www.aclweb.org/anthology/P15-2097.

Courtney Napoles, Keisuke Sakaguchi, and Joel Tetreault. 2017. JFLEG: A fluency corpus and benchmark for grammatical error correction. In *Proceedings of the 2017 Conference of the European Chapter of the Association for Computational Linguistics*. Association for Computational Linguistics, Valencia, Spain. https://arxiv.org/abs/1702.04066.

Hwee Tou Ng, Siew Mei Wu, Ted Briscoe, Christian Hadiwinoto, Raymond Hendy Susanto, and

289

Christopher Bryant. 2014. The CoNLL-2014 shared task on grammatical error correction. In *Proceedings of the Eighteenth Conference on Computational Natural Language Learning: Shared Task*. Association for Computational Linguistics, Baltimore, Maryland, pages 1–14. http://www.aclweb.org/anthology/W14-1701.

Hwee Tou Ng, Siew Mei Wu, Yuanbin Wu, Christian Hadiwinoto, and Joel Tetreault. 2013. The CoNLL-2013 shared task on grammatical error correction. In *Proceedings of the Seventeenth Conference on Computational Natural Language Learning: Shared Task*. Association for Computational Linguistics, Sofia, Bulgaria, pages 1–12. http://www.aclweb.org/anthology/W13-3601.

Franz Josef Och. 2003. Minimum error rate training in statistical machine translation. In *Proceedings of the 41st Annual Meeting on Association for Computational Linguistics - Volume 1*. Association for Computational Linguistics, Stroudsburg, USA, ACL '03, pages 160–167.

Alla Rozovskaya and Dan Roth. 2016. Grammatical error correction: Machine translation and classifiers. In *Proceedings of the 54th Annual Meeting of the Association for Computational Linguistics (Volume 1: Long Papers)*. Association for Computational Linguistics, Berlin, Germany, pages 2205–2215. http://www.aclweb.org/anthology/P16-1208.

Keisuke Sakaguchi, Matt Post, and Benjamin Van Durme. 2017. Grammatical error correction with neural reinforcement learning. In *Proceedings of the Eighth International Joint Conference on Natural Language Processing (Volume 2: Short Papers)*. Asian Federation of Natural Language Processing, Taipei, Taiwan, pages 366–372. http://www.aclweb.org/anthology/I17-2062.

Allen Schmaltz, Yoon Kim, Alexander Rush, and Stuart Shieber. 2017. Adapting sequence models for sentence correction. In *Proceedings of the 2017 Conference on Empirical Methods in Natural Language Processing*. Association for Computational Linguistics, Copenhagen, Denmark, pages 2807–2813. https://www.aclweb.org/anthology/D17-1298.

Rico Sennrich, Orhan Firat, Kyunghyun Cho, Alexandra Birch, Barry Haddow, Julian Hitschler, Marcin Junczys-Dowmunt, Samuel Läubli, Antonio Valerio Miceli Barone, Jozef Mokry, and Maria Nadejde. 2017. Nematus: a toolkit for neural machine translation. In *Proceedings of the Software Demonstrations of the 15th Conference of the European Chapter of the Association for Computational Linguistics*. Association for Computational Linguistics, Valencia, Spain, pages 65–68. http://aclweb.org/anthology/E17-3017.

Rico Sennrich, Barry Haddow, and Alexandra Birch. 2016a. Edinburgh neural machine translation systems for WMT 16. In *Proceedings of the First Conference on Machine Translation*. Association for Computational Linguistics, Berlin, Germany, pages 371–376. http://www.aclweb.org/anthology/W/W16/W16-2323.

Rico Sennrich, Barry Haddow, and Alexandra Birch. 2016b. Neural machine translation of rare words with subword units. In *Proceedings of the 54th Annual Meeting of the Association for Computational Linguistics (Volume 1: Long Papers)*. Association for Computational Linguistics, Berlin, Germany, pages 1715–1725. http://www.aclweb.org/anthology/P16-1162.

Ziang Xie, Anand Avati, Naveen Arivazhagan, Dan Jurafsky, and Andrew Y Ng. 2016. Neural language correction with character-based attention. *arXiv preprint arXiv:1603.09727* .

Helen Yannakoudakis, Marek Rei, Øistein E. Andersen, and Zheng Yuan. 2017. Neural sequence-labelling models for grammatical error correction. In *Proceedings of the 2017 Conference on Empirical Methods in Natural Language Processing*. Association for Computational Linguistics, Copenhagen, Denmark, pages 2785–2796. https://www.aclweb.org/anthology/D17-1296.

Zheng Yuan and Ted Briscoe. 2016. Grammatical error correction using neural machine translation. In *Proceedings of the 2016 Conference of the North American Chapter of the Association for Computational Linguistics: Human Language Technologies*. Association for Computational Linguistics, San Diego, California, pages 380–386.

Strong Baselines for Simple Question Answering over Knowledge Graphs with and without Neural Networks

Salman Mohammed, Peng Shi, and Jimmy Lin

David R. Cheriton School of Computer Science

University of Waterloo

smohammed1993@gmail.com, {peng.shi,jimmylin}@uwaterloo.ca

Abstract

We examine the problem of question answering over knowledge graphs, focusing on simple questions that can be answered by the lookup of a single fact. Adopting a straightforward decomposition of the problem into entity detection, entity linking, relation prediction, and evidence combination, we explore simple yet strong baselines. On the popular SIMPLEQUESTIONS dataset, we find that basic LSTMs and GRUs plus a few heuristics yield accuracies that approach the state of the art, and techniques that do not use neural networks also perform reasonably well. These results show that gains from sophisticated deep learning techniques proposed in the literature are quite modest and that some previous models exhibit unnecessary complexity.

1 Introduction

There has been significant recent interest in *simple* question answering over knowledge graphs, where a natural language question such as "Where was Sasha Vujacic born?" can be answered via the lookup of a simple fact—in this case, the "place of birth" property of the entity "Sasha Vujacic". Analysis of an existing benchmark dataset (Yao, 2015) and real-world user questions (Dai et al., 2016; Ture and Jojic, 2017) show that such questions cover a broad range of users' needs.

Most recent work on the simple QA task involves increasingly complex neural network (NN) architectures that yield progressively smaller gains over the previous state of the art (see §2 for more details). Lost in this push, we argue, is an understanding of what exactly contributes to the effectiveness of a particular NN architecture. In many cases, the lack of rigorous ablation studies further compounds difficulties in interpreting results and credit assignment. To give two related examples: Melis et al. (2017) reported that standard LSTM architectures, when properly tuned, outperform some more recent models; Vaswani et al. (2017) showed that the dominant approach to sequence transduction using complex encoder–decoder networks with attention mechanisms work just as well with the attention module only, yielding networks that are far simpler and easier to train.

In line with an emerging thread of research that aims to improve empirical rigor in our field by focusing on knowledge and insights, as opposed to simply "winning" (Sculley et al., 2018), we take the approach of peeling away unnecessary complexity until we arrive at the simplest model that works well. On the SIMPLEQUESTIONS dataset, we find that baseline NN architectures plus simple heuristics yield accuracies that approach the state of the art. Furthermore, we show that a combination of simple techniques that do not involve neural networks can still achieve reasonable accuracy. These results suggest that while NNs do indeed contribute to meaningful advances on this task, some models exhibit unnecessary complexity and that the best models yield at most modest gains over strong baselines.

2 Related Work

The problem of question answering on knowledge graphs dates back at least a decade, but the most relevant recent work in the NLP community comes from Berant et al. (2013). This thread of work focuses on semantic parsing, where a question is mapped to its logical form and then translated to a structured query, cf. (Berant and Liang, 2014; Reddy et al., 2014). However, the more recent SIMPLEQUESTIONS dataset (Bordes et al., 2015) has emerged as the de facto benchmark for evaluating simple QA over knowledge graphs.

The original solution of Bordes et al. (2015) featured memory networks, but over the past several

Proceedings of NAACL-HLT 2018, pages 291–296

New Orleans, Louisiana, June 1 - 6, 2018. ©2018 Association for Computational Linguistics

years, researchers have applied many NN architectures for tackling this problem: Golub and He (2016) proposed a character-level attention-based encoder-decoder framework; Dai et al. (2016) proposed a conditional probabilistic framework using BiGRUs. Lukovnikov et al. (2017) used a hierarchical word/character-level question encoder and trained a neural network in an end-to-end manner. Yin et al. (2016) applied a character-level CNN for entity linking and a separate word-level CNN with attentive max-pooling for fact selection. Yu et al. (2017) used a hierarchical residual BiLSTM for relation detection, the results of which were combined with entity linking output. These approaches can be characterized as exploiting increasingly sophisticated modeling techniques (e.g., attention, residual learning, etc.).

In this push toward complexity, we do not believe that researchers have adequately explored baselines, and thus it is unclear how much various NN techniques actually help. To this end, our work builds on Ture and Jojic (2017), who adopted a straightforward problem decomposition with simple NN models to argue that attention-based mechanisms don't really help. We take this one step further and examine techniques that do not involve neural networks. Establishing strong baselines allows us to objectively quantify the contribution of various deep learning techniques.

3   Approach

We begin with minimal preprocessing on questions: downcasing and tokenizing based on the Penn TreeBank. As is common in the literature, we decompose the simple QA problem into four tasks: entity detection, entity linking, relation prediction, and evidence integration, detailed below. All our code is available open source on GitHub.[1]

3.1   Entity Detection

Given a question, the goal of entity detection is to identify the entity being queried. This is naturally formulated as a sequence labeling problem, where for each token, the task is to assign one of two tags, either ENTITY or NOTENTITY.

Recurrent Neural Networks (RNNs): The most obvious NN model for this task is to use RNNs; we examined both bi-directional LSTM and GRU variants over an input matrix comprised of word embeddings from the input question. Following

standard practice, the representation of each token is a concatenation of the hidden states from the forward and backward passes. This representation is then passed through a linear layer, followed by batch normalization, ReLU activation, dropout, and a final layer that maps into the tag space. Note that since we're examining baselines, we do *not* layer a CRF on top of the BiLSTM (Lample et al., 2016; Ma and Hovy, 2016).

Conditional Random Fields (CRFs): Prior to the advent of neural techniques, CRFs represented the state of the art in sequence labeling, and therefore it makes sense to explore how well this method works. We specifically adopt the approach of Finkel et al. (2005), who used features such as word positions, POS tags, character n-grams, etc.

3.2   Entity Linking

The output of entity detection is a sequence of tokens representing a candidate entity. This still needs to be linked to an actual node in the knowledge graph. In Freebase, each node is denoted by a Machine Identifier, or MID. Our formulation treats this problem as fuzzy string matching and does not use neural networks.

For all the entities in the knowledge graph (Freebase), we pre-built an inverted index over n-grams $n \in \{1, 2, 3\}$ in an entity's name. At linking time, we generate all corresponding n-grams from the candidate entity and look them up in the inverted index for all matches. Candidate entity MIDs are retrieved from the index and appended to a list, and an early termination heuristic similar to Ture and Jojic (2017) is applied. We start with $n = 3$ and if we find an exact match for an entity, we do not further consider lower-order n-grams, backing off otherwise. Once all candidate entities have been gathered, they are then ranked by Levenshtein Distance to the MID's canonical label.

3.3   Relation Prediction

The goal of relation prediction is to identify the relation being queried. We view this as classification over the entire question.

RNNs: Similar to entity detection, we explored BiLSTM and BiGRU variants. Since relation prediction is over the entire question, we base the classification decision only on the hidden states (forward and backward passes) of the final token, but otherwise the model architecture is the same as for entity detection.

Convolutional Neural Networks (CNNs): Another natural model is to use CNNs, which have been shown to perform well for sentence classification. We adopt the model of Kim (2014), albeit slightly simplified in that we use a single static channel instead of multiple channels. Feature maps of widths two to four are applied over the input matrix comprised of input tokens transformed into word embeddings, followed by max pooling, a fully-connected layer and softmax to output the final prediction. Note this is a "vanilla" CNN without any attention mechanism.

Logistic Regression (LR): Before the advent of neural networks, the most obvious solution to sentence classification would be to apply logistic regression. We experimented with two feature sets over the questions: (1) tf-idf on unigrams and bigrams and (2) word embeddings + relation words. In (2), we averaged the word embeddings of each token in the question, and to that vector, we concatenated the one-hot vector comprised of the top 300 most frequent terms from the names of the relations (e.g., people/person/place_of_birth), which serve as the dimensions of the one-hot vector. The rationale behind this hybrid representation is to combine the advantages of word embeddings in capturing semantic similarity with the ability of one-hot vectors to clearly discriminate strong "cue" tokens in the relation names.

3.4 Evidence Integration

Given the top m entities and r relations from the previous components, the final task is to integrate evidence to arrive at a single (entity, relation) prediction. We begin by generating $m \times r$ (entity, relation) tuples whose scores are the product of their component scores. Since both entity detection/linking and relation prediction are performed independently, many combinations are meaningless (e.g., no such relation exists for an entity in the knowledge graph); these are pruned.

After pruning, we observe many scoring ties, which arise from nodes in the knowledge graph that share the exact same label, e.g., all persons with the name "Adam Smith". We break ties by favoring more "popular" entities, using the number of incoming edges to the entity in the knowledge graph (i.e., entity in-degree) as a simple proxy. We further break ties by favoring entities that have a mapping to Wikipedia, and hence are "popular". Note that these heuristics for breaking scoring ties

are based on the structure of the knowledge graph, as neither of these signals are available from the surface lexical forms of the entities.

4   Experimental Setup

We conducted evaluations on the SIMPLEQUESTIONS dataset (Bordes et al., 2015), comprised of 75.9k/10.8k/21.7k training/validation/test questions. Each question is associated with a (subject, predicate, object) triple from a Freebase subset that answers the question. The subject is given as an MID, but the dataset does not identify the entity in the question, which is needed for our formulation of entity detection. For this, we used the names file by Dai et al. (2016) to backproject the entity names onto the questions to annotate each token as either ENTITY or NOTENTITY. This introduces some noise, as in some cases there are no exact matches—for these, we back off to fuzzy matching and project the entity onto the n-gram sequence with the smallest Levenshtein Distance to the entity name. As with previous work, we report results over the 2M-subset of Freebase.

For entity detection, we evaluate by extracting every sequence of contiguous ENTITY tags and compute precision, recall, and F1 against the ground truth. For both entity linking and relation prediction, we evaluate recall at N (R@N), i.e., whether the correct answer appears in the top N results. For end-to-end evaluation, we follow the approach of Bordes et al. (2015) and mark a prediction as correct if both the entity and the relation exactly match the ground truth. The main metric is accuracy, which is equivalent to R@1.

Our models were implemented in PyTorch v0.2.0 with CUDA 8.0 running on an NVIDIA GeForce GTX 1080 GPU. GloVe embeddings (Pennington et al., 2014) of size 300 served as the input to our models. We used negative log likelihood loss to optimize model parameters using Adam, with an initial learning rate of 0.0001. We performed random search over hyperparameters, exploring a range that is typical of NNs for NLP applications; the hyperparameters were selected based on the development set. In our final model, all LSTM and GRU hidden states sizes and MLP hidden sizes were set to 300. For the CNNs, we used a size 300 output channel. Dropout rate for the CNNs was 0.5 and 0.3 for the RNNs. For the CRF implementation, we used the Stanford NER tagger (Finkel et al.,

R@N	BiLSTM	CRF
1	67.8 [67.5 68.0]	66.6
5	82.6 [82.3 82.7]	81.3
20	88.7 [88.5 88.8]	87.4
50	91.0 [90.8 91.1]	89.8

Table 1: Results for entity linking on the validation set, given the underlying entity detection model.

Model	R@1	R@5
BiGRU	82.3 [82.0 82.5]	95.9 [95.7 96.1]
CNN	82.8 [82.5 82.9]	95.8 [95.7 96.1]
LR (tf-idf)	72.4	87.6
LR (GloVe+rel)	74.7	92.2
Ture and Jojic (2017)	81.6	-

Table 2: Results for relation prediction on the validation set using different models.

5 Results

We begin with results on individual components. To alleviate the effects of parameter initialization, we ran experiments with n different random seeds ($n = 20$ for entity detection and $n = 50$ for relation prediction). Following Reimers and Gurevych (2017), and due to questions about assumptions of normality, we simply report the mean as well as the minimum and maximum scores achieved in square brackets.

For entity detection, on the validation set, the BiLSTM (which outperforms the BiGRU) achieves 93.1 [92.8 93.4] F1, compared to the CRF at 90.2. Entity linking results (R@N) are shown in Table 1 for both the BiLSTM and the CRF. We see that entity linking using the CRF achieves comparable accuracy, even though the CRF performs slightly worse on entity detection alone; entity linking appears to be the bottleneck. Error analysis shows that there is a long tail of highly-ambiguous entities—that is, entities in the knowledge graph that have the same label—and that even at depth 50, we are unable to identify the correct entity (MID) more than 10% of the time.

Results of relation prediction are shown in Table 2 on the validation set. Ture and Jojic (2017) conducted the same component-level evaluation, the results of which we report (but none else that

Entity	Relation	Acc.
BiLSTM	BiGRU	74.9 [74.6 75.1]
BiLSTM	CNN	74.7 [74.5 74.9]
BiLSTM	LR (tf-idf)	68.3 [68.2 68.5]
BiLSTM	LR (GloVe+rel)	70.9 [70.8 71.1]
CRF	BiGRU	73.7 [73.4 73.9]
CRF	CNN	73.6 [73.4 73.7]
CRF	LR (tf-idf)	67.3
CRF	LR (GloVe+rel)	69.9
Previous Work		
Bordes et al. (2015)		62.7
Golub and He (2016)		70.9
Lukovnikov et al. (2017)		71.2
Dai et al. (2016)		75.7
Yin et al. (2016)		76.4
Yu et al. (2017)		77.0
Ture and Jojic (2017)		86.8

Table 3: End-to-end answer accuracy on the test set with different model combinations, compared to a selection of previous results reported in the literature.

we could find). We are able to achieve slightly better accuracy. Interestingly, we see that the CNN slightly outperforms the BiGRU (which beats the BiLSTM slightly; not shown) on R@1, but both give essentially the same results for R@5. Compared to LR, it seems clear that for this task NNs form a superior solution.

Finally, end-to-end results on the test set are shown in Table 3 for various combinations of entity detection/linking and relation prediction. We found that crossing 50 candidate entities with five candidate relations works the best. To compute the [min, max] scores, we crossed 10 randomly-selected entity models with 10 relation models. The best model combination is BiLSTM (for entity detection/linking) and BiGRU (for relation prediction), which achieves an accuracy of 74.9, competitive with a cluster of recent top results. Ture and Jojic (2017) reported a much higher accuracy, but we have not been able to replicate their results (and their source code does not appear to be available online). Setting aside that work, we are two points away from the next-highest reported result in the literature.

Replacing the BiLSTM with the CRF for entity detection/linking yields 73.7, which is only a 1.2 absolute decrease in end-to-end accuracy. Replacing the BiGRU with the CNN for relation prediction has only a tiny effect on accuracy (0.2 decrease at most). Results show that the baselines that don't use neural networks (CRF + LR) perform surprisingly well: combining LR (GloVe+rel) or LR (td-idf) for relation prediction

2005). For LR, we used the scikit-learn package in Python. For Levenshtein Distance, we used the `ratio` function in the "fuzzywuzzy" Python package. Evidence integration involves crossing m candidate entities with r candidate relations, tuned on the validation set.

with CRFs for entity detection/linking achieves
69.9 and 67.3, respectively. Arguably, the former
still takes advantages of neural networks since it
uses word embeddings, but the latter is unequivo-
cally a "NN-free" baseline. We note that this figure is still higher than the original Bordes et al.
(2015) paper. Cast in this light, our results suggest that neural networks have indeed contributed
to real and meaningful improvements in the state
of the art according to this benchmark dataset, but
that the improvements directly attributable to neural networks are far more modest than previous papers may have led readers to believe.

One should further keep in mind an important caveat in interpreting the results in Table 3:
As Reimers and Gurevych (2017) have discussed,
non-determinism associated with training neural
networks can yield significant differences in accuracy. Crane (2018) further demonstrated that for
answer selection in question answering, a range
of mundane issues such as software versions can
have a significant impact on accuracy, and these
effects can be larger than incremental improvements reported in the literature. We adopt the
emerging best practice of reporting results from
multiple trials, but this makes comparison to previous single-point results difficult.

It is worth emphasizing that all NN models
we have examined can be characterized as "Deep
Learning 101": easily within the grasp of a student
after taking an intro NLP course. Yet, our strong
baselines compare favorably with the state of the
art. It seems that some recent models exhibit unnecessary complexity, in that they perform *worse*
than our baseline. State-of-the-art NN architectures only improve upon our strong baselines modestly, and at the cost of introducing significant
complexity—i.e., they are "doing a lot" for only
limited gain. In real-world deployments, there are
advantages to running simpler models even if they
may perform slightly worse. Sculley et al. (2014)
warned that machine-learned solutions have a tendency to incur heavy technical debt in terms of on-
going maintenance costs at the systems level. The
fact that Netflix decided not to deploy the winner
of the Netflix Prize (a complex ensemble of many
different models) is a real-world example.

6   Conclusions

Moving forward, we are interested in more formally characterizing complexity–accuracy trade-

offs and their relation to the amount of training
data necessary to learn a model. It is perhaps
self-evident that our baseline CNNs and RNNs
are "less complex" than other recent models described in the literature, but how can we compare
model complexity objectively in a general way?
The number of model parameters provides only a
rough measure, and does not capture the fact that
particular arrangements of architectural elements
make certain linguistic regularities much easier to
learn. We seek to gain a better understanding of
these tradeoffs. One concrete empirical approach
is to reintroduce additional NN architectural elements in a controlled manner to isolate their contributions. With a strong baseline to build on, we
believe that such studies can be executed with sufficient rigor to yield clear generalizations.

To conclude, we offer the NLP community three
points of reflection: First, at least for the task of
simple QA over knowledge graphs, in our rush
to explore ever sophisticated deep learning techniques, we have not adequately examined simple,
strong baselines in a rigorous manner. Second, it
is important to consider baselines that do not involve neural networks, even though it is easy to
forget that NLP existed before deep learning. Our
experimental results show that, yes, deep learning
is exciting and has certainly advanced the state of
the art, but the actual improvements are far more
modest than the literature suggests. Finally, in our
collective frenzy to improve results on standard
benchmarks, we may sometimes forget that the ultimate goal of science is knowledge, not owning
the top entry in a leaderboard.

7   Acknowledgments

This research was supported by the Natural Sciences and Engineering Research Council
(NSERC) of Canada.

References

Jonathan Berant, Andrew Chou, Roy Frostig, and Percy
Liang. 2013. Semantic parsing on Freebase from
question–answer pairs. In *Proceedings of the 2013
Conference on Empirical Methods in Natural Language Processing (EMNLP 2013)*. Seattle, Washington, pages 1533–1544.

Jonathan Berant and Percy Liang. 2014. Semantic
parsing via paraphrasing. In *Proceedings of the
52nd Annual Meeting of the Association for Computational Linguistics (ACL 2014)*. Baltimore, Maryland, pages 1415–1425.

Antoine Bordes, Nicolas Usunier, Sumit Chopra, and Jason Weston. 2015. Large-scale simple question answering with memory networks. *arXiv:1506.02075v1*.

Matt Crane. 2018. Questionable answers in question answering research: Reproducibility and variability of published results. *Transactions of the Association for Computational Linguistics* 6, *to appear*.

Zihang Dai, Lei Li, and Wei Xu. 2016. CFO: Conditional focused neural question answering with large-scale knowledge bases. In *Proceedings of the 54th Annual Meeting of the Association for Computational Linguistics (ACL 2016)*. Berlin, Germany, pages 800–810.

Jenny Rose Finkel, Trond Grenager, and Christopher Manning. 2005. Incorporating non-local information into information extraction systems by Gibbs sampling. In *Proceedings of the 43rd Annual Meeting of the Association for Computational Linguistics (ACL 2005)*. Ann Arbor, Michigan, pages 363–370.

David Golub and Xiaodong He. 2016. Character-level question answering with attention. In *Proceedings of the 2016 Conference on Empirical Methods in Natural Language Processing (EMNLP 2016)*. Austin, Texas, pages 1598–1607.

Yoon Kim. 2014. Convolutional neural networks for sentence classification. In *Proceedings of the 2014 Conference on Empirical Methods in Natural Language Processing (EMNLP 2014)*. Doha, Qatar, pages 1746–1751.

Guillaume Lample, Miguel Ballesteros, Sandeep Subramanian, Kazuya Kawakami, and Chris Dyer. 2016. Neural architectures for named entity recognition. In *Proceedings of the 15th Annual Conference of the North American Chapter of the Association for Computational Linguistics: Human Language Technologies (NAACL/HLT 2016)*. San Diego, California, pages 260–270.

Denis Lukovnikov, Asja Fischer, Jens Lehmann, and Sören Auer. 2017. Neural network-based question answering over knowledge graphs on word and character level. In *Proceedings of the 26th International World Wide Web Conference (WWW 2017)*. Perth, Australia, pages 1211–1220.

Xuezhe Ma and Eduard Hovy. 2016. End-to-end sequence labeling via bi-directional LSTM-CNNs-CRF. In *Proceedings of the 54th Annual Meeting of the Association for Computational Linguistics (ACL 2016)*. Berlin, Germany, pages 1064–1074.

Gábor Melis, Chris Dyer, and Phil Blunsom. 2017. On the state of the art of evaluation in neural language models. *arXiv:1707.05589v2*.

Jeffrey Pennington, Richard Socher, and Christopher D. Manning. 2014. GloVe: Global vectors for word representation. In *Proceedings of the 2014 Conference on Empirical Methods in Natural Language Processing (EMNLP 2014)*. Doha, Qatar, pages 1532–1543.

Siva Reddy, Mirella Lapata, and Mark Steedman. 2014. Large-scale semantic parsing without question-answer pairs. *Transactions of the Association for Computational Linguistics* 2:377–392.

Nils Reimers and Iryna Gurevych. 2017. Reporting score distributions makes a difference: Performance study of LSTM-networks for sequence tagging. In *Proceedings of the 2017 Conference on Empirical Methods in Natural Language Processing (EMNLP 2017)*. Copenhagen, Denmark, pages 338–348.

D. Sculley, Gary Holt, Daniel Golovin, Eugene Davydov, Todd Phillips, Dietmar Ebner, Vinay Chaudhary, and Michael Young. 2014. Machine learning: The high-interest credit card of technical debt. In *Proceedings of the NIPS 2014 Workshop on Software Engineering for Machine Learning*. Montreal, Quebec, Canada.

D. Sculley, Jasper Snoek, Alex Wiltschko, and Ali Rahimi. 2018. Winner's curse? On pace, progress, and empirical rigor. In *Proceedings of the 6th International Conference on Learning Representations, Workshop Track (ICLR 2018)*.

Ferhan Ture and Oliver Jojic. 2017. No need to pay attention: Simple recurrent neural networks work! (for answering "simple" questions). In *Proceedings of the 2017 Conference on Empirical Methods in Natural Language Processing (EMNLP 2017)*. Copenhagen, Denmark, pages 2856–2862.

Ashish Vaswani, Noam Shazeer, Niki Parmar, Jakob Uszkoreit, Llion Jones, Aidan N. Gomez, Lukasz Kaiser, and Illia Polosukhin. 2017. Attention is all you need. *arXiv:1706.03762v5*.

Xuchen Yao. 2015. Lean question answering over Freebase from scratch. In *Proceedings of the 2015 Conference of the North American Chapter of the Association for Computational Linguistics: Demonstrations (NAACL/HLT 2015)*. Denver, Colorado, pages 66–70.

Wenpeng Yin, Mo Yu, Bing Xiang, Bowen Zhou, and Hinrich Schütze. 2016. Simple question answering by attentive convolutional neural network. In *Proceedings of the 26th International Conference on Computational Linguistics (COLING 2016)*. Osaka, Japan, pages 1746–1756.

Mo Yu, Wenpeng Yin, Kazi Saidul Hasan, Cicero dos Santos, Bing Xiang, and Bowen Zhou. 2017. Improved neural relation detection for knowledge base question answering. In *Proceedings of the 55th Annual Meeting of the Association for Computational Linguistics (ACL 2017)*. Vancouver, British Columbia, Canada, pages 571–581.

Looking for structure in lexical and acoustic-prosodic entrainment behaviors

Andreas Weise
Dept. of Computer Science
The Graduate Center, CUNY
365 5th Ave, New York, NY 10016
aweise@gradcenter.cuny.edu

Rivka Levitan
Dept. of Computer and Information Science
Brooklyn College, CUNY
2900 Bedford Ave, Brooklyn, NY 11210
rlevitan@brooklyn.cuny.edu

Abstract

Entrainment has been shown to occur for various linguistic features individually. Motivated by cognitive theories regarding linguistic entrainment, we analyze speakers' overall entrainment behaviors and search for an underlying structure. We consider various measures of both acoustic-prosodic and lexical entrainment, measuring the latter with a novel application of two previously introduced methods in addition to a standard high-frequency word measure. We present a negative result of our search, finding no meaningful correlations, clusters, or principal components in various entrainment measures, and discuss practical and theoretical implications.

1 Introduction

Entrainment, also called accommodation or alignment, is the tendency of human interlocutors to adapt their behavior to each other to become more similar. This affects many linguistic features such as referring expressions (Brennan and Clark, 1996), phonetics (Pardo, 2006), syntax (Reitter et al., 2006), linguistic style (Niederhoffer and Pennebaker, 2002), turn-taking (Levitan et al., 2011), and prosody (Levitan and Hirschberg, 2011) as well as non-linguistic behavior (Chartrand and Bargh, 1999). It has also been linked to external aspects of the conversation such as task success (Reitter and Moore, 2007; Nenkova et al., 2008) and social factors (Ireland et al., 2011; Levitan et al., 2012).

The study of entrainment thus far has been fragmented, with researchers considering numerous individual features and measuring similarity in various ways, but few searching for correlations or other structure. For instance, both Ward and Litman (2007) and Fusaroli and Tylén (2016) measured lexical as well as acoustic-prosodic entrainment but neither paper investigated correlations between these measures. There are two recent exceptions to this overall pattern. Mukherjee et al. (2017) found a correlation between speakers' prosodies becoming more similar over time and their fundamental frequencies varying in synchrony. Rahimi et al. (2017) also showed correlations, between lexical and acoustic-prosodic entrainment in group conversations. However, neither considered more complex structure and Rahimi et al., while including lexical features, focus on high-frequency and topic words alone.

We take a broad view of entrainment, analyzing 18 sets of measurements in four different ways on two corpora to uncover structure, hoping to find higher-level behaviors that explain observed variability between speakers. This is motivated by several cognitive theories that purport to explain linguistic entrainment. Pickering and Garrod (2004), for instance, claim that it serves dialog success and that "alignment at one level leads to alignment at other levels". According to Chartrand and Bargh (1999), entrainment is based on a link between perception and behavior and correlates with "greater perceptual activity directed at the other person". Giles et al. (1991), lastly, argue that adaptive behavior is meant to increase or decrease "interpersonal differences" of the interlocutors. All these theories implicitly postulate that entrainment can be considered a single latent behavior or a structured collection of behaviors. Here, we look for evidence that entrainment behaviors can be explained by an underlying structure, particularly one that spans multiple features. Practically, it would be useful for downstream analysis to need to consider only a small set of higher-level behaviors rather than each basic entrainment measure in the search for interactions with quality metrics.

Our analysis is based on two corpora of dyadic conversation. The first is the Objects Games por-

Proceedings of NAACL-HLT 2018, pages 297–302
New Orleans, Louisiana, June 1 - 6, 2018. ©2018 Association for Computational Linguistics

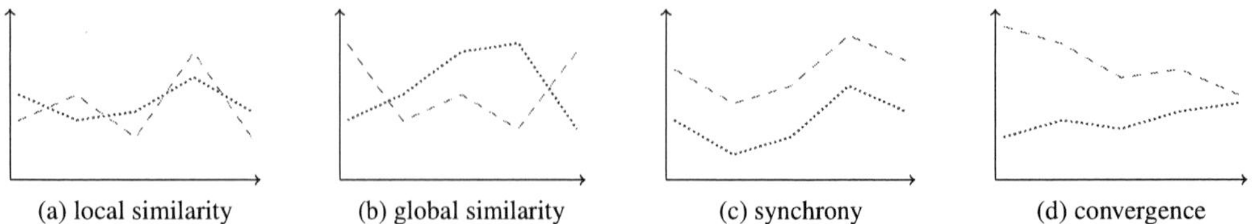

Figure 1: Depictions of measures of acoustic-prosodic entrainment, following (Levitan and Hirschberg, 2011). The axes represent time (x) and feature value (y), blue and red lines two speakers in conversation.

Linguistic Level	Measure	Reference
Prosody (pitch, rate, intensity)	local similarity and convergence global similarity and convergence synchrony	Levitan and Hirschberg (2011)
Lexical	Perplexity (*PPL*) Kullback-Leibler divergence (*KLD*)	Gravano et al. (2014)
	High-frequency words (*HFW*)	Nenkova et al. (2008)

Table 1: Overview of our entrainment measures, five per acoustic-prosodic feature, three lexical ones.

tion of the Columbia Games Corpus (Gravano and Hirschberg, 2011), **CGC**, which comprises 12 sessions with 14 identical tasks each, a total of about four hours of speech. Second, we use the Switchboard Corpus (Godfrey and Holliman, 1993), **SBC**, which contains over 2000 free conversations about given topics with a total of more than 200 hours of speech. Both corpora are fully orthographically transcribed and acoustic-prosodic features were extracted using Praat (Boersma and Weenink, 2001).

2 Methods

2.1 Acoustic-prosodic entrainment

We consider three acoustic-prosodic features: *pitch* (fundamental frequency in Hz), *intensity* (loudness in dB), and *speech rate* (in syllables per second). The arithmetic mean for each feature is determined at the level of an interpausal unit (IPU), a maximal segment of speech by a single speaker without a pause of 50ms or more. A maximal sequence of IPUs by one speaker, without interruption by the other, is called a turn.

The measures of acoustic-prosodic entrainment we use were defined by Levitan and Hirschberg (2011). Two speakers exhibit **local similarity** if their feature values differ little at turn exchanges and **local convergence** if that difference decreases over time. **Global similarity** is defined by a small difference in mean feature values over an entire task or session while **global convergence** is a decreasing difference in means from the first to the

second half of a session. **Synchrony**, lastly, exists if both speakers' feature values rise and fall together at turn exchanges. Figure 1 illustrates these different types of entrainment. Each allows us to numerically quantify a type of likeness of the speakers' prosodies. Those numeric values are then normalized and finally correlated, treated as coordinates in a feature space, etc.

2.2 Lexical entrainment

We apply three different measures of similarity based on the lemmata, i.e., canonical forms, of the words each speaker used throughout a session. The first two measures were used by Gravano et al. (2014) to compare ToBI annotations of **CGC** but, to our knowledge, have not been used before in the context of lexical entrainment. The third was defined by Nenkova et al. (2008) and shown to correlate with task success in **CGC** and perceived naturalness in **SBC**.

For the **perplexity** measure, *PPL*, we use SRILM (Stolcke, 2002) to build a trigram language model for each speaker, predict their partner's utterances with it, and compute the negated perplexity. For the second measure, *KLD*, we compute the negated **Kullback-Leibler divergence** between pairs of unigram distributions of partners' words. Lastly, for the **high-frequency words** measure, *HFW*, we compute, for each word w out of the 25 most frequent words in the respective overall corpus, the fraction of each speaker's words which are w. The sum of the negated absolute differences for the 25 pairs of fractions is our third measure of similarity for a pair of speakers. Table 1 gives an overview of all our entrainment measures.

2.3 Normalization

We apply z-score normalization by gender to our acoustic-prosodic features. That is, for each feature value we subtract the gender mean and then divide by gender standard deviation.

We normalize local similarity at each turn exchange using similarity of either IPU at the exchange with 10 randomly chosen, non-adjacent IPUs from the same session as a baseline. Similarly, global similarity and the lexical measures are normalized using similarity with non-partner speech as a baseline. For each speaker A we compare their similarity with partner B with the similarity with all non-partners C with whom A was never paired and who had the same role (**CGC**) or talked about the same topic (**SBC**) as B.

To control for the effect of complexity of speech on the lexical measures, we weight the non-partner similarities by how closely the entropy of the non-partner's language model matches that of the actual partner.

2.4 Analysis

The main purpose of our analysis is to look for structure in an array of entrainment measures. However, we first check whether similarity is significantly greater for partners than non-partners for our lexical measures since *PPL* and *KLD* have not previously been used for lexical entrainment and Nenkova et al. (2008) did not report a significance test for *HFW*.

We look for structure in our entrainment measures in four different ways. At the simplest level, we check for pairwise linear correlations by computing Pearson's correlation coefficient between each pair of entrainment behaviors. Second, we treat each entrainment behavior as binary (present if the speaker is more similar to the partner than to the baseline), and use χ^2 tests to investigate whether certain behaviors are disproportionately likely to co-occur. Third, we represent each speaker as a point in a continuous space defined by our entrainment measures and attempt to cluster these points to identify common complex entrainment behaviors. Fourth, we apply principal component analysis (PCA).

3 Results

3.1 Lexical entrainment significance

For each of our lexical entrainment measures, we use t-tests to check whether partner similarities are significantly greater than non-partner similarities, which we consider to be evidence of entrainment. For **CGC**, we find significance for *PPL* ($p < .001$) and *KLD* ($p < .01$) but not for *HFW* ($p > .25$) while for **SBC** we find all three to be highly significant ($p < 10^{-6}$). It is worth mentioning that the greater significance for **SBC** is attributable to the size of the corpus alone, as the average differences in similarities are comparable in both corpora. That is, even though conversations in **SBC** are less restricted than in **CGC**, the partner vs. non-partner comparison is still "fair".

3.2 Pearson correlation coefficients between entrainment measures

To check for simple linear correlations, we compute Pearson's r for each pair of entrainment measures. Due to the large number of correlation tests, we control for false discovery rate (FDR) (Benjamini and Hochberg, 1995) at .05 to reduce the probability of Type I error.

In both corpora we find strong correlations between local similarity and synchrony for each acoustic-prosodic feature (r between $+0.64$ and $+0.95$). This simply results from the measures' definitions: close feature values at turn exchanges throughout a session imply synchronous variation. In **CGC**, we find no other significant correlations.

In **SBC**, more results are significant due to the greater number of samples. Most correlations, however, are very weak, with only a few reaching $|r| > 0.1$, all between pairs of measurements on the same feature. Specifically, we find correlations between local and global *convergence* for each prosodic feature ($+0.14 \leq r \leq +0.47$) and local and global *similarity* on pitch ($r = +0.16$) and intensity ($r = +0.26$). We also find our lexical measures to be correlated with each other ($+0.16 \leq r \leq +0.58$).

We conclude that, contrary to our expectations, entrainment does not correlate across features and even within features this simplest kind of structure is barely present. We note that Rahimi et al. (2017), controlling less strictly for Type I error, did find correlations between lexical and acoustic-prosodic measures.

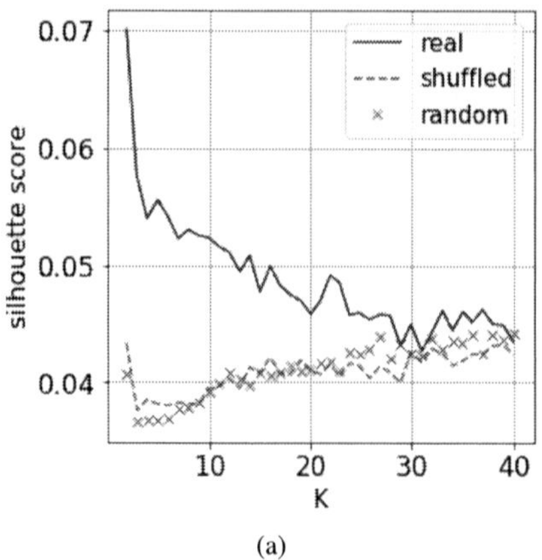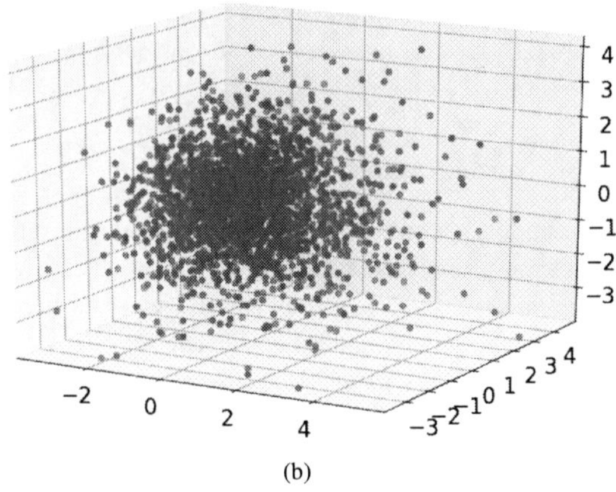

(a)   (b)

Figure 2: Silhouette scores for k-means clustering for $2 \leq k \leq 40$ (a) and 3D projection based on first three principal components (b) of 2433 **SBC** sessions in 18D space defined by entrainment measures.

3.3 χ^2 tests

To check for co-occurrence of different entrainment behaviors, we note, for each conversation: whether local and global partner similarity are greater than the respective non-partner similarity; whether the Pearson r defining synchrony and convergence is positive or not; whether global similarity is greater in the second half than in the first; and whether each of the lexical similarity measures between partners is greater than between non-partners. Then we use χ^2 tests to check whether some behaviors are disproportionately likely to co-occur.

For **SBC**, we consider all of our entrainment measures at the session level. For **CGC**, we analyze conversations at the task level as only this gives us a sufficient number of samples (149 usable tasks after excluding 19 with too little speech by at least one speaker). We also do not analyze local or global convergence for this corpus since they are not meaningful at the task level and do not consider the lexical measures because there are too few utterances per task to make use of them.

We find significant deviations from expected frequencies only for those few pairs of measurements which we found to be correlated according to Pearson's r in Section 3.2. We conclude that there is no significant co-occurrence of entrainment across features.

3.4 Clustering of entrainment measures

Next, we attempt to find structure in entrainment behavior through clustering of measurements. We analyze the same measurements as in Section 3.3, treating each task/session as a point in a continuous 9D/18D space, respectively, and use k-means clustering to group points in this space. In addition to the normalization described in Section 2.3, we apply z-score normalization per measure before clustering, which is a best practice.

Figure 2a shows the silhouette scores for various numbers of clusters k (solid line) for **SBC**. This score, which ranges from -1 to +1, compares the similarity of points in the same cluster with those in other clusters, with higher values for greater similarity within than across clusters. For comparison, we compute clusters after shuffling within columns of our data to remove correlations and cluster dummy data randomly sampled from standard normal distributions, the same distribution as our real data after normalization. The silhouette score is low for all values of k but for low values of k the scores achieved for the real data are greater than for the control data. The same pattern is present in **CGC**, with a maximum score for $k = 2$ of .165 versus .13 for the shuffled data.

For $k = 2$, we find that the clusters significantly separate gender pairs, for both corpora, according to χ^2 analysis. However, the same can be achieved with many randomly chosen cluster centroids. Because of this and the low silhouette scores, we conclude that the entrainment behaviors explored here cannot be meaningfully grouped into clusters.

3.5 Principal component analysis

Lastly, we use PCA on the same data as in Section 3.4. We find that all nine dimensions are needed to retain 99% of the variance in **CGC**, seven to retain 95% and six to retain 90%. For **SBC**, we find that all 18 dimensions are needed to retain 99% of variance, 15 for 95% and 13 for 90%. These reductions can mostly be attributed to the correlations between local similarity and synchrony per feature and between the lexical measures. Thus, the analysis again confirms a lack of correlation across features since more significant dimensionality reduction would otherwise be possible. A plot of our **SBC** data in 3D, shown in Figure 2b, retains 31% of the variance and visually confirms our finding of a lack of clusters.

4   Discussion and Conclusion

We present a corpus analysis using four different approaches to discover an underlying structure or collection of latent behaviors in 18 measures of acoustic-prosodic and lexical entrainment across two corpora. We find virtually no evidence of links between entrainment on different features, whether in the form of correlations or other common, complex behaviors.

While it is difficult to prove a negative, our results are strong enough to rule out at least the existence of any clear and strong structure. This is contrary to the expectations we had based on cognitive theory. It appears that entrainment, rather than a single behavior or a structured collection of behaviors, is a set of behaviors which are only loosely linked and perhaps independently explained by the competing theories. Practically, we had hoped to simplify and motivate downstream uses of entrainment measures, but our findings suggest that they must be considered separately.

Although we expected to find complex behavior, at least the absence of entrainment across *all* features simultaneously can be explained with past research. As far as entrainment is based on "attention", as Chartrand and Bargh (1999) suggest, this attention seems to be targeted and does not appear to result in entrainment on several features together. Alternatively, the absence of correlations may be explained by the fact that not all perception necessarily leads to a change in production, as Kraljic et al. (2008) found. Moreover, it has long been known that "too much" entrainment can be perceived negatively as mocking or patronizing (Giles and Smith, 1979). Furthermore, entrainment may be constrained by the need to achieve the communicative goal. Fusaroli and Tylén (2016), for instance, speculate based on their findings that "interpersonal synergies such as procedural scripts and routines [. . .] guide and constrain other central linguistic processes such as alignment". Lastly, there might be cognitive and physiological limits to speakers' ability to vary each feature individually or all at the same time.

Nonetheless, it remains surprising that we find a more general lack of structure, so the potential reasons warrant discussion. Entrainment is measured in various ways, even with regard to the same features. Therefore, it would be possible to continue our search using different entrainment measures on our features. However, all our measures meaningfully and diversely capture entrainment. Thus, it seems unlikely that alternative measures would yield fundamentally different outcomes, such as strong correlations across features. Similarly, we believe the analytical tools we employ are well-suited and further analysis of the same features and measures would not produce disparate results. Since we only considered low-level features, it is, however, conceivable that more latent structure might yet be found for entrainment at higher levels, such as emotional coloring and linguistic style.

Despite the fact that our result is negative, we consider it a starting point of inquiry, not an end. We intend to investigate higher-level features and perhaps additional corpora to confirm or qualify our findings. Beyond that, our result raises the question which principles govern the emergence of entrainment on one feature over another in a given conversation. As a first attempt to find an answer, we plan to use asymmetrical, speaker-specific measures of entrainment and analyze the consistency of each individual's entrainment behavior across sessions.

Acknowledgments

This material is based upon work supported in part by the PSC-CUNY Research Award Program under Grant No. 60604-00 48. We would also like to thank Julia Hirschberg, Štefan Beňuš, and Agustín Gravano for their helpful suggestions and Alyssa Caputo for her help with the project.

References

Yoav Benjamini and Yosef Hochberg. 1995. Controlling the false discovery rate: a practical and powerful approach to multiple testing. *Journal of the Royal Statistical Society, Series B* 57(1):289–300.

Paul Boersma and David Weenink. 2001. Praat, a system for doing phonetics by computer 5:341–345.

Susan E. Brennan and Herbert H. Clark. 1996. Conceptual pacts and lexical choice in conversation. *Experimental psychology: Learning, memory, and cognition* 22(6):1482–1493. https://doi.org/10.1037/0278-7393.22.6.1482.

Tanya L. Chartrand and John A. Bargh. 1999. The chameleon effect: The Perception-Behavior Link and Social Interaction. *Journal of Personality and Social Psychology* 76(6):893–910.

Riccardo Fusaroli and Kristian Tylén. 2016. Investigating Conversational Dynamics: Interactive Alignment, Interpersonal Synergy, and Collective Task Performance. *Cognitive Science* 40(1):145–171.

Howard Giles, Nikolas Coupland, and Justine Coupland. 1991. Accommodation theory: Communication, context, and consequence. In *Contexts of accommodation: Developments in applied sociolinguistics*, pages 1–68. https://doi.org/10.1017/CBO9780511663673.001.

Howard Giles and P.M. Smith. 1979. Accommodation theory: Optimal levels of convergence. In *Language and Social Psychology*, pages 45–65.

John J. Godfrey and Edward Holliman. 1993. Switchboard-1 Release 2 LDC97S62. Web download. Linguistic Data Consortium, Philadelphia.

Agustín Gravano, Štefan Beňuš, Rivka Levitan, and Julia Hirschberg. 2014. Three ToBI-based measures of prosodic entrainment and their correlations with speaker engagement. In *Spoken Language Technology (SLT), 2014 IEEE Workshop on*. pages 578–583.

Agustín Gravano and Julia Hirschberg. 2011. Turn-taking cues in task-oriented dialogue. *Computer Speech and Language* 25(3):601–634. https://doi.org/10.1016/j.csl.2010.10.003.

Molly E. Ireland, Richard B. Slatcher, Paul W. Eastwick, Lauren E. Scissors, Eli J. Finkel, and James W. Pennebaker. 2011. Language Style Matching Predicts Relationship Initiation and Stability. *Psychological Science* 22(1):39–44. https://doi.org/10.1177/0956797610392928.

Tanya Kraljic, Susan E. Brennan, and Arthur G. Samuel. 2008. Accommodating Variation: Dialects, Idiolects, and Speech Processing. *Cognition* 107(1):54–81.

Rivka Levitan, Agustín Gravano, and Julia Hirschberg. 2011. Entrainment in Speech Preceding Backchannels. In *ACL HLT*. pages 113–117.

Rivka Levitan and Julia Hirschberg. 2011. Measuring acoustic-prosodic entrainment with respect to multiple levels and dimensions. In *Interspeech 2011*. pages 3081–3084.

Rivka Levitan, Laura Willson, Agustín Gravano, Štefan Beňuš, Julia Hirschberg, and Ani Nenkova. 2012. Acoustic-Prosodic Entrainment and Social Behavior. In *NAACL HLT*. pages 11–19.

Sankar Mukherjee, Alessandro D'Ausilio, Noël Nguyen, Luciano Fadiga, and Leonardo Badino. 2017. The Relationship Between F0 Synchrony and Speech Convergence in Dyadic Interaction. *Interspeech 2017* pages 2341–2345. https://doi.org/10.21437/Interspeech.2017-795.

Ani Nenkova, Agustín Gravano, and Julia Hirschberg. 2008. High Frequency Word Entrainment in Spoken Dialogue. In *ACL HLT*. pages 169–172.

Kate G. Niederhoffer and James W. Pennebaker. 2002. Linguistic Style Matching in Social Interaction. *Journal of Language and Social Psychology* 21(4):337–360. https://doi.org/10.1177/026192702237953.

Jennifer S. Pardo. 2006. On phonetic convergence during conversational interaction. *The Journal of the Acoustical Society of America* 119(4):2382–2393. https://doi.org/10.1121/1.2178720.

Martin J. Pickering and Simon Garrod. 2004. Toward a mechanistic psychology of dialogue. *The Behavioral and brain sciences* 27(2):169–190. https://doi.org/10.1017/S0140525X04000056.

Zahra Rahimi, Anish Kumar, Diane Litman, Susannah Paletz, and Mingzhi Yu. 2017. Entrainment in Multi-Party Spoken Dialogues at Multiple Linguistic Levels. *Interspeech 2017* pages 1696–1700. https://doi.org/10.21437/Interspeech.2017-1568.

David Reitter and Johanna D. Moore. 2007. Predicting Success in Dialogue. In *Proceedings of the 45th Annual Meeting of the Association of Computational Linguistics*. pages 808–815. http://hdl.handle.net/1842/4165.

David Reitter, Johanna D. Moore, and Frank Keller. 2006. Priming of Syntactic Rules in Task-Oriented Dialogue and Spontaneous Conversation. In *CogSci 2006*. pages 685–690.

Andreas Stolcke. 2002. Srilm - an extensible language modeling toolkit. In *ICSLP*. pages 901–904.

Arthur Ward and Diane Litman. 2007. Automatically measuring lexical and acoustic / prosodic convergence in tutorial dialog corpora. In *Proceedings of the Workshop on Speech and Language Technology in Education (SLaTE)*. pages 57–60.

Modeling Semantic Plausibility by Injecting World Knowledge

Su Wang[1,2]   Greg Durrett[3]   Katrin Erk[1]

[1]Department of Linguistics
[2]Department of Statistics and Data Science
[3]Department of Computer Science
The University of Texas at Austin

shrekwang@utexas.edu   gdurrett@cs.utexas.edu   katrin.erk@mail.utexas.edu

Abstract

Distributional data tells us that a man can swallow candy, but not that a man can swallow a paintball, since this is never attested. However both are physically plausible events. This paper introduces the task of semantic plausibility: recognizing plausible but possibly novel events. We present a new crowdsourced dataset of semantic plausibility judgments of single events such as *man swallow paintball*. Simple models based on distributional representations perform poorly on this task, despite doing well on selection preference, but injecting manually elicited knowledge about entity properties provides a substantial performance boost. Our error analysis shows that our new dataset is a great testbed for semantic plausibility models: more sophisticated knowledge representation and propagation could address many of the remaining errors.

1   Introduction

Intuitively, a *man* can *swallow* a *candy* or *paintball* but not a *desk*. Equally so, one cannot plausibly *eat* a *cake* and then *hold* it. What kinds of semantic knowledge are necessary for distinguishing a physically plausible event (or event sequence) from an implausible one? *Semantic plausibility* stands in stark contrast to the familiar *selectional preference* (Erk and Padó, 2010; Van de Cruys, 2014) which is concerned with the *typicality* of events (Table 1). For example, *candy* is a typical entity for *man-swallow-** but *paintball* is not, even though both events are plausible physically. Also, some events are physically plausible but are never stated because humans avoid stating the obvious. Critically, semantic plausibility is sensitive to certain properties such as relative object size that are not explicitly encoded by selectional preferences (Bagherinezhad et al., 2016). Therefore, it is crucial that we learn to model these dimensions in addition to using classical distributional signals.

*man-swallow-**	PREFERRED?	PLAUSIBLE?
-candy	✓	✓
-paintball	✗	✓
-desk	✗	✗

Table 1: Distinguishing *semantic plausibility* from *selectional preference*. *candy* is selectionally preferred because it is distributionally common patient in the event *man-swallow-**, as opposed to the bizarre and rarely seen (if at all) patient *paintball*. However both are semantically plausible according to our world knowledge: they are small-sized objects that are swallowable by a man. *desk* is both distributionally unlikely and implausible (i.e. oversized for swallowing).

Semantic plausibility is pertinent and crucial in a multitude of interesting NLP tasks put forth previously, such as narrative schema (Chambers, 2013), narrative interpolation (Bowman et al., 2016), story understanding (Mostafazadeh et al., 2016), and paragraph reconstruction (Li and Jurafsky, 2017). Existing methods for these tasks, however, draw predominantly (if not only) on distributional data and produce rather weak performance. Semantic plausibility over *subject-verb-object* triples, while simpler than these other tasks, is a key building block that requires many of the same signals and encapsulates complex world knowledge in a binary prediction problem.

In this work, we show that world knowledge injection is necessary and effective for the semantic plausibility task, for which we create a robust, high-agreement dataset (details in section 3). Employing methods inspired by the recent work on world knowledge propagation through distributional context (Forbes and Choi, 2017; Wang et al., 2017), we accomplish the goal with minimal effort in manual annotation. Finally, we perform an in-depth error analysis to point to future directions of work on semantic plausibility.

Proceedings of NAACL-HLT 2018, pages 303–308
New Orleans, Louisiana, June 1 - 6, 2018. ©2018 Association for Computational Linguistics

2 Related Work

Simple events (i.e. S-V-O) have seen thorough investigation from the angle of selectional preference. While early works are resource-based (Resnik, 1996; Clark and Weir, 2001), later work shows that unsupervised learning with distributional data yields strong performance (O'Seaghdha, 2010; Erk and Padó, 2010), which has recently been further improved upon with neural approaches (Van de Cruys, 2014; Tilk et al., 2016). Distribution-only models however, as will be shown, fail on the semantic plausibility task we propose.

Physical world knowledge modeling appears frequently in more closely related work. Bagherinezhad et al. (2016) combine computer vision and text-based information extraction to learn the relative sizes of objects; Forbes and Choi (2017) crowdsource physical knowledge along specified dimensions and employ belief propagation to learn relative physical attributes of object pairs. Wang et al. (2017) propose a multimodal LDA to learn the definitional properties (e.g. *animal, four-legged*) of entities. Zhang et al. (2017) study the role of common-sense knowledge in natural language inference, which is inherently between-events rather than single-event focused. Prior work does not specifically handles the (single-event) semantic plausibility task and related efforts do not necessarily adapt well to this task, as we will show, suggesting that new approaches are needed.

3 Data

To study the semantic plausibility of S-V-O events, specifically *physical* semantic plausibility, we create a dataset[1] through Amazon Mechanical Turk with the following criteria in mind: (i) *Robustness*: Strong inter-annotator agreement; (ii) *Diversity*: A wide range of typical/atypical, plausible/implausible events; (iii) *Balanced*: Equal number of plausible and implausible events.

In creating physical events, we work with a fixed vocabulary of 150 concrete verbs and 450 concrete nouns from Brysbaert et al. (2014)'s word list, with a concreteness threshold of 4.95 (scale: 0-5). We take the following steps:

---

[1]Link: `https://github.com/suwangcompling/Modeling-Semantic-Plausibility-NAACL18/tree/master/data`.

(a) Have Turkers write down plausible or implausible S-V and V-O selections;

(b) Randomly generate S-V-O triples from collected S-V and V-O pairs;

(c) Send resulting S-V-O triples to Turkers to filter for ones with high agreement (by majority vote).

(a) ensures diversity and the cleanness of data (compared with noisy selectional preference data collected unsupervised from free text): the Turkers are instructed (with examples) to (i) consider both typical and atypical selections (e.g. *man-swallow-** with *candy* or *paintball*); (ii) disregard metaphorical uses (e.g. *feel-blue* or *fish-idea*). 2,000 pairs are collected in the step, balancing typical and atypical pairs. In (b), we manually filter error submissions in triple generation. For (c), 5 Turkers provide labels, and we only keep the ones that have $\geq$ 3 majority votes, resulting with 3,062 triples (of 4,000 annotated triples, plausible-implausible balanced), with **100% $\geq$ 3 agreement, 95% $\geq$ 4 agreement, and 90% 5 agreement**.

To empirically show the failure of distribution-only methods, we run Van de Cruys (2014)'s neural net classifier (hereforth **NN**), which is one of the strongest models designed for selectional preference (Figure 1, left-box). Let x be the concatenation of the embeddings of the three words in an S-V-O triple. The prediction $P(y|x)$ is computed as follows:

$$P(y = 1|x) = \sigma_2(W_2\sigma_1(W_1x)) \qquad (1)$$

where σ is a nonlinearity, W are weights, and we use 300D pretrained GloVe vectors (Pennington et al., 2014). The model achieves an accuracy of 68% (logistic regression baseline: 64%) after fine-tuning, verifying the intuition that distributional data alone cannot satisfactorily capture the semantics of physical plausibility.

4 World Knowledge Features

Recognizing that a distribution-alone method lacks necessary information, we collect a set of world knowledge features. The feature types derive from inspecting the high agreement event triples for knowledge missing in distributional selection (e.g. relative sizes in *man-swallow-paintball/desk*). Previously, Forbes and Choi (2017) proposed a three level (3-LEVEL) featurization scheme, where an object-pair can take 3 values for, e.g. relative size: $\{-1, 0, 1\}$ (i.e. lesser, similar, greater). This method, however, does not explain many cases we observed. For instance, *man-hug-cat/ant*, *man* is larger than both *cat* and *ant*, but the latter event is implausible. 3-LEVEL is also inefficient: k objects incur $O(k^2)$ elicitations. We thus propose a binning-by-landmark method, which is sufficiently fine-grained while still being efficient and easy for the annotator: given an entity n, the Turker decides to which of the landmarks n is closest to. E.g., for SIZE, we have the landmarks $\{$*watch, book, cat, person, jeep, stadium*$\}$, in ascending sizes. If $n = dog$, the Turker may put n in the bin corresponding to *cat*. The features[2] are listed with their landmarks as follows:

- SENTIENCE: *rock, tree, ant, cat, chimp, man.*
- MASS-COUNT: *milk, sand, pebbles, car.*
- PHASE: *smoke, milk, wood.*
- SIZE: *watch, book, cat, person, jeep, stadium.*
- WEIGHT: *watch, book, dumbbell, man, jeep, stadium.*
- RIGIDITY: *water, skin, leather, wood, metal.*

5 Turkers provide annotations for all 450 nouns, and we obtained **93% $\geq$ 3 agreement, 85% $\geq$ 4 agreement, and 79% 5 agreement**.

Our binning is sufficiently granular, which is crucial for semantic plausibility of an event in many cases. E.g. for *man-hug-cat/ant*, *man*, *cat* and *ant* fall in the $4^{th}, 3^{rd}$ and 1st bin, which suffices to explain why *man-hug-cat* is plausible while *man-hug-ant* is not. Compared to past work (Forbes and Choi, 2017), it is efficient. Each entity only needs one assignment in comparison to the landmarks to be located in a "global scale" (e.g. from the smallest to the largest objects), and even for extreme granularity, it only takes $O(k \log k)$ comparisons. It is also intuitive: differences in bins capture the intuition that one can *hug* smaller objects as long as those objects are not too small.

5 Models

We answer two questions: (i) Does world knowledge improve the accuracy of semantic plausibility classification? (ii) Can we minimize effort in knowledge feature annotation by learning from a

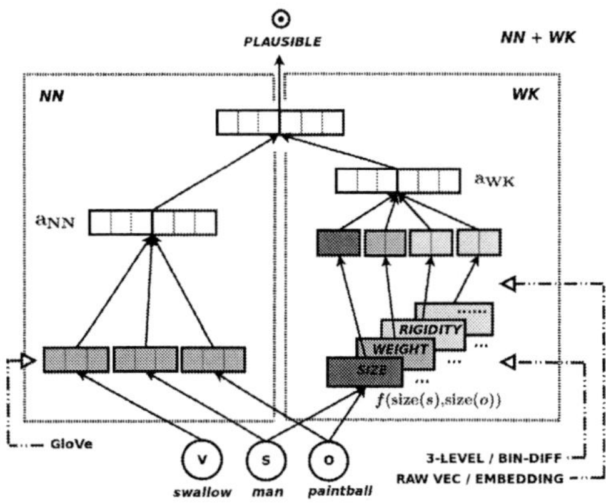

Figure 1: Model architecture (example input: *man-swallow-paintball*). Left box: Van de Cruys (2014)'s neural net (NN, embeddings only); Right box: world knowledge feature net **WK** with different modeling choices (Section 5). Only SIZE, WEIGHT, RIGIDITY are shown; the rest receive the same treatment. **NN + WK**: embedding and world knowledge combined.

small amount of training data?

For question (i), we experiment with various methods to incorporate the features on top of the embedding-only NN (Section 3). Our architecture[3] is outlined in Figure 1, where we ensemble the NN (left-box) and another feedforward net for features (**WK**, right-box) to produce the final prediction. For the feature net, the relative physical attributes of the subject-object pair can be encoded in **3-LEVEL** (Section 4) or the bin difference (**BIN-DIFF**) scheme.[4] For BIN-DIFF, given the two entities in an S-V-O event (i.e. S, O) *ant* and *man*, which are in the bins of the landmark *watch* (i.e. the 1st) and that of *person* (i.e. the 4th), the pair *ant-man* gets a BIN-DIFF value of $1 - 4 = -3$. Exemplifying the featurization function $f(s, o)$ with SIZE:

$$f_{\text{3-L}}(\text{SIZE}(s), \text{SIZE}(o)) \in \{-1, 0, 1\} \qquad (2)$$
$$f_{\text{BIN}}(\text{SIZE}(s), \text{SIZE}(o)) = \text{BIN}(s) - \text{BIN}(o) \qquad (3)$$

Then, given a featurization scheme, we may feed raw feature values (**RAW VEC**, for 3-LEVEL, e.g. concatenation of -1, 0 or 1 of all feature types, in that order, and in one-hot format), or feature embeddings (**EMBEDDING**, e.g. concatenation of embeddings looked up with feature values). Fi-

---

[2] We experimented with numerous feature types, e.g. size, temperature, shape, etc. and kept the subset that contributes most substantially to semantic plausibility classification. More details on the feature types in supplementary material (https://github.com/suwangcompling/Modeling-Semantic-Plausibility-NAACL18/tree/master/supplementary).

[3] More configuration details in supplementary material.

[4] We also tried using *bin numbers* directly, however it does not produce ideal results (classification accuracy between 3-LEVEL and BIN-DIFF). Thus for brevity we drop this setup.

MODELS	5%	20%
Label Spreading (Zhu et al., 2004)	0.56	0.59
Factor Graph (Forbes and Choi, 2017)	0.69	0.71
Multi-LDA (Wang et al., 2017)	0.64	0.72
Logistic Regression	0.72	0.83
Factor Graph (initialized with our LR)	0.72	0.84
Ordinal-LR	**0.76**	**0.88**

MODELS	5%		20%	
	3-L	BIN	3-L	BIN
Logistic Regression	0.61	0.21	0.68	0.26
Ordinal-LR	**0.66**	**0.32**	**0.76**	**0.40**

Table 2: Feature Propagation. Top-table: results on Forbes and Choi (2017)'s 2.5k object pair data; Bottom-table: results on our 10k object pair data.

nally, let $a_{\text{NN}}, a_{\text{WK}}$ be the penultimate-layer vectors of **NN** and **WK** (see Figure 1), we affine transform their concatenation to predict label $\hat{y}$ with argmax on the final softmax layer:

$$\hat{y} = \operatorname*{argmax}_{y} \operatorname{softmax}(\sigma(W[a_{\text{NN}}; a_{\text{WK}}] + b)) \quad (4)$$

where σ is a ReLU nonlinearity. We will only report the results from the best-performing model configuration, which has BIN-DIFF + EMBEDDING. The model will be listed below as **NN + WK-GOLD** (i.e. with **GOLD**, Turker-annotated World Knowledge features).

For question (ii), we select a data-efficient feature learning model. Following Forbes and Choi (2017) we evaluate the models with 5% or 20% of training data. We experiment with several previously proposed techniques: (a) *label spreading*; (b) *factor graph*; (c) *multi-LDA*. As a baseline we employ a simple but well-tuned logistic regressor (LR). We also initialize the factor graph with this LR, on account of its unexpectedly strong performance.[5] Finally, observing that the feature types are inherently ordinal (e.g. SIZE from small to large), we also run *ordinal logistic regression* (Adeleke and Adepoju, 2010). For model selection we first evaluate the object-pair attribute data collected by Forbes and Choi (2017), 2.5k pairs labeled in the 3-LEVEL scheme. We then compared the the LR and Ordinal-LR (our strongest models[6] in this experiment) on 10k randomly generated object-pairs from our annotated nouns. The results are summarized in Table 2, where we see

---

[5]We verified our setup with the authors and they attributed the higher performance of our LR to hyperparameter choices.
[6]Because the factor graph + LR gives very slight improvement, for simplicity we choose LR instead.

MODELS	ACCURACY			
Random	0.50			
LR baseline	0.64			
NN (Van de Cruys, 2014)	0.68			
NN + WK-GOLD	**0.76**			
	5%		20%	
NN + WK-PROP	3-L	BIN	3-L	BIN
	0.69	0.70	0.71	0.74

Table 3: Semantic Plausibility (binary) Classification. The average of 10-fold CV (splitting on the total 3,062 entries). The neural classifier injected with full annotation of world knowledge (i.e. **NN + WK-GOLD**) performs substantially better, and the performance retainment is rather strong with propagated features (by Ordinal-LR) from small fractions of gold annotation (i.e. in **NN + WK-PROP**).

(i) 3-LEVEL propagation is much easier; (ii) our object-pairs are more challenging, likely due to sparsity with larger vocabulary size; (iii) ordinality information contributes substantially to performance. The model that uses propagated features (w/ Ordinal-LR) will be listed as **NN + WK-PROP**.

6 Semantic Plausibility Results

We evaluate the models on the task of classifying our 3,062 S-V-O triples by semantic plausibility (10-fold CV, taking the average over 20 runs with the same random seed). We compare our three models in the 3-LEVEL and BIN-DIFF schemes, with **NN + WK-PROP** evaluated in 5% and 20% training conditions. The results are outlined in Table 3. Summarizing our findings: (i) world knowledge undoubtedly leads to a strong performance boost ($\sim$8%); (ii) BIN-DIFF scheme works much better than 3-LEVEL — it manages to outperform the latter even with much weaker propagation accuracy; (iii) the accuracy loss with propagated features seems rather mild with 20% labeled training and the best scheme.

7 Error Analysis

To understand what challenges remain in this task, we run the models above 200 times (10-fold CV, random shuffle at each run), and inspect the top 200 most frequently misclassified cases. The percentage statistics below are from counting the error cases.

In the cases where **NN** misclassifies while **NN + WK-GOLD** correctly classifies, 60% relates to SIZE and WEIGHT (e.g. missing *man-hug-ant* (bad) or *dog-pull-paper* (good)). PHASE takes up 18% (e.g. missing *monkey-puff-smoke* (good)). This validates the intuition that distributional contexts do not encode these types of world knowledge.

For cases often misclassified by *all* the models, we observe two main types of errors: (i) data sparsity; (ii) highly-specific attributes.

Data sparsity (32%). *man-choke-ant*, e.g., is a singleton big-object-choke-small-object instance, and there are no distributionally similar verbs that can help (e.g. *suffocate*); For *sun-heat-water*, because the majority of the actions in the data are limited to solid objects, the models tend to predict implausible for whenever a gas/liquid appears as the object.

Highly-specific attributes (68%). "long-tailed" physical attributes which are absent from our feature set are required. To exemplify a few:[7]

- *edibility* (21%). **-fry-egg* (plausible) and **-fry-cup* (implausible) are hard to distinguish because *egg* and *cup* are similar in SIZE/WEIGHT/..., however introducing large free-text data to help learn edibility misguides our model to mind selectional preference, causing mislabeling of other events.

- *natural vs. artificial* (18%). Turkers often think creating natural objects like *moon* or *mountain* is implausible but creating an equally big (but artificial) object like *skyscraper* is plausible.

- *hollow objects* (15%). *plane-contain-shell* and *purse-contain-scissors* are plausible, but the hollow-object-can-contain-things attribute is failed to be captured.

- *forefoot dexterity* (5%). *horse-hug-man* is implausible but *bear-hug-man* is plausible; For **-snatch-watch*, *girl* is a plausible subject, but not *pig*. Obviously the dexterity of the forefoot of the agent matters here.

The analysis shows that the task and the dataset highlights the necessity for more sophisticated knowledge featurization and cleverer learning techniques (e.g. features from computer vision, propagation methods with stronger capacity to generalize) to reduce the cost of manual annotation.

---

[7]Percentages calculated with the 68% as the denominator. Full list in supplementary material.

8 Conclusion

We present the novel task of *semantic plausibility*, which forms the foundation of various interesting and complex NLP tasks in event semantics (Bowman et al., 2016; Mostafazadeh et al., 2016; Li and Jurafsky, 2017). We collected a high-quality dedicated dataset, showed empirically that the conventional, distribution data only model fails on the task, and that clever world knowledge injection can help substantially with little annotation cost, which lends initial empirical support for the scalability of our approach in practical applications, i.e. labeling little but propagating well approximates performance with full annotation. Granted that annotation-based injection method does not cover the full spectrum of leverageable world knowledge information (alternative/complementary sources being images and videos, e.g. Bagherinezhad et al. 2016), it is indeed irreplaceable in some cases (e.g. features such as WEIGHT or RIGIDITY are not easily learnable through visual modality), and in other cases presents a low-cost and effective option. Finally, we also discovered the limitation of existing methods through a detailed error analysis, and thereby invite cross-area effort (e.g. multimodal knowledge features) in the future exploration in automated methods for semantic plausibility learning.

Acknowledgments

This research was supported by NSF grant IIS 1523637. Further, this material is based on research sponsored by DARPA under agreement number FA8750-18- 2-0017. The U.S. Government is authorized to reproduce and distribute reprints for Governmental purposes notwithstanding any copyright notation thereon. We acknowledge the Texas Advanced Computing Center for providing grid resources that contributed to these results. We would also like to thank our reviewers for their insightful comments.

References

K.A. Adeleke and A.A. Adepoju. 2010. Ordinal Logistic Regression Model: An Application to Pregnancy Outcomes. *Journal of Mathematics and Statistics* 6(3):279–285.

Hessam Bagherinezhad, Hannaneh Hjishirzi, Yejin Choi, and Ali Farhadi. 2016. Are Elephants Bigger

Than Butterflies? Reasoning about Sizes of Objects. In *Proceedings of AAAI*.

Samuel R. Bowman, Luke Vilnis, Oriol Vinyals, Andrew M. Dai, Rafal Jozefowicz, and Samy Bengio. 2016. Generating Sentences from a Continuous Space. In *Proceedings of CoNLL*.

M Brysbaert, A.B. Warriner, and V. Kuperman. 2014. Concreteness Ratings for 40 Thousand Generally Known English Word Lemmas. *Behavior Research Methods* 46:904–911.

Nathanael Chambers. 2013. Event schema induction with a probabilistic entity-driven model. In *Proceedings of EMNLP*.

Stephen Clark and David Weir. 2001. Class-based probability estimation using a semantic hierarchy. In *Proceedings of NAACL*.

Katrin Erk and Sebastian Padó. 2010. Exemplar-Based Models for Word Meaning in Context. In *Proceedings of ACL*.

Maxwell Forbes and Yejin Choi. 2017. VERB PHYSICS: Relative Physical Knowledge of Actions and Objects. In *Proceedings of ACL*.

Jiwei Li and Daniel Jurafsky. 2017. Neural Net Models of Open-domain Discourse Coherence. In *Proceedings of EMNLP*.

Nasrin Mostafazadeh, Nathanael Chambers, Xiaodong He, Devi Parikh, Dhruv Batra, Lucy Vanderwende, Pushmeet Kohli, and James Allen. 2016. A Corpus and Cloze Evaluation for Deeper Understanding of Commonsense Stories. In *Proceedings of NAACL*.

Diarmiuid O'Seaghdha. 2010. Latent variable models of selectional preference. In *Proceedings of ACL*.

Jeffrey Pennington, Richard Socher, and Christopher D. Manning. 2014. GloVe: Global Vectors for Word Embeddings. In *Proceedings of EMNLP*.

Philip Resnik. 1996. Selectional Constraints: An Information-Theoretic Model and Its Computational Realization. *Cognition* 61:127–159.

Ottokar Tilk, Vera Demberg, Asad Sayeed, Dietrich Klakow, and Stefan Thater. 2016. Event Participant Modeling with Neural Networks. In *Proceedings of EMNLP*.

Tim Van de Cruys. 2014. A Neural Network Approach to Selectional Preference Acquisition. In *Proceedings of EMNLP*.

Su Wang, Stephen Roller, and Katrin Erk. 2017. Distributional Modeling on a Diet: Learning Word Properties from Text Only. In *Proceedings of IJCNLP*.

Sheng Zhang, Rachel Rudinger, Kevin Duh, and Benjamin Van Durme. 2017. Ordinal Common-sense Inference. *TACL* 5:379–395.

Dengyong Zhu, Olivier Bousquet, Thomas Navin Lal, Jason Weston, and Bernhard Schölkopf. 2004. Learning with Local and Global Consistency. In *Proceedings of NIPS*.

A Bi-model based RNN Semantic Frame Parsing Model for Intent Detection and Slot Filling

Yu Wang **Yilin Shen** **Hongxia Jin**

Samsung Research America

{yu.wang1, yilin.shen, hongxia.jin}@samsung.com

Abstract

Intent detection and slot filling are two main tasks for building a spoken language understanding(SLU) system. Multiple deep learning based models have demonstrated good results on these tasks . The most effective algorithms are based on the structures of sequence to sequence models (or "encoder-decoder" models), and generate the intents and semantic tags either using separate models((Yao et al., 2014; Mesnil et al., 2015; Peng and Yao, 2015; Kurata et al., 2016; Hahn et al., 2011)) or a joint model ((Liu and Lane, 2016a; Hakkani-Tür et al., 2016; Guo et al., 2014)). Most of the previous studies, however, either treat the intent detection and slot filling as two separate parallel tasks, or use a sequence to sequence model to generate both semantic tags and intent. Most of these approaches use one (joint) NN based model (including encoder-decoder structure) to model two tasks, hence may not fully take advantage of the cross-impact between them. In this paper, new Bi-model based RNN semantic frame parsing network structures are designed to perform the intent detection and slot filling tasks jointly, by considering their cross-impact to each other using two correlated bidirectional LSTMs (BLSTM). Our Bi-model structure with a decoder achieves state-of-the-art result on the benchmark ATIS data (Hemphill et al., 1990; Tur et al., 2010), with about 0.5% intent accuracy improvement and 0.9 % slot filling improvement.

1 Introduction

The research on spoken language understanding (SLU) system has progressed extremely fast during the past decades. Two important tasks in an SLU system are intent detection and slot filling. These two tasks are normally considered as parallel tasks but may have cross-impact on each other. The intent detection is treated as an utterance classification problem, which can be modeled using conventional classifiers including regression, support vector machines (SVMs) or even deep neural networks (Haffner et al., 2003; Sarikaya et al., 2011). The slot filling task can be formulated as a sequence labeling problem, and the most popular approaches with good performances are using conditional random fields (CRFs) and recurrent neural networks (RNN) as recent works (Xu and Sarikaya, 2013).

Some works also suggested using one joint RNN model for generating results of the two tasks together, by taking advantage of the sequence to sequence(Sutskever et al., 2014) (or encoder-decoder) model, which also gives decent results as in literature(Liu and Lane, 2016a).

In this paper, Bi-model based RNN structures are proposed to take the cross-impact between two tasks into account, hence can further improve the performance of modeling an SLU system. These models can generate the intent and semantic tags concurrently for each utterance. In our Bi-model structures, two task-networks are built for the purpose of intent detection and slot filling. Each task-network includes one BLSTM with or without a LSTM decoder (Hochreiter and Schmidhuber, 1997; Graves and Schmidhuber, 2005).

The paper is organized as following: In section 2, a brief overview of existing deep learning approaches for intent detection and slot fillings are given. The new proposed Bi-model based RNN approach will be illustrated in detail in section 3. In section 4, two experiments on different datasets will be given. One is performed on the ATIS benchmark dataset, in order to demonstrate a state-of-the-art result for both semantic parsing tasks. The other experiment is tested on our internal multi-domain dataset by comparing our new algorithm with the current best performed RNN based joint model in literature for intent detection and slot filling.

Proceedings of NAACL-HLT 2018, pages 309–314

New Orleans, Louisiana, June 1 - 6, 2018. ©2018 Association for Computational Linguistics

2 Background

In this section, a brief background overview on using deep learning and RNN based approaches to perform intent detection and slot filling tasks is given. The joint model algorithm is also discussed for further comparison purpose.

2.1 Deep neural network for intent detection

Using deep neural networks for intent detection is similar to a standard classification problem, the only difference is that this classifier is trained under a specific domain. For example, all data in ATIS dataset is under the flight reservation domain with 18 different intent labels. There are mainly two types of models that can be used: one is a feed-forward model by taking the average of all words' vectors in an utterance as its input, the other way is by using the recurrent neural network which can take each word in an utterance as a vector one by one (Xu and Sarikaya, 2014).

2.2 Recurrent Neural network for slot filling

The slot filling task is a bit different from intent detection as there are multiple outputs for the task, hence only RNN model is a feasible approach for this scenario. The most straight-forward way is using single RNN model generating multiple semanctic tags sequentially by reading in each word one by one (Liu and Lane, 2015; Mesnil et al., 2015; Peng and Yao, 2015). This approach has a constrain that the number of slot tags generated should be the same as that of words in an utterance. Another way to overcome this limitation is by using an encoder-decoder model containing two RNN models as an encoder for input and a decoder for output (Liu and Lane, 2016a). The advantage of doing this is that it gives the system capability of matching an input utterance and output slot tags with different lengths without the need of alignment. Besides using RNN, It is also possible to use the convolutional neural network (CNN) together with a conditional random field (CRF) to achieve slot filling task (Xu and Sarikaya, 2013).

2.3 Joint model for two tasks

It is also possible to use one joint model for intent detection and slot filling (Guo et al., 2014; Liu and Lane, 2016a,b; Zhang and Wang, 2016; Hakkani-Tür et al., 2016). One way is by using one encoder with two decoders, the first decoder will generate sequential semantic tags and the second decoder generates the intent. Another approach is by consolidating the hidden states information from an RNN slot filling model, then generates its intent using an attention model (Liu and Lane, 2016a). Both of the two approaches demonstrates very good results on ATIS dataset.

3 Bi-model RNN structures for joint semantic frame parsing

Despite the success of RNN based sequence to sequence (or encoder-decoder) model on both tasks, most of the approaches in literature still use one single RNN model for each task or both tasks. They treat the intent detection and slot filling as two separate tasks. In this section, two new Bi-model structures are proposed to take their cross-impact into account, hence further improve their performance. One structure takes the advantage of a decoder structure and the other doesn't. An asynchronous training approach based on two models' cost functions is designed to adapt to these new structures.

3.1 Bi-model RNN Structures

A graphical illustration of two Bi-model structures with and without a decoder is shown in Figure 1. The two structures are quite similar to each other except that Figure 1a contains a LSTM based decoder, hence there is an extra decoder state s_t to be cascaded besides the encoder state h_t.

Remarks:

The concept of using information from multiple-model/multi-modal to achieve better performance has been widely used in deep learning (Dean et al., 2012; Wang, 2017; Ngiam et al., 2011; Srivastava and Salakhutdinov, 2012), system identification (Murray-Smith and Johansen, 1997; Narendra et al., 2014, 2015) and also reinforcement learning field recently (Narendra et al., 2016; Wang and Jin, 2018). Instead of using collective information, in this paper, our work introduces a totally new approach of training multiple neural networks asynchronously by sharing their internal state information.

3.1.1 Bi-model structure with a decoder

The Bi-model structure with a decoder is shown as in Figure 1a. There are two inter-connected bidirectional LSTMs (BLSTMs) in the structure, one is for intent detection and the other is for slot filling. Each BLSTM reads in the input utterance sequences $(x_1, x_2, \cdots, x_n)$ forward and backward, and generates two sequences of hidden states hf_t and hb_t. A concatenation of hf_t and hb_t forms a

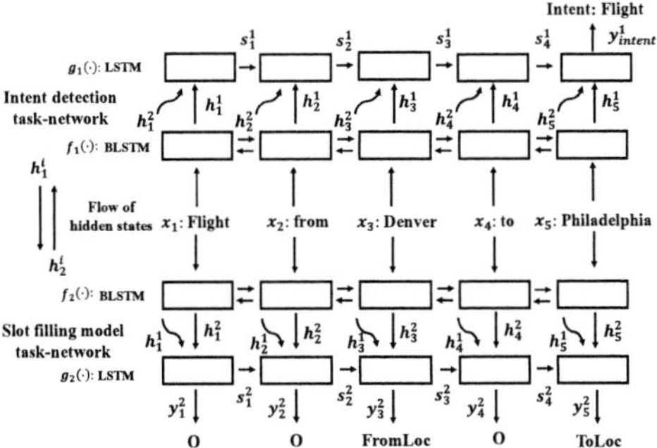

(a) Bi-model structure with a decoder

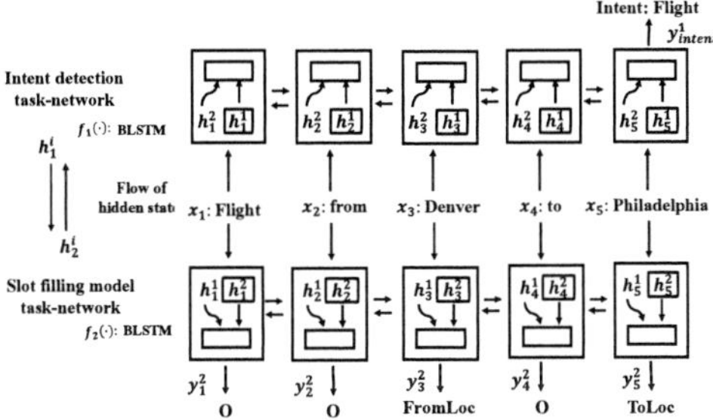

(b) Bi-model structure without a decoder

Figure 1: Bi-model structure

final BLSTM state $h_t = [hf_t, hb_t]$ at time step t. Hence, Our bidirectional LSTM $f_i(\cdot)$ generates a sequence of hidden states $(h_1^i, h_2^i, \cdots, h_n^i)$, where $i = 1$ corresponds the network for intent detection task and $i = 2$ is for the slot filling task.

In order to detect intent, hidden state h_t^1 is combined together with h_t^2 from the other bidirectional LSTM $f_2(\cdot)$ in slot filling task-network to generate the state of $g_1(\cdot)$, s_t^1, at time step t:

$$s_t^1 = \phi(s_{t-1}^1, h_{n-1}^1, h_{n-1}^2)$$
$$y_{intent}^1 = \arg\max_{\hat{y}_n^1} P(\hat{y}_n^1 | s_{n-1}^1, h_{n-1}^1, h_{n-1}^2) \quad (1)$$

where $\hat{y}_n^1$ contains the predicted probabilities for all intent labels at the last time step n.

For the slot filling task, a similar network structure is constructed with a BLSTM $f_2(\cdot)$ and a LSTM $g_2(\cdot)$. $f_2(\cdot)$ is the same as $f_1(\cdot)$, by reading in the a word sequence as its input. The difference is that there will be an output y_t^2 at each time step t for $g_2(\cdot)$, as it is a sequence labeling problem. At each step t:

$$s_t^2 = \psi(h_{t-1}^2, h_{t-1}^1, s_{t-1}^2, y_{t-1}^2)$$
$$y_t^2 = \arg\max_{\hat{y}_t^2} P(\hat{y}_t^2 | h_{t-1}^1, h_{t-1}^2, s_{t-1}^2, y_{t-1}^2) \quad (2)$$

where y_t^2 is the predicted semantic tags at time step t.

3.1.2 Bi-Model structure without a decoder

The Bi-model structure without a decoder is shown as in Figure 1b. In this model, there is no LSTM decoder as in the previous model.

For the intent task, only one predicted output label y_{intent}^1 is generated from BLSTM $f_1(\cdot)$ at the last time step n, where n is the length of the utterance. Similarly, the state value h_t^1 and output intent label are generated as:

$$h_t^1 = \phi(h_{t-1}^1, h_{t-1}^2)$$
$$y_{intent}^1 = \arg\max_{\hat{y}_n^1} P(\hat{y}_n^1 | h_{n-1}^1, h_{n-1}^2) \quad (3)$$

For the slot filling task, the basic structure of BLSTM $f_2(\cdot)$ is similar to that for the intent detection task $f_1(\cdot)$, except that there is one slot tag label y_t^2 generated at each time step t. It also takes the hidden state from two BLSTMs $f_1(\cdot)$ and $f_2(\cdot)$, i.e. h_{t-1}^1 and h_{t-1}^2, plus the output tag y_{t-1}^2 together to generate its next state value h_t^2 and also the slot tag y_t^2. To represent this as a function mathematically:

$$h_t^2 = \psi(h_{t-1}^2, h_{t-1}^1, y_{t-1}^2)$$
$$y_t^2 = \arg\max_{\hat{y}_t^2} P(\hat{y}_t^2 | h_{t-1}^1, h_{t-1}^2, y_{t-1}^2) \quad (4)$$

3.1.3 Asynchronous training

One of the major differences in the Bi-model structure is its asynchronous training, which trains two task-networks based on their own cost functions in an asynchronous manner. The loss function for intent detection task-network is $\mathcal{L}_1$, and for slot filling is $\mathcal{L}_2$. $\mathcal{L}_1$ and $\mathcal{L}_2$ are defined using cross entropy as:

$$\mathcal{L}_1 \triangleq -\sum_{i=1}^{k} \hat{y}_{intent}^{1,i} \log(y_{intent}^{1,i}) \quad (5)$$

and

$$\mathcal{L}_2 \triangleq -\sum_{j=1}^{n}\sum_{i=1}^{m} \hat{y}_j^{2,i} \log(y_j^{2,i}) \quad (6)$$

where k is the number of intent label types, m is the number of semantic tag types and n is the number of words in a word sequence. In each training iteration, both intent detection and slot filling networks will generate a groups of hidden states h^1 and h^2 from the models in previous iteration. The intent detection task-network reads in a batch of input data x_i and hidden states h^2, and generates the estimated intent labels $\hat{y}^1_{intent}$. The intent detection task-network computes its cost based on function $\mathcal{L}_1$ and trained on that. Then the same batch of data x_i will be fed into the slot filling task-network together with the hidden state h^1 from intent task-network, and further generates a batch of outputs y^2_i for each time step. Its cost value is then computed based on cost function $\mathcal{L}_2$, and further trained on that.

The reason of using asynchronous training approach is because of the importance of keeping two separate cost functions for different tasks. Doing this has two main advantages:
1. It filters the negative impact between two tasks in comparison to using only one joint model, by capturing more useful information and overcoming the structural limitation of one model.
2. The cross-impact between two tasks can only be learned by sharing hidden states of two models, which are trained using two cost functions separately.

4 Experiments

In this section, our new proposed Bi-model structures are trained and tested on two datasets, one is the public ATIS dataset (Hemphill et al., 1990) containing audio recordings of flight reservations, and the other is our self-collected datset in three different domains: Food, Home and Movie. The ATIS dataset used in this paper follows the same format as in (Liu and Lane, 2015; Mesnil et al., 2015; Xu and Sarikaya, 2013; Liu and Lane, 2016a). The training set contains 4978 utterance and the test set contains 893 utterance, with a total of 18 intent classes and 127 slot labels. The number of data for our self-collected dataset will be given in the corresponding experiment sections with a more detailed explanation. The performance is evaluated based on the classification accuracy for intent detection task and F1-score for slot filling task.

4.1 Training Setup

The layer sizes for both the LSTM and BLSTM networks in our model are chosen as 200. Based on the size of our dataset, the number of hidden layers is chosen as 2 and Adam optimization is used as in (Kingma and Ba, 2014). The size of word embedding is 300, which are initialized randomly at the beginning of experiment.

4.2 Performance on the ATIS dataset

Our first experiment is conducted on the ATIS benchmark dataset, and compared with the current existing approaches, by evaluating their intent detection accuracy and slot filling F1 scores. A

Model	F1 Score	Intent Accuracy
Recursive NN (Guo et al., 2014)	93.96%	95.4%
Joint model with recurrent intent and slot label context (Liu and Lane, 2016b)	94.47%	98.43%
Joint model with recurrent slot label context (Liu and Lane, 2016b)	94.64%	98.21%
RNN with Label Sampling (Liu and Lane, 2015)	94.89%	NA
Hybrid RNN (Mesnil et al., 2015)	95.06%	NA
RNN-EM (Peng and Yao, 2015)	95.25%	NA
CNN CRF (Xu and Sarikaya, 2013)	95.35%	NA
Encoder-labeler Deep LSTM (Kurata et al., 2016)	95.66%	NA
Joint GRU Model (W) (Zhang and Wang, 2016)	95.49%	98.10%
Attention Encoder-Decoder NN (Liu and Lane, 2016a)	95.87%	98.43%
Attention BiRNN (Liu and Lane, 2016a)	95.98%	98.21%
Bi-model without a decoder	**96.65%**	**98.76%**
Bi-model with a decoder	**96.89%**	**98.99%**

Table 1: Performance of Different Models on ATIS Dataset

detailed comparison is given in Table 1. Some of the models are designed for single slot filling task, hence only F1 scores are given. It can be observed that the new proposed Bi-model structures outperform the current state-of-the-art results on both intent detection and slot filling tasks, and the Bi-model with a decoder also outperform that without a decoder on our ATIS dataset. The current Bi-model with a decoder shows the state-of-the-art performance on ATIS benchmark dataset with 0.9% improvement on F1 score and 0.5% improvement on intent accuracy.
Remarks:
1. It is worth noticing that the complexities of encoder-decoder based models are normally higher than the models without using encoder-decoder structures, since two networks are used and more parameters need to be updated. This is another reason why we use two models with/without using encoder-decoder structures to demonstrate the new bi-model structure design. It can also be observed that the model with a decoder gives a better result due to its higher complexity.
2. It is also shown in the table that the joint model in (Liu and Lane, 2015, 2016a) achieves

better performance on intent detection task with slight degradation on slot filling, so a joint model is not necessary always better for both tasks. The bi-model approach overcomes this issue by generating two tasks' results separately.
3. Despite the absolute improvement of intent accuracy and F1 scores are only 0.5% and 0.9% on ATIS dataset, the relative improvement is not small. For intent accuracy, the number of wrongly classified utterances in test dataset reduced from 14 to 9, which gives us the 35.7% relative improvement on intent accuracy. Similarly, the relative improvement on F1 score is 22.63%.

4.3 Performance on multi-domain data

In this experiment, the Bi-model structures are further tested on an internal collected dataset from our users in three domains: food, home and movie. There are 3 intents for each domain, 15 semantic tags in food domain, 16 semantic tags in home domain, 14 semantic tags in movie domain. The data size of each domain is listed as in Table 2, and the split is 70% for training, 10% for validation and 20% for test.

Due to the space limitation, only the best performed semantic frame parsing model on ATIS dataset in literature,i.e. attention based BiRNN (Liu and Lane, 2016a) is used for comparison with our Bi-model structures. Table 2 shows a perfor-

Domain	SLU model	Size	F1 Score	Accuracy
Movie	Attention BiRNN	979	92.1%	92.86%
	Bi-model without a decoder	979	93.3%	94.89%
	Bi-model with a decoder	979	**93.8%**	**95.91%**
Food	Attention BiRNN	983	92.3%	98.48%
	Bi-model without a decoder	983	93.6%	98.98%
	Bi-model with a decoder	983	**95.8%**	**99.49%**
Home	Attention BiRNN	689	96.5%	97.83%
	Bi-model without a decoder	689	97.8%	98.55%
	Bi-model with a decoder	689	**98.2%**	**99.27%**

Table 2: Performance Comparison between Bi-model Structures and Attention BiRNN

mance comparison in three domains of data. The Bi-model structure with a decoder gives the best performance in all cases based on its intent accuracy and slot filling F1 score. The intent accuracy has at least 0.5% improvement, the F1 score improvement is around 1% to 3% for different domains.

5 Conclusion

In this paper, a novel Bi-model based RNN semantic frame parsing model for intent detection and slot filling is proposed and tested. Two substructures are discussed with the help of a decoder or not. The Bi-model structures achieve state-of-the-art performance for both intent detection and slot filling on ATIS benchmark data, and also surpass the previous best SLU model on the multi-domain data. The Bi-model based RNN structure with a decoder also outperforms the Bi-model structure without a decoder on both ATIS and multi-domain data.

References

Jeffrey Dean, Greg Corrado, Rajat Monga, Kai Chen, Matthieu Devin, Mark Mao, Andrew Senior, Paul Tucker, Ke Yang, Quoc V Le, et al. 2012. Large scale distributed deep networks. In *Advances in neural information processing systems*. pages 1223–1231.

Alex Graves and Jürgen Schmidhuber. 2005. Framewise phoneme classification with bidirectional lstm and other neural network architectures. *Neural Networks* 18(5):602–610.

Daniel Guo, Gokhan Tur, Wen-tau Yih, and Geoffrey Zweig. 2014. Joint semantic utterance classification and slot filling with recursive neural networks. In *Spoken Language Technology Workshop (SLT), 2014 IEEE*. IEEE, pages 554–559.

Patrick Haffner, Gokhan Tur, and Jerry H Wright. 2003. Optimizing svms for complex call classification. In *Acoustics, Speech, and Signal Processing, 2003. Proceedings.(ICASSP'03). 2003 IEEE International Conference on*. IEEE, volume 1, pages I–I.

Stefan Hahn, Marco Dinarelli, Christian Raymond, Fabrice Lefevre, Patrick Lehnen, Renato De Mori, Alessandro Moschitti, Hermann Ney, and Giuseppe Riccardi. 2011. Comparing stochastic approaches to spoken language understanding in multiple languages. *IEEE Transactions on Audio, Speech, and Language Processing* 19(6):1569–1583.

Dilek Hakkani-Tür, Gökhan Tür, Asli Celikyilmaz, Yun-Nung Chen, Jianfeng Gao, Li Deng, and Ye-Yi Wang. 2016. Multi-domain joint semantic frame parsing using bi-directional rnn-lstm. In *INTERSPEECH*. pages 715–719.

Charles T Hemphill, John J Godfrey, George R Doddington, et al. 1990. The atis spoken language systems pilot corpus. In *Proceedings of the DARPA speech and natural language workshop*. pages 96–101.

Sepp Hochreiter and Jürgen Schmidhuber. 1997. Long short-term memory. *Neural computation* 9(8):1735–1780.

Diederik Kingma and Jimmy Ba. 2014. Adam: A method for stochastic optimization. *arXiv preprint arXiv:1412.6980* .

Gakuto Kurata, Bing Xiang, Bowen Zhou, and Mo Yu. 2016. Leveraging sentence-level information with encoder lstm for semantic slot filling. In *Proceedings of the 2016 Conference on Empirical Methods in Natural Language Processing*. pages 2077–2083.

Bing Liu and Ian Lane. 2015. Recurrent neural network structured output prediction for spoken language understanding. In *Proc. NIPS Workshop on Machine Learning for Spoken Language Understanding and Interactions*.

Bing Liu and Ian Lane. 2016a. Attention-based recurrent neural network models for joint intent detection and slot filling. *Interspeech 2016* pages 685–689.

Bing Liu and Ian Lane. 2016b. Joint online spoken language understanding and language modeling with recurrent neural networks. In *17th Annual Meeting of the Special Interest Group on Discourse and Dialogue*. page 22.

Grégoire Mesnil, Yann Dauphin, Kaisheng Yao, Yoshua Bengio, Li Deng, Dilek Hakkani-Tur, Xiaodong He, Larry Heck, Gokhan Tur, Dong Yu, et al. 2015. Using recurrent neural networks for slot filling in spoken language understanding. *IEEE/ACM Transactions on Audio, Speech and Language Processing (TASLP)* 23(3):530–539.

Roderick Murray-Smith and T Johansen. 1997. *Multiple model approaches to nonlinear modelling and control*. CRC press.

Kumpati S Narendra, Yu Wang, and Wei Chen. 2014. Stability, robustness, and performance issues in second level adaptation. In *American Control Conference (ACC), 2014*. IEEE, pages 2377–2382.

Kumpati S Narendra, Yu Wang, and Wei Chen. 2015. Extension of second level adaptation using multiple models to siso systems. In *American Control Conference (ACC), 2015*. IEEE, pages 171–176.

Kumpati S Narendra, Yu Wang, and Snehasis Mukhopadhay. 2016. Fast reinforcement learning using multiple models. In *Decision and Control (CDC), 2016 IEEE 55th Conference on*. IEEE, pages 7183–7188.

Jiquan Ngiam, Aditya Khosla, Mingyu Kim, Juhan Nam, Honglak Lee, and Andrew Y Ng. 2011. Multimodal deep learning. In *Proceedings of the 28th international conference on machine learning (ICML-11)*. pages 689–696.

Baolin Peng and Kaisheng Yao. 2015. Recurrent neural networks with external memory for language understanding. *arXiv preprint arXiv:1506.00195* .

Ruhi Sarikaya, Geoffrey E Hinton, and Bhuvana Ramabhadran. 2011. Deep belief nets for natural language call-routing. In *Acoustics, Speech and Signal Processing (ICASSP), 2011 IEEE International Conference on*. IEEE, pages 5680–5683.

Nitish Srivastava and Ruslan R Salakhutdinov. 2012. Multimodal learning with deep boltzmann machines. In *Advances in neural information processing systems*. pages 2222–2230.

Ilya Sutskever, Oriol Vinyals, and Quoc V Le. 2014. Sequence to sequence learning with neural networks. In *Advances in neural information processing systems*. pages 3104–3112.

Gokhan Tur, Dilek Hakkani-Tür, and Larry Heck. 2010. What is left to be understood in atis? In *Spoken Language Technology Workshop (SLT), 2010 IEEE*. IEEE, pages 19–24.

Yu Wang. 2017. A new concept using lstm neural networks for dynamic system identification. In *American Control Conference (ACC), 2017*. IEEE, pages 5324–5329.

Yu Wang and Hongxia Jin. 2018. A boosting-based deep neural networks algorithm for reinforcement learning. In *American Control Conference (ACC), 2018*. IEEE.

Puyang Xu and Ruhi Sarikaya. 2013. Convolutional neural network based triangular crf for joint intent detection and slot filling. In *Automatic Speech Recognition and Understanding (ASRU), 2013 IEEE Workshop on*. IEEE, pages 78–83.

Puyang Xu and Ruhi Sarikaya. 2014. Contextual domain classification in spoken language understanding systems using recurrent neural network. In *Acoustics, Speech and Signal Processing (ICASSP), 2014 IEEE International Conference on*. IEEE, pages 136–140.

Kaisheng Yao, Baolin Peng, Yu Zhang, Dong Yu, Geoffrey Zweig, and Yangyang Shi. 2014. Spoken language understanding using long short-term memory neural networks. In *Spoken Language Technology Workshop (SLT), 2014 IEEE*. IEEE, pages 189–194.

Xiaodong Zhang and Houfeng Wang. 2016. A joint model of intent determination and slot filling for spoken language understanding. In *Proceedings of the Twenty-Fifth International Joint Conference on Artificial Intelligence*. AAAI Press, pages 2993–2999.

A Comparison of Two Paraphrase Models for Taxonomy Augmentation

Vassilis Plachouras[*]
Facebook
1 Rathbone Square, London, UK
vplachouras@fb.com

Fabio Petroni
Thomson Reuters
Corporate Research & Development
30 South Colonnade, London, UK
fabio.petroni@tr.com

Timothy Nugent
Thomson Reuters
Corporate Research & Development
30 South Colonnade, London, UK
tim.nugent@tr.com

Jochen L. Leidner
Thomson Reuters
Corporate Research & Development
30 South Colonnade, London, UK
jochen.leidner@tr.com

Abstract

Taxonomies are often used to look up the concepts they contain in text documents (for instance, to classify a document). The more comprehensive the taxonomy, the higher recall the application has that uses the taxonomy. In this paper, we explore automatic taxonomy augmentation with paraphrases. We compare two state-of-the-art paraphrase models based on Moses, a statistical Machine Translation system, and a sequence-to-sequence neural network, trained on a paraphrase datasets with respect to their abilities to add novel nodes to an existing taxonomy from the risk domain. We conduct component-based and task-based evaluations. Our results show that paraphrasing is a viable method to enrich a taxonomy with more terms, and that Moses consistently outperforms the sequence-to-sequence neural model. To the best of our knowledge, this is the first approach to augment taxonomies with paraphrases.

1 Introduction

Taxonomies are resources for organizing knowledge and are often used in a wide range of tasks such as document classification, search and natural language understanding, among others. Since developing taxonomies is a time consuming process, there has been a significant body of work on their automatic construction. However, even with the application of automatic methods, a taxonomy may not cover all concepts of interest due to issues in bootstrapping the automatic construction, for example the selection of seed terms, the coverage of the data used for mining the taxonomy, or balancing the trade-off between quality and recall.

In this work, we investigate the automatic augmentation of an existing taxonomy using generative paraphrasing. We train a statistical machine translation model and a sequence-to-sequence neural network based model on a subset of the Paraphrase Database (PPDB 2.0). We use the two models to augment an automatically mined taxonomy of risk terms based on (Leidner and Schilder, 2010).

The research questions we address in this work are the following:

- **RQ1** Can the models generate high quality paraphrases for automatically augmenting a taxonomy?

- **RQ2** How much does the coverage of the taxonomy increase?

- **RQ3** Which model is best for generating paraphrases?

We answer these research questions by assessing the quality of the generated risk phrases and quantifying the number of additional sentences that the generated paraphrases match in a large corpus of news articles.

2 Related Work

Paraphrase Generation. Identifying and generating paraphrases has received significant attention, being useful in applications ranging from natural language understanding, to query expansion for example (Madnani and Dorr, 2010; Androutsopoulos and Malakasiotis, 2010).

A number of works treat paraphrase generation as a special case of machine translation, learning to generate paraphrases based on a large number of

---

[*]work conducted whilst the author was at Thomson Reuters.

Proceedings of NAACL-HLT 2018, pages 315–320
New Orleans, Louisiana, June 1 - 6, 2018. ©2018 Association for Computational Linguistics

aligned sentence pairs from news articles (Quirk et al., 2004), extracting paraphrases from a bilingual parallel corpus (Bannard and Callison-Burch, 2005), or training statistical machine translation models on news headlines (Wubben et al., 2010).

Building on the recent advances in neural networks for machine translation, seq2seq models with attention representing input as a sequence of characters (Hasan et al., 2016), or with more layers and residual connections (Prakash et al., 2016) have been trained to generate paraphrases. Mallinson, Sennrich and Lapata (2017) applied the bilingual pivoting approach (Bannard and Callison-Burch, 2005) with neural machine translation, where the input sequence is mapped to a number of translations in different languages, and then these translations are mapped back to the original language.

Taxonomy Construction & Expansion Since manually creating knowledge structures, such as taxonomies, is a time consuming process, there exist several methods to automate it (Medelyan et al., 2013). Meng et al. (2015) employ techniques for automatically mining taxonomies in combination with crowd-sourcing to achieve greater coverage. Subramaniam, Nanavati and Mukherjea (2010) study the problem of merging one ontology into another one, thus asymmetrically extending one of the taxonomies. Harpy (Grycner and Weikum, 2014) addresses the sparsity of subsumption hierarchy of Patty, a large repository of relational paraphrases (Nakashole et al., 2013). Wang et al. (2014) automatically extend a taxonomy by identifying missing categories and predict the optimal structure based on a hierarchical Dirichlet model. The automatic placement of new concepts in a taxonomy has also been investigated as a shared task in SemEval 2016 (Jurgens and Pilehvar, 2016). However, to the best of our knowledge, there is no work that applies generative paraphrasing to expand a taxonomy.

3   Paraphrase Generation

In this work we approach the task of generating phrasal paraphrases as monolingual translation and we train two state-of-the-art models (Section 3.1) on an existing corpus of English phrasal paraphrases (Section 3.2).

3.1   Models

The two models we train for paraphrase generation are based on Moses (Koehn et al., 2007) and attention-based sequence-to-sequence (seq2seq) neural networks (Bahdanau et al., 2015).

Moses is an open-source implementation of statistical machine translation models. While it supports the use of additional structure such as dependency trees, we focus on phrase-based translation in this work and a tri-gram language model learned from the set of target paraphrases.

The attention-based seq2seq model consists of a bi-directional LSTM encoder and an LSTM decoder which uses an attention mechanism to learn which input words are the most important for each output word.

3.2   Training and Evaluation

For training the paraphrase generation models, we use a subset of the Paraphrase Database (PPDB 2.0) corpus. The PPDB 2.0 data set is a large-scale phrasal paraphrase data set that has been mined automatically based on (Bannard and Callison-Burch, 2005), and refined with machine learning based ranking of paraphrases based on human generated ground-truth and assignment of textual entailment labels for each paraphrase pair. In this work, we used the large pack of lexical (single word to single word) and phrasal (multi-word to single or multi-word) paraphrases[1]. Because the data set was automatically generated, some of the paraphrase pairs are not true paraphrases. In our experiments, we kept only pairs that do not contain numeric digits. We also use the textual entailment labels with which paraphrase pairs in the data set are annotated and keep the pairs labeled as equivalent. We split the remaining data in 757,300 training data points and 39,325 test data points. The splitting is performed by first creating a graph where phrases are nodes and edges exist between the two phrases in a paraphrase pair. In this graph, we identify connected components and we assign all data points within each connected component to either the training or the test sets. This process guarantees independence between the training and the test sets.

To train Moses, we precomputed a tri-gram language from the target phrases in the training data

---

[1]PPDB 2.0 is made available in packs of increasing size, where each pack contains a list of paraphrases, ordered in decreasing order of the score described in (Pavlick et al., 2015).

set and used the MERT optimizer. To train the seq2seq model, we used a batch size of 256 training samples, 100-unit LSTM cells for both the encoder and the decoder, dropout with keep probability 0.8 at the output of cells, a bidirectional encoder, greedy 1-best search output generation criteria, and an additive attention function (Bahdanau et al., 2015). For representing words, we used 100 dimensional pre-trained GloVe embeddings (Pennington et al., 2014). We trained using the Adam optimizer and a learning rate of 0.001 and let the models train for 200,000 steps (a step is an iteration over a batch of training points).

For evaluation we used the BLEU score (Papineni et al., 2002; Chen and Cherry, 2014). BLEU is calculated on tokenized data using the implementation provided in the *nltk* framework[2] with NIST geometric sequence smoothing. Moses achieved a BLEU score of 0.4098 compared to 0.3156 obtained by the seq2seq model. The difference in BLEU score shows that Moses is substantially better than the seq2seq model for the subset of PPDB 2.0 we used.

4 Taxonomy Augmentation Evaluation

After training the paraphrase generation models, we focus on augmenting the taxonomy of risks. The risk taxonomy has been automatically mined based on the method described in (Leidner and Schilder, 2010) and subsequently has been manually filtered to keep high quality risk terms, resulting in 2,824 terms.

For each term in the risk taxonomy, we apply the two paraphrase generation models to obtain a maximum of top 10 paraphrased risk terms. Figure 1 shows the number of generated paraphrases that are also in the original list of risk phrases. While our end goal is to generate phrases that are not in the original list of phrases, a large number of generations already appearing in the list of high-quality and manually filtered list of risk phrases is an indication of the quality of the paraphrases. As we can see from Figure 1, Moses outperforms with a wide margin the seq2seq model in generating paraphrases already in the taxonomy. Table 1 shows examples of generated paraphrases by Moses and seq2seq.

Furthermore, we have manually annotated the top-1 generated paraphrases that were not already in the original risk taxonomy. Each paraphrased

[2]http://www.nltk.org/

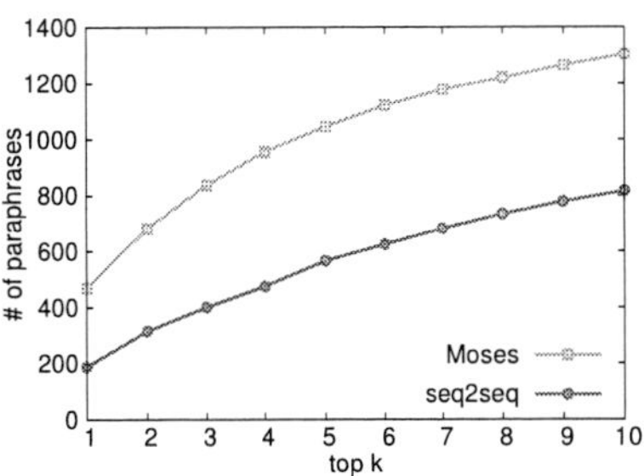

Figure 1: Number of top-k generated paraphrases already in the list of risk phrases.

risk term was annotated as *valid* when it can directly replace the original risk term, *noisy* when the meaning of the paraphrase is close to the meaning of the original term or the paraphrase has additional terms, and *invalid* when the paraphrase is not suitable for substituting the original risk term. Table 2 shows for both models the number of paraphrases that were not in the original taxonomy and that were annotated with a given label.

Even though both the BLEU score and the number of paraphrases that were already in the original risk taxonomy demonstrate that Moses performs better than seq2seq in our setting, we have also looked how often a paraphrase generated with seq2seq was annotated as being better than the paraphrase generated by Moses. For example, this is the case when one model generates a paraphrase that is annotated as *valid* and the other model generates for the input risk term a paraphrase that is annotated as *noisy* or *invalid*. We have observed that in 1211 cases, the paraphrase generated by Moses was better than the paraphrase generated by seq2seq. On the other hand, seq2seq was better only in 58 cases.

We have also looked at the lexical diversity of the generated paraphrases. We define lexical diversity as the fraction of tokens in a paraphrase that were not in the original risk phrase. Table 3 shows that the seq2seq model results in higher lexical diversity than Moses for both the valid and noisy paraphrases.

Finally, we have looked at the number of sentences matched by the original risk phrases and the generated paraphrases in large corpus of approximately 14 million news articles. The original list of risk phrases matches 23,110,506 sentences. As Table 4 demonstrates, the *valid* paraphrases generated by Moses match an additional 5.2M sentences that were not matched by any entry in the

Risk Term	Moses	seq2seq
wind-blown debris	wind-blown rubble	buildings
unexpected entry of competitors	unpredicted entrance of competitors	accident
trafficked people	trafficking in persons	victims of human trafficking
demolished	razed	demolition
committed fraud	fraud committed	the fight against fraud
genetically modified food	gm food	genetically engineered

Table 1: Examples of paraphrases generated by Moses and seq2seq.

Model	Valid	Noisy	Invalid
Moses	1,337	337	327
seq2seq	419	175	2,042

Table 2: Number of generated paraphrases annotated as valid, noisy or invalid.

Model	Diversity (valid)	Diversity (noisy)
Moses	0.5455 (1,337)	0.3952 (337)
seq2seq	0.6991 (419)	0.6969 (175)

Table 3: Lexical diversity of generated valid and noisy paraphrases in terms of fraction of tokens that are not in the original risk phrase.

Model	Valid	Noisy
Moses	5,197,781	1,868,734
seq2seq	1,751,745	749,886

Table 4: The number of sentences from the news archive matching at least one of the generated valid or noisy risk paraphrases, which were not already matched by a risk phrase in the original taxonomy.

original taxonomy, corresponding to an expansion of coverage by 22%. The *valid* paraphrases generated by seq2seq match 1.8M additional sentences, expanding coverage by 7.6%. A smaller increase in coverage can be achieved if we consider *noisy* paraphrases as well, 8.1% for Moses and 3.2% for seq2seq. However, these additional sentences may contain significantly more noise.

Overall, we have seen that the application of paraphrase generation can expand an existing taxonomy of risk terms with high quality phrases, where 67% of the added terms by Moses have been assessed as valid paraphrases (**RQ1**). This has led to an increase of the coverage of the taxonomy by 22% (**RQ2**). The experimental results also demonstrate that Moses outperforms the neural network-based model in this setting (**RQ3**).

5 Discussion

Domain-specific paraphrases. During the annotation of the generated paraphrases by the two models, we have observed a number of cases, which were annotated as *invalid* because the generated paraphrase, although it was grammatically correct and meaningful, it did not correspond to the original term in the domain of risk management. For example, the phrase "screening risk", which refers to risks in the process of performing background checks, was paraphrased to "projection risk" by one of the models. Even though the latter is a grammatically correct phrase, it does not have the same meaning in the context of risk management. Similarly, the word *concentrations* has been replaced by the word *levels* in the phrase "sector concentrations", which may be more appropriate as a replacement in the domain of chemistry. A more appropriate word to replace *level* would be *focus*. To address this issue of domain specific paraphrasing, one possible solution is to use a domain-specific corpus to train the language model used in Moses, or to pre-train the weights of the LSTM cells in the encoder and decoder of seq2seq in the context of a language modelling task (Dai and Le, 2015).

Grammatical diversity. We have quantified lexical diversity as the fraction of new words in the generated paraphrases. Another aspect of diversity, however, is grammatical diversity. For example, it would be interesting to quantify diversity in terms of the number of the classes of paraphrasing phenomena defined by Bhagat and Hovy (2013).

6 Conclusions

In this work we have looked at the problem of automatically augmenting a taxonomy by generating paraphrases of the terms in the taxonomy. Using a subset of PPDB 2.0, a data set of paraphrases, we have trained a statistical machine translation model based on Moses and a second one based on sequence-to-sequence neural network-based models. Our evaluation results show that Moses out-performs seq2seq in our setting and it augments the taxonomy with 67% of high quality terms, leading to an increase of coverage by 22%.

For future work, we want to investigate the impact of using pre-trained weights to initialize the LSTM cells in the seq2seq model from a language modelling task, as well the grammatical diversity of generated paraphrases.

References

Ion Androutsopoulos and Prodromos Malakasiotis. 2010. A survey of paraphrasing and textual entailment methods. *J. Artif. Int. Res.* 38(1):135–187.

Dzmitry Bahdanau, Kyung Hyun Cho, and Yoshua Bengio. 2015. Neural machine translation by jointly learning to align and translate. In *Proceedings of the International Conference on Learning Representations (ICLR)*.

Colin Bannard and Chris Callison-Burch. 2005. Paraphrasing with bilingual parallel corpora. In *Proceedings of the 43rd Annual Meeting on Association for Computational Linguistics*. ACL '05, pages 597–604.

Rahul Bhagat and Eduard Hovy. 2013. What is a paraphrase? *Computational Linguistics* 39:463–472.

Boxing Chen and Colin Cherry. 2014. A systematic comparison of smoothing techniques for sentence-level bleu. *ACL 2014* page 362.

Andrew M Dai and Quoc V Le. 2015. Semi-supervised sequence learning. In C. Cortes, N. D. Lawrence, D. D. Lee, M. Sugiyama, and R. Garnett, editors, *Advances in Neural Information Processing Systems 28*, Curran Associates, Inc., pages 3079–3087. http://papers.nips.cc/paper/5949-semi-supervised-sequence-learning.pdf.

Adam Grycner and Gerhard Weikum. 2014. Harpy: Hypernyms and alignment of relational paraphrases. In *Proceedings of COLING 2014, the 25th International Conference on Computational Linguistics: Technical Papers*. Dublin City University and Association for Computational Linguistics, pages 2195–2204. http://www.aclweb.org/anthology/C14-1207.

Sadid A. Hasan, Bo Liu, Joey Liu, Ashequl Qadir, Kathy Lee, Vivek Datla, Aaditya Prakash, and Oladimeji Farri. 2016. Neural clinical paraphrase generation with attention. In *Proceedings of the Clinical Natural Language Processing Workshop (ClinicalNLP)*. pages 42–53.

David Jurgens and Mohammad Taher Pilehvar. 2016. Semeval-2016 task 14: Semantic taxonomy enrichment. In *Proceedings of the 10th International Workshop on Semantic Evaluation (SemEval-2016)*. Association for Computational Linguistics, pages 1092–1102. https://doi.org/10.18653/v1/S16-1169.

Philipp Koehn, Hieu Hoang, Alexandra Birch, Chris Callison-Burch, Marcello Federico, Nicola Bertoldi, Brooke Cowan, Wade Shen, Christine Moran, Richard Zens, Chris Dyer, Ondrej Bojar, Alexandra Constantin, and Evan Herbst. 2007. Moses: Open source toolkit for statistical machine translation. In *Proceedings of the 45th Annual Meeting of the Association for Computational Linguistics Companion Volume Proceedings of the Demo and Poster Sessions*. Association for Computational Linguistics, pages 177–180. http://www.aclweb.org/anthology/P07-2045.

Jochen L. Leidner and Frank Schilder. 2010. Hunting for the black swan: Risk mining from text. In *Proceedings of the ACL 2010 System Demonstrations*. Association for Computational Linguistics, Stroudsburg, PA, USA, ACLDemos '10, pages 54–59. http://dl.acm.org/citation.cfm?id=1858933.1858943.

Nitin Madnani and Bonnie J. Dorr. 2010. Generating phrasal and sentential paraphrases: A survey of data-driven methods. *Comput. Linguist.* 36(3):341–387.

Jonathan Mallinson, Rico Sennrich, and Mirella Lapata. 2017. Paraphrasing revisited with neural machine translation. In *Proceedings of the 15th Conference of the European Chapter of the Association for Computational Linguistics: Volume 1, Long Papers*. EACL '17, pages 881–893.

Olena Medelyan, Ian H. Witten, Anna Divoli, and Jeen Broekstra. 2013. Automatic construction of lexicons, taxonomies, ontologies, and other knowledge structures. *Wiley Interdisciplinary Reviews: Data Mining and Knowledge Discovery* 3(4):257–279. https://doi.org/10.1002/widm.1097.

R. Meng, Y. Tong, L. Chen, and C. C. Cao. 2015. Crowdtc: Crowdsourced taxonomy construction. In *2015 IEEE International Conference on Data Mining*. pages 913–918. https://doi.org/10.1109/ICDM.2015.77.

Ndapandula Nakashole, Gerhard Weikum, and Fabian Suchanek. 2013. Discovering semantic relations from the web and organizing them with patty. *SIGMOD Rec.* 42(2):29–34. https://doi.org/10.1145/2503792.2503799.

Kishore Papineni, Salim Roukos, Todd Ward, and Wei-Jing Zhu. 2002. Bleu: A method for automatic evaluation of machine translation. In *Proceedings of the 40th Annual Meeting on Association for Computational Linguistics*. ACL '02, pages 311–318.

Ellie Pavlick, Johan Bos, Malvina Nissim, Charley Beller, Benjamin Van Durme, and Chris Callison-Burch. 2015. Adding semantics to data-driven paraphrasing. In *Proceedings of the 53rd Annual Meeting of the Association for Computational Linguistics and the 7th International Joint Conference on Natural Language Processing (Volume 1: Long Papers)*. Association for Computational Linguistics, pages 1512–1522. `https://doi.org/10.3115/v1/P15-1146`.

Jeffrey Pennington, Richard Socher, and Christopher Manning. 2014. Glove: Global vectors for word representation. In *Proceedings of the 2014 Conference on Empirical Methods in Natural Language Processing*. EMNLP '14, pages 1532–1543.

Aaditya Prakash, Sadid A. Hasan, Kathy Lee, Vivek Datla, Ashequl Qadir, Joey Liu, and Oladimeji Farry. 2016. Neural paraphrase generation with stacked residual lstm networks. In *Proceedings of the 26th International Conference on Computational Linguistics: Technical Papers*. COLING '16, pages 2923–2934.

Chris Quirk, Chris Brockett, and William B. Dolan. 2004. Monolingual machine translation for paraphrase generation. In *Proceedings of the 2004 Conference on Empirical Methods in Natural Language Processing*. EMNLP '04, pages 142–149.

L. V. Subramaniam, A. A. Nanavati, and S. Mukherjea. 2010. Enriching one taxonomy using another. *IEEE Transactions on Knowledge and Data Engineering* 22(10):1415–1427. `https://doi.org/10.1109/TKDE.2009.189`.

Jingjing Wang, Changsung Kang, Yi Chang, and Jiawei Han. 2014. A hierarchical dirichlet model for taxonomy expansion for search engines. In *Proceedings of the 23rd International Conference on World Wide Web*. ACM, New York, NY, USA, WWW '14, pages 961–970. `https://doi.org/10.1145/2566486.2568037`.

Sander Wubben, Antal van den Bosch, and Emiel Krahmer. 2010. Paraphrase generation as monolingual translation: Data and evaluation. In *Proceedings of the 6th International Natural Language Generation Conference*. INLG '10, pages 203–207.

A Laypeople Study on Terminology Identification
across Domains and Task Definitions

Anna Hätty
Robert Bosch GmbH
IMS, University of Stuttgart
`anna.haetty@de.bosch.com`

Sabine Schulte im Walde
Institute for Natural Language Proessing (IMS),
University of Stuttgart
`schulte@ims.uni-stuttgart.de`

Abstract

This paper introduces a new dataset of term annotation. Given that even experts vary significantly in their understanding of termhood, we offer a novel perspective to explore the common, natural understanding of what constitutes a term: Laypeople annotate single-word and multi-word terms, across four domains and across four task definitions. Analyses based on inter-annotator agreement offer insights into differences in term specificity, term granularity and subtermhood.

1 Introduction

Terms are linguistic units which characterize a specific topic domain, and their identification is relevant for a number of NLP tasks, such as information retrieval and automatic translation. Not only the automatic extraction of terms is a challenging task, but also their manual definition and identification: while we find a range of gold standard corpora for the evaluation of term extraction systems for English (Kim et al., 2003; Bernier-Colborne and Drouin, 2014; Zadeh and Schumann, 2016) and to a lesser extent also for German (Arcan et al., 2014; Arcan, 2017; Hätty et al., 2017), these benchmark datasets vary hugely in terms of granularity of term definition, topic and thematic focus. All datasets have in common that they have been annotated by domain experts and/or by terminologists, which is considered a necessary requirement for term evaluation (Castellví, 1999; Gouws et al., 2007). However, Estopà (2001) shows that even experts with different perspectives on terminology (e.g., terminologists, domain experts, translators and documentalists) vary significantly in their annotation of terms. Moreover, although individual studies describe different layers of terminology (Trimble, 1985; Roelcke, 1999), there is a lack of empirical

studies. This raises the question whether there is a common, natural understanding of what constitutes a term, and to what extent this term is associated to a domain.

In this study, we examine the concept of terminology from a new perspective. Differently to previous annotation studies, we investigate judgments of laypeople, rather than experts, and specify on analyzing their (dis-)agreements on common assumptions and core issues in term identification: the word classes of terms, the identification of ambiguous terms, and the relations between complex terms and possibly included subterms. To ensure a broad understanding of term identification, we designed four different tasks to address the granularities of term concepts, and we performed all annotations across four different domains in German: diy, cooking, hunting, chess. Finally, we compare the annotations to the output of an unsupervised hybrid term extraction system.

2 Material and Tasks

Domains The data for term identification comprise German open-source texts from the websites *wikiHow*[1], *Wikibooks*[2] and *Wikipedia*. All texts have been pos-tagged with the *Tree Tagger* (Schmid, 1994); compound splitting was performed with *Compost* (Cap, 2014) and manually post-edited. In total, the text basis consists of 20 texts (five per domain) with ≈ 5 sentences each. All texts together contain 3,075 words, distributed over the following four domains:

- diy: *"do it yourself"* (708 words)
- cooking (624 words)
- hunting (900 words)
- chess (843 words)

---

[1] `https://de.wikihow.com/`
[2] `https://www.wikibooks.org/`

Proceedings of NAACL-HLT 2018, pages 321–326
New Orleans, Louisiana, June 1 - 6, 2018. ©2018 Association for Computational Linguistics

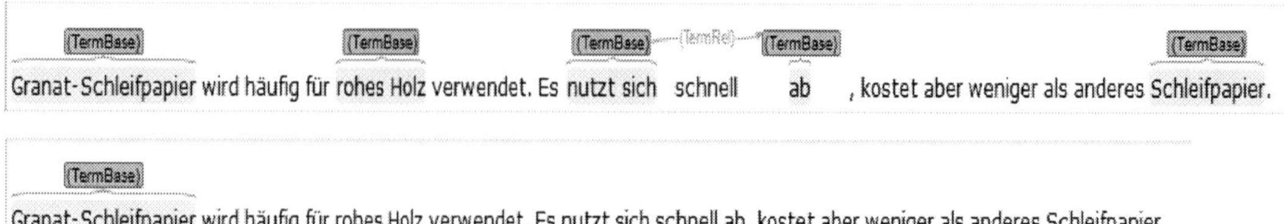

Figure 1: Example of WebAnno annotation for DS (top) and GL (bottom).

Term Identification Tasks In order to investigate the effect of term definition on their identification, we specified the following four tasks:

- highlight domain-specific phrases (**DS**)
- create an index (**IND**)
- define unknown words for creating a translation lexicon (**TR**)
- create a glossary (**GL**)

We assumed the four tasks to provide different strengths of associating the terms with the domains: DS and IND were expected to demand a broad range of terms that characterize the domains. TR and GL were expected to have a focus on unknown and ambiguous terms.

20 annotators were asked to perform only one of the identification tasks, which resulted in five annotations per task. In addition, we asked two annotators to perform all four tasks, to check whether the inter-annotator agreement differs in the two setups. Since the latter annotation setup did not exhibit systematic differences to the original setup, we merged the results of all seven annotations.

Annotation was done using *WebAnno* (Yimam et al., 2013), a general-purpose web-based annotation tool. We allowed annotations of single words, multi-words, and links between terms in case of nonadjacent term constituents. An example of two annotations is shown in figure 1. In addition to the actual annotation, annotators were asked to rate their knowledge about the respective domains. Overall, cooking was rated as best-known domain, with a mean of 6.86 on a scale from 1 (unknown) to 10 (well-known), followed by diy (5.18), chess (4.05) and hunting (1.90).

3 Analyses of Term Identification

In the following, we analyze word forms annotated as terms, across tasks and across domains. As the central means in our analyses, we make use of the *agreement* between annotators. We rely on simple agreement (how many of the 7 annotators per task agreed?), the Jaccard index and the chance-corrected agreement measure Fleiss' κ (Fleiss, 1971). We start with various single-word type-based evaluations in sections 3.1 and 3.2, and then explore multi-words in section 3.3.

3.1 Agreement across Tasks and Domains

Table 1 shows the number of type-based term annotations per task with the highest agreements, i.e. where all annotators (7) or most annotators (6 or 5) agreed. In line with our intuition, the number of identified terms is highest for DS, and lowest for GL, with IND and TR in between.

task	DS	IND	TR	GL
agree = 7 (*all*)	203	66	94	27
agree ≥ 6	315	111	173	68
agree ≥ 5	400	148	247	117

Table 1: Number of identified terms per task.

This trend is still obvious when including all annotated terms (i.e., all term types annotated by at least one annotator): Figure 2 shows the Jaccard index across tasks and domains, i.e., the intersection of the annotations divided by their union. DS again receives the highest values, GL the lowest. DS and GL thus seem to represent the extremes of the tasks, with DS providing the broadest and GL the narrowest definition of terminology.

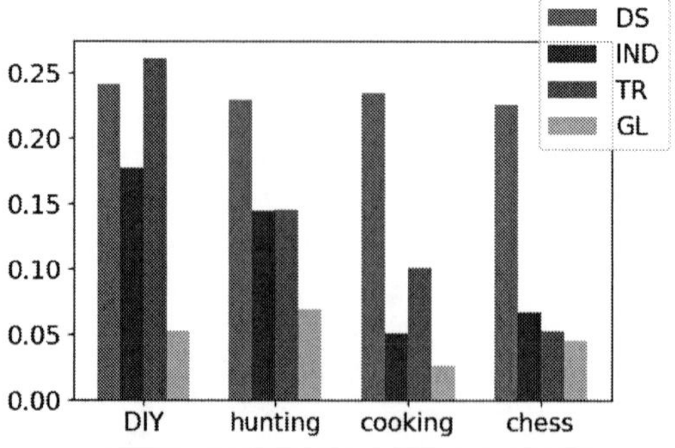

Figure 2: Jaccard index across tasks and domains.

Across the tasks and different scopes of the terms, there is a clear tendency for the same terms to receive high vs. low agreement. This effect is shown in figure 3, where all annotated term types are depicted in a four-dimensional space (x-, y- and z-axis plus the 4th dimension in colour). Each dimension represents one task, the value in each dimension represents the agreement on terms for this task (max. 7). We clearly observe an upward-moving tendency for term agreement across all dimensions, i.e., across the four tasks, annotators (dis-)agreed on the same terms to a similar degree. We conclude that annotators have similar intuitions about a term's domain specificity regardless of the term identification task.

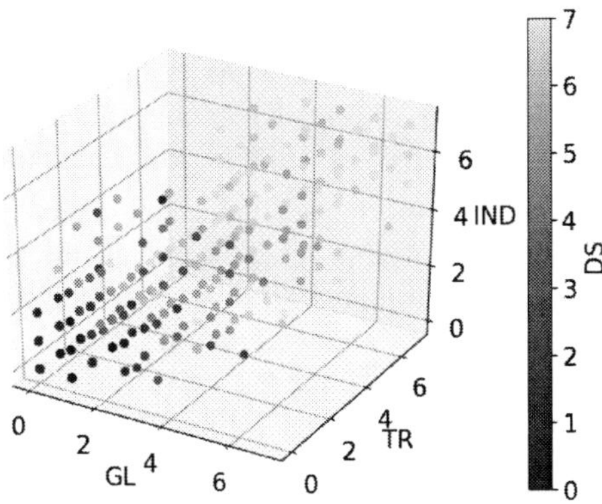

Figure 3: Term agreement across tasks.

Figure 4 depicts the interaction between tasks and domains even more clearly: While Fleiss' κ for DS is in general very high across domains, and also IND and TR are well-agreed upon for diy (and TR for hunting), the κ values for GL are particularly low, and so is IND for cooking and chess, and TR for chess.

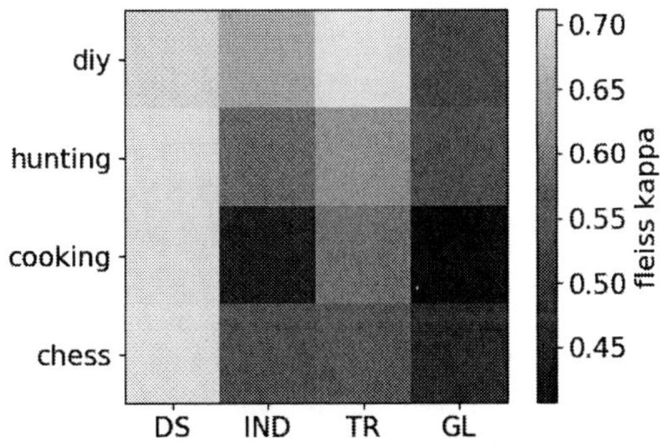

Figure 4: Fleiss' κ across tasks and domains.

3.2 Term Identification across Word Classes

Traditionally, mostly nouns are perceived as terms (Bourigault, 1992; Justeson and Katz, 1995), and consequently annotation and extraction of terms is often restricted to noun phrases (Bernth et al., 2003; Kim et al., 2003). However, according to Estopà (2001) and others, terminology should not be restricted to noun phrases. Figure 5 shows that both views have a point. The figure shows the number of term type annotations for nouns, verbs and adjectives across the 28 annotated datasets (7 annotators $\times$ 4 domains). For example, roughly 300 noun types received a total of 5 term annotations across the four tasks DS, IND, TR and GL.

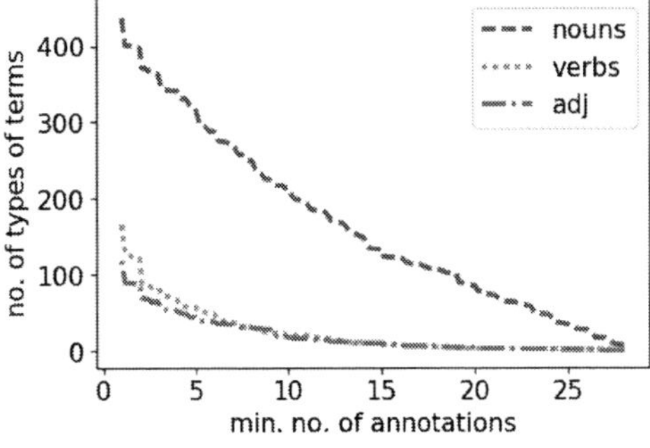

Figure 5: Annotations per part-of-speech.

We can see that in our dataset nouns are indeed preferred by our non-expert annotators. However, when looking at a smaller amount of annotations, the number of annotated verbs and adjectives increases. Looking into the data revealed that 70% and 58% of the annotated verbs and adjectives appear in multi-word terms (MWTs). One reason for this is their participation in annotated activities such as *großes Loch reparieren* ('repair a big hole') or *Eigelb schaumig schlagen* ('beat the egg yolk until fothy').

3.3 Complex Terms and Subterms

The fact that multi-word terms often contain subterms is a distinct attribute, frequently exploited by automatic term extraction methods relying on term constituent phrases for computing a termhood score (Frantzi et al., 1998; Nakagawa and Mori, 2003). In our study, 468 single-word terms, 138 closed compounds and 692 MWT types were annotated across annotators. Since German contains many closed compounds, treating them separately from MWTs (consisting of several separated words) is especially interesting: a compound term candidate is either annotated completely or not at all. Regarding MWTs, it is possible that only a subterm is annotated. For example, the compound *Rohholz* ('raw wood') cannot be separated, while annotators might mark only *Holz* as subterm of the MWT *rohes Holz*.

Table 2 shows aspects of multi-word and compound term types in relation to their number of annotations (7 annotators $\times$ 4 domains, i.e. a maximum of 28 annotations), across tasks and domains. We group the number of annotations into three categories: no concordance (<2), minimum concordance (≥ 2) and majority concordance (>14). For most MWTs (426), there is no concordance, and only a few MWTs were found in the majority of the 28 annotations (11). Compound terms show the opposite behaviour. Slightly more than half of the compounds (76) were found in the majority of the 28 annotations, while only 6 compounds appeared in only one annotation. Thus, annotators are confident in identifying compound terms, but not MWTs.

no. of annotations	<2	≥ 2	> 14
MWTs	426	266	11
compounds	6	132	76

Table 2: Annotation of compounds and MWTs.

We then analysed the annotation concordance of complex term components, and their likelihood to represent a subterm, cf. table 3. For that, we extracted all annotated single-word terms (SWTs) which were not also annotated as part of a complex term. We thus obtained the number of annotations for the SWTs only. While for MWTs the proportion of subterms is relatively high across categories (45.83–49.23%), the number of compound subterms is rather low for low-concordance cases (16.67%) and increases radically for higher-concordance cases (up to 40.37%).

no. of annotations	<2	≥ 2	> 14
MWTs			
% of subterms	49.23	57.40	45.83
$\varnothing$ annot. on subterms	7.53	7.26	6.0
compounds			
% of subterms	16.67	31.76	40.37
$\varnothing$ annot. on subterms	1.0	9.59	10.23

Table 3: Annotation of compound and MWT subterms.

Table 3 also illustrates that the average number of annotations per subterm drops for MWTs with an increasing concordance. Compounds, again, behave in the opposite way. Thus, the less confidence there is for an MWT, the more confidence we find in its subterms. For the closed compounds, this effect cannot be perceived.

3.4 Ambiguity

A peculiarity of many terminologies are general-language words with a specialized meaning in one or more domains. For example, the English noun *solution* has a general-language sense as well as domain-specific senses in mathematics and chemistry (Baker, 1988). Ambiguous vocabulary is also present across our domains, e.g., *Fuchsschwanz* ('ripsaw' vs. 'foxtail') in diy and *ansprechen* ('identify game' vs. 'address so.') in hunting.

In order to analyze the identification of ambiguous terms, we first looked up the general-language and domain-specific senses of all hunting and chess terms from our dataset in *Wiktionary*[3], *Duden*[4], and the *Wikipedia* disambiguation pages. We did this for hunting and chess, because only these domains are consistently specified in the sense definitions. We identified 18 terms for hunting and 15 for chess.

Table 4 shows the average agreement on these ambiguous words, across tasks. For example, on average 5.32 annotators out of 7 agreed on the 18 hunting term types in the DS task. The table shows that the average agreement is higher for DS than for the other three tasks.

domain	DS	IND	TR	GL
hunting	5.32	3.74	4.12	3.44
chess	5.08	3.72	3.75	2.93

Table 4: Average agreement on ambiguous words.

We conclude that when it comes to a stricter sense of termhood the domain-specific sense might be perceived by the annotators, but the general-language sense impedes them to accept the same strength of termhood for the ambiguous term as for other, more domain-specific terms.

---

[3] http://www.wiktionary.org/
[4] https://www.duden.de/

4 Automatic Term Extraction

In a final step, we compared the identification of terms in our dataset against the identification done by state-of-the-art term extraction approaches. We used the hybrid term-candidate extractor for the diy domain described in Schäfer et al. (2015) and Rösiger et al. (2016). After lemmatization and pos-tagging, the system extracts terms with predefined linguistic filters. For term candidate ranking, standard termhood measures are applied, cf. an overview in Schäfer et al. (2015).

Approximately half of our annotated terms were found by the term extractor (due to predefined linguistic patterns for extraction). Based on the measure scores, we applied Spearman's rank-order correlation coefficient ρ (Siegel and Castellan, 1988) to compare against a ranking based on annotator agreement. The best ρ values were 0.51 and 0.44 for two corpus-comparison extraction methods; these are statistically significant (p< 0.01).

When inspecting the ranked list, we observed that the term extractors rank compounds and MWTs higher than the laypeople do. Although the automatic extractors only use statistics over the whole word forms, ρ increases when adding subterm scores to compounds and MWTs. This again indicates the importance of subterms within complex terms for an annotator's decision.

5 Conclusion

This paper presented a new dataset of term annotation and a study about term identification by laypeople, across four domains and four task definitions. We found that laypeople generally share a common understanding of termhood and term association with domains, as reflected by inter-annotator agreement. Furthermore,

1. high inter-annotator variance for more specific tasks,

2. little awareness of the degree of termhood of ambiguous terms, and

3. low agreement on multi-word terms with high reliance on subterms

showed that laypeople's judgments deteriorate for specific and potentially unknown terms.

The dataset with the lapeople term annotations is publicly available at `www.ims.uni-stuttgart.de/data/term-annotation-laypeople`.

Acknowledgments

The research was supported by the DFG Collaborative Research Centre SFB 732. We would like to thank Michael Dorna for his helpful comments and reviews.

References

Mihael Arcan. 2017. *Machine Translation of Domain-Specific Expressions within Ontologies and Documents*. Ph.D. thesis, Insight Centre for Data Analytics, National University of Ireland, Galway.

Mihael Arcan, Marco Turchi, Sara Tonelli, and Paul Buitelaar. 2014. Enhancing statistical machine translation with bilingual terminology in a CAT environment. *Proceedings of the 11th Biennial Conference of the Association for Machine Translation in the Americas (AMTA)* pages 54–68.

Mona Baker. 1988. Sub-technical vocabulary and the esp teacher: An analysis of some rhetorical items in medical journal articles. *Reading in a Foreign Language* 4(2):91–105.

Gabriel Bernier-Colborne and Patrick Drouin. 2014. Creating a test corpus for term extractors through term annotation. *Terminology. International Journal of Theoretical and Applied Issues in Specialized Communication* 20(1):50–73.

Arendse Bernth, Michael McCord, and Kara Warburton. 2003. Terminology extraction for global content management. *Terminology. International Journal of Theoretical and Applied Issues in Specialized Communication* 9(1):51–69.

Didier Bourigault. 1992. Surface grammatical analysis for the extraction of terminological noun phrases. In *Proceedings of the 15th International Conference on Computational Linguistics*. Nantes, France, pages 977–981.

Fabienne Cap. 2014. *Morphological processing of compounds for statistical machine translation*. Dissertation, Institute for Natural Language Processing (IMS), University of Stuttgart.

M. Teresa Cabré Castellví. 1999. *Terminology: Theory, methods and applications*, volume 1. John Benjamins Publishing.

Rosa Estopà. 2001. Les unités de signification spécialisées: élargissant l'objet du travail en terminologie. *Terminology. International Journal of Theoretical and Applied Issues in Specialized Communication* 7(2):217–237.

J.L. Fleiss. 1971. Measuring nominal scale agreement among many raters. *Psychological Bulletin* 76(5):378–382.

Katerina T. Frantzi, Sophia Ananiadou, and Jun-ichi Tsujii. 1998. The c-value/nc-value method of automatic recognition for multi-word terms. In *Proceedings of the 2nd European Conference on Research and Advanced Technology for Digital Libraries*. London, UK, pages 585–604.

Rufus H. Gouws, Ulrich Heid, Wolfgang Schweickard, and Herbert Ernst Wiegand. 2007. Dictionaries. An international encyclopedia of lexicography. *Supplementary Volume: Recent Developments with special focus on Computational Lexicography* .

Anna Hätty, Simon Tannert, and Ulrich Heid. 2017. Creating a gold standard corpus for terminological annotation from online forum data. In *Proceedings of the EACL Workshop on Language, Ontology, Terminology and Knowledge Structures*.

John S. Justeson and Slava M. Katz. 1995. Technical terminology: Some linguistic properties and an algorithm for identification in text. *Natural Language Engineering* 1(1):9–27.

J.-D. Kim, Tomoko Ohta, Yuka Tateisi, and Junichi Tsujii. 2003. GENIA corpus – A semantically annotated corpus for bio-textmining. *Bioinformatics* 19(1):180–182.

Hiroshi Nakagawa and Tatsunori Mori. 2003. Automatic term recognition based on statistics of compound nouns and their components. *Terminology* 9(2):201–219.

Thorsten Roelcke. 1999. *Fachsprachen*. Grundlagen der Germanistik. Erich Schmidt Verlag.

Ina Rösiger, Julia Bettinger, Johannes Schäfer, Michael Dorna, and Ulrich Heid. 2016. Acquisition of semantic relations between terms: How far can we get with standard NLP tools? In *Proceedings of the 5th International Workshop on Computational Terminology*.

Johannes Schäfer, Ina Rösiger, Ulrich Heid, and Michael Dorna. 2015. Evaluating noise reduction strategies for terminology extraction. In *Proceedings of TIA 2015*.

Helmut Schmid. 1994. Probabilistic part-of-speech tagging using decision trees. In *Proceedings of the International Conference on New Methods in Language Processing*. Manchester, UK, pages 44–49.

Sidney Siegel and N. John Castellan. 1988. *Nonparametric Statistics for the Behavioral Sciences*. McGraw-Hill, Boston, MA.

Louis Trimble. 1985. *English for Science and Technology: A Discourse Approach*. Cambridge University Press.

Seid Muhie Yimam, Iryna Gurevych, Richard Eckart de Castilho, and Chris Biemann. 2013. WebAnno: A flexible, web-based and visually supported system for distributed annotations. In *Proceedings of the 51st Annual Meeting of the Association for Computational Linguistics: System Demonstrations*. Sofia, Bulgaria, pages 1–6.

Behrang Qasemi Zadeh and Anne-Kathrin Schumann. 2016. The ACL RD-TEC 2.0: A language resource for evaluating term extraction and entity recognition methods. In *Proceedings of the 10th International Conference on Language Resources and Evaluation*. Portoroz, Slovenia.

A Novel Embedding Model for Knowledge Base Completion Based on Convolutional Neural Network

Dai Quoc Nguyen[1], Tu Dinh Nguyen[1], Dat Quoc Nguyen[2], Dinh Phung[1]
[1] Deakin University, Geelong, Australia, Centre for Pattern Recognition and Data Analytics
{dai.nguyen,tu.nguyen,dinh.phung}@deakin.edu.au
[2] The University of Melbourne, Australia
dqnguyen@unimelb.edu.au

Abstract

In this paper, we propose a novel embedding model, named ConvKB, for knowledge base completion. Our model ConvKB advances state-of-the-art models by employing a convolutional neural network, so that it can capture global relationships and transitional characteristics between entities and relations in knowledge bases. In ConvKB, each triple *(head entity, relation, tail entity)* is represented as a 3-column matrix where each column vector represents a triple element. This 3-column matrix is then fed to a convolution layer where multiple filters are operated on the matrix to generate different feature maps. These feature maps are then concatenated into a single feature vector representing the input triple. The feature vector is multiplied with a weight vector via a dot product to return a score. This score is then used to predict whether the triple is valid or not. Experiments show that ConvKB achieves better link prediction performance than previous state-of-the-art embedding models on two benchmark datasets WN18RR and FB15k-237.

1 Introduction

Large-scale knowledge bases (KBs), such as YAGO (Suchanek et al., 2007), Freebase (Bollacker et al., 2008) and DBpedia (Lehmann et al., 2015), are usually databases of triples representing the relationships between entities in the form of fact *(head entity, relation, tail entity)* denoted as *(h, r, t)*, e.g., *(Melbourne, cityOf, Australia)*. These KBs are useful resources in many applications such as semantic searching and ranking (Kasneci et al., 2008; Schuhmacher and Ponzetto, 2014; Xiong et al., 2017), question answering (Zhang et al., 2016; Hao et al., 2017) and machine reading (Yang and Mitchell, 2017). However, the KBs are

still incomplete, i.e., missing a lot of valid triples (Socher et al., 2013; West et al., 2014). Therefore, much research work has been devoted towards *knowledge base completion* or *link prediction* to predict whether a triple *(h, r, t)* is valid or not (Bordes et al., 2011).

Many embedding models have proposed to learn vector or matrix representations for entities and relations, obtaining state-of-the-art (SOTA) link prediction results (Nickel et al., 2016a). In these embedding models, valid triples obtain lower implausibility scores than invalid triples. Let us take the well-known embedding model TransE (Bordes et al., 2013) as an example. In TransE, entities and relations are represented by k-dimensional vector embeddings. TransE employs a transitional characteristic to model relationships between entities, in which it assumes that if *(h, r, t)* is a valid fact, the embedding of head entity h plus the embedding of relation r should be close to the embedding of tail entity t, i.e. $v_h + v_r \approx v_t$ (here, v_h, v_r and v_t are embeddings of h, r and t respectively). That is, a TransE score $\|v_h + v_r - v_t\|_p$ of the valid triple *(h, r, t)* should be close to 0 and smaller than a score $\|v_{h'} + v_{r'} - v_{t'}\|_p$ of an invalid triple *(h', r', t')*. The transitional characteristic in TransE also implies the global relationships among same dimensional entries of v_h, v_r and v_t.

Other transition-based models extend TransE to additionally use projection vectors or matrices to translate head and tail embeddings into the relation vector space, such as: TransH (Wang et al., 2014), TransR (Lin et al., 2015b), TransD (Ji et al., 2015), STransE (Nguyen et al., 2016b) and TranSparse (Ji et al., 2016). Furthermore, DISTMULT (Yang et al., 2015) and ComplEx (Trouillon et al., 2016) use a tri-linear dot product to compute the score for each triple. Recent research

327

Proceedings of NAACL-HLT 2018, pages 327–333
New Orleans, Louisiana, June 1 - 6, 2018. ©2018 Association for Computational Linguistics

has shown that using relation paths between entities in the KBs could help to get contextual information for improving KB completion performance (Lin et al., 2015a; Luo et al., 2015; Guu et al., 2015; Toutanova et al., 2016; Nguyen et al., 2016a). See other embedding models for KB completion in Nguyen (2017).

Recently, convolutional neural networks (CNNs), originally designed for computer vision (LeCun et al., 1998), have significantly received research attention in natural language processing (Collobert et al., 2011; Kim, 2014). CNN learns non-linear features to capture complex relationships with a remarkably less number of parameters compared to fully connected neural networks. Inspired from the success in computer vision, Dettmers et al. (2018) proposed ConvE—the first model applying CNN for the KB completion task. In ConvE, only v_h and v_r are reshaped and then concatenated into an input matrix which is fed to the convolution layer. Different filters of the same 3×3 shape are operated over the input matrix to output feature map tensors. These feature map tensors are then vectorized and mapped into a vector via a linear transformation. Then this vector is computed with v_t via a dot product to return a score for *(h, r, t)*. See a formal definition of the ConvE score function in Table 1. It is worth noting that ConvE focuses on the local relationships among different dimensional entries in each of v_h or v_r, i.e., *ConvE does not observe the global relationships among same dimensional entries of an embedding triple (v_h, v_r, v_t)*, so that ConvE ignores the transitional characteristic in transition-based models, which is one of the most useful intuitions for the task.

In this paper, we present ConvKB—an embedding model which proposes a novel use of CNN for the KB completion task. In ConvKB, each entity or relation is associated with an unique k-dimensional embedding. Let v_h, v_r and v_t denote k-dimensional embeddings of h, r and t, respectively. For each triple *(h, r, t)*, the corresponding triple of k-dimensional embeddings (v_h, v_r, v_t) is represented as a $k \times 3$ input matrix. This input matrix is fed to the convolution layer where different filters of the same 1×3 shape are used to extract the global relationships among same dimensional entries of the embedding triple. That is, these filters are repeatedly operated over every row of the input matrix to produce different

Model	The score function $f(h, r, t)$
TransE	$\|v_h + v_r - v_t\|_p$
DISTMULT	$\langle v_h, v_r, v_t \rangle$
ComplEx	$\mathrm{Re}\left(\langle v_h, v_r, \overline{v}_t \rangle\right)$
ConvE	$g\left(\mathrm{vec}\left(g\left(\mathrm{concat}\left(\widehat{v}_h, \widehat{v}_r\right) * \Omega\right)\right) W\right) \cdot v_t$
ConvKB	$\mathrm{concat}\left(g\left([v_h, v_r, v_t] * \Omega\right)\right) \cdot \mathbf{w}$

Table 1: The score functions in previous SOTA models and in our ConvKB model. $\|v\|_p$ denotes the p-norm of v. $\langle v_h, v_r, v_t \rangle = \sum_i v_{h_i} v_{r_i} v_{t_i}$ denotes a tri-linear dot product. g denotes a non-linear function. $*$ denotes a convolution operator. $\cdot$ denotes a dot product. concat denotes a concatenation operator. $\widehat{v}$ denotes a 2D reshaping of v. Ω denotes a set of filters.

feature maps. The feature maps are concatenated into a single feature vector which is then computed with a weight vector via a dot product to produce a score for the triple *(h, r, t)*. This score is used to infer whether the triple *(h, r, t)* is valid or not.

Our contributions in this paper are as follows:

- We introduce ConvKB—a novel embedding model of entities and relationships for knowledge base completion. ConvKB models the relationships among same dimensional entries of the embeddings. This implies that ConvKB generalizes transitional characteristics in transition-based embedding models.

- We evaluate ConvKB on two benchmark datasets: WN18RR (Dettmers et al., 2018) and FB15k-237 (Toutanova and Chen, 2015). Experimental results show that ConvKB obtains better link prediction performance than previous SOTA embedding models. In particular, ConvKB obtains the best mean rank and the highest Hits@10 on WN18RR, and produces the highest mean reciprocal rank and highest Hits@10 on FB15k-237.

2 Proposed ConvKB model

A knowledge base $\mathcal{G}$ is a collection of valid factual triples in the form of *(head entity, relation, tail entity)* denoted as (h, r, t) such that $h, t \in \mathcal{E}$ and $r \in \mathcal{R}$ where $\mathcal{E}$ is a set of entities and $\mathcal{R}$ is a set of relations. Embedding models aim to define a *score function f* giving an implausibility score for each triple (h, r, t) such that valid triples receive lower scores than invalid triples. Table 1 presents score functions in previous SOTA models.

We denote the dimensionality of embeddings by k such that each embedding triple (v_h, v_r, v_t) are

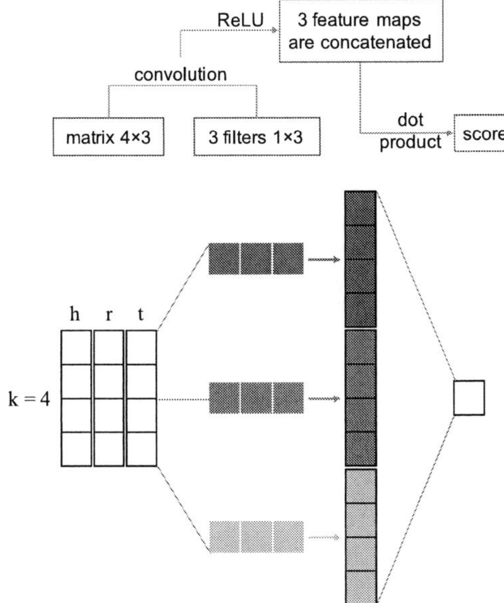

Figure 1: Process involved in ConvKB (with the embedding size $k = 4$, the number of filters $\tau = 3$ and the activation function $g = $ ReLU for illustration purpose).

viewed as a matrix $A = [v_h, v_r, v_t] \in \mathbb{R}^{k \times 3}$. And $A_{i,:} \in \mathbb{R}^{1 \times 3}$ denotes the i-th row of A. Suppose that we use a filter $\omega \in \mathbb{R}^{1 \times 3}$ operated on the convolution layer. ω is not only aimed to examine the global relationships between same dimensional entries of the embedding triple (v_h, v_r, v_t), but also to generalize the transitional characteristics in the transition-based models. ω is repeatedly operated over every row of A to finally generate a feature map $v = [v_1, v_2, ..., v_k] \in \mathbb{R}^k$ as:

$$v_i = g\left(\omega \cdot A_{i,:} + b\right)$$

where $b \in \mathbb{R}$ is a bias term and g is some activation function such as ReLU.

Our ConvKB uses different filters $\in \mathbb{R}^{1 \times 3}$ to generate different feature maps. Let Ω and τ denote the set of filters and the number of filters, respectively, i.e. $\tau = |\Omega|$, resulting in τ feature maps. These τ feature maps are concatenated into a single vector $\in \mathbb{R}^{\tau k \times 1}$ which is then computed with a weight vector $\mathbf{w} \in \mathbb{R}^{\tau k \times 1}$ via a dot product to give a score for the triple (h, r, t). Figure 1 illustrates the computation process in ConvKB.

Formally, we define the ConvKB score function f as follows:

$$f(h, r, t) = \text{concat}\left(g\left([v_h, v_r, v_t] * \Omega\right)\right) \cdot \mathbf{w}$$

where Ω and $\mathbf{w}$ are shared parameters, indepen-

Dataset	$|\mathcal{E}|$	$|\mathcal{R}|$	#Triples in train/valid/test		
WN18RR	40,943	11	86,835	3,034	3,134
FB15k-237	14,541	237	272,115	17,535	20,466

Table 2: Statistics of the experimental datasets.

dent of h, r and t; $*$ denotes a convolution operator; and concat denotes a concatenation operator.

If we only use one filter ω (i.e. using $\tau = 1$) with a fixed bias term $b = 0$ and the activation function $g(x) = |x|$ or $g(x) = x^2$, and fix $\omega = [1, 1, -1]$ and $\mathbf{w} = \mathbf{1}$ during training, ConvKB reduces to the plain TransE model (Bordes et al., 2013). So our ConvKB model can be viewed as an extension of TransE to further model global relationships.

We use the Adam optimizer (Kingma and Ba, 2014) to train ConvKB by minimizing the loss function $\mathcal{L}$ (Trouillon et al., 2016) with L_2 regularization on the weight vector $\mathbf{w}$ of the model:

$$\mathcal{L} = \sum_{(h,r,t) \in \{\mathcal{G} \cup \mathcal{G}'\}} \log\left(1 + \exp\left(l_{(h,r,t)} \cdot f(h, r, t)\right)\right)$$
$$+ \frac{\lambda}{2} \|\mathbf{w}\|_2^2$$

$$\text{in which, } l_{(h,r,t)} = \begin{cases} 1 \text{ for } (h, r, t) \in \mathcal{G} \\ -1 \text{ for } (h, r, t) \in \mathcal{G}' \end{cases}$$

here $\mathcal{G}'$ is a collection of invalid triples generated by corrupting valid triples in $\mathcal{G}$.

3 Experiments

3.1 Datasets

We evaluate ConvKB on two benchmark datasets: WN18RR (Dettmers et al., 2018) and FB15k-237 (Toutanova and Chen, 2015). WN18RR and FB15k-237 are correspondingly subsets of two common datasets WN18 and FB15k (Bordes et al., 2013). As noted by Toutanova and Chen (2015), WN18 and FB15k are easy because they contain many reversible relations. So knowing relations are reversible allows us to easily predict the majority of test triples, e.g. state-of-the-art results on both WN18 and FB15k are obtained by using a simple reversal rule as shown in Dettmers et al. (2018). Therefore, WN18RR and FB15k-237 are created to not suffer from this reversible relation problem in WN18 and FB15k, for which the knowledge base completion task is more realistic. Table 2 presents the statistics of WN18RR and FB15k-237.

Method	WN18RR			FB15k-237		
	MR	MRR	H@10	MR	MRR	H@10
IRN (Shen et al., 2017)	–	–	–	211	–	46.4
KBGAN (Cai and Wang, 2018)	–	0.213	48.1	–	0.278	45.8
DISTMULT (Yang et al., 2015) [⋆]	5110	0.43	49	254	0.241	41.9
ComplEx (Trouillon et al., 2016) [⋆]	5261	0.44	51	339	0.247	42.8
ConvE (Dettmers et al., 2018)	5277	**0.46**	48	246	0.316	49.1
TransE (Bordes et al., 2013) (our results)	3384	0.226	50.1	347	0.294	46.5
Our ConvKB model	**2554**	0.248	**52.5**	257	**0.396**	**51.7**
KB_{LRN} (García-Durán and Niepert, 2017)	–	–	–	209	0.309	49.3
R-GCN+ (Schlichtkrull et al., 2017)	–	–	–	–	0.249	41.7
Neural LP (Yang et al., 2017)	–	–	–	–	0.240	36.2
Node+LinkFeat (Toutanova and Chen, 2015)	–	–	–	–	0.293	46.2

Table 3: Experimental results on WN18RR and FB15k-237 test sets. MRR and H@10 denote the mean reciprocal rank and Hits@10 (in %), respectively. [⋆]: Results are taken from Dettmers et al. (2018) where Hits@10 and MRR are rounded to 2 decimal places on WN18RR. The last 4 rows report results of models that exploit information about relation paths (KB_{LRN}, R-GCN+ and Neural LP) or textual mentions derived from a large external corpus (Node+LinkFeat). The best score is in **bold**, while the second best score is in <u>underline</u>.

3.2 Evaluation protocol

In the KB completion or link prediction task (Bordes et al., 2013), the purpose is to predict a missing entity given a relation and another entity, i.e, inferring h given (r, t) or inferring t given (h, r). The results are calculated based on ranking the scores produced by the score function f on test triples.

Following Bordes et al. (2013), for each valid test triple (h, r, t), we replace either h or t by each of other entities in $\mathcal{E}$ to create a set of corrupted triples. We use the "**Filtered**" setting protocol (Bordes et al., 2013), i.e., not taking any corrupted triples that appear in the KB into accounts. We rank the valid test triple and corrupted triples in ascending order of their scores. We employ three common evaluation metrics: mean rank (MR), mean reciprocal rank (MRR), and Hits@10 (i.e., the proportion of the valid test triples ranking in top 10 predictions). Lower MR, higher MRR or higher Hits@10 indicate better performance.

3.3 Training protocol

We use the common Bernoulli trick (Wang et al., 2014; Lin et al., 2015b) to generate the head or tail entities when sampling invalid triples. We also use entity and relation embeddings produced by TransE to *initialize* entity and relation embeddings in ConvKB. We employ a TransE implementation available at: https://github.com/datquocnguyen/STransE. We train TransE using a grid search of hyper-parameters: the dimensionality of embeddings $k \in \{50, 100\}$, SGD learning rate $\in \{1e^{-4}, 5e^{-4}, 1e^{-3}, 5e^{-3}\}$, l_1-norm or l_2-norm, and margin $\gamma \in \{1, 3, 5, 7\}$. The highest Hits@10 scores on the validation set are when using l_1-norm, learning rate at $5e^{-4}$, $\gamma = 5$ and $k = 50$ for WN18RR, and using l_1-norm, learning rate at $5e^{-4}$, $\gamma = 1$ and k = 100 for FB15k-237.

To learn our model parameters including entity and relation embeddings, filters ω and the weight vector **w**, we use Adam (Kingma and Ba, 2014) and select its initial learning rate $\in \{5e^{-6}, 1e^{-5}, 5e^{-5}, 1e^{-4}, 5e^{-4}\}$. We use ReLU as the activation function g. We fix the batch size at 256 and set the L_2-regularizer λ at 0.001 in our objective function. The filters ω are initialized by a truncated normal distribution or by $[0.1, 0.1, -0.1]$. We select the number of filters $\tau \in \{50, 100, 200, 400, 500\}$. We run ConvKB up to 200 epochs and use outputs from the last epoch for evaluation. The highest Hits@10 scores on the validation set are obtained when using $k = 50$, $\tau = 500$, the truncated normal distribution for filter initialization, and the initial learning rate at $1e^{-4}$ on WN18RR; and k = 100, $\tau = 50$, $[0.1, 0.1, -0.1]$ for filter initialization, and the initial learning rate at $5e^{-6}$ on FB15k-237.

3.4 Main experimental results

Table 3 compares the experimental results of our ConvKB model with previous published results, using the same experimental setup. Table 3 shows that ConvKB obtains the best MR and highest Hits@10 scores on WN18RR and also the highest

MRR and Hits@10 scores on FB15k-237.

ConvKB does better than the closely related model TransE on both experimental datasets, especially on FB15k-237 where ConvKB gains significant improvements of $347 - 257 = 90$ in MR (which is about 26% relative improvement) and $0.396 - 0.294 = 0.102$ in MRR (which is 34+% relative improvement), and also obtains $51.7 - 46.5 = 5.2\%$ absolute improvement in Hits@10. Previous work shows that TransE obtains very competitive results (Lin et al., 2015a; Nickel et al., 2016b; Trouillon et al., 2016; Nguyen et al., 2016a). However, when comparing the CNN-based embedding model ConvE with other models, Dettmers et al. (2018) did not experiment with TransE. We reconfirm previous findings that TransE in fact is a strong baseline model, e.g., TransE obtains better MR and Hits@10 than ConvE on WN18RR.

ConvKB obtains better scores than ConvE on both datasets (except MRR on WN18RR and MR on FB15k-237), thus showing the usefulness of taking transitional characteristics into accounts. In particular, on FB15k-237, ConvKB achieves improvements of $0.394 - 0.316 = 0.078$ in MRR (which is about 25% relative improvement) and $51.7 - 49.1 = 2.6\%$ in Hits@10, while both ConvKB and ConvE produce similar MR scores. ConvKB also obtains 25% relatively higher MRR score than the relation path-based model KB_{LRN} on FB15k-237. In addition, ConvKB gives better Hits@10 than KB_{LRN}, however, KB_{LRN} gives better MR than ConvKB. We plan to extend ConvKB with relation path information to obtain better link prediction performance in future work.

4 Conclusion

In this paper, we propose a novel embedding model ConvKB for the knowledge base completion task. ConvKB applies the convolutional neural network to explore the global relationships among same dimensional entries of the entity and relation embeddings, so that ConvKB generalizes the transitional characteristics in the transition-based embedding models. Experimental results show that our model ConvKB outperforms other state-of-the-art models on two benchmark datasets WN18RR and FB15k-237. Our code is available at: https://github.com/daiquocnguyen/ConvKB.

We also plan to extend ConvKB for a new application where we could formulate data in the form of triples. For example, inspired from the work by Vu et al. (2017) for search personalization, we can also apply ConvKB to model *user*-oriented relationships between submitted *queries* and *documents* returned by search engines, i.e. modeling triple representations (query, user, document).

Acknowledgments

This research was partially supported by the Australian Research Council (ARC) Discovery Grant Project DP160103934.

References

Kurt Bollacker, Colin Evans, Praveen Paritosh, Tim Sturge, and Jamie Taylor. 2008. Freebase: A collaboratively created graph database for structuring human knowledge. In *Proceedings of the 2008 ACM SIGMOD International Conference on Management of Data*, pages 1247–1250.

Antoine Bordes, Nicolas Usunier, Alberto García-Durán, Jason Weston, and Oksana Yakhnenko. 2013. Translating Embeddings for Modeling Multi-relational Data. In *Advances in Neural Information Processing Systems 26*, pages 2787–2795.

Antoine Bordes, Jason Weston, Ronan Collobert, and Yoshua Bengio. 2011. Learning Structured Embeddings of Knowledge Bases. In *Proceedings of the Twenty-Fifth AAAI Conference on Artificial Intelligence*, pages 301–306.

Liwei Cai and William Yang Wang. 2018. KBGAN: Adversarial Learning for Knowledge Graph Embeddings. In *Proceedings of The 16th Annual Conference of the North American Chapter of the Association for Computational Linguistics: Human Language Technologies*, page to appear.

Ronan Collobert, Jason Weston, Léon Bottou, Michael Karlen, Koray Kavukcuoglu, and Pavel Kuksa. 2011. Natural language processing (almost) from scratch. *Journal of Machine Learning Research*, 12:2493–2537.

Tim Dettmers, Pasquale Minervini, Pontus Stenetorp, and Sebastian Riedel. 2018. Convolutional 2D Knowledge Graph Embeddings. In *Proceedings of the 32nd AAAI Conference on Artificial Intelligence*, page to appear.

Alberto García-Durán and Mathias Niepert. 2017. KBLRN: End-to-end learning of knowledge base representations with latent, relational, and numerical features. *arXiv preprint abs/1709.04676*.

Kelvin Guu, John Miller, and Percy Liang. 2015. Traversing Knowledge Graphs in Vector Space. In *Proceedings of the 2015 Conference on Empirical Methods in Natural Language Processing*, pages 318–327.

Yanchao Hao, Yuanzhe Zhang, Kang Liu, Shizhu He, Zhanyi Liu, Hua Wu, and Jun Zhao. 2017. An end-to-end model for question answering over knowledge base with cross-attention combining global knowledge. In *Proceedings of the 55th Annual Meeting of the Association for Computational Linguistics (Volume 1: Long Papers)*, pages 221–231.

Guoliang Ji, Shizhu He, Liheng Xu, Kang Liu, and Jun Zhao. 2015. Knowledge Graph Embedding via Dynamic Mapping Matrix. In *Proceedings of the 53rd Annual Meeting of the Association for Computational Linguistics and the 7th International Joint Conference on Natural Language Processing (Volume 1: Long Papers)*, pages 687–696.

Guoliang Ji, Kang Liu, Shizhu He, and Jun Zhao. 2016. Knowledge Graph Completion with Adaptive Sparse Transfer Matrix. In *Proceedings of the Thirtieth Conference on Artificial Intelligence*, pages 985–991.

Gjergji Kasneci, Fabian M Suchanek, Georgiana Ifrim, Maya Ramanath, and Gerhard Weikum. 2008. Naga: Searching and ranking knowledge. In *Proceedings of the 24th IEEE International Conference on Data Engineering*, pages 953–962.

Yoon Kim. 2014. Convolutional Neural Networks for Sentence Classification. In *Proceedings of the 2014 Conference on Empirical Methods in Natural Language Processing*, pages 1746–1751.

Diederik Kingma and Jimmy Ba. 2014. Adam: A method for stochastic optimization. *arXiv preprint arXiv:1412.6980*.

Yann LeCun, Léon Bottou, Yoshua Bengio, and Patrick Haffner. 1998. Gradient-based learning applied to document recognition. *Proceedings of the IEEE*, 86:2278–2324.

Jens Lehmann, Robert Isele, Max Jakob, Anja Jentzsch, Dimitris Kontokostas, Pablo N Mendes, Sebastian Hellmann, Mohamed Morsey, Patrick Van Kleef, Sören Auer, et al. 2015. DBpedia–a large-scale, multilingual knowledge base extracted from Wikipedia. *Semantic Web*, 6:167–195.

Yankai Lin, Zhiyuan Liu, Huanbo Luan, Maosong Sun, Siwei Rao, and Song Liu. 2015a. Modeling Relation Paths for Representation Learning of Knowledge Bases. In *Proceedings of the 2015 Conference on Empirical Methods in Natural Language Processing*, pages 705–714.

Yankai Lin, Zhiyuan Liu, Maosong Sun, Yang Liu, and Xuan Zhu. 2015b. Learning Entity and Relation Embeddings for Knowledge Graph Completion. In *Proceedings of the Twenty-Ninth AAAI Conference on Artificial Intelligence Learning*, pages 2181–2187.

Yuanfei Luo, Quan Wang, Bin Wang, and Li Guo. 2015. Context-Dependent Knowledge Graph Embedding. In *Proceedings of the 2015 Conference on Empirical Methods in Natural Language Processing*, pages 1656–1661.

Dat Quoc Nguyen. 2017. An overview of embedding models of entities and relationships for knowledge base completion. *arXiv preprint*, arXiv:1703.08098.

Dat Quoc Nguyen, Kairit Sirts, Lizhen Qu, and Mark Johnson. 2016a. Neighborhood Mixture Model for Knowledge Base Completion. In *Proceedings of The 20th SIGNLL Conference on Computational Natural Language Learning*, pages 40–50.

Dat Quoc Nguyen, Kairit Sirts, Lizhen Qu, and Mark Johnson. 2016b. STransE: a novel embedding model of entities and relationships in knowledge bases. In *Proceedings of the 2016 Conference of the North American Chapter of the Association for Computational Linguistics: Human Language Technologies*, pages 460–466.

Maximilian Nickel, Kevin Murphy, Volker Tresp, and Evgeniy Gabrilovich. 2016a. A Review of Relational Machine Learning for Knowledge Graphs. *Proceedings of the IEEE*, 104(1):11–33.

Maximilian Nickel, Lorenzo Rosasco, and Tomaso Poggio. 2016b. Holographic Embeddings of Knowledge Graphs. In *Proceedings of the Thirtieth AAAI Conference on Artificial Intelligence*, pages 1955–1961.

Michael Schlichtkrull, Thomas Kipf, Peter Bloem, Rianne van den Berg, Ivan Titov, and Max Welling. 2017. Modeling relational data with graph convolutional networks. *arXiv preprint arXiv:1703.06103*.

Michael Schuhmacher and Simone Paolo Ponzetto. 2014. Knowledge-based graph document modeling. In *Proceedings of the 7th ACM International Conference on Web Search and Data Mining*, pages 543–552.

Yelong Shen, Po-Sen Huang, Ming-Wei Chang, and Jianfeng Gao. 2017. Traversing knowledge graph in vector space without symbolic space guidance. *arXiv preprint arXiv:1611.04642v4*.

Richard Socher, Danqi Chen, Christopher D Manning, and Andrew Ng. 2013. Reasoning With Neural Tensor Networks for Knowledge Base Completion. In *Advances in Neural Information Processing Systems 26*, pages 926–934.

Fabian M. Suchanek, Gjergji Kasneci, and Gerhard Weikum. 2007. Yago: A core of semantic knowledge. In *Proceedings of the 16th International Conference on World Wide Web*, pages 697–706.

Kristina Toutanova and Danqi Chen. 2015. Observed Versus Latent Features for Knowledge Base and Text Inference. In *Proceedings of the 3rd Workshop on Continuous Vector Space Models and their Compositionality*, pages 57–66.

Kristina Toutanova, Xi Victoria Lin, Wen tau Yih, Hoifung Poon, and Chris Quirk. 2016. Compositional Learning of Embeddings for Relation Paths in Knowledge Bases and Text. In *Proceedings of the 54th Annual Meeting of the Association for Computational Linguistics*, pages 1434–1444.

Théo Trouillon, Johannes Welbl, Sebastian Riedel, Éric Gaussier, and Guillaume Bouchard. 2016. Complex Embeddings for Simple Link Prediction. In *Proceedings of the 33nd International Conference on Machine Learning*, pages 2071–2080.

Thanh Vu, Dat Quoc Nguyen, Mark Johnson, Dawei Song, and Alistair Willis. 2017. Search Personalization with Embeddings. In *Proceedings of the 39th European Conference on Information Retrieval*, pages 598–604.

Zhen Wang, Jianwen Zhang, Jianlin Feng, and Zheng Chen. 2014. Knowledge Graph Embedding by Translating on Hyperplanes. In *Proceedings of the Twenty-Eighth AAAI Conference on Artificial Intelligence*, pages 1112–1119.

Robert West, Evgeniy Gabrilovich, Kevin Murphy, Shaohua Sun, Rahul Gupta, and Dekang Lin. 2014. Knowledge Base Completion via Search-based Question Answering. In *Proceedings of the 23rd International Conference on World Wide Web*, pages 515–526.

Chenyan Xiong, Russell Power, and Jamie Callan. 2017. Explicit semantic ranking for academic search via knowledge graph embedding. In *Proceedings of the 26th International Conference on World Wide Web*, pages 1271–1279.

Bishan Yang and Tom Mitchell. 2017. Leveraging knowledge bases in lstms for improving machine reading. In *Proceedings of the 55th Annual Meeting of the Association for Computational Linguistics (Volume 1: Long Papers)*, pages 1436–1446.

Bishan Yang, Wen-tau Yih, Xiaodong He, Jianfeng Gao, and Li Deng. 2015. Embedding Entities and Relations for Learning and Inference in Knowledge Bases. In *Proceedings of the International Conference on Learning Representations*.

Fan Yang, Zhilin Yang, and William W Cohen. 2017. Differentiable Learning of Logical Rules for Knowledge Base Reasoning. pages 2316–2325.

Yuanzhe Zhang, Kang Liu, Shizhu He, Guoliang Ji, Zhanyi Liu, Hua Wu, and Jun Zhao. 2016. Question answering over knowledge base with neural attention combining global knowledge information. *arXiv preprint arXiv:1606.00979*.

Cross-language Article Linking using
Cross-Encyclopedia Entity Embedding

Chun-Kai Wu
Department of Computer Science
National Tsinghua University
Hsinchu, Taiwan
s106062851@m106.nthu.edu.tw

Richard Tzong-Han Tsai[*]
Department of CSIE
National Central University
Chungli, Taiwan
thtsai@csie.ncu.edu.tw

Abstract

Cross-language article linking (CLAL) is the task of finding corresponding article pairs of different languages across encyclopedias. This task is a difficult disambiguation problem in which one article must be selected among several candidate articles with similar titles and contents. Existing works focus on engineering text-based or link-based features for this task, which is a time-consuming job, and some of these features are only applicable within the same encyclopedia. In this paper, we address these problems by proposing cross-encyclopedia entity embedding. Unlike other works, our proposed method does not rely on known cross-language pairs. We apply our method to CLAL between English Wikipedia and Chinese Baidu Baike. Our features improve performance relative to the baseline by 29.62%. Tested 30 times, our system achieved an average improvement of 2.76% over the current best system (26.86% over baseline), a statistically significant result.

1 Introduction

Online encyclopedias now make vast amounts of information and human knowledge available to internet users around the world in various languages. However, information resources are not evenly distributed across all languages. To facilitate international knowledge sharing, the task of cross-language article linking (CLAL) aims to create links between encyclopedia articles in different languages that describe the same content. CLAL has been applied in several fields such as named entity translation (Lee and Hwang, 2013), cross-language information retrieval (Nguyen et al., 2009), and multilingual knowledge base creation (Lehmann et al., 2015).

Much CLAL research has been carried out on Wikipedia, one of the largest multilingual online encyclopedias. Articles in Wikipedia are partly structured, usually containing a title, table of contents, main context, related images, media files, categories, and infoboxes (structured metadata tables). Wikipedia articles may also have inter-language links to corresponding articles in other language versions. However, these links are manually created, so some articles lack inter-language links. Several approaches (Sorg and Cimiano, 2008; Oh et al., 2008; Bennacer et al., 2015) have been proposed to automatically generate inter-language links between different language versions of Wikipedia. The main challenge in this task is the distinction of ambiguous candidate articles with similar titles or contents. Most previous work on CLAL has used hand-crafted features for each encyclopedia, which is unscalable.

In this paper, we propose a method to learn cross-encyclopedia entity embedding (CEEE) on English Wikipedia and Chinese Baidu Baike. Every article (entity) in the two encyclopedias is represented by an embedding so that corresponding articles are placed closer together in the vector space. To acquire the training data without human annotation, we also offer a way to discover article correspondence among different encyclopedias. A set of evaluations carried out on the CLAL task between English Wikipedia and Chinese Baidu Baike show that our embedding method improves performance relative to the baseline by 29.62%, which represents a statistically significant improvement over the current best system (26.86% relative improvement). To the best of our knowledge, this is the first work to learn cross-encyclopedia bilingual entity embedding without relying on existing manually labeled cross-language links.

---

*Corresponding author

Proceedings of NAACL-HLT 2018, pages 334–339
New Orleans, Louisiana, June 1 - 6, 2018. ©2018 Association for Computational Linguistics

2 Related Work

2.1 Cross-language article linking

Previous Wikipedia-only CLAL studies have relied on existing inter-language links and have focused on using text-based features or link-based features in classifiers. For example, Wang et al.'s (2012) cross-language link similarity work can only be used for linking cross-language Wikipedia articles. Sorg and Cimiano (2008) assumed that given a cross-language pair a and b, the articles linked to a in encyclopedia A are more likely to be linked to the articles linked to b in encyclopedia B. They then designed link-based features on that assumption. Oh et al. (2008) relied on text-based features. They first constructed a translation dictionary from cross-language links. They then translated English terms into Japanese and designed features based on edit distance. Bennacer et al. (2015) used BabelNet (Navigli and Ponzetto, 2012) to select candidate articles with similar semantics in the target language. They then ranked the candidates based on cross-language link similarity. Unlike the above studies, we aim to carry out CLAL between different encyclopedia platforms, English and Baidu Baike; therefore we cannot use existing inter-language links.

Because much of the previous Wikipedia-only CLAL research cannot be directly applied to cross-platform linking, Wang et al. (2014) developed an SVM-based approach with content-similarity-based features to link articles in Wikipedia and Baidu Baike. In this work, they relied on Google Translate to translate Chinese terms into English. They then designed title-based and content-based features based on both the English and translated Chinese articles.

2.2 Entity Embedding

With recent work on word embedding, there has also been more interest in learning entity embedding. Hu et al. (2015) modeled Wikipedia's category structure in their entity embedding. Li et al. (2016) extended Hu et al.'s (2015) work to include category embedding in addition to entity embedding. They further extended the model by integrating category structure to capture meaningful semantic relationships between entities and categories. Yamada et al. (2016) learned joint embedding for words and entities. Tsai and Roth (2016) proposed a way to learn multilingual embedding of words and entities. They first learned

monolingual entity and word embedding from the Wikipedia corpus with the skip-gram word embedding model by replacing entity mentions with special symbols. They then used canonical correlation analysis (CCA) to project different embeddings on the same space, learning the CCA model using the existing Wikipedia cross-language links as the training data.

3 Methods

Given an article from a knowledge base (KB), CLAL aims to find the article's corresponding article in another KB of a different language. Corresponding articles are defined as articles describing the same entity in different languages. We base our CLAL system on Wang et al.'s (2014) work because theirs is the only previous CLAL system designed for a cross-encyclopedia setting.

Following Wang et al.'s (2014) example, we also divide CLAL into two stages: candidate selection and candidate ranking. The candidates for each Wikipedia article are selected with the Lucene search engine, and the queries and documents are translated with the Google Translate API. We then train an SVM classifier with the same features described in Wang et al.'s (2014) paper. The given English Wikipedia article and a candidate Baidu article are denoted as w and b. Wang et al.'s (2014) features are as follows:

- BM25: w's title is translated into Chinese and then used as a query to retrieve articles from Baidu Baike with the Lucene search engine. The returned BM25 score corresponding to b is treated as the value of b's BM25 feature.

- Hypernym translation (HT): Supposing the given English title is e and that e's hypernym is h, this feature is defined as the log frequency of h's Chinese translation in the candidate Chinese article.

- English title occurrence (ETO): Whether or not w's title appears in the first sentence of b is regarded as the value of b's ETO feature.

After replicating Wang et al.'s (2014) system, we add our proposed cross-encyclopedia entity embedding (CEEE) feature, the construction of which is detailed in the following sections.

3.1 Cross-Encyclopedia Entity Embedding Model

Similar to (Mikolov et al., 2013), our model learns the entity representation that are useful for predicting the target entity given the context entity. Within an online encyclopedia, each entity is linked with one or more other entities by hyperlinks. For example, the "Food" article in English Wikipedia is linked with the "Plant" article. We treat every article as context entity and the hyper-linked article in a context entity as target entity. Given a set of target-context entity pairs $E_{\mathcal{ST}} = \{(t,c)\}$ where every context entity c comes from the encyclopedia $\mathcal{S}$ and every target entity t comes from the encyclopedia $\mathcal{T}$, we learn the embeddings of entities by maximizing the training objective:

$$\mathcal{L}_{\mathcal{ST}} = \frac{1}{|E_{\mathcal{ST}}|}\Sigma_{(t,c)\in E_{\mathcal{ST}}}logP(t|c). \quad (1)$$

The probability of a target entity given a certain context entity is defined with the softmax function to represent the probability distribution over the entity space ε of the online encyclopedia which the target entity t is residing in:

$$P(t|c) = \frac{exp(v_t \odot v_c)}{\Sigma_{e\in\varepsilon}exp(v_e \odot v_c)}, \quad (2)$$

where $v_t, v_c \subset \mathbb{R}^d$ is the embedding of an entity, d is the size of the embedding and $\odot$ is the dot product operation. Using the link structure of Wikipedia and Baidu Baike, we have compiled two sets of entity pairs, $E_{\mathcal{WW}}$ and $E_{\mathcal{BB}}$, for training Wikipedia and Baidu entity embeddings, respectively.

3.2 Training Data Compilation for Cross-Encyclopedia Entity Embedding

To acquire the training data for cross-encyclopedia bilingual entity embeddings, we first translate all categories of Baidu Baike into English and then collect a set of common category labels between English Wikipedia and Baidu Baike by exact string match. There are 6,297 common categories between Wikipedia and Baidu. If there is no common category then the category is labeled as null. Next, we compile a set of entity pairs from Wikipedia and Baidu articles that share at least 1 common category label. The intuition behind the proposed method is that semantically correlated entities tend to share common category labels, and so do cross-lingual entities.

We then compile another two sets of entity pairs, $E_{\mathcal{WB}}$ and $E_{\mathcal{BW}}$ to learn meaningful cross-encyclopedia entity embeddings. The entity pairs in both sets are identical, except the roles are changed. Specifically, in $E_{\mathcal{BW}}$ the Wikipedia entity is the target while the Baidu entity is the context, and in $E_{\mathcal{WB}}$ the roles are reversed.

3.3 Learning Cross-Encyclopedia Entity Embedding

Since there are millions of entities in both Wikipedia and Baidu, we adopt negative sampling to speed up the training process. We set the negative sample size to 100 during training. We further filter out entities that are only linked to 9 or fewer other entities. Given the two embedding matrices $m^{\mathcal{W}} \subset \mathbb{R}^{|\mathcal{W}|\times d}$ and $m^{\mathcal{B}} \subset \mathbb{R}^{|\mathcal{B}|\times d}$, corresponding to Wikipedia and Baidu, we train the CEEE model with the following 4 tasks: (1) to predict any Baidu article given a Wikipedia article as context by optimizing $\mathcal{L}_{\mathcal{WB}}$, (2) to predict any Wikipedia article given a Baidu article as context by optimizing $\mathcal{L}_{\mathcal{BW}}$, (3) to predict any Wikipedia article given another Wikipedia article as context by optimizing $\mathcal{L}_{\mathcal{WW}}$, and (4) to predict any Baidu article given another Baidu article as context by optimizing $\mathcal{L}_{\mathcal{BB}}$. During task (3), only $m^{\mathcal{W}}$ is updated, and during task (4), only $m^{\mathcal{B}}$ is updated. Every task iterates through its corresponding set of entity pairs. The four tasks repeat 50 times each. The embeddings are updated by stochastic gradient descent with a batch size of 1280 entity pairs. The learning rate is set to 0.1, and entity embeddings are randomly initialized. We also normalize the embeddings to the unit vector every 10 batches during training as Xing et al. (2015) did to improve entity similarity measurement. We set the embedding size d to 100 for the following experiments.

After training, the learned embedding matrices are ready to be used. The similarity score of a Wikipedia entity and a Baidu entity is obtained by calculating the cosine value of their corresponding vectors in the learned embedding matrices. Supposing the embedding vectors corresponding to the English Wikipedia article and the Baidu article are v_w and v_b, the feature value is defined as follows:

$$\begin{cases} \frac{v_w \cdot v_b}{|v_w||v_b|} & \textit{if both } v_w \textit{ and } v_b \textit{ are available} \\ -1 & \textit{otherwise} \end{cases} \quad (3)$$

Table 1: Cross-language article linking performance the first dataset. "MRR (adding CEEE)" column shows the MRR and performance gain. The last column shows *t*-values. The *p*-value of every configuration is less than 0.001. Hence, we conclude that CEEE is effective in improving performance.

Configuration	MRR	MRR (adding CEEE)	
BM25	.6146	.7418(**+.1272**)	-29.6
BM25 + HT	.7457	.7944(+.0487)	-16.5
BM25 + ETO	.6469	.7604(+.1135)	-34.1
BM25 + HT + ETO	**.7542**	**.7967**(+.0425)	-14.9

Table 2: Cross-language article linking performance of the second dataset. "MRR (adding CEEE)" column shows the MRR and performance gain. The last column shows *t*-values. The *p*-value of every configuration is less than 0.001.

Configuration	MRR	MRR (adding CEEE)	
BM25	.6093	.6762(**+.0669**)	-11.3
BM25 + HT	**.6611**	.6918(+.0307)	-9.1
BM25 + ETO	.6466	.6933(+.0467)	-13.8
BM25 + HT + ETO	.6606	**.6989**(+.0383)	-13.5

Table 3: Performance comparison of CLAL methods. The mean MRR of our system is significantly greater than that of Wang et al.'s (2014), *t*-value $= -7.6$ and $= -4.5$, respectively. The *p*-values are less than 0.001 for both datasets.

Dataset	System	MRR	Relative Improvement
	BM25 (Baseline)	.6146	
1st	Our system	**.7967**	**29.62%**
	Wang et al. 2014	.7797	26.86%
	BM25 (Baseline)	.6093	
2nd	Our system	**.6989**	**14.70%**
	Wang et al. 2014	.6874	12.81%

4 Experiments

Following the same procedure used in (Wang et al., 2014), we downloaded the entire English Wikipedia dump and obtained 4M entities and 0.9M categories. We also crawled 6M Baidu Baike articles, which contain 50 thousand distinct category labels. Within Wikipedia and Baidu, there are 68M training pairs for Wikipedia and 20M for Baidu. After matching common categories, we extracted 54M bilingual entity pairs. To generate the gold standard evaluation sets of correct English and Chinese article pairs, we automatically collect English-Chinese inter-language links from Wikipedia. For pairs that have both English and Chinese articles, the Chinese article title is regarded as the translation of the English one. Next, we check if there is a Chinese article in Baidu Baike with exactly the same ti-

tle as the one in Chinese Wikipedia. If so, the corresponding English Wikipedia article and the Baidu Baike article are paired in the gold standard. We create two different datasets for our experiments. For the first dataset, we select the top 500 English-Chinese article pairs with the highest page view counts in Baidu Baike. This set represents the articles people in China are most interested in. The second dataset is based on random selection. We first randomly select 3500 Wikipedia articles and link them to Baidu Baike articles using English-Chinese Wikipedia inter-links and redirect pages. To eliminate rarely-viewed articles, the 3500 English-Chinese article pairs are sorted in decreasing order based on click count statistics of the article in English Wikipedia in 2012. The top 1000 English-Baidu article pairs are retained as the second dataset. For statistical generality, the data set is randomly split 4:1 (training:test) 30 times. The final evaluation results are calculated as the mean of the average of these 30 sets.

4.1 Cross-language article linking

The recall scores of the two datasets are 0.8953 and 0.8383, which is the upper bound of the system's performance. Since the candidate selection process relies heavily on translation, we think the difference between the two recall scores is due to the poor translation of unpopular content. We report the performance of ranking in terms of mean reciprocal rank (MRR).In Table 1, Column 2 (MRR) shows the performance of four feature configurations in the first dataset, BM25(Baseline), BM25+HT, BM25+ETO, and BM25+HT+ETO. To show CEEE's effectiveness, we list the performance before and after adding CEEE, including performance gain in parentheses. For the first dataset, we can see that CEEE boosts the baseline configuration by a significant margin. Using all three features, BM25+HT+ETO, the system achieves an MRR of 0.7967, which is the best score among all configurations. All configurations achieve statistically significant performance gains after adding CEEE.

Since the second dataset consists of seldom-read articles, we assume that some of the translations will be incorrect due to lack of popularity, and this may negatively impact system performance. Looking at the results of the second dataset in Table 2, we can see that HT and CEEE do not make the same improvement as they did in the first dataset, since both of them heavily rely on Google Translate results. The MRR/recall ratio of the second dataset is slightly better than that of the first dataset with the BM25 configuration. We believe this is because there are more ambiguous articles in the first dataset than in the second dataset. For example, "The Hunger Games" is an article describing the trilogy of novels in Wikipedia. But its Baike candidates include several articles with identical titles, such as the first novel of the trilogy, the movies series, and video games. The results suggest that translation quality affects our system's performance, and that the candidate selection process is also impacted by the popularity of the query article.

In Table 3, we compare our work with the state-of-the-art system developed by (Wang et al., 2014). Our features improve performance relative to the baseline by 29.62% and 14.70% for the first and second datasets, respectively, which represents a statistically significant improvement over Wang et al.'s (2014) best system (26.86% and 12.81% relative improvement for the two datasets). It's worth noting that (Wang et al., 2014) utilized another feature based on topic models which requires known cross-language links.

All the experiments above treat the cosine similarity between the query and each candidate embedding as a feature for the SVM classifier. Next, we show the results on the first dataset when using the embedding vector as the feature vector for the SVM classifier. More specifically, the CEEE feature is a vector of 200 dimensions. We get an MRR of 0.6352 when the classifier only takes the embedding vector as input, which is a significant gain compared to the MRR of BM25. However, when CEEE is used to measure query-candidate cosine similarity, we only get an MRR of 0.4629. This suggests that CEEE has learned a sufficiently accurate mapping between Wikipedia and Baidu Baike, but there is still room for improvement.

5   Discussion

According to (Wang et al., 2014), one common CLAL error type is due to several articles having the same title. These same-title articles are entities belonging to different categories or one entity with several duplicate articles. Our best system configuration with the CEEE similarity feature fixed 21 such errors made by Wang et al.'s (2014) system. For example, for the English article Frankenstein

(novel), Wang's system ranks the Chinese article 科学怪人(movie) as number one, but our system ranks the correct Chinese article 弗兰肯斯坦(novel) first. We then refer the set of these 21 errors as "Successfully corrected set (SCS)." Although our proposed CEEE feature can effectively disambiguate articles with the same title, it still failed to correct 90 of Wang's errors and generated 6 new ones. The set of the 90 uncorrected errors and the set of the six new errors are referred to as "Uncorrected set (US)" and "Mistakenly corrected set (MCS)," respectively. For example, the English article "British Museum" is still mistakenly linked to "英国科学博物馆(Science Museum, London)", when the correct corresponding article is in fact "大英博物馆".

We propose that the farther a concept is from the bilingual pairs used to train CEEE, the more likely it is to be linked to a non-corresponding article. To test this hypothesis, we calculated the link distance between each of the pairs above to the nearest training pair. Then, we calculate the average distance for SCS, US, and MCS. The results show that SCS has the least link distance, followed by US, and then MCS, which is consistent with our hypothesis. This finding suggests that in order to improve CLAL performance, we can introduce more cross-lingual pairs into the training data. In our future work, we plan to apply other lexical resources such as WordNet to find synonyms instead of simple string matching.

6   Conclusion

We describe a method to learn bilingual entity embedding for cross-encyclopedia CLAL. The embedding model is designed to encode both monolingual and bilingual entity structure so that related entities will be close to each other in the vector space. To acquire the training data without human annotation, we also offer a way to discover article correspondence among different encyclopedias. Our results show that using our proposed embedding outperforms the current best cross-encyclopedia CLAL system by statistically significant margin. Further investigations suggest that the proposed embedding can help to disambiguate candidates with the same title.

References

Nacéra Bennacer, Mia Johnson Vioulès, Maximiliano Ariel López, and Gianluca Quercini. 2015. *A

Multilingual Approach to Discover Cross-Language Links in Wikipedia. Springer.

Zhiting Hu, Poyao Huang, Yuntian Deng, Yingkai Gao, and Eric P. Xing. 2015. Entity hierarchy embedding. In *Proceedings of the 53rd Annual Meeting of the Association for Computational Linguistics and the 7th International Joint Conference on Natural Language Processing (Volume 1: Long Papers)*, pages 1292–1300.

Taesung Lee and Seung-won Hwang. 2013. Bootstrapping entity translation on weakly comparable corpora. In *Proceedings of the 52nd Annual Meeting of the Association for Computational Linguistics (Volume 1: Long Papers)*, pages 631–640. Association for Computational Linguistics.

Jens Lehmann, Robert Isele, Max Jakob, Anja Jentzsch, Dimitris Kontokostas, Pablo N Mendes, Sebastian Hellmann, Mohamed Morsey, Patrick Van Kleef, Sören Auer, et al. 2015. Dbpedia–a large-scale, multilingual knowledge base extracted from wikipedia. *Semantic Web*, 6(2):167–195.

Yuezhang Li, Ronghuo Zheng, Tian Tian, Zhiting Hu, Rahul Iyer, and Katia Sycara. 2016. Joint embedding of hierarchical categories and entities for concept categorization and dataless classification. *arXiv preprint arXiv:1607.07956*.

Tomas Mikolov, Ilya Sutskever, Kai Chen, Greg S. Corrado, and Jeff Dean. 2013. Distributed representations of words and phrases and their compositionality. In *Proceedings of the 2013 Conference on Neural Information Processing Systems (NIPS)*, pages 3111–3119.

Roberto Navigli and Simone Paolo Ponzetto. 2012. BabelNet: The automatic construction, evaluation and application of a wide-coverage multilingual semantic network. *Artificial Intelligence*, 193:217–250.

Dong Nguyen, Arnold Overwijk, Claudia Hauff, Dolf R. B. Trieschnigg, Djoerd Hiemstra, and Franciska de Jong. 2009. *WikiTranslate: Query Translation for Cross-Lingual Information Retrieval Using Only Wikipedia*.

Jong-Hoon Oh, Daisuke Kawahara, Kiyotaka Uchimoto, Jun'ichi Kazama, and Kentaro Torisawa. 2008. Enriching multilingual language resources by discovering missing cross-language links in wikipedia. In *Proceedings of the 2008 IEEE/WIC/ACM International Conference on Web Intelligence and Intelligent Agent Technology*, volume 1, pages 322–328.

Philipp Sorg and Philipp Cimiano. 2008. Enriching the crosslingual link structure of wikipedia-a classification-based approach. In *Proceedings of the AAAI 2008 Workshop on Wikipedia and Artifical Intelligence*, pages 49–54.

Chen-Tse Tsai and Dan Roth. 2016. Cross-lingual wikification using multilingual embeddings. In *Proceedings of the 2016 Conference of the North American Chapter of the Association for Computational Linguistics: Human Language Technologies*, pages 589–598.

Yu-Chun Wang, Chun-Kai Wu, and Richard Tzong-Han Tsai. 2014. Cross-language and cross-encyclopedia article linking using mixed-language topic model and hypernym translation. In *Proceedings of the 52nd Annual Meeting of the Association for Computational Linguistics (Volume 2: Short Papers)*, pages 586–591. Association for Computational Linguistics.

Zhichun Wang, Juanzi Li, Zhigang Wang, and Jie Tang. 2012. Cross-lingual knowledge linking across wiki knowledge bases. In *Proceedings of the 21st international conference on World Wide Web*, pages 459–468.

Chao Xing, Dong Wang, Chao Liu, and Yiye Lin. 2015. Normalized word embedding and orthogonal transform for bilingual word translation. In *Proceedings of the 2015 Conference of the North American Chapter of the Association for Computational Linguistics: Human Language Technologies*, pages 1006–1011.

Ikuya Yamada, Hiroyuki Shindo, Hideaki Takeda, and Yoshiyasu Takefuji. 2016. Joint learning of the embedding of words and entities for named entity disambiguation. *arXiv preprint arXiv:1601.01343*.

Identifying the Most Dominant Event in a News Article by Mining Event Coreference Relations

Prafulla Kumar Choubey, Kaushik Raju, Ruihong Huang
Department of Computer Science and Engineering
Texas A&M University
(prafulla.choubey, kaushik.raju, huangrh)@tamu.edu

Abstract

Identifying the most dominant and central event of a document, which governs and connects other foreground and background events in the document, is useful for many applications, such as text summarization, storyline generation and text segmentation. We observed that the central event of a document usually has many coreferential event mentions that are scattered throughout the document for enabling a smooth transition of subtopics. Our empirical experiments, using gold event coreference relations, have shown that the central event of a document can be well identified by mining properties of event coreference chains. But the performance drops when switching to system predicted event coreference relations. In addition, we found that the central event can be more accurately identified by further considering the number of sub-events as well as the realis status of an event.

1 Introduction

According to the grounding principles (Grimes, 1975), a document consists of foreground events that form the skeleton of the story and move the story forward, and background events that add supportive information. Studies have shown that a foreground event tends to be the most important event in a sentence, which is usually the event that appears in the main clause, is active voiced, and has a high transitivity[1] (Decker, 1985). But among multiple foreground events, which one is most central to the overall story? We propose a new task of detecting the most dominant event in a news article, which is an event assumed to govern and connect other foreground events and background events. In other words, removal of the central event can break the entirety of a document and

---

[1]High transitivity events have certain properties, are volitional, affirmative, realis etc.

Figure 1: An example document to illustrate the central event of a document. Red colored words are foreground events, blue colored words are background events and mentions of the central event are in bold.

decompose the document into sections describing disjoint sets of situations. Identifying the central event of a document is clearly important for a wide range of NLP applications, including text summarization, storyline generation and text segmentation.

The intuitive observation is that the central event of a document usually has a large number of coreferential event mentions and those coreferential mentions are spread throughout the document. In Figure 1, the paragraphs 1-4 each describe a relatively independent subtopic and the repeated mentions of the central event "demonstration" throughout the document enable a smooth flow of information. For the same reason, identifying the central event facilitates partitioning text into coherent segments. But note that, the central event may not be the most newsworthy event that serves as the trigger for writing an article, and thus may not appear in the title or in the first sentence of a new article. As illustrated in this example, the trigger event is "protesters leave capitol", while

Proceedings of NAACL-HLT 2018, pages 340–345
New Orleans, Louisiana, June 1 - 6, 2018. ©2018 Association for Computational Linguistics

the central event is "demonstration", the event that effectively connects other foreground events and background events and makes the story an entirety.

To systematically verify these observations, we annotated central events in news articles taken from two publicly available datasets, the richer event description (RED) (O'Gorman et al., 2016) and KBP 2015 (Mitamura et al., 2015) corpora. While whether each news article has only one central event is arguable, our two annotators agreed on the same central event in 97 out of 104 (93%) documents that we annotated. We then designed several rule-based methods to identify the central event by exploiting human annotated event coreference relations. Experimental results showed that indeed in around 75% of the documents in both corpora, the central event either has the largest number of coreferential event mentions or has the largest stretch size (i.e., the number of sentences between the first mention and the last mention of the central event) in the discourse. In addition, we found that the central event can be more accurately identified by further considering the number of sub-events as well as the realis status of an event, which indicate if an event is an actual specific event or a generic event etc. The evaluation shows that the insightful rules outperform several strong baseline approaches, including several heuristic based methods and random walk based event ranking methods, as well as two regression classifiers that integrate these rules as features.

2   Related Work

Many previous works studied the parameters that determine the overall quality of an individual event, including actualization (Tasaku, 1981), transitivity (Hopper and Thompson, 1980; Tsunoda, 1985) and the broader concept of eventiveness (Monahan and Brunson, 2014). However, these atomic qualities defined for an individual event are inadequate in distinguishing the key foreground event in a document.

In concurrent works, Decker (1985); Kay and Aylett (1996) focused on distinguishing foreground events from background events in a sentence and proposed that the most important event within a sentence is usually the event that appears in the main clause, is active voiced, and has a high transitivity. Upadhyay et al. (2016) applied these rules to identifying the trigger event of a news article by identifying the most important event in a

human-generated document summary.

Recognizing document-level central events has been shown important for text summarization. Filatova and Hatzivassiloglou (2004a,b) used normalized frequencies of co-referential event mentions as parameters to prioritize events to be included in a summary and found that this helped in generating better text summaries, despite its being an elementary measure. Our experiments showed that in addition to the number of co-referential event mentions, discourse layout features including both the stretch of an event chain and early presences of event mentions are key factors in identifying the central event of a document.

Graph-based methods (Mihalcea and Tarau, 2004) have been widely used to identify keywords and phrases in a document by constructing a word/ phrase graph and applying random walk algorithms (Brin and Page, 2012) on the graph. We implemented random walk based methods for identifying the central event as well, which however did not perform well. Mainly, the random walk based ranking strategy determines the importance of an events based on the importance of its related events in a document graph, which does not effectively capture discourse layout features of co-referential event mentions, which are important for identifying the central event of a document.

3   Central Event Annotations

We annotated central events for 30 news articles from the RED corpus[2] and 74 news articles from the KBP 2015 corpus[3]. We asked two annotators to identify the most dominant event that connects other foreground and background events. Both the documents and the gold event mentions for each document inherited from the previous RED and KBP annotations were provided to annotators. The annotators were instructed to select only one event as the central event. For 26 documents from the RED corpus and 71 documents from the KBP

---

[2]The RED corpus contains 95 documents in total. However, 65 documents are news summaries, discussion forum posts or web posts. The central event as defined should only be considered for natural coherent texts, therefore, the annotations were only conducted for the 30 news articles in the corpus.

[3]The KBP 2015 corpus contains 158 documents, where 81 are news articles and the remaining are discussion forum posts. Then in 7 out of the 81 news articles, annotators unanimously found that the central event was not of one of the interested event types in KBP and was not tagged in the KBP annotations. Therefore, our annotators skipped the 7 documents.

corpus, both annotators identified the same central event. For the other 7 documents, where the two annotators disagreed on the central event, we kept the annotations from the first annotator.

4 Characteristics of Central Events

We analyzed the distributional properties of central events in the first 10 documents from the RED corpus. The findings are summarized below.

Frequent and Extended Repetitions: As shown in Figure 1, the central event is usually repeated throughout the document. This observation can also be accounted to the way humans produce and comprehend language. Language is inherently sequential and a writer repeats the same event to remind the readers about the main event. Therefore, the frequent and extended repetitions of the central event facilitate to minimize the cognitive effort needed by the reader for understanding a text.

Early Presences: News articles mostly begin with a summary of important events and continue to elaborate them in subsequent paragraphs. To some extent, the objective of initial paragraphs is to direct readers' attention toward the main subject. Therefore, while the central event may not always appear in the title or in the first sentence of a new article, the central event often appears early in the beginning paragraphs.

Sub-events: Being the most dominant event in a document, the central event often has many sub-events that are present to elaborate and support the central event.

Event Realis Status: Central events are usually specific and have actually occurred. This event attribute has been defined as the contextual modality in RED corpus[4] and realis status in KBP corpus[5] and we observed that this attribute is "Actual" for the majority of central events.

5 Central Event Identification

Inspired by the identified characteristics of central events, we designed rule-based classifiers that rely on the following four ranking critera.

Size Rank: calculated using the number of coreferential event mentions in a event coreference chain. The event having the largest number of coreferential mentions is ranked the highest.

---

[4]defines 4 types of contextual modality, namely, actual, hypothetical, uncertain/ hedged and generic

[5]defines 3 realis status types, namely, actual, generic and other

Stretch Rank: based on the number of sentences between the first and the last mention of an event. The event with the largest stretch size is ranked the highest.

Position Rank: based on the sentence number in which an event was first mentioned. This measure is to capture the characteristic that central events tend to appear early in a document.

Enriched Size Rank: This rank is based on the sum of the number of coreferential mentions for an event and the number of its sub-events.

$$
\begin{aligned}
&\textbf{Input}: \text{central event candidates,} \ E_Z, E_T, E_P, E_E, E_R \\
&\textbf{Output}: E_{center} \\
&E_{center} := \phi \\
&\underline{\text{Coreference}} \\
&E_{center} := E_Z \cap E_T \cap E_P \\
&\text{if } E_{center} == \phi: \quad E_{center} := (E_Z \cup E_T) \cap E_P \\
&\text{if } E_{center} == \phi: \quad E_{center} := E_P \\
&\text{return } E_{center} \\
&\underline{\text{Coreference + Subevent}} \\
&E_{center} := E_Z \cap E_T \cap E_P \cap E_E \\
&\text{if } E_{center} == \phi: \quad E_{center} := (E_Z \cup E_T) \cap E_P \cap E_E \\
&\text{if } E_{center} == \phi: \quad E_{center} := E_P \cap E_E \\
&\text{if } E_{center} == \phi: \quad E_{center} := E_P \\
&\text{return } E_{center} \\
&\underline{\text{Coreference + Subevent + Realis}} \\
&E_{center} := E_Z \cap E_T \cap E_P \cap E_E \cap E_R \\
&\text{if } E_{center} == \phi: \quad E_{center} := (E_Z \cup E_T) \cap E_P \cap E_E \cap E_R \\
&\text{if } E_{center} == \phi: \quad E_{center} := E_P \cap E_E \cap E_R \\
&\text{if } E_{center} == \phi: \quad E_{center} := E_P \cap E_E \\
&\text{if } E_{center} == \phi: \quad E_{center} := E_P \\
&\text{return } E_{center}
\end{aligned}
$$

5.1 Rule Based Classifiers

First, we identify central event candidates by requiring their size rank in the top three positions. Note that more than three events may be selected if there are ties in any of the top three positions. Then, we identify the central event in the candidate set by requiring different combinations of the highest ranks, including the highest size rank E_Z, highest stretch rank E_T, highest position rank E_P and highest enriched size rank E_E. In addition, we identify an event set E_R which includes events whose contextual modality or realis status is "Actual" and use the set for constraining central event identification. Specifically, we define three rule based classifiers which begin with strict rules followed by relaxed rules in subsequent passes. The system **Coreference** uses size, stretch and position ranks, **Coreference + Subevent** considers enriched size rank as well, and **Coreference + Subevent + Realis** further combines realis status with each rank in favor of specific events.

5.2 Statistical Regression Classifiers

We trained a linear as well as a nonlinear regression classifier to integrate the same set of ranking rules as features for identifying central events, by using the standard ordinary least squares **linear regression** (Galton, 1886) model and the epsilon-support vector regression (**SVR**) (Vapnik, 1995) model with radial basis function kernel respectively. Input to both the linear and nonlinear regression classifiers consists of 20 (19) dimensional vector, 4 dimensional categorical vector for each of the size, stretch, position and enriched size ranks and 4 (3) dimensional categorical vector for realis attribute for RED (KBP) corpus. The models were implemented using scikit-learn module (Pedregosa et al., 2011). The SVR classifier uses **rbf** kernel with γ coefficient of 0.05 and all other parameters are left to be the default values.

5.3 Coreference: Predicted

We further used system predicted coreference relations to calculate size, stretch and position ranks and used them to identify central events, where coreference relations were predicted by a neural network based pairwise classifier using event lemmas, parts-of-speech tags and event arguments as features. The classifier was trained on the corpus used in the Event Nugget Detection and Coreference task in the TAC KBP 2016 (Ellis et al., 2015).

Specifically, the classifier uses a common neural layer shared between two event mentions that embed event lemma and parts-of-speech tags and then calculates cosine similarity, absolute and euclidean distances between two event embeddings. Classifier also includes a neural layer component to embed event arguments that are overlapped between the two event mentions. Its output layer takes the calculated cosine similarity, euclidean and absolute distances between event mention embeddings as well as the embedding of the overlapped event arguments as input, and output a confidence score to indicate the similarity of the two event mentions[6]. We used 300 dimensional word embeddings (Pennington et al., 2014) and one hot 37^7 dimensional pos tag embeddings. In addition, we used (Lewis et al., 2015) for semantic role labeling to obtain event arguments.

---

[6]We implemented our classifier using the Keras library (Chollet, 2015)

[7]Corresponding to the unique 36 POS tags based on the Stanford POS tagger (Toutanova et al., 2003) and an additional 'padding'.

6 Evaluation

6.1 Baseline Systems

Three Heuristics Based Classifiers: The three systems *Main event: Headline, First event: First sentence* and *Main event: First sentence* chose the main event (syntactic root) in headline, the first event in the first sentence and the main event (syntactic root) in the first sentence as the center event respectively.

Random Walk Based Ranking Systems: implemented the random walk based vertex ranking algorithm (Mihalcea and Tarau, 2004) on graphs generated using human annotated event relations. The motivation is to decide the importance of an event mention within an event graph of a document[8] based on the importance of its related event mentions[9]. The system *Random walk: All Relations* uses coreference, sub-event, set/ member, temporal and causal relations to build the graph while the system *Random walk: Coref+SE* only considers event coreference and sub-event relations. We evaluate both systems on documents from the RED corpus only as it extensively annotates event relations which yields a connected graph for each document. However, the graphs generated for documents in the KBP corpus often contain many disconnected components and thus are not suitable for these systems.

6.2 Results

We evaluated all the systems using the rest 20 documents from the RED corpus and all the 74 docu-

---

[8]We build an event graph for a document by using undirected edges for coreference relations and directed edges for other relations including set/ member, sub-event, temporal and causal relations. This is mainly meant to retain the symmetrical property of coreference relations. Moreover, since coreference link can easily create cycles in the graph, we utilize its transitivity property and link all the coreferent event mentions to its first instance in the document only.

[9]We rank event mentions by using the vertex scoring algorithm proposed in Brin and Page (2012).

$$S(V_i) = (1 - d) + d \sum_{j=IN(V_i)} \frac{1}{|OUT(V_j)|} S(V_j) \quad (1)$$

where $IN(V_i)$ and $OUT(V_j)$ represent the set of event mentions that are predecessors and successors to V_i respectively. Also, d is a damping vector that is kept 0.85 in our experiments. We initially assign random values to all the event mentions in an event graph and then update scores for all event nodes using equation 1 after each iteration. Computation stops when the sum of differences between the scores computed for all event mentions at two successive iterations reduces below 0.01.

Model	Rec	Prec	F1
Richer Event Description (RED)			
Main event: Headline	45.0	45.0	45.0
First event: First sentence	10.0	10.0	10.0
Main event: First sentence	40.0	40.0	40.0
Random walk: All Relations	40.0	40.0	40.0
Random walk: Coref+SM	45.0	45.0	45.0
Coreference	75.0	55.55	63.82
Coreference + Subevent	75.0	62.5	68.18
Coreference + Subevent + Realis	80.0	66.67	72.73
Linear Regression	63.33	63.33	63.33
SVR	66.67	66.67	66.67
Coreference: Predicted	45.0	45.0	45.0
KBP 2015			
Main event: Headline	45.94	45.94	45.94
First event: First sentence	39.19	39.19	39.19
Main event: First sentence	39.19	39.19	39.19
Coreference	77.03	54.81	64.04
Coreference + Subevent	77.03	60.0	67.46
Coreference + Subevent + Realis	78.37	66.67	72.05
Linear Regression	66.21	61.25	63.63
SVR	67.56	62.5	64.93
Coreference: Predicted	48.65	45.56	47.05

Table 1: Experimental Results.

ments from the KBP 2015 corpus. The two regression classifiers were evaluated using 5-fold cross-validation on each corpus. We expect a system to identify only one central event for each document. If a system predicts more than one central event, we will penalize the system on precision strictly and treat each wrongly predicted event as a false hit. Table 1 shows the comparison results.

The heuristic based systems obtained a low recall on both corpora, which indicates that simple heuristics miss a large proportion of cases. Both random walk based systems suffered from a low recall of 40-45% as well when applied to the RED corpus, due to the fact that graph-based ranking models do not effectively capture discourse layout features of co-referential event mentions.

In contrast, the rule based system **Coreference** achieved the recall above 75% on both corpora when using annotated event coreference relations. The system **Coreference + Subevent + Realis** further improves the precision of central event identification by over 11% on both corpora after considering subevents and the realis status in the rules, which facilitate accurate identification of the central event among multiple foreground events. The high recall and precision indicate that the insightful rules exploiting properties of event chains are able to capture the overall texture in the discourse. Then compared with rule based

systems, the two statistical classifiers that integrate the same set of rules as features do not further improve the central event identification performance. But when using system predicted noisy event coreference relations, the rule based system **Coreference: Predicted** performed dramatically worse than its counterpart using gold event chains (system **Coreference + Subevent + Realis**). This is unsurprising though considering the relatively low performance of current event coreference resolution systems.

6.3 Analysis

To gain a better understanding of how noise in system predicted event coreference links influences central event identification performance, we analyzed the documents where the system **Coreference: Predicted** failed to identify the central event. We found that both types of event coreference resolution errors, missed coreference links as well as wrong links, cause problems, especially in calculating the Size Rank and the Stretch Rank for an event. Specifically, the first type of errors can demote both ranks of the correct central event while the second type of errors can wrongly promote one of the two ranks for non-central events.

7 Conclusions

We have presented a new task of identifying the central event for a document. Based on our annotations, we discussed the role of central events in enabling a coherent discourse and the distributional characteristics of central events. We especially emphasized on the importance of event coreference in identifying central events. Inspired by these observations, we designed a rule-based classifier that achieved high recall and precision in identifying central events. The low performance of the classifier using system predicted event coreference relations indicates that significant efforts are needed to further improve event coreference resolution performance in the future.

Acknowledgments

This work was partially supported by the National Science Foundation via NSF Award IIS-1755943. Disclaimer: the views and conclusions contained herein are those of the authors and should not be interpreted as necessarily representing the official policies or endorsements, either expressed or implied, of NSF or the U.S. Government.

References

Sergey Brin and Lawrence Page. 2012. Reprint of: The anatomy of a large-scale hypertextual web search engine. *Computer networks* 56(18):3825–3833.

François Chollet. 2015. Keras. `https://github.com/fchollet/keras`.

Nan Decker. 1985. The use of syntactic clues in discourse processing. In *Proceedings of the 23rd annual meeting on Association for Computational Linguistics*. Association for Computational Linguistics, pages 315–323.

Joe Ellis, Jeremy Getman, Dana Fore, Neil Kuster, Zhiyi Song, Ann Bies, and Stephanie Strassel. 2015. Overview of linguistic resources for the tac kbp 2015 evaluations: Methodologies and results. In *Proceedings of TAC KBP 2015 Workshop, National Institute of Standards and Technology*. pages 16–17.

Elena Filatova and Vasileios Hatzivassiloglou. 2004a. Event-based extractive summarization. In *Proceedings of ACL Workshop on Summarization*. Barcelona, Spain., volume 111.

Elena Filatova and Vasileios Hatzivassiloglou. 2004b. A formal model for information selection in multi-sentence text extraction. In *Proceedings of the 20th international conference on Computational Linguistics*. Association for Computational Linguistics, page 397.

Francis Galton. 1886. Regression towards mediocrity in hereditary stature. *The Journal of the Anthropological Institute of Great Britain and Ireland* 15:246–263.

Joseph Evans Grimes. 1975. *The thread of discourse*, volume 207. Walter de Gruyter.

Paul J Hopper and Sandra A Thompson. 1980. Transitivity in grammar and discourse. *language* pages 251–299.

Roderick Kay and Ruth Aylett. 1996. Transitivity and foregrounding in news articles: Experiments in information retrieval and automatic summarising. In *Proceedings of the 34th Annual Meeting on Association for Computational Linguistics*. Association for Computational Linguistics, Stroudsburg, PA, USA, ACL '96, pages 369–371. `https://doi.org/10.3115/981863.981918`.

Mike Lewis, Luheng He, and Luke Zettlemoyer. 2015. Joint a* ccg parsing and semantic role labelling. In *EMNLP*. pages 1444–1454.

Rada Mihalcea and Paul Tarau. 2004. Textrank: Bringing order into text. In *EMNLP*. volume 4, pages 404–411.

Teruko Mitamura, Zhengzhong Liu, and Eduard Hovy. 2015. Overview of tac kbp 2015 event nugget track. In *Text Analysis Conference*.

Sean Monahan and Mary Brunson. 2014. Qualities of eventiveness. In *Proceedings of the Second Workshop on EVENTS: Definition, Detection, Coreference, and Representation*. pages 59–67.

Tim O'Gorman, Kristin Wright-Bettner, and Martha Palmer. 2016. Richer event description: Integrating event coreference with temporal, causal and bridging annotation. *Computing News Storylines* page 47.

F. Pedregosa, G. Varoquaux, A. Gramfort, V. Michel, B. Thirion, O. Grisel, M. Blondel, P. Prettenhofer, R. Weiss, V. Dubourg, J. Vanderplas, A. Passos, D. Cournapeau, M. Brucher, M. Perrot, and E. Duchesnay. 2011. Scikit-learn: Machine learning in Python. *Journal of Machine Learning Research* 12:2825–2830.

Jeffrey Pennington, Richard Socher, and Christopher D Manning. 2014. Glove: Global vectors for word representation. In *EMNLP*. volume 14, pages 1532–1543.

Tsunoda Tasaku. 1981. Split case-marking patterns in verb-types and tense/aspect/mood. *Linguistics* 19(5-6):389–438.

K. Toutanova, D. Klein, C. Manning, and Y. Singer. 2003. Feature-Rich Part-of-Speech Tagging with a Cyclic Dependency Network. In *Proceedings of HLT-NAACL 2003*.

Tasaku Tsunoda. 1985. Remarks on transitivity. *Journal of linguistics* pages 385–396.

Shyam Upadhyay, Christos Christodoulopoulos, and Dan Roth. 2016. " making the news": Identifying noteworthy events in news articles. In *Proceedings of the Fourth Workshop on Events*. pages 1–7.

Vladimir N. Vapnik. 1995. *The Nature of Statistical Learning Theory*. Springer-Verlag New York, Inc., New York, NY, USA.

Improve Neural Entity Recognition via Multi-Task Data Selection and Constrained Decoding

Huasha Zhao[1], Yi Yang[1,2][*], Qiong Zhang[1], and Luo Si[1]

[1]Alibaba Group, San Mateo, CA
{huasha.zhao, qz.zhang, luo.si}@alibaba-inc.com
[2]Nanjing University, Nanjing, Jiangsu, China
yangyi868@gmail.com

Abstract

Entity recognition is a widely benchmarked task in natural language processing due to its massive applications. The state-of-the-art solution applies a neural architecture named BiLSTM-CRF to model the language sequences. In this paper, we propose an entity recognition system that improves this neural architecture with two novel techniques. The first technique is Multi-Task Data Selection, which ensures the consistency of data distribution and labeling guidelines between source and target datasets. The other one is constrained decoding using knowledge base. The decoder of the model operates at the document level, and leverages global and external information sources to further improve performance. Extensive experiments have been conducted to show the advantages of each technique. Our system achieves state-of-the-art results on the English entity recognition task in KBP 2017 official evaluation, and it also yields very strong results in other languages.

1 Introduction

Entity Recognition (ER) is a fundamental task in Natural Language Processing (NLP). The task includes named entity recognition and nominal entity recognition. ER is the building blocks for higher level applications such as natural language understanding, question answering, machine reading comprehension, etc. They are usually treated as sequence labeling problems. Although the topics have been studied extensively for the past several decades, development of neural network and deep learning based methods in recent years (Lample et al., 2016; Ma and Hovy, 2016; Yang et al., 2017; Kenton Lee and Zettlemoyer, 2017; Xinchi Chen, 2017) significantly improves the previous state-of-the-art.

A popular neural architecture for ER is BiLSTM-CRF (Lample et al., 2016). The architecture has been shown to achieve best performance on many sequence labeling tasks. In addition, the architecture can be easily extended to model different sources of training data. In real world applications, it is important to include external data sources for model training, because using only domain-specific data for training is usually not enough to achieve best performance. For example, in the case of KBP 2016 tracks, both the 1*st* and the 2*nd* teams (ranking in the NERC evaluation) use external data source (Liu et al., 2016; Xu et al., 2017) for model training. The challenge here is to transfer knowledge from external data source to target data source. Multi-Task (MT) BiLSTM-CRF architecture (Yang et al., 2017) is designed for this knowledge transfer.

In this work, we develop an ER model based on the MT BiLSTM-CRF architecture, with additional entity embeddings and domain adaption. Two novel methods are proposed to further improve the model performance.

Multi-Task Data Selection

To ensure homogeneity between source and target training data, adaptive training data selection is applied to source data during multi-task learning, to filter out instances with different distribution and misaligned annotation guideline. Data selection is interleaved with model training iteratively, and this training process terminates until convergence.

Constrained Decoding using Knowledge Base

Knowledge-based constraints are enforced at decoding time. The goal is to capture document level contexts given those knowledge. For example, a phrase is likely to be an entity if it is detected in another sentence in the same document. It also helps detect related mentions, such as the mention

---

* Work was done while doing internship at Alibaba.

Proceedings of NAACL-HLT 2018, pages 346–351
New Orleans, Louisiana, June 1 - 6, 2018. ©2018 Association for Computational Linguistics

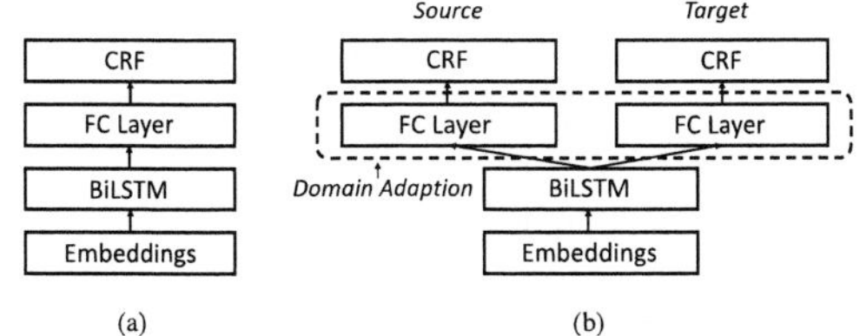

Figure 1: Neural architectures for mention detection and classification. a) Single-task model. b) Multi-task model with domain adaptions.

apple is more likely to be a ORG when it occurs in the same discussion forum with *Apple Inc*.

2 Related Works

There are many works in literature applying neural networks to ER problems (Lample et al., 2016; Ma and Hovy, 2016; Yang et al., 2017; Peng and Dredze, 2016). The baseline model of this work is mostly closed to (Yang et al., 2017). However, we introduce additional channel in the embedding layer(Peng and Dredze, 2016).

The idea of multi-task data selection is derived from topics of data selection (Moore and Lewis, 2010) and instance weighting (Jiang and Zhai, 2007) from the transfer learning community. Different from previous work, we propose an adaptive selection approach interleaved with MT BiLSTM-CRF model training. Decoding with global constraints has been studied in (Yarowsky, 1993; Krishnan and Manning, 2006). Here we share similar ideas with previous work, but explore the use of external knowledge base (Radford et al., 2015) as constraints.

3 Approach

This section describes the baseline model used for the ER task. We first describe a slight variant of BiLSTM-CRF and its MT version for transfer learning. For the sake of brevity, discussions of the basis theory of MT learning are skipped and more details can be found in (Zhang and Yang, 2017). Then we present in details how data selection and constrained decoding are applied to further improve the model performance.

3.1 BiLSTM-CRF

BiLSTM-CRF is a widely adopted neural architecture for sequence labeling problems including ER. BiLSTM-CRF is a hierarchical model and the architecture is illustrated in Figure 1(a).

The first layer of the model maps words to their embeddings. Let $\mathbf{x} = (x_1, \cdots, x_n)$ denote a sentence composed of n words in a sequence, with $x_i's$ as their word/character embedding combinations. In the second layer, word embeddings are encoded using a bidirectional-LSTM network, and the output is $\mathbf{h} = (h_1, \cdots, h_n)$, where $h_t = BiLSTM(\mathbf{x}, t)$. The encodings are further passed to a fully connection network, to compute CRF features $\phi(\mathbf{x}) = G \cdot \mathbf{h}$, and finally objective to optimize is the CRF likelihood defined as the following,

$$p(\mathbf{y}|\mathbf{x}; \theta) = \frac{\prod_{i=1}^{n} \exp(\theta \cdot f(y_{i-1}, y_i, \phi(\mathbf{x})))}{Z},$$

where $\mathbf{y}$ are predicted labels and Z is the normalizing constant.

3.1.1 Entity Embeddings

We extend the BiLSTM-CRF model by adding entity embedding channel to the embedding layer. As a result, x_i is the concatenation of word embedding, character embedding and its entity embedding, $x_i = [\omega_i, c_i, g_i]$. Entity embeddings are derived from a noisy gazetteer created using Wikipedia articles. The gazetteer is derived from the word-entity statistics from (Pan et al., 2017). More specifically, each coordinate of the entity embedding is the probability distribution of a word occurring as the corresponding entity type.

3.1.2 Domain Adaption

To explore external datasets, we apply MT BiLSTM-CRF with domain adaptions, as illustrated in Figure 1(b). The fully connection layer are adapted to different datasets. The CRF features are computed separately, i.e. $\phi^{\mathcal{T}}(\mathbf{x}) = G^{\mathcal{T}} \cdot \mathbf{h}$, $\phi^{\mathcal{S}}(\mathbf{x}) = G^{\mathcal{S}} \cdot \mathbf{h}$ for target and source dataset respectively. The loss function $p(\mathbf{y}|\mathbf{x}; \theta^{\mathcal{T}})$ and $p(\mathbf{y}|\mathbf{x}; \theta^{\mathcal{S}})$ are optimized in alternating order.

3.2 Multi-task Data Selection

Multi-task training can alleviate some of the problem caused by data heterogeneity between target and source. This section presents an adaptive data selection algorithm during multi-task training that further removes noisy data from source dataset.

The data selection procedure is described in details in Algorithm 1. At each iteration, data selection from the source domain is interleaved with model parameter updates. Training data is selected

Algorithm 1 Multi-task Data Selection

Input: Target training dataset $(\mathbf{x}, \mathbf{y}) \in \mathcal{T}$, source training dataset $(\mathbf{x}', \mathbf{y}') \in \mathcal{S}$.

Initialize: $\mathcal{S}_{train} \leftarrow \mathcal{S}$; $\mathcal{X}^S = \{\mathbf{x}' : (\mathbf{x}', \mathbf{y}') \in \mathcal{S}\}$.

Repeat:

1. Train the model for one iteration, by optimizing the following instance weighted object function,

$$J = \sum_{(\mathbf{x},\mathbf{y}) \in \mathcal{T}} p(\mathbf{y}|\mathbf{x}; \theta^{\mathcal{T}}) + \sum_{(\mathbf{x}',\mathbf{y}') \in \mathcal{S}_{train}} p(\mathbf{y}'|\mathbf{x}'; \theta^{\mathcal{S}});$$

2. Compute consistency score for each training example in $\mathcal{S}$,

$$s(\mathbf{x}) = \max_i \sum_j p(x_i = j) \log \frac{p(x_i = j)}{q(x_i = j)},$$

where $p(x_i) \sim softmax(\phi^{\mathcal{T}}(x_i))$ and $q(x_i) \sim softmax(\phi^{\mathcal{S}}(x_i))$;

3. Construct $\mathcal{S}_{same}$, $\mathcal{S}_{diff}$ by the following,
$\mathcal{S}_{same} = \{\mathbf{x} \in \mathcal{X}^S : s(\mathbf{x}) < \alpha\}$ and
$\mathcal{S}_{diff} = \{\mathbf{x} \in \mathcal{X}^S : s(\mathbf{x}) > \beta\}$;
Thresholds α and β are manually set that determine the selection/exclusion of a data point.

4. Update source training set $\mathcal{S}_{train}$,
$\mathcal{S}_{train} \leftarrow \mathcal{S}_{train} \cup \mathcal{S}_{same} \setminus \mathcal{S}_{diff}$.
In the new training set, data with different distributions are eliminated.

Until: $|\mathcal{S}_{diff}| < k$
Return: the final BiLSTM-CRF model.

---

based on a *consistency score*, which measures the similarity between target and source data distribution. Specifically, the consistency score is derived from the KL divergence between $\phi^{\mathcal{T}}(\mathbf{x})$ and $\phi^{\mathcal{S}}(\mathbf{x})$ for every word in the sentence in the source training data. According to step 4, data that are not *consistent* with the target are eliminated from the training dataset. The iterations terminate until there is few additional data to filter out, up to a manually-tuned threshold.

3.3 Constrained Decoding using Knowledge Base

It has been well studied that non-local information can be used to help improve entity recognition performance (Radford et al., 2015) (Krishnan and Manning, 2006). Here we describe a globally constrained decoding (Graves et al., 2012) method used in our model. In particular, we use external knowledge information to guide the decoding process at the document level.

3.3.1 Knowledge Base

An external knowledge base is built from Wikipedia articles (Radford et al., 2015) (Dalton et al., 2014). For each Wikipedia entity, we first extract all its aliases from the redirects, and then build a cluster of the mentions for the this entity which includes all its aliases. Our goal is that given a document mentions *Microsoft*, the knowledge base can help identify the other mentions such as *MS Corp*. The knowledge base can be naturally extended to include related entities (using anchor texts), instead of only aliases of the same entity, in the cluster; we leave this to the future works.

Then we apply global decoding with constraint C, such that all mentions that belong to the same cluster should be labeled as the same entity type within a single document,

$$\mathbf{y}_{1:\mathbf{N}} = \underset{C}{\operatorname{argmax}}\, p(\mathbf{y}_{1:\mathbf{N}}|\mathbf{x}_{1:\mathbf{N}}; \theta),$$

where subscripts $1 : N$ are indices of sentences within the same document. We use a greedy algorithm for decoding.

4 Experiments

This section presents experiments results of our methods on the KBP 2016 and 2017 evaluation datasets. We focus on Engilsh (ENG) and Mandarin Chinese (CMN) ER tasks, which include both named entity recognition (NAM) and nominal entity recognition (NOM). The neural models are implemented using Tensorflow (Abadi et al., 2016). Dropout and gradient clipping are applied when necessary to avoid numerical issues during training. Performance numbers are reported using the NERC F_1 score as defined in (Ji et al., 2016).

4.1 Datasets

KBP 2015 data is used for evaluation on the 2016 evaluation dataset. Both datasets are used for training for KBP 2017 evaluation. We also leverage external data sources to improve model performance. Unlike (Liu et al., 2016), manual annotation is not feasible to us due to budget limit, we instead use ACE (Walker et al., 2006) and ERE

Method	NAM	NOM	Overall
baseline (ENG)	0.809	0.587	0.748
+ EE (ENG)	0.842	0.587	0.770
baseline (CMN)	0.822	0.305	0.727
+ EE (CMN)	0.851	0.305	0.752

Table 1: Effectiveness of additional entity embeddings (EE) in model embedding layer.

(Song et al., 2015) entity annotations as source datasets. It is worth noting that annotation guidelines are different from one dataset to another, especially for nominal entity annotations.

4.2 Baseline

The baseline is a BiLSTM-CRF model with word and character embeddings which simply combines source and target data as training data. GloVe vectors (Pennington et al., 2014) are used as word embeddings. NAM and NOM models are trained separately with individually tuned parameters.

4.3 Results

First, we examine the performance impact of entity embedding. As shown in Table 1, entity embedding is very useful for both NAM and NOM prediction tasks, and for both languages. It provides an overall performance improvement of 2.2 F_1 points. Since the entity embeddings are derived from soft gazetteer features, this experiment confirms again the usefulness of gazetteer even in neural network models. In theory, the entity embeddings should have been already captured by the model itself; the additional predictability of the entity embeddings actually comes from the external dataset (Wikipedia) where the embeddings are derived from.

Next the effectiveness of Multi-Task Data Selection is evaluated. Results in Table 2 show that both MT and MTDS can significantly improve NOM detection over the baseline, and adaptive data selection in MTDS further improves over the MT model. However, there is no gain at all for NAM detection for both languages. We manually evaluate the source and target datasets, and find that the annotation guideline and data distribution of NAM data are quite the similar while there are some significant differences for NOM data. Notably, many of the plural form nouns are marked as nominal entities in the ACE dataset while in our target KBP tasks plural nouns are not labeled as

Method	NAM	NOM	Overall
baseline+EE (ENG)	0.842	0.587	0.770
+MT (ENG)	0.842	0.626	0.786
+MTDS (ENG)	0.842	0.634	0.788
baseline+EE (CMN)	0.851	0.305	0.752
+MT (CMN)	0.851	0.351	0.756
+MTDS (CMN)	0.851	0.364	0.758

Table 2: Effectiveness of Multi-Task Data Selection (MTDS).

entities in general.

Table 3 presents the performance impact of knowledge based constrained decoding. It is worth noting that the performance gain in the Chinese language is more limited in comparison with English. The primary reason behind this is that the English Wikipedia site is more comprehensive than its Chinese counterpart. Constrained decoding does not change the NOM performance because only name mentions are included in the knowledge base.

Method	NAM	NOM	Overall
baseline+EE (ENG)	0.842	0.587	0.770
+CD (ENG)	0.851	0.587	0.778
baseline+EE (CMN)	0.851	0.305	0.752
+CD (CMN)	0.855	0.305	0.754

Table 3: Effectiveness of Constrained Decoding (CD) using Knowledge Base.

Finally, we use model ensemble to further improve model scores. Four models are combined together for final evaluation. Majority vote is applied to produce final results. We presents the evaluation results on both KBP 2016 and 2017 datasets in Table 4, and compare them with state-of-the-art scores (Ji et al., 2016) (Ji et al., 2017). Our system ranks 1st in the English entity recognition task in the official evaluation in 2017. We also perform very strongly in the Chinese language as well: the best team applies many hand-tuned rules in the evaluation (Ji et al., 2017), while our model is free of rules. It also can be concluded from the table that the additional training data for KBP 2016 increases the overall model performance by 0.7 F_1 points.

Year/Language	Our F1	Best F1
2016/ENG	0.804	0.772
2017/ENG (Official evaluation)	0.811	0.811
2017/CMN	0.769	0.780

Table 4: Performance comparison between 2016 and 2017 datasets.

5 Conclusion and Future Works

This paper presents novel methods to improve neural entity recognition tasks. Multi-task data selection removes noise from training data, while constrained decoding further improves the model by exploiting global and external information sources. Extensive experiments show the effectiveness of the methods. Work needs to be done to justify in theoretic foundation the adaptive data selection algorithm. Furthermore, runtime and computational complexity of the system should be studied. We also plan to extend the knowledge base cluster to include related entities.

References

Martín Abadi, Paul Barham, Jianmin Chen, Zhifeng Chen, Andy Davis, Jeffrey Dean, Matthieu Devin, Sanjay Ghemawat, Geoffrey Irving, Michael Isard, et al. 2016. Tensorflow: A system for large-scale machine learning. In *OSDI*. volume 16, pages 265–283.

Jeffrey Dalton, Laura Dietz, and James Allan. 2014. Entity query feature expansion using knowledge base links. In *Proceedings of the 37th international ACM SIGIR conference on Research & development in information retrieval*. ACM, pages 365–374.

Alex Graves et al. 2012. *Supervised sequence labelling with recurrent neural networks*, volume 385. Springer.

Heng Ji, Joel Nothman, Hoa Trang Dang, and Sydney Informatics Hub. 2016. Overview of tac-kbp2016 tri-lingual edl and its impact on end-to-end cold-start kbp. *Proceedings of TAC* .

Heng Ji, Xiaoman Pan, Boliang Zhang, Joel Nothman, James Mayfield, Paul McNamee, and Cash Costello. 2017. Overview of tac-kbp2017 13 languages entity discovery and linking. *Proceedings of TAC* .

Jing Jiang and ChengXiang Zhai. 2007. Instance weighting for domain adaptation in nlp. In *ACL*. volume 7, pages 264–271.

Luheng He Mike Lewis Kenton Lee and Luke Zettlemoyer. 2017. End-to-end neural coreference resolution. In *EMNLP*. pages 188–197.

Vijay Krishnan and Christopher D Manning. 2006. An effective two-stage model for exploiting non-local dependencies in named entity recognition. In *Proceedings of the 21st International Conference on Computational Linguistics and the 44th annual meeting of the Association for Computational Linguistics*. Association for Computational Linguistics, pages 1121–1128.

Guillaume Lample, Miguel Ballesteros, Sandeep Subramanian, Kazuya Kawakami, and Chris Dyer. 2016. Neural architectures for named entity recognition. *arXiv preprint arXiv:1603.01360* .

Dan Liu, Wei Lin, Shiliang Zhang, Si Wei, and Hui Jiang. 2016. The ustc nelslip systems for trilingual entity detection and linking tasks at tac kbp 2016 .

Xuezhe Ma and Eduard Hovy. 2016. End-to-end sequence labeling via bi-directional lstm-cnns-crf. *arXiv preprint arXiv:1603.01354* .

Robert C Moore and William Lewis. 2010. Intelligent selection of language model training data. In *Proceedings of the ACL 2010 conference short papers*. Association for Computational Linguistics, pages 220–224.

Xiaoman Pan, Boliang Zhang, Jonathan May, Joel Nothman, Kevin Knight, and Heng Ji. 2017. Cross-lingual name tagging and linking for 282 languages. In *ACL*.

Nanyun Peng and Mark Dredze. 2016. Multi-task multi-domain representation learning for sequence tagging. *arXiv preprint arXiv:1608.02689* .

Jeffrey Pennington, Richard Socher, and Christopher Manning. 2014. Glove: Global vectors for word representation. In *Proceedings of the 2014 conference on empirical methods in natural language processing (EMNLP)*. pages 1532–1543.

Will Radford, Xavier Carreras, and James Henderson. 2015. Named entity recognition with document-specific kb tag gazetteers. In *EMNLP*. pages 512–517.

Zhiyi Song, Ann Bies, Stephanie Strassel, Tom Riese, Justin Mott, Joe Ellis, Jonathan Wright, Seth Kulick, Neville Ryant, and Xiaoyi Ma. 2015. From light to rich ere: annotation of entities, relations, and events. In *Proceedings of the 3rd Workshop on EVENTS at the NAACL-HLT*. pages 89–98.

Christopher Walker, Stephanie Strassel, Julie Medero, and Kazuaki Maeda. 2006. Ace 2005 multilingual training corpus. *Linguistic Data Consortium, Philadelphia* 57.

Zhan Shi Xipeng Qiu Xuanjing Huang Xinchi Chen. 2017. Adversarial multi-criteria learning for chinese word segmentation. In *ACL*.

Mingbin Xu, Hui Jiang, and Sedtawut Watcharawittayakul. 2017. A local detection approach for named entity recognition and mention detection. In *Proceedings of the 55th Annual Meeting of the Association for Computational Linguistics (Volume 1: Long Papers)*. volume 1, pages 1237–1247.

Zhilin Yang, Ruslan Salakhutdinov, and William W Cohen. 2017. Transfer learning for sequence tagging with hierarchical recurrent networks. *ICLR* .

David Yarowsky. 1993. One sense per collocation. Technical report, PENNSYLVANIA UNIV PHILADELPHIA DEPT OF COMPUTER AND INFORMATION SCIENCE.

Yu Zhang and Qiang Yang. 2017. A survey on multitask learning. *arXiv preprint arXiv:1707.08114* .

Keep your bearings: Lightly-supervised Information Extraction with Ladder Networks that avoids Semantic Drift

Ajay Nagesh
Dept. of Computer Science
University of Arizona
ajaynagesh@email.arizona.edu

Mihai Surdeanu
Dept. of Computer Science
University of Arizona
surdeanu@email.arizona.edu

Abstract

We propose a novel approach to semi-supervised learning for information extraction that uses ladder networks (Rasmus et al., 2015). In particular, we focus on the task of named entity classification, defined as identifying the correct label (e.g., person or organization name) of an entity mention in a given context. Our approach is simple, efficient and has the benefit of being robust to semantic drift, a dominant problem in most semi-supervised learning systems. We empirically demonstrate the superior performance of our system compared to the state-of-the-art on two standard datasets for named entity classification. We obtain between 62% and 200% improvement over the state-of-art baseline on these two datasets.

1 Introduction

Training machine learning systems with limited supervision is one of the fundamental challenges in natural language processing (NLP), as annotated data is often scarce and generating it requires costly human supervision. Semi-supervised learning addresses this challenge by combining limited supervision with a large, unannotated dataset, thereby mitigating the supervision cost.

For NLP, bootstrapping is a popular approach to semi-supervised learning due its relative simplicity coupled with reasonable performance (Abney, 2007). However, a crucial limitation of bootstrapping, which is typically iterative, is that, as learning advances, the task often *drifts semantically* into a related but different space, e.g., from learning women names into learning flower names (McIntosh, 2010; Yangarber, 2003).

In this paper, we propose an effective technique for semi-supervised learning for information extraction (IE), which obviates the need for an iterative approach, thereby mitigating the problem of semantic drift. Our technique is based on the recently proposed ladder networks (LNs) (Rasmus et al., 2015; Valpola, 2014). Ladder networks are deep denoising auto-encoders which have skip connections and reconstruction targets in the intermediate layers. Ladder networks are closely related to hierarchical latent variable models (Rasmus et al., 2015; Valpola, 2014). The lateral skip connections relieve the pressure on lower layers of the encoder to encode all latent information, thereby making the architecture modular in design, similar to a factor graph. The integration of the encoder-decoder framework as a neural network, allows one to use backpropagation for training, thereby not having to rely on intractable inference as in a standard graphical model. Furthermore, LNs have been shown to achieve state-of-the-art performance in image recognition tasks (Rasmus et al., 2015).

To the best of our knowledge, our work is one of the first applications of LN to any NLP task. Specifically, our contributions are as follows:

(1) We provide a novel application of LNs to an IE task, in particular semi-supervised named entity classification (NEC). Our approach is simple: we concatenate embeddings of entity mentions with that of its context[1] and feed the resulting vectors into the LN's denoising auto-encoder.

(2) We empirically demonstrate, for the task of semi-supervised NEC on two standard datasets – CoNLL (Tjong Kim Sang and De Meulder, 2003) and Ontonotes (Pradhan et al., 2013) – that we obtain a classification accuracy of 66.11% and 63.12% with minimal supervision on only 0.3% and 0.6% of the data, respectively. These results compare favorably against the accuracy of state-of-the-art bootstrapping algorithms of 40.74% and 21.06% on the same datasets. Further, in our experiments we observed an almost 7-fold decrease

---

[1]A context consists of all the patterns of n-grams within a certain window around the corresponding entity mention.

Proceedings of NAACL-HLT 2018, pages 352–358
New Orleans, Louisiana, June 1 - 6, 2018. ©2018 Association for Computational Linguistics

in training time compared to an iterative bootstrapping system.

(3) Lastly, we also provide empirical evidence that our approach is robust to the phenomenon of semantic drift. We obtain consistently better accuracy compared to traditional bootstrapping algorithms and label propagation, when initialized with identical supervision. We also demonstrate the reduction in semantic drift by measuring the purity of the entity pools with respect to a category as the algorithm advances (§4).

2 Related Work

There is a long line of work in semi-supervised learning for NLP (Zhu, 2005; Abney, 2007). This encompasses many different types of techniques such as self-training or bootstrapping (Carlson et al., 2010a,b; McIntosh, 2010; Gupta and Manning, 2015, inter alia), co-training (Blum and Mitchell, 1998), or graph-based methods such as label propagation (Delalleau et al., 2005). Perhaps the most popular approach among them is self-training, or bootstrapping, which has been used in many applications, including information extraction (Carlson et al., 2010a; Gupta and Manning, 2014, 2015), lexicon acquisition (Neelakantan and Collins, 2015), named entity classification (Collins and Singer, 1999) and sentiment analysis (Rao and Ravichandran, 2009). However, most of these approaches are iterative, and suffer from semantic drift (Komachi et al., 2008).

Auto-encoder frameworks have been getting a lot of attention in the machine learning community recently. Such framewoks include recursive auto-encoders (Socher et al., 2011), denoising auto-encoders (Vincent et al., 2008), etc. They are primarily used as a pre-training mechanism before supervised training. Recently, such networks have also been used for semi-supervised learning as they are more amenable to combining supervised and unsupervised components of the objective functions (Zhai and Zhang, 2015).

Ladder networks (LN) are stacked denoising auto-encoders with skip-connections in the intermediate layers (Rasmus et al., 2015; Valpola, 2014). LNs have been shown to produce state-of-the-art performance on both supervised and semi-supervised tasks on the MNIST dataset in image processing. Our work is among the first to apply LNs to NLP. While similar in spirit to Zhang et al. (2017), the only other work we found that applies a denoising auto-encoder to a semi-supervised spelling correction task, our work is much simpler, since it uses a multi-layer perceptron instead of convolution-deconvolution operations. Further, we demonstrate that LNs perform very well on a complex IE task, considerably outperforming several state-of-the-art approaches.

3 Approach

We apply the proposed semi-supervised learning approach to the task of NEC, defined as identifying the correct label of an entity mention in a given context. In our setting, the context of a mention is defined as all the patterns that match the specific mention. Please refer to the right half of Figure 1 for an example sentence snippet, an entity mention (in boldface) and its context. Using these as input, the classifier must infer that the mention's correct label is person.[2]

For the NEC task, the embedding of a mention and its context is concatenated to produce X which is input to the ladder network to predict a label y for the particular entity mention.

Initializing the network

We initialize the words in the entities and patterns around them with pre-trained word embeddings. To obtain a single embedding for an entity mention and its context we: (a) average word embeddings to obtain a single embedding for the entity mention and each of its patterns; and (b) average the resulting pattern embeddings to produce the embedding of the corresponding context. We then concatenate the mention's embedding and context embedding to be given as input to the ladder network. This process is depicted schematically in the right part of Figure 1.

Architecture of the ladder network

Ladder Network (Rasmus et al., 2015) is a neural network architecture designed to use unsupervised learning as a scaffolding for the supervised task. It is a denoising autoencoder (DAE) with noise introduced in every layer. It consists of two sets of encoders, a clean one and another corrupted with noise, and a decoder. In addition, there

---

[2]Note that the NEC task can be defined at mention level, as defined above, or at entity level, i.e., identify all labels that apply to all mentions of a given entity. (e.g., "Washington" = {person, location}. Here we focus on mention classification, although in some of our evaluations we revert to entity classification, to be able to compare against other approaches.

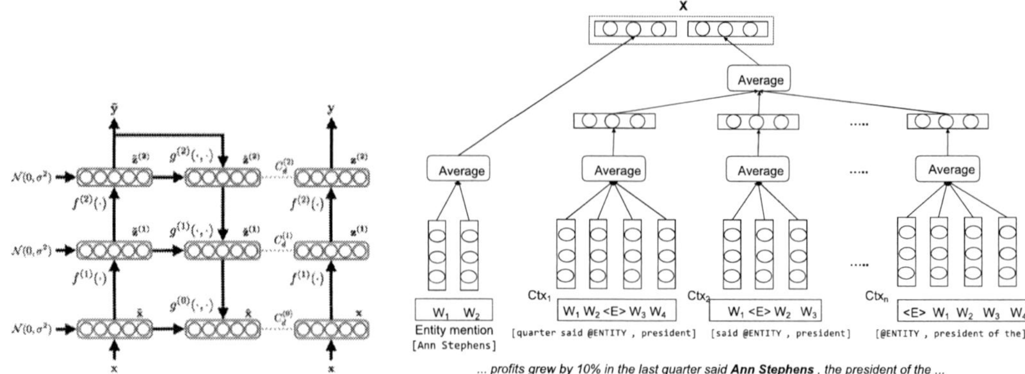

Figure 1: Architecture of the ladder network (Rasmus et al., 2015) (left) and of the network initialization component for the NEC task (right). LN is a deep denoising auto-encoder with lateral skip connections between the layers. The input to our LN is an entity mention along with its context, averaged and concatenated vector initialized with pre-trained embeddings for every token (§3). We introduce noise in the network by perturbing the embeddings with standard Gaussian noise with fixed stdev.

are skip connections between the encoder and decoder. The ladder network is defined as follows:

$$\tilde{X}, \tilde{Z}^{(1)}, \ldots \tilde{Z}^{(L)}, \tilde{y} = f_{corr}(X) \tag{1}$$

$$X, Z^{(1)}, \ldots Z^{(L)}, y = f_{clean}(X) \tag{2}$$

$$\hat{X}, \hat{Z}^{(1)}, \ldots \hat{Z}^{(L)} = g(\tilde{Z}^{(1)}, \ldots \tilde{Z}^{(L)}) \tag{3}$$

where X, $\tilde{X}$ and $\hat{X}$ is an input datapoint, its corrupted version, and its reconstruction, respectively; $Z^{(l)}$ and $\tilde{Z}^{(l)}$ are clean and corrupted hidden representations in the l-th layer; and, lastly, y, $\tilde{y}$ are the clean and corrupted activations, converted to a probability distribution over the label set (using a softmax layer). For our NEC task, X is the concatenation of an entity mention and its context embedding vectors generated as mentioned previously, and y represents one of the predicted mention labels (e.g. `person`).

We introduce noise in this architecture by perturbing the embeddings with a standard Gaussian noise with a fixed standard deviation.

The objective function is a combination of a supervised training cost and unsupervised reconstruction costs at each layer (including the hidden layers):

$$Cost = -\sum_{n=1}^{N} logP(\tilde{y}_n = y_n^* | X_n) +$$

$$\sum_{n=N+1}^{M} \sum_{l=1}^{L} \lambda_l ReconstCost(Z_n^{(l)}, \hat{Z}_n^{(l)}) \tag{4}$$

where the first term is the supervised cross-entropy based on the N labeled datapoints $(X_1, y_1^*), (X_2, y_2^*), \ldots (X_N, y_n^*)$, and the second term is the reconstruction loss on the M unlabeled datapoints $X_{N+1}, X_{N+2}, \ldots X_{N+M}$, for each layer l. Typically $M \gg N$.

Pezeshki et al. (2016) analyze the different architectural aspects of LN and note that the lateral connections and corresponding reconstruction costs (second term in Eq. 4) are critical for semi-supervised learning. In other words, it is important for unlabeled data to be used for regularization to be able to learn good abstractions in the different layers. We have similar observations for the NEC task (see Experiments). The overall architecture of LN is shown in the left part of Figure 1.

4 Experiments

Datasets: We used two datasets, the CoNLL-2003 shared task dataset (Tjong Kim Sang and De Meulder, 2003), which contains 4 entity types, and the OntoNotes dataset (Pradhan et al., 2013), which contains 11[3], both of which are benchmark datasets for supervised named entity recognition (NER). These datasets contain marked entity boundaries with labels for each marked entity. Here we only use the entity boundaries but *not* the labels of these entities during the training of our bootstrapping systems. To simulate learning from large texts, we tuned hyper parameters on development, but ran the actual experiments on the *train* partitions.

Baselines: We compared against 2 baselines:

Explicit Pattern-based Bootstrapping (EPB): this system is our implementation of the state-of-the-art bootstrapping system of Gupta and Manning (2015), adapted to NEC. The algorithm grows a pool of known entities and patterns for

---

[3]We excluded numerical categories such as DATE.

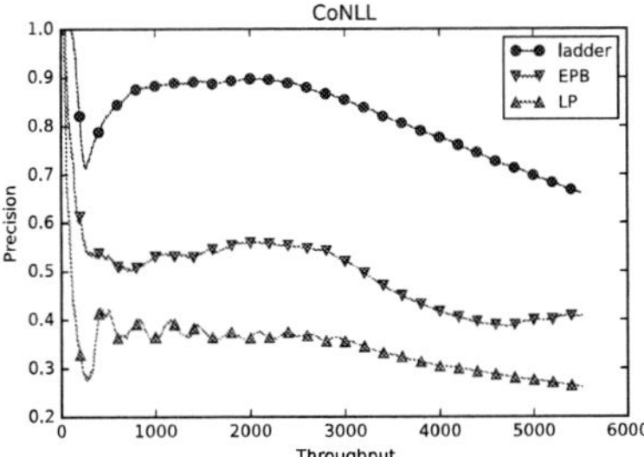
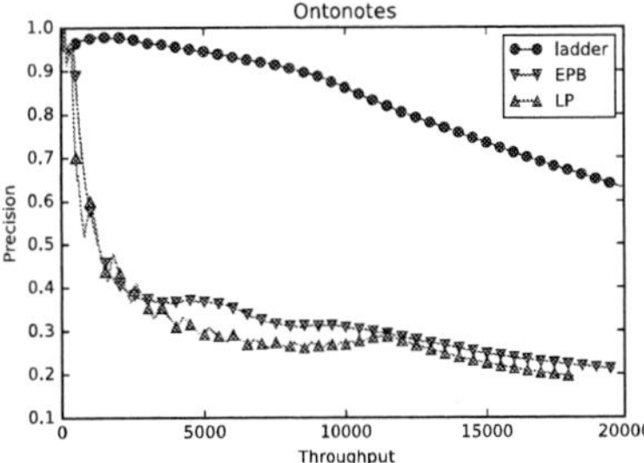

Figure 2: Overall results on the CoNLL (left) and Ontonotes (right) datasets. Throughput is the number of entities classified, and precision is the proportion of entities that were classified correctly.

each category of interest, from a few seed examples per category, by iterating between pattern promotion and entity promotion. The former is implemented using a ranking formula driven by the point-wise mutual information (PMI) between each pattern with the corresponding category; the top ranked patterns are promoted to the pattern pool in each iteration. The latter component promotes entities using a classifier that estimates the likelihood of an entity belonging to each class. Our feature set includes, for each category c: (a) edit distance between the candidate entity e and known entities for c; (b) the PMI (with c) of the patterns in the pool of c that matched e in the training documents; and (c) similarity between e and entities in c's pool in some semantic space.[4] Entities classified with the highest confidence for each class are promoted to the corresponding pool after each epoch.

Label Propagation (LP): we used the implementation available in the `scikit-learn` package of the LP algorithm (Zhu and Ghahramani, 2002).[5] In each bootstrapping epoch, we run LP, select the entities with the lowest entropy, and add them to their top category. Each entity is represented by a feature vector that contains the co-occurrence counts of the entity and each of the patterns that matches it in text.[6]

Settings: For each entity mention, we consider a n-gram window of size 4 on either side as a pattern. We initialized the mention and contexts embeddings input to the ladder network as well as the baseline system with pre-trained embeddings from Levy and Goldberg (2014) (size 300d) as this

gave us improved results on the baseline compared to vanilla `word2vec` initialization. We used a 600d dimensional embedding for each datapoint (300 each from entity and context concatenated). We used a 3-layer ladder network with dimensions 600-500-K where K is the number of labels present in the dataset. Further, we used a standard Gaussian noise with stdev = 0.3 for the corrupted encoder and reconstruction cost for the 3-layers were 1000-10-0.1. We set the supervised examples (mentions along their corresponding contexts and labels) randomly. For CoNLL we used 40 and Ontonotes 440 examples, with equal representation from their labels' set. To compare with the baselines, which classify entities rather than mentions, we sorted the predictions returned by the LN in decreasing order of their activation scores and chose the most confident entity label (when all its mention scores were averaged). We ran the baselines until they predicted labels for all the entities. For the baselines, in each iteration we promoted 100 entities per category.[7] For a fair comparison, we used the same set of entity mentions as seeds (selected randomly) for each of our experiments.

Figure 2 shows the precision vs. throughput curves for the baselines and our LN approach. We see that on both the datasets the LN outperforms the baselines by a large margin. Further we notice that the LN is reasonably stable for most of the precision/recall curve whereas EPB degrades quickly. Iterative bootstrapping approaches inherently suffer from semantic drift: as the iterations progress the learned model begins to drift into a different semantic space due to incomplete statistics and ambiguity (McIntosh, 2010; Yangarber, 2003). These results parallel other previous observations that semantic drift is an inherent problem in iterative bootstrapping approaches (Komachi

---

[4]We used pre-trained word representations, averaged for multi-word entities, to compute cosine similarities between pairs of entities.

[5]`http://scikit-learn.org/stable/modules/generated/sklearn.semi_supervised.LabelPropagation.html`

[6]We experimented with other feature values, e.g., pattern PMI scores, but all performed worse than raw counts.

[7]We also ran a cautious approach of promoting 10 entities per category per iteration and noticed that the former had better performance.

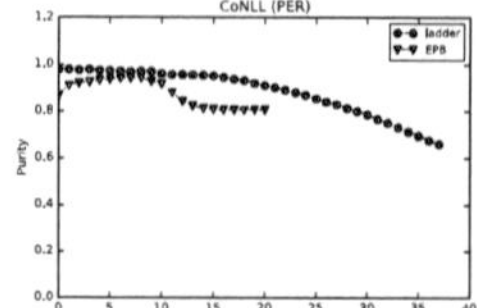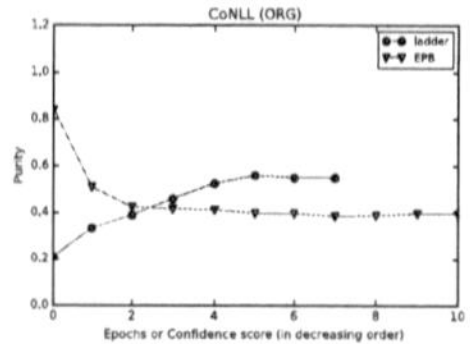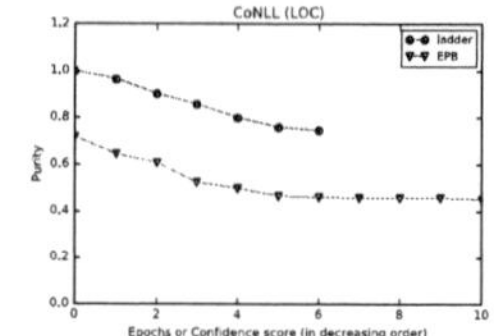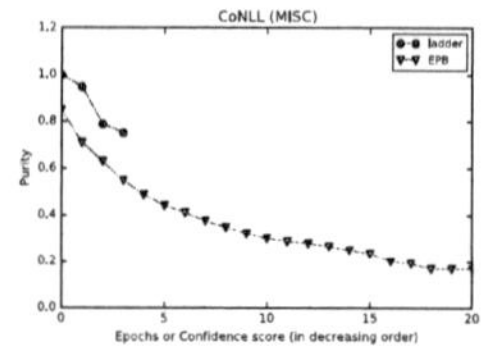

Figure 3: Avoiding semantic drift: Comparison of pool purity between ladder and EPB on the CoNLL dataset.

et al., 2008). The figure empirically demonstrates that, in contrast, the paradigm of semi-supervised learning based on ladder networks is more effective in combating semantic drift. Further, we empirically observed a speedup of almost 7x in training a ladder network compared to an iterative bootstrapping approach.

Table 1 lists the accuracy of the LN approach on all the data points, as we varied the amount of supervision. As expected, as we increase the amount of supervision, we observe improvements in accuracy. More importantly, the table shows that LN outperforms the overall accuracy of EPB (rightmost points in Figure 2) with much fewer annotations (e.g., with 55 annotations in OntoNotes, LN outperforms the performance of EPB with 440 annotated examples).

Figure 3 shows the purity of entity pools for a given label vs. confidence scores of the entity predictions sorted in decreasing order for the CoNLL dataset.[8] Purity is defined here as the precision of an entity pool for a given category. In the EPB setting, this is equivalent to computing the precision at the stage of entity promotion in a particular epoch. In LNs, we sort the entity predictions in decrease order of their confidence scores and create bins of size 100 for this comparison.We notice that for every category, LN maintains a higher overall purity over EPB, the best iterative bootstrapping baseline, demonstrating that the entity pools are less polluted by noisy entries, thereby reducing semantic drift. It is also important to observe that LN inherently captures the bias in the training data, by predicting more entities in the PER category, as this is the most frequently occurring label in the dataset.

5   Conclusion

We discussed a novel application of ladder networks to the task of lightly supervised named entity classification. Our approach concatenates embeddings of entity mentions with their contexts

CoNLL		OntoNotes	
Num. labels	Accuracy	Num. labels	Accuracy
20	46.46	55	26.04
40	66.46	110	48.53
80	75.37	220	59.66
160	81.11	440	73.10
320	80.94	880	73.58
640	82.51	1760	73.23
1280	81.22	3520	73.77
2560	81.34	7040	73.31
5120	81.26	14080	82.47
10240	81.91	28160	83.32

Table 1: Num. of annotated labels vs. overall accuracy. # of mention labels - CoNLL: 13200; OntoNotes: 67000

and feeds the resulting vectors into the LN's denoising auto-encoder. We demonstrate that our system outperforms state-of-the-art iterative bootstrapping approaches by approximately 62% and 200% on two benchmark datasets. Furthermore, our approach mitigates the issue of semantic drift as it is not iterative in nature, unlike traditional bootstrapping.

As part of future investigation, we will experiment with other types of encoders such as convolutional and recurrent networks. Furthermore, we aim to scale this approach to larger datasets. The approach presented in the paper is broad in scope. Application of this framework to other tasks in natural language processing such as relation extraction, sentiment analysis, and fine-grained entity typing, where obtaining supervised training data is hard, is another interesting avenue for further research. For example, relation extraction can be modeled similarly to the NEC task described here, as a feed forward network over embeddings of the entity mentions participating in the relation and of the lexico-syntactic patterns connecting them.

Acknowledgements

Mihai declares a financial interest in lum.ai. This interest has been properly disclosed to the University of Arizona Institutional Review Committee and is managed in accordance with its conflict of interest policies. This work was funded by the DARPA Big Mechanism program under ARO contract W911NF-14-1-0395 and by the Bill and Melinda Gates Foundation HBGDki Initiative.

---

[8]In the appendix, a similar analysis is presented on the Ontonotes dataset.

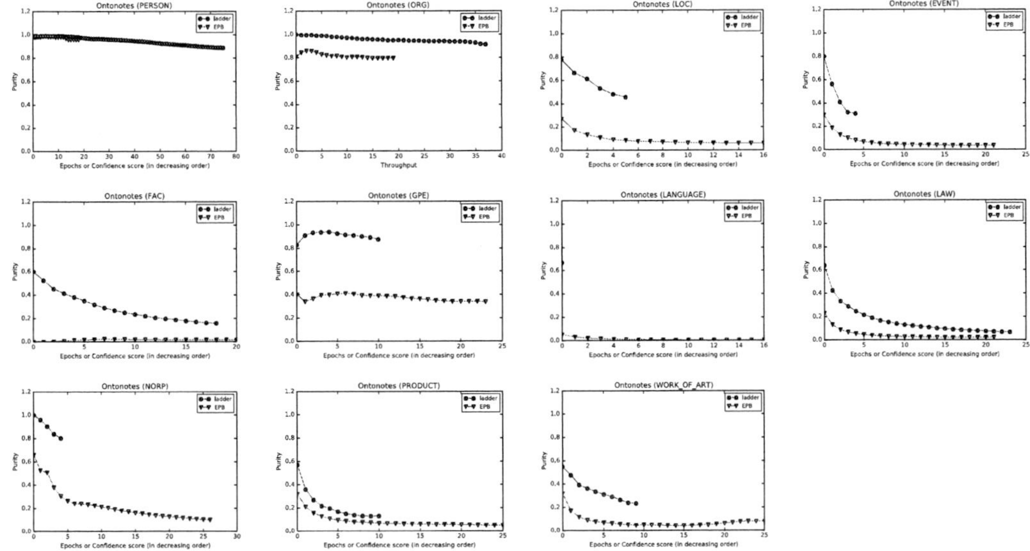

Figure 4: Avoiding semantic drift: Comparison of pool purity between ladder and EPB on the Ontonotes dataset.

References

Steven Abney. 2007. *Semisupervised Learning for Computational Linguistics*. Chapman & Hall/CRC, 1st edition.

Avrim Blum and Tom Mitchell. 1998. Combining labeled and unlabeled data with co-training. In *Proceedings of the Eleventh Annual Conference on Computational Learning Theory*. ACM, New York, NY, USA, COLT' 98, pages 92–100. https://doi.org/10.1145/279943.279962.

Andrew Carlson, Justin Betteridge, Bryan Kisiel, Burr Settles, Estevam R. Hruschka Jr., and Tom M. Mitchell. 2010a. Toward an architecture for never-ending language learning. In *Proceedings of the Twenty-Fourth Conference on Artificial Intelligence (AAAI 2010)*.

Andrew Carlson, Justin Betteridge, Richard C Wang, Estevam R Hruschka Jr, and Tom M Mitchell. 2010b. Coupled semi-supervised learning for information extraction. In *Proceedings of the third ACM international conference on Web search and data mining*. ACM, pages 101–110.

Michael Collins and Yoram Singer. 1999. Unsupervised models for named entity classification. In *Proceedings of the Conference on Empirical Methods in Natural Language Processing*.

Olivier Delalleau, Yoshua Bengio, and Nicolas Le Roux. 2005. Efficient non-parametric function induction in semi-supervised learning. In Robert G. Cowell and Zoubin Ghahramani, editors, *Proceedings of the Tenth International Workshop on Artificial Intelligence and Statistics (AISTATS'05)*. Society for Artificial Intelligence and Statistics, pages 96–103. http://www.iro.umontreal.ca/~lisa/pointeurs/semisup_aistats2005.pdf.

Sonal Gupta and Christopher D Manning. 2014. Improved pattern learning for bootstrapped entity extraction. In *CoNLL*. pages 98–108.

Sonal Gupta and Christopher D. Manning. 2015. Distributed representations of words to guide bootstrapped entity classifiers. In *Proceedings of the Conference of the North American Chapter of the Association for Computational Linguistics*.

Mamoru Komachi, Taku Kudo, Masashi Shimbo, and Yuji Matsumoto. 2008. Graph-based analysis of semantic drift in espresso-like bootstrapping algorithms. In *Proceedings of the Conference on Empirical Methods in Natural Language Processing*. Association for Computational Linguistics, Stroudsburg, PA, USA, EMNLP '08, pages 1011–1020. http://dl.acm.org/citation.cfm?id=1613715.1613847.

Omer Levy and Yoav Goldberg. 2014. Dependency-based word embeddings. In *Proceedings of the 52nd Annual Meeting of the Association for Computational Linguistics (Volume 2: Short Papers)*. Association for Computational Linguistics, Baltimore, Maryland, pages 302–308. http://www.aclweb.org/anthology/P14-2050.

Tara McIntosh. 2010. Unsupervised discovery of negative categories in lexicon bootstrapping. In *Proceedings of the 2010 Conference on Empirical Methods in Natural Language Processing*. Association for Computational Linguistics, pages 356–365.

Arvind Neelakantan and Michael Collins. 2015. Learning dictionaries for named entity recognition using minimal supervision. *CoRR* abs/1504.06650. http://arxiv.org/abs/1504.06650.

Mohammad Pezeshki, Linxi Fan, Philemon Brakel, Aaron Courville, and Yoshua Bengio. 2016. Deconstructing the ladder network architecture. In Maria Florina Balcan and Kilian Q. Weinberger, editors, *Proceedings of The 33rd International Conference on Machine Learning*. PMLR, New York, New York, USA, volume 48 of *Proceedings of Machine Learning Research*, pages 2368–2376. http://proceedings.mlr.press/v48/pezeshki16.html.

Sameer Pradhan, Alessandro Moschitti, Nianwen Xue, Hwee Tou Ng, Anders Bjrkelund, Olga Uryupina, Yuchen Zhang, and Zhi Zhong. 2013. Towards robust linguistic analysis using ontonotes. In *Proceedings of the Seventeenth Conference on Computational Natural Language Learning*. Association for Computational Linguistics, Sofia, Bulgaria, pages 143–152. http://www.aclweb.org/anthology/W13-3516.

Delip Rao and Deepak Ravichandran. 2009. Semi-supervised polarity lexicon induction. In *Proceedings of the 12th Conference of the European Chapter of the Association for Computational Linguistics*. Association for Computational Linguistics, Stroudsburg, PA, USA, EACL '09, pages 675–682. http://dl.acm.org/citation.cfm?id=1609067.1609142.

Antti Rasmus, Mathias Berglund, Mikko Honkala, Harri Valpola, and Tapani Raiko. 2015. Semi-supervised learning with ladder networks. In C. Cortes, N. D. Lawrence, D. D. Lee, M. Sugiyama, and R. Garnett, editors, *Advances in Neural Information Processing Systems 28*, Curran Associates, Inc., pages 3546–3554.

Richard Socher, Jeffrey Pennington, Eric H. Huang, Andrew Y. Ng, and Christopher D. Manning. 2011. Semi-Supervised Recursive Autoencoders for Predicting Sentiment Distributions. In *Proceedings of the 2011 Conference on Empirical Methods in Natural Language Processing (EMNLP)*.

Erik F. Tjong Kim Sang and Fien De Meulder. 2003. Introduction to the CoNLL-2003 shared task: Language-independent named entity recognition. In Walter Daelemans and Miles Osborne, editors, *Proceedings of CoNLL-2003*. Edmonton, Canada, pages 142–147.

Harri Valpola. 2014. From neural PCA to deep unsupervised learning. *CoRR* abs/1411.7783. http://arxiv.org/abs/1411.7783.

Pascal Vincent, Hugo Larochelle, Yoshua Bengio, and Pierre-Antoine Manzagol. 2008. Extracting and composing robust features with denoising autoencoders. In *Proceedings of the 25th International Conference on Machine Learning*. ACM, New York, NY, USA, ICML '08, pages 1096–1103. https://doi.org/10.1145/1390156.1390294.

Roman Yangarber. 2003. Counter-training in discovery of semantic patterns. In *Proceedings of the Annual Meeting of the Association for Computational Linguistics*.

Shuangfei Zhai and Zhongfei Zhang. 2015. Semisupervised autoencoder for sentiment analysis. *CoRR* abs/1512.04466. http://arxiv.org/abs/1512.04466.

Yizhe Zhang, Dinghan Shen, Guoyin Wang, Zhe Gan, Ricardo Henao, and Lawrence Carin. 2017. Deconvolutional paragraph representation learning. *CoRR* abs/1708.04729. http://arxiv.org/abs/1708.04729.

X. Zhu and Z. Ghahramani. 2002. Learning from labeled and unlabeled data with label propagation. Technical Report CMU-CALD-02-107, Carnegie Mellon University. citeseer.ist.psu.edu/zhu02learning.html.

Xiaojin Zhu. 2005. Semi-supervised learning literature survey. Technical Report 1530, Computer Sciences, University of Wisconsin-Madison.

A Purity on Ontonotes

Figure 4 shows the purity of the entity pools on the Ontonotes dataset (Purity is defined in §4). From these graphs, we can observe that LN has a higher overall purity compared to EPB for all categories, which indicates that it suffers less from the problem of semantic drift. Further, we observe that LN predicts more PERSON and ORG entities as these as the most frequently appearing types in this dataset. In other words, LN follows closely the underlying distribution of the data when making predictions, unlike EPB.

Semi-Supervised Event Extraction with Paraphrase Clusters

James Ferguson, Colin Lockard, Daniel S. Weld, and Hannaneh Hajishirzi
University of Washington
`{jfferg, lockardc, weld, hannaneh}@cs.washington.edu`

Abstract

Supervised event extraction systems are limited in their accuracy due to the lack of available training data. We present a method for self-training event extraction systems by bootstrapping additional training data. This is done by taking advantage of the occurrence of multiple mentions of the same event instances across newswire articles from multiple sources. If our system can make a high-confidence extraction of some mentions in such a cluster, it can then acquire diverse training examples by adding the other mentions as well. Our experiments show significant performance improvements on multiple event extractors over ACE 2005 and TAC-KBP 2015 datasets.

1 Introduction

Event extraction is a challenging task, which aims to discover event triggers in a sentence and classify them by type. Training an event extraction system requires a large dataset of annotated event triggers and their types in a sentence. Unfortunately, because of the large amount of different event types, each with its own set of annotation rules, such manual annotation is both time-consuming and expensive. As a result, popular event datasets, such as ACE (Walker et al., 2006) and TAC-KBP (Mitamura et al., 2015), are small (*e.g.*, the median number of positive examples per subtype is only 65 and 86, respectively) and biased towards frequent event types, such as Attack.

When an event occurs, there are often multiple parallel descriptions of that event (Figure 1) available somewhere on the Web due to the large number of different news sources. Some descriptions are simple, explaining in basic language the event that occurred. These are often easier for existing extraction systems to identify. Meanwhile,

1) **LSU** *fires* head coach **Les Miles** after 12 seasons.
2) **Les Miles** is *out* at **LSU** after 12 seasons in Baton Rouge.
3) On Sunday morning, **LSU** athletic director Joe Alleva told **Les Miles** that the coach would *no longer represent* Louisiana State.

Figure 1: Example of a cluster of paraphrases. Shared entities are bolded, and the triggers are italicized. Some, such as the first sentence, are very simple. Others, like the third sentence are more difficult.

other descriptions might use more complex language that falls outside the scope of typical event extractors, but which, if identified, could serve as valuable training data for said systems.

We automatically generate labeled training data for event trigger identification leveraging this wealth of event descriptions[1]. Specifically, we first group together paraphrases of event mentions. We then use the simple examples in each cluster to assign a label to the entire cluster. This simplifies the task of extracting events from difficult examples; rather than having to identify whether an event occurs, and which word serves as a trigger for that event, our system needs only to identify the most likely trigger for the given event. Finally, we combine the new examples with the original training set and retrain the event extractor.

Our experiments show that this data can be used with limited amounts of gold data to achieve significant improvement over both standard and neural event extraction systems. In particular, it achieves 1.1 and 1.3 point F1 improvements over a state-of-the-art system in trigger identification on TAC-KBP and ACE data respectively. Moreover, we show how the benefit of our method varies as a function of the amount of fully-supervised training data and the number of additional heuristically-labeled examples.

---

[1] The generated data and our code can be found at https://github.com/jferguson144/NewsCluster

Proceedings of NAACL-HLT 2018, pages 359–364
New Orleans, Louisiana, June 1 - 6, 2018. ©2018 Association for Computational Linguistics

2   Approach

Our goal is to automatically add high quality labeled examples, which can then be used as additional training data to improve the performance of any event extraction model. Our data generation process has three steps. The first is to identify clusters of news articles all describing the same event. The second step is to run a baseline system over the sentences in these clusters to identify events found in each cluster. Finally, once we have identified an event in one article in a cluster, our system scans through the other articles in that cluster choosing the most likely trigger in each article for the given event type.

Cluster Articles   In order to identify groups of articles describing the same event instance, we use an approach inspired by the NewsSpike idea introduced in Zhang et al. (2015). The main intuition is that rare entities that are mentioned a lot on a single date are more indicative that two articles are covering the same event. We assign a score, S, to each pair of articles, (a_i, a_j) appearing on the same day, for whether or not they cover the same event, as follows:

$$S(a_i, a_j) = \sum_{e \in E_{a_i} \cap E_{a_j}} \frac{\text{count}(e, \text{date}_{a_i, a_j})}{\text{count}(e, \text{corpus})}, \quad (1)$$

where E_a is the list of named entities for the article a, and count is the number of times the entity appears on the given date, or in the whole corpus. This follows from the intuition above by reducing the weight given to common entities. For example, *United States* appears 367k times in the corpus, so it is not uncommon for it to appear hundreds of times on a single day, and articles mentioning it could be covering completely different topics. Meanwhile *Les Miles* appears only 1.6k times in the corpus, so when there are hundreds of mentions involving *Les Miles* on a single day, it is much more likely that he participated in some event. Accumulating these counts over all shared entities between two articles thus indicates whether the articles are covering the same event. We then group all articles that cover the same event according to this score into clusters.

Label Clusters   Then, given clusters of articles, we run a baseline extractor which was trained on what limited amount of fully-supervised training data is available. The hope is that one or more of a cluster's sentences will use language similar enough to our training data that the extractor can make an accurate prediction. Our system keeps any cluster in which the baseline system identifies at least some threshold, θ_{event}, of event mentions for a single event type, and labels those clusters with the identified type.

Assign Triggers   After labeling, the event clusters are comprised of articles in which at least one sentence should contain event mentions of the labeled type. Because most current event extraction systems require labeled event triggers for sentences, we identify those sentences and the event triggers therein so that we can run the baseline systems. For each sentence we identify the most likely trigger by checking the similarity of the word embeddings to the canonical vector for that event. This vector is computed as the average of the embeddings of the event triggers, v_t, in the gold training data: $v_{event} = \frac{1}{|T_{event}|} \sum_{t \in T_{event}} v_t$, where T_{event} is the set of triggers for this event in the gold training data. If the maximum similarity is greater than some threshold, θ_{sim}, the sentence and the corresponding trigger are added to the training data.

Event Trigger Identification Systems   Event extraction tasks such as ACE and TAC-KBP have frequently been approached with supervised machine learning systems based on hand-crafted features, such as the system adapted from Li et al. (2013) which we make use of here. Recently, state-of-the-art results have been obtained with neural-network-based systems (Nguyen et al., 2016; Chen et al., 2015; Feng et al., 2016). Here, we make use of two systems whose implementations are publicly available and show that adding additional data would improve their performance.

The first system is the joint recurrent neural net (JRNN) introduced by Nguyen et al. (2016). This model uses a bi-directional GRU layer to encode the input sentence. It then concatenates that with the vectors of words in a window around the current word, and passes the concatenated vectors into a feed-forward network to predict trigger types for each token. Because we are only classifying triggers, and not arguments, we don't include the memory vectors/matrices, which primarily help improve argument prediction, or the argument role prediction steps of that model.

The second is a conditional random field (CRF) model with the trigger features introduced by Li et al. (2013). These include lexical features, such as tokens, part-of-speech tags, and lemmas, syntactic features, such as dependency types and arcs associated with each token, and entity features, including unigrams/bigrams normalized by entity types, and the nearest entity in the sentence. In particular, we use the Evento system from Ferguson et al. (2017).

3 Experimental Setup

Labeled Datasets We make use of two labeled datasets: ACE-2005 and TAC-KBP 2015. For the ACE data, we use the same train/development/test split as has been previously used in (Li et al., 2013), consisting of 529 training documents, 30 development documents, and a test set consisting of 40 newswire articles containing 672 sentences. For the TAC-KBP 2015 dataset, we use the official train/test split as previously used in Peng et al. (2016) consisting of 158 training documents and 202 test documents. ACE contains 33 event types, and TAC-KBP contains 38 event types.

For our approach, we use a collection of news articles scraped from the web. These articles were scraped following the approach described in Zhang and Weld (2013). The process involves collecting article titles from RSS news seeds, and then querying the Bing news search with these titles to collect additional articles. This process was repeated on a daily basis between January 2013 and February 2015, resulting in approximately 70 million sentences from 8 million articles. Although the seed titles were collected during that two year period, the search results include articles from prior years with similar titles, so the articles range from 1970 to 2015.

Evaluation We report the micro-averaged F1 scores over all events. A trigger is considered correctly labeled if both its offsets and event type match those of a reference trigger.

Implementation details For creating the automatically-generated data, we set thresholds θ_{event} and θ_{sim} to 2 and 0.4 respectively, which were selected according to validation data. We use CoreNLP (Manning et al., 2014) for named entity recognition, and we use a pre-trained Word2Vec model (Mikolov et al., 2013) for the vector representations.

For the JRNN model, we follow the parameter settings of (Nguyen et al., 2016) and use a context window of 2 for context words, and a feed-forward neural network with one hidden layer for trigger

		ACE			TAC-KBP		
		P	R	F1	P	R	F1
CRF	0%	62.9	70.0	66.3	53.5	52.3	52.9
	10%	64.5	69.8	67.0	**59.9**	49.3	**54.1***
	20%	**65.1**	**70.2**	**67.6***	59.3	49.2	53.8
	30%	**65.1**	69.9	67.4	58.1	**49.4**	53.4
JRNN	0%	65.7	72.9	69.1	**68.8**	49.2	57.3
	10%	67.4	72.7	69.9	65.4	52.1	58.0
	20%	**67.6**	**73.5**	**70.4***	65.3	52.8	**58.4***
	30%	67.5	73.3	70.3	64.7	**52.9**	58.2
HNN		84.6	64.9	73.4	-	-	-
SSED		-	-	-	69.9	48.8	57.5

Table 1: Results after adding varying amounts of automatically-generated news data. Percentages indicate the amount of additional data relative to the size of the gold training data. Using a modest amount of semi-supervised data improves extractor performance on both ACE & TAC-KBP events. * indicates that the difference in F1 relative to training with just the gold data is statistically significant ($p < 0.05$).

prediction with hidden layer size of 300. Finally, for training, We apply the stochastic gradient descent algorithm with mini-batches of size 50 and the AdaDelta update rule (Zeiler, 2012) with L_2 regularization. For the CRF model, we maximize the conditional log likelihood of the training data with a loss function via softmax-margin (Gimpel and Smith, 2010). We optimize using AdaGrad (Duchi et al., 2011) with L_2 regularization.

4 Experiments

Varying Amounts of Additional Data In this section we show that the addition of automatically-generated training examples improves the performance of both systems we tested it on. We sample examples from the automatically-generated data, limiting the total number of positive examples to a specific number. In order to avoid biasing the system in favor of a specific event type, we ensure that the additional data has a uniform distribution of event types. We run 10 trials at each point, and report average results.

Table 1 reports the results of adding varying amounts of our generated data to both CRF and JRNN systems. We observe that that adding any amount of heuristically-generated data improves performance. Optimal performance, however, is achieved fairly early in both datasets. This is likely due to the domain mismatch between the gold and additional data. For reference purposes, we also include the result of using the HNN model from (Feng et al., 2016) and the SSED system from

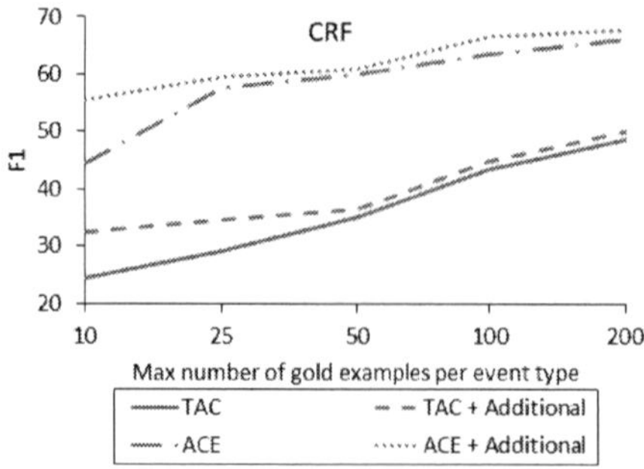

Figure 2: Adding a reasonable amount (200 examples per event) of semi-supervised data on top of limited amounts of gold training data improves performance across the board, but the gain is dramatic when the number of supervised examples is extremely small.

(Sammons et al., 2015), which are the best reported results on the ACE-2005 and TAC-KBP 2015 corpora respectively. These systems could also benefit from our additional data since our approach is system independent.

Varying Amounts of Supervised Data In this section we evaluate how the benefit of adding semi-supervised data varies given different amounts of gold (supervised) data to start. We conjecture that semi-supervision will be more beneficial when gold data is very limited, but the conclusion isn't obvious, since semi-supervision is more likely to add noisy examples in this case. Specifically, we limit the number of positive gold examples for each event by randomly sampling the overall set. We then add in the same amount of automatically-generated data to each trial. We again run 10 trials for each size, and report the average.

The results for this experiment using the CRF model can be seen in figure 2: training with large amounts of semi-supervised data improves performance considerably when limited gold training data is available, but those gains diminish with more high-quality supervised data. We observe the same trend for the JRNN system as well.

Discussion We randomly selected 100 examples from the automatically-generated data and manually annotated them. For each example that did not contain a correctly labeled event mention, we further annotated where in the pipeline an error occurred to cause the incorrect labeling. This breakdown can be seen in table 2. As observed in the table, the errors are mainly due to the incorrect event identification or trigger assignment.

Correct		72
Incorrect	clustering	5
	event identification	13
	trigger assignment	10

Table 2: The results of manually labeling 100 examples that were automatically-generated using JRNN as the supervised system.

Incorrect clustering refers to cases in which a sentence does not cover the same topic as other sentences in its cluster. This was primarily caused by entities participating in multiple events around the same time period. For example, this occurred in sentences from the 2012 US presidential election coverage involving Barack Obama and Mitt Romney.

Incorrect event identification refers to clusters that were incorrectly labeled by the supervised system. The primary reason for these errors is due to domain mismatch between the news articles and the gold data. For example, our system identifies the token *shot* in *Bubba Watson shot a 67 on Friday* as an attack event trigger. Because the gold data does not contain examples involving sports, the baseline system mistakenly identifies a paraphrase of the above sentence as an attack event, and our system is not able to fix that mistake. However, this problem can be solved by training the baseline extractor on the same domain as the additional data.

Incorrect trigger assignment refers to errors in which a sentence is correctly identified as containing an event mention, but the wrong token is selected as a trigger. The most common source of this error is tokens that are strongly associated with multiple events. For example, *shooting* is strongly associated with both attack and die events, but only actually indicates an attack event.

Looking through the correct examples, the data collection process is able to identify uncommon triggers that do not show up in the baseline training data. For example, it correctly identifies "offload" as a trigger for Transfer-Ownership in *Barclays is to offload part of its Spanish business to Caixabank*. Despite the trigger identification step having no context awareness, the process is also able to correctly identify triggers that rely on context, such as "contributions" triggering Transfer-Money in *Chatwal made $188,000 of illegal campaign contributions to three U.S. candidates via straw donors*.

5 Related Work

A challenge in event extraction is the relatively small number of labeled training examples available. Researchers have dealt with this by framing event extraction in a way that allows them to rely heavily on systems built for dependency parsing (McClosky et al., 2011) and semantic role labeling (Peng et al., 2016). Unlike these researchers, we join a line of work that attempts to directly harvest additional training examples for use in traditional event extraction systems.

Distant supervision is one source of additional data that has been successfully applied to relation extraction tasks (Riedel et al., 2010; Hoffmann et al., 2011; Mintz et al., 2009), which align a background knowledge base to an accompanying corpus of natural language documents. For event extraction, such data sources are not as easily available since there are no pre-existing stores of tuples of attacks, movements or meetings.

Other work has generated additional data by using a pattern-based model of event mentions and bootstrapping on top of a small set of seed examples. Huang and Riloff (2012) begin with a set of nouns that are specific to certain event roles and extract patterns based on the contexts in which those words appear. Li et al. (2014) extracted additional patterns using various event inference mechanisms.

The work most similar to ours is that of Liao and Grishman (2010, 2011) to identify articles from a corpus which described the same event instances found in training examples. These articles are then used in self-training an ACE-trained system after being filtered to select passages with consistent roles and triggers. Their method provides a 2.7 point boost to F1, but their baseline system results are much lower than ours (54.1 vs 69.1) and it is unclear what improvement their method would have on a state-of-the-art extractor. In addition, their system attempts to identify relevant articles that describe event instances already present in their training data, while we attempt to find clusters of sentences describing a common event, at least one of which we can confidently label.

The use of parallel news streams to acquire event extraction training data in an unsupervised fashion was explored in (Zhang et al., 2015), whose clustering methods we have adapted here. Unlike Zhang *et al.*, we have a defined event ontology for which we are acquiring data, rather than attempting to learn event types from the data. Furthermore, we use an extractor trained on fully-supervised examples to filter clusters, in contrast to Zhang *et al.*, whose method is completely unsupervised, which allows us to relax some of the assumptions made by Zhang *et al.* and consider "spikes" of individual entities as opposed to pairs.

6 Conclusion

We present a method for self-training event extraction systems by taking advantage of parallel mentions of the same event instance in newswire text. By examining clusters of sentences which produce at least two extractions of the same event type and assigning a trigger label to each sentence via word embedding similarity, we add diverse training examples to our dataset. Our experiments show a 1.3 point F1 increase in trigger labeling for a state-of-the-art baseline system on ACE, and a 1.1 point increase on TAC-KBP. For future research, this work can be applied to arbitrary event extraction models to improve performance, or make up for a lack of training data. The code and data are publicly available at our github repository.

Acknowledgements

This research was supported in part by ONR grants N00014-11-1-0294 and N00014-15-1-2774, DARPA contract FA8750-13-2- 0019, NSF (IIS-1616112, IIS-1420667, IIS-1703166), ARO grant W911NF13-1-0246 and the WRF/T.J. Cable Professorship. We would like to thank Stephen Soderland for many helpful discussions and our anonymous reviewers for their comments.

References

Yubo Chen, Liheng Xu, Kang Liu, Daojian Zeng, and Jun Zhao. 2015. Event extraction via dynamic multi-pooling convolutional neural networks. In *ACL*.

John Duchi, Elad Hazan, and Yoram Singer. 2011. Adaptive subgradient methods for online learning and stochastic optimization. In *Journal of Machine Learning Research*.

Xiaocheng Feng, Lifu Huang, Duyu Tang, Heng Ji, Bing Qin, and Ting Liu. 2016. A language-independent neural network for event detection. In *ACL*.

James Ferguson, Colin Lockard, Natalie Hawkins, Stephen Soderland, Hannaneh Hajishirzi, and Daniel S. Weld. 2017. University of washington tac-kbp 2016 system description. In *TAC-KBP*.

Kevin Gimpel and Noah A. Smith. 2010. Softmax-margin crfs: Training log-linear models with cost functions. In *HLT-NAACL*.

Raphael Hoffmann, Congle Zhang, Xiao Ling, Luke S. Zettlemoyer, and Daniel S. Weld. 2011. Knowledge-based weak supervision for information extraction of overlapping relations. In *ACL*.

Ruihong Huang and Ellen Riloff. 2012. Bootstrapped training of event extraction classifiers. In *EACL*.

Peifeng Li, Qiaoming Zhu, and Guodong Zhou. 2014. Employing event inference to improve semi-supervised chinese event extraction. In *COLING*.

Qi Li, Heng Ji, and Liang Huang. 2013. Joint event extraction via structured prediction with global features. In *ACL*.

Shasha Liao and Ralph Grishman. 2010. Filtered ranking for bootstrapping in event extraction. In *COLING*.

Shasha Liao and Ralph Grishman. 2011. Can document selection help semi-supervised learning? a case study on event extraction. In *ACL*.

Christopher D. Manning, Mihai Surdeanu, John Bauer, Jenny Finkel, Steven J. Bethard, and David Mc-Closky. 2014. The Stanford CoreNLP natural language processing toolkit. In *Association for Computational Linguistics (ACL) System Demonstrations*, pages 55–60.

David McClosky, Mihai Surdeanu, and Christopher D. Manning. 2011. Event extraction as dependency parsing. In *ACL*.

Tomas Mikolov, Ilya Sutskever, Kai Chen, Gregory S. Corrado, and Jeffrey Dean. 2013. Distributed representations of words and phrases and their compositionality. *CoRR*, abs/1310.4546.

Mike Mintz, Steven Bills, Rion Snow, and Daniel Jurafsky. 2009. Distant supervision for relation extraction without labeled data. In *ACL/IJCNLP*.

Teruko Mitamura, Yukari Yamakawa, Susan Holm, Zhiyi Song, Ann Bies, Seth Kulick, and Stephanie Strassel. 2015. Event nugget annotation: Processes and issues.

Thien Huu Nguyen, Kyunghyun Cho, and Ralph Grishman. 2016. Joint event extraction via recurrent neural networks. In *HLT-NAACL*.

Haoruo Peng, Yangqiu Song, and Dan Roth. 2016. Event detection and co-reference with minimal supervision. In *EMNLP*.

Sebastian Riedel, Limin Yao, and Andrew McCallum. 2010. Modeling relations and their mentions without labeled text. In *ECML/PKDD*.

Mark Sammons, Haoruo Peng, Yangqiu Song, Shyam Upadhyay, Chen-Tse Tsai, Pavankumar Reddy, Subhro Roy, and Dan Roth. 2015. Illinois ccg tac 2015 event nugget, entity discovery and linking, and slot filler validation systems. In *TAC*.

Christopher Walker, Stephanie Strassel, Julie Medero, and Kazuaki Maeda. 2006. *ACE 2005 Multilingual Training Corpus LDC2006T06*. Linguistic Data Consortium, Philadelphia.

Matthew D. Zeiler. 2012. ADADELTA: an adaptive learning rate method. *CoRR*, abs/1212.5701.

Congle Zhang, Stephen Soderland, and Daniel S. Weld. 2015. Exploiting parallel news streams for unsupervised event extraction. *TACL*, 3:117–129.

Congle Zhang and Daniel S. Weld. 2013. Harvesting parallel news streams to generate paraphrases of event relations. In *EMNLP*.

Structure Regularized Neural Network for Entity Relation Classification for Chinese Literature Text

Ji Wen[1], Xu Sun[1,2], Xuancheng Ren[1], Qi Su[3]

[1]MOE Key Lab of Computational Linguistics, School of EECS, Peking University
[2]Deep Learning Lab, Beijing Institute of Big Data Research, Peking University
[3]School of Foreign Languages, Peking University
`{wenjics, xusun, renxc, sukia}@pku.edu.cn`

Abstract

Relation classification is an important semantic processing task in the field of natural language processing. In this paper, we propose the task of relation classification for Chinese literature text. A new dataset of Chinese literature text is constructed to facilitate the study in this task. We present a novel model, named Structure Regularized Bidirectional Recurrent Convolutional Neural Network (SR-BRCNN), to identify the relation between entities. The proposed model learns relation representations along the shortest dependency path (SDP) extracted from the structure regularized dependency tree, which has the benefits of reducing the complexity of the whole model. Experimental results show that the proposed method significantly improves the F_1 score by 10.3, and outperforms the state-of-the-art approaches on Chinese literature text[1].

1 Introduction

Relation classification is the task of identifying the semantic relation holding between two nominal entities in text. Recently, neural networks are widely used in relation classification. Wang et al. (2016) proposes a convolutional neural network with two levels of attention. Zhang et al. (2015) uses bidirectional long short-term memory networks to model the sentence with sequential information. Bunescu and Mooney (2005) first uses SDP between two entities to capture the predicate-argument sequences. Wang et al. (2017) explores the idea of incorporating syntactic parse tree into neural networks. Liu et al. (2017) proposes a noise-tolerant method to deal with wrong labels in distant-supervised relation extraction with soft labels. In recent years, we

have seen a move towards deep learning architectures. Liu et al. (2015) develops dependency-based neural networks. Xu et al. (2015) applies long short term memory (LSTM) (Hochreiter and Schmidhuber, 1997) based recurrent neural networks (RNNs) along with the SDP.

In this paper, we focus on relation classification of Chinese literature text, which to our knowledge has not been studied before, due to the challenge. Chinese literature text tends to express intuitions and feelings. It has a wide range of topics. Many literature articles express feelings in a subtle and special way, making it more difficult to recognize entities. Chinese literature text is not organized very logically, whether among paragraphs or sentences. They tend to use various and flexible forms of sentences to create free feelings. The sentences are not associated with each other by evident conjunctions. Besides, Chinese is a topic-prominent language, the subject is usually covert and the usage of words is relatively flexible.

In short, sentences of Chinese literature text contain many non-essential words, and embody very complex and flexible structures. Existing methods make intensive use of the syntactical information, such as part-of-speech tags, and dependency relations. However, the automatically generated information is not reliable and of poor quality for Chinese literature text. It is of great challenge for the existing methods to achieve satisfying performance.

To mitigate the noisy syntactical information, we propose to apply structure regularization to the structures used in relation classification. Recently, many existing systems on structured prediction focus on increasing the level of structural dependencies within the model. However, the theoretical and experimental study of Sun (2014a) suggests that complex structures are tend to increase the overfitting risk, and can potentially be harm-

---

[1]The Chinese literature text corpus for relation classification, developed and used by this paper, is available at `https://github.com/lancopku/Chinese-Literature-NER-RE-Dataset`

Proceedings of NAACL-HLT 2018, pages 365–370
New Orleans, Louisiana, June 1 - 6, 2018. ©2018 Association for Computational Linguistics

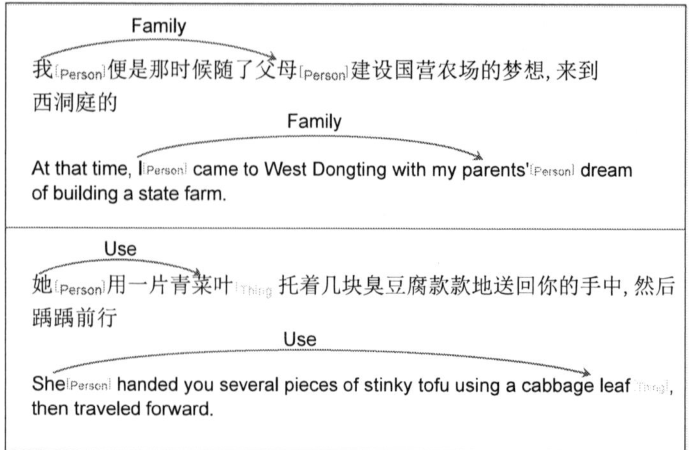

Figure 1: Examples from the Chinese literature text corpus.

ful to the model accuracy. As pointed out by Sun (2014a), complex structural dependencies have a drawback of increasing the generalization risk, because more complex structures are easier to suffer from overfitting.

In this paper, we focus on the study of applying structure regularization to the relation classification task of Chinese literature text. To summarize, the contributions of this paper are as follows:

- To our knowledge, we are the first to develop a corpus of Chinese literature text for relation classification. The corpus contains 837 articles. It helps alleviate the dilemma of the lack of corpus in Chinese Relation Classification.

- We develop the tree-based structure regularization methods and make progress on the task of relation classification. The method of structure regularization is normally used on the structure of sequences, while we find a way to realize it on the structure of trees. Comparing to the original model, applying structure regularization substantially improves the F_1 score by 10.3.

2 Chinese Literature Text Corpus

In Figure 1, we show two examples from the annotated corpus. We label the entities and relations of the text on a sentence level. There are 6 kinds of entities and 9 kinds of relations. Details of the tags are shown in Table 1. The task aims at predicting the labels of these relations, given the sentences as well as the entities and their types. The corpus is part of the work of Xu et al. (2017).

We obtain over 1,000 Chinese prose articles from the Internet and then filter and extract 837 articles. Articles that are too short or too noisy are not included. Due to the difficulty of tagging Chinese prose text, we divide the annotation process into three steps.

First, we attempt to annotate the raw articles based on defined entity and relation tags. Second, we design several generic disambiguation rules to ensure the consistency of annotation guidelines. For example, remove all adjective words and only tag "entity header" when tagging entities (e.g., change "a girl in red cloth" to "girl"). In this stage, we re-annotate all articles and correct all inconsistency entities based on the heuristic rules. Even though the heuristic tagging process significantly improves dataset quality, it is too hard to handle all inconsistency cases based on limited heuristic rules. Finally, we introduce a machine auxiliary tagging method. The core idea is to train a model to learn annotation guidelines on the subset of the corpus and produce predicted tags on the rest data. The predicted tags are used to be compared with the gold tags to discovery inconsistent entities, which largely reduce annotators' efforts. After all annotation steps, we also manually check all entities and relations to ensure the correctness of corpus.

In prior work, Chinese literature text corpus is very rare. Many tasks cannot achieve a satisfying result on Chinese literature text compared to other corpus. However, understanding Chinese literature text is of great importance to Chinese literature research.

Tag	Description	Example	%
Located	locate in	幽兰(orchid)-山谷(valley)	37.43
Part-Whole	be a part of	花(flower)-仙人掌(cactus)	23.76
Family	be family members	母亲(mother)-奶奶(grandmother)	10.25
General-Special	be a general range and a special kind of it	鱼(fish)-鲫鱼(carp)	6.99
Social	be socially related	母亲(mother)-邻里(neighbour)	6.02
Ownership	be in possession of	村民(villager)-旧屋(house)	5.10
Use	do something with	爷爷(grandfather)-毛笔(brush)	4.76
Create	make happen or exist	男人(man)-陶器(pottery)	2.93
Near	a short distance away	山(hill)-县城(town)	2.76

Table 1: The set of relation tags. The last column indicates each tag's relative frequency in the full annotated data.

3 Structure Regularized BRCNN

3.1 Basic BRCNN

The Bidirectional Recurrent Convolutional Neural Network (BRCNN) model is used to learn representations with bidirectional information along the shortest dependency path (SDP).

Given a sentence and its dependency tree, we build our neural network on its SDP extracted from tree. Along the SDP, recurrent neural networks are applied to learn hidden representations of words and dependency relations, respectively. A convolution layer is applied to capture local features from hidden representations of every two neighbor words and the dependency relations between them. A max pooling layer thereafter gathers information from local features of the SDP and the inverse SDP. We have a softmax output layer after pooling layer for classification in the unidirectional model RCNN.

On the basis of RCNN model, we build a bidirectional architecture BRCNN taking the SDP and the inverse SDP of a sentence as input. During the training stage of a (K+1)-relation task, two fine-grained softmax classifiers of RCNNs do a (2K+1)-class classification respectively. The pooling layers of two RCNNs are concatenated and a coarse-grained softmax output layer is followed to do a (K+1)-class classification. The final (2K+1)-class distribution is the combination of two (2K+1)-class distributions provided by fine grained classifiers during the testing stage.

We use two bidirectional LSTMs to capture the features of words and relations separately. After we obtain representations of words and relations, we concatenate them to get a representation of a complete dependency unit. The hidden state of a relation is denoted as r_{ab}. Words on its sides have the hidden states denoted as h_a and h_b. [h_a h_{ab} h_b] denotes the representation of a dependency unit L_{ab}. Then we utilize a convolution layer upon the concatenation. We have

$$L_{ab} = f(W_{con} \cdot [h_a \oplus h'_{ab} \oplus h_b] + b_{con}) \quad (1)$$

where W_{con} is the weight matrix and b_{con} is a bias term. We choose $tanh$ as our activation function and apply max pooling following the activation.

Two RCNNs pick up information along the SDP and its reverse. A coarse-grained softmax classifier is applied on the global representations $\overrightarrow{G}$ and $\overleftarrow{G}$. Two fine-grained softmax classifier are applied to to give a more detailed prediction of 2K+1 class.

$$\overrightarrow{y} = softmax(W_f \cdot \overrightarrow{G} + b_f) \quad (2)$$

$$\overleftarrow{y} = softmax(W_f \cdot \overleftarrow{G} + b_f) \quad (3)$$

During training, our objective is the penalized cross-entropy of three classifiers. Formally,

$$J = \sum_{i=1}^{2K+1} \overrightarrow{t_i} \log \overrightarrow{y_i} + \sum_{i=1}^{2K+1} \overleftarrow{t_i} \log \overleftarrow{y_i}$$
$$+ \sum_{i=1}^{K} t_i \log y_i + \lambda \cdot \|\theta\|^2 \quad (4)$$

When decoding, the final prediction is a combination of $\overrightarrow{y}$ and $\overleftarrow{y}$

$$y_{test} = \alpha \cdot \overrightarrow{y} + (1 - \alpha) \cdot z(\overleftarrow{y}) \quad (5)$$

where α is the fraction of the composition of distributions. We apply a function z to transform $\overleftarrow{y}$ to a corresponding forward distribution like $\overrightarrow{y}$.

3.2 Structure Regularized BRCNN

The basic BRCNN model can handle the task to some extent, but there still remains some weakness, especially dealing with long sentences with

	Models	Information	F_1 Score
Baselines	SVM (Hendrickx et al., 2010)	Word embeddings, NER, WordNet, HowNet, POS, dependency parse, Google n-gram	48.9
	RNN (Socher et al., 2011)	Word embeddings	48.3
		+ POS, NER, WordNet	49.1
	CNN (Zeng et al., 2014)	Word embeddings	47.6
		+ word position embeddings, NER, WordNet	52.4
	CR-CNN (dos Santos et al., 2015)	Word embeddings	52.7
		+ word position embeddings	54.1
	SDP-LSTM (Xu et al., 2015)	Word embeddings	54.9
		+ POS + NER + WordNet	55.3
	DepNN (Liu et al., 2015)	Word embeddings, WordNet	55.2
	BRCNN (Cai et al., 2016)	Word embeddings	55.0
		+ POS, NER, WordNet	55.6
Our Model	**SR-BRCNN**	Word embeddings	**65.2 (+9.6)**
		+ POS, NER, WordNet	**65.9 (+10.3)**

Table 2: Comparison of relation classification systems on Chinese literature text.

complicated structures. The SDP generated from a more complicated dependency tree consists more irrelevant words. Sun (2014b) shows both theoretically and empirically that structure regularization can effectively control overfitting risk and lead to better performance. Sun et al. (2017a) and Sun et al. (2017b) also show that complex structure models are prone to the structure-based overfitting. Therefore, we propose the structure regularized BRCNN.

We conduct structure regularization on the dependency tree of the sentences. Based on the heuristic rules, several nodes in the dependency tree are selected. The subtrees of these selected nodes are cut from the whole dependency tree. With these selected nodes as the roots, these subtrees form a forest. The forest will be connected by lining the roots of the trees of the forest. Traditional SDP is extracted directly from the dependency tree, while in our model, the SDP is extracted from the final forest. We call these kinds of SDPs as SR-SDPs. We build our BRCNN model on the SR-SDP.

3.3 Various Structure Regularization Methods

We experiment with three kinds of regularization rules. First, the punctuation is a natural break point of the sentence. The resulting subtrees usually keep similar syntax to traditional dependency trees. Another popular method to regularize the structure is to decompose the structure randomly. In our model, we randomly select several nodes in the dependency tree and then cut the subtrees under these nodes. Finally we decide to cut the dependency tree by prepositions. Especially in Chi-

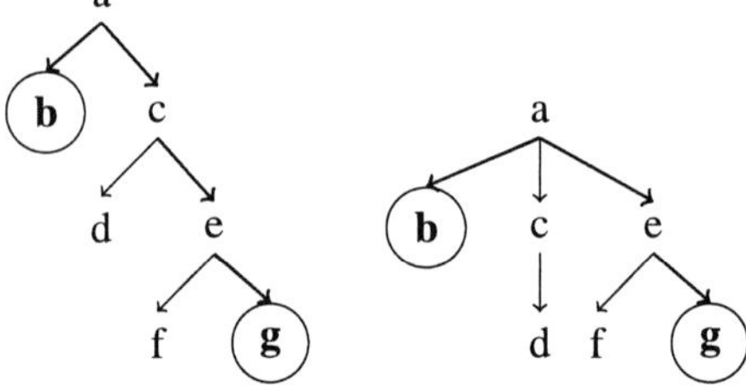

(a) The dependency tree and the SDP before flattening.

(b) The dependency tree and the SDP after flattening.

Figure 2: An example of the proposed method. The two words in circles are the entities, and the thick edges form the SDP. By flattening the dependency tree, the path becomes shorter.

nese literature text, there usually are many decorations to describe the entities, and the using of prepositional phrases is very common for that purpose. So we also try to decompose the dependency trees using prepositions.

4 Experiments

We evaluate our model on the Chinese literature text corpus. It contains 9 distinguished types of relations among 837 articles. The dataset contains 695 articles for training, 58 for validation, and 84 for testing.

4.1 Experiment settings

We use pre-trained word embeddings, which are trained on Gigaword with word2vec (Mikolov et al., 2013). Word embeddings are 200-dimensional. The embeddings of relation are initialized randomly and are 50-dimensional. The hidden layers of LSTMs to extract information from entities and relations are the same as the embedding dimension of entities and relations. We applied L2 regularization to weights in neural networks and dropout to embeddings with a keep probability 0.5. AdaDelta (Zeiler, 2012) is used for optimization.

4.2 Experimental Results

Table 2 compares our SR-BRCNN model with other state-of-the-art methods on the corpus of Chinese literature text, including the basic BRCNN method (Cai et al., 2016). Structure regularization helps improve the result substantially. The method of structure regularization could prevent the overfitting of poor quality SDPs.

4.3 Analysis: Effect of SR

Figure 2a and Figure 2b show an example of structure regularized SDP. The relation is between the two circled elements. The main idea of the method is to avoid the incorrect structure from the dependency trees generated by the parser. The SDP in Figure 2a is longer than the SR-SDP in Figure 2b. However, the dependency tree of the example is not completely correct. The longer the SDP is, the more incorrect information the model learns.

The structure regularized BRCNN has shown obvious improvements. We attribute the improvements to the simplified structures that generated by structure regularization. The internal relations of components of a sentence are more obscure due to the feature of Chinese literature text. By conducting structure regularization on the dependency tree, we get several subtrees with simpler structure, and then we extract SDP from the lined forests. In most cases, the distance between two entities will be shortened along the new SR-SDP. Without the redundant information along the original SDP. The model that benefits from the intensive dependencies will capture more effective information for classification.

4.4 Analysis: Effect of Different Regularization Methods

The punctuation is a natural break point of the sentence, which makes subtrees more like the traditional dependency trees in the aspect of integrity. However, the original dependency trees cannot be sufficiently regularized. Despite its drawbacks, this method still shows obvious improvements on the model and leads to further experiments.

Classifier	F_1 score
BRCNN	55.6
SR by punctuation	59.7
SR by random	62.4
SR by preposition	65.9

Table 3: Different structure regularization results on Chinese literature text.

Regularizing the structure by decomposing the structure randomly will solve the insufficient decomposition problems. The method of structure regularization has shown that the degree of loss of information is not a serious problem. It gives a slightly better result compared to cutting dependency trees by punctuations.

A more elaborate method is to cut the dependency tree by prepositions. In Chinese literature text, prepositional phrases are used frequently. Cutting by prepositions will regularize the tree more sufficiently. Meanwhile, the subtrees under the prepositional nodes are usually internally linked.

5 Conclusions

In this paper, we present a novel model, Structure Regularized BRCNN, to classify the relation of two entities in a sentence. We demonstrate that tree-based structure regularization can help improve the results, while the method is normally used in sequence-based models before. The proposed structure regularization method makes the SDP shorter and contain less noise from the unreliable parse trees. This leads to substantial improvements on the relation classification results. The results also show how different ways of regularization act in the model of BRCNN.

We also develop a corpus on Chinese literature text focusing on the task of Relation Classification. The new corpus is large enough for us to train models and verify the models.

Acknowledgements

This work was supported in part by National Natural Science Foundation of China (No. 61673028), National High Technology Research and Development Program of China (863 Program, No. 2015AA015404), and the National Thousand Young Talents Program. Xu Sun is the corresponding author of this paper.

References

Razvan Bunescu and Raymond Mooney. 2005. A shortest path dependency kernel for relation extraction. In *Proceedings of Human Language Technology Conference and Conference on Empirical Methods in Natural Language Processing*, pages 724–731.

Rui Cai, Xiaodong Zhang, and Houfeng Wang. 2016. Bidirectional recurrent convolutional neural network for relation classification. In *Proceedings of the 54th Annual Meeting of the Association for Computational Linguistics (Volume 1: Long Papers)*, pages 756–765.

Iris Hendrickx, Su Nam Kim, Zornitsa Kozareva, Preslav Nakov, Diarmuid Ó. Séaghdha, Sebastian Padó, Marco Pennacchiotti, Lorenza Romano, and Stan Szpakowicz. 2010. Semeval-2010 task 8: Multi-way classification of semantic relations between pairs of nominals. In *Proceedings of the 5th International Workshop on Semantic Evaluation*, pages 33–38.

Sepp Hochreiter and Jürgen Schmidhuber. 1997. Long short-term memory. *Neural computation*, 9(8):1735–1780.

Tianyu Liu, Kexiang Wang, Baobao Chang, and Zhifang Sui. 2017. A soft-label method for noise-tolerant distantly supervised relation extraction. In *Proceedings of the 2017 Conference on Empirical Methods in Natural Language Processing*, pages 1790–1795.

Yang Liu, Furu Wei, Sujian Li, Heng Ji, Ming Zhou, and Houfeng WANG. 2015. A dependency-based neural network for relation classification. In *Proceedings of the 53rd Annual Meeting of the Association for Computational Linguistics and the 7th International Joint Conference on Natural Language Processing (Volume 2: Short Papers)*, pages 285–290.

Tomas Mikolov, Ilya Sutskever, Kai Chen, Greg S Corrado, and Jeff Dean. 2013. Distributed representations of words and phrases and their compositionality. In *Advances in neural information processing systems*, pages 3111–3119.

Cicero dos Santos, Bing Xiang, and Bowen Zhou. 2015. Classifying relations by ranking with convolutional neural networks. In *Proceedings of the 53rd Annual Meeting of the Association for Computational Linguistics and the 7th International Joint Conference on Natural Language Processing (Volume 1: Long Papers)*, pages 626–634.

Richard Socher, Jeffrey Pennington, Eric H. Huang, Andrew Y. Ng, and Christopher D. Manning. 2011. Semi-supervised recursive autoencoders for predicting sentiment distributions. In *Proceedings of the 2011 Conference on Empirical Methods in Natural Language Processing*, pages 151–161.

Xu Sun. 2014a. Structure regularization for structured prediction. In *Advances in Neural Information Processing Systems 27: Annual Conference on Neural Information Processing Systems 2014*, pages 2402–2410.

Xu Sun. 2014b. Structure regularization for structured prediction: Theories and experiments. *CoRR*, abs/1411.6243.

Xu Sun, Xuancheng Ren, Shuming Ma, Bingzhen Wei, Wei Li, and Houfeng Wang. 2017a. Training simplification and model simplification for deep learning: A minimal effort back propagation method. *CoRR*, abs/1711.06528.

Xu Sun, Weiwei Sun, Shuming Ma, Xuancheng Ren, Yi Zhang, Wenjie Li, and Houfeng Wang. 2017b. Complex structure leads to overfitting: A structure regularization decoding method for natural language processing. *CoRR*, abs/1711.10331.

Linlin Wang, Zhu Cao, Gerard de Melo, and Zhiyuan Liu. 2016. Relation classification via multi-level attention CNNs. In *Proceedings of the 54th Annual Meeting of the Association for Computational Linguistics (Volume 1: Long Papers)*, pages 1298–1307.

Yizhong Wang, Sujian Li, Jingfeng Yang, Xu Sun, and Houfeng Wang. 2017. Tag-enhanced tree-structured neural networks for implicit discourse relation classification. In *Proceedings of the Eighth International Joint Conference on Natural Language Processing (Volume 1: Long Papers)*, pages 496–505.

Ji Wen. 2017. Structure regularized bidirectional recurrent convolutional neural network for relation classification. *CoRR*, abs/1711.02509.

Jingjing Xu, Ji Wen, Xu Sun, and Qi Su. 2017. A discourse-level named entity recognition and relation extraction dataset for chinese literature text. *CoRR*, abs/1711.07010.

Yan Xu, Lili Mou, Ge Li, Yunchuan Chen, Hao Peng, and Zhi Jin. 2015. Classifying relations via long short term memory networks along shortest dependency paths. In *Proceedings of the 2015 Conference on Empirical Methods in Natural Language Processing*, pages 1785–1794.

Matthew D. Zeiler. 2012. ADADELTA: an adaptive learning rate method. *CoRR*, abs/1212.5701.

Daojian Zeng, Kang Liu, Siwei Lai, Guangyou Zhou, and Jun Zhao. 2014. Relation classification via convolutional deep neural network. In *Proceedings of COLING 2014, the 25th International Conference on Computational Linguistics: Technical Papers*, pages 2335–2344.

Shu Zhang, Dequan Zheng, Xinchen Hu, and Ming Yang. 2015. Bidirectional long short-term memory networks for relation classification. In *Proceedings of the 29th Pacific Asia Conference on Language, Information and Computation*, pages 73–78.

Syntactic Patterns Improve Information Extraction for Medical Search

Roma Patel[12]**, Yinfei Yang**,* **Iain Marshall**[3]**, Ani Nenkova**[1] **and Byron C. Wallace**[4]

[1]Department of Computer and Information Science, University of Pennsylvania
[2]Department of Computer Science, Rutgers University-Camden
[3]Department of Primary Care and Public Health Sciences, Kings College London
[4]College of Computer and Information Science, Northeastern University

Abstract

Medical professionals search the published literature by specifying the type of *patients*, the medical *intervention(s)* and the *outcome* measure(s) of interest. In this paper we demonstrate how features encoding syntactic patterns improve the performance of state-of-the-art sequence tagging models (both linear and neural) for information extraction of these medically relevant categories. We present an analysis of the type of patterns exploited, and the semantic space induced for these, i.e., the distributed representations learned for identified multi-token patterns. We show that these learned representations differ substantially from those of the constituent unigrams, suggesting that the patterns capture contextual information that is otherwise lost.

1 Introduction

The efficacy of medical treatments depends on patient characteristics, treatment administration details (e.g., dosage) and the measures or outcomes used to quantify treatment success. These criteria should be precisely defined when searching the medical literature (Richardson et al., 1995; Heneghan and Badenoch, 2013; Miller and Forrest, 2001). Unfortunately, these aspects are not usually described in a structured way. Abstracts with explicit category headings (Nakayama et al., 2005) partially address this, but these are not standardized nor uniform. Automated solutions are thus emerging to better support medical search, including methods for: identifying sentences containing key pieces of clinical information (Wallace et al., 2016); summarization (Sarker et al., 2016); identifying contradictory claims in medical articles (Alamri and Stevenson, 2016); and information retrieval system prototypes that harness this type of information (Boudin et al., 2010a,b).

Several studies have assessed the use of the PICO framework (Huang et al., 2006; Demner-Fushman and Lin, 2007). Our task is also to identify spans of text describing *PICO elements* i.e., the participants (P), interventions (I)/comparators (C), and outcomes (O) in the abstracts of articles reporting findings from randomized controlled trails (RCTs). We exploit the availability of structured abstracts in the medical domain: from these coarse (multi-)sentence labels we derive patterns typically used in bootstrap methods for entity recognition and relation extraction (Carlson et al., 2010). We incorporate these patterns into supervised sequence labeling models to improve the identification of P, I and O spans in new texts. Below we show examples of each extraction type: patterns are bolded and target PICO description spans italicized. The extracted patterns disambiguate fairly well the type of information expressed in the segment when individual words (e.g., "children"), do not. **(P)** The trial included *230* **children with** *Stage-IV lymphoblastic leukemia ...*

(I) In Group I, the **children were treated** with *prednisone ...*

(O) .. reported that Group 2 **children underwent** fewer *isolated bone marrow relapses ..*

We explore three strategies for exploiting extracted patterns in a state-of-the-art LSTM-CRF sequence tagging model (Lample et al., 2016; Ma and Hovy, 2016): as additional features at the CRF layer; as one-hot indicators concatenated to distributed representations of words; and as individual units embedded in a semantic space shared with words. The second representation improves recall for two extraction tasks, and the third improves precision for all three tasks. We analyze the induced semantic space to show that patterns capture contextual information that is otherwise lost.

---

* now at Google Inc.

Proceedings of NAACL-HLT 2018, pages 371–377
New Orleans, Louisiana, June 1 - 6, 2018. ©2018 Association for Computational Linguistics

2   Data

For training sequence tagging models we use a corpus of 4,741 medical article abstracts with manual crowd-sourced annotations for P, I, and O sequences. For testing we use a set of 191 abstracts annotated for P, I, and O by medical professionals. There are 18,849 (831), 44,329 (1,808), 41,454 (1,711) variable length sequences for P, I, and O in the training (testing) data.[1]

For minimally supervised extraction of n-gram patterns, we use structured abstracts in which the authors describe different aspects of their work under targeted headings. We retrieved the headings and associated sections automatically from abstracts in XML format (downloaded from PubMed[2]). In general abstracts are structured idiosyncratically (often as Introduction, Methods, Results, Discussion). We capitalized on the minority of abstracts that used the explicit Participants, Intervention and Outcome headings. We obtained 50,000 segments for each of these three categories.

3   Patterns extraction and analysis

We extract syntactic patterns associated with each of the extraction types using AutoSlog-TS (Riloff, 1996), which consumes two sets of text: one relevant to an extraction domain and one irrelevant. In our case the relevant sets are the 50K P, I, and O sections, respectively, from the structured abstracts described above. The irrelevant set is a mix of 25K of the other two categories.

AutoSlog-TS generates n-gram patterns from input texts that capture the context of all noun phrases appearing as subject, direct and indirect object, or in a prepositional phrase. Each of these patterns is scored with the estimated probability that it occurred in an instance from the relevant set (out of all occurrences of the pattern), scaled by the number of times the pattern occurs (Riloff and Phillips, 2004). Common patterns that tend to occur in relevant sentences thus receive relatively high scores. We filter out patterns that contain digits, and those that occur fewer than 10 times in the structured abstract texts. Of the remaining patterns, we preserve those with probability 0.8 or

higher of occurring with the relevant class. This yields 3,499, 3,898 and 2,386 patterns associated with P, I and O, respectively.

The vast majority of patterns are bigrams: 90% for P, 81% for I and 86% O. Fewer than 0.5% of the n-grams for each type are trigrams, and the remaining are unigrams. Examples of extracted patterns include: *women_who*, *years_of* and *diagnosed_with* for P; *patients_received* and *performed_after* for I; and *scale_of*, *patients_reported* and *rate_of* for O.

The majority (82.86%) of the extracted n-gram patterns comprise a combination of a content word and a function/stopword token.[3] For example, the patterns *patients_with, patients_who* or *patients_from* are associated with the condition that a patient had, while *patients_were, patients_in* or *patients_received* describe the treatment they received. Function words provide disambiguating context for otherwise ambiguous words; this aids text classification and information retrieval (Riloff, 1995), and here we use them to improve sequence tagging models.

4   Patterns + linear CRF

For supervised IE models, we first consider including n-gram patterns as features in a linear-chain CRF (Lafferty et al., 2001). The standard set of token-level features used in the model include word identity, POS tag (from CoreNLP), and a list of binary features indicating whether the token is a digit, title (i.e., the first token only is uppercase), uppercase word, hyphenated word, or if the token is a punctuation mark (colon, fullstop or another symbol). In addition, features for the current token include the identity of the previous and next words, and the immediately preceding and following bi- and trigrams.

For the pattern-augmented CRF (**CRF-Pattern**), we add nine binary features that indicate if the current token and the immediately preceding/following bigrams are one of the AutoSlog-TS patterns associated with a given extraction type.[4] There are three indicators, for P, I and O respectively. For the context bigrams, a feature is 1 if the bigram is one of the bigram patterns associated with this extraction type, 0 otherwise. The remaining three indicators have value 1 if the current token is one of the

---

[1]The complete details of the corpus, along with inter-annotator analysis and links for download of the full corpus will be described in a forthcoming paper and eventually made available here: `http://www.byronwallace.com/EBM_abstracts_data`.

[2]`https://www.nlm.nih.gov/databases/download/pubmed_medline.html`

[3]We use stopwords from CoreNLP (Manning et al., 2014).

[4]We ignore trigram patterns as they constitute <0.5% of identified patterns.

Model	Precision			Recall			F1		
	P	I	O	P	I	O	P	I	O
CRF	70.29	47.01	64.78	38.75	43.89	10.47	49.95	45.39	18.02
CRF-Pattern	**73.3**	**52.1**	**66.37**	**40.62**	**45.41**	**44.07**	**52.27**	**48.52**	**52.96**
LSTM-CRF	62.27	52.37	**47.91**	49.48	40.49	**36.16**	55.14	45.67	**41.21**
LSTM-CRF-Pattern (best)	**76.10**	**58.25**	44.66	**64.75**	**43.39**	35.20	**69.97**	**49.74**	39.69
Before CRF	61.87	38.65	46.27	41.45	23.8	37.27	49.64	29.55	41.28
Before BiLSTM	**76.10**	**58.25**	44.66	**64.75**	43.39	35.20	**69.97**	**49.74**	39.69
Embedding	55.18	51.07	44.30	54.24	**47.41**	**41.60**	54.71	49.17	**42.91**

Table 1: Models for extracting **P**articipants, **I**ntervention and **O**utcomes with and without pattern features, evaluated via token-level precision, recall and F1 scores. The first and second groups of rows report results for CRF and LSTM-CRF models without and with pattern features. The bottom group reports results achieved using different means of incorporating pattern features in neural models.

unigram patterns associated with a given type. For example, the nine features for the token "chronic" in the sequence *patients with chronic sinus issues* will be [1,0,0—0,0,0—0,0,0] because *patients_with* is one of the bigrams associated with the P type, the word "chronic" does not match any of the unigram patterns and "sinus issues" does not match any of the bigram patterns. Table 1 (top) reports the performance on the test data of the original CRF model, and the one augmented with pattern features. Including patterns yields consistent and considerable improvements in both precision and recall.

5 Patterns + LSTM-CRF

LSTM-CRF models (Lample et al., 2016; Ma and Hovy, 2016) for sequence tagging are general in that they do not require feature engineering. Instead, the features representing each token in the CRF are generated by a bi-directional LSTM. To generate this representation the LSTM consumes distributed word representations as input and outputs vector representations describing words *in context* (the bi-LSTM runs one LSTM in each direction, concatenating outputs). This vector is passed to a CRF layer for prediction. Character-level information for each word is incorporated by running a bi-LSTM over the characters of each word (Lample et al., 2016). We used the IO tagging scheme. We set the hidden state dimensions to 200 and dropout to 0.5. We did not perform gradient clipping. We used the Adam optimizer (Kingma and Ba, 2014) with learning rate = 0.001.

We consider three alternatives for extending this model with patterns. The first two use the indicator features describing the presence of patterns in the context, similar to those we described above for the linear CRF model. The difference is where these features are introduced: immediately before the CRF layer, concatenated with the output of the

LSTMs (**Before CRF**), or as part of the input to the LSTM, concatenated to the distributed word and character representations (**Before LSTM**). We use Moen and Ananiadou (2013)'s release of 200 dimensional word vectors trained over 5.5 billion words from medical articles as pre-trained word embeddings as input to the LSTM. We use the same set of hyperparamaters for the LSTM as used in Lample et al. (2016), and do not optimize these for the present extraction tasks. The third alternative (**Embedding**) treats the patterns as collocations; we derive embedded representations for them as a unit, the way collocations are treated in Mikolov et al. (2013b). In training and during prediction each occurrence of a pattern in the input is treated as a single token with a corresponding distributed representation. Character-level representations are concatenated to word representations and the output of the LSTM cells is passed to the CRF to make predictions (as above).

For these embeddings, we collected 6 million PubMed abstracts (~1.4 billion words) filtering for only Human RCTs and used this to train word vectors using the Word2Vec tool (Mikolov et al., 2013a), inducing 200-dimensional vectors using the Skip-Gram model, where our vocabulary now consists of the learned n-gram patterns as single units, along with other unigrams. We then test these embedding representations by using them as input to our neural model for the structured prediction task.

6 Discussion of results

Table 1 reports the performance of the LSTM-CRF model achieved using each of the three strategies for incorporating pattern features discussed above. Inserting the pattern indicator features before the CRF layer yields the worst performance. Compared to the generic LSTM-CRF model, its F-measure is lower or the same for all three ex-

n-gram	similar to n-gram	similar to unigram
have_children	1: *marry* 2: *conceive* 3: *breast-feed* 4: *be_pregnant* 5: *have_surgery*	1: *adults* 2: *adolescents* 3: *toddlers* 4: *youngsters* 5: *school-age*
condition_at	1: *status_at* 2: *features_at* 3: *outcome_at* 4: *qol_at* 5: *outcomes*	1: *circumstance* 2: *conditions* 3: *malady* 4: *ailment* 5: *situation*
filled_with	1: *covered_with* 2: *mixed_with* 3: *sealed_with* 4: *suspended* 5: *immersed_in*	1: *sealed* 2: *obturated* 3: *enclosed* 4: *enclosing* 5: *fill*
side_**effects**	1: *toxicities* 2: *side-effect* 3: *complications* 4: *AEs* 5: *nausea*	1: *effect* 2: *Effects* 3: *action* 4: *impact* 5: *influence*

Table 2: Example illustrating the shift in semantic space realized using pattern embeddings. For each of the listed n-grams, we report the top 5 most similar words to: (1) the n-gram pattern embedding, and, (2) the most relevant constituent n-gram i.e., the word in bold font.

traction categories, P, I, O.

Including the pattern features as input to the LSTM or as part of the embedding leads to substantial improvements over the baseline model, and this despite the smaller dataset over which pattern embeddings were learned: compared to the LSTM-CRF without pattern features, the former markedly improves precision for P and I, while the latter improves the recall for all three types. In terms of F-measure, best results for P and I are achieved by inserting the pattern features as input to the LSTM, with about 15% and 4% absolute improvement. For O, the best F-measure is achieved by incorporating patterns as part of the embeddings, yielding 1% absolute improvement.

The linear CRF and its variant enriched with pattern feature has the best precision, outperforming the LSTM-CRF models, but worse recall. It may still be useful for scenarios in which high precision extraction is needed.

7 Semantics of pattern embeddings

We established that syntactic patterns can markedly improve the extraction of patient, intervention and outcome descriptions in medical abstracts. We now turn to an analysis of how the patterns fit into the semantic space of word embeddings. Our goal is to quantify the extent to which including pattern representations changes which words will be considered similar to the pattern, but not to the words that compose it.

To this end, we find the ten words most similar (under cosine similarity) to each pattern, and those most similar to the individual words these comprise, in the embedding space. We analyze the size of the intersection of these two sets for all patterns (∼10,000). To simplify the comparison we consider only the constituent word that has the largest intersection of similar words with the pattern of interest. The size of the intersection theoretically ranges from 0 to 10, but on average there is only

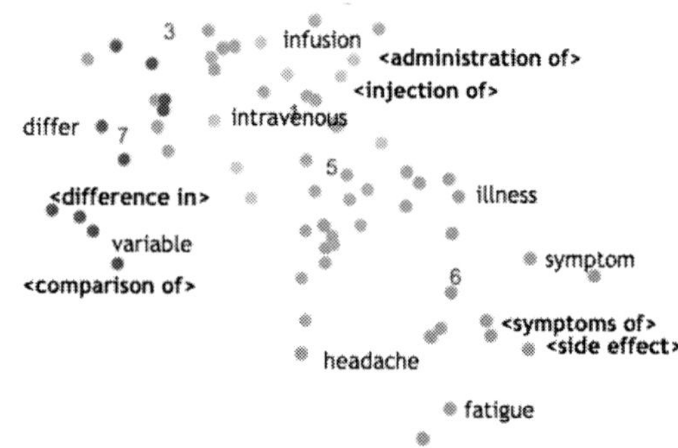

Figure 1: Scatter of PCA-reduced embeddings clustered using K-means. <> brackets show the syntactic pattern n-grams given by Autoslog-TS that are embedding in the same space as unigrams.

one word overlap between the words most similar with the pattern and those most similar with the constituent word. For the majority (61%) of the pattern–constituent word pairs, there is no overlap between the top 10 most similar words. To make this discussion more concrete, Table 2 provides examples of the top 5 most similar words to select bigram patterns and the constituent unigram with greatest overlap, shown in italics. The patterns encode disambiguating context that was previously lost in unigram representations.

Finally, we present a scatter of learned embeddings, reduced via IncrementalPCA[5] in Figure 1. Embedded patterns cluster more intuitively than their content words alone. For example, the patterns *injection_of* and *administration_of* cluster together, along with other topically similar unigrams such as *infusion* and *intravenous* that may all correspond to Intervention terms. Similarly, *side_effect* is very different from its constituent words *side* or *effect*, and moreover, clusters with actual side effects like *headache* and *fatigue* that patients may suffer from in the course of a trial.

---

[5] We use the implementation in *scikit-learn* (Pedregosa et al., 2011).

Model	Precision			Recall			F1		
	P	I	O	P	I	O	P	I	O
LSTM-CRF	62.27	52.37	**47.91**	49.48	40.49	36.16	55.14	45.67	**41.21**
LSTM-CRF (Bigrams)	64.41	53.37	43.20	50.33	41.24	**37.32**	59.91	46.52	40.04
LSTM-CRF (Autoslog)	**76.10**	**58.25**	44.66	**64.75**	**43.39**	35.20	**69.97**	**49.74**	39.69

Table 3: Results to illustrate syntactic nature of Autoslog bigrams. Row 1 shows results of baseline model with no added features. Row 2 shows results of the model that uses all bigrams as features and Row 3 shows results of the model that uses only Autoslog extracted bigrams as features. Features are added before the LSTM, as incorporated in the best working model from Table 1.

8 Syntactic patterns vs bigrams

Our experiments show that using these bigram features extracted by AutoSlog improves model predictions. AutoSlog takes a fundamentally syntax-driven approach to identifying patterns, which suggests the discovered patterns (and associated performance boost) is due to exploiting syntax. However, the performance gains could also be due to additional contextual information that bigrams and larger n-grams provide over unigrams alone, rather than their syntactic properties.

We therefore performed an experiment to assess the influence of the syntactic AutoSlog bigrams, as compared to general bigram features. We consider the same data used as input to AutoSlog, i.e., 50,000 segments for the three categories P, I, and O. In the same setup, we decompose sentences within each category into bigrams, and collect bigram counts in the respective categories. We calculate precision for each category by collapsing the other two categories, similar to the AutoSlog procedure. We use the same threshold values as AutoSlog for filtering, i.e., we remove bigrams that occur fewer than 10 times or that have a score <0.8 of occuring with the target class out of all occurrences. This procedure for identifying predictive bigrams yields a notably larger number of bigrams (30k) than AutoSlog ($\sim$10K). Table 3 shows that while using generic bigrams as features sometimes leads to small improvements, the AutoSlog induced pattern bigrams result in substantially better performance. This suggests that the exploitation of syntactic structure in identifying patterns is indeed important. We also compare the performance of word2vec embeddings for unigrams and bigrams, and extended with collocations and syntactic patterns, trained on exactly the same data. In the experiments reported in Table 1, the unigram embeddings are trained on a larger dataset of generic medical text while the patterns are trained on a smaller set of medical abstracts describing RCTs. In addition here we compare the AutoSlog patterns with collocations discovered by word2vec. Representing collocations leads to markedly lower F-score (Table 4). Representing bigrams leads to prediction performance better than that with collocations, but worse than unigrams.

Standard unigram representations that we trained work better than the off-the-shelf medical representations, possibly because they were trained specifically on abstracts of papers reporting the conduct and results of RCTs and thus better fit the abstracts we are analyzing. Most importantly, the LSTM-CRF with syntactic pattern embeddings results in the best observed performance.

Embedding	Vocabulary	P	I	O
Unigram	947,670	54.31	46.19	**42.68**
Bigram	9,326,144	52.01	43.71	38.77
collocation	1,254,863	50.31	40.21	40.21
Pattern	949,112	**54.71**	**47.68**	42.27

Table 4: LSTM-CRF predictions on word embeddings trained on the same 6 million documents. Column 1 shows the type of embedding, column 2 shows the size of the vocabulary and columns 3-5 show F1 score.

9 Conclusions

We presented a method for exploiting abundant unlabeled biomedical texts to generate minimally supervised extraction patterns that improve generic supervised models for sequence tagging in this domain. We explored alternative ways to incorporating the patterns in both linear and neural tagging models. In the latter, we analyzed the changes in semantic space that likely explain the observed gains in predictive performance.

10 Acknowledgements

This work was supported in part by the National Cancer Institute (NCI) of the National Institutes of Health (NIH), award number UH2CA203711 and the National Science Foundation (NSF), award number CCF-1433220.

References

Abdulaziz Alamri and Mark Stevenson. 2016. A corpus of potentially contradictory research claims from cardiovascular research abstracts. *Journal of biomedical semantics* 7(1):36.

Florian Boudin, Jian-Yun Nie, and Martin Dawes. 2010a. Clinical information retrieval using document and PICO structure. In *Human Language Technologies: Conference of the North American Chapter of the Association of Computational Linguistics, Proceedings, June 2-4, 2010, Los Angeles, California, USA.* pages 822–830.

Florian Boudin, Lixin Shi, and Jian-Yun Nie. 2010b. Improving medical information retrieval with PICO element detection. In *Advances in Information Retrieval, 32nd European Conference on IR Research, ECIR 2010, Milton Keynes, UK, March 28-31, 2010. Proceedings.* pages 50–61.

Andrew Carlson, Justin Betteridge, Bryan Kisiel, Burr Settles, Estevam R. Hruschka Jr., and Tom M. Mitchell. 2010. Toward an architecture for never-ending language learning. In *Proceedings of the Twenty-Fourth AAAI Conference on Artificial Intelligence, AAAI 2010, Atlanta, Georgia, USA, July 11-15, 2010.*

Dina Demner-Fushman and Jimmy Lin. 2007. Answering clinical questions with knowledge-based and statistical techniques. *Computational Linguistics* 33(1):63–103.

Carl Heneghan and Douglas Badenoch. 2013. *Evidence-based medicine toolkit.* John Wiley & Sons.

Xiaoli Huang, Jimmy Lin, and Dina Demner-Fushman. 2006. Evaluation of pico as a knowledge representation for clinical questions. In *AMIA annual symposium proceedings.* American Medical Informatics Association, volume 2006, page 359.

Diederik P Kingma and Jimmy Ba. 2014. Adam: A method for stochastic optimization. *arXiv preprint arXiv:1412.6980* .

John Lafferty, Andrew McCallum, and Fernando CN Pereira. 2001. Conditional random fields: Probabilistic models for segmenting and labeling sequence data .

Guillaume Lample, Miguel Ballesteros, Sandeep Subramanian, Kazuya Kawakami, and Chris Dyer. 2016. Neural architectures for named entity recognition. In *Proceedings of NAACL-HLT.* pages 260–270.

Xuezhe Ma and Eduard Hovy. 2016. End-to-end sequence labeling via bi-directional lstm-cnns-crf. In *Proceedings of the 54th Annual Meeting of the Association for Computational Linguistics (Volume 1: Long Papers).* Association for Computational Linguistics, Berlin, Germany, pages 1064–1074. http://www.aclweb.org/anthology/P16-1101.

Christopher D. Manning, Mihai Surdeanu, John Bauer, Jenny Rose Finkel, Steven Bethard, and David McClosky. 2014. The stanford corenlp natural language processing toolkit. In *Proceedings of the 52nd Annual Meeting of the Association for Computational Linguistics, ACL 2014, June 22-27, 2014, Baltimore, MD, USA, System Demonstrations.* pages 55–60.

Tomas Mikolov, Kai Chen, Greg Corrado, and Jeffrey Dean. 2013a. Efficient estimation of word representations in vector space. corr abs/1301.3781 (2013).

Tomas Mikolov, Ilya Sutskever, Kai Chen, Greg S Corrado, and Jeff Dean. 2013b. Distributed representations of words and phrases and their compositionality. In *Advances in neural information processing systems.* pages 3111–3119.

Syrene A Miller and Jane L Forrest. 2001. Enhancing your practice through evidence-based decision making: PICO, learning how to ask good questions. *Journal of Evidence Based Dental Practice* 1(2):136–141.

SPFGH Moen and Tapio Salakoski2 Sophia Ananiadou. 2013. Distributional semantics resources for biomedical text processing.

Takeo Nakayama, Nobuko Hirai, Shigeaki Yamazaki, and Mariko Naito. 2005. Adoption of structured abstracts by general medical journals and format for a structured abstract. *Journal of the Medical Library Association* 93(2):237.

F. Pedregosa, G. Varoquaux, A. Gramfort, V. Michel, B. Thirion, O. Grisel, M. Blondel, P. Prettenhofer, R. Weiss, V. Dubourg, J. Vanderplas, A. Passos, D. Cournapeau, M. Brucher, M. Perrot, and E. Duchesnay. 2011. Scikit-learn: Machine learning in Python. *Journal of Machine Learning Research* 12:2825–2830.

W Scott Richardson, Mark C Wilson, Jim Nishikawa, and Robert SA Hayward. 1995. The well-built clinical question: a key to evidence-based decisions. *ACP journal club* 123(3):A12–A12.

Ellen Riloff. 1995. Little words can make a big difference for text classification. In *Proceedings of the 18th annual international ACM SIGIR conference on Research and development in information retrieval.* ACM, pages 130–136.

Ellen Riloff. 1996. Automatically generating extraction patterns from untagged text. In *Proceedings of the Thirteenth National Conference on Artificial Intelligence - Volume 2.* AAAI Press, AAAI'96, pages 1044–1049. http://dl.acm.org/citation.cfm?id=1864519.1864542.

Ellen Riloff and William Phillips. 2004. An introduction to the sundance and autoslog systems. Technical report.

Abeed Sarker, Diego Mollá, and Cecile Paris. 2016. Query-oriented evidence extraction to support evidence-based medicine practice. *Journal of biomedical informatics* 59:169–184.

Byron C. Wallace, Joël Kuiper, Aakash Sharma, Mingxi (Brian) Zhu, and Iain James Marshall. 2016. Extracting PICO sentences from clinical trial reports using supervised distant supervision. *Journal of Machine Learning Research* 17:132:1–132:25.

Syntactically Aware Neural Architectures for Definition Extraction

Luis Espinosa-Anke and **Steven Schockaert**
School of Computer Science and Informatics
Cardiff University
{espinosa-ankel,schockaertsl}@cardiff.ac.uk

Abstract

Automatically identifying definitional knowledge in text corpora (Definition Extraction or DE) is an important task with direct applications in, among others, Automatic Glossary Generation, Taxonomy Learning, Question Answering and Semantic Search. It is generally cast as a binary classification problem between definitional and non-definitional sentences. In this paper we present a set of neural architectures combining Convolutional and Recurrent Neural Networks, which are further enriched by incorporating linguistic information via syntactic dependencies. Our experimental results in the task of sentence classification, on two benchmarking DE datasets (one generic, one domain-specific), show that these models obtain consistent state of the art results. Furthermore, we demonstrate that models trained on clean Wikipedia-like definitions can successfully be applied to more noisy domain-specific corpora.

1 Introduction

Dictionaries and glossaries are among the most important sources of meaning for humankind. Compiling, updating and translating them has traditionally been left mostly to domain experts and professional lexicographers. However, the last two decades have witnessed a growing interest in automating the construction of lexicographic resources.

Analogously, in Natural Language Processing (NLP), lexicographic resources have proven useful for a myriad of tasks, for example Word Sense Disambiguation (Banerjee and Pedersen, 2002; Navigli and Velardi, 2005; Agirre and Soroa, 2009; Camacho-Collados et al., 2015), Taxonomy Learning (Velardi et al., 2013; Espinosa-Anke et al., 2016b) or Information Extraction (Richardson et al., 1998; Delli Bovi et al., 2015). Moreover,

lexicographic information such as definitions constitutes the cornerstone of important language resources for NLP, such as WordNet (Miller et al., 1990), BabelNet (Navigli and Ponzetto, 2012), Wikidata (Vrandečić and Krötzsch, 2014) and basically any Wikipedia-derived resource.

In this context, systems able to address the problem of *Definition Extraction* (DE), i.e., identifying definitional information spanning in free text, are of great value both for computational lexicography and for NLP. In the early days of DE, rule-based approaches leveraged linguistic cues observed in definitional data (Rebeyrolle and Tanguy, 2000; Klavans and Muresan, 2001; Malaisé et al., 2004; Saggion and Gaizauskas, 2004; Storrer and Wellinghoff, 2006). However, in order to deal with problems like language dependence and domain specificity, machine learning was incorporated in more recent contributions (Del Gaudio et al., 2013), which focused on encoding informative lexico-syntactic patterns in feature vectors (Cui et al., 2005; Fahmi and Bouma, 2006; Westerhout and Monachesi, 2007; Borg et al., 2009), both in supervised and semi-supervised settings (Reiplinger et al., 2012; Faralli and Navigli, 2013).

On the other hand, while encoding definitional information using deep learning techniques has been addressed in the past (Hill et al., 2015; Noraset et al., 2016), to the best of our knowledge no previous work has tackled the problem of DE by reconciling both the linguistic lessons learned in the past decades (e.g., the importance of lexico syntactic patterns or long-distance relations between *definiendum* and *definiens*)[1] and the processing potential of neural networks.

Thus, we propose to bridge this gap by learning high level features over candidate definitions

---

[1] Traditionally, a *definienidum* is a term being defined, whereas the *definiens* refers to its differentiable characteristics.

378

Proceedings of NAACL-HLT 2018, pages 378–385
New Orleans, Louisiana, June 1 - 6, 2018. ©2018 Association for Computational Linguistics

via convolutional filters, and then apply recurrent neural networks to learn long term dependencies over these feature maps. Without preprocessing and only taking pretrained embeddings as input, it is already possible to consistently obtain state of the art results in two benchmarking datasets for DE (one generic, one domain-specific). Further improvements over this simple model are obtained by incorporating syntactic information by composing and embedding head-modifier syntactic dependencies and dependency labels. One interesting side result of our experiments is the observation that a model trained only on canonical wikipedia-like definitions performs significantly better in a domain-specific academic setting than a model that has been trained on that domain, which somewhat contradicts previously assumed notions about the creativity of academic authors when presenting and describing novel terminology.[2]

2 Method

The impact of deep learning methods in NLP is today indisputable. The utilization of neural networks has improved the state of the art almost systematically in a wide number of tasks, from language modeling (Bengio et al., 2003; Yih et al., 2011; Mikolov et al., 2013) to text classification (Kim, 2014) or machine translation (Bahdanau et al., 2014), among many others.

In this paper we leverage two of the most popular architectures in deep learning for NLP with the goal to predict, given an input sentence, its probability of including definitional knowledge. In our best performing model we take advantage of Convolutional Neural Networks (CNNs) to learn local features via convolved filters (LeCun et al., 1998), and then apply to the learned feature maps a Bidirectional Long Short Term Memory (blstm) network (Hochreiter and Schmidhuber, 1997). In this way, we aim at capturing ngram-wise features (Zhou et al., 2015), which may be strong indicators of definitional patterns (e.g., the classic *X is a Y* pattern), combined with the learning of long-term sequential dependencies over these learned feature maps.

Following standard notation for sentence modeling via CNNs (Kim, 2014), we let $x_i \in \mathbb{R}^k$ be the k-dimensional word vector associated to the i-th word in an input sentence **S**. We use as pre-

trained embeddings the *word2vec* (Mikolov et al., 2013) vectors trained with negative sampling on the Google News corpus[3]. Each sentence is represented as an $n \times k$ matrix $\mathcal{S}$, where n is the size of the longest sentence in the corpus (using padding where necessary). The convolution layer applies a filter $\mathbf{w_j} \in \mathbb{R}^{(h+1)k}$ to each ngram window of $h+1$ tokens. Specifically, writing $\mathbf{x_{i:i+h}}$ for the concatenation of the word vectors $\mathbf{x_i}, \mathbf{x_{i+1}}, ..., \mathbf{x_{i+h}}$, we have:

$$c_j^i = f\left(\mathbf{w_j} \cdot \mathbf{x_{i:i+h}} + b_j\right)$$

where $b_j \in \mathbb{R}$ is a bias term and f is the ReLu activation function (Nair and Hinton, 2010). In total, we use 100 such convolutional features, i.e. we use the vector $\mathbf{c^i} = \left[c_1^i, c_2^i, \cdots, c_{100}^i\right]$ to encode the ith ngram. We empirically set the length $h+1$ of each ngram to 3. To reduce the size of the representation, we then use a max pooling layer with a pool size of 4. Let us write $\mathbf{d^i} = \left[d_1^i, d_2^i, \cdots, d_{97}^i\right]$, where $d_j^i = \max(d_j^i, d_j^{i+1}, d_j^{i+2}, d_j^{i+3})$. The input sentence S is then represented as the sequence $\mathbf{d^1}, \mathbf{d^5}, \mathbf{d^9}, ..., \mathbf{d^{n-3}}$, which is used as the input to a bidirectional LSTM (BLSTM) layer. Finally, the output vectors of the final states for both directions of this BLSTM are connected to a single neuron with a sigmoid activation function. In all the experiments reported in this paper, we classify a sentence as definitional when the output of this neuron yields a value which is at least 0.5.

2.1 Incorporating Syntactic Information

The role of syntax has been extensively studied for improving semantic modeling of domain terminologies. Examples where syntactic cues are leveraged include medical acronym expansion (Pustejovsky et al., 2001), hyponym-hypernym extraction and detection (Hearst, 1992; Shwartz et al., 2016), and definition extraction either from the web (Saggion and Gaizauskas, 2004), scholarly articles (Reiplinger et al., 2012), and more recently from Wikipedia-like definitions (Boella et al., 2014).

However, the interplay between syntactic information and the generalization potential of neural networks remains unexplored in definition modeling, although intuitively it seems reasonable to assume that a syntax-informed architecture should have more tools at its disposal for discriminating

---

[2]Code available at `bitbucket.org/ luisespinosa/neural_de`

[3]`code.google.com/archive/p/word2vec/`

between definitional and non-definitional knowledge. As an example of the importance of syntax in encyclopedic definitions, among the definitions contained in the WCL definition corpus (see Section 3.1), 71% of them include the lexico-syntactic pattern $\text{noun} \xleftarrow{\text{subj}} \text{is} \xrightarrow{\text{dobj}} \text{noun}$. To explore the potential of syntactic information, we represent dependency-based phrases by embedding them in the same vector space as the pretrained word embeddings introduced above. This approach draws from previous work on modeling phrases by composing their parts and the relations that link them (Socher et al., 2011, 2013, 2014).

Specifically, let $\mathcal{S}_d$ be the list of head-modifier relations obtained by parsing[4] sentence **S**. Each relation r in $\mathcal{S}_d$ is a head-modifier tuple $\langle h, m, l \rangle$. Here l denotes the dependency label of the relation (e.g., *nsubj*), which we represent as the vector $\mathbf{r} = \frac{1}{2}(\mathbf{h} + \mathbf{m})$, with $\mathbf{h}$ and $\mathbf{m}$ the vector representations of words h and m respectively. This setting for composing first-order head-modifier relations is similar to the one proposed in Dyer et al. (2015) for dependency parsing. This leads to a represention of the sentence as a sequence $\mathbf{r_1}, ..., \mathbf{r_{|\mathcal{S}_d|}}$, which preserves the original order of head words. The intuition is that this "coarser" grained sorting[5] provides integrated semantic-syntactic information that can be leveraged both by the convolutional feature extraction step, and more importantly, by the sequential BLSTM module.

Then, for each sentence we concatenate the dependency-based representation $\mathbf{r_1}, ..., \mathbf{r_{|\mathcal{S}_d|}}$ to the word vector sequence $\mathbf{x_1}, ..., \mathbf{x_n}$, to obtain the input to the convolutional layer of our model. It is worth mentioning that we tried different merging schemes (concatenation, but also dot product and averaging) at different layers, and found that the best way to inform our neural definition extractor is to encode this syntactic information explicitly at input time. Finally, we also explore the effect of enriching the input representation with the information of the dependency label. For each sentence, we enrich each head-modifier mean vector $\mathbf{r_i}$ by concatenating them a one-hot representation of their corresponding dependency label. The search space of these labels is 46 (e.g., *nsubj* or *dobj*). An illustrative diagram of our proposed architecture is provided in Figure 1.

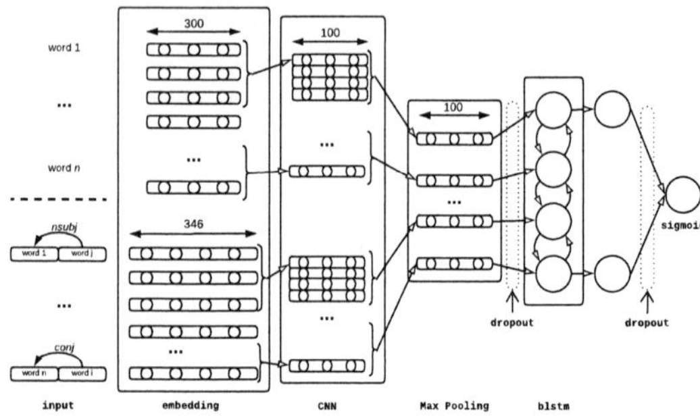

Figure 1: Architecture of our proposed definition extraction model. Input may be either simple pretrained embeddings or syntactically enriched representations (separated by the dotted line).

3 Evaluation

3.1 Evaluation data

WCL: The WCL (World-Class Lattices) dataset (Navigli et al., 2010) consists of manually annotated Wikipedia definitions and distractors (1,871 and 2,847 respectively). These distractors are sentences that also include the term (i.e., the Wikpedia page title) and are what the authors call "syntactically plausible false definitions". The style of the definitions is fairly consistent, and follows in most cases the Aristotelian *genus et differentia* structure of a definition (A is a B which C). We list below both an example definition and one of its distractors:

✓ *The **Amiga** is a family of personal computers originally developed by Amiga Corporation.*

✗ *Development on the **Amiga** began in 1982 with Jay Miner as the principal hardware designer.*

W00: Introduced in Jin et al. (2013), this corpus consists of a collection of 731 definition sentences compiled from the ACL-ARC anthology (Bird et al., 2008), and 1454 distractors. Their style is different[6], as they are used mostly for introducing and describing novel terminology in NLP research papers. Let us show an example for each sentence class:

---

[4]We use the dependency parser provided in the SpaCy NLP library: `spacy.io`.

[5]It is coarser because in a dependency tree modifiers naturally lose their original order.

[6]In lexicographic terms, most definitions in this dataset would be classified either as *extensional* (definition without hypernym) or *functional* (define something by *what it does*, instead of what it is).

✓ *Our system, **SNS** (pronounced "essence"), retrieves documents related to an unrestricted user query and summarizes a subset of them as selected by the user.*

✗ *The **senses** with the highest confidence scores are the senses that contribute the most to the maximization function for the set .*

3.2 Baselines

Let us provide a succint description of each competing baseline. **(1) WCL**: An algorithm that learns word-class lattices for modeling higher-level features over shallow parsing and part of speech (Navigli and Velardi, 2010). **(2) DefMiner**: A CRF-based sequential modeling system trained with lexical, terminological and structural (e.g., document position) features (Jin et al., 2013). **(3) B&DC**: A binary classifier trained with dependency paths over input sentences (Boella et al., 2014). **(4) E&S**: A system based on more complex dependency-based features (Espinosa-Anke and Saggion, 2014). **(5) LSTM-POS**: An LSTM-based system which represents each sentence as a mixture of infrequent words and frequent words' associated part-of-speech (Li et al., 2016).

As for our proposed models, we include results for a CNN architecture alone (**CNN**), as well as for the proposed CNN and BLSTM (**C-BLSTM**) combination. For both architectures, subscripts d or l denote the syntactically informed variant without and with one-hot label encoding information, respectively. Finally, among the many hyperparameters that can be explored, we report the impact of the dimensionality of the output vectors of the BLSTM layer, with sizes of 100 and 300. We did not attempt to tune the other hyperparameters.

Experiment 1: In-domain 10-fold CV

In this experiment, we compare the performance of different configurations of our proposed model with previous contributions in a 10-fold cross validation (CV) setting. The experimental results, listed in Table 1, show that a fairly simple CNN architecture with no preprocessing already achieves remarkably strong results, especially for the WCL dataset. Among our proposed systems, the overall best performance in Wikipedia definitions is obtained by the CNN_l configuration. However, incorporating a BLSTM layer contributes towards the best performing model on the NLP-specific

	WCL			W00		
	P	R	F1	P	R	F1
WCL	**98.8**	60.7	75.2	-	-	-
DefMiner	92.0	79.0	85.0	-	-	-
B&DC	88.0	76.0	81.6	-	-	-
E&S	85.9	85.3	85.4	-	-	-
LSTM-POS	90.4	92.0	91.2	-	-	-
CNN	91.1	92.0	91.5	33.5	68.7	44.8
CNN_d	90.6	90.9	90.7	34.2	**69.4**	45.8
CNN_l	94.2	**94.2**	**94.2**	42.8	65.5	51.3
C-BLSTM100	93.3	91.8	92.5	46.1	68.7	54.5
$C\text{-}BLSTM100_d$	93.2	92.2	92.6	**52.0**	67.6	**57.4**
$C\text{-}BLSTM100_l$	93.2	92.7	92.9	51.7	66.2	57.3
C-BLSTM300	93.4	92.3	92.7	48.9	64.5	54.0
$C\text{-}BLSTM300_d$	94.3	91.0	92.6	47.3	64.0	51.9
$C\text{-}BLSTM300_l$	94.0	90.7	92.5	50.0	64.5	53.8

Table 1: Comparative results between previous contributions and different configurations of our proposed contribution.

dataset ($C\text{-}BLSTM100_d$). Several conclusions can be drawn from these results. First, CNNs are capable of capturing a great deal of Wikipedia-like definitional information. This probably owes to the fairly recurrent linguistic structure of these definitions. On the contrary, however, LSTMs seem necessary in more complex scenarios, e.g., in those presented in the W00 dataset. Here, we argue that long term dependencies may play an important role, for example, for capturing cases where a full-fledged definitions appear spanning only over the last tokens of a sentence. Finally, syntax seems to help for most configurations, and for both datasets, although the difference is more pronounced in the more challenging W00 dataset.

These differences in performance are, however, small enough to make it difficult to draw strong conclusions other than that neural network architectures are a sensible choice for this task, and that syntax can play an important role depending on the type of data to be processed. It is important to highlight, finally, that depending on the application, one may be more interested in having an almost perfect precision (as in the system described in Navigli and Velardi (2010)). For automatic glossary generation from text, on the other hand, having a more balanced model, with high recall at the expense of only slightly lower precision, may be preferred, as automatic glossaries usually undergo a human post-editing and revision step.

Experiment 2: Cross-domain DE

In this experiment we assess the performance of a cross-domain model on the W00 dataset (cf. Section 3.1). The main goal is to verify to what extent a model trained only on Wikipedia-like definitions can do well in a domain-specific setting. To this end, we apply our best performing configuration trained on the whole WCL corpus to the W00 dataset (**WCL>W00**), and compare it with the performance of our best configuration as per 10-fold CV (**C-BLSTM100$_d$**, see Table 1). This experiment is important, for example, for learning what would be more appropriate if we were to aim at constructing domain-specific glossaries or at extracting highly specific semantic relations from a domain terminology.

System	Precision	Recall	F-Score
C-BLSTM100$_d$	52.0	67.6	57.4
WCL>W00	**69.0**	**71.0**	**70.0**

Table 2: Results of our proposed model (with two different training schemes) on the NLP-specific W00 definition dataset.

The results in Table 2 reveal that, despite differences in style, a system modeled over encyclopedic definitions outperforms a neural model trained only on these idiosyncratic definitions. This might be due to several reasons. First, because of the slightly smaller size of this dataset. And second, the more noisy nature of the corpus may pose a stronger challenge for a neural model to identify recurrent definitional patterns. Still, our experimental results seem to suggest that these patterns do exist, as evidenced by the strong performance of the Wikipedia-trained model.

Qualitative Evaluation

We run our best performing model over a subset of the ACL-ARC anthology (Bird et al., 2008), specifically the subcorpus described in (Espinosa-Anke et al., 2016a), which removed noisy sentences as produced by the pdf to text conversion.

In Table 3 we show three high quality definitions discovered by our model, as well as three false positives. We may highlight the somewhat surprising remarkable capacity of the model to identify definitions beyond the is-a pattern (e.g.,

using the verb 'mean') and with long-distance dependencies between subject and object. As for the incorrect cases, we find that for this model to be used in the automatic glossary construction task, in addition to further refinement, it would have to be coupled with a term extraction system so that only definitions associated to meaningful domain terms are extracted.

```
compositional grammar means that the
semantics of a a phrase is composed of
the semantics of the subphrases
```
```
f-score is the harmonic mean of recall
(r) and precision (p) percentages
```
```
silc is a language and encoding
identification system developed by
the rali laboratory at the university
of montreal
```
```
the main lesson is that complex
sentences are analysed with a proper
understanding without sacrificing
efficiency
```
```
a simple spell correction is a part
of the system (essentially 1 character
errors)
```
```
the segmentation of a translation
memory is a key feature for our system
```

Table 3: Examples of extracted definitions with over 0.9 confidence from a subset of the ACL-ARC corpus.

4 Conclusion

We have presented and evaluated a neural model based on CNNs and Bidirectional LSTMs which obtains state of the art results on two well known *definition extraction* datasets. From our experiments, it stems that: (1) Neural network architectures perform well for identifying definitional text snippets in corpora, more so with syntactic information; (2) A model trained on Wikipedia is competitive even in a domain-specific setting; and (3) More complex linguistic structures seem to be better captured with more complex models. As for future work, it would be interesting to explore whether meaningful further gains can be obtained by performing hyperparameter tuning.

Acknowledgments

We thank the anonymous reviewers for their helpful comments. We would also like to thank Miguel Ballesteros for fruitful discussions. This work was supported by ERC Starting Grant 637277.

References

Eneko Agirre and Aitor Soroa. 2009. Personalizing pagerank for word sense disambiguation. In *Proceedings of the 12th Conference of the European Chapter of the Association for Computational Linguistics*. Association for Computational Linguistics, pages 33–41.

Dzmitry Bahdanau, Kyunghyun Cho, and Yoshua Bengio. 2014. Neural machine translation by jointly learning to align and translate. *arXiv preprint arXiv:1409.0473*.

Satanjeev Banerjee and Ted Pedersen. 2002. An adapted lesk algorithm for word sense disambiguation using wordnet. In *International Conference on Intelligent Text Processing and Computational Linguistics*. Springer, pages 136–145.

Yoshua Bengio, Réjean Ducharme, Pascal Vincent, and Christian Jauvin. 2003. A neural probabilistic language model. *Journal of machine learning research* 3(Feb):1137–1155.

Steven Bird, Robert Dale, Bonnie Dorr, Bryan Gibson, Mark Joseph, Min-Yen Kan, Dongwon Lee, Brett Powley, Dragomir Radev, and Yee Fan Tan. 2008. The ACL Anthology reference corpus: A reference dataset for bibliographic research in computational linguistics. In *Proceedings of the Sixth International Conference on Language Resources and Evaluation (LREC-08)*. European Language Resources Association (ELRA), Marrakech, Morocco. ACL Anthology Identifier: L08-1005.

Guido Boella, Luigi Di Caro, Alice Ruggeri, and Livio Robaldo. 2014. Learning from syntax generalizations for automatic semantic annotation. *Journal of Intelligent Information Systems* pages 1–16.

Claudia Borg, Michael Rosner, and Gordon Pace. 2009. Evolutionary algorithms for definition extraction. In *Proceedings of the 1st Workshop in Definition Extraction*.

José Camacho-Collados, Mohammad Taher Pilehvar, and Roberto Navigli. 2015. A unified multilingual semantic representation of concepts. In *ACL (1)*. pages 741–751.

Hang Cui, Min-Yen Kan, and Tat-Seng Chua. 2005. Generic soft pattern models for definitional question answering. In *Proceedings of the 28th annual international ACM SIGIR conference on Research and development in information retrieval*. ACM, pages 384–391.

Rosa Del Gaudio, Gustavo Batista, and António Branco. 2013. Coping with highly imbalanced datasets: A case study with definition extraction in a multilingual setting. *Natural Language Engineering* pages 1–33.

Claudio Delli Bovi, Luca Telesca, and Roberto Navigli. 2015. Large-scale information extraction from textual definitions through deep syntactic and semantic analysis. *TACL* 3:529–543.

Chris Dyer, Miguel Ballesteros, Wang Ling, Austin Matthews, and Noah A Smith. 2015. Transition-based dependency parsing with stack long short-term memory. *arXiv preprint arXiv:1505.08075*.

Luis Espinosa-Anke, Roberto Carlini, Horacio Saggion, and Francesco Ronzano. 2016a. Defext: A semi supervised definition extraction tool. In *Globalex,*.

Luis Espinosa-Anke and Horacio Saggion. 2014. Applying dependency relations to definition extraction. In *Natural Language Processing and Information Systems*, Springer, pages 63–74.

Luis Espinosa-Anke, Horacio Saggion, Francesco Ronzano, and Roberto Navigli. 2016b. Extasem! extending, taxonomizing and semantifying domain terminologies. In *Proceedings of the 30th Conference on Artificial Intelligence (AAAI16)*.

Ismail Fahmi and Gosse Bouma. 2006. Learning to identify definitions using syntactic features. In *Proceedings of the EACL workshop on Learning Structured Information in Natural Language Applications*.

Stefano Faralli and Roberto Navigli. 2013. Growing multi-domain glossaries from a few seeds using probabilistic topic models. In *EMNLP*. pages 170–181.

Marti A Hearst. 1992. Automatic acquisition of hyponyms from large text corpora. In *Proceedings of the 14th conference on Computational linguistics*. pages 539–545.

Felix Hill, Kyunghyun Cho, Anna Korhonen, and Yoshua Bengio. 2015. Learning to understand phrases by embedding the dictionary. *arXiv preprint arXiv:1504.00548*.

Sepp Hochreiter and Jürgen Schmidhuber. 1997. Long short-term memory. *Neural Computation* 9(8):1735–1780.

Yiping Jin, Min-Yen Kan, Jun-Ping Ng, and Xiangnan He. 2013. Mining scientific terms and their definitions: A study of the ACL anthology. In *Proceedings of the 2013 Conference on Empirical Methods in Natural Language Processing*. Association for Computational Linguistics, Seattle, Washington, USA, pages 780–790.

Yoon Kim. 2014. Convolutional neural networks for sentence classification. *arXiv preprint arXiv:1408.5882*.

Judith Klavans and Smaranda Muresan. 2001. Evaluation of the DEFINDER system for fully automatic glossary construction. In *Proceedings of the AMIA*

Symposium. American Medical Informatics Association, page 324.

Yann LeCun, Léon Bottou, Yoshua Bengio, and Patrick Haffner. 1998. Gradient-based learning applied to document recognition. *Proceedings of the IEEE* 86(11):2278–2324.

SiLiang Li, Bin Xu, and Tong Lee Chung. 2016. Definition extraction with lstm recurrent neural networks. In *China National Conference on Chinese Computational Linguistics*. Springer, pages 177–189.

Véronique Malaisé, Pierre Zweigenbaum, and Bruno Bachimont. 2004. Detecting semantic relations between terms in definitions. In *CompuTerm 2004 - 3rd International Workshop on Computational Terminology*. pages 55–62.

Tomas Mikolov, Wen-tau Yih, and Geoffrey Zweig. 2013. Linguistic regularities in continuous space word representations. In *HLT-NAACL*. pages 746–751.

George A Miller, Richard Beckwith, Christiane Fellbaum, Derek Gross, and Katherine J Miller. 1990. Introduction to WordNet: An on-line lexical database. *International journal of lexicography* 3(4):235–244.

Vinod Nair and Geoffrey E Hinton. 2010. Rectified linear units improve restricted boltzmann machines. In *Proceedings of the 27th international conference on machine learning (ICML-10)*. pages 807–814.

Roberto Navigli and Simone Paolo Ponzetto. 2012. BabelNet: The automatic construction, evaluation and application of a wide-coverage multilingual semantic network. *Artificial Intelligence* 193:217–250.

Roberto Navigli and Paola Velardi. 2005. Structural semantic interconnections: a knowledge-based approach to word sense disambiguation. *IEEE Transactions on pattern analysis and machine intelligence* 27(7):1075–1086.

Roberto Navigli and Paola Velardi. 2010. Learning word-class lattices for definition and hypernym extraction. In *ACL*. pages 1318–1327.

Roberto Navigli, Paola Velardi, and Juana María Ruiz-Martínez. 2010. An annotated dataset for extracting definitions and hypernyms from the web. In *Proceedings of LREC'10*. Valletta, Malta.

Thanapon Noraset, Chen Liang, Larry Birnbaum, and Doug Downey. 2016. Definition modeling: Learning to define word embeddings in natural language. *arXiv preprint arXiv:1612.00394* .

James Pustejovsky, J Castano, Jason Zhang, M Kotecki, and B Cochran. 2001. Robust relational parsing over biomedical literature: Extracting inhibit relations. In *Proceedings of the Pacific symposium on biocomputing*. volume 7, pages 362–373.

Josette Rebeyrolle and Ludovic Tanguy. 2000. Repérage automatique de structures linguistiques en corpus : le cas des énoncés définitoires. *Cahiers de Grammaire* 25:153–174.

Melanie Reiplinger, Ulrich Schäfer, and Magdalena Wolska. 2012. Extracting glossary sentences from scholarly articles: A comparative evaluation of pattern bootstrapping and deep analysis. In *Proceedings of the ACL-2012 Special Workshop on Rediscovering 50 Years of Discoveries*. Association for Computational Linguistics, Jeju Island, Korea, pages 55–65.

Stephen D Richardson, William B Dolan, and Lucy Vanderwende. 1998. Mindnet: acquiring and structuring semantic information from text. In *Proceedings of the 36th Annual Meeting of the Association for Computational Linguistics and 17th International Conference on Computational Linguistics-Volume 2*. Association for Computational Linguistics, pages 1098–1102.

Horacio Saggion and Robert Gaizauskas. 2004. Mining on-line sources for definition knowledge. In *17th FLAIRS*. Miami Bearch, Florida.

Vered Shwartz, Yoav Goldberg, and Ido Dagan. 2016. Improving hypernymy detection with an integrated path-based and distributional method. In *Proceedings of the 54th Annual Meeting of the Association for Computational Linguistics, ACL 2016, August 7-12, 2016, Berlin, Germany, Volume 1: Long Papers*.

Richard Socher, Eric H Huang, Jeffrey Pennin, Christopher D Manning, and Andrew Y Ng. 2011. Dynamic pooling and unfolding recursive autoencoders for paraphrase detection. In *Advances in Neural Information Processing Systems*. pages 801–809.

Richard Socher, Andrej Karpathy, Quoc V Le, Christopher D Manning, and Andrew Y Ng. 2014. Grounded compositional semantics for finding and describing images with sentences. *Transactions of the Association for Computational Linguistics* 2:207–218.

Richard Socher, Alex Perelygin, Jean Wu, Jason Chuang, Christopher D Manning, Andrew Ng, and Christopher Potts. 2013. Recursive deep models for semantic compositionality over a sentiment treebank. In *Proceedings of the 2013 conference on empirical methods in natural language processing*. pages 1631–1642.

Angelika Storrer and Sandra Wellinghoff. 2006. Automated detection and annotation of term definitions in German text corpora. In *Conference on Language Resources and Evaluation (LREC)*.

Paola Velardi, Stefano Faralli, and Roberto Navigli. 2013. OntoLearn Reloaded: A graph-based algorithm for taxonomy induction. *Computational Linguistics* 39(3):665–707.

Denny Vrandečić and Markus Krötzsch. 2014. Wikidata: A free collaborative knowledge base. *Communications of the ACM* 57(10):78–85.

Eline Westerhout and Paola Monachesi. 2007. Combining pattern-based and machine learning methods to detect definitions for elearning purposes. In *Proceedings of RANLP 2007 Workshop Natural Language Processing and Knowledge Representation for eLearning Environments*.

Wen-tau Yih, Kristina Toutanova, John C Platt, and Christopher Meek. 2011. Learning discriminative projections for text similarity measures. In *Proceedings of the Fifteenth Conference on Computational Natural Language Learning*. Association for Computational Linguistics, pages 247–256.

Chunting Zhou, Chonglin Sun, Zhiyuan Liu, and Francis Lau. 2015. A c-lstm neural network for text classification. *arXiv preprint arXiv:1511.08630* .

A Dynamic Oracle for Linear-Time 2-Planar Dependency Parsing

Daniel Fernández-González and **Carlos Gómez-Rodríguez**
Universidade da Coruña
FASTPARSE Lab, LyS Research Group, Departamento de Computación
Campus de Elviña, s/n, 15071 A Coruña, Spain
`d.fgonzalez@udc.es, carlos.gomez@udc.es`

Abstract

We propose an efficient dynamic oracle for training the 2-Planar transition-based parser, a linear-time parser with over 99% coverage on non-projective syntactic corpora. This novel approach outperforms the static training strategy in the vast majority of languages tested and scored better on most datasets than the arc-hybrid parser enhanced with the Swap transition, which can handle unrestricted non-projectivity.

1 Introduction

Linear-time greedy transition-based parsers such as *arc-eager*, *arc-standard* and *arc-hybrid* (Nivre, 2003, 2004; Kuhlmann et al., 2011) are widely used for dependency parsing due to their efficiency and performance, but they cannot deal with non-projective syntax. To address this, various extensions have been proposed, involving new transitions (Attardi, 2006; Nivre, 2009; Fernández-González and Gómez-Rodríguez, 2012), data structures (Gómez-Rodríguez and Nivre, 2010; Pitler and McDonald, 2015) or pre and postprocessing (Nivre and Nilsson, 2005). Among these extensions, the 2-Planar parser (Gómez-Rodríguez and Nivre, 2010) has attractive properties, as it (1) keeps the original worst-case linear time, (2) has close to full coverage of non-projective phenomena, and (3) needs no pre- or post-processing.

Dynamic oracles (Goldberg and Nivre, 2012) are known to improve the accuracy of greedy parsers by enabling more robust training, by exploring configurations beyond the gold path. While dynamic oracles have been defined for many transition-based algorithms (Goldberg and Nivre, 2013; Goldberg et al., 2014; Gómez-Rodríguez et al., 2014; Gómez-Rodríguez and Fernández-González, 2015; de Lhoneux et al., 2017), none is available so far for the 2-Planar system. The lack of the arc-decomposability property, which can be used to derive dynamic oracles for parsers that have it, makes the obtention of one non-trivial.

To fill this gap, we define an efficient dynamic oracle for the 2-Planar transition-based parser, using similar loss calculation techniques as described in (Gómez-Rodríguez and Fernández-González, 2015) for the non-arc-decomposable Covington parser (Covington, 2001). Training the 2-Planar parser with this novel strategy achieves accuracy gains in the vast majority of datasets tested. In addition, we empirically compare our novel approach to the most similar existing alternative:[1] the arc-hybrid parser with a swap transition trained with a static-dynamic oracle, recently introduced by de Lhoneux et al. (2017); which can handle unrestricted non-projective dependencies in $O(n^2)$ worst-case time in theory, but expected linear time in practice (Nivre, 2009). Our approach outperforms this swap-based system on average over a standard set of dependency treebanks.

2 The 2-Planar parser

We briefly sketch the 2-Planar transition system, which was defined by Gómez-Rodríguez and Nivre (2010, 2013) under the transition-based parsing framework (Nivre, 2008) and is based on the arc-eager algorithm (Nivre, 2003), keeping its linear time complexity. It works by building, in a single pass, two non-crossing graphs (called *planes*) whose union provides a dependency parse in the set of 2-planar (or pagenumber-2) graphs, which is known to cover over 99% of parses in a large number of real treebanks (Gómez-Rodríguez and Nivre, 2010; Gómez-Rodríguez, 2016).

Parser configurations have the form $c =$

---

[1] Although the two-register parser by Pitler and McDonald (2015) is even closer to ours in terms of the transition system (being based on arc-eager and running in linear time), no dynamic oracle is known for it, to the best of our knowledge.

386

Proceedings of NAACL-HLT 2018, pages 386–392
New Orleans, Louisiana, June 1 - 6, 2018. ©2018 Association for Computational Linguistics

$\langle \Sigma_1, \Sigma_2, B, A \rangle$, where Σ_1 and Σ_2 are, respectively, the *active stack* and *inactive stack* and are tied to each of the planes or pages of the output graph, B is a *buffer* of unread words, and A the set of dependency arcs built so far. For an input string $w_1 \cdots w_n$, the parser starts at configuration $c_s(w_1 \ldots w_n) = \langle [\,], [\,], [w_1 \ldots w_n], \emptyset \rangle$, applying transitions until a terminal configuration $\langle \Sigma_1, \Sigma_2, [\,], A \rangle$ is reached, and A yields the output.

Figure 1 shows the parser's transitions. The Shift transition pops the first (leftmost) word in the buffer, and pushes it to both stacks; the Reduce transition pops the top word from the active stack, implying that we have added all arcs to or from it on the plane tied to that stack; and the Left-Arc and Right-Arc transitions create a leftward or rightward dependency arc connecting the first word in the buffer to the top of the active stack. Finally, the Switch transition makes the active stack inactive and vice versa, changing the plane the parser is working with. Transitions that violate the single-head or acyclicity constraints are disallowed, so that the output is a forest. Finally, to guarantee the termination of the parsing process, two consecutive Switch transitions are not allowed.

3   A dynamic oracle

We now define an efficient dynamic oracle to train the 2-Planar algorithm, which operates under the assumption of a fixed assignment of arcs to planes.

Following Goldberg and Nivre (2013), if the Hamming loss ($\mathcal{L}$) between trees t and t_G is the amount of words with a different head in t and t_G, then implementing a dynamic oracle reduces to defining a loss function $\ell(c)$ which, given a parser configuration c and a gold tree t_G, computes the minimum loss between t_G and a tree reachable from c.[2] We call this the minimum loss of configuration c, $\ell(c) = \min_{t|c \rightsquigarrow t} \mathcal{L}(t, t_G)$. A correct dynamic oracle will return the set of transitions τ that do not increase this loss (i.e., $\ell(\tau(c)) - \ell(c) = 0$), thus leading to the best parse reachable from c.

For parsers that are *arc-decomposable*[3], $\ell(c)$ can be obtained by counting gold arcs that are *not* individually reachable from c, which is trivial in most parsers. Unfortunately, the 2-Planar parser

is non-arc-decomposable. To show this, it suffices to consider any configuration where an incorrect arc created in A forms a cycle together with a set of otherwise reachable gold arcs, just as in the proof of non-arc-decomposability for Covington provided by Gómez-Rodríguez and Fernández-González (2015). In fact, the same counter-example provided there also works for this parser.

Note, however, that non-arc-decomposability in the 2-Planar parser not only comes from cycles (as in Covington) but also from situations where, due to a poor assignment of planes to already-built arcs, no possible plane assignment allows building a set of pending gold arcs. Thus, the loss calculation technique of the Covington dynamic oracle is not directly applicable to the 2-Planar parser.

However, if we statically choose a canonical plane assignment and we calculate loss with respect to that assignment (i.e., creating a correct arc in the non-canonical plane incurs loss), then the Covington technique, based on counting individually unreachable arcs and then correcting for the presence of cycles, works for the 2-Planar parser. This is the idea of our dynamic oracle, which therefore is a correct dynamic oracle only with respect to a preset criterion for plane assignment, and not for all the possible plane assignments that would produce the gold dependency structure.

In particular, given a 2-planar gold dependency tree whose set of arcs is t_G, we need to divide it into two gold arc sets t_G^1 and t_G^2, associated with each plane.[4] In this paper, we take as canonical the division provided by the static oracle of Gómez-Rodríguez and Nivre (2010), which prefers to build arcs in the active plane to minimize the number of Switch transitions needed.[5]

Once the plane assignment is set, we can associate individually unreachable arcs to a plane. Then, we can calculate configuration loss as:

$$\ell(c) = |\mathcal{U}_1(c, t_G^1) \cup \mathcal{U}_2(c, t_G^2)|$$
$$+ n_c(A \cup (\mathcal{I}_1(c, t_G^1) \cup \mathcal{I}_2(c, t_G^2)))$$

---

[2] We say that an arc set X is *reachable* from configuration c, and we write $c \rightsquigarrow X$, if there is some (possibly empty) path of transitions from c to some configuration $c' = \langle \Sigma_1, \Sigma_2, B, A' \rangle$, with $X \subseteq A'$.

[3] i.e., if every individual arc of X is reachable from a given configuration c, the set X as a whole is reachable from c.

[4] In practice, for gold parses that are not 2-planar, some arcs will need to be discarded, so that $t_G^1 \cup t_G^2$ will be a 2-planar subset of t_G. Note that in this case, our oracle is correct with respect to this 2-planar subset, but it does not guarantee minimum loss with respect to the original non-2-planar graph (in the same way as existing projective dynamic oracles do not guarantee it with respect to non-projective trees).

[5] Our dynamic oracle can work with any plane assignment criterion. We chose this one for simplicity, for direct comparability to the existing static oracle, and because it has been shown to be learnable in practice.

Shift: $\langle \Sigma_1, \Sigma_2, w_i | B, A \rangle \Rightarrow \langle \Sigma_1 | w_i, \Sigma_2 | w_i, B, A \rangle$

Reduce: $\langle \Sigma_1 | w_i, \Sigma_2, B, A \rangle \Rightarrow \langle \Sigma_1, \Sigma_2, B, A \rangle$

Left-Arc: $\langle \Sigma_1 | w_i, \Sigma_2, w_j | B, A \rangle \Rightarrow \langle \Sigma_1 | w_i, \Sigma_2, w_j | B, A \cup \{ w_j \rightarrow w_i \} \rangle$
only if $\nexists w_k \mid w_k \rightarrow w_i \in A$ (single-head) and $w_i \rightarrow^* w_j \notin A$ (acyclicity).

Right-Arc: $\langle \Sigma_1 | w_i, \Sigma_2, w_j | B, A \rangle \Rightarrow \langle \Sigma_1 | w_i, \Sigma_2, w_j | B, A \cup \{ w_i \rightarrow w_j \} \rangle$
only if $\nexists w_k \mid w_k \rightarrow w_j \in A$ (single-head) and $w_j \rightarrow^* w_i \notin A$ (acyclicity).

Switch: $\langle \Sigma_1, \Sigma_2, B, A \rangle \Rightarrow \langle \Sigma_2, \Sigma_1, B, A \rangle$

Figure 1: Transitions of the 2-Planar dependency parser. The notation $w_i \rightarrow^* w_j \in A$ means that there is a (possibly empty) directed path from w_i to w_j in A.

where for $i \in \{1, 2\}$, each set $\mathcal{I}_i(c, t_G^i) = \{x \rightarrow y \in t_G^i \mid c \rightsquigarrow (x \rightarrow y)\}$ is the set of *individually reachable arcs* of t_G^i from configuration c; $\mathcal{U}_i(c, t_G^i)$ is the set of *individually unreachable arcs* of t_G^i from c, defined as $t_G^i \setminus \mathcal{I}_i(c, t_G^i)$; and $n_c(G)$ denotes the number of cycles in a graph G.

To compute the sets of individually unreachable arcs $\mathcal{U}_i(c, t_G^i)$ from a configuration $c = \langle \Sigma_1, \Sigma_2, B, A \rangle$, we examine gold arcs. A gold arc $x \rightarrow y \in t_G^i$ will be in $\mathcal{U}_i(c, t_G^i)$ if it is not in $A \cap t_G^i$ (the set of already-built arcs from the plane of interest), and at least one of the following holds:

- $\min(x, y) \notin \Sigma_i \cup B \lor \max(x, y) \notin B$, (i.e., $\min(x, y)$ must be in plane i's stack or in the buffer, and $\max(x, y)$ must be in the buffer so that the arc $x \rightarrow y$ can still be built),

- there is some $z \neq 0, z \neq x$ such that $z \rightarrow y \in A$, (i.e., we cannot create $x \rightarrow y$ because it would violate the single-head constraint),

- x and y are on the same weakly connected component of A (i.e., we cannot create $x \rightarrow y$ due to the acyclicity constraint).

- $x \rightarrow y \in A \cap t_G^{3-i}$ (i.e., the arc was already erroneously created in the other plane and, therefore, is unreachable in plane i).

Once we have $\mathcal{U}_i(c, t_G^i)$ for each of the two planes, $\mathcal{I}_i(c, t_G^i)$ can be obtained as $t_G^i \setminus \mathcal{U}_i(c, t_G^i)$. Finally, since the graph $A \cup \mathcal{I}_1(c, t_G^1) \cup \mathcal{I}_2(c, t_G^2)$ has in-degree 1, the algorithm by Tarjan (1972) can be used to implement the function n_c to count its cycles in $O(n)$ time. For this reason, the full loss calculation runs in linear time as well.[6]

Given a plane assignment, $\ell(c)$ is an exact expression of the loss of a configuration of the 2-Planar parser as expressed in Figure 1, without the control constraint that forbids two consecutive Switch transitions. This can be proven using the same reasoning as for the Covington loss expression of (Gómez-Rodríguez and Fernández-González, 2015). Thus, the computation of $\ell(c)$ provides a complete and correct dynamic oracle for this parser under a given plane assignment, by directly evaluating $\ell(\tau(c)) - \ell(c)$ for each transition τ. However, to make the oracle correct for the practical version, where consecutive Switch transitions are disallowed, we need to modify the cost calculation for the Switch transition.

In particular, applying a Switch transition does not affect the loss, so $\ell(\mathsf{Switch}(c)) - \ell(c)$ is always 0. Indeed, if Switch transitions are always allowed, their cost is zero because they can always be undone and thus never affect the reachability of any arcs. However, when consecutive Switch transitions are banned to ensure parser termination, choosing to Switch can have consequences as, in the resulting configuration, the parser will be forced to take one of the other four transitions, which may lead to suboptimal outcomes compared to not having switched.

To address this, we compute the cost of Switch transitions instead as $min(\{\ell(\tau(\mathsf{Switch}(c))) - \ell(c) | \tau \neq \mathsf{Switch}\})$, i.e., the minimum number of gold arcs missed after being forced to apply one of the other four transitions after Switch (if this cost is 0, then switching stacks is an optimal choice). Adding this modification makes the dynamic oracle correct for the practical version of the parser

_____

[6]The check for acyclicity using weakly connected components has no impact on the complexity: when weakly connected components are represented using path compression and union by rank, the relevant operations run in amortized inverse Ackermann time, meaning that they behave as constant time for all practical purposes, like in (Gómez-Rodríguez and Nivre, 2013)

that disallows consecutive Switch transitions.

Regularization While the above dynamic oracle is theoretically correct, we noticed experimentally that the Switch transition tends to switch stacks very frequently during training, due to exploration. This leads the parser to learn unnecessarily long and complex transition sequences that change planes more than needed, harming accuracy.

To avoid this, we add a regularization term to $\ell(c)$ representing the transition sequence length from c to its minimum-loss reachable tree(s), to discourage unnecessarily long sequences. This amounts to penalizing the Switch transition if there is any zero-cost transition available in the active plane and changing planes will delay its application. Thus, arcs assigned to the currently active plane will be built before switching if possible, enforcing a global arc creation order. This is similar to the prioritization of monotonic paths in (Honnibal et al., 2013, §6), as they also penalize unneeded actions that will need to be undone later.

4 Experiments

4.1 Data and Evaluation

We conduct our experiments on the commonly-used non-projective benchmark compounded of nine datasets from the CoNLL-X shared task (Buchholz and Marsi, 2006) and all datasets from the CoNLL-XI shared task (Nivre et al., 2007).[7] We also use the Stanford Dependencies (de Marneffe and Manning, 2008) conversion (using the Stanford parser v3.3.0)[8] of the WSJ Penn Treebank (PTB-SD) (Marcus et al., 1993) with standard splits. Labelled and Unlabelled Attachment Scores (LAS and UAS) are computed including punctuation for all datasets except for the PTB where, following common practice, the punctuation is excluded. We train our system for 15 iterations and choose the best model according to development set accuracy. Statistical significance is calculated using a paired test with 10,000 bootstrap samples.

4.2 Model

We implement both the static oracle and the dynamic oracle with aggressive exploration for the

2-Planar parser under the neural network architecture proposed by Kiperwasser and Goldberg (2016). We also add the static-dynamic arc-hybrid parser with Swap transition (de Lhoneux et al., 2017), implemented under the same framework to perform a fair comparison.

The neural network architecture used in this paper is taken from Kiperwasser and Goldberg (2016). We use the same BiLSTM-based featurization method that concatenates the representations of the top 3 words on the active stack and the leftmost word in the buffer for the arc-hybrid and 2-Planar algorithms, and we add the top 2 words on the inactive stack for the latter. Following Kiperwasser and Goldberg (2016), we also include the BiLSTM vectors of the rightmost and leftmost modifiers of words from the stacks, as well as the leftmost modifier of the first word in the buffer. We initialize word embeddings with 100-dimensional GloVe vectors (Pennington et al., 2014) for English and use 300-dimensional Facebook vectors (Bojanowski et al., 2016) for other languages. The other parameters of the neural network keep the same values as in (Kiperwasser and Goldberg, 2016).

4.3 Results

Table 1 shows that the 2-Planar parser trained with a dynamic oracle outperforms the static training strategy in terms of UAS in 15 out of 20 languages, with 8 of these improvements statistically significant ($\alpha = .05$), and one statistically significant decrease. When comparing with the enhanced arc-hybrid system in Table 2, our approach provides a better UAS in 12 out of 20 datasets tested, achieving statistically significant ($\alpha = .05$) gains in accuracy on 7 of them, and significant losses on 3 of them.

We could not find a clear pattern to explain why the 2-Planar algorithm outperforms arc-hybrid plus Swap in some languages and vice versa. The latter seems to work better on treebanks with less non-projectivity such as the English, Chinese and Japanese datasets, and worse on those with higher amounts like Turkish, Dutch or Basque. However, some cases like Czech or Catalan go against this trend. From (Gómez-Rodríguez and Nivre, 2010), we also know that the Dutch and German treebanks have a relatively high proportion of non-2-planar trees, but the 2-Planar parser seems to be a better option on them than the extended arc-

---

[7]We use for evaluation the latest version for each language, i.e., if a language appeared in both CoNLL-X and CoNLL-XI, we use the CoNLL-XI dataset.

[8]`https://nlp.stanford.edu/software/lex-parser.shtml`

	2-Planar static		2-Planar dynamic	
Language	UAS	LAS	UAS	LAS
Arabic	**83.20**	**73.48**	82.96	73.24
Basque	77.61	69.94	**78.11**	**70.11**
Catalan	92.50	87.92	**93.70***	**88.48***
Chinese	85.95	80.97	**87.08***	**81.73***
Czech	84.67	78.56	**85.29**	**79.40**
English	89.57	88.69	**90.87***	**90.03***
Greek	81.93	74.23	**82.06**	**74.79**
Hungarian	81.50	75.94	**82.48***	**76.97***
Italian	86.85	82.36	**87.24**	**82.38**
Turkish	**81.68**	73.59	81.48	**73.61**
Bulgarian	93.14	89.74	**93.23**	**89.97**
Danish	88.31	84.23	**88.57**	**84.76**
Dutch	85.51	81.63	**86.50***	**82.70***
German	**90.80**	**88.71**	90.71	88.51
Japanese	92.51	90.56	**93.19***	**90.65***
Portugue.	88.68	85.12	**89.02***	**85.92***
Slovene	78.67	70.49	**79.30**	**70.86**
Spanish	**83.63***	**79.79***	82.42	78.68
Swedish	**89.92**	**85.48**	89.83	85.40
PTB-SD	93.59	91.60	**93.96***	**92.06***
Average	86.51	81.65	**86.90**	**82.01**

Table 1: Parsing accuracy of the 2-Planar parser trained with static and dynamic oracles on CoNLL-XI (first block), CoNLL-X (second block) and PTB-SD (third block) datasets. Best results for each language are shown in boldface. Statistically significant improvements ($\alpha = .05$) are marked with *.

	2-Planar dynamic		AHybrid$_{Swap}$ static-dynamic	
Language	UAS	LAS	UAS	LAS
Arabic	**82.96***	**73.24***	80.74	70.69
Basque	**78.11***	**70.11***	75.60	68.70
Catalan	**93.70***	**88.48**	93.12	88.06
Chinese	87.08	81.73	**87.31**	**82.02**
Czech	85.29	79.40	**85.71***	**80.08***
English	90.87	90.03	**91.37**	**90.37**
Greek	82.06	74.79	**83.72***	**76.33***
Hungarian	**82.48**	**76.97**	82.20	76.88
Italian	**87.24***	**82.38***	86.24	81.48
Turkish	**81.48***	**73.61***	77.44	69.22
Bulgarian	**93.23**	**89.97**	93.17	89.62
Danish	88.57	**84.76**	**88.65**	84.60
Dutch	**86.50***	**82.70***	84.24	81.04
German	**90.71**	**88.51**	90.60	88.39
Japanese	93.19	90.65	**93.40**	**91.47***
Portugue.	**89.02**	**85.92**	88.78	85.48
Slovene	**79.30***	**70.86**	77.68	70.61
Spanish	82.42	78.68	**83.98***	**80.15***
Swedish	89.83	**85.40**	**89.92**	85.18
PTB-SD	**93.96**	**92.06**	93.83	91.93
Average	**86.90**	**82.01**	86.39	81.62

Table 2: Parsing accuracy of the 2-Planar parser trained with the dynamic oracle and the arc-hybrid parser with the Swap transition trained with a static-dynamic oracle on CoNLL-XI (first block), CoNLL-X (second block) and PTB-SD (third block) datasets. Best results for each language are in boldface. Statistically significant improvements ($\alpha = .05$) are marked with *.

hybrid system that can handle unrestricted non-projectivity. The reasons, beyond the scope of this research, might be related to different dependency length distributions or non-projective topologies.

We noticed that, in general, the 2-Planar parser has higher precision on non-projective arcs and the enhanced arc-hybrid parser has a better recall.

5 Conclusion

We present an efficient dynamic oracle to train the 2-Planar transition-based parser, which is correct with respect to a given plane assignment, and results in notable gains in accuracy. The parser trained with this dynamic oracle performs better on average than an expected linear-time parser supporting unrestricted non-projectivity.

Acknowledgments

This work has received funding from the European Research Council (ERC), under the European Union's Horizon 2020 research and innovation programme (FASTPARSE, grant agreement No 714150), from the TELEPARES-UDC project (FFI2014-51978-C2-2-R) and the ANSWER-ASAP project (TIN2017-85160-C2-1-R) from MINECO, and from Xunta de Galicia (ED431B 2017/01).

References

Giuseppe Attardi. 2006. Experiments with a multi-anguage non-projective dependency parser. In *Proceedings of the 10th Conference on Computational Natural Language Learning (CoNLL)*. pages 166–170.

Piotr Bojanowski, Edouard Grave, Armand Joulin, and Tomas Mikolov. 2016. Enriching word vectors with subword information. *arXiv preprint arXiv:1607.04606* .

Sabine Buchholz and Erwin Marsi. 2006. CoNLL-X shared task on multilingual dependency parsing. In *Proceedings of the 10th Conference on Computational Natural Language Learning (CoNLL)*. pages 149–164. http://www.aclweb.org/anthology/W06-2920.

Michael A. Covington. 2001. A fundamental algorithm for dependency parsing. In *Proceedings of the 39th Annual ACM Southeast Conference*. ACM, New York, NY, USA, pages 95–102.

Miryam de Lhoneux, Sara Stymne, and Joakim Nivre. 2017. Arc-hybrid non-projective dependency parsing with a static-dynamic oracle. In *Proceedings of the The 15th International Conference on Parsing Technologies (IWPT)..* Pisa, Italy.

Marie-Catherine de Marneffe and Christopher D. Manning. 2008. The stanford typed dependencies representation. In *Coling 2008: Proceedings of the Workshop on Cross-Framework and Cross-Domain Parser Evaluation*. Association for Computational Linguistics, Stroudsburg, PA, USA, CrossParser '08, pages 1–8. http://dl.acm.org/citation.cfm?id=1608858.1608859.

Daniel Fernández-González and Carlos Gómez-Rodríguez. 2012. Improving transition-based dependency parsing with buffer transitions. In *Proceedings of the 2012 Joint Conference on Empirical Methods in Natural Language Processing and Computational Natural Language Learning*. Association for Computational Linguistics, pages 308–319. http://aclweb.org/anthology/D/D12/D12-1029.pdf.

Yoav Goldberg and Joakim Nivre. 2012. A dynamic oracle for arc-eager dependency parsing. In *Proceedings of COLING 2012*. Association for Computational Linguistics, Mumbai, India, pages 959–976. http://www.aclweb.org/anthology/C12-1059.

Yoav Goldberg and Joakim Nivre. 2013. Training deterministic parsers with non-deterministic oracles. *Transactions of the Association for Computational Linguistics* 1:403–414. http://anthology.aclweb.org/Q/Q13/Q13-1033.pdf.

Yoav Goldberg, Francesco Sartorio, and Giorgio Satta. 2014. A tabular method for dynamic oracles in transition-based parsing. *Transactions of the Association for Computational Linguistics* 2:119–130.

Carlos Gómez-Rodríguez. 2016. Restricted non-projectivity: Coverage vs. efficiency. *Comput. Linguist.* 42(4):809–817. https://doi.org/10.1162/COLI_a_00267.

Carlos Gómez-Rodríguez and Daniel Fernández-González. 2015. An efficient dynamic oracle for

unrestricted non-projective parsing. In *Proceedings of the 53rd Annual Meeting of the Association for Computational Linguistics and the 7th International Joint Conference on Natural Language Processing of the Asian Federation of Natural Language Processing, ACL 2015, July 26-31, 2015, Beijing, China, Volume 2: Short Papers*. pages 256–261. http://aclweb.org/anthology/P/P15/P15-2042.pdf.

Carlos Gómez-Rodríguez and Joakim Nivre. 2010. A transition-based parser for 2-planar dependency structures. In *Proceedings of the 48th Annual Meeting of the Association for Computational Linguistics*. Association for Computational Linguistics, Stroudsburg, PA, USA, ACL '10, pages 1492–1501. http://dl.acm.org/citation.cfm?id=1858681.1858832.

Carlos Gómez-Rodríguez and Joakim Nivre. 2013. Divisible transition systems and multiplanar dependency parsing. *Comput. Linguist.* 39(4):799–845. https://doi.org/10.1162/COLI_a_00150.

Carlos Gómez-Rodríguez, Francesco Sartorio, and Giorgio Satta. 2014. A polynomial-time dynamic oracle for non-projective dependency parsing. In *Proceedings of the 2014 Conference on Empirical Methods in Natural Language Processing (EMNLP)*. Association for Computational Linguistics, pages 917–927. http://aclweb.org/anthology/D14-1099.

Matthew Honnibal, Yoav Goldberg, and Mark Johnson. 2013. A non-monotonic arc-eager transition system for dependency parsing. In *Proceedings of the Seventeenth Conference on Computational Natural Language Learning, CoNLL 2013, Sofia, Bulgaria, August 8-9, 2013*. pages 163–172. http://aclweb.org/anthology/W/W13/W13-3518.pdf.

Eliyahu Kiperwasser and Yoav Goldberg. 2016. Simple and accurate dependency parsing using bidirectional LSTM feature representations. *TACL* 4:313–327. https://transacl.org/ojs/index.php/tacl/article/view/885.

Marco Kuhlmann, Carlos Gómez-Rodríguez, and Giorgio Satta. 2011. Dynamic programming algorithms for transition-based dependency parsers. In *Proceedings of the 49th Annual Meeting of the Association for Computational Linguistics: Human Language Technologies - Volume 1*. Association for Computational Linguistics, Stroudsburg, PA, USA, HLT '11, pages 673–682. http://dl.acm.org/citation.cfm?id=2002472.2002558.

Mitchell P. Marcus, Beatrice Santorini, and Mary Ann Marcinkiewicz. 1993. Building a large annotated corpus of English: The Penn Treebank. *Computational Linguistics* 19:313–330.

Joakim Nivre. 2003. An efficient algorithm for projective dependency parsing. In *Proceedings of the 8th International Workshop on Parsing Technologies (IWPT 03)*. ACL/SIGPARSE, pages 149–160.

Joakim Nivre. 2004. Incrementality in deterministic dependency parsing. In *Proceedings of the Workshop on Incremental Parsing: Bringing Engineering and Cognition Together (ACL)*. pages 50–57.

Joakim Nivre. 2008. Algorithms for Deterministic Incremental Dependency Parsing. *Computational Linguistics* 34(4):513–553. https://doi.org/10.1162/coli.07-056-R1-07-027.

Joakim Nivre. 2009. Non-projective dependency parsing in expected linear time. In *Proceedings of the Joint Conference of the 47th Annual Meeting of the ACL and the 4th International Joint Conference on Natural Language Processing of the AFNLP (ACL-IJCNLP)*. pages 351–359.

Joakim Nivre, Johan Hall, Sandra Kübler, Ryan McDonald, Jens Nilsson, Sebastian Riedel, and Deniz Yuret. 2007. The CoNLL 2007 shared task on dependency parsing. In *Proceedings of the CoNLL Shared Task Session of EMNLP-CoNLL 2007*. pages 915–932. http://www.aclweb.org/anthology/D/D07/D07-1096.pdf.

Joakim Nivre and Jens Nilsson. 2005. Pseudo-projective dependency parsing. In *ACL '05: Proceedings of the 43rd Annual Meeting of the Association for Computational Linguistics*. Association for Computational Linguistics, Morristown, NJ, USA, pages 99–106.

Jeffrey Pennington, Richard Socher, and Christopher D. Manning. 2014. Glove: Global vectors for word representation. In *Empirical Methods in Natural Language Processing (EMNLP)*. pages 1532–1543. http://www.aclweb.org/anthology/D14-1162.

Emily Pitler and Ryan McDonald. 2015. A linear-time transition system for crossing interval trees. In *Proceedings of the 2015 Conference of the North American Chapter of the Association for Computational Linguistics: Human Language Technologies*. Association for Computational Linguistics, Denver, Colorado, pages 662–671. http://www.aclweb.org/anthology/N15-1068.

Robert Endre Tarjan. 1972. Depth-first search and linear graph algorithms. *SIAM J. Comput.* 1(2):146–160. http://dblp.uni-trier.de/db/journals/siamcomp/siamcomp1.html.

Are Automatic Methods for Cognate Detection Good Enough for Phylogenetic Reconstruction in Historical Linguistics?

Taraka Rama♠   Johann-Mattis List◇   Johannes Wahle♡   Gerhard Jäger♡

♠Department of Informatics, University of Oslo, Norway
◇Department of Linguistic and Cultural Evolution, MPI-SHH, Jena, Germany
♡Department of Linguistics, University of Tübingen, Germany

tarakark@ifi.uio.no, list@shh.mpg.de, {johannes.wahle,gerhard.jaeger}@uni-tuebingen.de

Abstract

We evaluate the performance of state-of-the-art algorithms for automatic cognate detection by comparing how useful automatically inferred cognates are for the task of phylogenetic inference compared to classical manually annotated cognate sets. Our findings suggest that phylogenies inferred from automated cognate sets come close to phylogenies inferred from expert-annotated ones, although on average, the latter are still superior. We conclude that future work on phylogenetic reconstruction can profit much from automatic cognate detection. Especially where scholars are merely interested in exploring the bigger picture of a language family's phylogeny, algorithms for automatic cognate detection are a useful complement for current research on language phylogenies.

1 Introduction

The task of *cognate detection*, i.e., the search for genetically related words in different languages, has traditionally been regarded as a task that is barely automatable. During the last decades, however, automatic cognate detection approaches since Covington (1996) have been constantly improved following the work of Kondrak (2002), both regarding the quality of the inferences (List et al., 2017b; Jäger et al., 2017), and the sophistication of the methods (Hauer and Kondrak, 2011; Rama, 2016; Jäger et al., 2017), which have been expanded to account for the detection of partial cognates (List et al., 2016b), language specific sound-transition weights (List, 2012) or the search of cognates in whole dictionaries (St Arnaud et al., 2017).

Despite the progress, none of the automated cognate detection methods have been used for the purpose of inferring phylogenetic trees using modern Bayesian phylogenetic methods (Yang

and Rannala, 1997) from computational biology. Phylogenetic trees are hypotheses of how sets of related languages evolved in time. They can in turn be used for testing additional hypotheses of language evolution, such as the age of language families (Gray and Atkinson, 2003; Chang et al., 2015), their spread (Bouckaert et al., 2012; Gray et al., 2009), the rates of lexical change (Greenhill et al., 2017), or as a proxy for tasks like cognate detection and linguistic reconstruction (Bouchard-Côté et al., 2013). By plotting shared traits on a tree and testing how they could have evolved, trees can even be used to test hypotheses independent from language evolution, such as the universality of typological statements (Dunn et al., 2011), or the ancestry of cultural traits (Jordan et al., 2009).

In the majority of these approaches, scholars infer phylogenetic trees with help of *expert-annotated cognate sets* which serve as input to the phylogenetic software which usually follows a Bayesian likelihood framework. Unfortunately, expert cognate judgments are only available for a small number of language families which look back on a long tradition of classical comparative linguistic research (Campbell and Poser, 2008). Despite the claims that automatic cognate detection is useful for linguists working on less well studied language families, none of the papers actually tested, if automated cognates can be used instead as well for the important downstream task of Bayesian phylogenetic inference. So far, scholars have only tested distance-based approaches to phylogenetic reconstruction (Wichmann et al., 2010; Rama and Borin, 2015; Jäger, 2013), which employ aggregated linguistic distances computed from string similarity algorithms to infer phylogenetic trees.

In order to test whether automatic cognate detection is useful for phylogenetic inference, we collected multilingual wordlists for five different

393

Proceedings of NAACL-HLT 2018, pages 393–400
New Orleans, Louisiana, June 1 - 6, 2018. ©2018 Association for Computational Linguistics

language families (230 languages, cf. section 2.1) and then applied different cognate detection methods (cf. section 2.2) to infer cognate sets. We then applied the Bayesian phylogenetic inference procedure (cf. section 3) to the automated and the expert-annotated cognate sets in order to infer phylogenetic trees. These trees were then evaluated against the *family gold standard trees*, based on external linguistic knowledge (Hammarström et al., 2017), using the *Generalized Quartet Distance* (cf. section 4.1). The results are provided in table 3 and the paper is concluded in section 5.

To the best of our knowledge, this is the first study in which the performance of several automatic cognate detection methods on the downstream task of phylogenetic inference is compared. While we find that on average the trees inferred from the expert-annotated cognate sets come closer to the gold standard trees, the trees inferred from automated cognate sets come surprisingly close to the trees inferred from the expert-annotated ones.

Dataset	Mngs.	Lngs.	AMC
Austronesian	210	45	0.79
Austro-Asiatic	200	58	0.90
Indo-European	208	42	0.95
Pama-Nyungan	183	67	0.89
Sino-Tibetan	110	64	0.91

Table 1: Datasets used in our study. The second, third, and fourth columns show the number of number of meanings, languages and average mutual coverage for each language family respectively.

2 Materials and Methods

2.1 Datasets

Our wordlists were extracted from publicly available datasets from five different language families: Austronesian (Greenhill et al., 2008), Austro-Asiatic (Sidwell, 2015), Indo-European (Dunn, 2012), Pama-Nyungan (Bowern and Atkinson, 2012), and Sino-Tibetan (Peiros, 2004). In order to make sure that the datasets were amenable for automatic cognate detection, we had to make sure that the transcriptions employed are readily recognized, and that the data is sufficient for those methods which rely on the identification of regular sound correspondences. The problem of transcriptions was solved by applying intensive semi-automatic cleaning. In order to guarantee an optimal data size, we selected a subset of languages from each dataset, which would guarantee a high *average mutual coverage* (AMC). AMC is calculated as the average proportion of words shared by all language pairs in a given dataset. All analyses were carried out with version 2.6.2 of LingPy (List et al., 2017a). Table 1 gives an overview on the number of languages, concepts, and the AMC score for all datasets.[1]

2.2 Automatic Cognate Detection

The basic workflow for automatic cognate detection methods applied to multilingual wordlists has been extensively described in the literature (Hauer and Kondrak, 2011; List, 2014). The workflow can be divided into two major steps: (a) word similarity calculation, and (b) cognate set partitioning. In the first step, similarity or distance scores for all word pairs in the same concept slot in the data are computed. In the second step, these scores are used to partition the words into sets of presumably related words. Since the second step is a mere clustering task for which many solutions exist, the most crucial differences among algorithms can be noted for step (a).

For our analysis, we tested six different methods for cognate detection: The Consonant-Class-Matching (CCM) Method (Turchin et al., 2010), the Normalized Edit Distance (NED) approach (Levenshtein, 1965), the Sound-Class-Based Aligmnent (SCA) method (List, 2014), the LexStat-Infomap method (List et al., 2017b), the SVM method (Jäger et al., 2017), and the Online PMI approach (Rama et al., 2017).

The **CCM** approach first reduces the size of the alphabets in the phonetic transcriptions by mapping consonants to *consonant classes* and discarding vowels. Assuming that different sounds which share the same sound class are likely to go back to the same ancestral sound, words which share the first two consonant classes are judged to be cognate, while words which differ regarding their first two classes are regarded as non-cognate.

---

[1] In order to allow for an easy re-use of our datasets, we linked all language varieties to Glottolog (Hammarström et al., 2017) and all concepts to Concepticon (List et al., 2016a). In addition to the tabular data formats required to run the analyses with our software tools, we also provide the data in form of the format specifications suggested by the Cross-Linguistic Data Formats initiative (Forkel et al., 2017). Data and source code are provided along with the supplementary material accompanying this paper.

The **NED** approach first computes the *normalized edit distance* (Nerbonne and Heeringa, 1997) for all word pairs in given semantic slot and then clusters the words into cognate sets using a flat version of the UPGMA algorithm (Sokal and Michener, 1958) and a user-defined threshold of maximal distance among the words. We follow List et al. (2017b) in setting this threshold to 0.75.

The **SCA** approach is very similar to NED, but the pairwise distances are computed with help of the Sound-Class-Based Phonetic Alignment algorithm (List, 2014) which employs an extended sound-class model and a linguistically informed scoring function. Following List et al. (2017b), we set the threshold for this approach to 0.45.

The **LexStat-Infomap** method builds on the SCA method by employing the same sound-class model, but individual scoring functions are inferred from the data for each language pair by applying a permutation method and computing the *log-odds scores* (Eddy, 2004) from the expected and the attested distribution of sound matches (List, 2014). While SCA and NED employ flat UGPMA clustering for step 2 of the workflow, LexStat-Infomap further uses the Infomap community detection algorithm (Rosvall and Bergstrom, 2008) to partition the words into cognate set. Following List et al. (2017b), we set the threshold for LexStat-Infomap to 0.55.

The **OnlinePMI** approach (Rama et al., 2017) estimates the sound-pair PMI matrix using the online procedure described in Liang and Klein (2009). The approach starts with an empty PMI matrix and a list of synonymous word pairs from all the language pairs. The approach proceeds by calculating the PMI matrix from alignments calculated for each minibatch of word pairs using the current PMI matrix. Then the calculated PMI matrix for the latest minibatch is combined with the current PMI matrix. This procedure is repeated for a fixed number of iterations. We employ the final PMI matrix to calculate pairwise word similarity matrix for each meaning. In an additional step, the similarity score was transformed into a distance score using the sigmoid transformation: $1.0 - (1 + \exp(-x))^{-1}$ The word distance matrix is then supplied as an input to the Label Propagation algorithm (Raghavan et al., 2007) to infer cognate clusters. We set the threshold for the algorithm to be 0.5.

For the **SVM** approach (Jäger et al., 2017) a linear SVM classifier was trained with PMI similarity (Jäger, 2013), LexStat distance, mean word length, distance between the languages as features on cognate and non-cognate pairs extracted from word lists from Wichmann and Holman (2013) and List (2014). The details of the training dataset are given in table 1 in Jäger et al. (2017). We used the same training settings as reported in the paper to train our SVM model. The trained SVM model is then employed to compute the probability that a word pair is cognate or not. The word pair probability matrix is then given as input to InfoMap algorithm for inferring word clusters. The threshold for InfoMap algorithm is set to 0.57 after cross-validation experiments on the training data.

We evaluate the quality of the inferred cognate sets using the above described methods using B-cubed F-score (Amigó et al., 2009) which is widely used in evaluating the quality of automatically inferred cognate clusters (Hauer and Kondrak, 2011). We present the cognate evaluation results in table 2. The SVM system is the best in the case of Austro-Asiatic and Pama-Nyungan whereas LexStat algorithm performs the best in the case of rest of the datasets. This is surprising since LexStat scores are used as features for SVM and we expect the SVM system to perform better than LexStat in all the language families. On the other hand, both OnlinePMI and SCA systems perform better than the algorithmically simpler systems such as CCM and NED. Given these F-scores, we hypothesize that the cognate sets output from the best cognate identification systems would also yield the high quality phylogenetic trees. However, we find the opposite in our phylogenetic experiments.

3 Bayesian Phylogenetic Inference

The objective of Bayesian phylogenetic inference is based on the Bayes rule in 1.

$$f(\tau, v, \theta | X) = \frac{f(X | \tau, v, \theta) f(\tau, v, \theta)}{f(X)} \quad (1)$$

where X is the data matrix, τ is the topology of the tree, v is the vector of branch lengths, and θ is the substitution model parameters. The data matrix X is a binary matrix of dimensions $N \times C$ where N is the number of languages and C is the number of cognate clusters in a language family. The posterior distribution $f(\tau, v, \theta | X)$ is difficult to calculate analytically since one has to sum over

Method	Austro-Asiatic	Austronesian	Indo-European	Pama-Nyungan	Sino-Tibetan
CCM	0.71	0.7	0.75	0.74	0.48
NED	0.73	0.77	0.69	0.53	0.49
SCA	0.76	0.78	0.81	0.71	0.56
LexStat	0.76	0.84	0.83	0.84	0.6
OnlinePMI	0.76	0.81	0.82	0.72	0.56
SVM	0.82	0.81	0.79	0.86	0.5

Table 2: B-cubed F-scores for different cognate detection methods across the language families.

all the possible topologies ($\frac{(2N-3)!}{2^{N-2}(N-2)!}$) to compute the marginal in the denominator. However, posterior probability of all the parameters of interest (here, $\Psi = \{\tau, v, \theta\}$) can be computed from samples drawn using a Markov chain Monte Carlo (MCMC) method. Typically, Metropolis-Hastings (MH) algorithm is the MCMC algorithm used to sample phylogenies from the posterior distribution (Huelsenbeck et al., 2001).

The MH algorithm constructs a Markov chain of the parameters' states by proposing change to a single parameter or a block of parameters in Ψ. The current state Ψ in the Markov chain has a parameter θ and a new value θ^* is proposed from a distribution $q(\theta^*|\theta)$, then θ^* is accepted with a probability

$$r = \frac{f(X|\tau, v, \theta^*)}{f(X|\tau, v, \theta)} \frac{f(\theta^*)}{f(\theta)} \frac{q(\theta|\theta^*)}{q(\theta^*|\theta)} \quad (2)$$

The likelihood of the data $f(X|\Psi)$ is computed using the Felsenstein's pruning algorithm (Felsenstein, 1981) also known as sum-product algorithm (Jordan et al., 2004). We assume that τ, θ, v are independent of each other.

4 Experiments

In this section, we report the experimental settings, the evaluation measure, and the results of our experiments.

All our Bayesian analyses use binary datasets with states 0 and 1. We employ the Generalized Time Reversible Model (Yang, 2014, chapter 1) for computing the transition probabilities between individual states. The rate variation across sites is modeled using a four category discrete Γ distribution (Yang, 1994). We follow Lewis (2001) and Felsenstein (1992) in correcting the likelihood calculation for ascertainment bias resulting from unobserved 0 patterns. We used a uniform tree prior (Ronquist et al., 2012) in all our analyses which constructs a rooted tree and draws internal node heights from uniform distribution. In our analysis,

we assumes a Independent Gamma Rates relaxed clock model (Lepage et al., 2007) where the rate for a branch j of length b_j in the tree is drawn from a Gamma distribution with mean 1 and variance σ_{IG}^2/b_j where σ_{IG}^2 is a parameter sampled in the MCMC analysis.

We infer τ, v, θ from two independent random starting points and sample every 1000th state in the chain until the phylogenies from the two independent runs do not differ beyond 0.01. For each dataset, we ran the chains for 15 million generations and threw away the initial 50% of the chain's states as part of burnin. After that we computed the generalized quartet distance from each of the posterior trees to the gold standard tree described in subsection 4.1. All our experiments are performed using MrBayes 3.2.6 (Zhang et al., 2015).

4.1 GQD

Pompei et al. (2011) introduced Generalized Quartet Distance (GQD) as an extension to Quartet Distance (QD) in order to compare binary trees with a polytomous tree, since gold standard trees can have non-binary internal nodes. It was widely used for comparing inferred language phylogenies with gold standard phylogenies (Greenhill et al., 2010; Wichmann et al., 2011; Jäger, 2013).

QD measures the distance between two trees in terms of the number of different quartets (Estabrook et al., 1985). A quartet is defined as a set of four leaves selected from a set of leaves without replacement. A tree with n leaves has $\binom{n}{4}$ quartets in total. A quartet defined on four leaves a, b, c, d can have four different topologies: $ab|cd$, $ac|bd$, $ad|bc$, and $ab \times cd$. The first three topologies have an internal edge separating two pairs of leaves. Such quartets are called as *butterflies*. The fourth quartet has no internal edge and as such is known as star quartet. Given a tree τ with n leaves, the quartets can be partitioned into sets of butterflies, $B(\tau)$, and sets of stars, $S(\tau)$. Then, the QD between τ and τ_g is defined

Method	Austro-Asiatic	Austronesian	Indo-European	Pama-Nyungan	Sino-Tibetan
Expert cognate sets	**0.0081 ± 0.001**	0.1056 ± 0.0118	**0.0249 ± 0.0079**	**0.1384 ± 0.0225**	**0.0561 ± 0.0123**
CCM	0.0243 ± 0.018	0.0854 ± 0.0176	0.0369 ± 0.0148	0.1617 ± 0.0162	0.1424 ± 0.027
NED	0.0265 ± 0.007	0.0458 ± 0.0152	0.046 ± 0.0132	0.196 ± 0.0166	0.1614 ± 0.0282
SCA	0.0152 ± 0.0035	0.0514 ± 0.013	0.0256 ± 0.009	0.166 ± 0.0153	0.0704 ± 0.0206
LexStat	0.0267 ± 0.0085	0.0848 ± 0.0226	0.0314 ± 0.0091	0.1507 ± 0.0143	0.0786 ± 0.0209
OnlinePMI	0.0158 ± 0.0048	0.1056 ± 0.0198	0.0457 ± 0.0135	0.1717 ± 0.0185	0.1184 ± 0.031
SVM	0.0146 ± 0.0039	0.0989 ± 0.0224	0.0452 ± 0.011	0.1827 ± 0.0237	0.1199 ± 0.0269

Table 3: The mean and standard deviation for each method and family is computed from 7500 posterior trees. The automatic methods which comes closest to the gold standard phylogeny is shaded in gray, and where the expert cognate sets perform best, this is indicated with a **bold** font.

as $1 - \frac{|S(\tau) \cap S(\tau_g)| + |B(\tau) \cap B(\tau_g)|}{\binom{n}{4}}$. The QD formulation counts the butterflies in an inferred tree τ as errors. The tree τ should not be penalized if an internal node in the gold standard tree τ_g is m-ary. To this end, Pompei et al. (2011) defined a new measure known as GQD to discount the presence of star quartets in τ_g. GQD is defined as $DB(\tau, \tau_g)/B(\tau_g)$ where $DB(.)$ is the number of different butterflies between τ, τ_g.

We extracted gold standard trees from Glottolog (Hammarström et al., 2017) for the purpose of evaluating the inferred posterior trees from each automated cognate identification system. We note that the Bayesian inference procedure produces rooted trees with branch lengths whereas the gold standard trees do not have any branch lengths. Although there exist other linguistic phylogenetic inference algorithms such as those of Ringe et al. (2002) we do not test the algorithms due to the non-availability and scalability of the software to datasets with more than twenty languages.

4.2 Results

The results of our experiments are given in table 3. A average lower GQD score implies that the inferred trees are closer to the gold standard phylogeny than a higher average GQD score. Except for Austronesian, Bayesian inference based on expert cognate sets yields trees that are very close to the gold standard tree. Surprisingly, algorithmically simple systems such as NED and CCM show better performance than the machine-learned SVM model except from Sino-Tibetan. SCA is a subsystem of LexStat but emerges as the winner in two language families (Indo-European and Sino-Tibetan). Given that SCA is outperformed by SVM and LexStat in automatic cognate detection, this is very surprising, and further research is needed to find out, why the simpler models

perform well on phylogenetic reconstruction. Although our results indicate that expert-coded cognate sets are generally more suitable for phylogenetic reconstruction, we can also see that the difference to trees inferred from automated cognate sets is not very large.

5 Conclusion

In this paper, we carried out a preliminary evaluation of the usefulness of automated cognate detection methods for phylogenetic inference. Although the cognate sets predicted by automated cognate detection methods yield phylogenetic trees that come close to expert trees, there is still room for improvement, and future research is needed to further enhance automatic cognate detection methods. However, as our experiments show, expert-annotated cognate sets are also not free from errors, and it seems likewise useful to investigate, how the consistency of cognate coding by experts could be further improved.

As future work, we intend to create a cognate identification system that combines the output of different algorithms in a more systematic way. We intend to infer cognate sets from the combined system and use them to infer phylogenies and evaluate the inferred phylogenies against the gold standard trees.

Acknowledgments

This research was supported by the ERC Advanced Grant 324246 EVOLAEMP (GJ, JW), the DFG-KFG 2237 Words, Bones, Genes, Tools (GJ), the ERC Starting Grant 715618 CALC (JML), and the BIGMED project (TR). We thank our anonymous reviewers for helpful comments, Mei-Shin Wu for helping with Sino-Tibetan data, Claire Bowern and Tiago Tresoldi for helping with Pama-Nyungan data, Paul Sidwell for helping with Austro-Asiatic data, as well as the audience at the CESC 2017 conference (MPI-SHH, Jena) for their helpful comments on an earlier version of the paper.

References

Enrique Amigó, Julio Gonzalo, Javier Artiles, and Felisa Verdejo. 2009. A comparison of extrinsic clustering evaluation metrics based on formal constraints. *Information retrieval*, 12(4):461–486.

Alexandre Bouchard-Côté, David Hall, Thomas L. Griffiths, and Dan Klein. 2013. Automated reconstruction of ancient languages using probabilistic models of sound change. *Proceedings of the National Academy of Sciences*, 110(11):4224–4229.

Remco Bouckaert, Philippe Lemey, Michael Dunn, Simon J. Greenhill, Alexander V. Alekseyenko, Alexei J. Drummond, Russell D. Gray, Marc A. Suchard, and Quentin D. Atkinson. 2012. Mapping the origins and expansion of the Indo-European language family. *Science*, 337(6097):957–960.

Claire Bowern and Quentin D. Atkinson. 2012. Computational phylogenetics of the internal structure of Pama-Nguyan. *Language*, 88:817–845.

Lyle Campbell and William J. Poser. 2008. *Language classification: History and Method*. Cambridge University Press.

Will Chang, Chundra Cathcart, David Hall, and Andrew Garrett. 2015. Ancestry-constrained phylogenetic analysis supports the Indo-European steppe hypothesis. *Language*, 91(1):194–244.

Michael A. Covington. 1996. An algorithm to align words for historical comparison. *Computational Linguistics*, 22(4):481–496.

Michael Dunn. 2012. Indo-European lexical cognacy database (IELex).

Michael Dunn, Simon J. Greenhill, Stephen C. Levinson, and Russell D. Gray. 2011. Evolved structure of language shows lineage-specific trends in word-order universals. *Nature*, 473(7345):79–82.

Sean R. Eddy. 2004. Where did the BLOSUM62 alignment score matrix come from? *Nature Biotechnology*, 22(8):1035–1036.

George F Estabrook, FR McMorris, and Christopher A Meacham. 1985. Comparison of undirected phylogenetic trees based on subtrees of four evolutionary units. *Systematic Biology*, 34(2):193–200.

Joseph Felsenstein. 1981. Evolutionary trees from DNA sequences: A maximum likelihood approach. *Journal of Molecular Evolution*, 17(6):368–376.

Joseph Felsenstein. 1992. Phylogenies from restriction sites: A maximum-likelihood approach. *Evolution*, 46(1):159–173.

Robert Forkel, Johann-Mattis List, Michael Cysouw, and Simon J. Greenhill. 2017. *CLDF. Cross-Linguistic Data Formats. Version 1.0*. Max Planck Institute for the Science of Human History, Jena.

Russell D. Gray and Quentin D. Atkinson. 2003. Language-tree divergence times support the Anatolian theory of Indo-European origin. *Nature*, 426(6965):435–439.

Russell D Gray, Alexei J Drummond, and Simon J Greenhill. 2009. Language phylogenies reveal expansion pulses and pauses in pacific settlement. *science*, 323(5913):479–483.

Simon J. Greenhill, Robert Blust, and Russell D. Gray. 2008. The Austronesian Basic Vocabulary Database: From bioinformatics to lexomics. *Evolutionary Bioinformatics*, 4:271–283.

Simon J. Greenhill, Alexei J. Drummond, and Russell D. Gray. 2010. How accurate and robust are the phylogenetic estimates of Austronesian language relationships? *PloS one*, 5(3):e9573.

Simon J Greenhill, Chieh-Hsi Wu, Xia Hua, Michael Dunn, Stephen C Levinson, and Russell D Gray. 2017. Evolutionary dynamics of language systems. *Proceedings of the National Academy of Sciences*, 114(42):E8822–E8829.

Harald Hammarström, Robert Forkel, and Martin Haspelmath. 2017. *Glottolog*. Max Planck Institute for Evolutionary Anthropology, Leipzig.

Bradley Hauer and Grzegorz Kondrak. 2011. Clustering semantically equivalent words into cognate sets in multilingual lists. In *Proceedings of 5th International Joint Conference on Natural Language Processing*, pages 865–873, Chiang Mai, Thailand. Asian Federation of Natural Language Processing.

John P Huelsenbeck, Fredrik Ronquist, Rasmus Nielsen, and Jonathan P Bollback. 2001. Bayesian inference of phylogeny and its impact on evolutionary biology. *science*, 294(5550):2310–2314.

Gerhard Jäger. 2013. Phylogenetic inference from word lists using weighted alignment with empirically determined weights. *Language Dynamics and Change*, 3(2):245–291.

Gerhard Jäger, Johann-Mattis List, and Pavel Sofroniev. 2017. Using support vector machines and state-of-the-art algorithms for phonetic alignment to identify cognates in multi-lingual wordlists. In *Proceedings of the 15th Conference of the European Chapter of the Association for Computational Linguistics. Long Papers*, pages 1204–1215, Valencia. Association for Computational Linguistics.

Fiona M. Jordan, Russell D. Gray, Simon J. Greenhill, and Ruth Mace. 2009. Matrilocal residence is ancestral in Austronesian societies. *Proceedings of the Royal Society B: Biological Sciences*, 276(1664):1957–1964.

Michael I Jordan et al. 2004. Graphical models. *Statistical Science*, 19(1):140–155.

Grzegorz Kondrak. 2002. *Algorithms for language reconstruction*. Ph.D. thesis, University of Toronto, Ontario, Canada.

Thomas Lepage, David Bryant, Hervé Philippe, and Nicolas Lartillot. 2007. A general comparison of relaxed molecular clock models. *Molecular biology and evolution*, 24(12):2669–2680.

Vladimir I Levenshtein. 1965. Binary codes capable of correcting spurious insertions and reversals. *Cybernetics and Control Theory*, 10:707–710.

Paul O. Lewis. 2001. A likelihood approach to estimating phylogeny from discrete morphological character data. *Systematic Biology*, 50(6):913–925.

Percy Liang and Dan Klein. 2009. Online em for unsupervised models. In *Proceedings of human language technologies: The 2009 annual conference of the North American chapter of the association for computational linguistics*, pages 611–619. Association for Computational Linguistics.

Johann-Mattis List. 2012. LexStat: Automatic detection of cognates in multilingual wordlists. In *Proceedings of the EACL 2012 Joint Workshop of LINGVIS & UNCLH*, pages 117–125, Avignon, France. Association for Computational Linguistics.

Johann-Mattis List. 2014. *Sequence comparison in historical linguistics*. Düsseldorf University Press, Düsseldorf.

Johann-Mattis List, Michael Cysouw, and Robert Forkel. 2016a. Concepticon. A resource for the linking of concept lists. In *Proceedings of the Tenth International Conference on Language Resources and Evaluation*, pages 2393–2400. European Language Resources Association (ELRA).

Johann-Mattis List, Simon Greenhill, and Robert Forkel. 2017a. *LingPy. A Python library for quantitative tasks in historical linguistics*. Max Planck Institute for the Science of Human History, Jena.

Johann-Mattis List, Simon J. Greenhill, and Russell D. Gray. 2017b. The potential of automatic word comparison for historical linguistics. *PLOS ONE*, 12(1):1–18.

Johann-Mattis List, Philippe Lopez, and Eric Bapteste. 2016b. Using sequence similarity networks to identify partial cognates in multilingual wordlists. In *Proceedings of the 54th Annual Meeting of the Association for Computational Linguistics (Volume 2: Short Papers)*, pages 599–605, Berlin, Germany. Association for Computational Linguistics.

John Nerbonne and Wilbert Heeringa. 1997. Measuring dialect distance phonetically. In *Proceedings of SIGPHON-97: 3rd Meeting of the ACL Special Interest Group in Computational Phonology*.

Ilia Peiros. 2004. *[Dataset on Sino-Tibetan languages encoded in STARLING in the file] sintib.exe*. Russian State University for the Humanities, Moscow.

Simone Pompei, Vittorio Loreto, and Francesca Tria. 2011. On the accuracy of language trees. *PloS one*, 6(6):e20109.

Usha Nandini Raghavan, Réka Albert, and Soundar Kumara. 2007. Near linear time algorithm to detect community structures in large-scale networks. *Physical review E*, 76(3):036106.

Taraka Rama. 2016. Siamese convolutional networks for cognate identification. In *Proceedings of COLING 2016, the 26th International Conference on Computational Linguistics: Technical Papers*, pages 1018–1027.

Taraka Rama and Lars Borin. 2015. Comparative evaluation of string similarity measures for automatic language classification. In Ján Mačutek and George K. Mikros, editors, *Sequences in Language and Text*, pages 203–231. Walter de Gruyter.

Taraka Rama, Johannes Wahle, Pavel Sofroniev, and Gerhard Jäger. 2017. Fast and unsupervised methods for multilingual cognate clustering. *arXiv preprint arXiv:1702.04938*.

Don Ringe, Tandy Warnow, and Ann Taylor. 2002. Indo-European and computational cladistics. *Transactions of the Philological Society*, 100(1):59–129.

Fredrik Ronquist, Seraina Klopfstein, Lars Vilhelmsen, Susanne Schulmeister, Debra L. Murray, and Alexandr P. Rasnitsyn. 2012. A total-evidence approach to dating with fossils, applied to the early radiation of the hymenoptera. *Systematic Biology*, 61(6):973–999.

Martin Rosvall and Carl T Bergstrom. 2008. Maps of random walks on complex networks reveal community structure. *Proceedings of the National Academy of Sciences*, 105(4):1118–1123.

Paul Sidwell. 2015. Austroasiatic dataset for phylogenetic analysis: 2015 version. *Mon-Khmer Studies (Notes, Reviews, Data-Papers)*, 44:lxviii–ccclvii.

Robert. R. Sokal and Charles. D. Michener. 1958. A statistical method for evaluating systematic relationships. *University of Kansas Scientific Bulletin*, 28:1409–1438.

Adam St Arnaud, David Beck, and Grzegorz Kondrak. 2017. Identifying cognate sets across dictionaries of related languages. In *Proceedings of the 2017 Conference on Empirical Methods in Natural Language Processing*, pages 2509–2518.

Peter Turchin, Ilja Peiros, and Murray Gell-Mann. 2010. Analyzing genetic connections between languages by matching consonant classes. *Journal of Language Relationship*, 3:117–126.

Søren Wichmann and Eric W Holman. 2013. Languages with longer words have more lexical change. In *Approaches to Measuring Linguistic Differences*, pages 249–281. Mouton de Gruyter.

Søren Wichmann, Eric W. Holman, Dik Bakker, and Cecil H. Brown. 2010. Evaluating linguistic distance measures. *Physica A: Statistical Mechanics and its Applications*, 389:3632–3639.

Søren Wichmann, Eric W. Holman, Taraka Rama, and Robert S. Walker. 2011. Correlates of reticulation in linguistic phylogenies. *Language Dynamics and Change*, 1(2):205–240.

Ziheng Yang. 1994. Maximum likelihood phylogenetic estimation from DNA sequences with variable rates over sites: Approximate methods. *Journal of Molecular evolution*, 39(3):306–314.

Ziheng Yang. 2014. *Molecular evolution: A statistical approach*. Oxford University Press, Oxford.

Ziheng Yang and Bruce Rannala. 1997. Bayesian phylogenetic inference using DNA sequences: a Markov Chain Monte Carlo method. *Molecular biology and evolution*, 14(7):717–724.

Chi Zhang, Tanja Stadler, Seraina Klopfstein, Tracy A Heath, and Fredrik Ronquist. 2015. Total-evidence dating under the fossilized birth–death process. *Systematic biology*, page syv080.

A   Supplemental Material

The code and data used in this paper are uploaded as a zip file. In addition, they are available for download via Zenodo at `https://doi.org/10.5281/zenodo.1218060`.

Automatically Selecting the Best Dependency Annotation Design with Dynamic Oracles

Guillaume Wisniewski[1], **Ophélie Lacroix**[2] and **François Yvon**[1]
[1]LIMSI, CNRS, Univ. Paris-Sud, Université Paris-Saclay, F-91405 Orsay, France
[2]Siteimprove, Sankt Annæ Plads 28, DK-1250 Copenhagen, Denmark
`wisniews@limsi.fr, ola@siteimprove.com, yvon@limsi.fr`

Abstract

This work introduces a new strategy to compare the numerous conventions that have been proposed over the years for expressing dependency structures and discover the one for which a parser will achieve the highest parsing performance. Instead of associating each sentence in the training set with a single gold reference, we propose to consider a set of references encoding alternative syntactic representations. Training a parser with a dynamic oracle will then automatically select among all alternatives the reference that will be predicted with the highest accuracy. Experiments on the UD corpora show the validity of this approach.

1 Introduction

Multiple annotation conventions have been proposed over the years for representing dependency structures (Hajič et al., 2001; De Marneffe et al., 2014). The divergence between annotation guidelines can result from the theoretical linguistic principles governing the choices of head status and dependency inventories, the tree-to-dependency conversion scheme or arbitrary decisions regarding closed class words, such as interjections or discursive markers, the syntactic role of which is debatable. Several works have shown that the choice of a dependency structure can have a large impact on parsing performance (Silveira and Manning, 2015; de Lhoneux and Nivre, 2016; Kohita et al., 2017) and on the performance of downstream applications (Elming et al., 2013).

A natural way to decide which syntactic representation is the best is to choose the one for which a standard parser will achieve the highest parsing performance (Schwartz et al., 2012; Husain and Agrawal, 2012; Noro et al., 2005). Implementing this general principle faces two challenges: *i)* defining a learning criterion that can predict which dependency structure will be the easiest to learn *ii)*

finding a way to explore a potentially large number of annotation schemes that describe all combinations of several design decisions.

This work shows that the dynamic oracle of Goldberg and Nivre (2013) can straightforwardly uncover the most *learnable* dependency representation among a predefined set of possible references.[1] Rather than associating each sentence in the training set to a single reference, we propose to consider a set of references encoding alternative syntactic representations. Training a parser with a dynamic oracle will then automatically select among all alternatives the reference that will be predicted with the highest accuracy.

This article is organized as follows: we first review standard structural transformations studied in the literature that will be used to build a treebank annotated with multiple references (§2). We then show how the dynamic oracle of Goldberg and Nivre (2013) can be used to train a parser when each sentence is associated to a set of references and explain how it can be used to define a learnability criteria (§3). An experimental evaluation of our approach is presented in §4.

2 Dependency Transformations

In this section, we explain how to automatically transform the reference UD treebanks (Nivre et al., 2016), to build corpora in which each sentence is annotated by a set of possible trees.

The UD project aims at developing cross-linguistically consistent treebank annotations for many languages by harmonizing annotation schemes between languages and converting existing treebanks to this new scheme. Several recent papers (Kohita et al., 2017; de Lhoneux and Nivre, 2016; Silveira and Manning, 2015; Popel et al.,

---

[1]Contrary to unsupervised parsing, our approach does not aim at discovering a dependency structure and rather relies on the existence of several hand-crafted references.

401

Proceedings of NAACL-HLT 2018, pages 401–406
New Orleans, Louisiana, June 1 - 6, 2018. ©2018 Association for Computational Linguistics

2013) have investigated whether the choices made to increase the sharing of structures between languages hurt parsing performance and have identified a variety of choice points in which more than one design could be advocated. Most of these points are related to the issue of headness: contrary to most works in theoretical linguistic, UD assumes that function words should be categorically subordinated to content words to maximize the similarity of dependency trees across languages (Osborne and Maxwell, 2015).

The alternative representations we consider are summarized in Table 1. They mostly consist in demoting the lexical head and making it dependent on a functional head. We designed a set of handcrafted rules[2] to convert dependencies between these two schemes. Each application of a rule creates a new tree in the set of references that is being built. As shown in Figure 1, the resulting set of references encodes all possible combinations of the considered transformations.

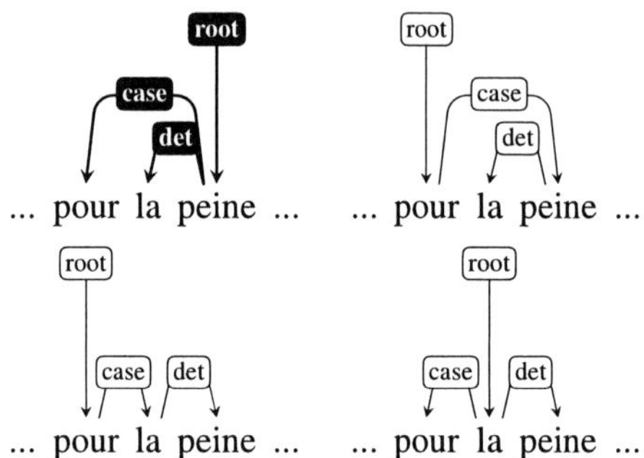

Figure 1: Examples of all the annotations generated by applying the rules of Table 1. The UD reference is in solid black.

3 Training a Dependency Parser with Multiple References

Dynamic Oracle In a transition-based parser (Nivre, 2008), a parse is computed by performing a sequence of *transitions* building the parse tree in an incremental fashion. A partially built dependency tree is represented by a *configuration* c; when in c, applying a transition t results in the parser moving to a new configuration denoted $c \circ t$.

At each step of the parsing process, every possible transition is scored by a classifier (e.g. a linear model), given a feature representation of c and

---

Algorithm 1: Training on one sentence with multiple references (see text for notations).

Input: W the input sentence, $\mathcal{T}$ the set of gold trees
1   $c \leftarrow \textsc{Initial}(W)$
2   **while** $\neg\textsc{Terminal}(c)$ **do**
3    $\textsc{Correct} \leftarrow \{t | \exists T \in \mathcal{T}, \textsc{Oracle}(t, c, T) = 0\}$
4    $t_p \leftarrow \arg\max_{t \in \textsc{Legal}(c)} \mathbf{w} \cdot \phi(c, t)$
5    $t_o \leftarrow \arg\max_{t \in \textsc{Correct}(c)} \mathbf{w} \cdot \phi(c, t)$
6   **if** $t_p \notin \textsc{Correct}$ **then**
7     $\textsc{Update}(\mathbf{w}, \phi(c, t_o), \phi(c, t_p))$
8     $t_{\text{next}} \leftarrow t_o$
9   **else**
10     $t_{\text{next}} \leftarrow t_p$
11    $\mathcal{T} \leftarrow \{T \in \mathcal{T} | \textsc{Oracle}(t_{\text{next}}, c, T) = 0\}$
12    $c \leftarrow c \circ t_{\text{next}}$

---

model parameters $\mathbf{w}$; the score of a *derivation* (a sequence of transitions) generating a given parse tree is the sum of its transition scores. Parsing thus amounts to finding, starting from the initial configuration $\textsc{Initial}(W)$, the derivation having the highest score, typically using greedy or beam search.[3]

Algorithm 1 formalizes the training procedure when the dynamic[4] oracle of Goldberg and Nivre (2013) is used: for each sentence, a parse tree is built incrementally and at each step, if the predicted transition prevents the creation of a gold dependency, the parameters are updated, according, for instance, to the perceptron rule (l.7). Erroneous transitions can efficiently be found using the $\textsc{Oracle}(t, c, T)$ function formally defined in (Goldberg and Nivre, 2013) as computing the number of dependencies of a gold parse tree T that can no longer be predicted when a transition t is applied in configuration c.

During training, it often happens that several transitions are equally good: in such situations, the training algorithm breaks ties among oracle transitions according to the model current prediction (l.5). As suggested in the imitation learning literature (Daumé III and Marcu, 2005; Ross and Bagnell, 2010), this strategy enables to sample those configurations that will be the most similar to the ones seen when predicting a new dependency tree:

---

[2]A more detailed description of the transformations can be found in (Wisniewski and Lacroix, 2017). The source code is freely available on the first author web site.

[3]In this work we only consider greedy parsers. Extending the proposed approach to beam parsers would prevent discarding a reference because one of the its transition is too hard to predict (i.e. has a very low score), which would, intuitively, results in even better predictions.

[4]Algorithm 1 only uses the non-deterministic property of the oracle and not its completeness. Even if we use the most common term, 'dynamic oracle', our approach only requires the former property.

Syntactic Functions		Annotation Scheme	
Relation	**UD labels**	**UD**	**Alternative**
Clause subordinates	`mark`	to read	to read
Determiners	`det`	the book	the book
Noun sequences	`mwe+goeswith, name`	John Jr. Doe	John Jr. Doe
Case marking	`case`	of Earth	of Earth
Coordinations	`cc+conj`	me and you	me and you
Copulas	`cop+auxpass`	is nice	is nice

Table 1: Annotation schemes in the UD treebanks and standard alternatives.

it is a way to let the parser explore more specifically the part of the search space it prefers and is more likely to see at test time (Aufrant et al., 2017). Using a dynamic oracle usually results in substantial improvements in accuracy compared to static oracles.

Considering Multiple References Implementing the training algorithm described above only requires the ability to detect whether a transition will cause an erroneous dependency. It can naturally be extended to the case of multiple references: a transition is considered correct as long as it can predict at least one of the gold trees; when moving to a new configuration, trees that can no longer be generated are removed from the set of references, in order to make sure the parser will not mix the dependencies of two gold trees (l.11).

Upon full completion of parsing, there will remain only one surviving reference that has been selected *according to the model current predictions*. This reference corresponds to the dependency structure that is the most similar to the hypothesis the parser would have predicted at test time and can therefore be described as the reference the parser prefers: intuitively, Algorithm 1 will thus identify the reference that will be predicted with the highest accuracy.

4 Experiments

Data We separately apply to the 7 dependencies considered the transformations described in Section 2 on the 38 languages of the UD project (v1.3), resulting in 266 transformed corpora.[5] To evaluate the ability of the proposed method to identify the 'best' dependency structure, we consider fully as well as partially transformed sentences: a sentence with n dependencies of interest will generate 2^n references.

For each condition (i.e. a language and a transformation), a dependency parser is trained using (a) the original data annotated with UD convention, (b) 'transformed' data in which each sentence is associated to a reference in which all dependencies of interest have been transformed and (c) the data associated with a set of reference containing all the partially transformed references (including the original and transformed references).

Parser We use our own implementation of an arc-eager unlabeled dependency parser with a dynamic oracle and an averaged perceptron, using the features described in (Zhang and Nivre, 2011) which have been designed for English and have not been adapted to the specificities of the other languages.[6] Training stops when the UAS estimated on the validation set has converged.

Impact of Transformations Figure 2 shows the distribution of differences in UAS between a parser trained on the original data (setting (a)) and a parser trained on the transformed data (setting (b)). To evaluate the proposed transformations, we follow the approach introduced in (Schwartz et al.,

---

[5] 44 transformed corpora were identical to the original corpora as the transformation can not be applied (e.g. there are no multi-word expression in Chinese).

[6] Note that the proposed approach can be apply to other transition systems and classifiers.

2012) consisting in comparing the original and the transformed data on their respective references.

As expected, the annotation scheme has a large impact on the quality of the prediction, with an average difference in scores of 0.66 UAS points and variations as large as 8.1 UAS points. These results show that, contrary to general belief (Schwartz et al., 2012; Kohita et al., 2017), the UD scheme is not sub-optimal for monolingual parsing: the difference in UAS is negative in 93 conditions and positive in 129. Table 2 details for each dependency the when the UD scheme results in better predictions.

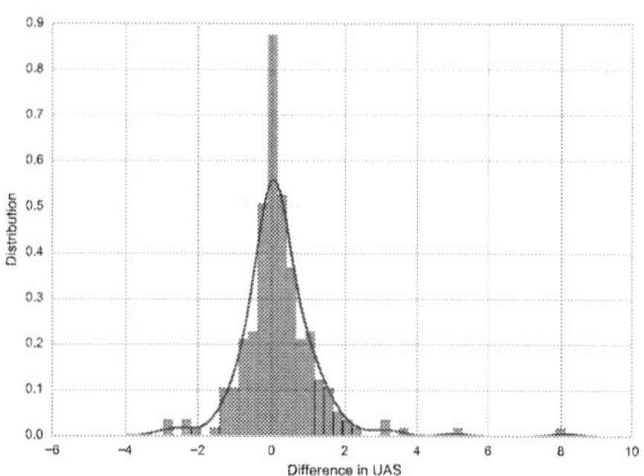

Figure 2: Distribution of differences between the UAS achieved on the UD and transformed corpora. Positive values indicate better prediction performance with UD annotations.

case	44.7%	mark	58.3%	det	80.5%
cc	89.4%	mwe	50.0%	name	45.8%
cop	25.0%				

Table 2: Percentage of times a parser trained and evaluated on UD data (setting (a)) outperforms a parser trained and evaluated on transformed data (setting (b)).

Training with Multiple References To assess the impact of training with multiple references (setting (c)), we first evaluate the capacity of Algorithm 1 to consistently select a single annotation scheme during training. We count, in each conditions, the number of times the reference that has survived training was following the original scheme and the number of times it was following the transformed scheme. For 74.7% of the conditions, the reference that has survived training was following the same annotation scheme for more than 70% of the training examples. This observation proves the ability of the parser to commit itself to a single annotation scheme.

Learnability Criterion The training procedure proposed in this article was designed to uncover the dependency structure that will optimize parsing accuracy. In this section we evaluate whether this goal is achieved, by counting the number of conditions in which the annotation scheme that has survived training the most often (in setting (c)) is indeed the one that achieves the best performance on the test set, as evaluated by testing a parser in settings (a) and (b).

We will consider, as baselines, two measures of the 'learnability' of a treebank, the *predictability* of an annotation scheme (Schwartz et al., 2012) and the *derivation perplexity* (Søgaard and Haulrich, 2010). Contrary to our approach, these two measures aims at deciding which of two annotations schemes will achieve the best parsing accuracy without actually training and testing a parser. The predictability is defined as the entropy of the conditional distribution of the dependent PoS knowing the head PoS. The derivation perplexity is the perplexity of 3-gram language model estimated on a corpus in which the words of a sentence appear in the order in which they are attached to their head.[7]

Table 3 reports the number of times, averaged over languages and transformations, that each measure of learnability is able to predict which of two competing annotation schemes will yield the best parsing performance. These results clearly show that the approach we propose to evaluate the 'learnability' of an annotation scheme outperforms existing criteria and is able to select the annotation convention that achieves the highest parsing performance.

metric	learnability
predictability	64.8%
derivation complexity	62.6%
multiple references	76.3%

Table 3: Number of times a given learnability measure is able to predict which annotation scheme will result in the best parsing performance. 'multiple references' corresponds to the approach proposed in this work.

---

[7]Similarly to (Søgaard and Haulrich, 2010), we consider a trigram language model but use Witten-Bell smoothing as many corpora are too small to use Kneser-Ney smoothing.

5 Conclusion

This work introduces a new strategy to compare the numerous representations that have been proposed over the years for expressing dependency structures and discover the one that is easiest to learn. Experiments with the popular transition-based parser on the UD corpora show the validity of the proposed approach.

In future work, we would like to evaluate the impact of annotation conventions on other kind of parsers and to find the properties of a dependency tree that facilitate its prediction. We also plan to find ways to easily annotate sentences with multiple references (e.g. by indicating that the head of word can be chosen arbitrarily) and eliminate the constraint that references should be trees.

Acknowledgments

This work has been partly funded by the *Agence Nationale de la Recherche* under ParSiTi project (ANR-16-CE33-0021) and MultiSem project (ANR-16-CE33-0013).

References

Lauriane Aufrant, Guillaume Wisniewski, and François Yvon. 2017. Don't stop me now! Using global dynamic oracles to correct training biases of transition-based dependency parsers. In *Proceedings of the 15th Conference of the European Chapter of the Association for Computational Linguistics: Volume 2, Short Papers*. Association for Computational Linguistics, Valencia, Spain, pages 318–323. http://www.aclweb.org/anthology/E17-2051.

Hal Daumé III and Daniel Marcu. 2005. Learning as search optimization: approximate large margin methods for structured prediction. In *ICML '05: Proceedings of the 22nd international conference on Machine learning*. ACM Press, New York, NY, USA, pages 169–176. https://doi.org/http://doi.acm.org/10.1145/1102351.1102373.

Miryam de Lhoneux and Joakim Nivre. 2016. Should Have, Would Have, Could Have. Investigating Verb Group Representations for Parsing with Universal Dependencies. In *Proceedings of the Workshop on Multilingual and Cross-lingual Methods in NLP*. Association for Computational Linguistics, San Diego, California, pages 10–19. http://www.aclweb.org/anthology/W16-1202.

Marie-Catherine De Marneffe, Timothy Dozat, Natalia Silveira, Katri Haverinen, Filip Ginter, Joakim Nivre, and Christopher D. Manning. 2014. Universal stanford dependencies: a cross-linguistic typology. In Nicoletta Calzolari (Conference Chair), Khalid Choukri, Thierry Declerck, Hrafn Loftsson, Bente Maegaard, Joseph Mariani, Asuncion Moreno, Jan Odijk, and Stelios Piperidis, editors, *Proceedings of the Ninth International Conference on Language Resources and Evaluation (LREC'14)*. European Language Resources Association (ELRA), Reykjavik, Iceland.

Jakob Elming, Anders Johannsen, Sigrid Klerke, Emanuele Lapponi, Hector Martinez Alonso, and Anders Søgaard. 2013. Down-stream effects of tree-to-dependency conversions. In *Proceedings of the 2013 Conference of the North American Chapter of the Association for Computational Linguistics: Human Language Technologies*. Association for Computational Linguistics, Atlanta, Georgia, pages 617–626. http://www.aclweb.org/anthology/N13-1070.

Yoav Goldberg and Joakim Nivre. 2013. Training deterministic parsers with non-deterministic oracles. *Transactions of the Association for Computational Linguistics* 1:403–414. https://transacl.org/ojs/index.php/tacl/article/view/145.

Jan Hajič, Barbora Vidová-Hladká, and Petr Pajas. 2001. The Prague Dependency Treebank: Annotation Structure and Support. In *Proceedings of the IRCS Workshop on Linguistic Databases*. University of Pennsylvania, Philadelphia, USA, pages 105–114.

Samar Husain and Bhasha Agrawal. 2012. Analyzing parser errors to improve parsing accuracy and to inform tree banking decisions. *Linguistic Issues in Language Technology* 7.

Ryosuke Kohita, Hiroshi Noji, and Yuji Matsumoto. 2017. Multilingual back-and-forth conversion between content and function head for easy dependency parsing. In *Proceedings of the 15th Conference of the European Chapter of the Association for Computational Linguistics: Volume 2, Short Papers*. Association for Computational Linguistics, Valencia, Spain, pages 1–7. http://www.aclweb.org/anthology/E17-2001.

Joakim Nivre. 2008. Algorithms for deterministic incremental dependency parsing. *Comput. Linguist.* 34(4):513–553. https://doi.org/10.1162/coli.07-056-R1-07-027.

Joakim Nivre, Željko Agić, Lars Ahrenberg, Maria Jesus Aranzabe, Masayuki Asahara, Aitziber Atutxa, Miguel Ballesteros, John Bauer, Kepa Bengoetxea, Yevgeni Berzak, Riyaz Ahmad Bhat, Cristina Bosco, Gosse Bouma, Sam Bowman, Gülşen Cebirolu Eryiit, Giuseppe G. A. Celano, Çar Çöltekin, Miriam Connor, Marie-Catherine de Marneffe, Arantza Diaz de Ilarraza, Kaja Dobrovoljc, Timothy Dozat, Kira Droganova, Tomaž Erjavec, Richárd

Farkas, Jennifer Foster, Daniel Galbraith, Sebastian Garza, Filip Ginter, Iakes Goenaga, Koldo Gojenola, Memduh Gokirmak, Yoav Goldberg, Xavier Gómez Guinovart, Berta Gonzáles Saavedra, Normunds Grūzītis, Bruno Guillaume, Jan Hajič, Dag Haug, Barbora Hladká, Radu Ion, Elena Irimia, Anders Johannsen, Hüner Kaşkara, Hiroshi Kanayama, Jenna Kanerva, Boris Katz, Jessica Kenney, Simon Krek, Veronika Laippala, Lucia Lam, Alessandro Lenci, Nikola Ljubešić, Olga Lyashevskaya, Teresa Lynn, Aibek Makazhanov, Christopher Manning, Cătălina Mărănduc, David Mareček, Héctor Martínez Alonso, Jan Mašek, Yuji Matsumoto, Ryan McDonald, Anna Missilä, Verginica Mititelu, Yusuke Miyao, Simonetta Montemagni, Keiko Sophie Mori, Shunsuke Mori, Kadri Muischnek, Nina Mustafina, Kaili Müürisep, Vitaly Nikolaev, Hanna Nurmi, Petya Osenova, Lilja Øvrelid, Elena Pascual, Marco Passarotti, Cenel-Augusto Perez, Slav Petrov, Jussi Piitulainen, Barbara Plank, Martin Popel, Lauma Pretkalnia, Prokopis Prokopidis, Tiina Puolakainen, Sampo Pyysalo, Loganathan Ramasamy, Laura Rituma, Rudolf Rosa, Shadi Saleh, Baiba Saulīte, Sebastian Schuster, Wolfgang Seeker, Mojgan Seraji, Lena Shakurova, Mo Shen, Natalia Silveira, Maria Simi, Radu Simionescu, Katalin Simkó, Kiril Simov, Aaron Smith, Carolyn Spadine, Alane Suhr, Umut Sulubacak, Zsolt Szántó, Takaaki Tanaka, Reut Tsarfaty, Francis Tyers, Sumire Uematsu, Larraitz Uria, Gertjan van Noord, Viktor Varga, Veronika Vincze, Jing Xian Wang, Jonathan North Washington, Zdeněk Žabokrtský, Daniel Zeman, and Hanzhi Zhu. 2016. Universal dependencies 1.3. LINDAT/CLARIN digital library at Institute of Formal and Applied Linguistics, Charles University in Prague. http://hdl.handle.net/11234/1-1699.

Tomoya Noro, Chimato Koike, Taiichi Hashimoto, Takenobu Tokunaga, and Hozumi Tanaka. 2005. Evaluation of a japanese cfg derived from a syntactically annotated corpus with respect to dependency measures. In *Proceedings of the Fifth Workshop on Asian Language Resources (ALR-05) and First Symposium on Asian Language Resources Network (ALRN)*. http://aclweb.org/anthology/I/I05/I05-4002.pdf.

Timothy Osborne and Daniel Maxwell. 2015. A historical overview of the status of function words in dependency grammar. In *Proceedings of the Third International Conference on Dependency Linguistics (Depling 2015)*. Uppsala University, Uppsala, Sweden, Uppsala, Sweden, pages 241–250. http://www.aclweb.org/anthology/W15-2127.

Martin Popel, David Mareček, Jan Štpánek, Daniel Zeman, and Zdnk Žabokrtský. 2013. Coordination structures in dependency treebanks. In *Proceedings of the 51st Annual Meeting of the Association for Computational Linguistics (Volume 1: Long Papers)*. Association for Computational Linguistics, Sofia, Bulgaria, pages 517–527. http://www.aclweb.org/anthology/P13-1051.

Stephane Ross and J. Andrew (Drew) Bagnell. 2010. Efficient reductions for imitation learning. In *Proceedings of the 13th International Conference on Artificial Intelligence and Statistics (AISTATS)*. pages 661–668.

Roy Schwartz, Omri Abend, and Ari Rappoport. 2012. Learnability-based syntactic annotation design. In *Proceedings of COLING 2012*. The COLING 2012 Organizing Committee, Mumbai, India, pages 2405–2422. http://www.aclweb.org/anthology/C12-1147.

Natalia Silveira and Christopher Manning. 2015. Does Universal Dependencies need a parsing representation? An investigation of English. *Depling 2015* 310.

Anders Søgaard and Martin Haulrich. 2010. On the derivation perplexity of treebanks. In *Proceedings of Treebanks and Linguistic Theories 9*.

Guillaume Wisniewski and Ophélie Lacroix. 2017. A systematic comparison of syntactic representations of dependency parsing. In *Proceedings of the NoDaLiDa 2017 Workshop on Universal Dependencies (UDW 2017)*. Association for Computational Linguistics, Gothenburg, Sweden, pages 146–152. http://www.aclweb.org/anthology/W17-0419.

Yue Zhang and Joakim Nivre. 2011. Transition-based Dependency Parsing with Rich Non-local Features. In *Proceedings of ACL 2011, the 49th Annual Meeting of the Association for Computational Linguistics: Human Language Technologies*. Association for Computational Linguistics, Portland, Oregon, USA, pages 188–193. http://www.aclweb.org/anthology/P11-2033.

Consistent CCG Parsing over Multiple Sentences
for Improved Logical Reasoning

Masashi Yoshikawa[1]

yoshikawa.masashi.yh8@is.naist.jp

Hiroshi Noji[3]

hiroshi.noji@aist.go.jp

Koji Mineshima[2]

mineshima.koji@ocha.ac.jp

Daisuke Bekki[2]

bekki@is.ocha.ac.jp

[1]Nara Institute of Science and Technology, Nara, Japan
[2]Ochanomizu University, Tokyo, Japan
[3]Artificial Intelligence Research Center, AIST, Tokyo, Japan

Abstract

In formal logic-based approaches to Recognizing Textual Entailment (RTE), a Combinatory Categorial Grammar (CCG) parser is used to parse input premises and hypotheses to obtain their logical formulas. Here, it is important that the parser processes the sentences consistently; failing to recognize a similar syntactic structure results in inconsistent predicate argument structures among them, in which case the succeeding theorem proving is doomed to failure. In this work, we present a simple method to extend an existing CCG parser to parse a set of sentences consistently, which is achieved with an inter-sentence modeling with Markov Random Fields (MRF). When combined with existing logic-based systems, our method always shows improvement in the RTE experiments on English and Japanese languages.

1 Introduction

While today's neural network-based syntactic parsers (Dyer et al., 2016; Dozat and Manning, 2017; Yoshikawa et al., 2017) have proven successful on sentence level modeling, it is still challenging to accurately process texts that go beyond a single sentence (e.g. coreference resolution, discourse structure analysis). In this work we focus, among others, on the consistent analysis of multiple sentences in a document. This is as an important problem in reasoning tasks as other document analysis.

RTE is an elemental technology for semantic analysis of multiple sentences, where, given a text (T) and a hypothesis (H), a system determines if T entails H. Existing methods based on formal logic (Bos, 2008; Martínez-Gómez et al., 2017; Abzianidze, 2017) obtain logical formulas for T and H using an off-the-shelf CCG parser, and then feed them to a theorem prover. The standard approach to mapping CCG trees onto logical formulas is to assign λ-terms to the words in a sentence

(a) An example semantic template:
$$V \vdash S\backslash NP : \lambda F.(\exists x.(F(x) \land \exists e.V(e, x)))$$

(b) **T:**

$$\frac{\displaystyle \frac{\text{A man}}{NP} \quad \frac{\displaystyle \frac{\text{is}}{(S\backslash NP)/(S\backslash NP)} \quad \frac{\text{exercising}}{S\backslash NP}}{S\backslash NP}{>}}{S : \exists x.(\mathtt{man}(x) \land \exists e.\mathtt{exercise}(e, x))}{<}$$

H:

$$\frac{\displaystyle \frac{\text{There}}{NP} \quad \frac{\text{is}}{S\backslash NP/NP} \quad \frac{\text{a}}{NP/N} \quad \frac{\displaystyle \frac{\text{man}}{N/N} \quad \frac{\text{exercising}}{N}}{\vdots}}{S : \exists x.(\mathtt{man}(x) \land \mathtt{exercise}(x))}$$

Figure 1: (a) An example semantic template for verbs V that associates a CCG category $S\backslash NP$ with a λ-term. (b) A logical formula of a sentence is obtained at the root of a tree by composing λ-terms of all words following CCG combinatory rules. In this Figure, hypothesis H is wrongly parsed (See the text for details).

and combine them in a bottom-up fashion (Figure 1a). Here, when the parser fails to make consistent analyses for T and H, the succeeding inference component is also doomed to failure. In Figure 1b, when the parser wrongly analyzes "*man exercising*" in H as "*man*" modifying "*exercising*", the entailment relation cannot be established, due to the different argument structures of `exercise` in the resulting formulas.

While it is ideal to enhance the overall performance of a parser, it is not cheaply obtainable. Additionally, neural network-based parsers are susceptible to subtle changes in the input and thus hard to inspect and modify its parameters to change its prediction. Due to this, we cannot expect that a particular pair of words across multiple sentences be always analyzed in a consistent manner.

In this work, we solve the inconsistency prob-

Proceedings of NAACL-HLT 2018, pages 407–412
New Orleans, Louisiana, June 1 - 6, 2018. ©2018 Association for Computational Linguistics

lem above by adapting the inter-sentence model of Rush et al. (2012) to CCG parsing. Their motivation is to exploit the similarities among test sentences to overcome situations where the amount of the training data is scarce or its domain is different from the test data. The method based on dual decomposition tries to find parse trees for a set of sentences that agree with an MRF, which encourages the assignment of a similar structure to similar contexts.

In our approach, we aim to eliminate wrong logical formulas such as in Figure 1 by rewarding consistent CCG parses across sentences. This, in turn, is achieved by rewarding the consistent assignment of categories to the terminals. This works for CCG parsing, as its derivation is mostly determined by the terminal categories. The key of our approach is that by combining A* parsing of Yoshikawa et al. (2017) with dual decomposition, we can keep small the latency incurred by the use of the iterative algorithm.

We conducted experiments using two state-of-the-art logic-based systems (Martínez-Gómez et al., 2017; Abzianidze, 2017) and two RTE datasets for English and Japanese languages. Our method always shows improvement compared to the baselines.

2 Method

We describe our approach of modeling the inter-consistencies among CCG trees $Y = \langle y_1, \ldots, y_N \rangle$ for sentences $X = \langle x_1, \ldots, x_N \rangle$ (§2.1), [1] A* parsing method for each y_i (§2.2) and joint decoding of the MRF and A* parsing using dual decomposition (§2.3).

2.1 Document Consistencies with MRF

To model inter-consistencies among CCG parses, we adapt the global MRF model of Rush et al. (2012). See Figure 2 for an example MRF. Our MRF encourages the assignment of similar categories to the words appearing in similar contexts.

Firstly we construct a graphical representation of an MRF. For each context (unigram surface form in the case of Figure 2) $c \in C$, we have a set W_c of indices $\langle s, t \rangle$ that appear in c, where s is a sentence index and t a word index on sentence

---

[1] In this work, we focus on the inconsistency problem of premises and hypotheses of RTE task, and thus X does not contain sentences from any "training data", as was done in Rush et al. (2012). Exploiting external resources in the same manner is also an interesting future direction.

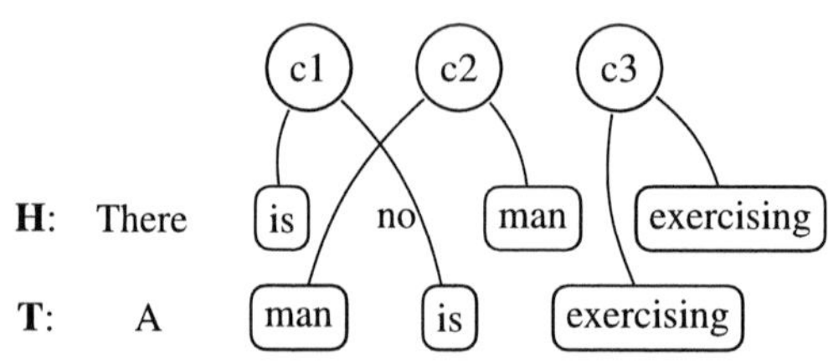

Figure 2: An MRF graph is made up of cliques each consisting of one *context node* ($\in C$; circles) and *word nodes* ($\in W$; rectangles) instantiating that context. As such, each clique expresses the interdependencies among words appearing across sentences.

s. Let $W = \bigcup_{c \in C} W_c$. We define an undirected graph $G = \langle V, E \rangle$, whose vertices are $V = C \cup W$ and edges $E = \{\langle w, c \rangle : c \in C, w \in W_c\}$. See Figure 2 for an MRF graph constructed for an example RTE problem.

We assign to each node in the graph a label from a set of CCG categories $\mathcal{T}$, so as to maximize the global consistency score g. By combining g with local CCG parsing for each y, we aim to obtain globally consistent trees Y (§2.3). We define label assignment z to nodes in V as $z = \langle z_1, \ldots, z_{|W|}, z'_1, \ldots, z'_{|C|} \rangle \in \mathcal{T}^{|W|} \times \mathcal{T}'^{|C|}$, where $\mathcal{T}' = \mathcal{T} \cup \{NULL\}$. In the following, z_w denotes the element in z at the index corresponding to $w \in W$ (similarly z'_c for $c \in C$). Following Rush et al. (2012), we allow $NULL$ label for context nodes. This works as a switch to "turn off" the consistency constraints to the connected nodes. Then, in the set $\mathcal{Z}(X)$ of all possible zs for X, we look for $z^* = \arg\max_{z \in \mathcal{Z}(X)} g(z)$, where $g(z)$ is[2]:

$$g(z) = \sum_{w \in W} f_w(z_w) + \sum_{(w,c) \in E} f_{w,c}(z_w, z'_c).$$

To reward the consistent assignment of categories among connected nodes, $f_{w,c}$ is defined as follow:

$$f_{w,c}(z_w, z'_c) = \begin{cases} \delta_1 & \text{if } z_w = z'_c \\ \delta_2 & \text{if } \texttt{simpl}(z_w) = \texttt{simpl}(z'_c) \\ \delta_3 & \text{if } z'_c = NULL \\ 0 & \text{otherwise,} \end{cases}$$

where $\delta_1 \geq \delta_2 \geq \delta_3$ and $\texttt{simpl}$ removes feature values from a category (e.g. $\texttt{simpl}(S_{dcl} \backslash NP) = S \backslash NP$). for f_w, we use $\log P_{tag}$ obtained by CCG

---

[2] We omit unary terms f_c for $c \in C$, as we set them 0.

parser (§2.2). We tune δ_is based on the RTE performance on the development set.

Since the above MRF $g(z)$ has a simple naïve Bayes structure, we can compute $argmax$ using dynamic programming.

2.2 A* CCG Parsing

To parse a sentence, we use the state-of-the-art A* parsing method of Yoshikawa et al. (2017), which treats a CCG tree y as a tuple $\langle c, h \rangle$ of categories $c = \langle c_1, \ldots, c_M \rangle$ and dependency structure $h = \langle h_1, \ldots, h_M \rangle$, where each h_i is a head index. They model a tree with a locally factored model; the probability of a CCG tree is the product of the probabilities of the categories p_{tag} and the dependency heads p_{dep} of all words in x:

$$p(y|x) = \prod_{i \in [1,M]} p_{tag}(c_i|x) \prod_{i \in [1,M]} p_{dep}(h_i|x).$$

Note that the most computationally heavy part of their method is the calculation of $P_{tag|dep}$, which needs to be done only once in our extension with dual decomposition. The additional computational cost of our method is rather small, as it depends on the number of times to run A* algorithm on the precomputed $P_{tag|dep}$, which is quite efficient.[3]

The probability $P(Y|X)$ of parses Y for X under this model is simply the product of all y_is:

$$Y^* = \underset{Y \in \mathcal{Y}(X)}{\arg\max} P(Y|X)$$
$$= \underset{Y \in \mathcal{Y}(X)}{\arg\max} \sum_{y_i \in Y} \log p(y_i|x_i),$$

where $\mathcal{Y}(X)$ is the space of all possible parses for X.

2.3 Dual Decomposition

To obtain CCG parses Y for sentences X that are optimal in terms of both the global consistency model (§2.1) and the local parsing model (§2.2), we solve the following problem using dual decomposition:

$$(Y^*, z^*) = \underset{Y \in \mathcal{Y}(X), z \in \mathcal{Z}(X)}{\arg\max} P(Y|X) + g(z)$$
$$\text{s.t. } \forall \langle s, t \rangle \in W \ z_{s,t} = c_{s,t},$$

Algorithm 1 Joint CCG parsing and global MRF decoding

$\triangleright$ J: a set of pairs of word nodes and categories in MRF
$\triangleright$ α: step size $(0.0 < \alpha \leq 1.0)$
Let $J = \{\langle w, c \rangle | w \in W, c \in \mathcal{T}\}$
Let $\mathbb{1}_c(z) = 1$ if z equals to c else 0
$u_{w,c}^{(1)} \leftarrow 0 \ \forall \langle w, c \rangle \in J$
for $k = 1, \ldots, K$ **do**
$\quad z^{(k)} \leftarrow \underset{z \in \mathcal{Z}(X)}{\arg\max} g(z) + \sum_{\langle w,c \rangle \in J} u_{w,c}^{(k)} \mathbb{1}_c(z_w)$
$\quad Y^{(k)} \leftarrow \underset{Y \in \mathcal{Y}(X)}{\arg\max} P(Y|X) - \sum_{\langle w,c \rangle \in J} u_{w,c}^{(k)} \mathbb{1}_c(c_w)$
$\quad$ **if** $z_w^{(k)} = c_w^{(k)}$ for all $w \in W$ **then**
$\quad\quad$ **return** $\langle z^{(k)}, Y^{(k)} \rangle$
$\quad u_{w,c}^{(k+1)} \leftarrow u_{w,c}^{(k)} + \alpha(\mathbb{1}_c(z_w^{(k)}) - \mathbb{1}_c(c_w^{(k)})) \ \forall \langle w, c \rangle \in J$
return $\langle z^{(K)}, Y^{(K)} \rangle$

---

where $c_{s,t}$ is the category assigned on t'th word in y_s. The condition in the equation states that the decoded Y^* and z^* must agree in the category assignment to word nodes in the MRF. Alg. 1 shows the pseudocode for dual decomposition applied to our method. Note that all the decoding subproblems can be kept intact even when added the Lagrangian multiplier u of dual decomposition.

3 Experiments

3.1 Experimental Settings

English In English experiment, we test the performance of ccg2lambda (Martínez-Gómez et al., 2017) and LangPro (Abzianidze, 2017) on SICK dataset (Marelli et al., 2014)[4]. As mentioned earlier, these systems try to prove whether T entails H, by applying a theorem prover to the logical formulas converted from the CCG trees. We report results for ccg2lambda with the default settings (with SPSA abduction; Martínez-Gómez et al. (2017)) and results for two versions of LangPro, one which is described in Abzianidze (2015) (henceforth we refer to it as LangPro15) and the other in Abzianidze (2017) (LangPro17).[5] Briefly, the difference between the two versions is that LangPro17 is more robust to parse errors. See the paper for the detail. For the CCG parser in §2.2, we use depccg[6] with an MRF in §2.1. We

---

[3] The supertagger of depccg processes 54 sentences per second while its A* decoder 2463 sentences per second. This is measured on SICK test set consisting of 9854 sentences using 2.20 GHz Intel Xeon CPUs with 16 cores.

[4] We also conducted experiments on FraCaS dataset (Cooper et al., 1996). For ccg2lambda, we found no improvements in RTE performance with our MRF, while for LangPro, we found that MRF guides to solve additional two problems.

[5] We report the scores for LangPro improved from the reviewed version, which we obtained from the author through the personal communication after the acceptance.

[6] https://github.com/masashi-y/depccg

Method	Accuracy	Precision	Recall
LangPro15 (Abzianidze, 2015)			
EasyCCG	79.05	**98.00**	52.67
depccg	80.37	97.94	55.81
depccg + MRF	**80.88**	97.91	**57.03**
LangPro17 (Abzianidze, 2017)			
EasyCCG	81.04	97.47	57.69
depccg	81.53	97.51	58.81
depccg + MRF	**81.61**	**97.52**	**59.00**
ccg2lambda (Martínez-Gómez et al., 2017)			
EasyCCG	81.59	**97.73**	58.48
depccg	81.95	97.19	59.98
depccg + MRF	**82.86**	97.14	**62.18**

Table 1: RTE results on test section of SICK

Method	Accuracy	Precision	Recall
jigg	75.0	92.7	65.4
depccg	67.87	88.34	56.77
depccg + MRF	71.31	88.88	62.24

Table 2: RTE results using ccg2lambda on JSeM

3.2 Results and Error Analysis

We show the results on SICK in Table 1. Our MRF consistently contributes to the improvement of the accuracies for both ccg2lambda and LangPro. We observe the same tendency in the scores for all systems; with MRF, both the accuracy and recall for the systems moderately improve and the systems using depccg have higher recall and lower precision compared to the ones with EasyCCG (with LangPro17 it marks higher precision as well).

In SICK, there are many instances of the construction shown in Figure 1 ("*There is no man exercising*", "*There is no dog barking*", etc.), whose correct reading is that the last verb (e.g. *exercising*) is a present participle modifying a noun (e.g. *man*). EasyCCG and default depccg wrongly parse the last phrase (*man exercising*) as $N/N\ N$, where *man* modifies *exercising*. Our method correctly predicts $N\ S_{ng}\backslash NP$, by utilizing the paired sentence (e.g. "*A man is exercising*"), in which the role of *exercising* is less ambiguous.

Given that the strength of LangPro17 is its robustness to parse errors such as PP-attachment, the larger gain in the accuracy for LangPro15 (roughly 0.5 versus 0.1 point up) indicates that our method is also robust in handling well-known difficult parsing problems. The example (a) in Table 3 is a case of coordinate construction. Baseline depccg wrongly coordinates *crocheting* with a noun *sofa*, while our method successfully resolves the correct coordinate structure by assigning $S_{ng}\backslash NP$ to the word (hence attaching it to *sitting*). Example (b) is one of the cases of PP-attachment that our method successfully resolved. Our method relocates the two PPs in T in their correct places. As in the example in Figure 1, our method corrects cases like (a) and (b) by using the structure of the less ambiguous counterpart as a guide. In the case of (c), the existing parsers misclassify *outdoors* in T as a noun and turns the verb *run* into a transitive verb. With our method, intransitive verb *run* in H works as a soft constraint on the verb in T and corrects its structure successfully. However, there are some cases where using only surface forms as a cue forces the assignment of categories which is

compare our results with depccg without the MRF and baselines reported in the above papers that use EasyCCG (Lewis and Steedman, 2014).

In MRF, a context node is constructed when two or more words from both T and H share the same surface form. Exceptionally, some pairs of categories are allowed to be aligned with score δ_1: a pair of noun modifier (N/N) and verb tense ($S_{ng}\backslash NP$), which are categories for present participles, and a pair of nominal modifier (N/N) and noun (N). In the experiment using ccg2lambda the pairs of categories of transitive and intransitive verbs, $((S_X\backslash NP)/NP, S_X\backslash NP)$ and $((S_X\backslash NP)/PP, S_X\backslash NP)$, for any feature X are also allowed with δ_1.

For the hyperparamters, we conducted grid search over $[0.0, 0.1, \ldots, 0.9]$ for each δ_i in the MRF s.t. $\delta_1 \geq \delta_2 \geq \delta_3$ and found that $\delta_1 = 0.9, \delta_2 = 0.1, \delta_3 = 0.0$ works the best on SICK trial set. We set $\alpha = 0.0002$ and $K = 500$ in Alg. 1. We decay α by 0.9 in every iteration.

Japanese In Japanese experiment, we evaluate ccg2lambda's performance on JSeM dataset (Kawazoe et al., 2017). To construct an MRF graph, we processed RTE problems with kuromoji[7] and made a context node for a noun or a verb followed by an adverb. The reason why we use bigram POS tag-based context is that the graph construction based on the surface form has resulted in poor RTE performance, by overgenerating MRF constraints. This may be due to the fact that Japanese sentences are usually tokenized into smaller units. We used depccg and the same hyperparameters as English experiment.

---

[7] http://www.atilika.org/

Sentences

(a)		T: The girl is sitting on the couch and is $[_{S_{ng}\backslash NP}$ crocheting]
		H: The girl is sitting on the sofa and **crocheting**
		crocheting: ✗ $N \rightsquigarrow$ ✓ $S_{ng}\backslash NP$
(b)		T: A veteran is showing different things **from** a war **to** some people
		H: Different things $[_{(NP\backslash NP)/NP}$ **from**] a war are being shown $[_{((S\backslash NP)\backslash(S\backslash NP))/NP}$ **to**] some people by a veteran
		from: ✗ $((S\backslash NP)\backslash(S\backslash NP))/NP \rightsquigarrow$ ✓ $(NP\backslash NP)/NP$
		to: ✗ $(NP\backslash NP)/NP \rightsquigarrow$ ✓ $((S\backslash NP)\backslash(S\backslash NP))/NP$
(c)		T: A few man in a competition are $[_{S_{ng}\backslash NP}$ **running**] outside
		H: A few man in a competition are **running** outdoors
		running: ✗ $(S_{ng}\backslash NP)/NP \rightsquigarrow$ ✓ $S_{ng}\backslash NP$
(d)		T: A man is $[_{(S_{ng}\backslash NP)/NP}$ **eating**] some food
		H: The person is **eating**
		eating: ✓ $S_{ng}\backslash NP \rightsquigarrow$ ✗ $(S_{ng}\backslash NP)/NP$

Table 3: Example parse results in SICK test set. (a), (b), (c) With the global MRF model, words in bold font previously assigned a wrong category (✗) have been assigned a correct one (✓). (d) is a case where the MRF is too strict and leads to the wrong assignment.

consistent but not desirable. In example (d), *eat* is used as a transitive verb in T and as an intransitive verb in H; thus it should have different categories.

We show the results on JSeM in Table 2. The RTE performance for Japanese language has improved consistently across all the scores when we add an MRF. However all the scores with depccg (with or without MRF) lag behind the scores reported in Mineshima et al. (2016), which uses a CCG parser implemented in Jigg (Noji and Miyao, 2016). We hypothesize that this is due to the fact that the previous work created the semantic templates for this language by analyzing parse outputs by Jigg and this resulted in a kind of "overfitting" in the templates.

In the above experiments, our method worked well, mainly due to the fact that the sentences in these datasets have comparably simple structure. However, in other datasets, there are naturally more complex cases as in Table 3 (d), where we want different syntactic analyses for occurences of words with the same surface form. We can counter these cases by simply extending the definition of "context" by N-grams or the use of POS tag as we did in the Japanese experiment. Developing a machine learning-based method that selects which contexts to use and set δ_is automatically is also an important future work.

4 Conclusion and Future Work

In this work, by modeling the inter-consistencies of multiple sentences in CCG parsing, we have successfully improved the performance of the formal logic-based methods to RTE. Still, there can be pairs of words in more complex RTE problems that should not have the same category but that our method wrongly force them to. This is mainly due to the fact that we hand-tuned rules to construct context nodes. In future work, we extend the method so that it learns when to set an MRF constraint.

Acknowledgments

First of all, we thank the three anonymous reviewers for their insightful comments. We are also grateful to Lasha Abzianidze for conducting in-depth experiments and for detailed discussion about LangPro. This work was supported by JST CREST Grant Number JPMJCR1301, Japan.

References

Lasha Abzianidze. 2015. A tableau prover for natural logic and language. In *Proceedings of the 2015 Conference on Empirical Methods in Natural Language Processing*. Association for Computational Linguistics, Lisbon, Portugal, pages 2492–2502. http://aclweb.org/anthology/D15-1296.

Lasha Abzianidze. 2017. LangPro: Natural Language Theorem Prover. In *Proceedings of the 2017 Conference on Empirical Methods in Natural Language Processing: System Demonstrations*. Association for Computational Linguistics, Copenhagen, Denmark, pages 115–120. http://www.aclweb.org/anthology/D17-2020.

Johan Bos. 2008. Wide-coverage Semantic Analysis with Boxer. In *Proceedings of the 2008 Conference on Semantics in Text Processing*. Association for Computational Linguistics, Stroudsburg, PA, USA, STEP '08, pages 277–286.

http://dl.acm.org/citation.cfm?id=
1626481.1626503.

Robin Cooper, Dick Crouch, Jan Van Eijck, Chris Fox, Josef Van Genabith, Jan Jaspars, Hans Kamp, David Milward, Manfred Pinkal, Massimo Poesio, Steve Pulman, Ted Briscoe, Holger Maier, and Karsten Konrad. 1996. FraCaS: A Framework for Computational Semantics. Deliverable D16.

Timothy Dozat and Christopher D. Manning. 2017. Deep Biaffine Attention for Neural Dependency Parsing. *In Proc. of ICLR* https://arxiv.
org/abs/1611.01734.

Chris Dyer, Adhiguna Kuncoro, Miguel Ballesteros, and Noah A. Smith. 2016. Recurrent Neural Network Grammars. In *Proceedings of the 2016 Conference of the North American Chapter of the Association for Computational Linguistics: Human Language Technologies*. Association for Computational Linguistics, San Diego, California, pages 199–209. http://www.aclweb.
org/anthology/N16-1024.

Ai Kawazoe, Ribeka Tanaka, Koji Mineshima, and Daisuke Bekki. 2017. An inference problem set for evaluating semantic theories and semantic processing systems for japanese. In Mihoko Otake, Setsuya Kurahashi, Yuiko Ota, Ken Satoh, and Daisuke Bekki, editors, *New Frontiers in Artificial Intelligence: JSAI-isAI 2015 Workshops, LENLS, JURISIN, AAA, HAT-MASH, TSDAA, ASD-HR, and SKL, Kanagawa, Japan, November 16-18, 2015, Revised Selected Papers*. Springer International Publishing, Cham, pages 58–65. https://doi.
org/10.1007/978-3-319-50953-2_5.

Mike Lewis and Mark Steedman. 2014. A* CCG Parsing with a Supertag-factored Model. In *Proceedings of the 2014 Conference on Empirical Methods in Natural Language Processing (EMNLP)*. Association for Computational Linguistics, pages 990–1000. https://doi.org/10.3115/v1/
D14-1107.

Marco Marelli, Stefano Menini, Marco Baroni, Luisa Bentivogli, Raffaella bernardi, and Roberto Zamparelli. 2014. A SICK cure for the evaluation of compositional distributional semantic models. In Nicoletta Calzolari, Khalid Choukri, Thierry Declerck, Hrafn Loftsson, Bente Maegaard, Joseph Mariani, Asuncion Moreno, Jan Odijk, and Stelios Piperidis, editors, *Proceedings of the Ninth International Conference on Language Resources and Evaluation (LREC'14)*. European Language Resources Association (ELRA), Reykjavik, Iceland, pages 216–223. ACL Anthology Identifier: L14-1314. http:
//www.lrec-conf.org/proceedings/
lrec2014/pdf/363_Paper.pdf.

Pascual Martínez-Gómez, Koji Mineshima, Yusuke Miyao, and Daisuke Bekki. 2017. On-demand Injection of Lexical Knowledge for Recognising Textual Entailment. In *Proceedings of the 15th Conference of the European Chapter of the Association for Computational Linguistics: Volume 1, Long Papers*. Association for Computational Linguistics, Valencia, Spain, pages 710–720. http://www.
aclweb.org/anthology/E17-1067.

Koji Mineshima, Ribeka Tanaka, Pascual Martínez-Gómez, Yusuke Miyao, and Daisuke Bekki. 2016. Building compositional semantics and higher-order inference system for a wide-coverage Japanese CCG parser. In *Proceedings of the 2016 Conference on Empirical Methods in Natural Language Processing*. Association for Computational Linguistics, Austin, Texas, pages 2236–2242. https:
//aclweb.org/anthology/D16-1242.

Hiroshi Noji and Yusuke Miyao. 2016. Jigg: A Framework for an Easy Natural Language Processing Pipeline. In *Proceedings of ACL-2016 System Demonstrations*. Association for Computational Linguistics, pages 103–108. https://doi.
org/10.18653/v1/P16-4018.

Alexander Rush, Roi Reichart, Michael Collins, and Amir Globerson. 2012. Improved Parsing and POS Tagging Using Inter-Sentence Consistency Constraints. In *Proceedings of the 2012 Joint Conference on Empirical Methods in Natural Language Processing and Computational Natural Language Learning*. Association for Computational Linguistics, Jeju Island, Korea, pages 1434–1444. http://www.aclweb.org/
anthology/D12-1131.

Masashi Yoshikawa, Hiroshi Noji, and Yuji Matsumoto. 2017. A* CCG Parsing with a Supertag and Dependency Factored Model. In *Proceedings of the 55th Annual Meeting of the Association for Computational Linguistics (Volume 1: Long Papers)*. Association for Computational Linguistics, Vancouver, Canada, pages 277–287. http://aclweb.
org/anthology/P17-1026.

Exploiting Dynamic Oracles to Train Projective Dependency Parsers on Non-Projective Trees

Lauriane Aufrant[1,2]**, Guillaume Wisniewski**[1] and **François Yvon**[1]

[1]LIMSI, CNRS, Univ. Paris-Sud, Université Paris-Saclay, F-91405 Orsay, France
[2]DGA, 60 boulevard du Général Martial Valin, 75 509 Paris, France
{lauriane.aufrant,guillaume.wisniewski,francois.yvon}@limsi.fr

Abstract

Because the most common transition systems are projective, training a transition-based dependency parser often implies to either ignore or rewrite the non-projective training examples, which has an adverse impact on accuracy. In this work, we propose a simple modification of dynamic oracles, which enables the use of non-projective data when training projective parsers. Evaluation on 73 treebanks shows that our method achieves significant gains (+2 to +7 UAS for the most non-projective languages) and consistently outperforms traditional projectivization and pseudo-projectivization approaches.

1 Introduction

Because of their efficiency and ease of implementation, transition-based parsers are the most common systems for dependency parsing. However, efficiency comes at a price, namely a loss in expressivity: while graph-based parsers are able to produce any tree spanning the input sentence, many transition-based systems are restricted to projective trees. Informally, a dependency tree is *non-projective* if at least one dependency crosses another arc (see Figure 1).

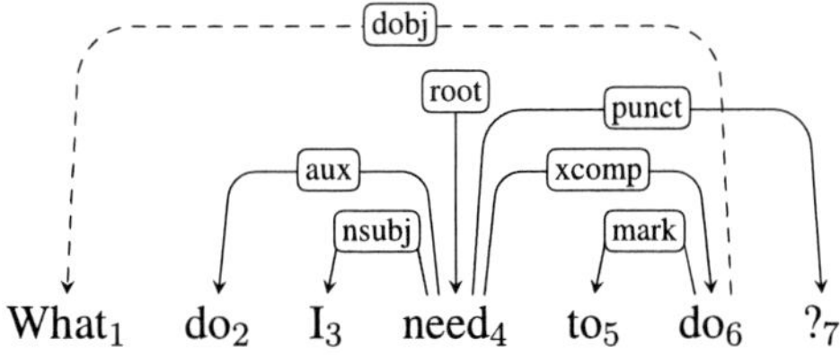

Figure 1: An example of non-projectivity: the tree is made non-projective by the dependency *What⌢do*.

The inability to generate non-projective trees is an obvious issue for accuracy: at test time, a projective parser is guaranteed to be wrong for all the non-projective dependencies, a limitation already pointed out several times (Nivre, 2009; Lacroix and Béchet, 2014). In this paper, we show that the impact can also be severe *at training time*. This is because the standard training procedure assumes that the reference tree is within reach of the parser, which is not the case for non-projective examples. Therefore, projective parsers cannot make any use of such samples and common practice is to filter them out, thereby wasting potentially valuable training material. Depending on the annotation schemes and languages, between 5 and 10% of the training set are typically discarded.[1]

Several strategies have been proposed to overcome the projectivity constraint. One line of research is to sacrifice parsing efficiency and introduce special transition systems capable to build non-projective dependencies (Covington, 2001; Nivre, 2009). Another approach introduces non-projective dependencies by post-processing the output projective trees. This is the case of the pseudo-projectivization method (Nivre and Nilsson, 2005), which encodes crossings in augmented relation labels and makes all examples projective. The accuracy on projective dependencies alone can also be maximized by projectivizing all training examples prior to training, using Eisner (1996)'s decoder.

In this work, we propose an alternative strategy: we show (§3) that it is possible, with a small modification of the dynamic oracle of Goldberg and Nivre (2012), to directly train a projective parser with non-projective examples. While our approach remains unable to produce non-projective trees, it still results in significant improvements

---

[1]In UD 1.2, examples with non-projective dependencies represent 4.96% of trees (0.48% of dependencies) for English, 12.45% (0.83%) for French, 8.19% (0.33%) for Arabic. However, the numbers rise for some languages such as Dutch (30.87%, 4.10%) or Ancient Greek (63.22%, 9.78%). See Straka et al. (2015) for complete data on 37 treebanks.

Proceedings of NAACL-HLT 2018, pages 413–419
New Orleans, Louisiana, June 1 - 6, 2018. ©2018 Association for Computational Linguistics

on the overall UAS (§4), and consistently outperforms the (pseudo-)projectivization approaches.

2 Training transition-based parsers

2.1 Parsing with a transition system

In transition-based parsing (Nivre, 2003), dependency trees are built incrementally, in a shift-reduce manner: to parse a sentence, a sequence of transitions (the *derivation*) is applied on the internal state of the parser (the *configuration*), consisting typically in a stack and a buffer of unprocessed words. In the ARCEAGER transition system (Nivre, 2004), four actions are available, one for each possible transition (see Table 1).

At parsing time, each transition to follow is predicted in turn by a classifier, typically an averaged perceptron (Collins and Roark, 2004) or a neural network (Chen and Manning, 2014; Dyer et al., 2015; Andor et al., 2016), based on features extracted from the current parser configuration.

Compared to other parsing frameworks, such as graph-based parsing (McDonald et al., 2005), a major advantage of transition-based parsing is its computational efficiency: the processing time of a sentence is linear in its length.

2.2 Training with dynamic oracles

The classifier used to predict the actions is typically trained in an online fashion, using a dataset consisting of input sentences and reference parse trees. Various strategies have been envisioned to generate, based on that data, pairs of positive (gold) and negative (predicted) parser configurations with which to update the model. A recent and successful proposal uses so-called *dynamic oracles* (Goldberg and Nivre, 2012): the training example is parsed by the model, and for each predicted configuration in the resulting derivation, the dynamic oracle computes a reference action, tailored to the current configuration.

In practice, the reference is defined as an action which does not degrade the accuracy on that sentence: if a transition prevents a gold arc from being produced later (such as attaching a token to the wrong head), it is incorrect, but no error is flagged if that arc was already unreachable (for instance if the true head was already removed from the stack).

Formally, if each configuration is associated with a UAS_{max}, the maximum UAS value that can be achieved by any of its successor derivations, then the *action cost* is defined as the difference between the current UAS_{max} and the future UAS_{max} (once the corresponding action has been applied). The best decision in that situation is the one which ensures the best future UAS, ie. which leaves UAS_{max} unchanged and has zero cost. By definition of UAS_{max}, in all configurations at least one action has zero cost; there may even be several in case of spurious ambiguities. Hence, when asked for a reference action, the dynamic oracle simply returns the set of zero-cost actions.

The core of the method is thus the computation of action costs. In order to simplify it, Goldberg and Nivre (2013) introduce the concept of *arc decomposition*: a transition system is *arc-decomposable* if in every configuration, all the gold dependencies that are still reachable can be reached simultaneously by the same derivation. It ensues that for such systems, the action cost is simply the number of gold arcs that the action explicitly forbids, which are in general straightforward to enumerate. For instance in ARCEAGER, the REDUCE action (which pops the topmost stack element s) has a cost of 1 for each child of s still in the buffer, since they no longer can get their true head (Goldberg and Nivre, 2013).

Arc-decomposability does not always hold, however, in which case there are extra costs to take into account: by definition of non-arc-decomposable systems, some arcs are incompatible (they are not unreachable, they can simply not be reached together). Therefore, at some point, adding a gold arc will imply renouncing to another gold arc, thereby inserting an error. It is however incorrect to assign this cost to the given action, since it is due to a much earlier action which introduced the incompatibility.[2] As exemplified by Goldberg et al. (2014) and Gómez-Rodríguez and Fernández-González (2015), it is not impossible to derive dynamic oracles for non-arc-decomposable systems, but taking this kind of incompatibilities into account makes the computation of their action

---

[2] A straightforward example of non-arc-decomposable system is the ARCSTANDARD system (Nivre, 2003). It consists in three actions: SHIFT (the same as in ARCEAGER), and LEFT and RIGHT actions, which link the two topmost stack elements in either direction, and then remove the child from the stack. For the reference tree 'The $\frown$ bag $\frown$ fell', in the configuration where the buffer is empty and the stack is [*The bag fell*], the only way to output the *bag* $\frown$ *fell* dependency is consequently to attach (and pop) '*bag*' immediately, thereby renouncing to its child '*The*', even tough it is currently reachable (with RIGHT+LEFT). In this configuration all decisions seem to degrade the UAS, but the actual error was done when SHIFTing '*fell*' before attaching '*The*'.

SHIFT	[S]	$(\sigma,$	$b\|\beta,$	$P)$	$\Rightarrow$	$(\sigma\|b,$	$\beta,$	$P)$	if b is a word
LEFT	[L]	$(\sigma\|s,$	$b\|\beta,$	$P)$	$\Rightarrow$	$(\sigma,$	$b\|\beta,$	$P + (b \to s))$	if s is a word and s is unattached
RIGHT	[R]	$(\sigma\|s,$	$b\|\beta,$	$P)$	$\Rightarrow$	$(\sigma\|s\|b,$	$\beta,$	$P + (s \to b))$	
REDUCE	[RE]	$(\sigma\|s,$	$\beta,$	$P)$	$\Rightarrow$	$(\sigma,$	$\beta,$	$P)$	if s is attached

Table 1: The ARCEAGER transition system: semantics and preconditions of each action. σ stands for the stack, s for the topmost stack element, β stands for the buffer, b for the first buffer element, and P is the partially built tree.

costs much more complex.

3 Using dynamic oracles to train on non-projective data

The reason why dynamic oracles can help solving the non-projectivity issue is that non-projective examples, in this framework, are not different from projective ones: the cost is well-defined for any action, and by definition there is always at least one zero-cost action. So, all training examples are usable by design, regardless of their projectivity. The issue rather resides in deriving a sound definition of the cost, which covers non-projective cases;[3] in the current state of the art, the dynamic oracles derived for projective systems are only sound for projective examples, though (see Figure 2).

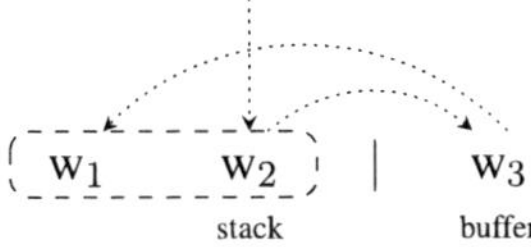

Figure 2: A configuration where all actions have non-zero cost (thereby contradicting its definition), for a non-projective reference tree (see dotted edges), when using the standard ARCEAGER dynamic oracle. The action cost is 2 for SHIFT (only w_2 can be correctly attached, by applying L+L+L afterwards), 2 for LEFT (L+S+L correctly attaches w_1 only) and 1 for RIGHT (RE+L+L correctly attaches both w_2 and w_3).

One way to look at non-projective examples is as a set of configurations containing arc incompatibilities: when two crossing edges are reachable, only one can actually belong to the final output. Yet, this is a known setting: with non-arc-decomposable systems, some erroneous configurations face the same issue. Hence, from the oracle point of view, the initial empty configuration already comes with embedded 'past errors' (the incompatibilities due to edge crossings). As in non-arc-decomposable systems, the cost incurred by these incompatibilities is not due to actions to

come, but should be attributed to previous actions, taken in a fictive history before the initial configuration. As such, the natural behavior of dynamic oracles is to ignore this cost. Hence, using the same methodology as for non-arc-decomposable systems, it is formally possible to define dynamic oracles for non-projective examples. But it implies enumerating all non-projective arc incompatibilities in an arbitrary parser configuration (and proving exhaustivity), which is a difficult task and remains, to date, an open question.

Instead of deriving exact costs, we propose here a straightforward strategy which *approximates* the action costs for non-projective examples: using the usual cost computation, but defining the oracles as *minimum-cost* actions instead of zero-cost ones. Indeed, when the parser ends up in a configuration where all decisions appear erroneous, the part of the cost which is common to all actions should in fact have been taken care of in the past; with this minimum-cost approach, it is ignored. In Figure 2, the RIGHT action is chosen as reference by the minimum-cost criterion, thereby acknowledging the fact that non-projectivity by itself incurs a cost of 1. This oracle generalizes the zero-cost one, as they are equivalent on projective trees.

Compared to an exact oracle, this approximated cost biases the oracle towards delaying the resolution of incompatibilities (like the SHIFT action in Figure 3). A few updates are consequently unsound, but empirically their impact remains small compared to the benefits of making more examples usable, as will be assessed in the next section.

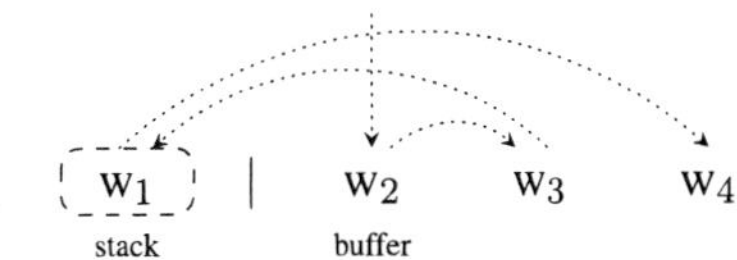

Figure 3: A configuration where action cost is poorly approximated, for a non-projective reference tree (see dotted edges). All gold arcs are reachable, but at most two can be reached simultaneously. The cost computed for LEFT is 2, 1 for RIGHT and 0 for SHIFT, even though all actions lead to a tree with two gold arcs.

---

[3]Exhaustive search would be a straightforward strategy to compute exact action costs in any setting, but it is computationally too expensive.

	μ	% non-projective sentences				# training sentences	
		> 50%	25-50%	10-25%	< 10%	> 500	< 500
# corresponding treebanks:	[73]	[1]	[9]	[32]	[31]	[57]	[16]
PANPARSER – greedy ARCEAGER							
Static oracle (only projective snt.)	78.28	56.23	76.22	75.49	82.47	81.34	67.37
Static oracle + projectivized snt.	+0.31	+2.12	+1.54	+0.15	+0.06	+0.50	-0.36
Dynamic oracle (only projective snt.)	78.94	57.75	76.99	76.26	82.97	81.92	68.34
Dynamic oracle + projectivized snt.	+0.32	+1.06	+1.04	+0.52	-0.11	+0.24	+0.61
Dynamic oracle + pseudo-proj. snt.	+0.26	+2.01	+1.49	+0.19	-0.07	+0.47	-0.45
Dynamic oracle + non-projective snt.	+0.48	+2.43	+1.83	+0.44	+0.07	+0.52	+0.36
PANPARSER – beam ARCEAGER							
Global dynamic oracle (only projective snt.)	79.77	57.12	78.28	76.83	83.96	83.12	67.84
Global dynamic oracle + non-projective snt.	80.40	61.49	80.11	77.54	84.04	83.63	68.87
	+0.63	+4.38	+1.84	+0.71	+0.07	+0.51	+1.03
PANPARSER – greedy ARCHYBRID							
Static oracle (only projective snt.)	75.71	53.08	73.66	73.19	79.63	78.29	66.51
Dynamic oracle (only projective snt.)	76.51	54.23	74.61	73.96	80.41	79.23	66.81
Dynamic oracle + non-projective snt.	+0.55	+3.08	+2.16	+0.33	+0.22	+0.53	+0.61
MALTPARSER – greedy ARCEAGER							
Baseline (only projective snt.)	72.88	57.88	71.74	69.99	76.68	76.82	58.87
+ pseudo-projectivized sentences	+0.37	+5.84	+1.41	+0.19	+0.08	+0.48	-0.01
+ non-proj. output (pseudo-proj. + deproj.)	+0.45	+6.83	+1.69	+0.25	+0.09	+0.59	-0.04
UDPIPE – tuned hyperparameters							
Baseline (proj. and non-proj. parsers)	79.47	66.99	81.20	75.51	83.45	83.67	64.48

Table 2: Comparison on Universal Dependencies 2.0 of various strategies to handle non-projective training examples, depending on the non-projectivity rate and on treebank size. We report the average UAS over the corresponding sets of languages. All UAS gains are computed with respect to their '*only projective snt.*' baseline.

4 Experiments

The benefits of non-projective examples for training projective parsers are evaluated on the 73 treebanks of the UD 2.0 (Nivre et al., 2017b,a). Three methods to exploit non-projective trees (instead of discarding them) are contrasted: learning on the trees projectivized using Eisner (1996)'s algorithm, learning on pseudo-projectivized examples (Nivre and Nilsson, 2005) and learning on the non-projective trees, with the minimum-cost oracle described in §3. Projectivization is based on Yoav Goldberg's code.[4] For pseudo-projectivization, the MALTPARSER 1.9 implementation is used, with the `head` encoding scheme. For parsing, we use PANPARSER (Aufrant and Wisniewski, 2016), our own open source[5] implementation of a greedy ARCEAGER parser (using an averaged perceptron and a dynamic oracle).

As shown in Table 2, it is empirically better to handle non-projective sentences with minimum-cost dynamic oracles than to discard them all; but this strategy also outperforms projectivization and pseudo-projectivization. As expected, the gains of all methods increase when the proportion of non-projectivity increases, i.e. when more examples would have been discarded.

The minimum-cost technique is notably effective on the least projective treebanks, which correspond to ancient languages like Ancient Greek (63% of non-projective examples, with a gain of +2.4 UAS, compared to +1.1 and +2.0 for projectivization and pseudo-projectivization) and Latin (41%, +2.0 vs +0.4/+2.8); but it also achieves large improvements for modern languages with less non-projectivity, such as Dutch-LassySmall (30%, +7.0 vs +5.7/+3.3), Belarusian (17%, +5.2 vs +2.2/+4.4) and Turkish (11%, +2.3 vs +1.9/+1.3).

Apart from higher gains on average, the advantage of the minimum-cost strategy is that

---

[4]https://www.cs.bgu.ac.il/~yoavg/
software/projectivize

[5]https://perso.limsi.fr/aufrant

it is consistently beneficial, whereas pseudo-projectivization is detrimental for small treebanks. A plausible explanation is that arbitrarily rewriting the trees introduces inconsistencies in the training material, which are only alleviated when data is large enough. In that regard, the opposite effects of projectivization (detrimental with a static oracle, beneficial with a dynamic one) highlight the limited reliability of such transformations.

The minimum-cost strategy is also applied to an improved version of PANPARSER, using beam search and a dynamic oracle extended to global training (Aufrant et al., 2017), with a beam of size 8 and the max-violation strategy. The minimum-cost criterion appears particularly fit for that setting, with even larger gains (+0.63 UAS on average) despite a higher baseline.

Comparison with other parsers For illustrative purposes, similar experiments are conducted with other parsing systems: the ARCHYBRID version of PANPARSER, MALTPARSER and UDPIPE. MALTPARSER is the original implementation of the ARCEAGER system, but differs from ours in several ways, notably feature templates and the oracle (which is not dynamic, but precomputed statically); to help comparison, additional results are reported for PANPARSER without dynamic oracles. UDPIPE is a state-of-the-art neural parser including both projective and non-projective parsing systems; we use version 1.1 (Straka and Straková, 2017) with Straka (2017)'s set of tuned hyperparameters, but without their pre-trained word embeddings, for fair comparison.

The ARCHYBRID results show that the gains achieved by the minimum-cost criterion are not specific to the ARCEAGER system: despite different baseline scores, the proposed strategy yields similar improvements.

Compared to MALTPARSER, our ARCEAGER baseline appears much stronger (+5.4 UAS) on the downsized datasets; but the gains achieved when exploiting the non-projective trees (with pseudo-projectivization) are similar in both implementations. There is one exception, Ancient Greek (the only treebank with more than 50% non-projective sentences), for which the MALTPARSER gains are way larger than those of PANPARSER; but this treebank seems particular in several regards[6]

and consequently does not question the superiority of the minimum-cost oracle over the pseudo-projectivization strategy, measured even in Ancient Greek for PANPARSER.

Table 2 also reports the gains achieved by MALTPARSER when pseudo-projectivization is followed by deprojectivization of the output. Plain comparison of this line with the minimum-cost strategy is delicate, because it does not result from better training only, but also from a gain in expressivity: it is able to retrieve even non-projective dependencies. But it is interesting to see that deprojectivization only marginally improves over pseudo-projectivization alone: most of the gain actually resides in the treebank augmentation rather than in retrieving non-projective dependencies. Besides, the minimum-cost strategy outperforms even the deprojectivized results.

Finally, measures with UDPIPE reveal that, even though it benefits a lot from its higher expressivity (as it uses non-projective systems for the most non-projective treebanks), it achieves low accuracies on small treebanks and is thus outperformed on average by the beam version of PANPARSER (+0.30 UAS) – and the minimum-cost criterion significantly widens that gap (+0.97 UAS).

5 Conclusion

This work has addressed the restriction of projective parsers to train only on projective examples. We have explained how the dynamic oracle framework can help overcoming this issue, and shown that a simple modification of the framework (using minimum-cost actions as references instead of zero-cost ones) enables a seamless use of non-projective examples. Compared to the traditional (pseudo-)projectivization approaches, this method provides higher and more reliable improvements over the filtering baseline.

Acknowledgments

This work has been partly funded by the French *Direction générale de l'armement* and by the *Agence Nationale de la Recherche* under ParSiTi project (ANR-16-CE33-0021) and MultiSem project (ANR-16-CE33-0013).

---

[6]The baseline MALTPARSER already behaves differently for that language: it slightly outperforms the baseline PANPARSER instead of underperforming it by a large margin. The explanation may simply lie in other differences between implementations, for instance MALTPARSER's feature templates may be particularly suited to Ancient Greek.

References

Daniel Andor, Chris Alberti, David Weiss, Aliaksei Severyn, Alessandro Presta, Kuzman Ganchev, Slav Petrov, and Michael Collins. 2016. Globally Normalized Transition-Based Neural Networks. In *Proceedings of the 54th Annual Meeting of the Association for Computational Linguistics (Volume 1: Long Papers)*, pages 2442–2452, Berlin, Germany. Association for Computational Linguistics.

Lauriane Aufrant and Guillaume Wisniewski. 2016. PanParser: a Modular Implementation for Efficient Transition-Based Dependency Parsing. Technical report, LIMSI-CNRS.

Lauriane Aufrant, Guillaume Wisniewski, and François Yvon. 2017. Don't Stop Me Now! Using Global Dynamic Oracles to Correct Training Biases of Transition-Based Dependency Parsers. In *Proceedings of the 15th Conference of the European Chapter of the Association for Computational Linguistics: Volume 2, Short Papers*, pages 318–323, Valencia, Spain. Association for Computational Linguistics.

Danqi Chen and Christopher Manning. 2014. A Fast and Accurate Dependency Parser using Neural Networks. In *Proceedings of the 2014 Conference on Empirical Methods in Natural Language Processing (EMNLP)*, pages 740–750, Doha, Qatar. Association for Computational Linguistics.

Michael Collins and Brian Roark. 2004. Incremental Parsing with the Perceptron Algorithm. In *Proceedings of the 42nd Meeting of the Association for Computational Linguistics (ACL'04), Main Volume*, pages 111–118, Barcelona, Spain.

Michael A. Covington. 2001. A Fundamental Algorithm for Dependency Parsing. In *Proceedings of the 39th annual ACM southeast conference*, pages 95–102.

Chris Dyer, Miguel Ballesteros, Wang Ling, Austin Matthews, and Noah A. Smith. 2015. Transition-Based Dependency Parsing with Stack Long Short-Term Memory. In *Proceedings of the 53rd Annual Meeting of the Association for Computational Linguistics and the 7th International Joint Conference on Natural Language Processing (Volume 1: Long Papers)*, pages 334–343, Beijing, China. Association for Computational Linguistics.

Jason M Eisner. 1996. Three new probabilistic models for dependency parsing: An exploration. In *Proceedings of the 16th conference on Computational linguistics-Volume 1*, pages 340–345. Association for Computational Linguistics.

Yoav Goldberg and Joakim Nivre. 2012. A Dynamic Oracle for Arc-Eager Dependency Parsing. In *Proceedings of COLING 2012*, pages 959–976, Mumbai, India. The COLING 2012 Organizing Committee.

Yoav Goldberg and Joakim Nivre. 2013. Training Deterministic Parsers with Non-Deterministic Oracles. *Transactions of the Association for Computational Linguistics*, 1:403–414.

Yoav Goldberg, Francesco Sartorio, and Giorgio Satta. 2014. A Tabular Method for Dynamic Oracles in Transition-Based Parsing. *Transactions of the Association for Computational Linguistics*, 2:119–130.

Carlos Gómez-Rodríguez and Daniel Fernández-González. 2015. An Efficient Dynamic Oracle for Unrestricted Non-Projective Parsing. In *Proceedings of the 53rd Annual Meeting of the Association for Computational Linguistics and the 7th International Joint Conference on Natural Language Processing (Volume 2: Short Papers)*, pages 256–261, Beijing, China. Association for Computational Linguistics.

Ophélie Lacroix and Denis Béchet. 2014. A Three-Step Transition-Based System for Non-Projective Dependency Parsing. In *Proceedings of COLING 2014, the 25th International Conference on Computational Linguistics: Technical Papers*, pages 224–232, Dublin, Ireland. Dublin City University and Association for Computational Linguistics.

Ryan McDonald, Fernando Pereira, Kiril Ribarov, and Jan Hajic. 2005. Non-Projective Dependency Parsing using Spanning Tree Algorithms. In *Proceedings of Human Language Technology Conference and Conference on Empirical Methods in Natural Language Processing*, pages 523–530, Vancouver, British Columbia, Canada. Association for Computational Linguistics.

Joakim Nivre. 2003. An Efficient Algorithm for Projective Dependency Parsing. In *Proceedings of the 8th International Workshop on Parsing Technologies*, IWPT 2003, Nancy, France.

Joakim Nivre. 2004. Incrementality in Deterministic Dependency Parsing. In *Proceedings of the ACL Workshop Incremental Parsing: Bringing Engineering and Cognition Together*, pages 50–57, Barcelona, Spain. Association for Computational Linguistics.

Joakim Nivre. 2009. Non-Projective Dependency Parsing in Expected Linear Time. In *Proceedings of the Joint Conference of the 47th Annual Meeting of the ACL and the 4th International Joint Conference on Natural Language Processing of the AFNLP*, pages 351–359, Suntec, Singapore. Association for Computational Linguistics.

Joakim Nivre, Željko Agić, Lars Ahrenberg, Lene Antonsen, Maria Jesus Aranzabe, Masayuki Asahara, Luma Ateyah, Mohammed Attia, Aitziber Atutxa, Elena Badmaeva, Miguel Ballesteros, Esha Banerjee, Sebastian Bank, John Bauer, Kepa Bengoetxea, Riyaz Ahmad Bhat, Eckhard Bick, Cristina Bosco, Gosse Bouma, Sam Bowman, Aljoscha Burchardt, Marie Candito, Gauthier Caron, Gülşen

Cebirolu Eryiit, Giuseppe G. A. Celano, Savas Cetin, Fabricio Chalub, Jinho Choi, Yongseok Cho, Silvie Cinková, Çar Çöltekin, Miriam Connor, Marie-Catherine de Marneffe, Valeria de Paiva, Arantza Diaz de Ilarraza, Kaja Dobrovoljc, Timothy Dozat, Kira Droganova, Marhaba Eli, Ali Elkahky, Tomaž Erjavec, Richárd Farkas, Hector Fernandez Alcalde, Jennifer Foster, Cláudia Freitas, Katarína Gajdošová, Daniel Galbraith, Marcos Garcia, Filip Ginter, Iakes Goenaga, Koldo Gojenola, Memduh Gökrmak, Yoav Goldberg, Xavier Gómez Guinovart, Berta Gonzáles Saavedra, Matias Grioni, Normunds Grūzītis, Bruno Guillaume, Nizar Habash, Jan Hajič, Jan Hajič jr., Linh Hà M, Kim Harris, Dag Haug, Barbora Hladká, Jaroslava Hlaváčová, Petter Hohle, Radu Ion, Elena Irimia, Anders Johannsen, Fredrik Jørgensen, Hüner Kaşkara, Hiroshi Kanayama, Jenna Kanerva, Tolga Kayadelen, Václava Kettnerová, Jesse Kirchner, Natalia Kotsyba, Simon Krek, Sookyoung Kwak, Veronika Laippala, Lorenzo Lambertino, Tatiana Lando, Phng Lê Hng, Alessandro Lenci, Saran Lertpradit, Herman Leung, Cheuk Ying Li, Josie Li, Nikola Ljubešić, Olga Loginova, Olga Lyashevskaya, Teresa Lynn, Vivien Macketanz, Aibek Makazhanov, Michael Mandl, Christopher Manning, Ruli Manurung, Cătălina Mărănduc, David Mareček, Katrin Marheinecke, Héctor Martínez Alonso, André Martins, Jan Mašek, Yuji Matsumoto, Ryan McDonald, Gustavo Mendonça, Anna Missilä, Verginica Mititelu, Yusuke Miyao, Simonetta Montemagni, Amir More, Laura Moreno Romero, Shunsuke Mori, Bohdan Moskalevskyi, Kadri Muischnek, Nina Mustafina, Kaili Müürisep, Pinkey Nainwani, Anna Nedoluzhko, Lng Nguyn Th, Huyn Nguyn Th Minh, Vitaly Nikolaev, Rattima Nitisaroj, Hanna Nurmi, Stina Ojala, Petya Osenova, Lilja Øvrelid, Elena Pascual, Marco Passarotti, Cenel-Augusto Perez, Guy Perrier, Slav Petrov, Jussi Piitulainen, Emily Pitler, Barbara Plank, Martin Popel, Lauma Pretkalnia, Prokopis Prokopidis, Tiina Puolakainen, Sampo Pyysalo, Alexandre Rademaker, Livy Real, Siva Reddy, Georg Rehm, Larissa Rinaldi, Laura Rituma, Rudolf Rosa, Davide Rovati, Shadi Saleh, Manuela Sanguinetti, Baiba Saulīte, Yanin Sawanakunanon, Sebastian Schuster, Djamé Seddah, Wolfgang Seeker, Mojgan Seraji, Lena Shakurova, Mo Shen, Atsuko Shimada, Muh Shohibussirri, Natalia Silveira, Maria Simi, Radu Simionescu, Katalin Simkó, Mária Šimková, Kiril Simov, Aaron Smith, Antonio Stella, Jana Strnadová, Alane Suhr, Umut Sulubacak, Zsolt Szántó, Dima Taji, Takaaki Tanaka, Trond Trosterud, Anna Trukhina, Reut Tsarfaty, Francis Tyers, Sumire Uematsu, Zdeňka Urešová, Larraitz Uria, Hans Uszkoreit, Gertjan van Noord, Viktor Varga, Veronika Vincze, Jonathan North Washington, Zhuoran Yu, Zdeněk Žabokrtský, Daniel Zeman, and Hanzhi Zhu. 2017a. Universal Dependencies 2.0 – CoNLL 2017 Shared Task Development and Test Data. LINDAT/CLARIN digital library at the Institute of Formal and Applied Linguistics, Charles University.

Joakim Nivre, Željko Agić, Lars Ahrenberg, et al. 2017b. Universal Dependencies 2.0. LINDAT/CLARIN digital library at the Institute of Formal and Applied Linguistics, Charles University, Prague.

Joakim Nivre and Jens Nilsson. 2005. Pseudo-Projective Dependency Parsing. In *Proceedings of the 43rd Annual Meeting of the Association for Computational Linguistics (ACL'05)*, pages 99–106, Ann Arbor, Michigan. Association for Computational Linguistics.

Milan Straka. 2017. CoNLL 2017 Shared Task - UDPipe Baseline Models and Supplementary Materials. LINDAT/CLARIN digital library at the Institute of Formal and Applied Linguistics, Charles University.

Milan Straka, Jan Hajič, Jana Straková, and Jan Hajič jr. 2015. Parsing Universal Dependency Treebanks Using Neural Networks and Search-Based Oracle. In *International Workshop on Treebanks and Linguistic Theories (TLT14)*, pages 208–220.

Milan Straka and Jana Straková. 2017. Tokenizing, POS Tagging, Lemmatizing and Parsing UD 2.0 with UDPipe. In *Proceedings of the CoNLL 2017 Shared Task: Multilingual Parsing from Raw Text to Universal Dependencies*, pages 88–99, Vancouver, Canada. Association for Computational Linguistics.

Improving Coverage and Runtime Complexity for Exact Inference in Non-Projective Transition-Based Dependency Parsers

Tianze Shi
Cornell University
tianze@cs.cornell.edu

Carlos Gómez-Rodríguez
Universidade da Coruña
carlos.gomez@udc.es

Lillian Lee
Cornell University
llee@cs.cornell.edu

Abstract

We generalize Cohen, Gómez-Rodríguez, and Satta's (2011) parser to a family of non-projective transition-based dependency parsers allowing polynomial-time exact inference. This includes novel parsers with better coverage than Cohen et al. (2011), and even a variant that reduces time complexity to $O(n^6)$, improving on prior bounds. We hope that this piece of theoretical work inspires design of novel transition systems with better coverage and better run-time guarantees.

1 Introduction

Non-projective dependency trees are those containing crossing edges. They account for 12.59% of all training sentences in the annotated Universal Dependencies (UD) 2.1 data (Nivre et al., 2017), and more than 20% in each of 10 languages among the 54 in UD 2.1 with training treebanks. But modeling non-projectivity is computationally costly (McDonald and Satta, 2007).

Some transition-based dependency parsers have deduction systems that use dynamic programming to enable *exact* inference in polynomial time and space (Huang and Sagae, 2010; Kuhlmann et al., 2011). For non-projective parsing, though, the only tabularization of a transition-based parser is, to our knowledge, that of Cohen et al. (2011). They define a deduction system for (an isomorphic variant of) Attardi's (2006) transition system, which covers a subset of non-projective trees. The exact inference algorithm runs in $O(n^7)$ time, where n denotes sentence length.

In this paper, we show how Cohen et al.'s (2011) system can be modified to generate a new family of deduction systems with corresponding transition systems. In particular, we present three novel variants of the degree-2 Attardi parser, summarized in Fig. 1 (our technique can also be applied to generalized Attardi (2006) systems; see

§3.2). The first two bring non-projective coverage for UD 2.1 to as high as 95.99% by adding extra transitions, and yet retain the same time complexity. The third reduces time complexity for exact inference to $O(n^6)$ and space complexity from $O(n^5)$ to $O(n^4)$, while still improving empirical coverage from 87.24% to 93.16%.[1] Code and full statistics for all treebanks can be found at https://github.com/tzshi/nonproj-dp-variants-naacl2018.

These theoretical improvements are a step towards making recent state-of-the-art results in transition-based parsing with exact inference (Shi et al., 2017) extensible to practical non-projective parsing, by exemplifying the design of transition systems with better coverage on highly non-projective datasets and, for one variant, bringing the runtime complexity one level closer to feasibility.

2 Transition-based Parsing

We first introduce necessary definitions and notation.

2.1 A General Class of Transition Systems

A *transition system* is given by a 4-tuple (C, T, c^s, C_τ), where C is a set of configurations, T is a set of transition functions between configurations, c^s is an initialization function mapping an input sentence to an initial configuration, and $C_\tau \subset C$ defines a set of terminal configurations.

---

[1] Faster exact inference algorithms have been defined for some sets of mildly non-projective trees (e.g. Pitler et al. (2013); see Gómez-Rodríguez (2016) for more), but lack an underlying transition system. Having one has the practical advantage of allowing generative models, as in Cohen et al. (2011), and transition-based scoring functions, which have yielded good projective-parsing results (Shi et al., 2017); plus the theoretical advantage of providing a single framework supporting greedy, beam-search, and exact inference.

Proceedings of NAACL-HLT 2018, pages 420–425
New Orleans, Louisiana, June 1 - 6, 2018. ©2018 Association for Computational Linguistics

System	Reduce Transitions	Non-proj. Coverage	Time Complexity	Max. Degree
Attardi (2006)	$\sigma \quad s_2 \quad s_1 \quad s_0 \quad | \quad b_0 \quad \beta$ (stack / buffer)	87.24%	$O(n^7)$	2
Var. 1: ALLDEG1	$\sigma \quad s_2 \quad s_1 \quad s_0 \quad | \quad b_0 \quad \beta$	93.32%	$O(n^7)$	2
Var. 2: ALL	$\sigma \quad s_2 \quad s_1 \quad s_0 \quad | \quad b_0 \quad \beta$	**95.99%**	$O(n^7)$	3
Var. 3: ALL$s_0 s_1$	$\sigma \quad s_2 \quad s_1 \quad s_0 \quad | \quad b_0 \quad \beta$	93.16%	$\boldsymbol{O(n^6)}$	2

Figure 1: Attardi's (2006) transition system of degree 2 and our variants. Solid arrows denote the inventory of reduce transitions; each arrow points from the head to the modifier of the edge created by that transition. The *degree* of a transition is the distance between the head and modifier. Green highlights the single degree-3 transition. Thick arrows and gray dotted arrows represent additional and deleted transitions with respect to the original Attardi (2006) system. Coverage refers to the percentage of non-projective sentences (a total of 76,084 extracted from 604,273 training sentences in UD 2.1) that the systems are able to handle.

We employ a tripartite representation for configurations: (σ, β, A), where the three elements are as follows. σ and β are disjoint lists called the *stack* and *buffer*, respectively. Each dependency arc (h, m) in the *resolved arcs set* A has head h and modifier m. For a length-n input sentence w, the initial configuration is $c^s(w) = ([], [0, 1, ..., n], \varnothing)$ where the 0 in the initial buffer denotes a special node representing the root of the parse tree. All terminal configurations have an empty buffer and a stack containing only 0.

Indexing from 0, we write s_i and b_j to denote item i on the stack (starting from the right) and item j on the buffer (from the left), respectively. We use vertical bars to separate different parts of the buffer or stack. For example, when concerned with the top three stack items and the first item on the buffer, we may write $\sigma|s_2|s_1|s_0$ and $b_0|\beta$.

2.2 Attardi's (2006) System

We now introduce the widely-used Attardi (2006) system, which includes transitions that create arcs between non-consecutive subtrees, thus allowing it to produce some non-projective trees. To simplify exposition, here we present Cohen et al.'s (2011) isomorphic version.

The set of transitions consists of a shift transition (sh) and four reduce transitions (re). A *shift* moves the first buffer item onto the stack:

$$\mathsf{sh}[(\sigma, b_0|\beta, A)] = (\sigma|b_0, \beta, A).$$

A *reduce* transition $\mathsf{re}_{h,m}$ creates a dependency arc between h (head) and m (modifier) and reduces m. For example,

$$\mathsf{re}_{s_0,s_1}[(\sigma|s_1|s_0, \beta, A)] = (\sigma|s_0, \beta, A \cup \{(s_0, s_1)\}).$$

Row 1 of Fig. 1 depicts the four Attardi reduces.

The distance between h and m in a $\mathsf{re}_{h,m}$ transition is called its *degree*. A system limited to degree-1 transitions can only parse projective sentences. As shown in Fig. 1, Attardi's (2006) system has two degree-2 transitions (re_{s_0,s_2} and re_{s_2,s_0}) that allow it to cover 87.24% of the *non-projective trees* in UD 2.1. More generally, an Attardi system of degree D adds re_{s_0,s_D} and re_{s_D,s_0} to the system of degree $D - 1$.

3 Improving Coverage

A key observation is that a degree-D Attardi system does not contain all possible transitions of degree within D. Since prior empirical work has ascertained that transition systems using more transitions with degree greater than 1 can handle more non-projective treebank trees (Attardi, 2006; Gómez-Rodríguez, 2016), we hypothesize that adding some of these "missing" reduce transitions into the system's inventory should increase coverage. The challenge is to simultaneously maintain run-time guarantees, as there exists a known trade-off between coverage and complexity (Gómez-Rodríguez, 2016). We want to use Cohen et al.'s (2011)'s exact-inference algorithm for Attardi-based degree-D non-projective dependency parsing systems, which was previously analyzed as having $O(n^{3D+1})$ time complexity.[2] **Our contribution** *is systems that improve the degree-2 Attardi (2006) system's non-projective coverage, and yet (i) one has degree* **3** *but still the same* $O(n^7)$ *runtime as Cohen et al. (2011), rather than* $O(n^{3\cdot3+1})$*; and (ii) another has degree 2 but better* *runtime than Cohen et al.'s (2011) system.*

Here, we first sketch the existing exact inference algorithm,[3] and then present our variants.

3.1 Cohen et al.'s (2011) Exact Inference

The main idea of the algorithm is to group transition sequences into equivalence classes and construct longer sequences from shorter ones. Formally, for $m \geq 1$, Cohen et al. (2011) define a length-m *computation* as a sequence of m applications of transitions to configurations: $c_0 \xrightarrow{t_1} c_1 \cdots \xrightarrow{t_m} c_m$, where $t_i \in T$ and $t_i(c_{i-1}) = c_i$ for $i \in 1..m$. As depicted in Fig. 2, a length-m *I-computation* $[h_1, i, h_2, h_3, j]$ is any length-m computation where (1) $c_0 = (\sigma|h_1, i|\beta, A)$ and $c_m = (\sigma|h_2|h_3, j|\beta', A')$ for some σ, β, β', A, and A'; and (2) for all $k \in 1..m$, c_k's stack has σ as base and length at least $|\sigma| + 2$. Only condition (1) is relevant to this paper:[4] it states that the net effect of an I-computation is to replace the rightmost item h_1 on the stack with items h_2 and h_3, while advancing the buffer-start from i to j.

The dynamic programming algorithm is specified as a deduction system, where each transition corresponds to a deduction rule. The shift rule is:

$$\text{sh} : \frac{[h_1, i, h_2, h_3, j]}{[h_3, j, h_3, j, j+1]}.$$

Each reduce rule combines two I-computations into a larger I-computation, e.g. (see Fig. 3):

$$\text{re}_{s_0,s_1} : \frac{[h_1, i, h_2, h_3, k] \quad [h_3, k, h_4, h_5, j]}{[h_1, i, h_2, h_5, j]},$$

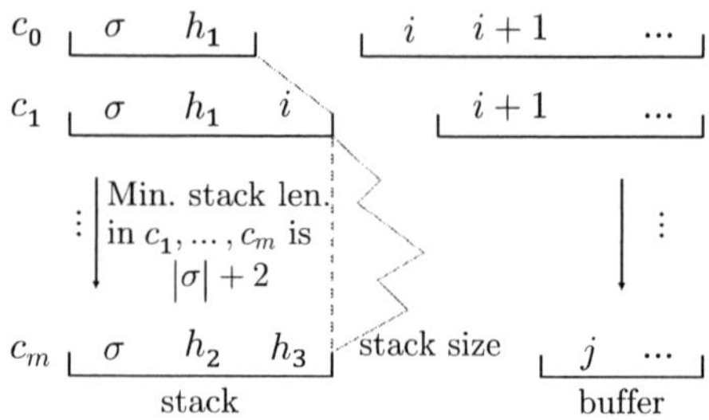

Figure 2: From Cohen et al. (2011, Fig. 2): schematic of I-computation $[h_1, i, h_2, h_3, j]$.

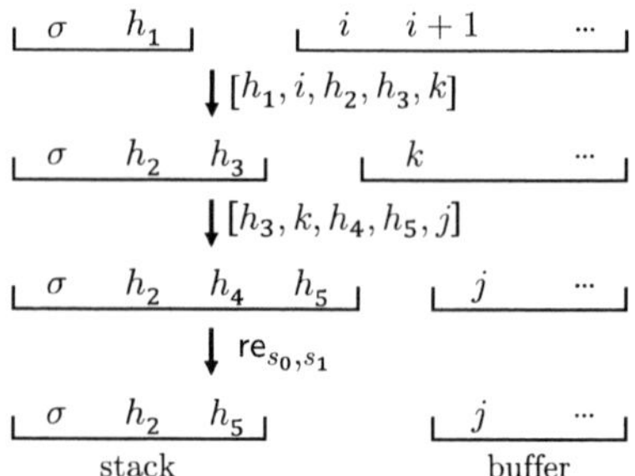

Figure 3: Illustration of deduction rule re_{s_0,s_1}.

with the side condition that h_4 modifies h_5.[5] Other reduce transitions have similar deduction rules, with the same two premises, but a different conclusion depending on the reduced stack item. As an illustration:

$$\text{re}_{s_2,s_0} : \frac{[h_1, i, h_2, h_3, k] \quad [h_3, k, h_4, h_5, j]}{[h_1, i, h_2, h_4, j]}.$$

The goal of deduction is to produce the I-computation $[\epsilon, 0, \epsilon, 0, \epsilon]$, using the shift and reduce deduction rules starting from the axiom $[\epsilon, 0, \epsilon, 0, 1]$, corresponding to the first and mandatory shift transition moving the root node from buffer to stack. ϵ stands for an empty stack or buffer. As analyzed by Cohen et al. (2011), direct tabularization for this deduction system takes $O(n^5)$ space and $O(n^8)$ time. With adaptation of the "hook trick" described in Eisner and Satta (1999), we can reduce the running time to $O(n^7)$.

3.2 Our New Variants

In this section, we modify Cohen et al.'s (2011) set of reduce deduction rules to improve coverage or

---

[2] While $O(n^7)$ or $O(n^{10})$ is not practical, the result is still impressive, since the search space is exponential. Cohen et al. (2011) were inspired by Huang and Sagae's (2010) and Kuhlmann et al.'s (2011) dynamic-programming approach for projective systems.

[3] See Cohen et al. (2011) for full description.

[4] Condition (2) is used for proving completeness of the deduction system (Cohen et al., 2011).

[5] This side condition can be interpreted as a grammar rule (for a recognizer) or as an edge to be scored and added to the parse tree (for a parser).

time complexity. Since each such deduction rule corresponds to a reduce transition, each revision to the deduction system yields a variant of Attardi's (2006) parser. In other words, generalization of the deduction system gives rise to a family of non-projective transition-based dependency parsers.

We first explain why there are exactly nine reduce transitions $\mathcal{R} = \{\text{re}_{s_0,s_1}, \text{re}_{s_1,s_0}, \text{re}_{s_0,s_2}, \text{re}_{s_2,s_0}, \text{re}_{s_1,s_2}, \text{re}_{s_2,s_1}, \text{re}_{b_0,s_0}, \text{re}_{b_0,s_1}, \text{re}_{b_0,s_2}\}$ that can be used in Cohen et al.'s (2011) exact inference algorithm, without allowing a reduction with head b_i for $i \geq 1$.[6] (Note that Cohen et al.'s (2011) reduce rules are precisely the first four elements of $\mathcal{R}$.) From Fig. 3 we infer that the concatenation of I-computations $[h_1, i, h_2, h_3, k]$ and $[h_3, k, h_4, h_5, j]$ yields a configuration of the form $(\sigma|h_2|h_4|h_5, j|\beta, A)$. For the application of a reduce rule to yield a valid I-computation, by condition (1) of the I-computation definition, first, the head and modifier must be selected from the "exposed" elements h_2, h_4, h_5, and j, corresponding to s_2, s_1, s_0, b_0, respectively; and second, the modifier can only come from the stack. $\mathcal{R}$ is precisely the set of rules satisfying these criteria. Further, every reduce transition from $\mathcal{R}$ is compatible with Eisner and Satta's (1999) "hook trick". This gives us the satisfactory result that the $O(n^7)$ running time upper bound still holds for transitions in $\mathcal{R}$, even though one of them has degree 3.

Next, we consider three notable variants within the family of $\mathcal{R}$-based non-projective transition-based dependency parsers. They are given in Fig. 1, along with their time complexities and empirical coverage statistics. The latter is computed using static oracles (Cohen et al., 2012) on the UD 2.1 dataset (Nivre et al., 2017).[7] We report the global coverage over the 76,084 non-projective sentences from all the training treebanks.

One might assume that adding more degree-1 transitions wouldn't improve coverage of trees with non-crossing edges. On the other hand, since their addition doesn't affect the asymptotic run-time, we define **ALLDEG1** to include all five degree-1 transitions from $\mathcal{R}$ into the Attardi (2006) system. Surprisingly, using ALLDEG1 improves non-projective coverage from 87.24% to 93.32%.

Furthermore, recall that we argued above that,

by construction, using any of the transitions in $\mathcal{R}$ still preserves the original $O(n^7)$ run-time upper bound for Cohen et al.'s (2011) exact inference algorithm. We therefore define **ALL** to include all 9 reduce transitions in $\mathcal{R}$; it runs in time $O(n^7)$ despite the fact that $\text{re}_{b_0,s_2} \in \mathcal{R}$ has degree 3, a significant improvement over the best previously-known bound for degree-3 systems of $O(n^{10})$. Moreover, as shown in Fig. 1, this variant improves non-projective coverage to 95.54%.

Now, if our goal is to reduce run-time, we can start with an Attardi (2006) system of degree 1 instead of 2, which, as previously mentioned, can only handle projective sentences, but which has runtime $O(n^{(3 \cdot 1)+1}) = O(n^4)$. Reasoning about the analog of $\mathcal{R}$ with respect to Kuhlmann et al.'s (2011) exact inference algorithm — the projective predecessor of Cohen et al. (2011) — brings us to the degree-2 set of reduce rules $\{\text{re}_{s_0,s_1}, \text{re}_{s_1,s_0}, \text{re}_{b_0,s_1}\}$. This system, however, can only handle leftward non-projective arcs.

Instead, we return to ALL, but discard transitions reducing s_2, thus deriving **ALL**s_0s_1, which still produces both left and right non-projective arcs, but has a run-time lower than $O(n^7)$, which we show as follows. Since s_2 cannot be reduced, when concatenating $[h_1, i, h_2, h_3, k]$ and $[h_3, k, h_4, h_5, j]$, the larger I-computation we deduce will be either $[h_1, i, h_2, h_4, j]$ or $[h_1, i, h_2, h_5, j]$, so that the first three indices of the conclusion item remain the same as those of the first premise. In addition, the only remaining deduction rule, a shift, produces deduction items of the form $[h_1, j, h_1, j, j + 1]$. Hence, all derivable items will be of the form $[h_1, i, h_1, h_3, j]$, with only four unique indices, instead of five. It follows that the exact inference algorithm for this variant runs in $O(n^6)$ time, improving from $O(n^7)$. The tabularization takes $O(n^4)$ space, a reduction from the original $O(n^5)$ as well. In terms of empirical coverage, this new system can handle 93.16% of the non-projective sentences in UD 2.1, more than Attardi's (2006) system, but fewer than our other two variants.

Generally, for a *degree-D* Attardi (2006)-based system, one may apply our first two variants to improve its non-projective coverage while maintaining the previously-analyzed $O(n^{3D+1})$ time complexity, or the third variant to reduce its time complexity down to $O(n^{3D})$, and space complexity from $O(n^{2D+1})$ to $O(n^{2D})$.

---

[6] Such reductions might prove interesting in the future.

[7] We also compare results from symbolic execution of the dynamic programming algorithms on short sentences as a double check.

4   Conclusion

We have introduced a family of variants of Cohen et al.'s (2011) Attardi-based transition system and its associated dynamic programming algorithm. Among these, we have highlighted novel
algorithms that (1) increase non-projective coverage without affecting computational complexity
for exact inference, and (2) improve the time and
space complexity for exact inference, even while
providing better coverage than the original parser.
Specifically, our $\text{ALL}s_0s_1$ runs in $O(n^6)$ time and
$O(n^4)$ space (improving from $O(n^7)$ and $O(n^5)$,
respectively) while providing coverage of 93.16%
of the non-projective sentences in UD 2.1.

Exact inference for transition-based parsers has
recently achieved state-of-the-art results in projective parsing (Shi et al., 2017). The complexity improvements achieved in this paper are a step towards making their exact-inference, projective approach extensible to practical, wide-coverage non-
projective parsing.

Acknowledgments

We thank the reviewers for their time and careful reading, and reviewer 2 for suggestions that
improved our presentation.   TS and LL were
supported in part by a Google Focused Research Grant to Cornell University.   CG has received funding from the European Research Council (ERC), under the European Union's Horizon
2020 research and innovation programme (FAST-
PARSE, grant agreement No 714150), from the
TELEPARES-UDC project (FFI2014-51978-C2-
2-R) and the ANSWER-ASAP project (TIN2017-
85160-C2-1-R) from MINECO, and from Xunta
de Galicia (ED431B 2017/01). LL was also supported in part by NSF grant SES-1741441. Any
opinions, findings, and conclusions or recommendations expressed in this material are those of the
author(s) and do not necessarily reflect the views
of the National Science Foundation or other sponsors.

References

Giuseppe Attardi. 2006. Experiments with a multilanguage non-projective dependency parser. In *Proceedings of the Tenth Conference on Computational
Natural Language Learning (CoNLL-X)*, pages 166–
170, New York City, New York, USA.

Shay B. Cohen, Carlos Gómez-Rodríguez, and Giorgio Satta. 2011.   Exact inference for generative
probabilistic non-projective dependency parsing. In
*Proceedings of the 2011 Conference on Empirical
Methods in Natural Language Processing (EMNLP)*,
pages 1234–1245, Edinburgh, Scotland, UK.

Shay B. Cohen, Carlos Gómez-Rodríguez, and Giorgio Satta. 2012.   Elimination of spurious ambiguity in transition-based dependency parsing.   *ArXiv
e-prints*, 1206.6735.

Jason Eisner and Giorgio Satta. 1999.   Efficient parsing for bilexical context-free grammars and head automaton grammars.   In *Proceedings of the 37th Annual Meeting of the Association for Computational
Linguistics (ACL)*, pages 457–464, College Park,
Maryland, USA.

Carlos Gómez-Rodríguez. 2016.   Restricted non-
projectivity: Coverage vs. efficiency.   *Computational Linguistics*, 42(4):809–817.

Liang Huang and Kenji Sagae. 2010.   Dynamic programming for linear-time incremental parsing.   In
*Proceedings of the 48th Annual Meeting of the Asso-
ciation for Computational Linguistics (ACL)*, pages
1077–1086, Uppsala, Sweden.

Marco Kuhlmann, Carlos Gómez-Rodríguez, and Giorgio Satta. 2011.   Dynamic programming algorithms
for transition-based dependency parsers.   In *Proceedings of the 49th Annual Meeting of the Association for Computational Linguistics: Human Language Technologies (ACL-HLT)*, pages 673–682,
Portland, Oregon, USA.

Ryan McDonald and Giorgio Satta. 2007. On the complexity of non-projective data-driven dependency
parsing. In *Proceedings of the Tenth International
Conference on Parsing Technologies (IWPT)*, pages
121–132, Prague, Czech Republic. Association for
Computational Linguistics.

Joakim Nivre, Željko Agić, Lars Ahrenberg, Lene
Antonsen, Maria Jesus Aranzabe, Masayuki Asa-
hara, Luma Ateyah, Mohammed Attia, Aitziber
Atutxa, Liesbeth Augustinus, Elena Badmaeva,
Miguel Ballesteros, Esha Banerjee, Sebastian Bank,
Verginica Barbu Mititelu, John Bauer, Kepa Ben-
goetxea, Riyaz Ahmad Bhat, Eckhard Bick, Victo-
ria Bobicev, Carl Börstell, Cristina Bosco, Gosse
Bouma, Sam Bowman, Aljoscha Burchardt, Marie
Candito, Gauthier Caron, Gülşen Cebiroğlu Eryiğit,
Giuseppe G. A. Celano, Savas Cetin, Fabri-
cio Chalub, Jinho Choi, Silvie Cinková, Çağrı
Çöltekin, Miriam Connor, Elizabeth Davidson,
Marie-Catherine de Marneffe, Valeria de Paiva,
Arantza Diaz de Ilarraza, Peter Dirix, Kaja Do-
brovoljc, Timothy Dozat, Kira Droganova, Puneet
Dwivedi, Marhaba Eli, Ali Elkahky, Tomaž Erjavec,
Richárd Farkas, Hector Fernandez Alcalde, Jennifer
Foster, Cláudia Freitas, Katarína Gajdošová, Daniel
Galbraith, Marcos Garcia, Moa Gärdenfors, Kim
Gerdes, Filip Ginter, Iakes Goenaga, Koldo Go-
jenola, Memduh Gökırmak, Yoav Goldberg, Xavier

Gómez Guinovart, Berta Gonzáles Saavedra, Matias Grioni, Normunds Grūzītis, Bruno Guillaume, Nizar Habash, Jan Hajič, Jan Hajič jr., Linh Hà Mỹ, Kim Harris, Dag Haug, Barbora Hladká, Jaroslava Hlaváčová, Florinel Hociung, Petter Hohle, Radu Ion, Elena Irimia, Tomáš Jelínek, Anders Johannsen, Fredrik Jørgensen, Hüner Kaşıkara, Hiroshi Kanayama, Jenna Kanerva, Tolga Kayadelen, Václava Kettnerová, Jesse Kirchner, Natalia Kotsyba, Simon Krek, Veronika Laippala, Lorenzo Lambertino, Tatiana Lando, John Lee, Phương Lê Hồng, Alessandro Lenci, Saran Lertpradit, Herman Leung, Cheuk Ying Li, Josie Li, Keying Li, Nikola Ljubešić, Olga Loginova, Olga Lyashevskaya, Teresa Lynn, Vivien Macketanz, Aibek Makazhanov, Michael Mandl, Christopher Manning, Cătălina Mărănduc, David Mareček, Katrin Marheinecke, Héctor Martínez Alonso, André Martins, Jan Mašek, Yuji Matsumoto, Ryan McDonald, Gustavo Mendonça, Niko Miekka, Anna Missilä, Cătălin Mititelu, Yusuke Miyao, Simonetta Montemagni, Amir More, Laura Moreno Romero, Shinsuke Mori, Bohdan Moskalevskyi, Kadri Muischnek, Kaili Müürisep, Pinkey Nainwani, Anna Nedoluzhko, Gunta Nešpore-Bērzkalne, Lương Nguyễn Thị, Huyền Nguyễn Thị Minh, Vitaly Nikolaev, Hanna Nurmi, Stina Ojala, Petya Osenova, Robert Östling, Lilja Øvrelid, Elena Pascual, Marco Passarotti, Cenel-Augusto Perez, Guy Perrier, Slav Petrov, Jussi Piitulainen, Emily Pitler, Barbara Plank, Martin Popel, Lauma Pretkalniņa, Prokopis Prokopidis, Tiina Puolakainen, Sampo Pyysalo, Alexandre Rademaker, Loganathan Ramasamy, Taraka Rama, Vinit Ravishankar, Livy Real, Siva Reddy, Georg Rehm, Larissa Rinaldi, Laura Rituma, Mykhailo Romanenko, Rudolf Rosa, Davide Rovati, Benoît Sagot, Shadi Saleh, Tanja Samardžić, Manuela Sanguinetti, Baiba Saulīte, Sebastian Schuster, Djamé Seddah, Wolfgang Seeker, Mojgan Seraji, Mo Shen, Atsuko Shimada, Dmitry Sichinava, Natalia Silveira, Maria Simi, Radu Simionescu, Katalin Simkó, Mária Šimková, Kiril Simov, Aaron Smith, Antonio Stella, Milan Straka, Jana Strnadová, Alane Suhr, Umut Sulubacak, Zsolt Szántó, Dima Taji, Takaaki Tanaka, Trond Trosterud, Anna Trukhina, Reut Tsarfaty, Francis Tyers, Sumire Uematsu, Zdeňka Urešová, Larraitz Uria, Hans Uszkoreit, Sowmya Vajjala, Daniel van Niekerk, Gertjan van Noord, Viktor Varga, Eric Villemonte de la Clergerie, Veronika Vincze, Lars Wallin, Jonathan North Washington, Mats Wirén, Tak-sum Wong, Zhuoran Yu, Zdeněk Žabokrtský, Amir Zeldes, Daniel Zeman, and Hanzhi Zhu. 2017. Universal Dependencies 2.1. LINDAT/CLARIN digital library at the Institute of Formal and Applied Linguistics (ÚFAL), Faculty of Mathematics and Physics, Charles University.

Emily Pitler, Sampath Kannan, and Mitchell Marcus. 2013. Finding optimal 1-endpoint-crossing trees. *Transactions of the Association of Computational Linguistics*, 1:13–24.

Tianze Shi, Liang Huang, and Lillian Lee. 2017. Fast(er) exact decoding and global training for transition-based dependency parsing via a minimal feature set. In *Proceedings of the 2017 Conference on Empirical Methods in Natural Language Processing (EMNLP)*, pages 12–23, Copenhagen, Denmark.

Towards a Variability Measure for Multiword Expressions

Caroline Pasquer and **Agata Savary** and **Jean-Yves Antoine**
University of Tours, France
`first.last@univ-tours.fr`

Carlos Ramisch
Aix Marseille Univ, Université de Toulon, CNRS, LIS, Marseille, France
`carlos.ramisch@lis-lab.fr`

Abstract

One of the outstanding properties of multiword expressions (MWEs), especially verbal ones (VMWEs), important both in theoretical models and applications, is their idiosyncratic variability. Some MWEs are always continuous, while some others admit certain types of insertions. Components of some MWEs are rarely or never modified, while some others admit either specific or unrestricted modification. This unpredictable variability profile of MWEs hinders modeling and processing them as "words-with-spaces" on the one hand, and as regular syntactic structures on the other hand. Since variability of MWEs is a matter of scale rather than a binary property, we propose a 2-dimensional language-independent measure of variability dedicated to verbal MWEs based on syntactic and discontinuity-related clues. We assess its relevance with respect to a linguistic benchmark and its utility for the tasks of VMWE classification and variant identification on a French corpus.

1 Introduction

Multiword expressions (MWEs), in particular verbal ones (VMWEs), are groups of words whose meaning does not derive from the meaning of their components and from their syntactic structure in a regular way (Gross, 1982), like **pay a visit** and **take the cake** 'be the most remarkable of its kind'. MWEs exhibit some degree of variability. On the one hand, they allow internal inflection (**paid many visits**), insertions (**pay annual visits**) and syntactic transformations (**visits paid** last month). On the other hand, they can block variation that is usual/typical for ordinary expressions with the same syntactic structure, such as inflection (#take a turn[1] vs. **take turns**), diathesis alternation (#he cast the die vs. **the die is cast** 'the point of no retreat is passed'), or adjunction of modifiers (#take

---

[1] We use # to signal a loss of idiomatic meaning.

the _sweet_ cake). This leads to variation schemes which are specific to subclasses of MWE, that is, MWE variability is idiosyncratic.

Variability, also known as flexibility, has been considered a key property of MWEs in linguistic studies (Gross, 1988; Tutin, 2016; Nunberg et al., 1994; Sheinfux et al., 2017). It was also highlighted as a major challenge in NLP models and applications (Constant et al., 2017). Variants are pervasive (Jacquemin, 2001) and hinder straightforward search of MWE citation forms in a corpus (Nissim and Zaninello, 2013). They introduce discontinuities which challenge sequence labeling approaches. Even when employing parsers to cope with discontinuities, MWE recognizers can still fail to capture some syntactic transformations such as complex determiners, which can break a direct link between a verb and a noun in a dependency tree (**pay a series of visits**). These facts have important implications for downstream tasks and applications, e.g. parsers can heavily suffer from incorrectly identified MWEs (Baldwin et al., 2004).

The restricted variability of MWEs as compared to their regular counterparts can also be seen as an advantage in their automatic discovery (Weller and Heid, 2010; Tsvetkov and Wintner, 2014; Buljan and Šnajder, 2017). Substitution-based MWE discovery techniques based on lexico-semantic variability have been largely explored (Pearce, 2001; Farahmand and Henderson, 2016). Morphological and syntactic variability, however, have rarely been studied for MWE discovery (Ramisch et al., 2008) and even less so for in-context identification (Fazly et al., 2009).

Given the importance of MWE variability (Constant et al., 2017) as well as its gradual nature, especially for VMWEs, we suggest that this phenomenon should be subject to measurement. This paper presents measures of VMWE variability based on variant-to-variant similarity, taking syn-

Proceedings of NAACL-HLT 2018, pages 426–432
New Orleans, Louisiana, June 1 - 6, 2018. ©2018 Association for Computational Linguistics

tactic variability and linear discontinuity into account (Sec. 2–3).[2] Our proposal is evaluated on a French corpus (Sec. 4). We assess the relevance of our measure with respect to a linguistic benchmark (Sec.5), and we study its usability for VMWE classification (Sec. 6) and variant identification (Sec. 7). Then, we conclude and sketch perspectives to extend our proposal to other languages and to an unsupervised framework (Sec. 8).

2 Variant-to-variant similarity

To capture the variability of a VMWE, we rely on pairwise comparison of its occurrences. Fig. 1 shows the dependency trees of sentences containing two variants, henceforth V_1 and V_2, of **prendre une décision** 'to take a decision'. V_1 and V_2 exhibit some common and some divergent syntactic and linear properties. For instance, the noun *decision* governs a determiner (*det*) and an adjectival modifier (*amod*) both in V_1 and in V_2, and a relative clause (*acl:relcl*) in V_2. The verb *take* governs a nominal subject (*nsubj*), an object (*obj*) and adverbial modifiers (*adv*) in both V_1 and V_2, and an auxiliary (*aux*) in V_2. External elements are inserted between the lexicalized ones in both variants. Their POS are *adv* (twice), *det* and *adj* in V_1, and *pron, propn, aux* and *adv* in V_2, i.e. one POS (*adv*) is shared.[3]

In order to measure both these common characteristics and discrepancies, we define the similarity of two VMWE variants on the basis of the similarity of their components and of the external inserted elements. A *lexicalized component*, or simply a *component*, of a VMWE E is the one which is realized by the same lexeme in any variant of E.[4] All variants of E necessarily have the same number of lexicalized components, which are lemmatized and lexicographically sorted, yielding a canonical form of $E = (C_1, C_2, \ldots, C_n)$ which uniquely represents it.[5] By C_i^j we denote the form that component i takes in variant j. For instance, in Fig. 1 C_1 = décision, C_2 = prendre, E = (décision, prendre), C_1^1 = décision, C_1^2 = décisions, C_2^1 = prennent and C_2^2 = prises. Similarity of objects (components or

VMWEs) is measured by the Sørensen–Dice coefficient, which is defined as $S(O_1, O_2) = 2 \times |P(O_1) \cap P(O_2)|/(|P(O_1)| + |P(O_2)|)$, where $P(O_1)$ and $P(O_2)$ denote the sets of (relevant) properties exhibited by objects O_1 and O_2. We now define two variant-to-variant similarity measures: syntactic – focusing on the outgoing dependencies – and linear – based on insertions.

2.1 Syntactic similarity

Syntactic similarity S^S is based on the dependencies between a VMWE and its external elements. It allows us to account for long-distance arguments and modifiers not necessarily included between the lexicalized components. The similarity of each pair of lexicalized components is calculated first, and then averaged for the whole VMWE. For each component, the set of outgoing dependencies is considered and relations of the same type are counted once. In the two sentences given in Fig. 1, the syntactic similarity of the noun C_1 and the verb C_2 is:

$$S^S(C_1^1, C_1^2) = \frac{2 \times |\{\text{amod,det}\}|}{|\{\text{acl:relcl,amod,det}\}| + |\{\text{amod,det}\}|}$$
$$= \frac{4}{5}$$

$$S^S(C_2^1, C_2^2) = \frac{2 \times |\{\text{adv,nsubj,obj}\}|}{|\{\text{adv,nsubj,obj}\}| + |\{\text{adv,aux,nsubj,obj}\}|}$$
$$= \frac{6}{7}$$

Variant-to-variant syntactic similarity is the weighted average of the per-component scores:

$$S^S(V_1, V_2) = \sum_{i=1}^{n} w_i \times S^S(C_i^1, C_i^2)$$

where weights $w_1, \ldots, w_n$ sum up to 1. For instance, with uniform weights $w_1 = w_2 = \frac{1}{2}$:

$$S^S(V_1, V_2) = \frac{1}{2} \times \frac{4}{5} + \frac{1}{2} \times \frac{6}{7} = \frac{29}{35}$$

2.2 Linear similarity

Linear similarity S^L is defined for two VMWE variants in terms of the POS of the elements inserted between the lexicalized components. The number of insertions for the same POS is disregarded. In this way we focus on the quality of admitting an insertion of a certain POS, rather than on their count. For example, the two *adv* insertions in V_1 (*vraiment* 'really' and *pas* 'NEG') are only counted once:

---

[2]Morphological variability is disregarded in this paper, as it did not prove influential in the experiments described here.

[3]POS, morphological features and dependencies from UD: http://universaldependencies.org.

[4]Lexicalized components are highlighted in bold.

[5] We neglect rare cases of VMWEs sharing a canonical form, e.g. **fermer les yeux** 'close the eyes' ⇒ 'pretend not to see' vs. **fermer l'oeil** 'close the eye' ⇒ 'have a nap'.

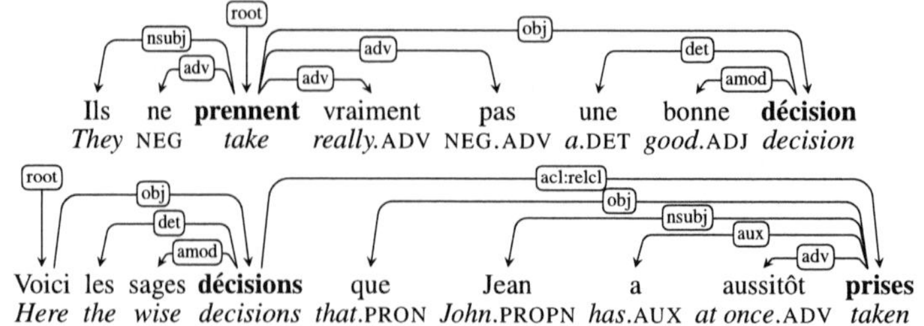

Figure 1: Two POS-tagged and dependency-parsed occurrences of ***prendre** une **décision*** 'take a decision'.

$$S^L(V_1, V_2) = \frac{2 \times |\{\text{adv}\}|}{|\{\text{adj,adv,det}\}| + |\{\text{adv,aux,pron,propn}\}|}$$
$$= \frac{2}{7}$$

3 VMWE variability

Given the two similarity measures S^S and S^L between variants V_1 and V_2 of a VMWE E, the *rigidity* scores of E are the averages of all pairs of E's variants. For example, if *take decision* occurs 6 times, we average the scores S^S and S^L of $\binom{6}{2} = 15$ pairs:

$$R^Y(E) = \frac{1}{\binom{m}{2}} \times \sum_{i=1}^{m-1} \sum_{j=i+1}^{m} S^Y(V_i(E), V_j(E))$$

where $Y \in \{S, L\}$, m is the number of E's variants in the corpus, and $V_i(E)$ is the i'th variant.

Note that the rigidity measures defined above range from 0 to 1. The *variability* of E can, thus, be defined as the complement of rigidity: $V_X^Y(E) = 1 - R_X^Y(E)$. Experiments were performed in order to estimate the relevance and utility of these measures. Parameter values were chosen empirically and are presented in Appendix A. In the long run, these parameters should be estimated experimentally, possibly in an application-specific manner.

4 Corpus

We use the French part of the PARSEME corpus[6] manually annotated for VMWEs in 18 languages (Savary et al., 2017). Among its 4 VMWE categories two are particularly relevant:

- *Light-verb constructions* (LVCs): combinations of the type Verb-(Adp)-(Det)-Noun where the verb is semantically void and the noun bears the meaning, e.g. ***faire** un **voeu*** 'make a wish'.

- *Idioms* (IDs): verbal phrases of various syntactic structures, often with non-compositional meaning and admitting both literal and idiomatic reading e.g. ***perdre** **pied*** 'lose foot' ⇒ 'lose self-confidence'

The VMWEs annotations in the corpus are accompanied by morphological and a syntactic layers, as shown in Fig. 1. In the morphological layer, lemmas, POS and morphological features are assigned to each token. The syntactic layer represents syntactic dependencies between tokens. Both result from manual annotation and use UD tagsets. The corpus is divided into a training corpus (TrC) and a test corpus (TeC). TrC contains 17,880 sentences, 450,221 tokens, and 4,462 VMWE occurrences, including 1,786 occurrences of 502 unique IDs and 1,362 occurrences of 672 unique LVCs. On average, each ID has 3.6 variants and each LVC has 2 variants. The frequency of individual VMWEs varies greatly (from 1 to 172) and so does the reliability of the variability estimation of each MWE. Hence, only the most frequent VMWEs are considered in Sec. 6.

5 Linguistic relevance

It order to estimate the relevance of our measures, we refer to an existing corpus study by Tutin (2016). There, 30 French VMWEs of the form Verb-(Det)-Noun are studied with respect to 5 morpho-syntactic variation types. This yields 6 *variability levels* depending on how many of the 5 variability types a VMWE exhibits. This is illustrated in Tab. 1 with three VMWEs which stand at distinct levels of the variability spectrum.

Tutin's variability types are defined in terms of complex linguistic phenomena, such as admitting passivization and relative constructions, which have to be validated manually. We, conversely, are in need of fully automatic procedures. Therefore we capture the VMWE variability in distinct ways. It is interesting to see how far both approaches agree on their conclusions.

---

[6] `http://hdl.handle.net/11372/LRT-2282`

Variability type	Examples
Noun's number inflection	**prendre** la/les **décision(s)** 'take the decision(s)' **fermer** la/les **porte(s)** 'close the door(s)' **donner lieu**/# lieux 'give place(s)'
Passivization	**décision prise** 'decision taken' **porte fermée** 'door closed' #**lieu donné** 'place given'
Noun's determiner variation	**prendre** la/ma/cette **décision** 'take the/my/this decision' #**fermer** une/ma/cette porte 'close the/my/this door' #**donner** un/mon/ce lieu 'give a/my/this place'
Relative construction	la **décision** qu'il **prend** 'the decision which he takes' #la porte qu'il ferme 'the door which he closes' #lieu qu'il donne 'place which it gives'
Adjunction of noun modifiers	**prendre** une grande **décision** 'take a great decision' #**fermer** la grande porte 'close the great door' #**donner** un grand lieu 'give a great place'

Table 1: Tutin's variability types for **prendre** une **décision** 'take a decision' ⇒ 'make a decision' (level 5), **fermer la porte** 'close the door' ⇒ 'hinder' (level 2), **donner lieu** 'give place' ⇒ 'lead to' (level 0).

Tutin's variability level	0	1	2	3	4	5	All
# TrC VMWEs	6	3	2	3	1	3	18
# TrC occurrences	69	114	8	18	7	54	270
Aggregated level	S_{0-1}		S_{2-4}			S_5	S

Table 2: Distribution of the VMWEs extracted from the PARSEME training corpus into Tutin's classes.

To this aim, we extract from TrC all occurrences of the 30 VMWEs covered by Tutin and retain those with at least 2 occurrences (measuring similarity requires two variants at least). Tab. 2 shows the distribution of the resulting set S of 18 VMWEs into Tutin's levels. While their corpus frequency is relatively high at levels 0, 1 and 5, it is low at levels 2, 3 and 4. Therefore we aggregate neighbor levels into 3 subsets: S_{0-1}, S_{2-4} and S_5. For each VMWE in S we calculate V^L and V^S with weight $w_i = 1$ for the noun and 0 for the verb and the determiner (if any). As shown by the corresponding boxplots in Fig. 2 (a–b), V^L tends to increase with Tutin's level. That is to say, the more variable VMWEs are (as judged by a linguist expert on the basis of a manual corpus study), the higher is their automatically calculated linear variability value. Tutin's extreme levels 0–1 and 5 are particularly well discriminated by V^L.[7] No interesting tendency could be observed for the syntactic variability of the noun. We hypothesize that different outgoing dependencies have different roles in modeling syntactic variability. For instance in **aller dans** le bon **sens** 'go to the right direction' ⇒ 'evolve positively', the dependency between the noun and the modifier bon 'good' probably tells us more about the rigidity of this VWME than its case-marking preposition dans 'in' or its

---

[7]Wilcoxon-Mann-Whitney (WMW) test confirms that S_5 differs from S_{0-1} with significance at $\alpha = 0.05$.

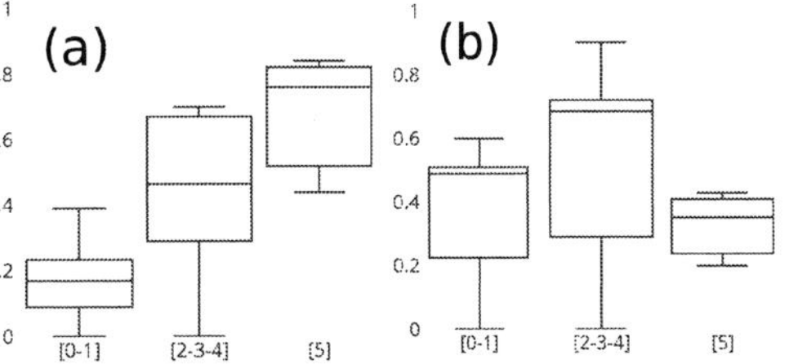

Figure 2: Tukey boxplots of V^L and V^S (y-axis) as a function of Tutin's levels (x-axis).

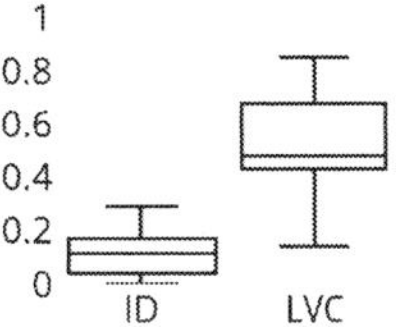

Figure 3: Tukey boxplots of V^L (y-axis) as a function of VMWE categories (x-axis).

determiner le 'the'. In future work, we would like to address experimental estimation of weights for different dependency relations in S^S.

6 VMWE classification

LVCs are known to have a relatively regular morphosyntactic behavior as compared to IDs, which tend to be more rigid. We expect our variability measures to help discriminate these categories. We selected those VMWEs whose frequency in TrC was higher than 9, i.e. 12 IDs and 17 LVCs.[8] We then calculated V^S and V^L for each selected VMWE. As shown in Fig. 3, a strong ID vs. LVC discriminative power can be attributed especially to V^L, given that the variability of IDs never exceeds 0.3, while it reaches 0.94 for LVCs.[9]

7 Identification of VMWE variants

As shown by Fazly et al. (2009), English MWEs exhibit lower variability than non-MWEs. Thus, variability measures can help identify MWEs in running text. We test this hypothesis for French using S^L and S^S, which model variant similarity differently from this seminal work. To this aim, we adapted the method proposed by Savary and

---

[8]This threshold is a trade-off between keeping enough variant pairs to be compared to capture the variability profile of a VMWE, and enough VMWEs to evaluate V^S and V^L. Increasing this value e.g. to 19 would yield at least 190 comparisons per VMWE (vs. 45 here) but keep only 8 VMWEs.

[9]These results are statistically significant at $\alpha = 0.01$ according to the WMW test.

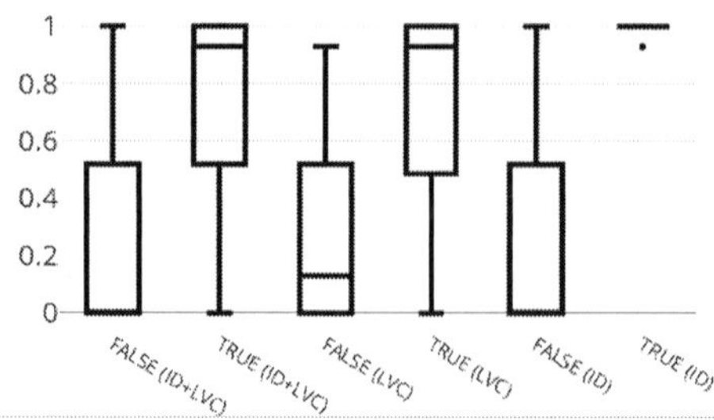

Figure 4: VMWE identification with S^L : Tukey boxplots of False vs. True positives

Cordeiro (2018) to consider all VMWEs of the form Verb-(Det)-Noun annotated in TrC and extract their candidate occurrences in TeC. For instance, if TrC contains the expression e **perdre pied** '*lose foot*' ⇒ '*lose self-confidence*', then the extracted TeC candidates, noted $Cand(e)$, contain true variants of e (e.g. *ces obstacles me font* **perdre pied** 'these obstacles make me lose my self-confidence'), literal readings of e (e.g. *il a perdu le pied gauche* '*he lost his left foot*'), and coincidental occurrences of e's components (e.g. *traces des pieds de l'enfant perdu* '*traces of the lost child's feet*'). Our hypothesis is that S^S and S^L should be able to distinguish true VMWEs from literal and accidental occurrences, thus being useful for supervised VMWE identification. More precisely, we hypothesise that the more a candidate resembles a known VMWE occurrence, the more chances it has to be a VMWE.

We extracted 195 candidates $c \in Cand(e)$ from TeC. For each candidate c, we calculated the minimum similarities $S^L(e, c)$, $S^S(e, c)$ and the average of both $S^{L-S}(e, c)$ over all occurrences of e in TrC.[10] Interesting results were obtained mainly with S^L. Fig. 4 shows pairwise comparison of the minimal value of $S^L(e, c)$ when IDs and LVCs are considered jointly (boxplots 1–2), or separately (boxplots 3–6). In each case S^L clearly delimits false from true positives.[11]

8   Conclusions and future work

We defined syntactic and linear measures of VMWE variability. They use pairwise similarity based on expert linguistic knowledge. We showed their statistically significant correlation with a linguistic benchmark. We also discovered that linear

similarity proves useful in VMWE classification and identification, which is particularly interesting in comparison to the seminal work by Fazly et al. (2009), who do not consider this kind of similarity.

These definitions and estimations should be further improved to deal with other MWE categories, not only verb-noun combinations. Our similarity measures rely on language-independent assumptions: they can be applied to any MWE-annotated corpus containing POS tags and dependency trees. If these morphosyntactic annotations use the unified UD tagsets, cross-language MWE variability studies can be carried out. Therefore, our experiments will be extended to all languages accounted for in the PARSEME corpus. Task-specific parameter tuning should show which parameters are shared by all/many languages and/or tasks, and which have to be language- and task-specific. Morphological variability, including both inflection and derivation (as in **refaire appel** '<u>re</u>-make appeal' ⇒ 'to call on again'), temporarily abandoned for French, could be examined in a multilingual context. Finally, the measures should be adapted to an unsupervised context, to scale them up to larger VMWE vocabularies and languages with no MWE-annotated corpora. For instance, MWE variant candidates could be extracted from automatically parsed text, using lists of known MWE lemmas (Savary and Cordeiro, 2018).

We believe that with these extensions our variability measures will offer a unified framework for describing variability profiles of MWEs, which should be useful both in theoretical and applied research. They could help: (i) disambiguate literal vs. idiomatic readings of VMWEs, (ii) conflate variants of the same MWE to reduce information variation in text, (iii) measure the sensitivity of NLP tools to variability, (iv) define variability-specific evaluation measures in MWE identification to boost the efficient recognition of variants.

Acknowledgments

This work was funded by the French PARSEME-FR grant (ANR-14-CERA-0001). We are grateful to Silvio Cordeiro for sharing the script for VMWE candidate extraction and for his helpful assistance. We also thank the anonymous reviewers for their useful comments.

---

[10]In this section, all similarities S are estimated as the average of the four coefficients presented in App. B.

[11]This is confirmed by the WMW test with significancy at $\alpha = 0.01$ for both IDs and LVCs.

References

Timothy Baldwin, Emily M. Bender, Dan Flickinger, Ara Kim, and Stephan Oepen. 2004. Road-testing the English Resource Grammar over the British National Corpus. In *Fourth International Conference on Language Resources and Evaluation (LREC 2004)*. Lisbon, Portugal.

Maja Buljan and Jan Šnajder. 2017. Combining Linguistic Features for the Detection of Croatian Multiword Expressions. In *Proceedings of the 13th Workshop on Multiword Expressions (MWE 2017)*. Association for Computational Linguistics, Valencia, Spain.

Mathieu Constant, Gülşen Eryiğit, Johanna Monti, Lonneke van der Plas, Carlos Ramisch, Michael Rosner, and Amalia Todirascu. 2017. Multiword expression processing: A survey. *Computational Linguistics* 43(4):837–892. https://doi.org/10.1162/COLI_a_00302.

Meghdad Farahmand and James Henderson. 2016. Modeling the non-substitutability of multiword expressions with distributional semantics and a log-linear model. In *Proc. of the ACL 2016 Workshop on MWEs*. Berlin, pages 61–66. http://anthology.aclweb.org/W16-1809.

Afsaneh Fazly, Paul Cook, and Suzanne Stevenson. 2009. Unsupervised type and token identification of idiomatic expressions. *Computational Linguistics* 35(1):61–103. https://doi.org/10.1162/coli.08-010-R1-07-048.

Gaston Gross. 1988. Degré de figement des noms composés. *Langages* 90:57–72.

Maurice Gross. 1982. Une classification des phrases "figées" du français. *Revue québécoise de linguistique* 11(2).

Christian Jacquemin. 2001. *Spotting and Discovering Terms through Natural Language Processing*, The MIT Press.

Malvina Nissim and Andrea Zaninello. 2013. Modelling the internal variability of multiword expressions through a pattern-based method. In *ACM Transactions on Speech and Language Processing , Special issue on Multiword Expressions*. volume 10.

Geoffrey Nunberg, Ivan A. Sag, and Thomas Wasow. 1994. Idioms. *Language* 70:491–538.

Darren Pearce. 2001. Synonymy in collocation extraction. In *Proc. of the NAACL 2001 Workshop on WordNet and Other Lexical Resources*. Pittsburgh, PA, pages 41–46.

Carlos Ramisch, Paulo Schreiner, Marco Idiart, and Aline Villavicencio. 2008. An evaluation of methods for the extraction of multiword expressions. In *Proc. of the LREC 2008 Workshop on MWEs*. Marrakech, pages 50–53.

Agata Savary and Silvio Ricardo Cordeiro. 2018. Literal readings of multiword expressions: as scarce as hen's teeth. In *Proceedings of the 16th Workshop on Treebanks and Linguistic Theories (TLT 16)*. Prague, Czech Republic.

Agata Savary, Carlos Ramisch, Silvio Cordeiro, Federico Sangati, Veronika Vincze, Behrang QasemiZadeh, Marie Candito, Fabienne Cap, Voula Giouli, Ivelina Stoyanova, and Antoine Doucet. 2017. The PARSEME Shared Task on Automatic Identification of Verbal Multiword Expressions. In *Proceedings of the 13th Workshop on Multiword Expressions (MWE 2017)*. Association for Computational Linguistics, Valencia, Spain, pages 31–47. http://www.aclweb.org/anthology/W/W17/W17-1704.

Livnat Herzig Sheinfux, Tali Arad Greshler, Nurit Melnik, and Shuly Wintner. 2017. *Verbal MWEs: Idiomaticity and flexibility*, Language Science Press, to appear, pages 5–38.

Yulia Tsvetkov and Shuly Wintner. 2014. Identification of multiword expressions by combining multiple linguistic information sources. *Computational Linguistics* 40(2):449–468. https://doi.org/10.1162/COLI_a_00177.

Agnès Tutin. 2016. Comparing morphological and syntactic variations of support verb constructions and verbal full phrasemes in French: a corpus based study. In *PARSEME COST Action. Relieving the pain in the neck in natural language processing: 7th final general meeting*. Dubrovnik, Croatia.

Marion Weller and Ulrich Heid. 2010. Extraction of German multiword expressions from parsed corpora using context features. In *Proc. of LREC 2010*. Valletta, pages 3195–3201.

A Parameter weights

Weigths of lexicalized components : 'VERB': 0 'NOUN': 1 'DET': 0

Features for S^L : 'ADJ': 1 'ADV': 1 'INTJ': 1 'NOUN': 1 'CCONJ': 1 'NUM': 1 'PROPN': 1 'VERB': 1 'AUX': 1 'SCONJ': 1 'ADP': 1 'PRON': 1 'X': 1 'PART': 1 'SYM': 1 'DET': 1 '_': 0 'PUNCT': 0

Features for S^S : 'aux:pass': 1 'nmod:poss': 1 'nummod': 1 'det': 1 'nsubj:pass': 1 'acl:relcl': 1 'amod': 1 'acl': 1 'expl': 0 'xcomp': 0 'root': 0 'iobj': 0 'goeswith': 0 'advcl': 0 'appos': 0 'compound': 0 'fixed': 0 'obl': 0 'mark': 0 'parataxis': 0 'punct': 0 'csubj': 0 'nmod': 0 'flat:name': 0 'orphan': 0 'discourse': 0 '_': 0 'flat:foreign': 0 'dep': 0 'cop': 0 'aux': 0 'dislocated': 0 'obj': 0 'advmod': 0 'conj': 0 'vocative': 0 'reparandum': 0 'nsubj': 0 'case': 0 'cc': 0 'ccomp': 0

B Similarity coefficients used in the variant-to-variant similarity

Similarity between two datasets X and Y is given by the following formulae:

$$\text{card}(X \cap Y) = a$$

$$\text{card}(X \cup Y) = a + b + c$$

$$\text{card}(X) = a + b$$

$$\text{card}(Y) = a + c$$

$$\text{Jaccard} : \frac{a}{a+b+c}$$

$$\text{Sørensen-Dice} : \frac{2a}{2a+b+c}$$

$$\text{Sneath-Sokal} : \frac{a}{a+2(b+c)}$$

$$\text{Cosinus} : \frac{a}{\sqrt{((a+b).(a+c))}}$$

The variant-to-variant similarity defined in Sec. 7 uses the arithmetic mean of these four coefficients.

Defoiling Foiled Image Captions

Pranava Madhyastha, Josiah Wang and **Lucia Specia**
Department of Computer Science
University of Sheffield, UK
{p.madhyastha, j.k.wang, l.specia}@sheffield.ac.uk

Abstract

We address the task of detecting foiled image captions, i.e. identifying whether a caption contains a word that has been deliberately replaced by a semantically similar word, thus rendering it inaccurate with respect to the image being described. Solving this problem should in principle require a fine-grained understanding of images to detect linguistically valid perturbations in captions. In such contexts, encoding sufficiently descriptive image information becomes a key challenge. In this paper, we demonstrate that it is possible to solve this task using simple, interpretable yet powerful representations based on explicit object information. Our models achieve state-of-the-art performance on a standard dataset, with scores exceeding those achieved by humans on the task. We also measure the upper-bound performance of our models using gold standard annotations. Our analysis reveals that the simpler model performs well even without image information, suggesting that the dataset contains strong linguistic bias.

1 Introduction

Models tackling vision-to-language (V2L) tasks, for example Image Captioning (IC) and Visual Question Answering (VQA), have demonstrated impressive results in recent years in terms of automatic metric scores. However, whether or not these models are actually learning to address the tasks they are designed for is questionable. For example, Hodosh and Hockenmaier (2016) showed that IC models do not understand images sufficiently, as reflected by the generated captions. As a consequence, in the last few years many diagnostic tasks and datasets have been proposed aiming at investigating the capabilities of such models in more detail to determine whether and how these models are capable of exploiting visual and/or linguistic information (Shekhar et al., 2017b; John-

son et al., 2017; Antol et al., 2015; Chen et al., 2015; Gao et al., 2015; Yu et al., 2015; Zhu et al., 2016).

FOIL (Shekhar et al., 2017b) is one such dataset. It was proposed to evaluate the ability of V2L models in understanding the interplay of objects and their attributes in the images and their relations in an image captioning framework. This is done by replacing a word in MSCOCO (Lin et al., 2014) captions with a 'foiled' word that is semantically similar or related to the original word (substituting *dog* with *cat*), thus rendering the image caption unfaithful to the image content, while yet linguistically valid. Shekhar et al. (2017b) report poor performance for V2L models in classifying captions as foiled (or not). They suggested that their models (using image embeddings as input) are very poor at encoding structured visual-linguistic information to spot the mismatch between a foiled caption and the corresponding content depicted in the image.

In this paper, we focus on the foiled captions classification task (Section 2), and propose the use of *explicit object detections* as salient image cues for solving the task. In contrast to methods from previous work that make use of word based information extracted from captions (Heuer et al., 2016; Yao et al., 2016; Wu et al., 2018), we use explicit object category information directly extracted from the images. More specifically, we use an interpretable *bag of objects* as image representation for the classifier. Our hypothesis is that, to truly 'understand' the image, V2L models should exploit information about *objects* and their relations in the image and not just global, low-level image embeddings as used by most V2L models.

Our main contributions are:

1. A model (Section 3) for foiled captions classification using a simple and interpretable

Proceedings of NAACL-HLT 2018, pages 433–438
New Orleans, Louisiana, June 1 - 6, 2018. ©2018 Association for Computational Linguistics

object-based representation, which leads to the best performance in the task (Section 4);

2. Insights on upper-bound performance for foiled captions classification using gold standard object annotations (Section 4);

3. An analysis of the models, providing insights into the reasons for their strong performance (Section 5).

Our results reveal that the FOIL dataset has a very strong linguistic bias, and that the proposed simple object-based models are capable of finding salient patterns to solve the task.

2 Background

In this section we describe the foiled caption classification task and dataset.

We combine the tasks and data from Shekhar et al. (2017b) and Shekhar et al. (2017a). Given an image and a caption, in both cases the task is to learn a model that can distinguish between a **REAL** caption that describes the image, and a **FOIL**ed caption where a word from the original caption is swapped such that it no longer describes the image accurately. There are several sets of 'foiled captions' where words from specific parts of speech are swapped:

- **Foiled Noun:** In this case a noun word in the original caption is replaced with another similar noun, such that the resultant caption is not the correct description for the image. The foiled noun is obtained from list of object annotations from MSCOCO (Lin et al., 2014) and nouns are constrained to the same super-category;

- **Foiled Verb:** Here, verb is foiled with a similar verb. The similar verb is extracted using external resources;

- **Foiled Adjective and Adverb:** Adjectives and adverbs are replaced with similar adjectives and adverbs. Here, the notion of similarity again is obtained from external resources;

- **Foiled Preposition:** Prepositions are directly replaced with functionally similar prepositions.

The Verb, Adjective, Adverb and Preposition subsets were obtained using a slightly different methodology (see Shekhar et al. (2017a)) than that used for Nouns (Shekhar et al., 2017b). Therefore, we evaluate these two groups separately.

3 Proposed Model

For the foiled caption classification task (Section 3.1), our proposed model uses information from explicit object detections as an object-based image representation along with textual representations (Section 3.2) as input to several different classifiers (Section 3.3).

3.1 Model definition

Let $y \in \{$REAL, FOIL$\}$ denote binary class labels. The objective is to learn a model that computes $P(y|I;C)$, where I and C correspond to the image and caption respectively. Our model seeks to maximize a scoring function θ:

$$y = \arg \max \theta(I;C) \tag{1}$$

3.2 Representations

Our scoring function θ takes in image features and text features (from captions) and concatenates them. We experiment with various types of features.

For the image side, we propose a *bag of objects* representation for 80 pre-defined MSCOCO categories. We consider two variants: (a) **Object Mention**: A binary vector where we encode the presence/absence of instances of each object category for a given image; (b) **Object Frequency**: A histogram vector where we encode the *number* of instances of each object category in a given image.

For both features, we use **Gold** MSCOCO object annotations as well as **Predict**ed object detections using YOLO (Redmon and Farhadi, 2017) pre-trained on MSCOCO to detect instances of the 80 categories.

As comparison, we also compute a standard **CNN**-based image representation, using the POOL5 layer of a ResNet-152 (He et al., 2016) CNN pre-trained on ImageNet. We posit that our object-based representation will better capture semantic information corresponding to the text compared to the CNN embeddings used directly as a feature by most V2L models.

For the language side, we explore two features: (a) a simple **bag of words (BOW)** representation for each caption; (b) an **LSTM** classifier based model trained on the training part of the dataset.

PoS Type	Train^{foil}	Test^{foil}	Total Train	Total Test
Noun	153,229	75,278	306,458	150,556
Verb	6,314	2,788	60,262	33,616
Adjective	15,640	9,009	73,057	42,163
Adverb	1,011	451	53,381	30,738
Preposition	8,733	5,551	77,002	46,018

Table 1: Dataset statistics for different foiled parts of speech. The superscript $foil$ indicates the number of foiled captions.

Our intuition is that an image description/caption is essentially a result of the interaction between important objects in the image (this includes spatial relations, co-occurrences, etc.). Thus, representations explicitly encoding object-level information are better suited for the foiled caption classification task.

3.3 Classifiers

Three types of classifiers are explored: (a) **Multilayer Perceptron (MLP)**: For BOW-based text representations, a two 100-dimensional hidden layer MLP with ReLU activation function is used with cross-entropy loss, and is optimized with Adam (learning rate 0.001); (b) **LSTM Classifier**: For LSTM-based text representations, a uni-directional LSTM classifier is used with 100-dimensional word embeddings and 200-dimensional hidden representations. We train it using cross-entropy loss and optimize it using Adam (learning rate 0.001). Image representations are appended to the final hidden state of the LSTM; (c) **Multimodal LSTM (MM-LSTM) Classifier**: As above, except that we initialize the LSTM with the image representation instead of appending it to its output. This can also be seen as am image grounded LSTM based classifier.

4 Experiments

Data: We use the dataset for nouns from Shekhar et al. (2017b)[1] and the datasets for other parts of speech from Shekhar et al. (2017a) [2]. Statistics about the dataset are given in Table 1. The evaluation metric is accuracy per class and the average (overall) accuracy over the two classes.

Performance on nouns: The results of our experiments with foiled nouns are summarized in Table 2. First, we note that the models that use **Gold**

---

[1] https://foilunitn.github.io/

[2] The authors have kindly provided us the datasets.

Feats	Overall	Real	Foil
Blind (LSTM only)[†]	55.62	86.20	25.04
HieCoAtt[†]	64.14	91.89	36.38
CNN + BOW MLP	88.42	86.89	89.97
Predict Mention + BOW MLP	94.94	95.68	94.23
Predict Freq + BOW MLP	95.14	95.82	94.48
Gold Mention + BOW MLP	95.83	96.30	95.36
Gold Freq + BOW MLP	96.45	96.04	96.85
CNN + LSTM	87.45	86.78	88.14
Predict Freq + LSTM	85.99	85.17	86.81
Gold Freq + LSTM	87.38	86.62	88.18
Predict Freq + MM-LSTM	87.90	86.73	88.95
Gold Freq + MM-LSTM	89.02	88.35	89.72
Human (majority)[†]	92.89	91.24	94.52

Table 2: Accuracy on Nouns dataset. [†] are taken directly from Shekhar et al. (2017b). HieCoAtt is the state of the art reported in the paper.

bag of objects information are the best performing models across classifiers. We also note that the performance is better than human performance. We hypothesize the following reasons for this: (a) human responses were crowd-sourced, which could have resulted in some noisy annotations; (b) our gold object-based features closely resembles the information used for data-generation as described in Shekhar et al. (2017b) for the foil noun dataset. The models using **Predict**ed bag of objects from a detector are very close to the performance of **Gold**. The performance of models using simple bag of words (**BOW**) sentence representations and an **MLP** is better than that of models that use **LSTM**s. Also, the accuracy of the bag of objects model with **Frequency** counts is higher than with the binary **Mention** vector, which only encodes the presence of objects. The Multimodal LSTM (**MM-LSTM**) has a slightly better performance than **LSTM** classifiers. In all cases, we observe that the performance is on par with human-level accuracy. Our overall accuracy is substantially higher than that reported in Shekhar et al. (2017b). Interestingly, our implementation of **CNN+LSTM** produced better results than their equivalent model (they reported 61.07% vs. our 87.45%). We investigate this further in Section 5.

Performance on other parts of speech: For other parts of speech, we fix the image representation to **Gold Frequency**, and compare results using the **BOW**-based **MLP** and **MM-LSTM**. We also compare the scores to the state of the art reported in Shekhar et al. (2017a). Note that this

	Classifier	Overall	Real	Foil
VB	Gold Freq + BOW MLP	84.03	97.38	70.68
	Gold Freq + MM-LSTM	87.90	99.48	76.32
	HieCoAtt[†]	81.79	-	57.94
ADJ	Gold Freq + BOW MLP	87.74	96.96	78.52
	Gold Freq + MM-LSTM	92.29	85.82	98.77
	HieCoAtt[†]	86.00	-	80.05
ADV	Gold Freq + BOW MLP	54.99	98.49	11.48
	Gold Freq + MM-LSTM	56.55	99.45	13.65
	HieCoAtt[†]	53.40	-	14.73
PREP	Gold Freq + BOW MLP	75.53	92.61	58.45
	Gold Freq + MM-LSTM	89.74	95.59	83.89
	HieCoAtt[†]	74.91	-	61.92

Table 3: Accuracy on Verb, Adjective, Adverb and Preposition datasets, using **Gold Frequency** as the image representation. [†] is the best performing model as reported in Shekhar et al. (2017a).

model does not use gold object information and may thus not be directly comparable – we however recall that only a slight drop in accuracy was found for our models when using predicted object detections rather than gold ones. Our findings are summarized in Table 3. The classification performance is not as high as it was for the nouns dataset. Noteworthy is the performance on adverbs, which is significantly lower than the performance across other parts of speech. We hypothesize that this is because of the imbalanced distribution of foiled and real captions in the dataset. We also found that the performance of **LSTM**-based models on other parts of speech datasets are almost always better than **BOW**-based models, indicating the necessity of more sophisticated features.

5 Analysis

In this section, we attempt to better understand why our models achieve such a high accuracy.

5.1 Ablation Analysis

We first perform ablation experiments with our proposed models over the Nouns dataset (FOIL). We compute image-only models (**CNN** or **Gold Frequency**) and text-only models (**BOW** or **LSTM**), and investigate which components of our model (text or image/objects) contribute to the strong classification performance (Table 4). As expected, we cannot classify foiled captions given only image information (global or object-level), resulting in chance-level performance.

On the other hand, text-only models achieve a

very high accuracy. This is a central finding, suggesting that foiled captions are easy to detect even without image information. We also observe that the performance of **BOW** improves by adding object **Frequency** image information, but not **CNN** image embeddings. We posit that this is because there is a tighter correspondence between the bag of objects and bag of word models. In the case of LSTMs, adding either image information helps slightly. The accuracy of our models is substantially higher than that reported in Shekhar et al. (2017b), even for equivalent models.

We note, however, that while the trends of image information is similar for other parts of speech datasets, the performance of **BOW** based models are lower than the performance of **LSTM** based models. The anomaly of improved performance of **BOW** based models seems heavily pronounced in the nouns dataset. Thus, we further analyze our model in the next section to shed light on whether the high performance is due to the models or the dataset itself.

	Image	Text	Overall	Real	Foil
	CNN	-	50.01	64.71	35.31
	Gold Freq	-	50.04	53.10	47.00
MLP	-	BOW	89.33	88.32	90.34
	CNN	BOW	88.42	86.89	89.97
	Gold Freq	BOW	96.45	96.04	96.85
LSTM	-	LSTM	85.07	85.52	84.66
	CNN	LSTM	87.38	86.62	88.18
	Gold Freq	LSTM	87.45	86.78	88.14

Table 4: Ablation study on FOIL (Nouns).

5.2 Feature Importance Analysis

We apply Local Interpretable Model-agnostic Explanations (Ribeiro et al., 2016) to further understand the strong performance of our simple classifier on the Nouns dataset (FOIL) without any image information. We present an example in Figure 1. We use **MLP** with **BOW** only (no image information) as our classifier. As the caption is correctly predicted to be foiled, we observe that the most important feature for classification is the information on the word *ball*, which also happens to be the foiled word. We further analyzed the chances of this happening on the entire test set. We found that 96.56% of the time the most important classification feature happens to be the foiled word. This firmly indicates that there is a very strong linguistic bias in the training data, despite

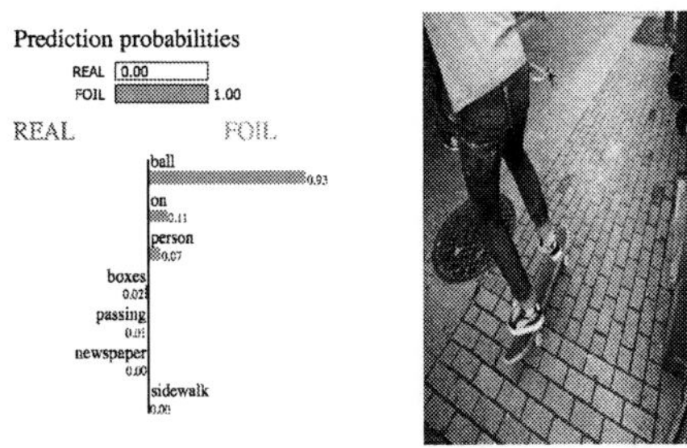

Figure 1: Classifier's prediction for the foiled caption: The classifier is able to correctly classify the foiled caption and uses the foiled word as the trigger for classification.

the claim in Shekhar et al. (2017b) that special attention was paid to avoid linguistic biases in the dataset.[3] We note that we were not able to detect the linguistic bias in the other parts of speech datasets.

6 Conclusions

We presented an object-based image representation derived from explicit object detectors/gold annotations to tackle the task of classifying foiled captions. The hypothesis was that such models provide the necessary semantic information for the task, while this informaiton is not explicitly present in CNN image embeddings commonly used in V2L tasks. We achieved state-of-the-art performance on the task, and also provided a strong upper-bound using gold annotations. A significant finding is that our simple models, especially for the *foiled noun* dataset, perform well even without image information. This could be partly due to the strong linguistic bias in the foiled noun dataset, which was revealed by our analysis on our interpretable object-based models. We release our analysis and source code at `https://github.com/sheffieldnlp/foildataset.git`.

Acknowledgments

This work is supported by the MultiMT project (H2020 ERC Starting Grant No. 678017). The authors also thank the anonymous reviewers for their valuable feedback on an earlier draft of the paper.

---

[3]Shekhar et al. (2017b) have acknowledged about the bias in our personal communications and are currently working on a fix

References

Stanislaw Antol, Aishwarya Agrawal, Jiasen Lu, Margaret Mitchell, Dhruv Batra, C. Lawrence Zitnick, and Devi Parikh. 2015. VQA: Visual question answering. In *Proceedings of the IEEE International Conference on Computer Vision (ICCV)*, pages 2425–2433. IEEE.

Jianfu Chen, Polina Kuznetsova, David Warren, and Yejin Choi. 2015. Déjà image-captions: A corpus of expressive descriptions in repetition. In *Proceedings of the North American Chapter of the Association for Computational Linguistics: Human Language Technologies (NAACL-HLT)*, pages 504–514. Association for Computational Linguistics.

Haoyuan Gao, Junhua Mao, Jie Zhou, Zhiheng Huang, Lei Wang, and Wei Xu. 2015. Are you talking to a machine? Dataset and methods for multilingual image question. In C. Cortes, N. D. Lawrence, D. D. Lee, M. Sugiyama, and R. Garnett, editors, *Advances in Neural Information Processing Systems 28*, pages 2296–2304. Curran Associates, Inc.

Kaiming He, Xiangyu Zhang, Shaoqing Ren, and Jian Sun. 2016. Deep residual learning for image recognition. In *Proceedings of the IEEE Conference on Computer Vision & Pattern Recognition (CVPR)*, pages 770–778. IEEE.

Hendrik Heuer, Christof Monz, and Arnold W. M. Smeulders. 2016. Generating captions without looking beyond objects. In *ECCV Workshop on Storytelling with Images and Videos*.

Micah Hodosh and Julia Hockenmaier. 2016. Focused evaluation for image description with binary forced-choice tasks. In *Proceedings of the 5th Workshop on Vision and Language*, pages 19–28. Association for Computational Linguistics.

Justin Johnson, Bharath Hariharan, Laurens van der Maaten, Li Fei-Fei, C. Lawrence Zitnick, and Ross Girshick. 2017. CLEVR: A diagnostic dataset for compositional language and elementary visual reasoning. In *Proceedings of the IEEE Conference on Computer Vision & Pattern Recognition (CVPR)*, pages 1988–1997. IEEE.

Tsung-Yi Lin, Michael Maire, Serge Belongie, James Hays, Pietro Perona, Deva Ramanan, Piotr Dollár, and C. Lawrence Zitnick. 2014. Microsoft COCO: Common objects in context. In *Proceedings of the European Conference on Computer Vision (ECCV)*, pages 740–755. Springer International Publishing.

Joseph Redmon and Ali Farhadi. 2017. YOLO9000: Better, Faster, Stronger. In *Proceedings of the IEEE Conference on Computer Vision & Pattern Recognition (CVPR)*, pages 6517–6525. IEEE.

Marco Tulio Ribeiro, Sameer Singh, and Carlos Guestrin. 2016. "Why should I trust you?" Explaining the predictions of any classifier. In *Proceedings of the 22nd ACM SIGKDD International Conference on Knowledge Discovery and Data Mining*, KDD '16, pages 1135–1144. ACM.

Ravi Shekhar, Sandro Pezzelle, Aurelie Herbelot, Moin Nabi, Enver Sangineto, and Raffaella Bernardi. 2017a. Vision and language integration: Moving beyond objects. In *Proceedings of International Conference on Computational Semantics (IWCS)*.

Ravi Shekhar, Sandro Pezzelle, Yauhen Klimovich, Aurélie Herbelot, Moin Nabi, Enver Sangineto, and Raffaella Bernardi. 2017b. FOIL it! Find One mismatch between Image and Language caption. In *Proceedings of the Association for Computational Linguistics (ACL)*, pages 255–265. Association for Computational Linguistics.

Qi Wu, Chunhua Shen, Peng Wang, Anthony Dick, and Anton van den Hengel. 2018. Image captioning and visual question answering based on attributes and external knowledge. *Transactions on Pattern Analysis and Machine Intelligence*.

Li Yao, Nicolas Ballas, Kyunghyun Cho, John R. Smith, and Bengio Yoshua. 2016. Oracle performance for visual captioning. In *Proceedings of the British Machine Vision Conference (BMVC)*, pages 141.1–141.13. BMVA Press.

Licheng Yu, Eunbyung Park, Alexander C. Berg, and Tamara L. Berg. 2015. Visual Madlibs: Fill in the blank description generation and question answering. In *Proceedings of the IEEE International Conference on Computer Vision (ICCV)*, pages 2461–2469. IEEE.

Yuke Zhu, Oliver Groth, Michael Bernstein, and Li Fei-Fei. 2016. Visual7W: Grounded question aswering in images. In *Proceedings of the IEEE Conference on Computer Vision & Pattern Recognition (CVPR)*, pages 4995–5004. IEEE.

Pragmatically Informative Image Captioning
with Character-Level Inference

Reuben Cohn-Gordon , Noah Goodman , and Chris Potts

Stanford University
{reubencg, ngoodman, cgpotts}@stanford.edu

Abstract

We combine a neural image captioner with a Rational Speech Acts (RSA) model to make a system that is *pragmatically informative*: its objective is to produce captions that are not merely true but also distinguish their inputs from similar images. Previous attempts to combine RSA with neural image captioning require an inference which normalizes over the entire set of possible utterances. This poses a serious problem of efficiency, previously solved by sampling a small subset of possible utterances. We instead solve this problem by implementing a version of RSA which operates at the level of characters ("a","b","c",...) during the unrolling of the caption. We find that the utterance-level effect of referential captions can be obtained with only character-level decisions. Finally, we introduce an automatic method for testing the performance of pragmatic speaker models, and show that our model outperforms a non-pragmatic baseline as well as a word-level RSA captioner.

1 Introduction

The success of automatic image captioning (Farhadi et al., 2010; Mitchell et al., 2012; Karpathy and Fei-Fei, 2015; Vinyals et al., 2015) demonstrates compellingly that end-to-end statistical models can align visual information with language. However, high-quality captions are not merely *true*, but also *pragmatically informative* in the sense that they highlight salient properties and help distinguish their inputs from similar images. Captioning systems trained on single images struggle to be pragmatic in this sense, producing either very general or hyper-specific descriptions.

In this paper, we present a neural image captioning system[1] that is a *pragmatic speaker* as defined by the Rational Speech Acts (RSA) model (Frank and Goodman, 2012; Goodman and Stuhlmüller,

---

[1]The code is available at https://github.com/reubenharry/Recurrent-RSA

Figure 1: Captions generated by literal (S_0) and pragmatic (S_1) model for the target image (in green) in the presence of multiple distractors (in red).

2013). Given a set of images, of which one is the *target*, its objective is to generate a natural language expression which identifies the target in this context. For instance, the literal caption in Figure 1 could describe both the target and the top two distractors, whereas the pragmatic caption mentions something that is most salient of the target. Intuitively, the RSA speaker achieves this by reasoning not only about what is true but also about what it's like to be a listener in this context trying to identify the target.

This core idea underlies much work in referring expression generation (Dale and Reiter, 1995; Monroe and Potts, 2015; Andreas and Klein, 2016; Monroe et al., 2017) and image captioning (Mao et al., 2016a; Vedantam et al., 2017), but these models do not fully confront the fact that the agents must reason about all possible utterances, which is intractable. We fully address this problem by implementing RSA at the level of characters rather than the level of utterances or words: the neural language model emits individual characters, choosing them to balance pragmatic informativeness with overall well-formedness. Thus, the agents reason not about full utterances, but rather only about all possible character choices, a very small space. The result is that the information encoded recurrently in the neural model allows us

Proceedings of NAACL-HLT 2018, pages 439–443
New Orleans, Louisiana, June 1 - 6, 2018. ©2018 Association for Computational Linguistics

to obtain global pragmatic effects from local decisions. We show that such character-level RSA speakers are more effective than literal captioning systems at the task of helping a reader identify the target image among close competitors, and outperform word-level RSA captioners in both efficiency and accuracy.

2 Bayesian Pragmatics for Captioning

In applying RSA to image captioning, we think of captioning as a kind of reference game. The *speaker* and *listener* are in a shared context consisting of a set of images W, the speaker is privately assigned a target image $w^* \in W$, and the speaker's goal is to produce a caption that will enable the listener to identify w^*. U is the set of possible utterances. In its simplest form, the *literal speaker* is a conditional distribution $S_0(u|w)$ assigning equal probability to all true utterances $u \in U$ and 0 to all others. The pragmatic listener L_0 is then defined in terms of this literal agent and a prior $P(w)$ over possible images:

$$L_0(w|u) \propto \frac{S_0(u|w) * P(w)}{\sum_{w' \in W} S_0(u|w') * P(w')} \quad (1)$$

The pragmatic speaker S_1 is then defined in terms of this pragmatic listener, with the addition of a rationality parameter $\alpha > 0$ governing how much it takes into account the L_0 distribution when choosing utterances. $P(u)$ is here taken to be a uniform distribution over U:

$$S_1(u|w) \propto \frac{L_0(w|u)^\alpha * P(u)}{\sum_{u' \in U} L_0(w|u')^\alpha * P(u')} \quad (2)$$

As a result of this back-and-forth, the S_1 speaker is reasoning not merely about what is true, but rather about a listener reasoning about a literal speaker who reasons about truth.

To illustrate, consider the pair of images 2a and 2b in Figure 2. Suppose that $U = \{bus, red\ bus\}$. Then the literal speaker S_0 is equally likely to produce *bus* and *red bus* when the left image 2a is the target. However, L_0 breaks this symmetry; because *red bus* is false of the right bus, $L_0(2a|bus) = \frac{1}{3}$ and $L_0(2b|bus) = \frac{2}{3}$. The S_1 speaker therefore ends up favoring *red bus* when trying to convey 2a, so that $S_1(red\ bus|2a) = \frac{3}{4}$ and $S_1(bus|2a) = \frac{1}{4}$.

S_0 caption: a double decker bus
S_1 caption: a red double decker bus

Figure 2: Captions for the target image (in green).

3 Applying Bayesian Pragmatics to a Neural Semantics

To apply the RSA model to image captioning, we first train a neural model with a CNN-RNN architecture (Karpathy and Fei-Fei, 2015; Vinyals et al., 2015). The trained model can be considered an S_0-style distribution $P(caption|image)$ on top of which further listeners and speakers can be built. (Unlike the idealized S_0 described above, a neural S_0 will assign some probability to untrue utterances.)

The main challenge for this application is that the space of utterances (captions) U will be very large for any suitable captioning system, making the calculation of S_1 intractable due to its normalization over all utterances. The question, therefore, is how best to approximate this inference. The solution employed by Monroe et al. (2017) and Andreas and Klein (2016) is to sample a small subset of probable utterances from the S_0, as an approximate prior upon which exact inference can be performed. While tractable, this approach has the shortcoming of only considering a small part of the true prior, which potentially decreases the extent to which pragmatic reasoning will be able to apply. In particular, if a useful caption never appears in the sampled prior, it cannot appear in the posterior.

3.1 Step-Wise Inference

Inspired by the success of the "emittor-suppressor" method of Vedantam et al. (2017), we propose an incremental version of RSA. Rather than performing a single inference over utterances, we perform an inference *for each step of the unrolling of the utterance.*

We use a character-level LSTM, which defines a distribution over characters $P(u|pc, image)$, where *pc* ("partial caption") is a string of characters constituting the caption so far and u is the next character of the caption. This is now our S_0: given a partially generated caption and an image, it returns a distribution over which character should next be added to the caption. The advantage of using a character-level LSTM over a word-level one is that U is much smaller for the former (≈ 30 vs. $\approx 20,000$), making the ensuing RSA model much more efficient.

We use this S_0 to define an L_0 which takes a partial caption and a new character, and returns a distribution over images. The S_1, in turn, given a target image w^*, performs an inference over the set of possible characters to determine which is best with respect to the listener choosing w^*.

At timestep t of the unrolling, the listener L_0 takes as its prior over images the L_0 posterior from timestep $(t-1)$. The idea is that as we proceed with the unrolling, the L_0 priors on which image is being referred to may change, which in turn should affect the speaker's actions. For instance, the speaker, having made the listener strongly in favor of the target image, is less compelled to continue being pragmatic.

3.2 Model Definition

In our incremental RSA, speaker models take both a target image and a partial caption pc. Thus, S_0 is a neurally trained conditional distribution $S_0^t(u|w, pc_t)$, where t is the current timestep of the unrolling and u is a character.

We define the L_0^t in terms of the S_0^t as follows, where ip is a distribution over images representing the L_0 prior:

$$L_0^t(w|u, ip_t, pc_t) \propto S_0^t(u|w, pc_t) * ip_t(w) \quad (3)$$

Given an S_0^t and L_0^t, we define S_1^t and L_1^t as:

$$S_1^t(u|w, ip_t, pc_t) \propto$$
$$S_0^t(u|w, pc_t) * L_0^t(w|u, ip_t, pc_t)^\alpha \quad (4)$$

$$L_1^t(w|u, ip_t, pc_t) \propto$$
$$L_0^t(w|u, ip_t, pc_t) * S_0^t(u|w, pc_t) \quad (5)$$

Unrolling To perform greedy unrolling (though in practice we use a beam search) for either S_0 or S_1, we initialize the state as a partial caption pc_0 consisting of only the start token and a uniform prior over the images ip_0. Then, for $t > 0$, we use our incremental speaker model S_0 or S_1 to generate a distribution over the subsequent character $S^t(u|w, ip_t, pc_t)$, and add the character u with highest probability density to pc_t, giving us pc_{t+1}. We then run our listener model L_1 on u, to obtain a distribution $ip_{t+1} = L_1^t(w|u, ip_t, pc_t)$ over images that the L_0 can use at the next timestep.

This incremental approach keeps the inference itself very simple, while placing the complexity of the model in the recurrent nature of the unrolling.[2] While our S_0 is character-level, the same incremental RSA model works for a word-level S_0, giving rise to a word-level S_1. We compare character and word S_1s in section 4.2.

As well as being incremental, these definitions of S_1^t and L_1^t differ from the typical RSA described in section 2 in that S_1^t and L_1^t draw their priors from S_0^t and L_0^t respectively. This generalizes the scheme put forward for S_1 by Andreas and Klein (2016). The motivation is to have Bayesian speakers who are somewhat constrained by the S_0 language model. Without this, other methods are needed to achieve English-like captions, as in Vedantam et al. (2017), where their equivalent of the S_1 is combined in a weighted sum with the S_0.

4 Evaluation

Qualitatively, Figures 1 and 2 show how the S_1 captions are more informative than the S_0, as a result of pragmatic considerations. To demonstrate the effectiveness of our method quantitatively, we implement an automatic evaluation.

4.1 Automatic Evaluation

To evaluate the success of S_1 as compared to S_0, we define a listener $L_{eval}(image|caption) \propto P_{S_0}(caption|image)$, where $P_{S_0}(caption|image)$ is the total probability of S_0 incrementally generating *caption* given *image*. In other words, L_{eval} uses Bayes' rule to obtain from S_0 the posterior probability of each image w given a full caption u.

The neural S_0 used in the definition of L_{eval} must be trained on separate data to the neural S_0 used for the S_1 model which produces captions, since otherwise this S_1 production model effectively has access to the system evaluating it. As Mao et al. (2016b) note, "a model might 'com-

---

[2]The move from standard to incremental RSA can be understood as a switching of the order of two operations; instead of unrolling a character-level distribution into a sentence level one and then applying pragmatics, we apply pragmatics and then unroll. This generalizes to any recursive generation of utterances.

municate' better with itself using its own language than with others". In evaluation, we therefore split the training data in half, with one part for training the S_0 used in the caption generation model S_1 and one part for training the S_0 used in the caption evaluation model L_{eval}.

We say that the caption succeeds as a referring expression if the target has more probability mass under the distribution $L_{eval}(image|caption)$ than any distractor.

Dataset We train our production and evaluation models on separate sets consisting of regions in the Visual Genome dataset (Krishna et al., 2017) and full images in MSCOCO (Chen et al., 2015). Both datasets consist of over 100,000 images of common objects and scenes. MSCOCO provides captions for whole images, while Visual Genome provides captions for regions within images.

Our test sets consist of clusters of 10 images. For a given cluster, we set each image in it as the target, in turn. We use two test sets. Test set 1 (TS1) consists of 100 clusters of images, 10 for each of the 10 most common objects in Visual Genome.[3] Test set 2 (TS2) consists of regions in Visual Genome images whose ground truth captions have high word overlap, an indicator that they are similar. We again select 100 clusters of 10. Both test sets have 1,000 items in total (10 potential target images for each of 100 clusters).

Captioning System Our neural image captioning system is a CNN-RNN architecture[4] adapted to use a character-based LSTM for the language model.

Hyperparameters We use a beam search with width 10 to produce captions, and a rationality parameter of $\alpha = 5.0$ for the S_1.

4.2 Results

As shown in Table 1, the character-level S_1 obtains higher accuracy (68% on TS1 and 65.9% on TS2) than the S_0 (48.9% on TS1 and 47.5% on TS2), demonstrating that S_1 is better than S_0 at referring.

Advantage of Incremental RSA We also observe that 66% percent of the times in which the S_1 caption is referentially successful and the S_0

Model	TS1	TS2
Char S_0	48.9	47.5
Char S_1	**68.0**	**65.9**
Word S_0	57.6	53.4
Word S_1	60.6	57.6

Table 1: Accuracy on both test sets.

caption is not, for a given image, the S_1 caption is not one of the top 50 S_0 captions, as generated by the beam search unrolling at S_0. This means that in these cases the non-incremental RSA method of Andreas and Klein (2016) could not have generated the S_1 caption, if these top 50 S_0 captions were the support of the prior over utterances.

Comparison to Word-Level RSA We compare the performance of our character-level model to a word-level model.[5] This model is incremental in precisely the way defined in section 3.2, but uses a word-level LSTM so that $u \in U$ are words and U is a vocabulary of English. It is evaluated with an L_{eval} model that also operates on the word level.

Though the word S_0 performs better on both test sets than the character S_0, the character S_1 outperforms the word S_1, demonstrating the advantage of a character-level model for pragmatic behavior. We conjecture that the superiority of the character-level model is the result of the increased number of decisions where pragmatics can be taken into account, but leave further examination for future research.

Variants of the Model We further explore the effect of two design decisions in the character-level model. First, we consider a variant of S_1 which has a prior over utterances determined by an LSTM language model trained on the full set of captions. This achieves an accuracy of 67.2% on TS1. Second, we consider our standard S_1 but with unrolling such that the L_0 prior is drawn uniformly at each timestep rather than determined by the L_0 posterior at the previous step. This achieves an accuracy of 67.4% on TS1. This suggests that neither this change of S_1 nor L_0 priors has a large effect on the performance of the model.

---

[3] Namely, *man, person, woman, building, sign, table, bus, window, sky,* and *tree.*

[4] https://github.com/yunjey/ pytorch-tutorial/tree/master/tutorials/ 03-advanced/image_captioning

[5] Here, we use greedy unrolling, for reasons of efficiency due to the size of U for the word-level model, and set $\alpha = 1.0$ from tuning on validation data. For comparison, we note that greedy character-level S_1 achieves an accuracy of 61.2% on TS1.

5 Conclusion

We show that incremental RSA at the level of characters improves the ability of the neural image captioner to refer to a target image. The incremental approach is key to combining RSA with language models: as utterances become longer, it becomes exponentially slower, for a fixed n, to subsample $n\%$ of the utterance distribution and *then* perform inference (non-incremental approach). Furthermore, character-level RSA yields better results than word-level RSA and is far more efficient.

Acknowledgments

Many thanks to Hiroto Udagawa and Poorvi Bhargava, who were involved in early versions of this project. This material is based in part upon work supported by the Stanford Data Science Initiative and by the NSF under Grant No. BCS-1456077. This work is also supported by a Sloan Foundation Research Fellowship to Noah Goodman.

References

Jacob Andreas and Dan Klein. 2016. Reasoning about pragmatics with neural listeners and speakers. In *Proceedings of the 2016 Conference on Empirical Methods in Natural Language Processing*, pages 1173–1182. Association for Computational Linguistics.

Xinlei Chen, Hao Fang, Tsung-Yi Lin, Ramakrishna Vedantam, Saurabh Gupta, Piotr Dollár, and C Lawrence Zitnick. 2015. Microsoft COCO captions: Data collection and evaluation server. *arXiv preprint arXiv:1504.00325*.

Robert Dale and Ehud Reiter. 1995. Computational interpretations of the Gricean maxims in the generation of referring expressions. *Cognitive Science*, 19(2):233–263.

Ali Farhadi, Mohsen Hejrati, Mohammad Amin Sadeghi, Peter Young, Cyrus Rashtchian, Julia Hockenmaier, and David Forsyth. 2010. Every picture tells a story: Generating sentences from images. In *European Conference on Computer Vision*, pages 15–29. Springer.

Michael C. Frank and Noah D. Goodman. 2012. Predicting pragmatic reasoning in language games. *Science*, 336(6084):998.

Noah D Goodman and Andreas Stuhlmüller. 2013. Knowledge and implicature: Modeling language understanding as social cognition. *Topics in Cognitive Science*, 5(1):173–184.

Andrej Karpathy and Li Fei-Fei. 2015. Deep visual-semantic alignments for generating image descriptions. In *Proceedings of the IEEE Conference on Computer Vision and Pattern Recognition*, pages 3128–3137.

Ranjay Krishna, Yuke Zhu, Oliver Groth, Justin Johnson, Kenji Hata, Joshua Kravitz, Stephanie Chen, Yannis Kalantidis, Li-Jia Li, David A Shamma, et al. 2017. Visual genome: Connecting language and vision using crowdsourced dense image annotations. *International Journal of Computer Vision*, 123(1):32–73.

Junhua Mao, Jonathan Huang, Alexander Toshev, Oana Camburu, Alan L. Yuille, and Kevin Murphy. 2016a. Generation and comprehension of unambiguous object descriptions. In *Proceedings of the IEEE Conference on Computer Vision and Pattern Recognition*, pages 11–20. IEEE.

Junhua Mao, Jonathan Huang, Alexander Toshev, Oana Camburu, Alan L Yuille, and Kevin Murphy. 2016b. Generation and comprehension of unambiguous object descriptions. pages 11–20.

Margaret Mitchell, Jesse Dodge, Amit Goyal, Kota Yamaguchi, Karl Stratos, Xufeng Han, Alyssa Mensch, Alex Berg, Tamara Berg, and Hal Daume III. 2012. Midge: Generating image descriptions from computer vision detections. In *Proceedings of the 13th Conference of the European Chapter of the Association for Computational Linguistics*, pages 747–756. Association for Computational Linguistics.

Will Monroe, Robert X. D. Hawkins, Noah D. Goodman, and Christopher Potts. 2017. Colors in context: A pragmatic neural model for grounded language understanding. *Transactions of the Association for Computational Linguistics*, 5:325–338.

Will Monroe and Christopher Potts. 2015. Learning in the Rational Speech Acts model. In *Proceedings of 20th Amsterdam Colloquium*, Amsterdam. ILLC.

Ramakrishna Vedantam, Samy Bengio, Kevin Murphy, Devi Parikh, and Gal Chechik. 2017. Context-aware captions from context-agnostic supervision. *arXiv preprint arXiv:1701.02870*.

Oriol Vinyals, Alexander Toshev, Samy Bengio, and Dumitru Erhan. 2015. Show and tell: A neural image caption generator. In *Proceedings of the IEEE Conference on Computer Vision and Pattern Recognition*, pages 3156–3164.

Object Ordering with Bidirectional Matchings for Visual Reasoning

Hao Tan and **Mohit Bansal**
UNC Chapel Hill
{haotan, mbansal}@cs.unc.edu

Abstract

Visual reasoning with compositional natural language instructions, e.g., based on the newly-released Cornell Natural Language Visual Reasoning (NLVR) dataset, is a challenging task, where the model needs to have the ability to create an accurate mapping between the diverse phrases and the several objects placed in complex arrangements in the image. Further, this mapping needs to be processed to answer the question in the statement given the ordering and relationship of the objects across three similar images. In this paper, we propose a novel end-to-end neural model for the NLVR task, where we first use joint bidirectional attention to build a two-way conditioning between the visual information and the language phrases. Next, we use an RL-based pointer network to sort and process the varying number of unordered objects (so as to match the order of the statement phrases) in each of the three images and then pool over the three decisions. Our model achieves strong improvements (of 4-6% absolute) over the state-of-the-art on both the structured representation and raw image versions of the dataset.

1 Introduction

Visual Reasoning (Antol et al., 2015; Andreas et al., 2016; Bisk et al., 2016; Johnson et al., 2017) requires a sophisticated understanding of the compositional language instruction and its relationship with the corresponding image. Suhr et al. (2017) recently proposed a challenging new NLVR task and dataset in this direction with natural and complex language statements that have to be classified as true or false given a multi-image set (shown in Fig. 1). Specifically, each task instance consists of an image with three sub-images and a statement which describes the image. The model is asked to answer the question whether the given statement is consistent with the image or not.

To solve the task, the designed model needs to fuse the information from two different domains,

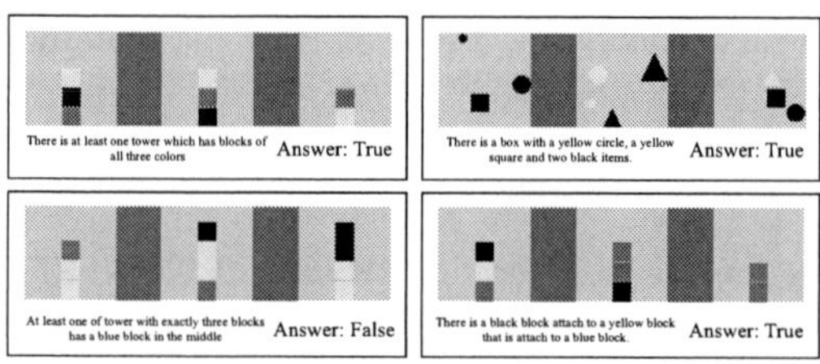

Figure 1: NLVR task: given an image with 3 sub-images and a statement, the model needs to predict whether the statement correctly describes the image or not. We show 4 such examples which our final BiATT-Pointer model correctly classifies but the strong baseline models do not (see Sec. 5).

the visual objects and the language, and learn accurate relationships between the two. Another difficulty is that the objects in the image do not have a fixed order and the number of objects also varies. Moreover, each statement reasons for truth over three sub-images (instead of the usual single image setup), which also breaks most of the existing models. In our paper, we introduce a novel end-to-end model to address these three problems, leading to strong gains over the previous best model. Our pointer network based LSTM-RNN sorts and learns recurrent representations of the objects in each sub-image, so as to match it better with the order of the phrases in the language statement. For this, it employs an RL-based policy gradient method with a reward extracted from the subsequent comprehension model. With these strong representations of the visual objects and the statement units, a joint-bidirectional attention flow model builds consistent, two-way matchings between the representations in different domains. Finally, since the scores computed by the bidirectional attention are about the three sub-images, a pooling combination layer over the three sub-image representations is required to give the final score of the whole image.

On the structured-object-representation version of the dataset, our pointer-based, end-to-end bidi-

Proceedings of NAACL-HLT 2018, pages 444–451
New Orleans, Louisiana, June 1 - 6, 2018. ©2018 Association for Computational Linguistics

rectional attention model achieves an accuracy of 73.9%, outperforming the previous (end-to-end) state-of-the-art method by 6.2% absolute, where both the pointer network and the bidirectional attention modules contribute significantly. We also contribute several other strong baselines for this new NLVR task based on Relation Networks (Santoro et al., 2017) and BiDAF (Seo et al., 2016). Furthermore, we also show the result of our joint bidirectional attention model on the raw-image version (with pixel-level, spatial-filter CNNs) of the NLVR dataset, where our model achieves an accuracy of 69.7% and outperforms the previous best result by 3.6%. On the unreleased leaderboard test set, our model achieves an accuracy of 71.8% and 66.1% on the structured and raw-image versions, respectively, leading to 4% absolute improvements on both tasks.

2   Related work

Besides the NLVR corpus with a focus on complex and natural compositional language (Suhr et al., 2017), other useful visual reasoning datasets have been proposed for navigation and assembly tasks (MacMahon et al., 2006; Bisk et al., 2016), as well as for visual Q&A tasks which focus more on complex real-world images (Antol et al., 2015; Johnson et al., 2017). Specifically for the NLVR dataset, previous models have incorporated property- and count-based features of the objects and the language (Suhr et al., 2017), or extra semantic parsing (logical form) annotations (Goldman et al., 2017) – we focus on end-to-end models for this visual reasoning task.

Attention mechanism (Bahdanau et al., 2014; Luong et al., 2015; Xu et al., 2015) has been widely used for conditioned language generation tasks. It is further used to learn alignments between different modalities (Lu et al., 2016; Wang and Jiang, 2016; Seo et al., 2016; Andreas et al., 2016; Chaplot et al., 2017). In our work, a bidirectional attention mechanism is used to learn a joint representation of the visual objects and the words by building matchings between them.

Pointer network (Vinyals et al., 2015) was introduced to learn the conditional probability of an output sequence. Bello et al. (2016) extended this to near-optimal combinatorial optimization via reinforcement learning. In our work, a policy gradient based pointer network is used to "sort" the objects conditioned on the statement, such that the sequence of ordered objects is sent to the subsequent comprehension model for a reward.

3   Model

The training datum for this task consists of the statement s, the structured-representation objects o in the image I, and the ground truth label y (which is 1 for true and 0 for false). Our BiATT-Pointer model (shown in Fig. 2) for the structured-representation task uses the pointer network to sort the object sequence (optimized by policy gradient), and then uses the comprehension model to calculate the probability $P(s, o)$ of the statement s being consistent with the image. Our CNN-BiATT model for the raw-image I dataset version is similar but learns the structure directly via pixel-level, spatial-filter CNNs – details in Sec. 5 and the appendix. In the remainder of this section, we first describe our BiATT comprehension model and then the pointer network.

3.1   Comprehension Model with Joint Bidirectional Attention

We use one bidirectional LSTM-RNN (Hochreiter and Schmidhuber, 1997) (denoted by LANG-LSTM) to read the statement $s = w_1, w_2, \ldots, w_T$, and output the hidden state representations $\{h_i\}$. A word embedding layer is added before the LSTM to project the words to high-dimension vectors $\{\tilde{w}_i\}$.

$$h_1, h_2, \ldots, h_T = \text{LSTM}\left(\tilde{w}_1, \tilde{w}_2, \ldots, \tilde{w}_T\right) \quad (1)$$

The raw features of the objects in the j-th sub-image are $\{o_k^j\}$ (since the NLVR dataset has 3 sub-images per task). A fully-connected (FC) layer without nonlinearity projects the raw features to object embeddings $\{e_k^j\}$. We then go through all the objects in random order (or some learnable order, e.g., via our pointer network, see Sec. 3.2) by another bidirectional LSTM-RNN (denoted by OBJ-LSTM), whose output is a sequence of vectors $\{g_k^j\}$ which is used as the (left plus right memory) representation of the objects (the objects in different sub-images are handled separately):

$$e_k^j = W\, o_k^j + b \quad (2)$$

$$g_1^j, g_2^j, \ldots, g_{N_j}^j = \text{LSTM}\left(e_1^j, e_2^j, \ldots, e_{N_j}^j\right) \quad (3)$$

where N_j is the number of the objects in jth sub-image. Now, we have two vector sequences for the representations of the words and the objects, using which the bidirectional attention then calculates the score measuring the correspondence be-

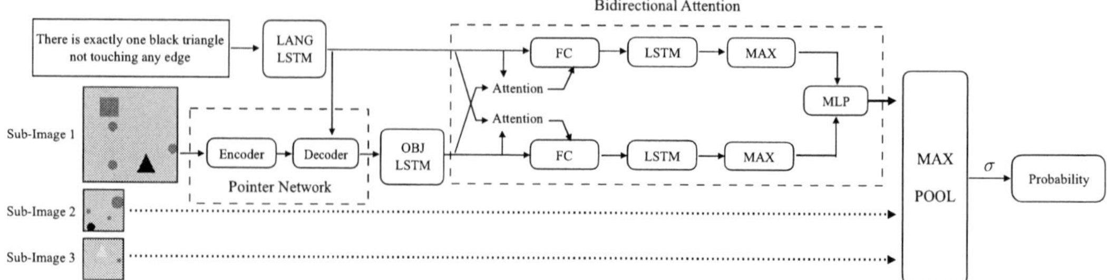

Figure 2: Our BiATT-Pointer model with a pointer network and a joint bidirectional attention module.

tween the statement and the image's object structure. To simplify the notation, we will ignore the sub-image index j. We first merge the LANG-LSTM hidden outputs $\{h_i\}$ and the object-aware context vectors $\{c_i\}$ together to get the joint representation $\{\hat{h}_i\}$. The object-aware context vector c_i for a particular word w_i is calculated based on the bilinear attention between the word representation h_i and the representations of the objects $\{g_k\}$:

$$\alpha_{i,k} = \text{softmax}_k \left(h_i^\intercal B_1 g_k \right) \quad (4)$$

$$c_i = \sum_k \alpha_{i,k} \cdot g_k \quad (5)$$

$$\hat{h}_i = \text{relu} \left(W_{\text{LANG}} \left[h_i; c_i; h_i - c_i; h_i \circ c_i \right] \right) \quad (6)$$

where the symbol $\circ$ denotes element-wise multiplication.

Improvement over BiDAF The BiDAF model of Seo et al. (2016) does not use a full object-to-words attention mechanism. The query-to-document attention module in BiDAF added the attended-context vector to the document representation instead of the query representation. However, the inverse attention from the objects to the words is important in our task because the representation of the object depends on its corresponding words. Therefore, different from the BiDAF model, we create an additional 'symmetric' attention to merge the OBJ-LSTM hidden outputs $\{g_k\}$ and the statement-aware context vectors $\{d_k\}$ together to get the joint representation $\{\hat{g}_k\}$. The improvement (6.1%) of our BiATT model over the BiDAF model is shown in Table 1.

$$\beta_{k,i} = \text{softmax}_i \left(g_k^\intercal B_2 h_i \right) \quad (7)$$

$$d_k = \sum_i \beta_{k,i} \cdot h_i \quad (8)$$

$$\hat{g}_k = \text{relu} \left(W_{\text{OBJ}} \left[g_k; d_k; g_k - d_k; g_k \circ d_k \right] \right) \quad (9)$$

These above vectors $\{\hat{h}_i\}$ and $\{\hat{g}_k\}$ are the representations of the words and the objects which

are aware of each other bidirectionally. To make the final decision, two additional bidirectional LSTM-RNNs are used to further process the above attention-based representations via an additional memory-based layer. Lastly, two max pooling layers over the hidden output states create two single-vector outputs for the statement and the sub-image, respectively:

$$\bar{h}_1, \bar{h}_2, \ldots, \bar{h}_T = \text{LSTM}(\hat{h}_1, \hat{h}_2, \ldots, \hat{h}_T) \quad (10)$$

$$\bar{g}_1, \bar{g}_2, \ldots, \bar{g}_N = \text{LSTM}(\hat{g}_1, \hat{g}_2, \ldots, \hat{g}_N) \quad (11)$$

$$\bar{h} = \underset{i}{\text{ele max}} \left\{ \bar{h}_i \right\} \quad (12)$$

$$\bar{g} = \underset{k}{\text{ele max}} \left\{ \bar{g}_k \right\} \quad (13)$$

where the operator ele max denotes the element-wise maximum over the vectors. The final scalar score for the sub-image is given by a 2-layer MLP over the concatenation of $\bar{h}$ and $\bar{g}$ as follows:

$$score = W_2 \tanh \left(W_1 [\bar{h}; \bar{g}] + b_1 \right) \quad (14)$$

Max-Pooling over Sub-Images In order to address the 3 sub-images present in each NLVR task, a max-pooling layer is used to combine the above-defined scores of the sub-images. Given that the sub-images do not have any specific ordering among them (based on the data collection procedure (Suhr et al., 2017)), a pooling layer is suitable because it is permutation invariant. Moreover, many of the statements are about the existence of a special object or relationship in one sub-image (see Fig. 1) and hence the max-pooling layer effectively captures the meaning of these statements. We also tried other combination methods (mean-pooling, concatenation, LSTM, early pooling on the features/vectors, etc.); the max pooling (on scores) approach was the simplest and most effective method among these (based on the dev set).

The overall probability that the statement correctly describes the full image (with three sub-images) is the sigmoid of the final max-pooled

446

score. The loss of the comprehension model is the negative log probability (i.e., the cross entropy):

$$P(s,o) = \sigma \left(\max_j score^j \right) \tag{15}$$

$$\begin{aligned} L(s,o,y) = &-y \log P(s,o) \\ &-(1-y) \log(1-P(s,o)) \end{aligned} \tag{16}$$

where y is the ground truth label.

3.2 Pointer Network

Instead of randomly ordering the objects, humans look at the objects in an appropriate order w.r.t. their reading of the given statement and after the first glance of the image. Following this idea, we use an additional pointer network (Vinyals et al., 2015) to find the best object ordering for the subsequent language comprehension model. The pointer network contains two RNNs, the encoder and the decoder. The encoder reads all the objects in a random order. The decoder then learns a permutation π of the objects' indices, by recurrently outputting a distribution over the objects based on the attention over the encoder hidden outputs. At each time step, an object is sampled without replacement following this distribution. Thus, the pointer network models a distribution $p(\pi \mid s, o)$ over all the permutations:

$$p(\pi \mid s, o) = \prod_i p\left(\pi(i) \mid \pi(< i), s, o\right) \tag{17}$$

Furthermore, the appropriate order of the objects depends on the language statement, and hence the decoder importantly attends to the hidden outputs of the LANG-LSTM (see Eqn. 1).

The pointer network is trained via reinforcement learning (RL) based policy gradient optimization. The RL loss $L_{RL}(s,o,y)$ is defined as the expected comprehension loss (expectation over the distribution of permutations):

$$L_{RL}(s,o,y) = E_{\pi \sim p(\cdot|s,o)} L(s, o[\pi], y) \tag{18}$$

where $o[\pi]$ denotes the permuted input objects for permutation π, and L is the loss function defined in Eqn. 16. Suppose that we sampled a permutation π^* from the distribution $p(\pi|s,o)$; then the above RL loss could be optimized via policy gradient methods (Williams, 1992). The reward R is the negative loss of the subsequent comprehension model $L(s, o[\pi^*], y)$. A baseline b is subtracted from the reward to reduce the variance (we use the self-critical baseline of Rennie et al. (2016)). The gradient of the loss L_{RL} could then be approximated as:

$$R = -L(s, o[\pi^*], y) \tag{19}$$

$$\begin{aligned} \nabla_\theta L_{RL}(s,o,y) \approx &-(R-b)\nabla_\theta \log p(\pi^* \mid s, o) \\ &+ \nabla_\theta L(s, o[\pi^*], y) \end{aligned} \tag{20}$$

This overall BiATT-Pointer model (for the structured-representation task) is shown in Fig. 2.

4 Experimental Setup

We evaluate our model on the NLVR dataset (Suhr et al., 2017), for both the structured and raw-image versions. All model tuning was performed on the dev set. Given the fact that the dataset is balanced (the number of true labels and false labels are roughly the same), the accuracy of the whole corpus is used as the metric. We only use the raw features of the statement and the objects with minimal standard preprocessing (e.g., tokenization and UNK replacement; see appendix for reproducibility training details).

5 Results and Analysis

Results on Structured Representations Dataset: Table 1 shows our primary model results. In terms of previous work, the state-of-the-art result for end-to-end models is 'MAXENT', shown in Suhr et al. (2017).[1] Our proposed BiATT-Pointer model (Fig. 2) achieves a 6.2% improvement on the public test set and a 4.0% improvement on the unreleased test set over this SotA model. To show the individual effectiveness of our BiATT and Pointer components, we also provide two ablation results: (1) the bidirectional attention BiATT model without the pointer network; and (2) our BiENC baseline model without any attention or the pointer mechanisms. The BiENC model uses the similarity between the last hidden outputs of the LANG-LSTM and the OBJ-LSTM as the score (Eqn. 14).

Finally, we also reproduce some recent popular frameworks, i.e., Relationship Network (Santoro et al., 2017) and BiDAF model (Seo et al., 2016), which have been proven to be successful in other machine comprehension and visual reasoning tasks. The results of these models are weaker than our proposed model. Reimplementation details are shown in the appendix.

---

[1] There is also recent work by Goldman et al. (2017), who use extra, manually-labeled semantic parsing data to achieve a released/unreleased test accuracy of 80.4%/83.5%, resp.

Model	Dev	Test-P	Test-U
STRUCTURED REPRESENTATIONS DATASET			
MAXENT (Suhr et al., 2017)	68.0%	67.7%	67.8%
MLP (Suhr et al., 2017)	67.5%	66.3%	65.3%
ImageFeat+RNN (Suhr et al., 2017)	57.7%	57.6%	56.3%
RelationNet (Santoro et al., 2017)	65.1%	62.7%	-
BiDAF (Seo et al., 2016)	66.5%	68.4%	-
BiENC Model	65.1%	63.4%	-
BiATT Model	72.6%	72.3%	-
BiATT-Pointer Model	**74.6%**	**73.9%**	**71.8%**
RAW IMAGE DATASET			
CNN+RNN (Suhr et al., 2017)	56.6%	58.0%	56.3%
NMN (Suhr et al., 2017)	63.1%	66.1%	62.0%
CNN-BiENC Model	58.7%	58.7%	-
CNN-BiATT Model	**66.9%**	**69.7%**	**66.1%**

Table 1: Dev, Test-P (public), and Test-U (unreleased) results of our model on the structured-representation and raw-image datasets, compared to the previous SotA results and other reimplemented baselines.

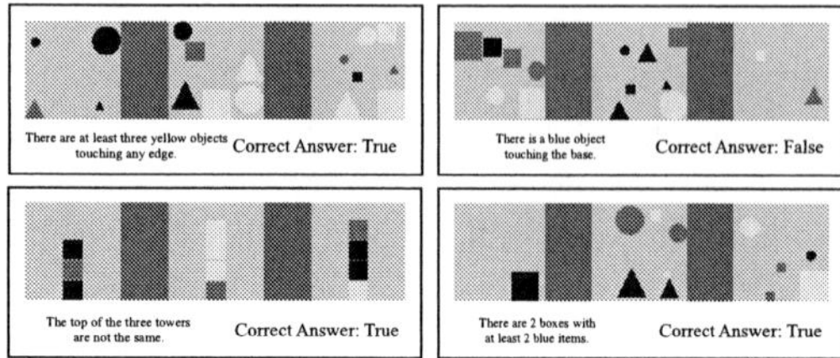

Figure 3: Incorrectly-classified examples.

Results on Raw Images Dataset: To further show the effectiveness of our BiATT model, we apply this model to the raw image version of the NLVR dataset, with minimal modification. We simply replace each object-related LSTM with a visual feature CNN that directly learns the structure via pixel-level, spatial filters (instead of a pointer network which addresses an unordered sequence of structured object representations). As shown in Table 1, this CNN-BiATT model outperforms the neural module networks (NMN) (Andreas et al., 2016) previous-best result by 3.6% on the public test set and 4.1% on the unreleased test set. More details and the model figure are in the appendix.

Output Example Analysis: Finally, in Fig. 1, we show some output examples which were successfully solved by our BiATT-Pointer model but failed in our strong baselines. The left two examples in Fig. 1 could not be handled by the Bi-ENC model. The right two examples are incorrect for the BiATT model without the ordering-based pointer network. Our model can quite successfully understand the complex meanings of the attributes and their relationships with the diverse objects, as well as count the occurrence of and reason over objects without any specialized features.

Next, in Fig. 3, we also show some negative examples on which our model fails to predict the correct answer. The top two examples involve com-plex high-level phrases e.g., "touching any edge" or "touching the base", which are hard for an end-to-end model to capture, given that such statements are rare in the training data. Based on the result of the validation set, the max-pooling layer is selected as the combination method in our model. The max-pooling layer will choose the highest score from the sub-images as the final score. Thus, the layer could easily handle statements about single-subimage-existence based reasoning (e.g., the 4 positively-classified examples in Fig. 1). However, the bottom two negatively-classified examples in Fig. 3 could not be resolved because of the limitation of the max-pooling layer on scenarios that consider multiple-subimage-existence. We did try multiple other pooling and combination methods, as mentioned in Sec. 3.1. Among these methods, the concatenation, early pooling and LSTM-fusion approaches might have the ability to solve these particular bottom-two failed statements. In our future work, we are addressing multiple types of pooling methods jointly.

6 Conclusion

We presented a novel end-to-end model with joint bidirectional attention and object-ordering pointer networks for visual reasoning. We evaluate our model on both the structured-representation and raw-image versions of the NLVR dataset and achieve substantial improvements over the previous end-to-end state-of-the-art results.

Acknowledgments

We thank the anonymous reviewers for their helpful comments. This work was supported by a Google Faculty Research Award, a Bloomberg Data Science Research Grant, an IBM Faculty Award, and NVidia GPU awards.

References

Jacob Andreas, Marcus Rohrbach, Trevor Darrell, and Dan Klein. 2016. Neural module networks. In *Proceedings of the IEEE Conference on Computer Vision and Pattern Recognition*, pages 39–48.

Stanislaw Antol, Aishwarya Agrawal, Jiasen Lu, Margaret Mitchell, Dhruv Batra, C Lawrence Zitnick, and Devi Parikh. 2015. Vqa: Visual question answering. In *Proceedings of the IEEE International Conference on Computer Vision*, pages 2425–2433.

Dzmitry Bahdanau, Kyunghyun Cho, and Yoshua Bengio. 2014. Neural machine translation by jointly learning to align and translate. *arXiv preprint arXiv:1409.0473*.

Irwan Bello, Hieu Pham, Quoc V Le, Mohammad Norouzi, and Samy Bengio. 2016. Neural combinatorial optimization with reinforcement learning. *arXiv preprint arXiv:1611.09940*.

Yonatan Bisk, Deniz Yuret, and Daniel Marcu. 2016. Natural language communication with robots. In *HLT-NAACL*, pages 751–761.

Devendra Singh Chaplot, Kanthashree Mysore Sathyendra, Rama Kumar Pasumarthi, Dheeraj Rajagopal, and Ruslan Salakhutdinov. 2017. Gated-attention architectures for task-oriented language grounding. *arXiv preprint arXiv:1706.07230*.

Omer Goldman, Veronica Latcinnik, Udi Naveh, Amir Globerson, and Jonathan Berant. 2017. Weakly-supervised semantic parsing with abstract examples. *arXiv preprint arXiv:1711.05240*.

Kaiming He, Xiangyu Zhang, Shaoqing Ren, and Jian Sun. 2016. Identity mappings in deep residual networks. In *European Conference on Computer Vision*, pages 630–645. Springer.

Sepp Hochreiter and Jürgen Schmidhuber. 1997. Long short-term memory. *Neural computation*, 9(8):1735–1780.

Justin Johnson, Bharath Hariharan, Laurens van der Maaten, Li Fei-Fei, C Lawrence Zitnick, and Ross Girshick. 2017. Clevr: A diagnostic dataset for compositional language and elementary visual reasoning. In *2017 IEEE Conference on Computer Vision and Pattern Recognition (CVPR)*, pages 1988–1997. IEEE.

Jiasen Lu, Jianwei Yang, Dhruv Batra, and Devi Parikh. 2016. Hierarchical question-image co-attention for visual question answering. In *Advances In Neural Information Processing Systems*, pages 289–297.

Minh-Thang Luong, Hieu Pham, and Christopher D Manning. 2015. Effective approaches to attention-based neural machine translation. *arXiv preprint arXiv:1508.04025*.

Matt MacMahon, Brian Stankiewicz, and Benjamin Kuipers. 2006. Walk the talk: Connecting language, knowledge, and action in route instructions. *Def*, 2(6):4.

Steven J Rennie, Etienne Marcheret, Youssef Mroueh, Jarret Ross, and Vaibhava Goel. 2016. Self-critical sequence training for image captioning. *arXiv preprint arXiv:1612.00563*.

Adam Santoro, David Raposo, David GT Barrett, Mateusz Malinowski, Razvan Pascanu, Peter Battaglia, and Timothy Lillicrap. 2017. A simple neural network module for relational reasoning. *arXiv preprint arXiv:1706.01427*.

Minjoon Seo, Aniruddha Kembhavi, Ali Farhadi, and Hannaneh Hajishirzi. 2016. Bidirectional attention flow for machine comprehension. *arXiv preprint arXiv:1611.01603*.

Alane Suhr, Mike Lewis, James Yeh, and Yoav Artzi. 2017. A corpus of natural language for visual reasoning. In *55th Annual Meeting of the Association for Computational Linguistics, ACL*.

Oriol Vinyals, Meire Fortunato, and Navdeep Jaitly. 2015. Pointer networks. In *Advances in Neural Information Processing Systems*, pages 2692–2700.

Shuohang Wang and Jing Jiang. 2016. Machine comprehension using match-lstm and answer pointer. *arXiv preprint arXiv:1608.07905*.

Ronald J Williams. 1992. Simple statistical gradient-following algorithms for connectionist reinforcement learning. In *Reinforcement Learning*, pages 5–32. Springer.

Kelvin Xu, Jimmy Ba, Ryan Kiros, Kyunghyun Cho, Aaron Courville, Ruslan Salakhudinov, Rich Zemel, and Yoshua Bengio. 2015. Show, attend and tell: Neural image caption generation with visual attention. In *International Conference on Machine Learning*, pages 2048–2057.

A Supplementary Material

A.1 CNN-BiATT Model Details

As shown in Fig. 4, we apply our BiATT model to the raw image dataset with minimal modification. The visual input of the model for this task is changed from the unordered structured representation set of objects o to the raw image pixels I. Hence, we replace all object-related LSTMs (e.g., the OBJ-LSTM and the LSTM-RNN in the bidirectional attention in Fig. 2) with visual feature convolutional neural networks (CNNs) that directly learn the structure via pixel-level, spatial filters (instead of a pointer network which addresses an unordered sequence of structured object representations).

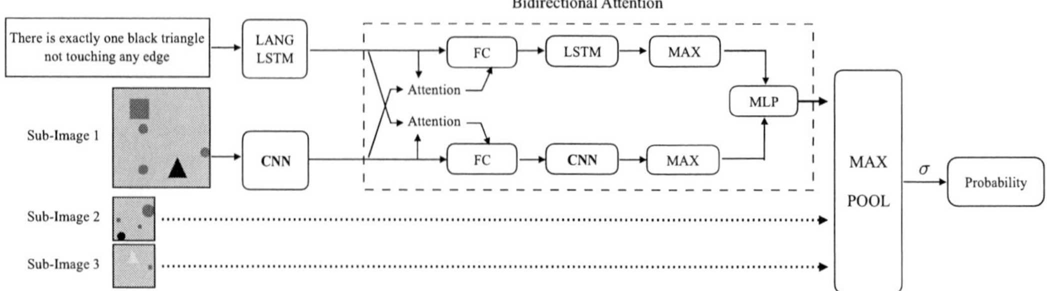

Figure 4: Our CNN-BiATT model for the raw-image dataset version replaces every object-related LSTM-RNN with a spatial-filter convolutional neural network (CNN). The CNN for the raw image-pixels is a pretrained ResNet-v2-101. A 3-layers CNN with relu activation is used in the bidirectional attention.

The training datum for the NLVR raw-image version consists of the statement s, the image I and the ground truth label y. The image I contains three sub-images x^1, x^2 and x^3. We will use x to indicate any sub-image. The superscript which indicates the index of the sub-image is ignored to simplify the notation. The representation of the statement $\{h_i\}$ is calculated by the LANG-LSTM as before. For the image representation, we project the sub-image to a sequence of feature vectors (i.e., the feature map) $\{a_l : l = 1, \ldots, L\}$ corresponding to the different image locations. $L = m \times m$ is the size of the features and m is the width and height of the feature map. The projection consists of ResNet-V2-101 (He et al., 2016) and a following fully-connected (FC) layer. We only use the blocks in the ResNet before the average pooling layer and the output of the ResNet is a feature map of size $m \times m \times 2048$.

$$f_1, \ldots, f_L = \text{ResNet}(x) \tag{21}$$
$$a_l = \text{relu}(W_x\, f_l + b_x) \tag{22}$$

The joint-representation of the statement $\{\hat{h}_i\}$ is the combination of the LANG-LSTM hidden output states $\{h_i\}$ and the image-aware context vectors $\{c_i\}$:

$$\alpha_{i,l} = \text{softmax}_l \left(h_i^\mathsf{T} B_1\, a_l \right) \tag{23}$$
$$c_i = \sum_l \alpha_{i,l} \cdot a_l \tag{24}$$
$$\hat{h}_i = \text{relu} \left(W_{\text{LANG}} [h_i;\, c_i;\, h_i{-}c_i;\, h_i{\circ}c_i] \right) \tag{25}$$

The joint-representation of the image $\{\hat{a}_l\}$ is cal-

culated in the same way:

$$\beta_{l,i} = \text{softmax}_i \left(a_l^\mathsf{T} B_2\, h_i \right) \tag{26}$$
$$d_l = \sum_i \beta_{l,i} \cdot h_i \tag{27}$$
$$\hat{a}_l = \text{relu} \left(W_{\text{IMG}} [a_l;\, d_l;\, a_l{-}d_l;\, a_l{\circ}d_l] \right) \tag{28}$$

The joint-representation of the statement is further processed by a LSTM-RNN. Different from our BiATT model, a 3-layers CNN is used for modeling the joint-representation of the image $\{\hat{a}_l\}$. The output of the CNN layer is another feature map $\{\bar{a}_l\}$. Each CNN layer has kernel size 3×3 and uses relu as the activation function, and then we finally use element-wise max operator similar to Sec. 3.1:

$$\bar{h}_1, \bar{h}_2, \ldots, \bar{h}_T = \text{LSTM}(\hat{h}_1, \hat{h}_2, \ldots, \hat{h}_T) \tag{29}$$
$$\bar{a}_1, \bar{a}_2, \ldots, \bar{a}_{L'} = \text{CNN}(\hat{a}_1, \hat{a}_2, \ldots, \hat{a}_L) \tag{30}$$
$$\bar{h} = \text{ele} \max_i \{\bar{h}_i\} \tag{31}$$
$$\bar{a} = \text{ele} \max_l \{\bar{a}_l\} \tag{32}$$

At last, we use the same method as our BiATT model to calculate the score and the loss function:

$$score(s, x) = W_2 \tanh \left(W_1 [\bar{h};\, \bar{a}] + b_1 \right) \tag{33}$$
$$P(s, I) = \sigma \left(\max_j\, score(s, x^j) \right) \tag{34}$$
$$\begin{aligned} L(s, I, y) = &- y \log P(s, I) \\ &- (1 - y) \log(1 - P(s, I)) \end{aligned} \tag{35}$$

A.2 Reimplementation Details for Relationship Network and BiDAF Models

We reimplement a Relationship Network (Santoro et al., 2017), using a three-layer MLP with

256 units per layer in the G-net and a three-layer MLP consisting of 256, 256 (with 0.3 dropout), and 1 units with ReLU nonlinearities for F-net. We also reimplement a BiDAF model (Seo et al., 2016) using 128-dimensional word embedding, 256-dimensional LSTM-RNN and 0.3 dropout rate. A max pooling layer on top of the modeling layer of BiDAF is used to merge the hidden outputs to a single vector.

A.3 Experimental Setup and Training Details for Our BiATT-Pointer, BiENC, and CNN-BiATT Models

A.3.1 BiATT-Pointer

For preprocessing, we replace the words whose occurrence is less than 3 with the "UNK" token. We create a 9 dimension vector as the feature of each object. This feature contains the location (x, y) in 2D coordinate, the size of the object and two 3-dimensional hot vectors for the shape and the color. The (x, y) coordinates are normalized to the range $[-1, 1]$.

For the model hyperparameters (all lightly tuned on dev set), the dimension of the word embedding is 128, and the number of units in an LSTM cell is 256. The word embedding is trained from scratch. The object feature is projected to a 64-dimensional vector. The dimensions of joint representation $\hat{h}_i$ and $\hat{g}_k$ are both 512. The first fully-connected layer in calculating the sub-images score has 512 units. All the trainable variables are initialized with the Xavier initializer. To regularize the training process, we add a dropout rate 0.3 to the hidden output of the LSTM-RNNs and before the last MLP layer which calculates the score for sub-images. We also clip the gradients by their norm to avoid gradient exploding. The losses are optimized by a single Adam optimizer and the learning rate is fixed at 1e-4.

For the pointer network, we sample the objects following the distribution of the objects at each decoder step during training. In inference, we select the object with maximum probability. We use the self-critical baseline (Rennie et al., 2016) to stabilize the RL training, where the final score in inference (choosing object with maximum probability) is subtracted from the reward. To reduce the number of parameters, we share the weight of the fully-connected layer which projects the raw object feature to the high dimensional vector in the pointer encoder, the pointer decoder, and the OBJ-LSTM. The pointer decoder attends to the hidden outputs of the LANG-LSTM using bilinear attention (Luong et al., 2015).

A.3.2 CNN-BiATT

We initialize our model with weights of the public pretrained ResNet-V2-101 (based on the ImageNet dataset) and freeze it during training. The ResNet projects the sub-image to a feature map of $10 \times 10 \times 2048$. The feature map is normalized to a mean of 0 and a standard deviation of 1 before feeding into the FC layer. The fully connected layer after the ResNet has 512 units. Each layer of the 3-layers CNN in the bidirectional attention has kernel size 3×3 with 512 filters and no padding.

A.3.3 BiENC

The BiENC model uses LANG-LSTM and OBJ-LSTM to read the statement and the objects. A bilinear form calculates the similarity between the last hidden outputs of the two LSTM-RNNs. The similarity is directly used as the score of the sub-image. The CNN-BiENC model replaces the OBJ-LSTM with a CNN.

Contextual Augmentation:
Data Augmentation by Words with Paradigmatic Relations

Sosuke Kobayashi
Preferred Networks, Inc., Japan
`sosk@preferred.jp`

Abstract

We propose a novel data augmentation for labeled sentences called *contextual augmentation*. We assume an invariance that sentences are natural even if the words in the sentences are replaced with other words with paradigmatic relations. We stochastically replace words with other words that are predicted by a bi-directional language model at the word positions. Words predicted according to a context are numerous but appropriate for the augmentation of the original words. Furthermore, we retrofit a language model with a label-conditional architecture, which allows the model to augment sentences without breaking the label-compatibility. Through the experiments for six various different text classification tasks, we demonstrate that the proposed method improves classifiers based on the convolutional or recurrent neural networks.

1 Introduction

Neural network-based models for NLP have been growing with state-of-the-art results in various tasks, e.g., dependency parsing (Dyer et al., 2015), text classification (Socher et al., 2013; Kim, 2014), machine translation (Sutskever et al., 2014). However, machine learning models often overfit the training data by losing their generalization. Generalization performance highly depends on the size and quality of the training data and regularizations. Preparing a large annotated dataset is very time-consuming. Instead, automatic data augmentation is popular, particularly in the areas of vision (Simard et al., 1998; Krizhevsky et al., 2012; Szegedy et al., 2015) and speech (Jaitly and Hinton, 2015; Ko et al., 2015). Data augmentation is basically performed based on human knowledge on invariances, rules, or heuristics, e.g., "even if a picture is flipped, the class of an object should be unchanged".

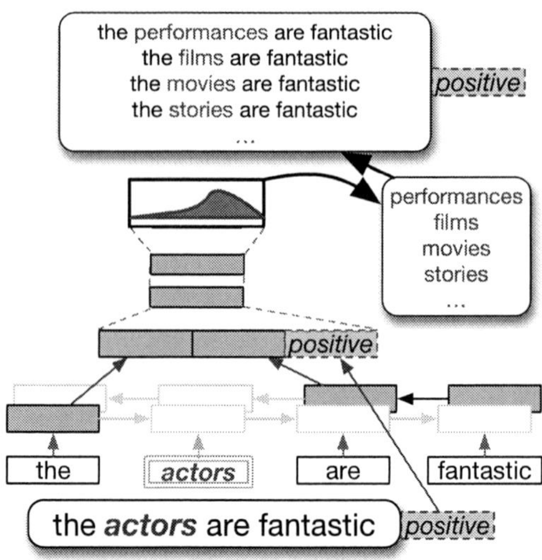

Figure 1: Contextual augmentation with a bi-directional RNN language model, when a sentence *"the actors are fantastic"* is augmented by replacing only *actors* with words predicted based on the context.

However, usage of data augmentation for NLP has been limited. In natural languages, it is very difficult to obtain universal rules for transformations which assure the quality of the produced data and are easy to apply automatically in various domains. A common approach for such a transformation is to replace words with their synonyms selected from a handcrafted ontology such as WordNet (Miller, 1995; Zhang et al., 2015) or word similarity calculation (Wang and Yang, 2015). Because words having exactly or nearly the same meanings are very few, synonym-based augmentation can be applied to only a small percentage of the vocabulary. Other augmentation methods are known but are often developed for specific domains with handcrafted rules or pipelines, with the loss of generality.

In this paper, we propose a novel data aug-

Proceedings of NAACL-HLT 2018, pages 452–457
New Orleans, Louisiana, June 1 - 6, 2018. ©2018 Association for Computational Linguistics

mentation method called *contextual augmentation*. Our method offers a wider range of substitute words by using words predicted by a bi-directional language model (LM) according to the context, as shown in Figure 1. This contextual prediction suggests various words that have paradigmatic relations (Saussure and Riedlinger, 1916) with the original words. Such words can also be good substitutes for augmentation. Furthermore, to prevent word replacement that is incompatible with the annotated labels of the original sentences, we retrofit the LM with a label-conditional architecture. Through the experiment, we demonstrate that the proposed conditional LM produces good words for augmentation, and contextual augmentation improves classifiers using recurrent or convolutional neural networks (RNN or CNN) in various classification tasks.

2 Proposed Method

For performing data augmentation by replacing words in a text with other words, prior works (Zhang et al., 2015; Wang and Yang, 2015) used synonyms as substitute words for the original words. However, synonyms are very limited and the synonym-based augmentation cannot produce numerous different patterns from the original texts. We propose *contextual augmentation*, a novel method to augment words with more varied words. Instead of the synonyms, we use words that are predicted by a LM given the context surrounding the original words to be augmented, as shown in Figure 1.

2.1 Motivation

First, we explain the motivation of our proposed method by referring to an example with a sentence from the Stanford Sentiment Treebank (SST) (Socher et al., 2013), which is a dataset of sentiment-labeled movie reviews. The sentence, *"the actors are fantastic."*, is annotated with a positive label. When augmentation is performed for the word (position) *"actors"*, how widely can we augment it? According to the prior works, we can use words from a synset for the word *actor* obtained from WordNet (*histrion, player, thespian,* and *role_player*). The synset contains words that have meanings similar to the word *actor* on average.[1] However, for data augmentation, the word

actors can be further replaced with non-synonym words such as *characters, movies, stories,* and *songs* or various other nouns, while retaining the positive sentiment and naturalness. Considering the generalization, training with maximum patterns will boost the model performance more.

We propose using numerous words that have the paradigmatic relations with the original words. A LM has the desirable property to assign high probabilities to such words, even if the words themselves are not similar to the original word to be replaced.

2.2 Word Prediction based on Context

For our proposed method, we requires a LM for calculating the word probability at a position i based on its context. The context is a sequence of words surrounding an original word w_i in a sentence S, i.e., cloze sentence $S \backslash \{w_i\}$. The calculated probability is $p(\cdot | S \backslash \{w_i\})$. Specifically, we use a bi-directional LSTM-RNN (Hochreiter and Schmidhuber, 1997) LM. For prediction at position i, the model encodes the surrounding words individually rightward and leftward (see Figure 1). As well as typical uni-directional RNN LMs, the outputs from adjacent positions are used for calculating the probability at target position i. The outputs from both the directions are concatenated and fed into the following feed-forward neural network, which produces words with a probability distribution over the vocabulary.

In contextual augmentation, new substitutes for word w_i can be smoothly sampled from a given probability distribution, $p(\cdot | S \backslash \{w_i\})$, while prior works selected top-K words conclusively. In this study, we sample words for augmentation at each update during the training of a model. To control the strength of augmentation, we introduce temperature parameter τ and use an annealed distribution $p_\tau(\cdot | S \backslash \{w_i\}) \propto p(\cdot | S \backslash \{w_i\})^{1/\tau}$. If the temperature becomes infinity ($\tau \to \infty$), the words are sampled from a uniform distribution.[2] If it becomes zero ($\tau \to 0$), the augmentation words are always words predicted with the highest probability. The sampled words can be obtained at one time at each word position in the sentences. We replace each word simultaneously with a probability

---

[1] Actually, the word *actor* has another synset containing other words such as *doer* and *worker*. Thus, this synonym-based approach further requires word sense disambiguation or some rules for selecting ideal synsets.

[2] Bengio et al. (2015) reported that stochastic replacements with uniformly sampled words improved a neural encoder-decoder model for image captioning.

as well as Wang and Yang (2015) for efficiency.

2.3 Conditional Constraint

Finally, we introduce a novel approach to address the issue that context-aware augmentation is not always compatible with annotated labels. For understanding the issue, again, consider the example, *"the actors are fantastic."*, which is annotated with a positive label. If contextual augmentation, as described so far, is simply performed for the word (position of) *fantastic*, a LM often assigns high probabilities to words such as *bad* or *terrible* as well as *good* or *entertaining*, although they are mutually contradictory to the annotated labels of positive or negative. Thus, such a simple augmentation can possibly generate sentences that are implausible with respect to their original labels and harmful for model training.

To address this issue, we introduce a conditional constraint that controls the replacement of words to prevent the generated words from reversing the information related to the labels of the sentences. We alter a LM to a label-conditional LM, i.e., for position i in sentence S with label y, we aim to calculate $p_\tau(\cdot|y, S\backslash\{w_i\})$ instead of the default $p_\tau(\cdot|S\backslash\{w_i\})$ within the model. Specifically, we concatenate each embedded label y with a hidden layer of the feed-forward network in the bi-directional LM, so that the output is calculated from a mixture of information from both the label and context.

3 Experiment

3.1 Settings

We tested combinations of three augmentation methods for two types of neural models through six text classification tasks. The corresponding code is implemented by Chainer (Tokui et al., 2015) and available [3].

The benchmark datasets used are as follows: (1, 2) SST is a dataset for sentiment classification on movie reviews, which were annotated with five or two labels (SST5, SST2) (Socher et al., 2013). (3) Subjectivity dataset (Subj) was annotated with whether a sentence was subjective or objective (Pang and Lee, 2004). (4) MPQA is an opinion polarity detection dataset of short phrases rather than sentences (Wiebe et al., 2005). (5) RT is another movie review sentiment dataset (Pang

and Lee, 2005). (6) TREC is a dataset for classification of the six question types (e.g., person, location) (Li and Roth, 2002). For a dataset without development data, we use 10% of its training set for the validation set as well as Kim (2014).

We tested classifiers using the LSTM-RNN or CNN, and both have exhibited good performances. We used typical architectures of classifiers based on the LSTM or CNN with dropout using hyperparameters found in preliminary experiments. [4] The reported accuracies of the models were averaged over eight models trained from different seeds.

The tested augmentation methods are: (1) synonym-based augmentation, and (2, 3) contextual augmentation with or without a label-conditional architecture. The hyperparameters of the augmentation (temperature τ and probability of word replacement) were also selected by a grid-search using validation set, while retaining the hyperparameters of the models. For contextual augmentation, we first pretrained a bi-directional LSTM LM without the label-conditional architecture, on WikiText-103 corpus (Merity et al., 2017) from a subset of English Wikipedia articles. After the pretraining, the models are further trained on each labeled dataset with newly introduced label-conditional architectures.

3.2 Results

Table 1 lists the accuracies of the models with or without augmentation. The results show that our contextual augmentation improves the model performances for various datasets from different domains more significantly than the prior synonym-based augmentation does. Furthermore, our label-conditional architecture boosted the performances on average and achieved the best accuracies. Our methods are effective even for datasets with more than two types of labels, SST5 and TREC.

---

[4] An RNN-based classifier has a single layer LSTM and word embeddings, whose output is fed into an output affine layer with the softmax function. A CNN-based classifier has convolutional filters of size $\{3, 4, 5\}$ and word embeddings (Kim, 2014). The concatenated output of all the filters are applied with a max-pooling over time and fed into a two-layer feed-forward network with ReLU, followed by the softmax function. For both the architectures, training was performed by Adam and finished by early stopping with validation at each epoch.

The hyperparameters of the models and training were selected by a grid-search using baseline models without data augmentation in each task's validation set individually. We used the best settings from the combinations by changing the learning rate, unit or filter size, embedding dimension, and dropout ratio.

---

[3] https://github.com/pfnet-research/contextual_augmentation

Models	STT5	STT2	Subj	MPQA	RT	TREC	Avg.
CNN	41.3	79.5	92.4	86.1	75.9	90.0	77.53
w/ synonym	40.7	80.0	92.4	86.3	76.0	89.6	77.50
w/ context	41.9	80.9	92.7	86.7	75.9	90.0	78.02
+ label	42.1	80.8	93.0	86.7	76.1	90.5	**78.20**
RNN	40.2	80.3	92.4	86.0	76.7	89.0	77.43
w/ synonym	40.5	80.2	92.8	86.4	76.6	87.9	77.40
w/ context	40.9	79.3	92.8	86.4	77.0	89.3	77.62
+ label	41.1	80.1	92.8	86.4	77.4	89.2	**77.83**

Table 1: Accuracies of the models for various benchmarks. The accuracies are averaged over eight models trained from different seeds.

For investigating our label-conditional bi-directional LM, we show in Figure 2 the top-10 word predictions by the model for a sentence from the SST dataset. Each word in the sentence is frequently replaced with various words that are not always synonyms. We present two types of predictions depending on the label fed into the conditional LM. With a positive label, the word "fantastic" is frequently replaced with *funny, honest, good,* and *entertaining*, which are also positive expressions. In contrast, with a negative label, the word "fantastic" is frequently replaced with *tired, forgettable, bad*, and *dull*, which reflect a negative sentiment. At another position, the word "the" can be replaced with "no" (with the seventh highest probability), so that the whole sentence becomes "no actors are fantastic.", which seems negative as a whole. Aside from such inversions caused by labels, the parts unrelated to the labels (e.g., "actors") are not very different in the positive or negative predictions. These results also demonstrated that conditional architectures are effective.

4 Related Work

Some works tried text data augmentation by using synonym lists (Zhang et al., 2015; Wang and Yang, 2015), grammar induction (Jia and Liang, 2016), task-specific heuristic rules (Fürstenau and Lapata, 2009; Kafle et al., 2017; Silfverberg et al., 2017), or neural decoders of autoencoders (Bergmanis et al., 2017; Xu et al., 2017; Hu et al., 2017) or encoder-decoder models (Kim and Rush, 2016; Sennrich et al., 2016; Xia et al., 2017). The works most similar to our research are Kolomiyets et al. (2011) and Fadaee et al. (2017). In a task of time expression recognition, Kolomiyets et al. replaced only the headwords under a task-specific assumption that temporal trigger words usually occur as headwords. They selected substitute words with top-K scores

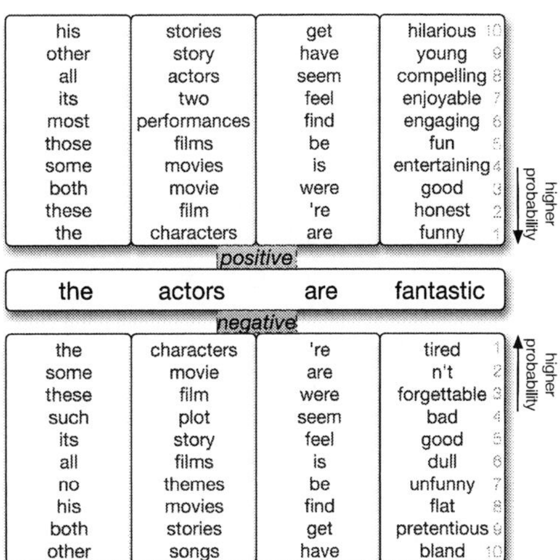

Figure 2: Words predicted with the ten highest probabilities by the conditional bi-directional LM applied to the sentence *"the actors are fantastic"*. The squares above the sentence list the words predicted with a positive label. The squares below list the words predicted with a negative label.

given by the Latent Words LM (Deschacht and Moens, 2009), which is a LM based on fixed-length contexts. Fadaee et al. (2017), focusing on the rare word problem in machine translation, replaced words in a source sentence with only rare words, which both of rightward and leftward LSTM LMs independently predict with top-K confidences. A word in the translated sentence is also replaced using a word alignment method and a rightward LM. These two works share the idea of the usage of language models with our method. We used a bi-directional LSTM LM which captures variable-length contexts with considering both the directions jointly. More importantly, we proposed a label-conditional architecture and demonstrated its effect both qualitatively and quantitatively. Our method is independent of any task-specific knowledge, and effective for classification tasks in various domains.

We use a label-conditional fill-in-the-blank context for data augmentation. Neural models using the fill-in-the-blank context have been invested in other applications. Kobayashi et al. (2016, 2017) proposed to extract and organize information about each entity in a discourse using the context. Fedus et al. (2018) proposed GAN (Goodfellow et al., 2014) for text generation and demonstrated that the mode collapse and training instability can be relieved by in-filling-task training.

5 Conclusion

We proposed a novel data augmentation using numerous words given by a bi-directional LM, and further introduced a label-conditional architecture into the LM. Experimentally, our method produced various words compatibly with the labels of original texts and improved neural classifiers more than the synonym-based augmentation. Our method is independent of any task-specific knowledge or rules, and can be generally and easily used for classification tasks in various domains.

On the other hand, the improvement by our method is sometimes marginal. Future work will explore comparison and combination with other generalization methods exploiting datasets deeply as well as our method.

Acknowledgments

I would like to thank the members of Preferred Networks, Inc., especially Takeru Miyato and Yuta Tsuboi, for helpful comments. I would also like to thank anonymous reviewers for helpful comments.

References

Samy Bengio, Oriol Vinyals, Navdeep Jaitly, and Noam Shazeer. 2015. Scheduled sampling for sequence prediction with recurrent neural networks. In *NIPS*, pages 1171–1179.

Toms Bergmanis, Katharina Kann, Hinrich Schütze, and Sharon Goldwater. 2017. Training data augmentation for low-resource morphological inflection. In *CoNLL SIGMORPHON*, pages 31–39.

Koen Deschacht and Marie-Francine Moens. 2009. Semi-supervised semantic role labeling using the latent words language model. In *EMNLP*, pages 21–29.

Chris Dyer, Miguel Ballesteros, Wang Ling, Austin Matthews, and Noah A. Smith. 2015. Transition-based dependency parsing with stack long short-term memory. In *ACL*, pages 334–343.

Marzieh Fadaee, Arianna Bisazza, and Christof Monz. 2017. Data augmentation for low-resource neural machine translation. In *ACL*, pages 567–573.

William Fedus, Ian Goodfellow, and Andrew M. Dai. 2018. MaskGAN: Better text generation via filling in the ______. In *ICLR*.

Hagen Fürstenau and Mirella Lapata. 2009. Semi-supervised semantic role labeling. In *EACL*, pages 220–228.

Ian Goodfellow, Jean Pouget-Abadie, Mehdi Mirza, Bing Xu, David Warde-Farley, Sherjil Ozair, Aaron Courville, and Yoshua Bengio. 2014. Generative adversarial nets. In *NIPS*, pages 2672–2680.

Sepp Hochreiter and Jürgen Schmidhuber. 1997. Long short-term memory. *Neural computation*, 9(8):1735–1780.

Zhiting Hu, Zichao Yang, Xiaodan Liang, Ruslan Salakhutdinov, and Eric P. Xing. 2017. Toward controlled generation of text. In *ICML*, pages 1587–1596.

Navdeep Jaitly and Geoffrey E Hinton. 2015. Vocal tract length perturbation (vtlp) improves speech recognition. In *ICML*.

Robin Jia and Percy Liang. 2016. Data recombination for neural semantic parsing. In *ACL*, pages 12–22.

Kushal Kafle, Mohammed Yousefhussien, and Christopher Kanan. 2017. Data augmentation for visual question answering. In *INLG*, pages 198–202.

Yoon Kim. 2014. Convolutional neural networks for sentence classification. In *EMNLP*, pages 1746–1751.

Yoon Kim and Alexander M. Rush. 2016. Sequence-level knowledge distillation. In *EMNLP*, pages 1317–1327.

Tom Ko, Vijayaditya Peddinti, Daniel Povey, and Sanjeev Khudanpur. 2015. Audio augmentation for speech recognition. In *INTERSPEECH*, pages 3586–3589.

Sosuke Kobayashi, Naoaki Okazaki, and Kentaro Inui. 2017. A neural language model for dynamically representing the meanings of unknown words and entities in a discourse. In *IJCNLP*, pages 473–483.

Sosuke Kobayashi, Ran Tian, Naoaki Okazaki, and Kentaro Inui. 2016. Dynamic entity representation with max-pooling improves machine reading. In *Proceedings of NAACL-HLT*, pages 850–855.

Oleksandr Kolomiyets, Steven Bethard, and Marie-Francine Moens. 2011. Model-portability experiments for textual temporal analysis. In *ACL*, pages 271–276.

Alex Krizhevsky, Ilya Sutskever, and Geoffrey E Hinton. 2012. Imagenet classification with deep convolutional neural networks. In *NIPS*, pages 1097–1105.

Xin Li and Dan Roth. 2002. Learning question classifiers. In *COLING*, pages 1–7.

Stephen Merity, Caiming Xiong, James Bradbury, and Richard Socher. 2017. Pointer sentinel mixture models. In *ICLR*.

George A. Miller. 1995. Wordnet: A lexical database for english. *Commun. ACM*, 38(11):39–41.

Bo Pang and Lillian Lee. 2004. A sentimental education: Sentiment analysis using subjectivity summarization based on minimum cuts. In *ACL*.

Bo Pang and Lillian Lee. 2005. Seeing stars: Exploiting class relationships for sentiment categorization with respect to rating scales. In *ACL*, pages 115–124.

Charles Bally Albert Sechehaye Saussure, Ferdinand de and Albert Riedlinger. 1916. *Cours de linguistique generale*. Lausanne: Payot.

Rico Sennrich, Barry Haddow, and Alexandra Birch. 2016. Improving neural machine translation models with monolingual data. In *ACL*, pages 86–96.

Miikka Silfverberg, Adam Wiemerslage, Ling Liu, and Lingshuang Jack Mao. 2017. Data augmentation for morphological reinflection. In *CoNLL SIGMORPHON*, pages 90–99.

Patrice Y. Simard, Yann A. LeCun, John S. Denker, and Bernard Victorri. 1998. *Transformation Invariance in Pattern Recognition — Tangent Distance and Tangent Propagation*. Springer Berlin Heidelberg.

Richard Socher, Alex Perelygin, Jean Wu, Jason Chuang, Christopher D. Manning, Andrew Ng, and Christopher Potts. 2013. Recursive deep models for semantic compositionality over a sentiment treebank. In *EMNLP*, pages 1631–1642.

Ilya Sutskever, Oriol Vinyals, and Quoc V Le. 2014. Sequence to sequence learning with neural networks. In *NIPS*, pages 3104–3112.

Christian Szegedy, Wei Liu, Yangqing Jia, Pierre Sermanet, Scott Reed, Dragomir Anguelov, Dumitru Erhan, Vincent Vanhoucke, and Andrew Rabinovich. 2015. Going deeper with convolutions. In *CVPR*.

Seiya Tokui, Kenta Oono, Shohei Hido, and Justin Clayton. 2015. Chainer: a next-generation open source framework for deep learning. In *Proceedings of Workshop on LearningSys in NIPS 28*.

William Yang Wang and Diyi Yang. 2015. That's so annoying!!!: A lexical and frame-semantic embedding based data augmentation approach to automatic categorization of annoying behaviors using #petpeeve tweets. In *EMNLP*, pages 2557–2563.

Janyce Wiebe, Theresa Wilson, and Claire Cardie. 2005. Annotating expressions of opinions and emotions in language. *Language Resources and Evaluation*, 39(2):165–210.

Yingce Xia, Tao Qin, Wei Chen, Jiang Bian, Nenghai Yu, and Tie-Yan Liu. 2017. Dual supervised learning. In *ICML*, pages 3789–3798.

Weidi Xu, Haoze Sun, Chao Deng, and Ying Tan. 2017. Variational autoencoder for semi-supervised text classification. In *AAAI*, pages 3358–3364.

Xiang Zhang, Junbo Zhao, and Yann LeCun. 2015. Character-level convolutional networks for text classification. In *NIPS*, pages 649–657.

Cross-lingual Learning-to-Rank with Shared Representations

Shota Sasaki[1], Shuo Sun[2], Shigehiko Schamoni[3], Kevin Duh[2], Kentaro Inui[1,4]
[1]Tohoku University, [2]Johns Hopkins University, [3]Heidelberg University, [4]RIKEN AIP
`{sasaki.shota,inui}@ecei.tohoku.ac.jp`, `ssun32@jhu.edu`,
`schamoni@cl.uni-heidelberg.de`, `kevinduh@cs.jhu.edu`

Abstract

Cross-lingual information retrieval (CLIR) is a document retrieval task where the documents are written in a language different from that of the user's query. This is a challenging problem for data-driven approaches due to the general lack of labeled training data. We introduce a large-scale dataset derived from Wikipedia to support CLIR research in 25 languages. Further, we present a simple yet effective neural learning-to-rank model that shares representations across languages and reduces the data requirement. This model can exploit training data in, for example, Japanese-English CLIR to improve the results of Swahili-English CLIR.

1 Introduction

Multilingual document collections are becoming prevalent. Thus an important application is cross-lingual information retrieval (CLIR), i.e. document retrieval which assumes that the language of the user's query does not match that of the documents. For example, imagine an investor who wishes to monitor consumer sentiment of an international brand in Twitter conversations around the world. She might issue a query string in English, and desire all relevant tweets in any language.

There are two main approaches to building CLIR systems. The *modular approach* involves a pipeline of two components: translation (machine translation or bilingual dictionary look-up) and monolingual information retrieval (IR). These approaches may be further divided into the *document translation* and *query translation* approaches (Nie, 2010). In the former, one translates all foreign-language documents to the language of the user query prior to IR indexing; in the latter, one indexes foreign-language documents and translates the query. In both, the idea is to solve the translation problem separately, so that CLIR becomes document retrieval in the monolingual setting.

A distinctly different way to build CLIR systems is what may be called the *direct modeling approach* (Bai et al., 2010; Sokolov et al., 2013). This assumes the availability of CLIR training examples of the form (q, d, r), where q is an English query, d is a foreign-language document, a r is the corresponding relevance judgment for d with respect to q. One directly builds a retrieval model $S(q, d)$ that scores the query-document pair. While q and d are in different languages, the model directly learns both translation and retrieval relevance on the CLIR training data. Compared to the modular approach, direct modeling is advantageous in that it focuses on learning translations that are beneficial for retrieval, rather than translations that preserve sentence meaning/structure in bitext.

However, there exist no large-scale CLIR dataset that can support direct modeling approaches in a wide variety of languages. To obtain relevance judgments, one typically needs a bilingual speaker who can read a foreign-language document and assess whether it is relevant for a given English query. This can be an expensive process. Here, we present a large-scale dataset that is automatically constructed from Wikipedia: it can support training and evaluation of CLIR systems between English queries and documents in 25 other languages (Section 2). The data is of sufficient size for direct modeling, and can also serve as an wide-coverage evaluation data for the modular approaches.[1]

To demonstrate the utility of the data, we further present experiments for CLIR in low-resource languages. First, we introduce a neural CLIR model based on the direct modeling approach (Section

---

[1]To facilitate CLIR research, the dataset is publicly available at `http://www.cs.jhu.edu/~kevinduh/a/wikiclir2018/`.

Proceedings of NAACL-HLT 2018, pages 458–463
New Orleans, Louisiana, June 1 - 6, 2018. ©2018 Association for Computational Linguistics

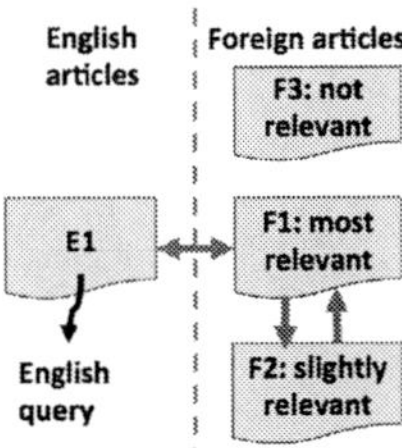

Figure 1: CLIR data construction process: From an English article (E1), we extract the English query. Using the inter-language link, we obtain the *most relevant* foreign-language document (F1). Any article that has mutual links to and from F1 are labeled as *slightly relevant* (F2). All other articles are *not relevant* (F3). The data is a set of tuples: (English query q, foreign document d, relevance judgment r), where $r \in \{0, 1, 2\}$ represents the three levels of relevance.

3.1). We then show how we can bootstrap CLIR models for languages with less training data by an appropriate use of paramater sharing among different language pairs (Section 3.2). For example, using the training data for Japanese-English CLIR, we can improve the Mean Average Precision (MAP) results of a Swahili-English CLIR system by 5-7 points (Section 4).

2 Large-Scale CLIR Dataset

We construct a large-scale CLIR data from Wikipedia. The idea is to exploit *inter-language links*: from an English page, we extract a sentence as query, and label the linked foreign-document pages as relevant. See Figure 1 for an illustration.

This data construction process is similar to (Schamoni et al., 2014) who made an English-German CLIR dataset, but ours is at a larger scale. Specifically, we use Wikipedia dumps released on August 23, 2017. English queries are obtained by extracting the first sentence of every English Wikipedia article. The intuition is that the first sentence is usually a well-defined summary of its corresponding article and should be thematically related for articles linked to it from another language. Similar to (Schamoni et al., 2014), title words from the query sentences are removed, because they may be present across different language editions. This deletion prevents the task from becoming an easy keyword matching task.

For practical purposes, each document is limited to the first 200 words of the article. Empty documents and category pages are filtered. Currently, our dataset consists of more than 2.8 mil-

Language	#Doc	#Query	#SR
Arabic	535	324	194
Catalan	548	339	625
Chinese	951	463	462
Czech	386	233	720
Dutch	1908	687	1646
Finnish	418	273	665
French	1894	1089	4048
German	2091	938	4612
Italian	1347	808	2635
Japanese	1071	426	2912
Korean	394	224	343
Norwegian-Nynorsk	133	99	150
Norwegian-Bokmål	471	299	663
Polish	1234	693	1777
Portuguese	973	611	1130
Romanian	376	199	251
Russian	1413	664	1656
Simple English	127	114	135
Spanish	1302	781	2113
Swahili	37	22	35
Swedish	3785	639	1430
Tagalog	79	48	23
Turkish	295	185	195
Ukrainian	704	348	565
Vietnamese	1392	354	257
(All numbers are in units of one thousand)			

Table 1: CLIR dataset statistics. For each language X, we show the total number of documents in language X and the number of English queries. The number of "most relevant" documents is by definition equal to #Query. The number of "slightly relevant" documents is shown in the column #SR.

lion English queries and relevant documents from 25 other selected languages (see Table 1).

In sum, we have created a CLIR dataset that is large-scale in terms of both the amount of examples as well as the number of languages. This can be used in two scenarios: (1) one mixed-language collection where an English query may retrieve relevant documents in multiple languages. (2) 25 independent datasets for training and evaluating CLIR on English queries against one foreign language collection. In the experiments in Section 4, we will utilize the dataset in terms of scenario (2).[2]

---

[2] For extensibility purposes, these experiments use only half of the data, randomly sampled by query (the held-out data is reserved for other uses). Also it only considers binary relevance (*most relevant* vs *not relevant*) for simplicity. The exact data splits will be provided along with the data release.

3 Direct Modeling for CLIR

3.1 Neural Ranking Model

Given an English query q and a foreign-language document d, our models compute the relevance score $S(q, d)$. First, we represent each word as n-dimensional vectors, so q and d are represented as matrices $\mathbf{Q} \in \mathbb{R}^{n \times |q|}$ and $\mathbf{D} \in \mathbb{R}^{n \times |d|}$, where $|q|$ and $|d|$ are the numbers of tokens in q and d:

$$\mathbf{Q} = [E_q(q_1); E_q(q_2); ...; E_q(q_{|q|})]$$
$$\mathbf{D} = [E_d(d_1); E_d(d_2); ...; E_d(d_{|d|})]$$

q_i and d_i denote the i-th term in q and d. E is embedding function which transforms each term to a dense n-dimensional vector as its representation. ; is the concatenation operator. Then, we apply convolutional feature map[3] to these matrices, followed by tanh activation and average-pooling to obtain each representation vector $\hat{q}$ and $\hat{d}$.

$$\hat{q} = CNN_q(\mathbf{Q}); \quad \hat{d} = CNN_d(\mathbf{D}) \quad (1)$$

Next, we define two variations in calculating $S(q, d)$. The first is a *cosine model* which computes cosine similarity between $\hat{q}$ and $\hat{d}$:

$$S_{cos}(q, d) = cossim(\hat{q}, \hat{d}) \quad (2)$$

The second is a *deep model* with a fully connected layer on top of the concatenation of $\hat{q}$ and $\hat{d}$ (a 200-dimensional vector):

$$S_{deep}(q, d) = tanh(O \cdot h_{vec}^{\mathrm{T}}) \quad (3)$$
$$= tanh(O \cdot relu(W \cdot [\hat{q}; \hat{d}]^{\mathrm{T}}))$$

Here, $O \in \mathbb{R}^{1 \times h}$ and $W \in \mathbb{R}^{h \times 200}$ are the deep model parameters, and h is the number of dimensions of the hidden state, $h_{vec} \in \mathbb{R}^{1 \times h}$. For regularization, we set dropout rate as 0.5 (Srivastava et al., 2014) at the hidden layer.

In the training phase, we minimize pairwise ranking loss, which is widely used for learning-to-rank (Pang et al., 2016; Guo et al., 2016; Hui et al., 2017; Xiong et al., 2017; Dehghani et al., 2017), defined as follows:

$$L = max\left\{0, 1 - (S(q, d^+) - S(q, d^-))\right\} \quad (4)$$

where d^+ and d^- are relevant and non-relevant document respectively. We fix only the word embeddings and tune the other parameters.

---

[3]The $n \times 4$ convolution window has filter size of 100 and takes a stride of 1.

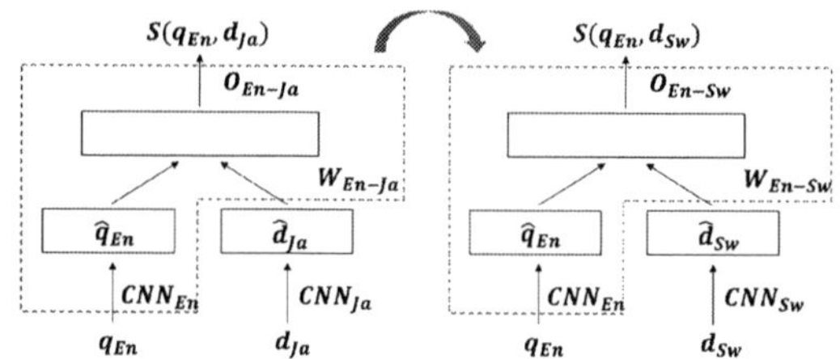

Figure 2: Illustration of the proposed method. On low resource dataset (e.g. Swahili-English), the parameters of the CNN for encoding query (CNN_{En}) and the parameters of the fully connected layer (O_{En-Sw}, W_{En-Sw}) are initialized by the ones pre-trained on high resource dataset (e.g. Japanese-English).

	Ja	De	Fr
$S_{cos}(q, d)$: cos	59/74	49/66	55/70
$S_{deep}(q, d)$: h=100	61/75	64/77	69/81
$S_{deep}(q, d)$: h=200	68/80	67/79	74/84
$S_{deep}(q, d)$: h=300	70/82	70/81	74/84
$S_{deep}(q, d)$: h=400	**73/83**	**71/82**	75/85
$S_{deep}(q, d)$: h=500	**73/84**	70/81	**76/85**

Table 2: P@1/MAP performance (0-100 range, in percent) of the cosine model and the deep model with different hidden state size on **high resource datasets**. Best value in each column is highlighted in bold.

We note there are many other ranking models that can be adapted to CLIR (Huang et al., 2013; Shen et al., 2014; Xiong et al., 2017; Mitra et al., 2017); they have a common framework in extracting features from both query and document and optimizing scores $S(q, d)$ via some ranking loss.

3.2 Sharing Representations

Training a network like the deep model generally requires a nontrivial amount of data. To address the data requirement for low-resource languages, we propose a simple yet effective method that shares representations across CLIR models trained in different language-pairs. Basically, we use the same architecture as the deep model ($S_{deep}(q, d)$, Equation 3). However, we use the parameters trained on a high-resource dataset (e.g Japanese-English) to initialize the parameters for a low-resource language-pair (e.g. Swahili-English).

Figure 2 illustrates the idea: Concretely, we initialize the parameters of the CNN for encoding query (CNN_q) and the parameters of the fully connected layer (O, W) by using the pre-trained parameters. When training on low-resource data,

	Tl			Sw			De (subsample)			Fr (subsample)		
	In	Sh	Δ	In	Sh	Δ	In	Sh	Δ	In	Sh	Δ
cos	51/68	50/67	-/-	51/67	49/65	-/-	40/59	38/56	-/-	46/63	43/60	-/-
h=100	34/50	48/62	+/+	46/62	46/62	=/=	39/55	46/62	+/+	40/57	46/62	+/+
h=200	44/58	55/67	+/+	47/63	52/67	+/+	41/57	48/63	+/+	43/60	51/66	+/+
h=300	42/57	49/63	+/+	50/65	58/70	+/+	44/60	50/65	+/+	49/65	51/66	+/+
h=400	49/63	**57/69**	+/+	51/66	**60/73**	+/+	45/61	**51/66**	+/+	47/64	**56/70**	+/+
h=500	51/64	54/67	+/+	53/68	56/69	+/+	44/60	49/65	+/+	47/63	51/66	+/+

Table 3: P@1/MAP performances on **low resource datasets**. Δ columns show the comparison between the basic deep models with in-language training (In) and the deep models with sharing parameters (Sh); + indicates Sh outperforms In, and - indicates the In outperforms Sh. Best value in each dataset is highlighted in bold.

we fix only the word embedding, and tune the parameters of CNNs and the fully connected layer.

The intuition behind this is that our direct modeling approach enforces $\hat{q}$ and $\hat{d}$ to become language-independent representations of the query and document. The parameters O and W in the deep layer can therefore be used for any language-pair. Note for the cosine model, we can also share parameters for CNN_q.

4 Experiment Results

Setup: We use datasets of 3 high-resource languages (Japanese [Ja], German [De], French [Fr]) and 2 low-resource languages (Tagalog [Tl], Swahili [Sw]). We also subsample German and French data to be equivalent to the size of Swahili, in order to compare training size effects. Word embedding with dimension 100 for each language is trained on Wikipedia corpus, using word2vec SGNS (Mikolov et al., 2013). The size of hidden states in the deep model is $\{100, 200, 300, 400, 500\}$. We adopt Adam (Kingma and Ba, 2014) for optimization, train for 20 epochs and pick the best epoch based on development set loss. For the proposed method of parameter sharing, we use the weight parameters pre-trained on Japanese-English dataset to initialize parameters.

High-resource results: Table 2 shows the P@1 (precision at top position) and MAP (mean average precision) for datasets consisting of on the order of 100k+ training queries. The deep models outperformed the cosine models under all conditions, suggesting that the fully connected layer can exploit the large training set in learning more expressive scoring functions.

Low-resource results: Table 3 shows the results on the low resource datasets under two conditions: training on only the language-pair of interest (in-

language), or additionally sharing parameters using a pre-trained Japanese-English model. For the in-language case, we observe the cosine model outperforms the deep model. In contrast to the high-resource results, this implies that deep models, which have a lot of parameters, only become effective if provided with sufficient training data.

For the sharing case, the deep models with parameter sharing outperformed the basic deep models trained only on in-language data under almost all conditions. This indicates that our sharing method reduces training data requirement. Importantly, by sharing parameters, the deep models are now able to outperform the cosine model and achieve the best results on all datasets.[4]

5 Conclusion and Future Work

We introduce a large-scale CLIR dataset in 25 languages. This enables the training and evaluation of direct modeling approaches in CLIR. We also present a neural ranking model with shared representations, and demonstrate its effectiveness in bootstrapping CLIR in low-resource languages.

Future work includes: (a) expansion of the dataset to more languages, (b) extraction of different types of queries and relevant judgments from Wikipedia, and (c) development of other ranking models. Importantly, we also plan to evaluate our models on standard CLIR test sets such as TREC (Schäuble and Sheridan, 1997), NTCIR (2007), FIRE (2013) and CLEF (2016). This will help answer the question of whether knowledge

---

[4]Sharing representations with the cosine models did not help; we hypothesize that cross-lingual sharing only works if given sufficient model expressiveness. We also tried the shared deep models on high resource datasets (e.g. using Japanese parameters on the full French dataset without subsampling). As expected, results did not change significantly.

learned from automatically-generated datasets can be transferred to a wide range of CLIR problems.

Acknowledgments

This work was supported by Cooperative Laboratory Study Program (COLABS-Outbound), JSPS KAKENHI Grant Number 15H0170 and JST CREST Grant Number JPMJCR1513, Japan. Sun and Duh are supported in part by the Office of the Director of National Intelligence (ODNI), Intelligence Advanced Research Projects Activity (IARPA), via contract # FA8650-17-C-9115. The views and conclusions contained herein are those of the authors and should not be interpreted as necessarily representing the official policies, either expressed or implied, of ODNI, IARPA, or the U.S. Government. The U.S. Government is authorized to reproduce and distribute reprints for governmental purposes notwithstanding any copyright annotation therein.

References

2007. NII test collection for IR systems project. http://research.nii.ac.jp/ntcir/ntcir-ws6/ws-en.html.

2013. Forum for information retrieval evaluation. https://www.isical.ac.in/~fire/2013/index.html.

2016. Conference and labs of the evaluation forum. http://clef2016.clef-initiative.eu/.

Bing Bai, Jason Weston, David Grangier, Ronan Collobert, Kunihiko Sadamasa, Yanjun Qi, Olivier Chapelle, and Kilian Weinberger. 2010. Learning to rank with (a lot of) word features. *Information Retrieval* 13(3):291–314.

Mostafa Dehghani, Hamed Zamani, Aliaksei Severyn, Jaap Kamps, and W. Bruce Croft. 2017. Neural ranking models with weak supervision. In *Proceedings of the 40th International ACM SIGIR Conference on Research and Development in Information Retrieval*. ACM, pages 65–74.

Jiafeng Guo, Yixing Fan, Qingyao Ai, and W. Bruce Croft. 2016. A deep relevance matching model for ad-hoc retrieval. In *Proceedings of the 25th ACM International on Conference on Information and Knowledge Management*. ACM, pages 55–64.

Po-Sen Huang, Xiaodong He, Jianfeng Gao, Li Deng, Alex Acero, and Larry Heck. 2013. Learning deep structured semantic models for web search using clickthrough data. In *Proceedings of the 22nd ACM international conference on Conference on information & knowledge management*. ACM, pages 2333–2338.

Kai Hui, Andrew Yates, Klaus Berberich, and Gerard de Melo. 2017. PACRR: A position-aware neural ir model for relevance matching. In *Proceedings of the 2017 Conference on Empirical Methods in Natural Language Processing*. Association for Computational Linguistics, pages 1049–1058.

Diederik Kingma and Jimmy Ba. 2014. Adam: A method for stochastic optimization. *arXiv preprint arXiv:1412.6980* .

Tomas Mikolov, Ilya Sutskever, Kai Chen, Greg Corrado, and Jeffrey Dean. 2013. Distributed representations of words and phrases and their compositionality. In *Proceedings of the 26th International Conference on Neural Information Processing Systems - Volume 2*. Curran Associates Inc., pages 3111–3119.

Bhaskar Mitra, Fernando Diaz, and Nick Craswell. 2017. Learning to match using local and distributed representations of text for web search. In *Proceedings of the 26th International Conference on World Wide Web*. International World Wide Web Conferences Steering Committee, pages 1291–1299.

Jian-Yun Nie. 2010. *Cross-Language Information Retrieval*. Morgan & Claypool Publishers.

Liang Pang, Yanyan Lan, Jiafeng Guo, Jun Xu, and Xueqi Cheng. 2016. A study of match pyramid models on ad-hoc retrieval. In *Neu-IR16 SIGIR Workshop on Neural Information Retrieval*.

Shigehiko Schamoni, Felix Hieber, Artem Sokolov, and Stefan Riezler. 2014. Learning translational and knowledge-based similarities from relevance rankings for cross-language retrieval. In *Proceedings of the 52 Annual Meeting of the Association for Computational Linguistics*.

P. Schäuble and P. Sheridan. 1997. Cross-language information retrieval (CLIR) track overview. In *Proceedings of TREC Conference*.

Yelong Shen, Xiaodong He, Jianfeng Gao, Li Deng, and Grégoire Mesnil. 2014. A latent semantic model with convolutional-pooling structure for information retrieval. In *Proceedings of the 23rd ACM International Conference on Conference on Information and Knowledge Management*. ACM, pages 101–110.

Artem Sokolov, Laura Jehl, Felix Hieber, and Stefan Riezler. 2013. Boosting cross-language retrieval by learning bilingual phrase associations from relevance rankings. In *Proceedings of the 2013 Conference on Empirical Methods in Natural Language Processing*. Association for Computational Linguistics, pages 1688–1699.

Nitish Srivastava, Geoffrey Hinton, Alex Krizhevsky, Ilya Sutskever, and Ruslan Salakhutdinov. 2014. Dropout: A simple way to prevent neural networks from overfitting. *Journal of machine learning research* 15(1):1929–1958.

Chenyan Xiong, Zhuyun Dai, Jamie Callan, Zhiyuan Liu, and Russell Power. 2017. End-to-end neural ad-hoc ranking with kernel pooling. In *Proceedings of the 40th International ACM SIGIR Conference on Research and Development in Information Retrieval*. ACM, pages 55–64.

Self-Attention with Relative Position Representations

Peter Shaw
Google
petershaw@google.com

Jakob Uszkoreit
Google Brain
usz@google.com

Ashish Vaswani
Google Brain
avaswani@google.com

Abstract

Relying entirely on an attention mechanism, the Transformer introduced by Vaswani et al. (2017) achieves state-of-the-art results for machine translation. In contrast to recurrent and convolutional neural networks, it does not explicitly model relative or absolute position information in its structure. Instead, it requires adding representations of absolute positions to its inputs. In this work we present an alternative approach, extending the self-attention mechanism to efficiently consider representations of the relative positions, or distances between sequence elements. On the WMT 2014 English-to-German and English-to-French translation tasks, this approach yields improvements of 1.3 BLEU and 0.3 BLEU over absolute position representations, respectively. Notably, we observe that combining relative and absolute position representations yields no further improvement in translation quality. We describe an efficient implementation of our method and cast it as an instance of relation-aware self-attention mechanisms that can generalize to arbitrary graph-labeled inputs.

1 Introduction

Recent approaches to sequence to sequence learning typically leverage recurrence (Sutskever et al., 2014), convolution (Gehring et al., 2017; Kalchbrenner et al., 2016), attention (Vaswani et al., 2017), or a combination of recurrence and attention (Bahdanau et al., 2014; Cho et al., 2014; Luong et al., 2015; Wu et al., 2016) as basic building blocks. These approaches incorporate information about the sequential position of elements differently.

Recurrent neural networks (RNNs) typically compute a hidden state h_t, as a function of their input at time t and a previous hidden state h_{t-1}, capturing relative and absolute positions along the time dimension directly through their sequential structure. Non-recurrent models do not necessarily consider input elements sequentially and may hence require explicitly encoding position information to be able to use sequence order.

One common approach is to use position encodings which are combined with input elements to expose position information to the model. These position encodings can be a deterministic function of position (Sukhbaatar et al., 2015; Vaswani et al., 2017) or learned representations. Convolutional neural networks inherently capture relative positions within the kernel size of each convolution. They have been shown to still benefit from position encodings (Gehring et al., 2017), however.

For the Transformer, which employs neither convolution nor recurrence, incorporating explicit representations of position information is an especially important consideration since the model is otherwise entirely invariant to sequence ordering. Attention-based models have therefore used position encodings or biased attention weights based on distance (Parikh et al., 2016).

In this work we present an efficient way of incorporating relative position representations in the self-attention mechanism of the Transformer. Even when entirely replacing its absolute position encodings, we demonstrate significant improvements in translation quality on two machine translation tasks.

Our approach can be cast as a special case of extending the self-attention mechanism of the Transformer to considering arbitrary relations between any two elements of the input, a direction we plan to explore in future work on modeling labeled, directed graphs.

Proceedings of NAACL-HLT 2018, pages 464–468
New Orleans, Louisiana, June 1 - 6, 2018. ©2018 Association for Computational Linguistics

2 Background

2.1 Transformer

The Transformer (Vaswani et al., 2017) employs an encoder-decoder structure, consisting of stacked encoder and decoder layers. Encoder layers consist of two sublayers: self-attention followed by a position-wise feed-forward layer. Decoder layers consist of three sublayers: self-attention followed by encoder-decoder attention, followed by a position-wise feed-forward layer. It uses residual connections around each of the sublayers, followed by layer normalization (Ba et al., 2016). The decoder uses masking in its self-attention to prevent a given output position from incorporating information about future output positions during training.

Position encodings based on sinusoids of varying frequency are added to encoder and decoder input elements prior to the first layer. In contrast to learned, absolute position representations, the authors hypothesized that sinusoidal position encodings would help the model to generalize to sequence lengths unseen during training by allowing it to learn to attend also by relative position. This property is shared by our relative position representations which, in contrast to absolute position representations, are invariant to the total sequence length.

Residual connections help propagate position information to higher layers.

2.2 Self-Attention

Self-attention sublayers employ h attention heads. To form the sublayer output, results from each head are concatenated and a parameterized linear transformation is applied.

Each attention head operates on an input sequence, $x = (x_1, \ldots, x_n)$ of n elements where $x_i \in \mathbb{R}^{d_x}$, and computes a new sequence $z = (z_1, \ldots, z_n)$ of the same length where $z_i \in \mathbb{R}^{d_z}$.

Each output element, z_i, is computed as weighted sum of a linearly transformed input elements:

$$z_i = \sum_{j=1}^{n} \alpha_{ij}(x_j W^V) \tag{1}$$

Each weight coefficient, α_{ij}, is computed using a softmax function:

$$\alpha_{ij} = \frac{\exp e_{ij}}{\sum_{k=1}^{n} \exp e_{ik}}$$

And e_{ij} is computed using a compatibility function that compares two input elements:

$$e_{ij} = \frac{(x_i W^Q)(x_j W^K)^T}{\sqrt{d_z}} \tag{2}$$

Scaled dot product was chosen for the compatibility function, which enables efficient computation. Linear transformations of the inputs add sufficient expressive power.

$W^Q, W^K, W^V \in \mathbb{R}^{d_x \times d_z}$ are parameter matrices. These parameter matrices are unique per layer and attention head.

3 Proposed Architecture

3.1 Relation-aware Self-Attention

We propose an extension to self-attention to consider the pairwise relationships between input elements. In this sense, we model the input as a labeled, directed, fully-connected graph.

The edge between input elements x_i and x_j is represented by vectors $a_{ij}^V, a_{ij}^K \in \mathbb{R}^{d_a}$. The motivation for learning two distinct edge representations is that a_{ij}^V and a_{ij}^K are suitable for use in eq. (3) and eq. (4), respectively, without requiring additional linear transformations. These representations can be shared across attention heads. We use $d_a = d_z$.

We modify eq. (1) to propagate edge information to the sublayer output:

$$z_i = \sum_{j=1}^{n} \alpha_{ij}(x_j W^V + a_{ij}^V) \tag{3}$$

This extension is presumably important for tasks where information about the edge types selected by a given attention head is useful to downstream encoder or decoder layers. However, as explored in 4.3, this may not be necessary for machine translation.

We also, importantly, modify eq. (2) to consider edges when determining compatibility:

$$e_{ij} = \frac{x_i W^Q (x_j W^K + a_{ij}^K)^T}{\sqrt{d_z}} \tag{4}$$

The primary motivation for using simple addition to incorporate edge representations in eq. (3) and eq. (4) is to enable an efficient implementation described in 3.3.

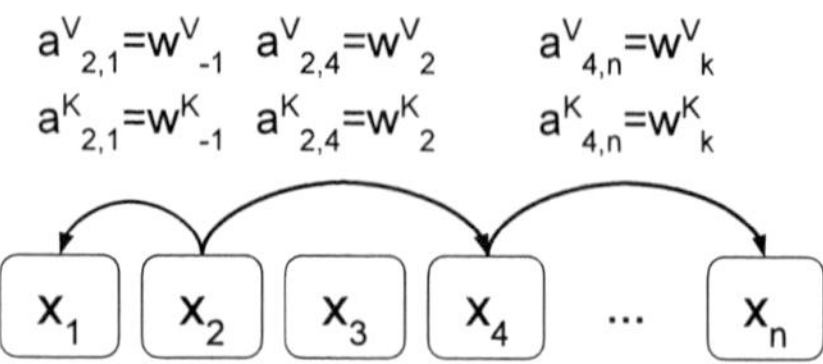

Figure 1: Example edges representing relative positions, or the distance between elements. We learn representations for each relative position within a clipping distance k. The figure assumes $2 <= k <= n - 4$. Note that not all edges are shown.

3.2 Relative Position Representations

For linear sequences, edges can capture information about the relative position differences between input elements. The maximum relative position we consider is clipped to a maximum absolute value of k. We hypothesized that precise relative position information is not useful beyond a certain distance. Clipping the maximum distance also enables the model to generalize to sequence lengths not seen during training. Therefore, we consider $2k + 1$ unique edge labels.

$$a^K_{ij} = w^K_{\mathrm{clip}(j-i,k)}$$
$$a^V_{ij} = w^V_{\mathrm{clip}(j-i,k)}$$
$$\mathrm{clip}(x,k) = \max(-k, \min(k, x))$$

We then learn relative position representations $w^K = (w^K_{-k}, \ldots, w^K_k)$ and $w^V = (w^V_{-k}, \ldots, w^V_k)$ where $w^K_i, w^V_i \in \mathbb{R}^{d_a}$.

3.3 Efficient Implementation

There are practical space complexity concerns when considering edges between input elements, as noted by Veličković et al. (2017), which considers unlabeled graph inputs to an attention model.

For a sequence of length n and h attention heads, we reduce the space complexity of storing relative position representations from $O(hn^2d_a)$ to $O(n^2d_a)$ by sharing them across each heads. Additionally, relative position representations can be shared across sequences. Therefore, the overall self-attention space complexity increases from $O(bhnd_z)$ to $O(bhnd_z + n^2d_a)$. Given $d_a = d_z$, the size of the relative increase depends on $\frac{n}{bh}$.

The Transformer computes self-attention efficiently for all sequences, heads, and positions in a batch using parallel matrix multiplication operations (Vaswani et al., 2017). Without relative position representations, each e_{ij} can be computed using bh parallel multiplications of $n \times d_z$ and $d_z \times n$ matrices. Each matrix multiplication computes e_{ij} for all sequence positions, for a particular head and sequence. For any sequence and head, this requires sharing the same representation for each position across all compatibility function applications (dot products) with other positions.

When we consider relative positions the representations differ with different pairs of positions. This prevents us from computing all e_{ij} for all pairs of positions in a single matrix multiplication. We also want to avoid broadcasting relative position representations. However, both issues can be resolved by splitting the computation of eq. (4) into two terms:

$$e_{ij} = \frac{x_i W^Q (x_j W^K)^T + x_i W^Q (a^K_{ij})^T}{\sqrt{d_z}} \quad (5)$$

The first term is identical to eq. (2), and can be computed as described above. For the second term involving relative position representations, tensor reshaping can be used to compute n parallel multiplications of $bh \times d_z$ and $d_z \times n$ matrices. Each matrix multiplication computes contributions to e_{ij} for all heads and batches, corresponding to a particular sequence position. Further reshaping allows adding the two terms. The same approach can be used to efficiently compute eq. (3).

For our machine translation experiments, the result was a modest 7% decrease in steps per second, but we were able to maintain the same model and batch sizes on P100 GPUs as Vaswani et al. (2017).

4 Experiments

4.1 Experimental Setup

We use the tensor2tensor [1] library for training and evaluating our model.

We evaluated our model on the WMT 2014 machine translation task, using the WMT 2014 English-German dataset consisting of approximately 4.5M sentence pairs and the 2014 WMT English-French dataset consisting of approximately 36M sentence pairs.

---

[1] The tensor2tensor library is available at https://github.com/tensorflow/tensor2tensor.

Model	Position Information	EN-DE BLEU	EN-FR BLEU
Transformer (base)	Absolute Position Representations	26.5	38.2
Transformer (base)	Relative Position Representations	**26.8**	**38.7**
Transformer (big)	Absolute Position Representations	27.9	41.2
Transformer (big)	Relative Position Representations	**29.2**	**41.5**

Table 1: Experimental results for WMT 2014 English-to-German (EN-DE) and English-to-French (EN-FR) translation tasks, using newstest2014 test set.

For all experiments, we split tokens into a 32,768 word-piece vocabulary (Wu et al., 2016). We batched sentence pairs by approximate length, and limited input and output tokens per batch to 4096 per GPU. Each resulting training batch contained approximately 25,000 source and 25,000 target tokens.

We used the Adam optimizer (Kingma and Ba, 2014) with $\beta_1 = 0.9$, $\beta_2 = 0.98$, and $\epsilon = 10^{-9}$. We used the same warmup and decay strategy for learning rate as Vaswani et al. (2017), with 4,000 warmup steps. During training, we employed label smoothing of value $\epsilon_{ls} = 0.1$ (Szegedy et al., 2016). For evaluation, we used beam search with a beam size of 4 and length penalty $\alpha = 0.6$ (Wu et al., 2016).

For our base model, we used 6 encoder and decoder layers, $d_x = 512$, $d_z = 64$, 8 attention heads, 1024 feed forward inner-layer dimensions, and $P_{dropout} = 0.1$. When using relative position encodings, we used clipping distance $k = 16$, and used unique edge representations per layer and head. We trained for 100,000 steps on 8 K40 GPUs, and did not use checkpoint averaging.

For our big model, we used 6 encoder and decoder layers, $d_x = 1024$, $d_z = 64$, 16 attention heads, 4096 feed forward inner-layer dimensions, and $P_{dropout} = 0.3$ for EN-DE and $P_{dropout} = 0.1$ for EN-FR. When using relative position encodings, we used $k = 8$, and used unique edge representations per layer. We trained for 300,000 steps on 8 P100 GPUs, and averaged the last 20 checkpoints, saved at 10 minute intervals.

4.2 Machine Translation

We compared our model using only relative position representations to the baseline Transformer (Vaswani et al., 2017) with sinusoidal position encodings. We generated baseline results to isolate the impact of relative position representations from any other changes to the underlying library and experimental configuration.

For English-to-German our approach improved performance over our baseline by 0.3 and 1.3 BLEU for the base and big configurations, respectively. For English-to-French it improved by 0.5 and 0.3 BLEU for the base and big configurations, respectively. In our experiments we did not observe any benefit from including sinusoidal position encodings in addition to relative position representations. The results are shown in Table 1.

4.3 Model Variations

We performed several experiments modifying various aspects of our model. All of our experiments in this section use the base model configuration without any absolute position representations. BLEU scores are calculated on the WMT English-to-German task using the development set, newstest2013.

We evaluated the effect of varying the clipping distance, k, of the maximum absolute relative position difference. Notably, for $k \geq 2$, there does not appear to be much variation in BLEU scores. However, as we use multiple encoder layers, precise relative position information may be able to propagate beyond the clipping distance. The results are shown in Table 2.

k	EN-DE BLEU
0	12.5
1	25.5
2	25.8
4	25.9
16	25.8
64	25.9
256	25.8

Table 2: Experimental results for varying the clipping distance, k.

We also evaluated the impact of ablating each of the two relative position representations defined in section 3.1, a_{ij}^V in eq. (3) and a_{ij}^K in eq. (4). Including relative position representations solely when determining compatibility between elements may be sufficient, but further work is needed to determine whether this is true for other tasks. The results are shown in Table 3.

a_{ij}^V	a_{ij}^K	EN-DE BLEU
Yes	Yes	25.8
No	Yes	25.8
Yes	No	25.3
No	No	12.5

Table 3: Experimental results for ablating relative position representations a_{ij}^V and a_{ij}^K.

5 Conclusions

In this paper we presented an extension to self-attention that can be used to incorporate relative position information for sequences, which improves performance for machine translation.

For future work, we plan to extend this mechanism to consider arbitrary directed, labeled graph inputs to the Transformer. We are also interested in nonlinear compatibility functions to combine input representations and edge representations. For both of these extensions, a key consideration will be determining efficient implementations.

References

Jimmy Lei Ba, Jamie Ryan Kiros, and Geoffrey E Hinton. 2016. Layer normalization. *arXiv preprint arXiv:1607.06450* .

Dzmitry Bahdanau, Kyunghyun Cho, and Yoshua Bengio. 2014. Neural machine translation by jointly learning to align and translate. *arXiv preprint arXiv:1409.0473* .

Kyunghyun Cho, Bart Van Merriënboer, Caglar Gulcehre, Dzmitry Bahdanau, Fethi Bougares, Holger Schwenk, and Yoshua Bengio. 2014. Learning phrase representations using rnn encoder-decoder for statistical machine translation. *arXiv preprint arXiv:1406.1078* .

Jonas Gehring, Michael Auli, David Grangier, Denis Yarats, and Yann N Dauphin. 2017. Convolutional sequence to sequence learning. *arXiv preprint arXiv:1705.03122* .

Nal Kalchbrenner, Lasse Espeholt, Karen Simonyan, Aaron van den Oord, Alex Graves, and Koray Kavukcuoglu. 2016. Neural machine translation in linear time. *arXiv preprint arXiv:1610.10099* .

Diederik Kingma and Jimmy Ba. 2014. Adam: A method for stochastic optimization. *arXiv preprint arXiv:1412.6980* .

Minh-Thang Luong, Hieu Pham, and Christopher D Manning. 2015. Effective approaches to attention-based neural machine translation. *arXiv preprint arXiv:1508.04025* .

Ankur P Parikh, Oscar Täckström, Dipanjan Das, and Jakob Uszkoreit. 2016. A decomposable attention model for natural language inference. In *Empirical Methods in Natural Language Processing*.

Sainbayar Sukhbaatar, Jason Weston, Rob Fergus, et al. 2015. End-to-end memory networks. In *Advances in neural information processing systems*. pages 2440–2448.

Ilya Sutskever, Oriol Vinyals, and Quoc V Le. 2014. Sequence to sequence learning with neural networks. In *Advances in neural information processing systems*. pages 3104–3112.

Christian Szegedy, Vincent Vanhoucke, Sergey Ioffe, Jon Shlens, and Zbigniew Wojna. 2016. Rethinking the inception architecture for computer vision. In *Proceedings of the IEEE Conference on Computer Vision and Pattern Recognition*. pages 2818–2826.

Ashish Vaswani, Noam Shazeer, Niki Parmar, Jakob Uszkoreit, Llion Jones, Aidan N Gomez, Łukasz Kaiser, and Illia Polosukhin. 2017. Attention is all you need. In *Advances in Neural Information Processing Systems*. pages 6000–6010.

Petar Veličković, Guillem Cucurull, Arantxa Casanova, Adriana Romero, Pietro Liò, and Yoshua Bengio. 2017. Graph attention networks. *arXiv preprint arXiv:1710.10903* .

Yonghui Wu, Mike Schuster, Zhifeng Chen, Quoc V Le, Mohammad Norouzi, Wolfgang Macherey, Maxim Krikun, Yuan Cao, Qin Gao, Klaus Macherey, et al. 2016. Google's neural machine translation system: Bridging the gap between human and machine translation. *arXiv preprint arXiv:1609.08144* .

Text Segmentation as a Supervised Learning Task

Omri Koshorek[*] **Adir Cohen**[*] **Noam Mor** **Michael Rotman** **Jonathan Berant**
School of Computer Science
Tel-Aviv University, Israel
{omri.koshorek,adir.cohen,noam.mor,michael.rotman,joberant}@cs.tau.ac.il

Abstract

Text segmentation, the task of dividing a document into contiguous segments based on its
semantic structure, is a longstanding challenge
in language understanding. Previous work
on text segmentation focused on unsupervised
methods such as clustering or graph search,
due to the paucity in labeled data. In this
work, we formulate text segmentation as a
supervised learning problem, and present a
large new dataset for text segmentation that
is automatically extracted and labeled from
Wikipedia. Moreover, we develop a segmentation model based on this dataset and show
that it generalizes well to unseen natural text.

1   Introduction

Text segmentation is the task of dividing text into
segments, such that each segment is topically coherent, and cutoff points indicate a change of topic
(Hearst, 1994; Utiyama and Isahara, 2001; Brants
et al., 2002). This provides basic structure to a
document in a way that can later be used by downstream applications such as summarization and information extraction.

Existing datasets for text segmentation are small
in size (Choi, 2000; Glavaš et al., 2016), and are
used mostly for evaluating the performance of segmentation algorithms. Moreover, some datasets
(Choi, 2000) were synthesized automatically and
thus do not represent the natural distribution of
text in documents. Because no large labeled
dataset exists, prior work on text segmentation
tried to either come up with heuristics for identifying whether two sentences discuss the same
topic (Choi, 2000; Glavaš et al., 2016), or to model
topics explicitly with methods such as LDA (Blei
et al., 2003) that assign a topic to each paragraph
or sentence (Chen et al., 2009).

---

*Both authors contributed equally to this paper and the
order of authorship was determined randomly.

Recent developments in Natural Language Processing have demonstrated that casting problems
as supervised learning tasks over large amounts
of labeled data is highly effective compared to
heuristic-based systems or unsupervised algorithms (Mikolov et al., 2013; Pennington et al.,
2014). Therefore, in this work we (a) formulate
text segmentation as a supervised learning problem, where a label for every sentence in the document denotes whether it ends a segment, (b) describe a new dataset, WIKI-727K, intended for
training text segmentation models.

WIKI-727K comprises more than 727,000 documents from English Wikipedia, where the table
of contents of each document is used to automatically segment the document. Since this dataset
is large, natural, and covers a variety of topics,
we expect it to generalize well to other natural
texts. Moreover, WIKI-727K provides a better
benchmark for evaluating text segmentation models compared to existing datasets. We make WIKI-
727K and our code publicly available at https:
//github.com/koomri/text-segmentation.

To demonstrate the efficacy of this dataset, we
develop a hierarchical neural model in which a
lower-level bidirectional LSTM creates sentence
representations from word tokens, and then a
higher-level LSTM consumes the sentence representations and labels each sentence. We show that
our model outperforms prior methods, demonstrating the importance of our dataset for future
progress in text segmentation.

2   Related Work

2.1   Existing Text Segmentation Datasets

The most common dataset for evaluating performance on text segmentation was created by Choi
(2000). It is a synthetic dataset containing 920
documents, where each document is a concatena-

469

Proceedings of NAACL-HLT 2018, pages 469–473
New Orleans, Louisiana, June 1 - 6, 2018. ©2018 Association for Computational Linguistics

tion of 10 random passages from the Brown corpus. Glavaš et al. (2016) created a dataset of their own, which consists of 5 manually-segmented political manifestos from the Manifesto project.[1] (Chen et al., 2009) also used English Wikipedia documents to evaluate text segmentation. They defined two datasets, one with 100 documents about major cities and one with 118 documents about chemical elements. Table 1 provides additional statistics on each dataset.

Thus, all existing datasets for text segmentation are small and cannot benefit from the advantages of training supervised models over labeled data.

2.2 Previous Methods

Bayesian text segmentation methods (Chen et al., 2009; Riedl and Biemann, 2012) employ a generative probabilistic model for text. In these models, a document is represented as a set of topics, which are sampled from a topic distribution, and each topic imposes a distribution over the vocabulary. Riedl and Biemann (2012) perform best among this family of methods, where they define a coherence score between pairs of sentences, and compute a segmentation by finding drops in coherence scores between pairs of adjacent sentences.

Another noteworthy approach for text segmentation is GRAPHSEG (Glavaš et al., 2016), an unsupervised graph method, which performs competitively on synthetic datasets and outperforms Bayesian approaches on the Manifesto dataset. GRAPHSEG works by building a graph where nodes are sentences, and an edge between two sentences signifies that the sentences are semantically similar. The segmentation is then determined by finding maximal cliques of adjacent sentences, and heuristically completing the segmentation.

3 The WIKI-727K Dataset

For this work we have created a new dataset, which we name WIKI-727K. It is a collection of 727,746 English Wikipedia documents, and their hierarchical segmentation, as it appears in their table of contents. We randomly partitioned the documents into a train (80%), development (10%), and test (10%) set.

Different text segmentation use-cases require different levels of granularity. For example, for segmenting text by overarching topic it makes sense to train a model that predicts only top-level

segments, which are typically vary in topic – for example, *"History"*, *"Geography"*, and *"Demographics"*. For segmenting a radio broadcast into separate news stories, which requires finer granularity, it makes sense to train a model to predict sub-segments. Our dataset provides the entire segmentation information, and an application may choose the appropriate level of granularity.

To generate the data, we performed the following preprocessing steps for each Wikipedia document:

- Removed all photos, tables, Wikipedia template elements, and other non-text elements.
- Removed single-sentence segments, documents with less than three segments, and documents where most segments were filtered.
- Divided each segment into sentences using the PUNKT tokenizer of the NLTK library (Bird et al., 2009). This is necessary for the use of our dataset as a benchmark, as without a well-defined sentence segmentation, it is impossible to evaluate different models.

We view WIKI-727K as suitable for text segmentation because it is natural, open-domain, and has a well-defined segmentation. Moreover, neural network models often benefit from a wealth of training data, and our dataset can easily be further expanded at very little cost.

4 Neural Model for Text Segmentation

We treat text segmentation as a supervised learning task, where the input x is a document, represented as a sequence of n sentences $s_1, \ldots, s_n$, and the label $y = (y_1, \ldots, y_{n-1})$ is a segmentation of the document, represented by $n - 1$ binary values, where y_i denotes whether s_i ends a segment.

We now describe our model for text segmentation. Our neural model is composed of a hierarchy of two sub-networks, both based on the LSTM architecture (Hochreiter and Schmidhuber, 1997). The lower-level sub-network is a two-layer bidirectional LSTM that generates sentence representations: for each sentence s_i, the network consumes the words $w_1^{(i)}, \ldots, w_k^{(i)}$ of s_i one by one, and the final sentence representation e_i is computed by max-pooling over the LSTM outputs.

The higher-level sub-network is the segmentation prediction network. This sub-network takes a sequence of sentence embeddings $e_1, \ldots, e_n$ as input, and feeds them into a two-layer bidirectional

---

[1] https://manifestoproject.wzb.eu

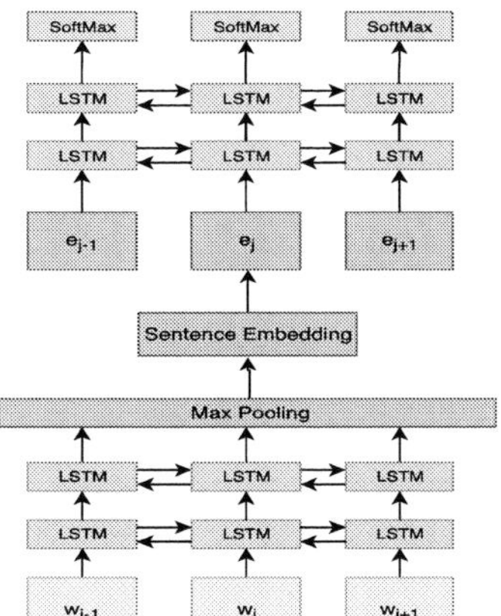

Figure 1: Our model contains a sentence embedding sub-network, followed by a segmentation prediction sub-network which predicts a cut-off probability for each sentence.

LSTM. We then apply a fully-connected layer on each of the LSTM outputs to obtain a sequence of n vectors in $\mathbb{R}^2$. We ignore the last vector (for e_n), and apply a *softmax* function to obtain $n - 1$ segmentation probabilities. Figure 1 illustrates the overall neural network architecture.

4.1 Training

Our model predicts for each sentence s_i, the probability p_i that it ends a segment. For an n-sentence document, we minimize the sum of cross-entropy errors over each of the $n - 1$ relevant sentences:

$$J(\Theta) = \sum_{i=1}^{n-1} \left[-y_i \log p_i - (1 - y_i) \log (1 - p_i) \right].$$

Training is done by stochastic gradient descent in an end-to-end manner. For word embeddings, we use the GoogleNews word2vec pre-trained model.

We train our system to only predict the top-level segmentation (other granularities are possible). In addition, at training time, we removed from each document the first segment, since in Wikipedia it is often a summary that touches many different topics, and is therefore less useful for training a segmentation model. We also omitted lists and code snippets tokens.

4.2 Inference

At test time, the model takes a sequence of word embeddings divided into sentences, and returns a vector p of cutoff probabilities between sentences. We use greedy decoding, i.e., we create a new segment whenever p_i is greater than a threshold τ. We optimize the parameter τ on our validation set, and use the optimal value while testing.

5 Experimental Details

We evaluate our method on the WIKI-727 test set, Choi's synthetic dataset, and the two small Wikipedia datasets (CITIES, ELEMENTS) introduced by Chen et al. (2009). We compare our model performance with those reported by Chen et al. (2009) and GRAPHSEG. In addition, we evaluate the performance of a random baseline model, which starts a new segment after every sentence with probability $\frac{1}{k}$, where k is the average segment size in the dataset.

Because our test set is large, it is difficult to evaluate some of the existing methods, which are computationally demanding. Thus, we introduce WIKI-50, a set of 50 randomly sampled test documents from WIKI-727K. We use WIKI-50 to evaluate systems that are too slow to evaluate on the entire test set. We also provide human segmentation performance results on WIKI-50.

We use the P_k metric as defined in Beeferman et al. (1999) to evaluate the performance of our model. P_k is the probability that when passing a sliding window of size k over *sentences*, the sentences at the boundaries of the window will be incorrectly classified as belonging to the same segment (or vice versa). To match the setup of Chen et al. (2009), we also provide the P_k metric for a sliding window over *words* when evaluating on the datasets from their paper. Following (Glavaš et al., 2016), we set k to half of the average segment size in the ground-truth segmentation. For evaluations we used the SEGEVAL package (Fournier, 2013).

In addition to segmentation accuracy, we also report runtime when running on a mid-range laptop CPU.

We note that segmentation results are not always directly comparable. For example, Chen et al. (2009) require that all documents in the dataset discuss the same topic, and so their method is not directly applicable to WIKI-50. Nevertheless, we attempt a comparison in Table 2.

5.1 Accuracy

Comparing our method to GRAPHSEG, we can see that GRAPHSEG gives better results on the synthetic Choi dataset, but this success does not carry over to the natural Wikipedia data, where they underperform the random baseline. We ex-

	WIKI-727K	CHOI	MANIFESTO	CITIES	ELEMENTS
Documents	727,746	920	5	100	118
Segment Length[2]	13.6 ± 20.3	7.4 ± 2.96	8.99 ± 10.8	5.15 ± 4.57	3.33 ± 3.05
Segments per document[2]	3.48 ± 2.23	9.98 ± 0.12	127 ± 42.9	12.2 ± 2.79	6.82 ± 2.57
Real-world	✓	✗	✓	✓	✓
Large variety of topics	✓	✗	✗	✗	✗

Table 1: Statistics on various text segmentation datasets.

P_k variant	WIKI-727K sentences	WIKI-50 sentences	CHOI sentences	CITIES sentences	CITIES words	ELEMENTS sentences	ELEMENTS words
(Chen et al., 2009)	-	-	-	-	22.1	-	**20.1**
GraphSeg	-	63.56	**5.6-7.2**	39.95	-	49.12	-
Our model	22.13	**18.24**	26.26[3]	**19.68**	18.14	**41.63**	33.82
Random baseline	53.09	52.65	49.43	47.14	44.14	50.08	42.80
Human performance	-	14.97	-	-	-	-	-

Table 2: P_k Results on the test set.

plain this by noting that since the dataset is synthetic, and was created by concatenating unrelated documents, even the simple word counting method in Choi (2000) can achieve reasonable success. GRAPHSEG uses a similarity measure between word embedding vectors to surpass the word counting method, but in a natural document, word similarity may not be enough to detect a change of topic within a single document. At the word level, two documents concerning completely different topics are much easier to differentiate than two sections in one document.

We compare our method to Chen et al. (2009) on the two small Wikipedia datasets from their paper. Our method outperforms theirs on CITIES and obtains worse results on ELEMENTS, where presumably our word embeddings were of lower quality, having been trained on Google News, where one might expect that few technical words from the domain of Chemistry are used. We consider this result convincing, since we did not exploit the fact that all documents have similar structure as Chen et al. (2009), and did not train specifically for these datasets, but still were able to demonstrate competitive performance.

Interestingly, human performance on WIKI-50 is only slightly better than our model. We assume that because annotators annotated only a small number of documents, they still lack familiarity with the right level of granularity for segmentation, and are thus at a disadvantage compared to the model that has seen many documents.

5.2 Run Time

Our method's runtime is linear in the number of words and the number of sentences in a docu-

ment. Conversely, GRAPHSEG has a much worse asymptotic complexity of $O(N^3 + V^k)$ where N is the length of the longest sentence, V the number of sentences, and k the largest clique size. Moreover, neural network models are highly parallelizable, and benefit from running on GPUs.

In practice, our method is much faster than GRAPHSEG. In Table 3 we report the average run time per document on WIKI-50 on a CPU.

	WIKI-50
Our model (CPU)	1.6
GRAPHSEG (CPU)	23.6

Table 3: Average run time in seconds per document.

6 Conclusions

In this work, we present a large labeled dataset, WIKI-727K, for text segmentation, that enables training neural models using supervised learning methods. This closes an existing gap in the literature, where thus far text segmentation models were trained in an unsupervised fashion.

Our text segmentation model outperforms prior methods on Wikipedia documents, and performs competitively on prior benchmarks. Moreover, our system has linear runtime in the text length, and can be run on modern GPU hardware. We argue that for text segmentation systems to be useful in the real world, they must be able to segment arbitrary natural text, and this work provides a path towards achieving that goal.

In future work, we will explore richer neural models at the sentence-level. Another important

---

[2]Statistics on top-level segments.
[3]We optimized τ by cross validation on the CHOI dataset.

direction is developing a structured global model that will take all local predictions into account and then perform a global segmentation decision.

Acknowledgements

We thank the anonymous reviewers for their constructive feedback. This work was supported by the Israel Science Foundation, grant 942/16.

References

Doug Beeferman, Adam Berger, and John Lafferty. 1999. Statistical models for text segmentation. *Machine learning* 34(1):177–210.

S. Bird, E. Loper, and E. Klein. 2009. *Natural Language Processing with Python*. OReilly Media Inc.

D. Blei, A. Ng, and M. I. Jordan. 2003. Latent Dirichlet allocation. *Journal of Machine Learning Research (JMLR)* 3:993–1022.

Thorsten Brants, Francine Chen, and Ioannis Tsochantaridis. 2002. Topic-based document segmentation with probabilistic latent semantic analysis. In *Proceedings of the eleventh international conference on Information and knowledge management*. ACM, pages 211–218.

Harr Chen, SRK Branavan, Regina Barzilay, and David R Karger. 2009. Global models of document structure using latent permutations. In *Proceedings of Human Language Technologies: The 2009 Annual Conference of the North American Chapter of the Association for Computational Linguistics*. Association for Computational Linguistics, pages 371–379.

Freddy YY Choi. 2000. Advances in domain independent linear text segmentation. In *Proceedings of the 1st North American chapter of the Association for Computational Linguistics conference*. Association for Computational Linguistics, pages 26–33.

Chris Fournier. 2013. Evaluating Text Segmentation using Boundary Edit Distance. In *Proceedings of 51st Annual Meeting of the Association for Computational Linguistics*. Association for Computational Linguistics, Stroudsburg, PA, USA, page to appear.

Goran Glavaš, Federico Nanni, and Simone Paolo Ponzetto. 2016. Unsupervised text segmentation using semantic relatedness graphs. Association for Computational Linguistics.

Marti A Hearst. 1994. Multi-paragraph segmentation of expository text. In *Proceedings of the 32nd annual meeting on Association for Computational Linguistics*. Association for Computational Linguistics, pages 9–16.

Sepp Hochreiter and Jürgen Schmidhuber. 1997. Long short-term memory. *Neural computation* 9(8):1735–1780.

T. Mikolov, W. Yih, and G. Zweig. 2013. Linguistic regularities in continuous space word representations. In *hlt-Naacl*. volume 13, pages 746–751.

Jeffrey Pennington, Richard Socher, and Christopher D. Manning. 2014. Glove: Global vectors for word representation. In *Empirical Methods in Natural Language Processing (EMNLP)*. pages 1532–1543. http://www.aclweb.org/anthology/D14-1162.

Martin Riedl and Chris Biemann. 2012. Topictiling: a text segmentation algorithm based on lda. In *Proceedings of ACL 2012 Student Research Workshop*. Association for Computational Linguistics, pages 37–42.

Masao Utiyama and Hitoshi Isahara. 2001. A statistical model for domain-independent text segmentation. In *Proceedings of the 39th Annual Meeting on Association for Computational Linguistics*. Association for Computational Linguistics, pages 499–506.

What's in a Domain?
Learning Domain-Robust Text Representations using Adversarial Training

Yitong Li and **Timothy Baldwin** and **Trevor Cohn**

School of Computing and Information Systems

The University of Melbourne, Australia

yitongl4@student.unimelb.edu.au, {tbaldwin,tcohn}@unimelb.edu.au

Abstract

Most real world language problems require learning from heterogenous corpora, raising the problem of learning robust models which generalise well to both similar (*in domain*) and dissimilar (*out of domain*) instances to those seen in training. This requires learning an underlying task, while not learning irrelevant signals and biases specific to individual domains. We propose a novel method to optimise both in- and out-of-domain accuracy based on joint learning of a structured neural model with domain-specific and domain-general components, coupled with adversarial training for domain. Evaluating on multi-domain language identification and multi-domain sentiment analysis, we show substantial improvements over standard domain adaptation techniques, and domain-adversarial training.

1 Introduction

Heterogeneity is pervasive in NLP, arising from corpora being constructed from different sources, featuring different topics, register, writing style, etc. An important, yet elusive, goal is to produce NLP tools that are capable of handling all types of texts, such that we can have, e.g., text classifiers that work well on texts from newswire to wikis to micro-blogs. A key roadblock is application to new domains, unseen in training. Accordingly, training needs to be robust to domain variation, such that domain-general concepts are learned in preference to domain-specific phenomena, which will not transfer well to out-of-domain evaluation. To illustrate, Bitvai and Cohn (2015) report learning formatting quirks of specific reviewers in a review text regression task, which are unlikely to prove useful on other texts.

This classic problem in NLP has been tackled under the guise of "domain adaptation", also known as unsupervised transfer learning, using feature-based methods to support knowledge transfer over multiple domains (Blitzer et al., 2007; Daumé III, 2007; Joshi et al., 2012; Williams, 2013; Kim et al., 2016). More recently, Ganin and Lempitsky (2015) proposed a method to encourage domain-general text representations, which transfer better to new domains.

Inspired by the above methods, in this paper we propose a novel technique for multitask learning of domain-general representations.[1] Specifically, we propose deep learning architectures for multi-domain learning, featuring a *shared* representation, and domain *private* representation. Our approach generalises the feature augmentation method of Daumé III (2007) to convolutional neural networks, as part of a larger deep learning architecture. Additionally, we use adversarial training such that the *shared* representation is explicitly discouraged from learning domain identifying information (Ganin and Lempitsky, 2015). We present two architectures which differ in whether domain is conditioned on or generated, and in terms of parameter sharing in forming private representations.

We primarily evaluate on the task of language identification ("LangID": Cavnar and Trenkle (1994)), using the corpora of Lui and Baldwin (2012), which combine large training sets over a diverse range of text domains. Domain adaptation is an important problem for this task (Lui and Baldwin, 2014; Jurgens et al., 2017), where text resources are collected from numerous sources, and exhibit a wide variety of language use. We show that while domain adversarial training overall improves over baselines, gains are modest. The same applies to twin shared/private architectures, but when the two methods are combined, we observe substantial improvements. Overall, our

---

[1]Code, data and evaluation scripts available at https://github.com/lrank/Domain_Robust_Text_Representation.git

Proceedings of NAACL-HLT 2018, pages 474–479

New Orleans, Louisiana, June 1 - 6, 2018. ©2018 Association for Computational Linguistics

methods outperform the state-of-the-art (Lui and Baldwin, 2012) in terms of out-of-domain accuracy. As a secondary evaluation, we use the Multi-Domain Sentiment Dataset (Blitzer et al., 2007), where we once again observe a clear advantage for our approaches, illustrating the potential of our technique more broadly in NLP.

2 Multi-domain Learning

A primary consideration when formulating models of multi-domain data is how best to use the domain. Basic methods might learn several separate models, or simply ignore the domain and learn a single model. Neither method is ideal: the former fails to share statistics between the models to capture the general concept, while the latter discards information that can aid classification, e.g., domain-specific vocabulary or class skew.

To address these issues, we propose two architectures as illustrated in Figure 1 (a and b), parameterised as a convolutional network (CNN) over the input instance, chosen based on the success of CNNs for text categorisation problems (Kim, 2014); note, however, that our method is general and can be applied with other network types. Both representations are based on the idea of twin representations of each instance,[2] denoted *shared* and *private* representations, which are trained to capture domain-general versus domain-specific concepts, respectively. This is achieved using various loss functions, most notably an adversarial loss to discourage learning of domain-specific concepts in the shared representations. The two architectures differ in whether the domain is provided as an input (COND) or an output (GEN). Below, we elaborate on the details of the two models.

2.1 Domain-Conditional Model (COND)

The first model, illustrated in Figure 1a, includes a collection of domain-specific CNNs, and for each training instance $\mathbf{x}$, the domain-specific $\text{CNN}^p_{d_i}$ is used to compute its private representation $\mathbf{h}^p$. In this manner, the model *conditions* on the domain identifier. The COND model also computes a shared representation, $\mathbf{h}^s$, directly from $\mathbf{x}$, using a shared CNN^s, and the two representations are concatenated together to form input to linear softmax classification function c for predicting class label y. Thus far, the approach resembles Daumé

---

[2]This differs from standard architectures, e.g., 'baseline' in Figure 1c, which uses a single representation.

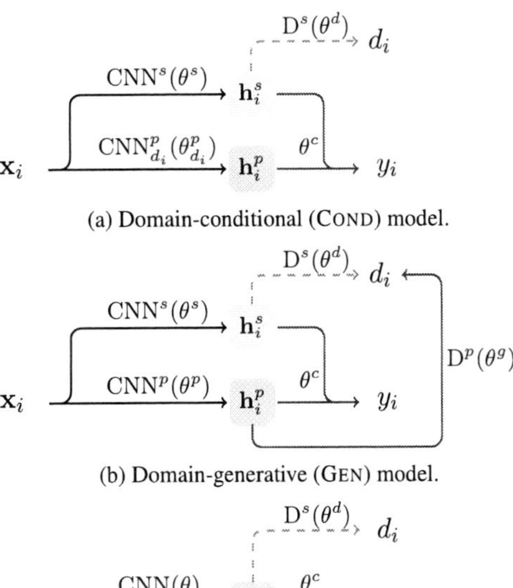

(a) Domain-conditional (COND) model.

(b) Domain-generative (GEN) model.

(c) Baseline CNN model with adversarial loss.

Figure 1: Proposed model architectures, showing a single training instance $(\mathbf{x}_i, y_i)$ with domain d_i, and baseline model with domain adversarial loss. CNN denotes a convolutional network, D indicates a discriminator (d for domain adversarial and g for domain generation), and red dashed and blue lines denote adversarial and standard loss, resp.

III (2007), a method for multitask learning based on feature augmentation in a linear model, which works by replicating the input features to create both general shared features, and domain-specific features. Note that the approaches differ in that our method uses deep learning to form the two representations, in place of feature replication.

Adversarial Supervision A key challenge for the COND model is that the 'shared' representation can be contaminated by domain-specific concepts. To address this, we borrow ideas from adversarial learning (Goodfellow et al., 2014; Ganin et al., 2016). The central idea is to learn a good general representation (suitable for the shared component) to maximize end task performance, yet obscure the domain information, as modelled by a discriminator, $\mathbf{D}^s$. This reduces the domain-specific information in the shared representation, however note that important domain-specific components can still be captured in the private representation.

Overall, this results in the training objective:

$$\mathcal{L}^{\text{COND}} = \min_{\theta^c, \theta^s, \{\theta^p\}} \max_{\theta^d} \mathcal{X}(\mathbf{y}|\mathbf{H}^s, \mathbf{H}^p, \mathbf{d}; \theta^c)$$
$$- \lambda_d \mathcal{X}(\mathbf{d}|\mathbf{H}^s; \theta^d) \tag{1}$$

where $\mathcal{X}$ denotes the cross-entropy classification loss, $\mathbf{H}^s = \{\mathbf{h}_i^s(\mathbf{x}_i)\}_{i=1}^n$ are the shared representations for the training set of n instances, and likewise $\mathbf{H}^p = \{\mathbf{h}_i^p(\mathbf{x}_i, d_i)\}_{i=1}^n$ are the private representations, which are both functions of θ^s and $\{\theta^p\}$, respectively. Note the negative sign of the adversarial loss (referred to as d), and the maximisation with respect to the discriminator parameters θ^d. This has the effect of learning a maximally accurate discriminator *wrt* θ^d, while making it maximally inaccurate *wrt* representation $\mathbf{H}^s$, and is implemented using a gradient reversal step during backpropagation (Ganin et al., 2016).

Minimum Entropy Inference As COND conditions on the domain, this imposes the requirement that the domain of the test data is known (and covered in training), which is incompatible with our goal of unsupervised adaptation. To deal with this situation, we consider each domain in the test set as belonging to one of the training domains, and then select the domain with the minimum entropy classification distribution. This is based on an assumption that a closely matching domain should be able to make confident predictions.[3]

2.2 Domain-Generative Model (GEN)

The second model is based on *generation* of, rather than *conditioning* on, the domain, which allows the model to learn domain signals that transfer across some, but not all, domains. Most components are common with the COND model as described in §2.1, including the use of private and shared representations, their use in the classification output, and the adversarial loss based on discriminating the domain from the shared representation. There are two key differences: (1) the private representation, $\mathbf{h}^p$, is computed using a single CNN^p, rather than several domain-specific CNNs, which confers benefits of domain-generalisation, a more compact model, and simpler test inference;[4] and (2) the private representation is used to positively predict the domain, which further encourages the split between domain general and domain-specific aspects of the representation.

GEN has the following training objective,

$$\mathcal{L}^{\text{GEN}} = \min_{\theta^c, \theta^s, \theta^p, \theta^g} \max_{\theta^d} \mathcal{X}(\mathbf{y}|\mathbf{H}^s, \mathbf{H}^p; \theta^c) \\ - \lambda_d \mathcal{X}(\mathbf{d}|\mathbf{H}^s; \theta^d) + \lambda_g \mathcal{X}(\mathbf{d}|\mathbf{H}^p; \theta^g) \tag{2}$$

where notation follows that used in §2.1, with the exception of $\mathbf{H}^p = \{\mathbf{h}_i^p(\mathbf{x}_i)\}_{i=1}^n$ that is redefined, with $\mathbf{h}_i^p(\mathbf{x}_i)$ a function of θ^p, and the addition of the last term to capture the generation loss g. The same gradient reversal method from §2.1 is used during training for the adversarial component.

3 Experiments

3.1 Language Identification

To evaluate our approach, we first consider the language identification task.

Data We follow the settings of Lui and Baldwin (2012), involving 5 training sets from 5 different domains with 97 languages in total: Debian, JRC-Acquis, Wikipedia, ClueWeb and RCV2, derived from Lui and Baldwin (2011).[5] We evaluate accuracy on seven holdout benchmarks: EuroGov, TCL, Wikipedia2[6] (all from Baldwin and Lui (2010)), EMEA (Tiedemann, 2009), EuroPARL (Koehn, 2005), T-BE (Tromp and Pechenizkiy, 2011), and T-SC (Carter et al., 2013).

Documents are tokenized as a byte sequence (consistent with Lui and Baldwin (2012)), and truncated or padded to a length of 1k bytes.[7]

Hyper-parameters We perform a grid search for the hyper-parameters, and selected the following settings to optimise accuracy over heldout data from each of the training domains. All byte tokens are mapped to byte embeddings, which are random initialized with size 300. We use the filter sizes of $2, 4, 8, 16$ and 32, with 128 filters for each, to capture n-gram features of different lengths. A dropout rate of 0.5 was applied to all the representation layers. We set the factors λ_d and λ_g to 10^{-3}. All the models are optimized using the Adam Optimizer (Kingma and Ba, 2015) with a learning rate of 10^{-4}.

---

[3]The minimum entropy method is quite effective, trailing oracle selection by only 0.8% accuracy.

[4]The domain need not be known for test examples, so the model can be used directly.

[5]As ClueWeb in Lui and Baldwin (2012) is not publicly accessible, we used a slightly different set of languages but comparable number of documents for training.

[6]Note that the two Wikipedia datasets have no overlap.

[7]We also tried different document length limits, such as 10k, but observed no substantial change in performance.

Models	EuroGov	TCL	Wikipedia2	EMEA	EuroPARL	T-BE	T-SC	ALL$_{out}$
baseline CNN	**99.9**	91.7	88.9	93.1	98.2	85.2	92.2	92.7
$+d$	**99.9**	92.4	88.4	90.2	98.2	87.7	93.1	92.8
$+g$	**99.9**	92.0	88.7	91.6	98.4	86.8	92.8	92.9
COND	**99.9**	91.3	88.2	92.0	98.7	91.5	94.5	93.7
$+d$	**99.9**	**93.5**	90.1	91.3	98.7	92.6	**97.9**	**94.9**
GEN	**99.9**	92.3	88.0	93.3	98.6	87.1	93.8	93.3
$+d+g$	**99.9**	93.1	88.7	92.5	99.1	91.2	96.1	94.4
LANGID.PY	98.7	90.4	**91.3**	**93.4**	**99.2**	**94.1**	88.6	93.6
CLD2	99.0	85.0	85.3	90.7	98.5	85.0	93.4	91.0

Table 1: Accuracy [%] of the different models over the seven heldout datasets, and the macro-averaged accuracy out-of-domain over the 7 test domains ("ALL$_{out}$"). The best result for each dataset is indicated in **bold**. Key: $+d$ = domain adversarial, $+g$ = domain generation component.

3.1.1 Results and Analysis

Baseline and comparisons For comparison, we implement a CNN baseline[8] which is trained using all the data without domain knowledge (i.e. the simple union of the different training datasets). We also employ adversarial learning (d) and generation (g) of domain to the baseline model to better understand the utility of these methods. Note that the baseline $+d$ is a multi-domain variant of Ganin and Lempitsky (2015), albeit trained without any text in the testing domains. For our models, we report results of configurations both with and without the d and g components. We also report the results for two state-of-the-art off-the-shelf LangID tools: (1) LANGID.PY[9] (Lui and Baldwin, 2012); and (2) Google's CLD2.[10]

Out-of-domain Results Our primary concern in terms of evaluating the ability of the different models to generalise, is out-of-domain performance. Table 1 provides a breakdown of out-of-domain results over the 7 holdout domains. The accuracy varies greatly between test domains, depending on the mix of languages, length of test documents, etc. Both our models, COND and GEN, achieve competitive performance, and are further improved by d and g.

For the baseline, applying either d or g results in mild improvements over the baseline, which is surprising as the two forms of supervision work in opposite directions. Overall the small change in performance means neither method appears to be a viable technique for domain adaptation.

Overall, the raw COND and GEN perform better than the baseline. Specifically, for COND, we observed performance gains on EuroPARL, T-BE and T-SC. These three datasets are notable in containing shorter documents, which benefit the most from shared learning. However, as discussed earlier, multi-domain data can introduce noise to the shared representation, causing the performance to drop over TCL, Wikipedia2 and EMEA. This observation demonstrates the necessity of applying adversarial learning to COND. On the other hand, it is a different story for GEN: vanilla GEN achieves accuracy gains relative to the baseline over 5 domains, but is slightly below COND for 4 domains, a result of parameter-sharing over the private representation.

In terms of the adversarial learning, we see that by adding an adversarial component ($+d$ or $+d+g$), COND and GEN realises substantial improvements out of domain, with the exception of EMEA. As we motivated, the domain adversarial part d can obscure the domain-specific information in the shared representation, which helps COND have better generalisation to other domains. Additionally, applying g to GEN helps the private representation to generalize better. These results demonstrate that both d and g are necessary components of multi-domain models. EMEA is noteworthy in that its pattern of results is overall different to the other domains, in that applying d hurts performance. For this domain, the baseline CNN performs very well, and GEN does much better than COND. We believe the reason is that, as a medical domain, EMEA is very much an outlier and does not align to any single training domain. Also, there is a lot of borrowing of terms such as drug and disease names verbatim between lan-

---

[8]The baseline here used a double capacity hidden representation, in order to better match the increased expressivity of the shared/private models.

[9]https://github.com/saffsd/langid.py

[10]https://github.com/CLD2Owners/cld2

Models	Deb	JRCA	Wiki	ClWb	RCV2	ALL$_{in}$
baseline CNN	96.6	99.8	97.8	90.7	97.9	96.6
baseline $+d$	96.5	99.8	97.8	90.7	97.0	96.4
COND	97.0	99.9	97.8	90.9	98.0	96.7
COND $+d$	97.0	**99.9**	**98.4**	90.8	98.1	96.8
GEN $+d+g$	**97.8**	99.9	98.0	91.1	97.9	96.9
LANGID.PY	97.4	99.8	97.6	**91.3**	**99.3**	**97.1**
CLD2	92.2	99.8	92.3	92.3	89.8	93.3

Table 2: Accuracy [%] of different models over five in-domain datasets using cross-validation evaluation and macro-averaged accuracy ("ALL$_{in}$").

guages, further complicating the task.

Overall, our best models (COND $+d$ and GEN $+d+g$) outperform both LANGID.PY and CLD2 in terms of average out-of-domain accuracy.

In-domain Results Table 2 reports the in-domain performance over the 5 training domains, using 5-fold cross validation, as well as the macro-averaged accuracy. Our proposed methods (COND $+d$ and COND $+d+g$) consistently achieve better performance than the baseline. Both COND and GEN achieve competitive performance with the state-of-the-art LANGID.PY in the in-domain scenario. Although LANGID.PY performs slightly better on average accuracy, our best model outperforms LANGID.PY for three of the five datasets.

3.2 Product Reviews

To evaluate the generalization of our methods to other tasks, we experiment with the Multi-Domain Sentiment Dataset (Blitzer et al., 2007).[11] We select the 20 domains with the most review instances, and discard the remaining 5 domains.

For model parameterization, we adopt the same basic hyper-parameter settings and training process as for LangID in §3.1, but change the filter sizes to 3, 4 and 5, use word-based tokenisation, and truncate sentences to 256 tokens, for better compatible with shorter documents.

We perform a out-of-domain evaluation over four target domains, "book" (B), "dvd" (D), "electronics" (E) and "kitchen & housewares" (K), as used in Blitzer et al. (2007). Our experimental setup differs from theirs, in that they train on a single domain and then evaluate on another, while we train over 16 domains, then evaluate on the four

[11]From `https://www.cs.jhu.edu/~mdredze/datasets/sentiment/`, using the positive and negative files from `unprocessed`, up to 2,000 instances per domain. For the four test domains we automatically aligned the reviews in the `processed` and `unprocessed`, such that we can compare results directly against prior work.

Models	B	D	E	K
baseline CNN	79.6	81.2	86.3	87.2
baseline $+d$	78.7	81.6	86.6	87.1
COND	79.2	81.8	85.8	87.2
COND $+d$	79.8	82.3	86.8	87.4
GEN $+d+g$	**80.2**	**82.4**	**87.3**	**87.8**
SCL_MI ♣	76.0	78.5	77.9	85.9
DANN ◇	72.3	78.4	84.3	85.4
IN DOMAIN ♣	82.4	80.4	84.4	87.7

Table 3: Accuracy [%] of different models over 4 domains (B, D, E and K) under out-of-domain evaluations on Multi Domain Sentiment Dataset. Key: ♣ from Blitzer et al. (2007); ◇ from Ganin and Lempitsky (2015).

test domains.

Table 3 presents the results. Overall, our proposed methods consistently outperform the baselines, with the GEN $+d+g$ approach a consistent winner over all other techniques. Note also the lacklustre performance when the baseline is trained with the adversarial loss, mirroring our findings for language identification in §3.1. For comparison, we also report the best results of SCL-MI and DANN, in both cases using an oracle selection of source domain. Our method consistently outperform these approaches, despite having no test oracle, although note that we use more diverse data sources for training.

4 Conclusions

We have proposed a novel deep learning method for multi-domain learning, based on joint learning of domain-specific and domain-general components, using either domain conditioning or domain generation. Based on our evaluation over multi-domain language identification and multi-domain sentiment analysis, we show our models to substantially outperform a baseline deep learning method, and set a new benchmark for state-of-the-art cross-domain LangID. Our approach has potential to benefit other NLP applications involving multi-domain data.

Acknowledgments

We thank the anonymous reviewers for their helpful feedback and suggestions, and the National Computational Infrastructure Australia for computation resources. This work was supported by the Australian Research Council (FT130101105).

References

Timothy Baldwin and Marco Lui. 2010. Language identification: The long and the short of the matter. In *Proceedings of Human Language Technologies: Conference of the North American Chapter of the Association of Computational Linguistics.* pages 229–237.

Zsolt Bitvai and Trevor Cohn. 2015. Non-linear text regression with a deep convolutional neural network. In *Proceedings of the 53rd Annual Meeting of the Association for Computational Linguistics and the 7th International Joint Conference on Natural Language Processing Short Papers.*

John Blitzer, Mark Dredze, and Fernando Pereira. 2007. Biographies, bollywood, boom-boxes and blenders: Domain adaptation for sentiment classification. In *Proceedings of the 45th Annual Meeting of the Association of Computational Linguistics.* pages 440–447.

Simon Carter, Wouter Weerkamp, and Manos Tsagkias. 2013. Microblog language identification: Overcoming the limitations of short, unedited and idiomatic text. *Language Resources and Evaluation* 47(1):195–215.

William B Cavnar and John M Trenkle. 1994. N-gram-based text categorization. In *Proceedings of the Third Symposium on Document Analysis and Information Retrieval.*

Hal Daumé III. 2007. Frustratingly easy domain adaptation. In *Proceedings of the 45th Annual Meeting of the Association for Computational Linguistics.* pages 256–263.

Yaroslav Ganin and Victor Lempitsky. 2015. Unsupervised domain adaptation by backpropagation. In *International Conference on Machine Learning 2015.* pages 1180–1189.

Yaroslav Ganin, Evgeniya Ustinova, Hana Ajakan, Pascal Germain, Hugo Larochelle, François Laviolette, Mario Marchand, and Victor Lempitsky. 2016. Domain-adversarial training of neural networks. *Journal of Machine Learning Research* 17:59:1–59:35.

Ian J. Goodfellow, Jean Pouget-Abadie, Mehdi Mirza, Bing Xu, David Warde-Farley, Sherjil Ozair, Aaron C. Courville, and Yoshua Bengio. 2014. Generative adversarial nets. In *Advances in Neural Information Processing Systems 27.* pages 2672–2680.

Mahesh Joshi, Mark Dredze, William W. Cohen, and Carolyn Penstein Rosé. 2012. Multi-domain learning: When do domains matter? In *Proceedings of the 2012 Joint Conference on Empirical Methods in Natural Language Processing and Computational Natural Language Learning.* pages 1302–1312.

David Jurgens, Yulia Tsvetkov, and Dan Jurafsky. 2017. Incorporating dialectal variability for socially equitable language identification. In *Proceedings of the 55th Annual Meeting of the Association for Computational Linguistics.* pages 51–57.

Yoon Kim. 2014. Convolutional neural networks for sentence classification. In *Proceedings of the 2014 Conference on Empirical Methods in Natural Language Processing.* pages 1746–1751.

Young-Bum Kim, Karl Stratos, and Ruhi Sarikaya. 2016. Frustratingly easy neural domain adaptation. In *Proceedings of COLING 2016, the 26th International Conference on Computational Linguistics: Technical Papers.* pages 387–396.

Diederik P. Kingma and Jimmy Ba. 2015. Adam: A method for stochastic optimization. In *Proceedings of the International Conference on Learning Representations.*

Philipp Koehn. 2005. Europarl: A parallel corpus for statistical machine translation. In *MT Summit 2005.* pages 79–86.

Marco Lui and Timothy Baldwin. 2011. Cross-domain feature selection for language identification. In *Fifth International Joint Conference on Natural Language Processing.* pages 553–561.

Marco Lui and Timothy Baldwin. 2012. langid.py: An off-the-shelf language identification tool. In *Proceedings of ACL 2012 System Demonstrations.* pages 25–30.

Marco Lui and Timothy Baldwin. 2014. Accurate language identification of Twitter messages. In *Proceedings of the 5th workshop on language analysis for social media.* pages 17–25.

Jörg Tiedemann. 2009. News from OPUS – a collection of multilingual parallel corpora with tools and interfaces. In *Recent Advances in Natural Language Processing.* volume 5, pages 237–248.

Erik Tromp and Mykola Pechenizkiy. 2011. Graph-based n-gram language identification on short texts. In *Proceedings of the 20th Machine Learning Conference of Belgium and The Netherlands.* pages 27–34.

Jason Williams. 2013. Multi-domain learning and generalization in dialog state tracking. In *Proceedings of the SIGDIAL 2013 Conference.* pages 433–441.

Automated Paraphrase Lattice Creation
for HyTER Machine Translation Evaluation

Marianna Apidianaki[*†], **Guillaume Wisniewski**[†],
Anne Cocos[*] and **Chris Callison-Burch**[*]

[†] LIMSI, CNRS, Univ. Paris Sud, Université Paris-Saclay, 91403 Orsay
[*] Computer and Information Science Department, University of Pennsylvania
{marapi,acocos,ccb}@seas.upenn.edu, guillaume.wisniewski@limsi.fr

Abstract

We propose a variant of a well-known machine translation (MT) evaluation metric, HyTER (Dreyer and Marcu, 2012), which exploits reference translations enriched with meaning equivalent expressions. The original HyTER metric relied on hand-crafted paraphrase networks which restricted its applicability to new data. We test, for the first time, HyTER with automatically built paraphrase lattices. We show that although the metric obtains good results on small and carefully curated data with both manually and automatically selected substitutes, it achieves medium performance on much larger and noisier datasets, demonstrating the limits of the metric for tuning and evaluation of current MT systems.

1 Introduction

Human translators and MT systems can produce multiple plausible translations for input texts. To reward meaning-equivalent but lexically divergent translations, MT evaluation metrics exploit synonyms and paraphrases, or multiple references (Papineni et al., 2002; Doddington, 2002; Denkowski and Lavie, 2010; Lo et al., 2012). The HyTER metric (Dreyer and Marcu, 2012) relies on massive reference networks encoding an exponential number of correct translations for parts of a given sentence, proposed by human annotators. The manually built networks attempt to encode the set of all correct translations for a sentence, and HyTER rewards high quality hypotheses by measuring their minimum edit distance to the set of possible translations.

HyTER spurred a lot of enthusiasm but the need for human annotations heavily reduced its applicability to new data. We propose to use an embedding-based lexical substitution model (Melamud et al., 2015) for building this type of reference networks and test, for the first time, the

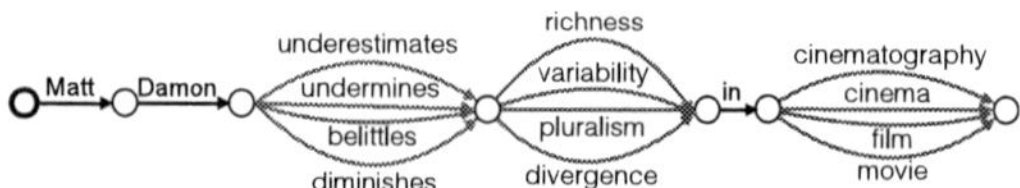

Figure 1: An English reference sentence enriched with substitutes selected by the embedding-based lexical substitution model.

metric with automatically generated lattices (hereafter HyTERA). We show that HyTERA strongly correlates with HyTER with hand-crafted lattices, and approximates the hTER score (Snover et al., 2006) as measured using post-edits made by human annotators. Furthermore, we generate lattices for standard datasets from a recent WMT Metrics Shared Task and perform the first evaluation of HyTER on large and noisier datasets. The results show that it still remains an interesting solution for MT evaluation, but highlight its limits when used to evaluate recent MT systems that make far less errors of lexical choice than older systems.

2 The Original HyTER Metric

The HyTER metric (Dreyer and Marcu, 2012) computes the similarity between a translation hypothesis and a reference lattice that compactly encodes millions of meaning-equivalent translations. Formally HyTER is defined as:

$$\text{HyTER}\,(x, \mathscr{Y}) = \underset{y \in \mathscr{Y}}{\arg\min} \frac{\text{LS}(x, y)}{\text{len}(y)} \qquad (1)$$

where $\mathscr{Y}$ is a set of references that can be encoded as a finite state automaton such as the one represented in Figure 1, x is a translation hypothesis and LS is the standard Levenshtein distance, defined as the minimum number of substitutions, deletions and insertions required to transform x into y. We use, in all our experiments, our own im-

Proceedings of NAACL-HLT 2018, pages 480–485
New Orleans, Louisiana, June 1 - 6, 2018. ©2018 Association for Computational Linguistics

plementation of HyTER[1] that relies on the Open-FST framework (Allauzen et al., 2007). Contrary to the original HyTER implementation, we do not consider permutations when transforming x into y as previous results (cf. Table 3 in (Dreyer and Marcu, 2012)) have shown that permutations have only very little impact while significantly increasing the computational complexity of HyTER computation.[2] We also use an exact search rather than a A* search to minimize Equation (1).

The HyTER metric has already been successfully used in MT evaluation but only with handcrafted lattices. To the best of our knowledge, this is the first time it is tested with lattices built automatically.

3 Automatic Lattice Creation

We propose an alternative to the costly manual annotation of reference translations which exploits an embedding-based model of lexical substitution proposed by Melamud et al. (2015) (called AddCos). The original AddCos implementation selects substitutes for words in context from the whole vocabulary. Here, we restrict candidate substitutes to paraphrases of words in the Paraphrase Database (PPDB) XXL package (Ganitkevitch et al., 2013).[3]

AddCos quantifies the fit of substitute word s for target word t in context C by measuring the semantic similarity of the substitute to the target, and the similarity of the substitute to the context:

$$\text{AddCos}(s,t,C) = \frac{\cos(s,t) + \sum_{c \in C} \cos(s,c)}{|C|+1} \quad (2)$$

The vectors s and t are word embeddings of the substitute and target generated by the *skip-gram with negative sampling* model (Mikolov et al., 2013b,a).[4] The context C is the set of context embeddings for words appearing within a fixed-width window of the target t in a sentence (we use

a window width of 1). The embeddings c are context embeddings generated by *skip-gram*.[5] In our implementation, we train 300-dimensional word and context embeddings over the 4B words in the Annotated Gigaword (AGiga) corpus (Napoles et al., 2012) using the gensim `word2vec` package (Mikolov et al., 2013b,a; Řehůřek and Sojka, 2010).[6]

Each content word token in a sentence is expanded to include all its possible substitutes selected by AddCos in this specific context, and the lattice can take any path from the expanded start token to the expanded end token. We filter the paraphrase candidates according to: a) their PPDB2.0 score, an *out-of-context* measure of paraphrase confidence which denotes the strength of the relation between the paraphrase and the target word (hereafter, PPDBSc) (Pavlick et al., 2015); b) the substitution score assigned to paraphrases in context by the AddCos model (hereafter, AddCosSc), which shows whether the paraphrase is a good fit for the target word *in a specific context*.[7] Figure 1 shows the four highest ranked paraphrases proposed by AddCos for words in the English reference sentence: *Matt Damon downplays diversity in filmmaking.* The sentences *Matt Damon underestimates richness in cinematography* and *Matt Damon belittles pluralism in cinema.* are included among the 48 references encoded in this lattice.

4 Evaluating HyTER with Automatic Substitutions

We assess the quality of HyTERA to evaluate the quality of MT output both at the sentence and the system level. We first use the setting of Dreyer and Marcu (2012), in Section § 5.1, to compare the score estimated by HyTER and HyTERA to hTER scores. In Section § 5.2, we explore whether HyTERA can reliably predict human translation quality scores from the WMT16 Metrics Shared Task.

---

[1] The code is available at `https://bitbucket.org/gwisniewski/hytera/`

[2] Note that as permutations of interest can be compactly encoded in a fine-state graph (Kumar and Byrne, 2005), the MOVE operation can be easily considered in our code by applying the substitutions to the permutation lattice rather than to the sentence.

[3] PPDB paraphrases come into packages of different sizes (going from S to XXXL): small packages contain high-precision paraphrases while larger ones have high coverage. All are available from `paraphrase.org`

[4] For the moment, we focus on individual content words. In future work, we plan to also annotate longer text segments in the references with multi-word PPDB paraphrases.

[5] In the original implementation, Melamud et al. (2015) use syntactic dependencies as contexts. We define context as a fixed-width window of words to avoid the need for dependency parsing.

[6] The `word2vec` training parameters we use are a context window of size 3, learning rate *alpha* from 0.025 to 0.0001, minimum word count 100, sampling parameter $1e^{-4}$, 10 negative samples per target word, and 5 training epochs.

[7] Our implementation of AddCos with PPDB substitutes can be found at `https://github.com/acocos/lexsub_addcos`

5 Comparing HyTER and HyTERA

5.1 Open MT NIST Evaluation

To evaluate the performance of HyTER, Dreyer and Marcu (2012) examine whether it can approximate the hTER score (Snover et al., 2006) that measures the number of edits required to change a system output into its post-edition. hTER scores are a good estimate of translation quality and usefulness, but require each translation hypothesis to be corrected by a human annotator. Dreyer and Marcu (2012) show that it can be closely approximated by HyTER scores. In this section, we reproduce their experiments with HyTERA to see whether it is possible to use automatically-built rather than hand-crafted references to approximate hTER scores.

Data Following Dreyer and Marcu (2012), we consider a subset of the 'progress set' used in the 2010 Open MT NIST evaluation.[8] This corpus is made of 102 Arabic and 102 Chinese sentences. Each sentence is automatically translated into English by five MT systems and these translation hypotheses are post-edited by experienced LDC annotators, allowing us to compute hTER scores. The corpus also contains four references and meaning-equivalent annotations which allow for direct comparison to the original HyTER.

Experimental Setting We build meaning-equivalent lattices by applying the lexical substitution method described in Section 3 to each of the four references associated with a sentence, and considering the union of the resulting lattices. We report results for two kinds of lattices: lattices encoding all lexical substitutes available for a word in PPDB (`allPars`) and lattices of substitutes with PPDBSc>2.3 (`allParsFiltered`) and AddCosSc$\geq$0. As expected, the `allPars` lattices are much larger than the manual and the filtered lattices (cf. Table 1). In all our experiments, all corpora are down-cased and tokenized using standard Moses scripts. hTER scores are computed using TERp (Snover et al., 2009).

Sentence Level Evaluation Table 2 reports the correlation between HyTER, HyTERA and hTER at the sentence level. We also include as a baseline the correlation with the sentence-level BLEU

	ar2en	zh2en
manual	$9,454,542$	7.8×10^9
`allPars`	1.8×10^{27}	8.5×10^{27}
`allParsFiltered`	$10,803$	3.3×10^{20}

Table 1: Median number of references generated by each method.

score, estimated by the arithmetic mean of 1 to 4-gram precisions.[9]

In all cases, there is a high correlation between HyTER, HyTERA and hTER, significantly higher than the correlation between BLEU and hTER. This observation shows that replacing the hand-crafted lattices with automatically built ones has only a moderate impact on the HyTER metric quality: automatic lattices result in a small drop of the correlation when evaluating hypotheses translated from Chinese, and slightly improve it for the Arabic to English condition. Overall HyTERA scores are highly correlated with HyTER scores ($\rho = 0.766$ for Arabic and $\rho = 0.756$ for Chinese). More importantly, considering the filtered lattices allows to significantly reduce computation time compared to the `allPars` ones without hurting the quality estimation capacity of the metric.

System Level Evaluation Figure 2 shows how the five MT systems are ranked by the different metrics we consider, when translating from Arabic to English. All metrics rank the systems in the same order, except from HyTER with `allParsFiltered` that only inverts two systems. Note that the tested systems were selected by NIST to cover a variety of system architectures (statistical, rule-based, hybrid) and performances (Dreyer and Marcu, 2012), which makes distinction between them an easy task for all metrics. The benefits of using a metric like HyTER, which focuses on the word level, are much clearer in the sentence-based evaluation (Table 2).

5.2 WMT Metrics Evaluation

In our second set of experiments, we explore the ability of HyTERA to predict direct human judgments at the sentence level using the setting of the WMT16 Metrics Shared Task (Bojar et al., 2016). We measure the correlation between ad-

---

[8]The corpus is available from LDC under reference `ldc2014t09`.

[9]More precisely: $\text{sBLEU} = \frac{1}{4} \cdot \sum_{i=1}^{4} p_i$ where p_i is the number of i-grams that appears both in the reference and in the hypothesis divided by the number of i-grams in the reference.

	ar → en	zh → en
HyTER	0.667	0.672
HyTERA(allPars)	0.673	0.616
HyTERA(allParsFiltered)	0.671	0.605
BLEU	-0.563	-0.556

Table 2: Correlation, calculated by Spearman's ρ, between the scores of translation hypotheses estimated by HyTER and hTER.

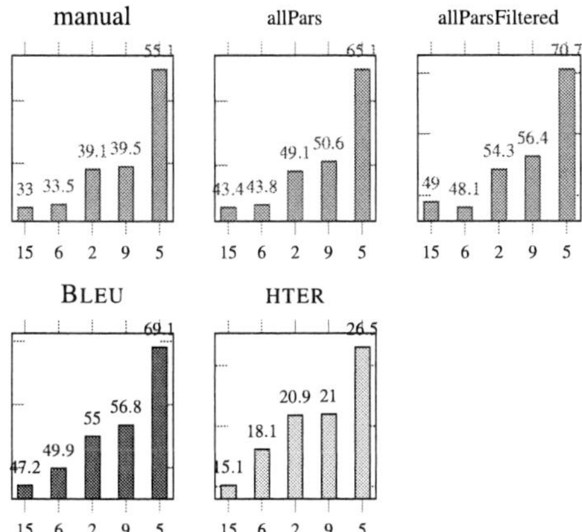

Figure 2: Five Arabic to English MT systems scored by different metrics.

equacy scores collected on Amazon Mechanical Turk following the method advocated by Graham et al. (2016) and the translation quality estimated by applying HyTERA to the official WMT reference. Table 3 reports the results achieved by HyTERA on the six language pairs of the WMT16 Shared Task and its rank among the other metrics tested in the competition.

HyTERA obtains medium performance on the WMT16 dataset, which is much larger and noisier than the dataset used for evaluation in (Dreyer and Marcu, 2012): it is made, for each language, of 560 translations sampled from outputs of all systems taking part in the WMT15 campaign. It is important to note that the hTER scores used in the initial HyTER evaluation were produced by experienced LDC annotators, while the WMT16 Direct Assessment (DA) adequacy judgments were collected from non-experts through crowd-sourcing (Bojar et al., 2016). HyTERA achieves higher performance than the SENTBLEU baseline in four language pairs (cs/de/ru/tr-en). It obtains slightly lower correlation than SENTBLEU for fi-en and ro-en, the language pairs in which correlation was lower for all metrics.

Among the metrics tested at the WMT16 shared task we find combination metrics, and metrics that have been tuned on a development dataset. The metric that performs best for most languages in the segment-level WMT16 evaluation, DPMFCOMB, combines 57 individual metrics (Yu et al., 2015). Similarly, the second highest ranked metric, METRICSF, combines BLEU, METEOR, the alignment-based metric UPF-COMBALT (Fomicheva et al., 2016), and fluency features. The BEER metric, found in fifth position, is a trained evaluation metric with a linear model that combines features capturing character n-grams and permutation trees (Stanojević and Sima'an, 2015).

We report the rank of HyTERA among all metrics (single and combined), and among the single ones. It is important to note that HyTERA needs no tuning, is straightforward to use and very fast to compute, especially with filtered lattices (on average 6s).

The lower performance of the metric on this dataset is also due to the different nature of the MT systems tested. While in the (Dreyer and Marcu, 2012) evaluation, the systems came from the 2010 Open MT NIST evaluation and were selected to cover a variety of architectures and performances, the systems that participated in WMT15 are, for the large part, neural MT systems (Bojar et al., 2015). As reported by Bentivogli et al. (2016), Neural MT systems make at least 17% fewer lexical choice errors than phrase-based systems, which limits the potential of HyTERA, primarily focused on capturing correct lexical choice.

6 Conclusion

We have proposed a method for automatic paraphrase lattice creation which makes the HyTER metric applicable to new datasets. We provide the first evaluation of HyTER on data from a recent

483

	HᴙTERA	SENTBleu	WMT All		WMT Single Metrics	
	r	r	best r	rank/15	best r	rank/13
cs → en	.599	.557	.713	10	.671	8
de → en	.498	.448	.601	6	.591	4
fi → en	.476	.484	.598	7	.554	5
ro → en	.483	.499	.662	9	.639	7
ru → en	.525	.502	.618	10	.618	8
tr → en	.540	.532	.663	10	.627	8

Table 3: Pearson correlation between HᴙTERA and human judgments at the segment level on WMT16 Metrics Shared Task data on different language pairs. We compare to the scores of the SENTBLEU baseline. We report the best correlation achieved by the participating metrics and the rank of HᴙTERA among all 15 participants, and among the single 13 metrics left after excluding combined ones.

WMT Metrics Shared task. We show that although the metric achieves high correlation with human judgments of translation quality on small and carefully curated data, with both manual and automatically constructed paraphrase networks, it obtains medium performance on recent WMT data. The lower performance is mainly due to the noisier nature of the data and to the higher quality lexical choices made by current neural MT systems, compared to phrase-based and transfer systems, which limits the potential of the metric for system evaluation and tuning.

In its current form, the paraphrase substitution mechanism supports only lexical substitutions. It would be straightforward to extend the AddCos method to handle multi-word paraphrases by training embeddings for multi-word phrases, keeping in mind that longer substitutions might require restructuring the produced sentences to preserve grammaticality.

7 Acknowledgments

We would like to thank Markus Dreyer for sharing with us the original HyTER code.

This work has been supported by the French National Research Agency under project ANR-16-CE33-0013. This material is based in part on research sponsored by DARPA under grant number FA8750-13-2-0017 (the DEFT program) and HR0011-15-C-0115 (the LORELEI program). The U.S. Government is authorized to reproduce and distribute reprints for Governmental purposes. The views and conclusions contained in this publication are those of the authors and should not be interpreted as representing official policies or endorsements of DARPA and the U.S. Government.

References

Cyril Allauzen, Michael Riley, Johan Schalkwyk, Wojciech Skut, and Mehryar Mohri. 2007. OpenFst: A General and Efficient Weighted Finite-State Transducer Library. In *Proceedings of the Ninth International Conference on Implementation and Application of Automata, (CIAA 2007)*. Springer, volume 4783 of *Lecture Notes in Computer Science*, pages 11–23.

Luisa Bentivogli, Arianna Bisazza, Mauro Cettolo, and Marcello Federico. 2016. Neural versus Phrase-Based Machine Translation Quality: a Case Study. In *Proceedings of the 2016 Conference on Empirical Methods in Natural Language Processing*. Austin, Texas, pages 257–267.

Ondřej Bojar, Rajen Chatterjee, Christian Federmann, Barry Haddow, Matthias Huck, Chris Hokamp, Philipp Koehn, Varvara Logacheva, Christof Monz, Matteo Negri, Matt Post, Carolina Scarton, Lucia Specia, and Marco Turchi. 2015. Findings of the 2015 Workshop on Statistical Machine Translation. In *Proceedings of the Tenth Workshop on Statistical Machine Translation*. Lisbon, Portugal, pages 1–46.

Ondřej Bojar, Yvette Graham, Amir Kamran, and Miloš Stanojević. 2016. Results of the WMT16 Metrics Shared Task. In *Proceedings of the First Conference on Machine Translation*. Berlin, Germany, pages 199–231.

Michael Denkowski and Alon Lavie. 2010. Extending the METEOR Machine Translation Evaluation Metric to the Phrase Level. In *Human Language Technologies: The 2010 Annual Conference of the North American Chapter of the Association for Computational Linguistics*. Los Angeles, California, USA, pages 250–253.

George Doddington. 2002. Automatic Evaluation of Machine Translation Quality Using N-gram Co-occurrence Statistics. In *Proceedings of the Second International Conference on Human Language Technology Research*. San Diego, California, pages 138–145.

Markus Dreyer and Daniel Marcu. 2012. HyTER: Meaning-Equivalent Semantics for Translation Evaluation. In *Proceedings of the 2012 Conference of the North American Chapter of the Association for Computational Linguistics: Human Language Technologies*. Montréal, Canada, pages 162–171.

Marina Fomicheva, Núria Bel, Lucia Specia, Iria da Cunha, and Anton Malinovskiy. 2016. CobaltF: A Fluent Metric for MT Evaluation. In *Proceedings of the First Conference on Machine Translation*. Berlin, Germany, pages 483–490.

Juri Ganitkevitch, Benjamin Van Durme, and Chris Callison-Burch. 2013. PPDB: The Paraphrase Database. In *Proceedings of the 2013 Conference of the North American Chapter of the Association for Computational Linguistics: Human Language Technologies*. Atlanta, Georgia, pages 758–764.

Yvette Graham, Timothy Baldwin, Alistair Moffat, and Justin Zobel. 2016. Can machine translation systems be evaluated by the crowd alone. *Natural Language Engineering* FirstView:1–28.

Shankar Kumar and William Byrne. 2005. Local Phrase Reordering Models for Statistical Machine Translation. In *Proceedings of Human Language Technology Conference and Conference on Empirical Methods in Natural Language Processing*. Vancouver, British Columbia, Canada, pages 161–168.

Chi-kiu Lo, Anand Karthik Tumuluru, and Dekai Wu. 2012. Fully Automatic Semantic MT Evaluation. In *Proceedings of the Seventh Workshop on Statistical Machine Translation*. Montréal, Canada, pages 243–252.

Oren Melamud, Omer Levy, and Ido Dagan. 2015. A Simple Word Embedding Model for Lexical Substitution. In *Proceedings of the 1st Workshop on Vector Space Modeling for Natural Language Processing*. Denver, Colorado, pages 1–7.

Tomas Mikolov, Kai Chen, Greg Corrado, and Jeffrey Dean. 2013a. Efficient estimation of word representations in vector space. *arXiv preprint arXiv:1301.3781* .

Tomas Mikolov, Ilya Sutskever, Kai Chen, Greg S Corrado, and Jeff Dean. 2013b. Distributed representations of words and phrases and their compositionality. In *Advances in neural information processing systems*. pages 3111–3119.

Courtney Napoles, Matthew Gormley, and Benjamin Van Durme. 2012. Annotated Gigaword. In *Proceedings of the Joint Workshop on Automatic Knowledge Base Construction and Web-scale Knowledge Extraction (AKBC-WEKEX)*. Montreal, Canada, pages 95–100.

Kishore Papineni, Salim Roukos, Todd Ward, and Wei-Jing Zhu. 2002. BLEU: a method for automatic evaluation of machine translation. In *Proceedings of 40th Annual Meeting of the Association for Computational Linguistics*. Philadelphia, Pennsylvania, USA, pages 311–318.

Ellie Pavlick, Pushpendre Rastogi, Juri Ganitkevitch, Benjamin Van Durme, and Chris Callison-Burch. 2015. PPDB 2.0: Better paraphrase ranking, fine-grained entailment relations, word embeddings, and style classification. In *Proceedings of the 53rd Annual Meeting of the Association for Computational Linguistics and the 7th International Joint Conference on Natural Language Processing (Volume 2: Short Papers)*. Beijing, China, pages 425–430.

Radim Řehůřek and Petr Sojka. 2010. Software Framework for Topic Modelling with Large Corpora. In *Proceedings of the LREC 2010 Workshop on New Challenges for NLP Frameworks*. Valletta, Malta, pages 45–50.

Matthew Snover, Bonnie Dorr, Richard Schwartz, Linnea Micciulla, and John Makhoul. 2006. A Study of Translation Edit Rate with Targeted Human Annotation. In *Proceedings of AMTA*. Cambridge, MA, USA, pages 223–231.

Matthew Snover, Nitin Madnani, Bonnie J. Dorr, and Richard Schwartz. 2009. Fluency, Adequacy, or HTER?: Exploring Different Human Judgments with a Tunable MT Metric. In *Proceedings of the Fourth Workshop on Statistical Machine Translation*. StatMT '09, pages 259–268.

Miloš Stanojević and Khalil Sima'an. 2015. BEER 1.1: ILLC UvA submission to metrics and tuning task. In *Proceedings of the Tenth Workshop on Statistical Machine Translation*. Lisbon, Portugal, pages 396–401.

Hui Yu, Qingsong Ma, Xiaofeng Wu, and Qun Liu. 2015. CASICT-DCU Participation in WMT2015 Metrics Task. In *Proceedings of the Tenth Workshop on Statistical Machine Translation*. Lisbon, Portugal, pages 417–421.

Exploiting Semantics in Neural Machine Translation with Graph Convolutional Networks

Diego Marcheggiani[1,2]   **Joost Bastings**[2]   **Ivan Titov**[1,2]

[1]ILCC, School of Informatics, University of Edinburgh
[2]ILLC, University of Amsterdam

marcheggiani@uva.nl   bastings@uva.nl   ititov@inf.ed.ac.uk

Abstract

Semantic representations have long been argued as potentially useful for enforcing meaning preservation and improving generalization performance of machine translation methods. In this work, we are the first to incorporate information about predicate-argument structure of source sentences (namely, semantic-role representations) into neural machine translation. We use Graph Convolutional Networks (GCNs) to inject a semantic bias into sentence encoders and achieve improvements in BLEU scores over the linguistic-agnostic and syntax-aware versions on the English–German language pair.

1   Introduction

It has long been argued that semantic representations may provide a useful linguistic bias to machine translation systems (Weaver, 1955; Bar-Hillel, 1960). Semantic representations provide an abstraction which can generalize over different surface realizations of the same underlying 'meaning'. Providing this information to a machine translation system, can, in principle, improve meaning preservation and boost generalization performance.

Though incorporation of semantic information into traditional statistical machine translation has been an active research topic (e.g., (Baker et al., 2012; Liu and Gildea, 2010; Wu and Fung, 2009; Bazrafshan and Gildea, 2013; Aziz et al., 2011; Jones et al., 2012)), we are not aware of any previous work considering semantic structures in neural machine translation (NMT). In this work, we aim to fill this gap by showing how information about predicate-argument structure of source sentences can be integrated into standard attention-based NMT models (Bahdanau et al., 2015).

We consider PropBank-style (Palmer et al., 2005) semantic role structures, or more specifi-

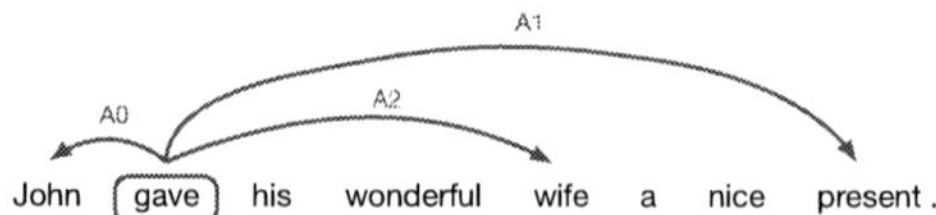

Figure 1:   An example sentence annotated with a semantic-role representation.

cally their dependency versions (Surdeanu et al., 2008). The semantic-role representations mark semantic arguments of predicates in a sentence and categorize them according to their *semantic roles*. Consider Figure 1, the predicate *gave* has three arguments:[1] *John* (semantic role A0, 'the giver'), *wife* (A2, 'an entity given to') and *present* (A1, 'the thing given'). Semantic roles capture commonalities between different realizations of the same underlying predicate-argument structures. For example, *present* will still be A1 in sentence *"John gave a nice present to his wonderful wife"*, despite different surface forms of the two sentences. We hypothesize that semantic roles can be especially beneficial in NMT, as 'argument switching' (flipping arguments corresponding to different roles) is one of frequent and severe mistakes made by NMT systems (Isabelle et al., 2017).

There is a limited amount of work on incorporating graph structures into neural sequence models. Though, unlike semantics in NMT, syntactically-aware NMT has been a relatively hot topic recently, with a number of approaches claiming improvements from using treebank syntax (Sennrich and Haddow, 2016; Eriguchi et al., 2016; Nadejde et al., 2017; Bastings et al., 2017; Aharoni and Goldberg, 2017), our graphs are different from syntactic structures. Unlike syntactic dependency graphs, they are not trees and thus

---

[1]We slightly abuse the terminology: formally these are syntactic heads of arguments rather than arguments.

Proceedings of NAACL-HLT 2018, pages 486–492
New Orleans, Louisiana, June 1 - 6, 2018. ©2018 Association for Computational Linguistics

cannot be processed in a bottom-up fashion as in Eriguchi et al. (2016) or easily linearized as in Aharoni and Goldberg (2017). Luckily, the modeling approach of Bastings et al. (2017) does not make any assumptions about the graph structure, and thus we build on their method.

Bastings et al. (2017) used Graph Convolutional Networks (GCNs) to encode syntactic structure. GCNs were originally proposed by Kipf and Welling (2016) and modified to handle labeled and automatically predicted (hence noisy) syntactic dependency graphs by Marcheggiani and Titov (2017). Representations of nodes (i.e. words in a sentence) in GCNs are directly influenced by representations of their neighbors in the graph. The form of influence (e.g., transition matrices and parameters of gates) are learned in such a way as to benefit the end task (i.e. translation). These linguistically-aware word representations are used within a neural encoder. Although recent research has shown that neural architectures are able to learn some linguistic phenomena without explicit linguistic supervision (Linzen et al., 2016; Vaswani et al., 2017), informing word representations with linguistic structures can provide a useful inductive bias.

We apply GCNs to the semantic dependency graphs and experiment on the English–German language pair (WMT16). We observe an improvement over the semantics-agnostic baseline (a BiRNN encoder; 23.3 vs 24.5 BLEU). As we use exactly the same modeling approach as in the syntactic method of Bastings et al. (2017), we can easily compare the influence of the types of linguistic structures (i.e., syntax vs. semantics). We observe that when using full WMT data we obtain better results with semantics than with syntax (23.9 BLEU for syntactic GCN). Using syntactic and semantic GCNs together, we obtain a further gain (24.9 BLEU) which suggests the complementarity of information encoded by the syntactic and semantic representations.

2 Model

2.1 Encoder-decoder Models

We use a standard attention-based encoder-decoder model (Bahdanau et al., 2015) as a starting point for constructing our model. In encoder-decoder models, the encoder takes as input the source sentence $\mathbf{x}$ and calculates a representation of each word x_t in $\mathbf{x}$. The decoder outputs a translation $\mathbf{y}$ relying on the representations of the source sentence. Traditionally, the encoder is parametrized as a Recurrent Neural Network (RNN), but other architectures have also been successful, such as Convolutional Neural Networks (CNN) (Gehring et al., 2017) and hierarchical self-attention models (Vaswani et al., 2017), among others. In this paper we experiment with RNN and CNN encoders. We explore the benefits of incorporating information about semantic-role structures into such encoders.

More formally, RNNs (Elman, 1990) can be defined as a function $\mathrm{RNN}(x_{1:t})$ that calculates the hidden representation h_t of a word x_t based on its left context. Bidirectional RNNs use two RNNs: one runs in the forward direction and another one in the backward direction. The forward $\mathrm{RNN}(x_{1:t})$ represents the left context of word x_t, whereas the backward $\mathrm{RNN}(x_{n:t})$ computes a representation of the right context. The two representations are concatenated in order to incorporate information about the entire sentence:

$$\mathrm{BiRNN}(\mathbf{x}, t) = \mathrm{RNN}(x_{1:t}) \circ \mathrm{RNN}(x_{n:t}).$$

In contrast to BiRNNs, CNNs (LeCun et al., 2001) calculate a representation of a word x_t by considering a window of words w around x_t, such as

$$\mathrm{CNN}(\mathbf{x}, t, w) = f(x_{t-\lfloor w/2 \rfloor}, .., x_t, .., x_{t+\lfloor w/2 \rfloor}),$$

where f is usually an affine transformation followed by a nonlinear function.

Once the sentence has been encoded, the decoder takes as input the induced sentence representation and generates the target sentence $\mathbf{y}$. The target sentence $\mathbf{y}$ is predicted word by word using an RNN decoder. At each step, the decoder calculates the probability of generating a word y_t conditioning on a context vector $\mathbf{c_t}$ and the previous state of the RNN decoder. The context vector $\mathbf{c_t}$ is calculated based on the representation of the source sentence computed by the encoder, using an attention mechanism (Bahdanau et al., 2015). Such a model is trained end-to-end on a parallel corpus to maximize the conditional likelihood of the target sentences.

2.2 Graph Convolutional Networks

Graph neural networks are a family of neural architectures (Scarselli et al., 2009; Gilmer et al., 2017) specifically devised to induce representation of nodes in a graph relying on its graph struc-

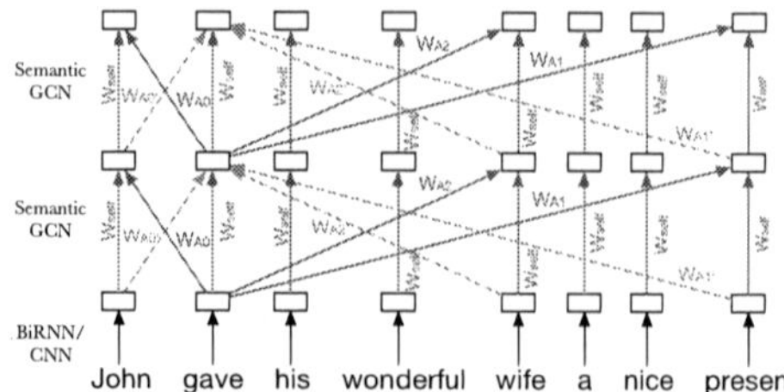

Figure 2: Two layers of semantic GCN on top of a (not shown) BiRNN or CNN encoder.

	BiRNN	CNN
Baseline (Bastings et al., 2017)	14.9	12.6
+Sem	15.6	13.4
+Syn (Bastings et al., 2017)	16.1	13.7
+Syn + Sem	15.8	14.3

Table 1: Test BLEU, En–De, News Commentary.

ture. Graph convolutional networks (GCNs) belong to this family. While GCNs were introduced for modeling undirected unlabeled graphs (Kipf and Welling, 2016), in this paper we use a formulation of GCNs for labeled directed graphs, where the direction and the label of an edge are incorporated. In particular, we follow the formulation of Marcheggiani and Titov (2017) and Bastings et al. (2017) for syntactic graphs and apply it to dependency-based semantic-role structures (Hajic et al., 2009) (as in Figure 1).

More formally, consider a directed graph $\mathcal{G} = (\mathcal{V}, \mathcal{E})$, where $\mathcal{V}$ is a set of nodes, and $\mathcal{E}$ is a set of edges. Each node $v \in \mathcal{V}$ is represented by a feature vector $\mathbf{x}_v \in \mathbb{R}^d$, where d is the latent space dimensionality. The GCN induces a new representation $\mathbf{h}'_v \in \mathbb{R}^d$ of a node v while relying on representations $\mathbf{h}_u$ of its neighbors:

$$\mathbf{h}'_v = \rho\Big(\sum_{u \in \mathcal{N}(v)} g_{u,v}\big(W_{dir(u,v)}\, \mathbf{h}_u + \mathbf{b}_{lab(u,v)}\big)\Big),$$

where $\mathcal{N}(v)$ is the set of neighbors of v, $W_{dir(u,v)} \in \mathbb{R}^{d \times d}$ is a direction-specific parameter matrix. There are three possible directions ($dir(u,v) \in \{in, out, loop\}$): self-loop edges were added in order to ensure that the initial representation of node $\mathbf{h}_v$ directly affects its new representation $\mathbf{h}'_v$. The vector $\mathbf{b}_{lab(u,v)} \in \mathbb{R}^d$ is an embedding of a semantic role label of the edge (u, v) (e.g., A0). The functions $g_{u,v}$ are scalar gates which weight the importance of each edge. Gates

	BiRNN
Baseline (Bastings et al., 2017)	23.3
+Sem	24.5
+Syn (Bastings et al., 2017)	23.9
+Syn + Sem	24.9

Table 2: Test BLEU, En–De, full WMT16.

are particularly useful when the graph is predicted and thus may contain errors, i.e., wrong edges. In this scenario gates can down weight the influence of potentially unreliable edges. The function ρ is a non-linearity (ReLU).[2]

As with CNNs, GCN layers can be stacked in order to incorporate higher order neighborhoods. In our experiments, we used GCNs on top of a standard BiRNN encoder and a CNN encoder (Figure 2). In other words, the initial representations of words fed into GCN were either RNN states or CNN representations.

3 Experiments

We experimented with the English-to-German WMT16 dataset ($\sim$4.5 million sentence pairs for training). We use its subset, News Commentary v11, for development and additional experiments ($\sim$226.000 sentence pairs). For all these experiments, we use `newstest2015` and `newstest2016` as a validation and test set, respectively.

We parsed the English partitions of these datasets with a syntactic dependency parser (Andor et al., 2016) and dependency-based semantic role labeler (Marcheggiani et al., 2017). We constructed the English vocabulary by taking all words with frequency higher than three, while for German we used byte-pair encodings (BPE) (Sennrich et al., 2016). All hyperparameter selection was performed on the validation set (see Appendix A). We measured the performance of the models with (cased) BLEU scores (Papineni et al., 2002). The settings and the framework (Neural Monkey (Helcl and Libovický, 2017)) used for experiments are the ones used in Bastings et al. (2017), which we use as baselines. As RNNs, we use GRUs (Cho et al., 2014).

We now discuss the impact that different architectures and linguistic information have on the translation quality.

---

[2]Refer to Marcheggiani and Titov (2017) and Bastings et al. (2017) for further details.

3.1 Results and Discussion

First, we start with experiments with the smaller News Commentary training set (see Table 1). As in Bastings et al. (2017), we used the standard attention-based encoder-decoder model as a baseline.

We tested the impact of semantic GCNs when used on top of CNN and BiRNN encoders. As expected, BiRNN results are stronger than CNN ones. In general, for both encoders we observe the same trend: using semantic GCNs leads to an improvement over the baseline model. The improvements is 0.7 BLEU for BiRNN and 0.8 for CNN. This is slightly surprising as the potentially non-local semantic information should in principle be more beneficial within a less powerful and local CNN encoder. The syntactic GCNs (Bastings et al., 2017) appear stronger than semantic GCNs. As exactly the same model and optimization are used for both GCNs, the differences should be due to the type of linguistic representations used.[3] Since syntax and semantic structures seem to be individually beneficial and, though related, capture different linguistic phenomena, it is natural to try combining them. When syntactic and semantic GCNs are stacked, we observe a further improvement with respect to the semantic GCN model, and a substantial improvement with respect to the syntactic GCN model with a CNN encoder.

Now we turn to the full WMT experiments. Though we expected the linguistic bias to be more valuable in the resource-poor setting, the improvement from using semantic-role structures is larger here (+1.2 BLEU). It is surprising but perhaps more data is beneficial for accurately modeling influence of semantics on the translation task. Interestingly, the semantic GCN now outperforms the syntactic one by 0.6 BLEU. Again, it is hard to pinpoint exact reasons for this. One may speculate though that, given enough data, RNNs were able to capture syntactic dependency and thus reducing the benefits from using treebank syntax, whereas (often less local and harder) semantic dependencies were more complementary. Finally, when the semantic GCN is stacked over the syntactic GCN, we obtain a further improvement reaching 24.9 BLEU. These results suggest that syntactic and se-

---

[3]Note that the SRL system we use (Marcheggiani et al., 2017) does not use syntax and is faster than the syntactic parser of Andor et al. (2016), so semantic GCNs may still be preferable from the engineering perspective even in this setting.

	BiRNN	CNN
Baseline (Bastings et al., 2017)	14.1	12.1
+Sem (1L)	14.3	12.5
+Sem (2L)	14.4	12.6
+Sem (3L)	14.4	12.7
+Syn (2L) (Bastings et al., 2017)	14.8	13.1
+SelfLoop (1L)	14.1	12.1
+SelfLoop (2L)	14.2	11.5
+SemSyn (1L)	14.1	12.7
+Syn (1L) + Sem (1L)	14.7	12.7
+Syn (1L) + Sem (2L)	14.6	12.8
+Syn (2L) + Sem (1L)	14.9	13.0
+Syn (2L) + Sem (2L)	14.9	13.5

Table 3: Validation BLEU, News commentary only

mantic dependency structures are complementary information when it comes to translation.

3.2 Ablations and Syntax-Semantics GCNs

We used the validation set to perform extra experiments, as well as to select hyper parameters (e.g., the number of GCN layers) for the experiments presented above. Table 3 presents the results. The annotation 1L, 2L and 3L refers to the number of GCN layers used.

First, we tested whether the gain we observed is an effect of an extra layer of non-linearity or an effect of the linguistic structures encoded with GCNs. In order to do so, we used the GCN layer without any structural information. In this way, only the self-loop edge is used within the GCN node updates. These results (e.g., BiRNN+SelfLoop) show that the linguistic-agnostic GCNs perform on par with the baseline, and thus using linguistic structure is genuinely beneficial in translation.

We compared stacking a semantic GCN on top of syntactic one (as done in section 3.1) against combining syntax and semantic in the same GCN layer (SemSyn).[4] With SemSyn we do not observe any improvement with respect to having semantic and syntactic information alone. We argue that the reason for this is that the two linguistic representations do not interact much as much as needed when encoded into the same GCN layer with a simple aggregation function. The stacking approach allows for more complex interaction and more successful. However, on this smaller dataset,

---

[4]We used distinct matrices W for syntax and semantics.

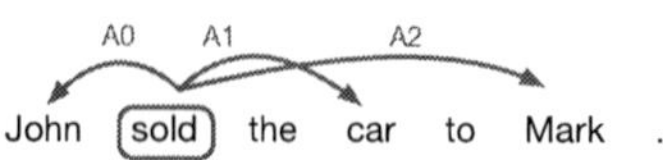

| BiRNN | John verkaufte das Auto nach Mark . |
| Sem | John verkaufte das Auto an Mark . |

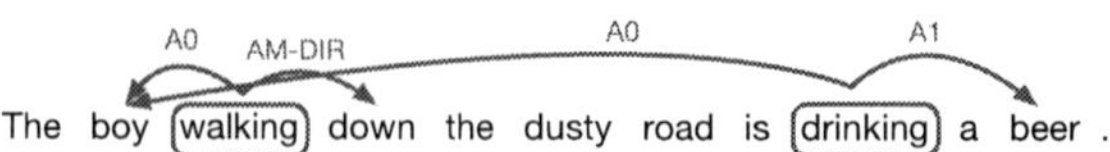

| BiRNN | Der Junge zu Fuß die staubige Straße ist ein Bier trinken . |
| Sem | Der Junge , der die staubige Straße hinunter geht , trinkt ein Bier . |

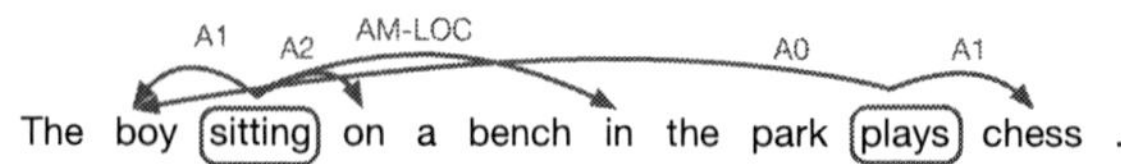

| BiRNN | Der Junge auf einer Bank im Park spielt Schach . |
| Sem | Der Junge sitzt auf einer Bank im Park Schach . |

Table 4: Qualitative analysis. The first two sentences are translations where the semantic structure helps. For the last sentence both translations are problematic but the BiRNN one is grammatical.

unlike full WMT (Table 1), we obtain smaller improvements over the single-representation models.

3.3 Qualitative Analysis

We analyzed the behavior of the BiRNN baseline and the semantic GCN model trained on the full WMT16 training set. In Table 4 we show three examples where there is a clear difference between translations produced by the two models. Besides the two translations, we show the dependency SRL structure predicted by the labeler and exploited by our GCN model.

In the first sentence, the only difference is in the choice of the preposition for the argument Mark. Note that the argument is correctly assigned to role A2 ('Buyer') by the semantic role labeler. The BiRNN model translates to with nach, which in German expresses directionality and would be a correct translation should the argument refer to a location. In contrast, semantic GCN correctly translates to as an. We hypothesize that the semantic structure, namely the assignment of the argument to A2 rather than AM-DIR ('Directionality'), helps the model to choose the right preposition. In the second sentence, the BiRNN's translation is ungrammatical, whereas semantic GCN is able to correctly translate the source sentence. Again, the arguments, correctly identified by semantic role labeler, may have been useful in translating this somewhat tricky sentence. Finally, in the third case, we can observe that both translations are problematic. BiRNN and Semantic GCN ignored verbs sit and play, respectively. However, BiRNN's translation for this sentence is preferable, as it is grammatically correct, even if not fluent or particularly precise.

4 Conclusions

In this work we propose injecting information about predicate-argument structures of sentences in NMT models. We observe that the semantic structures are beneficial for the English–German language pair. So far we evaluated the model performance in terms of BLEU only. It would be interesting in future work to both understand when semantics appears beneficial, and also to see which components of semantic structures play a role. Experiments on other language pairs are also left for future work.

Acknowledgments

We thank Stella Frank and Wilker Aziz for their suggestions and comments. The project was supported by the European Research Council (ERC StG BroadSem 678254), and the Dutch National Science Foundation (NWO VIDI 639.022.518). We thank NVIDIA for donating GPUs used for this research.

References

Roee Aharoni and Yoav Goldberg. 2017. Towards string-to-tree neural machine translation. In *Proceedings of the 55th Annual Meeting of the Association for Computational Linguistics, ACL.* pages 132–140. https://doi.org/10.18653/v1/P17-2021.

Daniel Andor, Chris Alberti, David Weiss, Aliaksei Severyn, Alessandro Presta, Kuzman Ganchev, Slav Petrov, and Michael Collins. 2016. Globally normalized transition-based neural networks. In *Proceedings of the 54th Annual Meeting of the Association for Computational Linguistics, ACL.* pages 2442–2452. https://doi.org/10.18653/v1/P16-1231.

Wilker Aziz, Miguel Rios, and Lucia Specia. 2011. Shallow semantic trees for SMT. In *Proceedings of the Sixth Workshop on Statistical Machine Translation, WMT@EMNLP.* pages 316–322. http://aclanthology.info/papers/W11-2136/shallow-semantic-trees-for-smt.

Dzmitry Bahdanau, Kyunghyun Cho, and Yoshua Bengio. 2015. Neural Machine Translation by Jointly Learning to Align and Translate. In *Proceedings of the International Conference on Learning Representations, ICLR.* http://arxiv.org/abs/1409.0473.

Kathrin Baker, Michael Bloodgood, Bonnie J. Dorr, Chris Callison-Burch, Nathaniel Wesley Filardo, Christine D. Piatko, Lori S. Levin, and Scott Miller. 2012. Modality and negation in SIMT use of modality and negation in semantically-informed syntactic MT. *Computational Linguistics* 38(2):411–438. https://doi.org/10.1162/COLI_a_00099.

Yehoshua Bar-Hillel. 1960. The present status of automatic translation of languages. *Advances in Computers* 1:91–163.

Joost Bastings, Ivan Titov, Wilker Aziz, Diego Marcheggiani, and Khalil Simaan. 2017. Graph convolutional encoders for syntax-aware neural machine translation. In *Proceedings of the 2017 Conference on Empirical Methods in Natural Language Processing, EMNLP.* pages 1957–1967. https://www.aclweb.org/anthology/D17-1209.

Marzieh Bazrafshan and Daniel Gildea. 2013. Semantic roles for string to tree machine translation. In *Proceedings of the 51st Annual Meeting of the Association for Computational Linguistics, ACL.* pages 419–423. http://aclweb.org/anthology/P/P13/P13-2074.pdf.

Kyunghyun Cho, Bart van Merrienboer, Caglar Gulcehre, Dzmitry Bahdanau, Fethi Bougares, Holger Schwenk, and Yoshua Bengio. 2014. Learning Phrase Representations using RNN Encoder–Decoder for Statistical Machine Translation. In *Proceedings of the 2014 Conference on Empirical Methods in Natural Language Processing, EMNLP.* pages 1724–1734. http://www.aclweb.org/anthology/D14-1179.

Jeffrey L Elman. 1990. Finding structure in time. *Cognitive science* 14(2):179–211.

Akiko Eriguchi, Kazuma Hashimoto, and Yoshimasa Tsuruoka. 2016. Tree-to-sequence attentional neural machine translation. In *Proceedings of the 54th Annual Meeting of the Association for Computational Linguistics, ACL.* pages 823–833. http://www.aclweb.org/anthology/P16-1078.

Jonas Gehring, Michael Auli, David Grangier, and Yann Dauphin. 2017. A convolutional encoder model for neural machine translation. In *Proceedings of the 55th Annual Meeting of the Association for Computational Linguistics, ACL.* pages 123–135. https://doi.org/10.18653/v1/P17-1012.

Justin Gilmer, Samuel S. Schoenholz, Patrick F. Riley, Oriol Vinyals, and George E. Dahl. 2017. Neural message passing for quantum chemistry. In *Proceedings of the 34th International Conference on Machine Learning, ICML.* pages 1263–1272. http://proceedings.mlr.press/v70/gilmer17a.html.

Jan Hajic, Massimiliano Ciaramita, Richard Johansson, Daisuke Kawahara, Maria Antònia Martí, Lluís Màrquez, Adam Meyers, Joakim Nivre, Sebastian Padó, Jan Stepánek, Pavel Stranák, Mihai Surdeanu, Nianwen Xue, and Yi Zhang. 2009. The conll-2009 shared task: Syntactic and semantic dependencies in multiple languages. In *Proceedings of the Thirteenth Conference on Computational Natural Language Learning: Shared Task, CoNLL.* pages 1–18. http://aclweb.org/anthology/W/W09/W09-1201.pdf.

Kaiming He, Xiangyu Zhang, Shaoqing Ren, and Jian Sun. 2016. Deep residual learning for image recognition. In *Proceedings of the IEEE Conference on Computer Vision and Pattern Recognition, CVPR.* pages 770–778. https://doi.org/10.1109/CVPR.2016.90.

Jindřich Helcl and Jindřich Libovický. 2017. Neural monkey: An open-source tool for sequence learning. *The Prague Bulletin of Mathematical Linguistics* (107):5–17. https://doi.org/10.1515/pralin-2017-0001.

Pierre Isabelle, Colin Cherry, and George F. Foster. 2017. A challenge set approach to evaluating machine translation. In *Proceedings of the 2017 Conference on Empirical Methods in Natural Language Processing, EMNLP.* pages 2486–2496. https://aclanthology.info/papers/D17-1263/d17-1263.

Bevan Jones, Jacob Andreas, Daniel Bauer, Karl Moritz Hermann, and Kevin Knight. 2012. Semantics-based machine translation with hyperedge replacement grammars. In *Proceedings of the 24th International Conference on Computational Linguistics, COLING*. pages 1359–1376. http://aclweb.org/anthology/C/C12/C12-1083.pdf.

Diederik P. Kingma and Jimmy Ba. 2015. Adam: A method for stochastic optimization. In *Proceedings of the International Conference on Learning Representations, ICLR*. http://arxiv.org/abs/1412.6980.

Thomas N. Kipf and Max Welling. 2016. Semi-supervised classification with graph convolutional networks. In *Proceedings of the International Conference on Learning Representations, ICLR*. http://arxiv.org/abs/1609.02907.

Yann LeCun, Leon Bottou, Yoshua Bengio, and Patrick Haffner. 2001. Gradient-based learning applied to document recognition. In *Proceedings of Intelligent Signal Processing*.

Tal Linzen, Emmanuel Dupoux, and Yoav Goldberg. 2016. Assessing the ability of lstms to learn syntax-sensitive dependencies. *Transactions of the Association for Computational Linguistics* 4:521–535. https://www.transacl.org/ojs/index.php/tacl/article/view/972.

Ding Liu and Daniel Gildea. 2010. Semantic role features for machine translation. In *Proceedings of the23rd International Conference on Computational Linguistics, COLING*. pages 716–724. http://aclweb.org/anthology/C10-1081.

Diego Marcheggiani, Anton Frolov, and Ivan Titov. 2017. A simple and accurate syntax-agnostic neural model for dependency-based semantic role labeling. In *Proceedings of the 21st Conference on Computational Natural Language Learning, CoNLL*. pages 411–420. https://doi.org/10.18653/v1/K17-1041.

Diego Marcheggiani and Ivan Titov. 2017. Encoding sentences with graph convolutional networks for semantic role labeling. In *Proceedings of the 2017 Conference on Empirical Methods in Natural Language Processing, EMNLP*. pages 1506–1515. https://aclanthology.info/papers/D17-1159/d17-1159.

Maria Nadejde, Siva Reddy, Rico Sennrich, Tomasz Dwojak, Marcin Junczys-Dowmunt, Philipp Koehn, and Alexandra Birch. 2017. Predicting target language CCG supertags improves neural machine translation. In *Proceedings of the Second Conference on Machine Translation, WMT*. pages 68–79. http://aclanthology.info/papers/W17-4707/w17-4707.

Martha Palmer, Paul Kingsbury, and Daniel Gildea. 2005. The proposition bank: An annotated corpus of semantic roles. *Computational Linguistics* 31(1):71–106. https://doi.org/10.1162/0891201053630264.

Kishore Papineni, Salim Roukos, Todd Ward, and Wei-Jing Zhu. 2002. Bleu: a method for automatic evaluation of machine translation. In *Proceedings of the 40th Annual Meeting of the Association for Computational Linguistics, ACL*. pages 311–318. http://www.aclweb.org/anthology/P02-1040.pdf.

Franco Scarselli, Marco Gori, Ah Chung Tsoi, Markus Hagenbuchner, and Gabriele Monfardini. 2009. The graph neural network model. *IEEE Trans. Neural Networks* 20(1):61–80. https://doi.org/10.1109/TNN.2008.2005605.

Rico Sennrich and Barry Haddow. 2016. Linguistic Input Features Improve Neural Machine Translation. In *Proceedings of the First Conference on Machine Translation, WMT*. pages 83–91. http://www.aclweb.org/anthology/W16-2209.

Rico Sennrich, Barry Haddow, and Alexandra Birch. 2016. Neural machine translation of rare words with subword units. In *Proceedings of the 54th Annual Meeting of the Association for Computational Linguistics, ACL*. pages 1715–1725. http://www.aclweb.org/anthology/P16-1162.

Mihai Surdeanu, Richard Johansson, Adam Meyers, Lluís Màrquez, and Joakim Nivre. 2008. The CoNLL 2008 shared task on joint parsing of syntactic and semantic dependencies. In *Proceedings of the Twelfth Conference on Computational Natural Language Learning, CoNLL*. pages 159–177. http://aclweb.org/anthology/W/W08/W08-2121.pdf.

Ashish Vaswani, Noam Shazeer, Niki Parmar, Jakob Uszkoreit, Llion Jones, Aidan N. Gomez, Lukasz Kaiser, and Illia Polosukhin. 2017. Attention is all you need. In *Advances in Neural Information Processing Systems 30: Annual Conference on Neural Information Processing Systems, NIPS*. pages 6000–6010. http://papers.nips.cc/paper/7181-attention-is-all-you-need.

Warren Weaver. 1955. Translation. *Machine translation of languages* 14:15–23.

Dekai Wu and Pascale Fung. 2009. Semantic roles for SMT: A hybrid two-pass model. In *Proceedings of the Human Language Technologies: Conference of the North American Chapter of the Association of Computational Linguistics, NAACL*. pages 13–16. http://www.aclweb.org/anthology/N09-2004.

Incremental Decoding and Training Methods for Simultaneous Translation in Neural Machine Translation

Fahim Dalvi[*]
faimaduddin@qf.org.qa

Nadir Durrani[*]
ndurrani@qf.org.qa

Hassan Sajjad
hsajjad@qf.org.qa

Stephan Vogel
svogel@qf.org.qa

Qatar Computing Research Institute – HBKU

Abstract

We address the problem of simultaneous translation by modifying the Neural MT decoder to operate with dynamically built encoder and attention. We propose a tunable agent which decides the best segmentation strategy for a user-defined BLEU loss and Average Proportion (AP) constraint. Our agent outperforms previously proposed Wait-if-diff and Wait-if-worse agents (Cho and Esipova, 2016) on BLEU with a lower latency. Secondly we proposed data-driven changes to Neural MT training to better match the incremental decoding framework.

1 Introduction

Simultaneous translation is a desirable attribute in Spoken Language Translation, where the translator is required to keep up with the speaker. In a lecture or meeting translation scenario where utterances are long, or the end of sentence is not clearly marked, the system must operate on a buffered sequence. Generating translations for such incomplete sequences presents a considerable challenge for machine translation, more so in the case of syntactically divergent language pairs (such as German-English), where the context required to correctly translate a sentence, appears much later in the sequence, and prematurely committing to a translation leads to significant loss in quality.

Various strategies to select appropriate segmentation points in a streaming input have been proposed (Fügen et al., 2007; Bangalore et al., 2012; Sridhar et al., 2013; Yarmohammadi et al., 2013; Oda et al., 2014). A downside of this approach is that the MT system translates sequences independent of each other, ignoring the context. Even if the segmenter decides perfect points to segment the input stream, an MT system requires lexical history to make the correct decision.

The end-to-end nature of the Neural MT architecture (Sutskever et al., 2014; Bahdanau et al., 2015) provides a natural mechanism[1] to integrate stream decoding. Specifically, the recurrent property of the encoder and decoder components provide an easy way to maintain historic context in a fixed size vector.

We modify the neural MT architecture to operate in an online fashion where i) the *encoder* and the *attention* are updated dynamically as new input words are added, through a READ operation, and ii) the *decoder* generates output from the available encoder states, through a WRITE operation. The decision of when to WRITE is learned through a tunable segmentation agent, based on user-defined thresholds. Our incremental decoder significantly outperforms the chunk-based decoder and restores the oracle performance with a deficit of ≤ 2 BLEU points across 4 language pairs with a moderate delay. We additionally explore whether modifying the Neural MT training to match the decoder can improve performance. While we observed significant restoration in the case of chunk decoding matched with chunk-based NMT training, the same was not found true with our proposed incremental training to match the incremental decoding framework.

The remaining paper is organized as follow: Section 2 describes modifications to the NMT decoder to enable stream decoding. Section 3 describes various agents to learn a READ/WRITE strategy. Section 4 presents evaluation and results. Section 5 describes modifications to the NMT training to mimic corresponding decoding strategy, and Section 6 concludes the paper.

---

[1]as opposed to the traditional phrase-based decoder (Moses), which requires pre-computation of phrase-table, future-cost estimation and separately maintaining each state-full feature (language model, OSM (Durrani et al., 2015) etc.)

---

*These authors contributed equally to this work

Proceedings of NAACL-HLT 2018, pages 493–499
New Orleans, Louisiana, June 1 - 6, 2018. ©2018 Association for Computational Linguistics

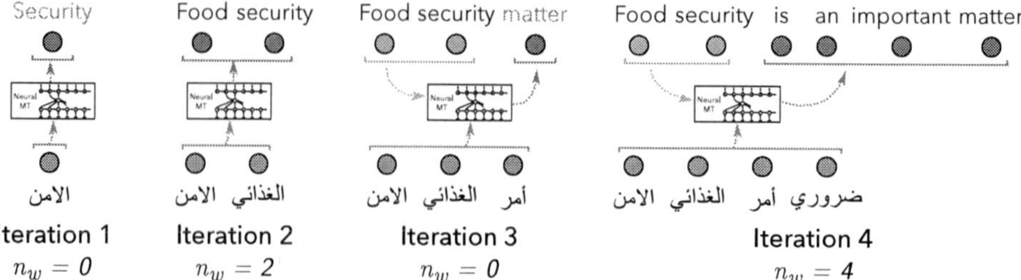

Figure 1: A decoding pass over a 4-word source sentence. n_w denotes the number of words the agent chose to commit. Green nodes = committed words, Blue nodes = newly generated words in the current iteration. Words marked in red are discarded, as the agent chooses to not commit them.

2 Incremental Decoding

Problem: In a stream decoding scenario, the entire source sequence is not readily available. The translator must either wait for the sequence to finish in order to compute the encoder state, or commit partial translations at several intermediate steps, potentially losing contextual information.

Chunk-based Decoder: A straight forward way to enable simultaneous translation is to chop the incoming input after every N-tokens. A drawback of these approaches is that the translation and segmentation process operate independently of each other, and the previous contextual history is not considered when translating the current chunk. This information is important to generate grammatically correct and coherent translations.

Incremental Decoding: The RNN-based NMT framework provides a natural mechanism to preserve context and accommodate streaming. The decoder maintains the entire target history through the previous decoder state alone. But to enable incremental neural decoding, we have to address the following constraints: i) how to dynamically build the encoder and attention with the streaming input? ii) what is the best strategy to pre-commit translations at several intermediate points? Inspired by Cho and Esipova (2016), we modify the NMT decoder to operate in a sequence of READ and WRITE operations. The former reads the next word from the buffered source sequence and translates it using the available context, and the latter is computed through an AGENT, which decides how many words should be committed from this generated translation. Note that, when a translation is generated in the READ operation, the already committed target words remain unchanged, i.e. the generation is continued from

Algorithm 1 Algorithm for incremental decoder

s, Source sequence
s', Available source sequence
t_c, Committed target sequence
t, Current decoded sequence for s'
n_w, Number of tokens to commit

$s' \leftarrow$ empty
for $token$ in s **do** ▷ READ operation
    $s' \leftarrow s' + token$
    $t \leftarrow$ NMTDECODER(s', t_c)
    if $s' \neq s$ **then**
        $n_w \leftarrow$ AGENT(s', t_c, t)
    else
        $n_w \leftarrow$ length$(t)-$ length(t_c)
    end if ▷ commit all new words if we have seen the
entire source
    $t'_c \leftarrow$ GETNEWTOKENS(t_c, t, n_w)
    $t_c \leftarrow t_c + t'_c$ ▷ WRITE operation
end for

function GETNEWTOKENS(t_c, t, n_w)
    $start \leftarrow$ length$(t_c) + 1$
    $end \leftarrow start + n_w$
    return $t[start : end]$
end function

the last committed target word using the saved decoder state. See Algorithm 1 for details. The AGENT decides how many target words to WRITE after every READ operation, and has complete control over the context each target word gets to see before being committed, as well as the overall delay incurred. Figure 1 shows the incremental decoder in action, where the agent decides to not commit any target words in iterations 1 and 3. The example shows an instance where the incorrectly translated words are discarded when more context becomes available. Given this generic framework, we describe several AGENTs in Section 3, trained to optimize the BLEU loss and latency.

Beam Search: Independent of the agent being used, the modified NMT architecture incurs some

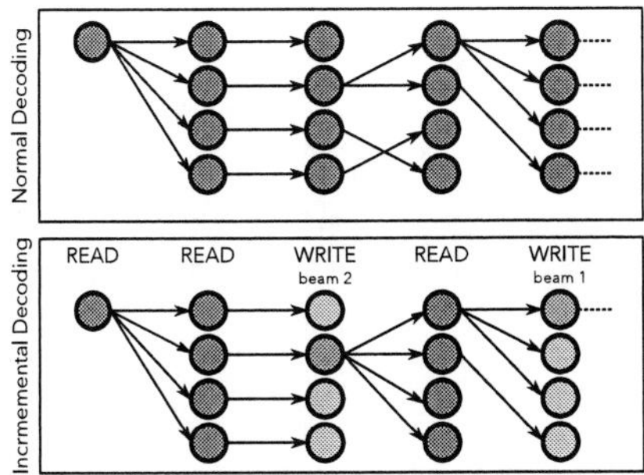

Figure 2: Beam Search in normal decoding vs incremental decoding. Green nodes indicate the hypothesis selected by the agent to WRITE. Since we cannot change what we have already committed, the other nodes (marked in yellow) are discarded and future hypotheses originate from the selected hypothesis alone. Normal beam search is executed for *consecutive* READ operations (blue nodes).

complexities for beam decoding. For example, if at some iteration the decoder generates 5 new words, but the agent decides to commit only 2 of these, the best hypothesis at the 2nd word may not be the same as the one at the 5th word. Hence, the agent has to re-rank the hypotheses at the last target word it decides to commit. Future hypotheses then continue from this selected hypothesis. See Figure 2 for a visual representation. The overall utility of beam decoding is reduced in the case of incremental decoding, because it is necessary to commit and retain only one beam at several points to start producing output with minimal delay.

3 Segmentation Strategies

In this section, we discuss different AGENTS that we evaluated in our modified incremental decoder. To measure latency in these agents, we use *Average Proportion* (AP) metric as defined by Cho and Esipova (2016). AP is calculated as the total number of source words each target word required before being committed, normalized by the product of the source and target lengths. It varies between 0 and 1 with lesser being better. See supplementary material for details.

Wait-until-end: The WUE agent waits for the entire source sentence before decoding, and serves as an upper bound on the performance of our agents, albeit with the worst $AP = 1$.

Wait-if-worse/diff: We reimplemented the baseline agents described in Cho and Esipova (2016). The **Wait-if-Worse** (WIW) agent WRITES

a target word if its probability does not decrease after a READ operation. The **Wait-if-Diff** (WID) agent instead WRITES a target word if the target word remains unchanged after a READ operation.

Static Read and Write: The STATIC-RW: agent is inspired from the chunk-based decoder and tries to resolve its shortcomings while maintaining its simplicity. The primary drawback of the chunk-based decoder is the loss of context across chunks. Our agent starts by performing $\mathcal{S}$ READ operations, followed by repeated $\mathcal{RW}$ WRITES and READS until the end of the source sequence. The number of WRITE and READ operations is the same to ensure that the gap between the source and target sequence does not increase with time. The initial $\mathcal{S}$ READ operations essentially create a buffer of $\mathcal{S}$ tokens, allowing some future context to be used by the decoder. Note that the latency induced by this agent in this case is only in the beginning, and remains constant for the rest of the sentence. This method actually introduces a class of AGENTS based on their $\mathcal{S},\mathcal{RW}$ values. We tune $\mathcal{S}$ and $\mathcal{RW}$ to select the specific AGENT with the user-defined BLEU-loss and AP thresholds.

4 Evaluation

Data: We trained systems for 4 language pairs: German-, Arabic-, Czech- and Spanish-English pairs using the data made available for IWSLT (Cettolo et al., 2014). See supplementary material for data stats. These language pairs present a diverse set of challenges for this problem, with Arabic and Czech being morphologically rich, German being syntactically divergent, and Spanish introducing local reorderings with respect to English.

NMT System: We trained a 2-layered LSTM encoder-decoder models with attention using the seq2seq-attn implementation (Kim, 2016). Please see supplementary material for settings.

Results: Figure 3 shows the results of various streaming agents. Our proposed STATIC-RW agent outperforms other methods while maintaining an AP $<$ 0.75 with a loss of less than 0.5 BLEU points on Arabic, Czech and Spanish. This was found to be consistent for all test-sets 2011-2014 (See under "small" models in Figure 4). In the case of German the loss at AP $<$ 0.75 was around 1.5 BLEU points. The syntactical divergence and rich morphology of German posits a

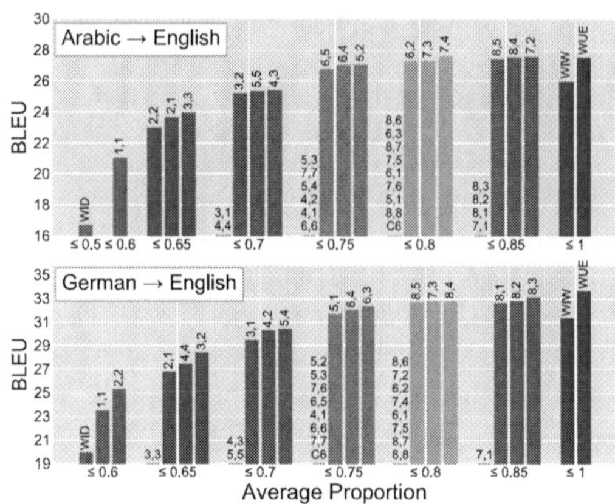 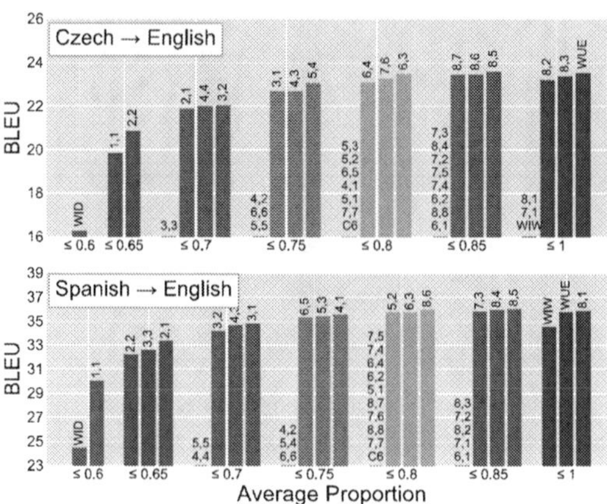

Figure 3: Results for various streaming AGENTS (WID, WIW, WUE, C6 (Chunk decoding with a N=6) and $\mathcal{S},\mathcal{RW}$ for STATIC-RW) on the tune-set. For each AP bucket, we only show the Agents with the top 3 BLEU scores in that bucket, with remaining listed in descending order of their BLEU scores.

bigger challenge and requires larger context than other language pairs. For example the conjugated verb in a German verb complex appears in the second position, while the main verb almost always occurs at the end of the sentence/phrase (Durrani et al., 2011). Our methods are also comparable to the more sophisticated techniques involving Reinforcement Learning to learn an agent introduced by Gu et al. (2017) and Satija and Pineau (2016), but without the overhead of expensive training for the agent.

Scalability: The preliminary results were obtained using models trained on the TED corpus only. We conducted further experiments by training models on larger data-sets (See the supplementary section again for data sizes) to see if our findings are scalable. We fine-tuned (Luong and Manning, 2015; Sajjad et al., 2017b) our models with the in-domain data to avoid domain disparity. We then re-ran our agents with the best $\mathcal{S},\mathcal{RW}$ values (with an AP under 0.75) for each language pair. Figure 4 ("large" models) shows that the BLEU loss from the respective oracle increased when the models were trained with bigger data sizes. This could be attributed to the increased lexical ambiguity from the large amount of out-domain data, which can only be resolved with additional contextual information. However our results were still better than the WIW agent, which also has an AP value above 0.8. Allowing similar AP, our STATIC-RW agents were able to restore the BLEU loss to be ≤ 1.5 for all language

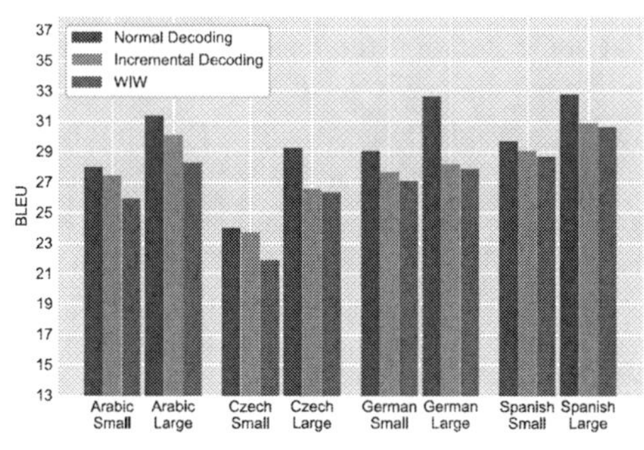

Figure 4: Averaged results on test-sets (2011-2014) using the models trained on small and large datasets using $AP \leq 0.75$. Detailed test-wise results are available in the supplementary material.

pairs except German-English. Detailed test results are available in the suplementary material.

5   Incremental Training

The limitation of previously described decoding approaches (chunk-based and incremental) is the mismatch between training and decoding. The training is carried on full sentences, however, at the test time, the decoder generates hypothesis based on incomplete source information. This discrepancy between training and decoding can be potentially harmful. In Section 2, we presented two methods to address the partial input sentence decoding problem, the *Chunk Decoder* and the *Incremental Decoder*. We now train models to match the corresponding decoding scenario.

5.1 Chunk Training

In chunk-based training, we simply split each training sentence into chunks of N tokens.[2] The corresponding target sentence for each chunk is generated by having a span of target words that are word-aligned[3] with the words in the source span. Chunking the data into smaller segments increases the training time significantly. To overcome this problem, we train a model on the full sentences using all the data and then fine-tune it with the in-domain chunked data.

5.2 Add-M Training

Next we formulate a training mechanism to match the incremental decoding described in Section 2. A way to achieve this is to force the attention on a local span of encoder states and block it from giving weight to the non-local (rightward) encoder states. The hope is that in the case of long-range dependencies, the model learns to predict these dependencies without the entire source context. Such a training procedure is non-trivial, as it requires dynamic inputs to the attention mechanism while training, including backpropagation where some encoder states which have been seen by the attention mechanism a greater number of times dynamically receiving more gradient inputs. We leave this idea as future work, while focusing on a data-driven technique to mimic this kind of training as described below.

We start with the first N words in a source sentence and generate target words that are aligned to these words. We then generate the next training instances with $N+M$, $N+2M$, $N+3M$ ... source words until the end of sentence has been reached.[4] The resulting training roughly mimics the decoding scenario where the source-side context is gradually built. The down-side of this method is that the data size increases quadratically, making the training infeasible. To overcome this, we fine-tune a model trained on full sentences with the in-domain corpus generated using this method.

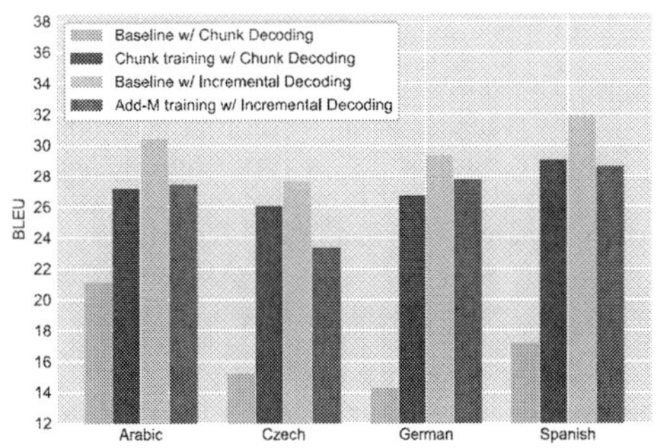

Figure 5: Averaged test set results on various training modifications

5.3 Results

The results in Figure 5 show that matching the chunk-decoding with corresponding chunk-based training significantly improves performance, with a gain of up to 12 BLEU points. However, we were not able to improve upon our incremental decoder, with the results deteriorating notably. One reason for this degradation is that the training/decoding scenarios are still not perfectly matched. The training pipeline in this case also sees the beginning of sentences much more often, which could lead to unnatural distributions being inferred within the model.

6 Conclusion

We addressed the problem of simultaneous translation by modifying the architecture in Neural MT decoder. We presented a tunable agent which decides the best segmentation strategy based on user-defined BLEU loss and AP constraints. Our results showed improvements over previously established WIW and WID methods. We additionally modified the Neural MT training to match the incremental decoding, which significantly improved the chunk-based decoding, but we did not observe any improvement using *Add-M Training*. The code for our incremental decoder and agents has been made available.[5] While were able to significantly improve the the chunk-based decoder, we did not observe any improvement using the *Add-M Training*. In the future we would like to change the training model to dynamically build the encoder and the attention model in order to match our incremental decoder.

---

[2] Although randomly segmenting the source sentence based on number of tokens is a naïve approach that does not take into account the linguistic properties, our goal here was to exactly match the training with the chunk-based decoding scenario.

[3] We used fast-align (Dyer et al., 2013) for alignments.

[4] We trained with $N = 6$ and $M = 1$ for our experiments.

[5] https://github.com/fdalvi/seq2seq-attn-stream

References

Ahmed Abdelali, Kareem Darwish, Nadir Durrani, and Hamdy Mubarak. 2016. Farasa: A fast and furious segmenter for arabic. In *Proceedings of the 2016 Conference of the North American Chapter of the Association for Computational Linguistics: Demonstrations*. Association for Computational Linguistics, San Diego, California, pages 11–16. http://www.aclweb.org/anthology/N16-3003.

Dzmitry Bahdanau, Kyunghyun Cho, and Yoshua Bengio. 2015. Neural machine translation by jointly learning to align and translate. In *ICLR*. http://arxiv.org/pdf/1409.0473v6.pdf.

Srinivas Bangalore, Vivek Kumar Rangarajan Sridhar, Prakash Kolan, Ladan Golipour, and Aura Jimenez. 2012. Real-time incremental speech-to-speech translation of dialogs. In *Proceedings of the 2012 Conference of the North American Chapter of the Association for Computational Linguistics: Human Language Technologies*. Association for Computational Linguistics, Montréal, Canada, pages 437–445.

Mauro Cettolo, Jan Niehues, Sebastian Stüker, Luisa Bentivogli, and Marcello Federico. 2014. Report on the 11th IWSLT Evaluation Campaign. *Proceedings of the International Workshop on Spoken Language Translation, Lake Tahoe, US* .

Kyunghyun Cho and Masha Esipova. 2016. Can neural machine translation do simultaneous translation? *CoRR* abs/1606.02012.

Nadir Durrani, Helmut Schmid, and Alexander Fraser. 2011. A Joint Sequence Translation Model with Integrated Reordering. In *Proceedings of the Association for Computational Linguistics: Human Language Technologies (ACL-HLT'11)*. Portland, OR, USA.

Nadir Durrani, Helmut Schmid, Alexander Fraser, Philipp Koehn, and Hinrich Schütze. 2015. The Operation Sequence Model – Combining N-Gram-based and Phrase-based Statistical Machine Translation. *Computational Linguistics* 41(2):157–186.

Chris Dyer, Victor Chahuneau, and Noah A. Smith. 2013. A simple, fast, and effective reparameterization of ibm model 2. In *Proceedings of NAACL'13*.

Andreas Eisele and Yu Chen. 2010. MultiUN: A Multilingual Corpus from United Nation Documents. In *Proceedings of the Seventh conference on International Language Resources and Evaluation*. Valleta, Malta.

Christian Fügen, Alex Waibel, and Muntsin Kolss. 2007. Simultaneous translation of lectures and speeches. *Machine Translation* 21(4):209–252.

Jiatao Gu, Graham Neubig, Kyunghyun Cho, and Victor O.K. Li. 2017. Learning to translate in real-time with neural machine translation. In *Proceedings of the 15th Conference of the European Chapter of the Association for Computational Linguistics: Volume 1, Long Papers*. Association for Computational Linguistics, Valencia, Spain, pages 1053–1062.

Yoon Kim. 2016. Seq2seq-attn. https://github.com/harvardnlp/seq2seq-attn.

Philipp Koehn, Hieu Hoang, Alexandra Birch, Chris Callison-Burch, Marcello Federico, Nicola Bertoldi, Brooke Cowan, Wade Shen, Christine Moran, Richard Zens, Chris Dyer, Ondrej Bojar, Alexandra Constantin, and Evan Herbst. 2007. Moses: Open source toolkit for statistical machine translation. In *Proceedings of the ACL 2007*. Prague, Czech Republic.

Minh-Thang Luong and Christopher D. Manning. 2015. Stanford Neural Machine Translation Systems for Spoken Language Domains. In *Proceedings of the International Workshop on Spoken Language Translation*. Da Nang, Vietnam.

Yusuke Oda, Graham Neubig, Sakriani Sakti, Tomoki Toda, and Satoshi Nakamura. 2014. Optimizing segmentation strategies for simultaneous speech translation. In *Proceedings of the 52nd Annual Meeting of the Association for Computational Linguistics (Volume 2: Short Papers)*. Association for Computational Linguistics, Baltimore, Maryland, pages 551–556. http://www.aclweb.org/anthology/P14-2090.

Hassan Sajjad, Fahim Dalvi, Nadir Durrani, Ahmed Abdelali, Yonatan Belinkov, and Stephan Vogel. 2017a. Challenging Language-Dependent Segmentation for Arabic: An Application to Machine Translation and Part-of-Speech Tagging. In *Proceedings of the 55th Annual Meeting of the Association for Computational Linguistics*. Association for Computational Linguistics, Vancouver, Canada.

Hassan Sajjad, Nadir Durrani, Fahim Dalvi, Yonatan Belinkov, and Stephan Vogel. 2017b. Neural Machine Translation Training in a Multi-Domain Scenario. In *Proceedings of the 14th International Workshop on Spoken Language Technology (IWSLT-14)*.

Harsh Satija and Joelle Pineau. 2016. Simultaneous machine translation using deep reinforcement learning. In *Abstraction in Reinforcement Learning Workshop*. International Conference on Machine Learning, New York, USA.

Rico Sennrich, Barry Haddow, and Alexandra Birch. 2016. Neural machine translation of rare words with subword units. In *Proceedings of the 54th Annual Meeting of the Association for Computational Linguistics (Volume 1: Long Papers)*. Association for Computational Linguistics, Berlin, Germany, pages 1715–1725. http://www.aclweb.org/anthology/P16-1162.

Rangarajan Sridhar, Vivek Kumar, John Chen, Srinivas Bangalore, Andrej Ljolje, and Rathinavelu Chengalvarayan. 2013. Segmentation strategies for streaming speech translation. In *Proceedings of the 2013 Conference of the North American Chapter of the Association for Computational Linguistics: Human Language Technologies*. Association for Computational Linguistics, Atlanta, Georgia, pages 230–238. `http://www.aclweb.org/anthology/N13-1023`.

Ilya Sutskever, Oriol Vinyals, and Quoc VV Le. 2014. Sequence to Sequence Learning with Neural Networks. In *Advances in neural information processing systems*. pages 3104–3112.

Mahsa Yarmohammadi, Vivek Kumar Rangarajan Sridhar, Srinivas Bangalore, and Baskaran Sankaran. 2013. Incremental segmentation and decoding strategies for simultaneous translation. In *Proceedings of the Sixth International Joint Conference on Natural Language Processing*. Asian Federation of Natural Language Processing, Nagoya, Japan, pages 1032–1036. `http://www.aclweb.org/anthology/I13-1141`.

Learning Hidden Unit Contribution for Adapting Neural Machine Translation Models

David Vilar

Amazon Research

Berlin, Germany

dvilar@amazon.com

Abstract

In this paper we explore the use of *Learning Hidden Unit Contribution* for the task of neural machine translation. The method was initially proposed in the context of speech recognition for adapting a general system to the specific acoustic characteristics of each speaker. Similar in spirit, in a machine translation framework we want to adapt a general system to a specific domain. We show that the proposed method achieves improvements of up to 2.6 BLEU points over a general system, and up to 6 BLEU points if the initial system has only been trained on out-of-domain data, a situation which may easily happen in practice. The good performance together with its short training time and small memory footprint make it a very attractive solution for domain adaptation.

1 Introduction

Domain adaptation for neural machine translation (NMT) is starting to get more attention from the scientific community. Often researchers and machine translation practitioners want to improve the performance of their systems on a domain for which they were not explicitly optimized. Due to the high training times needed to develop NMT systems, often up to several weeks, efficient methods for improving an existing system for a specific domain can have important practical applications.

In this paper we review "Learning Hidden Unit Contribution" (§ 3), a method developed initially for speaker adaptation in speech recognition systems, and apply it to the task of neural machine translation (§§ 4 and 5). We show that it improves translation quality on in-domain data, while at the same time keeping the translation quality of out-of-domain data intact (§ 6). Due to its small memory footprint and short training time it can be realistically applied to adapt large, general domain systems in order to improve their performance on specific domains.

2 Neural Machine Translation

In this section we will provide a short overview of NMT. For a more detailed description the reader is referred to existing literature. An NMT system is mainly composed of two parts. The first one, called the encoder, produces a sequence of vectors which constitute a representation of the input sentence in a continuous vector space. The decoder takes this sequence of vectors and generates a new sequence of words in the target language, which corresponds to the translation of the given sentence. An additional attention mechanism helps guiding the translation process.

Most NMT systems are based on recurrent networks, usually LSTMs or GRUs (Bahdanau et al., 2014), although recently new approaches to neural machine translation have been proposed (Vaswani et al., 2017; Gehring et al., 2017) which are not based on recurrent networks, but keep the encoder-decoder structure. All the approaches described in this paper are equally applicable to these models.

3 Learning Hidden Unit Contribution

Learning Hidden Unit Contribution (LHUC) is a method first introduced by Swietojanski and Renals (2014) and Swietojanski et al. (2016) for speaker adaptation in neural speech recognition systems. The goal of speaker adaptation is to tailor an existing speech recognition system to the specific acoustic characteristics of a given speaker. In normal conditions, the amount of training data available for one speaker is rather limited; therefore, the authors' goal was to develop a method that would be able to adapt with a small sample size. Additionally, when adapting a system, there is the danger that the system's performance on the

Proceedings of NAACL-HLT 2018, pages 500–505

New Orleans, Louisiana, June 1 - 6, 2018. ©2018 Association for Computational Linguistics

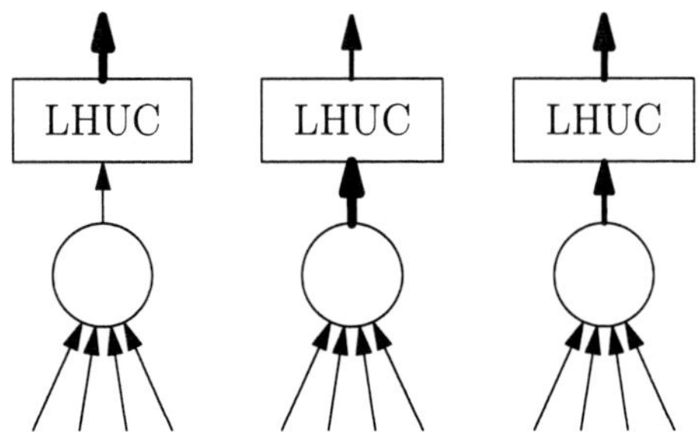

Figure 1: Illustration of the LHUC approach. Three units of a hidden layer are depicted. Each unit has an additional component that can scale the value of the original output. The number of additional parameters is linear in the number of hidden units (see Eq. 2).

general domain degrades significantly due to over-fitting, what in neural network literature is sometimes called "catastrophic forgetting" (McCloskey and Cohen, 1989; Ratcliff, 1990).

The intuition behind LHUC is that different network units specialize on different aspects of the task, and thus, when shifting domain the importance of each unit may change from the original domain on which the system was trained. An example of this behaviour (unrelated to translation) is shown by Radford et al. (2017). They trained a character-level language model on product review texts and found out that one specific neuron provided a quite accurate representation of the sentiment (positive or negative) of the text. While this neuron can provide valuable information for this task, it may not be so relevant for other domains where sentiment is not as important (e.g. news). At the same time, other neurons may become more important (e.g. ensuring a more formal style of the text).

LHUC introduces an additional multiplicative amplitude element to the output of each hidden unit in the network. As such the contribution of the hidden unit can be amplified (values greater than 1) for the units that are more relevant to the task, or dampened (values close to 0) for units that are not as important. The approach is illustrated in Figure 1. Coming back to the sentiment neuron example above, for tasks where sentiment is important (product reviews), LHUC will assign a high weight to the sentiment neuron, while for other tasks (news), the corresponding weight will be low. The weights are learned automatically from the available in-domain data.

More formally, let

$$\mathbf{h}^{(l)} = \phi_\theta(\mathbf{h}^{(l-1)}, \dots) \tag{1}$$

be a general equation for the output of a layer in a neural network, parametrized by the set θ. In case of a feed-forward layer, ϕ would be an affine transformation followed by a non-linearity, θ would be the parameter matrix of the linear transformation and the bias vector, and no additional arguments would be required. Other models like LSTM layers (Hochreiter and Schmidhuber, 1997) have a more complex structure and a memory state as an additional argument.

As the LHUC method is very general, the actual form of the layer activations does not need to be specified in complete detail; it is only important to note that it produces a vector, and is dependent of the previous layer. LHUC modifies the activation function by introducing a multplicative element

$$\mathbf{h}_{\text{LHUC}}^{(l)} = a(\boldsymbol{\rho}^{(l)}) \circ \phi_\theta(\mathbf{h}_{\text{LHUC}}^{(l-1)}, \dots) \tag{2}$$

where $\boldsymbol{\rho}^{(l)}$ is a layer-dependent vector of new parameters (independent of θ), of the same dimension as $\mathbf{h}^{(l)}$, and $\circ$ denotes element-wise vector multiplication. The $a(\cdot)$ function is a scaled element-wise sigmoid function. The range of the scaled sigmoid is limited to the interval $[0, 2]$[1]

$$a(\mathbf{x}) = \frac{2}{1 + e^{-\mathbf{x}}}. \tag{3}$$

The parameter vectors $\boldsymbol{\rho}^{(l)}$ are trained using standard backpropagation, keeping the initial parameter set θ constant during the LHUC training pass. As can be seen, the number of parameters grows only linearly in the number of units in each layer, instead as the usual quadratic growth for the number of parameters in most neural models.

4 Domain Adaptation for NMT

Domain adaptation for phrase-based and related approaches to machine translation has been extensively investigated, e.g. (Schwenk, 2008; Axelrod et al., 2011; Carpuat et al., 2013). Neural machine translation, being a relatively new approach to MT, has not seen so many works going into this direction yet. Previous methods can of course still be applied as long as they are model-independent, e.g. data selection methods as shown

---

[1] The value of 2 is chosen as to be able to amplify the value (it can be doubled) but without overshadowing the value of the other units, which could happen with bigger values.

in (van der Wees et al., 2017) or self-training approaches like (Bertoldi and Federico, 2009), of which back-translation (Sennrich et al., 2015) can be considered a special case.

Specific for neural machine translation, Freitag and Al-Onaizan (2016) present a really simple method, where the parameters of an already trained system are taken as the starting point of another training run using only in-domain data. This simple method achieves good results and has the advantage that no additional implementation work has to be carried out. Chu et al. (2017) propose a refinement of this method where the in-domain data is mixed with the out-of-domain data.

Chen et al. (2017) propose to use a domain classifier to weight the cost of the training data differently according to the similarity to the in-domain data, in what can be considered a tighter integration of previous data-selection methods.

Sennrich et al. (2016) introduce a simple method for controlling the politeness of an NMT system, which can also be used for domain adaptation. They add a special tag to the source sentence denoting the politeness level of the source sentence and the system is able to use this information to improve the translation output. This technique can be extended to domain adaptation by combining the text of the different domains and marking them with a specific, domain-dependent tag. Johnson et al. (2016) use this technique in an "extreme" domain adaptation setting, where the domains are actually different languages.

5   LHUC for Domain Adaptation of NMT

In this paper we propose to use LHUC for domain adaptation of NMT systems. For this, we first train a system on the general domain data. Once such a system is available, we add the LHUC component and adapt it for the characteristics of the domain, similar to the adaptation to the acoustic characteristics of a speaker in the case of speech recognition.

We will explore two different scenarios, in the first one all the data, both in-domain and out-of-domain, is available from the beginning. As such the initial system already has seen in-domain examples at training time and the domain adaptation step is mainly a "fine tuning" step.

In the second scenario we will assume that the initial system has been trained only on out-of-domain data. This system will then be adapted

Corpus	Sents	Words	Voc
WMT	5M	135M/141M	1.8M/877K
IWSLT	197K	3.7M/4M	122K/55K

Table 1: Training corpora statistics. "Sents" denotes number of sentences, "Words" refers to number of running words after tokenization and "Voc" is the size of the vocabulary, e.g. the number of unique words in the corresponding corpus.

for the new in-domain data, which has not been seen at the initial training stage. This scenario has an important role in practical applications, e.g. a general domain system has been trained and tuned to offer general domain translation, but it needs to be adapted to specific domains in order to provide better quality. In some cases, the time necessary for adapting such a system may also play a critical role on the applicability of the method.

LHUC provides an elegant solution for domain adaptation. Due to its reduced number of parameters it can be trained in a much shorter time than a full system. Furthermore, because it is an "add-on" for an already existing system it can be activated or de-activated on-demand. This effectively solves the catastrophic forgetting effect found in other adaptation techniques, as the general system can still be accessed at any time.

6   Experimental Results

Similar to Freitag and Al-Onaizan (2016), we present results on the IWSLT 2016[2] German to English TED dataset (Cettolo et al., 2016), consisting of transcribed and translated TED talks. As out-of-domain data we use the same year's WMT data (Bojar et al., 2016). We report results on the TED 2013 and TED 2014 (the newest ones with provided references) and additionally on the newstest 2016 dataset for measuring the performance on out-of-domain data. Statistics for the training corpora are given in Table 1. It can be seen that the WMT data (out-of-domain) is an order of magnitude bigger that the in-domain IWSLT data.

Our system is a recurrent encoder-decoder NMT model, with one bidirectional LSTM layer with 1024 units in the encoder and one layer with 1024 units in the decoder. The data has been BPE-encoded using 32K merge operations, and the em-

---

[2]Freitag and Al-Onaizan (2016) used an older version of the corpora.

bedding layer has a dimension of 512. Training has been performed with the Adam algorithm (Kingma and Ba, 2014). The provided TED dev set was used as stopping criterion (or newstest14 for the case of a WMT-only system). Experiments have been carried out using Sockeye (Hieber et al., 2017), and the LHUC code has been open sourced as part of it.

For LHUC experiments, both the encoder and decoder hidden units have been expanded with the additional scaling.

As discussed in Section 5 we will differentiate two conditions: in the "full training data" condition, both the out-of-domain and in-domain data are available for training the initial system. In the "growing training data" condition, the initial system is trained only on out-of-domain data.

We will compare the performance of the LHUC method with the "continuation of training" proposed by Freitag and Al-Onaizan (2016). Both methods can start from an already trained system and refine the training on the in-domain data. For the full training data condition we also explore the tagging technique similar to the one proposed by Sennrich et al. (2016).

6.1 Full Training Data Condition

In this data condition, both the WMT and IWSLT training data have been combined together. Each mini-batch in training is selected randomly, so that potentially samples from both domains are presented to the system. In this way there is no implicit domain adaptation effect due to the presentation of the data.

The results, in terms of BLEU score, can be seen in Table 2. Even when the in-domain data is already included in the set used for training the original system, the domain adaptation techniques are able to increase translation quality. Using continuation of training we are able to improve the performance by up to 1.2% absolute. However if we look at the translation quality on the out-of-domain data set we see the catastrophic forgetting effect, with a drop of 1.7 BLEU points.

LHUC achieves an even bigger improvement in translation quality: up to 2.6%. If we would blindly apply the LHUC enhanced system to the out-of-domain data we would again observe the catastrophic forgetting effect, in fact even more pronounced as with continuation of training (number in parenthesis in the corresponding column in

Table 2). However in practice this is a non-issue, as the LHUC can easily be deactivated, as discussed in Section 5.

Adding labels to the training data also proves to be an efficient domain adaptation method, with the advantage that it can be combined with the other methods. The improvements due to continuation of training or LHUC are not as big in this case.

For reference, the results of training on in-domain data only have also been included.

6.2 Growing Training Data Condition

In this condition the initial system has only been trained on WMT data. It is also worth noting that this also applies to the BPE vocabulary. It is trained only on the WMT data and then applied to the IWSLT data for the adaptation techniques.

In this case we see even bigger improvements with respect to the baseline system, up to 6 BLEU points. This is mainly due to the baseline system being trained only on out-of-domain data. In this way, in the domain adaptation step, new, unseen training data is added to system. The results are reported in Table 3. Interestingly, the absolute scores of the adapted systems are very close to those reported in Table 2, showing that the domain adaptation techniques can efficiently include new information into the original model. The catastrophic forgetting effect is also more pronounced in this data condition, but we note again that it does not effect the LHUC method.

It is also interesting to note that the performance of the baseline systems on out-of-domain data in both data conditions is the same, indicating that the in-domain data does not really help for the out-of-domain set. This is also indicated by the low score of the in-domain only system on out-of-domain data. Both effects can be explained by comparing the relative sizes of the datasets, as shown in Table 1.

6.3 Efficiency Considerations

As pointed out before, the number of parameters is linear in the number of units in the network. In our specific case we have a total of 2048 units in the encoder (a bidirectional layer with 1024 units in each direction) and 1024 units in the decoder. Using a 32-bit float representation, the overhead of LHUC amounts to just 12KB. For comparison a full model stored on disk in compressed npz format needs 335MB. This shows that LHUC can realistically be used for storing a large amount of

	newstest16 (OOD)	TED 2013 (ID)	TED 2014 (ID)
WMT (OOD) + IWSLT (ID)	33.7	35.9	30.5
+ continuation (ID)	32.0	36.7	31.7
+ LHUC (ID)	33.7 (30.8)	37.9	33.1
OOD + ID labelled	34.4	36.8	32.7
+ continuation (ID)	31.6	37.8	32.9
+ LHUC (ID)	34.4 (32.4)	38.4	33.6
IWSLT only (ID)	16.7	32.4	27.5

Table 2: BLEU scores [%] for the Full Training Data condition. "OOD" denotes out-of-domain data, "ID" denotes in-domain data. For LHUC results, the number in parenthesis shows the result of applying the adapted system to the out-of-domain data (which would not be applied in practice).

	newstest16 (OOD)	TED 2013 (ID)	TED 2014 (ID)
WMT only (OOD)	33.7	31.7	27.3
+ continuation (ID)	30.1	36.8	32.2
+ LHUC (ID)	33.7 (29.7)	37.7	32.8
IWSLT only (ID)	16.7	32.4	27.5

Table 3: BLEU scores [%] for the Growing Training Data condition.

adapted systems.

As for training time, in most experiments the best parameters for LHUC were already achieved in the first checkpoints. On a K80 GPU the best parameter can be found in under one hour for our datasets (continuation needs close to 2h).

7 Conclusions

We have shown how to effectively apply LHUC, a technique first proposed for speaker adaptation in speech recognition, for adapting neural machine translation systems. LHUC achieves good results compared to other domain adaptation methods and due to its low memory footprint and efficient training time can be realistically applied for on-demand adaptation of big systems. In addition it does not suffer the catastrophic forgetting effect, as the LHUC component can be activated or deactivated as needed.

References

Amittai Axelrod, Xiaodong He, and Jianfeng Gao. 2011. Domain adaptation via pseudo in-domain data selection. In *Proceedings of the conference on empirical methods in natural language processing*. Association for Computational Linguistics, pages 355–362.

Dzmitry Bahdanau, Kyunghyun Cho, and Yoshua Bengio. 2014. Neural Machine Translation by Jointly Learning to Align and Translate. *CoRR* abs/1409.0473.

Nicola Bertoldi and Marcello Federico. 2009. Domain adaptation for statistical machine translation with monolingual resources. In *Proceedings of the fourth workshop on statistical machine translation*. Association for Computational Linguistics, pages 182–189.

Ondřej Bojar, Rajen Chatterjee, Christian Federmann, Yvette Graham, Barry Haddow, Matthias Huck, Antonio Jimeno Yepes, Philipp Koehn, Varvara Logacheva, Christof Monz, et al. 2016. Findings of the 2016 conference on machine translation. In *Proceedings of the First Conference on Machine Translation: Volume 2, Shared Task Papers*. volume 2, pages 131–198.

Marine Carpuat, Hal Daume III, Katharine Henry, Ann Irvine, Jagadeesh Jagarlamudi, and Rachel Rudinger. 2013. Sensespotting: Never let your parallel data tie you to an old domain. In *Proceedings of the 51st Annual Meeting of the Association for Computational Linguistics (Volume 1: Long Papers)*. volume 1, pages 1435–1445.

Mauro Cettolo, Jan Niehues, Sebastian Stüker, Luisa Bentivogli, Roldano Cattoni, and Marcello Federico. 2016. The IWSLT 2016 Evaluation Campaign. In

Proceedings of the Internation Workshop on Spoken Language Translation.

Boxing Chen, Colin Cherry, George Foster, and Samuel Larkin. 2017. Cost weighting for neural machine translation domain adaptation. In *Proceedings of the First Workshop on Neural Machine Translation.* pages 40–46.

Chenhui Chu, Raj Dabre, and Sadao Kurohashi. 2017. An empirical comparison of domain adaptation methods for neural machine translation. In *Proceedings of the 55th Annual Meeting of the Association for Computational Linguistics (Volume 2: Short Papers).* Association for Computational Linguistics, pages 385–391. `https://doi.org/10.18653/v1/P17-2061.`

Markus Freitag and Yaser Al-Onaizan. 2016. Fast domain adaptation for neural machine translation. *arXiv preprint arXiv:1612.06897 .*

Jonas Gehring, Michael Auli, David Grangier, Denis Yarats, and Yann N. Dauphin. 2017. Convolutional sequence to sequence learning. *CoRR* abs/1705.03122. `http://arxiv.org/abs/1705.03122.`

Felix Hieber, Tobias Domhan, Michael Denkowski, David Vilar, Artem Sokolov, Ann Clifton, and Matt Post. 2017. Sockeye: A Toolkit for Neural Machine Translation. *ArXiv e-prints .*

Sepp Hochreiter and Jürgen Schmidhuber. 1997. Long short-term memory. *Neural computation* 9(8):1735–1780.

Melvin Johnson, Mike Schuster, Quoc V Le, Maxim Krikun, Yonghui Wu, Zhifeng Chen, Nikhil Thorat, Fernanda Viégas, Martin Wattenberg, Greg Corrado, et al. 2016. Google's multilingual neural machine translation system: enabling zero-shot translation. *arXiv preprint arXiv:1611.04558 .*

Diederik P. Kingma and Jimmy Ba. 2014. Adam: A method for stochastic optimization. *CoRR* abs/1412.6980.

Michael McCloskey and Neal J Cohen. 1989. Catastrophic interference in connectionist networks: The sequential learning problem. *Psychology of learning and motivation* 24:109–165.

Alec Radford, Rafal Jozefowicz, and Ilya Sutskever. 2017. Learning to generate reviews and discovering sentiment. *arXiv preprint arXiv:1704.01444 .*

Roger Ratcliff. 1990. Connectionist models of recognition memory: Constraints imposed by learning and forgetting functions. *Psychological review* 97(2):285–308.

Holger Schwenk. 2008. Investigations on large-scale lightly-supervised training for statistical machine translation. In *Proceedings of the Internation Workshop on Spoken Language Translation.* pages 182–189.

Rico Sennrich, Barry Haddow, and Alexandra Birch. 2015. Improving neural machine translation models with monolingual data. *arXiv preprint arXiv:1511.06709 .*

Rico Sennrich, Barry Haddow, and Alexandra Birch. 2016. Controlling politeness in neural machine translation via side constraints. In *Proceedings of the 2016 Conference of the North American Chapter of the Association for Computational Linguistics: Human Language Technologies.* Association for Computational Linguistics, San Diego, California, pages 35–40. `http://www.aclweb.org/anthology/N16-1005.`

Pawel Swietojanski, Jinyu Li, and Steve Renals. 2016. Learning hidden unit contributions for unsupervised acoustic model adaptation. *IEEE/ACM Transactions on Audio, Speech, and Language Processing* 24(8):1450–1463.

Pawel Swietojanski and Steve Renals. 2014. Learning hidden unit contributions for unsupervised speaker adaptation of neural network acoustic models. In *Spoken Language Technology Workshop (SLT), 2014 IEEE.* IEEE, pages 171–176.

Marlies van der Wees, Arianna Bisazza, and Christof Monz. 2017. Dynamic data selection for neural machine translation. *CoRR* abs/1708.00712.

Ashish Vaswani, Noam Shazeer, Niki Parmar, Jakob Uszkoreit, Llion Jones, Aidan N. Gomez, Lukasz Kaiser, and Illia Polosukhin. 2017. Attention is all you need. *CoRR* abs/1706.03762. `http://arxiv.org/abs/1706.03762.`

Neural Machine Translation Decoding with Terminology Constraints

Eva Hasler[1], Adrià de Gispert[1,2], Gonzalo Iglesias[1], Bill Byrne[1,2]

[1]SDL Research, Cambridge, UK
[2]Department of Engineering, University of Cambridge, UK
`{ehasler,agispert,giglesias,bbyrne}@sdl.com`

Abstract

Despite the impressive quality improvements yielded by neural machine translation (NMT) systems, controlling their translation output to adhere to user-provided terminology constraints remains an open problem. We describe our approach to constrained neural decoding based on finite-state machines and multi-stack decoding which supports target-side constraints as well as constraints with corresponding aligned input text spans. We demonstrate the performance of our framework on multiple translation tasks and motivate the need for constrained decoding with attentions as a means of reducing misplacement and duplication when translating user constraints.

1 Introduction

Adapting an NMT system with domain-specific data is one way to adjust its output vocabulary to better match the target domain (Luong and Manning, 2015; Sennrich et al., 2016). Another way to encourage the beam decoder to produce certain words in the output is to explicitly reward n-grams provided by an SMT system (Stahlberg et al., 2017) or language model (Gulcehre et al., 2017) or to modify the vocabulary distribution of the decoder with suggestions from a terminology (Chatterjee et al., 2017). While providing lexical guidance to the decoder, these methods do not strictly enforce a terminology. This is a requisite, however, for companies wanting to ensure that brand-related information is rendered correctly and consistently when translating web content or manuals and is often more important than translation quality alone. Although domain adaptation and guided decoding can help to reduce errors in these use cases, they do not provide reliable solutions.

Another recent line of work strictly enforces a given set of words in the output (Anderson et al., 2017; Hokamp and Liu, 2017; Crego et al., 2016).

Anderson et al. address the task of image captioning with *constrained beam search* where constraints are given by image tags and constraint permutations are encoded in a finite-state acceptor (FSA). Hokamp and Liu propose *grid beam search* to enforce target-side constraints for domain adaptation via terminology. However, since there is no correspondence between constraints and the source words they cover, correct constraint placement is not guaranteed and the corresponding source words may be translated more than once. Crego et al. replace entities with special tags that remain unchanged during translation and are replaced in a post-processing step using attention weights. Given good alignments, this method can translate entities correctly but it requires training data with entity tags and excludes the entities from model scoring.

We address decoding with constraints to produce translations that respect the terminologies of corporate customers while maintaining the high quality of unconstrained translations. To this end, we apply the constrained beam search of Anderson et al. to machine translation and propose to employ alignment information between target-side constraints and their corresponding source words. The lack of explicit alignments in NMT systems poses an extra challenge compared to statistical MT where alignments are given by translation rules. We address the problem of *constraint placement* by expanding constraints when the NMT model is attending to the correct source span. We also reduce *output duplication* by masking covered constraints in the NMT attention model.

2 Constrained Beam Search

A naive approach to decoding with constraints would be to use a large beam size and select from the set of complete hypotheses the best that satis-

506

fies all constraints. However, this is infeasible in practice because it would require searching a potentially very large space to ensure that even hypotheses with low model score due to the inclusion of a constraint would be part of the set of outputs. A better strategy is to force the decoder to produce hypotheses that satisfy the constraints regardless of their score and thus guide the decoder into the right area of the search space. We follow Anderson et al. (2017) in organizing our beam search into multiple stacks corresponding to subsets of satisfied constraints as defined by FSA states.

2.1 Finite-state Acceptors for Constraints

Before decoding, we build an FSA defining the constrained target language for an input sentence. It contains all permutations of constraints interleaved with loops over the remaining vocabulary.

Phrase Constraints: Constraints consisting of multiple tokens are encoded by one state per token. We refer to states within a phrase as intermediate states and restrict their outgoing vocabulary to the next token in the phrase.

Alternative Constraints: Synonyms of constraints can be defined as alternatives and encoded as different arcs connecting the same states. When alternatives consist of multiple tokens, the alternative paths will contain intermediate states.

Figure 1 shows an FSA with constraints C_1 and C_2 where C_1 is a phrase (yielding intermediate states s_1, s_4) and C_2 consists of two single-token alternatives. Both permutations $C_1 C_2$ and $C_2 C_1$ lead to final state s_5 with both constraints satisfied.

2.2 Multi-Stack Decoding

When extending a hypothesis to satisfy a constraint which is not among the top-k vocabulary items in the current beam, the overall likelihood may drop and the hypothesis may be pruned in subsequent steps. To prevent this, the extended hypothesis is placed on a new stack along with other hypotheses that satisfy the same set of constraints. Each stack maps to an acceptor state which helps to keep track of the permitted extensions for hypotheses on this stack. The stack where a hypothesis should be placed is found by following the appropriate arc leaving the current acceptor state. The stack mapping to the final state is used to generate complete hypotheses. At each time step, all stacks are pruned to the beam size k and therefore the actual beam size for constrained decoding depends on the number of acceptor states.

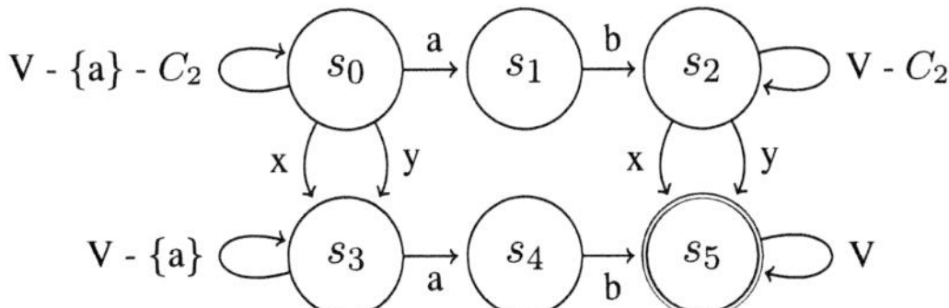

Figure 1: Example of FSA for two constraints $C_1 = ab$ and $C_2 = \{x, y\}$.

2.3 Decoding with Attentions

Since an acceptor encoding c single-token constraints has 2^c states, the constrained search of Anderson et al. (2017) can be inefficient for large numbers of constraints. In particular, all unsatisfied constraints are expanded at each time step t which increases decoding complexity from $\mathcal{O}(tk)$ for normal beam search to $\mathcal{O}(tk2^c)$. Hokamp and Liu (2017) organize their grid beam search into beams that group hypotheses with the same number of constraints, thus their decoding time is $\mathcal{O}(tkc)$. However, this means that different constraints will compete for completion of the same hypothesis and their placement is determined locally. We assume that a target-side constraint can come with an aligned source phrase which is encoded as a span in source sentence S and stored with the acceptor arc label:

$$s_0 \xrightarrow{C \text{ [i,j]}} s_1 \qquad j > i, \quad 0 \leq i, j \leq |S|$$

Because the attention weights in attention-based decoders function as soft alignments from the target to the source sentence (Alkhouli and Ney, 2017), we use them to decide at which position a constraint should be inserted in the output. At each time step in a hypothesis, we determine the source position with the maximum attention. If it falls into a constrained source span and this span matches an outgoing arc in the current acceptor state, we extend the current hypothesis with the arc label. Thus, the outgoing arcs in non-intermediate states are active or inactive depending on the current attentions. This reduces the complexity from $\mathcal{O}(tk2^c)$ to $\mathcal{O}(tkc)$ by ignoring all but one constraint permutation and in practice, disabling vocabulary loops saves extra time.

State-specific Attention Mechanism: Once a constraint has been completed, we need to ensure that its source span will not be translated again. We force the decoder to respect covered constraints by masking their spans during all future expansions of the hypothesis. This is done by zeroing out the attention weights on covered positions to exclude them from the context vector computed by the attention mechanism.

Implications: Constrained decoding with aligned source phrases relies on the quality of the source-target pairs. Over- and under-translation can occur as a result of incomplete source or target phrases in the terminology.

Special Cases: Monitoring the source position with the maximum attention is a relatively strict criterion to decide where a constraint should be placed in the output. It turns out that depending on the language pair, the decoder may produce translations of neighbouring source tokens when attending to a constrained source span.[1] The strict requirement of only producing constraint tokens can be relaxed to accommodate such cases, for example by allowing extra tokens before (s_1) or after (s_2) constraint C while attending to span $[i, j]$,

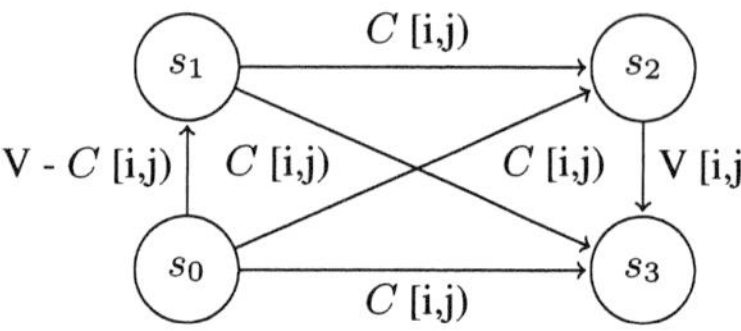

Conversely, the decoder may never place the maximum attention on a constraint span which can lead to empty translations. Relaxing this requirement using thresholding on the attention weights to determine positions with secondary attention can help in those cases.

3 Experimental Setup

We build attention-based neural machine translation models (Bahdanau et al., 2015) using the Blocks implementation of van Merriënboer et al. (2015) for English-German and English-Chinese translation in both directions. We combine three models per language pair as ensembles and further combine the NMT systems with n-grams extracted from SMT lattices using Lattice minimum Bayes-risk as described by Stahlberg et al. (2017), referred to as LNMT. We decode with a beam size of 12 and length normalization (Johnson et al., 2017) and back off to constrained decoding without attentions when decoding with attentions fails.[2] We report lowercase BLEU using mteval-v13.pl.

---

[1] For example, to produce an article before a noun when the constrained source span includes just the noun.

[2] This usually applies to less than 2% of the inputs.

3.1 Data

Our models are trained on the data provided for the 2017 Workshop for Machine Translation (Bojar et al., 2017). We tokenize and truecase the English-German data and apply compound splitting when the source language is German. The training data for the NMT systems is augmented with backtranslation data (Sennrich et al., 2016). For English-Chinese, we tokenize and lowercase the data. We apply byte-pair encoding (Sennrich et al., 2017) to all data.

3.2 Terminology Constraints

We run experiments with two types of constraints to evaluate our constrained decoder.

Gold Constraints: For each input sentence, we extract up to two tokens from the reference which were not produced by the baseline system, favouring rarer words. This aims at testing the performance in a setup where users may provide corrections to the NMT output which are to be incorporated into the translation. These reference tokens may consist of one or more subwords. Similarly, we extract phrases of up to five subwords surrounding a reference token missing from the baseline output. We do not have access to aligned source words for gold constraints.

Dictionary Constraints: We automatically extract bilingual dictionary entries using terms and phrases from the reference translations as candidates in order to ensure that the entries are relevant for the inputs. In a real setup, the dictionaries would be provided by customers and would be expected to contain correct translations without ambiguity. We apply a filter of English stop words and verbs to the candidates and look them up in a pruned phrase table to find likely pairs, resulting in entries as shown below:[3]

English	German
ICJ	IGH
The Wall Street Journal	The Wall Street Journal
Dead Sea	Tote Meer|Toten Meer

For evaluation purposes, we ensure that dictionary entries match the reference when applying them to an input sentence.

4 Results

The results for decoding with terminology constraints are shown in Table 1a and 1b where each

---

[3] Our dictionaries are available on request.

	dev (lr)	rep	test15	test16	test17
eng-ger-wmt17					
LNMT	24.9 (1.00)	443	28.1	34.7	27.0
+ 2 gold tokens	29.2 (1.14)	1141	33.4	40.9	32.3
+ 1 gold phrase	36.8 (1.09)	880	40.5	46.7	39.6
+ dictionary (v1)	26.4 (1.03)	610	29.6	36.4	28.8
+ dictionary (v2)	26.6 (1.02)	471	29.9	37.0	29.1
ger-eng-wmt17					
LNMT	31.2 (1.01)	307	33.5	40.7	34.6
+ 2 gold tokens	34.6 (1.14)	745	37.7	44.8	38.5
+ 1 gold phrase	42.3 (1.08)	550	45.7	51.3	46.4
+ dictionary (v1)	32.4 (1.02)	353	34.7	41.8	36.2
+ dictionary (v2)	32.5 (1.01)	320	34.6	41.9	36.0

(a) Results for English-German language pairs

	dev (lr)	test17
eng-chi-wmt17		
LNMT	30.8 (0.95)	31.0
+ 2 gold tokens	33.8 (1.10)	34.2
+ 1 gold phrase	40.6 (1.06)	41.2
+ dictionary (v1)	34.0 (1.01)	33.7
+ dictionary (v2)	33.9 (0.98)	34.1
chi-eng-wmt17		
LNMT	21.2 (1.00)	23.5
+ 2 gold tokens	23.3 (1.13)	25.5
+ 1 gold phrase	30.1 (1.09)	32.3
+ dictionary (v1)	23.0 (1.06)	25.5
+ dictionary (v2)	23.4 (1.03)	25.4

(b) Results for English-Chinese language pairs

Table 1: BLEU scores and dev length ratios for decoding with gold constraints (without attentions) followed by results for dictionary constraints without (v1) or with (v2) attentions. The column *rep* shows the number of character 7-grams that occur more than once within a sentence of the dev set, see Section 4.3.

section contains the results for gold constraints followed by dictionary constraints.

4.1 Results with Gold Constraints

Decoding with gold constraints yields large BLEU gains over LNMT for all language pairs. However, the length ratio on the dev set increases significantly. Inspecting the output reveals that this is often caused by constraints being translated more than once which can lead to whole passages being retranslated. Phrase constraints seem to integrate better into the output than single token constraints which may be due to the longer gold context being fed back to the NMT state.

4.2 Results with Dictionary Constraints

Decoding with up to two dictionary constraints per sentence yields gains of up to 3 BLEU. This is partly because we do not control whether LNMT already produced the constraint tokens and because not all sentences have dictionary matches. The length ratios are better compared to the gold experiments which we attribute to our filtering of tokens such as verbs which tend to influence the general word order more than nouns, for example.

Decoding with or without attentions yields similar BLEU scores overall and a consistent improvement for English-German. Note that decoding with attentions is sensitive to errors in the automatically extracted dictionary entries.

Output Duplication The first three examples in Table 2 show English↔German translations where decoding without attentions has generated both the target side of the constraint and the translation preferred by the NMT system. When using the attentions, each constraint is only translated once.

Constraint Placement The fourth example demonstrates the importance of tying constraints to source words. Decoding without attentions fails to translate *Zeichen* as *signs* because the alternative *sign* already appears in the translation of *Zeichensprache* as *sign language*. When using the attentions, *signs* is generated at the correct position in the output.

4.3 Output length ratio and repetitions

To back up our hypothesis that increases in length ratio are related to output duplication, Table 1a column *rep* shows the number of repeated character 7-grams within a sentence of the dev set, ignoring stop words and overlapping n-grams. This confirms that constrained decoding with attentions reduces the number of repeated n-grams in the output. While this does not account for alignments to the source or capture duplicated translations with unrelated surface forms, it provides evidence that the outputs are not just shorter than for decoding without attentions but in fact contain fewer repetitions and likely fewer duplicated translations.

4.4 Comparison of decoding speeds

To evaluate the speed of constrained decoding with and without attentions, we decode newstest-

eng-ger-wmt17	Example 1	Example 2
Source	It already has the **budget** ...	And it often costs over a hundred dollars to obtain the required **identity card**.
Constraints	Budget [4,5)	Ausweis [12,14)
LNMT	Es hat bereits den **Haushalt**...	Und es kostet oft mehr als hundert Dollar, um die erforderliche **Personalausweis** zu erhalten.
+ dictionary (v1)	Das **Budget** hat bereits den **Haushalt**...	Und es kostet oft mehr als hundert Dollar, um den **Ausweis** zu erhalten, um die erforderliche **Personalausweis** zu erhalten.
+ dictionary (v2)	Es verfügt bereits über das **Budget**...	Und es kostet oft mehr als hundert Dollar, um den gewünschten **Ausweis** zu erhalten.

ger-eng-wmt17	Example 3	Example 4
Source	Der **Pokal** war die einzige **Möglichkeit** , etwas zu gewinnen .	Aber es ist keine typische Zeichensprache – sagt sie . Edmund hat einige **Zeichen** alleine erfunden .
Constraints	cup [1,2), chance [5,6)	sign|signs [13,14)
LNMT	The **trophy** was the only **way** to win something.	But it's not a typical sign language – says, Edmund invented some **characters** alone.
+ dictionary (v1)	The **cup** was the only **way** to get something to win a **chance**.	But it's not a typical sign language – says, Edmund invented some **characters** alone.
+ dictionary (v2)	The **cup** was the only **chance** to win something.	But it is not a typical sign language – she says, Edmund invented some **signs** alone.

Table 2: English↔German translation outputs for constrained decoding.

	BLEU/speed ratio		
eng-ger-wmt17	c=2	c=3	c=4
LNMT	26.7 1.00	26.7 1.00	26.7 1.00
+ dict (v1)	28.2 0.20	28.4 0.14	28.5 0.11
+ dict (v2*)	27.8 0.69	28.0 0.66	28.1 0.59
+ A	28.0 0.65	28.2 0.61	28.2 0.54
+ B	28.4 0.27	28.6 0.24	28.7 0.21
+ C	28.5 0.21	28.6 0.19	28.7 0.17

Table 3: BLEU scores and speed ratios relative to unconstrained LNMT for production system with up to c constraints per sentence (newstest2017). A: secondary attention, B, C: allow 1 or 2 extra tokens, respectively (Section 2.3). *Dict (v2*)* refers to decoding with attentions but without A, B or C.

2017 on a single GPU using our English-German production system (Iglesias et al., 2018) which in comparison to the systems described in Section 3 uses a beam size of 4 and an early pruning strategy similar to that described in Johnson et al. (2017), amongst other differences. About 89% of the sentences have at least one dictionary match and we allow up to two, three or four matches per sentence. Because the constraints result from dictionary application, the number of constraints per sentence varies and not all sentences contain the maximum number of constraints.

Tab. 3 reports BLEU and speed ratios for different decoding configurations. Rows two and three confirm that the reduced computational complexity of our approach yields faster decoding speeds than the approach of Anderson et al. (2017) while incurring a small decrease in BLEU. Moreover, it compares favourably for larger numbers of constraints per sentence: v2* is 3.5x faster than v1 for c=2 and more than 5x faster for c=4. Relaxing the restrictions of decoding with attentions improves the BLEU scores but increases runtime. However, the slowest v2 configuration is still faster than v1. The optimal trade-off between quality and speed is likely to differ for each language pair.

5 Conclusion

We have presented our approach to NMT decoding with terminology constraints using decoder attentions which enables reduced output duplication and better constraint placement compared to existing methods. Our results on four language pairs demonstrate that terminology constraints as provided by customers can be respected during NMT decoding while maintaining the overall translation quality. At the same time, empirical results confirm that our improvements in computational complexity translate into faster decoding speeds. Future work includes the application of our approach to more recent architectures such as Vaswani et al. (2017) which will involve extracting attentions from multiple decoding layers and attention heads.

Acknowledgments

This work was partially supported by U.K. EPSRC grant EP/L027623/1.

References

Tamer Alkhouli and Hermann Ney. 2017. Biasing Attention-Based Recurrent Neural Networks Using External Alignment Information. In *Proceedings of the Conference on Machine Translation (WMT), Volume 1: Research Papers*. Association for Computational Linguistics, pages 108–117. http://www.statmt.org/wmt17/pdf/WMT11.pdf.

Peter Anderson, Basura Fernando, Mark Johnson, and Stephen Gould. 2017. Guided Open Vocabulary Image Captioning with Constrained Beam Search. In *Proceedings of the 2017 Conference on Empirical Methods in Natural Language Processing*. Association for Computational Linguistics, pages 936–945. https://aclweb.org/anthology/D17-1098.

Dzmitry Bahdanau, KyungHyun Cho, and Yoshua Bengio. 2015. Neural Machine Translation by Jointly Learning to Align and Translate. In *Proceedings of ICLR 2015*. https://arxiv.org/pdf/1409.0473.pdf.

Ondrej Bojar, Rajen Chatterjee, Christian Federmann, Yvette Graham, Barry Haddow, Shujian Huang, Matthias Huck, Philipp Koehn, Qun Liu, Varvara Logacheva, Christof Monz, Matteo Negri, Matt Post, Raphael Rubino, Lucia Specia, and Marco Turchi. 2017. Findings of the 2017 Conference on Machine Translation (WMT17). In *Proceedings of the Conference on Machine Translation (WMT), Volume 2: Shared Task Papers*. Association for Computational Linguistics, pages 169–214. http://www.statmt.org/wmt17/pdf/WMT17.pdf.

Rajen Chatterjee, Matteo Negri, Marco Turchi, Marcello Federico, Lucia Specia, and Frédéric Blain. 2017. Guiding Neural Machine Translation Decoding with External Knowledge. In *Proceedings of the Conference on Machine Translation (WMT), Volume 1: Research Papers*. Association for Computational Linguistics, pages 157–168. https://aclweb.org/anthology/W17-4716.

Josep Crego, Jungi Kim, Guillaume Klein, Anabel Rebollo, Kathy Yang, Jean Senellart, Egor Akhanov, Patrice Brunelle, Aurélien Coquard, Yongchao Deng, Satoshi Enoue, Chiyo Geiss, Joshua Johanson, Ardas Khalsa, Raoum Khiari, Byeongil Ko, Catherine Kobus, Jean Lorieux, Leidiana Martins, Dang-Chuan Nguyen, Alexandra Priori, Thomas Riccardi, Natalia Segal, Christophe Servan, Cyril Tiquet, Bo Wang, Jin Yang, Dakun Zhang, Jing Zhou, and Peter Zoldan. 2016. SYSTRAN's Pure Neural Machine Translation Systems. Arxiv preprint. https://arxiv.org/pdf/1610.05540v1.pdf.

Caglar Gulcehre, Orhan Firat, Kelvin Xu, Kyunghyun Cho, and Yoshua Bengio. 2017. On integrating a language model into neural machine translation. *Computer Speech & Language* 45:137–148. https://doi.org/10.1016/j.csl.2017.01.014.

Chris Hokamp and Qun Liu. 2017. Lexically Constrained Decoding for Sequence Generation Using Grid Beam Search. In *Proceedings of the 55th Annual Meeting of the Association for Computational Linguistics*. Association for Computational Linguistics, pages 1535–1546. https://doi.org/10.18653/v1/P17-1141.

Gonzalo Iglesias, William Tambellini, Adrià de Gispert, Eva Hasler, and Bill Byrne. 2018. Accelerating NMT Batched Beam Decoding with LMBR Posteriors for Deployment. In *Proceedings of the North American Chapter of the Association for Computational Linguistics: Human Language Technologies (Industry Track)*. Association for Computational Linguistics.

Melvin Johnson, Mike Schuster, Quoc V. Le, Maxim Krikun, Yonghui Wu, Zhifeng Chen, Nikhil Thorat, Fernanda Viégas, Martin Wattenberg, Greg Corrado, Macduff Hughes, and Jeffrey Dean. 2017. Google's Multilingual Neural Machine Translation System: Enabling Zero-Shot Translation. *Transactions of the Association for Computational Linguistics* 5:339–351. https://aclweb.org/anthology/Q17-1024.

Minh-Thang Luong and Christopher D Manning. 2015. Stanford Neural Machine Translation Systems for Spoken Language Domains. In *Proceedings of the 12th International Workshop on Spoken Language Translation*. pages 76–79. https://nlp.stanford.edu/pubs/luong-manning-iwslt15.pdf.

Rico Sennrich, Barry Haddow, and Alexandra Birch. 2016. Improving Neural Machine Translation Models with Monolingual Data. In *Proceedings of the 54th Annual Meeting of the Association for Computational Linguistics*. pages 86–96. https://aclweb.org/anthology/P16-1009.

Rico Sennrich, Barry Haddow, and Alexandra Birch. 2017. Neural Machine Translation of Rare Words with Subword Units. In *Proceedings of the 54th Annual Meeting of the Association for Computational Linguistics*. Association for Computational Linguistics, pages 1715–1725. https://aclweb.org/anthology/P16-1162.

Felix Stahlberg, Adrià de Gispert, Eva Hasler, and Bill Byrne. 2017. Neural Machine Translation by Minimising the Bayes-risk with Respect to Syntactic Translation Lattices. In *Proceedings of the 15th Conference of the European Chapter of the Association for Computational Linguistics: Volume 2, Short Papers*. Association for Computational Linguistics, pages 362–368. https://aclweb.org/anthology/E/E17/E17-2058.pdf.

Bart van Merriënboer, Dzmitry Bahdanau, Vincent Dumoulin, Dmitriy Serdyuk, David Warde-Farley, Jan Chorowski, and Yoshua Bengio. 2015. Blocks and Fuel: Frameworks for deep learning. In *Proceedings of ICLR 2015*. Arxiv preprint. https://arxiv.org/abs/1506.00619.

Ashish Vaswani, Noam Shazeer, Niki Parmar, Jakob Uszkoreit, Llion Jones, Aidan N Gomez, Ł ukasz Kaiser, and Illia Polosukhin. 2017. Attention is all you need. In I. Guyon, U. V. Luxburg, S. Bengio, H. Wallach, R. Fergus, S. Vishwanathan, and R. Garnett, editors, *Advances in Neural Information Processing Systems 30*, Curran Associates, Inc., pages 5998–6008. `http://papers.nips.cc/paper/7181-attention-is-all-you-need.pdf`.

On the Evaluation of Semantic Phenomena in Neural Machine Translation Using Natural Language Inference

Adam Poliak[1]   Yonatan Belinkov[2]   James Glass[2]   Benjamin Van Durme[1]

[1]Center for Language and Speech Processing
Johns Hopkins University, Baltimore, MD 21218
[2]Computer Science and Artificial Intelligence Laboratory
Massachusetts Institute of Technology, Cambridge, MA 02139
{azpoliak,vandurme}@cs.jhu.edu, {belinkov,glass}@mit.edu

Abstract

We propose a process for investigating the extent to which sentence representations arising from neural machine translation (NMT) systems encode distinct semantic phenomena. We use these representations as features to train a natural language inference (NLI) classifier based on datasets recast from existing semantic annotations. In applying this process to a representative NMT system, we find its encoder appears most suited to supporting inferences at the syntax-semantics interface, as compared to anaphora resolution requiring world-knowledge. We conclude with a discussion on the merits and potential deficiencies of the existing process, and how it may be improved and extended as a broader framework for evaluating semantic coverage.[1]

1. Introduction

What do neural machine translation (NMT) models learn about semantics? Many researchers suggest that state-of-the-art NMT models learn representations that capture the meaning of sentences (Gu et al., 2016; Johnson et al., 2017; Zhou et al., 2017; Andreas and Klein, 2017; Neubig, 2017; Koehn, 2017). However, there is limited understanding of how specific semantic phenomena are captured in NMT representations beyond this broad notion. For instance, how well do these representations capture Dowty (1991)'s thematic proto-roles? Are these representations sufficient for understanding paraphrastic inference? Do the sentence representations encompass complex anaphora resolution? We argue that existing semantic annotations recast as Natural Language Inference (NLI) can be leveraged to investigate whether sentence representations encoded by NMT models capture these semantic phenomena.

DPR	Sara adopted Jill, *she* wanted a child Sara adopted Jill, *Jill* wanted a child	✗
FN+	Iran *possesses* five research reactors Iran *has* five research reactors	✓
SPR	Berry Rejoins WPP Group Berry was *sentient*	✓

Figure 1: Example sentence pairs for the different semantic phenomena. DPR deals with complex anaphora resolution, FN+ is concerned with paraphrastic inference, and SPR covers Reisinger et al. (2015)'s semantic proto-roles. ✓ / ✗ indicates that the first sentence entails / does not entail the second.

We use sentence representations from pretrained NMT encoders as features to train classifiers for NLI, the task of determining if one sentence (a *hypothesis*) is supported by another (a *context*).[2] If the sentence representations learned by NMT models capture distinct semantic phenomena, we hypothesize that those representations should be sufficient to perform well on NLI datasets that test a model's ability to capture these phenomena. Figure 1 shows example NLI sentence pairs with their respective labels and semantic phenomena.

We evaluate NMT sentence representations of 4 NMT models from 2 domains on 4 different NLI datasets to investigate how well they capture different semantic phenomena. We use White et al. (2017)'s *Unified Semantic Evaluation Framework* (USEF) that recasts three semantic phenomena NLI: 1) semantic proto-roles, 2) paraphrastic inference, 3) and complex anaphora resolution. Additionally, we evaluate the NMT sentence representations on 4) Multi-NLI, a recent extension of the Stanford Natural Language Inference dataset (SNLI) (Bowman et al., 2015) that includes multiple genres and domains (Williams et al.,

---

[1]Code developed and data used are available at `https://github.com/boknilev/nmt-repr-analysis`.

[2]Sometimes referred to as recognizing textual entailment (Dagan et al., 2006, 2013).

Proceedings of NAACL-HLT 2018, pages 513–523
New Orleans, Louisiana, June 1 - 6, 2018. ©2018 Association for Computational Linguistics

2017). We contextualize our results with a standard neural encoder described in Bowman et al. (2015) and used in White et al. (2017).

Based on the recast NLI datasets, our investigation suggests that NMT encoders might learn more about semantic proto-roles than anaphora resolution or paraphrastic inference. We note that the target-side language affects how an NMT source-side encoder captures these semantic phenomena.

2. Motivation

Why use recast NLI? We focus on NLI, as opposed to a wide range of NLP taks, as a unified framework that can capture a variety of semantic phenomena based on arguments by White et al. (2017). Their recast dataset enables us to study whether NMT encoders capture "distinct types of semantic reasoning" under just one task. We choose these specific semantic phenomena for two reasons. First, a long term goal is to understand how combinations of different corpora and neural architectures can contribute to a system's ability to perform general language understanding. As humans can understand (annotate consistently) the sentence pairs used in our experiments, we would similarly like our final system to have this same capability. We posit that it is necessary but not necessarily sufficient for a language understanding system to be able to capture the semantic phenomena considered here. Second, we believe these semantic phenomena might be relevant for translation. We demonstrate this with a few examples.

Anaphora Anaphora resolution connects tokens, typically pronouns, to their referents. Anaphora resolution should occur when translating from morphologically poor languages into some morphologically rich languages. For example, when translating "The parent fed the child because she was hungry," a Spanish translation should describe *the child* as *la niña (fem.)* and not *el niño (masc.)* since *she* refers to *the child*. Because world knowledge is often required to perform anaphora resolution (Rahman and Ng, 2012; Javadpour, 2013), this may enable evaluating whether an NMT encoder learns world knowledge. In this example, *she* refers to *the child* and not *the parent* since world knowledge dictates that parents often feed children when children are hungry.

Proto-roles Dowty (1991)'s proto-roles may be expressed differently in different languages, and

so correctly identifying them can be important for translation. For example, English does not usually explicitly mark *volition*, a proto-role, except by using adverbs like *intentionally* or *accidentally*. Other languages mark volitionality by using special affixes (e.g., Tibetan and Sesotho, a Bantu language), case marking (Hindi, Sinhalese), or auxiliaries (Japanese).[3] Correctly generating these markers may require the MT system to encode volitionality on the source side.

Paraphrases Callison-Burch (2007) discusses how paraphrases help statistical MT (SMT) when alignments from source words to target-language words are unknown. If the alignment model can map a paraphrase of the source word to a word in the target language, then the SMT model can translate the original word based on its paraphrase.[4] Paraphrases are also used by professional translators to deal with non-equivalence of words in the source and target languages (Baker, 2018).

3. Methodology

We use NMT models based on bidirectional long short-term memory (Bi-LSTM) encoder-decoders with attention (Sutskever et al., 2014; Bahdanau et al., 2015), trained on a parallel corpus. Given an NLI context-hypothesis pair, we pass each sentence independently through a trained NMT encoder to extract their respective vector representations. We represent each sentence by concatenating the last hidden state from the forward and backward encoders, resulting in $\mathbf{v}$ and $\mathbf{u}$ (in $\mathbb{R}^{2d}$) for the context and hypothesis.[5] We follow the common practice of feeding the concatenation $(\mathbf{v}, \mathbf{u}) \in \mathbb{R}^{4d}$ to a classifier (Rocktäschel et al., 2016; Bowman et al., 2015; Mou et al., 2016; Liu et al., 2016; Cheng et al., 2016; Munkhdalai and Yu, 2017).

Sentence pair representations are fed into a classifier with a softmax layer that maps onto the number of labels. Experiments with both linear and non-linear classifiers have not shown major differences, so we report results with the linear classifier unless noted otherwise. We report implementation details in Appendix B.

---

[3] For references and examples, see: `en.wikipedia.org/wiki/Volition_(linguistics)`.

[4] Using paraphrases can help NMT models generate text in the target language in some settings (Sekizawa et al., 2017).

[5] We experimented with other sentence representations and their combinations, and did not see differences in overall conclusions. See Appendix A for these experiments.

Train \ Test	DPR: 50.0					SPR: 65.4					FN+: 57.5				
	ar	es	zh	de	USEF	ar	es	zh	de	USEF	ar	es	zh	de	USEF
DPR	49.8	**50.0**	**50.0**	**50.0**	49.5	45.4	57.1	47.0	43.9	**65.2**	48.0	**55.9**	51.0	46.8	19.2
SPR	50.1	50.3	50.1	49.9	**50.7**	72.1	74.2	73.6	73.1	**80.6**	56.3	57.0	56.9	56.1	**65.8**
FN+	50.0	50.0	**50.4**	50.0	49.5	57.3	**63.6**	54.5	60.7	60.0	56.2	56.1	54.3	55.5	**80.5**

Table 1: Accuracy on NLI with representations generated by encoders of English→{ar,es,zh,de} NMT models. Rows correspond to the training and validation sets and major columns correspond to the test set. The column labeled "USEF" refers to the test accuracies reported in White et al. (2017). The numbers on the top row represents each dataset's majority baseline. Bold numbers indicate the highest performing model for the given dataset.

4. Data

MT data We train NMT models on four language pairs: English → {Arabic (ar), Spanish (es), Chinese (zh), and German (de)}. See Appendix B for training details. The first three pairs use the United Nations parallel corpus (Ziemski et al., 2016) and for English-German, we use the WMT dataset (Bojar et al., 2014). Although the entailment classifier only uses representations extracted from the English-side encoders as features, using multiple language pairs allows us to explore whether different target languages affect what semantic phenomena are captured by an NMT encoder.

Natural Language Inference data We use four distinct datasets to train classifiers: Multi-NLI (Williams et al., 2017), a recent expansion of SNLI containing a broad array of domains that was used in the 2017 RepEval shared task (Nangia et al., 2017), and three recast NLI datasets from The JHU Decompositional Semantics Initiative (`Decomp`)[6] released by White et al. (2017). Sentence-pairs and labels were recast, i.e. automatically converted, from existing semantic annotations: FrameNet Plus (FN+) (Pavlick et al., 2015), Definite Pronoun Resolution (DPR) (Rahman and Ng, 2012), and Semantic Proto-Roles (SPR) (Reisinger et al., 2015). The FN+ portion contains sentence pairs based on paraphrastic inference, DPR's sentence pairs focus on identifying the correct antecedent for a definite pronoun, and SPR's sentence pairs test whether the semantic proto-roles from Reisinger et al. (2015) apply based on a given sentence.[7] Recasting makes it easy to determine how well an NLI method captures the fine-grained semantics inspired by Dowty (1991)'s thematic proto-roles, paraphrastic inference, and complex anaphora resolutions. Table 2 includes the datasets' statistics.

	DPR	SPR	FN+	MNLI
Train	2K	123K	124K	393K
Dev	.4K	15K	15K	9K
Test	1K	15K	14K	9K

Table 2: Number of sentences in NLI datasets.

5. Results

Table 1 shows results of NLI classifiers trained on representations from different NMT encoders. We also report the majority baseline and the results of Bowman et al.'s 3-layer deep 200 dimensional neural network used by White et al. ("USEF").

Paraphrastic entailment (FN+) Our classifiers predict FN+ entailment worse than the majority baseline, and drastically worse than USEF when trained on FN+'s training set. Since FN+ tests paraphrastic inference and NMT models have been shown to be useful to generate sentential paraphrase pairs (Wieting and Gimpel, 2017; Wieting et al., 2017), it is surprising that our classifiers using the representations from the NMT encoder perform poorly. Although the sentences in FN+ are much longer than in the other datasets, sentence length does not seem to be responsible for the poor FN+ results. The classifiers do not noticeably perform better on shorter sentences than longer ones, as noted in Appendix C.

Upon manual inspection, we noticed that in many *not-entailed* examples, swapped paraphrases had different part-of-speech (POS) tags. This begs the question of whether different POS tags for swapped paraphrases affects the accuracies. Using Stanford CoreNLP (Manning et al., 2014), we partition our validation set based on whether the paraphrases share the same POS tag. Table 3 reports dev set accuracies using classifiers trained on FN+. Classifiers using features from NMT encoders trained on the three languages from the UN corpus noticeably perform better on cases where paraphrases have different POS tags compared to paraphrases with the same POS tags. These dif-

---

⁶`decomp.net`

⁷We refer the reader to White et al. (2017) for detailed discussion on how the existing datasets were recast as NLI.

	ar	es	zh	de
Same Tag	52.9	52.6	52.6	50.2
Different Tag	55.8	59.1	53.4	46.0

Table 3: Accuracies on FN+'s dev set based on whether the swapped paraphrases share the same POS tag.

ferences might suggest that the recast FN+ might not be an ideal dataset to test how well NMT encoders capture paraphrastic inference. The sentence representations may be impacted more by ungrammaticality caused by different POS tags as opposed to poor paraphrases.

Anaphora entailment (DPR) The low accuracies for predicting NLI targeting anaphora resolution are similar to White et al. (2017)'s findings. They suggest that the model has difficulty in capturing complex anaphora resolution. By using contrastive evaluation pairs, Bawden et al. (2017) recently suggested as well that NMT models are poorly suited for co-reference resolution. Our results are not surprising given that DPR tests whether a model contains common sense knowledge (Rahman and Ng, 2012). In DPR, syntactic cues for co-reference are purposefully balanced out as each pair of pro-nouns appears in at least two context-hypothesis pairs (Table 9). This forces the model's decision to be informed by semantics and world knowledge – a model cannot use syntactic cues to help perform anaphora resolution.[8] Although the poor performance of NMT representations may be explained by a variety of reasons, e.g. training data, architectures, etc., we would still like ideal MT systems to capture the semantics of co-reference, as evidenced in the example in §2.

Even though the classifiers perform poorly when predicting paraphrastic entailment, they surprisingly outperform USEF by a large margin (around 25–30 %) when using a model trained on DPR.[9] This might suggest that an NMT encoder can pick up on how pronouns may be used as a type of lexical paraphrase (Bhagat and Hovy, 2013).

Proto-role entailment (SPR) When predicting SPR entailments using a classifier trained on SPR data, we noticeably outperform the majority baseline but are below USEF. Both ours and USEF's accuracies are lower than Teichert et al. (2017)'s best reported numbers. This is not surprising as Teichert et al. condition on observed semantic role labels when predicting proto-role labels.

---

[8]Appendix D includes some illustrative examples.
[9]This is seen in the last columns of the top row in Table 1.

Proto-Role	ar	es	zh	de	avg	MAJ
physically existed	70.6	70.8	**77.2**	70.8	72.4[†]	65.9
sentient	78.5	**82.2**	80.5	81.7	80.7[†]	75.5
aware	75.9	**77.0**	76.6	76.7	76.6[†]	60.9
volitional	74.3	**76.8**	74.7	73.7	74.9[†]	64.5
existed before	68.4	**70.5**	66.5	68.4	68.5[†]	64.8
caused	69.4	**74.1**	72.2	72.7	72.1[†]	63.4
changed	64.2	62.4	63.8	62.0	63.1	**65.1**
location	91.1	90.1	90.4	90.2	90.4	**91.7**
moved	90.6	88.8	90.1	90.3	89.9	**93.3**
used in	34.9	38.1	31.8	34.2	34.7	**55.2**
existed after	62.7	69.0	65.6	65.2	65.7	**69.7**
chang. state	61.8	60.7	60.9	60.7	61.0	**65.2**
chang. possession	89.6	88.6	89.9	88.3	89.1	**93.9**
stationary during	86.3	84.4	90.5	86.0	86.8	**96.3**
physical contact	85.0	82.0	84.5	84.4	84.0	**85.8**
existed during	59.3	71.8	60.8	64.4	64.1	**84.7**

Table 4: Accuracies on the SPR test set broken down by each proto-role. "avg" represents the score for the proto-role averaged across target languages. Bold and [†] respectively indicate the best results for each proto-role and whether all of our classifiers outperformed the proto-role's majority baseline.

Table 4 reports accuracies for each proto-role. Whenever one of the classifiers outperforms the baseline for a proto-role, all the other classifiers do as well. The classifiers outperform the majority baseline for 6 of the reported 16 proto-roles. We observe these 6 properties are more associated with proto-agents than proto-patients.

The larger improvements over the majority baseline for SPR compared to FN+ and DPR is not surprising. Dowty (1991) posited that proto-agent, and -patient should correlate with English syntactic subject, and object, respectively, and empirically the *necessity of [syntactic] parsing for predicate argument recognition* has been observed in practice (Gildea and Palmer, 2002; Punyakanok et al., 2008). Further, recent work is suggestive that LSTM-based frameworks implicitly may encode syntax based on certain learning objectives (Linzen et al., 2016; Shi et al., 2016; Belinkov et al., 2017b). It is unclear whether NMT encoders capture semantic proto-roles specifically or just underlying syntax that affects the proto-roles.

NMT target language Our experiments show differences based on which target language was used to train the NMT encoder, in capturing semantic proto-roles and paraphrastic inference. In Table 1, we notice a large improvement using sentence representations from an NMT encoder that was trained on en-es parallel text. The improvements are most profound when a classifier trained on DPR data predicts entailment focused on se-

	ar	es	zh	de	MAJ
MNLI-1	45.9	45.7	46.6	48.0	35.6
MNLI-2	46.6	46.7	48.2	48.9	36.5

Table 5: Accuracies for MNLI test sets. MNLI-1 refers to the matched case and MNLI-2 is the mismatched.

mantic proto-roles or paraphrastic inference. We also note that using the NMT encoder trained on en-es parallel text results in the highest results in 5 of the 6 proto-roles in the top portion of Table 4. When using other sentence representations (Appendix A), we notice that using representations from English-German encoders consistently outperforms using the other encoders (Tables 6 and 7). This prevents us from making generalizations regarding specific target side languages.

NLI across multiple domains Though our main focus is exploring what NMT encoders learn about distinct semantic phenomena, we would like to know how useful NMT models are for general NLI across multiple domains. Therefore, we also evaluate the sentence representations with Multi-NLI. As indicated by Table 5, the representations perform noticeably better than a majority baseline. However, our results are not competitive with state-of-the-art systems trained specifically for Multi-NLI (Nangia et al., 2017).

6. Related Work

In concurrent work, Poliak et al. (2018) explore whether NLI datasets contain statistical irregularities by training a model with access to only hypotheses. Their model significantly outperforms the majority baseline and our results on Multi-NLI, SPR, and FN+. They suggest that these, among other NLI datasets, contain statistical irregularities. Their findings illuminate issues with the recast datasets we consider, but do not invalidate our approach of using recast NLI to determine whether NMT encoders capture distinct semantic phenomena. Instead, they force us to re-evaluate the majority baseline as an indicator of whether encoders learn distinct semantics and to what extent we can make conclusions based on these recast datasets.

Prior work has focused on the relationship between semantics and machine translation. MEANT and its extension XMEANT evaluate MT systems based on semantics (Lo and Wu, 2011; Lo et al., 2014). Others have focused on incorporating semantics directly in MT. Chan et al. (2007) use word sense disambiguation to help statistical MT,

Gao and Vogel (2011) add semantic-roles to improve phrase-based MT, and Carpuat et al. (2017) demonstrate how filtering parallel sentences that are not parallel in meaning improves translation. Recent work explores how representations learned by NMT systems can improve semantic tasks. Mc-Cann et al. (2017) show improvements in many tasks by using contextualized word vectors extracted from a LSTM encoder trained for MT. Their goal is to use NMT to improve other tasks while we focus on using NLI to determine what NMT models learn about different semantic phenomena.

Researchers have explored what NMT models learn about other linguistic phenomena, such as morphology (Dalvi et al., 2017; Belinkov et al., 2017a), syntax (Shi et al., 2016), and lexical semantics (Belinkov et al., 2017b), including word senses (Marvin and Koehn, 2018; Liu et al., 2018)

7. Conclusion and Future Work

Researchers suggest that NMT models learn sentence representations that capture meaning. We inspected whether distinct types of semantics are captured by NMT encoders. Our experiments suggest that NMT encoders might learn the most about semantic proto-roles, do not focus on anaphora resolution, and may poorly capture paraphrastic inference. We conclude by suggesting that target-side language affects how well an NMT encoder captures these semantic phenomena.

In future work, we would like to study how well NMT encoders capture other semantic phenomena, possibly by recasting other datasets. Comparing how semantic phenomena are represented in different NMT architectures, e.g. purely convolutional (Gehring et al., 2017) or attention-based (Vaswani et al., 2017), may shed light on whether different architectures may better capture semantic phenomena. Finally, investigating how multilingual systems learn semantics can bring a new perspective to questions of universality of representation (Schwenk and Douze, 2017).

Acknowledgements

This work was supported by JHU-HLTCOE, DARPA LORELEI, and Qatar Computing Research Institute. We thank anonymous reviewers. Views and conclusions contained in this publication are those of the authors and should not be interpreted as representing official policies or endorsements of DARPA or the U.S. Government.

References

Jacob Andreas and Dan Klein. 2017. Analogs of linguistic structure in deep representations. In *Proceedings of the 2017 Conference on Empirical Methods in Natural Language Processing*. Association for Computational Linguistics, pages 2893–2897.

Dzmitry Bahdanau, Kyunghyun Cho, and Yoshua Bengio. 2015. Neural machine translation by jointly learning to align and translate. In *International Conference on Learning Representations (ICLR)*.

Mona Baker. 2018. *In other words: A coursebook on translation*. Routledge.

Rachel Bawden, Rico Sennrich, Alexandra Birch, and Barry Haddow. 2017. Evaluating discourse phenomena in neural machine translation. *arXiv preprint arXiv:1711.00513* .

Yonatan Belinkov, Nadir Durrani, Fahim Dalvi, Hassan Sajjad, and James Glass. 2017a. What do Neural Machine Translation Models Learn about Morphology? In *Proceedings of the 55th Annual Meeting of the Association for Computational Linguistics (Volume 1: Long Papers)*. Association for Computational Linguistics, pages 861–872. `https://doi.org/10.18653/v1/P17-1080`.

Yonatan Belinkov, Lluís Màrquez, Hassan Sajjad, Nadir Durrani, Fahim Dalvi, and James Glass. 2017b. Evaluating Layers of Representation in Neural Machine Translation on Part-of-Speech and Semantic Tagging Tasks. In *Proceedings of the Eighth International Joint Conference on Natural Language Processing (Volume 1: Long Papers)*. Asian Federation of Natural Language Processing, Taipei, Taiwan, pages 1–10.

Rahul Bhagat and Eduard Hovy. 2013. What is a paraphrase? *Computational Linguistics* 39(3):463–472.

Ondrej Bojar, Christian Buck, Christian Federmann, Barry Haddow, Philipp Koehn, Johannes Leveling, Christof Monz, Pavel Pecina, Matt Post, Herve Saint-Amand, Radu Soricut, Lucia Specia, and Aleš Tamchyna. 2014. Findings of the 2014 workshop on statistical machine translation. In *Proceedings of the Ninth Workshop on Statistical Machine Translation*. Association for Computational Linguistics, Baltimore, Maryland, USA, pages 12–58.

Samuel R. Bowman, Gabor Angeli, Christopher Potts, and Christopher D. Manning. 2015. A large annotated corpus for learning natural language inference. In *Proceedings of the 2015 Conference on Empirical Methods in Natural Language Processing (EMNLP)*. Association for Computational Linguistics.

Chris Callison-Burch. 2007. *Paraphrasing and Translation*. Ph.D. thesis, University of Edinburgh, Edinburgh, Scotland. `http://cis.upenn.edu/~ccb/publications/callison-burch-thesis.pdf`.

Marine Carpuat, Yogarshi Vyas, and Xing Niu. 2017. Detecting cross-lingual semantic divergence for neural machine translation. In *Proceedings of the First Workshop on Neural Machine Translation*. Association for Computational Linguistics, pages 69–79. `http://aclweb.org/anthology/W17-3209`.

Seng Yee Chan, Tou Hwee Ng, and David Chiang. 2007. Word Sense Disambiguation Improves Statistical Machine Translation. In *Proceedings of the 45th Annual Meeting of the Association of Computational Linguistics*. Association for Computational Linguistics, pages 33–40.

Jianpeng Cheng, Li Dong, and Mirella Lapata. 2016. Long short-term memory-networks for machine reading. In *Proceedings of the 2016 Conference on Empirical Methods in Natural Language Processing*. Association for Computational Linguistics, Austin, Texas, pages 551–561.

Kyunghyun Cho, Bart van Merrienboer, Dzmitry Bahdanau, and Yoshua Bengio. 2014. On the properties of neural machine translation: Encoder–decoder approaches. In *Proceedings of SSST-8, Eighth Workshop on Syntax, Semantics and Structure in Statistical Translation*. Association for Computational Linguistics, Doha, Qatar, pages 103–111. `http://www.aclweb.org/anthology/W14-4012`.

Ronan Collobert, Koray Kavukcuoglu, and Clément Farabet. 2011. Torch7: A Matlab-like Environment for Machine Learning. In *BigLearn, NIPS workshop*. EPFL-CONF-192376.

Alexis Conneau, Douwe Kiela, Holger Schwenk, Loïc Barrault, and Antoine Bordes. 2017. Supervised learning of universal sentence representations from natural language inference data. In *Proceedings of the 2017 Conference on Empirical Methods in Natural Language Processing*. Association for Computational Linguistics, pages 670–680. `http://aclweb.org/anthology/D17-1070`.

Ido Dagan, Oren Glickman, and Bernardo Magnini. 2006. The pascal recognising textual entailment challenge. In *Machine learning challenges. evaluating predictive uncertainty, visual object classification, and recognising tectual entailment*, Springer, pages 177–190.

Ido Dagan, Dan Roth, Mark Sammons, and Fabio Massimo Zanzotto. 2013. Recognizing textual entailment: Models and applications. *Synthesis Lectures on Human Language Technologies* 6(4):1–220.

Fahim Dalvi, Nadir Durrani, Hassan Sajjad, Yonatan Belinkov, and Stephan Vogel. 2017. Understanding and improving morphological learning in the neural machine translation decoder. In *Proceedings of the Eighth International Joint Conference on Natural Language Processing (Volume 1: Long Papers)*. Asian Federation of Natural Language Processing, Taipei, Taiwan, pages 142–151.

David Dowty. 1991. Thematic proto-roles and argument selection. *Language* pages 547–619.

Qin Gao and Stephan Vogel. 2011. Utilizing Target-Side Semantic Role Labels to Assist Hierarchical Phrase-based Machine Translation. In *Proceedings of Fifth Workshop on Syntax, Semantics and Structure in Statistical Translation*. Association for Computational Linguistics, pages 107–115.

Jonas Gehring, Michael Auli, David Grangier, Denis Yarats, and Yann N. Dauphin. 2017. Convolutional Sequence to Sequence Learning. In Doina Precup and Yee Whye Teh, editors, *Proceedings of the 34th International Conference on Machine Learning*. PMLR, International Convention Centre, Sydney, Australia, volume 70 of *Proceedings of Machine Learning Research*, pages 1243–1252.

Daniel Gildea and Martha Palmer. 2002. The necessity of parsing for predicate argument recognition. In *Proceedings of the 40th Annual Meeting on Association for Computational Linguistics*. Association for Computational Linguistics, pages 239–246.

Jiatao Gu, Zhengdong Lu, Hang Li, and Victor O.K. Li. 2016. Incorporating copying mechanism in sequence-to-sequence learning. In *Proceedings of the 54th Annual Meeting of the Association for Computational Linguistics (Volume 1: Long Papers)*. Association for Computational Linguistics, Berlin, Germany, pages 1631–1640.

Seyedeh Leili Javadpour. 2013. *Resolving pronominal anaphora using commonsense knowledge*. Ph.D. thesis, Louisiana State University.

Melvin Johnson, Mike Schuster, Quoc Le, Maxim Krikun, Yonghui Wu, Zhifeng Chen, Nikhil Thorat, Fernand a ViÃ©gas, Martin Wattenberg, Greg Corrado, Macduff Hughes, and Jeffrey Dean. 2017. Google's multilingual neural machine translation system: Enabling zero-shot translation. *Transactions of the Association for Computational Linguistics* 5:339–351.

Philipp Koehn. 2017. Neural machine translation. *arXiv preprint arXiv:1709.07809* .

Tal Linzen, Emmanuel Dupoux, and Yoav Goldberg. 2016. Assessing the Ability of LSTMs to Learn Syntax-Sensitive Dependencies. *Transactions of the Association of Computational Linguistics* 4(1):521–535.

Frederick Liu, Han Lu, and Graham Neubig. 2018. Handling Homographs in Neural Machine Translation. In *Proceedings of the 16th Annual Conference of the North American Chapter of the Association for Computational Linguistics: Human Language Technologies*.

Yang Liu, Chengjie Sun, Lei Lin, and Xiaolong Wang. 2016. Learning natural language inference using bidirectional lstm model and inner-attention. *arXiv preprint arXiv:1605.09090* .

Chi-kiu Lo, Meriem Beloucif, Markus Saers, and Dekai Wu. 2014. Xmeant: Better semantic mt evaluation without reference translations. In *Proceedings of the 52nd Annual Meeting of the Association for Computational Linguistics (Volume 2: Short Papers)*. volume 2, pages 765–771.

Chi-kiu Lo and Dekai Wu. 2011. Meant: an inexpensive, high-accuracy, semi-automatic metric for evaluating translation utility via semantic frames. In *Proceedings of the 49th Annual Meeting of the Association for Computational Linguistics: Human Language Technologies-Volume 1*. Association for Computational Linguistics, pages 220–229.

Christopher D. Manning, Mihai Surdeanu, John Bauer, Jenny Finkel, Steven J. Bethard, and David McClosky. 2014. The Stanford CoreNLP natural language processing toolkit. In *Association for Computational Linguistics (ACL) System Demonstrations*. pages 55–60. http://www.aclweb.org/anthology/P/P14/P14-5010.

Rebecca Marvin and Philipp Koehn. 2018. Exploring Word Sense Disambiguation Abilities of Neural Machine Translation Systems. In *Proceedings of the 13th Conference of The Association for Machine Translation in the Americas (Volume 1: Research Track*. pages 125–131.

Bryan McCann, James Bradbury, Caiming Xiong, and Richard Socher. 2017. Learned in translation: Contextualized word vectors. In I. Guyon, U. V. Luxburg, S. Bengio, H. Wallach, R. Fergus, S. Vishwanathan, and R. Garnett, editors, *Advances in Neural Information Processing Systems 30*, Curran Associates, Inc., pages 6297–6308.

Lili Mou, Rui Men, Ge Li, Yan Xu, Lu Zhang, Rui Yan, and Zhi Jin. 2016. Natural language inference by tree-based convolution and heuristic matching. In *Proceedings of the 54th Annual Meeting of the Association for Computational Linguistics (Volume 2: Short Papers)*. Association for Computational Linguistics, Berlin, Germany, pages 130–136. http://anthology.aclweb.org/P16-2022.

Tsendsuren Munkhdalai and Hong Yu. 2017. Neural tree indexers for text understanding. In *Proceedings of the 15th Conference of the European Chapter of the Association for Computational Linguistics: Volume 1, Long Papers*. Association for Computational Linguistics, Valencia, Spain, pages 11–21.

Nikita Nangia, Adina Williams, Angeliki Lazaridou, and Samuel Bowman. 2017. The repeval 2017 shared task: Multi-genre natural language inference with sentence representations. In *Proceedings of the 2nd Workshop on Evaluating Vector Space Representations for NLP*. pages 1–10.

Graham Neubig. 2017. Neural machine translation and sequence-to-sequence models: A tutorial. *arXiv preprint arXiv:1703.01619* .

Ellie Pavlick, Travis Wolfe, Pushpendre Rastogi, Chris Callison-Burch, Mark Dredze, and Benjamin Van Durme. 2015. Framenet+: Fast paraphrastic tripling of framenet. In *Proceedings of the 53rd Annual Meeting of the Association for Computational Linguistics and the 7th International Joint Conference on Natural Language Processing (Volume 2: Short Papers)*. Association for Computational Linguistics, Beijing, China, pages 408–413.

Adam Poliak, Jason Naradowsky, Aparajita Haldar, Rachel Rudinger, and Benjamin Van Durme. 2018. Hypothesis only baselines for natural language inference. In *The Seventh Joint Conference on Lexical and Computational Semantics (*SEM)*.

Vasin Punyakanok, Dan Roth, and Wen-tau Yih. 2008. The importance of syntactic parsing and inference in semantic role labeling. *Computational Linguistics* 34(2):257–287.

Altaf Rahman and Vincent Ng. 2012. Resolving complex cases of definite pronouns: The winograd schema challenge. In *Proceedings of the 2012 Joint Conference on Empirical Methods in Natural Language Processing and Computational Natural Language Learning*. Association for Computational Linguistics, Jeju Island, Korea, pages 777–789. http://www.aclweb.org/anthology/D12-1071.

Drew Reisinger, Rachel Rudinger, Francis Ferraro, Craig Harman, Kyle Rawlins, and Benjamin Van Durme. 2015. Semantic proto-roles. *Transactions of the Association for Computational Linguistics* 3:475–488.

Tim Rocktäschel, Edward Grefenstette, Karl Moritz Hermann, Tomas Kocisky, and Phil Blunsom. 2016. Reasoning about entailment with neural attention. In *International Conference on Learning Representations (ICLR)*.

Holger Schwenk and Matthijs Douze. 2017. Learning joint multilingual sentence representations with neural machine translation. In *Proceedings of the 2nd Workshop on Representation Learning for NLP*. pages 157–167.

Yuuki Sekizawa, Tomoyuki Kajiwara, and Mamoru Komachi. 2017. Improving japanese-to-english neural machine translation by paraphrasing the target language. In *Proceedings of the 4th Workshop on Asian Translation (WAT2017)*. Asian Federation of Natural Language Processing, Taipei, Taiwan, pages 64–69.

Xing Shi, Inkit Padhi, and Kevin Knight. 2016. Does string-based neural mt learn source syntax? In *Proceedings of the 2016 Conference on Empirical Methods in Natural Language Processing*. Association for Computational Linguistics, Austin, Texas, pages 1526–1534. https://aclweb.org/anthology/D16-1159.

Ilya Sutskever, Oriol Vinyals, and Quoc V Le. 2014. Sequence to sequence learning with neural networks. In *Advances in neural information processing systems*. pages 3104–3112.

Adam Teichert, Adam Poliak, Benjamin Van Durme, and Matthew R Gormley. 2017. Semantic proto-role labeling. In *Thirty-First AAAI Conference on Artificial Intelligence (AAAI-17)*.

Ashish Vaswani, Noam Shazeer, Niki Parmar, Jakob Uszkoreit, Llion Jones, Aidan N Gomez, Ł ukasz Kaiser, and Illia Polosukhin. 2017. Attention is All you Need. In I. Guyon, U. V. Luxburg, S. Bengio, H. Wallach, R. Fergus, S. Vishwanathan, and R. Garnett, editors, *Advances in Neural Information Processing Systems 30*, Curran Associates, Inc., pages 5998–6008.

Aaron Steven White, Pushpendre Rastogi, Kevin Duh, and Benjamin Van Durme. 2017. Inference is everything: Recasting semantic resources into a unified evaluation framework. In *Proceedings of the Eighth International Joint Conference on Natural Language Processing (Volume 1: Long Papers)*. Asian Federation of Natural Language Processing, Taipei, Taiwan, pages 996–1005.

John Wieting and Kevin Gimpel. 2017. Pushing the limits of paraphrastic sentence embeddings with millions of machine translations. *arXiv preprint arXiv:1711.05732* .

John Wieting, Jonathan Mallinson, and Kevin Gimpel. 2017. Learning paraphrastic sentence embeddings from back-translated bitext. In *Proceedings of the 2017 Conference on Empirical Methods in Natural Language Processing*. Association for Computational Linguistics, Copenhagen, Denmark, pages 274–285. https://www.aclweb.org/anthology/D17-1026.

Adina Williams, Nikita Nangia, and Samuel R Bowman. 2017. A broad-coverage challenge corpus for sentence understanding through inference. *arXiv preprint arXiv:1704.05426* .

Hao Zhou, Zhaopeng Tu, Shujian Huang, Xiaohua Liu, Hang Li, and Jiajun Chen. 2017. Chunk-based bi-scale decoder for neural machine translation. In *Proceedings of the 55th Annual Meeting of the Association for Computational Linguistics (Volume 2: Short Papers)*. Association for Computational Linguistics, pages 580–586. https://doi.org/10.18653/v1/P17-2092.

Michał Ziemski, Marcin Junczys-Dowmunt, and Bruno Pouliquen. 2016. The united nations parallel corpus v1.0. In Nicoletta Calzolari (Conference Chair), Khalid Choukri, Thierry Declerck, Sara Goggi, Marko Grobelnik, Bente Maegaard, Joseph Mariani, Helene Mazo, Asuncion Moreno, Jan Odijk, and Stelios Piperidis, editors, *Proceedings of the Tenth International Conference on Language Resources and Evaluation (LREC 2016)*. European Language Resources Association (ELRA), Paris, France.

A. Sentence Representations

In the experiments reported in the main paper, we used a simple sentence representation, the first and last hidden states of the forward and backward encoders. We concatenated them for both the context and the hypothesis and fed to a linear classifier. Here we compare the results of `InferSent` (Conneau et al., 2017), a more involved representation that was found to provide a good sentence representation based on NLI data. Specifically, we concatenate the forward and backward encodings for each sentence, and max-pool over the length of the sentence, resulting in $\mathbf{v}$ and $\mathbf{u}$ (in $\mathbb{R}^{2d}$) for the context and hypothesis. The `InferSent` representation is defined by

$$\left(\mathbf{u}, \mathbf{v}, |\mathbf{u} - \mathbf{v}|, \mathbf{u} * \mathbf{v}\right) \in \mathbb{R}^{8d}$$

where the product and subtraction are carried element-wise and commas denote vector-concatenation.

The pair representation is fed into a multi-layered perceptron (MLP) with one hidden layer and a ReLU non-linearity. We set the hidden layer size to 500 dimensions, similarly to Conneau et al. (2017). The softmax layer maps onto the number of labels, which is either 2 or 3 depending on the dataset.

InferSent results Table 6 shows the results of the classifier trained on NMT representations with the InferSent architecture. Here, the representations from NMT encoders trained on the English-German parallel corpus slightly outperforms the others. Since this data used a different corpus compared to the other language pairs, we cannot determine whether the improved results are due to the different target side language or corpus. The main difference with respects to the simpler sentence representation (Concat) is improved results on FN+. Table 7 shows the results on Multi-NLI. It is interesting to note that, when using the sentence representations from NMT encoders, concatenating the sentence vectors outperformed the `InferSent` method on Multi-NLI.

B. Implementation & Experimental Details

We use 4-layer NMT systems with 500-dimensional word embeddings and LSTM states (i.e., $d = 500$). The vocabulary size is 75K words.

		FN+	DPR	SPRL
NMT Concat	en-ar	56.2	49.8	72.1
	en-es	56.1	50.0	74.2
	en-zh	54.3	50.0	73.1
	en-de	55.5	50.0	73.1
NMT InferSent	en-ar	57.9	50.0	73.6
	en-es	58.0	50.0	72.7
	en-zh	57.8	49.8	72.4
	en-de	58.3	50.1	73.7
Majority		57.5	50.0	65.4
(White et al., 2017)		80.5	49.5	80.6

Table 6: NLI results on fine-grained semantic phenomena. FN+ = paraphrases; DPR = pronoun resolution; SPRL = proto-roles. NMT representations are combined with either a simple concatenation (results copied from Table 2) or the `InferSent` representation. State-of-the-art (SOTA) is from White et al. (2017).

		MNLI-1	MNLI-2
NMT Concat	en-ar	45.9	46.6
	en-es	45.7	46.7
	en-zh	46.6	48.2
	en-de	48.0	48.9
NMT InferSent	en-ar	40.1	41.8
	en-es	44.9	40.8
	en-zh	43.7	42.1
	en-de	41.3	41.1
Majority		35.6	36.5
SOTA		81.10	83.21

Table 7: Results on language inference on MultiNLI (Williams et al., 2017), matched/mismatched scenario (MNLI1/2).

We train NMT models until convergence and take the models that performed best on the development set for generating representations to feed into the entailment classifier. We use the hidden states from the top encoding layer for obtaining sentence representations since it has been hypothesized that higher layers focus on word meaning, as opposed to syntax (Belinkov et al., 2017a,b). We remove long sentences (> 50 words) when training both the classifier and the NMT model, as is common NMT practice (Cho et al., 2014). During testing, we use all test sentences regardless of sentence length. Our implementation extends Belinkov et al. (2017a)'s implementation in Torch (Collobert et al., 2011).

We train English→Arabic/Spanish/Chinese NMT models on the first 2 million sentences of the United Nations parallel corpus training set (Ziemski et al., 2016), and the English→German model on the WMT dataset (Bojar et al., 2014). We use the official training/development/test splits.

In our NLI experiments, we do not train on Multi-NLI and test on the recast datasets, or vice-versa, since Multi-NLI since Multi-NLI uses a 3-way classification (*entailment*, *neutral*, and *contradictions*) while the recast datasets use just two labels (*entailed* and *not-entailed*). In preliminary experiments, we also used a 3-layered MLP. Although the results slightly improved, we noted similar trends to the linear classifier.

C.   Sentence length

The average sentence in the FN+ test dataset is 31 words and almost 10% of the test sentences are longer than 50 words. In SPR and DPR, each premise sentence has on average 21 and 15 words respectively and only 1% of sentences in SPR have more than 50 words. No DPR sentences have > 50 words.

Table 8 reports accuracies for ranges of sentence lengths in FN+'s development set. When trained on sentence representations form an English→Chinese,German NMT encoder, the NLI accuracies steadily decrease. When using English→Arabic, the accuracies stay consistent until sentences have between 70–80 tokens while the results from English→Spanish quickly drops from 0–10 to 10–20 but then stays relatively consistent.

D.   World Knowledge in DPR

When released, Rahman and Ng (2012)'s DPR dataset confounded the best co-reference models because "its difficulty stems in part from its reliance on sophisticated knowledge sources." Table 9 includes examples that demonstrate how world knowledge is needed to accurately predict these recast NLI sentence-pairs.

Sentence length	ar	es	zh	de	total
0-10	46.8	63.7	66.0	65.4	526
10-20	49.0	53.3	57.4	56.5	2739
20-30	48.4	54.0	53.2	54.9	4889
30-40	48.4	54.1	51.2	53.9	4057
40-50	47.7	59.0	55.0	58.7	2064
50-60	49.1	56.1	54.5	57.5	877
60-70	46.4	53.6	43.9	44.1	444
70-80	59.9	51.6	43.3	43.3	252

Table 8: Accuracies on FN+'s dev set based on sentence length. The first column represents the range of sentences length: first number is inclusive and second is exclusive. The last column represents how many context sentences have lengths that are in the given row's range.

Chris was running after John, because he stole his watch	
▶ Chris was running after John, because John stole his watch	✓
▶ Chris was running after John, because Chris stole his watch	✗
Chris was running after John, because he wanted to talk to him	
▶ Chris was running after John, because Chris wanted to talk to him	✓
▶ Chris was running after John, because John wanted to talk to him	✗
The plane shot the rocket at the target, then it hit the target	
▶ The plane shot the rocket at the target, then the rocket hit the target	✓
▶ The plane shot the rocket at the target, then the target hit the target	✗
Professors do a lot for students, but they are rarely thankful	
▶ Professors do a lot for students, but students are rarely thankful	✓
▶ Professors do a lot for students, but Professors are rarely thankful	✗
MIT accepted the students, because they had good grades	
▶ MIT accepted the students, because the students had good grades	✓
▶ MIT accepted the students, because MIT had good grades	✗
Obama beat John McCain, because he was the better candidate	
▶ Obama beat John McCain, because Obama was the better candidate	✓
▶ Obama beat John McCain, because John McCain was the better candidate	✗
Obama beat John McCain, because he failed to win the majority of the electoral votes	
▶ Obama beat John McCain, because John McCain failed to win the majority of the electoral votes	✓
▶ Obama beat John McCain, because Obama failed to win the majority of the electoral vote	✗

Table 9: Examples from DPR's dev set. The first line in each section is a context and lines with ▶ are corresponding hypotheses. ✓ (✗) in the last column indicates whether the hypothesis is entailed (or not) by the context.

Using Word Vectors to Improve Word Alignments for Low Resource Machine Translation

Nima Pourdamghani, Marjan Ghazvininejad, Kevin Knight
Information Sciences Institute & Department of Computer Science
University of Southern California
{damghani,ghazvini,knight}@isi.edu

Abstract

We present a method for improving word alignments using word similarities. This method is based on encouraging common alignment links between semantically similar words. We use word vectors trained on monolingual data to estimate similarity. Our experiments on translating fifteen languages into English show consistent BLEU score improvements across the languages.

1 Introduction

Word alignments are essential for statistical machine translation (MT), especially in low-resource settings where neural MT systems often do not compete with phrase-based and syntax-based MT (Koehn and Knowles, 2017). The most widely used word alignment method (Brown et al., 1993) works by estimating the parameters of IBM models from training data using the Expectation Maximization (EM) algorithm. However, EM works poorly for low-frequency words as they do not appear enough in the training data for confident parameter estimation. This problem is even worse in low-resource settings where a large portion of word types appear infrequently in the parallel data. In this paper we improve word alignments and consequently machine translation in low resource settings by improving the alignments of infrequent tokens.

Works that deal with the rare-word problem in word alignment include those that alter the probability distribution of IBM models' parameters by adding prior distributions (Vaswani et al., 2012; Mermer and Saraçlar, 2011), smoothing the probabilities (Moore, 2004; Zhang and Chiang, 2014; Van Bui and Le, 2016) or introducing symmetrization (Liang et al., 2006; Pourdamghani et al., 2014). These works, although effective, merely rely on the information extracted from the paral-

lel data. Another branch adds linguistic knowledge like word stems, orthography (Hermjakob, 2009) morphological analysis (De Gispert et al., 2006; Lee, 2004), syntactic constraints (Fossum et al., 2008; Cherry and Lin, 2006; Toutanova et al., 2002) or a mixture of such clues (Tiedemann, 2003). These methods need language-specific knowledge or tools like morphological analyzers or syntax parsers that is costly and time consuming to obtain for any given language.

A less explored branch that can help aligning rare words is adding semantic information. The motivation behind this branch is simple: Words with similar meanings should have similar translations. Previously, Ma et al. (2011) cluster words using monolingual data and substitute each word with its cluster representative to get alignments. They then duplicate their parallel data and use both regular alignments and alignments on word classes for training MT. Kočiský et al. (2014) simultaneously learn alignments and word representations from bilingual data. Their method does not benefit from monolingual data and requires large parallel data for training. Songyot and Chiang (2014) define a word-similarity model that can be trained from monolingual data using a feed-forward neural network, and alter the implementation of IBM models in Giza++ (Och and Ney, 2003) to use the word similarity inside their EM. They require large monolingual data for both source language and English. While English monolingual data is abundant, availability of large and reliable monolingual data for many low resource languages is not guaranteed.

All these previous works define their own word similarity models, which similar to the more widely used distributed word representation methods (Mikolov et al., 2013; Pennington et al., 2014), assign high similarity to substitutable words in a given context; however, substitutability does not

524

Proceedings of NAACL-HLT 2018, pages 524–528
New Orleans, Louisiana, June 1 - 6, 2018. ©2018 Association for Computational Linguistics

always imply synonymy. For instance *tea* and *coffee*, or *Pakistan* and *Afghanistan* will be similar in these models but do not share translations.

In this paper we propose a simple method to use off-the-shelf distributed representation methods to improve word alignments for low-resource machine translation (Section 2). Our model is based on encouraging common alignment links between semantically similar words. We do this by extracting a bilingual lexicon, as a subset of the translation tables trained by IBM models and adding it to the parallel data. For instance, the rare word *obliterated* and its semantically similar word *destroyed*, have a common entry *destruida* in the English/Spanish translation table. We add a new (*obliterated*, *destruida*) pair to the parallel data to encourage aligning *obliterated* to *destruida*.

The simplicity of our method makes it easy to be widely used. Our work addresses a major problem of previous works, which is taking substitutability for synonymy without discrimination. Finally, the lexicon can be extracted either with or without help of word vectors trained on foreign language monolingual data. Large and reliable foreign monolingual data can help our alignments, but we still get good improvements over baseline for languages with small monolingual data where we only use English word vectors (Section 4).

We test our method on both alignment f-score and machine translation BLEU (Section 4). Alignment accuracy is tested on Arabic-English, Chinese-English and Farsi-English gold alignments. Machine translation accuracy is tested on fifteen languages were we show a consistent BLEU score improvement.

2 Proposed Method

We improve the alignment of rare words by encouraging them to align to what their semantic neighbors align to. For instance we encourage the rare word *obliterated* to align to what *destroyed* aligns to. However, we should be careful in this process. Distributed word representation methods like (Mikolov et al., 2013; Pennington et al., 2014) often define word similarity as the ability to substitute one word for another given a context. This does not always imply having same translations. Multiple reasons contribute to this problem. First, word vectors are noisy, especially when monolingual data is small. Second, some words might have multiple meanings and a semantically simi-

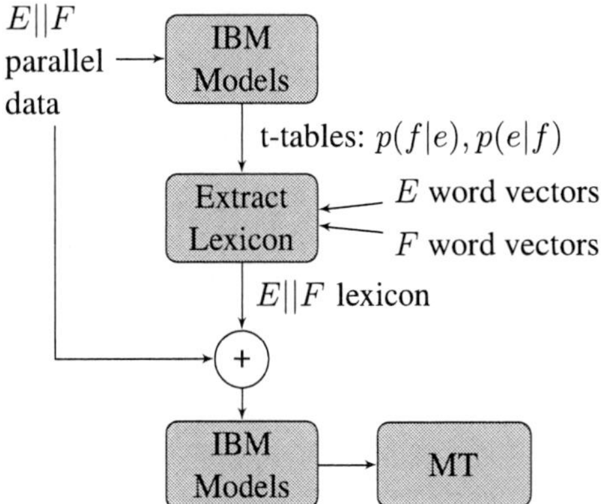

Figure 1: Word vectors trained on monolingual data are used to extract a bilingual lexicon out of translation tables. This lexicon is added to the parallel data, resulting in improved alignments for machine translation.

lar word might share only part of these meanings. Finally, some words do not have synonyms, especially proper names. Word vectors often group such entities together as they are substitutable, but this similarity should not be used for alignments.

We bring a simple three-fold solution to these problems. First, we split the use of English and foreign word vectors in the method, so that if foreign monolingual data is small or unreliable, we can fall back to only using English word vectors. Second, and more importantly, we limit the effect of a semantic neighbor on the alignments of a token to the common alignment links between them. This removes the effect of a semantic neighbor which is not a synonym (like effect of *tea* on alignments of *coffee*) and irrelevant meanings of a semantic neighbor (like multiple meanings of *bow* on alignments of token *crossbow*) as we only encourage an alignment link if it appears as a potential translation for both the neighbors. Third, we note that using similarities based on distributed representations only hurts alignments for proper names. For these cases we encourage alignment to transliterations if applicable.

Figure 1 shows the outline of the proposed method. We provide the initial parallel data to the IBM models and train the translate tables $p(f|e)$ and $p(e|f)$. We then use the word vectors trained on English and foreign language monolingual data to extract a bilingual lexicon from these tables. This lexicon is added to the original parallel data and used to re-train the alignments. The lexicon contains both common alignment links and transliteration links that are extracted from the translation table. Next we will describe how each section of the lexicon is generated.

2.1 Extracting Semantically Similar Tokens

Assume an infrequent English token e (w.r.t. the parallel data), and its semantic neighbor e'. If e and e' have a common t-table entry—some f, where $p(f|e) > 0$ and $p(f|e') > 0.1$ we encourage the translation of e to f by adding this pair to the parallel data for re-alignment. We limit the lexicon entries to non-common words. We only add entries where $freq(e) \leq 100$ and $freq(f) \leq 100$. The translation table is trained by 5 iterations of each of IBM models 1, HMM, and 4.

We add each (e,f) pair multiple times to the lexicon proportional to $p(f|e')$, the cosine distance of e and e', and the frequency of e. More precisely, for each neighbor e', each (e, f) pair appears $\lceil min(freq(e) \times dist(e, e') \times p(f|e'), \frac{freq(e)}{4}) \rceil$ times in the lexicon.

To measure similarity, we use cosine distance of word vectors trained on monolingual data using an implementation of continues bag-of-words (CBOW) algorithm.[1] English word vectors are trained on the one-billion-word language modeling benchmark (Chelba et al., 2013). Foreign language word vectors are trained on the monolingual data described in Section 3. All vectors are trained with window size 6 and dimension 300. For each word we consider its two nearest neighbors according to the cosine distance.

In a similar manner, we extract a lexicon from the $p(e|f)$ translation table as well. For each foreign rare token f and its semantic neighbor f', we add (e, f) pair to the lexicon if $p(e|f) > 0$ and $p(e|f') > 0.1$. However, as discussed in Section 4, it is better to use this lexicon only if the foreign language word vectors are trained on more than 10 million tokens of monolingual data.

2.2 Extracting Transliterations

For any infrequent English token e (w.r.t. the parallel data) and its translation table entry f, if f is a transliteration of e we add the (e, f) pair to the lexicon. Similarly we extract transliteration pairs from the $p(e|f)$ translation table. Each transliteration pair is added once to the lexicon.

In order to decide whether two tokens are transliterations, we compute the normalized edit distance of their romanizations. We use uro-

man,[2] a universal romanizer that converts text in any script to its romanized version (Latin alphabet). We say two tokens are transliterations if $dist(rom(e), rom(f)) \leq 0.25$, where $dist$ is the normalized Levenshtein distance and $rom(.)$ is the output of the romanizer.

3 Data

We use data from fifteen languages for our machine translation experiments.[3] These languages include Amheric, Arabic, Bengali, Mandarin, Farsi, Hausa, Somali, Spanish, Tamil, Thai, Turkish, Uighur, Urdu, Uzbek and Yoruba. Table 1 shows the size of training, development, test and monolingual data for each language. In addition, we use hand aligned data[4] for Arabic/English ($77.3K+119.5K$ tokens), Chinese/English ($240.2K+305.2K$ tokens), and Farsi/English ($0.9K+0.8K$ tokens) for word alignment experiments. We lowercase and tokenize all data using Moses (Koehn et al., 2007) scripts.

	train	dev.	test	mono.
amh	2.1M	39.8K	19.5K	4.3M
ara	3.8M	39.1K	19.8K	230.4M
ben	0.9M	41.9K	21.0K	2.5M
cmn	10.6M	41.7K	20.5K	33.2M
fas	4.3M	47.7K	24.2K	271.2M
hau	2.1M	48.0K	24.1K	3.9M
som	2.8M	46.8K	23.5K	13.5M
spa	24.1M	49.4K	24.3K	14.7M
tam	0.5M	39.0K	11.4K	1.0M
tha	0.7M	39.1K	23.1K	39.7M
tur	4.1M	40.2K	19.9K	483.0M
uig	5.2M	8.6K	4.3K	33.8M
urd	1.1M	46.7K	23.2K	14.4M
uzb	4.2M	42.5K	21.7K	60.3M
yor	2.1M	47.9K	24.5K	7.0M

Table 1: Data split and size of monolingual data (tokens) for different languages. For parallel data, size refers to the number of English plus foreign language tokens.

---

[1] https://code.google.com/archive/p/word2vec/

[2] https://www.isi.edu/ ulf/uroman.html

[3] LDC2015E13, LDC2015E14, LDC2015E83, LDC2015E84, LDC2016E57, and LDC2016E86 to LDC2016E105

[4] LDC2012E51, LDC2012E24, (Pilevar et al., 2011)

4 Experiments

4.1 Machine Translation

We perform end-to-end machine translation experiments on 15 different languages described in Section 3. We use Giza++ (Och and Ney, 2003) to get the alignments and Moses (Koehn et al., 2007) to train and decode phrase based machine translation (PBMT) systems. The parallel data is stemmed to the first 4 characters for training the alignments but not for the PBMT system. We use 5 iterations of each of IBM models 1, HMM and 4 to train the alignments both before and after adding the lexicons. In order to reduce the effect of randomness, we tune and test each system three times and report the average scores. Our baseline is the system before adding the lexicons. We test both the effect of only adding the lexicon extracted from $p(f|e)$ translation table using the English word vectors (L_e), and adding both the lexicons ($L_e + L_f$). Table 2 shows the BLEU scores of running different experiments. The languages are sorted by the size of their monolingual data. The first five languages have less than $10M$ tokens of monolingual data.

	baseline	L_e	$L_e + L_f$	improve
tam	19.2	**19.3**	19.2	0.1
ben	8.1	**8.2**	8.0	0.1
hau	19.4	**19.6**	19.9	0.2
amh	11.5	**11.9**	11.2	0.4
yor	14.2	**14.6**	14.3	0.4
som	18.7	19.1	**18.9**	0.2
urd	15.6	15.2	**16.2**	0.6
spa	**40.0**	40.0	**40.0**	0.0
cmn	12.5	12.7	**12.7**	0.2
uig	12.8	14.3	**14.0**	1.2
tha	20.3	20.1	**20.5**	0.2
uzb	13.2	13.5	**13.9**	0.7
ara	**18.2**	18.1	18.0	-0.2
fas	19.2	19.3	**19.4**	0.2
tur	14.7	15.4	**15.4**	0.7

Table 2: Machine translation experiments (BLEU). For languages with less than $10M$ monolingual tokens (first five) we only use L_e, otherwise we use both lexicons $L_e + L_f$. This way we improve baseline for almost all languages.

We see that it is generally better to only use L_e for languages with small monolingual data and use both L_e and L_f for others. If we put the threshold at $10M$ tokens of monolingual data, we improve the BLEU score over baseline for almost all languages, up to 1.2 points for Uighur. The exceptions are Arabic and Spanish. However, the Spanish experiment is hardly within the low resource settings as it has about $24M$ tokens of parallel data.

4.2 Alignments

In addition, we perform word alignment experiments on Arabic/English, Chinese/English, and Farsi/English, for which we have access to gold alignment data (Section 3). We append the test sentences to the existing parallel training data for each language (Table 1) and use it to get the alignments. Baseline and proposed methods are defined as in the machine translation experiments above (Section 4.1). Note that word vectors for these three languages are trained on more than 10M tokens, so we use both lexicons in the proposed method. Table 3 presents the precision, recall, and f-score of the alignments compared to the gold alignments.

	baseline	$L_e + L_f$
ara	63.1/58.1/60.5	63.8/58.4/61.0
cmn	66.5/61.6/63.9	66.7/61.6/64.1
fas	52.7/66.7/58.9	54.3/68.5/60.6

Table 3: Word alignment experiments (alignment precision/recall/f-score). The proposed method ($L_e + L_f$) improves baseline in all cases.

The proposed method gets better precision, recall, and f-score for all three languages.

5 Conclusion

In this paper we present a method for improving word alignments using word similarities. The method is simple and yet efficient. We use off-the-shelf distributed word representation tools to encourage a subset of translation table entries that are common between semantically similar words. End-to-end experiments on translating 15 languages into English, as well as alignment-accuracy experiments for three languages, show consistent improvement over the baseline.

Acknowledgments

This work was supported by DARPA contract HR0011-15-C-0115. The authors would like to thank Ulf Hermjakob, Jonathan May, and Michael Pust for their comments and suggestions.

References

Peter F. Brown, Vincent J. Della Pietra Stephen A. Della Pietra, and Robert L. Mercer. 1993. The mathematics of statistical machine translation: Parameter estimation. *Computational linguistics* 19(2).

Ciprian Chelba, Tomas Mikolov, Mike Schuster, Qi Ge, Thorsten Brants, Phillipp Koehn, and Tony Robinson. 2013. One billion word benchmark for measuring progress in statistical language modeling. *arXiv preprint arXiv:1312.3005* .

Colin Cherry and Dekang Lin. 2006. Soft syntactic constraints for word alignment through discriminative training. In *Proc. COLING*.

Adrià De Gispert, Deepa Gupta, Maja Popović, Patrik Lambert, Jose B Marino, Marcello Federico, Hermann Ney, and Rafael Banchs. 2006. Improving statistical word alignments with morpho-syntactic transformations. In *Advances in Natural Language Processing*.

Victoria Fossum, Kevin Knight, and Steven Abney. 2008. Using syntax to improve word alignment precision for syntax-based machine translation. In *Proc. Workshop on Statistical Machine Translation*.

Ulf Hermjakob. 2009. Improved word alignment with statistics and linguistic heuristics. In *Proc. EMNLP*.

Tomáš Kočiskỳ, Karl Moritz Hermann, and Phil Blunsom. 2014. Learning bilingual word representations by marginalizing alignments. *arXiv preprint arXiv:1405.0947* .

Philipp Koehn, Hieu Hoang, Alexandra Birch, Chris Callison-Burch, Marcello Federico, Nicola Bertoldi, Brooke Cowan, Wade Shen, Christine Moran, Richard Zens, et al. 2007. Moses: Open source toolkit for statistical machine translation. In *Proc. ACL, interactive poster and demonstration sessions*.

Philipp Koehn and Rebecca Knowles. 2017. Six challenges for neural MT. In *Proc. Workshop on Neural Machine Translation*.

Young-Suk Lee. 2004. Morphological analysis for statistical machine translation. In *Proc. NAACL*.

Percy Liang, Ben Taskar, and Dan Klein. 2006. Alignment by agreement. In *Proc. NAACL*.

Jeff Ma, Spyros Matsoukas, and Richard Schwartz. 2011. Improving low-resource statistical machine translation with a novel semantic word clustering algorithm. *Proc. MT Summit XIII* .

Coşkun Mermer and Murat Saraçlar. 2011. Bayesian word alignment for statistical machine translation. In *Proc. ACL*.

Tomas Mikolov, Kai Chen, Greg Corrado, and Jeffrey Dean. 2013. Efficient estimation of word representations in vector space. *arXiv preprint arXiv:1301.3781* .

Robert C Moore. 2004. Improving IBM word-alignment model 1. In *Proc. ACL*.

Franz Josef Och and Hermann Ney. 2003. A systematic comparison of various statistical alignment models. *Computational linguistics* 29(1).

Jeffrey Pennington, Richard Socher, and Christopher Manning. 2014. Glove: Global vectors for word representation. In *Proc. EMNLP*.

Mohammad Taher Pilevar, Heshaam Faili, and Abdol Hamid Pilevar. 2011. Tep: Tehran English-Persian parallel corpus. In *Proc. CICLing*.

Nima Pourdamghani, Yang Gao, Ulf Hermjakob, and Kevin Knight. 2014. Aligning English strings with abstract meaning representation graphs. In *Proc. EMNLP*.

Theerawat Songyot and David Chiang. 2014. Improving word alignment using word similarity. In *Proc. EMNLP*.

Jörg Tiedemann. 2003. Combining clues for word alignment. In *Proc. EACL*.

Kristina Toutanova, H Tolga Ilhan, and Christopher D Manning. 2002. Extensions to HMM-based statistical word alignment models. In *Proc. EMNLP*.

Vuong Van Bui and Cuong Anh Le. 2016. Smoothing parameter estimation framework for IBM word alignment models. *arXiv preprint arXiv:1601.03650* .

Ashish Vaswani, Liang Huang, and David Chiang. 2012. Smaller alignment models for better translations: unsupervised word alignment with the l0-norm. In *Proc. ACL*.

Hui Zhang and David Chiang. 2014. Kneser-Ney smoothing on expected counts. In *Proc. ACL*.

When and Why are Pre-trained Word Embeddings Useful for Neural Machine Translation?

Ye Qi, Devendra Singh Sachan, Matthieu Felix,
Sarguna Janani Padmanabhan, Graham Neubig
Language Technologies Institute, Carnegie Mellon University, USA
{yeq,dsachan,matthief,sjpadman,gneubig}@andrew.cmu.edu

Abstract

The performance of Neural Machine Translation (NMT) systems often suffers in low-resource scenarios where sufficiently large-scale parallel corpora cannot be obtained. Pre-trained word embeddings have proven to be invaluable for improving performance in natural language analysis tasks, which often suffer from paucity of data. However, their utility for NMT has not been extensively explored. In this work, we perform five sets of experiments that analyze when we can expect pre-trained word embeddings to help in NMT tasks. We show that such embeddings can be surprisingly effective in some cases – providing gains of up to 20 BLEU points in the most favorable setting.[1]

1 Introduction

Pre-trained word embeddings have proven to be highly useful in neural network models for NLP tasks such as sequence tagging (Lample et al., 2016; Ma and Hovy, 2016) and text classification (Kim, 2014). However, it is much less common to use such pre-training in NMT (Wu et al., 2016), largely because the large-scale training corpora used for tasks such as WMT[2] tend to be several orders of magnitude larger than the annotated data available for other tasks, such as the Penn Treebank (Marcus et al., 1993). However, for low-resource languages or domains, it is not necessarily the case that bilingual data is available in abundance, and therefore the effective use of monolingual data becomes a more desirable option.

Researchers have worked on a number of methods for using monolingual data in NMT systems (Cheng et al., 2016; He et al., 2016; Ramachandran et al., 2016). Among these, pre-trained word embeddings have been used either in standard

translation systems (Neishi et al., 2017; Artetxe et al., 2017) or as a method for learning translation lexicons in an entirely unsupervised manner (Conneau et al., 2017; Gangi and Federico, 2017). Both methods show potential improvements in BLEU score when pre-training is properly integrated into the NMT system.

However, from these works, it is still not clear as to *when* we can expect pre-trained embeddings to be useful in NMT, or *why* they provide performance improvements. In this paper, we examine these questions more closely, conducting five sets of experiments to answer the following questions:

Q1 Is the behavior of pre-training affected by language families and other linguistic features of source and target languages? (§3)

Q2 Do pre-trained embeddings help more when the size of the training data is small? (§4)

Q3 How much does the similarity of the source and target languages affect the efficacy of using pre-trained embeddings? (§5)

Q4 Is it helpful to align the embedding spaces between the source and target languages? (§6)

Q5 Do pre-trained embeddings help more in multilingual systems as compared to bilingual systems? (§7)

2 Experimental Setup

In order to perform experiments in a controlled, multilingual setting, we created a parallel corpus from TED talks transcripts.[3] Specifically, we prepare data between English (EN) and three pairs of languages, where the two languages in the pair are similar, with one being relatively low-resourced compared to the other: Galician (GL) and Portuguese (PT), Azerbaijani (AZ) and Turkish (TR), and Belarusian (BE) and Russian (RU).

---

[1] Scripts/data to replicate experiments are available at https://github.com/neulab/word-embeddings-for-nmt

[2] http://www.statmt.org/wmt17/

[3] https://www.ted.com/participate/translate

Proceedings of NAACL-HLT 2018, pages 529–535
New Orleans, Louisiana, June 1 - 6, 2018. ©2018 Association for Computational Linguistics

Dataset	train	dev	test
Gl → En	10,017	682	1,007
Pt → En	51,785	1,193	1,803
Az → En	5,946	671	903
Tr → En	182,450	4,045	5,029
Be → En	4,509	248	664
Ru → En	208,106	4,805	5,476

Table 1: Number of sentences for each language pair.

The languages in each pair are similar in vocabulary, grammar and sentence structure (Matthews, 1997), which controls for language characteristics and also improves the possibility of transfer learning in multi-lingual models (in §7). They also represent different language families – Gl/Pt are Romance; Az/Tr are Turkic; Be/Ru are Slavic – allowing for comparison across languages with different caracteristics. Tokenization was done using `Moses` tokenizer[4] and hard punctuation symbols were used to identify sentence boundaries. Table 1 shows data sizes.

For our experiments, we use a standard 1-layer encoder-decoder model with attention (Bahdanau et al., 2014) with a beam size of 5 implemented in `xnmt`[5] (Neubig et al., 2018). Training uses a batch size of 32 and the Adam optimizer (Kingma and Ba, 2014) with an initial learning rate of 0.0002, decaying the learning rate by 0.5 when development loss decreases (Denkowski and Neubig, 2017). We evaluate the model's performance using BLEU metric (Papineni et al., 2002).

We use available pre-trained word embeddings (Bojanowski et al., 2016) trained using `fastText`[6] on Wikipedia[7] for each language. These word embeddings (Mikolov et al., 2017) incorporate character-level, phrase-level and positional information of words and are trained using CBOW algorithm (Mikolov et al., 2013). The dimension of word embeddings is set to 300. The embedding layer weights of our model are initialized using these pre-trained word vectors. In baseline models without pre-training, we use Glorot and Bengio (2010)'s uniform initialization.

3 Q1: Efficacy of Pre-training

In our first set of experiments, we examine the efficacy of pre-trained word embeddings across the various languages in our corpus. In addition to

| **Src →** | std | pre | std | pre |
→ Trg	std	std	pre	pre
Gl → En	2.2	**13.2**	2.8	12.8
Pt → En	26.2	**30.3**	26.1	**30.8**
Az → En	1.3	**2.0**	1.6	**2.0**
Tr → En	14.9	17.6	14.7	**17.9**
Be → En	1.6	2.5	1.3	**3.0**
Ru → En	18.5	**21.2**	18.7	**21.1**

Table 2: Effect of pre-training on BLEU score over six languages. The systems use either random initialization (`std`) or pre-training (`pre`) on both the source and target sides.

providing additional experimental evidence supporting the findings of other recent work on using pre-trained embeddings in NMT (Neishi et al., 2017; Artetxe et al., 2017; Gangi and Federico, 2017), we also examine whether pre-training is useful across a wider variety of language pairs and if it is more useful on the source or target side of a translation pair.

The results in Table 2 clearly demonstrate that pre-training the word embeddings in the source and/or target languages helps to increase the BLEU scores to some degree. Comparing the second and third columns, we can see the increase is much more significant with pre-trained source language embeddings. This indicates that the majority of the gain from pre-trained word embeddings results from a better encoding of the source sentence.

The gains from pre-training in the higher-resource languages are consistent: ≈3 BLEU points for all three language pairs. In contrast, for the extremely low-resource languages, the gains are either quite small (Az and Be) or very large, as in Gl which achieves a gain of up to 11 BLEU points. This finding is interesting in that it indicates that word embeddings may be particularly useful to bootstrap models that are on the threshold of being able to produce reasonable translations, as is the case for Gl in our experiments.

4 Q2: Effect of Training Data Size

The previous experiment had interesting implications regarding available data size and effect of pre-training. Our next series of experiments examines this effect in a more controlled environment by down-sampling the training data for the higher-resource languages to 1/2, 1/4 and 1/8 of their original sizes.

From the BLEU scores in Figure 1, we can see

---

[4]https://github.com/moses-smt/mosesdecoder/blob/master/scripts/tokenizer/tokenizer.perl

[5]https://github.com/neulab/xnmt/

[6]https://github.com/facebookresearch/fastText/

[7]https://dumps.wikimedia.org/

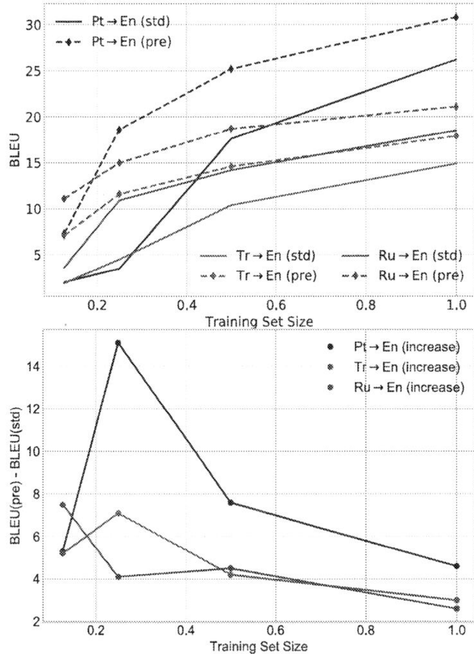

Figure 1: BLEU and BLEU gain by data size.

Dataset	Lang. Family	std	pre
Es → Pt	West-Iberian	17.8	24.8 (+**7.0**)
Fr → Pt	Western Romance	12.4	18.1 (+5.7)
It → Pt	Romance	14.5	19.2 (+4.7)
Ru → Pt	Indo-European	2.4	8.6 (+6.2)
He → Pt	*No Common*	3.0	11.9 (+**8.9**)

Table 3: Effect of linguistic similarity and pre-training on BLEU. The language family in the second column is the most recent common ancestor of source and target language.

that for all three languages the gain in BLEU score demonstrates a similar trend to that found in GL in the previous section: the gain is highest when the baseline system is poor but not too poor, usually with a baseline BLEU score in the range of 3-4. This suggests that at least a moderately effective system is necessary before pre-training takes effect, but once there is enough data to capture the basic characteristics of the language, pre-training can be highly effective.

5 Q3: Effect of Language Similarity

The main intuitive hypothesis as to why pre-training works is that the embedding space becomes more consistent, with semantically similar words closer together. We can also make an additional hypothesis: if the two languages in the translation pair are more linguistically similar, the semantic neighborhoods will be more similar between the two languages (i.e. semantic distinctions or polysemy will likely manifest themselves in more similar ways across more similar languages). As a result, we may expect that the gain from pre-training of embeddings may be larger when the source and target languages are more similar. To examine this hypothesis, we selected Portuguese as the target language, which when following its language family tree from top to bottom, belongs to Indo-European, Romance,

Western Romance, and West-Iberian families. We then selected one source language from each family above.[8] To avoid the effects of training set size, all pairs were trained on 40,000 sentences.

From Table 3, we can see that the BLEU scores of Es, Fr, and It do generally follow this hypothesis. As we move to very different languages, Ru and He see larger accuracy gains than their more similar counterparts Fr and It. This can be largely attributed to the observation from the previous section that systems with larger headroom to improve tend to see larger increases; Ru and He have very low baseline BLEU scores, so it makes sense that their increases would be larger.

6 Q4: Effect of Word Embedding Alignment

Until now, we have been using embeddings that have been trained independently in the source and target languages, and as a result there will not necessarily be a direct correspondence between the embedding spaces in both languages. However, we can postulate that having consistent embedding spaces across the two languages may be beneficial, as it would allow the NMT system to more easily learn correspondences between the source and target. To test this hypothesis, we adopted the approach proposed by Smith et al. (2017) to learn orthogonal transformations that convert the word embeddings of multiple languages to a single space and used these aligned embeddings instead of independent ones.

From Table 4, we can see that somewhat surprisingly, the alignment of word embeddings was not beneficial for training, with gains or losses essentially being insignificant across all languages. This, in a way, is good news, as it indicates that *a priori* alignment of embeddings may not be neces-

---

[8] English was excluded because the TED talks were originally in English, which results in it having much higher BLEU scores than the other languages due to it being direct translation instead of pivoted through English like the others.

531

Dataset	unaligned	aligned
GL → EN	12.8	11.5 (−1.3)
PT → EN	30.8	30.6 (−0.2)
AZ → EN	2.0	2.1 (+0.1)
TR → EN	17.9	17.7 (−0.2)
BE → EN	3.0	3.0 (+0.0)
RU → EN	21.1	21.4 (+0.3)

Table 4: Correlation between word embedding alignment and BLEU score in bilingual translation task.

Train	Eval	bi	std	pre	align
GL + PT	GL	2.2	17.5	20.8	**22.4**
AZ + TR	AZ	1.3	5.4	5.9	**7.5**
BE + RU	BE	1.6	**10.0**	7.9	9.6

Table 5: Effect of pre-training on multilingual translation into English. `bi` is a bilingual system trained on only the eval source language and all others are multi-lingual systems trained on two similar source languages.

sary in the context of NMT, since the NMT system can already learn a reasonable projection of word embeddings during its normal training process.

7 Q5: Effect of Multilinguality

Finally, it is of interest to consider pre-training in multilingual translation systems that share an encoder or decoder between multiple languages (Johnson et al., 2016; Firat et al., 2016), which is another promising way to use additional data (this time from another language) as a way to improve NMT. Specifically, we train a model using our pairs of similar low-resource and higher-resource languages, and test on only the low-resource language. For those three pairs, the similarity of GL/PT is the highest while BE/RU is the lowest.

We report the results in Table 5. When applying pre-trained embeddings, the gains in each translation pair are roughly in order of their similarity, with GL/PT showing the largest gains, and BE/RU showing a small decrease. In addition, it is also interesting to note that as opposed to previous section, aligning the word embeddings helps to increase the BLEU scores for all three tasks. These increases are intuitive, as a single encoder is used for both of the source languages, and the encoder would have to learn a significantly more complicated transform of the input if the word embeddings for the languages were in a semantically separate space. Pre-training and alignment ensures that the word embeddings of the two source languages are put into similar vector spaces, allowing the model to learn in a similar fashion as it would if training on a single language.

Interestingly, BE → EN does not seem to benefit from pre-training in the multilingual scenario, which hypothesize is due to the fact that: 1) Belarusian and Russian are only partially mutually intelligible (Corbett and Comrie, 2003), i.e., they are not as similar; 2) the Slavic languages have comparatively rich morphology, making sparsity in the trained embeddings a larger problem.

8 Analysis

8.1 Qualitative Analysis

Finally, we perform a qualitative analysis of the translations from GL → EN, which showed one of the largest increases in quantitative numbers. As can be seen from Table 6, pre-training not only helps the model to capture rarer vocabulary but also generates sentences that are more grammatically well-formed. As highlighted in the table cells, the best system successfully translates a person's name ("*chris*") and two multi-word phrases ("*big lawyer*" and "*patent legislation*"), indicating the usefulness of pre-trained embeddings in providing a better representations of less frequent concepts when used with low-resource languages.

In contrast, the bilingual model without pre-trained embeddings substitutes these phrases for common ones ("*i*"), drops them entirely, or produces grammatically incorrect sentences. The incomprehension of core vocabulary causes deviation of the sentence semantics and thus increases the uncertainty in predicting next words, generating several phrasal loops which are typical in NMT systems.

8.2 Analysis of Frequently Generated n-grams.

We additionally performed pairwise comparisons between the top 10 n-grams that each system (selected from the task GL → EN) is better at generating, to further understand what kind of words pre-training is particularly helpful for.[9] The results displayed in Table 7 demonstrate that pre-training helps both with words of low frequency in the training corpus, and even with function words such as prepositions. On the other hand, the improvements in systems without pre-trained embed-

---

[9] Analysis was performed using `compare-mt.py` from https://github.com/neubig/util-scripts/.

`source`	(*risos*) e é que **chris** é un grande avogado , pero non sabía case nada sobre lexislación de patentes e absolutamente nada sobre xenética .
`reference`	(*laughter*) now **chris** is a really brilliant lawyer , but he knew almost nothing about patent law and certainly nothing about genetics .
`bi:std`	(*laughter*) and **i** 'm not a little bit of a little bit of a little bit of and (laughter) and i 'm going to be able to be a lot of years .
`multi:pre-align`	(*laughter*) and **chris** is a big lawyer , but i did n't know almost anything about patent legislation and absolutely nothing about genetic .

Table 6: Example translations of GL → EN.

`bi:std`		`bi:pre`			`multi:std`		`multi:pre+align`	
) so	2/0	about	0/53		here	6/0	on the	0/14
(laughter) i	2/0	people	0/49		again ,	4/0	like	1/20
) i	2/0	or	0/43		several	4/0	should	0/9
laughter) i	2/0	these	0/39		you 're going	4/0	court	0/9
) and	2/0	with	0/38		've	4/0	judge	0/7
they were	1/0	because	0/37		we 've	4/0	testosterone	0/6
have to	5/2	like	0/36		you 're going to	4/0	patents	0/6
a new	1/0	could	0/35		people ,	4/0	patent	0/6
to do ,	1/0	all	0/34		what are	3/0	test	0/6
`` and then	1/0	two	0/32		the room	3/0	with	1/12

(a) Pairwise comparison between two bilingual models   (b) Pairwise comparison between two multilingual models

Table 7: Top 10 n-grams that one system did a better job of producing. The numbers in the figure, separated by a slash, indicate how many times each n-gram is generated by each of the two systems.

dings were not very consistent, and largely focused on high-frequency words.

8.3 F-measure of Target Words

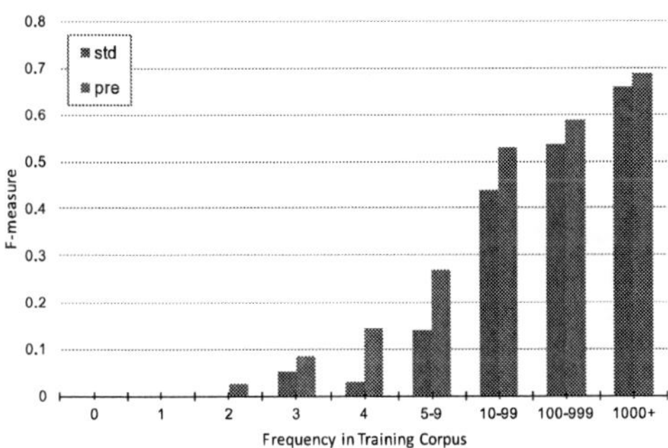

Figure 2: The f-measure of target words in bilingual translation task PT → EN

Finally, we performed a comparison of the f-measure of target words, bucketed by frequency in the training corpus. As displayed in Figure 2, this shows that pre-training manages to improve the accuracy of translation for the entire vocabulary, but particularly for words that are of low frequency in the training corpus.

9   Conclusion

This paper examined the utility of considering pre-trained word embeddings in NMT from a number of angles. Our conclusions have practical effects on the recommendations for when and why pre-trained embeddings may be effective in NMT, particularly in low-resource scenarios: (1) there is a sweet-spot where word embeddings are most effective, where there is very little training data but not so little that the system cannot be trained at all, (2) pre-trained embeddings seem to be more effective for more similar translation pairs, (3) *a priori* alignment of embeddings may not be necessary in bilingual scenarios, but is helpful in multi-lingual training scenarios.

Acknowledgements

Parts of this work were sponsored by Defense Advanced Research Projects Agency Information Innovation Office (I2O). Program: Low Resource Languages for Emergent Incidents (LORELEI). Issued by DARPA/I2O under Contract No. HR0011-15-C-0114. The views and conclusions contained in this document are those of the authors and should not be interpreted as representing the official policies, either expressed or implied, of the U.S. Government. The U.S. Government is authorized to reproduce and distribute reprints for Government purposes notwithstanding any copyright notation here on.

References

Mikel Artetxe, Gorka Labaka, Eneko Agirre, and Kyunghyun Cho. 2017. Unsupervised neural machine translation. *arXiv preprint arXiv:1710.11041* .

Dzmitry Bahdanau, Kyunghyun Cho, and Yoshua Bengio. 2014. Neural machine translation by jointly learning to align and translate. *arXiv e-prints* abs/1409.0473. https://arxiv.org/abs/1409.0473.

Piotr Bojanowski, Edouard Grave, Armand Joulin, and Tomas Mikolov. 2016. Enriching word vectors with subword information. *arXiv preprint arXiv:1607.04606* .

Yong Cheng, Wei Xu, Zhongjun He, Wei He, Hua Wu, Maosong Sun, and Yang Liu. 2016. Semisupervised learning for neural machine translation. *arXiv preprint arXiv:1606.04596* .

Alexis Conneau, Guillaume Lample, Marc'Aurelio Ranzato, Ludovic Denoyer, and Hervé Jégou. 2017. Word translation without parallel data. *arXiv preprint arXiv:1710.04087* .

Greville Corbett and Bernard Comrie. 2003. *The Slavonic Languages*. Routledge.

Michael Denkowski and Graham Neubig. 2017. Stronger baselines for trustable results in neural machine translation. *arXiv preprint arXiv:1706.09733* .

Orhan Firat, Kyunghyun Cho, and Yoshua Bengio. 2016. Multi-way, multilingual neural machine translation with a shared attention mechanism. *arXiv preprint arXiv:1601.01073* .

Mattia Antonino Di Gangi and Marcello Federico. 2017. Monolingual embeddings for low resourced neural machine translation. In *International Workshop on Spoken Language Translation (IWSLT)*.

Xavier Glorot and Yoshua Bengio. 2010. Understanding the difficulty of training deep feedforward neural networks. In *Proceedings of the Thirteenth International Conference on Artificial Intelligence and Statistics*. pages 249–256.

Di He, Yingce Xia, Tao Qin, Liwei Wang, Nenghai Yu, Tieyan Liu, and Wei-Ying Ma. 2016. Dual learning for machine translation. In *Advances in Neural Information Processing Systems*. pages 820–828.

Melvin Johnson et al. 2016. Google's multilingual neural machine translation system: Enabling zero-shot translation. *arXiv preprint arXiv:1611.04558* .

Yoon Kim. 2014. Convolutional neural networks for sentence classification. In *In EMNLP*. Citeseer.

Diederik Kingma and Jimmy Ba. 2014. Adam: A method for stochastic optimization. *arXiv preprint arXiv:1412.6980* .

Guillaume Lample, Miguel Ballesteros, Sandeep Subramanian, Kazuya Kawakami, and Chris Dyer. 2016. Neural architectures for named entity recognition. In *HLT-NAACL*.

Xuezhe Ma and Eduard Hovy. 2016. End-to-end sequence labeling via bi-directional lstm-cnns-crf. In *Proceedings of the 54th Annual Meeting of the Association for Computational Linguistics (Volume 1: Long Papers)*. Association for Computational Linguistics, Berlin, Germany, pages 1064–1074. http://www.aclweb.org/anthology/P16-1101.

Mitchell P Marcus, Mary Ann Marcinkiewicz, and Beatrice Santorini. 1993. Building a large annotated corpus of english: The penn treebank. *Computational linguistics* 19(2):313–330.

P.H. Matthews. 1997. *The Concise Oxford Dictionary of Linguistics..* Oxford Paperback Reference / Oxford University Press, Oxford. Oxford University Press, Incorporated. https://books.google.com/books?id=aYoYAAAAIAAJ.

Tomas Mikolov, Edouard Grave, Piotr Bojanowski, Christian Puhrsch, and Armand Joulin. 2017. Advances in pre-training distributed word representations .

Tomas Mikolov, Ilya Sutskever, Kai Chen, Greg S Corrado, and Jeff Dean. 2013. Distributed representations of words and phrases and their compositionality. In *Advances in neural information processing systems*. pages 3111–3119.

Masato Neishi, Jin Sakuma, Satoshi Tohda, Shonosuke Ishiwatari, Naoki Yoshinaga, and Masashi Toyoda. 2017. A bag of useful tricks for practical neural machine translation: Embedding layer initialization and large batch size. In *Proceedings of the 4th Workshop on Asian Translation (WAT2017)*. Asian Federation of Natural Language Processing, Taipei, Taiwan, pages 99–109.

Graham Neubig, Matthias Sperber, Xinyi Wang, Matthieu Felix, Austin Matthews, Sarguna Padmanabhan, Ye Qi, Devendra Singh Sachan, Philip Arthur, Pierre Godard, John Hewitt, Rachid Riad, and Liming Wang. 2018. XNMT: The extensible neural machine translation toolkit. In *Conference of the Association for Machine Translation in the Americas (AMTA) Open Source Software Showcase*. Boston.

Kishore Papineni, Salim Roukos, Todd Ward, and Wei-Jing Zhu. 2002. Bleu: a method for automatic evaluation of machine translation. In *Proceedings of the 40th annual meeting on association for computational linguistics*. Association for Computational Linguistics, pages 311–318.

Prajit Ramachandran, Peter J Liu, and Quoc V Le. 2016. Unsupervised pretraining for sequence to sequence learning. *arXiv preprint arXiv:1611.02683* .

Samuel L Smith, David HP Turban, Steven Hamblin, and Nils Y Hammerla. 2017. Offline bilingual word vectors, orthogonal transformations and the inverted softmax. *arXiv preprint arXiv:1702.03859* .

Yonghui Wu, Mike Schuster, Zhifeng Chen, Quoc V. Le, Mohammad Norouzi, Wolfgang Macherey, Maxim Krikun, Yuan Cao, Qin Gao, Klaus Macherey, Jeff Klingner, Apurva Shah, Melvin Johnson, Xiaobing Liu, Lukasz Kaiser, Stephan Gouws, Yoshikiyo Kato, Taku Kudo, Hideto Kazawa, Keith Stevens, George Kurian, Nishant Patil, Wei Wang, Cliff Young, Jason Smith, Jason Riesa, Alex Rudnick, Oriol Vinyals, Gregory S. Corrado, Macduff Hughes, and Jeffrey Dean. 2016. Google's neural machine translation system: Bridging the gap between human and machine translation. *CoRR* abs/1609.08144.

Are All Languages Equally Hard to Language-Model?

Ryan Cotterell[1] and **Sebastian J. Mielke**[1] and **Jason Eisner**[1] and **Brian Roark**[2]
[1] Department of Computer Science, Johns Hopkins University   [2] Google
{ryan.cotterell@,sjmielke@,jason@cs.}jhu.edu   roark@google.com

Abstract

For general modeling methods applied to diverse languages, a natural question is: how well should we expect our models to work on languages with differing typological profiles? In this work, we develop an evaluation framework for fair cross-linguistic comparison of language models, using translated text so that all models are asked to predict approximately the same information. We then conduct a study on 21 languages, demonstrating that in some languages, the textual expression of the information is harder to predict with both n-gram and LSTM language models. We show complex inflectional morphology to be a cause of performance differences among languages.

1 Introduction

Modern natural language processing practitioners strive to create modeling techniques that work well on all of the world's languages. Indeed, most methods are portable in the following sense: Given appropriately annotated data, they should, in principle, be trainable on any language. However, despite this crude cross-linguistic compatibility, it is unlikely that all languages are equally easy, or that our methods are equally good at all languages.

In this work, we probe the issue, focusing on *language modeling*. A fair comparison is tricky. Training corpora in different languages have different sizes, and reflect the disparate topics of discussion in different linguistic communities, some of which may be harder to predict than others. Moreover, bits per character, a standard metric for language modeling, depends on the vagaries of a given orthographic system. We argue for a fairer metric based on the bits per utterance using utterance-aligned multi-text. That is, we train and test on "the same" set of utterances in each language, modulo translation. To avoid discrepancies in out-of-vocabulary handling, we evaluate open-vocabulary models.

We find that under standard approaches, text tends to be harder to predict in languages with fine-grained inflectional morphology. Specifically, language models perform worse on these languages, in our controlled comparison. Furthermore, this performance difference essentially vanishes when we remove the inflectional markings.[1]

Thus, in highly inflected languages, either the utterances have more content or the models are worse. (1) Text in highly inflected languages may be *inherently harder to predict* (higher entropy per utterance) if its extra morphemes carry additional, unpredictable information. (2) Alternatively, perhaps the extra morphemes are *predictable in principle*—for example, redundant marking of grammatical number on both subjects and verbs, or marking of object case even when it is predictable from semantics or word order—and yet our current language modeling technology fails to predict them. This might happen because (2a) the technology is biased toward modeling words or characters and fails to discover intermediate morphemes, or because (2b) it fails to capture the syntactic and semantic predictors that govern the appearance of the extra morphemes. We leave it to future work to tease apart these hypotheses.

2 Language Modeling

A traditional closed-vocabulary, word-level language model operates as follows: Given a fixed set of words $\mathcal{V}$, the model provides a probability distribution over sequences of words with parameters to be estimated from data. Most fixed-vocabulary language models employ a distinguished symbol UNK that represents all words not present in $\mathcal{V}$; these words are termed out-of-vocabulary (OOV).

Choosing the set $\mathcal{V}$ is something of a black art: Some practitioners choose the k most com-

---

[1] One might have expected *a priori* that some difference would remain, because most highly inflected languages can also vary word order to mark a topic-focus distinction, and this (occasional) marking is preserved in our experiment.

Proceedings of NAACL-HLT 2018, pages 536–541
New Orleans, Louisiana, June 1 - 6, 2018. ©2018 Association for Computational Linguistics

mon words (e.g., Mikolov et al. (2010) choose $k = 10000$) and others use all those words that appear at least twice in the training corpus. In general, replacing more words with UNK artificially improves the perplexity measure but produces a less useful model. OOVs present something of a challenge for the cross-linguistic comparison of language models, especially in morphologically rich languages, which simply have more word forms.

2.1 The Role of Inflectional Morphology

Inflectional morphology can explode the base vocabulary of a language. Compare, for instance, English and Turkish. The nominal inflectional system of English distinguishes two forms: a singular and plural. The English lexeme BOOK has the singular form *book* and the plural form *books*. In contrast, Turkish distinguishes at least 12: *kitap, kitablar, kitabı, kitabın*, etc.

To compare the degree of morphological inflection in our evalation languages, we use **counting complexity** (Sagot, 2013). This crude metric counts the number of inflectional categories distinguished by a language (e.g., English includes a category of 3rd-person singular present-tense verbs). We count the categories annotated in the language's UniMorph (Kirov et al., 2018) lexicon. See Table 1 for the counting complexity of evaluated languages.

2.2 Open-Vocabulary Language Models

To ensure comparability across languages, we require our language models to predict every character in an utterance, rather than skipping some characters because they appear in words that were (arbitrarily) designated as OOV in that language. Such models are known as "open-vocabulary" LMs.

Notation. Let $\cup$ denote disjoint union, i.e., $A \cup B = C$ iff $A \cup B = C$ and $A \cap B = \emptyset$. Let Σ be a discrete alphabet of characters, including a distinguished unknown-character symbol $\star$.[2] A character LM then defines $p(\boldsymbol{c}) = \prod_{i=1}^{|c|+1} p(c_i \mid \boldsymbol{c}_{<i})$, where we take $c_{|c|+1}$ to be a distinguished end-of-string symbol EOS. In this work, we consider two open-vocabulary LMs, as follows.

Baseline n-gram LM. We train "flat" hybrid word/character open-vocabulary n-gram models (Bisani and Ney, 2005), defined over strings Σ^+

from a vocabulary Σ with mutually disjoint subsets: $\Sigma = W \cup C \cup S$, where single characters $c \in C$ are distinguished in the model from single character full words $w \in W$, e.g., a versus the word a. Special symbols $S = \{\text{EOW}, \text{EOS}\}$ are end-of-word and end-of-string, respectively. N-gram histories in H are either word-boundary or word-internal (corresponding to a whitespace tokenization), i.e., $H = H_b \cup H_i$. String-internal word boundaries are always separated by a single whitespace character.[3] For example, if foo, baz $\in W$ but bar $\notin W$, then the string foo bar baz would be generated as: foo b a r EOW baz EOS. Possible 3-gram histories in this string would be, e.g., [foo b] $\in H_i$, [r EOW] $\in H_b$, and [EOW baz] $\in H_b$.

Symbols are generated from a multinomial given the history h, leading to a new history h' that now includes the symbol and is truncated to the Markov order. Histories $h \in H_b$ can generate symbols $s \in W \cup C \cup \{\text{EOS}\}$. If $s = \text{EOS}$, the string is ended. If $s \in W$, it has an implicit EOW and the model transitions to history $h' \in H_b$. If $s \in C$, it translitions to $h' \in H_i$. Histories $h \in H_i$ can generate symbols $s \in C \cup \{\text{EOW}\}$ and transition to $h' \in H_b$ if $s = \text{EOW}$, otherwise to $h' \in H_i$.

We use standard Kneser and Ney (1995) model training, with distributions at word-internal histories $h \in H_i$ constrained so as to only provide probability mass for symbols $s \in C \cup \{\text{EOW}\}$. We train 7-gram models, but prune n-grams hs where the history $h \in W^k$, for $k > 4$, i.e., 6- and 7-gram histories must include at least one $s \notin W$. To establish the vocabularies W and C, we replace exactly one instance of each word type with its spelled out version. Singleton words are thus excluded from W, and character sequence observations from all types are included in training. Note any word $w \in W$ can also be generated as a character sequence. For perplexity calculation, we sum the probabilities for each way of generating the word.

LSTM LM. While neural language models can also take a hybrid approach (Hwang and Sung, 2017; Kawakami et al., 2017), recent advances indicate that full character-level modeling is now competitive with word-level modeling. A large part of this is due to the use of recurrent neural networks (Mikolov et al., 2010), which can generalize about

---

[2] The set of graphemes in these languages can be assumed to be closed, but external graphemes may on rare occasion appear in random text samples. These are rare enough to not materially affect the metrics.

[3] The model can be extended to handle consecutive whitespace characters or punctuation at word boundaries; for this paper, the tokenization split punctuation from words and reduced consecutive whitespaces to one, hence the simpler model.

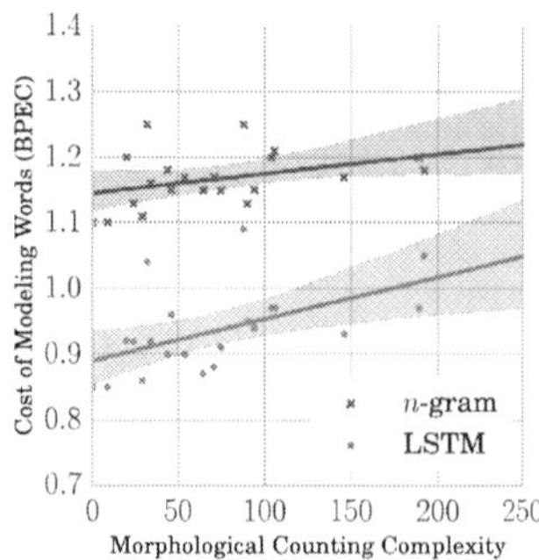

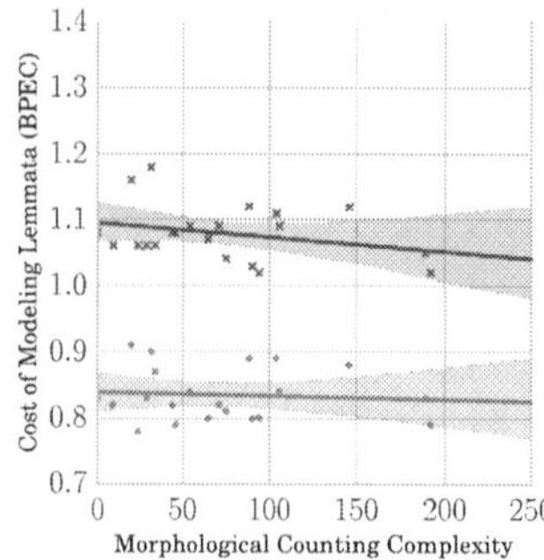

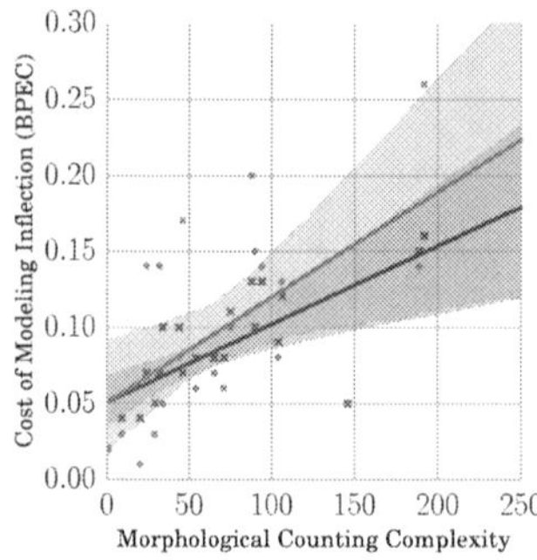

(a) BPEC performance of n-gram (blue) and LSTM (green) LMs over word sequences. Lower is better.

(b) BPEC performance of n-gram (blue) and LSTM (green) LMs over lemma sequences. Lower is better.

(c) Difference in BPEC performance of n-gram (blue) and LSTM (green) LMs between words and lemmata.

Figure 1: The primary findings of our paper are evinced in these plots. Each point is a language. While the LSTM outperforms the hybrid n-gram model, the relative performance on the highly inflected languages compared to the more modestly inflected languages is almost constant; to see this point, note that the regression lines in Fig. 1c are almost identical. Also, comparing Fig. 1a and Fig. 1b shows that the correlation between LM performance and morphological richness disappears after lemmatization of the corpus, indicating that inflectional morphology is the origin for the lower BPEC.

how the distribution $p(c_i \mid c_{<i})$ depends on $c_{<i}$.

We use a long short-term memory (LSTM) LM (Sundermeyer et al., 2012), identical to that of Zaremba et al. (2014), but at the character-level. To achieve the hidden state $\mathbf{h}_i \in \mathbb{R}^d$ at time step i, one feeds the left context c_{i-1} to the LSTM: $\mathbf{h}_i = \mathrm{LSTM}\,(c_1, \ldots, c_{i-1})$ where the model uses a learned vector to represent each character type. This involves a recursive procedure described in Hochreiter and Schmidhuber (1997). Then, the probability distribution over the ith character is $p(c_t \mid c_{<i}) = \mathrm{softmax}\,(\mathbf{W}\,\mathbf{h}_i + \mathbf{b})$, where $\mathbf{W} \in \mathbb{R}^{|\Sigma| \times d}$ and $\mathbf{b} \in \mathbb{R}^{|\Sigma|}$ are parameters.

Parameters for all models are estimated on the training portion and model selection is performed on the development portion. The neural models are trained with SGD (Robbins and Monro, 1951) with gradient clipping, such that each component has a maximum absolute value of 5. We optimize for 100 iterations and perform early stopping (on the development portion). We employ a character embedding of size 1024 and 2 hidden layers of size 1024.[4] The implementation is in PyTorch.

3 A Fairer Evaluation: Multi-Text

Effecting a cross-linguistic study on LMs is complicated because different models could be trained and tested on incomparable corpora. To avoid this problem, we use **multi-text**: k-way translations of the same semantic content.

What's wrong with bits per character? Open-vocabulary language modeling is most commonly evaluated under **bits per character** (BPC) $= \frac{1}{|c|+1} \sum_{i=1}^{|c|+1} \log p(c_i \mid c_{<i})$.[5] Even with multi-text, comparing BPC is not straightforward, as it relies on the vagaries of individual writing systems. Consider, for example, the difference in how Czech and German express the phoneme /tʃ/: Czech uses *č*, whereas German *tsch*. Now, consider the Czech word *puč* and its German equivalent *Putsch*. Even if these words are both predicted with the *same* probability in a given context, German will end up with a lower BPC.[6]

Bits per English Character. Multi-text allows us to compute a fair metric that is invariant to the orthographic (or phonological) changes discussed above: **bits per English character** (BPEC). $\mathrm{BPEC} = \frac{1}{|c_{English}|+1} \sum_{i=1}^{|c|+1} \log p(c_i \mid c_{<i})$, where $c_{English}$ is the English character sequence in the utterance aligned to c. The choice of English is arbitrary, as any other choice of language would simply scale the values by a constant factor.

Note that this metric is essentially capturing the overall *bits per utterance*, and that normalizing using English characters only makes numbers independent of the overall utterance length; it is not critical to the analysis we perform in this paper.

---

[4]As Zaremba et al. (2014) indicate, increasing the number of parameters may allow us to achieve better performance.

[5]To aggregate this over an entire test corpus, we replace the denominator and also the numerator by summations over all utterances c.

[6]Why not work with *phonological* characters, rather than orthographic ones, obtaining /putʃ/ for both Czech and German? Sadly this option is also fraught with problems as many languages have perfectly predictable phonological elements that will artificially lower the score.

| | data (M) | | BPEC / ΔBPC ($\cdot$e-2) | | | |
| | | | hybrid n-gram | | LSTM | |
lang	wds / ch	MCC	form	lemma	form	lemma
bg	0.71/4.3	96	1.13/ 4	1.03/ 1	0.95/ 3	0.80/ 1
cs	0.65/3.9	195	1.20/ -8	1.05/-12	0.97/ -6	0.83/ -9
da	0.70/4.1	15	1.10/ -1	1.06/ -4	0.85/ -1	0.82/ -3
de	0.74/4.8	38	1.25/ 17	1.18/ 13	1.04/ 14	0.90/ 10
el	0.75/4.6	50	1.18/ 13	1.08/ 5	0.90/ 10	0.82/ 4
en	0.75/4.1	6	1.10/ 0	1.08/ -3	0.85/ 0	0.83/ -3
es	0.81/4.6	71	1.15/ 12	1.07/ 7	0.87/ 9	0.80/ 5
et*	0.55/3.9	110	1.20/ -8	1.11/-15	0.97/ -6	0.89/-12
fi*	0.52/4.2	198	1.18/ 2	1.02/-11	1.05/ 1	0.79/ -9
fr	0.88/4.9	30	1.13/ 17	1.06/ 13	0.92/ 14	0.78/ 10
hu*	0.63/4.3	94	1.25/ 5	1.12/ -9	1.09/ 5	0.89/ -7
it	0.85/4.8	52	1.15/ 16	1.08/ 14	0.96/ 14	0.79/ 10
lt	0.59/3.9	152	1.17/ -6	1.12/ -7	0.93/ -5	0.88/ -6
lv	0.61/3.9	81	1.15/ -6	1.04/ -9	0.91/ -5	0.81/ -7
nl	0.75/4.5	26	1.20/ 11	1.16/ 4	0.92/ 8	0.91/ 4
pl	0.65/4.3	112	1.21/ 6	1.09/ -1	0.97/ 5	0.84/ -1
pt	0.89/4.8	77	1.17/ 16	1.09/ 9	0.88/ 12	0.82/ 7
ro	0.74/4.4	60	1.17/ 8	1.09/ 0	0.90/ 6	0.84/ 0
sk	0.64/3.9	40	1.16/ -6	1.06/-11	0.92/ -5	0.87/ -9
sl	0.64/3.8	100	1.15/-10	1.02/-10	0.90/ -8	0.80/ -7
sv	0.66/4.1	35	1.11/ -2	1.06/ -8	0.86/ -2	0.83/ -7

Table 1: Results for all configurations and the typological profile of the 21 Europarl languages. All languages are Indo-European, except for those marked with * which are Uralic. Morpholical counting complexity (MCC) is given for each language, along with bits per English character (BPEC) and the ΔBPC, which is BPEC minus bits per character (BPC). This is blue if BPEC > BPC and red if BPEC < BPC.

A Potential Confound: Translationese. Working with multi-text, however, does introduce a new bias: all of the utterances in the corpus have a source language and 20 translations of that source utterance into target languages. The characteristics of translated language has been widely studied and exploited, with one prominent characteristic of translations being simplification (Baker, 1993).

Note that a significant fraction of the original utterances in the corpus are English. Our analysis may then have underestimated the BPEC for other languages, to the extent that their sentences consist of simplified "translationese." Even so, English had the lowest BPEC from among the set of languages.

4 Experiments and Results

Our experiments are conducted on the 21 languages of the Europarl corpus (Koehn, 2005). The corpus consists of utterances made in the European parliament and are aligned cross-linguistically by a unique utterance id. With the exceptions (noted in Table 1) of Finnish, Hungarian and Estonian, which are Uralic, the languages are Indo-European.

While Europarl does not contain quite our desired breadth of typological diversity, it serves our purpose by providing large collections of aligned data across many languages. To create our experimental data, we extract all utterances and randomly sort them into train-development-test splits such that roughly 80% of the data are in train and 10% in development and test, respectively.[7] We also perform experiments on *lemmatized* text, where we replace every word with its lemma using the UD-Pipe toolkit (Straka et al., 2016), stripping away its inflectional morphology. We report two evaluation metrics: BPC and BPEC (see §3). Our BPEC measure always normalizes by the length of the original, not lemmatized, English.

Experimentally, we want to show: (i) When evaluating models in a controlled environment (multitext under BPEC), the models achieve lower performance on certain languages and (ii) inflectional morphology is the primary culprit for the performance differences. However, we repeat that we do not in this paper tease apart whether the models are at fault, or that certain languages inherently encode more information.

5 Discussion and Analysis

We display the performance of the n-gram LM and the LSTM LM under BPC and BPEC for each of the 21 languages in Fig. 1 with full numbers listed in Table 1. There are several main take-aways.

The Effect of BPEC. The first major take-away is that BPEC offers a cleaner cross-linguistic comparison than BPC. Were we to rank the languages by BPC (lowest to highest), we would find that English was in the middle of the pack, which is surprising as new language models are often only tuned on English itself. For example, BPC surprisingly suggests that French is easier to model than English. However, ranking under BPEC shows that the LSTM has the easiest time modeling English itself. Scandinavian languages Danish and Swedish have BPEC closest to English; these languages are typologically and genetically similar to English.

n-gram versus LSTM. As expected, the LSTM outperforms the baseline n-gram models across the board. In addition, however, n-gram modeling yields relatively poor performance on some languages, such as Dutch, with only modestly more complex inflectional morphology than English.

---

[7]Characters appearing < 100 times in train are ⋆.

Other phenomena—e.g., perhaps, compounding—may also be poorly modeled by n-grams.

The Impact of Inflectional Morphology. Another major take-away is that rich inflectional morphology is a difficulty for both n-gram and LSTM LMs. In this section we give numbers for the LSTMs. Studying Fig. 1a, we find that Spearman's rank correlation between a language's BPEC and its counting complexity (§2.1) is quite high ($\rho = 0.59$, significant at $p < 0.005$). This clear correlation between the level of inflectional morphology and the LSTM performance indicates that character-level models do not automatically fix the problem of morphological richness. If we lemmatize the words, however (Fig. 1b), the correlation becomes insignificant and in fact slightly negative ($\rho = -0.13$, $p \approx 0.56$). The difference of the two previous graphs (Fig. 1c) shows more clearly that the LM penalty for modeling inflectional endings is greater for languages with higher counting complexity. Indeed, this penalty is arguably a more appropriate measure of the complexity of the inflectional system. See also Fig. 2.

The differences in BPEC among languages are reduced when we lemmatize, with standard deviation dropping from 0.065 bits to 0.039 bits. Zooming in on Finnish (see Table 1), we see that Finnish forms are harder to model than English forms, but Finnish lemmata are *easier* to model than English ones. This is strong evidence that it was primarily the inflectional morphology, which lemmatization strips, that caused the differences in the model's performance on these two languages.

6   Related Work

Recurrent neural language models can effectively learn complex dependencies, even in open-vocabulary settings (Hwang and Sung, 2017; Kawakami et al., 2017). Whether the models are able to learn particular syntactic interactions is an intriguing question, and some methodologies have been presented to tease apart under what circumstances variously-trained models encode attested interactions (Linzen et al., 2016; Enguehard et al., 2017). While the sort of detailed, construction-specific analyses in these papers is surely informative, our evaluation is language-wide.

MT researchers have investigated whether an English sentence contains enough information to predict the fine-grained inflections used in its foreign-language translations (see Kirov et al., 2017).

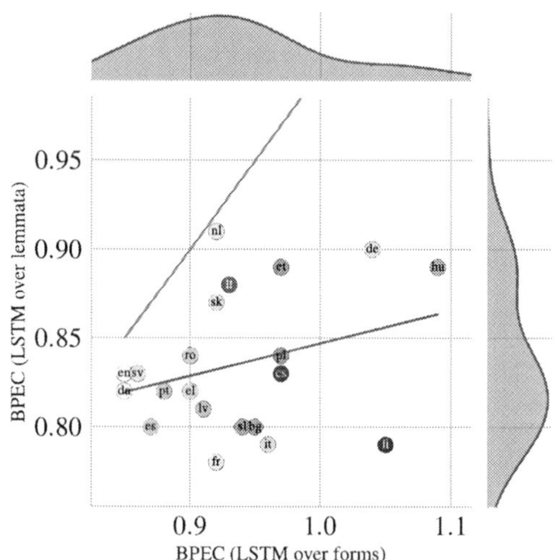

Figure 2: Each dot is a language, and its coordinates are the BPEC values for the LSTM LMs over words and lemmata. The top and right margins show kernel density estimates of these two sets of BPEC values. All dots follow the blue regression, but stay below the green line ($y = x$), and the darker dots—which represent languages with higher counting complexity—tend to fall toward the right but not toward the top, since counting complexity is correlated only with the BPEC over words.

Sproat et al. (2014) present a corpus of close translations of sentences in typologically diverse languages along with detailed morphosyntactic and morphosemantic annotations, as the means for assessing linguistic complexity for comparable messages, though they expressly do not take an information-theoretic approach to measuring complexity. In the linguistics literature, McWhorter (2001) argues that certain languages are less complex than others: he claims that Creoles are simpler. Müller et al. (2012) compare LMs on EuroParl, but do not compare performance across languages.

7   Conclusion

We have presented a clean method for the cross-linguistic comparison of language modeling: We assess whether a language modeling technique can compress a sentence and its translations equally well. We show an interesting correlation between the morphological richness of a language and the performance of the model. In an attempt to explain causation, we also run our models on lemmatized versions of the corpora, showing that, upon the removal of inflection, no such correlation between morphological richness and LM performance exists. It is still unclear, however, whether the performance difference originates from the inherent difficulty of the languages or with the models.

References

Mona Baker. 1993. Corpus linguistics and translation studies: Implications and applications. *Text and Technology: In Honour of John Sinclair* 233:250.

Maximilian Bisani and Hermann Ney. 2005. Open vocabulary speech recognition with flat hybrid models. In *INTERSPEECH*. pages 725–728.

Émile Enguehard, Yoav Goldberg, and Tal Linzen. 2017. Exploring the syntactic abilities of RNNs with multi-task learning. In *Proceedings of the 21st Conference on Computational Natural Language Learning (CoNLL 2017)*. Association for Computational Linguistics, pages 3–14. https://doi.org/10.18653/v1/K17-1003.

Sepp Hochreiter and Jürgen Schmidhuber. 1997. Long short-term memory. *Neural Computation* 9(8):1735–1780.

Kyuyeon Hwang and Wonyong Sung. 2017. Character-level language modeling with hierarchical recurrent neural networks. In *International Conference on Acoustics, Speech and Signal Processing (ICASSP)*. IEEE, pages 5720–5724.

Kazuya Kawakami, Chris Dyer, and Phil Blunsom. 2017. Learning to create and reuse words in open-vocabulary neural language modeling. In *Proceedings of the 55th Annual Meeting of the Association for Computational Linguistics (ACL)*. Association for Computational Linguistics, Vancouver, Canada, pages 1492–1502. http://aclweb.org/anthology/P17-1137.

Christo Kirov, Ryan Cotterell, John Sylak-Glassman, Géraldine Walther, Ekaterina Vylomova, Patrick Xia, Manaal Faruqui, Arya McCarthy, Sebastian J. Mielke, Sandra Kübler, David Yarowsky, Jason Eisner, and Mans Hulden. 2018. Unimorph 2.0: Universal morphology. In *Proceedings of the Ninth International Conference on Language Resources and Evaluation (LREC)*. European Language Resources Association (ELRA).

Christo Kirov, John Sylak-Glassman, Rebecca Knowles, Ryan Cotterell, and Matt Post. 2017. A rich morphological tagger for English: Exploring the cross-linguistic tradeoff between morphology and syntax. In *Proceedings of the 15th Conference of the European Chapter of the Association for Computational Linguistics: Volume 2, Short Papers*. Association for Computational Linguistics, pages 112–117. http://aclweb.org/anthology/E17-2018.

Reinhard Kneser and Hermann Ney. 1995. Improved backing-off for m-gram language modeling. In *International Conference on Acoustics, Speech, and Signal Processing, ICASSP*. pages 181–184.

Philipp Koehn. 2005. Europarl: A parallel corpus for statistical machine translation. In *MT Summit*. volume 5, pages 79–86.

Tal Linzen, Emmanuel Dupoux, and Yoav Goldberg. 2016. Assessing the ability of LSTMs to learn syntax-sensitive dependencies. *Transactions of the Association of Computational Linguistics* 4:521–535. http://www.aclweb.org/anthology/Q16-1037.

John McWhorter. 2001. The worlds simplest grammars are creole grammars. *Linguistic Typology* 5(2):125–66.

Tomas Mikolov, Martin Karafiát, Lukás Burget, Jan Cernocký, and Sanjeev Khudanpur. 2010. Recurrent neural network based language model. In *INTERSPEECH 2010, 11th Annual Conference of the International Speech Communication Association*. pages 1045–1048. http://www.isca-speech.org/archive/interspeech_2010/i10_1045.html.

Thomas Müller, Hinrich Schütze, and Helmut Schmid. 2012. A comparative investigation of morphological language modeling for the languages of the European Union. In *Proceedings of the 2012 Conference of the North American Chapter of the Association for Computational Linguistics: Human Language Technologies*. Association for Computational Linguistics, Montréal, Canada, pages 386–395. http://www.aclweb.org/anthology/N12-1043.

Herbert Robbins and Sutton Monro. 1951. A stochastic approximation method. *The Annals of Mathematical Statistics* pages 400–407.

Benoît Sagot. 2013. Comparing complexity measures. In *Computational Approaches to Morphological Complexity*.

Richard Sproat, Bruno Cartoni, HyunJeong Choe, David Huynh, Linne Ha, Ravindran Rajakumar, and Evelyn Wenzel-Grondie. 2014. A database for measuring linguistic information content. In *LREC*.

Milan Straka, Jan Hajič, and Jana Straková. 2016. UDPipe: Trainable pipeline for processing CoNLL-U files performing tokenization, morphological analysis, POS tagging and parsing. In *LREC*.

Martin Sundermeyer, Ralf Schlüter, and Hermann Ney. 2012. LSTM neural networks for language modeling. In *Thirteenth Annual Conference of the International Speech Communication Association*.

Wojciech Zaremba, Ilya Sutskever, and Oriol Vinyals. 2014. Recurrent neural network regularization. *CoRR* abs/1409.2329. http://arxiv.org/abs/1409.2329.

The Computational Complexity of Distinctive Feature Minimization in Phonology

Hubie Chen
Computer Science and Information Systems
Birkbeck, University of London
`hubie@dcs.bbk.ac.uk`

Mans Hulden
Department of Linguistics
University of Colorado
`mans.hulden@colorado.edu`

Abstract

We analyze the complexity of the problem of determining whether a set of phonemes forms a natural class and, if so, that of finding the minimal feature specification for the class. A standard assumption in phonology is that finding a minimal feature specification is an automatic part of acquisition and generalization. We find that the natural class decision problem is tractable (i.e. is in $\mathcal{P}$), while the minimization problem is not; the decision version of the problem which determines whether a natural class can be defined with k features or less is $\mathcal{NP}$-complete. We also show that, empirically, a greedy algorithm for finding minimal feature specifications will sometimes fail, and thus cannot be assumed to be the basis for human performance in solving the problem.

1 Introduction

The **distinctive feature** is held by many phonologists, independently of theoretical orientation, to be the fundamental unit of analysis of sound patterns in language. The underlying working assumption of most phonological approaches is that a single sound or a set of sounds is expressed through a combination of positive or negative features and that these features are in some sense universal across languages (Mielke, 2008a). The exact makeup of the feature set employed has varied over time, ranging from the limited, more acoustic-oriented features of Jakobson et al. (1951), to the richer model presented in Chomsky and Halle (1968), to more complex hierarchically organized features in Clements (1985). The concept of **natural class** is intimately tied to such feature systems and is taken to be any set of segments that share some number of distinctive features. Furthermore, phonological alternations that do not target natural classes are hypothesized not to occur.

Another assumption that is found in phonological literature—often less explicit—is that whenever a phonological process targets a group of sounds, that group is to be expressed nonredundantly by the *minimum number of features* required to do so. In general, one can find a multitude of ways in which a set of phonemes can be specified using positive or negative features. For example, using the feature system shown in Table 1, the set $\{m,n\}$ has the obvious minimal description [+nas], since m and n are the only nasals. But that set could also be specified non-minimally as:

$$\begin{bmatrix} \text{+cons} \\ \text{-cnt} \\ \text{-hi} \\ \text{-bk} \\ \text{+voi} \\ \text{+son} \end{bmatrix} \tag{1}$$

The potential complexity of this problem, finding a minimal specification, is not addressed in the phonological literature. Yet, finding such a minimal specification is not trivial. Using more realistic feature systems such as the ones given in Hayes (2011), there are, for example, 208 distinct solutions to specifying the set $\{e,i\}$ in English, only four of which have the minimum length of 3 features. While such modern feature systems work with 25–30 features, one can actually assume more features are needed to cover more cross-linguistically exotic contrasts such as those produced by including click consonants (Miller, 2011). The P-base 3 resource (Mielke, 2008b) lists 398 features over 8 feature systems, covering 629 languages.

The general notion of **feature economy** has a long tradition in phonology (Jakobson, 1942; Martinet, 1955; Clements, 2003), mostly targeting entire feature systems in a language, i.e. advocating

Proceedings of NAACL-HLT 2018, pages 542–547
New Orleans, Louisiana, June 1 - 6, 2018. ©2018 Association for Computational Linguistics

that on the grammar level, individual languages make maximal use of the feature inventory available (Fant, 1966). Equally prominent is the assumption that any specification of phonological alternations be made with the minimal number of features necessary: "one should use the minimum number of features required to specify all and only the sounds in the class." (Zsiga, 2012, p.282). Hayes (2011), among others, argues, following Ockham's Razor, that this is how generalization can take place and that phonological hypotheses are made in precisely this way—witnessing alternations that target a set of sounds, learners find the minimal feature specification that is consistent with the alternating sounds, generalizing from there to other sounds that may enter the language. Halle (1962) also proposes a mechanism of "feature counting" as a methodology to rule out spurious generalizations one might propose—a process which implicitly includes the capability of feature minimization.

Similar arguments of feature minimization are used to perform an optimization of an entire phonological grammar. In Radical Underspecification, Archangeli (1984) refers to what is termed FEATURE MINIMIZATION PRINCIPLE: "A grammar is most highly valued when underlying representations include the minimal number of features necessary to make the different phonemes of the language" (Archangeli, 1984, p. 48).

Given such claims concerning acquisition and phonological analysis, it is of some interest to assess the actual computational complexity of feature minimization. This entails answering how difficult it is in the worst case to determine whether a set of segments represents a natural class, and also how to find the minimal feature specification.

2 Overview

We will assume a set of phonemes P—the phoneme inventory—and another set Q, our target set that we want to express through a combination of features, and a feature system $\mathcal{F}$ such as the one shown in Table 1. The first problem we address is that of determining whether a set of phonemes Q forms a *natural class*, which we call the *feature description problem*. We show that this is decidable in polynomial time. Further, we will show that a minimization version of the problem, which we call the *feature minimization problem* is $\mathcal{NP}$-complete (Garey and Johnson, 1979; Sipser,

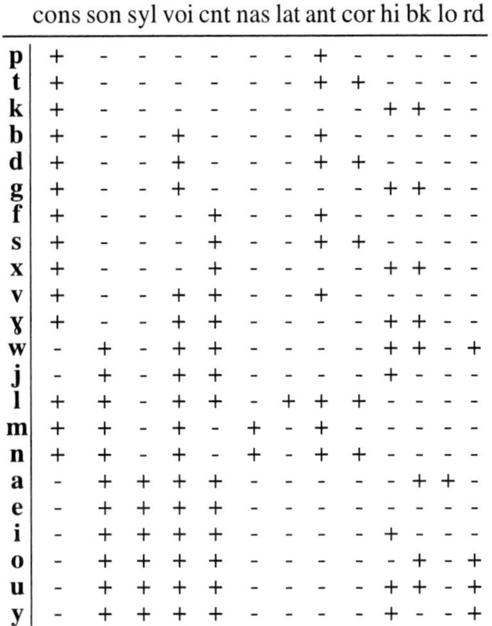

	cons	son	syl	voi	cnt	nas	lat	ant	cor	hi	bk	lo	rd
p	+	-	-	-	-	-	-	+	-	-	-	-	-
t	+	-	-	-	-	-	-	+	+	-	-	-	-
k	+	-	-	-	-	-	-	-	-	+	+	-	-
b	+	-	-	+	-	-	-	+	-	-	-	-	-
d	+	-	-	+	-	-	-	+	+	-	-	-	-
g	+	-	-	+	-	-	-	-	-	+	+	-	-
f	+	-	-	-	+	-	-	+	-	-	-	-	-
s	+	-	-	-	+	-	-	+	+	-	-	-	-
x	+	-	-	-	+	-	-	-	-	+	+	-	-
v	+	-	-	+	+	-	-	+	-	-	-	-	-
ɣ	+	-	-	+	+	-	-	-	-	+	+	-	-
w	-	+	-	+	+	-	-	-	-	+	+	-	+
j	-	+	-	+	+	-	-	-	-	+	-	-	-
l	+	+	-	+	+	-	+	+	+	-	-	-	-
m	+	+	-	+	-	+	-	+	-	-	-	-	-
n	+	+	-	+	-	+	-	+	+	-	-	-	-
a	-	+	+	+	+	-	-	-	-	-	+	+	-
e	-	+	+	+	+	-	-	-	-	-	-	-	-
i	-	+	+	+	+	-	-	-	-	+	-	-	-
o	-	+	+	+	+	-	-	-	-	-	+	-	+
u	-	+	+	+	+	-	-	-	-	+	+	-	+
y	-	+	+	+	+	-	-	-	-	+	-	-	+

Table 1: An example typical feature system (truncated to 13 features).

2013). We will show this by reduction from the well known set covering problem (Karp, 1972).

Many phonologists espouse a combination of binary (equipollent) and privative (univalent) features (Trubetzkoy, 1969; Ewen and van der Hulst, 1985; Goldsmith, 1985). The rationale is that, for example, the feature [±labial] has rarely, if ever, been found to play a role in a phonological system as [−labial], i.e. phonological processes that target non-labials seem to be absent. Hence, many phonologists favor the use of a single possibility [LABIAL] in a specification that includes the labials. For this reason, we analyze separately both the complexity of using only such privative features (positive features only), which we call the *positive feature description problem* (is Q a natural class if we only use positive features?) and the corresponding *positive feature minimization problem*.

3 Notation and terms

Throughout, when A is a set, we use $\wp(A)$ to denote the power set of A.

Relative to a set P of phonemes, we define a *feature system* to be a subset $\mathcal{F} \subseteq \wp(P)$. When $Q \subseteq P$, we define a $\mathcal{F}$-*description of* Q to be a sequence $G_1, \ldots, G_m \subseteq P$ such that there exist pairwise distinct elements $F_1, \ldots, F_m \in \mathcal{F}$ where:

- each G_i is equal to either F_i or $P \setminus F_i$, and

- $Q = G_1 \cap \cdots \cap G_m$.

We refer to m as the *size* of the description. We say that such a description is *positive* if each G_i is an element of $\mathcal{F}$.

We define the *feature description problem* as follows. An instance consists of a set P of phonemes, a feature system $\mathcal{F}$, and a non-empty subset $Q \subseteq P$; the problem is to decide whether or not there exists a $\mathcal{F}$-description of Q.

We define the *feature minimization problem* as follows. An instance consists of a tuple $(P, \mathcal{F}, Q, k)$ where P, $\mathcal{F}$, and Q are an instance of the feature description problem, and $k \geq 1$ is a natural number. The problem is to decide whether or not there exists a $\mathcal{F}$-description of Q having size less than or equal to k.

We define the *positive feature description problem* to have the same instances as the *feature description problem*, but where the problem is to decide whether or not there exists a positive $\mathcal{F}$-description of Q. Analogously, we define the *positive feature minimization problem* to have the same instances as the *feature minimization problem*, but where the problem is to decide whether or not there exists a positive $\mathcal{F}$-description of Q obeying the size restriction.

3.1 The feature description problems

We will first show that the feature description problems are decidable in polynomial time.

Proposition 1. *The feature description problem and the positive feature description problem are each polynomial-time decidable.*

Proof. The algorithm for the feature description problem is as follows. Given an instance $(P, \mathcal{F}, Q)$, compute a set $\mathcal{C} \subseteq \wp(P)$ as follows. For each $F \in \mathcal{F}$, place F in $\mathcal{C}$ if $Q \subseteq F$, and place $P \setminus F$ in $\mathcal{C}$ if $Q \subseteq P \setminus F$. Then, check if $\bigcap \mathcal{C} = Q$; if so, accept, otherwise, reject. It suffices to argue that if there exists a $\mathcal{F}$-description of Q, then the elements of $\mathcal{C}$ constitute such a description. If there exists a $\mathcal{F}$-description of Q, say, $G_1, \ldots, G_m$, we have $Q \subseteq G_i$ for each i; thus, $G_1, \ldots, G_m \in \mathcal{C}$ and we have

$$Q \subseteq \bigcap \mathcal{C} \subseteq G_1 \cap \cdots \cap G_m = Q,$$

implying that the elements of $\mathcal{C}$ provide a $\mathcal{F}$-description of Q.

For the positive feature description problem, the algorithm computes $\mathcal{C}^+$ to contain each $F \in \mathcal{F}$ such that $Q \subseteq F$, and accepts if and only if $\bigcap \mathcal{C}^+ = Q$. The proof of correctness is similar to that given for the general feature description problem. $\square$

3.2 The minimization problems

An instance $(U, \mathcal{S}, k)$ of the set cover problem consists of a non-empty set U, a subset $\mathcal{S} \subseteq \wp(U)$, and a natural number $k \geq 1$. A *set cover* $S_1, \ldots, S_m$ is a sequence of sets from $\mathcal{S}$ such that $S_1 \cup \cdots \cup S_m = U$; m is said to be its size. The problem is to decide whether or not there exists a set cover of size less than or equal to k (Karp, 1972). We prove that both the feature minimization problem and the positive feature minimization problem are $\mathcal{NP}$-complete, by reducing from set cover.

The reduction is the same for both of these problems, and is as follows. Given an instance $(U, \mathcal{S}, k)$ of set cover, let x be a fresh element not in U.

Define

$$P = U \cup \{x\}$$
$$\mathcal{F} = \{(U \setminus S) \cup \{x\} \mid S \in \mathcal{S}\}$$
$$Q = \{x\}$$

The resulting instance is $(P, \mathcal{F}, Q, k)$.

The following establishes the correctness of this reduction.

Proposition 2. *The following are equivalent:*

1. There exists a size m set cover of U.

2. The set $Q = \{x\}$ has a positive $\mathcal{F}$-description of size m.

3. The set $Q = \{x\}$ has a $\mathcal{F}$-description of size m.

Proof. $1 \Rightarrow 2$: Let (S_i) be such a set cover, so that $S_1 \cup \cdots \cup S_m = U$. Then, by DeMorgan's laws, $(U \setminus S_1) \cap \cdots \cap (U \setminus S_m) = \emptyset$, and so $((U \setminus S_1) \cup \{x\}) \cap \cdots \cap ((U \setminus S_m) \cup \{x\}) = \{x\}$.

$2 \Rightarrow 3$ is immediate.

$3 \Rightarrow 1$: Suppose that $G_1, \ldots, G_m$ is such a description. Since $x \in G_i$ for each i, it follows that each G_i is an element of $\mathcal{F}$. Define $S_1, \ldots, S_m$ to be the sets such that $G_i = (U \setminus S_i) \cup \{x\}$. By reversing the argumentation in the $1 \Rightarrow 2$ case, we obtain that $S_1, \ldots, S_m$ is a set cover of U. $\square$

In the just-given reduction, the parameter k is not changed. We show that there in fact exists a reduction in the other direction, from set cover to each of the minimization problems, that likewise does not change the parameter k. This indicates a tight relationship between these minimization problems and the set cover problem.

Proposition 3. *Let $(P, \mathcal{F}, Q, k)$ be an instance of the feature minimization problem; let $\mathcal{C}$ be the set (from Proposition 1). The mapping which, upon being given this instance, returns $(U, \mathcal{S}, k)$ where $U = P \setminus Q$ and $\mathcal{S} = \{\overline{G \setminus Q} \mid G \in \mathcal{C}\}$, is a reduction to the set cover problem; here, the complement is with respect to U. Likewise, one obtains a reduction from the positive feature minimization problem to the set cover problem, by using $\mathcal{C}^+$ in place of $\mathcal{C}$.*

Proof. We argue this for the feature minimization problem as follows (the positive minimization case is analogous). It was seen in the proof of Proposition 1 that $(P, \mathcal{F}, Q, k)$ is a 'yes' instance if and only if there exist $G_1, \ldots, G_m \in \mathcal{C}$, with $m \leq k$, such that $G_1 \cap \cdots \cap G_m = Q$. This equality holds if and only if $(G_1 \setminus Q) \cap \cdots \cap (G_m \setminus Q) = \emptyset$, which holds if and only if $\overline{(G_1 \setminus Q)} \cup \cdots \cup \overline{(G_m \setminus Q)} = U$. □

Parametrized complexity The set cover problem, with the value k taken to be parameter, is known to be W[2]-complete in parameterized complexity theory (Cygan et al., 2015, Theorem 13.21). As we have given polynomial-time reductions between set cover and each of the minimization problems that do not change the value k, we obtain the following.

Proposition 4. *Both the feature minimization problem and the positive feature minimization problem are W[2]-complete, when viewed as parameterized problems with k taken to be the parameter.*

4   Empirical concerns

Many $\mathcal{NP}$-hard problems can in practice often be solved by either a greedy algorithm (Chvatal, 1979) or a branch-and-bound algorithm (Land and Doig, 1960) that recursively explores the search space, terminating search branches as soon as some defined limit is exceeded.

Greedy Search We have implemented a greedy search strategy that starts with no features, and

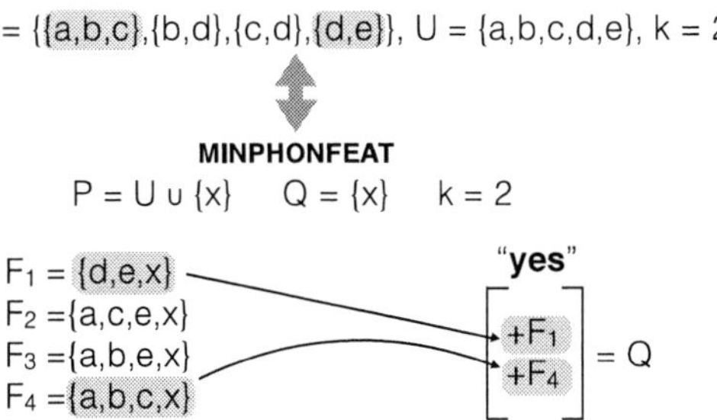

Figure 1: Illustration of the reduction from SETCOVERING: we can solve an instance of the set cover problem (SETCOVERING) by a call to a solver for the feature minimization problem (MINPHONFEAT). There are reductions both from and to the set cover problem.

then picks a single ($\pm$) feature from the known, possibly non-minimal description $\mathcal{C}$ discussed in §3.1 in such a way as to rule out the majority of phonemes not in the desired set Q. Features are added to the description until only the set Q is described. For example, in describing the set $\{m\}$ using the example in Table 1, the greedy approach would first pick the feature [+nas] since this cuts down the number of corresponding phonemes to just two (m and n), less than any other feature choice. This is essentially an analogue to the well-known greedy approximation algorithm for set cover (Chvatal, 1979).

This greedy algorithm, however, in many practical cases fails to find the correct minimal specification, and is therefore not a viable candidate for efficient feature minimization. A simple example is finding the featural specification for the set $\{ə\}$ in English under the fairly standard featural system provided in Hayes (2011) and van Vugt and Hayes (2012): the algorithm recovers the features [-tense, -back, -front, -coronal] while the minimal specification is [-back, -front, -coronal].

Branch & Bound We also implemented a branch-and-bound algorithm with a recursive component that explores, exhaustively, all combinations of features in the full description $\mathcal{C}$, bounding the search whenever the current search tree contains more features than in the shortest solution found so far. The branch-and-bound algorithm is efficient in practice in finding minimal feature specifications, but still needs to explore a reasonably large search space (see Table 2).

Set	$\{h\}$	$\{i,e\}$	$\{r\}$	$\{j\}$	$\{m,n\}$	$\{p,t,k\}$
BF	32,768	262,144	131,072	524,288	2048	4,096
B&B	3,432	11,482	3,444	4,790	1,450	1,315

Table 2: The number of search nodes explored during a brute-force search (BF) for finding a minimal solution for various sets of phonemes, or a branch-and-bound search (B&B). The feature inventory is one used for English (van Vugt and Hayes, 2012; Hayes, 2011).

5 Discussion

Humans have been noted to outperform simple, low-polynomial time heuristic algorithms for some intractable problems such as the traveling salesman problem (MacGregor and Ormerod, 1996) using intuition and visual inspection of the problem structure. It is, however, unclear if such performance carries over to other problems of a different structure, such as MINPHONFEAT, or whether the hypothesis that a phonological acquisition process should include this type of minimization is too strong.

An important point to address in the complexity analysis is whether we are operating in a bounded domain. With a fixed, finite set of features to choose from and a fixed finite phoneme inventory, the problem can be considered static and solvable in constant time by memorizing or pre-calculating all the possible patterns of feature combinations and their corresponding phoneme sets. Such counter-arguments have been leveled (Kornai, 2006) at other $\mathcal{NP}$-completeness analyses, such as those that have shown that Optimality Theory is potentially intractable (Eisner, 2000; Idsardi, 2006). In the case at hand, however, such an argument has less traction since the domain in question is rather large (potentially hundreds of features) and it seems inevitable that some search method must be used by speakers (or phonologists) to discover the minimum number of features required. The fact that simple greedy algorithms do not always find the minimum specification, and that branch-and-bound algorithms, while efficient for practical computational use, still need to explore a large search space, prompts the question whether some alternative strategy would work particularly well with phonological feature structures proposed in the literature. This could address the problem that this intractability poses to phonological learning.

6 Conclusion

We have shown that one of the commonly assumed subtasks of acquisition of phonological generalizations—distinctive feature minimization—is computationally intractable. The decision version of the minimization problem is $\mathcal{NP}$-complete, and it follows that the optimization version $\mathcal{NP}$-hard. This is true even if one limits oneself to using only positive features, i.e. a privative feature system. Furthermore, a simple greedy strategy for solving the problem can not be attributed to purported human performance in finding minimal feature specifications since such a strategy will sometimes fail to find a minimal description with commonly proposed feature systems and phonological inventories. The problem of simply deciding whether a set of phonemes constitutes a natural class—the feature description problem—is solvable in polynomial time.

Reproducibility

Our feature systems data and code for the feature description and minimization problems is available at `https://github.com/mhulden/minphonfeat`.

Acknowledgements

Chen was partially supported by the Spanish Project TIN2017-86727-C2-2-R. We wish to thank Miikka Silfverberg for comments on an earlier version on the paper. Thanks also to participants in LING 5410 (Phonology) and LING 7410 (Phonological Theory) at The University of Colorado, whose work and feedback on various feature minimization problems prompted part of this research.

References

Diana Bennett Archangeli. 1984. *Underspecification in Yawelmani phonology and morphology*. Ph.D. thesis, Massachusetts Institute of Technology.

Noam Chomsky and Morris Halle. 1968. *The Sound Pattern of English*. Harper & Row.

Vasek Chvatal. 1979. A greedy heuristic for the set-covering problem. *Mathematics of operations research*, 4(3):233–235.

George N. Clements. 1985. The geometry of phonological features. *Phonology*, 2(1):225–252.

George N Clements. 2003. Feature economy in sound systems. *Phonology*, 20(03):287–333.

Marek Cygan, Fedor V. Fomin, Lukasz Kowalik, Daniel Lokshtanov, Dániel Marx, Marcin Pilipczuk, Michal Pilipczuk, and Saket Saurabh. 2015. *Parameterized Algorithms*. Springer.

Jason Eisner. 2000. Easy and hard constraint ranking in optimality theory. In *Proceedings of the 5th Workshop of the ACL Special Interest Group in Computational Phonology (SIGPHON)*, pages 22–33.

Colin J. Ewen and Harry van der Hulst. 1985. Single-valued features and the nonlinear analysis of vowel harmony. *Linguistics in the Netherlands*, pages 39–48.

Gunnar Fant. 1966. The nature of distinctive features. *STL-QPSR*, 4(1966):1.

Michael R. Garey and David S. Johnson. 1979. Computers and intractability: A guide to the theory of NP-completeness.

John Goldsmith. 1985. Vowel harmony in Khalkha Mongolian, Yaka, Finnish and Hungarian. *Phonology*, 2(1):253–275.

Morris Halle. 1962. Phonology in generative grammar. *Word*, 18(1-3):54–72.

Bruce Hayes. 2011. *Introductory Phonology*. John Wiley & Sons.

William J. Idsardi. 2006. A simple proof that optimality theory is computationally intractable. *Linguistic Inquiry*, 37(2):271–275.

Roman Jakobson. 1942. The concept of phoneme. In Linda R. Waugh and Monique Moville-Burston, editors, *On Language*, pages 218–241. Harvard Univ. Press, Cambridge, MA.

Roman Jakobson, C. Gunnar M. Fant, and Morris Halle. 1951. *Preliminaries to Speech Analysis. The distinctive features and their correlates*. MIT Press, Cambridge, MA.

Richard M. Karp. 1972. Reducibility among combinatorial problems. In *Complexity of computer computations*, pages 85–103. Springer.

András Kornai. 1993. The generative power of feature geometry. *Annals of Mathematics and Artificial Intelligence*, 8(1-2):37.

András Kornai. 2006. Is OT NP-hard? *Rutgers Optimality Archive (ROA)*.

Ailsa H. Land and Alison G. Doig. 1960. An automatic method of solving discrete programming problems. *Econometrica: Journal of the Econometric Society*, pages 497–520.

James N. MacGregor and Tom Ormerod. 1996. Human performance on the traveling salesman problem. *Attention, Perception, & Psychophysics*, 58(4):527–539.

André Martinet. 1955. *Économie des changements phonétiques*. A. Francke, Bern, Switzerland.

Jeff Mielke. 2008a. *The Emergence of Distinctive Features*. Oxford University Press.

Jeff Mielke. 2008b. P-base 3. `http://pbase.phon.chass.ncsu.edu/`. Accessed: 2017-10-01.

Amanda Miller. 2011. The representation of clicks. In Mark van Oostendorp, Colin J. Ewen, Elizabeth Hume, and Keren Rice, editors, *The Blackwell Companion to Phonology*, volume 1, pages 416–439. Blackwell.

Michael Sipser. 2013. *Introduction to the Theory of Computation*, 2nd edition. Cengage Learning.

Nikolai Sergeevich Trubetzkoy. 1969. *Principles of phonology*. Univ. of California Press, Berkeley.

Florian van Vugt and Bruce Hayes. 2012. Pheatures speadsheet: User's manual. Technical report, UCLA.

Elizabeth C. Zsiga. 2012. *The sounds of language: An introduction to phonetics and phonology*. John Wiley & Sons.

Unsupervised Disambiguation of Syncretism in Inflected Lexicons

Ryan Cotterell and **Christo Kirov** and **Sebastian J. Mielke** and **Jason Eisner**
Department of Computer Science, Johns Hopkins University
`{ryan.cotterell@,ckirov1@,sjmielke@,jason@cs}.jhu.edu`

Abstract

Lexical ambiguity makes it difficult to compute various useful statistics of a corpus. A given word form might represent any of several morphological feature bundles. One can, however, use unsupervised learning (as in EM) to fit a model that probabilistically disambiguates word forms. We present such an approach, which employs a neural network to smoothly model a prior distribution over feature bundles (even rare ones). Although this basic model does not consider a token's context, that very property allows it to operate on a simple list of unigram type counts, partitioning each count among different analyses of that unigram. We discuss evaluation metrics for this novel task and report results on 5 languages.

1 Introduction

Inflected lexicons—lists of morphologically inflected forms—are commonplace in NLP. Such lexicons currently exist for over 100 languages in a standardized annotation scheme (Kirov et al., 2018), making them one of the most multi-lingual annotated resources in existence. These lexicons are typically annotated at the type level, i.e., each word type is listed with its *possible* morphological analyses, divorced from sentential context.

One might imagine that most word types are unambiguous. However, many inflectional systems are replete with a form of ambiguity termed syncretism—a systematic merger of morphological slots. In English, some verbs have five distinct inflected forms, but regular verbs (the vast majority) merge two of these and so distinguish only four. The verb *sing* has the past tense form sang but the participial form sung; the verb *talk*, on the other hand, employs talked for both functions. The form talked is, thus, said to be syncretic. Our task is to partition the count of talked in a corpus between the past-tense and participial readings, respectively.

	SG	PL	SG	PL
NOM	**Wort**	Wörter	Herr	Herren
GEN	Wortes	Wörter	**Herrn**	Herren
ACC	**Wort**	Wörter	**Herrn**	Herren
DAT	Worte	Wörtern	**Herrn**	Herren

Table 1: Full paradigms for the German nouns *Wort* ("word") and *Herr* ("gentleman") with abbreviated and tabularized UniMorph annotation. The syncretic forms are bolded and colored by ambiguity class. Note that, while in the plural the nominative and accusative are always syncretic across all paradigms, the same is not true in the singular.

In this paper, we model a generative probability distribution over *annotated* word forms, and fit the model parameters using the token counts of *unannotated* word forms. The resulting distribution predicts how to partition each form's token count among its possible annotations. While our method actually deals with all ambiguous forms in the lexicon, it is particularly useful for syncretic forms because syncretism is often systematic and pervasive.

In English, our unsupervised procedure learns from the counts of irregular pairs like sang–sung that a verb's past tense tends to be more frequent than its past participle. These learned parameters are then used to disambiguate talked. The method can also learn from regular paradigms. For example, it learns from the counts of pairs like runs–run that singular third-person forms are common. It then uses these learned parameters to guess that tokens of run are often singular or third-person (though never both at once, because the lexicon does not list that as a possible analysis of run).

Proceedings of NAACL-HLT 2018, pages 548–553
New Orleans, Louisiana, June 1 - 6, 2018. ©2018 Association for Computational Linguistics

2 Formalizing Inflectional Morphology

We adopt the framework of word-based morphology (Aronoff, 1976; Spencer, 1991). In the present paper, we consider only inflectional morphology. An **inflected lexicon** is a set of word types. Each **word type** is a 4-tuple of a part-of-speech tag, a lexeme, an inflectional slot, and a surface form.

A **lexeme** is a discrete object (represented by an arbitrary integer or string, which we typeset in *cursive*) that indexes the word's core meaning and part of speech. A **part-of-speech (POS) tag** is a coarse syntactic category such as VERB. Each POS tag allows some set of lexemes, and also allows some set of inflectional **slots** such as "1st-person present singular." Each allowed ⟨tag, lexeme, slot⟩ triple is realized—in only one way—as an inflected **surface form**, a string over a fixed phonological or orthographic alphabet Σ. In this work, we take Σ to be an orthographic alphabet.

A **paradigm** $\pi(t, \ell)$ is the mapping from tag t's slots to the surface forms that "fill" those slots for lexeme ℓ. For example, in the English paradigm $\pi(\text{VERB}, \textit{talk})$, the past-tense slot is said to be filled by talked, meaning that the lexicon contains the tuple ⟨VERB, *talk*, PAST, talked⟩.[1]

We will specifically work with the UniMorph annotation scheme (Sylak-Glassman, 2016). Here each slot specifies a morpho-syntactic bundle of inflectional features (also called a morphological tag in the literature), such as tense, mood, person, number, and gender. For example, the German surface form Wörtern is listed in the lexicon with tag NOUN, lemma *Wort*, and a slot specifying the feature bundle $[\text{NUM}=\text{PL}, \text{CASE}=\text{DAT}]$. An example of UniMorph annotation is found in Table 1.

2.1 What is Syncretism?

We say that a surface form f is **syncretic** if two slots $s_1 \neq s_2$ exist such that some paradigm $\pi(t, \ell)$ maps both s_1 and s_2 to f. In other words, a single form fills multiple slots in a paradigm: syncretism may be thought of as intra-paradigmatic ambiguity. This definition does depend on the exact annotation scheme in use, as some schemes collapse syncretic slots. For example, in German nouns, *no* lexeme distinguishes the nominative, accusative and genitive plurals. Thus, a

human-created lexicon might employ a single slot $[\text{NUM}=\text{PL}, \text{CASE}=\text{NOM}/\text{ACC}/\text{GEN}]$ and say that Wörter fills just this slot rather than three separate slots. For a discussion, see Baerman et al. (2005).

2.2 Inter-Paradigmatic Ambiguity

A different kind of ambiguity occurs when a surface form belongs to more than one paradigm. A form f is inter-paradigmatically ambiguous if $\langle t_1, \ell_1, s_1, f \rangle$ and $\langle t_2, \ell_2, s_2, f \rangle$ are both in the lexicon for lexemes $\langle t_1, \ell_1 \rangle \neq \langle t_2, \ell_2 \rangle$.

For example, talks belongs to the English paradigms $\pi(\text{VERB}, \textit{talk})$ and $\pi(\text{NOUN}, \textit{talk})$. The model we present in §3 will resolve both syncretism and inter-paradigmatic ambiguity. However, our exposition focuses on the former, as it is cross-linguistically more common.

2.3 Disambiguating Surface Form Counts

The previous sections §2.1 and §2.2 discussed two types of ambiguity found in inflected lexicons. The goal of this paper is the *disambiguation* of raw surface form counts, taken from an unannotated text corpus. In other words, given such counts, we seek to impute the fractional counts for individual lexical entries (4-tuples), which are unannotated in raw text. Let us assume that the word talked is observed $c(\text{talked})$ times in a raw English text corpus. We do not know which instances of talked are participles and which are past tense forms. However, given a probability distribution $p_{\boldsymbol{\theta}}(t, \ell, s \mid f)$, we may disambiguate these counts in expectation, i.e., we attribute a count of

$$c(\text{talked}) \cdot p_{\boldsymbol{\theta}}(\text{VERB}, \textit{talk}, \text{PAST\_PART} \mid \text{talked})$$

to the past participle of the VERB *talk*. Our aim is the construction and unsupervised estimation of the distribution $p_{\boldsymbol{\theta}}(t, \ell, s \mid f)$.

While the task at hand is novel, what applications does it have? We are especially interested in *sampling* tuples $\langle t, \ell, s, f \rangle$ from an inflected lexicon. Sampling is a necessity for creating train-test splits for evaluating morphological inflectors, which has recently become a standard task in the literature (Durrett and DeNero, 2013; Hulden et al., 2014; Nicolai et al., 2015; Faruqui et al., 2016), and has seen two shared tasks (Cotterell et al., 2016, 2017). Creating train-test splits for training inflectors involves sampling *without replacement* so that all test types are unseen. Ideally, we would like more frequent word types in the training portion and less

---

[1]Lexicographers will often refer to a paradigm by its **lemma**, which is the surface form that fills a certain designated slot such as the infinitive. We instead use lexemes because lemmas may be ambiguous: bank is the lemma for at least two nominal and two verbal paradigms.

549

frequent ones in the test portion. This is a realistic evaluation: a training lexicon for a new language would tend to contain frequent types, so the system should be tested on its ability to extrapolate to rarer types that could not be looked up in that lexicon, as discussed by Cotterell et al. (2015). To make the split, we sample N word types without replacement, which is equivalent to collecting the first N distinct forms from an annotated corpus generated from the same unigram distribution.

The fractional counts that our method estimates may also be useful for corpus linguistics—for example, tracking the frequency of specific lexemes over time, or comparing the rate of participles in the work of two different authors.

Finally, the fractional counts can aid the training of NLP methods that operate on a raw corpus, such as distributional embedding of surface form types into a vector space. Such methods sometimes consider the morphological properties (tags, lexemes, and slots) of nearby context words. When the morphological properties of a context word f are ambiguous, instead of tagging (which may not be feasible) one could *fractionally* count the occurrences of the possible analyses according to $p_\theta(t, \ell, s \mid f)$, or else characterize f's morphology with a single *soft* indicator vector whose elements are the probabilities of the properties according to $p_\theta(t, \ell, s \mid f)$.

3   A Neural Latent Variable Model

In general, we will only observe unannotated word forms f. We model these as draws from a distribution over form types $p_\theta(f)$, which marginalizes out the unobserved structure of the lexicon—which tag, lexeme and slot generated each form. Training the parameters of this latent-variable model will recover the posterior distribution over analyses of a form, $p_\theta(t, \ell, s \mid f)$, which allows us to disambiguate counts at the type level.

The latent-variable model is a Bayesian network,

$$p_\theta(f) = \sum_{\langle t, \ell, s \rangle \in \mathcal{T} \times \mathcal{L} \times \mathcal{S}} p_\theta(t)\, p_\theta(\ell \mid t)\, p_\theta(s \mid t)\, \delta(f \mid t, \ell, s)$$

$$(1)$$

where $\mathcal{T}, \mathcal{L}, \mathcal{S}$ range over the possible tags, lexemes, and slots of the language, and $\delta(f \mid t, \ell, s)$ returns 1 or 0 according to whether the lexicon lists f as the (unique) realization of $\langle t, \ell, s \rangle$. We fix $p_\theta(s \mid t) = 0$ if the lexicon lists no tuples of the

form $\langle t, \cdot, s, \cdot \rangle$, and otherwise model

$$p_\theta(s \mid t) \propto \exp\left(\mathbf{u}^\top \tanh\left(\mathbf{W} \cdot \mathbf{v}_{t,s}\right)\right) > 0 \quad (2)$$

where $\mathbf{v}_{t,s}$ is a multi-hot vector whose "1" components indicate the morphological features possessed by $\langle t, s \rangle$: namely attribute-value pairs such as POS=VERB and NUM=PL. Here $\mathbf{u} \in \mathbb{R}^d$ and $\mathbf{W}$ is a conformable matrix of weights. This formula specifies a neural network with d hidden units, which can learn to favor or disfavor specific soft conjunctions of morphological features. Finally, we define $p_\theta(t) \propto \exp \omega_t$ for $t \in \mathcal{T}$, and $p_\theta(\ell \mid t) \propto \exp \omega_{t,\ell}$ or 0 if the lexicon lists no tuples of the form $\langle t, \ell, \cdot, \cdot \rangle$. The model's parameter vector θ specifies $\mathbf{u}, \mathbf{W}$, and the ω values.

3.1   Inference and Learning

We maximize the regularized log-likelihood

$$\sum_{f \in \mathcal{F}} c(f) \log p_\theta(f) + \frac{\lambda}{2} \|\theta\|_2^2 \quad (3)$$

where $\mathcal{F}$ is the set of surface form types and $p_\theta(f)$ is defined by (1). It is straightforward to use a gradient-based optimizer, and we do. However, (3) could also be maximized by an intuitive EM algorithm: at each iteration, the E-step uses the current model parameters to partition each count $c(f)$ among possible analyses, as in (2.3), and then the M step improves the parameters by following the gradient of *supervised* regularized log-likelihood as if it had observed those fractional counts.

On each iteration, either algorithm loops through all listed (t, s) pairs, all listed (t, ℓ) pairs, and all observed forms f, taking time at most proportional to the size of the lexicon. In practice, training completes within a few minutes on a modern laptop.

3.2   Baseline Models

To the best of our knowledge, this disambiguation task is novel. Thus, we resort to comparing three variants of our model in lieu of a previously published baseline. We evaluate three simplifications of the slot model, to investigate whether the complexity of equation (2) is justified.

UNIF: $p(s \mid t)$ is uniform over the slots s that are listed with t. This involves no learning.

FREE: $p(s \mid t) \propto \exp \omega_{t,s}$: a model with a single parameter $\omega_{t,s} \in \mathbb{R}$ per slot. This can capture any distribution, but it has less inductive bias:

slots that share morphological features do not share parameters.

LINEAR: $p(s \mid t) \propto \exp(\mathbf{u}^\top \mathbf{v}_{t,s})$: a linear model with no conjunctions between morphological features. This chooses the features orthogonally, in the sense that (e.g.) if verbal paradigms have a complete 3-dimensional grid of slots indexed by their PERSON, NUM, and TENSE attributes, then sampling from $p(s \mid \text{VERB})$ is equivalent to independently sampling these three coordinates. Moreover, $p(\text{NUM=PL} \mid \text{NOUN}) = p(\text{NUM=PL} \mid \text{VERB})$.

4 Experiments

4.1 Computing Evaluation Metrics

We first evaluate **perplexity**. Since our model is a tractable generative model, we may easily evaluate its perplexity on held-out tokens. For each language, we randomly partition the observed surface tokens into 80% training, 10% development, and 10% test. We then estimate the parameters of our model by maximizing (3) on the counts from the training portion, selecting hyperparameters such that the estimated parameters[2] minimize perplexity on the development portion. We then report perplexity on the test portion.

Using the same hyperparameters, we now train our latent-variable model p_θ *without* supervision on 100% of the observed surface forms f. We now measure how poorly, for the average surface form type f, we recovered the maximum-likelihood distribution $\hat{p}(t, \ell, s \mid f)$ that would be estimated *with* supervision in terms of **KL-divergence**:

$$\sum_f \hat{p}(f)\, \text{KL}(\hat{p}(\cdot \mid f) \,\|\, p_\theta(\cdot \mid f)) \qquad (4)$$

$$= \frac{1}{N} \sum_{i=1}^{N} \log_2 \frac{\hat{p}(t_i, \ell_i, s_i \mid f_i)}{p_\theta(t_i, \ell_i, s_i \mid f_i)}$$

We can see that this formula reduces to a simple average over disambiguated tokens i.

4.2 Training Details and Hyperparameters

We optimized on training data using batch gradient descent with a fixed learning rate. We used perplexity on development data to jointly choose the learning rate, the initial random θ (from among several random restarts), the regularization coefficient $\lambda \in \{10^{-1}, 10^{-2}, 10^{-3}, 10^{-4}\}$ and the neural network architecture. The NEURAL architecture shown in eq. (2) has 1 hidden layer, but we actually generalized this to consider networks with $k \in \{1, 2, 3, 4\}$ hidden layers of $d = 100$ units each. In some cases, the model selected on development data had k as high as 3. Note that the LINEAR model corresponds to $k = 0$.

4.3 Datasets

Each language constitutes a separate experiment. In each case we obtain our lexicon from the UniMorph project and our surface form counts from Wikipedia. To approximate supervised counts to estimate $\hat{p}$ in the KL evaluation, we analyzed the surface form tokens in Wikipedia (in context) using the tool in Straka et al. (2016), as trained on the disambiguated Universal Dependencies (UD) corpora (Nivre et al., 2016). We wrote a script[3] to convert the resulting analyses from UD format into $\langle t, \ell, s, f \rangle$ tuples in UniMorph format for five languages—Czech (cs), German (de), Finnish (fi), Hebrew (he), Swedish (sv)—each of which displays both kinds of ambiguity in its UniMorph lexicon. Lexicons with these approximate supervised counts are provided as supplementary material.

4.4 Results

Our results are graphed in Fig. 1, exact numbers are found in Table 2. We find that the NEURAL model slightly outperforms the other baselines on languages except for German. The LINEAR model is quite competitive as well.

	NEURAL NET		FREE		LINEAR		UNIFORM	
lang	perp	KL	perp	KL	perp	KL	perp	KL
cs	**621**	**0.56**	643	0.58	637	0.67	896	1.19
de	776	2.39	**775**	**2.25**	776	2.33	813	3.03
fi	**300**	**0.99**	319	1.18	304	1.03	889	2.61
he	**96**	**0.27**	130	0.69	97	0.29	675	3.69
sv	**547**	**0.06**	565	0.14	568	0.08	1025	1.5

Table 2: Results for the best performing neural network (hyperparameters selected on dev) and the three baselines under both performance metrics. Best are bolded.

UNIF would have a KL divergence of 0 bits if all forms were either unambiguous or uniformly ambiguous. Its higher value means the unsupervised task is nontrivial. Our other models substantially

---

[2] Our vocabulary and parameter set are determined from the *lexicon*. Thus we create a regularized parameter ω_ℓ, yielding a smoothed estimate $p(\ell)$, even if the training count $c(\ell) = 0$.

[3] The script discarded up to 31% of the tokens because the UD analysis could not be successfully converted into an UniMorph analysis that was present in the lexicon.

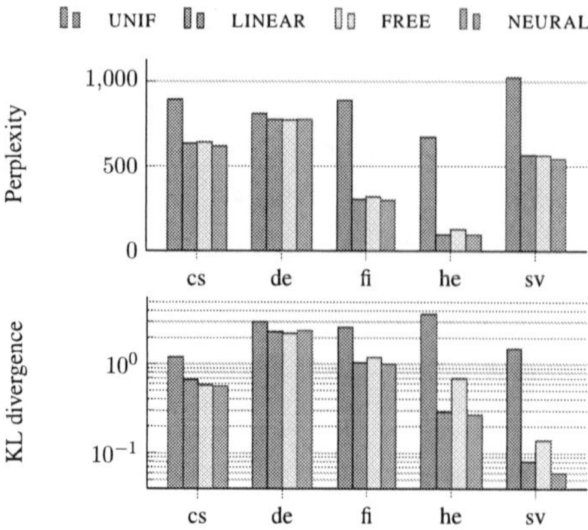

Figure 1: Unsupervised and supervised test results under each model, averaged over 50 training-dev-test splits.

outperform UNIF. NEURAL matches the supervised distributions reasonably closely, achieving an average KL of < 1 bit on all languages but German.

5 Related Work

By far the closest work to ours is the seminal paper of Baayen and Sproat (1996), who asked the following question: "Given a form that is previously unseen in a sufficiently large training corpus, and that is morphologically n-ways ambiguous [...] what is the best estimator for the lexical prior probabilities for the various functions of the form?" While we address the same task, i.e., estimation of a lexical prior, Baayen and Sproat (1996) assume supervision in the form of an disambiguated corpus. We are the first to treat the specific task in an unsupervised fashion. We discuss other work below.

Supervised Morphological Tagging. Morphological tagging is a common task in NLP; the state of the art is currently held by neural models (Heigold et al., 2017). This task is distinct from the problem at hand. Even if a tagger obtains the possible analyses from a lexicon, it is still trained in a supervised manner to choose among analyses.

Unsupervised POS Tagging. Another vein of work that is similar to ours is that of unsupervised part-of-speech (POS) tagging. Here, the goal is map sequences of forms into coarse-grained syntactic categories. Christodoulopoulos et al. (2010) provide a useful overview of previous work. This task differs from ours on two counts. First, we are interested in finer-grained morphological distinctions: the universal POS tagset (Petrov et al., 2012) makes 12 distinctions, whereas UniMorph

has languages expressing hundreds of distinctions. Second, POS tagging deals with the induction of syntactic categories from sentential context.

We note that purely unsupervised morphological tagging, has yet to be attempted to the best of our knowledge.

6 Conclusion

We have presented a novel generative latent-variable model for resolving ambiguity in unigram counts, notably due to syncretism. Given a lexicon, an unsupervised model partitions the corpus count for each ambiguous form among its analyses listed in a lexicon. We empirically evaluated our method on 5 languages under two evaluation metrics. The code is availabile at `https://sjmielke.com/papers/syncretism`, along with type-disambiguated unigram counts for all lexicons provided by the UniMorph project (100+ languages).

References

Mark Aronoff. 1976. *Word Formation in Generative Grammar*. Number 1 in Linguistic Inquiry Monographs. MIT Press, Cambridge, MA.

Harald Baayen and Richard Sproat. 1996. Estimating lexical priors for low-frequency morphologically ambiguous forms. *Computational Linguistics*, 22(2):155–166.

Matthew Baerman, Dunstan Brown, and Greville G. Corbett. 2005. *The Syntax-Morphology Interface: A study of Syncretism*, volume 109. Cambridge University Press.

Christos Christodoulopoulos, Sharon Goldwater, and Mark Steedman. 2010. Two decades of unsupervised POS induction: How far have we come? In *Proceedings of the Conference on Empirical Methods in Natural Language Processing (EMNLP)*, pages 575–584, Cambridge, MA. Association for Computational Linguistics.

Ryan Cotterell, Christo Kirov, John Sylak-Glassman, Géraldine Walther, Ekaterina Vylomova, Patrick Xia, Manaal Faruqui, Sandra Kübler, David Yarowsky, Jason Eisner, and Mans Hulden. 2017. The CoNLL-SIGMORPHON 2017 shared task: Universal morphological reinflection in 52 languages. In *Proceedings of the CoNLL-SIGMORPHON 2017 Shared Task: Universal Morphological Reinflection*, Vancouver, Canada. Association for Computational Linguistics.

Ryan Cotterell, Christo Kirov, John Sylak-Glassman, David Yarowsky, Jason Eisner, and Mans Hulden. 2016. The SIGMORPHON 2016 shared task— morphological reinflection. In *Proceedings of the*

14th SIGMORPHON Workshop on Computational Research in Phonetics, Phonology, and Morphology, pages 10–22, Berlin, Germany. Association for Computational Linguistics.

Ryan Cotterell, Nanyun Peng, and Jason Eisner. 2015. Modeling word forms using latent underlying morphs and phonology. *Transactions of the Association for Computational Linguistics*, 3:433–447.

Greg Durrett and John DeNero. 2013. Supervised learning of complete morphological paradigms. In *Proceedings of the Conference of the North American Chapter of the Association for Computational Linguistics: Human Language Technologies (NAACL)*, pages 1185–1195, Atlanta, Georgia. Association for Computational Linguistics.

Manaal Faruqui, Yulia Tsvetkov, Graham Neubig, and Chris Dyer. 2016. Morphological inflection generation using character sequence to sequence learning. In *Proceedings of the Conference of the North American Chapter of the Association for Computational Linguistics: Human Language Technologies (NAACL)*, pages 634–643, San Diego, California. Association for Computational Linguistics.

Georg Heigold, Guenter Neumann, and Josef van Genabith. 2017. An extensive empirical evaluation of character-based morphological tagging for 14 languages. In *Proceedings of the Conference of the European Chapter of the Association for Computational Linguistics (EACL)*, pages 505–513, Valencia, Spain. Association for Computational Linguistics.

Mans Hulden, Markus Forsberg, and Malin Ahlberg. 2014. Semi-supervised learning of morphological paradigms and lexicons. In *Proceedings of the Conference of the European Chapter of the Association for Computational Linguistics*, pages 569–578, Gothenburg, Sweden. Association for Computational Linguistics.

Christo Kirov, Ryan Cotterell, John Sylak-Glassman, Géraldine Walther, Ekaterina Vylomova, Patrick Xia, Manaal Faruqui, Sebastian Mielke, Arya McCarthy, Sandra Kübler, David Yarowsky, Jason Eisner, and Mans Hulden. 2018. Unimorph 2.0: Universal morphology. In *Proceedings of the Ninth International Conference on Language Resources and Evaluation (LREC)*. European Language Resources Association (ELRA).

Garrett Nicolai, Colin Cherry, and Grzegorz Kondrak. 2015. Inflection generation as discriminative string transduction. In *Proceedings of the Conference of the North American Chapter of the Association for Computational Linguistics: Human Language Technologies (NAACL)*, pages 922–931, Denver, Colorado. Association for Computational Linguistics.

Joakim Nivre, Marie-Catherine de Marneffe, Filip Ginter, Yoav Goldberg, Jan Hajic, Christopher D. Manning, Ryan McDonald, Slav Petrov, Sampo Pyysalo, Natalia Silveira, Reut Tsarfaty, and Daniel Zeman. 2016. Universal dependencies v1: A multilingual treebank collection. In *Proceedings of the Tenth International Conference on Language Resources and Evaluation (LREC)*, Paris, France. European Language Resources Association (ELRA).

Slav Petrov, Dipanjan Das, and Ryan McDonald. 2012. A universal part-of-speech tagset. In *Proceedings of the Eight International Conference on Language Resources and Evaluation (LREC)*, Istanbul, Turkey. European Language Resources Association (ELRA).

Andrew Spencer. 1991. *Morphological Theory: An Introduction to Word Structure in Generative Grammar*. Wiley-Blackwell.

Milan Straka, Jan Hajič, and Jana Straková. 2016. UDPipe: Trainable pipeline for processing CoNLL-U files performing tokenization, morphological analysis, POS tagging and parsing. In *LREC*.

John Sylak-Glassman. 2016. The composition and use of the universal morphological feature schema (Unimorph schema). Technical report, Johns Hopkins University.

Contextualized Word Representations for Reading Comprehension

Shimi Salant
Tel-Aviv University
shimi.salant@cs.tau.ac.il

Jonathan Berant
Tel-Aviv University
joberant@cs.tau.ac.il

Abstract

Reading a document and extracting an answer to a question about its content has attracted substantial attention recently. While most work has focused on the interaction between the question and the document, in this work we evaluate the importance of context when the question and document are processed independently. We take a standard neural architecture for this task, and show that by providing rich contextualized word representations from a large pre-trained language model as well as allowing the model to choose between context-dependent and context-independent word representations, we can obtain dramatic improvements and reach performance comparable to state-of-the-art on the competitive SQUAD dataset.

1 Introduction

Reading comprehension (RC) is a high-level task in natural language understanding that requires reading a document and answering questions about its content. RC has attracted substantial attention over the last few years with the advent of large annotated datasets (Hermann et al., 2015; Rajpurkar et al., 2016; Trischler et al., 2016; Nguyen et al., 2016; Joshi et al., 2017), computing resources, and neural network models and optimization procedures (Weston et al., 2015; Sukhbaatar et al., 2015; Kumar et al., 2015).

Reading comprehension models must invariably represent word tokens contextually, as a function of their encompassing sequence (document or question). The vast majority of RC systems encode contextualized representations of words in both the document and question as hidden states of bidirectional RNNs (Hochreiter and Schmidhuber, 1997; Schuster and Paliwal, 1997; Cho et al., 2014), and focus model design and capacity around question-document *interaction*, carry-

ing out calculations where information from both is available (Seo et al., 2016; Xiong et al., 2017b; Huang et al., 2017; Wang et al., 2017).

Analysis of current RC models has shown that models tend to react to simple word-matching between the question and document (Jia and Liang, 2017), as well as benefit from explicitly providing matching information in model inputs (Hu et al., 2017; Chen et al., 2017; Weissenborn et al., 2017). In this work, we hypothesize that the still-relatively-small size of RC datasets drives this behavior, which leads to models that make limited use of context when representing word tokens.

To illustrate this idea, we take a model that carries out only basic question-document interaction and prepend to it a module that produces token embeddings by explicitly gating between contextual and non-contextual representations (for both the document and question). This simple addition already places the model's performance on par with recent work, and allows us to demonstrate the importance of context.

Motivated by these findings, we turn to a semi-supervised setting in which we leverage a language model, pre-trained on large amounts of data, as a sequence encoder which forcibly facilitates context utilization. We find that model performance substantially improves, reaching accuracy comparable to state-of-the-art on the competitive SQuAD dataset, showing that contextual word representations captured by the language model are beneficial for reading comprehension. [1]

2 Contextualized Word Representations

Problem definition We consider the task of *extractive* reading comprehension: given a paragraph of text $\mathbf{p} = (p_1, \ldots, p_n)$ and a question $\mathbf{q} =$

---

[1] Our complete code base is available at http://github.com/shimisalant/CWR.

Proceedings of NAACL-HLT 2018, pages 554–559
New Orleans, Louisiana, June 1 - 6, 2018. ©2018 Association for Computational Linguistics

$(q_1, \ldots, q_m)$, an answer span $(p_l, \ldots, p_r)$ is to be extracted, i.e., a pair of indices $1 \leq l \leq r \leq n$ into **p** are to be predicted.

When encoding a word token in its encompassing sequence (question or passage), we are interested in allowing extra computation over the sequence and evaluating the extent to which context is utilized in the resultant representation. To that end, we employ a *re-embedding* component in which a contextual and a non-contextual representation are explicitly combined per token. Specifically, for a sequence of word-embeddings $w_1, \ldots, w_k$ with $w_t \in \mathbb{R}^{d_w}$, the re-embedding of the t-th token w'_t is the result of a Highway layer (Srivastava et al., 2015) and is defined as:

$$w'_t = g_t \odot w_t + (1 - g_t) \odot z_t$$
$$g_t = \sigma(W_g x_t + U_g u_t)$$
$$z_t = tanh(W_z x_t + U_z u_t)$$

where x_t is a function strictly of the word-type of the t-th token, u_t is a function of the enclosing sequence, W_g, W_z, U_g, U_z are parameter matrices, and $\odot$ the element-wise product operator. We set $x_t = [w_t; c_t]$, a concatenation of w_t with $c_t \in \mathbb{R}^{d_c}$ where the latter is a character-based representation of the token's word-type produced via a CNN over character embeddings (Kim, 2014). We note that word-embeddings w_t are pre-trained (Pennington et al., 2014) and are kept fixed during training, as is commonly done in order to reduce model capacity and mitigate overfitting. We next describe different formulations for the contextual term u_t.

RNN-based token re-embedding (TR) Here we set $\{u_1, \ldots, u_k\} = \text{BiLSTM}(x_1, \ldots, x_k)$ as the hidden states of the top layer in a stacked BiLSTM of multiple layers, each uni-directional LSTM in each layer having d_h cells and $u_k \in \mathbb{R}^{2d_h}$.

LM-augmented token re-embedding (TR+LM) The simple module specified above allows better exploitation of the context that a token appears in, if such exploitation is needed and is not learned by the rest of the network, which operates over $w'_1, \ldots, w'_k$. Our findings in Section 4 indicate that context is crucial but that in our setting it may be utilized to a limited extent.

We hypothesize that the main determining factor in this behavior is the relatively small size of the data and its distribution, which does not require using long-range context in most examples. Therefore, we leverage a strong language model

that was pre-trained on large corpora as a fixed encoder which supplies additional contextualized token representations. We denote these representations as $\{o_1, \ldots, o_k\}$ and set $u_t = [u'_t; o_t]$ for $\{u'_1, \ldots, u'_k\} = \text{BiLSTM}(x_1, \ldots, x_k)$.

The LM we use is from Józefowicz et al. (2016),[2] trained on the One Billion Words Benchmark dataset (Chelba et al., 2013). It consists of an initial layer which produces character-based word representations, followed by two stacked LSTM layers and a softmax prediction layer. The hidden state outputs of each LSTM layer are projected down to a lower dimension via a bottleneck layer (Sak et al., 2014). We set $\{o_1, \ldots, o_k\}$ to either the projections of the first layer, referred to as TR + LM(L1), or those of the second one, referred to as TR + LM(L2).

With both re-embedding schemes, we use the resulting representations $w'_1, \ldots, w'_k$ as a drop-in replacement for the word-embedding inputs fed to a standard model, described next.

3 Base model

We build upon Lee et al. (2016), who proposed the RaSoR model. For word-embedding inputs $q_1, \ldots, q_m$ and $p_1, \ldots, p_n$ of dimension d_w, RaSoR consists of the following components:

Passage-independent question representation The question is encoded via a BiLSTM $\{v_1, \ldots, v_m\} = \text{BiLSTM}(q_1, \ldots, q_m)$ and the resulting hidden states are summarized via attention (Bahdanau et al., 2015; Parikh et al., 2016): $q^{indep} = \sum_{j=1}^{m} \alpha_j v_j \in \mathbb{R}^{2d_h}$. The attention coefficients α are normalized logits $\{\alpha_1, \ldots, \alpha_m\} = \text{softmax}(s_1, \ldots, s_m)$ where $s_j = w_q^T \cdot \text{FF}(v_j)$ for a parameter vector $w_q \in \mathbb{R}^{d_f}$ and $\text{FF}(\cdot)$ a single layer feed-forward network.

Passage-aligned question representations For each passage position i, the question is encoded via attention operated over its word-embeddings $q_i^{align} = \sum_{j=1}^{m} \beta_{ij} q_j \in \mathbb{R}^{d_w}$. The coefficients β_i are produced by normalizing the logits $\{s_{i1}, \ldots, s_{im}\}$, where $s_{ij} = \text{FF}(q_j)^T \cdot \text{FF}(p_i)$.

Augmented passage token representations Each passage word-embedding p_i is concatenated with its corresponding q_i^{align} and with the independent q^{indep} to produce $p_i^* = [p_i; q_i^{align}; q^{indep}]$,

---

[2]Named BIG LSTM+CNN INPUTS in that work and available at `http://github.com/tensorflow/models/tree/master/research/lm_1b`.

and a BiLSTM is operated over the resulting vectors: $\{h_1, \ldots, h_n\} = \text{BiLSTM}(p_1^*, \ldots, p_n^*)$.

Span representations A candidate answer span $a = (l, r)$ with $l \leq r$ is represented as the concatenation of the corresponding augmented passage representations: $h_a^* = [h_l; h_r]$. In order to avoid quadratic runtime, only spans up to length 30 are considered.

Prediction layer Finally, each span representation h_a^* is transformed to a logit $s_a = w_c^T \cdot \text{FF}(h_a^*)$ for a parameter vector $w_c \in \mathbb{R}^{d_f}$, and these logits are normalized to produce a distribution over spans. Learning is performed by maximizing the log-likelihood of the correct answer span.

4 Evaluation and Analysis

We evaluate our contextualization scheme on the SQuAD dataset (Rajpurkar et al., 2016) which consists of 100,000+ paragraph-question-answer examples, crowdsourced from Wikipedia articles.

Importance of context We are interested in evaluating the effect of our RNN-based re-embedding scheme on the performance of the downstream base model. However, the addition of the re-embedding module incurs additional depth and capacity for the resultant model. We therefore compare this model, termed RaSoR + TR, to a setting in which re-embedding is non-contextual, referred to as RaSoR + TR(MLP). Here we set $u_t = \text{MLP}(x_t)$, a multi-layered perceptron on x_t, allowing for the additional computation to be carried out on word-level representations without any context and matching the model size and hyperparameter search budget of RaSoR + TR. In Table 1 we compare these two variants over the development set and observe superior performance by the contextual one, illustrating the benefit of contextualization and specifically per-sequence contextualization which is done separately for the question and for the passage.

Context complements rare words Our formulation lends itself to an inspection of the different dynamic weightings computed by the model for interpolating between contextual and noncontextual terms. In Figure 1 we plot the average gate value g_t for each word-type, where the average is taken across entries of the gate vector and across all occurrences of the word in both passages

Model	EM	F1
RaSoR (base model)	70.6	78.7
RaSoR + TR(MLP)	72.5	79.9
RaSoR + TR	75.0	82.5
RaSoR + TR + LM(emb)	75.8	83.0
RaSoR + TR + LM(L1)	**77.0**	**84.0**
RaSoR + TR + LM(L2)	76.1	83.3

Table 1: Results on SQuAD's development set. The EM metric measures an exact-match between a predicted answer and a correct one and the F1 metric measures the overlap between their bag of words.

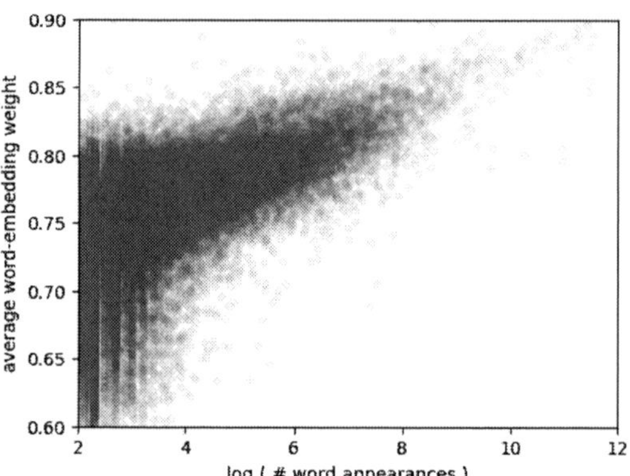

Figure 1: Average gate activations.

and questions. This inspection reveals the following: On average, the less frequent a word-type is, the smaller are its gate activations, i.e., the re-embedded representation of a rare word places less weight on its fixed word-embedding and more on its contextual representation, compared to a common word. This highlights a problem with maintaining fixed word representations: albeit pretrained on extremely large corpora, the embeddings of rare words need to be complemented with information emanating from their context. Our specific parameterization allows observing this directly, but it may very well be an implicit burden placed on any contextualizing encoder such as a vanilla BiLSTM.

Incorporating language model representations Supplementing the calculation of token re-embeddings with the hidden states of a strong language model proves to be highly effective. In Table 1 we list development set results for using either the LM hidden states of the first stacked LSTM layer or those of the second one. We additionally evaluate the incorporation of that model's

Model	EM	F1
BiDAF + Self Attention + ELMo [1]	78.6	85.8
RaSoR + TR + LM(L1) [2]	77.6	84.2
SAN [3]	76.8	84.4
r-net [4]	76.5	84.3
FusionNet [5]	76.0	83.9
Interactive AoA Reader+ [6]	75.8	83.8
RaSoR + TR [7]	75.8	83.3
DCN+ [8]	75.1	83.1
Conductor-net [9]	73.2	81.9
...		
RaSoR (base model) [10]	70.8	78.7

Table 2: Single-model results on SQuAD's test set.[3] [1] Peters et al. (2018) [2,7] This work. [3] Liu et al. (2017b) [4] Wang et al. (2017) [5] Huang et al. (2017) [6] Cui et al. (2017) [8] Xiong et al. (2017a) [9] Liu et al. (2017a) [10] Lee et al. (2016)

word-type representations (referred to as RaSoR + TR + LM(emb)), which are based on character-level embeddings and are naturally unaffected by context around a word-token.

Overall, we observe a significant improvement with all three configurations, effectively showing the benefit of training a QA model in a semi-supervised fashion (Dai and Le, 2015) with a large language model. Besides a crosscutting boost in results, we note that the performance due to utilizing the LM hidden states of the first LSTM layer significantly surpasses the other two variants. This may be due to context being most strongly represented in those hidden states as the representations of LM(emb) are non-contextual by definition and those of LM(L2) were optimized (during LM training) to be similar to parameter vectors that correspond to word-types and not to word-tokens.

In Table 2 we list the top-scoring single-model published results on SQuAD's test set, where we observe RaSoR + TR + LM(L1) ranks second in EM, despite having only minimal question-passage interaction which is a core component of other works. An additional evaluation we carry out is following Jia and Liang (2017), which demonstrated the proneness of current QA models to be fooled by distracting sentences added to the paragraph. In Table 3 we list the single-model results reported thus far and observe that the utilization of LM-based representations carried out by RaSoR + TR + LM(L1) results in improved robustness to adversarial examples.

<hr>

[3]From SQuAD's leaderboard per Dec 13, 2017. `http://rajpurkar.github.io/SQuAD-explorer`

Model	AddSent	AddOneSent
RaSoR + TR + LM(L1) [1]	47.0	57.0
Mnemonic Reader [2]	46.6	56.0
RaSoR + TR [3]	44.5	53.9
MPCM [4]	40.3	50.0
RaSoR (base model) [5]	39.5	49.5
ReasoNet [6]	39.4	50.3
jNet [7]	37.9	47.0

Table 3: Single-model F1 on adversarial SQuAD. [1,3] This work. [2] Hu et al. (2017) [4] Wang et al. (2016) [5] Lee et al. (2016) [6] Shen et al. (2017) [7] Zhang et al. (2017)

5 Experimental setup

We use pre-trained GloVe embeddings (Pennington et al., 2014) of dimension $d_w = 300$ and produce character-based word representations via $d_c = 100$ convolutional filters over character embeddings as in Seo et al. (2016). For all BiLSTMs, hyper-parameter search included the following values, with model selection being done according to validation set results (underlined): number of stacked BiLSTM layers $(1, \underline{2}, 3)$, number of cells d_h $(50, 100, \underline{200})$, dropout rate over input $(0.4, 0.5, \underline{0.6})$, dropout rate over hidden state $(0.05, \underline{0.1}, 0.15)$. To further regularize models, we employed word dropout (Iyyer et al., 2015; Dai and Le, 2015) at rate $(0.05, 0.1, \underline{0.15})$ and couple LSTM input and forget gate as in Greff et al. (2016). All feed-forward networks and the MLP employed the ReLU non-linearity (Nair and Hinton, 2010) with dropout rate $(\underline{0.2}, 0.3)$, where the single hidden layer of the FFs was of dimension $d_f = (50, \underline{100})$ and the best performing MLP consisted of 3 hidden layers of dimensions 865, 865 and 400. For optimization, we used Adam (Kingma and Ba, 2015) with batch size 80.

6 Related Work

Our use of a Highway layer with RNNs is related to Highway LSTM (Zhang et al., 2016) and Residual LSTM (Kim et al., 2017). The goal in those works is to effectively train many stacked LSTM layers and so highway and residual connections are introduced into the definition of the LSTM function. Our formulation is external to that definition, with the specific goal of gating between LSTM hidden states and fixed word-embeddings.

Multiple works have shown the efficacy of semi-supervision for NLP tasks (Søgaard, 2013).

Pre-training a LM in order to initialize the weights of an encoder has been reported to improve generalization and training stability for sequence classification (Dai and Le, 2015) as well as translation and summarization (Ramachandran et al., 2017).

Similar to our work, Peters et al. (2017) utilize the same pre-trained LM from Józefowicz et al. (2016) for sequence tagging tasks, keeping encoder weights fixed during training. Their formulation includes a backward LM and uses the hidden states from the top-most stacked LSTM layer of the LMs, whereas we also consider reading the hidden states of the bottom one, which substantially improves performance. In parallel to our work, Peters et al. (2018) have successfully leveraged pre-trained LMs for several tasks, including RC, by utilizing representations from all layers of the pre-trained LM.

In a transfer-learning setting, McCann et al. (2017) pre-train an attentional encoder-decoder model for machine translation and show improvements across a range of tasks when incorporating the hidden states of the encoder as additional fixed inputs for downstream task training.

7   Conclusion

In this work we examine the importance of context for the task of reading comprehension. We present a neural module that gates contextual and non-contextual representations and observe gains due to context utilization. Consequently, we inject contextual information into our model by integrating a pre-trained language model through our suggested module and find that it substantially improves results, reaching state-of-the-art performance on the SQuAD dataset.

Acknowledgements

We thank the anonymous reviewers for their constructive comments and suggestions. This work was supported by the Israel Science Foundation, grant 942/16.

References

Dzmitry Bahdanau, Kyunghyun Cho, and Yoshua Bengio. 2015. Neural machine translation by jointly learning to align and translate. In *ICLR*.

Ciprian Chelba, Tomas Mikolov, Mike Schuster, Qi Ge, Thorsten Brants, and Phillipp Koehn. 2013. One billion word benchmark for measuring progress in statistical language modeling. *CoRR* abs/1312.3005.

Danqi Chen, Adam Fisch, Jason Weston, and Antoine Bordes. 2017. Reading wikipedia to answer open-domain questions. In *ACL*.

Kyunghyun Cho, Bart van Merrienboer, Dzmitry Bahdanau, and Yoshua Bengio. 2014. On the properties of neural machine translation: Encoder-decoder approaches. In *EMNLP*.

Yiming Cui, Zhipeng Chen, Si Wei, Shijin Wang, Ting Liu, and Guoping Hu. 2017. Attention-over-attention neural networks for reading comprehension. In *ACL*.

Andrew M. Dai and Quoc V. Le. 2015. Semi-supervised sequence learning. In *NIPS*.

Klaus Greff, Rupesh Kumar Srivastava, Jan Koutník, Bas R. Steunebrink, and Jurgen Schmidhuber. 2016. Lstm: A search space odyssey. In *IEEE Transactions on Neural Networks and Learning Systems*.

Karl Moritz Hermann, Tomás Kociský, Edward Grefenstette, Lasse Espeholt, Will Kay, Mustafa Suleyman, and Phil Blunsom. 2015. Teaching machines to read and comprehend. *CoRR* abs/1506.03340.

S. Hochreiter and J. Schmidhuber. 1997. Long short-term memory. *Neural Computation* 9(8):1735–1780.

Minghao Hu, Yuxing Peng, and Xipeng Qiu. 2017. Mnemonic reader for machine comprehension. *CoRR* abs/1705.02798.

Hsin-Yuan Huang, Chenguang Zhu, Yelong Shen, and Weizhu Chen. 2017. Fusionnet: Fusing via fully-aware attention with application to machine comprehension. *CoRR* abs/1711.07341.

Mohit Iyyer, Varun Manjunatha, Jordan L. Boyd-Graber, and Hal Daumé III. 2015. Deep unordered composition rivals syntactic methods for text classification. In *ACL*.

Robin Jia and Percy Liang. 2017. Adversarial examples for evaluating reading comprehension systems. In *EMNLP*. pages 2011–2021.

Mandar Joshi, Eunsol Choi, Daniel S. Weld, and Luke Zettlemoyer. 2017. Triviaqa: A large scale distantly supervised challenge dataset for reading comprehension. In *ACL*.

Rafal Józefowicz, Oriol Vinyals, Mike Schuster, Noam Shazeer, and Yonghui Wu. 2016. Exploring the limits of language modeling. *CoRR* abs/1602.02410.

Jaeyoung Kim, Mostafa El-Khamy, and Jungwon Lee. 2017. Residual LSTM: design of a deep recurrent architecture for distant speech recognition. *CoRR* abs/1701.03360.

Yoon Kim. 2014. Convolutional neural networks for sentence classification. In *EMNLP*.

Diederik P. Kingma and Jimmy Lei Ba. 2015. Adam: A method for stochastic optimization. In *ICLR*.

Ankit Kumar, Ozan Irsoy, Jonathan Su, James Bradbury, Robert English, Brian Pierce, Peter Ondruska, Ishaan Gulrajani, and Richard Socher. 2015. Ask me anything: Dynamic memory networks for natural language processing. *CoRR* abs/1506.07285.

Kenton Lee, Shimi Salant, Tom Kwiatkowski, Ankur P. Parikh, Dipanjan Das, and Jonathan Berant. 2016. Learning recurrent span representations for extractive question answering. *CoRR* abs/1611.01436.

Rui Liu, Wei Wei, Weiguang Mao, and Maria Chikina. 2017a. Phase conductor on multi-layered attentions for machine comprehension. *CoRR* abs/1710.10504.

Xiaodong Liu, Yelong Shen, Kevin Duh, and Jianfeng Gao. 2017b. Stochastic answer networks for machine reading comprehension. *CoRR* abs/1712.03556.

Bryan McCann, James Bradbury, Caiming Xiong, and Richard Socher. 2017. Learned in translation: Contextualized word vectors. In *NIPS*.

Vinod Nair and Geoffrey E. Hinton. 2010. Rectified linear units improve restricted boltzmann machines. In *ICML*.

Tri Nguyen, Mir Rosenberg, Xia Song, Jianfeng Gao, Saurabh Tiwary, Rangan Majumder, and Li Deng. 2016. MS MARCO: A human generated machine reading comprehension dataset. In *NIPS Workshop on Cognitive Computation*.

Ankur P. Parikh, Oscar Täckström, Dipanjan Das, and Jakob Uszkoreit. 2016. A decomposable attention model for natural language inference. In *EMNLP*.

Jeffrey Pennington, Richard Socher, and Christopher D. Manning. 2014. Glove: Global vectors for word representation. In *EMNLP*.

Matthew E. Peters, Waleed Ammar, Chandra Bhagavatula, and Russell Power. 2017. Semi-supervised sequence tagging with bidirectional language models. *CoRR* abs/1705.00108.

Matthew E. Peters, Mark Neumann, Mohit Iyyer, Matt Gardner, Christopher Clark, Kenton Lee, and Luke Zettlemoyer. 2018. Deep contextualized word representations. *CoRR* abs/1802.05365.

Pranav Rajpurkar, Jian Zhang, Konstantin Lopyrev, and Percy Liang. 2016. Squad: 100, 000+ questions for machine comprehension of text. In *EMNLP*.

Prajit Ramachandran, Peter J. Liu, and Quoc V. Le. 2017. Unsupervised pretraining for sequence to sequence learning. In *EMNLP*.

Hasim Sak, Andrew W. Senior, and Françoise Beaufays. 2014. Long short-term memory recurrent neural network architectures for large scale acoustic modeling. In *INTERSPEECH*.

Mike Schuster and Kuldip K. Paliwal. 1997. Bidirectional recurrent neural networks. *IEEE Trans. Signal Processing* 45(11):2673–2681.

Min Joon Seo, Aniruddha Kembhavi, Ali Farhadi, and Hannaneh Hajishirzi. 2016. Bidirectional attention flow for machine comprehension. *CoRR* abs/1611.01603.

Yelong Shen, Po-Sen Huang, Jianfeng Gao, and Weizhu Chen. 2017. Reasonet: Learning to stop reading in machine comprehension. In *SIGKDD*.

Anders Søgaard. 2013. Semi-supervised learning and domain adaptation for nlp .

Rupesh Kumar Srivastava, Klaus Greff, and Jrgen Schmidhuber. 2015. Highway networks. In *ICML 2015 Deep Learning workshop*.

Sainbayar Sukhbaatar, Arthur Szlam, Jason Weston, and Rob Fergus. 2015. End-to-end memory networks. In *NIPS*.

Adam Trischler, Tong Wang, Xingdi Yuan, Justin Harris, Alessandro Sordoni, Philip Bachman, and Kaheer Suleman. 2016. Newsqa: A machine comprehension dataset. *CoRR* abs/1611.09830.

Wenhui Wang, Nan Yang, Furu Wei, Baobao Chang, and Ming Zhou. 2017. Gated self-matching networks for reading comprehension and question answering. In *ACL*.

Zhiguo Wang, Haitao Mi, Wael Hamza, and Radu Florian. 2016. Multi-perspective context matching for machine comprehension. *CoRR* abs/1612.04211.

Dirk Weissenborn, Georg Wiese, and Laura Seiffe. 2017. Making neural QA as simple as possible but not simpler. In *CoNLL*.

Jason Weston, Antoine Bordes, Sumit Chopra, and Tomas Mikolov. 2015. Towards ai-complete question answering: A set of prerequisite toy tasks. *CoRR* abs/1502.05698.

Caiming Xiong, Victor Zhong, and Richard Socher. 2017a. DCN+: mixed objective and deep residual coattention for question answering. *CoRR* abs/1711.00106.

Caiming Xiong, Victor Zhong, and Richard Socher. 2017b. Dynamic coattention networks for question answering. In *ICLR*.

Junbei Zhang, Xiao-Dan Zhu, Qian Chen, Li-Rong Dai, Si Wei, and Hui Jiang. 2017. Exploring question understanding and adaptation in neural-network-based question answering. *CoRR* abs/1703.04617.

Yu Zhang, Guoguo Chen, Dong Yu, Kaisheng Yao, Sanjeev Khudanpur, and James R. Glass. 2016. Highway long short-term memory RNNS for distant speech recognition. In *ICASSP*.

Crowdsourcing Question-Answer Meaning Representations

Julian Michael,[1] Gabriel Stanovsky,[*,1,3] Luheng He,[1] Ido Dagan,[2] and Luke Zettlemoyer[1]

[1]Paul G. Allen School of Computer Science & Engineering, University of Washington, Seattle, WA
[2]Bar-Ilan University Computer Science Department, Ramat Gan, Israel
[3]Allen Institute for Artificial Intelligence, Seattle, WA
{julianjm,luheng,lsz}@cs.washington.edu
gabriel.stanovsky@gmail.com, dagan@cs.biu.ac.il

Abstract

We introduce Question-Answer Meaning Representations (QAMRs), which represent the predicate-argument structure of a sentence as a set of question-answer pairs. We develop a crowdsourcing scheme to show that QAMRs can be labeled with very little training, and gather a dataset with over 5,000 sentences and 100,000 questions. A qualitative analysis demonstrates that the crowd-generated question-answer pairs cover the vast majority of predicate-argument relationships in existing datasets (including PropBank, Nom-Bank, and QA-SRL) along with many previously under-resourced ones, including implicit arguments and relations. We also report baseline models for question generation and answering, and summarize a recent approach for using QAMR labels to improve an Open IE system. These results suggest the freely available[1] QAMR data and annotation scheme should support significant future work.

1 Introduction

Predicate-argument relationships form a key part of sentential meaning representations, and support answering basic questions such as *who did what to whom*. Resources for predicate-argument structure are well-developed for verbs (e.g. Prop-Bank (Palmer et al., 2005)) and there have been efforts to study other parts of speech (e.g. Nom-Bank (Meyers et al., 2004) and FrameNet (Baker et al., 1998)) and introduce whole-sentence structures (e.g. AMR (Banarescu et al., 2013)). However, highly skilled and trained annotators are re-

---

*Work performed while at Bar-Ilan University.
[1]github.com/uwnlp/qamr

Pierre Vinken, 61 years old, will join the board as a nonexecutive director Nov. 29.

Who will **join** as **nonexecutive director**? - Pierre Vinken
What is **Pierre**'s last name? - Vinken
Who is **61 years old**? - Pierre Vinken
How **old** is **Pierre Vinken**? - 61 years old
What will he **join**? - the board
What will he **join the board** as? - nonexecutive director
What type of **director** will **Vinken** be? - nonexecutive
What day will **Vinken join the board**? - Nov. 29

Figure 1: Example QAMR.

quired to label data within these formulations for each new domain, and it takes significant effort to model each new type of relationship (e.g., noun arguments in NomBank). We propose a new method to annotate relatively complete representations of the predicate-argument structure of a sentence, which can be done easily by non-experts.

We introduce Question-Answer Meaning Representations (QAMRs), which represent the predicate-argument structure of a sentence as a set of question-answer pairs (see Figure 1). Following the QA-SRL formalism (He et al., 2015), each question-answer pair corresponds to a predicate-argument relationship. There is no need for a carefully curated ontology and the labels are highly interpretable. However, we differ from QA-SRL in focusing on *all words* in the sentence rather than just verbs, and allowing *free form* questions instead of using templates.

The QAMR formulation provides a new way of thinking about predicate-argument structure. Any form of sentence meaning—from a vector of real numbers to a logical form—should support the challenge of determining which questions are answerable by the sentence, and what the answers are. A QAMR sidesteps intermediate formal representations by surfacing those questions and an-

Proceedings of NAACL-HLT 2018, pages 560–568
New Orleans, Louisiana, June 1 - 6, 2018. ©2018 Association for Computational Linguistics

swers *as* the representation. As with any other representation, this can then be reprocessed for downstream tasks. Indeed, the question-answer format facilitates reprocessing for tasks that are similar in form, for example Open IE (see Section 4).

A key advantage of QAMRs is that they can be annotated with crowdsourcing. The main challenge is coverage, as it can be difficult for a single annotator to write all possible QA pairs for a sentence. Instead, we distribute the work between multiple annotators in a novel crowdsourcing scheme, which we use to gather a dataset of over 100,000 QA pairs for 5,000 sentences in Newswire and Wikipedia domains.

Although QAMR questions' free-form nature is crucial for our approach, it means that predicates are not explicitly marked. However, with a simple predicate-finding heuristic, we can align QAMR to PropBank, NomBank, and QA-SRL and show high coverage of predicate-argument structure, including more than 90% of non-discourse relationships. Further analysis reveals that QAMRs also capture many phenomena that are not modeled in traditional representations of predicate-argument structure, including coreference, implicit and inferred arguments, and implicit relations (for example, with noun adjuncts).

Finally, we report simple neural baselines for QAMR question generation and answering. We also highlight a recent result (Stanovsky et al., 2018) showing that QAMR data can be used to improve performance on a challenging task: Open Information Extraction. Together, these results show that there is significant potential for follow up work on developing innovative uses of QAMR and modeling their relatively comprehensive and complex predicate-argument relationships.

2 Crowdsourcing

We gather QAMRs with a two-stage crowdsourcing pipeline[2] using monetary incentives and crowd-driven quality control to ensure high coverage of predicate-argument structure. *Generation* workers write QA pairs and *validation* workers answer or reject the generated questions. Full details of our setup are given in Appendix A.

Generation Workers receive an English sentence with up to four *target words*. They are asked to write as many QA pairs as possible containing

	PTB	Train	Dev	Test
Sentences	253	3,938	499	480
Annotators	5	1	3	3
QA Pairs	27,082	73,561	27,535	26,994
Filtered	18,789	51,063	19,069	18,959
Cost	$2,862	$7,879	$2,919	$2,919
Cost/token	$0.44	$0.08	$0.25	$0.25

Table 1: Summary of the data gathered.

each target word in the question or answer, subject to light constraints (for example, the question must contain a word from the sentence and be answered in the sentence, and they must highlight the answer in the sentence). Workers must write at least one QA pair for each target word to receive the base pay of 20c. An increasing bonus of $3(k+1)$ cents is paid for each k-th additional QA pair they write that passes the validation stage.

Validation Workers receive a sentence and a batch of questions written by an annotator in the first stage (with no marked target words or answers). The worker must mark each question as *invalid* or *redundant* with another question, or highlight its answer in the sentence. Two workers validate and answer each set of questions. They are paid a base rate of 10c for each batch, with an extra 2c for each question past four.

Quality control Question writers are disqualified if the percentage of valid judgments on their questions falls below 75%. Validators need to pass a qualification test and maintain above 70% agreement with others, where overlapping answer spans are considered to agree.

2.1 Data Preparation and Annotation

We drew our data from 1,000 Wikinews articles from 2012–2015 and 1,000 articles from Wikipedia's 1,000 core topics,[3] partitioned by document into train, dev, and test, and preprocessed using the Stanford CoreNLP tools (Manning et al., 2014). We also annotated 253 sentences from the Penn Treebank (Marcus et al., 1993) chosen to overlap with existing resources for comparison (see Section 3).

For each sentence, we group its non-stopwords sequentially into groups of 3 or 4 target words, removing sentences with no content words. By presenting workers with nearly-contiguous lists of

---

[2]Built using Amazon Mechanical Turk: www.mturk.com

[3]https://en.wikipedia.org/wiki/Wikipedia:1,000_core_topics

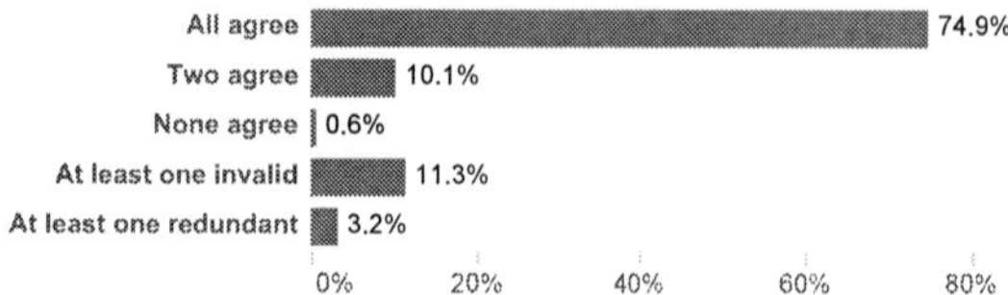

Figure 2: Agreement and validation statistics on all data gathered. Answers were considered to agree if their spans overlapped. High agreement on answers indicates that questions were generally interpretable and answers were consistent.

target words, enforcing non-redundancy, and providing bonuses, we encourage exhaustiveness over all possible QA pairs. By allowing the target word to appear in the question *or* the answer, we make the requirements flexible enough that there is almost always some QA pair that can be written.

Figure 2 shows agreement statistics for question validation. We removed questions either validator counted invalid or redundant, as well as questions not beginning with a wh-word,[4] which we found to be of low quality. We also annotated the partitions at different levels of redundancy to allow for more exhaustive dev, test, and comparison sets. See Table 1 for statistics.

3   Data Analysis

In this section, we show that QAMR has high coverage of predicate-argument structure and uses a rich vocabulary to label fine-grained and implicit semantic relations.

Coverage   To show that QAMR captures the same kinds of predicate-argument relations as existing formalisms, we compare our data to PropBank, NomBank, and QA-SRL. Since predicates in the questions are not explicitly marked, we use a simple predicate-finding heuristic to help align to other formalisms: for each minimal span that appears in the QAMR questions and answers (i.e., none of its subspans appear independently of it elsewhere in the QAMR), we compute its *predicate score* as the proportion of its appearances that are in a question rather than in an answer.[5] We then choose the span with the highest predicate score in each question as its predicate.

We measure recall on the shared Penn Treebank sentences for each resource by randomly sampling n annotators out of 5 for each group of target

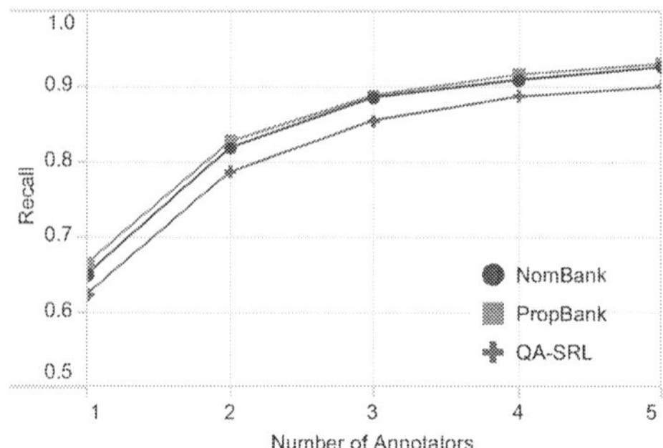

Figure 3: Recall of predicate-argument relations for sentences shared with each of our reference datasets, with increasing number of annotators.

words, which simulates the situation for the training set (1 annotator) and the dev/test sets (3 annotators). For each n we took the mean of 10 runs. Full details of our comparison are in Appendix B.

Results are shown in Figure 3. Single annotators cover over 60% of relationships, and coverage quickly increases with the number of annotators, reaching over 90% with all five. This shows that QAMR's representational capacity covers the vast majority of relevant predicate-argument relations in existing resources. However, coverage in our training set is low due to low annotation density.

For a qualitative analysis, we sample 150 QA pairs (see Table 2 for examples).[6] Of our sample, over 90% of question-answer pairs correspond to a predicate-argument relation expressed in the sentence,[7] including arguments and modifiers of nouns and verbs as well as relationships like those within proper names (Table 2, ex. 2c, 3a) and coreference (ex. 3c, 4c). Questions that do not align to predicate-argument structure often target shallow inferences (ex. 3b, 7c).

Rich vocabulary   Annotators use the open question format to introduce a large vocabulary of *external phrases* which do not appear in the sentence. Overall, 5,687 different external phrases are introduced (excluding stopwords), appearing 25,952 times in 38.7% of the questions (see Figure 4). These include typing words like *state* and *country* (Table 2, ex. 5), most often directly after the *wh*-word, and relation-denoting phrases like *work for* (ex. 2b), *last name* (ex. 3a), and *victim*

---

[4] *who, what, when, where, why, how, which,* and *whose*

[5] This follows the intuition that predicates are more likely to appear in the question; for example, see **join** in Figure 1.

[6] This sample, and statistics for the remainder of this section, were taken from the filtered train and development sets, with a total of about 70k QA pairs.

[7] We assume a QA pair targets the relation corresponding to the semantic role of the wh-word in the question.

Sentence	Ann.	Question	Answers
(1) Climate change affects distribution of weeds, pests, and diseases.	VAR	(a) What affects distribution of diseases? (b) What is affected?	Climate change distribution of... / distribution
(2) Baruch ben Neriah, Jeremiah's scribe, used this alphabet to create the later scripts of the Old Testament.	SYN ROLE	(a) Who wrote the scripts? (b) Who did Baruch work for? (c) What is old?	Baruch ben Neriah Jeremiah Testament / the Old Testament
(3) Mahlunga has said he did nothing wrong and Judge Horn said he "failed to express genuine remorse".	ROLE INF CO	(a) What is the Judge's last name? (b) Who doubted his remorse was genuine? (c) Who didn't express genuine remorse?	Horn Judge Horn Mahlunga
(4) In Byron's later memoirs, "Mary Chaworth is portrayed as the first object of his adult sexual feelings."	IMP VAR	(a) Who is portrayed in the work? (b) Who was the object of his sexual feelings? (c) Who was Mary the object of sexual feelings for?	Mary Chaworth Mary Chaworth Byron
(5) Volunteers are presently renovating the former post office in the town of Edwards, Mississippi, United States for the doctor to have an office.	IMP VAR	(a) What town is the post office in? (b) What state is the post office in? (c) What country are the volunteers renovating in? (d) What country is the city of Edwards in?	Edwards Mississippi United States United States
(6) The ossicles are the malleus (hammer), incus (anvil), and the stapes (stirrup).	VAR	(a) What is the malleus one of?	The ossicles / ossicles
(7) Liam "had his whole life in front of him", said Detective Inspector Andy Logan, who was the senior investigator of his murder.	ROLE ROLE INF	(a) Who is the murder victim Logan is investigating? (b) What rank of investigator is Andy Logan? (c) Who was Detective Logan speaking about?	Liam Detective Inspector / senior Liam
(8) This cemetery dates from the time of Menkaure (Junker) or earlier (Reisner), and contains several stone-built mastabas dating from as late as the 6th dynasty.	INF IMP	(a) How old are the stone-built mastabas? (b) What period was earlier than Menkaure? (c) What dates from the 6th dynasty?	dating from as late as the 6th dynasty / from as late as the 6th dynasty Reisner mastabas / several stone-built mastabas

Table 2: Examples of question-answer pairs capturing various semantic relations, annotated with interesting phenomena they exhibit: syntactic variation (VAR), synonym use (SYN), explicit role names for implicit relations (ROLE), coreference (CO), implicit arguments (IMP), and inferred relations (INF).

Figure 4: Novel phrases appearing more than 50 times. Darker phrases appear more commonly after *who, which,* or *how.* The vast majority of external phrases are used to denote entity/event types or semantic relations.

(ex. 7a). Despite the open format, synonyms are not a major issue, obscuring the semantic relation in only 2% of our sample (ex. 2a).

We also find verbal paraphrases of noun compounds, as proposed by Nakov (2008). For example, where *Gallup poll* appears in the text, one annotator has written *Who conducted the poll?*, which explicates the relationship between *Gallup* and *poll.* Similarly, *Who received the bailouts?* is written for the phrase *bank bailouts.*

Semantics, not just syntax Only 63% of QA pairs characterize their predicate-argument relation using the same syntactic relationship as in the sentence. 5% have answers coreferent with the

syntactic argument (Table 2, ex. 3c, 4c); 17% exhibit syntactic variation, using different prepositions (ex. 4c, 6a), alternating between active and passive (ex. 1b), or changing between the noun and verb form of the predicate (ex. 8a); 6% ask about implicit arguments (ex. 4b, 5c, 8b); and 6% ask about inferred relations (ex. 3b).

4   Models

To establish initial baselines, we apply existing neural models for QAMR question generation and answering. We also briefly summarize a recent end task result, where QAMR annotations were used to improve an Open IE system.

Question generation In question generation (QG), we learn a mapping from a sentence $\mathbf{w}$ to a set of questions $q_1, \ldots, q_m$. We enumerate pairs of words (w_q, w_a) from the sentence to seed the generator. During training, outputs are questions q and inputs are tuples $(\mathbf{w}, w_q, w_a)$, where $w_q \in q$ and w_a is in q's answer. We also add negative samples where the output is a special token and the input has w_q, w_a that never appear together.

We use an encoder-decoder model with a copying mechanism (Zhou et al., 2017) to generate a question from an input sentence with tagging features for part of speech, w_q, and w_a. At test time, we run all pairs of content words (w_i, w_j) where $|i - j| \leq 5$ through the model to yield a set of questions. On the QAMR test set, this achieves 28% precision and 24% recall with fuzzy matching (multi-BLEU[8] > 0.8).

Question answering The format of QAMRs allows us to apply an existing question-answering model (Seo et al., 2016) designed for the SQuAD (Rajpurkar et al., 2016) reading comprehension task to answer QAMR questions. Training and testing with the SQuAD metrics on QAMR, the model achieves 70.8% exact match and 79.7% F1 score. We further improve performance to 75.7% exact match and 83.9% F1 by pooling our training set with the SQuAD training data. The relative ease of QA in comparison to QG suggests that in QAMR, most of the information is contained in the questions.

Open IE Finally, we also expect that the predicate-argument relationships represented in QAMRs will be useful for many end tasks. Such a result was recently shown for Open IE (Stanovsky et al., 2018), using our QAMR corpus. Open IE involves extracting tuples of natural language phrases that express the propositions asserted by a sentence. They show that, using a syntactic dependency parser, a QAMR can be converted to a list of Open IE extractions. Augmenting their training data with a conversion of our QAMR dataset yields state-of-the-art performance on several Open IE benchmarks (Stanovsky and Dagan, 2016b; Xu et al., 2013; de Sá Mesquita et al., 2013; Schneider et al., 2017). The gains come largely from the extra extractions (e.g., with nominal predicates) that QAMRs support over traditional resources focusing on verbal predications.

5   Related Work

In addition to the semantic formalisms (Palmer et al., 2005; Meyers et al., 2004; Banarescu et al., 2013; He et al., 2015) we have already discussed, FrameNet (Baker et al., 1998) also focuses predicate-argument structure, but has more fine-grained argument types. Gerber and Chai (2010) target implicit nominal arguments. Stanovsky and Dagan (2016a) annotate non-restrictive noun phrase modifiers on top of QA-SRL. Other linguistically motivated annotation schemes include

UCCA (Abend and Rappoport, 2013), HSPG treebanks (Flickinger et al., 2017), and the Groningen meaning bank (Basile et al., 2012).

Crowdsourcing has also been applied to gather annotations of structure in the setup of multiple choice questions, for example, for Dowty's semantic proto-roles (Reisinger et al., 2015; White et al., 2016) and human-in-the-loop parsing and classification (He et al., 2016; Duan et al., 2016; Werling et al., 2015), while Wang et al. (2017) use crowdsourcing with question-answer pairs to annotate some PropBank roles directly. Our approach recovers paraphrases of noun compounds similar to those crowdsourced by Nakov (2008).

More broadly, non-expert annotation has been used extensively to gather question-answer pairs over natural language texts, for example in reading comprehension (Rajpurkar et al., 2016; Richardson et al., 2013; Nguyen et al., 2016) and visual question answering (Antol et al., 2015). However, while these treat question answering as an end task, we regard it as a representation of predicate-argument structure, and focus annotators on a smaller selection of text (a few target words in a single sentence, rather than a paragraph) aiming to achieve high coverage.

6   Conclusion

QAMR provides a new way of thinking about meaning representation: using open-ended natural language annotation to represent rich semantic structure. This paradigm allows for representing a broad range of semantic phenomena with data easily gathered from native speakers. Our dataset has already been used to improve the performance of an Open IE system, and how best to leverage the data and model its complex phenomena is an open challenge which our annotation scheme could support studying at a relatively large scale.

Acknowledgments

This work was supported in part by grants from the MAGNET program of the Israeli Office of the Chief Scientist (OCS); the German Research Foundation through the German-Israeli Project Cooperation (DIP, grant DA 1600/1-1); the Israel Science Foundation (grant No. 1157/16); the US NSF (IIS1252835,IIS-1562364); and an Allen Distinguished Investigator Award.

---

[8]An average of the BLEU1–BLEU4 scores.

References

Omri Abend and Ari Rappoport. 2013. Universal conceptual cognitive annotation (ucca). In *Proceedings of the 51st Annual Meeting of the Association for Computational Linguistics*.

Stanislaw Antol, Aishwarya Agrawal, Jiasen Lu, Margaret Mitchell, Dhruv Batra, C. Lawrence Zitnick, and Devi Parikh. 2015. VQA: Visual Question Answering. In *International Conference on Computer Vision (ICCV)*.

Collin F Baker, Charles J Fillmore, and John B Lowe. 1998. The berkeley framenet project. In *Proceedings of the 17th International Conference on Computational Linguistics*.

Laura Banarescu, Claire Bonial, Shu Cai, Madalina Georgescu, Kira Griffitt, Ulf Hermjakob, Kevin Knight, Philipp Koehn, Martha Palmer, and Nathan Schneider. 2013. Abstract meaning representation for sembanking. In *Proceedings of the Linguistic Annotation Workshop*.

Valerio Basile, Johan Bos, Kilian Evang, and Noortje Venhuizen. 2012. Developing a large semantically annotated corpus. In *Proceedings of the 2012 International Conference on Language Resources and Evaluation*.

Manjuan Duan, Ethan Hill, and Michael White. 2016. Generating disambiguating paraphrases for structurally ambiguous sentences. In *Proceedings of the 10th Linguistic Annotation Workshop*.

Dan Flickinger, Stephan Oepen, and Emily M. Bender. 2017. *Sustainable Development and Refinement of Complex Linguistic Annotations at Scale*.

Matthew Gerber and Joyce Y Chai. 2010. Beyond nombank: A study of implicit arguments for nominal predicates. In *Proceedings of the 48th Annual Meeting of the Association for Computational Linguistics*, pages 1583–1592. Association for Computational Linguistics.

Luheng He, Mike Lewis, and Luke Zettlemoyer. 2015. Question-answer driven semantic role labeling: Using natural language to annotate natural language. In *Proceedings of the 2015 Conference on Empirical Methods in Natural Language Processing*.

Luheng He, Julian Michael, Mike Lewis, and Luke Zettlemoyer. 2016. Human-in-the-loop parsing.

Christopher D. Manning, Mihai Surdeanu, John Bauer, Jenny Finkel, Steven J. Bethard, and David McClosky. 2014. The Stanford CoreNLP natural language processing toolkit. In *Association for Computational Linguistics (ACL) System Demonstrations*, pages 55–60.

Mitchell P Marcus, Mary Ann Marcinkiewicz, and Beatrice Santorini. 1993. Building a large annotated corpus of english: The penn treebank. *Computational Linguistics*.

Adam Meyers, Ruth Reeves, Catherine Macleod, Rachel Szekely, Veronika Zielinska, Brian Young, and Ralph Grishman. 2004. The nombank project: An interim report. In *HLT-NAACL 2004 workshop: Frontiers in corpus annotation*.

Preslav Nakov. 2008. *Noun Compound Interpretation Using Paraphrasing Verbs: Feasibility Study*. Springer Berlin Heidelberg, Berlin, Heidelberg.

Tri Nguyen, Mir Rosenberg, Xia Song, Jianfeng Gao, Saurabh Tiwary, Rangan Majumder, and Li Deng. 2016. MS MARCO: A human generated machine reading comprehension dataset. In *Advances in Neural Information Processing Systems*.

Martha Palmer, Daniel Gildea, and Paul Kingsbury. 2005. The proposition bank: An annotated corpus of semantic roles. *Computational Linguistics*.

Pranav Rajpurkar, Jian Zhang, Konstantin Lopyrev, and Percy Liang. 2016. Squad: 100,000+ questions for machine comprehension of text. *arXiv preprint arXiv:1606.05250*.

Drew Reisinger, Rachel Rudinger, Francis Ferraro, Craig Harman, Kyle Rawlins, and Benjamin Van Durme. 2015. Semantic proto-roles. *Transactions of the Association for Computational Linguistics*.

Matthew Richardson, Christopher JC Burges, and Erin Renshaw. 2013. MCTest: A challenge dataset for the open-domain machine comprehension of text. In *EMNLP*, pages 193–203.

Filipe de Sá Mesquita, Jordan Schmidek, and Denilson Barbosa. 2013. Effectiveness and efficiency of open relation extraction. In *Proceedings of the 2013 Conference on Empirical Methods in Natural Language Processing, EMNLP 2013, 18-21 October 2013, Grand Hyatt Seattle, Seattle, Washington, USA, A meeting of SIGDAT, a Special Interest Group of the ACL*, pages 447–457.

Rudolf Schneider, Tom Oberhauser, Tobias Klatt, Felix A. Gers, and Alexander Loser. 2017. Analysing errors of open information extraction systems. *CoRR*, abs/1707.07499.

Minjoon Seo, Aniruddha Kembhavi, Ali Farhadi, and Hannaneh Hajishirzi. 2016. Bidirectional attention flow for machine comprehension. *arXiv preprint arXiv:1611.01603*.

Gabriel Stanovsky and Ido Dagan. 2016a. Annotating and predicting non-restrictive noun phrase modifications. In *Proceedings of the 54rd Annual Meeting of the Association for Computational Linguistics (ACL 2016)*.

Gabriel Stanovsky and Ido Dagan. 2016b. Creating a large benchmark for open information extraction. In *Proceedings of the 2016 Conference on Empirical Methods in Natural Language Processing (EMNLP)*, Austin, Texas. Association for Computational Linguistics.

Gabriel Stanovsky, Julian Michael, Luke Zettlemoyer, and Ido Dagan. 2018. Supervised open information extraction. In *Proceedings of the 2018 Conference of the North American Chapter of the Association for Computational Linguistics: Human Language Technologies*. Association for Computational Linguistics.

Chenguang Wang, Alan Akbik, laura chiticariu, Yunyao Li, Fei Xia, and Anbang Xu. 2017. Crowd-in-the-loop: A hybrid approach for annotating semantic roles. In *Proceedings of the 2017 Conference on Empirical Methods in Natural Language Processing*, pages 1914–1923. Association for Computational Linguistics.

Keenon Werling, Arun Tejasvi Chaganty, Percy S Liang, and Christopher D Manning. 2015. On-the-job learning with bayesian decision theory. In *Advances in Neural Information Processing Systems*.

Aaron Steven White, Drew Reisinger, Sakaguchi Tim Vieira, Sheng Zhang Rachel Rudinger Kyle Rawlins, and Benjamin Van Durme. 2016. Universal decompositional semantics on universal dependencies.

Ying Xu, Mi-Young Kim, Kevin Quinn, Randy Goebel, and Denilson Barbosa. 2013. Open information extraction with tree kernels. In *Proceedings of the 2013 Conference of the North American Chapter of the Association for Computational Linguistics: Human Language Technologies*, pages 868–877, Atlanta, Georgia. Association for Computational Linguistics.

Qingyu Zhou, Nan Yang, Furu Wei, Chuanqi Tan, Hangbo Bao, and Ming Zhou. 2017. Neural question generation from text: A preliminary study. *arXiv preprint arXiv:1704.01792*.

A Crowdsourcing Details

In this section we provide full details of the data collection methodology described in Section 2. For the exact text of the instructions shown to workers, and code to reproduce the annotation or demo the interface, see `github.com/uwnlp/qamr`.

Stages Data collection proceeded in two stages: *generation* and *validation*. These were run as two types of HITs (Human Intelligence Tasks) on the Amazon Mechanical Turk platform. Workers wrote questions and answers for the generation task, and those questions would be immediately uploaded as new HITs for the validation task, which ran concurrently. Two workers would validate each question. The worker writing the question would be assessed based on the validators' judgments, and the validators would be assessed

based on their agreement. In this way, the quality of workers in either stage could be quickly assessed so spammers or low-quality workers could be disqualified before causing much damage.

Question constraints In both stages, we define a *valid* question to

(1) contain at least one word from the sentence,

(2) be about the sentence's meaning,

(3) be answered obviously and explicitly in the sentence,

(4) not be a yes/no question, and

(5) not be *redundant*,

where we define two questions as being redundant by the informal criterion of "having the same meaning" and the same answer. These requirements are illustrated with examples.

Workers in the generation phase are instructed only to write valid questions, while workers in the validation phase are instructed only to answer valid questions (marking the rest invalid or redundant).

When we ask that the question contains a word from the sentence, we allow for changing forms of the word through inflectional or derivational morphology (with examples of both). The only constraint on questions that is strictly enforced by the interface is a length limit of 50 characters.

Target words In the generation task, each sentence is presented to the worker with several underlined *target words*. They are required to write at least one QA pair for each target word, where the target word must appear either in the question or the answer. We choose sets of target words by chunking consecutive words (ignoring stopwords) into groups of 3 or 4 (or fewer for very short sentences). Because the target words shown to a single worker are close to each other—and often share a constituent—it restricts the set of QA pairs they write to relate to a certain part of the sentence. However, asking that the target word appears either in the question *or* the answer makes it flexible enough so that the worker is almost never stuck with no reasonable question to write. We identified this approach after some experimentation, finding that together with the monetary incentives described below, it struck the appropriate

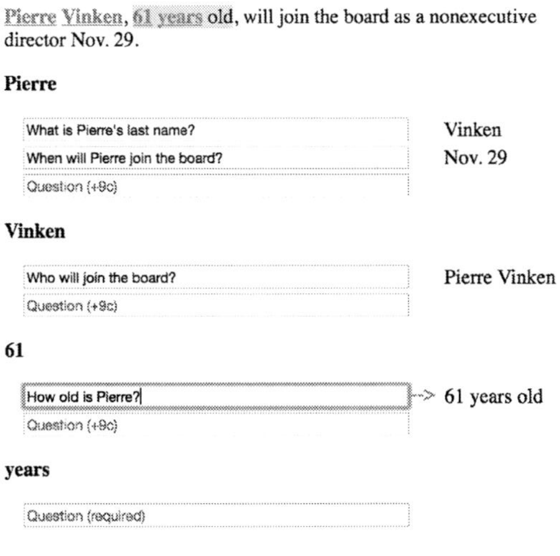

Figure 5: Annotation interface for generation.

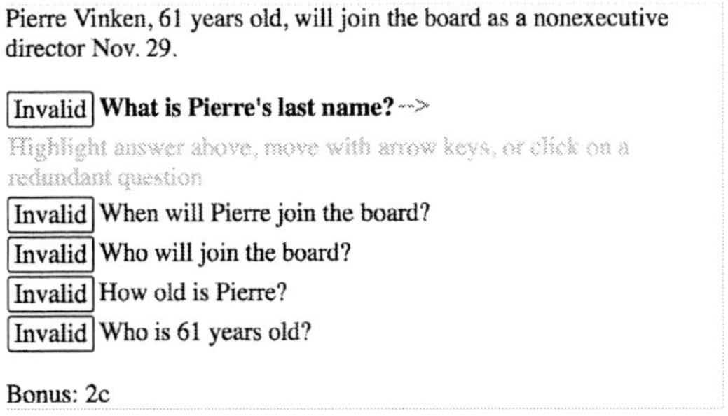

Figure 6: Annotation interface for validation.

balance of scope that was small enough to get exhaustive annotation, but not so small that it cornered workers into writing awkward questions or getting frustrated.

Interface   In the generation stage, below the sentence, each target word is listed with a text field below it where they write a question for that target word. While the text field is focused, they highlight the answer tokens in the sentence using custom implemented highlighting functionality. The highlighted tokens then appear next to the focused question. The answer tokens need not be a contiguous span in our interface (though they almost always are in practice). Once a question is written and answered, a new text field appears directly below it for another question, allowing the annotator to write as many questions as they can. See Figure 5 for a screenshot of the generation task interface.

In the validation stage, no target words are indicated to the user; they only see a list of questions written in a single HIT by a worker in the generation stage. They use the arrow keys to switch between the questions, and use the mouse to assess them: either highlighting the answer in the sentence, clicking another question to mark the selected one redundant, or clicking the *invalid* button to mark a question invalid. See Figure 6.

Incentives and payment   Base pay for the generation stage was 20c, with a bonus of $3(k + 1)$ cents for each question beyond the number required (so, the first extra question would reward them 6c, the next 9c, and so on). However, their

bonuses were only calculated based on the number of questions considered valid by annotators. So if a worker in the generation task wrote 2 extra questions, but any 2 (or 3, or more) of their questions were judged invalid, then they would receive no bonus.

In the validation stage, workers were paid 10c plus a bonus of 2c per question beyond four.

Quality control   We used Mechanical Turk's quality control mechanisms in several ways. First, we used the built-in Locale qualification to limit the tasks to workers based in the United States as a proxy for English proficiency. Second, we wrote a multiple-choice qualification test for the validation task, which tested workers' understanding of the definitions of question validity and redundancy. Workers were required to get a score of 75% on this test before working on the validation task.

Finally, we used Mechanical Turk's built-in qualification mechanism to keep track of worker accuracy and agreement ratings. Before working on either task, a worker would have to request a qualification which stored their accuracy or agreement value. Then as they worked, it would be updated over time and they could check its value in their Mechanical Turk account to see how they were doing. In the generation task, accuracy was calculated as the proportion of all judgments (aggregating those from both validators) that were not *invalid* or *redundant*, and accuracy had to remain above 75% to avoid disqualification. In the validation task, agreement was calculated by treating answer spans as agreeing if they had any overlap, and *redundant* judgments agreeing if their targets had agreeing answer spans. A worker's agreement had to stay above 70% for them to remain qualified.

If a worker's accuracy or agreement rating

dropped within 5% of the threshold, the worker was automatically sent an email with a warning and a list of common mistakes and tips they might use to improve.

Implementation All of our code was written in Scala, using the Java AWS SDK on the backend to interface with Mechanical Turk, Akka Actors and Akka HTTP to implement the web server and quality control logic, and Scala.js with React to implement the user interface.

Dataset Our dataset was gathered over the course of 1 month from 330 unique workers. See Section 2.1 for details.

B SRL Comparison

In this section we provide the full details of the comparison of QAMR to PropBank, NomBank, and QA-SRL given in Section 3.

Preprocessing For each of these resources, there were certain predicate-argument relationships that we filtered out of the comparison for being out of scope.

For PropBank, we filter out predicates and arguments that are auxiliary verbs, as well as reference (R-) roles since aligning these properly is difficult and their function is primarily syntactic. We also remove discourse (-DIS) arguments such as *but* and *instead*: these may be regarded as involved in *discourse* structure separately from the predicate-argument structure we are investigating. 78% of the original dependencies remain.

For NomBank, we also remove auxiliaries, and we remove arguments that include the predicate— which are present for words like *salesman* and *teacher*—leaving 83% of the original dependencies.

For QA-SRL, we use all dependencies, and where multiple answers were provided to a question, we take the union of the answer spans to be the argument span.

Alignment Because QAMR does not mark predicates explicitly, we use a simple predicate-finding heuristic to align the QA pairs in a QAMR to the predicate-argument relations in each resource independently.

For each QAMR, we identify every *minimal span* appearing in its questions and answers, i.e., a span from the sentence where none of its subspans appear independently of it in the QAMR.

We then calculate a *predicate score* for each span, as the proportion of times it appeared in a question versus an answer. Then for each QA pair, we identify the span in the question with highest predicate score as its *predicate span*, and the answer as its argument span. This is then aligned to the predicate-argument arc in the chosen resource with the greatest non-zero argument overlap such that the predicate is contained within the question's predicate span. If there is no such alignment, we check for an opposite-direction alignment where the predicate is in the answer of a QA pair and the argument completely contains the question's predicate span.

Results See Section 3 for a description of the results. With 1 annotator, we get around 60% recall, but it begins to level off over 85% with 3 annotators.

We manually examined 25 sentences to study sources of coverage loss in the 5-annotator case. In comparison to PropBank and NomBank, the missing dependencies are due to missing QA pairs (44%), mistakes in our alignment heuristic (28%), and subtle modifiers/idiomatic uses (28%). For example, annotators sometimes overlook phrases such as *so far* (marked as a temporal modifier in PropBank) or *let's* (where *'s* is marked as a core verbal argument). Comparing to QA-SRL, 60% of the missed relations are inferred/ambiguous relations that are common in that dataset. Missed QA pairs in QA-SRL account for another 20%.

In aggregate, these analyses show that the QAMR labels capture the same kinds of predicate-argument structures as existing resources. However, while our development and test sets can be expected to have reasonable coverage, where we have labels from only one annotator for each target word (as in our training set), the recall low compared to expert-annotated structures, which may pose challenges to learning.

Leveraging Context Information for Natural Question Generation

Linfeng Song[1]*, **Zhiguo Wang**[2], **Wael Hamza**[2], **Yue Zhang**[3] **and Daniel Gildea**[1]
[1]Department of Computer Science, University of Rochester, Rochester, NY 14627
[2]IBM T.J. Watson Research Center, Yorktown Heights, NY 10598
[3]Singapore University of Technology and Design

Abstract

The task of natural question generation is to generate a corresponding question given the input passage (fact) and answer. It is useful for enlarging the training set of QA systems. Previous work has adopted sequence-to-sequence models that take a passage with an additional bit to indicate answer position as input. However, they do not explicitly model the information between answer and other context within the passage. We propose a model that matches the answer with the passage before generating the question. Experiments show that our model outperforms the existing state of the art using rich features.

1 Introduction

The task of natural question generation (NQG) is to generate a fluent and relevant question given a passage and a target answer. Recently NQG has received increasing attention from both the industrial and academic communities because of its values for improving QA systems by automatically increasing the training data. It can also be used for educational purposes such as language learning (Heilman and Smith, 2010).

One example is shown in Table 1, where a question "when was nikola tesla born ?" is generated given a passage and a fact "1856". Existing work for NQG uses a sequence-to-sequence model (Sutskever et al., 2014), which takes a passage as input for generating a question. They either entirely ignore the target answer (Du et al., 2017), or directly hard-code answer positions (Zhou et al., 2017; Yang et al., 2017; Subramanian et al., 2017; Tang et al., 2017; Wang et al., 2017a; Yuan et al., 2017). These methods can neglect rich potential

---

Passage: nikola tesla (serbian cyrillic : Никола Тесла ; 10 july <u>1856</u> – 7 january 1943) was a serbian american inventor , electrical engineer , mechanical engineer , physicist , and futurist best known for his contributions to the design of the modern alternating current (ac) electricity supply system .
Question: when was nikola tesla born ?

Table 1: A QG example, where answer is underlined.

---

interactions between the passage and the target answer. In addition, they fail when the target answer does not occur in the passage verbatim. In Table 1 the answer "1856" is the year when nikola tesla was born. This can be easily determined by leveraging the contextual information of "10 july 1856 – 7 january 1943", while it is relatively hard when only the answer position information is adopted.

We investigate explicit interaction between the target answer and the passage, so that contextual information can be better considered by the encoder. In particular, matching is used between the target answer and the passage for collecting relevant contextual information. We adopt the multi-perspective context matching (MPCM) algorithm (Wang et al., 2017b), which takes two texts as input before producing a vector of numbers, representing similarity under different perspectives.

Results on SQuAD (Rajpurkar et al., 2016) show that our model gives better BLEU scores than the state of the art. Furthermore, the questions generated by our model help to improve a strong extractive QA system. Our code is available at https://github.com/freesunshine0316/MPQG.

---

* Work done during an internship at IBM.

569

Proceedings of NAACL-HLT 2018, pages 569–574
New Orleans, Louisiana, June 1 - 6, 2018. ©2018 Association for Computational Linguistics

2   Baseline: sequence-to-sequence

Our baseline is a sequence-to-sequence model
(Bahdanau et al., 2015) with the copy mechanism
(Gulcehre et al., 2016; Gu et al., 2016). It uses an
LSTM encoder to encode a passage and an LSTM
decoder to synthesize a question.

2.1   Encoder

The encoder is a bi-directional LSTM (Hochreiter and Schmidhuber, 1997), whose input x_j at
step j is $[e_j; b_j]$, the concatenation of the current
word embedding e_j with additional bit b_j indicating whether it belongs to the answer.

2.2   Decoder with the copy mechanism

The decoder is an attentional LSTM model, with
the attention memory H being the concatenation
of all encoder states. Each encoder state h_j is the
concatenation of two bi-directional LSTM states:

$$h_j = [\overleftarrow{h_j}; \overrightarrow{h_j}] \tag{1}$$
$$H = [h_0; \ldots; h_N], \tag{2}$$

where N is the number of encoder states. At each
step t, the decoder state s_t and context vector c_t are
generated from the previous decoder state s_{t-1},
context vector c_{t-1} and output x_{t-1} in the same
way as Bahdanau et al. (2015). The output distribution over a vocabulary is calculated via:

$$P_{vocab} = \text{softmax}(V_1[s_t; c_t] + b_1),$$

where V_1 and b_1 are model parameters, and the
number of rows in V_1 is the size of the vocabulary.

Since many passage words also appear in the
question, we adopt the copy mechanism (Gulcehre
et al., 2016; Gu et al., 2016), which integrates the
attention over input words into the final vocabulary distribution. The probability distribution is
defined as the interpolation:

$$P_{final} = g_t P_{vocab} + (1 - g_t) P_{attn},$$

where g_t is the switch for controlling generating
a word from the vocabulary or directly copying it
from the passage. P_{vocab} is the vocabulary probability distribution as defined above, and P_{attn} is
calculated based on the current attention distribution by merging probabilities of duplicated words.
Finally, g_t is defined as:

$$g_t = \sigma(w_c^T c_t + w_s^T s_t + w_x^T x_{t-1} + b_2),$$

where the vectors w_c, w_s, w_x and scalar b_2 are
model parameters.

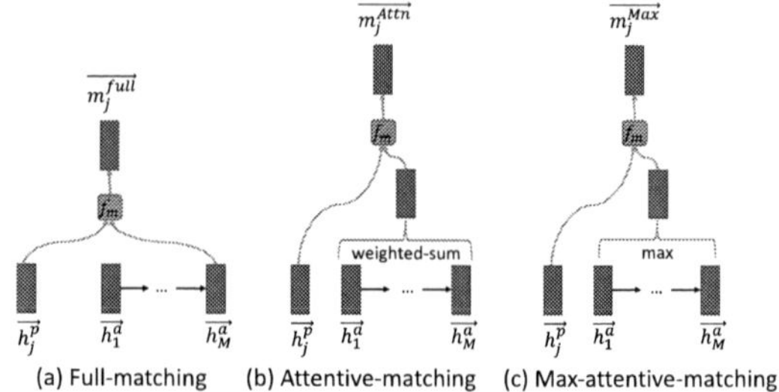

Figure 1: Matching strategies.

3   Method

Our model follows the baseline encoder-decoder
framework. The encoder reads a passage $P = (p_1, \ldots, p_N)$ and an answer $A = (a_1, \ldots, q_M)$;
the decoder generates a question $Q = (q_1, \ldots, q_L)$
word by word.

3.1   Multi-perspective encoder

Different from the baseline, we first encode both
the passage and the answer by using two separate
bi-directional LSTMs:

$$h_j^p = [\overleftarrow{h_j^p}, \overrightarrow{h_j^p}] = \text{BiLSTM}(\overleftarrow{h_{j+1}^p}, \overrightarrow{h_{j-1}^p}, p_j)$$
$$h_i^a = [\overleftarrow{h_i^a}, \overrightarrow{h_i^a}] = \text{BiLSTM}(\overleftarrow{h_{i+1}^a}, \overrightarrow{h_{i-1}^a}, a_i)$$

We use the multi-perspective context matching
algorithm (Wang et al., 2017b) on top of the BiL-
STM outputs, matching each hidden state h_j^p of the
passage against all hidden states $h_1^a \ldots h_M^a$ of the
answer. The goal is to detect whether each passage word belongs to the relevant context of the
answer. Shown in Figure 1, we adopt three strategies to match the passage with the answer, each
investigating different sources of information.

Full-matching considers the last hidden state of
the answer, which encodes all words and the word
order. *Attentive-matching* synthesizes a vector by
computing a weighted sum of all answer states
against the passage state, then compares the vector with the passage state. It also considers all
words in the answer but without word order. Finally, *max-attentive-matching* only considers the
most relevant answer state to the passage state.

Multi-perspective matching   These strategies
require a function f_m to match two vectors v_1 and
v_2. It is defined as:

$$m = f_m(v_1, v_2; \mathbf{W}),$$

where $\mathbf{W}$ is a tunable weight matrix. Each row
$W_k \in \mathbf{W}$ represents the weights associated with

one perspective, and the similarity according to that perspective is defined as:

$$m_k = \cos(W_k \odot v_1, W_k \odot v_2),$$

where $\odot$ is the element-wise multiplication operation. So $f_m(v_1, v_2; \mathbf{W})$ represents the matching results between v_1 and v_2 from all perspectives. Intuitively, each *perspective* calculates the cosine similarity between two reweighted input vectors, associated with a weight vector trained to highlight different dimensions of the input vectors. This can be regarded as considering a different part of the semantics captured in the vector.

The final matching vector m_j for the j-th word in the passage is the concatenation of the matching results of all three strategies. We employ another BiLSTM layer on top of the matching layer:

$$h_j^m = \overleftarrow{h_j^m}, \overrightarrow{h_j^m} = \mathrm{BiLSTM}(\overleftarrow{h_{j+1}^m}, \overrightarrow{h_{j-1}^m}, m_j)$$

Comparison with the baseline The encoder states (h_j) of the baseline only contains the answer position information in addition to the passage content. The matching states (h_j^m) of our model includes the matching information of all passage words, and potentially contains the answer position information. The rich matching information can guide the decoder to generate more accurate questions.

3.2 Decoder with the copy mechanism

The decoder is identical to the one described in Section 2.2, except that matching information ($\overleftarrow{h_j^m}, \overrightarrow{h_j^m}$) is added to the attention memory:

$$h_j = [\overleftarrow{h_j^p}; \overrightarrow{h_j^p}; \overleftarrow{h_j^m}; \overrightarrow{h_j^m}] \tag{3}$$

$$H = [h_0; \ldots; h_N] \tag{4}$$

The attention memory contains not only the passage content, but also the matching information, which helps generate more accurate questions.

4 Experiments

Following existing work (Du et al., 2017; Zhou et al., 2017), experiments are conducted on the publically accessible part of SQuAD (Rajpurkar et al., 2016). The dataset contains 536 articles and over 100k questions, and around 10% is held by the organizer for fair evaluation.

Models	BLEU
M2S+cp	12.63
w/o full-matching	11.57
w/o attentive-matching	11.78
w/o max-attentive-matching	12.11

Table 2: Ablation results for matching strategies.

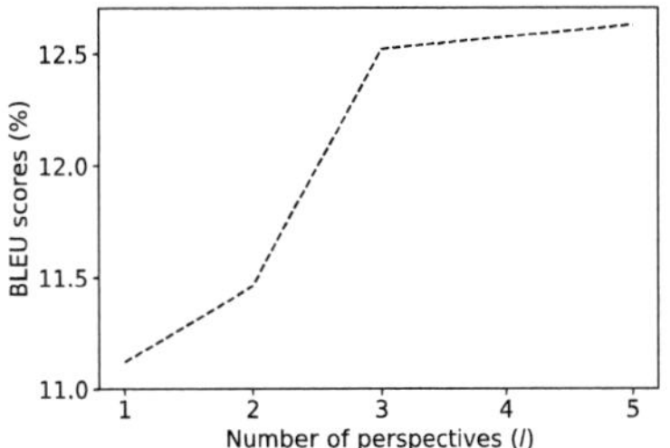

Figure 2: Effectiveness on the number of perspectives.

4.1 Settings

We evaluate our model for question quality against gold questions, as well as their effectiveness in improving an extractive QA system. Since Du et al. (2017) and Zhou et al. (2017) conducted their experiments using different training/dev/test split, we conduct experiments on both splits, and compare with their reported performance. For improving an extractive QA system, we use the data split of Du et al. (2017), and conduct experiments on low-resource settings, where only (10%, 20%, or 50%) of the human-labeled questions in the training data are available. We choose Wang et al. (2016) as the extractive QA system.

Both the baseline and our model are trained with cross-entropy loss. Greedy search is adopted for generating questions.

4.2 Development experiments

Matching strategies In Table 2, we analyze the importance of each matching strategy by performing an ablation experiment on the devset according to the data split of Du et al. (2017). We can see that there is a performance decrease when removing each of the three matching strategies, which means that all three strategies are complementary. In addition, *w/o max-attentive-matching* shows the least performance decrease. One likely reason is that *max-attentive-matching* considers only the most similar hidden state of the answer, while the other two consider all hidden states. Finally, *w/o full-matching* shows more performance decrease than *w/o attentive-matching*. A reason

Models	Split 1			Split 2
	BLEU	METEOR	ROUGE-L	BLEU
S2S-ans	12.28	16.62	39.75	–
S2S+cp+f	–	–	–	13.29
S2S+cp	12.22	17.38	39.03	12.59
M2S+cp	**13.98**	**18.77**	**42.72**	**13.91**

Table 3: Test results.

may be that *full-matching* captures word order information, while *attentive-matching* does not.

Number of perspectives Figure 2 shows the performance changes with different numbers of perspectives. There is a large performance improvement when increasing the number from 1 to 3, which becomes small when further increasing the number from 3 to 5. This shows that our multi-perspective matching algorithm is effective, as we do not need a large number of perspectives for reaching our reported performance.

4.3 Results

In Table 3, we compare our model with the previous state of the art: *S2S-ans* (Du et al., 2017) and *S2S+cp+f* (Zhou et al., 2017). Both methods use the sequence-to-sequence model. *S2S-ans* encodes only the passage, yet does not use answer position information. *S2S+cp+f* uses both answer position and rich features (NE and POS tags) by concatenating their embeddings with the word embedding on the encoder side (Peng et al., 2016), adopting the copy mechanism for their decoder. *S2S+cp* is our sequence-to-sequence baseline with the copy mechanism, and *M2S+cp* is our model, which further uses multi-perspective encoder.

M2S+cp outperforms *S2S+cp* on both data splits, showing that modeling contextual information is helpful for generating better questions. In addition, only taking word embedding features, *M2S+cp* shows better performance than *S2S+cp+f*. Both multi-perspective matching and rich features play a similar role of leveraging more information than the answer position information. However, *M2S+cp* can be applied to low-resource languages and domains, where there is not sufficient labeled data for training the taggers for generating rich features. *M2S+cp* is also free from feature engineering, which is necessary for *S2S+cp+f* on new domains.

Finally, unlike *S2S-ans*, *S2S+cp+f* and *S2S+cp*, *M2S+cp* can be useful when the answer is not explicitly contained in the passage, as it matches the target answer against the passage rather than using

Passage: nikola tesla (serbian cyrillic : Никола Тесла ; 10 july <u>1856</u> – 7 january 1943) was a serbian american inventor , electrical engineer , mechanical engineer , physicist , and futurist best known for his contributions to the design of the modern alternating current (ac) electricity supply system . **Reference:** when was nikola tesla born ? **S2S+cp:** when was nikola tesla 's inventor ? **M2S+cp:** when was nikola tesla born ?
Passage: zhèng (chinese : 正) meaning " right " , " just " , or " true " , would have received the mongolian adjectival modifiers , creating " jenggis " , which in medieval romanization would be written " genghis " . **Reference:** what does zhèng mean ? **S2S+cp:** what are the names of the " jenggis " ? **M2S+cp:** what does zhèng mean ?
Passage: the university of chicago (uchicago , chicago , or u of c) is a private research university in chicago . **Answer:** <u>in illinois</u> **M2S+cp:** where is the university of chicago located ?

Table 4: QG example, where answers are underlined.

the answer position information.

4.4 Example Output

Table 4 shows example outputs of *M2S+cp* and *S2S+cp*. For the first case, *M2S+cp* recognizes that "1856" is the year when "nikola tesla" is born, while *S2S+cp* fails to. The matching algorithm of *M2S+cp* gives high matching numbers for the phrase "10 july 1856 – 7 january 1943" with "1856" having the highest matching number, while *S2S+cp* only highlights "1856". Simply highlighting "1856" can be ambiguous, while recognizing a pattern "day month year – day month year" with the first year being the answer is more definite. It is similar in the second case, where *M2S+cp* recognize "zhèng meaning right", which fits into the pattern "*A* meaning *B*" with *B* being the answer.

The third example is a case where the answer is not explicitly contained in the passage.[1] *M2S+cp* generates a precise question, even though the answer "in illinois" does not appear in the passage. On the other hand, *S2S+cp* fails in this case, as the answer position information can not be obtained from the input.

4.5 Question generation for extractive QA

Table 5 shows data augmentation results for extractive QA, where the gold questions of only a part of the training data are available. *Only-gold* uses only the available gold questions to train the

---

[1]This is modified from SQuAD, as all the original answers in the SQuAD dataset are explicitly contained in the passage.

Methods	Exact Match (EM)			F1 score		
	10%	20%	50%	10%	20%	50%
only-gold	47.87	57.98	63.60	59.64	68.05	73.02
S2S+cp	57.80	60.26	64.79	67.01	69.71	73.74
M2S+cp	**59.11**	**61.40**	**65.95**	**67.73**	**70.60**	**75.08**

Table 5: Results on improving extractive QA with automatically generated questions.

extractive QA model, while *S2S+cp* and *M2S+cp* use all training data, adopting the model-generated questions if the gold question is not available. For evaluation metrics, *F1 score* treats the prediction and ground-truth answer as bags of tokens, and compute their F1 score; *Exact Match* measures the percentage of predictions that match the ground truth answer exactly (Rajpurkar et al., 2016).

M2S+cp is consistently better than *S2S+cp* both under F1 score and Exact Match, showing that contextual information helps to generate more accurate questions. Besides, using 10% gold data, the automatically generated questions from *M2S+cp* help to reach a better performance than that using only 20% gold data, and it is 11 points better than that using only 10% gold data.

5 Conclusion

We demonstrated that natural question generation can benefit from contextual information. Leveraging a multi-perspective matching algorithm, our model outperforms the existing state of the art, and our automatically generated questions help to improve a strong extractive QA system.

Acknowledgments

We would like to thank the anonymous reviewers for their feedback.

References

Dzmitry Bahdanau, Kyunghyun Cho, and Yoshua Bengio. 2015. Neural machine translation by jointly learning to align and translate. In *ICLR 2015*.

Xinya Du, Junru Shao, and Claire Cardie. 2017. Learning to ask: Neural question generation for reading comprehension. In *Proceedings of the 55th Annual Meeting of the Association for Computational Linguistics (ACL 2017)*. pages 1342–1352.

Jiatao Gu, Zhengdong Lu, Hang Li, and Victor O.K. Li. 2016. Incorporating copying mechanism in sequence-to-sequence learning. In *Proceedings of the 54th Annual Meeting of the Association for Computational Linguistics (ACL 2016)*.

Caglar Gulcehre, Sungjin Ahn, Ramesh Nallapati, Bowen Zhou, and Yoshua Bengio. 2016. Pointing the unknown words. In *Proceedings of the 54th Annual Meeting of the Association for Computational Linguistics (ACL 2016)*. Berlin, Germany.

Michael Heilman and Noah A. Smith. 2010. Good Question! Statistical ranking for question generation. In *The 2010 Annual Conference of the North American Chapter of the Association for Computational Linguistics (NAACL-2010)*. pages 609–617.

Sepp Hochreiter and Jürgen Schmidhuber. 1997. Long short-term memory. *Neural computation* 9(8):1735–1780.

Xi Peng, Rogerio S Feris, Xiaoyu Wang, and Dimitris N Metaxas. 2016. A recurrent encoder-decoder network for sequential face alignment. In *European Conference on Computer Vision*. pages 38–56.

Pranav Rajpurkar, Jian Zhang, Konstantin Lopyrev, and Percy Liang. 2016. SQuAD: 100,000+ questions for machine comprehension of text. In *Proceedings of EMNLP 2016*. Austin, Texas, pages 2383–2392.

Sandeep Subramanian, Tong Wang, Xingdi Yuan, and Adam Trischler. 2017. Neural models for key phrase detection and question generation. *arXiv preprint arXiv:1706.04560* .

Ilya Sutskever, Oriol Vinyals, and Quoc V Le. 2014. Sequence to sequence learning with neural networks. In *NIPS 2014*. pages 3104–3112.

Duyu Tang, Nan Duan, Tao Qin, and Ming Zhou. 2017. Question answering and question generation as dual tasks. *arXiv preprint arXiv:1706.02027* .

Tong Wang, Xingdi Yuan, and Adam Trischler. 2017a. A joint model for question answering and question generation. *arXiv preprint arXiv:1706.01450* .

Zhiguo Wang, Wael Hamza, and Radu Florian. 2017b. Bilateral multi-perspective matching for natural language sentences. In *IJCAI 2017*.

Zhiguo Wang, Haitao Mi, Wael Hamza, and Radu Florian. 2016. Multi-perspective context matching for machine comprehension. *arXiv preprint arXiv:1612.04211* .

Zhilin Yang, Junjie Hu, Ruslan Salakhutdinov, and William Cohen. 2017. Semi-supervised QA with generative domain-adaptive nets. In *Proceedings of the 55th Annual Meeting of the Association for*

Computational Linguistics (ACL-2017). Vancouver, Canada, pages 1040–1050.

Xingdi Yuan, Tong Wang, Caglar Gulcehre, Alessandro Sordoni, Philip Bachman, Saizheng Zhang, Sandeep Subramanian, and Adam Trischler. 2017. Machine comprehension by text-to-text neural question generation. In *Proceedings of the 2nd Workshop on Representation Learning for NLP*. Vancouver, Canada, pages 15–25.

Qingyu Zhou, Nan Yang, Furu Wei, Chuanqi Tan, Hangbo Bao, and Ming Zhou. 2017. Neural question generation from text: A preliminary study. *arXiv preprint arXiv:1704.01792* .

Robust Machine Comprehension Models via Adversarial Training

Yicheng Wang and **Mohit Bansal**
University of North Carolina at Chapel Hill
{yicheng, mbansal}@cs.unc.edu

Abstract

It is shown that many published models for the Stanford Question Answering Dataset (Rajpurkar et al., 2016) lack robustness, suffering an over 50% decrease in F1 score during adversarial evaluation based on the AddSent (Jia and Liang, 2017) algorithm. It has also been shown that retraining models on data generated by AddSent has limited effect on their robustness. We propose a novel alternative adversary-generation algorithm, AddSentDiverse, that significantly increases the variance within the adversarial training data by providing effective examples that punish the model for making certain superficial assumptions. Further, in order to improve robustness to AddSent's semantic perturbations (e.g., antonyms), we jointly improve the model's semantic-relationship learning capabilities in addition to our AddSentDiverse-based adversarial training data augmentation. With these additions, we show that we can make a state-of-the-art model significantly more robust, achieving a 36.5% increase in F1 score under many different types of adversarial evaluation while maintaining performance on the regular SQuAD task.

1 Introduction

We explore the task of reading comprehension based question answering (Q&A), where we focus on the Stanford Question Answering Dataset (SQuAD) (Rajpurkar et al., 2016), in which models answer questions about paragraphs taken from Wikipedia. Significant progress has been made with deep end to end neural-attention models, with some achieving above human level performance on the test set (Wang and Jiang, 2017; Seo et al., 2017; Wang et al., 2017; Huang et al., 2018; Peters et al., 2018). However, as shown recently by Jia and Liang (2017), these models are very fragile when presented with adversarially gener-

ated data. They proposed AddSent, which creates a semantically-irrelevant sentence containing a fake answer that resembles the question syntactically, and appends it to the context. Many state-of-the-art models exhibit a nearly 50% reduction in F1 score on AddSent, showing their over-reliance on syntactic similarity and limited semantic understanding.

Importantly, this is in part due to the nature of the SQuAD dataset. Most questions in the dataset have answer spans embedded in sentences that are syntactically similar to the question. Thus during training, the model is rarely punished for answering questions based on syntactic similarity, and learns it as a reliable approach to Q&A. This correlation between syntactic similarity and correctness is of course not true in general: the adversaries generated by AddSent (Jia and Liang, 2017) are syntactically similar to the question but do not answer them. The models' failures on AddSent demonstrates their ignorance of this aspect of the task. Jia and Liang (2017) presented some initial attempts to fix this problem by retraining the BiDAF model (Seo et al., 2017) with adversaries generated with AddSent. But they showed that the method is not very effective, as slight modifications (e.g., different positioning of the distractor sentence in the paragraph and different fake answer set) to the adversary generation algorithm at test time have drastic impact on the retrained model's performance.

In this paper, we show that their method of adversarial training failed because the specificity of the AddSent algorithm along with the lack of naturally-occurring counterexamples allow models to learn superficial clues regarding what is a 'distractor' and subsequently ignore it; thus significantly limiting their robustness. Instead, we first introduce a novel algorithm, AddSentDiverse, for generating adversarial examples with signifi-

575

Proceedings of NAACL-HLT 2018, pages 575–581
New Orleans, Louisiana, June 1 - 6, 2018. ©2018 Association for Computational Linguistics

cantly higher variance (by varying the locations where the distractors are placed and expanding the set of fake answers), so that the model is punished during training time for making these superficial assumptions about the distractor. We show that an AddSentDiverse-based adversarially-trained model beats an AddSent-trained model across 3 different adversarial test sets, showing an average improvement of 24.22% in F1 score, demonstrating a general increase in robustness.

However, even with our diversified adversarial training data, the model is still not fully resilient to AddSent-style attacks, e.g., its antonymy-style semantic perturbations. Hence, we next add semantic relationship features to the model to let it directly identify such relationships between the context and question. Interestingly, we see that these additions only increase model robustness when trained adversarially, because intuitively in the non-adversarially-trained setup, there are not enough negative (adversarial) examples for the model to learn how to use its semantic features.

Overall, we demonstrate that with our adversarial training method and model improvement, we can increase the performance of a state-of-the-art model by 36.46% on the AddSent evaluation set. Although we focused on the AddSent adversary (Jia and Liang, 2017), our method of effective adversarial training by eliminating superficial statistical correlations (with joint model capability improvements) are generalizable to other similar insertion-based adversaries for Q&A tasks.[1]

2 Related Work

Adversarial Evaluation In computer vision, adversarial examples are frequently used to punish model oversensitivity, where semantic-preserving perturbations (usually in the form of small noise vectors) are added to an image to fool the classifier into giving it a different label (Szegedy et al., 2014; Goodfellow et al., 2015).

In the field of Q&A, Jia and Liang (2017) introduced the AddSent algorithm, which generates adversaries that punish model failure in the other direction: overstability, or the inability to detect semantic-altering noise. It does so by generating distractor sentences that only resemble the questions syntactically and appending them to the context paragraphs (detailed description included in

Sec. 3). When tested on these adversarial examples, Jia and Liang (2017) showed that even the most 'robust' amongst published models (the Mnemonic Reader (Hu et al., 2017)) only achieved 46.6% F1 (compared to 79.6% F1 on the regular task). Since then, the FusionNet model (Huang et al., 2018) used history-of-word representations and multi-level attention mechanism to obtain an improved 51.4% F1 score under adversarial evaluation, but that is still a 30% decrease from the model's performance on the regular task. We show, however, that one can make a pre-existing model significantly more robust by simply retraining it with better, higher variance adversarial training data, and improve it further with minor semantic feature additions to its inputs.

Adversarial Training It has been shown in the field of image classification that training with adversarial examples produces more robust and error-resistant models (Goodfellow et al., 2015; Kurakin et al., 2017). In the field of Q&A, Jia and Liang (2017) attempted to retrain the BiDAF (Seo et al., 2017) model with data generated with AddSent algorithm. Despite performing well when evaluated on AddSent, the retrained model suffers a more than 30% decrease in F1 performance when tested on a slightly different adversarial dataset generated by AddSentMod (which differs from AddSent in two superficial ways: using a different set of fake answers and prepending instead of appending the distractor sentence to the context). We show that using AddSent to generate adversarial training data introduces new superficial trends for a model to exploit; and instead we propose the AddSentDiverse algorithm that generates highly varied data for adversarial training, resulting in more robust models.

3 Methods

Our 'AddSentDiverse' algorithm is a modified version of AddSent (Jia and Liang, 2017), aimed at producing good adversarial examples for robust training purposes. For each {context, question, answer} triple, AddSent does the following: (1) Several antonym and named-entity based semantic altering perturbations (swapping) are applied to the question; (2) A fake answer is generated that matches the 'type' of the original answer (e.g., Prague $\rightarrow$ Chicago, etc.); (3) The fake answer and the altered question are combined into a distractor statement based on a set of manually

---

[1] We release our AddSentDiverse-based adversarial training dataset for SQuAD at `https://goo.gl/qdSNDr`.

defined rules; (4) Errors in grammar are fixed by crowd-workers; (5) The finalized distractor is appended to the end of the context. The specificity of the algorithm creates new superficial cues that a model can learn and use during training and never get punished for: (1) a model can learn that it is unlikely for the last sentence to contain the real answer; (2) a model can learn that the fixed set of fake answers should not be picked. These nullify the effectiveness of the distractors as the model will learn to simply ignore them. We thus introduce the AddSentDiverse algorithm, which adds two modifications to AddSent that allows for generating higher-variance adversarial examples. Namely, we randomize the distractor placement (Sec. 3.1) and we diversity the set of fake answers used (Sec. 3.2). Lastly, to address the antonym-style semantic perturbations used in AddSent, we show that we need to improve model capabilities by adding indicator features for semantic relationships (but only when) in tandem with the addition of diverse adversarial data (Sec. 3.3).

3.1 Random Distractor Placement

Given a paragraph P containing n sentences, let X, Y be random variables representing the location of the sentence containing the correct answer counting from the front and back.[2] Let P' represent the paragraph with the inserted distractor, and X' and Y' represent the updated location of the sentence with the correct answer. As shown in Fig. 1, their distribution is highly dependent on the strategy used to insert the distractor. During training done by Jia and Liang (2017), the distractor is always added as the last sentence, creating a very skewed distribution for Y'. This resulted in the model learning to ignore the last sentence, as it was never punished for doing so. This, in turn, caused the retrained model to fail on AddSent-Mod, where the distractor is inserted to the front instead of the back of the context paragraph (this is shown by our experiments as well). However, Fig. 1 shows that when the distractor is inserted randomly, the distributions of X' and Y' are almost identical to that of X and Y, indicating that no new correlation between the location of a sentence and its likelihood to contain the correct answer is introduced by the distractors, hence forcing the model to learn to discern them from the

---

[2] Note that for any fixed n, $Y = n - X$, but for our purposes it is easier to keep them separate since the length of the paragraph is also a random variable.

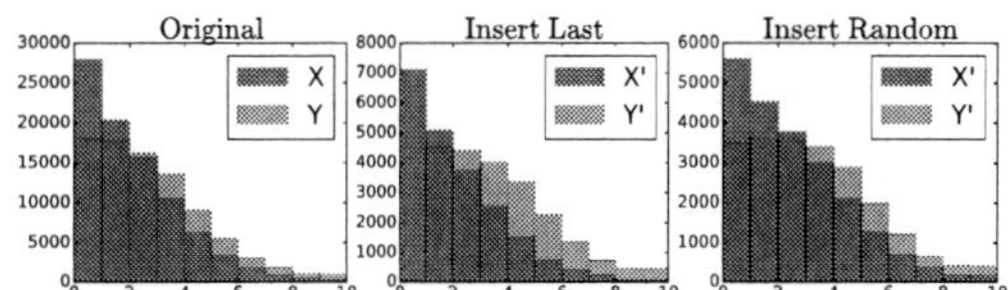

Figure 1: Left: Distribution of X and Y for the original SQuAD training set. Middle: Distribution of X' and Y' when the distractor is inserted at the end of the context. Right: Distribution of X' and Y' when the distractor is inserted randomly into the context.

real answers by other, deeper means.

3.2 Dynamic Fake Answer Generation

To prevent the model from superficially deciding what is a distractor based on certain specific words, we dynamically generate the fake answers instead of using AddSent's pre-defined set. Let S be the set that contains all the answers in the SQuAD training data, tagged by their type (e.g., person, location, etc.). For each answer a, we generate the fake answer dynamically by randomly selecting another answer $a' \neq a$ from S that has the same type as a, as opposed to AddSent (Jia and Liang, 2017), which uses a pre-defined fake answer for each type (e.g., "Chicago" for any location). This creates a much larger set of fake answers, thus decreasing the correlation between any text and its likelihood of being a part of a distractor, forcing the model to become more robust.

3.3 Semantic Feature Enhanced Model

In previous sections, we prevented the model from identifying distractors based on superficial clues such as location and fake answer identity by eliminating these correlations within the training data. But even if we force the model to learn some deeper methods for identifying/discarding the distractors, it only has limited ability in recognizing semantic differences because its current inputs do not capture crucial aspects of lexical semantics such as antonymy (which were inserted by Jia and Liang (2017) when generating the AddSent adversaries; see Sec. 3). Most current models use pre-trained word embeddings (e.g., GloVE (Pennington et al., 2014) and ELMo (Peters et al., 2018)) as input, which are usually calculated based on the distributional hypothesis (Harris, 1954), and do not capture lexical semantic relations such as antonymy (Geffet and Dagan, 2005). These shortcomings are reflected by our results in Sec. 4.6, where we see that we can't resolve all AddSent-

Training	Original-SQuAD-Dev	AddSent	AddSentPrepend	AddSentRandom	AddSentMod	Average
Original-SQuAD	**84.65**	42.45	41.46	40.48	41.96	50.20
AddSent	83.76	**79.55**	51.96	59.03	46.85	64.23
AddSentDiverse	83.49	76.95	**77.45**	**76.02**	**77.06**	**78.19**

Table 1: F1 performance of the BSAE model trained and tested on different regular/adversarial datasets.

Training	AddSent	AddSentPrepend	Average
InsFirst	60.22	**79.81**	70.02
InsLast	**79.54**	51.96	65.75
InsMid	74.74	74.33	74.54
InsRandom	76.33	77.38	**76.85**

Table 2: F1 performance of the BSAE model trained on datasets with different distractor placement strategies.

style adversaries by diversifying the training data alone. For the model to be robust to semantics-based (e.g., antonym-style) attacks, it needs extra knowledge of lexical semantic relations. Hence, we augment the input of each word in the question/context with two indicator features indicating the existence of its synonym and antonym (using WordNet (Fellbaum, 1998)) in the context/question, allowing the model to use lexical semantics directly instead of learned statistical correlations of the word embeddings.

4 Experiments And Results

4.1 Model and Training Details

We use the architecture and hyperparameters of the strong BiDAF + Self-Attn + ELMo (BSAE) model (Peters et al., 2018), currently (as of January 10, 2018) the third highest performing single-model on the SQuAD leaderboard.[3]

4.2 Evaluation Details

Models are evaluated on the original SQuAD dev set and 4 adversarial datasets: AddSent, the adversarial evaluation set by Jia and Liang (2017), and 3 variations of AddSent: AddSentPrepend, where the distractor is prepended to the context, AddSentRandom, where the distractor is randomly inserted into the context,[4] and AddSentMod (Jia and Liang, 2017), where a different set of fake answers is used and the distractor is prepended to the context. Experiments measure the soft F1 score and all of the adversarial evaluations are model-dependent, following the style of AddSent, where multiple adversaries are generated for each exam-

ple in the evaluation set and the model's worst performance among the variants is recorded.

4.3 Primary Experiment Results

In our main experiment, we compare the BSAE model's performance on different test sets when trained with three different training sets: the original SQuAD data (Original-SQuAD), SQuAD data augmented with AddSent generated adversaries (similar to adversarial training conducted by Jia and Liang (2017)), and SQuAD data augmented with our AddSentDiverse generated adversaries. For the latter two, we run the respective adversarial generation algorithms on the training set, and add randomly selected adversarial examples such that they make up 20% of the total training data. The results are shown in Table 1. First, as shown, the AddSent-trained model is not able to perform well on test sets where the distractors are not inserted at the end, e.g., the AddSentRandom adversarial test set.[5] On the other hand, it can be seen that retraining with AddSentDiverse boosts performance of the model significantly across all adversarial datasets, indicating a general increase in robustness.

4.4 Distractor Placement Results

We also conducted experiments studying the effect of different distractor placement strategies on the trained models' robustness. The BSAE model was trained on 4 variations of AddSentDiverse-augmented training set, with the only difference between them being the location of the distractor within the context: InsFirst, where the distractor is prepended, InsLast, where the distractor is appended, InsMid, where the distractor is inserted in the middle and InsRandom, where the distractor is randomly placed. The retrained models are tested on AddSent and AddSentPrepend, whose only difference is where the distractor is located. The result is shown in Table 2. It is clear that when trained under InsFirst and InsLast, the model only

---

[3] https://rajpurkar.github.io/SQuAD-explorer/

[4] Note that since the distractor was randomly inserted, the model cannot identify/ignore the distractor reliably based on location. Thus, high performance on AddSentRandom serves as a better indicator for robustness to semantic-based attacks.

[5] For this 59.03% accuracy, i.e., in the remaining 40.96% errors, we found that in 77.0% of these errors, the model still predicted a span within the randomly inserted distractor; indicating that it has not learned to fully recognize semantic-altering perturbations.

Training	AddSentPrepend	AddSentMod
Fixed-FakeAns	77.37	73.65
Dynamic-FakeAns	**77.45**	**77.06**

Table 3: F1 performance of the BSAE model trained on datasets with different answer generation strategies.

Model/Training	Original-SQuAD-Dev	AddSent
BSAE/Reg.	**84.65**	42.45
BSAE/Adv.	83.49	76.95
BSAE+SA/Reg.	84.62	44.60
BSAE+SA/Adv.	84.49	**78.91**

Table 4: Regular and adversarial training with BSAE and BSAE+SA (with synonym/antonym features).

performs well on test sets created by a similar distractor placement strategy, indicating that they are exploiting superficial trends instead of learning to process the semantics. It is also shown that InsRandom gives optimal performance on both evaluation datasets. Further investigations regarding distractor placement can be found in the appendix.

4.5 Fake Answer Generation Results

We also conducted experiments studying the effect of training on data containing distractors with dynamically generated fake answers (Dynamic-FakeAns) instead of chosen from a predefined set (Fixed-FakeAns). The trained models are tested on AddSentPrepend and AddSentMod, whose only difference is that AddSentMod uses a different set of fake answers. The results are displayed in Table 3. It shows that the model trained on Fixed-FakeAns suffers an approximate 3% drop in performance when tested on a dataset with a different set of fake answers, but this gap does not exist for the model retrained on Dynamic-FakeAns.

4.6 Semantic Feature Enhancement Results

In Table 1, we see that despite improving performance on adversarial test sets, adversarial training on the BSAE model leads to a 1% decrease in its performance on the original SQuAD task (from 84.65% to 83.49%). Furthermore, there is still a 6.5% gap between its performance on adversarial datasets and the original SQuAD dev set (76.95% vs 83.49%). These point to the limitations of adversarial training without any model enhancements, especially for AddSent's antonymy style semantic perturbations (see details in Sec. 3.3). We thus conducted experiments to test the effectiveness of adding WordNet based synonymy/antonymy semantic-relation indicators in helping the model to better deal with semantics-based adversaries. We added the lexical semantic indicators to the BSAE model to create the BSAE+SA model. We trained and tested it in both the regular and adversarial setup. Its results, compared to the original BSAE model are shown in Table 4, where we see that unlike the BSAE model, adversarial training of the BSAE+SA model does not cause a decrease in its performance on the original SQuAD dataset, as the model can now learn lexical semantic relationships instead of statistical correlations. We also see that the BSAE+SA model, when trained in the normal setup, shows very similar performance as the BSAE model across all metrics. This is most likely because despite having the ability to recognize semantic relations, there are not enough negative examples in the regular SQuAD training set to teach the model how to use these features correctly, but this issue is solved via the addition of adversarial examples in adversarial training.

4.7 Error Analysis

Finally, we examined the errors of our final adversarially-trained BSAE+SA model on the AddSent dataset and found that out of the 21.09% remaining errors (Table 4), 33.3% (46 cases) of these erroneous predictions occurred within the inserted distractor, and 63.7% (88 cases) occurred on questions that the model got wrong in the original SQuAD dev set (without the inserted distractors). The former errors are mainly occurring within distractors created with named-entity replacements (which we haven't addressed directly in the current paper) or malformed distractors (that in fact do answer the question).

5 Conclusion

We demonstrate that we can overcome model overstability and increase their robustness by training on diverse adversarial data that eliminates latent data correlations. We further show that adversarial training is more effective when we jointly add useful semantic-relations knowledge to improve model capabilities. We hope that these robustness methods are generalizable to other insertion-based adversaries for Q&A tasks.

Acknowledgments

We thank the anonymous reviewers for their helpful comments. This work was supported by a Google Faculty Research Award, a Bloomberg Data Science Research Grant, an IBM Faculty Award, and NVidia GPU awards.

References

C. Fellbaum. 1998. Wordnet: An electronic lexical database. In *MIT Press*.

Maayan Geffet and Ido Dagan. 2005. The distributional inclusion hypotheses and lexical entailment. In *ACL*.

I. Goodfellow, J. Shlens, and C. Szegedy. 2015. Explaining and harnessing adversarial examples. In *International Conference on Learning Representations (ICLR)*.

Zellig S Harris. 1954. Distributional structure. *Word* 10(2-3):146–162.

Minghao Hu, Yuxing Peng, and Xipeng Qiu. 2017. Reinforced mnemonic reader for machine comprehension. *CoRR, abs/1705.02798* .

Hsin-Yuan Huang, Chenguang Zhu, Yelong Shen, and Weizhu Chen. 2018. Fusionnet: Fusing via fully-aware attention with application to machine comprehension. In *International Conference on Learning Representations (ICLR)*.

R. Jia and P. Liang. 2017. Adversarial examples for evaluating reading comprehension systems. In *Empirical Methods in Natural Language Processing (EMNLP)*.

A. Kurakin, I. Goodfellow, and S. Bengio. 2017. Adversarial machine learning at scale. In *International Conference on Learning Representations (ICLR)*.

Jeffrey Pennington, Richard Socher, and Christopher D. Manning. 2014. Glove: Global vectors for word representation. In *Empirical Methods in Natural Language Processing (EMNLP)*. pages 1532–1543.

Matthew E Peters, Mark Neumann, Mohit Iyyer, Matt Gardner, Christopher Clark, Kenton Lee, and Luke Zettlemoyer. 2018. Deep contextualized word representations. *NAACL* .

P. Rajpurkar, J. Zhang, K. Lopyrev, and P. Liang. 2016. Squad: 100,000+ questions for machine comprehension of text. In *Empirical Methods in Natural Language Processing (EMNLP) 2016*.

Minjoon Seo, Aniruddha Kembhavi, Ali Farhadi, and Hannaneh Hajishirzi. 2017. Bi-directional attention flow for machine comprehension. In *International Conference on Learning Representations (ICLR)*.

C. Szegedy, W. Zaremba, I. Sutskever, J. Bruna, D. Erhan, I. Goodfellow, and R. Fergus. 2014. Intriguing properties of neural networks. In *International Conference on Learning Representations (ICLR)*.

S. Wang and J. Jiang. 2017. Machine comprehension using match-lstm and answer pointer. In *International Conference on Learning Representations (ICLR)*.

Wenhui Wang, Nan Yang, Furu Wei, Baobao Chang, and Ming Zhou. 2017. Gated self-matching networks for reading comprehension and question answering. In *ACL*.

A   Appendix: Distractor Placement Strategies

This section provides a theoretical framework to predict a model's performance on adversarial test sets when trained on adversarial data generated by a specific distractor-insertion strategy.

Given a paragraph composed of n sentences (with the distractor inserted) $P = \{s_1, s_2, \ldots, s_n\}$, where s_i is the ith sentence counting from the front. Define random variables X and Y to represent the location of the distractor counting from the front and back, respectively. The distributions of X and Y are dependent upon the insertion strategy used to add the distractors, several examples of this are displayed in Fig. 2.

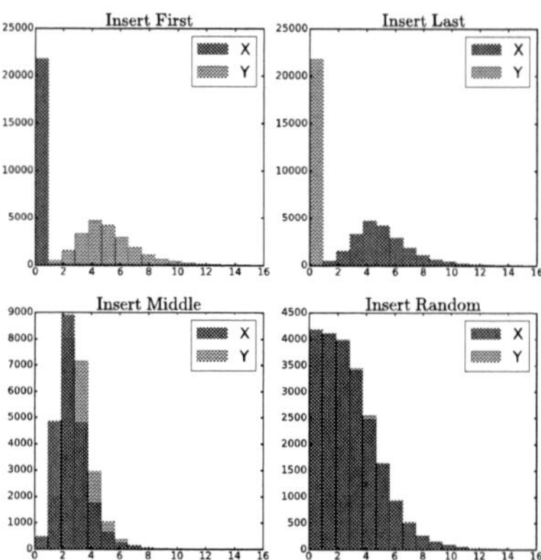

Figure 2: Distributions of X and Y in adversarially augmented SQuAD training data under different distractor-insertion strategies.

A bidirectional deep learning model, trained in a supervised setting, should be able to jointly learn X and Y. Thus, at test time, when given a paragraph of n sentences, the model can obtain the probability that the sentence s_a is the distractor, P_{s_a}, by computing $P(X = a) + P(Y = n - a)$. Ideally, we want the distribution of P_{s_a} to be uniform, as that means the model is not biased towards discarding any sentence as the distractor based on location. The actual distributions of P_{s_a} under different distractor-insertion strategies are displayed in Fig. 3 for $n = 3, 5$ and 7. We pick these n as they are typical lengths of contexts within the SQuAD dataset (the complete distribution of paragraph lengths in the SQuAD training set is shown in Fig. 4). We see that under random

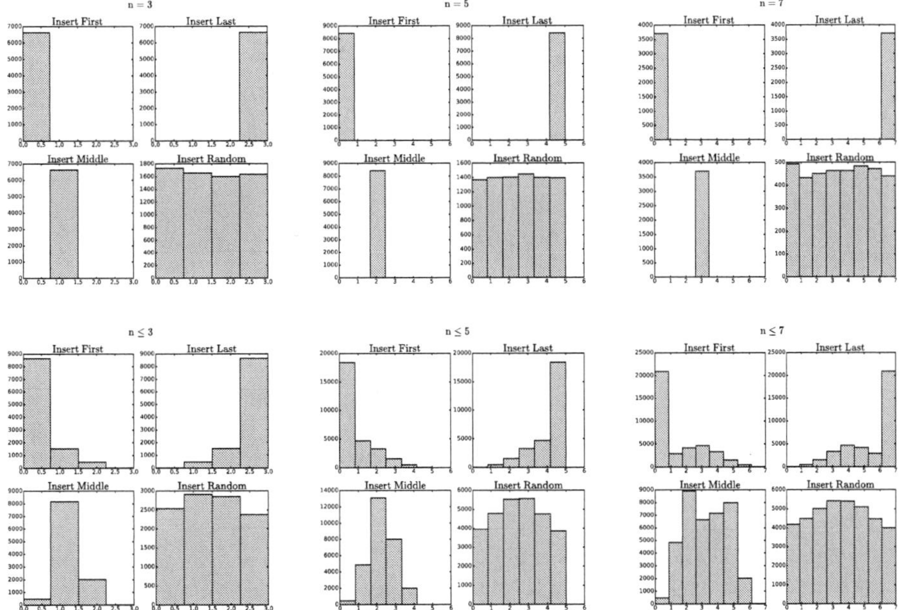

Figure 3: Learned distribution of P_{s_a} for different n.

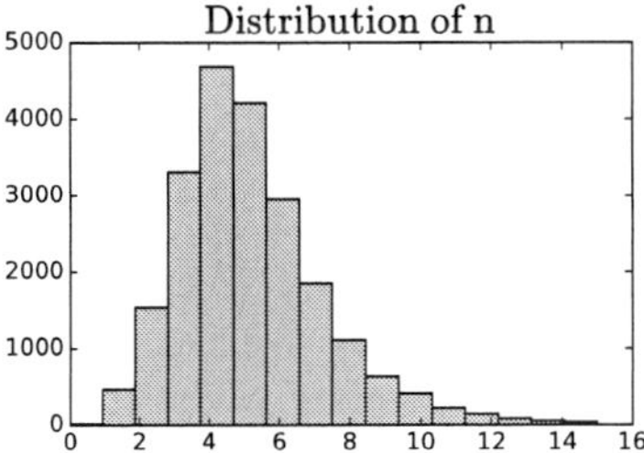

Figure 4: Distribution of length of paragraphs in the SQuAD training set.

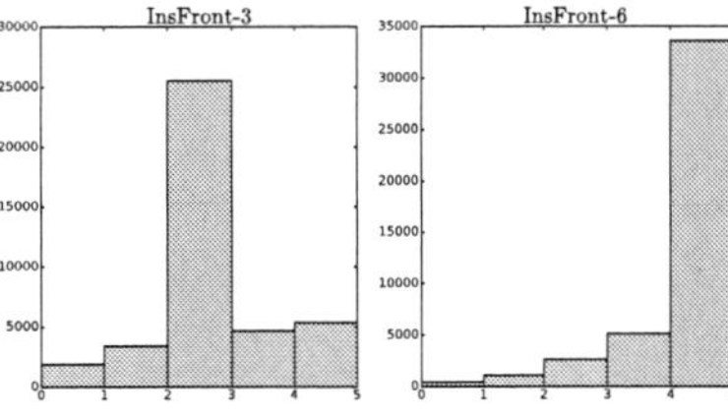

Figure 5: Distributions of P_{s_a} under InsFront-3 and InsFront-6 for $n \leq 5$.

Training	AddSent	AddSentPrepend	Average
InsFront-3	75.47	72.79	74.13
InsFront-6	77.73	64.42	71.10

Table 5: F1 Performance of the BSAE model trained on datasets with different distractor placement strategies.

insertion, the distribution is very close to uniform. Note that if we were to aggregate n and plot P_{s_a} for $n \leq 3$, 5 and 7, as shown in Fig. 3, the distributions of P_{s_a} created by inserting in the middle and inserting randomly are very similar, but the distribution of inserting in the middle is skewed against the beginnings and ends of the paragraphs. This explains why in our experiment studying the effect of distractor placement strategies (see Table 2), InsMid's performance was not skewed towards either AddSent or AddSentPrepend, but was worse on both when compared to InsRandom.

This method of calculating the distribution of P_{s_a} allows us to predict the model's performance when trained on datasets where the distractors are inserted at specific locations. To test this hypothesis, we created two datasets: InsFront-3 and InsFront-6 where the distractors were inserted as the 3rd and 6th sentence from the beginning and

measure the model's performance when trained on these two datasets. The distributions of P_{s_a} for these two datasets are shown in Fig. 5, from which we can predict that models trained on InsFront-3 should perform slightly better on adversarial sets where the distractors are appended (as opposed to prepended), whereas those trained on InsFront-6 will perform much better on such adversarial sets. These predictions are confirmed by the results in Table 5.

Simple and Effective Semi-Supervised Question Answering

Bhuwan Dhingra[*]   **Danish Pruthi**[*]   **Dheeraj Rajagopal**[*]
School of Computer Science
Carnegie Mellon University, Pittsburgh, USA
{bdhingra, ddanish, dheeraj}@cs.cmu.edu

Abstract

Recent success of deep learning models for the task of extractive Question Answering (QA) is hinged on the availability of large annotated corpora. However, large domain specific annotated corpora are limited and expensive to construct. In this work, we envision a system where the end user specifies a set of base documents and only a few labelled examples. Our system exploits the document structure to create cloze-style questions from these base documents; pre-trains a powerful neural network on the cloze style questions; and further fine-tunes the model on the labeled examples. We evaluate our proposed system across three diverse datasets from different domains, and find it to be highly effective with very little labeled data. We attain more than 50% F1 score on SQuAD and TriviaQA with less than a thousand labelled examples. We are also releasing a set of 3.2M cloze-style questions for practitioners to use while building QA systems[1].

1 Introduction

Deep learning systems have shown a lot of promise for extractive Question Answering (QA), with performance comparable to humans when large scale data is available. However, practitioners looking to build QA systems for specific applications may not have the resources to collect tens of thousands of questions on corpora of their choice. At the same time, state-of-the-art machine reading systems do not lend well to low-resource QA settings where the number of labeled question-answer pairs are limited (c.f. Table 2). Semi-supervised QA methods like (Yang et al., 2017) aim to improve this performance by leveraging unlabeled data which is easier to collect.

In this work, we present a semi-supervised QA system which requires the end user to specify a set of base documents and only a small set of question-answer pairs over a subset of these documents. Our proposed system consists of three stages. First, we construct cloze-style questions (predicting missing spans of text) from the unlabeled corpus; next, we use the generated clozes to pre-train a powerful neural network model for extractive QA (Clark and Gardner, 2017; Dhingra et al., 2017); and finally, we fine-tune the model on the small set of provided QA pairs.

Our cloze construction process builds on a typical writing phenomenon and document structure: an introduction precedes and summarizes the main body of the article. Many large corpora follow such a structure, including Wikipedia, academic papers, and news articles. We hypothesize that we can benefit from the un-annotated corpora to better answer various questions – at least ones that are lexically similar to the content in base documents and directly require factual information.

We apply the proposed system on three datasets from different domains – SQuAD (Rajpurkar et al., 2016), TriviaQA-Web (Joshi et al., 2017) and the BioASQ challenge (Tsatsaronis et al., 2015). We observe significant improvements in a low-resource setting across all three datasets. For SQuAD and TriviaQA, we attain an F1 score of more than 50% by merely using 1% of the training data. Our system outperforms the approaches for semi-supervised QA presented in Yang et al. (2017), and a baseline which uses the same unlabeled data but with a language modeling objective for pretraining. In the BioASQ challenge, we outperform the best performing system from previous year's challenge, improving over a baseline which does transfer learning from the SQuAD dataset. Our analysis reveals that questions which ask for factual information and match to specific parts of the context documents benefit the most from pretraining on automatically constructed clozes.

---

[*]Equal Contribution

[1]http://bit.ly/semi-supervised-qa

Proceedings of NAACL-HLT 2018, pages 582–587
New Orleans, Louisiana, June 1 - 6, 2018. ©2018 Association for Computational Linguistics

2 Related Work

Semi-supervised learning augments the labeled dataset L with a potentially larger unlabeled dataset U. Yang et al. (2017) presented a model, GDAN, which trained an auxiliary neural network to generate questions from passages by reinforcement learning, and augment the labeled dataset with the generated questions to train the QA model. Here we use a much simpler heuristic to generate the auxiliary questions, which also turns out to be more effective as we show superior performance compared to GDAN. Several approaches have been suggested for generating natural questions (Tang et al., 2017; Subramanian et al., 2017; Song et al., 2017), however none of them show a significant improvement of using the generated questions in a semi-supervised setting. Recent papers also use unlabeled data for QA by training large language models and extracting contextual word vectors from them to input to the QA model (Salant and Berant, 2017; Peters et al., 2018; McCann et al., 2017). The applicability of this method in the low-resource setting is unclear as the extra inputs increase the number of parameters in the QA model, however, our pretraining can be easily applied to these models as well.

Domain adaptation (and **Transfer learning**) leverage existing large scale datasets from a source domain (or task) to improve performance on a target domain (or task). For deep learning and QA, a common approach is to pretrain on the source dataset and then fine-tune on the target dataset (Chung et al., 2017; Golub et al., 2017). Wiese et al. (2017) used SQuAD as a source for the target BioASQ dataset, and Kadlec et al. (2016) used Book Test (Bajgar et al., 2016) as source for the target SQuAD dataset. Mihaylov et al. (2017) transfer learned model layers from the tasks of sequence labeling, text classification and relation classification to show small improvements on SQuAD. All these works use manually curated source datatset, which in themselves are expensive to collect. Instead, we show that it is possible to automatically construct the source dataset from the same domain as the target, which turns out to be more beneficial in terms of performance as well (c.f. Section 4). Several cloze datasets have been proposed in the literature which use heuristics for construction (Hermann et al., 2015; Onishi et al., 2016; Hill et al., 2016). We further see the usability of such a dataset in a semi-supervised setting.

3 Methodology

Our system comprises of following three steps:

Cloze generation: Most of the documents typically follow a template, they begin with an introduction that provides an overview and a brief summary for what is to follow. We assume such a structure while constructing our cloze style questions. When there is no clear demarcation, we treat the first $K\%$ (hyperparameter, in our case 20%) of the document as the introduction. While noisy, this heuristic generates a large number of clozes given any corpus, which we found to be beneficial for semi-supervised learning despite the noise.

We use a standard NLP pipeline based on Stanford CoreNLP[2] (for SQuAD, TrivaQA and PubMed) and the BANNER Named Entity Recognizer[3] (only for PubMed articles) to identify entities and phrases. Assume that a document comprises of introduction sentences $\{q_1, q_2, ...q_n\}$, and the remaining passages $\{p_1, p_2, ..p_m\}$. Additionally, let's say that each sentence q_i in introduction is composed of words $\{w_1, w_2, ...w_{l_{q_i}}\}$, where l_{q_i} is the length of q_i. We consider a match(q_i, p_j), if there is an exact string match of a sequence of words $\{w_k, w_{k+1}, ..w_{l_{q_i}}\}$ between the sentence q_i and passage p_j. If this sequence is either a noun phrase, verb phrase, adjective phrase or a named entity in p_j, as recognized by CoreNLP or BANNER, we select it as an answer span A. Additionally, we use p_j as the passage P and form a cloze question Q from the answer bearing sentence q_i by replacing A with a placeholder. As a result, we obtain passage-question-answer (P, Q, A) triples (Table 1 shows an example). As a post-processing step, we prune out (P, Q, A) triples where the word overlap between the question (Q) and passage (P) is less than 2 words (after excluding the stop words).

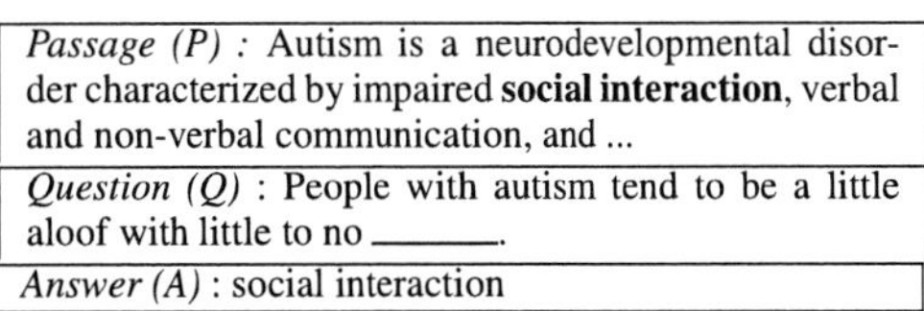

Passage (P) : Autism is a neurodevelopmental disorder characterized by impaired **social interaction**, verbal and non-verbal communication, and ...
Question (Q) : People with autism tend to be a little aloof with little to no _______.
Answer (A) : social interaction

Table 1: An example constructed cloze.

The process relies on the fact that answer candidates from the introduction are likely to be discussed in detail in the remainder of the article.

---

[2] https://stanfordnlp.github.io/CoreNLP/
[3] http://banner.sourceforge.net

In effect, the cloze question from the introduction and the matching paragraph in the body forms a question and context passage pair. We create two cloze datasets, one each from Wikipedia corpus (for SQuAD and TriviaQA) and PUBMed academic papers (for the BioASQ challenge), consisting of 2.2M and 1M clozes respectively. From analyzing the cloze data manually, we were able to answer 76% times for the Wikipedia set and 80% times for the PUBMed set using the information in the passage. In most cases the cloze paraphrased the information in the passage, which we hypothesized to be a useful signal for the downstream QA task.

We also investigate the utility of forming subsets of the large cloze corpus, where we select the top passage-question-answer triples, based on the different criteria, like i) jaccard similarity of answer bearing sentence in introduction and the passage ii) the tf-idf scores of answer candidates and iii) the length of answer candidates. However, we empirically find that we were better off using the entire set rather than these subsets.

Pre-training: We make use of the generated cloze dataset to pre-train an expressive neural network designed for the task of reading comprehension. We work with two publicly available neural network models – the GA Reader (Dhingra et al., 2017) (to enable comparison with prior work) and BiDAF + Self-Attention (SA) model from Clark and Gardner (2017) (which is among the best performing models on SQuAD and TriviaQA). After pretraining, the performance of BiDAF+SA on a dev set of the (Wikipedia) cloze questions is 0.58 F1 score and 0.55 Exact Match (EM) score. This implies that the cloze corpus is neither too easy, nor too difficult to answer.

Fine Tuning: We fine tune the pre-trained model, from the previous step, over a small set of labelled question-answer pairs. As we shall later see, this step is crucial, and it only requires a handful of labelled questions to achieve a significant proportion of the performance typically attained by training on tens of thousands of questions.

4 Experiments & Results

4.1 Datasets

We apply our system to three datasets from different domains. **SQuAD** (Rajpurkar et al., 2016) consists of questions whose answers are free form spans of text from passages in Wikipedia articles.

We follow the same setting as in (Yang et al., 2017), and split 10% of training questions as the test set, and report performance when training on subsets of the remaining data ranging from 1% to 90% of the full set. We also report the performance on the dev set when trained on the full training set (1* in Table 2). We use the same hyperparameter settings as in prior work. We compare and study four different settings: 1) the Supervised Learning (**SL**) setting, which is only trained on the supervised data, 2) the best performing **GDAN** model from Yang et al. (2017), 3) pretraining on a Language Modeling (**LM**) objective and finetuning on the supervised data, and 4) pretraining on the **Cloze** dataset and fine-tuning on the supervised data. The LM and Cloze methods use exactly the same data for pretraining, but differ in the loss functions used. We report F1 and EM scores on our test set using the official evaluation scripts provided by the authors of the dataset.

TriviaQA (Joshi et al., 2017) comprises of over 95K web question-answer-evidence triples. Like SQuAD, the answers are spans of text. Similar to the setting in SQuAD, we create multiple smaller subsets of the entire set. For our semi-supervised QA system, we use the BiDAF+SA model (Clark and Gardner, 2017) – the highest performing publicly available system for TrivaQA. Here again, we compare the supervised learning (**SL**) settings against the pretraining on **Cloze** set and fine tuning on the supervised set. We report F1 and EM scores on the dev set[4].

We also test on the **BioASQ 5b dataset**, which consists of question-answer pairs from PubMed abstracts. We use the publicly available system[5] from Wiese et al. (2017), and follow the exact same setup as theirs, focusing only on factoid and list questions. For this setting, there are only 899 questions for training. Since this is already a low-resource problem we only report results using 5-fold cross-validation on all the available data. We report Mean Reciprocal Rank (MRR) on the factoid questions, and F1 score for the list questions.

4.2 Main Results

Table 2 shows a comparison of the discussed settings on both SQuAD and TriviaQA. Without any

---

[4]We use a sample of dev questions, which is the default setting for the code by Clark and Gardner (2017). Since our goal is only to compare the models, this is not problematic.

[5]`https://github.com/georgwiese/biomedical-qa`

Model	Method	0		0.01		0.05		0.1		0.2		0.5		0.9		1	
		F1	EM	F1	EM	F1	EM	F1	EM	F1	EM	F1	EM	F1	EM	F1	EM
								SQuAD									
GA	SL	–	–	0.0882	0.0359	0.3517	0.2275	0.4116	0.2752	0.4797	0.3393	0.5705	0.4224	0.6125	0.4684	–	–
GA	GDAN	–	–	–	–	–	–	0.4840	0.3270	0.5394	0.3781	0.5831	0.4267	0.6102	0.4531	–	–
GA	LM	–	–	0.0957	0.0394	0.3141	0.1856	0.3725	0.2365	0.4406	0.2983	0.5111	0.3589	0.5520	0.3964	–	–
GA	Cloze	–	–	0.3090	0.1964	0.4688	0.3385	0.4937	0.3588	0.5575	0.4126	0.6086	0.4679	0.6302	0.4894	–	–
BiDAF+SA	SL	–	–	0.1926	0.1018	0.4764	0.3388	0.5639	0.4258	0.6484	0.5031	0.7044	0.5615	0.7287	0.5874	0.8069	0.7154
BiDAF+SA	Cloze	**0.0682**	**0.032**	**0.5042**	**0.3751**	**0.6324**	**0.4862**	**0.6431**	**0.4995**	**0.6839**	**0.5413**	**0.7151**	**0.5767**	**0.7369**	**0.6005**	**0.8080**	**0.7186**
								TRIVIA-QA									
BiDAF+SA	SL	–	–	0.2533	0.1898	0.4215	0.3566	0.4971	0.4318	0.5624	0.5077	0.6867	0.6239	0.7131	0.6617	0.7291	0.6786
BiDAF+SA	Cloze	**0.1182**	**0.0729**	**0.5521**	**0.4807**	**0.6245**	**0.5614**	**0.6506**	**0.5893**	**0.6849**	**0.6281**	**0.7196**	**0.6607**	**0.7381**	**0.6823**	**0.7461**	**0.6903**

Table 2: A holistic view of the performance of our system compared against baseline systems on SQuAD and TriviaQA. Column groups represent different fractions of the training set used for training.

fine-tuning (column 0) the performance is low, probably because the model never saw a real question, but we see significant gains with Cloze pretraining even with very little labeled data. The BiDAF+SA model, exceeds an F1 score of 50% with only 1% of the training data (454 questions for SQuAD, and 746 questions for TriviaQA), and approaches 90% of the best performance with only 10% labeled data. The gains over the SL setting, however, diminish as the size of the labeled set increases and are small when the full dataset is available.

Method	Factoid MRR	List F1
SL[*]	0.242	0.211
SQuAD pretraining	0.262	0.211
Cloze pretraining	**0.328**	**0.230**

Table 3: 5-fold cross-validation results on BioASQ Task 5b. [*]Our SL experiments showed better performance than what was reported in (Wiese et al., 2017).

Cloze pretraining outperforms the GDAN baseline from Yang et al. (2017) using the same SQuAD dataset splits. Additionally, we show improvements in the 90% data case unlike GDAN. Our approach is also applicable in the extremely low-resource setting of 1% data, which we suspect GDAN might have trouble with since it uses the labeled data to do reinforcement learning. Furthermore, we are able to use the same cloze dataset to improve performance on both SQuAD and TriviaQA datasets. When we use the same unlabeled data to pre-train with a language modeling objective, the performance is worse[6], showing the bias we introduce by constructing clozes is important.

On the BioASQ dataset (Table 3) we again see a significant improvement when pretraining with the cloze questions over the supervised baseline. The improvement is smaller than what we observe with SQuAD and TriviaQA datasets – we believe this is because questions are generally more difficult in BioASQ. Wiese et al. (2017) showed that pretraining on SQuAD dataset improves the downstream performance on BioASQ. Here, we show a much larger improvement by pretraining on cloze questions constructed in an *unsupervised* manner from the same domain.

4.3 Analysis

Regression Analysis: To understand which types of questions benefit from pre-training, we pre-specified certain features (see Figure 1 right) for each of the dev set questions in SQuAD, and then performed linear regression to predict the F1 score for that question from these features. We predict the F1 scores from the cloze pretrained model (y^{cloze}), the supervised model (y^{sl}), and the difference of the two ($y^{\text{cloze}} - y^{\text{sl}}$), when using 10% of labeled data. The coefficients of the fitted model are shown in Figure 1 (left) along with their std errors. Positive coefficients indicate that a high value of that feature is predictive of a high F1 score, and a negative coefficient indicates that a small value of that feature is predictive of a high F1 score (or a high difference of F1 scores from the two models in the case of $y^{\text{cloze}} - y^{\text{sl}}$).

The two strongest effects we observe are that a high lexical overlap between the question and the sentence containing the answer is indicative of high boost with pretraining, and that a high lexical overlap between the question and the whole passage is indicative of the opposite. This is hardly surprising, since our cloze construction process is biased towards questions which have a

---

[6]Since the GA Reader uses *bidirectional* RNN layers, when pretraining the LM we had to mask the inputs to the intermediate layers partially to avoid the model being exposed to the labels it is predicting. This results in a only a subset of the parameters being pretrained, which is why we believe this baseline performs poorly.

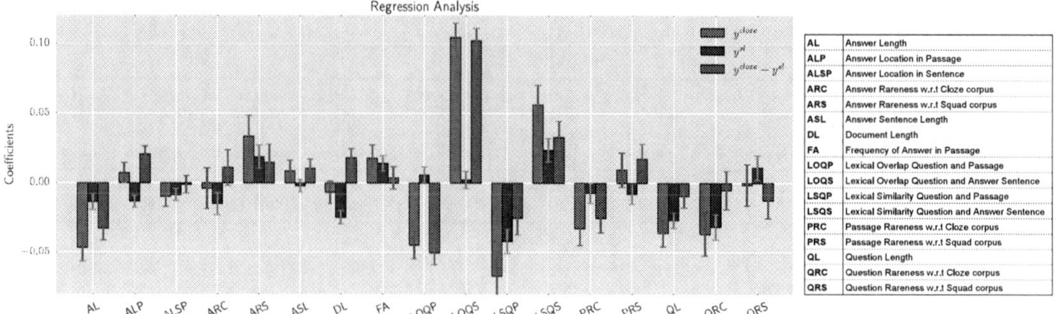

Figure 1: **Left:** Regression coefficients, along with std-errors, when predicting F1 score of *cloze* model, or *sl* model, or the difference of the two, from features computed from SQuAD dev set questions. **Right:** Descriptions of the features.

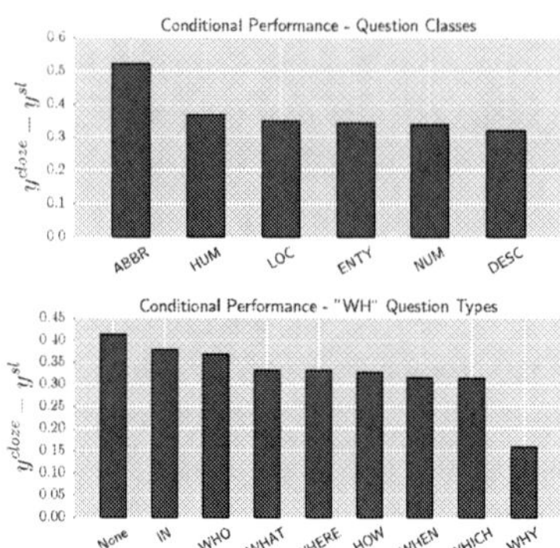

Figure 2: Performance gain with pretraining for different subsets of question types.

similar phrasing to the answer sentences in context. Hence, test questions with a similar property are answered correctly after pretraining, whereas those with a high overlap with the whole passage tend to have lower performance. The pretraining also favors questions with short answers because the cloze construction process produces short answer spans. Also passages and questions which consist of tokens infrequent in the SQuAD training corpus receive a large boost after pretraining, since the unlabeled data covers a larger domain.

Performance on question types: Figure 2 shows the average gain in F1 score for different types of questions, when we pretrain on the clozes compared to the supervised case. This analysis is done on the 10% split of the SQuAD training set. We consider two classifications of each question – one determined on the first word (usually a wh-word) of the question (Figure 2 (bottom)) and one based on the output of a separate question type classifier[7] adapted from (Li and Roth,

---

[7] https://github.com/brmson/question-classification

2002). We use the coarse grain labels namely Abbreviation (ABBR), Entity (ENTY), Description (DESC), Human (HUM), Location (LOC), Numeric (NUM) trained on a Logistic Regression classification system . While there is an improvement across the board, we find that abbreviation questions in particular receive a large boost. Also, "why" questions show the least improvement, which is in line with our expectation, since these usually require reasoning or world knowledge which cloze questions rarely require.

5   Conclusion

In this paper, we show that pre-training QA models with automatically constructed cloze questions improves the performance of the models significantly, especially when there are few labeled examples. The performance of the model trained only on the cloze questions is poor, validating the need for fine-tuning. Through regression analysis, we find that pretraining helps with questions which ask for factual information located in a specific part of the context. For future work, we plan to explore the active learning setup for this task – specifically, which passages and / or types of questions can we select to annotate, such that there is a maximum performance gain from fine-tuning. We also want to explore how to adapt cloze style pretraining to NLP tasks other than QA.

Acknowledgments

Bhuwan Dhingra is supported by NSF under grants CCF-1414030 and IIS-1250956 and by grants from Google. Danish Pruthi and Dheeraj Rajagopal are supported by the DARPA Big Mechanism program under ARO contract W911NF-14-1-0436.

References

Ondrej Bajgar, Rudolf Kadlec, and Jan Kleindienst. 2016. Embracing data abundance: Booktest dataset for reading comprehension. *arXiv preprint arXiv:1610.00956*.

Yu-An Chung, Hung-Yi Lee, and James Glass. 2017. Supervised and unsupervised transfer learning for question answering. *arXiv preprint arXiv:1711.05345*.

Christopher Clark and Matt Gardner. 2017. Simple and effective multi-paragraph reading comprehension. *arXiv preprint arXiv:1710.10723*.

Bhuwan Dhingra, Hanxiao Liu, Zhilin Yang, William W Cohen, and Ruslan Salakhutdinov. 2017. Gated-attention readers for text comprehension. *ACL*.

David Golub, Po-Sen Huang, Xiaodong He, and Li Deng. 2017. Two-stage synthesis networks for transfer learning in machine comprehension. *arXiv preprint arXiv:1706.09789*.

Karl Moritz Hermann, Tomas Kocisky, Edward Grefenstette, Lasse Espeholt, Will Kay, Mustafa Suleyman, and Phil Blunsom. 2015. Teaching machines to read and comprehend. In *Advances in Neural Information Processing Systems*, pages 1693–1701.

Felix Hill, Antoine Bordes, Sumit Chopra, and Jason Weston. 2016. The goldilocks principle: Reading children's books with explicit memory representations. *ICLR*.

Mandar Joshi, Eunsol Choi, Daniel S. Weld, and Luke Zettlemoyer. 2017. Triviaqa: A large scale distantly supervised challenge dataset for reading comprehension. In *Proceedings of the 55th Annual Meeting of the Association for Computational Linguistics*, Vancouver, Canada. Association for Computational Linguistics.

Rudolf Kadlec, Ondřej Bajgar, Peter Hrincar, and Jan Kleindienst. 2016. Finding a jack-of-all-trades: An examination of semi-supervised learning in reading comprehension.

Xin Li and Dan Roth. 2002. Learning question classifiers. In *Proceedings of the 19th international conference on Computational linguistics-Volume 1*, pages 1–7. Association for Computational Linguistics.

Bryan McCann, James Bradbury, Caiming Xiong, and Richard Socher. 2017. Learned in translation: Contextualized word vectors. *arXiv preprint arXiv:1708.00107*.

Todor Mihaylov, Zornitsa Kozareva, and Anette Frank. 2017. Neural skill transfer from supervised language tasks to reading comprehension. *arXiv preprint arXiv:1711.03754*.

Takeshi Onishi, Hai Wang, Mohit Bansal, Kevin Gimpel, and David McAllester. 2016. Who did what: A large-scale person-centered cloze dataset. *EMNLP*.

Matthew E Peters, Mark Neumann, Mohit Iyyer, Matt Gardner, Christopher Clark, Kenton Lee, and Luke Zettlemoyer. 2018. Deep contextualized word representations. *arXiv preprint arXiv:1802.05365*.

Pranav Rajpurkar, Jian Zhang, Konstantin Lopyrev, and Percy Liang. 2016. Squad: 100,000+ questions for machine comprehension of text. *EMNLP*.

Shimi Salant and Jonathan Berant. 2017. Contextualized word representations for reading comprehension. *arXiv preprint arXiv:1712.03609*.

Linfeng Song, Zhiguo Wang, and Wael Hamza. 2017. A unified query-based generative model for question generation and question answering. *arXiv preprint arXiv:1709.01058*.

Sandeep Subramanian, Tong Wang, Xingdi Yuan, and Adam Trischler. 2017. Neural models for key phrase detection and question generation. *arXiv preprint arXiv:1706.04560*.

Duyu Tang, Nan Duan, Tao Qin, and Ming Zhou. 2017. Question answering and question generation as dual tasks. *arXiv preprint arXiv:1706.02027*.

George Tsatsaronis, Georgios Balikas, Prodromos Malakasiotis, Ioannis Partalas, Matthias Zschunke, Michael R Alvers, Dirk Weissenborn, Anastasia Krithara, Sergios Petridis, Dimitris Polychronopoulos, et al. 2015. An overview of the bioasq large-scale biomedical semantic indexing and question answering competition. *BMC bioinformatics*, 16(1):138.

Georg Wiese, Dirk Weissenborn, and Mariana L. Neves. 2017. Neural question answering at bioasq 5b. In *BioNLP 2017, Vancouver, Canada, August 4, 2017*, pages 76–79.

Zhilin Yang, Junjie Hu, Ruslan Salakhutdinov, and William W Cohen. 2017. Semi-supervised qa with generative domain-adaptive nets. *ACL*.

TypeSQL: Knowledge-based Type-Aware Neural Text-to-SQL Generation

Tao Yu
Yale University
tao.yu@yale.edu

Zifan Li
Yale University
zifan.li@yale.edu

Zilin Zhang
Yale University
zilin.zhang@yale.edu

Rui Zhang
Yale University
r.zhang@yale.edu

Dragomir Radev
Yale University
dragomir.radev@yale.edu

Abstract

Interacting with relational databases through natural language helps users of any background easily query and analyze a vast amount of data. This requires a system that understands users' questions and converts them to SQL queries automatically. In this paper we present a novel approach, TYPESQL, which views this problem as a slot filling task. Additionally, TYPESQL utilizes type information to better understand rare entities and numbers in natural language questions. We test this idea on the WikiSQL dataset and outperform the prior state-of-the-art by 5.5% in much less time. We also show that accessing the content of databases can significantly improve the performance when users' queries are not well-formed. TYPESQL gets 82.6% accuracy, a 17.5% absolute improvement compared to the previous content-sensitive model.

1 Introduction

Building natural language interfaces to relational databases is an important and challenging problem (Li and Jagadish, 2014; Pasupat and Liang, 2015; Yin et al., 2016; Zhong et al., 2017; Yaghmazadeh et al., 2017; Xu et al., 2017; Wang et al., 2017a). It requires a system that is able to understand natural language questions and generate corresponding SQL queries. In this paper, we consider the WikiSQL task proposed by Zhong et al. (2017), a large scale benchmark dataset for the text-to-SQL problem. Given a natural language question for a table and the table's schema, the system needs to produce a SQL query corresponding to the question.

We introduce a knowledge-based type-aware text-to-SQL generator, TYPESQL. Based on the prior state-of-the-art SQLNet (Xu et al., 2017), TYPESQL employs a sketch-based approach and views the task as a slot filling problem (Figure 2). By grouping different slots in a reasonable way and capturing relationships between attributes, TYPESQL outperforms SQLNet by about 3.5% in half of the original training time.

Furthermore, natural language questions often contain rare entities and numbers specific to the underlying database. Some previous work (Agrawal and Srikant, 2003) already shows those words are crucial to many downstream tasks, such as infering column names and condition values in the SQL query. However, most of such key words lack accurate embeddings in popular pre-trained word embedding models. In order to solve this problem, TYPESQL assigns each word a type as an entity from either the knowledge graph, a column or a number. For example, for the question in Figure 1, we label "mort drucker" as PERSON according to our knowledge graph; "spoofed title," "artist" and "issue" as COLUMN since they are column names; and "88.5" as FLOAT. Incorporating this type information, TYPESQL further improves the state-of-the-art performance by about another 2% on the WikiSQL dataset, resulting in a final 5.5% improvement in total.

Moreover, most previous work assumes that user queries contain exact column names and entries. However, it is unrealistic that users always formulate their questions with exact column names and string entries in the table. To tackle this issue, when scaleability and privacy are not of a concern, the system needs to search databases to better understand what the user is querying. Our content-sensitive model TYPESQL + TC gains roughly 9% improvement compared to the content-insensitive model, and outperforms the previous content-sensitive model by 17.5%.

2 Related Work

Semantic parsing maps natural language to meaningful executable programs. The programs could

588

Proceedings of NAACL-HLT 2018, pages 588–594
New Orleans, Louisiana, June 1 - 6, 2018. ©2018 Association for Computational Linguistics

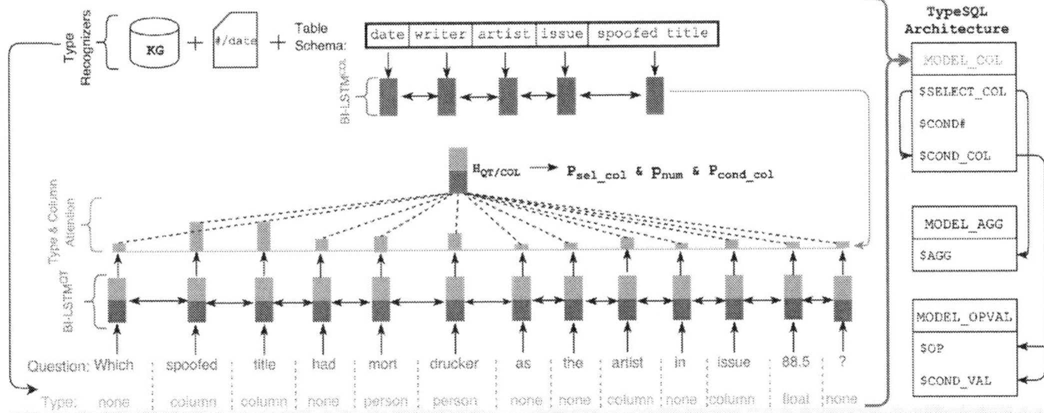

Figure 1: TYPESQL consists of three slot-filling models on the right. We only show MODEL_COL on the left for brevity. MODEL_AGG and MODEL_OPVAL have the similar pipelines.

be a range of representations such as logic forms (Zelle and Mooney, 1996; Zettlemoyer and Collins, 2005; Wong and Mooney, 2007; Das et al., 2010; Liang et al., 2011; Banarescu et al., 2013; Artzi and Zettlemoyer, 2013; Reddy et al., 2014; Berant and Liang, 2014; Pasupat and Liang, 2015). Another area close to our task is code generation. This task parses natural language descriptions into a more general-purpose programming language such as Python (Allamanis et al., 2015; Ling et al., 2016; Rabinovich et al., 2017; Yin and Neubig, 2017).

As a sub-task of semantic parsing, the text-to-SQL problem has been studied for decades (Warren and Pereira, 1982; Popescu et al., 2003, 2004; Li et al., 2006; Giordani and Moschitti, 2012; Wang et al., 2017b). The methods of the Database community (Li and Jagadish, 2014; Yaghmazadeh et al., 2017) involve more hand feature engineering and user interactions with the systems. In this work, we focus on recent neural network based approaches (Yin et al., 2016; Zhong et al., 2017; Xu et al., 2017; Wang et al., 2017a; Iyer et al., 2017). Dong and Lapata (2016) introduce a sequence-to-sequence approach to converting text to logical forms. Most of previous work focus on specific table schemas, which means they use a single database in both train and test. Thus, they don't generalize to new databases. Zhong et al. (2017) publish the WikiSQL dataset and propose a sequence-to-sequence model with reinforcement learning to generate SQL queries. In the problem definition of the WikiSQL task, the databases in the test set do not appear in the train and develop-

SELECT $AGG $SELECT_COL
WHERE $COND_COL $OP $COND_VAL
(**AND** $COND_COL $OP $COND_VAL)*

Figure 2: SQL Sketch. The tokens starting with "$" are slots to fill. "*" indicates zero or more **AND** clauses.

ment sets. Also, the task needs to take different table schemas into account. Xu et al. (2017) further improve the results by using a SQL sketch based approach employing a sequence-to-set model.

3 Methodology

Like SQLNet, we employ a sketch-based approach and format the task as a slot filling problem. Figure 2 shows the SQL sketch. Our model needs to predict all slots that begin with $ in Figure 2.

Figure 1 illustrates the architecture of TYPE-SQL on the right and a detailed overview of one of three main models MODEL_COL on the left. We first preprocess question inputs by type recognition (Section 3.1). Then we use two bi-directional LSTMs to encode words in the question with their types and the column names separately (Section 3.2). The output hidden states of LSTMs are then used to predict the values for the slots in the SQL sketch (Section 3.3).

3.1 Type Recognition for Input Preprocessing

In order to create one-to-one type input for each question, we, first, tokenize each question into n-grams of length 2 to 6, and use them to search over the table schema and label any column name appears in the question as COLUMN. Then, we assign numbers and dates in the question into four self-explanatory categories: INTEGER, FLOAT, DATE, and YEAR. To identify named entities, we search for five types of entities: PERSON, PLACE, COUNTRY, ORGANIZATION, and SPORT, on Freebase[1] using grams as keyword queries. The five categories cover a majority of entities in the dataset. Thus, we do not use other entity types provided by Freebase. Domain-specific knowledge graphs can be used for other applications.

In the case where the content of databases is available, we match words in the question with both the table schema and the content and labels of the columns as COLUMN and match the entry values as the corresponding column names. For example, the type in the Figure 1 would be [none, column, column, none, artist, artist, none, none, column, none, column, issue, none] in this case. Other parts in the Figure 1 keep the same as the content-insensitive approach.

3.2 Input Encoder

As shown in the Figure 1, our input encoder consists of two bi-directional LSTMs, BI-LSTM^{QT} and BI-LSTM^{COL}. To encode word and type pairs of the question, we concatenate embeddings of words and their corresponding types and input them to BI-LSTM^{QT}. Then the output hidden states are $\mathbf{H}_{\text{QT}}$ and $\mathbf{H}_{\text{COL}}$, respectively.

For encoding column names, SQLNet runs a bi-directional LSTM over each column name. We first average the embeddings of words in the column name. Then, we run a single BI-LSTM^{COL} between column names. This encoding method improves the result by 1.5% and cuts the training time by half. Even though the order of column names does not matter, we attribute this improvement to the fact that the LSTM can capture their occurrences and relationships.

3.3 Slot-Filling Model

Next, we predict values for the slots in the SQL sketch. For the slots in Figure 2, SQLNet has a separate model for each of them which do not share their trainable parameters. This creates five models for the five slots and one model for $COND# (12 BI-LSTMs in total). However, since the predict procedures of $SELECT_COL, $COND_COL, and $COND# are similar, we combine them into a single model. Additionally, $COND_COL depends on

the output of $SELECT_COL, which reduces errors of predicting the same column in these two slots $COND_COL Moreover, we group $OP and $COND_VAL together because both depend on the outputs of $COND_COL. Furthermore, we use one model for $AGG because we notice that the $AGG model converges much faster and suffers from overfitting when combined with other models. Finally, TYPESQL consists of three models (Figure 1 right):

- MODEL_COL for $SELECT_COL, $COND# and $COND_COL

- MODEL_AGG for $AGG

- MODEL_OPVAL for $OP and $COND_VAL

where the parameters of BI-LSTM^{QT} and BI-LSTM^{COL} are shared in each model (6 BI-LSTMs in total).

Since all three models use the same way to compute the weighted question and type representation $\mathbf{H}_{\text{QT/COL}}$ using the column attention mechanism proposed in SQLNet, we first introduce the following step in all three models:

$$\alpha_{\text{QT/COL}} = \textbf{softmax}(\mathbf{H}_{\text{COL}}\mathbf{W}_{ct}\mathbf{H}_{\text{QT}}^{\top})$$
$$\mathbf{H}_{\text{QT/COL}} = \alpha_{\text{QT/COL}}\mathbf{H}_{\text{QT}}$$

where **softmax** applies the softmax operator over each row of the input matrix, $\alpha_{\text{QT/COL}}$ is a matrix of attention scores, and $\mathbf{H}_{\text{QT/COL}}$ is the weighted question and type representation. In our equations, we use $\mathbf{W}$ and $\mathbf{V}$ to represent all trainable parameter matrices and vectors, respectively.

MODEL_COL-$SELECT_COL $\mathbf{H}_{\text{QT/COL}}$ is used to predict the column name in the $SELECT_COL:

$$s = \mathbf{V}^{sel}\textbf{tanh}(\mathbf{W}_c^{sel}\mathbf{H}_{\text{COL}}^{\top} + \mathbf{W}_{qt}^{sel}\mathbf{H}_{\text{QT/COL}}^{\top})$$
$$P_{sel\_col} = \textbf{softmax}(s)$$

MODEL_COL-$COND# Unlike SQLNet, we compute number of conditions in the WHERE in a simpler way:

$$P_{num} = \textbf{softmax}\left(\mathbf{V}^{num}\textbf{tanh}(\mathbf{W}_{qt}^{num}\textstyle\sum_i \mathbf{H}_{\text{QT/COL}_i}^{\top})\right)$$

We set the maximum number of conditions to 4.

---

[1] https://developers.google.com/freebase/

	Dev			Test		
	Acc_{lf}	Acc_{qm}	Acc_{ex}	Acc_{lf}	Acc_{qm}	Acc_{ex}
Content Insensitive						
Dong and Lapata (2016)	23.3%	-	37.0%	23.4%	-	35.9%
Augmented Pointer Network (Zhong et al., 2017)	44.1%	-	53.8%	42.8%	-	52.8%
Seq2SQL (Zhong et al., 2017)	49.5%	-	60.8%	48.3%	-	59.4%
SQLNet (Xu et al., 2017)	-	63.2%	69.8%	-	61.3%	68.0%
TypeSQL w/o type-awareness (ours)	-	66.5%	72.8%	-	64.9%	71.7%
TypeSQL (ours)	-	**68.0%**	**74.5%**	-	**66.7%**	**73.5%**
Content Sensitive						
Wang et al. (2017a)	59.6%	-	65.2%	59.5%	-	65.1%
TypeSQL+TC (ours)	-	**79.2%**	**85.5%**	-	**75.4%**	**82.6%**

Table 1: Overall results on WikiSQL. Acc_{lf}, Acc_{qm}, and Acc_{ex} denote the accuracies of exact string, canonical representation, and execute result matches between the synthesized SQL with the ground truth respectively. The top six results are content-insensitive, which means only the question and table schema are used as inputs. The bottom two are content-sensitive, where the models use the question, the table schema, and the content of databases.

	Dev			Test		
	Acc_{agg}	Acc_{sel}	$\text{Acc}_{\text{where}}$	Acc_{agg}	Acc_{sel}	$\text{Acc}_{\text{where}}$
Seq2SQL (Zhong et al., 2017)	90.0%	89.6%	62.1%	90.1%	88.9%	60.2%
SQLNet (Xu et al., 2017)	90.1%	91.5%	74.1%	90.3%	90.9%	71.9%
TypeSQL (ours)	90.3%	**93.1%**	**78.5%**	90.5%	**92.2%**	**77.8%**
TypeSQL+TC (ours)	90.3%	**93.5%**	**92.8%**	90.5%	**92.1%**	**87.9%**

Table 2: Breakdown results on WikiSQL. Acc_{agg}, Acc_{sel}, and $\text{Acc}_{\text{where}}$ are the accuracies of canonical representation matches on AGGREGATOR, SELECT COLUMN, and WHERE clauses between the synthesized SQL and the ground truth respectively.

MODEL_COL-\$COND_COL We find that SQLNet often selects the same column name in the $COND_COL as $SELECT_COL, which is incorrect in most cases. To avoid this problem, we pass the weighted sum of question and type hidden states conditioned on the column chosen in $SELECT_COL $\mathbf{H}_{\text{QT/SCOL}}$ (expended as the same shape of $\mathbf{H}_{\text{QT/COL}}$) to the prediction:

$$c = \mathbf{V}^{col}\tanh(\mathbf{W}_c^{col}\mathbf{H}_{\text{COL}}^{\top} + \mathbf{W}_{qt}^{col}\mathbf{H}_{\text{QT/COL}}^{\top} + \mathbf{W}_{qt}^{scol}\mathbf{H}_{\text{QT/SCOL}}^{\top})$$

$$P_{cond\_col} = \textbf{softmax}(c)$$

MODEL_AGG-\$AGG Given the weighted sum of question and type hidden states conditioned on the column chosen in $SELECT_COL $\mathbf{H}_{\text{QT/SCOL}}$, $AGG is chosen from {NULL, MAX, MIN, COUNT, SUM, AVG} in the same way as SQLNet:

$$P_{agg} = \textbf{softmax}\left(\mathbf{V}^{agg}\tanh(\mathbf{W}_{qt}^{agg}\mathbf{H}_{\text{QT/SCOL}}^{\top})\right)$$

MODEL_OPVAL-\$OP For each predicted condition column, we choose a $OP from $\{=, >, <\}$ by:

$$P_{op} = \textbf{softmax}\left(\mathbf{W}_t^{op}\tanh(\mathbf{W}_c^{op}\mathbf{H}_{\text{COL}}^{\top} + \mathbf{W}_{qt}^{op}\mathbf{H}_{\text{QT/COL}}^{\top})\right)$$

MODEL_OPVAL-\$COND_VAL Then, we need to generate a substring from the question for each predicted column. As in SQLNet, a bi-directional LSTM is used for the encoder. It employs a pointer network (Vinyals et al., 2015) to compute the distribution of the next token in the decoder. In particular, the probability of selecting the i-th token w_i in the natural language question as the next token in the substring is computed as:

$$v = \mathbf{V}_t^{val}\tanh(\mathbf{W}_{qt}^{val}\mathbf{H}_{\text{QT}}^{i} + \mathbf{W}_c^{val}\mathbf{H}_{\text{COL}} + \mathbf{W}_h^{val}\mathbf{h})$$

$$P_{cond\_val} = \textbf{softmax}(v)$$

where $\mathbf{h}$ is the hidden state of the previously generated token. The generation process continues until the ⟨END⟩ token is the most probable next token of the substring.

4 Experiments

Dataset We use the WikiSQL dataset (Zhong et al., 2017), a collection of 87,673 examples of questions, queries, and database tables built from 26,521 tables. It provides train/dev/test splits such that each table is only in one split. This requires model to generalize to not only new questions but new table schemas as well.

Implementation Details We implement our model based on SQLNet (Xu et al., 2017) in Py-

Torch (Paszke et al., 2017). We concatenate pretrained Glove (Pennington et al., 2014) and paraphrase (Wieting and Gimpel, 2017) embeddings. The dimensions and dropout rates of all hidden layers are set to 120 and 0.3 respectively. We use Adam (Kingma and Ba, 2015) with the default hyperparameters for optimization. The batch size is set to 64. The same loss functions in (Xu et al., 2017) are used. Our code is available at https://github.com/taoyds/typesql.

Results and Discussion   Table 1 shows the main results on the WikiSQL task. We compare our work with previous results using the three evaluation metrics used in (Xu et al., 2017). Table 2 provides the breakdown results on AGGREGATION, SELECTION, and WHERE clauses.

Without looking at the content of databases, our model outperforms the previous best work by 5.5% on execute accuracy. According to Table 2, TYPESQL improves the accuracy of SELECT by 1.3% and WHERE clause by 5.9%. By encoding column names and grouping model components in a simpler but reasonable way, TYPESQL achieves a much higher result on the most challenging subtask WHERE clause. Also, the further improvement of integrating word types shows that TYPESQL could encode the rare entities and numbers in a better way.

Also, if complete access to the database is allowed, TYPESQL can achieve 82.6% on execute accuracy, and improves the performance of the previous content-aware system by 17.5%. Although (Zhong et al., 2017) enforced some limitations when creating the WikiSQL dataset, there are still many questions that do not have any column name and entity indicator. This makes generating the right SQLs without searching the database content in such cases impossible. This is not a critical problem for WikiSQL but is so for most real-world tasks.

5   Conclusion and Future Work

We propose TYPESQL for text-to-SQL which views the problem as a slot filling task and uses type information to better understand rare entities and numbers in the input. TYPESQL can use the database content to better understand the user query if it is not well-formed. TYPESQL significantly improves upon the previous state-of-the-art on the WikiSQL dataset.

Although, unlike most of the previous work, the WikiSQL task requires model to generalize to new databases, the dataset does not cover some important SQL operators such as JOIN and GROUP BY. This limits the generalization of the task to other SQL components. In the future, we plan to advance this work by exploring other more complex datasets under the database-split setting. In this way, we can study the performance of a generalized model on a more realistic text-to-SQL task which includes many complex SQL and different databases.

Acknowledgement

We thank Alexander Fabbri for his help in reviewing.

References

Rakesh Agrawal and Ramakrishnan Srikant. 2003. Searching with numbers. *IEEE Trans. Knowl. Data Eng.*, 15(4):855–870.

Miltiadis Allamanis, Daniel Tarlow, Andrew D. Gordon, and Yi Wei. 2015. Bimodal modelling of source code and natural language. In *ICML*, volume 37 of *JMLR Workshop and Conference Proceedings*, pages 2123–2132. JMLR.org.

Yoav Artzi and Luke Zettlemoyer. 2013. Weakly supervised learning of semantic parsers for mapping instructions to actions. *Transactions of the Association for Computational Linguistics*.

Laura Banarescu, Claire Bonial, Shu Cai, Madalina Georgescu, Kira Griffitt, Ulf Hermjakob, Kevin Knight, Philipp Koehn, Martha Palmer, and Nathan Schneider. 2013. Abstract meaning representation for sembanking. In *Proceedings of the 7th Linguistic Annotation Workshop and Interoperability with Discourse*.

Jonathan Berant and Percy Liang. 2014. Semantic parsing via paraphrasing. In *Proceedings of the 52nd Annual Meeting of the Association for Computational Linguistics (Volume 1: Long Papers)*, pages 1415–1425, Baltimore, Maryland. Association for Computational Linguistics.

Dipanjan Das, Nathan Schneider, Desai Chen, and Noah A. Smith. 2010. Probabilistic frame-semantic parsing. In *NAACL*.

Li Dong and Mirella Lapata. 2016. Language to logical form with neural attention. In *Proceedings of the 54th Annual Meeting of the Association for Computational Linguistics, ACL 2016, August 7-12, 2016, Berlin, Germany, Volume 1: Long Papers*.

Alessandra Giordani and Alessandro Moschitti. 2012. Translating questions to sql queries with generative parsers discriminatively reranked. In *COLING (Posters)*, pages 401–410.

Srinivasan Iyer, Ioannis Konstas, Alvin Cheung, Jayant Krishnamurthy, and Luke Zettlemoyer. 2017. Learning a neural semantic parser from user feedback. *CoRR*, abs/1704.08760.

Diederik P. Kingma and Jimmy Ba. 2015. Adam: A method for stochastic optimization. *The 3rd International Conference for Learning Representations, San Diego.*

Fei Li and HV Jagadish. 2014. Constructing an interactive natural language interface for relational databases. *VLDB.*

Yunyao Li, Huahai Yang, and HV Jagadish. 2006. Constructing a generic natural language interface for an xml database. In *EDBT*, volume 3896, pages 737–754. Springer.

P. Liang, M. I. Jordan, and D. Klein. 2011. Learning dependency-based compositional semantics. In *Association for Computational Linguistics (ACL)*, pages 590–599.

Wang Ling, Phil Blunsom, Edward Grefenstette, Karl Moritz Hermann, Tomás Kociský, Fumin Wang, and Andrew Senior. 2016. Latent predictor networks for code generation. In *ACL (1)*. The Association for Computer Linguistics.

Panupong Pasupat and Percy Liang. 2015. Compositional semantic parsing on semi-structured tables. In *Proceedings of the 53rd Annual Meeting of the Association for Computational Linguistics and the 7th International Joint Conference on Natural Language Processing of the Asian Federation of Natural Language Processing, ACL 2015, July 26-31, 2015, Beijing, China, Volume 1: Long Papers*, pages 1470–1480.

Adam Paszke, Sam Gross, Soumith Chintala, Gregory Chanan, Edward Yang, Zachary DeVito, Zeming Lin, Alban Desmaison, Luca Antiga, and Adam Lerer. 2017. Automatic differentiation in pytorch. *NIPS 2017 Workshop.*

Jeffrey Pennington, Richard Socher, and Christopher D. Manning. 2014. Glove: Global vectors for word representation. In *EMNLP*, pages 1532–1543. ACL.

Ana-Maria Popescu, Alex Armanasu, Oren Etzioni, David Ko, and Alexander Yates. 2004. Modern natural language interfaces to databases: Composing statistical parsing with semantic tractability. In *Proceedings of the 20th international conference on Computational Linguistics*, page 141. Association for Computational Linguistics.

Ana-Maria Popescu, Oren Etzioni, and Henry Kautz. 2003. Towards a theory of natural language interfaces to databases. In *Proceedings of the 8th international conference on Intelligent user interfaces*, pages 149–157. ACM.

Maxim Rabinovich, Mitchell Stern, and Dan Klein. 2017. Abstract syntax networks for code generation and semantic parsing. In *ACL (1)*, pages 1139–1149. Association for Computational Linguistics.

Siva Reddy, Mirella Lapata, and Mark Steedman. 2014. Large-scale semantic parsing without question-answer pairs. *Transactions of the Association for Computational Linguistics*, 2:377–392.

Oriol Vinyals, Meire Fortunato, and Navdeep Jaitly. 2015. Pointer networks. In C. Cortes, N. D. Lawrence, D. D. Lee, M. Sugiyama, and R. Garnett, editors, *Advances in Neural Information Processing Systems 28*, pages 2692–2700. Curran Associates, Inc.

Chenglong Wang, Marc Brockschmidt, and Rishabh Singh. 2017a. Pointing out sql queries from text. *Technical Report.*

Chenglong Wang, Alvin Cheung, and Rastislav Bodik. 2017b. Synthesizing highly expressive sql queries from input-output examples. In *Proceedings of the 38th ACM SIGPLAN Conference on Programming Language Design and Implementation*, pages 452–466. ACM.

David HD Warren and Fernando CN Pereira. 1982. An efficient easily adaptable system for interpreting natural language queries. *Computational Linguistics*, 8(3-4):110–122.

John Wieting and Kevin Gimpel. 2017. Pushing the limits of paraphrastic sentence embeddings with millions of machine translations. *arXiv preprint arXiv:1711.05732.*

Yuk Wah Wong and Raymond J. Mooney. 2007. Learning synchronous grammars for semantic parsing with lambda calculus. In *Proceedings of the 45th Annual Meeting of the Association for Computational Linguistics (ACL-2007)*, Prague, Czech Republic.

Xiaojun Xu, Chang Liu, and Dawn Song. 2017. Sqlnet: Generating structured queries from natural language without reinforcement learning. *arXiv preprint arXiv:1711.04436.*

Navid Yaghmazadeh, Yuepeng Wang, Isil Dillig, and Thomas Dillig. 2017. Sqlizer: Query synthesis from natural language. *Proc. ACM Program. Lang.*, 1(OOPSLA):63:1–63:26.

Pengcheng Yin, Zhengdong Lu, Hang Li, and Ben Kao. 2016. Neural enquirer: Learning to query tables in natural language. In *Proceedings of the Twenty-Fifth International Joint Conference on Artificial Intelligence, IJCAI 2016, New York, NY, USA, 9-15 July 2016*, pages 2308–2314.

Pengcheng Yin and Graham Neubig. 2017. A syntactic neural model for general-purpose code generation. In *ACL (1)*, pages 440–450. Association for Computational Linguistics.

John M. Zelle and Raymond J. Mooney. 1996. Learning to parse database queries using inductive logic programming. In *AAAI/IAAI*, pages 1050–1055, Portland, OR. AAAI Press/MIT Press.

Luke S. Zettlemoyer and Michael Collins. 2005. Learning to map sentences to logical form: Structured classification with probabilistic categorial grammars. *UAI*.

Victor Zhong, Caiming Xiong, and Richard Socher. 2017. Seq2sql: Generating structured queries from natural language using reinforcement learning. *CoRR*, abs/1709.00103.

Community Member Retrieval on Social Media using Textual Information

Aaron Jaech, Shobhit Hathi, Mari Ostendorf
University of Washington
`{ajaech, shathi, ostendor}uw.edu`

Abstract

This paper addresses the problem of community membership detection using only text features in a scenario where a small number of positive labeled examples defines the community. The solution introduces an unsupervised proxy task for learning user embeddings: user re-identification. Experiments with 16 different communities show that the resulting embeddings are more effective for community membership identification than common unsupervised representations.

1 Introduction

Active users of social media often like identifying other users with common interests and values. Or, a user may want to find other users that share characteristics with specific accounts that they follow, e.g. cartoonists or local food trucks. Members of such communities of interest are often identifiable via their social network connections, and shared social connections are clearly important in recommendations. However, shared connections often reflect a subset of a person's interests, and there may be users of interest where any shared connections are distant. In addition, there may be scenarios where there is no explicit social graph, or the full graph is expensive to obtain. In such cases, the language of tweets, blogs, etc. is helpful in identifying users with particular interests.

In this paper, we represent users in terms of the text in their communications and introduce a scenario where a user can define a "community" by providing a small number of example accounts that are used to train a system for retrieving similar users. Note that our use of the term "community" differs from other online contexts, where members explicitly self-identify with a community (e.g. by joining a discussion forum or using a specific hashtag). The community is in the eye of the user issuing the query.

We frame the task of community membership detection as a retrieval problem. A small set of representative accounts selected by the user forms the query, and the system retrieves additional community members from a large index of accounts. The task is loosely related to entity set expansion (Pantel et al., 2009). We make no assumptions about the type of communities that can be handled, and no labeled data is available other than the query. Because the training set (query) is minimal, unsupervised learning is useful for the text representation. We propose the proxy task of person re-identification for learning a user embedding, where the goal is for two embeddings from the same user to be closer to each other than to the embedding of a random user. The hypothesis is that a representation useful for detecting similarities between posts from the same person made at different times will also do well at identifying similarities between people in the same community. This hypothesis stems from observations that people with shared interests often talk about topics related to these interests, and that they tend to have shared jargon and other similarities in language use (Nguyen and Rosé, 2011; Danescu-Niculescu-Mizil et al., 2013; Tran and Ostendorf, 2016).

In this paper, we demonstrate experimentally that the re-identification proxy task is useful with simple models that are suited to the retrieval scenario, and present analyses showing that the approach learns to emphasize words associated with individual interests and polarizing issues.

2 Model

The model for community detection includes: i) a mapping from a user's text (a collection of tweets) to a k-dimensional embedding, and ii) a binary classifier for detecting whether a candidate user belongs to the target community. The novel con-

595

Proceedings of NAACL-HLT 2018, pages 595–601
New Orleans, Louisiana, June 1 - 6, 2018. ©2018 Association for Computational Linguistics

tribution of the work is the proxy re-identification task for learning the user embedding.

User Embedding Model. The mapping from text to an embedding could leverage any document-level representation. We focus on a simple weighted bag-of-words neural model for direct comparison to other popular methods, motivated by the fact that many virtual communities form around shared interests in particular topics. Specifically, let $c_{p,i}$ denote the number of times person p uses word $v_i \in V$, where V is the vocabulary, and $w_{p,i} = \log(c_{p,i} + 1)$ be the log-scaled word count. Then the user embedding is

$$u_p = \frac{w_p^T \mathbf{E}}{||w_p^T \mathbf{E}||} \qquad (1)$$

where $w_p = [w_{p,1} \cdots w_{p,|V|}]$ and $\mathbf{E} \in \Re^{|V| \times k}$ is the matrix of word embeddings.

Person Re-identification Learning. The embedding matrix $\mathbf{E}$ is learned using a person re-identification objective that encourages embeddings from the same person to be closer than embeddings from different people. We build on the triplet loss function taken from Schroff et al. (2015) used to train a face recognition system. Specifically:

$$\mathbf{E} = \underset{\mathbf{E}}{\operatorname{argmin}} \sum_{p_1, p_2 \in \mathcal{P}} \operatorname{cost}(p_1, p_2), \qquad (2)$$

$$\operatorname{cost}(p_1, p_2) = (1 + \operatorname{d}(u_{p_1^1}, u_{p_1^2}) - \operatorname{d}(u_{p_1^1}, u_{p_2^1}))^+,$$

xwhere $\operatorname{d}(x, y)$ is the cosine distance between x and y. $u_{p_1^1}$ and $u_{p_1^2}$ are embeddings made from distinct subsets of a single person's Tweets, and $u_{p_2^1}$ is an embedding made from a subset of another person's Tweets. In practice, we estimate the loss function randomly sampling triplets (p_1^1, p_1^2, p_2^1) from a large training set.

Classifier. A logistic regression model with L2 regularization is used for the classifier, because it is simple but powerful and our scenario has little training data. Simplicity is important because the classifier should be trainable in real-time after receiving the query. The classifier objective is to discriminate the embeddings from the users in the query from a set of user embeddings from the general collection. For the i-th user, let $y_i \in \{0, 1\}$ be the binary label indicating whether the user belongs to a particular community and u_i be the user

embedding. The logistic regression model computes the probability that the user belongs to the community according to:

$$p(y_i = 1 | u_i) = \sigma(w^T u_i + b), \qquad (3)$$

where $\sigma(x) = 1/(1 - e^{-x})$. During evaluation, the users in the index are ranked according to the maximum log probability ratio

$$\underset{i}{\operatorname{argmax}} \log \frac{p(y_i = 1 | u_i)}{p(y_i = 0 | u_i)} = \underset{i}{\operatorname{argmax}} \, w^T u_i. \quad (4)$$

Because the classifier is linear, we can quickly retrieve the top matching users from the index using approximate nearest-neighbor search (Kushilevitz et al., 2000). The technique is scalable up to hundreds of millions of users and beyond.

3 Data

All data was collected using the Twitter API.[1] We used 1,035 randomly selected items from the list of trending topics in the USA during the period April-June 2017 to query for users and collected their most recent 2,000 tweets. Example trending topics are #Quantico, RonaldoCristiano, and #MayDay2017. (The full list is available with the data.) Each user had at least one Tweet that mentioned a trending topic but their other Tweets could be on any topic.

We refer to this collection as the "general population," because it was not targeted towards any particular community. In total, we collected around 80,000 such users and used roughly 36,000 for learning user embeddings, 1,000 for learning the community classifiers, and 43,000 for evaluation. The text is mostly in English, but some of it is in Spanish, French, or other languages. A list of the tweet IDs is available.[2]

To support evaluation with the community detection task, we conducted a second collection (contemporaneous with the first) targeting members that we had identified as belonging to one of 16 communities (Table 2). To define a "community," volunteers manually selected a set of users that fit with a theme that they had familiarity with. Thus, the specific 16 communities were determined based on themes of interest to the authors and their friends and colleagues, where we could

---

[1] http://developer.twitter.com/en/docs/api-reference-index
[2] http://github.com/ajaech/twittercommunities

be reasonably confident about membership decisions. In addition, we tried to avoid themes that might be biased towards well-known celebrities, and we made an effort to have diversity in the characteristics of the communities. The communities were selected to span a range of topics, sizes (6-130 accounts), individuals vs. organizations, and other characteristics. A few of the communities are comprised of organizations rather than individuals such as the high school drama departments and the Pittsburgh food truck communities. (The community names are invented by the authors for purposes of describing the data in this paper; they are not part of the retrieval task.)

The text is lower-cased and some punctuation is removed using regular expressions. Words are formed by splitting on white space. While this strategy will not work for languages that do not delimit words by spaces, these make up a negligible portion of the data. A 174k vocabulary was created by extracting the unique types that were seen in the tweets from the general population, as well as selected bigrams extracted using the open source Gensim library using a point-wise mutual information criteria (Řehůřek and Sojka, 2010). The vocabulary included roughly 49k bigrams, 36k usernames and 17k hashtags. Usernames, hashtags, and URLs are not treated specially and can be part of the vocabulary just like any other word if they occur frequently enough.

4 Experiments

4.1 Experiment Configuration

The experiments involved comparing different methods of learning user embeddings, all with a weighted bag-of-words modeling assumption:

- Weighted word2vec (W2V) using default[3] skip-gram training (Mikolov et al., 2013);
- Latent Dirichlet allocation (LDA) (Blei et al., 2003), using default settings from the Scikit Learn library (Pedregosa et al., 2011);
- Person re-identification with random initialization (RE-ID); and
- Person re-identification with W2V initialization (RE-ID, W2V init).

Both count-weighted W2V and LDA have been used as unsupervised representations in Twitter

---

[3]The default configuration uses a window of ± 7 words. We also tried using a window of 50 words, which roughly matches the context used in other methods, but community detection performance was significantly worse.

classification tasks, as noted in Section 5. Default configurations are used because there is insufficient data to have a separate validation set.

For all methods, the same vocabulary, final dimension (128), unit vector normalization strategy, and logistic regression model training were used. The embeddings are trained on the 36k user general data, randomly sampling pairs of users p_1 and p_2 and then sampling 50 tweets at a time without replacement to create $u_{p_1^1}$, $u_{p_1^2}$, and $u_{p_2^1}$. The logistic regression models are trained on the 1K user general training pool, using the 50 most recent tweets for each user. Because there are so few labeled examples for most communities, training and evaluation is done using a leave-one-out strategy with the positive samples but including all of the 1K negative samples. For each of the N classifiers (corresponding to N labeled samples), the test set is the left-out positive example and the 43K general user test pool. Also because of training limitations, there is no tuning of the regularization weight; the default weight of 1.0 is used. Tuning may be useful given a collection of training and testing communities. Performance is averaged over the N classifiers (corresponding to the N labeled samples). Two evaluation criteria are used: a retrieval metric (inverse mean reciprocal rank or 1/MRR) (Voorhees et al., 1999) and a detection metric (area under the curve or AUC).

4.2 Results

Table 1 shows retrieval results averaged across all communities. The RE-ID model outperforms the W2V and LDA baselines for both criteria, with substantial gains in 1/MRR (lower is better). Further, the version of RE-ID initialized with word2vec did better than the one that was initialized randomly even though the randomly initialized version was trained for twice as long.

Strategy	AUC	1/MRR
W2V	93.9	846
LDA	95.0	501
RE-ID (rand. init)	98.0	24
RE-ID (W2V init)	**98.5**	**12**

Table 1: Performance of different model variants.

A breakdown of the best model performance by community is given in Table 2. Sample size does not seem to be a good indicator of performance: the two smallest communities (Cartoonists, Fresno City Council) had the worst and one of the best results, respectively. Anecdotally, we observed that the sample of cartoonists were more likely to Tweet about topics outside their main interest (e.g., politics or sports). We hypothesize that the diversity of interests of the members of a community affects the difficulty of the retrieval task, but our test set is too small to confirm this hypothesis.

Community	Size	1/MRR
Cartoonists	8	58.1
Chess Stars	14	5.4
Conan Show Writers	12	4.7
Fashion Commentators	11	8.3
Fresno City Council	6	3.0
Hedge Fund Managers	11	25.7
H.S Drama Departments	18	2.3
Mathematicians	11	32.6
NLP Researchers	50	4.9
Pittsburgh Food Trucks	15	3.3
Police Dogs	16	2.7
Professional Economists	11	3.6
SCOTUS Reporters[4]	16	1.9
The Stranger Reporters[5]	11	8.3
Ultimate Frisbee Players	130	6.7
Ultramarathon Runners	28	14.6

Table 2: W2V+RE-ID results by community

These results may underestimate performance, because there is a chance that some users in the general population test data may actually belong to one or more of our test communities, i.e. there could be mislabeled data. To assess the potential impact, we manually checked the top ten false positives for each community for mislabeled users. We did discover some mislabeled examples for the economist, hedge fund manager, and ultramarathon runner communities. For the most part, the top ranked users from the general population tended to be people from related communities. For example, the top false ultimate frisbee users contained people who wrote about their participation in tournaments for other sports such as soccer.

4.3 Analysis

The finding that the W2V-initialized RE-ID model is significantly better than W2V raises the question: how do the embeddings learned by the re-identification task differ from the ones learned by the word2vec objective? To investigate this, we looked at the 1,000 words in the RE-ID model with embeddings that were farthest (in Euclidean distance) from its word2vec initialization. These top words disproportionately contain Twitter user handles, so some social network structure is captured. Using agglomerative clustering, we found groups of words that centered around frequent words used in particular regions (foreign words, dialects) or cultures (sociolects), associated with hobbies or interests (specific sports, music genres, gaming), or polarizing topics (political parties, controversial issues). At least one of the top tokens was the username of an account later identified as being sponsored by the Russian government to spread propaganda during the United States presidential election, e.g., "ten_gop" in Table 4 of the Appendix.

We also looked at which communities are closest in the embedding space. We represent a community with the average of the member embeddings and use a normalized cosine distance for similarity. The two nearest neighbors are Mathematicians and NLP researchers, which are also close to the next two nearest neighbors, Hedge Fund Managers and Professional Economists.

To interpret what the model as a whole captured, we found the top scoring tweets for each held-out user (creating an embedding for a single tweet) according to the logistic regression model. Representative examples include "recurrent neural_network grammars simplified and analyzed" for NLP Researchers, and "we're looking_forward to seeing you opening_night may 24th love the cast of high_school musical" for High School Drama clubs. Examples for additional communities are included in the appendix. The results provide insight into the community member identification decision.

5 Related Work

One notion of community detection involves discovering different communities within a collection of users (Chen et al., 2009; Di, 2011; Fani et al., 2017). A related task is making recommendations of friends or people to follow (Gupta et al., 2013; Yu et al., 2016). In contrast, our task involves identifying other members of a community, which is specified in terms of a set of example users. These tasks use different learning frameworks (our work uses supervised learning), but the features (social network and/or text cues)

---

[4]People who write news articles about the Supreme Court of the United States.

[5]The Stranger is a small weekly newspaper.

are relevant across tasks. Our task is perhaps more similar to using social media text to predict author characteristics such as personality (Golbeck et al., 2011), gang membership (Wijeratne et al., 2016), geolocation (Han et al., 2014), political affiliation (Makazhanov et al., 2014), occupational class (Preoţiuc-Pietro et al., 2015), and more. Again, a commonality across tasks is the frequent use of unsupervised representations of textual features.

In representing text, a common assumption is that community language reflects topical interests, so representations aimed at topic modeling have been used, including LDA (Pennacchiotti and Popescu, 2011) and tf-idf weighted word2vec embeddings (Boom et al., 2016; Wijeratne et al., 2016). Yu et al. (2016) compute a user embedding by averaging tweet embeddings. Other work investigates methods for learning embeddings that integrate text and social network (graph or text-based) features (Benton et al., 2016).

The work closest to ours is by Fani et al. (2017), which learns embeddings that are close for like-minded users, where like-minded pairs are identified by a deterministic algorithm that leverages timing of related posts. Our approach requires no additional heuristics for defining user similarity, but instead relies on an objective that maximizes self-similarity and minimizes similarity to other users randomly sampled from a large general pool.

Our person re-identification proxy task makes use of the triplet loss used to learn person embeddings for face recognition (Schroff et al., 2015). In image processing, person re-identification refers to the task of tracking people who have left the field of view of one camera and are later seen by another camera (Bedagkar-Gala and Shah, 2014). It is different from our proxy task and the methods are not the same.

6 Conclusion

In summary, this paper defines a task of community member retrieval based on their tweets, introduces a person re-identification task to allow community definition with a small number of examples, and shows that that the method gives very good results compared to word2vec and LDA baselines. Analyses show that the user embeddings learned efficiently represent user interests. The text embeddings are largely complementary to the social network features used in other studies, so performance gains can be expected from feature combination. While our experiments use a bag-of-words representation, as in most related work, the re-identification training objective proposed here can easily be used with other methods for deriving document embeddings, e.g. (Le and Mikolov, 2014; Kim, 2014).

Acknowledgements

The authors thank the anonymous reviewers for their feedback and helpful suggestions.

References

Apurva Bedagkar-Gala and Shishir Shah. 2014. A survey of approaches and trends in person re-identification. *Image and Vision Computing*, 32(4):270–216.

Adrian Benton, Raman Arora, and Mark Dredze. 2016. Learning multiview embeddings of Twitter users. In *Proc. ACL*, volume 2, pages 14–19.

David Blei, Andrew Ng, and Michael Jordan. 2003. Latent dirichlet allocation. *Journal of Machine Learning Research*, 3:993–1022.

Cedric De Boom, Steven Van Canneyt, Thomas Demeester, and Bart Dhoedt. 2016. Representation learning for very short texts using weighted word embedding aggregation. *Pattern Recognition Letters*, 80:150–156.

Jiyang Chen, Osmar R. Zaïane, and Randy Goebel. 2009. Local community identification in social networks. In *International Conference on Advances in Social Network Analysis and Mining*, pages 237–242.

Cristian Danescu-Niculescu-Mizil, Robert West, Dan Jurafsky, Jure Leskovec, and Christopher Potts. 2013. No country for old members: User lifecycle and linguistic change in online communities. In *Proc. WWW*.

Ying Di. 2011. Community detection: topological vs. topical. *Journal of Informatics*, 5(4):489–514.

Hossein Fani, Ebrahim Bagheri, and Weichang Du. 2017. Temporally like-minded user community identification through neural embeddings. In *Proc. ACM Conference on Information and Knowledge Management*, pages 577–586.

Jennifer Golbeck, Cristina Robles, Michon Edmondson, and Karen Turner. 2011. Predicting personality from twitter. In *Privacy, Security, Risk and Trust (PASSAT) and 2011 IEEE Third Inernational Conference on Social Computing (SocialCom), 2011 IEEE Third International Conference on*, pages 149–156. IEEE.

Pankaj Gupta, Ashish Goel, Jimmy Lin, Aneesh Sharma, Dong Wang, and Reza Zadeh. 2013. Wtf: The who to follow service at Twitter. In *Proc. WWW*, pages 505–514. ACM.

Bo Han, Paul Cook, and Timothy Baldwin. 2014. Text-based Twitter user geolocation prediction. *Journal of Artificial Intelligence Research*, 49:451–500.

Yoon Kim. 2014. Convolutional neural networks for sentence classification. In *Proc. EMNLP*, pages 1746–1751.

Eyal Kushilevitz, Rafail Ostrovsky, and Yuval Rabani. 2000. Efficient search for approximate nearest neighbor in high dimensional spaces. *SIAM Journal on Computing*, 30(2):457–474.

Quo Le and Tomas Mikolov. 2014. Distributed representations of sentences and documents. In *Proc. ICML*, pages 3104–3112.

Aibek Makazhanov, Davood Rafiei, and Muhammad Waqar. 2014. Predicting political preference of twitter users. *Social Network Analysis and Mining*, 4(1):1–15.

Tomas Mikolov, Ilya Sutskever, Kai Chen, Greg S Corrado, and Jeff Dean. 2013. Distributed representations of words and phrases and their compositionality. In *Proc. NIPS*, pages 3111–3119.

Dong Nguyen and Carolyn P. Rosé. 2011. Language use as a reflection of socialization in online communities. In *Proceedings of the Workshop on Languages in Social Media*, LSM '11, pages 76–85. Association for Computational Linguistics.

Patrick Pantel, Eric Crestan, Arkady Borkovsky, Ana-Maria Popescu, and Vishnu Vyas. 2009. Web-scale distributional similarity and entity set expansion. In *Proc. EMNLP*, pages 938–947. Association for Computational Linguistics.

F. Pedregosa, G. Varoquaux, A. Gramfort, V. Michel, B. Thirion, O. Grisel, M. Blondel, P. Prettenhofer, R. Weiss, V. Dubourg, J. Vanderplas, A. Passos, D. Cournapeau, M. Brucher, M. Perrot, and E. Duchesnay. 2011. Scikit-learn: Machine learning in Python. *Journal of Machine Learning Research*, 12:2825–2830.

Marco Pennacchiotti and Ana-Maria Popescu. 2011. A machine learning approach to Twitter user classification. In *ICWSM*.

Daniel Preoţiuc-Pietro, Vasileios Lampos, and Nikolaos Aletras. 2015. An analysis of the user occupational class through Twitter content. In *Proc. ACL-IJCNLP*, pages 1754–1764.

Radim Řehůřek and Petr Sojka. 2010. Software framework for topic modelling with large corpora. In *Proceedings of the LREC 2010 Workshop on New Challenges for NLP Frameworks*, pages 45–50, Valletta, Malta. ELRA. http://is.muni.cz/publication/884893/en.

Florian Schroff, Dmitry Kalenichenko, and James Philbin. 2015. Facenet: A unified embedding for face recognition and clustering. In *Proc. CVPR*, pages 815–823.

Trang Tran and Mari Ostendorf. 2016. Characterizing the language of online communities and its relation to community reception. In *Proc. EMNLP*.

Ellen M Voorhees et al. 1999. The TREC-8 question answering track report. In *Trec*, volume 99, pages 77–82.

Sanjaya Wijeratne, Lakshika Balasuriya, Derek Doran, and Amit Sheth. 2016. Word embeddings to enhance Twitter gang member profile identification. In *Proc. IJCAI Workshop on Semantic Machine Learning*.

Yang Yu, Xiaojun Wan, and Xinjie Zhu. 2016. User embedding for scholarly microblag recommendation. In *Proc. ACL*, pages 449–453.

Appendix: Supplementary Tables

Community	Selected Tweet
Chess Stars	@chesscom yep karpov well_done twittersphere
Professional Economists	#china real_estate as long as liquidity remains ample this will continue
Fashion Commentators	rihanna's fenty corp creative_director jahleel weaver styles the collection on 3 muses
Fresno City Council	gr8 resource developed by our local @citdfresno on how to export @city-offresno @fresnocountyedc lee_ann eager
High School Drama	we're looking_forward to seeing you opening_night may 24th love the cast of high_school musical
Mathematicians	forms of knowledge of advanced mathematics for teaching (i wrote a thing)
NLP Researchers	recurrent neural_network grammars simplified and analyzed
Police Dogs	when a trained police dog is placed with another handler they complete a re handling course to be licensed normally 2_weeks
SCOTUS Reporters	as supreme_court throws out two gop-drawn congressional_districts as unconstitutional racial gerrymanders
Ultramarathon Runners	we're covering the lake sonoma 50 mile live on saturday tell your friends spread the word and get ready

Table 3: Top tweets for selected communities. Underscore is used to join bigrams.

Interpretation	Top Words
Languages & Dialects	• à, ça, j'ai, quand, c'est, avec, sur, dans_le
	• é, não, melhor, tem, mesmo, só, mais, hoje, uma, tá, já
	• es_un, más, jugar, en_el, maduro, jajajaja
	• bruh, dawg, @iamakademiks, black_women, @chancetherapper, lmaooo, y'all, tryna
Sports	• @mlb, baseball, bullpen, @angels, mets, mlb
	• arsenal, mate, liverpool, @manutd, mourinho, #mufc
	• @nhl, hockey, nhl, leafs, @nhlblackhawks, @nhlonnbcsports
	• xd, @playoverwatch, #ps4share, anime, @keemstar, overwatch, twitch, @nintendoamerica, gaming
Music	• @niallofficial, @harry_styles, @louis_tomlinson, @ashton5sos, @shawnmendes, @ethandolan, @graysondolan, @michael5sos, @danisnotonfire
Political	• @indivisibleteam #resist, #trumpcare, @ezlusztig, @kurteichenwald, @georgetakei, @sarahkendzior, @repadamschiff, @malcolmnance, @lawrence
	• @mitchellvii, @prisonplanet, @realjameswoods, @jackposobiec, @bfraser747, @cernovich, @ten_gop, #maga
Other	• tories, labour, corbyn, #auspol, tory, mum, nhs, lads scotland

Table 4: Clusters of words that change the most between Word2Vec and the re-identification objective.

Cross-Domain Review Helpfulness Prediction based on Convolutional Neural Networks with Auxiliary Domain Discriminators

Cen Chen[1], Yinfei Yang[2], Jun Zhou[1], Xiaolong Li[1], Forrest Sheng Bao[3]

[1]Ant Financial Services Group, Hangzhou, China
[2]1600 Amphitheatre Pkwy, Mountain View, CA 94043 *
[3]Iowa State University, Ames, IA 50011
{chencen.cc, jun.zhoujun, xl.li}@antfin.com
{yangyin7, forrest.bao}@gmail.com

Abstract

With the growing amount of reviews in e-commerce websites, it is critical to assess the helpfulness of reviews and recommend them accordingly to consumers. Recent studies on review helpfulness require plenty of labeled samples for each domain/category of interests. However, such an approach based on close-world assumption is not always practical, especially for domains with limited reviews or the "out-of-vocabulary" problem. Therefore, we propose a convolutional neural network (CNN) based model which leverages both word-level and character-based representations. To transfer knowledge between domains, we further extend our model to jointly model different domains with auxiliary domain discriminators. On the Amazon product review dataset, our approach significantly outperforms the state of the art in terms of both accuracy and cross-domain robustness.

1 Introduction

Product reviews significantly help consumers finalize their purchasing decisions. With online reviews being ubiquitous, it is critical to examine the quality of reviews and present consumers more useful information. Both academia and industry have drawn close attention to the task of review helpfulness prediction (Liu et al., 2017a; Yang et al., 2015, 2016; Martin and Pu, 2014).

Recent studies on review helpfulness prediction have been shown effective by using hand-crafted features. For example, semantic features like LIWC, INQUIRER, and GALC (Yang et al., 2015; Martin and Pu, 2014), aspect- (Yang et al., 2016) and argument-based (Liu et al., 2017a) features. However, those methods require a large amount of labeled samples which is not always practical and yields models limited to product domains/categories of interests. For example, the

"Electronics" category used in our experiment from Amazon.com Review Dataset (McAuley and Leskovec, 2013) has more than 354k labeled reviews, while the "Watches" category has under 10k. For domains with limited data, labeled samples may be too few to build good estimators and the "out-of-vocabulary" (OOV) problem is often observed.

To alleviate the aforementioned issues, in this work, we propose an end-to-end approach for review helpfulness prediction requiring no prior knowledge nor manual feature crafting. In recent years, convolutional neural networks (CNNs), able to extract deep features from raw text contents, have demonstrated remarkable results in many tasks of natural language processing, for its high efficiency and performance comparable to Recurrent Neural Networks (RNNs) (Kim, 2014; Zhang et al., 2015). We thus employ CNNs as the basis of this work. As character-level representations are notably beneficial for alleviating the OOV problem for tasks such as text classification and machine translation (Ballesteros et al., 2015; Ling et al., 2015; Kim et al., 2016; Lee et al., 2017), we specifically enrich the word-level representation of CNNs by adding character-based representation. Experiments show that our CNN-based method significantly outperforms those using hand-crafted features and yields better results than the ensemble models.

To tackle the problem of insufficient data in some domains, we develop a cross-domain transfer learning (TL) approach to leverage knowledge from a domain with sufficient data. It is worth noting that, existing studies on this task only focus on a single product category or largely ignore the inter-domain correlations. Previous works also show that some features are domain-specific while others are sharable across domains. For example, image quality features are only useful for categories covering products like cameras (Yang et al.,

---

* Yinfei Yang is now with Google.

Proceedings of NAACL-HLT 2018, pages 602–607
New Orleans, Louisiana, June 1 - 6, 2018. ©2018 Association for Computational Linguistics

2016), while semantic features and argument-based features usually work for all domains (Yang et al., 2015; Liu et al., 2017a). Thus it is important for a TL approach to learn shared features for different domains. A typical TL model uses both a shared neural network (NN) and domain-specific NNs to derive shared and domain-specific features (Ganin et al., 2016; Taigman et al., 2017). Recently, Liu et al. (2017b) and Chen et al. (2017) apply adversarial loss and domain discriminators to specific shared models using RNNs for text classification and word segmentation tasks, respectively. Inspired by them, we study the cross-domain review helpfulness task with both adversarial loss and domain discriminators in a specific shared framework.

In a nutshell, our main novelty is in the first end-to-end cross-domain model for review helpfulness prediction. Our model consists of two components: a feature transformation network (CNN) to represent the input reviews and a transfer learning module to adapt domain knowledge. In addition, shared and specific-shared features are confined with adversarial and domain discrimination losses. Extensive experiments show that our model is able to transfer knowledge between domains, and outperforms the state of the arts.

The remainder of the paper is organized as follows. Section 2 formally defines the problem and presents our model. Section 3 illustrates the effectiveness of the proposed model in the experiments. Section 4 presents related work, and finally Section 5 concludes our paper.

2 Model

We define review helpfulness prediction as a regression task that predicts the helpfulness score of a given review. The ground truth of helpfulness is determined using the "a of b approach": a of b users think a review is helpful.

Formally, we consider a cross-domain review helpfulness prediction task where we have a set of labeled reviews from a source domain and a target domain. We seek to transfer knowledge from a source domain with adequate data to train a better model for a target domain, which has relatively insufficient amount of data. For a review $\mathbf{X}$, our goal is to predict its helpfulness score y.

As shown in Figure 1, our base model is a multi-granularity CNN, which combines both word-level and character-level representations.

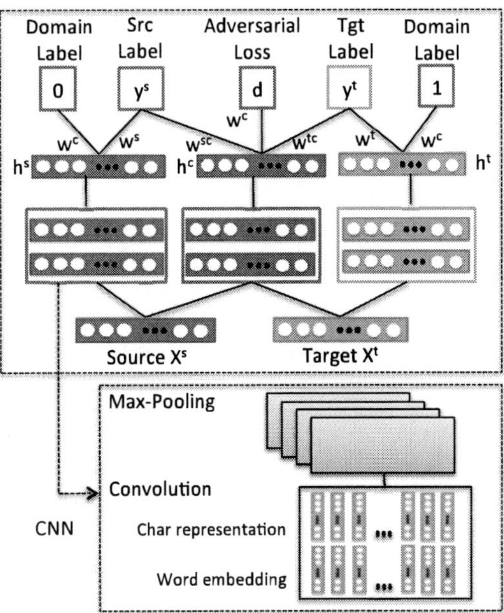

Figure 1: Our proposed end-to-end cross-domain model for review helpfulness prediction.

2.1 CNN with Character Representations

In many applications, such as text classification (Bojanowski et al., 2017) and machine reading comprehension (Seo et al., 2016), it is beneficial to enrich word embeddings with subword information. Inspired by that, we use a character embedding layer to enrich word representations.

Let $\mathbf{X}$ be a review, consisting of a sequence of words $(x_1, x_2, \ldots, x_m)$. Following the CNN model in (Kim, 2014), for words in a review $\mathbf{X}$, we first lookup the embeddings of all words $(\mathbf{e}_1, \mathbf{e}_2, \ldots, \mathbf{e}_m)$ from an embedding matrix $\mathbf{E} \in \mathbb{R}^{|\mathcal{V}| \times l}$ where $|\mathcal{V}|$ is the vocabulary size and l is the embedding dimension.

The characters of the i-th word x_i are embedded into vectors and then fed into a convolutional layer and a max-pooling layer to obtain a fixed-sized vector $\text{CharEmb}(x_i)$. This vector is concatenated with the original word embedding $\mathbf{e}_i$ to form a new word embedding. This representation is advantageous in two folds: it helps group words with shared subwords, and it alleviates the OOV problem. Hence, we obtain a review's final representation by concatenating the embeddings of words in the review: $\mathbf{e}_X = [\mathbf{e}'_1, \mathbf{e}'_2, \mathbf{e}'_3, \ldots, \mathbf{e}'_m]$ where $\mathbf{e}'_i = \text{CharEmb}(x_i) \oplus \mathbf{e}_i, \forall i \in [1..m]$, $\mathbf{e}'_i$ is a column vector, and $\oplus$ is a stacking operator.

Next, we stack two 2-D convolutional layers

and two 2-D max-pooling layers on the matrix $\mathbf{e}_X$ to obtain the hidden representation $\mathbf{h}_X$. Multiple filters are used here. For each filter, we obtain a hidden representation:

$$\mathbf{g}_f = \text{MaxPool}(\text{Conv}(\mathbf{e}_X, \text{filterSize} = [f, l, c]))$$

where $f \in \{2, 3, 4, 5\}$ is window size, l is embedding dimension, c is channel size, $\text{Conv}(\cdot)$ represents a convolution layer, $\text{MaxPool}(\cdot)$ is a max-pooling layer. All the representations are then concatenated to form the final representation $\mathbf{h}_X$, i.e., $\mathbf{h}_X = [\mathbf{g}_2, \mathbf{g}_3, \mathbf{g}_4, \mathbf{g}_5]$.

In all, for each input $\mathbf{X}$, our CNN model outputs a hidden feature representation $h_X = \text{CNN}(\mathbf{X})$.

2.2 Knowledge Transfer with Domain Discriminators

A typical transfer learning framework is to use both a shared neural network and domain-specific neural networks to learn shared and domain-specific features (Liu et al., 2017b). In our model, we use a shared CNN and domain-specific CNNs to derive shared features $\mathbf{h^c}$ and domain-specific features $\mathbf{h^s}$ and $\mathbf{h^t}$. The domain-specific output layers are defined as:

$$\hat{y}^k = \begin{cases} \sigma(\mathbf{W^{sc}h^c} + \mathbf{W^s h^s} + \mathbf{b^s}), & \text{if } k = 0 \\ \sigma(\mathbf{W^{tc}h^c} + \mathbf{W^t h^t} + \mathbf{b^t}), & \text{if } k = 1 \end{cases}$$

where $k \in \{0, 1\}$ is the domain label indicating whether a data instance is from the source domain (i.e., $k = 0$) or the target domain (i.e., $k = 1$). $\mathbf{W^{sc}}$, $\mathbf{W^{tc}}$, $\mathbf{W^s}$, and $\mathbf{W^t}$ are the weights for shared-source, shared-target, source, and target domains respectively, while $\mathbf{b^s}$ and $\mathbf{b^t}$ are the biases for source and target domains respectively. The $\sigma(\cdot)$ represents the sigmoid function.

Recent studies (Ganin et al., 2016; Taigman et al., 2017; Liu et al., 2017b) consider to apply domain discriminators on shared features to prevent domain-specific features from creeping into shared feature space. The main idea of using a domain discriminator $p(d \mid \mathbf{h^c})$ is to predict the domain label d on the shared features $\mathbf{h^c}$. Here the domain discriminator is defined as a fully connected layer with weights $\mathbf{W}^c$ and bias vector $\mathbf{b}^c$:

$$p(d \mid \mathbf{h^c}) = \text{softmax}(\mathbf{W^c h^c} + \mathbf{b^c}).$$

Since the goal is to encourage the shared feature space indiscriminate across two domains, we define the adversarial loss L_{adv} as:

$$L_{adv} = \frac{1}{n} \sum_{i=1}^{n} \sum_{k=0}^{1} p(d = k | \mathbf{h}_i^c) \log p(d = k | \mathbf{h}_i^c).$$

where $\mathbf{h}_i^c$ is the derived shared features from an input $\mathbf{X}_i$.

Furthermore, to encourage the specific feature space to discriminate between different domains, we consider applying domain discrimination losses on the two specific feature spaces. We further add two negative cross-entropy losses, L_s for the source domain and L_t for the target domain:

$$L_s = -\frac{1}{n_s} \sum_{i=1}^{n_s} \sum_{k=0}^{1} \mathbb{I}^{(d_i=k)} \log p(d = k | \mathbf{h}_i^s).$$

$$L_t = -\frac{1}{n_t} \sum_{i=1}^{n_t} \sum_{k=0}^{1} \mathbb{I}^{(d_i=k)} \log p(d = k | \mathbf{h}_i^t).$$

where $\mathbb{I}^{(d_i=k)}$ is an indicator function set to 1 when $d_i = k$ holds, or 0 otherwise, and $\mathbf{h}_i^s$ and $\mathbf{h}_i^t$ are the derived domain-specific features from an input $\mathbf{X}_i$ from source and target domains respectively.

Nevertheless, studies in (Bousmalis et al., 2016; Liu et al., 2017b) show that adding orthogonality constraints on learned shared features $\mathbf{H^c}$ and specific features $\mathbf{H^k}$ for each domain $k \in \{s, t\}$ can help learn domain-invariant features. We thus adopt the constraint $L_{orth} = \sum_{k \in \{s,t\}} \mathbf{H^c}^\top \mathbf{H^k}$ in our model. $\mathbf{H^c}$ and $\mathbf{H^k}$ are obtained by stacking the hidden features from all the input instances.

Finally, we obtain a combined loss as follows:

$$\mathcal{L} = \sum_{\mathbf{k} \in \mathbf{s}, \mathbf{t}} -\frac{1}{n_\mathbf{k}} \sum_{j=1}^{n_\mathbf{k}} \frac{1}{2}(y_j^k - \hat{y}_j^k)^2 + \frac{\lambda_1}{2} L_{adv}$$
$$+ \frac{\lambda_2}{2} L_s + \frac{\lambda_3}{2} L_t + \frac{\lambda_4}{2} L_{orth} + \frac{\lambda_5}{2} ||\mathbf{\Theta}||_F^2.$$

where all λ's are weights for different losses, and $\mathbf{\Theta}$ denotes model parameters.

3 Experiments

Following previous work (Yang et al., 2015, 2016), experiments are done on reviews from five categories of products in Amazon review dataset (McAuley and Leskovec, 2013). Data statistics are summarized in Table 1.

The empirical study is done in two steps. Without TL, Part 1 (Sections 3.1 and 3.2) shows that embedding-based feature of CNN outperforms hand-crafted features. After validating the advantage of the CNN-based model, we demonstrate that our TL approach (introduced in Section 2.2) is more effective in boosting the advantage farther than other TL approaches in Part 2 (Section 3.3). In Part 2, the same CNN-based model is used for all TL approaches.

General category	# of reviews with 5+ votes	Total # of reviews
Watches (Watch)	9,737	68,356
Cellphones (Phone)	18,542	78,930
Outdoor	72,796	510,991
Home	219,310	991,784
Electronics (Elec.)	354,301	1,241,778

Table 1: Amazon reviews from 5 different categories.

The lookup table E is initialized with pre-trained vectors from GloVe (Pennington et al., 2014) by setting $l = 100$. For CNNs, the activation function is ReLU, and the channel size is set to 128. We also set $\lambda_1 = \lambda_2 = \lambda_3 = \lambda_4 = 0.05$, and $\lambda_5 = 0.0008$. AdaGrad (Duchi et al., 2011) is used in training with an initial learning rate of 0.08. Fowllowing the previous work (Yang et al., 2015, 2016), ten-fold cross-validation is performed for all experiments and all the results are evaluated in correlation coefficients between the predicted helpfulness score and the ground truth score computed by "a of b approach" from the dataset.

3.1 Comparison with hand-crafted features

We first compare our base CNN model with regression baselines that use hand-crafted features which are STR, UGR, LIWC, INQUIRER (Yang et al., 2015), and aspect-based feature ASP (Yang et al., 2016), and the vanilla CNN (CNN) in (Kim, 2014). As shown in Table 2, both CNN-based models outperform the baselines, indicating CNN-based models have better expressiveness than these hand-crafted features for this task.

Our CNN-based model outperforms the vanilla CNN based one on relatively small domains (e.g., "Watches", "Cellphones") and achieves comparable results on large ones (e.g., "Electronics"). This is because the OOV problem is severe on small domains and our model with character-level representations can help more on them. In all, our CNN-based method shows better performance compared to the baselines.

	Watch	Phone	Outdoor	Home	Elec.
STR	0.276	0.349	0.277	0.222	0.338
UGR	0.425	0.466	0.412	0.309	0.355
LIWC	0.378	0.464	0.382	0.331	0.400
INQ	0.403	0.506	0.419	0.366	0.405
ASP	0.406	0.437	0.385	0.283	0.406
CNN	0.480	0.562	0.501	0.459	0.524
our CNN	**0.495**	**0.566**	**0.511**	**0.464**	**0.521**

Table 2: Comparison with linguistic features.

3.2 Comparison with ensemble features

We further compare our CNN-based model with two groups of ensemble features: Fusion_1 comprising of STR, UGR, LIWC, and INQUIRER features (Yang et al., 2015), and Fusion_2 further comprising of the ASP feature (Yang et al., 2016). As shown in Table 3.2, our CNN-based model consistently outperforms the models based on ensemble features.

	Watch	Phone	Outdoor	Home	Elec.
Fusion_1	0.488	0.539	0.497	0.432	0.484
Fusion_2	0.493	0.550	0.501	0.436	0.491
our CNN	**0.495**	**0.566**	**0.511**	**0.464**	**0.521**

Table 3: Comparison with ensemble features.

3.3 Comparison with TL models

To evaluate the effectiveness of our transfer learning approach, we compare our full model with three baselines: Src-only that uses only source data, Tgt-only that uses only target data, and TL-S that use both source and target data with the adversarial training as in (Liu et al., 2017b). For TL based approaches, we use the "Electronics" caterory as the source domain and all other categories as target domains.

	Watch	Phone	Outdoor	Home
Src-only	0.471	0.459	0.447	0.365
Tgt-only	0.495	0.566	0.511	0.464
TL-S	0.501	0.564	0.511	0.468
Ours	**0.515**	**0.571**	0.510	**0.472**

Table 4: Comparison of TL models.

According to Table 4, due to the domain shift, Src-only performs worse than Tgt-only. This is intuitive as those domains are related but different. Our model achieves better or comparable results than Tgt-only and TL-S. This supports the benefits of transfer learning and demonstrates the usefulness of adding domain discriminators on both source and target domains.

Last but not the least, our model shows less improvement over Tgt-only when target domain data size increases. For example, our model yields an improvement of 4% over Tgt-only on the smallest domain "Watches." But the improvement drops to 1.7% on the largest domain "Home." To investigate this, we pick the category "Outdoor" as the target domain and track how our TL approach looses its edge as the amount (in terms of percentage in Table 5) of data from the target domain used in training increases. The full set of data from the source domain "Electronics" is constantly used.

	10%	30%	50%	70%	100%
Tgt-only	0.425	0.463	0.475	0.493	0.511
Ours	0.454	0.481	0.491	0.497	0.510
Improve	6.8%	3.7%	3.4%	0.6%	-0.2%

Table 5: Comparison of TL with respect to the amount of training data of the "Outdoor" category.

According to Table 5, the more data from the target domain, the less advantage our approach has over the Tgt-only model. It is more beneficial to leverage knowledge from another relevant domain when there is less data in the target domain. This also demonstrates that our model is able to learn transferable features from a relevant domain to help the task on a target domain which often has limited data.

4 Related Work

Review Helpfulness Prediction: The recent studies on review helpfulness prediction focus on hand-crafted features from the review texts. For example, (Yang et al., 2015) and (Martin and Pu, 2014) examined semantic features like LIWC, INQUIRER, and GALC. Subsequently, aspect- (Yang et al., 2016) and argument-based (Liu et al., 2017a) features are demonstrated to improve the prediction performance. However, these methods rely on sufficient labeled data and may not perform ideally for domains with limited data. To alleviate this issue, we employ Convolutional Neural Networks (CNNs) (Kim, 2014; Zhang et al., 2015) as the base model and further considers character-level representations (Ballesteros et al., 2015; Ling et al., 2015; Kim et al., 2016; Lee et al., 2017).

Transfer Learning: Transfer learning (TL) has been extensively studied in the last decade, interested readers can refer to (Pan and Yang, 2010) for a detailed survey. With the popularity of deep learning, a great amount of Neural Network (NN) based methods are proposed for TL (Yosinski et al., 2014; Wang and Zheng, 2015; Mou et al., 2016; Yang et al., 2017; Liu et al., 2017b). A simple but widely used framework is referred to as *fine-tuning* approaches, which first use the parameters of the well-trained models on the source domain to initialize the model parameters of the target domain, and then fine-tune the parameters based on labeled data in the target domain (Yosinski et al., 2014; Mou et al., 2016). Another typical framework is to use a shared NN to learn shared features for both source and target domains (Mou et al., 2016; Yang et al., 2017; Qiu et al., 2017). On top of that, specific shared framework use both a shared NN and domain-specific NNs to derive shared and domain-specific features (Ganin et al., 2016; Taigman et al., 2017; Yu et al., 2018). However it may not be ideal to separate shared and specific features, recent studies (Ganin et al., 2016; Taigman et al., 2017; Liu et al., 2017b) consider the adversarial networks to learn more robust shared features across domains. Inspired by this, our method adopts adversarial network on the shared features. In the meanwhile, we also use domain discriminators on both source and target features to help learn domain-specific features.

To the best of our knowledge, our work is the first to study cross-domain review helpfulness prediction. Without any hand-crafted features, our CNN-based method achieves better results than the existing approaches.

5 Conclusion

In this work, we proposed a convolutional neural network (CNN) based approach that combines both word- and character-level representations, for review helpfulness prediction. We studied transfer learning for the task and used auxiliary domain discriminators on both shared and specific representations. Experiments showed our CNN-based models outperform the existing approaches. In the near future, we will look at multi-task helpfulness prediction to further transfer knowledge across domains. Meanwhile, it is also worth studying domain correlation in the transfer learning (Yu et al., 2018) or multi-task settings (Qiu et al., 2017).

Acknowledgments

Bao's work in this paper is partially sponsored by National Science Foundation under Grant No. 1616216.

References

Miguel Ballesteros, Chris Dyer, and Noah A. Smith. 2015. Improved transition-based parsing by modeling characters instead of words with lstms. In *EMNLP*. Association for Computational Linguistics, pages 349–359.

Piotr Bojanowski, Edouard Grave, Armand Joulin, and Tomas Mikolov. 2017. Enriching word vectors with subword information. *Transactions of the Association for Computational Linguistics* 5:135–146.

Konstantinos Bousmalis, George Trigeorgis, Nathan Silberman, Dilip Krishnan, and Dumitru Erhan. 2016. Domain separation networks. In *NIPS*. MIT Press, pages 343–351.

Xinchi Chen, Zhan Shi, Xipeng Qiu, and Xuanjing Huang. 2017. Adversarial multi-criteria learning for chinese word segmentation. In *ACL*. Association for Computational Linguistics, pages 1193–1203.

John Duchi, Elad Hazan, and Yoram Singer. 2011. Adaptive subgradient methods for online learning and stochastic optimization. *JMLR* 12(7):2121–2159.

Yaroslav Ganin, Evgeniya Ustinova, Hana Ajakan, Pascal Germain, Hugo Larochelle, François Laviolette, Mario Marchand, and Victor Lempitsky. 2016. Domain-adversarial training of neural networks. *JMLR* 17(59):1–35.

Yoon Kim. 2014. Convolutional neural networks for sentence classification. In *EMNLP*. Association for Computational Linguistics, pages 1746–1751.

Yoon Kim, Yacine Jernite, David Sontag, and Alexander M. Rush. 2016. Character-aware neural language models. In *AAAI*. AAAI Press, pages 2741–2749.

Jason Lee, Kyunghyun Cho, and Thomas Hofmann. 2017. Fully character-level neural machine translation without explicit segmentation. *Transactions of the Association for Computational Linguistics* 5:365–378.

Wang Ling, Isabel Trancoso, Chris Dyer, and Alan W Black. 2015. Character-based neural machine translation. *arXiv preprint arXiv:1511.04586* .

Haijing Liu, Yang Gao, Pin Lv, Mengxue Li, Shiqiang Geng, Minglan Li, and Hao Wang. 2017a. Using argument-based features to predict and analyse review helpfulness. In *EMNLP*. Association for Computational Linguistics, pages 1358–1363.

Pengfei Liu, Xipeng Qiu, and Xuanjing Huang. 2017b. Adversarial multi-task learning for text classification. In *ACL*. Association for Computational Linguistics, pages 1–10.

Lionel Martin and Pearl Pu. 2014. Prediction of Helpful Reviews Using Emotions Extraction. In *AAAI*. AAAI Press, pages 1551–1557.

Julian McAuley and Jure Leskovec. 2013. Hidden factors and hidden topics: understanding rating dimensions with review text. In *RecSys*. ACM, pages 165–172.

Lili Mou, Zhao Meng, Rui Yan, Ge Li, Yan Xu, Lu Zhang, and Zhi Jin. 2016. How transferable are neural networks in nlp applications? In *EMNLP*. Association for Computational Linguistics, pages 479–489.

Sinno Jialin Pan and Qiang Yang. 2010. A survey on transfer learning. *IEEE Transactions on Knowledge and Data Engineering* 22(10):1345–1359.

Jeffrey Pennington, Richard Socher, and Christopher Manning. 2014. Glove: Global vectors for word representation. In *EMNLP*. Association for Computational Linguistics, pages 1532–1543.

Minghui Qiu, Peilin Zhao, Ke Zhang, Jun Huang, Xing Shi, Xiaoguang Wang, and Wei Chu. 2017. A short-term rainfall prediction model using multi-task convolutional neural networks. In *ICDM*. IEEE, pages 395–404.

Min Joon Seo, Aniruddha Kembhavi, Ali Farhadi, and Hannaneh Hajishirzi. 2016. Bidirectional attention flow for machine comprehension. *CoRR* abs/1611.01603.

Yaniv Taigman, Adam Polyak, and Lior Wolf. 2017. Unsupervised cross-domain image generation. *ICLR* .

Dong Wang and Thomas Fang Zheng. 2015. Transfer learning for speech and language processing. In *APSIPA*. IEEE, pages 1225–1237.

Yinfei Yang, Cen Chen, and Forrest Sheng Bao. 2016. Aspect-based helpfulness prediction for online product reviews. In *ICTAI*. IEEE, pages 836–843.

Yinfei Yang, Yaowei Yan, Minghui Qiu, and Forrest Bao. 2015. Semantic analysis and helpfulness prediction of text for online product reviews. In *ACL-IJCNLP*. Association for Computational Linguistics, pages 38–44.

Zhilin Yang, Ruslan Salakhutdinov, and William W Cohen. 2017. Transfer learning for sequence tagging with hierarchical recurrent networks. *ICLR* .

Jason Yosinski, Jeff Clune, Yoshua Bengio, and Hod Lipson. 2014. How transferable are features in deep neural networks? In *NIPS 2014*. MIT Press, pages 3320–3328.

Jianfei Yu, Minghui Qiu, Jing Jiang, Jun Huang, Shuangyong Song, Wei Chu, and Haiqing Chen. 2018. Modelling domain relationships for transfer learning on retrieval-based question answering systems in e-commerce. In *WSDM*. ACM, pages 682–690.

Xiang Zhang, Junbo Zhao, and Yann LeCun. 2015. Character-level convolutional networks for text classification. In *NIPS*. MIT Press, pages 649–657.

Predicting Foreign Language Usage from English-Only Social Media Posts

Svitlana Volkova, Stephen Ranshous,* Lawrence Phillips
Data Sciences and Analytics, National Security Directorate
Pacific Northwest National Laboratory
902 Battelle Blvd, Richland, WA 99354
`firstname.lastname@pnnl.gov`

Abstract

Social media is known for its multi-cultural and multilingual interactions, a natural product of which is code-mixing. Multilingual speakers mix languages they tweet to address a different audience, express certain feelings, or attract attention. This paper presents a large-scale analysis of 6 million tweets produced by 27 thousand multilingual users speaking 12 other languages besides English. We rely on this corpus to build predictive models to infer non-English languages that users speak exclusively from their English tweets. Unlike native language identification task, we rely on large amounts of informal social media communications rather than ESL essays. We contrast the predictive power of the state-of-the-art machine learning models trained on lexical, syntactic, and stylistic signals with neural network models learned from word, character and byte representations extracted from English only tweets. We report that content, style and syntax are the most predictive of non-English languages that users speak on Twitter. Neural network models learned from byte representations of user content combined with transfer learning yield the best performance. Finally, by analyzing cross-lingual transfer – the influence of non-English languages on various levels of linguistic performance in English, we present novel findings on stylistic and syntactic variations across speakers of 12 languages in social media.

1 Introduction

Twitter is known for its diverse multi-cultural and multilingual interactions (Mocanu et al., 2013) where multilingual users play an important bridging role in global social network connectivity (Hale, 2014; Eleta and Golbeck, 2014).

Multilingual speakers often mix languages inside the tweet (e.g., intra-sentential code-switching) or across their tweets (e.g., inter-sentential code-mixing) to express their thoughts or feelings, to address a different audience, to attract attention or emphasize a point (Eldin, 2014; Nguyen and Doğruöz, 2013; Lignos and Marcus, 2013). Hidayat (2013) reported that 45 percent of code-switching on Facebook happened due to lexical need, 40 percent due to the choice of a topic.

This work focuses on inter-sentential code-mixing within multilingual user timelines. The goal of this work is introduce a task of predicting foreign (non-English) languages users speak exclusively from their English informal communications in social media. Unlike L1 identification task (Tetreault et al., 2013), we do not claim that non-English languages are native languages of multilingual speakers in our data. Moreover, we rely on large amounts of real-world communications on Twitter – informal and noisy rather than hundreds of essays generated by ESL learners (targeted student population). We experiment with the largest group of non-English languages analyzed so far.[1] Inspired by earlier work on native language identification (Smith, 2001; Koppel et al., 2005), we hypothesize that lexical, semantic, syntactic and stylistic choices in English portion of multilingual content have different predictive power on inferring non-English languages users speak. For that we first develop linguistic models to test our hypothesis, and then evaluate syntactic and stylistic similarities across speakers of non-English languages using the English portion of their multilingual content in social media. In addition, we contrast the state-of-the-art predic-

---

*This work was performed while the student was an intern at PNNL. Stephen Ranshous is a PhD student at North Carolina State University now.

[1]Multilingual Twitter dataset was acquired using the public Twitter API and analyzed over the period of 09/15 – 01/16. Multilingual user and tweet IDs are available at `http://www.cs.jhu.edu/~svitlana/`

Proceedings of NAACL-HLT 2018, pages 608–614
New Orleans, Louisiana, June 1 - 6, 2018. ©2018 Association for Computational Linguistics

	NON-ENGLISH			ENGLISH	
Lang	**Users**	**Tweets**	**O**	**Tweets**	**E**
Tagalog	11,681	864,344	74	1,199,933	102
Spanish	4,451	406,410	91	661,754	149
Portuguese	2,877	267,935	93	270,386	94
Indonesian	2,360	269,004	114	518,897	220
French	1,555	121,581	78	262,712	169
Korean	907	51,034	56	81,706	90
Italian	765	52,346	68	94,444	123
Hindi	755	50,091	66	104,121	138
German	677	107,426	158	252,954	374
Polish	584	41,577	71	106,177	182
Japanese	528	62,800	118	125,485	238
Russian	195	23,325	119	39,643	203

Table 1: Dataset statistics in terms of the number of users, tweets, and the average number of tweets per user in English (E) and non-English (O) languages.

tive models with neural networks trained on word, character and byte representations, social network interactions, and using transfer learning.

The proposed approach on inferring foreign languages users communicate on Twitter and the detailed analysis on cross-lingual variations have several important implications. Our findings can not only inform models in sociolinguistics and psycholinguistics, but also have broad applications in a variety of natural language processing (NLP) tasks including language identification (Tetreault et al., 2013), author profiling (Volkova et al., 2015) and English as a second language (ESL) error detection (Leacock et al., 2010).

2 Background

Multilinguality in Social Media Multilinguality and code-mixing in social media is the norm rather than an exception. While it has been studied extensively in formal and spoken contexts (Joshi, 1982; Solorio and Liu, 2008; Holmes, 2013), it remains under-examined in social media (Shafie and Nayan, 2013; Bock, 2013; Sihombing and Meisuri, 2014; Androutsopoulos, 2015).

Only a few corpora have been created to support studies on multilinguality and code-switching in informal communications (Cotterell et al., 2014; Maharjan et al., 2015). The majority of work in social media focused on word-level language identification (Solorio et al., 2014; Jain and Bhat, 2014) and automatic prediction of code-switching points (Nguyen and Doğruöz, 2013). Other studies investigated how language groups connect within a network of multilingual users (Eleta and Golbeck, 2014; Kim et al., 2014), the use of code-switched hashtags (Jurgens et al., 2014) and minority languages on Twitter (Nguyen et al., 2015).

Cross-Linguistic Transfer in ESL Texts Recent work by Berzak et al. (2014) measured cross-linguistic transfer using correlations between language similarities estimated from structured features of ESL texts and typological features of native languages. Similar to earlier work on language similarities by Georgi et al. (2010) they used the Word Atlas of Language Structures (WALS) topological features that include phonology, morphology, nominal categories, nominal syntax, verbal categories, word order, simple clauses, complex sentences and lexicon features.

Native Language Identification (L1) on ESL Speakers Earlier work on L1 identification (Koppel et al., 2005; Tsur and Rappoport, 2007; Brooke and Hirst, 2012; Wong and Dras, 2011; Tetreault et al., 2013) focused on identifying L1 in small corpora generated by ESL students. The proposed models relied on classifiers learned from lexical features over characters, words, and parts of speech tags, and the document structure.

Unlike previous work, this paper is a first large-scale study that focuses on cross-lingual syntactic and stylistic variations in informal multilingual communications in social media. We build models to predict non-English languages that users speak exclusively from their tweets in English and discuss cross-linguistic transfer from non-English to English in social media. Moreover, in contrast to earlier work on L1 identification in ESL essays (Tetreault et al., 2013) that reports models learning topical distinctions rather than differences in syntax, we found that stylistic and syntactic choices are predictive of foreign languages users communicate in social media.

3 Multilingual Twitter Dataset

We collected multilingual user timelines using the public Twitter API stream from September 2015 through January 2016. From the set of users who posted during that time, we only sampled users who produced at least 25 tweets in English and 25 tweets in any other language. Tweet-based language detection was obtained using the state-of-the-art language identification algorithm Lui and Baldwin (2011).[2] The resulting user and tweet distributions, the mean and the median number of tweets per user in English (EN) and Other (O) languages are reported in Table 1. In total, our

---

[2] http://support.gnip.com/enrichments/language_detection.html

dataset contains 6,036,085 tweets (3,718,212 in English and 2,317,873 in other languages) produced by 27,335 users who tweet in English and one or more of 12 other languages.[3]

4 Approach

4.1 Non-English Language Prediction

We evaluate the influence of different signals in English tweets on predicting non-English languages the users speak in a classification task. We use several classifiers including Logistic Regression, Random Forest and AdaBoost implemented in scikit-learn (Pedregosa et al., 2011). In addition, we developed a neural network architecture as shown in Figure 1 that relies on word, character and byte representations, social interactions (graph) and transfer learning from a much larger multilingual Twitter corpus. We validate out models using 10-fold cross-validation.

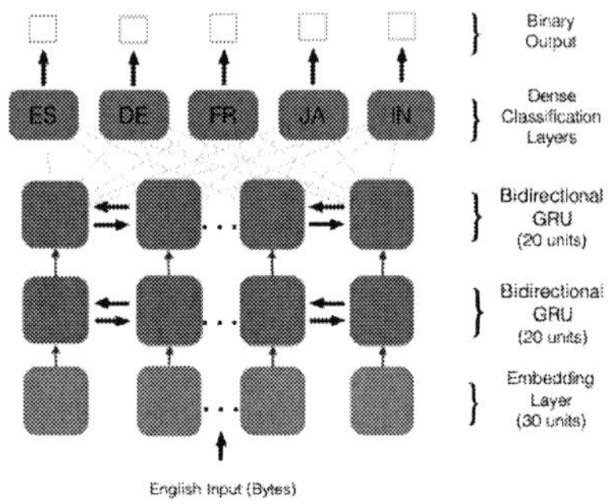

Figure 1: Neural network architecture for predicting non-English languages from English tweets.

For machine learning models, in addition to lexical, phonetic, syntactic and stylistic signals described in Section 4.2, we rely on pre-trained word embeddings – 300-dim Word2Vec (W2V) vectors trained on Google News (News W2V),[4] 100-dim GloVe[5] vectors (Twitter GloVe) trained on 2 billion tweets (Pennington et al., 2014) and Normalized Pointwise Mutual Information (Twitter NPMI) vectors released by Lampos et al. (2014). To construct 50-dim embedding vectors we learned word embeddings using a skip-gram model (Mikolov et al., 2013) from gensim package[6] on a corpus of one million English tweets.

For deep learning models, social network interactions are encoded as one-hot vectors over the vocabulary of `@mentions` similar to (Volkova et al., 2017). For transfer learning, we trained a language model on large Twitter dataset of 450 thousand users who speak 12 non-English languages, and transferred weights to 27,335 users.

4.2 Multilingual Timeline Analysis

Cross-Lingual Stylistic Analysis To measure cross-lingual stylistic similarities in English content (as incorporate stylistic features into our predictive models) we calculate tweet-level and word-level stylistic features that reflect user communication behavior and interaction style similar to (Volkova and Bell, 2017). For example, a style vector includes tweet length in words and characters; proportion of uppercased, elongated e.g., *Yaay, woow* and capitalized words; punctuation, hashtag, mention, url, emoticon and mixed punctuation rate e.g., *???!!!* etc. We tokenized tweets using the Twokenizer (Owoputi et al., 2013) for the majority of languages, except Korean,[7] Japanese,[8] and Hindi.[9]

Cross-Lingual Syntactic Analysis To estimate syntactic variations in English content given other foreign languages the users speak we focus on the part-of-speech use. We convert all English tweets to the corresponding part-of-speech (POS) tag vectors using the state-of-the-art POS tagger trained on Twitter data (Owoputi et al., 2013).

5 Classification Results

Table 2 presents classification results of non-English languages multilingual users speak predicted from their English tweets obtained using machine learning models. We found that tweet content – word embeddings or word ngrams are the most predictive of non-English languages that multilingual users tweet (F1=0.72, 12-way classification). Style is more predictive than syntax (F1=0.66 compared to F1=0.64). As expected, linguistic features – content, syntax and style features significantly outperform the baseline profile features. Logistic Regression and Random Forest models outperform AdaBoost classifier.

---

[3]If a user tweets in more that one foreign language, we predict the most used language.

[4]`https://code.google.com/archive/p/word2vec/`

[5]`http://nlp.stanford.edu/projects/glove/`

[6]`https://radimrehurek.com/gensim/`

`models/word2vec.html`

[7]`https://github.com/twitter/twitter-korean-text`

[8]`https://pypi.python.org/pypi/tinysegmenter`

[9]`http://www.nltk.org/`

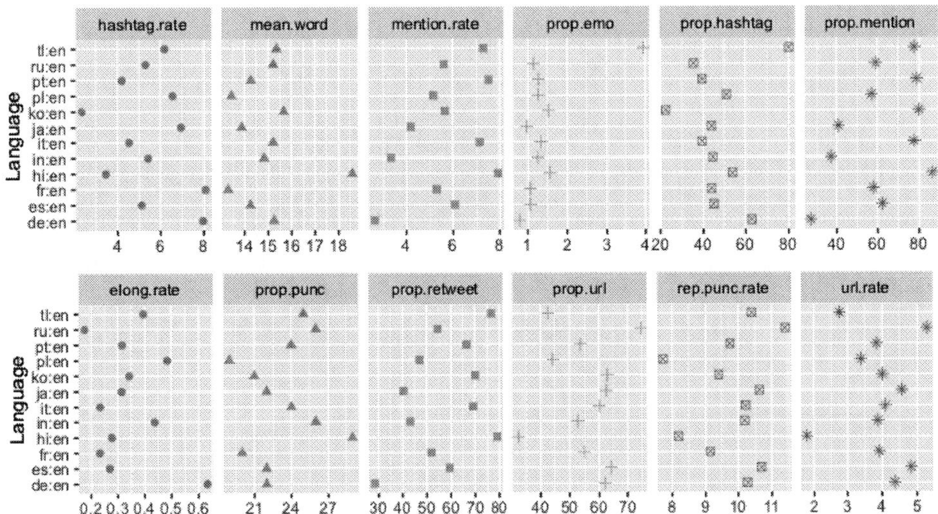

Figure 2: Cross-lingual stylistic variations in the English portion of multilingual content: "prop." is the proportion of tweets, ".rate" – the rate per word (ru:en stands for the English content of Russian speakers).

Feature	AdaBoost	LogReg	RandForest
SEMANTIC: EMBEDDINGS			
Twitter Glove	0.53	0.47	**0.57**
Twitter NPMI	**0.55**	0.53	0.52
News W2V	0.54	0.46	**0.56**
Twitter W2V	0.58	**0.67**	0.54
LEXICAL: WORDS			
Unigrams	0.53	**0.72**	0.64
Trigrams	0.53	**0.72**	0.65
PHONETIC: CHARACTERS			
Bigrams	0.53	0.55	**0.56**
Trigrams	0.42	**0.60**	0.59
Fivegrams	0.52	0.64	**0.66**
SYNTACTIC AND STYLISTIC			
Profile	0.48	0.41	**0.54**
Style	0.53	0.52	**0.66**
Syntax	0.52	**0.64**	0.46

Table 2: Prediction results (macro F1 weighted by support) of non-English languages users speak learned from syntax, style and lexical content in 3.7 million English tweets using AdaBoost, Random Forest, and Logistic Regression models.

Figure 3 presents foreign language classification results using neural network architectures trained on word, character, and byte representations (content), (b) social interactions encoded as one-hot `@mention` vectors (graph), (c) the combination of content and graph vectors, and (d)

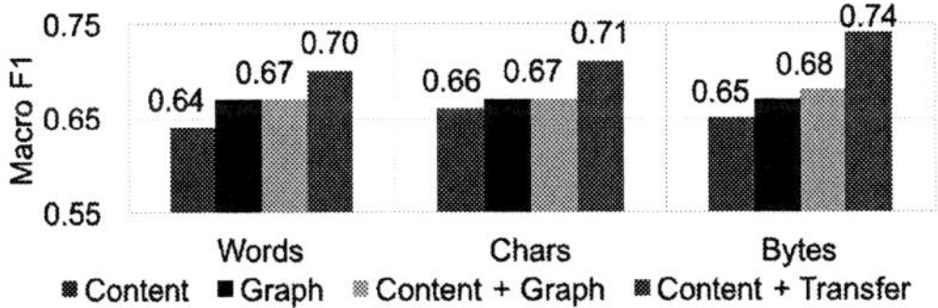

Figure 3: Foreign language classification results obtained using neural network models.

content with embedding weights initialized using transfer learning. Graph representations rely on one-hot encoding vectors of user interactions.

6 Stylistic and Syntactic Analysis

We summarize our novel findings on stylistic similarities in English content across multilingual user timelines in Figure 2 and discuss them below.

Language Complexity Hindi (highly phonetic) speakers generate the longest tweets in English – more than 18 words per tweet on average, but speakers of Polish and French produce English tweets with less than 14 words. Speakers of Hindi use punctuation more in their English tweets ($\geq$ 27% of tweets), whereas speakers of Polish and French use less ($\leq$ 20%).

Language Subjectivity Speakers of Tagalog use significantly more English tweets with emoticons (4%) compared to other languages ($\leq$ 1.5%). Speakers of Russian produce tweets with repeated punctuation the most (12%) whereas speakers of Polish the least (7%) compared to others. Elongations e.g., *Woooow* are used significantly more in English tweets generated by German speakers (0.6%) and less by Russian users ($\leq$ 0.2%).

Communication Behavior Speakers of French and German tend to use more hashtags per word (8%) in their English tweets compared to other languages. In contrast, speakers of Hindi (1%) and Korean (3.5%) use the least. Interestingly, the proportion of English tweets with hashtags is the highest ($\geq$ 80%) for Tagalog speakers. Users who

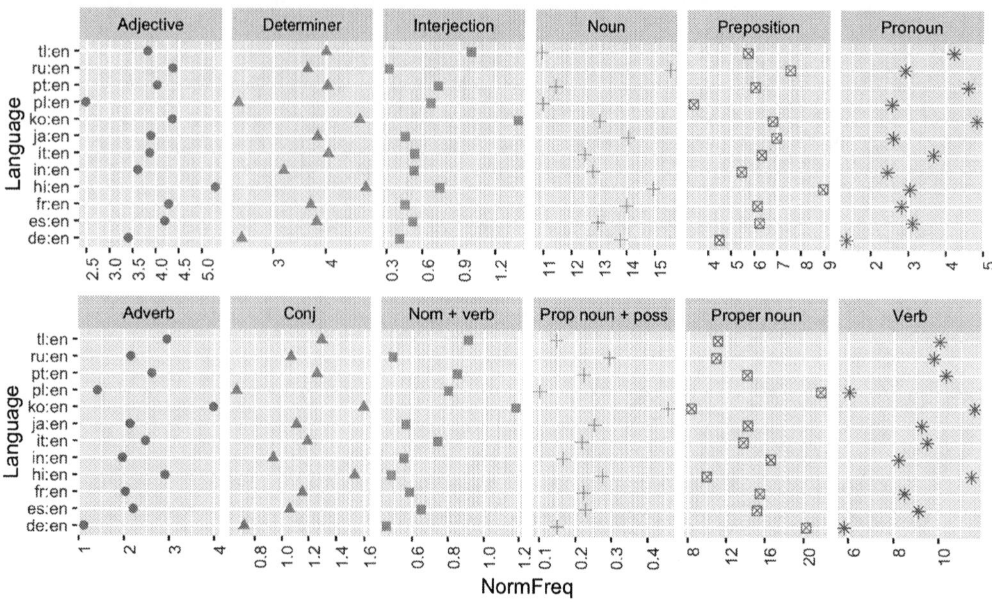

Figure 4: Cross-lingual syntactic variations in the English portion of multilingual content.

speak Tagalog, Portuguese, Italian and Hindi communicate through user mentions in English tweets the most compared to others – more than 80% of the tweets contain mentions. German users produce the least mentions per word ($\leq 3\%$) and the least tweets with mentions ($\leq 30\%$). German speakers retweet the least ($\leq 30\%$), Tagalog and Hindi speakers the most ($\geq 75\%$) in English. Russian speakers share URLs the most – more than 75% of tweets contain URLs in their English content, and Hindi speakers the least.

Syntactic Analysis Figure 4 presents preferences in part-of-speech tags used in English portion of multilingual content generated by speakers of 12 non-English languages. We discuss our findings below focusing on the most common ESL errors for non-English speakers defined by Rozovskaya and Roth (2010) that include determiners, prepositions, adverbs and pronouns.

We found that speakers of Hindi use more **adjectives** compared to other languages in their English content (5%), whereas speakers of German and Polish use less (3.5 and 2.5 percent respectively). We found that speakers of Korean and Hindi use more **determiners** (5%), but speakers of German and Polish use twice less articles. Speakers of Korean use the most interjections e.g., *lol, yaay!* and speakers of Russian use the least. However, speakers of Russian use more **nouns** (16%) compared to other languages and speakers of Tagalog and Polish use the least (11%). Rus-

sian and Hindi speakers generate more **prepositions** (7.5 and 9 percent), and Polish speakers use the least (3%). Korean, Portuguese and Tagalog speakers produce more **pronouns** (4 – 5%), but German speakers generate less (1%) in their English content. Korean users produce more **adverbs** (4%), German and Polish users generate less adverbs (1 – 1.5%). Speakers of Hindi and Korean use more **conjunctions** and **verbs** (1.5% and 12%) but speakers of Polish and German use less than 1% and 6%, respectively.

7 Conclusions

We presented an approach to identify foreign (non-English) language speakers from their English social media posts. We showed that lexical, syntactic and syntactic choices of users in their English posts are the most predictive of other non-English languages they speak. Furthermore, our analysis of cross-lingual transfer in informal communications revealed novel findings on stylistic and syntactic variations across speakers of 12 languages on Twitter.

8 Acknowledgements

This research was conducted at Pacific Northwest National Laboratory, a multiprogram national laboratory operated by Battelle for the U.S. The authors would like to thank Nathan Hodas and Eric Bell for their contribution to this project.

References

Jannis Androutsopoulos. 2015. Networked multilingualism: Some language practices on facebook and their implications. *International Journal of Bilingualism*, 19(2):185–205.

Yevgeni Berzak, Roi Reichart, and Boris Katz. 2014. Reconstructing native language typology from foreign language usage. *Proceedings of the Eighteenth Conference on Computational Language Learning*, pages 21–29.

Zannie Bock. 2013. Cyber socialising: Emerging genres and registers of intimacy among young south african students. *Language Matters*, 44(2):68–91.

Julian Brooke and Graeme Hirst. 2012. Robust, lexicalized native language identification. *Proceedings of COLING*, pages 391–408.

Ryan Cotterell, Adithya Renduchintala, Naomi Saphra, and Chris Callison-Burch. 2014. An algerian Arabic-French code-switched corpus. In *Workshop on Open-Source Arabic Corpora and Corpora Processing Tools Workshop Program*, pages 34–37.

Ahmad Abdel Tawwab Sharaf Eldin. 2014. Socio linguistic study of code switching of the Arabic language speakers on social networking. *International Journal of English Linguistics*, 4(6):78.

Irene Eleta and Jennifer Golbeck. 2014. Multilingual use of Twitter: Social networks at the language frontier. *Computers in Human Behavior*, 41:424–432.

Ryan Georgi, Fei Xia, and William Lewis. 2010. Comparing language similarity across genetic and typologically-based groupings. In *Proceedings of ACL*, pages 385–393.

Scott A Hale. 2014. Global connectivity and multilinguals in the twitter network. In *Proceedings of the SIGCHI Conference on Human Factors in Computing Systems*, pages 833–842.

Taofik Hidayat. 2013. *An Analysis of code switching used by Facebookers*. Ph.D. thesis.

Janet Holmes. 2013. *An introduction to sociolinguistics*. Routledge.

Naman Jain and Riyaz Ahmad Bhat. 2014. Language identification in code-switching scenario. In *Proceedings of the First Workshop on Computational Approaches to Code Switching*, pages 87–93.

Aravind K Joshi. 1982. Processing of sentences with intra-sentential code-switching. In *Proceedings of the 9th conference on Computational Linguistics*, pages 145–150.

David Jurgens, Stefan Dimitrov, and Derek Ruths. 2014. Twitter users# codeswitch hashtags!# moltoimportante# wow. In *Proceedings of the First Workshop on Computational Approaches to Code Switching*, pages 51–61.

Suin Kim, Ingmar Weber, Li Wei, and Alice Oh. 2014. Sociolinguistic analysis of Twitter in multilingual societies. In *Proceedings of the 25th ACM Conference on Hypertext and Social Media*, pages 243–248.

Moshe Koppel, Jonathan Schler, and Kfir Zigdon. 2005. Determining an author's native language by mining a text for errors. In *Proceedings of ACM SIGKDD*, pages 624–628.

Vasileios Lampos, Nikolaos Aletras, Daniel Preoţiuc-Pietro, and Trevor Cohn. 2014. Predicting and characterizing user impact on Twitter. In *Proceedings of EACL*, pages 405–413.

Claudia Leacock, Martin Chodorow, Michael Gamon, and Joel Tetreault. 2010. Automated grammatical error detection for language learners. *Synthesis lectures on Human Language Technologies*, 3(1):1–134.

Constantine Lignos and Mitch Marcus. 2013. Toward web-scale analysis of codeswitching. In *87th Annual Meeting of the Linguistic Society of America*.

Marco Lui and Timothy Baldwin. 2011. Cross-domain feature selection for language identification. In *Proceedings of 5th International Joint Conference on Natural Language Processing*, pages 553–561.

Suraj Maharjan, Elizabeth Blair, Steven Bethard, and Thamar Solorio. 2015. Developing language-tagged corpora for code-switching tweets. In *The 9th Linguistic Annotation Workshop*, pages 72–84.

Tomas Mikolov, Ilya Sutskever, Kai Chen, Greg S Corrado, and Jeff Dean. 2013. Distributed representations of words and phrases and their compositionally. In *Advances in Neural Information Processing Systems (NIPS)*, pages 3111–3119.

Delia Mocanu, Andrea Baronchelli, Nicola Perra, Bruno Gonçalves, Qian Zhang, and Alessandro Vespignani. 2013. The Twitter of babel: Mapping world languages through microblogging platforms. *PloS one*, 8(4):e61981.

Dong Nguyen and A Seza Doğruöz. 2013. Word level language identification in online multilingual communication. In *Proceedings of the 2013 Conference on Empirical Methods in Natural Language Processing*, pages 857–862.

Dong Nguyen, Dolf Trieschnigg, and Leonie Cornips. 2015. Audience and the use of minority languages on twitter. In *Proceedings of ICWSM*, pages 666–669.

Olutobi Owoputi, Brendan O'Connor, Chris Dyer, Kevin Gimpel, Nathan Schneider, and Noah A. Smith. 2013. Improved part-of-speech tagging for online conversational text with word clusters. In *Proceedings of NAACL*, pages 380–390.

Fabian Pedregosa, Gal Varoquaux, Alexandre Gramfort, Vincent Michel, Bertrand Thirion, Olivier Grisel, Mathieu Blondel, Peter Prettenhofer, Ron Weiss, Vincent Dubourg, Jake Vanderplas, Alexandre Passos, David Cournapeau, Matthieu Brucher, Matthieu Perrot, and Edouard Duchesnay. 2011. Scikit-learn: Machine Learning in Python. *Journal of Machine Learning Research*, 12:2825–2830.

Jeffrey Pennington, Richard Socher, and Christopher D Manning. 2014. Glove: Global vectors for word representation. In *Proceedings of EMNLP*, pages 1532–1543.

Alla Rozovskaya and Dan Roth. 2010. Annotating esl errors: Challenges and rewards. In *Proceedings of the 5th Workshop on Innovative Use of NLP for Building Educational Applications*, pages 28–36.

Latisha Asmaak Shafie and Surina Nayan. 2013. Languages, code-switching practice and primary functions of Facebook among university students. *Studies in English Language Teaching*, 1(1):187.

Riris Desnia Sihombing and Meisuri Meisuri. 2014. Code switching in social media Twitter. *LINGUISTICA*, 3(2).

Bernard Smith. 2001. *Learner English: A teacher's guide to interference and other problems*. Ernst Klett Sprachen.

Thamar Solorio, Elizabeth Blair, Suraj Maharjan, Steven Bethard, Mona Diab, Mahmoud Gohneim, Abdelati Hawwari, Fahad AlGhamdi, Julia Hirschberg, Alison Chang, et al. 2014. Overview for the first shared task on language identification in code-switched data. In *Proceedings of The First Workshop on Computational Approaches to Code Switching*, pages 62–72.

Thamar Solorio and Yang Liu. 2008. Part-of-speech tagging for English-Spanish code-switched text. In *Proceedings of EMNLP*, pages 1051–1060.

Joel Tetreault, Daniel Blanchard, and Aoife Cahill. 2013. A report on the first native language identification shared task. In *Proceedings of the 8th Workshop on Innovative Use of NLP for Building Educational Applications*, pages 48–57.

Oren Tsur and Ari Rappoport. 2007. Using classifier features for studying the effect of native language on the choice of written second language words. In *Proceedings of the Workshop on Cognitive Aspects of Computational Language Acquisition*, pages 9–16.

Svitlana Volkova, Yoram Bachrach, Michael Armstrong, and Vijay Sharma. 2015. Inferring latent user properties from texts published in social media. In *Proceedings of AAAI*, pages 4296–4297.

Svitlana Volkova and Eric Bell. 2017. Identifying effective signals to predict deleted and suspended accounts on twitter across languages. In *Proceedings of ICWSM*, pages 290–298.

Svitlana Volkova, Kyle Shaffer, Jin Yea Jang, and Nathan Hodas. 2017. Separating facts from fiction: Linguistic models to classify suspicious and trusted news posts on twitter. In *Proceedings of the 55th Annual Meeting of the Association for Computational Linguistics*, volume 2, pages 647–653.

Sze-Meng Jojo Wong and Mark Dras. 2011. Exploiting parse structures for native language identification. In *Proceedings of EMNLP*, pages 1600–1610.

A Discourse-Aware Attention Model for
Abstractive Summarization of Long Documents

Arman Cohan[†]   **Franck Dernoncourt**[⋆]   **Doo Soon Kim**[⋆]   **Trung Bui**[⋆]
Seokhwan Kim[⋆]   **Walter Chang**[⋆]   **Nazli Goharian**[†]

[†]Department of Computer Science, Georgetown University, Washington, DC
{arman,nazli}@ir.cs.georgetown.edu

[⋆]Adobe Research, San Jose, CA
{dernonco,dkim,bui,seokim,wachang}@adobe.com

Abstract

Neural abstractive summarization models have led to promising results in summarizing relatively short documents. We propose the first model for abstractive summarization of single, longer-form documents (e.g., research papers). Our approach consists of a new hierarchical encoder that models the discourse structure of a document, and an attentive discourse-aware decoder to generate the summary. Empirical results on two large-scale datasets of scientific papers show that our model significantly outperforms state-of-the-art models.

1 Introduction

Existing large-scale summarization datasets consist of relatively short documents. For example, articles in the CNN/Daily Mail dataset (Hermann et al., 2015) are on average about 600 words long. Similarly, existing neural summarization models have focused on summarizing sentences and short documents. In this work, we propose a model for effective abstractive summarization of longer documents. Scientific papers are an example of documents that are significantly longer than news articles (see Table 1). They also follow a standard discourse structure describing the problem, methodology, experiments/results, and finally conclusions (Suppe, 1998).

Most summarization works in the literature focus on extractive summarization. Examples of prominent approaches include frequency-based methods (Vanderwende et al., 2007), graph-based methods (Erkan and Radev, 2004), topic modeling (Steinberger and Jezek, 2004), and neural models (Nallapati et al., 2017). Abstractive summarization is an alternative approach where the generated summary may contain novel words and phrases and is more similar to how humans summarize documents (Jing, 2002). Recently, neural methods have led to encouraging results in abstractive summarization (Nallapati et al., 2016; See et al., 2017; Paulus et al., 2017; Li et al., 2017). These approaches employ a general framework of sequence-to-sequence (seq2seq) models (Sutskever et al., 2014) where the document is fed to an encoder network and another (recurrent) network learns to decode the summary. While promising, these methods focus on summarizing news articles which are relatively short. Many other document types, however, are longer and structured. Seq2seq models tend to struggle with longer sequences because at each decoding step, the decoder needs to learn to construct a context vector capturing relevant information from all the tokens in the source sequence (Shao et al., 2017).

Our main contribution is an abstractive model for summarizing scientific papers which are an example of long-form structured document types. Our model includes a hierarchical encoder, capturing the discourse structure of the document and a discourse-aware decoder that generates the summary. Our decoder attends to different discourse sections and allows the model to more accurately represent important information from the source resulting in a better context vector. We also introduce two large-scale datasets of long and structured scientific papers obtained from arXiv and PubMed to support both training and evaluating models on the task of long document summarization. Evaluation results show that our method outperforms state-of-the-art summarization models[1].

2 Background

In the seq2seq framework for abstractive summarization, an input document x is encoded using a Recurrent Neural Network (RNN) with $\mathbf{h}_i^{(e)}$ being the hidden state of the encoder at timestep i. The last step of the encoder is fed as input to another RNN which decodes the output one token

---

[1] Data/code: https://github.com/acohan/long-summarization

Proceedings of NAACL-HLT 2018, pages 615–621
New Orleans, Louisiana, June 1 - 6, 2018. ©2018 Association for Computational Linguistics

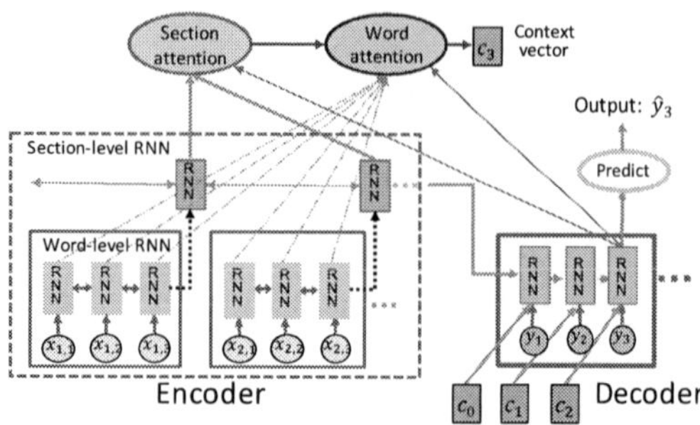

Figure 1: Overview of our model. The word-level RNN is shown in blue and section-level RNN is shown in green. The decoder also consists of an RNN (orange) and a "predict" network for generating the summary. At each decoding time step t (here $t=3$ is shown), the decoder forms a context vector c_t which encodes the relevant source context (c_0 is initialized as a zero vector). Then the section and word attention weights are respectively computed using the green "section attention" and the blue "word attention" blocks. The context vector is used as another input to the decoder RNN and as an input to the "predict" network which outputs the next word using a joint pointer-generator network.

at a time. Given an input document along with the corresponding ground-truth summary $\mathbf{y}$, the model is trained to output a summary $\hat{\mathbf{y}}$ that is close to $\mathbf{y}$. The output at timestep t is predicted using the decoder input $\mathbf{x}'_t$, decoder hidden state $\mathbf{h}_t^{(d)}$, and some information about the input sequence. This framework is the general seq2seq framework employed in many generation tasks including machine translation (Sutskever et al., 2014; Bahdanau et al., 2014) and summarization (Nallapati et al., 2016; Chopra et al., 2016).

Attentive decoding The attention mechanism maps the decoder state and the encoder states to an output vector, which is a weighted sum of the encoder states and is called context vector (Bahdanau et al., 2014). Incorporating this context vector at each decoding timestep (attentive decoding) is proven effective in seq2seq models. Formally, the context vector c_t is defined as: $\mathbf{c}_t = \sum_{i=1}^{N} \alpha_i^{(t)} \mathbf{h}_i^{(e)}$ where $\alpha_i^{(t)}$ are the attention weights calculated as follows:

$$\alpha_i^{(t)} = \operatorname*{softmax}_i(\operatorname{score}(\mathbf{h}_i^{(e)}, \mathbf{h}_{t-1}^{(d)})) \qquad (1)$$

where $\operatorname*{softmax}_i$ means that the denominator's sum in the softmax function is over i. The score function can be defined in bilinear, additive, or multiplicative ways (Luong et al., 2015). We use the additive scoring function:

$$\operatorname{score}(\mathbf{h}_i^{(e)}, \mathbf{h}_{t-1}^{(d)}) = \mathbf{v}_a^\top \tanh\left(\operatorname{linear}(\mathbf{h}_i^{(e)}, \mathbf{h}_{t-1}^{(d)})\right) \quad (2)$$

where $\mathbf{v}_a$ is a weight vector and linear is a linear mapping function. I.e.,

$$\operatorname{linear}(\mathbf{x}_1, \mathbf{x}_2) = \mathbf{w}_1\mathbf{x}_1 + \mathbf{w}_2\mathbf{x}_2 + \mathbf{b} \qquad (3)$$

where $\mathbf{w}_1$ and $\mathbf{w}_2$ are weight matrices and $\mathbf{b}$ is the bias vector.

3 Model

We now describe our discourse-aware summarization model (shown in Figure 1).

Encoder Our encoder extends the RNN encoder to a hierarchical RNN that captures the document discourse structure. We first encode each discourse section and then encode the document. Formally, we encode the document as a vector $\mathbf{d}$ according to the following:

$$\mathbf{d} = \operatorname{RNN}_{doc}\left(\{\mathbf{h}_1^{(s)}, ..., \mathbf{h}_N^{(s)}\}\right)$$

RNN(.) denotes a function which is a recurrent neural network whose output is the final state of the network encoding the entire sequence. N is the number of sections in the document and $\mathbf{h}_j^{(s)}$ is representation of section j in the document consisting of a sequence of tokens.

$$\mathbf{h}_j^{(s)} = \operatorname{RNN}_{sec}\left(\mathbf{x}_{(j,1)}, ...\mathbf{x}_{(j,M)}\}\right)$$

where $\mathbf{x}_{(j,i)}$ are dense embeddings corresponding to the tokens $w_{(j,i)}$ and M is the maximum section length. The parameters of RNN_{sec} are shared for all the discourse sections. We use a single layer bidirectional LSTM (following the LSTM formulation of Graves et al. (2013)) for both RNN_{doc} and RNN_{sec}; further extension to multilayer LSTMs is straightforward. We combine the forward and backward LSTM states to a single state using a simple feed-forward network:

$$\mathbf{h} = \operatorname{relu}(\mathbf{W}([\overrightarrow{\mathbf{h}}, \overleftarrow{\mathbf{h}}] + \mathbf{b})$$

where $[,]$ shows the concatenation operation. Throughout, when we mention the RNN (LSTM) state, we are referring to this combined state of both forward and backward RNNs (LSTMs).

Discourse-aware decoder When humans summarize a long structured document, depending on the domain and the nature of the document, they write about important points from different discourse sections of the document. For example, scientific paper abstracts typically include the description of the problem, discussion of the methods, and finally results and conclusions (Suppe, 1998). Motivated by this observation, we propose a discourse-aware attention method. Intuitively, at each decoding timestep, in addition to the words

616

in the document, we also attend to the relevant discourse section (the "section attention" block in Figure 1). Then we use the discourse-related information to modify the word-level attention function. Specifically, the context vector representing the source document is:

$$\mathbf{c}_t = \sum_{j=1}^{N} \sum_{i=1}^{M} \alpha_{(j,i)}^{(t)} \mathbf{h}_{(j,i)}^{(e)} \qquad (4)$$

where $\mathbf{h}_{(j,i)}^{(e)}$ shows the encoder state of word i in discourse section j and $\alpha_{(j,i)}^{(t)}$ shows the corresponding attention weight to that encoder state. The scalar weights $\alpha_{(j,i)}^{(t)}$ are obtained according to:

$$\alpha_{(j,i)}^{(t)} = \underset{(i,j)}{\mathrm{softmax}} \left(\beta_j^{(t)} \, \mathrm{score}(\mathbf{h}_{(j,i)}^{(e)}, \mathbf{h}_{t-1}^{(d)}) \right) \quad (5)$$

The score function is the additive attention function (Equation 2) and the weights $\beta_j^{(t)}$ are updated according to:

$$\beta_j^{(t)} = \underset{j}{\mathrm{softmax}}(\mathrm{score}(\mathbf{h}_j^{(s)}, \mathbf{h}_{t-1}^{(d)})) \qquad (6)$$

At each timestep t, the decoder state $\mathbf{h}_t^{(d)}$ and the context vector $\mathbf{c}_t$ are used to estimate the probability distribution of next word y_t:

$$p(y_t|y_{1:t-1}) = \mathrm{softmax} \left(\mathbf{V}^\top \, \mathrm{linear} \left(\mathbf{h}_t^{(d)}, \mathbf{c}_t \right) \right) \quad (7)$$

where $\mathbf{V}$ is a vocabulary weight matrix and softmax is over the entire vocabulary.

Copying from source There has been a surge of recent works in sequence learning tasks to address the problem of *unkown* token prediction by allowing the model to occasionally copy words directly from source instead of generating a new token (Gu et al., 2016; See et al., 2017; Paulus et al., 2017; Wiseman et al., 2017). Following these works, we add an additional binary variable z_t to the decoder, indicating generating a word from vocabulary (z_t=0) or copying a word from the source (z_t=1). The probability is learnt during training according to the following equation:

$$p(z_t{=}1|y_{1:t-1}) = \sigma(\mathrm{linear}(\mathbf{h}_t^{(d)}, \mathbf{c}_t, \mathbf{x}_t')) \quad (8)$$

Then the next word y_t is generated according to:

$$p(y_t|y_{1:t-1}) = \sum_z p(y_t, z_t{=}z|y_{1:t-1}); z = \{0,1\}$$

The joint probability is decomposed as:

$$p(y_t, z_t{=}z) = \begin{cases} p_c(y_t|y_{1:t-1})\, p(z_t{=}z|y_{1:t-1}), & z{=}1 \\ p_g(y_t|y_{1:t-1})\, p(z_t{=}z|y_{1:t-1}), & z{=}0 \end{cases}$$

p_g is the probability of generating a word from the vocabulary and is defined according to Equation 7.

p_c is the probability of copying a word from the source vector $\mathbf{x}$ and is defined as the sum of the word's attention weights. Specifically, the probability of copying a word x_ℓ is defined as:

$$p_c(y_t = x_\ell|y_{1:t-1}) = \sum_{(j,i):x_{(j,i)}=x_\ell} \alpha_{(j,i)}^{(t)} \quad (9)$$

Decoder coverage In long sequences, the neural generation models tend to repeat phrases where the softmax layer predicts the same phrase multiple times over multiple timesteps. To address this issue, following See et al. (2017), we track attention coverage to avoid repeatedly attending to the same steps. This is done with a coverage vector $\mathbf{cov}^{(t)}$, the sum of attention weight vectors at previous timesteps: $\mathrm{cov}_{(j,i)}^{(t)} = \sum_{k=0}^{t-1} \alpha_{(j,i)}^{(k)}$

The coverage implicitly includes information about the attended document discourse sections. We incorporate the decoder coverage as an additional input to the attention function:

$$\alpha_{(j,i)}^{(t)} = \underset{(i,j)}{\mathrm{softmax}} \left(\beta_j^{(t)} \, \mathrm{score}(\mathbf{h}_{(j,i)}^{(e)}, \mathrm{cov}_{(j,i)}^{(t)}, \mathbf{h}_{t-1}^{(d)}) \right)$$

4   Related work

Neural abstractive summarization models have been studied in the past (Rush et al., 2015; Chopra et al., 2016; Nallapati et al., 2016) and later extended by source copying (Miao and Blunsom, 2016; See et al., 2017), reinformcement learning (Paulus et al., 2017), and sentence salience information (Li et al., 2017). One model variant of Nallapati et al. (2016) is related to our model in using sentence-level information in attention. However, our model is different as it contains a hierarchical encoder, uses discourse sections in the decoding step, and has a coverage mechanism. Similarly, Ling and Rush (2017) proposed a coarse-to-fine attention model that uses hard attention to find the text chunks of importance and then only attend to words in that chunk. In contrast, we consider all the discourse sections using soft attention. The closest model to ours is that of See et al. (2017) and Paulus et al. (2017) who used a joint pointer-generator network for summarization. However, our model extends theirs by *(i)* a hierarchical encoder for modeling long documents and *(ii)* a discourse-aware decoder that captures the information flow from all discourse sections of the document. Finally, in a recent work, Liu et al. (2018) proposed a model based on the transformer network (Vaswani et al., 2017) for abstractive generation of Wikipedia articles. However, their focus

Datasets	# docs	avg. doc. length (words)	avg. summary length (words)
CNN	92K	656	43
Daily Mail	219K	693	52
NY Times	655K	530	38
PubMed (this work)	133K	3016	203
arXiv (this work)	215K	4938	220

Table 1: Statistics of our arXiv and PubMed datasets compared with existing large-scale summarization corpora, CNN and Daily Mail (Nallapati et al., 2016) and NY Times (Paulus et al., 2017).

is on multi-document summarization.

Our datasets are obtained from scientific papers. Scientific document summarization has been recently received extended attention (Qazvinian et al., 2013; Cohan and Goharian, 2015, 2017b,a). In contrast to ours, existing approaches are extractive and rely on external information such as citations, which may not be available for all papers.

5 Data

Seq2seq models typically have a large number of parameters and thus they require large training data with ground truth summaries. Researchers have constructed such training data from news articles (e.g., CNN, Daily Mail and New York Times articles), where the abstracts or highlights of news articles are considered as ground truth summaries (Nallapati et al., 2016; Paulus et al., 2017). However, news articles are relatively short and not suitable for the task of long-from document summarization. Following these works, we take scientific papers as an example of long documents with discourse information, where their abstracts can be used as ground-truth summaries. We introduce two datasets collected from scientific repositories, arXiv.org and PubMed.com.

The choice of scientific papers for our dataset is motivated by the fact that scientific papers are examples of long documents that follow a standard discourse structure and they already come with ground truth summaries, making it possible to train supervised neural models. We follow existing work in constructing large-scale summarization datasets that take news article abstracts as ground truth.

We remove the documents that are excessively long (e.g., theses) or too short (e.g., tutorial announcements), or do not have an abstract or discourse structure. We use the level-1 section headings as the discourse information. For arXiv, we use the LaTeX files and convert them to plain text

using Pandoc (https://pandoc.org) to preserve the discourse section information. We remove figures and tables using regular expressions to only preserve the textual information. We also normalize math formulas and citation markers with special tokens. We analyze the document section names and identify the most common concluding sections names (e.g. *conclusion, concluding remarks, summary*, etc). We only keep the sections up to the conclusion section of the document and we remove sections after the conclusion.

The statistics of our datasets are shown in Table 1. In our datasets, both document and summary lengths are significantly larger than the existing large-scale summarization datasets. We retain about 3% (5%) of PubMed (ArXiv) as validation data and about another 3% (5%) for test; the rest is used for training.

6 Experiments

Setup Similar to the majority of published research in the summarization literature (Chopra et al., 2016; Nallapati et al., 2016; See et al., 2017), evaluation was done using the ROUGE automatic summarization evaluation metric (Lin, 2004) with full-length F-1 ROUGE scores. We lowercase all tokens and perform sentence and word tokenization using spaCy (Honnibal and Johnson, 2015).

Implementation details We use Tensorflow 1.4 for implementing our models. We use the hyperparameters suggested by See et al. (2017). In particular, we use two bidirectional LSTMs with cell size of 256 and embedding dimensions of 128. Embeddings are trained from scratch and we did not find any gain using pre-trained embeddings. The vocabulary size is constrained to 50,000; using larger vocabulary size did not result in any improvement. We use mini-batches of size 16 and we limit the document length to 2000 and section length to 500 tokens, and number of sections to 4. We use batch-padding and dynamic unrolling to handle variable sequence lengths in LSTMs. Training was done using Adagrad optimizer with learning rate 0.15 and an initial accumulator value of 0.1. The maximum decoder size was 210 tokens which is in line with average abstract length in our datasets. We first train the model without coverage and added it at the last two epochs to help the model converge faster. We train the models on NVIDIA Titan X Pascal GPUs. Training is performed for about 10 epochs and each training step takes about 3.2 seconds. We used beam search at

	Summarizer	RG-1	RG-2	RG-3	RG-L
Extractive	SumBasic	29.47	6.95	2.36	26.30
	LexRank	33.85	10.73	**4.54**	28.99
	LSA	29.91	7.42	3.12	25.67
Abstractive	Attn-Seq2Seq	29.30	6.00	1.77	25.56
	Pntr-Gen-Seq2Seq	32.06	9.04	2.15	25.16
	This work	†‡**35.80**	†**11.05**	†**3.62**	†‡**31.80**

Table 2: Results on the arXiv dataset, RG: ROUGE. For our method † (‡) shows statistically significant improvement with $p<0.05$ over other abstractive methods (all other methods).

	Summarizer	RG-1	RG-2	RG-3	RG-L
Extractive	SumBasic	37.15	11.36	5.42	33.43
	LexRank	**39.19**	13.89	7.27	34.59
	LSA	33.89	9.93	5.04	29.70
Abstractive	Attn-Seq2Seq	31.55	8.52	7.05	27.38
	Pntr-Gen-Seq2Seq	35.86	10.22	7.60	29.69
	This work	†38.93	†‡**15.37**	†‡**9.97**	†‡**35.21**

Table 3: Results on PubMed dataset, RG:ROUGE. For our method, † (‡) shows statistically significant improvement with $p<0.05$ over abstractive methods (all other methods).

decoding time with beam size of 4. We train the abstractive baselines for about 250K iterations as suggested by their authors.

Comparison We compare our method with several well-known extractive baselines as well as state-of-the-art abstractive models using their open-sourced implementations, when available; we follow the same training setup described in the corresponding papers. The compared methods are: *LexRank* (Erkan and Radev, 2004), *SumBasic* (Vanderwende et al., 2007), *LSA* (Steinberger and Jezek, 2004), *Attn-Seq2Seq* (Nallapati et al., 2016; Chopra et al., 2016), *Pntr-Gen-Seq2Seq* (See et al., 2017). The first three are extractive models and last two are abstractive. *Pntr-Gen-Seq2Seq* extends *Attn-Seq2Seq* by using a joint pointer network during decoding. For *Pntr-Gen-Seq2Seq* we use their reported hyperparameters to ensure that the result differences are not due to hyperparameter tuning.

Results Our main results are shown in Tables 2 and 3. Our model significantly outperforms the state-of-the-art abstractive methods, showing its effectiveness on both datasets. We observe that in our ROUGE-1 score is respectively about 4 and 3 points higher than the abstractive model *Pntr-Gen-Seq2Seq* for the arXiv and PubMed datasets, providing a significant improvement. Our method also outperforms most of the extractive methods except for *LexRank* in one of the ROUGE scores. We note that since extractive methods copy salient sentences from the document, it is usually easier

Abstract: in this paper , the author proposes a series of multilevel double hashing schemes called cascade hash tables . they use several levels of hash tables . in each table , we use the common double hashing scheme . higher level hash tables work as fail - safes of lower level hash tables . by this strategy , it could effectively reduce collisions in hash insertion . thus it gains a constant worst case lookup time with a relatively high load factor (@xmath0) in random experiments . different parameters of cascade hash tables are tested .

Pntr-Gen-Seq2Seq: hash table is a common data structure used in large set of data storage and retrieval . it has an o(1) lookup time on average , but the worst case lookup time can be as bad as . is the size of the hash table . we present a set of hash table schemes called cascade hash tables . hash table data structures which consist of several of hash tables with different size .

Our method: cascade hash tables are a common data structure used in large set of data storage and retrieval . such a time variation is essentially caused by possibly many collisions during keys hashing . in this paper , we present a set of hash schemes called cascade hash tables which consist of several levels (@xmath2) of hash tables with different size . after constant probes , if an item ca 'nt find a free slot in limited probes in any hash table , it will try to find a cell in the second level , or subsequent lower levels . with this simple strategy , these hash tables will have descendant load factors , therefore lower collision probabilities .

Figure 2: Example of a generated summary

for them to achieve higher ROUGE scores.

Figure 2 illustrates the effectiveness of our model extensions in capturing various discourse information from the papers. It can be observed that the state-of-the-art *Pntr-Gen-Seq2Seq* model generates a summary that mostly focuses on introducing the problem, whereas our model generates a summary that includes more information about the methodology and impacts of the target paper. This indicates that the context vector in our model compared with *Pntr-Gen-Seq2Seq* is better able to capture important information from the source by attending to various discourse sections.

7 Conclusions and future work

This work was the first attempt at addressing neural abstractive summarization of single, long documents. We presented a neural sequence-to-sequence model that is able to effectively summarize long and structured documents such as scientific papers. While our results are encouraging, there is still much room for improvement for this challenging task; our new datasets can help the community to further explore this problem.

We note that following the convention in the summarization research, our quantitative evaluation is performed by ROUGE automatic metric. While ROUGE is an effective evaluation framework, nuances in the coherence or coverage of the summaries are not captured with it. It is non-trivial to evaluate such qualities especially for long document summarization; future work can design expert human evaluations to explore these nuances.

Acknowledgements

We thank the three anonymous reviewers for their comments and suggestions.

References

Dzmitry Bahdanau, Kyunghyun Cho, and Yoshua Bengio. 2014. Neural machine translation by jointly learning to align and translate. *arXiv preprint arXiv:1409.0473* .

Sumit Chopra, Michael Auli, Alexander M Rush, and SEAS Harvard. 2016. Abstractive sentence summarization with attentive recurrent neural networks. In *HLT-NAACL*. pages 93–98.

Arman Cohan and Nazli Goharian. 2015. Scientific article summarization using citation-context and article's discourse structure. In *Proceedings of the 2015 Conference on Empirical Methods in Natural Language Processing*. Association for Computational Linguistics, Lisbon, Portugal, pages 390–400. http://aclweb.org/anthology/D15-1045.

Arman Cohan and Nazli Goharian. 2017a. Contextualizing citations for scientific summarization using word embeddings and domain knowledge. *arXiv preprint arXiv:1705.08063* .

Arman Cohan and Nazli Goharian. 2017b. Scientific document summarization via citation contextualization and scientific discourse. *International Journal on Digital Libraries* pages 1–17. https://doi.org/10.1007/s00799-017-0216-8.

Günes Erkan and Dragomir R Radev. 2004. Lexrank: Graph-based lexical centrality as salience in text summarization. *Journal of Artificial Intelligence Research* 22:457–479.

Alex Graves, Abdel-rahman Mohamed, and Geoffrey Hinton. 2013. Speech recognition with deep recurrent neural networks. In *Acoustics, speech and signal processing (icassp), 2013 ieee international conference on*. IEEE, pages 6645–6649.

Jiatao Gu, Zhengdong Lu, Hang Li, and Victor O.K. Li. 2016. Incorporating copying mechanism in sequence-to-sequence learning. In *Proceedings of the 54th Annual Meeting of the Association for Computational Linguistics (Volume 1: Long Papers)*. Association for Computational Linguistics, Berlin, Germany, pages 1631–1640. http://www.aclweb.org/anthology/P16-1154.

Karl Moritz Hermann, Tomas Kocisky, Edward Grefenstette, Lasse Espeholt, Will Kay, Mustafa Suleyman, and Phil Blunsom. 2015. Teaching machines to read and comprehend. In *Advances in Neural Information Processing Systems*. pages 1693–1701.

Matthew Honnibal and Mark Johnson. 2015. An improved non-monotonic transition system for dependency parsing. In *Proceedings of the 2015 Conference on Empirical Methods in Natural Language Processing*. Association for Computational Linguistics, Lisbon, Portugal, pages 1373–1378. https://aclweb.org/anthology/D/D15/D15-1162.

Hongyan Jing. 2002. Using hidden markov modeling to decompose human-written summaries. *Computational linguistics* 28(4):527–543.

Piji Li, Wai Lam, Lidong Bing, Weiwei Guo, and Hang Li. 2017. Cascaded attention based unsupervised information distillation for compressive summarization. In *Proceedings of the 2017 Conference on Empirical Methods in Natural Language Processing*. pages 2071–2080.

Chin-Yew Lin. 2004. Rouge: A package for automatic evaluation of summaries. In *Text summarization branches out: Proceedings of the ACL-04 workshop*. Barcelona, Spain, volume 8.

Jeffrey Ling and Alexander Rush. 2017. Coarse-to-fine attention models for document summarization. In *Proceedings of the Workshop on New Frontiers in Summarization*. Association for Computational Linguistics, Copenhagen, Denmark, pages 33–42. http://www.aclweb.org/anthology/W17-4505.

Peter J. Liu, Mohammad Saleh, Etienne Pot, Ben Goodrich, Ryan Sepassi, Lukasz Kaiser, and Noam Shazeer. 2018. Generating wikipedia by summarizing long sequences. In *International Conference on Learning Representations*. https://openreview.net/forum?id=Hyg0vbWC-.

Minh-Thang Luong, Hieu Pham, and Christopher D Manning. 2015. Effective approaches to attention-based neural machine translation. *arXiv preprint arXiv:1508.04025* .

Yishu Miao and Phil Blunsom. 2016. Language as a latent variable: Discrete generative models for sentence compression. *arXiv preprint arXiv:1609.07317* .

Ramesh Nallapati, Feifei Zhai, and Bowen Zhou. 2017. Summarunner: A recurrent neural network based sequence model for extractive summarization of documents. *AAAI* 1:1.

Ramesh Nallapati, Bowen Zhou, Caglar Gulcehre, Bing Xiang, et al. 2016. Abstractive text summarization using sequence-to-sequence rnns and beyond. *arXiv preprint arXiv:1602.06023* .

Romain Paulus, Caiming Xiong, and Richard Socher. 2017. A deep reinforced model for abstractive summarization. *arXiv preprint arXiv:1705.04304* .

Vahed Qazvinian, Dragomir R Radev, Saif M Mohammad, Bonnie Dorr, David Zajic, Michael Whidby, and Taesun Moon. 2013. Generating extractive summaries of scientific paradigms. *Journal of Artificial Intelligence Research* 46:165–201.

Alexander M Rush, Sumit Chopra, and Jason Weston. 2015. A neural attention model for abstractive sentence summarization. *arXiv preprint arXiv:1509.00685* .

Abigail See, Christopher Manning, and Peter Liu. 2017. Get to the point: Summarization with pointer-generator networks. In *Association for Computational Linguistics*. https://arxiv.org/abs/1704.04368.

Yuanlong Shao, Stephan Gouws, Denny Britz, Anna Goldie, Brian Strope, and Ray Kurzweil. 2017. Generating high-quality and informative conversation responses with sequence-to-sequence models. In *Proceedings of the 2017 Conference on Empirical Methods in Natural Language Processing*. pages 2210–2219.

Josef Steinberger and Karel Jezek. 2004. Using latent semantic analysis in text summarization and summary evaluation. In *Proc. ISIM04*. pages 93–100.

Frederick Suppe. 1998. The structure of a scientific paper. *Philosophy of Science* 65(3):381–405.

Ilya Sutskever, Oriol Vinyals, and Quoc V Le. 2014. Sequence to sequence learning with neural networks. In *Advances in neural information processing systems*. pages 3104–3112.

Lucy Vanderwende, Hisami Suzuki, Chris Brockett, and Ani Nenkova. 2007. Beyond sumbasic: Task-focused summarization with sentence simplification and lexical expansion. *Information Processing & Management* 43(6):1606–1618.

Ashish Vaswani, Noam Shazeer, Niki Parmar, Jakob Uszkoreit, Llion Jones, Aidan N Gomez, Ł ukasz Kaiser, and Illia Polosukhin. 2017. Attention is all you need. In I. Guyon, U. V. Luxburg, S. Bengio, H. Wallach, R. Fergus, S. Vishwanathan, and R. Garnett, editors, *Advances in Neural Information Processing Systems 30*, Curran Associates, Inc., pages 6000–6010. http://papers.nips.cc/paper/7181-attention-is-all-you-need.pdf.

Sam Wiseman, Stuart M Shieber, and Alexander M Rush. 2017. Challenges in data-to-document generation. *arXiv preprint arXiv:1707.08052* .

A Mixed Hierarchical Attention based Encoder-Decoder Approach for Standard Table Summarization

Parag Jain[†] **Anirban Laha**[†*] **Karthik Sankaranarayanan**[†]
Preksha Nema[*] **Mitesh M. Khapra**[*‡] **Shreyas Shetty**[*]
[†]IBM Research [*]IIT Madras, India
[‡] Robert Bosch Center for Data Science and Artificial Intelligence, IIT Madras
{pajain34,anirlaha,kartsank}@in.ibm.com
{preksha,miteshk,shshett}@cse.iitm.ac.in

Abstract

Structured data summarization involves generation of natural language summaries from structured input data. In this work, we consider summarizing structured data occurring in the form of tables as they are prevalent across a wide variety of domains. We formulate the *standard table summarization* problem, which deals with tables conforming to a single predefined schema. To this end, we propose a *mixed hierarchical attention* based encoder-decoder model which is able to leverage the structure in addition to the content of the tables. Our experiments on the publicly available WEATHERGOV dataset show around 18 BLEU ($\sim 30\%$) improvement over the current state-of-the-art.

1 Introduction

Abstractive summarization techniques from structured data seek to exploit both structure and content of the input data. The type of structure on the input side can be highly varied ranging from key-value pairs (e.g. WIKIBIO (Lebret et al., 2016)), source code (Iyer et al., 2016), ontologies (Androutsopoulos et al., 2014; Colin et al., 2016), or tables (Wiseman et al., 2017), each of which require significantly varying approaches. In this paper, we focus on generating summaries from tabular data. Now, in most practical applications such as finance, healthcare or weather, data in a table are arranged in rows and columns where the schema is known beforehand. However, change in the actual data values can necessitate drastically different output summaries. Examples shown in the figure 1 have a predefined schema obtained from the WEATHERGOV dataset (Liang et al., 2009) and its corresponding weather report summary. Therefore, the problem that we seek to address in this paper is to generate abstractive summaries of tables conforming to a pre-

defined fixed schema (as opposed to cases where the schema is unknown). We refer to this setting as **standard table summarization** problem. Another problem that could be formulated is one in which the output summary is generated from multiple tables as proposed in a recent challenge (Wiseman et al., 2017) (this setting is out of the scope of this paper). Now, as the schema is fixed, simple rule based techniques (Konstas and Lapata, 2013) or template based solutions could be employed. However, due to the vast space of selection (which attributes to use in the summary based on the current value it takes) and generation (how to express these selected attributes in natural language) choices possible, such approaches are not scalable in terms of the number of templates as they demand hand-crafted rules for both selection and generation.

We attempt to solve the problem of standard table summarization by leveraging the hierarchical nature of fixed-schema tables. In other words, rows consist of a fixed set of attributes and a table is defined by a set of rows. We cast this problem into a **mixed hierarchical attention model** following the encode-attend-decode (Cho et al., 2015) paradigm. In this approach, there is static attention on the attributes to compute the row representation followed by dynamic attention on the rows, which is subsequently fed to the decoder. This formulation is theoretically more efficient than the fully dynamic hierarchical attention framework followed by Nallapati et al. (2016). Also, our model does not need sophisticated sampling or sparsifying techniques like (Ling and Rush, 2017; Deng et al., 2017), thus, retaining differentiability. To demonstrate the efficacy of our approach, we transform the publicly available WEATHERGOV dataset (Liang et al., 2009) into fixed-schema tables, which is then used for our experiments. Our proposed *mixed hierarchi-*

Proceedings of NAACL-HLT 2018, pages 622–627
New Orleans, Louisiana, June 1 - 6, 2018. ©2018 Association for Computational Linguistics

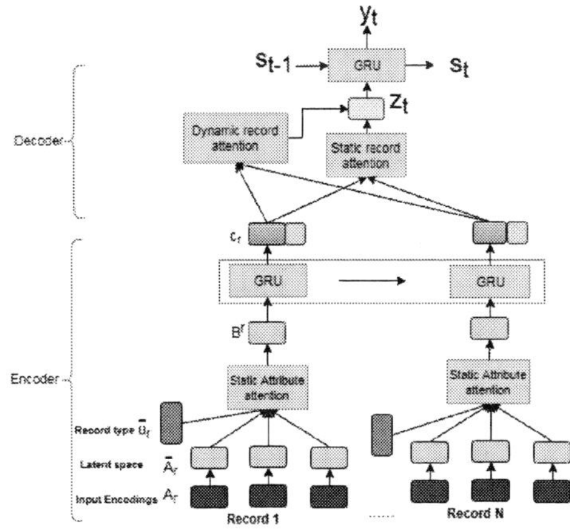

Input : Table 1

TYPE	TIME	MIN	MAX	MEAN	MODE	MB100-4	MB20-2
temperature	17-30	33	60	44	-	-	-
windChill	17-30	0	47	31	-	-	-
windSpeed	17-30	5	9	7	-	-	0-10
windDir	17-30	-	-	-	NNW	-	-
gust	17-30	0	0	0	-	-	-
skyCover	17-30	-	-	-	-	0-25	-
skyCover	17-21	-	-	-	-	0-25	-
skyCover	17-26	-	-	-	-	0-25	-
skyCover	21-30	-	-	-	-	0-25	-
skyCover	26-30	-	-	-	-	0-25	-
precipPotential	17-30	0	0	0	-	-	-

Input : Table 2

TYPE	TIME	MIN	MAX	MEAN	MODE	MB100-4	MB20-2
temperature	6-21	35	53	46	-	-	-
windChill	6-21	0	47	27	-	-	-
windSpeed	6-21	6	8	7	-	-	0-10
windDir	6-21	-	-	-	WSW	-	-
gust	6-21	0	0	0	-	-	-
skyCover	6-21	-	-	-	-	75-100	-
skyCover	6-9	-	-	-	-	75-100	-
skyCover	6-13	-	-	-	-	50-75	-
skyCover	9-21	-	-	-	-	75-100	-
skyCover	13-21	-	-	-	-	75-100	-
precipPotential	6-21	4	48	17	-	-	-
rainChance	13-21	-	-	-	Chc	-	-

Output : Summary 1

Output : Summary 2

Figure 1: Standard Table Summarization with fixed schema tables as input.

cal attention model provides an **improvement of around 18 BLEU (around 30%) over the current state-of-the-art result** by Mei et al. (2016).

2 Tabular Data Summarization

A standard table consist of set of records (or rows) $R = (r_1, r_2, ...r_T)$ and each record r has a fixed set of attributes (or columns) $A^r = (a_{r1}, a_{r2}, ...a_{rM})$. Tables in figure 1 have 7 columns (apart from 'TYPE') which correspond to different attributes. Also $U = (u_1, u_2, ...u_T)$ represents the type of each record where u_k is one-hot encoding for the record type for record r_k. Training data consists of instance pairs (X_i, Y_i) for $i = 1, 2, ..n$, where $X_i = (R_i, U_i)$ represents the input table and $Y_i = (y_1, ..., y_{T'})$ represents the corresponding natural language summary. In this paper, we propose an end-to-end model which takes in a table instance X to produce the output summary Y. This can be derived by solving in Y the following conditional probability objective:

$$Y^* = \arg\max_Y \prod_{t=1}^{T'} p(y_t | y_1, ..., y_{t-1}, X) \quad (1)$$

2.1 Mixed Hierarchical Attention Model (MHAM)

Our model is based on the *encode-attend-decode* paradigm as defined by Cho et al. (2015). It consists of an *encoder* RNN which encodes a variable length input sequence $\mathbf{x} = (x_1, ..., x_T)$ into a representation sequence $\mathbf{c} = (c_1, ..., c_T)$. Another decoder RNN generates sequence of output symbols

Figure 2: Proposed Architecture

$\mathbf{y} = (y_1, ..., y_{T'})$, attending to different combinations of c_i while generating different y_t.

As illustrated in figure 2, our encoder is not a single RNN. The encoder has a hierarchical structure to leverage the structural aspect of a *standard table*: a table consists of a set of records (or rows) and each record consists of values corresponding to a fixed set of attributes. We call it a *mixed hierarchical attention* based encoder, as it incorporates static attention and dynamic attention at two different levels of the encoder. At the record level, the attention over record representations is *dynamic* as it changes with each decoder time step. Whereas at the attribute level, since the schema is fixed, a record representation can be computed without the need of varying attention over attributes - thus *static* attention is used. For

623

example, with respect to WEATHERGOV dataset, a *temperature* record will always be defined by the attributes like min, max and mean irrespective of the decoder time step. So, attention over attributes can be static. On the other hand, while generating a word by the decoder, there can be a preference of focusing on a record type say, *temperature*, over some other type say, *windSpeed*. Thus, dynamic attention is used across records.

[!ht]

$$\bar{A}_j^r = W_j A_j^r, \ \forall j \in [1, M] \tag{2}$$

$$I_j^r = \bar{A}_j^r \odot \bar{u}_r \quad , \quad \bar{u}_r = W_0 u_r \tag{3}$$

$$\alpha_j^r = softmax_j(I^r) \tag{4}$$

$$B^r = \sum_j \alpha_j^r \bar{A}_j^r \tag{5}$$

$$c_r = [h_r; B^r] \quad , \quad h_r = GRU(B^r) \tag{6}$$

$$g_r = \sigma(q^T tanh(P c_r)) \tag{7}$$

$$\beta_t^r = v^T tanh(W_s s_{t-1} + W_c c_r) \tag{8}$$

$$w_t^r = softmax_r(\beta_t) \tag{9}$$

$$z_t = \sum_r \gamma_t^r c_r \quad , \quad \gamma_t^r = \frac{g_r w_t^r}{\sum_r g_r w_t^r} \tag{10}$$

$$s_t = GRU(z_t, s_{t-1}) \tag{11}$$

$$l_t = W_1 s_t + W_2 z_t + b_l \tag{12}$$

$$p_t = softmax(l_t) \tag{13}$$

Capturing attribute semantics: We learn record type embeddings and use them to calculate attentions over attributes. *For the trivial case of all records being same type, it boils down to having a single record type embedding.* Given attributes A^r for a record r, where each attribute a_i^r is encoded into a vector A_i^r based on the attribute type (discussed further in section 3), using equation 2 we embed each attribute where W_j is the embedding matrix for j^{th} attribute. We embed record type one-hot vector u_r through W_0, which is used to compute the importance score I_j^r for attribute j in record r according to equation 3.

Static Attribute attention: Not all attribute values contribute equally to the record. Hence, we introduce attention weights for attributes of each record. These attention weights are static and does not change with decoder time step. We calculate the attention probability vector α^r over attributes using the attribute importance vector I^r. The attention weights can then be used to calculate the

record representation B^r for record r by using equations 4 and 5.

Record Encoder: A GRU based RNN encoder takes as input a sequence of attribute attended records $B^{1:N}$ and returns a sequence of hidden states $h_{1:N}$, where h_r is the encoded vector for record B^r. We obtain the final record encoding c_r (equation 6) by concatenating the GRU hidden states with the embedded record encodings B^r.

Static Record attention: In a table, a subset of record types can always be more salient compared to other record types. This is captured by learning a static set of weights over all the records. These weights regulate the dynamic attention weights computed during decoding at each time step. Equation 7 performs this step where g_r is the static record attention weight for r^{th} record and q and P are weights to be learnt. We do not have any constraints on static attention vector.

Dynamic Record attention for Decoder: Our decoder is a GRU based decoder with dynamic attention mechanism similar to (Mei et al., 2016) with modifications to modulate attention weights at each time step using static record attentions. At each time step t attention weights are calculated using 8, 9, 10, where γ_t^r is the aggregated attention weight of record r at time step t. We use the *soft attention* over input encoder sequences c_r to calculate the weighted average, which is passed to the GRU. GRU hidden state s_t is used to calculate output probabilities p_t by using a softmax as described by equation 11, 12, 13, which is then used to get output word y_t.

Due to the static attention at attribute level, the time complexity of a single pass is $O(TM + TT')$, where T is the number of records, M is the number of attributes and T' is the number of decoder steps. In case of dynamic attention at both levels (as in Nallapati et al. (2016)), the time complexity is much higher $O(TMT')$. Thus, *mixed hierarchical attention* model is faster than fully dynamic hierarchical attention. For better understanding of the contribution of hierarchical attention(MHAM), we propose a simpler non-hierarchical (NHM) architecture with attention only at record level. In NHM, B^r is calculated by concatenating all the record attributes along with corresponding record type.

Input Table								Generated Output

TYPE	TIME	MIN	MAX	MEAN	MODE	MB100-4	MB20-2
temperature	17-30	27	36	29	-	-	-
windChill	17-30	14	26	18	-	-	-
windSpeed	17-30	14	20	16	-	-	10-20
windDir	17-30	-	-	-	SSW	-	-
gust	17-30	0	0	0	-	-	-
skyCover	17-30	-	-	-	-	75-100	-
skyCover	17-21	-	-	-	-	75-100	-
skyCover	17-26	-	-	-	-	75-100	-
skyCover	21-30	-	-	-	-	75-100	-
skyCover	26-30	-	-	-	-	75-100	-
precipPotential	17-30	26	58	43	-	-	-
rainChance	17-21	-	-	-	Lkly	-	-
snowChance	17-30	-	-	-	Chc	-	-
snowChance	17-26	-	-	-	Lkly	-	-

Reference: Periods of rain and possibly a thunderstorm . Some of the storms could produce heavy rain . Temperature rising to near 51 by 10am , then falling to around 44 during the remainder of the day . Breezy , with a north northwest wind between 10 and 20 mph . Chance of precipitation is 90 % . New rainfall amounts between one and two inches possible .

NHM:Periods of rain and possibly a thunderstorm . Some of the storms could produce heavy rain . Temperature rising to near 51 by 8am , then falling to around 6 during the remainder of the day . Breezy , with a north northwest wind 10 to 15 mph increasing to between 20 and 25 mph . Chance of precipitation is 90 % . New rainfall amounts between one and two inches possible .

MHAM: Periods of rain and possibly a *thunderstorm* . Some of the storms could produce *heavy rain* . Temperature rising to *near 51 by 8am* , then falling to *around 44* during the remainder of the day . Breezy , with a *north northwest wind* between *10 and 20 mph* . Chance of precipitation is *90 %* . New rainfall amounts between *one and two inches* possible.

TYPE	TIME	MIN	MAX	MEAN	MODE	MB100-4	MB20-2
temperature	17-30	27	36	29	-	-	-
windChill	17-30	14	26	18	-	-	-
windSpeed	17-30	14	20	16	-	-	10-20
windDir	17-30	-	-	-	SSW	-	-
gust	17-30	0	0	0	-	-	-
skyCover	17-30	-	-	-	-	75-100	-
skyCover	17-21	-	-	-	-	75-100	-
skyCover	17-26	-	-	-	-	75-100	-
skyCover	21-30	-	-	-	-	75-100	-
skyCover	26-30	-	-	-	-	75-100	-
precipPotential	17-30	26	58	43	-	-	-
rainChance	17-21	-	-	-	Lkly	-	-
snowChance	17-30	-	-	-	Chc	-	-
snowChance	17-26	-	-	-	Lkly	-	-

Reference: A chance of rain and snow . Snow level 5500 feet . Mostly cloudy , with a low around 31 . Calm wind becoming north northeast around 6 mph . Chance of precipitation is 40% .

NHM: A chance of rain and snow . Mostly cloudy , with a low around 31 . North northwest wind at 6 mph becoming east southeast . Chance of precipitation is 40% .

MHAM: A chance of *rain and snow* . Snow level *5800 feet lowering to 5300 feet* after midnight . Mostly cloudy , with a low *around 31* . *North northwest wind* at *6 mph* becoming south southwest . Chance of precipitation is *40%* .

TYPE	TIME	MIN	MAX	MEAN	MODE	MB100-4	MB20-2
temperature	17-30	27	36	29	-	-	-
windChill	17-30	14	26	18	-	-	-
windSpeed	17-30	14	20	16	-	-	10-20
windDir	17-30	-	-	-	SSW	-	-
gust	17-30	0	0	0	-	-	-
skyCover	17-30	-	-	-	-	75-100	-
skyCover	17-21	-	-	-	-	75-100	-
skyCover	17-26	-	-	-	-	75-100	-
skyCover	21-30	-	-	-	-	75-100	-
skyCover	26-30	-	-	-	-	75-100	-
precipPotential	17-30	26	58	43	-	-	-
rainChance	17-21	-	-	-	Lkly	-	-
snowChance	17-30	-	-	-	Chc	-	-
snowChance	17-26	-	-	-	Lkly	-	-

Reference: Rain and snow likely , becoming all snow after 8pm . Cloudy , with a low around 22 . South southwest wind around 15 mph . Chance of precipitation is 60% . New snow accumulation of less than one inch possible .

NHM : Rain or freezing rain likely before 8pm , then snow after 11pm , snow showers and sleet likely before 8pm , then a chance of rain or freezing rain after 3am . Mostly cloudy , with a low around 27 . South southeast wind between 15 and 17 mph . Chance of precipitation is 80% . Little or no ice accumulation expected . Little or no snow accumulation expected .

MHAM: Snow , and freezing rain , *snow after 9pm* . Cloudy , with a steady temperature *around 23* . Breezy , with a *south wind* between *15 and 20 mph* . Chance of precipitation is *60%* . New snow accumulation of *around an inch* possible .

Table 1: Anecdotal example. Records which contain all null attributes are not shown in the example. MB100-4 and MB20-2 correspond to mode-bucket-0-100-4 & mode-bucket-0-20-2 resp. in the dataset.

3   Experiments

Dataset and methodology: To evaluate our model we have used WEATHERGOV dataset (Liang et al., 2009) which is the standard benchmark dataset to evaluate tabular data summarization techniques. We compared the performance of our model against the state-of-the-art work of MBW (Mei et al., 2016), as well as two other baseline models KL (Konstas and Lapata, 2013) and ALK (Angeli et al., 2010). Dataset consists of a total of 29,528 tables (25000:1000:3528 ratio for train:validation:test splits) corresponding to scenarios created by collecting weather forecasts for 3,753 cities in the U.S.A over three days. There are 12 record types consisting of both numeric and categorical values. Each table contains 36 weather records (e.g., temperature, wind direction etc.) along with a corresponding natural language summary.

Input Encodings: Attributes were encoded based on the attribute type. Numbers are encoded in binary representation. Record type is encoded as a one-hot vector. Mode attribute is encoded using specific ordinal encodings for example 'Lkly',

'SChc', 'Chc' are encoded as '00100000000000', '00010000000000' and '00001000000000' respectively. Similar works for directions, for example 'NW', 'NNE' and 'NE' are encoded as '00000100000000', '00000011000000' and '00000001000000' resp. Time interval were also encoded as ordinal encodings, for example '6-21' is encoded as '111100' and '6-13' is encoded as '110000', the six bits corresponding to six atomic time intervals available in the dataset. Other attributes and words were encoded as one-hot vectors.

3.1   Training and hyperparameter tuning

We used TensorFlow (Abadi et al., 2015) for our experiments. Encoder embeddings were initialized by generating the values from a uniform distribution in the range [-1, 1). Other variables were initialized using Glorot uniform initialization (Glorot and Bengio, 2010). We tune each hyperparameter by choosing parameter from a ranges of values, and selected the model with best sBLEU score in validation set over 500 epochs. We did not use any regularization while training the model. For both the models, the hyperparameter tuning was separately performed to give both models a fair chance of performance. For both the models, Adam optimizer (Kingma and Ba, 2014) was used with learning rate set to 0.0001. We found embedding size of 100, GRU size of 400, static record attention size P of 150 to work best for MHAM model. We also experimented using bi-directional GRU in the encoder but there was no significant boost observed in the BLEU scores.

Evaluation metrics: To evaluate our models we employed BLEU and Rouge-L scores. In addition to the standard BLEU (sBleu) (Papineni et al., 2002), a customized BLEU (cBleu) (Mei et al., 2016) has also been reported. cBleu does not penalize numbers which differ by at most five; hence 20 and 18 will be considered same.

4   Results and Analyses

Table 2 describes the results of our proposed models (MHAM and NHM) along with the aforementioned baseline models. We observe a significant performance improvement of 16.6 cBleu score (24%) and 18.3 sBleu score (30%) compared to the current state-of-the-art model of MBW. MHAM also shows an improvement over NHM in all metrics demonstrating the importance of hierarchical attention.

Model	sBleu	cBleu	Rouge-L
KL	36.54	-	-
ALK	38.40	51.50	-
MBW	61.0	70.4	-
NHM	76.2	85.0	86.4
MHAM	**79.3**	**87.0**	**88.5**

Table 2: Overall results

Attention analysis: Analysis of figure 3 reveals that the learnt attention weights are reasonable. For example, as shown in figure 3(a), for the phrase 'with a high near 52', the model had a high attention on *temperature* before and while generating the number '52'. Similarly while generating 'mostly cloudy', the model had a high attention on *precipitation potential*. Attribute attentions are also learned as expected (in figure 3(b)). The *temperature*, *wind speed* and *gust* records have high weights on min/max/mean values which describe these records.

Qualitative analysis: Table 1 contains example table-summary pairs, with summary generated by the proposed hierarchical and non-hierarchical

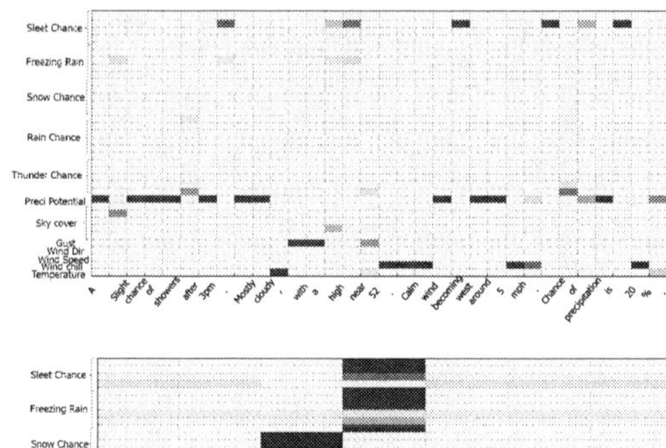
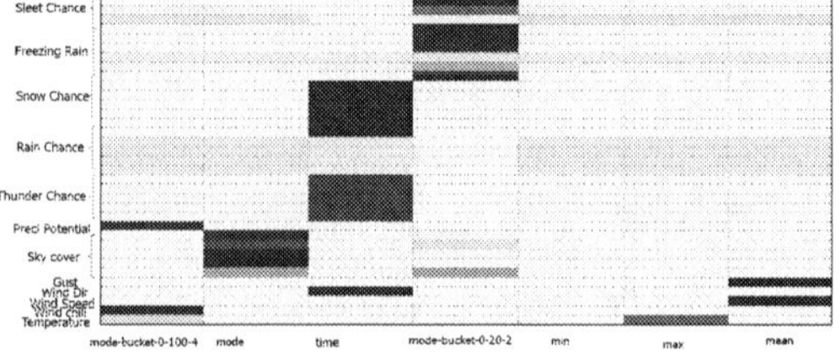

Figure 3: Heatmaps: (a) record level attention (top) and (b) attribute level attention (bottom).

versions. We observe that our model is able to generate numbers more accurately by enabling hierarchical attention. Our model is also able to capture weak signals like *snow accumulation*. Further, our proposed model MHAM is able to avoid repetition as compared to NHM.

5   Conclusion and Future Work

In this work, we have formulated the problem of *standard table summarization* where all the tables come from a predefined schema. Towards this, we proposed a novel mixed hierarchical attention based encoder-decoder approach. Our experiments on the publicly available WEATHERGOV benchmark dataset have shown significant improvements over the current state-of-the-art work. Moreover, this proposed method is theoretically more efficient compared to the current fully dynamic hierarchical attention model. As future work, we propose to tackle general tabular summarization where the schema can vary across tables in the whole dataset.

6   Acknowledgements

We would like to acknowledge Abhijit Mishra for his valuable feedback and comments.

References

Martín Abadi, Ashish Agarwal, Paul Barham, Eugene Brevdo, Zhifeng Chen, Craig Citro, Greg S. Corrado, Andy Davis, Jeffrey Dean, Matthieu Devin,

Sanjay Ghemawat, Ian Goodfellow, Andrew Harp, Geoffrey Irving, Michael Isard, Yangqing Jia, Rafal Jozefowicz, Lukasz Kaiser, Manjunath Kudlur, Josh Levenberg, Dan Mané, Rajat Monga, Sherry Moore, Derek Murray, Chris Olah, Mike Schuster, Jonathon Shlens, Benoit Steiner, Ilya Sutskever, Kunal Talwar, Paul Tucker, Vincent Vanhoucke, Vijay Vasudevan, Fernanda Viégas, Oriol Vinyals, Pete Warden, Martin Wattenberg, Martin Wicke, Yuan Yu, and Xiaoqiang Zheng. 2015. TensorFlow: Large-scale machine learning on heterogeneous systems. Software available from tensorflow.org.

Ion Androutsopoulos, Gerasimos Lampouras, and Dimitrios Galanis. 2014. Generating natural language descriptions from OWL ontologies: the naturalowl system. *CoRR*, abs/1405.6164.

Gabor Angeli, Percy Liang, and Dan Klein. 2010. A simple domain-independent probabilistic approach to generation. In *Proceedings of the 2010 Conference on Empirical Methods in Natural Language Processing*, pages 502–512. Association for Computational Linguistics.

KyungHyun Cho, Aaron C. Courville, and Yoshua Bengio. 2015. Describing multimedia content using attention-based encoder-decoder networks. *CoRR*, abs/1507.01053.

Emilie Colin, Claire Gardent, Yassine Mrabet, Shashi Narayan, and Laura Perez-Beltrachini. 2016. The webnlg challenge: Generating text from dbpedia data. In *INLG 2016 - Proceedings of the Ninth International Natural Language Generation Conference, September 5-8, 2016, Edinburgh, UK*, pages 163–167.

Yuntian Deng, Anssi Kanervisto, Jeffrey Ling, and Alexander M. Rush. 2017. Image-to-markup generation with coarse-to-fine attention. In *Proceedings of the 34th International Conference on Machine Learning, ICML 2017, Sydney, NSW, Australia, 6-11 August 2017*, pages 980–989.

Xavier Glorot and Yoshua Bengio. 2010. Understanding the difficulty of training deep feedforward neural networks. In *In Proceedings of the International Conference on Artificial Intelligence and Statistics (AISTATS10). Society for Artificial Intelligence and Statistics*.

Srinivasan Iyer, Ioannis Konstas, Alvin Cheung, and Luke Zettlemoyer. 2016. Summarizing source code using a neural attention model. In *Proceedings of the 54th Annual Meeting of the Association for Computational Linguistics (Volume 1: Long Papers)*, pages 2073–2083, Berlin, Germany. Association for Computational Linguistics.

Diederik Kingma and Jimmy Ba. 2014. Adam: A method for stochastic optimization. *arXiv preprint arXiv:1412.6980*.

Ioannis Konstas and Mirella Lapata. 2013. Inducing document plans for concept-to-text generation. In *EMNLP*.

Rémi Lebret, David Grangier, and Michael Auli. 2016. Neural text generation from structured data with application to the biography domain. In *Proceedings of the 2016 Conference on Empirical Methods in Natural Language Processing*, pages 1203–1213, Austin, Texas. Association for Computational Linguistics.

Percy Liang, Michael I. Jordan, and Dan Klein. 2009. Learning semantic correspondences with less supervision. In *Proceedings of the Joint Conference of the 47th Annual Meeting of the ACL and the 4th International Joint Conference on Natural Language Processing of the AFNLP: Volume 1 - Volume 1*, ACL '09, pages 91–99, Stroudsburg, PA, USA. Association for Computational Linguistics.

Jeffrey Ling and Alexander M. Rush. 2017. Coarse-to-fine attention models for document summarization. In *Proceedings of the Workshop on New Frontiers in Summarization, NFiS@EMNLP 2017, Copenhagen, Denmark, September 7, 2017*, pages 33–42.

Hongyuan Mei, Mohit Bansal, and Matthew R. Walter. 2016. What to talk about and how? selective generation using lstms with coarse-to-fine alignment. In *Proceedings of the 2016 Conference of the North American Chapter of the Association for Computational Linguistics: Human Language Technologies*, pages 720–730, San Diego, California. Association for Computational Linguistics.

Ramesh Nallapati, Bing Xiang, and Bowen Zhou. 2016. Sequence-to-sequence rnns for text summarization. *CoRR*, abs/1602.06023.

Kishore Papineni, Salim Roukos, Todd Ward, and Wei-Jing Zhu. 2002. Bleu: a method for automatic evaluation of machine translation. In *Proceedings of the 40th annual meeting on association for computational linguistics*, pages 311–318. Association for Computational Linguistics.

Sam Wiseman, Stuart M. Shieber, and Alexander M. Rush. 2017. Challenges in data-to-document generation. In *Proceedings of the 2017 Conference on Empirical Methods in Natural Language Processing, EMNLP 2017, Copenhagen, Denmark, September 9-11, 2017*, pages 2253–2263.

Effective Crowdsourcing for a New Type of Summarization Task

Youxuan Jiang, Catherine Finegan-Dollak, Jonathan K. Kummerfeld, Walter S. Lasecki
Computer Science & Engineering
University of Michigan, Ann Arbor
{lyjiang,cfdollak,jkummerf,wlasecki}@umich.edu

Abstract

Most summarization research focuses on summarizing the entire given text, but in practice readers are often interested in only one aspect of the document or conversation. We propose "targeted summarization" as an umbrella category for summarization tasks that intentionally consider only parts of the input data. This covers query-based summarization, update summarization, and a new task we propose where the goal is to summarize a particular aspect of a document. However, collecting data for this new task is hard because directly asking annotators (e.g., crowd workers) to write summaries leads to data with low accuracy when there are a large number of facts to include. We introduce a novel crowdsourcing workflow, Pin-Refine, that allows us to collect high-quality summaries for our task, a necessary step for the development of automatic systems.

1 Introduction

Our lives are increasingly dependent on information, but so much is generated every day that manually processing it is overwhelming (Jones et al., 2004). For decades, research in NLP has focused on automatic summarization as a solution to this problem (Nenkova and McKeown, 2012). However, most of that research has focused on generic summarization, where the summary aims to produce a shorter form of a document. Variants of this task, query-based summarization and update summarization, consider summarization focusing on certain parts of the document, but neither covers the situation when a user wants the summary to capture a particular aspect of a document. For example, a legal case document can contain multiple types of information, such as facts, procedural history, and legal reasoning – but a lawyer may only want a summary of the facts stated in the document, while leaving out procedural history and legal reasoning.

This paper makes two contributions: First, we propose a new hierarchy of summarization task types, which provides a framework for understanding how tasks relate to one another and where gaps exist currently. We define a new concept, *targeted summarization*, that contrasts with generic summarization. We then define a new category of summarization task, *aspect-based summarization*, that covers cases like the law example above.

Second, we present and evaluate a new crowdsourced data collection workflow pattern, *Pin-Refine*, that splits the summarization task into two stages: *choosing what to summarize* and *writing the summary*. We apply this approach to a dialog dataset, where questions are expressed over multiple turns, to collect summaries that concisely express each question. Our results show that when more facts need to be summarized, the Pin-Refine workflow produces significantly more accurate summaries compared to a baseline approach in which crowd workers read text and write summaries in a single step. Our method enables efficient creation of datasets for this new task and may be beneficial for other summarization tasks.

2 Related Work

Our work on targeted summarization is related to previous work in automatic summarization and crowdsourced corpus generation.

2.1 Automatic Summarization

In the most common form of summarization, generic summarization, summaries cover all the content in the given text (Gong and Liu, 2001). Specific variants of the task exist for certain domains, such as narrative (Mani, 2004) and email-thread summarization (Rambow et al., 2004).

Proceedings of NAACL-HLT 2018, pages 628–633
New Orleans, Louisiana, June 1 - 6, 2018. ©2018 Association for Computational Linguistics

In contrast, summaries for query-based summarization only cover parts of the text that are about the topic specified by a query (Rahman and Borah, 2015). Another alternative is update summarization, in which the summary should cover content in one set of documents, but not in another set that the user has already read (Dang and Owczarzak, 2008). The specific form of summarization we are interested in does not fit within either query-based or update summarization. To clarify the relationships between all of these different summarization tasks, we propose a new term, aspect-based summarization, and present a hierarchy of tasks.

In data mining, recent work has explored summarizing different aspects of graph data given domain context (Jin and Koutra, 2017). In NLP, previous summarization tasks have explored summarization based on information types in individual domains, such as opinion summarization (Condori and Pardo, 2017) and task-focused email summarization (Corston-Oliver et al., 2004). Performance on these tasks is usually lower than traditional summarization tasks due to the difficulty of identifying relevant information in noisy text. We introduce a new crowdsourcing workflow, Pin-Refine, that improves the quality of data collection for specialized summarization tasks.

2.2 Crowdsourced Corpus Generation

Large corpora are critical for training robust natural language processing systems, but traditional expert-driven data collection methods are both costly and time-consuming (Hovy et al., 2006). During the last decade, crowdsourcing has been broadly applied to collect natural language data at large scale with reasonable costs (Snow et al., 2008), including for translation (Zaidan and Callison-Burch, 2011), paraphrasing (Burrows et al., 2013; Jiang et al., 2017), dialog generation (Lasecki et al., 2013b,a), and annotation of corpora in tasks like sentiment classification (Hsueh et al., 2009).

Since individual workers' outputs are usually error-prone, aggregation mechanisms such as majority voting (Raykar et al., 2010) and quality verification tasks (Callison-Burch, 2009) have been developed to improve consistency. However, the results receiving the most votes may still miss information that should be included. To address this issue, crowdsourced iterative methods have been developed to divide a complicated task into

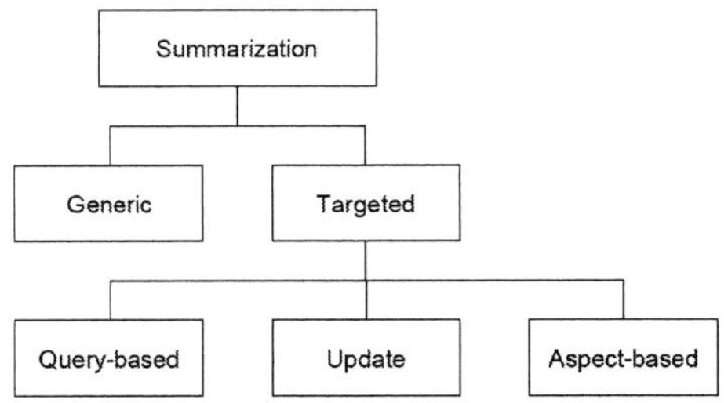

Figure 1: Proposed hierarchy of summarization tasks.

a series of micro-stages, each with a different focus (Little et al., 2010; Merritt et al., 2017). For example, Ouyang et al. (2017) developed a dataset of aligned extractive and abstractive summaries by creating separate tasks for summarization, alignment, and classification of changes. However, maintaining accuracy when the complexity of the given text increases has remained an open question. In our Pin-Refine workflow, workers first identified all text relevant to the given information type, which was aggregated across workers with a threshold, then wrote the summary using that information. This aggregation and priming helps maintain accuracy as text grows more complex.

3 Targeted and Aspect-Based Summarization

Traditionally, the NLP community has divided summarization tasks into generic summarization, which covers the entire text, query-based summarization, which covers only topics related to a query provided by the user (Nenkova and McKeown, 2012), and update summarization, which covers only topics that were not addressed in documents already presented to the user (Dang and Owczarzak, 2008). In query-based and update summarization, what should and should not be summarized depends on a topic (defined either by the query, or the already-read documents). This view omits cases where the user describes an information need using something other than topics.

We therefore re-categorize summarization tasks (Figure 1) as generic or *targeted*. We define the latter as the task of generating a summary that captures the part of a document relevant to the user's information request. It includes (1) query-based summarization, where the information request is a query indicating the desired topic, (2) update summarization, where the request is whether information is new, and (3) *aspect-based summarization* where the request is the desired information type,

Person A: I am a *CS major* and need to *schedule classes for next semester.*
Person B: It looks like you have most of your pre-requisites out of the way and you can start taking some more EECS classes.
Person A: Cool, I'm very *interested in Software Infrastructure Applications and web app.*

Figure 2: Example conversation for summarization. Targeted information units (TIUs) are in italics.

which can partially cover content of one or more topics. The information type targeted by aspect-based summarization varies based on users' needs. For example, meeting attendees might want a summary of a meeting transcript only including action items, while a supervisor evaluating an employee might need a summary of status updates the employee provided at the meeting.

This hierarchy shows the relationship among existing summarization tasks and provides a framework to understand how the aspect-based task and potential future tasks relate to each other.

4 Experimental Design

When developing datasets for summarization, we are concerned with two key properties: accuracy and fluency. We conducted experiments to investigate design options for crowdsourced aspect-based summarization, aiming to optimize both.

4.1 Conversation Generation

In this study, we focus on summarizing student questions regarding course selection from advising conversations. For such a question to be correctly expressed, the summary must include all relevant facts about the student's background and preferences that appear in the conversation, as shown in Figure 2. We call these facts *targeted information units* (TIU), because they are the pieces of information that must be part of the summary for the given information type.

In this paper, we tested our workflows on a course advising conversation dataset produced by undergraduates role-playing as students and advisors. The goal of the conversations was to determine what courses the students should take based on their needs, as shown in the example conversation in Figure 2. Each "advisor" received a list of course profiles, and each "student" received a made-up student profile, including courses they had taken. Participants were instructed to use the profiles they received while letting the conversation proceed as smoothly as possible.

Rewrite Questions

Please read each conversation below and rewrite ALL parts of Person A's question, so that Person B can answer it without seeing the conversation. For example:

Example Conversation

Person A: I wanted to talk about my classes for next semester.
Person B: Okay, great. How many credits are you planning to take?
Person A: I was hoping to have a relaxed semester, so I'm hoping to take 12 credits.

You may write: 'What classes can I take next semester if I want 12 credits?'

If one sentence is not enough, use multiple sentences.

Figure 3: Baseline task instructions and examples.

4.2 Conversation Selection

We selected 30 conversations from the dataset mentioned above. Each conversation focuses on answering one question, and the number of TIUs per conversation varies evenly between 1 and 6 among the 30 conversations. Three of the authors—two native English speakers and one fluent speaker—read each conversation and summarized each user question. The lead author then compared these summaries and chose one per conversation as the ground truth summary.

4.3 Conditions

Baseline We recruited crowd workers via LegionTools (Lasecki et al., 2014; Gordon et al., 2015) from Amazon Mechanical Turk, presenting them with instructions and an example as shown in Figure 3. Workers were shown 5 conversations, one at a time, and asked to write the question being asked, including all the details that need to be known in order to correctly answer the question. Each worker was paid 10 cents per conversation.

Highlight In this condition, workers were first asked to highlight all details in each conversation that must be known to correctly answer the question, then write the question being asked, including the details they highlighted. We hypothesize that workers were primed by the process of highlighting TIUs in conversations before writing the actual summaries. In this condition, workers were paid 15 cents per conversation[1].

---

[1]Payments in the Highlight and Pin-Refine conditions were higher than in the baseline, because those two conditions required workers to also do priming tasks.

| Targeted Units | Time (s) | | | Correct Intent (%) | | | Targeted Information Units Captured | | | | | | | | | | |
| | | | | | | | Recall | | | Precision | | | F_1 | | | Fluency (%) | | |
	b	h	p	b	h	p	b	h	p	b	h	p	b	h	p	b	h	p
1	26.5	**45**	**107**†	100	94	96	100	96	92	94	96	88	96	96	89	84	90	86
2	35	**46**	**131.5**†	98	96	100	86	87	92	93	99	95	88	91	93	78	78	94
3	48	**63**	**155.5**†	94	84	96	73	78	86	89	93	91	79	83	87	66	72	78
4	60	**82**	**161.5**†	86	84	96	69	76	**85**	91	87	91	76	79	**87**	76	62	82
5	76.5	**94.5**	**192**†	78	88	94	68	71	**88**†	88	90	92	75	78	**90**†	80	80	76
6	92.5	**116.5**	**230**†	84	94	94	70	69	**81**†	87	88	90	77	76	**85**†	72	68	64

Table 1: Performance for a range of metrics (defined in § 4.4) as the number of targeted information units and the condition vary (b: Baseline, h: Highlight, p: Pin-Refine). Bold indicates a statistically significant difference compared to the baseline at the 0.05 level, and a † indicates significance compared to the highlight condition at the 0.05 level, both after applying the Holm-Bonferroni method across each row (Holm, 1979).

Pin-Refine This condition had two separate steps: pin and refine. In the pin step, workers selected sections of the text as in the highlight case, and were paid 5 cents per conversation. Highlights from multiple workers for each conversation were automatically aggregated by keeping highlights if the percentage of workers who assigned them was above a threshold. In the refine step, a different worker was shown the conversation with highlights and asked to write a justification of each highlight, *then* write a summary. Each worker was paid 15 cents per conversation for the refine step.

To find and validate the correct threshold in the pin step, we repeated the data collection and aggregation of the pin step twice on the same set of conversations. In both attempts, all of the TIUs were covered by aggregated highlights at 40% agreement, and no completely irrelevant information was covered. While we used 40% agreement as our threshold, we also observed that coverage was robust to variation in this value. When very high agreement was required (70%) we still found on average 90% of correct phrases were covered (recall remains high), and when very low agreement was required (20%) only 7% of highlighted phrases were irrelevant (precision remains high).

4.4 Metrics

We evaluate question summaries on three metrics: *time* was measured directly; *accuracy* and *fluency* were independently rated by three of the authors. We used Fleiss' Kappa to measure the inter-annotator agreement between the three annotators before discussing each case of disagreement for consensus judgment. The kappa scores were .95 for intent accuracy, .86 for TIU accuracy (both near-perfect agreement), and .62 for fluency (substantial agreement) (Altman, 1990).

Accuracy An accurate question summary must ask for the information sought by the student (intent accuracy) and include all the information needed to define the question (TIU accuracy). Three authors rated the question intent in each summary and counted how many of the gold TIUs were present, as well as how many information units not in the gold appeared in the summary. To measure TIU accuracy, we calculated recall, precision, and F_1 score. We used Fisher's exact tests and Mann Whitney U tests to measure significance of intent and TIU accuracy (respectively) between each pair of conditions in our study.

Fluency A fluent summary is grammatically correct or correct but for minor errors of punctuation. Run-on sentences, sentences with grammatical errors that obscure their meanings, sentences missing words, and so on, are not fluent. We used a χ^2 test to measure significance.

Time To estimate time-to-completion and ensure fair payment, we measured and calculated the average time between when a worker submitted one summary and the next. Time spent on the first summary was excluded because it typically includes time spent reading the instructions and understanding the task, which would skew the data. We report the median time to avoid skewing due to outliers, such as a value of five minutes when a worker took a break, and used a Moods Median test to measure significance.

5 Results

We spent $153.50, including initial testing, to collect 900 summaries: 10 summaries for each of the 30 conversations in all 3 conditions. We have released this dataset as an attachment to this paper.

Table 1 shows the results accross all of our metrics. We find there was relatively little variation in correctness and fluency of summaries across conditions. For the baseline, accuracy and fluency of summaries decreases as the number of TIUs per conversation increases.

Aggregation and priming had a major impact on recall and F_1 when the number of TIUs was greater than three. After that point, the Pin-Refine condition achieved significant improvements in recall and F_1 compared to the baseline. There was no significant difference between accuracy of the baseline and highlight conditions, likely because workers were primed by their own mistakes and chose not to highlight information they believed was not important. Precision remains relatively high with no significant difference across all conditions, implying that workers' ability to effectively exclude information is not related to the targeted information type.

The time workers spent summarizing one conversation increases as the number of TIUs per conversation increases. The significant time increase between the baseline and the other two conditions was caused by the additional work involved in highlighting and writing justifications.

On average, workers spent significantly longer on the justification task in the Pin-Refine condition (65.37s) than the highlighting task in the highlight condition (36.68s). Workers' justifications include single words like "timestamp," short phrases like "why they want a specific course," and long sentences like "This shows what grade they're in, what related class they've taken, what their interest is, and what kind of help they need." One possibility is that simply encouraging workers to spend more time writing their summaries improved performance, but fitting a linear model we find the correlation coefficient between time and F_1 is -0.06, indicating no linear correlation between time and accuracy across conditions. Therefore, we believe that the significant accuracy improvement observed in the Pin-Refine condition is the result of active priming with aggregated TIUs.

6 Conclusion

In this paper, we have identified a previously unexplored summarization problem that targets specific information in a document instead of aiming to extract all key elements: aspect-based summarization. Then, to address the corresponding gap in techniques for data collection for this new problem, we proposed the Pin-Refine crowdsourcing workflow, which leverages input aggregation and worker priming effects. This approach leads to significantly higher summarization accuracy when the number of targeted information units (TIUs) is large. Our work provides methods and task design guidance for future data generation efforts, which are crucial for the development of robust summarization systems.

7 Acknowledgements

We would like to thank Sai Gouravajhala, Stephanie O'Keefe, and the anonymous reviewers for their helpful suggestions on this work, and all of our study participants for their work.

This material is based in part upon work supported by IBM under contract 4915012629. Any opinions, findings, conclusions or recommendations expressed above are those of the authors and do not necessarily reflect the views of IBM.

References

Douglas G Altman. 1990. *Practical statistics for medical research*. CRC press.

Steven Burrows, Martin Potthast, and Benno Stein. 2013. Paraphrase acquisition via crowdsourcing and machine learning. *ACM Transactions on Intelligent Systems and Technology (TIST)* 4(3):43. https://dl.acm.org/citation.cfm?id=2483676.

Chris Callison-Burch. 2009. Fast, cheap, and creative: evaluating translation quality using amazon's mechanical turk. In *Empirical Methods in Natural Language Processing: Volume 1-Volume 1*. pages 286–295. https://www.aclweb.org/anthology/D/D09/D09-1030.pdf.

Roque Enrique López Condori and Thiago Alexandre Salgueiro Pardo. 2017. Opinion summarization methods: Comparing and extending extractive and abstractive approaches. *Expert Systems with Applications* 78:124–134.

Simon Corston-Oliver, Eric Ringger, Michael Gamon, and Richard Campbell. 2004. Task-focused summarization of email. *ACL Workshop on Text Summarization Branches Out* http://aclweb.org/anthology/W/W04/W04-1008.pdf.

Hoa Trang Dang and Karolina Owczarzak. 2008. Overview of the tac 2008 update summarization task. In *Text Analysis Conference*. pages 10–23.

Yihong Gong and Xin Liu. 2001. Generic text summarization using relevance measure and latent semantic analysis. In *Research and Development in Information Retrieval*. ACM, pages 19–25. `https://dl.acm.org/citation.cfm?id=383955`.

Mitchell Gordon, Jeffrey P Bigham, and Walter S Lasecki. 2015. Legiontools: a toolkit+ ui for recruiting and routing crowds to synchronous real-time tasks. In *User Interface Software and Technology*. ACM, pages 81–82. `https://dl.acm.org/citation.cfm?id=2815729`.

Sture Holm. 1979. A simple sequentially rejective multiple test procedure. *Scandinavian Journal of Statistics* 6(2):65–70. `http://www.jstor.org/stable/4615733`.

Eduard Hovy, Mitchell Marcus, Martha Palmer, Lance Ramshaw, and Ralph Weischedel. 2006. Ontonotes: the 90% solution. In *Proceedings of the Human Language Technology Conference of the NAACL, Companion Volume: Short Papers*. pages 57–60. `https://dl.acm.org/citation.cfm?id=1614064`.

Pei-Yun Hsueh, Prem Melville, and Vikas Sindhwani. 2009. Data quality from crowdsourcing: a study of annotation selection criteria. In *NAACL HLT 2009 workshop on active learning for natural language processing*. pages 27–35. `https://dl.acm.org/citation.cfm?id=1564137`.

Youxuan Jiang, Jonathan K. Kummerfeld, and Walter S. Lasecki. 2017. Understanding task design trade-offs in crowdsourced paraphrase collection. In *Association for Computational Linguistics (Volume 2: Short Papers)*. pages 103–109. `http://aclweb.org/anthology/P17-2017`.

Di Jin and Danai Koutra. 2017. Exploratory analysis of graph data by leveraging domain knowledge. In *2017 IEEE International Conference on Data Mining (ICDM)*. IEEE, pages 187–196.

Quentin Jones, Gilad Ravid, and Sheizaf Rafaeli. 2004. Information overload and the message dynamics of online interaction spaces: A theoretical model and empirical exploration. *Information systems research* 15(2):194–210.

Walter S Lasecki, Mitchell Gordon, Danai Koutra, Malte F Jung, Steven P Dow, and Jeffrey P Bigham. 2014. Glance: Rapidly coding behavioral video with the crowd. In *User Interface Software and Technology*. ACM, pages 551–562. `https://dl.acm.org/citation.cfm?id=2647367`.

Walter S Lasecki, Ece Kamar, and Dan Bohus. 2013a. Conversations in the crowd: Collecting data for task-oriented dialog learning. In *First AAAI Conference on Human Computation and Crowdsourcing*.

Walter S Lasecki, Rachel Wesley, Jeffrey Nichols, Anand Kulkarni, James F Allen, and Jeffrey P Bigham. 2013b. Chorus: a crowd-powered conversational assistant. In *User Interface Software and Technology*. ACM, pages 151–162. `https://dl.acm.org/citation.cfm?id=2502057`.

Greg Little, Lydia B Chilton, Max Goldman, and Robert C Miller. 2010. Turkit: human computation algorithms on mechanical turk. In *User Interface Software and Technology*. ACM, pages 57–66. `https://dl.acm.org/citation.cfm?id=1866040`.

Inderjeet Mani. 2004. Narrative summarization. *Traitement Automatique des Langues* 45(1).

David Merritt, Jasmine Jones, Mark S Ackerman, and Walter S Lasecki. 2017. Kurator: Using the crowd to help families with personal curation tasks. In *Proceedings of the 2017 ACM Conference on Computer Supported Cooperative Work and Social Computing*. pages 1835–1849. `https://dl.acm.org/citation.cfm?id=2998358`.

Ani Nenkova and Kathleen McKeown. 2012. A survey of text summarization techniques. *Mining text data* pages 43–76.

Jessica Ouyang, Serina Chang, and Kathy McKeown. 2017. Crowd-sourced iterative annotation for narrative summarization corpora. In *European Chapter of the Association for Computational Linguistics: Volume 2, Short Papers*. pages 46–51. `http://aclweb.org/anthology/E/E17/E17-2008.pdf`.

Nazreena Rahman and Bhogeswar Borah. 2015. A survey on existing extractive techniques for query-based text summarization. In *Advanced Computing and Communication (ISACC), 2015 International Symposium on*. IEEE, pages 98–102.

Owen Rambow, Lokesh Shrestha, John Chen, and Chirsty Lauridsen. 2004. Summarizing email threads. In *Proceedings of HLT-NAACL 2004: Short Papers*. pages 105–108. `http://aclweb.org/anthology/N/N04/N04-4027.pdf`.

Vikas C Raykar, Shipeng Yu, Linda H Zhao, Gerardo Hermosillo Valadez, Charles Florin, Luca Bogoni, and Linda Moy. 2010. Learning from crowds. *Journal of Machine Learning Research* 11(Apr):1297–1322.

Rion Snow, Brendan O'Connor, Daniel Jurafsky, and Andrew Y Ng. 2008. Cheap and fast—but is it good?: evaluating non-expert annotations for natural language tasks. In *Empirical Methods in Natural Language Processing*. pages 254–263. `http://aclweb.org/anthology/D/D08/D08-1027.pdf`.

Omar F. Zaidan and Chris Callison-Burch. 2011. Crowdsourcing translation: Professional quality from non-professionals. In *Proceedings of the 49th Annual Meeting of the Association for Computational Linguistics: Human Language Technologies*. pages 1220–1229. `http://www.aclweb.org/anthology/P11-1122`.

Key2Vec: Automatic Ranked Keyphrase Extraction from Scientific Articles using Phrase Embeddings

Debanjan Mahata
Bloomberg
New York, U.S.A
dmahata@bloomberg.net

John Kuriakose
Infosys Limited
Pune, India
John_Kuriakose@infosys.com

Rajiv Ratn Shah
IIIT-Delhi
New Delhi, India
rajivratn@iiitd.ac.in

Roger Zimmermann
NUS-Singapore,
Singapore
rogerz@comp.nus.edu.sg

Abstract

Keyphrase extraction is a fundamental task in natural language processing that facilitates mapping of documents to a set of representative phrases. In this paper, we present an unsupervised technique (*Key2Vec*) that leverages phrase embeddings for ranking keyphrases extracted from scientific articles. Specifically, we propose an effective way of processing text documents for training multi-word phrase embeddings that are used for thematic representation of scientific articles and ranking of keyphrases extracted from them using theme-weighted PageRank. Evaluations are performed on benchmark datasets producing state-of-the-art results.

1 Introduction and Background

Keyphrases are single or multi-word linguistic units that represent the salient aspects of a document. The task of ranked keyphrase extraction from scientific articles is of great interest to scientific publishers as it helps to recommend articles to readers, highlight missing citations to authors, identify potential reviewers for submissions, and analyze research trends over time (Augenstein et al., 2017). Due to its widespread use, keyphrase extraction has received significant attention from researchers (Kim et al., 2010; Augenstein et al., 2017). However, the task is far from solved and the performances of the present systems are worse in comparison to many other NLP tasks (Liu et al., 2010). Some of the major challenges are the varied length of the documents to be processed, their structural inconsistency and developing strategies that can perform well in different domains (Hasan and Ng, 2014).

Methods for automatic keyphrase extraction are mainly divided into two categories: *supervised* and *unsupervised*. Supervised methods approach the problem as a binary classification problem

(Hasan and Ng, 2014), whereas the unsupervised methods are mostly based on TF-IDF, clustering, and graph-based ranking (Hasan and Ng, 2010; Mihalcea and Tarau, 2004). On the presence of domain-specific data, supervised methods have shown better performance. The unsupervised methods have the advantage of not requiring any training data and can produce results in any domain.

With recent advancements in deep learning techniques applied to natural language processing (NLP), the trend is to represent words as dense real-valued vectors, popularly known as word embeddings. These representations of words have been shown to equal or outperform other methods (e.g. LSA, SVD) (Baroni et al., 2014). The embedding vectors, are supposed to preserve the semantic and syntactic similarities between words. They have been shown to be useful for several NLP tasks, like part-of-speech tagging, chunking, named entity recognition, semantic role labeling, syntactic parsing, and speech processing, among others (Collobert et al., 2011). Some of the most popular approaches for training word embeddings are Word2Vec (Mikolov et al., 2013), Glove (Pennington et al., 2014) and Fasttext (Bojanowski et al., 2016).

Title: Identification of states of complex systems with estimation of admissible measurement errors on the basis of fuzzy information.
Abstract: The problem of identification of states of complex systems on the basis of fuzzy values of informative attributes is considered. Some estimates of a maximally admissible degree of measurement error are obtained that make it possible, using the apparatus of fuzzy set theory, to correctly identify the current state of a system.
Automatically identified keywords: *complex systems, fuzzy information, admissible measurement errors, fuzzy values, informative attributes measurement error, maximally admissible degree, fuzzy set theory*
Manually assigned keywords: *complex system state identification, admissible measurement errors, informative attributes, measurement errors fuzzy set theory*

Table 1: Keyphrases extracted by using *Key2Vec* from a sample research article abstract.

Word embeddings have already shown promis-

Proceedings of NAACL-HLT 2018, pages 634–639
New Orleans, Louisiana, June 1 - 6, 2018. ©2018 Association for Computational Linguistics

ing results in the process of keyphrase extraction from scientific articles (Wang et al., 2015, 2014). However, Wang *et al.* did not use domain-specific word embeddings and had suggested that training them might lead to improvements. This motivated us to experiment with domain-specific embeddings on scientific articles.

In this work, we represent candidate keyphrases extracted from a scientific article by domain-specific phrase embeddings and rank them using a *theme-weighted* PageRank algorithm (Langville and Meyer, 2004), such that the *thematic weight* of a candidate keyphrase indicate how similar it is to the *thematic representation* or the main theme of the article, which is also constructed using the same embeddings. Due to extensive use of phrase embeddings for representing the candidate keyphrases and ranking them, we name our method as *Key2Vec*. To our knowledge, using multi-word phrase embeddings for constructing *thematic representation* of a given document and to assign *thematic weights* to phrases have not been used for ranked keyphrase extraction, and this work is the first preliminary attempt to do so. Table 1. shows ranked keyphrases extracted using *Key2Vec* from a sample research abstract. Next, we present our methodology.

2 Methodology

Our methodology primarily uses three steps: *candidate selection*, *candidate scoring*, and *candidate ranking*, similar to other popular frameworks of ranked keyphrase extraction (Kim et al., 2013). All the steps depend on the choice of our text processing steps and a phrase embedding model that we train on a large corpus of scientific articles. We explain them next and give a detailed description of their implementations.

2.1 Text Processing

It has been shown (Mikolov et al., 2013), that the presence of multi-word phrases intermixed with unigram words increases the performance and accruacy of the embedding models trained using techniques such as *Word2Vec*. However, in our framework we take a different approach in detecting meaningful and cohesive chunk of phrases while preparing the text samples for training. Instead of relying on measures considering how often two or more words co-occur with each other, we rely on already trained dependency parsing and

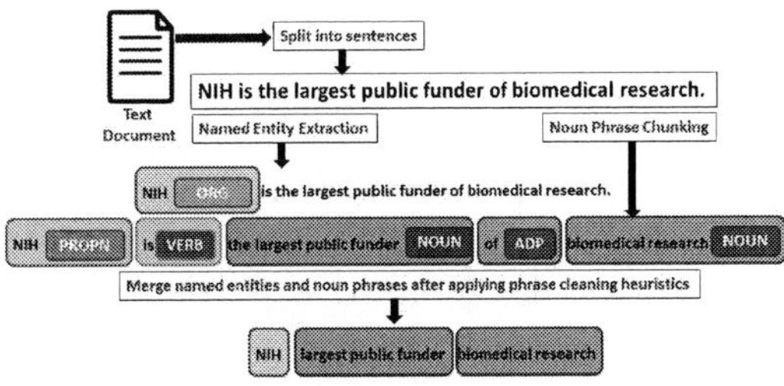

Figure 1: Text processing pipeline for preparing text samples used for training word embedding models.

named entity extraction models. For this work we use *Spacy*[1] as our NLP toolkit along with its default models. The choice of *Spacy* is just for convenience and is not driven by any other factor. We split a text document into sentences, tokenize a sentence into unigram tokens, as well as identify noun phrases and named entities from it. During this process if a named entity is detected at a particular offset in the sentence then a noun phrase appearing at the same offset is not considered.

We take steps in cleaning the individual single word and multi-word tokens that we obtain. Specifically, we filter out the following tokens.

- Noun phrases and named entities that are fully numeric.

- Named entities that belong to the following categories are filtered out : DATE, TIME, PERCENT, MONEY, QUANTITY, ORDINAL, CARDINAL. Refer, Spacy's named entity documentation[2] for details of the tags.

- Standard stopwords are removed.

- Punctuations are removed except '-'.

We also take steps to clean leading and ending tokens of a multi-word noun phrase and named entity.

- Common adjectives and reporting verbs are removed if they occur as the first or last token of a noun phrase/named entity.

- Determiners are removed from the first token of a noun phrase/named entity.

- First or last tokens of noun phrases/named entities belonging to following parts of

---

[1]https://spacy.io

[2]https://spacy.io/usage/linguistic-features#section-named-entities

speech: INTJ Interjection, AUX Auxiliary, CCONJ Coordinating Conjunction, ADP Adposition, DET Interjection, NUM Numeral, PART Particle, PRON Pronoun, SCONJ Subordinating Conjunction, PUNCT Punctutation, SYM Symbol, X Other, are removed. For a detailed reference of each of these POS tags please refer Spacy's documentation[3].

- Starting and ending tokens of a noun phrase/named entity is removed if they belong to a standard list of english stopwords and functional words.

Apart from relying on Spacy's parser we use hand crafted regexes for cleaning the final list of tokens obtained after the above data cleaning steps.

- Get rid of leading/trailing junk characters.

- Handle dangling/backwards parentheses. We don't allow '(' or ')' to appear without the other.

- Handle oddly separated hyphenated words.

- Handle oddly separated apostrophe'd words.

- Normalize whitespace.

The resultant unigram tokens and multi-word phrases are merged in the order they appeared in the original sentence. Figure 1, shows an example of how the text processing pipeline works on an example sentence for preparing the training samples that act as an input to the embedding algorithm.

2.2 Training Phrase Embedding Model

The methodology to a great extent relies on the underlying embeddings. We directly train multi-word phrase embeddings using *Fasttext*[4], rather than first training embedding models for unigram words and then combining their dense vectors to obtain vectors for multi-word phrases. Our training vocabulary consists of both unigram as well as multi-word phrases. We are aware of the existing procedures for training phrase embeddings (Yin and Schütze, 2014; Yu and Dredze, 2015), but

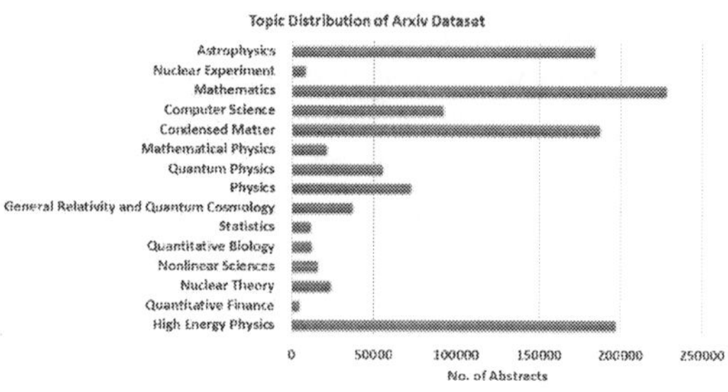

Figure 2: Frequency distribution of topics in the arxiv dataset used for training phrase embeddings.

refrain from using them in this preliminary work. We would like to use them in the future.

The main aim of the underlying embedding model is to capture semantic and syntactic similarities between textual units comprising of both single word and multi-word phrases. We chose *Fasttext* over other embedding techniques because it captures both the semantic and morphological similarities[5] between words. For example, if we have *breast cancer* in the content of the theme of a document then intuitively phrases like *breast cancer*, *breast cancer treatment*, should be assigned higher thematic weight than *prostrate cancer* or *lung cancer*, even though the document might mention other forms of cancer as well. Embedding techniques like *Word2Vec* and *Glove*, only takes into account the semantic similarity between words based on their occurrences in a similar context and will not display the desired property that we want to leverage. We would like to study the effects of other types of embeddings in the future.

Dataset: Since this work deals with the domain of scientific articles we train the embedding model on a collection of more than million scientific documents. We collect 1,147,000 scientific abstracts related to different areas (Fig 2) from arxiv.org[6]. For collecting data we use the API provided by arxiv.org that allows bulk access[7] to the articles uploaded in their portal. We also add the scientific documents present in the benchmark datasets (Sections 3), increasing the total number of documents to 1,149,244.

After processing the text of the documents as mentioned above, we train a *Fasttext-skipgram* model using *negative sampling* with a *context win-*

---

[3]https://spacy.io/api/annotation#pos-tagging
[4]https://fasttext.cc/

[5]https://rare-technologies.com/fasttext-and-gensim-word-embeddings/
[6]http://arxiv.org
[7]https://arxiv.org/help/bulk_data

dow size of 5, *dimension* of 100 and number of *epochs* set to 10. We would like to experiment further in the future on the selection of optimal parameters for the embedding model.

Candidate Selection: This step aids in chosing candidate keyphrases from the set of all phrases that can be extracted from a document, and is commonly used in most of the automated ranked keyphrase extraction systems. Not all the phrases are considered as candidates. Generally, unwanted and noisy phrases are eliminated in this process by using different heuristics (Section 2.1). We split a given document into sentences and to extract noun phrases and named entities as described previously. As an output of this step we get a set of unique phrases ($C_{d_i} = \{c_1, c_2, ..., c_n\}_{d_i}$) for a document d_i to be used later for scoring and ranking in the next two steps.

Candidate Scoring: In this step we assign a *theme vector* ($\hat{\tau}_{d_i}$) to a document (d_i). The *theme vector* can be tuned according to the type of documents that are being processed and the type of keyphrases that we want to get in our final results. In this work, we extract a *theme excerpt* from a given document and further extract a unique set of *thematic phrases* comprising of named entities, noun phrases and unigram words ($T_{d_i} = \{t_1, t_2, ..., t_m\}_{d_i}$) from it. For the *Inspec* dataset we use the first sentence of the document which consists its title, and for the *SemEval* dataset we use the title and the first ten sentences extracted from the beginning of the document, as the *theme excerpts*, respectively (see Section 3). The first ten sentences of a document from the *SemEval* dataset essentially captures the abstract and sometimes first few sentences of the introduction of a scientific article. We get the vector representation ($\hat{t}_j$) of each *thematic phrase* extracted from the *theme excerpt* using the phrase embedding model that we trained and perform vector addition in order to get the final *theme vector* ($\hat{\tau}_{d_i} = \sum_{j=1}^{m} \hat{t}_j$) of the document. The phrase embedding model is then used to get the vector representation ($\hat{c}_k; k \in \{1...n\}$) for each candidate keyphrase in C_{d_i}.

We calculate the *cosine distance* between the *theme vector* ($\hat{\tau}_{d_i}$) and vector for each candidate keyphrase ($\hat{c}_k$) and assign a score ($\kappa(\hat{x}, \hat{y}) \rightarrow [0, 1]$) to each candidate, with 1 indicating a complete similarity with the *theme vector* and 0 indicating a complete dissimilarity. To get the final *thematic weight* ($w_{c_j}^{d_i}$) for each candidate w.r.t.

a given document (d_i), the candidate scores are scaled again between 0 and 1 with a score of 1 assigned to the candidate semantically closest to the main theme of the document and 0 to the farthest.

Candidate Ranking: In order to perform final ranking of the candidate keyphrases we use weighted personalized PageRank algorithm. A directed graph G_{d_i} is constructed for a given document (d_i) with C_{d_i} as the vertices and E_{d_i} as the edges connecting two candidate keyphrases if they co-occur within a window size of 5. The edges are bidirectional. Weights $sr(c_j^{d_i}, c_k^{d_i})$ are calculated for the edges using the semantic similarity between the candidate keyphrases obtained from the phrase embedding model and their frequency of co-occurrence, as used by Wang *et al.* (Wang et al., 2015), and shown in equation 3. We use *cosine distance* ($\frac{1}{1-cosine(c_j^{d_i}, c_k^{d_i})}$) and *Point-wise Mutual Information* ($PMI(c_j^{d_i}, c_k^{d_i})$) for calculating $semantic(c_j^{d_i}, c_k^{d_i})$ (equation 1) and $cooccur(c_j^{d_i}, c_k^{d_i})$ (equation 2), respectively. The main intuition behind calculating semantic relatedness by using a phrase embedding model is to capture how well two phrases are related to each other in general. Whereas, the co-occurrence score captures the local relationship between the phrases within the context of the given document.

$$semantic(c_j^{d_i}, c_k^{d_i}) = \frac{1}{1 - cosine(c_j^{d_i}, c_k^{d_i})} \tag{1}$$

$$cooccur(c_j^{d_i}, c_k^{d_i}) = PMI(c_j^{d_i}, c_k^{d_i}) \tag{2}$$

$$sr(c_j^{d_i}, c_k^{d_i}) = semantic(c_j^{d_i}, c_k^{d_i}) \times cooccur(c_j^{d_i}, c_k^{d_i}) \tag{3}$$

Given graph G, if $\varepsilon(c_j^{d_i})$ be the set of all edges incident on the vertex $c_j^{d_i}$, and $w_{c_j}^{d_i}$ is the *thematic weight* of $c_j^{d_i}$ as calculated in the *candidate scoring* step, then the final PageRank score $R(c_j^{d_i})$ of a candidate keyphrase $c_j^{d_i}$ is calculated using equation 4, where $d = 0.85$ is the *damping factor* and $out(c_k^{d_i})$ is the out-degree of the vertex $c_k^{d_i}$.

$$R(c_j^{d_i}) = (1 - d)w_{c_j}^{d_i} + d \times \sum_{c_k^{d_i} \in \varepsilon(c_j^{d_i})} \left(\frac{sr(c_j^{d_i}, c_k^{d_i})}{\left|out(c_k^{d_i})\right|}\right) R(c_k^{d_i}) \tag{4}$$

Next, we evaluate the performance of *Key2Vec*.

	Micro Avg. Precision @5	Micro Avg. Recall @5	Micro Avg. F1 @5	Micro Avg. Precision @10	Micro Avg. Recall @10	Micro Avg. F1 @10	Micro Avg. Precision @15	Micro Avg. Recall @15	Micro Avg. F1 @15
Inspec	61.78 %	25.67 %	36.27 %	57.58 %	42.09 %	48.63 %	55.90 %	50.06 %	52.82 %
SemEval	41 %	14.37 %	21.28 %	35.29 %	24.67 %	29.04 %	34.39 %	32.48 %	33.41 %

Table 2: Performance of *Key2Vec* over combined *controlled* and *uncontrolled* annotated keyphrases for *Inspec* and *SemEval 2010* datasets.

Inspec (Combined)	Key2Vec	Wang et al., 2015	Liu et al., 2010	SGRank (Danesh et al., 2015)	TopicRank (Bougouin et al., 2013)
Micro Avg. F1@10	**48.63 %**	44.7 %	45.7 %	33.95 %	27.9 %

Table 3: Comparison of *Key2Vec* with some state-of-the-art systems (Liu et al., 2009; Danesh et al., 2015; Bougouin et al., 2013; Wang et al., 2015) for Avg. F1@10 on *Inspec* dataset.

SemEval 2010 (Combined)	Key2Vec	SGRank (Danesh et al., 2015)	HUMB (Lopez and Romary, 2010)	TopicRank (Bougouin et al., 2013)
Micro Avg. F1@10	**29.04 %**	26.07 %	22.50 %	12.1 %

Table 4: Comparison of *Key2Vec* with some state-of-the-art systems (Danesh et al., 2015; Bougouin et al., 2013; Lopez and Romary, 2010) for Avg. F1@10 on *SemEval 2010* dataset.

3 Experiments and Results

The final ranked keyphrases obtained using the *Key2Vec* methodology as described in the previous section is evaluated on the popular *Inspec* and *SemEval 2010* datasets. The Inspec dataset (Hulth, 2003) is composed of 2000 abstracts of scientific articles divided into sets of 1000, 500, and 500, as training, validation and test datasets respectively. Each document has two lists of keyphrases assigned by humans - *controlled*, which are assigned by the authors, and *uncontrolled*, which are freely assigned by the readers. The controlled keyphrases are mostly abstractive, whereas the uncontrolled ones are mostly extractive (Wang et al., 2015). The *Semeval 2010* dataset (Kim et al., 2010) consists of 284 full length ACM articles divided into a test set of size 100, training set of size 144 and trial set of size 40. Each article has two sets of human assigned keyphrases: the *author-assigned* and *reader-assigned* ones, equivalent to the *controlled* and *uncontrolled* categories, respectively of the *Inspec* dataset. We only use the test datasets for our evaluations and combine the annotated *controlled* and *uncontrolled* keyphrases.

The ranked keyphrases are evaluated using exact match evaluation metric as used in SemEval 2010 Task 5. We match the keyphrases in the annotated documents in the benchmark datasets with those generated by *Key2Vec*, and calculate micro-averaged precision, recall and F-score ($\beta = 1$),

respectively. In the evaluation, we check the performance over the top 5, 10 and 15 candidates returned by *Key2Vec*. The performance of *Key2Vec* on the metrics is shown in Table 2. Tables 3 and 4 shows a comparison of *Key2Vec* with some of the state-of-the-art systems giving best performances on the *Inspec* and *SemEval 2010* datasets, respectively.

4 Conclusion and Future Work

In this paper, we proposed a framework for automatic extraction and ranking of keyphrases from scientific articles. We showed an efficient way of training phrase embeddings, and showed its effectiveness in constructing thematic representation of scientific articles and assigning thematic weights to candidate keyphrases. We also introduced theme-weighted PageRank to rank the candidate keyphrases. Experimental evaluations confirm that our proposed technique of *Key2Vec* produces state-of-the-art results on benchmark datasets. In the future, we plan to use other existing procedures for training phrase embeddings and study their effects. We also plan to use *Key2Vec* in other domains such as news articles and extend the methodology for other related tasks like summarization.

References

Isabelle Augenstein, Mrinal Das, Sebastian Riedel, Lakshmi Vikraman, and Andrew McCallum. 2017. Semeval 2017 task 10: Scienceie-extracting keyphrases and relations from scientific publications. *arXiv preprint arXiv:1704.02853* .

Marco Baroni, Georgiana Dinu, and Germán Kruszewski. 2014. Don't count, predict! a systematic comparison of context-counting vs. context-predicting semantic vectors. In *ACL (1)*. pages 238–247.

Piotr Bojanowski, Edouard Grave, Armand Joulin, and Tomas Mikolov. 2016. Enriching word vectors with subword information. *arXiv preprint arXiv:1607.04606* .

Adrien Bougouin, Florian Boudin, and Béatrice Daille. 2013. Topicrank: Graph-based topic ranking for keyphrase extraction. In *International Joint Conference on Natural Language Processing (IJCNLP)*. pages 543–551.

Ronan Collobert, Jason Weston, Léon Bottou, Michael Karlen, Koray Kavukcuoglu, and Pavel Kuksa. 2011. Natural language processing (almost) from scratch. *Journal of Machine Learning Research* 12(Aug):2493–2537.

Soheil Danesh, Tamara Sumner, and James H Martin. 2015. Sgrank: Combining statistical and graphical methods to improve the state of the art in unsupervised keyphrase extraction. *Lexical and Computational Semantics (* SEM 2015)* page 117.

Kazi Saidul Hasan and Vincent Ng. 2010. Conundrums in unsupervised keyphrase extraction: making sense of the state-of-the-art. In *Proceedings of the 23rd International Conference on Computational Linguistics: Posters*. Association for Computational Linguistics, pages 365–373.

Kazi Saidul Hasan and Vincent Ng. 2014. Automatic keyphrase extraction: A survey of the state of the art. In *ACL (1)*. pages 1262–1273.

Anette Hulth. 2003. Improved automatic keyword extraction given more linguistic knowledge. In *Proceedings of the 2003 conference on Empirical methods in natural language processing*. Association for Computational Linguistics, pages 216–223.

Su Nam Kim, Olena Medelyan, Min-Yen Kan, and Timothy Baldwin. 2010. Semeval-2010 task 5: Automatic keyphrase extraction from scientific articles. In *Proceedings of the 5th International Workshop on Semantic Evaluation*. Association for Computational Linguistics, pages 21–26.

Su Nam Kim, Olena Medelyan, Min-Yen Kan, and Timothy Baldwin. 2013. Automatic keyphrase extraction from scientific articles. *Language resources and evaluation* 47(3):723–742.

Amy N Langville and Carl D Meyer. 2004. Deeper inside pagerank. *Internet Mathematics* 1(3):335–380.

Zhiyuan Liu, Wenyi Huang, Yabin Zheng, and Maosong Sun. 2010. Automatic keyphrase extraction via topic decomposition. In *Proceedings of the 2010 conference on empirical methods in natural language processing*. Association for Computational Linguistics, pages 366–376.

Zhiyuan Liu, Peng Li, Yabin Zheng, and Maosong Sun. 2009. Clustering to find exemplar terms for keyphrase extraction. In *Proceedings of the 2009 Conference on Empirical Methods in Natural Language Processing: Volume 1-Volume 1*. Association for Computational Linguistics, pages 257–266.

Patrice Lopez and Laurent Romary. 2010. Humb: Automatic key term extraction from scientific articles in grobid. In *Proceedings of the 5th international workshop on semantic evaluation*. Association for Computational Linguistics, pages 248–251.

Rada Mihalcea and Paul Tarau. 2004. Textrank: Bringing order into texts. Association for Computational Linguistics.

Tomas Mikolov, Ilya Sutskever, Kai Chen, Greg S Corrado, and Jeff Dean. 2013. Distributed representations of words and phrases and their compositionality. In *Advances in neural information processing systems*. pages 3111–3119.

Jeffrey Pennington, Richard Socher, and Christopher D Manning. 2014. Glove: Global vectors for word representation. In *EMNLP*. volume 14, pages 1532–1543.

Rui Wang, Wei Liu, and Chris McDonald. 2014. Corpus-independent generic keyphrase extraction using word embedding vectors. In *Software Engineering Research Conference*. volume 39.

Rui Wang, Wei Liu, and Chris McDonald. 2015. Using word embeddings to enhance keyword identification for scientific publications. In *Australasian Database Conference*. Springer, pages 257–268.

Wenpeng Yin and Hinrich Schütze. 2014. An exploration of embeddings for generalized phrases. In *ACL (Student Research Workshop)*. pages 41–47.

Mo Yu and Mark Dredze. 2015. Learning composition models for phrase embeddings. *Transactions of the Association for Computational Linguistics* 3:227–242.

Learning to Generate Wikipedia Summaries for Underserved Languages from Wikidata

Lucie-Aimée Kaffee[1†]   Hady Elsahar[2†]   Pavlos Vougiouklis[1†]
Christophe Gravier[2]   Frédérique Laforest[2]   Jonathon Hare[1]   Elena Simperl[1]

[1] School of Electronics and Computer Science, University of Southampton, UK
{kaffee, pv1e13, jsh2, e.simperl}@ecs.soton.ac.uk
[2] Laboratoire Hubert Curien, CNRS, UJM-Saint-Étienne, Université de Lyon, France
{hady.elsahar, christophe.gravier, frederique.laforest}@univ-st-etienne.fr

Abstract

While Wikipedia exists in 287 languages, its content is unevenly distributed among them. In this work, we investigate the generation of open domain Wikipedia summaries in underserved languages using structured data from Wikidata. To this end, we propose a neural network architecture equipped with copy actions that learns to generate single-sentence and comprehensible textual summaries from Wikidata triples. We demonstrate the effectiveness of the proposed approach by evaluating it against a set of baselines on two languages of different natures: Arabic, a morphological rich language with a larger vocabulary than English, and Esperanto, a constructed language known for its easy acquisition.

1 Introduction

Despite the fact that Wikipedia exists in 287 languages, the existing content is unevenly distributed. The content of the most under-resourced Wikipedias is maintained by a limited number of editors – they cannot curate the same volume of articles as the editors of large Wikipedia language-specific communities. It is therefore of the utmost social and cultural interests to address languages for which native speakers have only access to an impoverished Wikipedia. In this paper, we propose an automatic approach to generate textual summaries that can be used as a starting point for the editors of the involved Wikipedias. We propose an end-to-end trainable model that generates a textual summary given a set of KB triples as input. We apply our model on two languages that have a severe lack of both editors and articles on Wikipedia: Esperanto is an easily acquired artificially created language which makes it less data needy and a more suitable starting point

for exploring the challenges of this task. Arabic is a morphologically rich language that is much more challenging to work, mainly due to its significantly larger vocabulary. As shown in Table 1 both Arabic and Esperanto suffer a severe lack of content and active editors compared to the English Wikipedia which is currently the biggest one in terms of number of articles. Our research is mostly related to previous work on adapting the general encoder-decoder framework for the generation of Wikipedia summaries (Lebret et al., 2016; Chisholm et al., 2017; Vougiouklis et al., 2017). Nonetheless, all these approaches focus on task of biographies generation, and only in English – the language with the most language resources and knowledge bases available. In contrast with these works, we explore the generation of sentences in an open-domain, multilingual context. The model from (Lebret et al., 2016) takes the Wikipedia infobox as an input, while (Chisholm et al., 2017) uses a sequence of slot-value pairs extracted from Wikidata. Both models are only able to generate single-subject relationships. In our model the input triples go beyond the single-subject relationships of a Wikipedia infobox or a Wikidata page about a specific item (Section 2). Similarly to our approach, the model proposed by (Vougiouklis et al., 2017) accepts a set of triples as input, however, it leverages instance-type-related information from DBpedia in order to generate text that addresses rare or unseen entities. Our solution is much broader since it does not rely on the assumption that unseen triples will adopt the same pattern of properties and entities' instance types pairs as the ones that have been used for training. To this end, we use copy actions over the labels of entities in the input triples. This relates to previous works in machine translation which deals with rare or unseen word problem for translating names and numbers in text. (Luong et al., 2015)

[†] The authors contributed equally to this work.

Proceedings of NAACL-HLT 2018, pages 640–645
New Orleans, Louisiana, June 1 - 6, 2018. ©2018 Association for Computational Linguistics

	Arabic	Esperanto	English
# of Articles	541,166	241,901	5,483,928
# of Active Users	7,818	2,849	129,237
Vocab. Size	2.2M	1.5M	2.0M

Table 1: Recent page statistics and number of unique words (vocab. size) of Esperanto, Arabic and English Wikipedias.

propose a model that generates positional placeholders pointing to some words in source sentence and copy it to target sentence (*copy actions*). (Gulcehre et al., 2016) introduce separate trainable modules for copy actions to adapt to highly variable input sequences, for text summarisation. For text generation from tables, (Lebret et al., 2016) extend positional copy actions to copy values from fields in the given table. For Question Generation, (Serban et al., 2016) use a placeholder for the subject entity in the question to generalise to unseen entities.

We evaluate our approach by measuring how close our synthesised summaries can be to actual summaries in Wikipedia against two other baselines of different natures: a language model, and an information retrieval template-based solution. Our model substantially outperforms all the baselines in all evaluation metrics in both Esperanto and Arabic. In this work we present the following contributions: i) We investigate the task of generating textual summaries from Wikidata triples in underserved Wikipedia languages across multiple domains, and ii) We use an end-to-end model with copy actions adapted to this task. Our datasets, results, and experiments are available at: https://github.com/pvougiou/Wikidata2Wikipedia.

2   Model

Our approach is inspired by similar encoder-decoder architectures that have already been employed on similar text generative tasks (Serban et al., 2016; Vougiouklis et al., 2017).

2.1   Encoding the Triples

The encoder part of the model is a feed-forward architecture that encodes the set of input triples into a fixed dimensionality vector, which is subsequently used to initialise the decoder. Given a set of un-ordered triples $F_E = \{f_1, f_2, \ldots, f_R : f_j = (s_j, p_j, o_j)\}$, where s_j, p_j and o_j are the one-hot vector representations of the respective sub-

ject, property and object of the j-th triple, we compute an embedding h_{f_j} for the j-th triple by forward propagating as follows:

$$h_{f_j} = q(\mathbf{W_h}[\mathbf{W_{in}}s_j; \mathbf{W_{in}}p_j; \mathbf{W_{in}}o_j]) \ , \quad (1)$$

$$h_{F_E} = \mathbf{W_F}[h_{f_1}; \ldots ; h_{f_{R-1}}; h_{f_R}] \ , \quad (2)$$

where h_{f_j} is the embedding vector of each triple f_j, h_{F_E} is a fixed-length vector representation for all the input triples F_E. q is a non-linear activation function, $[\ldots ; \ldots]$ represents vector concatenation. $\mathbf{W_{in}}, \mathbf{W_h}, \mathbf{W_F}$ are trainable weight matrices. Unlike (Chisholm et al., 2017), our encoder is agnostic with respect to the order of input triples. As a result, the order of a particular triple f_j in the triples set does not change its significance towards the computation of the vector representation of the whole triples set, h_{F_E}.

2.2   Decoding the Summary

The decoder part of the architecture is a multi-layer RNN (Cho et al., 2014) with Gated Recurrent Units which generates the textual summary one token at a time. The hidden unit of the GRU at the first layer is initialised with h_{F_E}. At each timestep t, the hidden state of the GRU is calculated as follows:

$$h_t^l = \text{GRU}(h_{t-1}^l, h_t^{l-1}) \qquad (3)$$

The conditional probability distribution over each token y_t of the summary at each timestep t is computed as the softmax($\mathbf{W_{out}}h_t^L$) over all the possible entries in the summaries dictionary, where h_t^L is the hidden state of the last layer and $\mathbf{W_{out}}$ is a biased trainable weight matrix.

A summary consists of words and mentions of entity in the text. We adapt the concept of *surface form tuples* (Vougiouklis et al., 2017) in order to be able to learn an arbitrary number of different lexicalisations of the same entity in the summary (e.g. "aktorino", "aktoro"). Figure 1 shows the architecture of our generative model when it is provided with the three triples of the idealised example of Table 2.

2.3   Copy Actions

Following (Luong et al., 2015; Lebret et al., 2016) we model all the copy actions on the data level through a set of special tokens added to the basic vocabulary. Rare entities identified in text and existing in the input triples are being replaced by the token of the property of the relationship to which it

Triples	Q490900 (Floridia)	P31 (estas)	Q747074 (komunumo de Italio)
	Q490900 (Floridia)	P17 (ŝtato)	Q38 (Italio)
	Q30025755 (Floridia)	P1376 (ĉefurbo de)	Q490900 (Floridia)
Textual Summary	Floridia estas komunumo de Italio.		
Vocab. Extended	[[Q490900, Floridia]] estas komunumo de [[P17]].		

Table 2: Training example: a set of triples about *Floridia*. Subsequently, our system summarises the input set in the form of text. The vocabulary extended summary is the one on which we train our model.

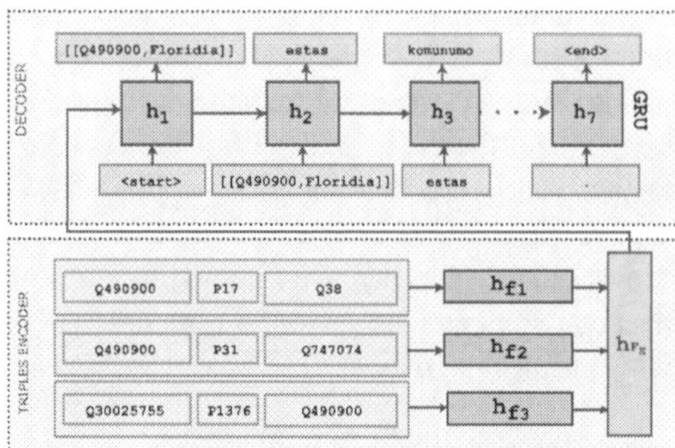

Figure 1: Model Overview

was matched. We refer to those tokens as *property placeholders*. In Table 2, [[P17]] in the vocabulary extended summary is an example of property placeholder – would it be generated by our model, it is replaced with the label of the object of the triple with which they share the same property (i.e. Q490900 (Floridia) P17 (ŝtato) Q38 (Italio)). When all the tokens of the summary are sampled, each property placeholder that is generated is mapped to the triple with which it shares the same property and is subsequently replaced with the textual label of the entity. We randomly choose an entity, in case there are more than one triple with the same property in the input triples set.

2.4 Implementation and Training Details

We implemented our neural network models using the Torch[1] package.

We included the $15,000$ and $25,000$ most frequent tokens (i.e. either words or entities) of the summaries in Esperanto and Arabic respectively for target vocabulary of the textual summaries. Using a larger size of target dictionary in Arabic is due to its greater linguistic variability – Arabic vocabulary is 47% larger than Esperanto vocabulary (cf. Table 1). We replaced any rare enti-

ties in the text that participate in relations in the aligned triples set with the corresponding property placeholder of the upheld relations. We include all property placeholders that occur at least 20 times in each training dataset. Subsequently, the dictionaries of the Esperanto and Arabic summaries are expanded by 80 and 113 property placeholders respectively. In case the rare entity is not matched to any subject or object of the set of corresponding triples it is replaced by the special <resource> token. Each summary is augmented with the respect start-of-summary <start> and end-of-summary <end> tokens.

For the decoder, we use 1 layer of GRUs. We set the dimensionality of the decoder's hidden state to 500 in Esperanto and 700 in Arabic. We initialise all parameters with random uniform distribution between -0.001 and 0.001, and we use Batch Normalisation before each non-linear activation function and after each fully-connected layer (Ioffe and Szegedy, 2015) on the encoder side (Vougiouklis et al., 2017). During training, the model tries to learn those parameters that minimise the sum of the negative log-likelihoods of a set of predicted summaries. The networks are trained using mini-batch of size 85. The weights are updated using Adam (Kingma and Ba, 2014) (i.e. it was found to work better than Stochastic Gradient Descent, RMSProp and AdaGrad) with a learning rate of 10^{-5}. An l_2 regularisation term of 0.1 over each network's parameters is also included in the cost function.

The networks converge after the 9th epoch in the Esperanto case and after the 11th in the Arabic case. During evaluation and testing, we do beam search with a beam size of 20, and we retain only the summary with the highest probability. We found that increasing the beam size resulted not only in minor improvements in terms of performance but also in a greater number of fully-completed generated summaries (i.e. summaries for which the special end-of-summary <end> to-

---

[1]Torch is a scientific computing package for Lua. It is based on the LuaJIT package.

	Arabic	**Esperanto**
Avg. # of Tokens per Summary	28.1 (±28.8)	26.4 (±22.7)
Avg. # of Triples per Summary	8.1 (±11.2)	11.0 (±13.8)
Avg. # of Linked Named Entities	2.2 (±1.0)	2.4 (±1.1)
Avg. # of Aligned Triples	0.1 (±0.4)	0.2 (±0.5)
Vocabulary Size	344,827	226,447
Total # of Summaries	255,741	126,714

Table 3: Dataset statistics in Arabic and Esperanto.

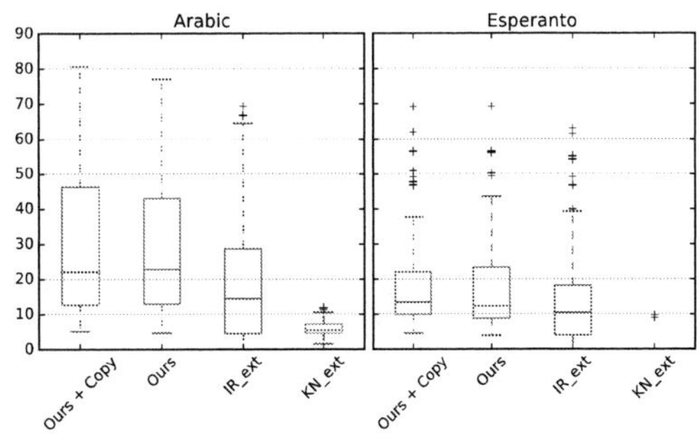

Figure 2: A box plot showing the distribution of BLEU 4 scores of all systems for each category of generated summaries.

ken is generated).

3 Dataset

In order to train our models to generate summaries from Wikidata triples, we introduce a new dataset for text generation from KB triples in a multilingual setting and align it with the triples of its corresponding Wikidata Item. For each Wikipedia article, we extract and tokenise the first introductory sentence and align it with triples where its corresponding item appears as a subject or an object in the Wikidata truthy dump. In order to create the *surface form tuples* (i.e. Section 2.3), we identify occurrences of entities in the text along with their verbalisations. We rely on keyword matching against labels from Wikidata expanded by the global language fallback chain introduced by Wikimedia[2] to overcome the lack of non-English labels in Wikidata (Kaffee et al., 2017).

For the *property placeholders*, we use the distant supervision assumption for relation extraction (Mintz et al., 2009). Entities that participate in relations with the main entity of the article are being replaced with their corresponding property placeholder tag. Table 3 shows statistics on the two corpora that we used for the training of our systems.

4 Baselines

To demonstrate the effectiveness of our approach, we compare it to two competitive systems.

KN is a 5-gram Kneser-Ney (KN) (Heafield et al., 2013) language model. KN has been used before as a baseline for text generation from structured data (Lebret et al., 2016) and provided competitive results on a single domain in English. We

also introduce a second KN model (KN_{ext}), which is trained on summaries with the special tokens for copy actions. During test time, we use beam search of size 10 to sample from the learned language model.

IR is an Information Retrieval (IR) baseline similar to those that have been used in other text generative tasks (Rush et al., 2015; Du et al., 2017). First, the baseline encodes the list of input triples using TF-IDF followed by LSA (Halko et al., 2011). For each item in the test set, we perform K-nearest neighbors to retrieve the vector from the training set that is the closest to this item and output its corresponding summary. Similar to KN baseline, we provide two versions of this baseline IR and IR_{ext}.

5 Results and Discussion

We evaluate the generated summaries from our model and each of the baselines against their original counterparts from Wikipedia. Triples sets whose generated summaries are incomplete[3] (i.e. summaries for which the special end-of-summary <end> token is generated) are excluded from the evaluation. We use a set of evaluation metrics for text generation: BLEU (Papineni et al., 2002), METEOR (Denkowski and Lavie, 2014) and $ROUGE_L$ (Lin, 2004). As displayed in Table 4, our model shows a significant enhancement compared to our baselines across the ma-

---

[2]https://meta.wikimedia.org/wiki/Wikidata/Notes/Language_fallback

[3]Around $\leq 1\%$ and 2% of the input validation and test triples sets in Arabic and Esperanto respectively led to the generation of summaries without the <end> token. We believe that this difference is explained by the limited size of the Esperanto dataset that increases the level of difficulty that the trained models (i.e. with or without Copy Actions) to generalise on unseen data.

	Model	BLEU 1		BLEU 2		BLEU 3		BLEU 4		ROUGE$_L$		METEOR	
		Valid.	Test	Valid.	Test	Valid.	Test	Valid.	Test	Valid.	Test	Valid.	Test
Arabic	KN	12.84	12.85	2.28	2.4	0.95	1.04	0.54	0.61	17.08	17.09	29.04	29.02
	KN$_{ext}$	28.93	28.84	21.21	21.16	16.78	16.76	13.42	13.42	28.57	28.52	30.47	30.43
	IR	41.39	41.73	34.18	34.58	29.36	29.72	25.68	25.98	43.26	43.58	32.99	33.33
	IR$_{ext}$	49.87	48.96	42.44	41.5	37.29	36.41	33.27	32.51	51.66	50.57	34.39	34.25
	Ours	53.61	54.26	47.38	48.05	42.65	43.32	38.52	39.20	64.27	64.64	45.89	45.99
	+ Copy	**54.10**	**54.40**	**47.96**	**48.27**	**43.27**	**43.60**	**39.17**	**39.51**	**64.60**	**64.69**	**46.09**	**46.17**
Esperanto	KN	18.12	17.8	6.91	6.64	4.18	4.0	2.9	2.79	37.48	36.9	31.05	30.74
	KN$_{ext}$	25.17	24.93	16.44	16.3	11.99	11.92	8.77	8.79	44.93	44.77	33.77	33.71
	IR	43.01	42.61	33.67	33.46	28.16	28.07	24.35	24.3	46.75	45.92	20.71	20.46
	IR$_{ext}$	**52.75**	**51.66**	43.57	42.53	37.53	36.54	33.35	32.41	58.15	57.62	31.21	31.04
	Ours	49.34	49.40	42.83	42.95	38.28	38.45	34.66	34.85	66.43	**67.02**	40.62	**41.13**
	+ Copy	50.22	49.81	**43.57**	**43.19**	**38.93**	**38.62**	**35.27**	**34.95**	**66.73**	66.61	**40.80**	40.74

Table 4: Automatic evaluation of our model against all other baselines using BLEU 1-4, ROUGE and METEOR for both Arabic and Esperanto Validation and Test set

jority of the evaluation metrics in both languages. We achieve at least an enhancement of at least 5.25 and 1.31 BLEU 4 score in Arabic and Esperanto respectively over the IR$_{ext}$, the strongest baseline. The introduction of the copy actions to our encoder-decoder architecture enhances our performance further by $0.61 - 1.10$ BLEU (using BLEU 4). In general, our copy actions mechanism benefits the performance of all the competitive systems.

Generalisation Across Domains. To investigate how well different models can generalise across multiple domains, we categorise each generated summary into one of 50 categories according to its main entity instance type (e.g. village, company, football player). We examine the distribution of BLEU-4 scores per category to measure how well the model generalises across domains (Figure 2). We show that i) the high performance of our system is not skewed towards some domains at the expense of others, and that ii) our model has a good generalisation across domains – better than any other baseline. Despite the fact that the Kneser-Ney template-based baseline (KN$_{ext}$) has exhibited competitive performance in a single-domain context (Lebret et al., 2016), it is failing to generalise in our multi-domain text generation scenario.

6 Conclusions

In this paper, we show that with the adaptation of the encoder-decoder neural network architecture for the generation of summaries we are able to overcome the challenges introduced by working with underserved languages. This is achieved by leveraging data from a structured knowledge base and careful data preparation in a multilingual fashion, which are of the utmost practical interest for our under-resourced task, that would have otherwise required a substantial additional amount of data. Our model was able to perform and generalise across domains better than a set of strong baselines.

Acknowledgements

This research is partially supported by the Answering Questions using Web Data (WDAqua) project, a Marie Skłodowska-Curie Innovative Training Network under grant agreement No 642795, part of the Horizon 2020 programme.

References

Andrew Chisholm, Will Radford, and Ben Hachey. 2017. Learning to generate one-sentence biographies from Wikidata. In *Proceedings of the 15th Conference of the European Chapter of the Association for Computational Linguistics: Volume 1, Long Papers*. Association for Computational Linguistics, Valencia, Spain, pages 633–642.

Kyunghyun Cho, Bart van Merrienboer, Çaglar Gülçehre, Fethi Bougares, Holger Schwenk, and Yoshua Bengio. 2014. Learning phrase representations using RNN encoder-decoder for statistical machine translation. *CoRR* abs/1406.1078.

Michael J. Denkowski and Alon Lavie. 2014. Meteor universal: Language specific translation evaluation for any target language. In *Proceedings of the Ninth Workshop on Statistical Machine Translation, WMT@ACL 2014, June 26-27, 2014, Baltimore, Maryland, USA*. pages 376–380.

Xinya Du, Junru Shao, and Claire Cardie. 2017. Learning to ask: Neural question generation for reading comprehension. In *Proceedings of the 55th Annual Meeting of the Association for Computational Linguistics, ACL 2017, Vancouver, Canada, July 30 - August 4, Volume 1: Long Papers*. pages 1342–1352.

Caglar Gulcehre, Marcin Moczulski, Misha Denil, and Yoshua Bengio. 2016. Noisy activation functions. In *International Conference on Machine Learning*. pages 3059–3068.

Nathan Halko, Per-Gunnar Martinsson, and Joel A. Tropp. 2011. Finding structure with randomness: Probabilistic algorithms for constructing approximate matrix decompositions. *SIAM Review* 53(2):217–288.

Kenneth Heafield, Ivan Pouzyrevsky, Jonathan H. Clark, and Philipp Koehn. 2013. Scalable modified Kneser-Ney language model estimation. In *Proceedings of the 51st Annual Meeting of the Association for Computational Linguistics, ACL 2013, 4-9 August 2013, Sofia, Bulgaria, Volume 2: Short Papers*. pages 690–696.

Sergey Ioffe and Christian Szegedy. 2015. Batch normalization: Accelerating deep network training by reducing internal covariate shift. In Francis Bach and David Blei, editors, *Proceedings of the 32nd International Conference on Machine Learning*. PMLR, Lille, France, volume 37 of *Proceedings of Machine Learning Research*, pages 448–456.

Lucie-Aimée Kaffee, Alessandro Piscopo, Pavlos Vougiouklis, Elena Simperl, Leslie Carr, and Lydia Pintscher. 2017. A Glimpse into Babel: An Analysis of Multilinguality in Wikidata. In *Proceedings of the 13th International Symposium on Open Collaboration*. ACM, page 14.

Diederik P. Kingma and Jimmy Ba. 2014. Adam: A method for stochastic optimization. *CoRR* abs/1412.6980. http://arxiv.org/abs/1412.6980.

Rémi Lebret, David Grangier, and Michael Auli. 2016. Neural text generation from structured data with application to the biography domain. In *Proceedings of the 2016 Conference on Empirical Methods in Natural Language Processing, EMNLP 2016, Austin, Texas, USA, November 1-4, 2016*. pages 1203–1213.

Chin-Yew Lin. 2004. Rouge: A package for automatic evaluation of summaries. In *Text summarization branches out: Proceedings of the ACL-04 workshop*. Barcelona, Spain, volume 8.

Thang Luong, Ilya Sutskever, Quoc V. Le, Oriol Vinyals, and Wojciech Zaremba. 2015. Addressing the rare word problem in neural machine translation. In *Proceedings of the 53rd Annual Meeting of the Association for Computational Linguistics and the 7th International Joint Conference on Natural Language Processing of the Asian Federation of Natural Language Processing, ACL 2015, July 26-31, 2015, Beijing, China, Volume 1: Long Papers*. pages 11–19.

Mike Mintz, Steven Bills, Rion Snow, and Daniel Jurafsky. 2009. Distant supervision for relation extraction without labeled data. In *ACL 2009, Proceedings of the 47th Annual Meeting of the Association for Computational Linguistics and the 4th International Joint Conference on Natural Language Processing of the AFNLP, 2-7 August 2009, Singapore*. pages 1003–1011.

Kishore Papineni, Salim Roukos, Todd Ward, and Wei-Jing Zhu. 2002. BLEU: A method for automatic evaluation of machine translation. In *Proceedings of the 40th Annual Meeting on Association for Computational Linguistics*. Association for Computational Linguistics, Stroudsburg, PA, USA, ACL '02, pages 311–318. https://doi.org/10.3115/1073083.1073135.

Alexander M. Rush, Sumit Chopra, and Jason Weston. 2015. A neural attention model for abstractive sentence summarization. In *Proceedings of the 2015 Conference on Empirical Methods in Natural Language Processing, EMNLP 2015, Lisbon, Portugal, September 17-21, 2015*. pages 379–389.

Iulian Vlad Serban, Alberto García-Durán, Çaglar Gülçehre, Sungjin Ahn, Sarath Chandar, Aaron C. Courville, and Yoshua Bengio. 2016. Generating factoid questions with recurrent neural networks: The 30m factoid question-answer corpus. In *Proceedings of the 54th Annual Meeting of the Association for Computational Linguistics, ACL 2016, August 7-12, 2016, Berlin, Germany, Volume 1: Long Papers*.

Pavlos Vougiouklis, Hady ElSahar, Lucie-Aimée Kaffee, Christophe Gravier, Frédérique Laforest, Jonathon S. Hare, and Elena Simperl. 2017. Neural wikipedian: Generating textual summaries from knowledge base triples. *CoRR* abs/1711.00155.

Multi-Reward Reinforced Summarization with Saliency and Entailment

Ramakanth Pasunuru and **Mohit Bansal**
UNC Chapel Hill
{ram, mbansal}@cs.unc.edu

Abstract

Abstractive text summarization is the task of compressing and rewriting a long document into a short summary while maintaining saliency, directed logical entailment, and non-redundancy. In this work, we address these three important aspects of a good summary via a reinforcement learning approach with two novel reward functions: ROUGE-Sal and Entail, on top of a coverage-based baseline. The ROUGESal reward modifies the ROUGE metric by up-weighting the salient phrases/words detected via a keyphrase classifier. The Entail reward gives high (length-normalized) scores to logically-entailed summaries using an entailment classifier. Further, we show superior performance improvement when these rewards are combined with traditional metric (ROUGE) based rewards, via our novel and effective multi-reward approach of optimizing multiple rewards simultaneously in alternate mini-batches. Our method achieves the new state-of-the-art results on CNN/Daily Mail dataset as well as strong improvements in a test-only transfer setup on DUC-2002.

1 Introduction

Abstractive summarization, the task of generating a natural short summary of a long document, is more challenging than the extractive paradigm, which only involves selection of important sentences or grammatical sub-sentences (Jing, 2000; Knight and Marcu, 2002; Clarke and Lapata, 2008; Filippova et al., 2015). Advent of sequence-to-sequence deep neural networks and large human summarization datasets (Hermann et al., 2015; Nallapati et al., 2016) made the abstractive summarization task more feasible and accurate, with recent ideas ranging from copy-pointer mechanism and redundancy coverage, to metric reward based reinforcement learning (Rush

et al., 2015; Chopra et al., 2016; Ranzato et al., 2015; Nallapati et al., 2016; See et al., 2017).

A good abstractive summary requires several important properties, e.g., it should choose the most salient information from the input document, be logically entailed by it, and avoid redundancy. Coverage-based models address the latter redundancy issue (Suzuki and Nagata, 2016; Nallapati et al., 2016; See et al., 2017), but there is still a lot of scope to teach current state-of-the-art models about saliency and logical entailment. Towards this goal, we improve the task of abstractive summarization via a reinforcement learning approach with the introduction of two novel rewards: 'ROUGESal' and 'Entail', and also demonstrate that these saliency and entailment skills allow for better generalizability and transfer.

Our ROUGESal reward gives higher weight to the important, salient words in the summary, in contrast to the traditional ROUGE metric which gives equal weight to all tokens. These weights are obtained from a novel saliency scorer, which is trained on a reading comprehension dataset's answer spans to give a saliency-based probability score to every token in the sentence. Our Entail reward gives higher weight to summaries whose sentences logically follow from the ground-truth summary. Further, we also add a length normalization constraint to our Entail reward, to importantly avoid misleadingly high entailment scores to very short sentences.

Empirically, we show that our new rewards with policy gradient approaches perform significantly better than a cross-entropy based state-of-the-art pointer-coverage baseline. We show further performance improvements by combining these rewards via our novel multi-reward optimization approach, where we optimize multiple rewards simultaneously in alternate mini-batches (hence avoiding complex scaling and weighting issues in

646

Proceedings of NAACL-HLT 2018, pages 646–653
New Orleans, Louisiana, June 1 - 6, 2018. ©2018 Association for Computational Linguistics

reward combination), inspired from how humans take multiple concurrent types of rewards (feedback) to learn a task. Overall, our methods achieve the new state-of-the-art on the CNN/Daily Mail dataset as well as strong improvements in a test-only transfer setup on DUC-2002. Lastly, we present several analyses of our model's saliency, entailment, and abstractiveness skills.

2 Related Work

Earlier summarization work was based on extraction and compression-based approaches (Jing, 2000; Knight and Marcu, 2002; Clarke and Lapata, 2008; Filippova et al., 2015), with more focus on graph-based (Giannakopoulos, 2009; Ganesan et al., 2010) and discourse tree-based (Gerani et al., 2014) models. Recent focus has shifted towards abstractive, rewriting-based summarization based on parse trees (Cheung and Penn, 2014; Wang et al., 2016), Abstract Meaning Representations (Liu et al., 2015; Dohare and Karnick, 2017), and neural network models with pointer-copy mechanism and coverage (Rush et al., 2015; Chopra et al., 2016; Chen et al., 2016; Nallapati et al., 2016; See et al., 2017), as well as reinforce-based metric rewards (Ranzato et al., 2015; Paulus et al., 2017). We also use reinforce-based models, but with novel reward functions and better simultaneous multi-reward optimization methods.

Recognizing Textual Entailment (RTE), the task of classifying two sentences as entailment, contradiction, or neutral, has been used for Q&A and IE tasks (Harabagiu and Hickl, 2006; Dagan et al., 2006; Lai and Hockenmaier, 2014; Jimenez et al., 2014). Recent neural network models and large datasets (Bowman et al., 2015; Williams et al., 2017) enabled stronger accuracies. Some previous work (Mehdad et al., 2013; Gupta et al., 2014) has explored the use of RTE by modeling graph-based relationships between sentences to select the most non-redundant sentences for summarization. Recently, Pasunuru and Bansal (2017) improved video captioning with entailment-corrected rewards. We instead directly use multi-sentence entailment knowledge (with additional length constraints) as a separate RL reward to improve abstractive summarization, while avoiding their penalty hyperparameter tuning.

For our saliency prediction model, we make use of the SQuAD reading comprehension dataset (Rajpurkar et al., 2016), where the answer

spans annotated by humans for important questions, serve as an interesting and effective proxy for keyphrase-style salient information in summarization. Some related previous work has incorporated document topic/subject classification (Isonuma et al., 2017) and webpage keyphrase extraction (Zhang et al., 2004) to improve saliency in summarization. Some recent work Subramanian et al. (2017) has also used answer probabilities in a document to improve question generation.

3 Models

3.1 Baseline Sequence-to-Sequence Model

Our abstractive text summarization model is a simple sequence-to-sequence single-layer bidirectional encoder and unidirectional decoder LSTM-RNN, with attention (Bahdanau et al., 2015), pointer-copy, and coverage mechanism – please refer to See et al. (2017) for details.

3.2 Policy Gradient Reinforce

Traditional cross-entropy loss optimization for sequence generation has an exposure bias issue and the model is not optimized for the evaluated metrics (Ranzato et al., 2015). Reinforce-based policy gradient approach addresses both of these issues by using its own distribution during training and by directly optimizing the non-differentiable evaluation metrics as rewards. We use the REINFORCE algorithm (Williams, 1992; Zaremba and Sutskever, 2015) to learn a policy p_θ defined by the model parameters θ to predict the next action (word) and update its internal (LSTM) states. We minimize the loss function $L_{\text{RL}} = -\mathbb{E}_{w^s \sim p_\theta}[r(w^s)]$, where w^s is the sequence of sampled words with w_t^s sampled at time step t of the decoder. The derivative of this loss function with approximation using a single sample along with variance reduction with a bias estimator is:

$$\nabla_\theta L_{\text{RL}} = -(r(w^s) - b_e)\nabla_\theta \log p_\theta(w^s) \quad (1)$$

There are several ways to calculate the baseline estimator; we employ the effective SCST approach (Rennie et al., 2016), as depicted in Fig. 1, where $b_e = r(w^a)$, is based on the reward obtained by the current model using the test time inference algorithm, i.e., choosing the arg-max word w_t^a of the final vocabulary distribution at each time step t of the decoder. We use the joint cross-entropy and reinforce loss so as to optimize the non-differentiable evaluation metric as reward

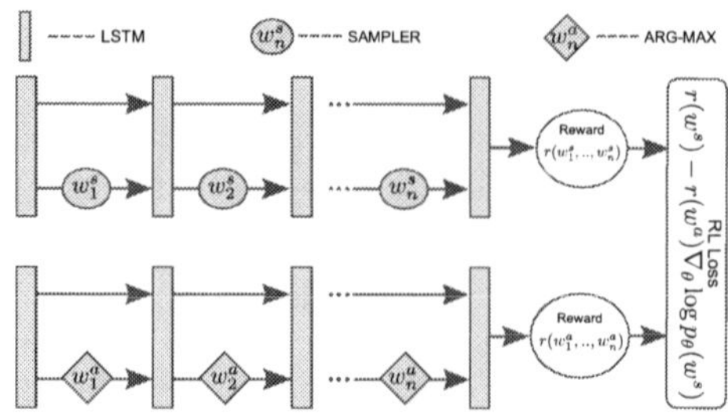

Figure 1: Our sequence generator with RL training.

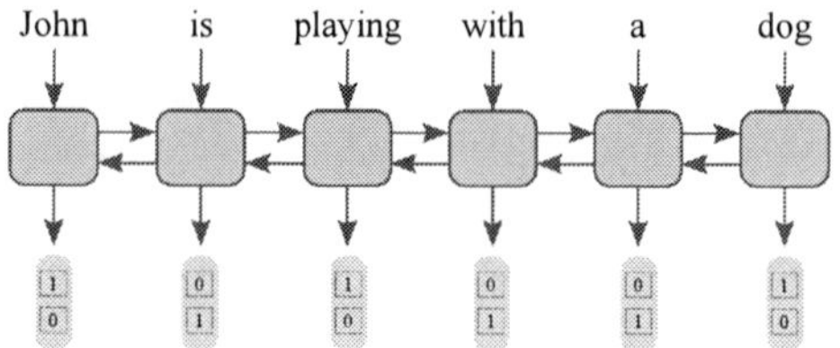

Figure 2: Overview of our saliency predictor model.

while also maintaining the readability of the generated sentence (Wu et al., 2016; Paulus et al., 2017; Pasunuru and Bansal, 2017), which is defined as $L_{\text{Mixed}} = \gamma L_{\text{RL}} + (1 - \gamma) L_{\text{XE}}$, where γ is a tunable hyperparameter.

3.3 Multi-reward Optimization

Optimizing multiple rewards at the same time is important and desired for many language generation tasks. One approach would be to use a weighted combination of these rewards, but this has the issue of finding the complex scaling and weight balance among these reward combinations. To address this issue, we instead introduce a simple multi-reward optimization approach inspired from multi-task learning, where we have different tasks, and all of them share all the model parameters while having their own optimization function (different reward functions in this case). If r_1 and r_2 are two reward functions that we want to optimize simultaneously, then we train the two loss functions of Eqn. 2 in alternate mini-batches.

$$
\begin{aligned}
L_{\text{RL}_1} &= -(r_1(w^s) - r_1(w^a))\nabla_\theta \log p_\theta(w^s) \\
L_{\text{RL}_2} &= -(r_2(w^s) - r_2(w^a))\nabla_\theta \log p_\theta(w^s)
\end{aligned}
\tag{2}
$$

4 Rewards

ROUGE Reward The first basic reward is based on the primary summarization metric of ROUGE package (Lin, 2004). Similar to Paulus et al. (2017), we found that ROUGE-L metric as a reward works better compared to ROUGE-1 and ROUGE-2 in terms of improving all the metric scores.[1] Since these metrics are based on simple phrase matching/n-gram overlap, they do not focus on important summarization factors such as salient phrase inclusion and directed logical entailment. Addressing these issues, we next introduce two new reward functions.

Saliency Rewards ROUGE-based rewards have no knowledge about what information is salient in the summary, and hence we introduce a novel reward function called 'ROUGESal' which gives higher weight to the important, salient words/phrases when calculating the ROUGE score (which by default assumes all words are equally weighted). To learn these saliency weights, we train our saliency predictor on sentence and answer spans pairs from the popular SQuAD reading comprehension dataset (Rajpurkar et al., 2016)) (Wikipedia domain), where we treat the human-annotated answer spans (avg. span length 3.2) for important questions as representative salient information in the document. As shown in Fig. 2, given a sentence as input, the predictor assigns a saliency probability to every token, using a simple bidirectional encoder with a *softmax* layer at every time step of the encoder hidden states to classify the token as salient or not. Finally, we use the probabilities given by this saliency prediction model as weights in the ROUGE matching formulation to achieve the final ROUGESal score (see appendix for details about our ROUGESal weighted precision, recall, and F-1 formulations).

Entailment Rewards A good summary should also be logically entailed by the given source document, i.e., contain no contradictory or unrelated information. Pasunuru and Bansal (2017) used entailment-corrected phrase-matching metrics (CIDEnt) to improve the task of video captioning; we instead directly use the entailment knowledge from an entailment scorer and its multi-sentence, length-normalized extension as our 'Entail' reward, to improve the task of abstractive text summarization. We train the entailment classifier (Parikh et al., 2016) on the SNLI (Bowman et al., 2015) and Multi-NLI (Williams et al., 2017) datasets and calculate the entailment probability score between the ground-truth (GT) summary (as premise) and each sentence of the generated summary (as hypothesis), and use avg. score as our

---

[1] For the rest of the paper, we mean ROUGE-L whenever we mention ROUGE-reward models.

Entail reward.[2] Finally, we add a length normalization constraint to avoid very short sentences achieving misleadingly high entailment scores:

$$\text{Entail} = \text{Entail} \times \frac{\text{\#tokens in generated summary}}{\text{\#tokens in reference summary}} \quad (3)$$

5 Experimental Setup

5.1 Datasets and Training Details

CNN/Daily Mail dataset (Hermann et al., 2015; Nallapati et al., 2016) is a collection of online news articles and their summaries. We use the non-anonymous version of the dataset as described in See et al. (2017). For test-only generalization experiments, we use the DUC-2002 single document summarization dataset[3]. For entailment reward classifier, we use a combination of the full Stanford Natural Language Inference (SNLI) corpus (Bowman et al., 2015) and the recent Multi-NLI corpus (Williams et al., 2017) training datasets. For our saliency prediction model, we use the Stanford Question Answering (SQuAD) dataset (Rajpurkar et al., 2016). All dataset splits and other training details (dimension sizes, learning rates, etc.) for reproducibility are in appendix.

5.2 Evaluation Metrics

We use the standard ROUGE package (Lin, 2004) and Meteor package (Denkowski and Lavie, 2014) for reporting the results on all of our summarization models. Following previous work (Chopra et al., 2016; Nallapati et al., 2016; See et al., 2017), we use the ROUGE full-length F1 variant.

6 Results

Baseline Cross-entropy Model Our abstractive summarization model has attention, pointer-copy, and coverage mechanism. First, we apply cross-entropy optimization and achieve comparable re-

Models	R-1	R-2	R-L	M
PREVIOUS WORK				
Nallapati (2016)*	35.46	13.30	32.65	-
See et al. (2017)	39.53	17.28	36.38	18.72
Paulus (2017) (XE)*	38.30	14.81	35.49	-
Paulus (2017) (RL)*	39.87	15.82	36.90	-
OUR MODELS				
Baseline (XE)	39.41	17.33	36.07	18.27
ROUGE (RL)	39.99	17.72	36.66	18.93
Entail (RL)	39.53	17.51	36.44	20.15
ROUGESal (RL)	40.36	17.97	37.00	19.84
ROUGE+Ent (RL)	40.37	17.89	37.13	19.94
ROUGESal+Ent (RL)	40.43	18.00	37.10	20.02

Table 1: Results on CNN/Daily Mail (non-anonymous). * represents previous work on anonymous version. 'XE': cross-entropy loss, 'RL': reinforce mixed loss (XE+RL). Columns 'R': ROUGE, 'M': METEOR.

sults on CNN/Daily Mail w.r.t. previous work (See et al., 2017).[4]

ROUGE Rewards First, using ROUGE-L as RL reward (shown as ROUGE in Table 1) improves the performance on CNN/Daily Mail in all metrics with stat. significant scores ($p < 0.001$) as compared to the cross-entropy baseline (and also stat. signif. w.r.t. See et al. (2017)). Similar to Paulus et al. (2017), we use mixed loss function (XE+RL) for all our reinforcement experiments, to ensure good readability of generated summaries.

ROUGESal and Entail Rewards With our novel ROUGESal reward, we achieve stat. signif. improvements in all metrics w.r.t. the baseline as well as w.r.t. ROUGE-reward results ($p < 0.001$), showing that saliency knowledge is strongly improving the summarization model. For our Entail reward, we achieve stat. signif. improvements in ROUGE-L ($p < 0.001$) w.r.t. baseline and achieve the best METEOR score by a large margin. See Sec. 7 for analysis of the saliency/entailment skills learned by our models.

Multi-Reward Results Similar to ROUGESal, Entail is a better reward when combined with the complementary phrase-matching metric information in ROUGE; Table 1 shows that the ROUGE+Entail multi-reward combination performs stat. signif. better than ROUGE-reward in ROUGE-1, ROUGE-L, and METEOR ($p < 0.001$), and better than Entail-reward in all

---

[2] Since the GT summary is correctly entailed by the source document, we directly (by transitivity) use this GT as premise for easier (shorter) encoding. We also tried using the full input document as premise but this didn't perform as well (most likely because the entailment classifiers are not trained on such long premises; and the problem with the sentence-to-sentence avg. scoring approach is discussed below). We also tried summary-to-summary entailment scoring (similar to ROUGE-L) as well as pairwise sentence-to-sentence avg. scoring, but we found that avg. scoring of ground-truth summary (as premise) w.r.t. each generated summary's sentence (as hypothesis) works better (intuitive because each sentence in generated summary might be a compression of multiple sentences of GT summary or source document).

[3] http://www-nlpir.nist.gov/projects/duc/guidelines/2002.html

[4] Our baseline is statistically equal to the paper-reported scores of See et al. (2017) (see Table 1) on ROUGE-1, ROUGE-2, based on the bootstrap test (Efron and Tibshirani, 1994). Our baseline is stat. significantly better ($p < 0.001$) in all ROUGE metrics w.r.t. the github scores (R-1: 38.82, R-2: 16.81, R-3: 35.71, M: 18.14) of See et al. (2017).

Models	R-1	R-2	R-L	M
Baseline (XE)	35.50	14.57	32.19	14.36
ROUGE (RL)	35.97	15.45	32.72	14.50
ROUGESal+Ent (RL)	38.95	17.05	35.52	16.47

Table 2: ROUGE F1 full length scores of our models on test-only DUC-2002 generalizability setup.

ROUGE metrics. Finally, we combined our two rewards ROUGESal+Entail to incorporate both saliency and entailment knowledge, and it gives the best results overall ($p < 0.001$ in all metrics w.r.t. both baseline and ROUGE-reward models), setting the new state-of-the-art.[5]

Test-Only Transfer (DUC-2002) Results Finally, we also tested our model's generalizability/transfer skills, where we take the models trained on CNN/Daily Mail and directly test them on DUC-2002 in a test-only setup. As shown in Table 2, our final ROUGESal+Entail multi-reward RL model is statistically significantly better than both the cross-entropy (pointer-generator + coverage) baseline as well as ROUGE reward RL model, in terms of all 4 metrics with a large margin (with $p < 0.001$). This demonstrates that our ROUGESal+Entail model learned better transferable and generalizable skills of saliency and logical entailment.

7 Output Analysis

Saliency Analysis We analyzed the output summaries generated by See et al. (2017), and our baseline, ROUGE-reward and ROUGESal-reward models, using our saliency prediction model (Sec. 4), and the scores are 27.95%, 28.00%, 28.80%, and 30.86%. We also used the original CNN/Daily Mail Cloze Q&A setup (Hermann et al., 2015) with the fill-in-the-blank answers treated as salient information, and the results are 60.66%, 59.36%, 60.67%, and 64.66% for the four models. Both these experiments illustrate that our ROUGESal reward model is stat. signif. better in saliency than the See et al. (2017), our baseline, and ROUGE-reward models ($p < 0.001$).

Entailment Analysis We also analyzed the entailment scores of the generated summaries from See et al. (2017), and our baseline, ROUGE-reward, and Entail-reward models, and the results are 27.33%, 27.21%, 28.23%, and 28.98%.[6]

Models	2-gram	3-gram	4-gram
See et al. (2017)	2.24	6.03	9.72
Baseline (XE)	2.23	5.58	8.81
ROUGE (RL)	2.69	6.57	10.23
ROUGESal (RL)	2.37	6.00	9.50
Entail (RL)	2.63	6.56	10.26

Table 3: Abstractiveness: novel n-gram percentage.

We observe that our Entail-reward model achieves stat. significant entailment scores ($p < 0.001$) w.r.t. all the other three models.

Abstractiveness Analysis In order to measure the abstractiveness of our models, we followed the 'novel n-gram overlap' approach suggested in See et al. (2017). First, we found that all our reward-based RL models have significantly ($p < 0.01$) more novel n-grams than our cross-entropy baseline (see Table 3). Next, the Entail-reward model 'maintains' stat. equal abstractiveness as the ROUGE-reward model, likely because it encourages rewriting to create logical subsets of information, while the ROUGESal-reward model does a bit worse, probably because it focuses on copying more salient information (e.g., names). Compared to previous work (See et al., 2017), our Entail-reward and ROUGE-reward models achieve statistically significant improvement ($p < 0.01$) while ROUGESal is comparable.

8 Conclusion

We presented a summarization model trained with novel RL reward functions to improve the saliency and directed logical entailment aspects of a good summary. Further, we introduced the novel and effective multi-reward approach of optimizing multiple rewards simultaneously in alternate mini-batches. We achieve the new state-of-the-art on CNN/Daily Mail and also strong test-only improvements on a DUC-2002 transfer setup.

Acknowledgments

We thank the reviewers for their helpful comments. This work was supported by DARPA (YFA17-D17AP00022), Google Faculty Research Award, Bloomberg Data Science Research Grant, and NVidia GPU awards. The views, opinions, and/or findings contained in this article are those of the authors and should not be interpreted as representing the official views or policies, either expressed or implied, of the funding agency.

---

[5]Our last three rows in Table 1 are all stat. signif. better in all metrics with $p < 0.001$ compared to See et al. (2017).

[6]Based on our ground-truth summary to output summary sentences' average entailment score (see Sec. 4); similar trends hold for document-to-summary entailment scores.

References

Dzmitry Bahdanau, Kyunghyun Cho, and Yoshua Bengio. 2015. Neural machine translation by jointly learning to align and translate. In *ICLR*.

Samuel R Bowman, Gabor Angeli, Christopher Potts, and Christopher D Manning. 2015. A large annotated corpus for learning natural language inference. In *EMNLP*.

Qian Chen, Xiaodan Zhu, Zhenhua Ling, Si Wei, and Hui Jiang. 2016. Distraction-based neural networks for modeling documents. In *IJCAI*.

Jackie Chi Kit Cheung and Gerald Penn. 2014. Unsupervised sentence enhancement for automatic summarization. In *EMNLP*. pages 775–786.

Sumit Chopra, Michael Auli, and Alexander M Rush. 2016. Abstractive sentence summarization with attentive recurrent neural networks. In *HLT-NAACL*.

James Clarke and Mirella Lapata. 2008. Global inference for sentence compression: An integer linear programming approach. *Journal of Artificial Intelligence Research* 31:399–429.

Ido Dagan, Oren Glickman, and Bernardo Magnini. 2006. The pascal recognising textual entailment challenge. In *Machine learning challenges. evaluating predictive uncertainty, visual object classification, and recognising tectual entailment*, Springer, pages 177–190.

Michael Denkowski and Alon Lavie. 2014. Meteor universal: Language specific translation evaluation for any target language. In *EACL*.

Shibhansh Dohare and Harish Karnick. 2017. Text summarization using abstract meaning representation. *arXiv preprint arXiv:1706.01678* .

Bradley Efron and Robert J Tibshirani. 1994. *An introduction to the bootstrap*. CRC press.

Katja Filippova, Enrique Alfonseca, Carlos A Colmenares, Lukasz Kaiser, and Oriol Vinyals. 2015. Sentence compression by deletion with lstms. In *EMNLP*. pages 360–368.

Kavita Ganesan, ChengXiang Zhai, and Jiawei Han. 2010. Opinosis: a graph-based approach to abstractive summarization of highly redundant opinions. In *Proceedings of the 23rd international conference on computational linguistics*. ACL, pages 340–348.

Shima Gerani, Yashar Mehdad, Giuseppe Carenini, Raymond T Ng, and Bita Nejat. 2014. Abstractive summarization of product reviews using discourse structure. In *EMNLP*. volume 14, pages 1602–1613.

George Giannakopoulos. 2009. Automatic summarization from multiple documents. *Ph. D. dissertation* .

Anand Gupta, Manpreet Kaur, Adarsh Singh, Aseem Goel, and Shachar Mirkin. 2014. Text summarization through entailment-based minimum vertex cover. *Lexical and Computational Semantics (* SEM 2014)* page 75.

Sanda Harabagiu and Andrew Hickl. 2006. Methods for using textual entailment in open-domain question answering. In *ACL*. pages 905–912.

Karl Moritz Hermann, Tomas Kocisky, Edward Grefenstette, Lasse Espeholt, Will Kay, Mustafa Suleyman, and Phil Blunsom. 2015. Teaching machines to read and comprehend. In *NIPS*. pages 1693–1701.

Masaru Isonuma, Toru Fujino, Junichiro Mori, Yutaka Matsuo, and Ichiro Sakata. 2017. Extractive summarization using multi-task learning with document classification. In *EMNLP*. pages 2091–2100.

Sergio Jimenez, George Duenas, Julia Baquero, Alexander Gelbukh, Av Juan Dios Bátiz, and Av Mendizábal. 2014. UNAL-NLP: Combining soft cardinality features for semantic textual similarity, relatedness and entailment. In *In SemEval*. pages 732–742.

Hongyan Jing. 2000. Sentence reduction for automatic text summarization. In *ANLP*.

Diederik Kingma and Jimmy Ba. 2015. Adam: A method for stochastic optimization. In *ICLR*.

Kevin Knight and Daniel Marcu. 2002. Summarization beyond sentence extraction: A probabilistic approach to sentence compression. *Artificial Intelligence* 139(1):91–107.

Alice Lai and Julia Hockenmaier. 2014. Illinois-LH: A denotational and distributional approach to semantics. *Proc. SemEval* 2:5.

Chin-Yew Lin. 2004. ROUGE: A package for automatic evaluation of summaries. In *Text Summarization Branches Out: Proceedings of the ACL-04 workshop*. volume 8.

Fei Liu, Jeffrey Flanigan, Sam Thomson, Norman Sadeh, and Noah A Smith. 2015. Toward abstractive summarization using semantic representations. In *NAACL: HLT*. pages 1077–1086.

Yashar Mehdad, Giuseppe Carenini, Frank W Tompa, and Raymond T Ng. 2013. Abstractive meeting summarization with entailment and fusion. In *Proc. of the 14th European Workshop on Natural Language Generation*. pages 136–146.

Ramesh Nallapati, Bowen Zhou, Caglar Gulcehre, Bing Xiang, et al. 2016. Abstractive text summarization using sequence-to-sequence rnns and beyond. In *CoNLL*.

Ankur P Parikh, Oscar Täckström, Dipanjan Das, and Jakob Uszkoreit. 2016. A decomposable attention model for natural language inference. In *EMNLP*.

Ramakanth Pasunuru and Mohit Bansal. 2017. Reinforced video captioning with entailment rewards. In *EMNLP*.

Romain Paulus, Caiming Xiong, and Richard Socher. 2017. A deep reinforced model for abstractive summarization. *arXiv preprint arXiv:1705.04304* .

Pranav Rajpurkar, Jian Zhang, Konstantin Lopyrev, and Percy Liang. 2016. Squad: 100,000+ questions for machine comprehension of text. In *EMNLP*.

Marc'Aurelio Ranzato, Sumit Chopra, Michael Auli, and Wojciech Zaremba. 2015. Sequence level training with recurrent neural networks. In *ICLR*.

Steven J Rennie, Etienne Marcheret, Youssef Mroueh, Jarret Ross, and Vaibhava Goel. 2016. Self-critical sequence training for image captioning. *arXiv preprint arXiv:1612.00563* .

Alexander M Rush, Sumit Chopra, and Jason Weston. 2015. A neural attention model for abstractive sentence summarization. In *CoRR*.

Abigail See, Peter J Liu, and Christopher D Manning. 2017. Get to the point: Summarization with pointer-generator networks. In *ACL*.

Sandeep Subramanian, Tong Wang, Xingdi Yuan, and Adam Trischler. 2017. Neural models for key phrase detection and question generation. *arXiv preprint arXiv:1706.04560* .

Jun Suzuki and Masaaki Nagata. 2016. Rnn-based encoder-decoder approach with word frequency estimation. In *EACL*.

Lu Wang, Hema Raghavan, Vittorio Castelli, Radu Florian, and Claire Cardie. 2016. A sentence compression based framework to query-focused multi-document summarization. *arXiv preprint arXiv:1606.07548* .

Adina Williams, Nikita Nangia, and Samuel R Bowman. 2017. A broad-coverage challenge corpus for sentence understanding through inference. *arXiv preprint arXiv:1704.05426* .

Ronald J Williams. 1992. Simple statistical gradient-following algorithms for connectionist reinforcement learning. *Machine learning* 8(3-4):229–256.

Yonghui Wu, Mike Schuster, Zhifeng Chen, Quoc V Le, Mohammad Norouzi, Wolfgang Macherey, Maxim Krikun, Yuan Cao, Qin Gao, Klaus Macherey, et al. 2016. Google's neural machine translation system: Bridging the gap between human and machine translation. *arXiv preprint arXiv:1609.08144* .

Wojciech Zaremba and Ilya Sutskever. 2015. Reinforcement learning neural turing machines. *arXiv preprint arXiv:1505.00521* 362.

Yongzheng Zhang, Nur Zincir-Heywood, and Evangelos Milios. 2004. World wide web site summarization. *Web Intelligence and Agent Systems: An International Journal* 2(1):39–53.

A Supplementary Material

A.1 Saliency Rewards

Here, we describe the ROUGE-L formulation at summary-level and later describe how we incorporate saliency information into it. Given a reference summary of u sentences containing a total of m tokens ($\{w_{r,k}\}_{k=1}^{m}$) and a generated summary of v sentences with a total of n tokens ($\{w_{c,k}\}_{k=1}^{n}$), let r_i be the reference summary sentence and c_j be the generated summary sentence. Then, the precision (P_{lcs}), recall (R_{lcs}), and F-score (F_{lcs}) for ROUGE-L are defined as follows:

$$P_{lcs} = \frac{\sum_{i=1}^{u} LCS_{\cup}(r_i, C)}{n} \tag{4}$$

$$R_{lcs} = \frac{\sum_{i=1}^{u} LCS_{\cup}(r_i, C)}{m} \tag{5}$$

$$F_{lcs} = \frac{(1+\beta^2)R_{lcs}P_{lcs}}{R_{lcs} + \beta^2 P_{lcs}} \tag{6}$$

where $LCS_{\cup}$ takes the *union* Longest Common Subsequence (LCS) between a reference summary sentence r_i and every generated summary sentence c_j ($c_j \in C$), and β is defined in Lin (2004). In the above ROUGE-L scores, we assume that every token has equal weight, i.e, 1. However, every summary has salient tokens which should be rewarded with more weight. Hence, we use the weights obtained from our novel saliency predictor to modify the ROUGE-L scores with salient information as follows:

$$P_{lcs}^s = \frac{\sum_{i=1}^{u} LCS_{\cup}^*(r_i, C)}{\sum_{k=1}^{n} \eta(w_{c,k})} \tag{7}$$

$$R_{lcs}^s = \frac{\sum_{i=1}^{u} LCS_{\cup}^*(r_i, C)}{\sum_{k=1}^{m} \eta(w_{r,k})} \tag{8}$$

$$F_{lcs}^s = \frac{(1+\beta^2)R_{lcs}^s P_{lcs}^s}{R_{lcs}^s + \beta^2 P_{lcs}^s} \tag{9}$$

where $\eta(w)$ is the weight assigned by the saliency predictor for token w, and β is defined in Lin (2004).[7] Let $\{w_k\}_{k=1}^{p}$ be the union LCS set, then $LCS_{\cup}^*(r_i, C)$ is defined as follows:

$$LCS_{\cup}^*(r_i, C) = \sum_{k=1}^{p} \eta(w_k) \tag{10}$$

---

[7]If a token is repeated at multiple times in the input sentence, we average the probabilities of those instances.

A.2 Experimental Setup

A.2.1 Datasets

CNN/Daily Mail Dataset CNN/Daily Mail dataset (Hermann et al., 2015; Nallapati et al., 2016) is a collection of online articles and their summaries. The summaries are based on the human written highlights of these articles. The dataset has $287,226$ training pairs, $13,368$ validation pairs, and $11,490$ test pairs. We use the non-anonymous version of the dataset as described in See et al. (2017).

DUC Test Corpus We use the DUC-2002 single document summarization dataset[8] as a test-only setup where we directly take the pretrained models trained on CNN/Daily Mail dataset and test them on DUC-2002, in order to check for our model's domain transfer capabilities. This corpus consists of 567 documents with one or two human annotated reference summaries.

SNLI and MultiNLI corpus We use the full Stanford Natural Language Inference (SNLI) corpus (Bowman et al., 2015) and the recent Multi-NLI corpus (Williams et al., 2017) data for building our entailment classifier. We use the standard splits following previous work.

SQuAD Dataset We use Stanford Question Answering Dataset (SQuAD) for our saliency prediction model. We process the SQuAD dataset to collect the sentence and their corresponding salient phrases pairs. Here again, we use the standard split following previous work.

A.2.2 Training Details

During training, all our LSTM-RNNs are set with hidden state size of 256. We use a vocabulary size of 50k, where word embeddings are represented in 128 dimension, and both the encoder and decoder share the same embedding for each word. We encode the source document using a 400 time-step unrolled LSTM-RNN and 100 time-step unrolled LSTM-RNN for decoder. We clip the gradients to a maximum gradient norm value of 2.0 and use Adam optimizer (Kingma and Ba, 2015) with a learning rate of 1×10^{-3} for pointer baseline and 1×10^{-4} while training along with coverage loss, and 1×10^{-6} for reinforcement learning. Following See et al. (2017), we add coverage mechanism to a converged pointer model. For mixed-

Models	Accuracy
Entailment Classifier	74.50%
Saliency Predictor	16.87%

Table 4: Performance of our entailment classifier and saliency predictor.

loss (XE+RL) optimization, we use the following γ values for various rewards: 0.9985 for ROUGE, 0.9999 for Entail and ROUGE+Entail, and 0.9995 for ROUGESal and ROUGESal+Entail. For reinforcement learning, we only use 5000 training samples ($< 2\%$ of the actual data) to speed up convergence, but we found it to work well in practice. During inference time, we use a beam search of size 4.

A.3 Results

A.3.1 Saliency and Entailment Scorer

Table 4 presents the performance of our saliency predictor (on the SQuAD-based dev set for answer span classification accuracy) and entailment classifier (on the Multi-NLI dev set accuracy). Our entailment classifier is comparable to the state-of-the-art models.[9]

---

[8] http://www-nlpir.nist.gov/projects/duc/guidelines/2002.html

[9] RepEval leaderboard: https://repeval2017.github.io/shared/

Objective Function Learning to Match Human Judgements for Optimization-Based Summarization

Maxime Peyrard and **Iryna Gurevych**

Research Training Group AIPHES and UKP Lab
Computer Science Department, Technische Universität Darmstadt
www.aiphes.tu-darmstadt.de, www.ukp.tu-darmstadt.de

Abstract

Supervised summarization systems usually rely on supervision at the sentence or n-gram level provided by automatic metrics like ROUGE, which act as noisy proxies for human judgments. In this work, we learn a summary-level scoring function θ including human judgments as supervision and automatically generated data as regularization. We extract summaries with a genetic algorithm using θ as a fitness function. We observe strong and promising performances across datasets in both automatic and manual evaluation.

1 Introduction

The task of extractive summarization can naturally be cast as a discrete optimization problem where the text source is considered as a set of sentences and the summary is created by selecting an optimal subset of the sentences under a length constraint (McDonald, 2007). This view entails defining an objective function which is to be maximized by some optimization technique. In the ideal case, this objective function would encode all the relevant quality aspects of a summary, such that by maximizing all these quality aspects we would obtain the best possible summary.

However, we find several issues with the objective function in previous work on optimization-based summarization. First, the choice of the objective function is based on ad-hoc assumptions about which quality aspects of a summary are relevant (Kupiec et al., 1995). This bias can be mitigated via supervised techniques guided by data. In practice, these approaches use signals at the sentence (Conroy and O'leary, 2001; Cao et al., 2015) or n-gram (Hong and Nenkova, 2014; Li et al., 2013) level and then define a combination function to estimate the quality of the whole summary (Carbonell and Goldstein, 1998; Ren et al., 2016).

This combination θ determines the trade-off between conflicting quality aspects (importance vs redundancy) encoded in the objective function by making simplistic assumptions to ensure convenient mathematical properties of θ like linearity or submodularity (Lin and Bilmes, 2011). This restriction comes from computational considerations without conceptual justifications. More importantly, the supervision signal comes from automatic metrics like ROUGE (Lin, 2004) which are convenient but noisy approximations for human judgment.

In this work, we propose to learn the objective function θ at the summary-level from a pool of manually annotated system summaries to ensure the extraction of summaries considered *good* by humans. This explicitly targets the extraction of high-quality summaries as measured by humans and limits undesired gaming of the target evaluation metric. However, the number of data points is relatively low and the learned θ might not be well-behaved (high θ scores for bad summaries) pushing the optimizer to explore regions of the feature space unseen during training where θ wrongly assumes high scores. To prevent this scenario, we rely on a large amount of noisy but automatic training data providing supervision on a larger span of the feature space. Intuitively, it can be viewed as a kind of regularization.

By defining θ directly at the summary-level, one has access to features like redundancy or global information content without the need to define a combination function from individual sentence scores. Any feature available at the sentence or n-gram level can be transferred to the summary-level (by summation), while the summary-level perspective provides access to new features capturing the interactions between sentences. Furthermore, recent works have demonstrated that global optimization using genetic algorithms without im-

Proceedings of NAACL-HLT 2018, pages 654–660
New Orleans, Louisiana, June 1 - 6, 2018. ©2018 Association for Computational Linguistics

posing any mathematical restrictions on θ is feasible (Peyrard and Eckle-Kohler, 2016).

In summary, our contributions are: (1) We propose to learn a summary-level scoring function θ and use human judgments as supervision. (2) We demonstrate a simple regularization strategy based on automatic data generation to improve the behavior of θ under optimization. (3) We perform both automatic and manual evaluation of the extracted summaries, which indicate competitive performances.

2 Approach

2.1 Learning setup

Let θ^* be the observed human judgments. θ^* can be manual Pyramid (Nenkova et al., 2007) or overall responsiveness on a 0 to 5 LIKERT scale. We learn a function θ_w with parameters w approximating θ^* based on a feature set Φ. $\Phi(S) \in \mathbb{R}^d$ is the feature representation of a summary S.

Let $\mathcal{T}$ be the set of topics in the training set, and $\mathcal{S}_T$ the set of scored summaries for the topic T. The learning problem consists in minimizing the following loss function:

$$\mathcal{L}_\omega = \sum_{T \in \mathcal{T}} \sum_{s \in \mathcal{S}_T} \|\theta_\omega(\Phi(S)) - \theta^*(S)\|^2 \qquad (1)$$

While any regression algorithm could be applied, we observed strong performances for the simple linear regression. It is particularly simple and not prone to overfitting.

2.2 Automatic data generation

Few annotated summaries are available (50 per topic) and they cover a small region of the feature space (low variability). θ may wrongly assume high scores in some parts of the feature space despite lack of evidence. The optimizer will explore these regions and output low-quality summaries.

To address this issue, we generate summaries distributed across the feature space. For each feature x, we sample a set of $k = 100$ summaries covering the range of possible values of x. For sampling, we use the genetic algorithm recently introduced by Peyrard and Eckle-Kohler (2016).[1] Their solver implements a Genetic Algorithm (**GA**) to create and iteratively optimize summaries over time. We use default values for the

reproduction and mutation rate and set the population size to 50. With x as fitness function, the resulting population is a set of summaries ranging from random to (close to) maximal value. After both maximization and minimization, we obtain 100 summaries covering the full range of x.

In total, we sample $m \cdot k$ summaries per topic, where m is the number of features. We score these summaries with ROUGE-2 recall (R2), which is a noisy approximation of human judgments but provides indications preventing bad regions from getting high scores.

2.3 Summary Extraction

We trained 3 different scoring functions: θ_{pyr} with manual pyramid annotations; θ_{resp} with responsiveness annotations; and θ_{R2} with our automatically generated data. [2] The final scoring function is a linear combination:

$$\theta(S) = \alpha_1 \cdot \theta_{pyr}(S) + \alpha_2 \cdot \theta_{resp}(S) + \alpha_3 \cdot \theta_{R2}(S)$$

Therefore θ_{R2} acts as a regularizer for the θ's learned with human judgments. [3] It is a simple form of model averaging which combine the different information of the 3 different models.

We didn't constrain θ to have specific properties like linearity with respect to sentence scores, thus extracting high scoring summaries cannot be done with Integer Linear Programming. Instead, we search an approximate solution by employing the same meta-heuristic solver we used for sampling with θ as the fitness function.

2.4 Features

Learning a scoring function at the summary-level gives us access to both n-gram/sentence-level features and summary-level features. Sentence-level features can be transferred to the summary-level, while new features capturing the interactions between sentences in the summary become available.

As sentence-level features, we used the standard: TF*IDF, n-gram frequency and overlap with the title. As new summary-level features, we used: number of sentences, summary-level redundancy and summary-level n-gram distributions: Jensen-Shannon (JS) divergence with n-gram distribution in the source (Louis and Nenkova, 2013).

---

[1] https://github.com/UKPLab/
coling2016-genetic-swarm-MDS

[2] We train these models separately because the different annotations do not lie on the same scale

[3] We didn't automatically tune the different values of α but observed that $[1, 0.5, 0.5]$ works well in practice.

N-gram Coverage. Each n-gram g_i in the documents has a frequency $tf(g_i)$, the summary S is scored by:

$$Cov_n(S) = \sum_{g \in S_n} tf(g_i)$$

Here S_n is the multiset of n-grams (with repetitions) composing S. Also, the frequency can be computed either by counting the number of occurrence of the n-gram or by counting the number of documents in which the n-gram appears. For both frequency computations, we extract features for unigrams, bigrams and trigrams.

TF*IDF. Each n-gram g_i is also associated its Inverse Document Frequence: $idf(g_i)$. The summary S is scored by:

$$TF * IDF_n(S) = \sum_{g \in S_n} tf(g_i) * idf(g_i)$$

Here S_n is the multiset of n-grams (with repetitions) composing the summary S. We also extract features for both frequency computations for unigrams, bigrams and trigrams.

Overlap with title. We measure the proportion of n-grams from the title that appear in the summary:

$$Overlap_n(S) = \frac{|T_n \cap S_n|}{T_n}$$

Where T_n is the multiset of n-grams in the title, and S_n is the multiset of n-grams in the summary. We compute it for unigrams, bigrams and trigrams.

Number of sentences. We also use the number of sentences in S as a feature because summaries with a lot of sentences tend to have very short and meaningless sentences.

Redundancy. Previous features were at the sentence-level, we obtained features for the whole summary by summation over sentences. However, the redundancy of S cannot be computed at the sentence-level. This is an example of features available at the summary-level but not available at the sentence-level. We define it as the number of unique n-gram types ($|U_n|$) in the summary divided by the total number of n-gram tokens (the length of S)

$$Red_n(S) = \frac{|U_n|}{|S_n|}$$

Where U_n is the set of n-grams (without repetitions) composing S and S_n is the multiset of n-grams (with repetitions).

Divergences. This is another feature that can only be computed at the summary-level inspired by Haghighi and Vanderwende (2009) and Peyrard and Eckle-Kohler (2016). We compute the KL divergence and JS divergence between n-gram probability distributions of the summaries and of the documents. The probability distributions are built from the two kinds of frequency distributions and for unigrams, bigrams and trigrams.

3 Experiments

Dataset We use two multi-document summarization datasets from the Text Analysis Conference (TAC) shared tasks: TAC-2008 and TAC-2009.[4] TAC-2008 and TAC-2009 contain 48 and 44 topics, respectively. Each topic consists of 10 news articles to be summarized in a maximum of 100 words. We use only the so-called initial summaries (A summaries), but not the update part.

We used these datasets because all system summaries and the 4 reference summaries were manually evaluated by NIST assessors for content selection (with Pyramid) and overall responsiveness. At the time of the shared tasks, 57 systems were submitted to TAC-2008 and 55 to TAC-2009. For our experiments, we use the Pyramid and the responsiveness annotations.

With our notations, for example with TAC-2009, we have $n = 55$ scored system summaries, $m = 44$ topics, $\mathcal{D}_i$ contains 10 documents and θ_i contains 4 reference summaries.

We also use the recently created German dataset DBS (Benikova et al., 2016) which contains 10 heterogeneous topics. For each topic, 5 summaries were evaluated by trained human annotators but only for content selection with Pyramid. The summaries have variable sizes and are about 500 words long.

Baselines (1) ICSI (Gillick and Favre, 2009) is a global linear optimization approach that extracts a summary by solving a maximum coverage problem considering the most frequent bigrams in the source documents. ICSI has been among the best systems in a standard ROUGE evaluation (Hong et al., 2014). (2) LexRank (Erkan

---

[4] http://tac.nist.gov/2009/
Summarization/, http://tac.nist.gov/2008/

	ρ	NDCG
Best-Baseline-R	.594	.505
θ_{R2}	**.663**	**.536**
Best-Baseline-Pyr	.492	.715
θ_{pyr}	**.554**	**.780**
Best-Baseline-Resp	.367	.710
θ_{resp}	**.391**	**.741**

Table 1: Performance of learned θ's compared to the best baselines for each type annotation types.

and Radev, 2004) is a graph-based approach computing sentence centrality based on the PageRank algorithm. (3) KL-Greedy (Haghighi and Vanderwende, 2009) minimizes the Kullback-Leibler (KL) divergence between the word distributions in the summary and the documents. (3) Peyrard and Eckle-Kohler (2016) optimize JS divergence with a genetic algorithm. (4) Finally, SFOUR is a supervised structured prediction approach that trains an end-to-end on a convex relaxation of ROUGE (Sipos et al., 2012).

Objective function learning In this section, we measure how well our models can predict human judgments. We train each θ in a leave-one-out cross-validation setup for each dataset and compare their performance to the summary scoring function of baselines like it was done previously (Peyrard and Eckle-Kohler, 2017). Each individual feature is also included in the baselines.

Correlations are measured with two complementary metrics: Spearman's ρ and Normalized Discounted Cumulative Gain (NDCG). Spearman's ρ is a rank correlation metric, which compares the ordering of systems induced by θ and the ordering of systems induced by human judgments. NDCG is a metric that compares ranked lists and puts more emphasis on the top elements with logarithmic decay weighting. Intuitively, it captures how well θ can recognize the best summaries. The optimization scenario benefits from high NDCG scores because only summaries with high θ scores are extracted.

The results are presented in Table 1. For simplicity, we report the average over the 3 datasets. Each θ is compared against the best performing baseline for the data annotation type it was trained on (R2, responsiveness or pyramid).[5] The trained models perform substantially and consistently bet-

ter than the best baselines. They have a high correlation with human judgments and are capable of identifying *good* summaries.

However, we need to test whether the combination of the three θ's is well behaved under optimization. For this, we perform an evaluation of the summaries extracted by the genetic optimizer.

Summaries Evaluation Now, we evaluate the summaries extracted by the genetic optimizer with θ as fitness function (noted (θ, Gen)). We still train θ with leave-one-out cross-validation.

To evaluate summaries, we report the ROUGE variant identified by Owczarzak et al. (2012) as strongly correlating with human evaluation methods: ROUGE-2 (R2) recall with stemming and stopwords not removed. We also report JS2, the Jensen-Shannon divergence between bigrams in the reference summaries and the candidate system summary (Lin et al., 2006). The last metric is S3 (Peyrard et al., 2017), a combination of several existing metrics trained explicitly to maximize its correlation with human judgments.

Finally, our approach aims at improving summarization systems based on human judgments, therefore we also set up a manual evaluation for the two English datasets. Two annotators were given the summaries of every system for 10 randomly selected topic of both TAC-2008 and TAC-2009. They annotated (with a Cohen's kappa of 0.73) summaries on a LIKERT scale following the responsiveness guidelines.

The results are reported in Table 2. We perform significance testing with *Approximate Random Testing* to compare differences between two means in cross-validation [6].

While θ's trained on human judgments have a high correlation with human judgments, they behave badly under optimization. This effect is much less visible for θ_{R2} because the data points have been sampled to cover the feature space. We observe the effectiveness of the regularization because each $\theta_{R2/pyr/resp}$ performs much worse individually than the combined θ. We also note that $(\theta_{R2}, \text{Gen})$ performs on par with the other supervised baseline SFOUR but both are outperformed by exploiting human judgments. (θ, Gen) is consistently and often significantly better than baselines across datasets and metrics. In particular, humans tend to prefer the summaries extracted by

---

[5]Best baseline for R2 and Responsiveness is: KL divergence on bigrams; for Pyramid: KL divergence on unigrams

[6]The symbol * indicates that the difference compared to the previous best baseline is significant with $p \leq 0.05$

	TAC-2008				TAC-2009				DBS		
	R2↑	JS2↓	S3↑	H↑	R2↑	JS2↓	S3↑	H↑	R2↑	JS2↓	S3↑
LexRank	.078	.635	.336	3.74	.090	.625	.360	3.75	.105	.594	.354
(KL, Greedy)	.068	.644	.294	3.42	.061	.648	.288	3.21	.078	.620	.293
(JS, Gen)	.098	.618	.376	3.99	.101	.618	.370	3.89	.112	**.584**	.362
SFOUR	.101	.623	.372	3.88	.101	.622	.367	3.85	.114	.591	.357
ICSI	.101	.620	.377	4.03	.103	.619	.369	3.91	.115	.586	.361
$(\theta_{R2}$, Gen)	.100	.620	.375	3.89	**.104**	.618	.373	3.82	.116	.585	.363
$(\theta_{pyr}$, Gen)	.096	.623	.369	3.65	.085	.631	.339	3.77	.078	.615	.312
$(\theta_{resp}$, Gen)	.096	.622	.364	3.78	.085	.635	.342	3.88	-	-	-
$(\theta$, Gen)	**.105**	**.615**[*]	**.382**	**4.09**[*]	**.104**	**.617**	**.376**	**4.03**[*]	**.117**	**.584**	**.367**[*]

Table 2: Comparison of systems across 3 datasets evaluated with ROUGE-2 recall; JS divergence on bigrams; S3 and Human annotations.

$(\theta$, Gen). Manual inspection of summaries reveals that $(\theta$, Gen) has lower redundancy than previous baselines thanks to summary-level features.

Important Features Since we used a linear regression, we can estimate the contribution of a feature by the amplitude of its associated weight. The two best features (n-gram distributions and redundancy) are summary-level features, which confirms the advantage of using a summary-level scoring function.

4 Related Work and Discussion

Supervised summarization started with Kupiec et al. (1995) who observed that there is no principled method to select and weight relevant features. Previous work focused on predicting sentence (Conroy and O'leary, 2001; Cao et al., 2015) or n-gram (Hong and Nenkova, 2014; Li et al., 2013) scores and then defining a composition function to get a score for the summary. This combination usually accounts for redundancy or coherence (Nishikawa et al., 2014) in an ad-hoc fashion (Carbonell and Goldstein, 1998; Ren et al., 2016). Structure prediction has been investigated to learn the composition function as well (Sipos et al., 2012; Takamura and Okumura, 2010). The supervision is always provided by automatic metrics, whereas we incorporate human judgments as supervision and learn from it directly at the summary-level. We note that He et al. (2006) and Peyrard and Eckle-Kohler (2016) have used a scoring function at the summary-level but these approaches are unsupervised.

One of the challenges we face is the lack of data with human judgments. We hope that this work will encourage efforts to create new and large datasets as they will be decisive for the progress of summarization. Indeed, systems trained only with automatic metrics can only be as good as the metrics are as a proxy for humans.

We used simple features but using more complex and semantic features is promising. Indeed, two syntactically similar but semantically different summaries cannot be distinguished by ROUGE, which diminishes the usefulness of semantic features. However, humans can distinguish them, thus inducing better usage of such features.

Another promising direction is to investigate more sophisticated ways of combining the human judgments with the automatically generated data. For example, by exploiting techniques from semi-supervised learning (Zhu et al., 2009) or by dynamically sampling unseen regions of the feature space with active learning (Settles, 2009).

5 Conclusion

We proposed an approach to learn a summary-level scoring function θ with human judgments as supervision and automatically generated data as regularization. The summaries subsequently extracted with a genetic algorithm are of high quality according to both automatic and manual evaluation. We hope this work will encourage more research directed towards the generation and usage of human judgment datasets.

Acknowledgements

This work has been supported by the German Research Foundation (DFG) as part of the Research Training Group "Adaptive Preparation of Information from Heterogeneous Sources" (AIPHES) under grant No. GRK 1994/1, and via the German-Israeli Project Cooperation (DIP, grant No. GU 798/17-1).

References

Darina Benikova, Margot Mieskes, Christian M. Meyer, and Iryna Gurevych. 2016. Bridging the Gap Between Extractive and Abstractive Summaries: Creation and Evaluation of Coherent Extracts from Heterogeneous Sources. In *Proceedings of the 26th International Conference on Computational Linguistics (COLING)*, pages 1039 – 1050.

Ziqiang Cao, Furu Wei, Sujian Li, Wenjie Li, Ming Zhou, and Houfeng Wang. 2015. Learning summary prior representation for extractive summarization. In *Proceedings of the 53rd Annual Meeting of the Association for Computational Linguistics and the 7th International Joint Conference on Natural Language Processing (IJCNLP)*, pages 829–833.

Jaime Carbonell and Jade Goldstein. 1998. The Use of MMR, Diversity-based Reranking for Reordering Documents and Producing Summaries. In *Proceedings of the 21st Annual International ACM SIGIR Conference on Research and Development in Information Retrieval*, pages 335–336.

John M. Conroy and Dianne P. O'leary. 2001. Text summarization via hidden markov models. In *Proceedings of the 24th Annual International ACM SIGIR Conference on Research and Development in Information Retrieval*, pages 406–407.

Günes Erkan and Dragomir R. Radev. 2004. LexRank: Graph-based Lexical Centrality As Salience in Text Summarization. *Journal of Artificial Intelligence Research*, pages 457–479.

Dan Gillick and Benoit Favre. 2009. A Scalable Global Model for Summarization. In *Proceedings of the Workshop on Integer Linear Programming for Natural Language Processing (ILP'09)*, pages 10–18.

Aria Haghighi and Lucy Vanderwende. 2009. Exploring Content Models for Multi-document Summarization. In *Proceedings of Human Language Technologies: The 2009 Annual Conference of the North American Chapter of the Association for Computational Linguistics*, pages 362–370.

Yan-xiang He, De-xi Liu, Dong-hong Ji, Hua Yang, and Chong Teng. 2006. MSBGA: A Multi-Document Summarization System Based on Genetic Algorithm. In *2006 International Conference on Machine Learning and Cybernetics*, pages 2659–2664.

Kai Hong, John Conroy, benoit Favre, Alex Kulesza, Hui Lin, and Ani Nenkova. 2014. A Repository of State of the Art and Competitive Baseline Summaries for Generic News Summarization. In *Proceedings of the Ninth International Conference on Language Resources and Evaluation (LREC'14)*, pages 1608–1616.

Kai Hong and Ani Nenkova. 2014. Improving the Estimation of Word Importance for News Multi-Document Summarization. In *Proceedings of the 14th Conference of the European Chapter of the Association for Computational Linguistics (EACL)*, pages 712–721.

Julian Kupiec, Jan Pedersen, and Francine Chen. 1995. A Trainable Document Summarizer. In *Proceedings of the 18th Annual International ACM SIGIR Conference on Research and Development in Information Retrieval*, pages 68–73.

Chen Li, Xian Qian, and Yang Liu. 2013. Using Supervised Bigram-based ILP for Extractive Summarization. In *Proceedings of the 51st Annual Meeting of the Association for Computational Linguistics (ACL)*, pages 1004–1013.

Chin-Yew Lin. 2004. ROUGE: A Package for Automatic Evaluation of summaries. In *Proceedings of ACL workshop on Text Summarization Branches Out*, pages 74–81, Barcelona, Spain.

Chin-Yew Lin, Guihong Cao, Jianfeng Gao, and Jian-Yun Nie. 2006. An Information-Theoretic Approach to Automatic Evaluation of Summaries. In *Proceedings of the Human Language Technology Conference at NAACL*, pages 463–470, New York City, USA.

Hui Lin and Jeff A. Bilmes. 2011. A Class of Submodular Functions for Document Summarization. In *Proceedings of the 49th Annual Meeting of the Association for Computational Linguistics (ACL)*, pages 510–520, Portland, Oregon.

Annie Louis and Ani Nenkova. 2013. Automatically Assessing Machine Summary Content Without a Gold Standard. *Computational Linguistics*, 39(2):267–300.

Ryan McDonald. 2007. A Study of Global Inference Algorithms in Multi-document Summarization. In *Proceedings of the 29th European Conference on Information Retrieval Research*, pages 557–564.

Ani Nenkova, Rebecca Passonneau, and Kathleen McKeown. 2007. The Pyramid Method: Incorporating Human Content Selection Variation in Summarization Evaluation. *ACM Transaction on Speech and Language Processing*, 4.

Hitoshi Nishikawa, Kazuho Arita, Katsumi Tanaka, Tsutomu Hirao, Toshiro Makino, and Yoshihiro Matsuo. 2014. Learning to generate coherent summary with discriminative hidden semi-markov model. In *Proceedings of the 25th International Conference on Computational Linguistics (COLING)*, pages 1648–1659.

Karolina Owczarzak, John M. Conroy, Hoa Trang Dang, and Ani Nenkova. 2012. An Assessment of the Accuracy of Automatic Evaluation in Summarization. In *Proceedings of Workshop on Evaluation Metrics and System Comparison for Automatic Summarization*, pages 1–9.

Maxime Peyrard, Teresa Botschen, and Iryna Gurevych. 2017. Learning to Score System Summaries for Better Content Selection Evaluation. In *Proceedings of the EMNLP workshop New Frontiers in Summarization*, pages 74–84.

Maxime Peyrard and Judith Eckle-Kohler. 2016. A General Optimization Framework for Multi-Document Summarization Using Genetic Algorithms and Swarm Intelligence. In *Proceedings of the 26th International Conference on Computational Linguistics (COLING)*, pages 247 – 257.

Maxime Peyrard and Judith Eckle-Kohler. 2017. A Principled Framework for Evaluating Summarizers: Comparing Models of Summary Quality against Human Judgments. In *Proceedings of the 55th Annual Meeting of the Association for Computational Linguistics (ACL 2017)*, volume Volume 2: Short Papers. Association for Computational Linguistics.

Pengjie Ren, Furu Wei, Zhumin Chen, Jun Ma, and Ming Zhou. 2016. A redundancy-aware sentence regression framework for extractive summarization. In *26th International Conference on Computational Linguistics, Proceedings of the Conference*, pages 33–43.

Burr Settles. 2009. Active Learning Literature Survey. Computer Sciences Technical Report 1648, University of Wisconsin–Madison.

Ruben Sipos, Pannaga Shivaswamy, and Thorsten Joachims. 2012. Large-margin Learning of Submodular Summarization Models. In *Proceedings of the 13th Conference of the European Chapter of the Association for Computational Linguistics (EACL)*, pages 224–233.

Hiroya Takamura and Manabu Okumura. 2010. Learning to Generate Summary as Structured Output. In *Proceedings of the 19th ACM international Conference on Information and Knowledge Management*, pages 1437–1440.

Xiaojin Zhu, Andrew B. Goldberg, Ronald Brachman, and Thomas Dietterich. 2009. *Introduction to Semi-Supervised Learning*. Morgan and Claypool Publishers.

Pruning Basic Elements for Better Automatic Evaluation of Summaries

Ukyo Honda[1]   **Tsutomu Hirao**[2]   **Masaaki Nagata**[2]

[1] Nara Institute of Science and Technology   [2] NTT Communication Science Laboratories

[1] honda.ukyo.hn6@is.naist.jp

[2] {hirao.tsutomu, nagata.masaaki}@lab.ntt.co.jp

Abstract

We propose a simple but highly effective automatic evaluation measure of summarization, pruned Basic Elements (pBE). Although the BE concept is widely used for the automated evaluation of summaries, its weakness is that it redundantly matches basic elements. To avoid this redundancy, pBE prunes basic elements by (1) disregarding frequency count of basic elements and (2) reducing semantically overlapped basic elements based on word similarity. Even though it is simple, pBE outperforms ROUGE in DUC datasets in most cases and achieves the highest rank correlation coefficient in TAC 2011 AESOP task.

1   Introduction

Automatic evaluation measures have a significant impact on the research on summarization. Since there is no other practical way to quickly evaluate the quality of system summaries, summarization studies work on raising the scores that are given by automatic evaluation measures.

Among the automatic evaluation measures, the most popular ones are ROUGE (Lin, 2004) and BE (Hovy et al., 2006). ROUGE/BE counts the number of ngrams/basic elements[1] that match those in manual reference summaries. ROUGE normally employs unigrams or bigrams while BE uses dependency triples (head|modifier|relation) as their units. It is known that both ROUGE and BE are well correlated with human judgment.

Their evaluation approach, however, is quite different from humans' in two ways: they score low-information units higher and ignore the semantic overlap of units. The first problem is

caused by scoring units according to their frequencies. We found that the units that occur multiple times in a summary are highly likely to be function-word bigrams (e.g., "of the") or basic elements that represent only single nouns (e.g., (house|the|det)); such units are less informative than units connected with verbs (e.g., "John went" and (went|John|nsubj)). The second problem is that ROUGE/BE sometimes gives scores twice or more to the units that are semantically overlapped but spelled differently. This is due to the fact that ROUGE/BE only considers the surface level of unit matching, which also yields inaccurate scoring of paraphrased units.

Our method is aimed at solving these problems by cutting back redundant units. We use BE, but with Universal Dependencies (UD) (Nivre et al., 2016), a more ideal form of annotation that is available for multiple languages, and introduce two steps to prune basic elements. The first step is to disregard the frequency count of basic elements, and the other one is to reduce semantically overlapped basic elements using word embeddings. We call this new measure pruned BE (pBE). Our experiments show that pBE outperforms ROUGE in most DUC datasets and achieves the highest rank correlation coefficient in TAC 2011 AESOP task.

2   Related Work

ROUGE-WE (Ng and Abrecht, 2015) and BEwT-E (Tratz and Hovy, 2008) are closely related to our method in that they aim to improve unit matching. ROUGE-WE exploits word embeddings to softly match ngrams based on their cosine similarities. Although this also takes semantic correspondence into consideration, it is different from pBE because it does not judge word similarity within one summary, but only between a target sum-

---

[1] We use "BE" to represent the evaluation method Basic Elements, "basic element(s)" to represent the fragments of Basic Elements and "unit" as a general term of ngrams and basic elements.

Proceedings of NAACL-HLT 2018, pages 661–666

New Orleans, Louisiana, June 1 - 6, 2018. ©2018 Association for Computational Linguistics

mary and its reference summaries. Furthermore, ROUGE-WE does not remove the frequency count of ngrams as pBE does. As a result, ROUGE-WE does not achieve our goal of reducing redundant units.

BEwT-E transforms basic elements to help in matching. However, it requires complex transformation rules, which are difficult to apply to languages other than English. pBE, on the other hand, needs no resources other than word embeddings and UD parsers, and so can be implemented in many other languages. BEwT-E was checked as to whether the frequency count of basic elements affected its performance. The focus, however, was not to prune basic elements and there was no clear explanation as to why disregarding frequency count was effective. Our contribution is that we have identified why disregarding frequency count is effective; it yields the pruning of low-information basic elements, and thus works well in combination with reducing semantic overlaps.

Syntactically and semantically richer structures are free from low-information units. In this sense, PEAK (Yang et al., 2016) is related to our method in that it tries to employ predicate-argument structures as primitive units for matching. However, the predicate-argument structures are more difficult to extract than dependency triples. It is reported that PEAK scored only about 0.7 in Pearson coefficient for the DUC 2006 dataset (Yang et al., 2016), whereas ROUGE achieved around 0.83.

3   pruned BE (pBE)[2]

In this section, we describe our implementation of BE and the two steps of pruning basic elements.

3.1   Our Implementation of BE

BE was proposed to compensate some of the shortcomings of ngrams (Hovy et al., 2006). ROUGE usually uses short ngrams such as unigrams and bigrams, but these can be low-information content because they are simply extracted without considering the syntactic relations of the words. For example, the sentence "John went to the store on foot" is decomposed into the bigrams ["John went", "went to", "to the", "the store", "store on", "on foot"]. The function-word pair "to the" bears almost no meaning but is frequently found since function words appear in sentences quite often. On the other hand, a dependency triple holds the syntactic information that the dependency of "to" is not "the" but "store". Although BE requires applying parsers to summaries, syntactic dependencies enable BE to avoid making low-information units[3].

Accordingly, while we use BE, the annotation is UD based, an approach not employed in previous studies. Since UD focuses on the relations between content words, UD triples are able to represent key components of sentences more directly. For example, the sentence above can be decomposed in UD as [(went|John|nsubj), (store|to|case), (store|the|det), (went|store|nmod:to), (foot|on|case), (went|foot|nmod:on)][4], while it is [(went|John|nsubj), (went|to|prep), (store|the|det), (to|store|pobj), (went|on|prep), (on|foot|pobj)] in Stanford Dependencies (de Marneffe et al., 2006). In UD, the predicate-object relation is directly expressed as (went|store|nmod:to), instead of having intermediate triples (went|to|prep) and (to|store|pobj). Moreover, UD has another key advantage, that it is available in many languages. This makes our method available for multiple languages other than English.

We use (head|modifier|relation) triples of UD v1 relations which correspond to narrow-sense dependencies and multiword expression (MWE) dependencies of UD v2[5]. One thing to note here is that we excluded auxpass and mwe relations. It is because the information of these is mostly contained in other relations such as nsubjpass, nmod and advcl. Auxpass is a special relation of aux, which indicates that a verb is passive. Aux indicates a verb's modality or tense, which is not mentioned by nsubj relation alone. Auxpass also indicates an important information of a verb, its voice. However, the information of voice is already contained in the relation of nsubjpass. Mwe is used for multiword expressions with function words that behave like a single function word.

---

[3]It can be pointed out that bigrams of function words can be avoided if we remove function words. However, this is just an ad hoc measure, which leads to another meaningless bigram "store foot".

[4]root relation triple is omitted because we do not include it in our basic elements. See the next footnote.

[5]That is, nsubj, nsubjpass, dobj, iobj, csubj, csubjpass, ccomp, xcomp, nmod, advcl, advmod, neg, vocative, discourse, expl, aux, cop, mark, nummod, appos, acl, amod, det, case, compound, name, foreign and dislocated.

[2]Code will be available at https://github.com/ukyh/prunedBE

The whole information of mwe, however, is generally contained in nmod or advcl relations in enhanced++ UD representation (Schuster and Manning, 2016) (e.g., (fruits|apple|nmod:such_as) and (bought|fixing|advcl:insted_of)). Counting these relations can lead to redundant unit matching. In fact, the performance was better when we excluded these relations.

3.2 Step 1: Disregard Frequency Count

ROUGE/BE score is defined as follows:

$$\text{ROUGE/BE}(\mathbf{R}, S) =$$

$$\frac{\sum_{k=1}^{K} \sum_{m=1}^{M_k} \min\{N(f_m^k, \mathbf{R}_k), N(f_m^k, S)\}}{\sum_{k=1}^{K} \sum_{m=1}^{M_k} \{N(f_m^k, \mathbf{R}_k)\}}. \quad (1)$$

Given K reference summaries $\mathbf{R} = \{\mathbf{R}_1, ..., \mathbf{R}_K\}$, target summary S, and the set of units that appear in $\mathbf{R}_k$ as $F_k = \{f_1^k, ..., f_{M_k}^k\}$ ($|F_k| = M_k$), ROUGE/BE counts how many times each f occurs in target summary S. Let $N(f_m^k, \mathbf{R}_k)$ be the frequency of f_m^k in $\mathbf{R}_k$ and $N(f_m^k, S)$ be the frequency of f_m^k in S. Unit f contributes to ROUGE/BE scores according to its frequency[6].

The problem is that the units found multiple times tend to be low-information units. ROUGE-2 often finds function-word bigrams, which leads to their overweighting. While BE is free from function-word bigrams, it still contains improperly weighted basic elements: compound and det. For example, in DUC 2003, 302 basic elements are returned more than 1 in $\min\{N(f_m^k, \mathbf{R}_k), N(f_m^k, S)\}$ of which 139 were compound and 96 were det; together they occupy about 78% of the total. This is because these relations represent only single nouns. Since they are not associated with verbs, which are key components of sentences, they appear in many sentences even within one summary[7]. It is not that compound and det are meaningless units, but that they should not be weighted more than other relations such as nsubj, dobj and iobj, which are associated with verbs.

Therefore, we simply get rid of the frequency count. We define our scoring function as follows:

$$\text{pBE}_{-\text{cnt}}(\mathbf{R}, S) =$$

$$\frac{\sum_{k=1}^{K} \sum_{m=1}^{M_k} \{O(f_m^k, S)\}}{\sum_{k=1}^{K} \sum_{m=1}^{M_k} \{O(f_m^k, \mathbf{R}_k)\}}. \quad (2)$$

Here $O(f_m^k, \mathbf{R}_k)$ and $O(f_m^k, S)$ are functions that return 1 if f_m^k is in $\mathbf{R}_k$ and S respectively, and otherwise return 0. This way, we can simplify equation (1) and avoid undue weighting.

3.3 Step 2: Cluster Basic Elements Using Word Embeddings

We are able to detect semantic correspondence. If we are given key points to be included in the summary, we can judge whether the key points are in the summary or not on the semantic level. ROGUE/BE, however, judges the correspondence of key points only on the surface level. Since the same content can be expressed in various surface forms, ROUGE/BE sometimes scores semantically overlapped units multiple times or does not score units that semantically correspond to each other but are significantly different on the surface level[8].

To deal with this problem, we put semantically identical words into one cluster based on word similarity. Our method only requires word embeddings trained with word2vec (Mikolov et al., 2013), and so offers multilingual capability.

Given K reference summaries $\mathbf{R} = \{\mathbf{R}_1, ..., \mathbf{R}_K\}$, target summary S, a set of all unigrams in $\mathbf{R}$ and S as $U = \{u_1, ..., u_P\}$, and a set of Q word embeddings for the unigrams as $V = \{v_1, ..., v_Q\}$ ($Q \leq P$), we put U into the set of cluster IDs $C = \{c_1, ..., c_N\}$ by hierarchical clustering using word similarities. The number of clusters, N, is a hyperparameter. Next, we convert the unigrams of $\mathbf{R}$ and S into the cluster ID c. If unigram u_i has no word embeddings, we leave it in its surface form. Let the converted reference summaries and target summary be $\mathbf{R}'$ and S', respectively. We define the set of basic elements in $\mathbf{R}'_k$ as $F'_k = \{f_1'^k, ..., f_{M_k}'^k\}$ ($|F'_k| = M_k$).

---

[6]In BE, it is optional to consider or disregard this frequency count (Tratz and Hovy, 2008). We describe why dispensing with the frequency count affects the results below.

[7]"Donald Trump" can be used in various sentences like "Donald Trump won the election." and "Donald Trump will visit China next week." But "Trump won" can only occur in the specific situation where Trump won something, which is unlikely to be described in a summary more than once.

[8]Suppose the phrases "John killed" and "John murdered" are in a target summary and each reference summaries. Here, the target summary gets double scores for the semantically same units. On the other hand, if "John killed" is only in the target summary and "John murdered" is only in the reference summaries, the target summary gets no score for the semantic correspondence.

	DUC03	DUC04	DUC05	DUC06	DUC06 pyr	DUC07	DUC07 pyr
ROUGE-2	.906/.821/.617	.909/.838/.691	**.932/.931/.792**	.836/.767/.584	**.905/.884/.740**	.880/.873/.715	.979/.989/.949
ROUGE-S4	.851/.791/.617	.876/.816/.647	.915/.889/.727	.829/.759/.574	.888/.880/.732	.850/.836/.646	.971/.956/.872
ROUGE-SU4	.782/.774/.600	.854/.772/.559	.925/.893/.731	.849/.790/.601	.885/.850/.706	.835/.832/.650	.961/.973/.897
BE	.928/.862/.700	.936/.868/.721	.897/.863/.706	.831/.757/.587	.881/.848/.688	.890/.890/.732	.982/.978/.923
pBE$_{-cnt}$	.930/**.871**/**.717**	.938/.873/.735	.904/.882/.723	.854/.793/.628	.894/.848/.714	**.902/.906/.760**	**.985**/.978/.923
pBE$_{+cls}$	.929/**.871**/**.717**	.940/.877/.735	.897/.862/.702	.834/.768/.601	.886/.849/.697	.890/.894/.736	.980/.967/.897
pBE$_{-cnt+cls}$	**.932/.871/.717**	**.943/.885/.765**	.905/.877/.718	**.859/.801/.631**	.898/.849/.714	**.902/.906**/.756	**.985/.995/.974**

Table 1: Correlation coefficients of pBE and ROUGE. The coefficients are written in the order of "Pearson/Spearman/Kendall".

	Pearson	Spearman	Kendall
ROUGE-SU4	**.981**	.894	.737
C_S_IIITH3	.965	.903	.758
ROUGE-WE-1	.949	.914	.753
pBE$_{-cnt+cls}$	.947	**.915**	**.774**

Table 2: Correlation coefficients of pBE and other participants with manual pyramid scores in TAC 2011. ROUGE-SU4/ROUGE-WE-1/C_S_IIITH3 (Kumar et al., 2011) achieved the highest correlation coefficient in Pearson/Spearman/Kendall correlation among the past results.

	Evaluation	Limit	Topic	Ref	System
DUC 2003	coverage	100	30	4	16
DUC 2004	coverage	100	50	4	17
DUC 2005	responsiveness	250	50	4 or 9	32
DUC 2006	responsiveness	250	50	4	35
	pyramid		20		22
DUC 2007	responsiveness	250	45	4	32
	pyramid		23		13
TAC 2011	pyramid	100	44	4	51

Table 3: The details of the datasets. "Evaluation" represents manual evaluation methods and "Limit" represents word limits of summarization.

Combined with step 1, fully pruned BE is defined as follows:

$$\text{pBE}_{-\text{cnt}+\text{cls}}(\mathbf{R}, S) =$$

$$\frac{\sum_{k=1}^{K} \sum_{m=1}^{M_k} \{O(f_m'^{k}, S')\}}{\sum_{k=1}^{K} \sum_{m=1}^{M_k} \{O(f_m'^{k}, \mathbf{R}'_k)\}}. \quad (3)$$

4 Experimental Setup

To assess the effectiveness of pBE, we computed the correlation coefficient between pBE scores and human judgments, as well as between the scores of other automatic evaluation measures and manual scores for comparison. We used multi-document summarization datasets DUC 2003 - 2007 and TAC 2011. The correlation was computed between all system summaries, excluding reference summaries.

Our first experiment compared the performance of pBE and ROUGE on DUC datasets. Since a dependency triple is a type of bigram/skip-bigram, we chose ROUGE-2 and ROUGE-S4 for comparison. We also examined ROUGE-SU4[9] because it is known as a strong baseline that outperforms most of other measures in TAC 2011 AESOP task (Owczarzak and Dang, 2011).

The second experiment was designed to see how well pBE worked compared with our related method ROUGE-WE. We chose the latest AESOP dataset, TAC 2011, for which ROUGE-WE achieved the highest Spearman coefficient (Ng and Abrecht, 2015).

The details of our experimental setup are given in Table 3 and below.

Parser: We used the neural-network dependency parser of Stanford CoreNLP (Manning et al., 2014). Dependencies were set to enhanced++ Universal Dependencies (Schuster and Manning, 2016).

Clustering: We employed hierarchical clustering, maximum distance method. The number of clusters, N, was set to $0.975 * Q$.

Word Embeddings: A set of pre-trained Google-News word embeddings[10]. It contains 3 million words, each of which has a word embedding of 300 dimensions.

5 Results and Discussion

Table 1 and 2 show the evaluation results on DUC and TAC data set, respectively.

Regardless of the diversity of datasets, pBE outperformed ROUGE in most cases (table 1). Interestingly, although step 2 itself sometimes did not work well, the combination of both steps gener-

---

[9]All three ROUGE here were run with stemming but with no removal of stopwords.

[10]https://code.google.com/archive/p/word2vec/

	Relation	BE	BE$_{+\text{cls}}$	Increased
DUC 2003	compound & det	235	281	46
	subj & obj	1	1	0
DUC 2004	compound & det	426	446	20
	subj & obj	10	10	0
DUC 2005	compound & det	2570	2750	180
	subj & obj	32	39	7
DUC 2006	compound & det	2969	3083	114
	subj & obj	26	49	23
DUC 2007	compound & det	3508	3622	114
	subj & obj	48	57	9

Table 4: The number of basic elements which returned more than 1 in $\min\{N(f_m^k, \mathbf{R}_k), N(f_m^k, S)\}$, before clustering (BE) and after clustering (BE$_{+\text{cls}}$), and the difference of the numbers, BE$_{+\text{cls}}$ − BE (Increased). The relation "subj & obj" includes nsubj, nsubjpass, csubj, csubjpass, iobj and dobj.

ally achieved the best performance. This is because clustering enhanced not only the matching of informative basic elements but also that of low-information basic elements. Table 4 shows how the number of compound and det triples increased, compared with that of subj (nsubj, nsubjpass, csubj and csubjpass) and obj (iobj and dobj) triples. In all datasets, the number of compound and det triples that returned more than 1 in $\min\{N(f_m^k, \mathbf{R}_k), N(f_m^k, S)\}$ increased much more than that of subj and obj, after converting unigrams into cluster IDs. Although clustering reduced semantic mismatches, it worsened the problem of redundant counting. Nonetheless, this problem can be easily solved by applying step 1. This is why the combination of step 1 and 2 was so synergistic.

Another problem with step 2 is that it sometimes makes inappropriate clusters. For example, numbers tend to be put in the same clusters since our word embeddings place them close to each other. In summaries, however, confusing quantitative information such as "two apples" and "five apples" must be avoided . It will be our future work to specify where clustering fails to work and to get rid of inappropriate clusters.

Table 2 shows that pBE achieved the best rank correlation among the other competitors in TAC 2011 and ROUGE-WE. Although its score was lower in Pearson coefficient, it should be noted that the Pearson correlation is based on some strict assumptions: Samples are normally distributed and are linearly related to each other. Since Spearman/Kendall correlation is free from these assumptions, the best rank correlation is a good evidence of pBE's performance.

6 Conclusion

We proposed an automatic evaluation measure of summarization, pBE. It is designed to prune redundant basic elements in two steps: (1) disregarding frequency count of basic elements and (2) using word similarity to reduce semantically overlapped basic elements. Our experiments show that pBE outperforms ROUGE in most cases and achieves the highest rank correlation coefficient in TAC 2011 AESOP task.

References

Marie-Catherine de Marneffe, Bill MacCartney, and Christopher D. Manning. 2006. Generating typed dependency parses from phrase structure parses. In *5th International Conference on Language Resources and Evaluation (LREC 2006)*.

Eduard H. Hovy, Chin-Yew Lin, Liang Zhou, and Junichi Fukumoto. 2006. Automated summarization evaluation with basic elements. In *Proceedings of the Fifth International Conference on Language Resources and Evaluation (LREC 06)*.

Niraj Kumar, Kannan Srinathan, and Vasudeva Varma. 2011. Using unsupervised system with least linguistic features for tac aesop task. In *Proceed- ings of the Text Analysis Conference (TAC)*.

Chin-Yew Lin. 2004. Rouge: A package for automatic evaluation of summaries. In *In Text Summarization Branches Out: Proceedings of the ACL-04 Workshop*. pages 74–81.

Christopher D. Manning, Mihai Surdeanu, John Bauer, Jenny Finkel, Steven J Bethard, and David McClosky. 2014. The Stanford CoreNLP natural language processing toolkit. In *Association for Computational Linguistics (ACL) System Demonstrations*. pages 55–60.

Tomas Mikolov, Ilya Sutskever, Kai Chen, Greg S Corrado, and Jeff Dean. 2013. Distributed representations of words and phrases and their compositionality. In *Proceedings of the 27th Annual Conference on Neural Information Processing Systems (NIPS)*. pages 3111–3119.

Jun-Ping Ng and Viktoria Abrecht. 2015. Better summarization evaluation with word embeddings for rouge. In *Proceedings of the 2015 Conference on Empirical Methods in Natural Language Processing*. Association for Computational Linguistics, Lisbon, Portugal, pages 1925–1930.

Joakim Nivre, Marie-Catherine de Marneffe, Filip Ginter, Yoav Goldberg, Jan Hajic, Christopher D. Manning, Ryan McDonald, Slav Petrov, Sampo Pyysalo,

Natalia Silveira, Reut Tsarfaty, and Daniel Zeman. 2016. Universal dependencies v1: A multilingual treebank collection. In *Proceedings of the Tenth International Conference on Language Resources and Evaluation (LREC-2016)*.

Karolina Owczarzak and Hoa Trang Dang. 2011. Overview of the TAC 2011 summarization track: Guided task and AESOP task. In *Proceedings of the Text Analysis Conference (TAC)*.

Sebastian Schuster and Christopher D. Manning. 2016. Enhanced English Universal Dependencies: An improved representation for natural language understanding tasks. In *Proceedings of the Tenth International Conference on Language Resources and Evaluation (LREC 2016)*.

Stephen Tratz and Eduard H. Hovy. 2008. Summarization evaluation using transformed basic elements. In *Proceedings of Text Analytics Conference (TAC)*.

Qian Yang, Rebecca J. Passonneau, and Gerard de Melo. 2016. PEAK: Pyramid evaluation via automated knowledge extraction. In *Proceedings of the 30th AAAI Conference on Artificial Intelligence (AAAI 2016)*. AAAI Press.

Unsupervised Keyphrase Extraction with Multipartite Graphs

Florian Boudin

LS2N, Université de Nantes, France

`florian.boudin@univ-nantes.fr`

Abstract

We propose an unsupervised keyphrase extraction model that encodes topical information within a multipartite graph structure. Our model represents keyphrase candidates and topics in a single graph and exploits their mutually reinforcing relationship to improve candidate ranking. We further introduce a novel mechanism to incorporate keyphrase selection preferences into the model. Experiments conducted on three widely used datasets show significant improvements over state-of-the-art graph-based models.

1 Introduction

Recent years have witnessed a resurgence of interest in automatic keyphrase extraction, and a number of diverse approaches were explored in the literature (Kim et al., 2010; Hasan and Ng, 2014; Gollapalli et al., 2015; Augenstein et al., 2017). Among them, graph-based approaches are appealing in that they offer strong performance while remaining completely unsupervised. These approaches typically involve two steps: 1) building a graph representation of the document where nodes are lexical units (usually words) and edges are semantic relations between them; 2) ranking nodes using a graph-theoretic measure, from which the top-ranked ones are used to form keyphrases.

Since the seminal work of Mihalcea and Tarau (2004), researchers have devoted a substantial amount of effort to develop better ways of modelling documents as graphs. Most if not all previous work, however, focus on either measuring the semantic relatedness between nodes (Wan and Xiao, 2008; Tsatsaronis et al., 2010) or devising node ranking functions (Tixier et al., 2016; Florescu and Caragea, 2017). So far, little atten-

tion has been paid to the use of different types of graphs. Yet, a key challenge in keyphrase extraction is to ensure topical coverage and diversity, which are not naturally handled by graph-of-words representations (Hasan and Ng, 2014).

Most attempts at using topic information in graph-based approaches involve biasing the ranking function towards topic distributions (Liu et al., 2010; Zhao et al., 2011; Zhang et al., 2013). Unfortunately, these models suffer from several limitations: they aggregate multiple topic-biased rankings which makes their time complexity prohibitive for long documents[1], they require a large dataset to estimate word-topic distributions that is not always available or easy to obtain, and they assume that topics are independent of one another, making it hard to ensure topic diversity. For the latter case, supervised approaches were proposed to optimize the broad coverage of topics (Bougouin et al., 2016; Zhang et al., 2017).

Another strand of work models documents as graphs of topics and selects keyphrases from the top-ranked ones (Bougouin et al., 2013). This higher level representation (see Figure 1a), in which topic relations are measured as the semantic relatedness between the keyphrase candidates they instantiate, was shown to improve the overall ranking and maximize topic coverage. The downside is that candidates belonging to a single topic are viewed as equally important, so that post-ranking heuristics are required to select the most representative keyphrase from each topic. Also, errors in forming topics propagate throughout the model severely impacting its performance.

Here, we build upon this latter line of work and propose a model that implicitly enforces topical diversity while ranking keyphrase candidates in a

---

[1]Recent work showed that comparable results can be achieved by computing a single topic specificity weight value for each word (Sterckx et al., 2015; Teneva and Cheng, 2017).

Proceedings of NAACL-HLT 2018, pages 667–672
New Orleans, Louisiana, June 1 - 6, 2018. ©2018 Association for Computational Linguistics

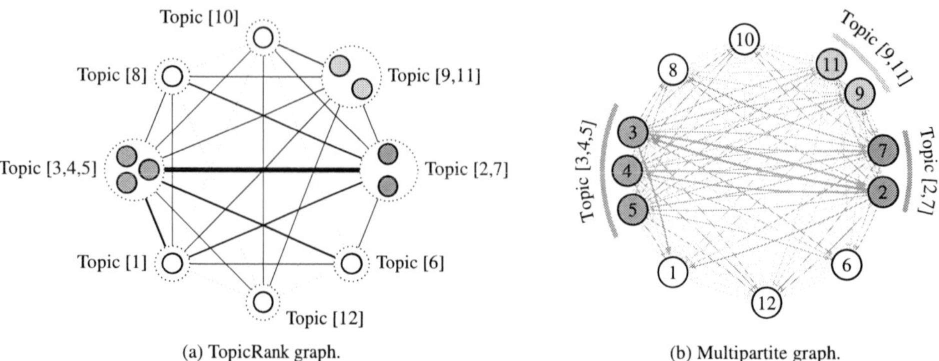

Figure 1: Comparison between TopicRank (Bougouin et al., 2013) and our multipartite graph representation for document 2040.abstr from the Hulth-2003 dataset. Nodes are topics (left) or keyphrase candidates (right), and edges represent co-occurrence relations.

single operation. To do this, we use a particular graph structure, called multipartite graph, to represent documents as tightly connected sets of topic related candidates (see Figure 1b). This representation allows for the seamless integration of any topic decomposition, and enables the ranking algorithm to make full use of the mutually reinforcing relation between topics and candidates.

Another contribution of this work is a mechanism to incorporate intra-topic keyphrase selection preferences into the model. It allows the ranking algorithm to go beyond semantic relatedness by leveraging information from additional salience features. Technically, keyphrase candidates that exhibit certain properties, e.g. that match a thesaurus entry or occur in specific parts of the document, are promoted in ranking through edge weight adjustments. Here, we show the effectiveness of this mechanism by introducing a bias towards keyphrase candidates occurring first in the document.

2 Proposed Model

Similar to previous work, our model operates in two steps. We first build a graph representation of the document (§2.1), on which we then apply a ranking algorithm to assign a relevance score to each keyphrase (§2.3). We further introduce an in-between step where edge weights are adjusted to capture position information (§2.2).

For direct comparability with Bougouin et al.

(2013), which served as the starting point for the work reported here, we follow their setup for identifying keyphrase candidates and topics. Keyphrase candidates are selected from the sequences of adjacent nouns with one or more preceding adjectives (/Adj*Noun+/). They are then grouped into topics based on the stem forms of the words they share using hierarchical agglomerative clustering with average linkage. Although simple, this method gives reasonably good results. There are many other approaches to find topics, including the use of knowledge bases or unsupervised probabilistic topic models. Here, we made the choice not to use them as they are not without their share of issues (e.g. limited coverage, parameter tuning), and leave this for future work.

2.1 Multipartite graph representation

A complete directed multipartite graph is built, in which nodes are keyphrase candidates that are connected only if they belong to different topics. Again, we follow (Bougouin et al., 2013) and weight edges according to the distance between two candidates in the document. More formally, the weight w_{ij} from node i to node j is computed as the sum of the inverse distances between the occurrences of candidates c_i and c_j:

$$w_{ij} = \sum_{p_i \in \mathcal{P}(c_i)} \sum_{p_j \in \mathcal{P}(c_j)} \frac{1}{|p_i - p_j|} \qquad (1)$$

where $\mathcal{P}(c_i)$ is the set of the word offset positions of candidate c_i. This weighting scheme achieves comparable results to window-based co-occurrence counts without any parameter tuning.

The resulting graph is a complete k-partite graph, whose nodes are partitioned into k different independent sets, k being the number of topics. As exemplified in Figure 1, our graph representation differs from the one of (Bougouin et al., 2013) in two significant ways. First, topics are encoded by partitioning candidates into sets of unconnected nodes instead of being subsumed in single nodes. Second, edges are directed which, as we will see in §2.2, allows to further control the incidence of individual candidates on the overall ranking.

The proposed representation makes no assumptions about how topics are obtained, and thus allows direct use of any topic decomposition. It implicitly promotes the number of topics covered in the selected keyphrases by dampening intra-topic recommendation, and captures the mutually reinforcing relationship between topics and keyphrase candidates. In other words, removing edges between candidates belonging to a single topic ensures that the overall recommendation of each topic is distributed throughout the entire graph. Also, a benefit of encoding topic related candidates differentially is that the ones that best underpin each topic are directly given by the model.

2.2 Graph weight adjustment mechanism

Selecting the most representative keyphrase candidates for each topic is a difficult task, and relying only on their importance in the document is not sufficient (Hasan and Ng, 2014). Among the features proposed to address this problem in the literature, the position of the candidate within the document is most reliable. In order to capture this in our model, we adjust the incoming edge weights of the nodes corresponding to the first occurring candidate of each topic.

More formally, candidates that occur at the beginning of the document are promoted according to the other candidates belonging to the same topic. Figure 2 gives an example of applying graph weight adjustment for promoting a given candidate. Note that the choice of the candidates to promote, i.e. the selection heuristic, can be adapted to fit other needs such as prioritising candidates from a thesaurus.

Incoming edge weights for the first occurring

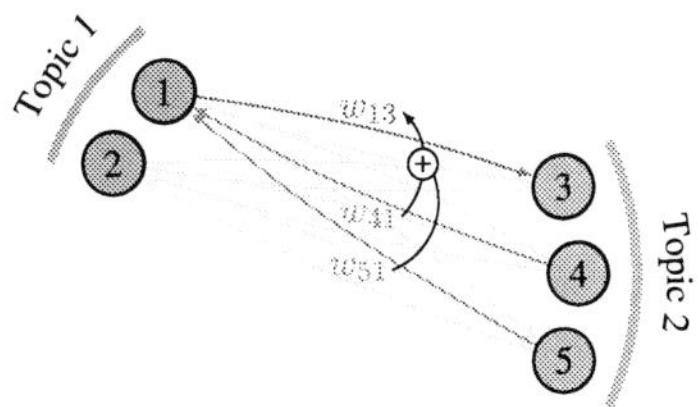

Figure 2: Illustration of the graph weight adjustment mechanism. Here, node 3 is promoted by increasing the weight of its incoming edge according to the outgoing edge weights of nodes 4 and 5.

candidate of each topic are modified by the following equation:

$$w_{ij} = w_{ij} + \alpha \cdot e^{\left(\frac{1}{p_i}\right)} \cdot \sum_{c_k \in \mathcal{T}(c_j) \setminus \{c_j\}} w_{ki} \qquad (2)$$

where w_{ij} is the edge weight between nodes c_i and c_j, $\mathcal{T}(c_j)$ is the set of candidates belonging to the same topic as c_j, p_i is the offset position of the first occurrence of candidate c_i, and α is a hyper-parameter that controls the strength of the weight adjustment.

2.3 Ranking and extraction

After the graph is built, keyphrase candidates are ordered by a graph-based ranking algorithm, and the top N are selected as keyphrases. Here, we adopt the widely used TextRank algorithm (Mihalcea and Tarau, 2004) in the form in which it leverages edge weights:

$$S(c_i) = (1 - \lambda) + \lambda \cdot \sum_{c_j \in \mathcal{I}(c_i)} \frac{w_{ij} \cdot S(c_j)}{\sum_{c_k \in \mathcal{O}(c_j)} w_{jk}} \qquad (3)$$

where $\mathcal{I}(c_i)$ is the set of predecessors of c_i, $\mathcal{O}(c_j)$ is the set of successors of c_j, and λ is a damping factor set to 0.85 as in (Mihalcea and Tarau, 2004). Note that other ranking algorithms can be applied. We use TextRank because it was shown to perform consistently well (Boudin, 2013).

3 Experiments

3.1 Datasets and evaluation measures

We carry out our experiments on three datasets:

SemEval-2010 (Kim et al., 2010), which is composed of scientific articles collected from the ACM Digital Library. We use the set of combined author- and reader-assigned keyphrases as reference keyphrases.

Model	SemEval-2010			Hulth-2003			Marujo-2012		
	F_1@5	F_1@10	MAP	F_1@5	F_1@10	MAP	F_1@5	F_1@10	MAP
(Bougouin et al., 2013)	9.7	12.3	7.3	25.3	29.3	24.3	12.1	17.6	14.6
(Sterckx et al., 2015)	9.3	10.5	7.4	21.9	30.2	25.3	11.7	16.4	16.1
(Florescu and Caragea, 2017)	10.6	12.2	8.9	23.5	30.3	26.0	10.9	17.2	16.1
Proposed model	12.2†	14.5†	11.8†	25.9†	30.6	29.2†	12.5	18.2	17.2†
w/o weight adjustment	8.8	12.4	9.4	21.1	26.8	25.2	12.2	17.8	16.9

Table 1: F_1-scores computed at the top 5, 10 extracted keyphrases and Mean Average Precision (MAP) scores. † indicate significance at the 0.05 level using Student's t-test.

Hulth-2003 (Hulth, 2003), which is made of paper abstracts about computer science and information technology. Reference keyphrases were assigned by professional indexers.

Marujo-2012 (Marujo et al., 2012) that contains news articles distributed over 10 categories (e.g. Politics, Sports). Reference keyphrases were assigned by readers via crowdsourcing.

We follow the common practice and evaluate the performance of our model in terms of f-measure (F_1) at the top N keyphrases, and apply stemming to reduce the number of mismatches. We also report the Mean Average Precision (MAP) scores of the ranked lists of keyphrases.

3.2 Baselines and parameter settings

We compare the performance of our model against that of three baselines. The first baseline is TopicRank (Bougouin et al., 2013) which is the model that is closest to ours. The second baseline is Single Topical PageRank (Sterckx et al., 2015), an improved version of Liu et al. (2010) that biases the ranking function towards topic distributions inferred by Latent Dirichlet Allocation (LDA). The third baseline is PositionRank (Florescu and Caragea, 2017), a model that, like ours, leverages additional features (word's position and its frequency) to improve ranking accuracy.

Over-generation errors[2] are frequent in models that rank keyphrases according to the sum of the weights of their component words (Hasan and Ng, 2014; Boudin, 2015). This is indeed the case for the second and third baselines, and we partially address this issue by normalizing candidate scores by their length, as proposed in (Boudin, 2013).

We use the parameters suggested by the authors for each model, and estimate LDA topic distributions on the training set of each dataset. Our model introduces one parameter, namely α, that controls the strength of the graph weight adjustment. This parameter is tuned on the training set of the SemEval-2010 dataset, and set to $\alpha = 1.1$ for all our experiments. For a fair and meaningful comparison, we use the same candidate selection heuristic (§2) across models.

3.3 Results

Results for the baselines and the proposed model are detailed in Table 1. Overall we observe that our model achieves the best results and significantly outperforms the baselines on most metrics. Relative improvements are smaller on the Hulth-2003 and Marujo-2012 datasets because they are composed of short documents, yielding a much smaller search space (Hasan and Ng, 2014). TopicRank obtains the highest precision among the baselines, suggesting that its –one keyphrase per topic– policy succeeds in filtering out topic-redundant candidates. On the other hand, TopicRank is directly affected by topic clustering errors as indicated by the lowest MAP scores, which supports the argument in favour of enforcing topical diversity implicitly. In terms of MAP, the best performing baseline is PositionRank, highlighting the positive effect of leveraging multiple features.

Additionally, we report the performance of our model without applying the weight adjustment mechanism. Results are higher or on-par with baselines that use topic information, and show that our model makes good use of the reinforcing relations between topics and the candidates they instantiate. We note that the drop-off in performance is more severe for F1@5 on the Semeval-2010 dataset, going from best to worst performance. Although further investigation is needed, we hypoth-

---

[2]These errors occur when a model correctly outputs a keyphrase because it contains an important word, but at the same time erroneously predicts other keyphrases because they contain the same word.

esise that our model struggles with selecting the most representative candidate from each topic using TextRank as a unique feature.

We also computed the topic coverage of the sets of keyphrases extracted by our model. With over 92% of the top-10 keyphrases assigned to different topics, our model successfully promotes diversity without the need of hard constraints. A manual inspection of the topic-redundant keyphrases reveals that a good portion of these are in fact clustering errors, that is, they have been wrongly assigned to the same topic (e.g. 'students' and 'student attitudes'). Some exhibit a hypernym-hyponym relation while both being in the gold references (e.g. 'model' and 'bayesian hierarch model' for document H-7 from the Semeval-2010 dataset), thus indicating inconsistencies in the gold data.

4 Conclusion

We introduced an unsupervised keyphrase extraction model that builds on a multipartite graph structure, and demonstrated its effectiveness on three public datasets. Our code and data are available at `https://github.com/boudinfl/pke`. In future work, we would like to apply ranking algorithms that leverage the specific structure of our graph representation, such as the one proposed in (Becker, 2013).

Acknowledgements

We thank the anonymous reviewers for their comments. This work was supported in part by the TALIAS project (grant of CNRS PEPS INS2I 2016). We also thank the members of the TALN team for their support.

References

Isabelle Augenstein, Mrinal Das, Sebastian Riedel, Lakshmi Vikraman, and Andrew McCallum. 2017. Semeval 2017 task 10: Scienceie - extracting keyphrases and relations from scientific publications. In *Proceedings of the 11th International Workshop on Semantic Evaluation (SemEval-2017)*. Association for Computational Linguistics, Vancouver, Canada, pages 546–555. `http://www.aclweb.org/anthology/S17-2091`.

N Becker. 2013. *Ranking on multipartite graphs*. Ph.D. thesis, Diploma thesis, Institute of Computer Science, LMU, Munich.

Florian Boudin. 2013. A comparison of centrality measures for graph-based keyphrase extraction. In *Proceedings of the Sixth International Joint Conference on Natural Language Processing*. Asian Federation of Natural Language Processing, Nagoya, Japan, pages 834–838. `http://www.aclweb.org/anthology/I13-1102`.

Florian Boudin. 2015. Reducing over-generation errors for automatic keyphrase extraction using integer linear programming. In *Proceedings of the ACL 2015 Workshop on Novel Computational Approaches to Keyphrase Extraction*. Association for Computational Linguistics, Beijing, China, pages 19–24. `http://www.aclweb.org/anthology/W15-3605`.

Adrien Bougouin, Florian Boudin, and Béatrice Daille. 2013. Topicrank: Graph-based topic ranking for keyphrase extraction. In *Proceedings of the Sixth International Joint Conference on Natural Language Processing*. Asian Federation of Natural Language Processing, Nagoya, Japan, pages 543–551. `http://www.aclweb.org/anthology/I13-1062`.

Adrien Bougouin, Florian Boudin, and Beatrice Daille. 2016. Keyphrase annotation with graph co-ranking. In *Proceedings of COLING 2016, the 26th International Conference on Computational Linguistics: Technical Papers*. The COLING 2016 Organizing Committee, Osaka, Japan, pages 2945–2955. `http://aclweb.org/anthology/C16-1277`.

Corina Florescu and Cornelia Caragea. 2017. Positionrank: An unsupervised approach to keyphrase extraction from scholarly documents. In *Proceedings of the 55th Annual Meeting of the Association for Computational Linguistics (Volume 1: Long Papers)*. Association for Computational Linguistics, Vancouver, Canada, pages 1105–1115. `http://aclweb.org/anthology/P17-1102`.

Sujatha Das Gollapalli, Cornelia Caragea, Xiaoli Li, and C. Lee Giles, editors. 2015. *Proceedings of the ACL 2015 Workshop on Novel Computational Approaches to Keyphrase Extraction*. Association for Computational Linguistics, Beijing, China. `http://www.aclweb.org/anthology/W15-36`.

Kazi Saidul Hasan and Vincent Ng. 2014. Automatic keyphrase extraction: A survey of the state of the art. In *Proceedings of the 52nd Annual Meeting of the Association for Computational Linguistics (Volume 1: Long Papers)*. Association for Computational Linguistics, Baltimore, Maryland, pages 1262–1273. `http://www.aclweb.org/anthology/P14-1119`.

Anette Hulth. 2003. Improved automatic keyword extraction given more linguistic knowledge. In *Proceedings of the 2003 Conference on Empirical Methods in Natural Language Processing*. Association for Computational Linguistics, Stroudsburg, PA, USA, EMNLP '03, pages 216–223. `https://doi.org/10.3115/1119355.1119383`.

Su Nam Kim, Olena Medelyan, Min-Yen Kan, and Timothy Baldwin. 2010. Semeval-2010 task 5 : Automatic keyphrase extraction from scientific articles. In *Proceedings of the 5th International Workshop on Semantic Evaluation*. Association for Computational Linguistics, Uppsala, Sweden, pages 21–26. http://www.aclweb.org/anthology/S10-1004.

Zhiyuan Liu, Wenyi Huang, Yabin Zheng, and Maosong Sun. 2010. Automatic keyphrase extraction via topic decomposition. In *Proceedings of the 2010 Conference on Empirical Methods in Natural Language Processing*. Association for Computational Linguistics, Cambridge, MA, pages 366–376. http://www.aclweb.org/anthology/D10-1036.

Lus Marujo, Anatole Gershman, Jaime Carbonell, Robert Frederking, and Joao P. Neto. 2012. Supervised topical key phrase extraction of news stories using crowdsourcing, light filtering and co-reference normalization. In Nicoletta Calzolari (Conference Chair), Khalid Choukri, Thierry Declerck, Mehmet Uur Doan, Bente Maegaard, Joseph Mariani, Asuncion Moreno, Jan Odijk, and Stelios Piperidis, editors, *Proceedings of the Eight International Conference on Language Resources and Evaluation (LREC'12)*. European Language Resources Association (ELRA), Istanbul, Turkey.

Rada Mihalcea and Paul Tarau. 2004. Textrank: Bringing order into texts. In Dekang Lin and Dekai Wu, editors, *Proceedings of EMNLP 2004*. Association for Computational Linguistics, Barcelona, Spain, pages 404–411. http://www.aclweb.org/anthology/W04-3252.

Lucas Sterckx, Thomas Demeester, Johannes Deleu, and Chris Develder. 2015. Topical word importance for fast keyphrase extraction. In *Proceedings of the 24th International Conference on World Wide Web*. ACM, New York, NY, USA, WWW '15 Companion, pages 121–122. https://doi.org/10.1145/2740908.2742730.

Nedelina Teneva and Weiwei Cheng. 2017. Salience rank: Efficient keyphrase extraction with topic modeling. In *Proceedings of the 55th Annual Meeting of the Association for Computational Linguistics (Volume 2: Short Papers)*. Association for Computational Linguistics, Vancouver, Canada, pages 530–535. http://aclweb.org/anthology/P17-2084.

Antoine Tixier, Fragkiskos Malliaros, and Michalis Vazirgiannis. 2016. A graph degeneracy-based approach to keyword extraction. In *Proceedings of the 2016 Conference on Empirical Methods in Natural Language Processing*. Association for Computational Linguistics, Austin, Texas, pages 1860–1870. https://aclweb.org/anthology/D16-1191.

George Tsatsaronis, Iraklis Varlamis, and Kjetil Nørvåg. 2010. Semanticrank: Ranking keywords and sentences using semantic graphs. In *Proceedings of the 23rd International Conference on Computational Linguistics (Coling 2010)*. Coling 2010 Organizing Committee, Beijing, China, pages 1074–1082. http://www.aclweb.org/anthology/C10-1121.

Xiaojun Wan and Jianguo Xiao. 2008. Collabrank: Towards a collaborative approach to single-document keyphrase extraction. In *Proceedings of the 22nd International Conference on Computational Linguistics (Coling 2008)*. Coling 2008 Organizing Committee, Manchester, UK, pages 969–976. http://www.aclweb.org/anthology/C08-1122.

Fan Zhang, Lian'en Huang, and Bo Peng. 2013. Wordtopic-multirank: A new method for automatic keyphrase extraction. In *Proceedings of the Sixth International Joint Conference on Natural Language Processing*. Asian Federation of Natural Language Processing, Nagoya, Japan, pages 10–18. http://www.aclweb.org/anthology/I13-1002.

Yuxiang Zhang, Yaocheng Chang, Xiaoqing Liu, Sujatha Das Gollapalli, Xiaoli Li, and Chunjing Xiao. 2017. Mike: Keyphrase extraction by integrating multidimensional information. In *Proceedings of the 2017 ACM on Conference on Information and Knowledge Management*. ACM, New York, NY, USA, CIKM '17, pages 1349–1358. https://doi.org/10.1145/3132847.3132956.

Xin Zhao, Jing Jiang, Jing He, Yang Song, Palakorn Achanauparp, Ee-Peng Lim, and Xiaoming Li. 2011. Topical keyphrase extraction from twitter. In *Proceedings of the 49th Annual Meeting of the Association for Computational Linguistics: Human Language Technologies*. Association for Computational Linguistics, Portland, Oregon, USA, pages 379–388. http://www.aclweb.org/anthology/P11-1039.

Where have I Heard this Story Before?: Identifying Narrative Similarity in Movie Remakes

Snigdha Chaturvedi
University of California
Santa Cruz
snigdha@ucsc.edu

Shashank Srivastava
Carnegie Mellon University
Pittsburgh
ssrivastava@cmu.edu

Dan Roth
University of Pennsylvania
Philadelphia
danroth@seas.upenn.edu

Abstract

People can identify correspondences between narratives in everyday life. For example, an analogy with the *Cinderella story* may be made in describing the unexpected success of an underdog in seemingly different stories. We present a new task and dataset for story understanding: identifying instances of similar narratives from a collection of narrative texts. We present an initial approach for this problem, which finds correspondences between narratives in terms of plot events, and resemblances between characters and their social relationships. Our approach yields an 8% absolute improvement in performance over an information-retrieval baseline on a novel dataset of plot summaries of 577 movie remakes from Wikipedia.

1 Introduction

The ability to automatically understand narratives has been a long-standing goal of AI. Humans routinely invoke narratives to share information, learn normative behavior, and to make sense of the world (Gottschall, 2012; Miller and Mitchell, 1983). They accept narratives that adhere to familiarity and personal experiences, and reinterpret those that appear unfamiliar (Herman, 2003). In this work, we present a new task for narrative understanding: identifying instances of similar narratives. The ability to recognize similar narratives can be valuable for tasks such as QA and information retrieval, and furnish tools towards analyzing collections of real or fictional narratives. For example, given a news story, a digital archives analyst might identify similar stories from the past.

A major bottleneck in computationally exploring narrative similarity is the limited availability of annotated data for analyses and evaluation. A contribution of this work is a dataset of plot summaries of movies, which include movie pairs that have been identified as remakes (see Sec. 3). Our

A Dutch couple, Rex and Saskia, are on holiday in France. Saskia enters a petrol station to buy drinks and does not return. Three years after Saskia's disappearance, Rex is still searching for her. Rex's new girlfriend, Lieneke, reluctantly helps him search for Saskia. Raymond confronts Rex and admits the kidnapping; he says he will reveal what happened to her if Rex comes with him. Raymond takes Rex to the rest area. He pours Rex a cup of drugged coffee, and tells him the only way to learn what happened to Saskia is to experience it himself. Rex drinks the coffee and awakens buried in a box underground ...

Jeff Harriman goes on vacation with his girlfriend Diane, who vanishes without a trace at a gas station. Three years later, Jeff is still obsessed with finding out what happened. One day, Barney Cousins arrives at Jeff's door and admits that he was responsible for her disappearance. Cousins promises to show Jeff what happened to Diane, but only if he agrees to go through exactly the same thing. Jeff is taken to the gas station and is told that if he drinks a cup of coffee, he will discover Diane's fate. He does, and wakes up to find he has been buried alive. Jeff's new girlfriend, Rita, traces him and his abductor, and discovers what has happened...

Figure 1: Example (condensed) movie summaries with similar narratives: *Spoorloos (1988)* (left) and *The Vanishing (1993)* (right). Note that (1) plot similarity and (2) characters and their relationships are significant elements in determining this similarity.

working hypothesis is that re-tellings of similar stories would retain prominent elements in terms of narrative theme, even while they look superficially different. Figure 1 shows an example of two such movie summaries, condensed here for brevity. Our approach for identifying similar narratives infers alignments between pairs of narratives using a *story-kernel* that takes into account two kinds of likenesses: (1) plot similarity (2) correspondences between characters in the narratives (based on attributes such as name, gender, prominence in the narrative, and social relationships with other characters).[1] While our data and problem formulation do not accommodate all aspects of narrative similarity, and our approach is relatively simple (for example, it doesn't model

---

[1] Our approach is unsupervised, but we use a development set to tune parameters

Proceedings of NAACL-HLT 2018, pages 673–678
New Orleans, Louisiana, June 1 - 6, 2018. ©2018 Association for Computational Linguistics

temporal or sentiment trajectories), we believe they capture many substantial aspects of the phenomenon and serve as a useful starting point for research into the problem.

Our contributions are:

1. We introduce the problem of characterizing narrative similarity in movie remakes, and formulate this as a ranking task.

2. We create a dataset of 577 narratives for this task, mined from plot summaries of movie remakes from Wikipedia.

3. We present a *story-kernel* that quantifies narrative similarity by considering correspondences between narratives using a character-centric approach. We empirically evaluate the *story-kernel* and its various components, and demonstrate its utility.

2 Related Work

The field of computational narratology has focused on algorithmic understanding and generation of narratives (Mani, 2012; Richards et al., 2009). Much previous work has attempted to understand narratives either from the perspective of their (i) *sequences of events* (Schank and Abelson, 1975; Chambers and Jurafsky, 2009) or plot units (McIntyre and Lapata, 2010; Goyal et al., 2010; Finlayson, 2012), or from the perspective of (ii) *characters* (Wilensky, 1978) or personas in a narrative (Propp, 1968; Bamman et al., 2013, 2014; Valls-Vargas et al., 2014). Elsner (2012) explore the plot structure of novels to distinguish original texts from novels from synthetically altered versions of the same. Some recent approaches have also focused on modeling relationships between literary characters (Chaturvedi, 2016; Iyyer et al., 2016; Chaturvedi et al., 2016), and their social networks (Elson et al., 2010; Agarwal et al., 2013; Krishnan and Eisenstein, 2015; Srivastava et al., 2016).

Other research has focused on characterizing narratives in terms of their structure. In particular, seminal formalisms such as plot units (Lehnert, 1981) and Story Grammars (Rumelhart, 1980) have been used to analyze story plots. A significant issue with almost all such frameworks is that they are either largely conceptual, or depend on careful manual annotations of features about narrative plot elements (Elsner, 2012; Elson, 2012; Finlayson and Henry Winston, 2006), which makes them unamenable to comprehensive

empirical analysis. While some of the above approaches explore prototypical patterns that characterize narratives (Nguyen et al., 2013) and narrative similarity (Fisseni and Löwe, 2012), they do not address the issue of automatically comparing narratives. Also noteworthy in this context is the Aarne-Thompson classification system (Aarne and Thompson, 1961), which has been extensively used in the analysis of folk-tales to organize types of stories, based on an index of motifs. Our work is most closely related to that of Nguyen et al. (2014) who attempt to understand the various dimensions that experts and non-experts consider while judging narrative similarity.

3 Movie Remakes Dataset

We present a dataset for evaluating narrative level similarity of texts. Our assumption is that movie remakes are re-tellings of the same story and retain prominent narrative elements. Hence, a good measure of narrative similarity should evaluate summaries of movie remakes as being similar to each other. To this end, we present a dataset of movie plots extracted from Wikipedia.

In particular, we scraped lists of movies from the *'Lists of film remakes'* page on Wikipedia, which consist of entries of movies considered remakes of previous movies. Since some movies have multiple remakes, we obtain clusters of movie plots, each of which share the same narrative theme. For each movie, we extract the text of its corresponding Wikipedia plot summary from the CMU Movie summary dataset (Bamman et al., 2013). In some cases, the remakes are close to the originals at a surface level, whereas in other cases, they diverge at a surface level, and may also significantly differ in the narrative. These clusters were then manually pruned to remove errors, and the statistics of the curated dataset are shown in Table 1. In particular, we observe that the average summary is quite long (564 words), which would make human annotations of similarity for such narratives difficult.

NLP pre-processing: We processed texts of movie summaries using the BookNLP pipeline (Bamman et al., 2014) to get dependency parses, and identify major characters. We also assigned a gender to each character which corresponded to the gender that is most frequently assigned to that character's mentions across the story using the Stanford Core NLP

Number of movies	577
Number of clusters	266
Max number of movies in a cluster	7
Avg number of words in a summary	564
Max number of words in a summary	2778
Min number of words in a summary	26

Table 1: Statistics for Movie Remakes dataset

system (Manning et al., 2014).

4 Identifying Narrative Similarity

Our approach's core consists of a *story-kernel*, $\mathbb{S}(s_i, s_j)$ that characterizes the similarity between two narratives, s_i and s_j. The story-kernel has the following two components: (i) Plot Kernel, which incorporates surface similarity between plots of the two stories (in terms of the principal events and entities), and (ii) Character Alignment Kernel, which considers correspondences in terms of character attributes and relationships.

Plot Kernel: A simple measure for narrative similarity can incorporate lexical similarities between textual descriptions of two narratives. However, our goal is to identify narratives that have similar plot structure, rather than incidental surface-level matches in their summaries. Therefore, we focus only on events, and entities and their properties. We model events mentioned in a story by identifying all verbs occurring in the text of the narrative. We capture entities and their properties by identifying nouns and the adjectives that modify them. As mentioned earlier, our approach specifically models characters as a separate component in the story-kernel. Hence, at this stage, we only consider text entities that do not represent a character mention. We represent the plot of a narrative using a bag-of-word representation of its events and entities (and their characteristics) as described above. We then define $\mathbb{S}_{plot}(s_i, s_j)$ as the cosine similarity between these representations for narratives s_i and s_j.

Character Alignment Kernel: This component compares two narratives by *aligning* characters of one with similar characters in the other. Specifically, we align each character, c_i, of a story, s_i, to a character, c_j, of the other story, s_j. This alignment is based on a similarity score, $\mathcal{S}(c_i, c_j)$, between the two characters (defined later). The goal of this joint alignment is to maximize the average alignment score of characters in the narrative pair:

$$\mathbb{S}_{char}(s_i, s_j) = \max_{x_{c_i c_j}; c_i \in s_i, c_j \in s_j} \frac{\sum x_{c_i c_j} \mathcal{S}(c_i, c_j)}{N}$$

subject to alignment constraints $\sum_{c_i} x_{c_i c_j} = 1, \forall c_j$ and $\sum_{c_j} x_{c_i c_j} = 1, \forall c_i$. Here, x is a binary matrix indicating character alignments, and N is the total number of aligned characters from the two narratives. These constraints ensure that each character is aligned to one, and only one, character from the other story. This combinatorial optimization can be solved in polynomial time by modifying the Hungarian assignment algorithm (Kuhn, 1955). When two stories have different number of characters, the extra unaligned characters are aligned to a special *null* character from the other story.

In the above description, the similarity between two (non-null) characters, $\mathcal{S}(c_i, c_j) \in [0, 1]$, is defined as a convex combination of their similarities along (i) name, (ii) gender, (iii) prominence in the story, and (iv) attributes and social relationships with other characters.

$$\begin{aligned}
\mathcal{S}(c_i, c_j) = \ & \lambda_1 \cdot \mathcal{S}_{name}(c_i, c_j) + \lambda_2 \cdot \mathcal{S}_{gender}(c_i, c_j) \\
+ \ & \lambda_3 \cdot \mathcal{S}_{prom}(c_i, c_j) \\
+ \ & (1 - \lambda_1 - \lambda_2 - \lambda_3) \cdot \mathcal{S}_{reln}(c_i, c_j)
\end{aligned}$$

Here, (1) $\mathcal{S}_{name}(c_i, c_j)$ is an indicator function that identifies if two character names are matching strings. It prefers aligning characters with same names, and can be a strong but shallow signal. (2) $\mathcal{S}_{gender}(c_i, c_j)$ prefers alignments of characters with the same gender; i.e. $\mathcal{S}_{gender}(c_i, c_j) = 1$ if gender of c_i is the same as of c_j, and 0 otherwise. (3) $\mathcal{S}_{prom}(c_i, c_j)$ aligns characters with similar prominence. E.g., it avoids matching a protagonist with a side-character. We compute the *prominence* of a character, $prom(c)$, as simply the fraction of mentions that refer to this character. We then define $\mathcal{S}_{prom}(c_i, c_j) = 1 - |prom(c_i) - prom(c_j)|$ (4) $\mathcal{S}_{reln}(c_i, c_j)$ considers how similar the two characters are in terms of attributes, and their relationship to other characters. For example, characters described with positive traits, or friends of the protagonist in one story are likely to be better matched to similar characters in other narratives.

We model the relationship between two characters (from the same narrative) by extracting features describing actions in which they participate and adjectives describing character attributes (Chaturvedi et al., 2017). E.g. we identify the actions using verbs that have the two character

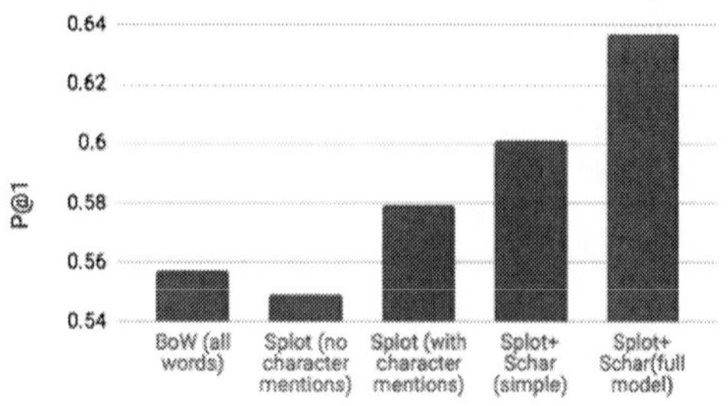

Figure 2: Performance of various approaches on Narrative Similarity task

Component	Weights
$\mathbb{S}_{plot}$	0.7
$\mathbb{S}_{character}$	0.3
$\mathbb{S}_{character}$ – name	0.4
$\mathbb{S}_{character}$ – gender	0.1
$\mathbb{S}_{character}$ – prominence	0.1
$\mathbb{S}_{character}$ – relationship	0.4

Table 2: Parameter values for various components of the story-kernel (tuned on development set)

mentions as their agents (identified using 'nsubj' and 'agent' dependency relations), and patients (using 'dobj' and 'nsubjpass' relations). We then represent a character's relationship with all other characters in the narrative using these features. Finally, we compute the relationship-based similarity, $\mathcal{S}_{reln}(c_i, c_j)$ between two characters, c_i and c_j as their cosine similarity in this feature space.

The **story kernel** is then defined as:

$$\mathbb{S}(s_i, s_j) = \alpha \, \mathbb{S}_{plot}(s_i, s_j) + (1 - \alpha) \, \mathbb{S}_{char}(s_i, s_j).$$

5 Evaluation

For our experiment, we tune parameters on 20% of the data and use the remaining data (466 movies) for the test set. In order to keep the test set completely distinct from the types of stories used for parameter tuning, this split was performed at the cluster level. Given a test story, we output the most similar story from the dataset. For evaluation, we compute P@1 (precision at 1) as follows: The output is deemed correct only if the predicted movie belongs to the same remake cluster, and incorrect otherwise.

Figure 2 shows the performance of our approach in identifying narrative similarity. Here, BoW refers to a baseline approach that uses all words in the movie summary (after stopword removal and lemmatization) as feature representation, and uses cosine similarity for retrieval. This approach achieves a P@1 performance of 0.558. The second column corresponds to using $\mathbb{S}_{plot}$ alone (does not include character mentions), and performs slightly worse than BoW, suggesting that character names do indicate remakes in our data. Adding character names in the plot kernel (third column) improves the performance significantly above BoW, indicating substantial value in focusing on narrative elements such as events and entities, rather than the entire text. The fourth column

shows an ablated variant of the approach that separately adds a character kernel score to $\mathbb{S}_{plot}$ based on character names alone, but does not incorporate correspondences based on gender, prominence and character relationships. We combine this alternative character-kernel with the plot-based kernel in the same manner (using a mixing parameter α tuned on the development set). This indicates that it helps to have a separate component dedicated to characters while solving this task. The final column shows the full model, which leads to a significant further improvement in performance to 0.637, reflecting an 8% absolute improvement over the baseline model. This indicates significant value in modeling multiple facets of character attributes and relationships. We observed similar trends on the development set.

Table 2 shows the weights for individual components of our kernel (tuned on the development set). These results validate our assumption that both plot and character similarity are distinct and important facets in evaluating narrative similarity.

Qualitative Results and Error Analysis: Figure 3 shows an illustrative example of character alignment using our *story-kernel* for the movie-summaries shown in Figure 1. Note that the stories do not share any character names. Our approach aligns the protagonists of the two narratives, Rex and Jeff. It also aligns their respective kidnapped girlfriends, Saskia and Diane, and their new girlfriends, Lieneke, and Rita. However, it aligns Saskia's kidnapper, Raymond, with a *null* character, even though the movie's summary mentions Diane's kidnapper, Barney Cousins. In this case, the NLP pipeline does not identify Barney Cousins as an animate character, possibly due to his unusual name. As a result, the method received as input a summary in which only three characters were identified for the story on the right. Nevertheless, it correctly identifies the story on the right

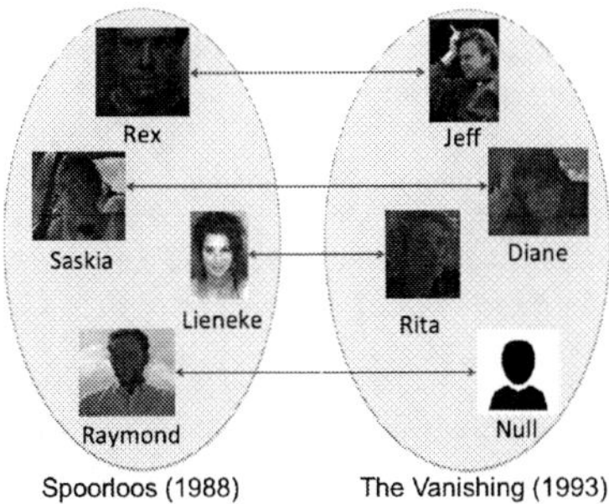

Figure 3: Example of aligned characters from the two movies in Figure 1

as most similar to the story on the left. An error analysis reveals that apart from missed character-identification, other NLP pipeline errors such as missed coreference, are major sources of errors.

6 Conclusion

We introduce an objective task, dataset and approach for quantitative evaluation of narrative similarity. Our approach, which compares narratives based on plot and character correspondences, takes a step towards addressing this problem. However, the general problem of narrative similarity can have further complexities. For example, narrative similarity can be abstract and rely on deeper reasoning (e.g., the subliminal resistance of temptation of power in 'The Lord of The Rings'). Such aspects are beyond the scope of current NLP tools, but may guide future explorations. Future work can also explore other domains (e.g., newswire and literary fiction) and evaluate character and event alignments between narratives based on established ground truths.

Acknowledgments

Most of this work was done while the first author was at the University of Illinois. This research was supported in part by the IBM-ILLINOIS Center for Cognitive Computing Systems Research (C3SR) - a research collaboration as part of the IBM AI Horizons Network and by a gift from Google. The authors thank the anonymous reviewers for their helpful comments and feedback.

References

A. Aarne and S. Thompson. 1961. *The types of the folktale: a classification and bibliography.* FF communications. Academia Scientarum Fennica.

Apoorv Agarwal, Anup Kotalwar, and Owen Rambow. 2013. Automatic extraction of social networks from literary text: A case study on alice in wonderland. In *Proceedings of IJCNLP 2013, Nagoya, Japan, October 14-18, 2013.* pages 1202–1208.

David Bamman, Brendan O'Connor, and Noah A. Smith. 2013. Learning latent personas of film characters. In *Proceedings of ACL (Volume 1: Long Papers).* Association for Computational Linguistics, Sofia, Bulgaria, pages 352–361.

David Bamman, Ted Underwood, and Noah A. Smith. 2014. A bayesian mixed effects model of literary character. In *Proceedings of ACL (Volume 1: Long Papers).* Association for Computational Linguistics, Baltimore, Maryland, pages 370–379.

Nathanael Chambers and Dan Jurafsky. 2009. Unsupervised learning of narrative schemas and their participants. In *Proceedings of the Joint Conference of ACL and AFNLP: Volume 2-Volume 2.* Association for Computational Linguistics, pages 602–610.

Snigdha Chaturvedi. 2016. *Structured Approaches for Exploring Interpersonal Relationships in Natural Language Text.* Ph.D. thesis, University of Maryland, College Park.

Snigdha Chaturvedi, Mohit Iyyer, and Hal Daumé III. 2017. Unsupervised Learning of Evolving Relationships Between Literary Characters. In *Proceedings of the Thirty First AAAI Conference on Artificial Intelligence.* AAAI'17.

Snigdha Chaturvedi, Shashank Srivastava, Hal Daumé III, and Chris Dyer. 2016. Modeling evolving relationships between characters in literary novels. In *Proceedings of the Thirtieth AAAI Conference on Artificial Intelligence, February 12-17, 2016, Phoenix, Arizona, USA..* AAAI'16, pages 2704–2710.

Micha Elsner. 2012. Character-based kernels for novelistic plot structure. In *Proceedings of EACL.* Association for Computational Linguistics, pages 634–644.

David K Elson. 2012. Detecting story analogies from annotations of time, action and agency. In *Proceedings of the LREC 2012 Workshop on Computational Models of Narrative.*

David K. Elson, Nicholas Dames, and Kathleen McKeown. 2010. Extracting Social Networks from Literary Fiction. In *Proceedings of ACL 2010.* pages 138–147.

Mark Finlayson and Patrick Henry Winston. 2006. Analogical retrieval via intermediate features: The goldilocks hypothesis. Technical report, MIT Computer Science and Artificial Intelligence Laboratory, Cambridge, MA.

Mark Alan Finlayson. 2012. *Learning Narrative Structure from Annotated Folktales.* Ph.D. thesis, Massachusetts Institute of Technology.

Bernhard Fisseni and Benedikt Löwe. 2012. Which dimensions of narratives are relevant for human judgments of story equivalence. In *The Third Workshop on Computational Models of Narrative*. pages 114–118.

Jonathan Gottschall. 2012. *The storytelling animal: How stories make us human*. Houghton Mifflin Harcourt.

Amit Goyal, Ellen Riloff, and Hal Daumé III. 2010. Automatically Producing Plot Unit Representations for Narrative Text. In *Proceedings of EMNLP 2010*. pages 77–86.

David Herman. 2003. *Narrative Theory and the Cognitive Sciences*. Stanford Univ Center for the Study.

Mohit Iyyer, Anupam Guha, Snigdha Chaturvedi, Jordan L. Boyd-Graber, and Hal Daumé III. 2016. Feuding families and former friends: Unsupervised learning for dynamic fictional relationships. In *Proceedings of NAACL HLT 2016, San Diego California, USA, June 12-17, 2016*. pages 1534–1544.

Vinodh Krishnan and Jacob Eisenstein. 2015. "You're Mr. Lebowski, I'm the Dude": Inducing Address Term Formality in Signed Social Networks. In *Proceedings of NAACL HLT 2015*. pages 1616–1626.

Harold W. Kuhn. 1955. The hungarian method for the assignment problem. *Naval Research Logistics Quarterly* 2:83–97.

Wendy G. Lehnert. 1981. Plot Units and Narrative Summarization. *Cognitive Science* 5(4):293–331.

Inderjeet Mani. 2012. *Computational Modeling of Narrative*. Synthesis Lectures on Human Language Technologies. Morgan & Claypool Publishers.

Christopher D. Manning, Mihai Surdeanu, John Bauer, Jenny Rose Finkel, Steven Bethard, and David McClosky. 2014. The stanford corenlp natural language processing toolkit. In *Proceedings of the 52nd Annual Meeting of the Association for Computational Linguistics, ACL 2014, June 22-27, 2014, Baltimore, MD, USA, System Demonstrations*. pages 55–60.

Neil McIntyre and Mirella Lapata. 2010. Plot Induction and Evolutionary Search for Story Generation. In *Proceedings of ACL 2010*. pages 1562–1572.

Owen Miller and WJT Mitchell. 1983. On narrative.

Dong Nguyen, Dolf Trieschnigg, and Mariët Theune. 2013. Folktale classification using learning to rank. In *ECIR*. Springer, pages 195–206.

Dong Nguyen, Dolf Trieschnigg, and Mariët Theune. 2014. Using crowdsourcing to investigate perception of narrative similarity. In *Proceedings of the 23rd ACM International Conference on Conference on Information and Knowledge Management, CIKM 2014, Shanghai, China, November 3-7, 2014*. pages 321–330.

Vladimir Iakovlevich Propp. 1968. *Morphology of the Folktale*. University of Texas.

Whitman Richards, Mark Alan Finlayson, and Patrick Henry Winston. 2009. Advancing computational models of narrative. *MIT Computer Science and Artificial Intelligence Laboratory, Cambridge, MA, Tech. Rep* 63:2009.

David E Rumelhart. 1980. On evaluating story grammars. *Cognitive Science* 4(3):313–316.

Roger C Schank and Robert P Abelson. 1975. Scripts, plans, and knowledge. In *IJCAI*. pages 151–157.

Shashank Srivastava, Snigdha Chaturvedi, and Tom M. Mitchell. 2016. Inferring interpersonal relations in narrative summaries. In *Proceedings of the Thirtieth AAAI Conference on Artificial Intelligence, February 12-17, 2016, Phoenix, Arizona, USA.*. pages 2807–2813.

Josep Valls-Vargas, Jichen Zhu, and Santiago Ontanón. 2014. Toward automatic role identification in unannotated folk tales. In *Proceedings of the Tenth AAAI Conference on Artificial Intelligence and Interactive Digital Entertainment*. AAAI Press, pages 188–194.

Robert Wilensky. 1978. *Understanding Goal-Based Stories*. Outstanding Dissertations in the Computer Sciences. Garland Publishing, New York.

Multimodal Emoji Prediction

Francesco Barbieri[◇] **Miguel Ballesteros**[♠] **Francesco Ronzano**[♡] **Horacio Saggion**[◇]
◇ Large Scale Text Understanding Systems Lab, TALN, UPF, Barcelona, Spain
♠IBM Research, U.S
♡ Integrative Biomedical Informatics Group, GRIB, IMIM-UPF, Barcelona, Spain

◇♡{name.surname}@upf.edu, ♠miguel.ballesteros@ibm.com

Abstract

Emojis are small images that are commonly included in social media text messages. The combination of visual and textual content in the same message builds up a modern way of communication, that automatic systems are not used to deal with. In this paper we extend recent advances in emoji prediction by putting forward a multimodal approach that is able to predict emojis in Instagram posts. Instagram posts are composed of pictures together with texts which sometimes include emojis. We show that these emojis can be predicted by using the text, but also using the picture. Our main finding is that incorporating the two synergistic modalities, in a combined model, improves accuracy in an emoji prediction task. This result demonstrates that these two modalities (text and images) encode different information on the use of emojis and therefore can complement each other.

1 Introduction

In the past few years the use of emojis in social media has increased exponentially, changing the way we communicate. The combination of visual and textual content poses new challenges for information systems which need not only to deal with the semantics of text but also that of images. Recent work (Barbieri et al., 2017) has shown that textual information can be used to predict emojis associated to text. In this paper we show that in the current context of multimodal communication where texts and images are combined in social networks, visual information should be combined with texts in order to obtain more accurate emoji-prediction models.

We explore the use of emojis in the social media platform Instagram. We put forward a multimodal approach to predict the emojis associated to an In-

stagram post, given its picture and text[1]. Our task and experimental framework are similar to (Barbieri et al., 2017), however, we use different data (Instagram instead of Twitter) and, in addition, we rely on images to improve the selection of the most likely emojis to associate to a post. We show that a multimodal approach (textual and visual content of the posts) increases the emoji prediction accuracy compared to the one that only uses textual information. This suggests that textual and visual content embed different but complementary features of the use of emojis.

In general, an effective approach to predict the emoji to be associated to a piece of content may help to improve natural language processing tasks (Novak et al., 2015), such as information retrieval, generation of emoji-enriched social media content, suggestion of emojis when writing text messages or sharing pictures online. Given that emojis may also mislead humans (Miller et al., 2017), the automated prediction of emojis may help to achieve better language understanding. As a consequence, by modeling the semantics of emojis, we can improve highly-subjective tasks like sentiment analysis, emotion recognition and irony detection (Felbo et al., 2017).

2 Dataset and Task

Dataset: We gathered Instagram posts published between July 2016 and October 2016, and geo-localized in the United States of America. We considered only posts that contained a photo together with the related user description of at least 4 words and exactly one emoji.

Moreover, as done by Barbieri et al. (2017), we considered only the posts which include *one and only one* of the 20 most frequent emojis (the

---

[1]In this paper we only utilize the first comment issued by the user who posted the picture.

679

Proceedings of NAACL-HLT 2018, pages 679–686
New Orleans, Louisiana, June 1 - 6, 2018. ©2018 Association for Computational Linguistics

most frequent emojis are shown in Table 3). Our dataset is composed of 299,809 posts, each containing a picture, the text associated to it and only one emoji. In the experiments we also considered the subsets of the 10 (238,646 posts) and 5 most frequent emojis (184,044 posts) (similarly to the approach followed by Barbieri et al. (2017)).

Task: We extend the experimental scheme of Barbieri et al. (2017), by considering also visual information when modeling posts. We cast the emoji prediction problem as a classification task: given an image or a text (or both inputs in the multimodal scenario) we select the most likely emoji that could be added to (thus used to label) such contents. The task for our machine learning models is, given the visual and textual content of a post, to predict the single emoji that appears in the input comment.

3   Models

We present and motivate the models that we use to predict an emoji given an Instagram post composed by a picture and the associated comment.

3.1   ResNets

Deep Residual Networks (ResNets) (He et al., 2016) are Convolutional Neural Networks which were competitive in several image classification tasks (Russakovsky et al., 2015; Lin et al., 2014) and showed to be one of the best CNN architectures for image recognition. ResNet is a feedforward CNN that exploits "residual learning", by bypassing two or more convolution layers (like similar previous approaches (Sermanet and Le-Cun, 2011)). We use an implementation of the original ResNet where the scale and aspect ratio augmentation are from (Szegedy et al., 2015), the photometric distortions from (Howard, 2013) and weight decay is applied to all weights and biases (instead of only weights of the convolution layers). The network we used is composed of 101 layers (ResNet-101), initialized with pretrained parameters learned on ImageNet (Deng et al., 2009). We use this model as a starting point to later finetune it on our emoji classification task. Learning rate was set to 0.0001 and we early stopped the training when there was not improving in the validation set.

3.2   FastText

Fastext (Joulin et al., 2017) is a linear model for text classification. We decided to employ FastText as it has been shown that on specific classification tasks, it can achieve competitive results, comparable to complex neural classifiers (RNNs and CNNs), while being much faster. FastText represents a valid approach when dealing with social media content classification, where huge amounts of data needs to be processed and new and relevant information is continuously generated. The FastText algorithm is similar to the CBOW algorithm (Mikolov et al., 2013), where the middle word is replaced by the label, in our case the emoji. Given a set of N documents, the loss that the model attempts to minimize is the negative log-likelihood over the labels (in our case, the emojis):

$$loss = -\frac{1}{N} \sum_{N}^{n=1} e_n \log(softmax(BA_{x_n}))$$

where e_n is the emoji included in the n-th Instagram post, represented as hot vector, and used as label. A and B are affine transformations (weight matrices), and x_n is the unit vector of the bag of features of the n-th document (comment). The bag of features is the average of the input words, represented as vectors with a look-up table.

3.3   B-LSTM Baseline

Barbieri et al. (2017) propose a recurrent neural network approach for the emoji prediction task. We use this model as baseline, to verify whether FastText achieves comparable performance. They used a Bidirectional LSTM with character representation of the words (Ling et al., 2015; Ballesteros et al., 2015) to handle orthographic variants (or even spelling errors) of the same word that occur in social media (e.g. *cooooool* vs *cool*).

4   Experiments and Evaluation

In order to study the relation between Instagram posts and emojis, we performed two different experiments. In the first experiment (Section 4.2) we compare the FastText model with the state of the art on emoji classification (B-LSTM) by Barbieri et al. (2017). Our second experiment (Section 4.3) evaluates the visual (ResNet) and textual (FastText) models on the emoji prediction task. Moreover, we evaluate a multimodal combination of both models respectively based on visual and

	top-5			top-10			top-20		
	P	**R**	**F1**	**P**	**R**	**F1**	**P**	**R**	**F1**
BW	61	61	61	45	45	45	34	36	32
BC	63	63	**63**	48	47	**47**	42	39	34
FT	61	62	61	47	49	46	38	39	**36**

Table 1: Comparison of B-LSTM with word modeling (BW), B-LSTM with character modeling (BC), and FastText (FT) on the same Twitter emoji prediction tasks proposed by Barbieri et al. (2017), using the same Twitter dataset.

textual inputs. Finally we discuss the contribution of each modality to the prediction task.

We use 80% of our dataset (introduced in Section 2) for training, 10% to tune our models, and 10% for testing (selecting the sets randomly).

4.1 Feature Extraction and Classifier

To model visual features we first finetune the ResNet (process described in Section 3.1) on the emoji prediction task, then extract the vectors from the input of the last fully connected layer (before the softmax). The textual embeddings are the bag of features shown in Section 3.2 (the x_n vectors), extracted after training the FastText model on the emoji prediction task.

With respect to the combination of textual and visual modalities, we adopt a middle fusion approach (Kiela and Clark, 2015): we associate to each Instagram post a multimodal embedding obtained by concatenating the unimodal representations of the same post (i.e. the visual and textual embeddings), previously learned. Then, we feed a classifier[2] with visual (ResNet), textual (FastText), or multimodal feature embeddings, and test the accuracy of the three systems.

4.2 B-LSTM / FastText Comparison

To compare the FastText model with the word and character based B-LSTMs presented by Barbieri et al. (2017), we consider the same three emoji prediction tasks they proposed: top-5, top-10 and top-20 emojis most frequently used in their Tweet datasets. In this comparison we used the same Twitter datasets. As we can see in Table 1 FastText model is competitive, and it is also able to outperform the character based B-LSTM in one of the emoji prediction tasks (top-20 emojis). This result suggests that we can employ FastText to represent Social Media short text (such as Twitter or Instragram) with reasonable accuracy.

---

[2]L2 regularized logistic regression

	top-5			top-10			top-20		
	P	**R**	**F1**	**P**	**R**	**F1**	**P**	**R**	**F1**
Maj	7.9	20.0	11.3	2.7	10.0	4.2	0.9	5.0	1.5
W.R.	20.1	20.0	20.1	9.8	9.8	9.8	4.6	4.8	4.7
Vis	38.6	31.1	31.0	26.3	20.9	20.5	20.3	17.5	16.1
Tex	56.1	54.4	54.9	41.6	37.5	38.3	36.7	29.9	31.3
Mul	57.4	56.3	**56.7**	42.3	40.5	**41.1**	36.6	35.2	**35.5**
%	2.3	3.5	3.3	1.7	8	7.3	-0.3	17.7	13.4

Table 2: Prediction results of top-5, top-10 and top-20 most frequent emojis in the Instagram dataset: Precision (P), Recall (R), F-measure (F1). Experimental settings: majority baseline, weighted random, visual, textual and multimodal systems. In the last line we report the percentage improvement of the multimodal over the textual system.

4.3 Multimodal Emoji Prediction

We present the results of the three emoji classification tasks, using the visual, textual and multimodal features (see Table 2).

The emoji prediction task seems difficult by just using the image of the Instagram post (**Visual**), even if it largely outperforms the majority baseline[3] and weighted random[4]. We achieve better performances when we use feature embeddings extracted from the text. The most interesting finding is that when we use a multimodal combination of visual and textual features, we get a nonnegligible improvement. This suggests that these two modalities embed different representations of the posts, and when used in combination they are synergistic. It is also interesting to note that the more emojis to predict, the higher improvement the multimodal system provides over the text only system (3.28% for top-5 emojis, 7.31% for top-10 emojis, and 13.42 for the top-20 emojis task).

4.4 Qualitative Analysis

In Table 3 we show the results for each class in the top-20 emojis task.

The emoji with highest F1 using the textual features is the most frequent one ♥ (0.62) and the US flag ▦ (0.52). The latter seems easy to predict since it appears in specific contexts: when the word USA/America is used (or when American cities are referred, like #NYC).

The hardest emojis to predict by the text only system are the two gestures ✌ (0.12) and 🙌 (0.13). The first one is often selected when the gold stan-

---

[3]Always predict ♥ since it is the most frequent emoji.
[4]Random keeping labels distribution of the training set

E	%	Tex	Vis	MM	E	%	Tex	Vis	MM
❤️	17.46	0.62	0.35	**0.69**	💜	3.68	0.22	0.15	**0.29**
😂	9.10	0.45	0.30	**0.47**	✌️	3.55	0.20	0.02	**0.26**
😍	8.41	0.32	0.15	**0.34**	🎶	3.54	0.13	0.02	**0.2**
💕	5.91	0.23	0.08	**0.26**	💯	3.51	0.26	0.17	**0.31**
✨	5.73	0.35	0.17	**0.36**	💪	3.31	0.43	0.25	**0.45**
🔥	4.58	0.45	0.24	**0.46**	😊	3.25	0.12	0.01	**0.16**
🇺🇸	4.31	0.52	0.23	**0.53**	👌	3.14	0.12	0.02	**0.15**
☀️	4.15	0.38	0.26	**0.49**	🙏	3.11	0.34	0.11	**0.36**
😎	3.84	0.19	0.1	**0.22**	🎄	2.91	0.36	0.04	**0.37**
🙌	3.73	0.13	0.03	**0.16**	🐶	2.82	0.45	0.54	**0.59**

Table 3: F-measure in the test set of the 20 most frequent emojis using the three different models. "%" indicates the percentage of the class in the test set

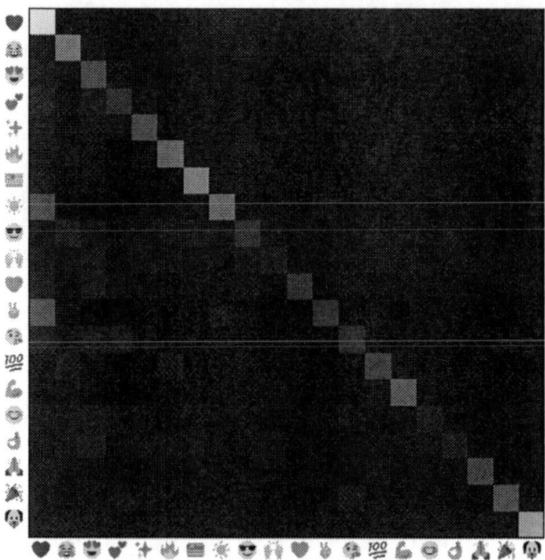

Figure 1: Confusion matrix of the multimodal model. The gold labels are plotted as y-axes and the predicted labels as x-axes. The matrix is normalized by rows.

dard emoji is the second one or 🙌 is often mispredicted by wrongly selecting 😍 or 😎.

Another relevant confusion scenario related to emoji prediction has been spotted by Barbieri et al. (2017): relying on Twitter textual data they showed that the emoji 💕 was hard to predict as it was used similarly to ❤️. Instead when we consider Instagram data, the emoji 💕 is easier to predict (0.23), even if it is often confused with 😍.

When we rely on visual contents (Instagram picture), the emojis which are easily predicted are the ones in which the associated photos are similar. For instance, most of the pictures associated to 🐶 are dog/pet pictures. Similarly, ☀️ is predicted along with very bright pictures taken outside. 💪 is correctly predicted along with pictures related to gym and fitness. The accuracy of 💪 is also high since most posts including this emoji are related to fitness (and the pictures are simply either selfies at the gym, weight lifting images, or protein food).

Employing a multimodal approach improves performance. This means that the two modalities are somehow complementary, and adding visual information helps to solve potential ambiguities that arise when relying only on textual content. In Figure 1 we report the confusion matrix of the multimodal model. The emojis are plotted from the most frequent to the least, and we can see that the model tends to mispredict emojis selecting more frequent emojis (the left part of the matrix is brighter).

4.4.1 Saliency Maps

In order to show the parts of the image most relevant for each class we analyze the global average pooling (Lin et al., 2013) on the convolutional feature maps (Zhou et al., 2016). By visually observing the image heatmaps of the set of Instagram post pictures we note that in most cases it is quite difficult to determine a clear association between the emoji used by the user and some particular portion of the image. Detecting the correct emoji given an image is harder than a simple object recognition task, as the emoji choice depends on subjective emotions of the user who posted the image. In Figure 2 we show the first four predictions of the CNN for three pictures, and where the network focuses (in red). We can see that in the first example the network selects the smile with sunglasses 😎 because of the legs in the bottom of the image, the dog emoji 🐶 is selected while focusing on the dog in the image, and the smiling emoji 😊 while focusing on the person in the back, who is lying on a hammock. In the second example the network selects again the 😊 due to the water and part of the kayak, the heart emoji ❤️ focusing on the city landscape, and the praying emoji 🙏 focusing on the sky. The same "praying" emoji is also selected when focusing on the luxury car in the third example, probably because the same emoji is used to express desire, i.e. "please, I want this awesome car".

It is interesting to note that images can give context to textual messages like in the following Instagram posts: (1)"Love my new home ☀️" (associated to a picture of a bright garden, outside) and (2) "I can't believe it's the first day of school!!!

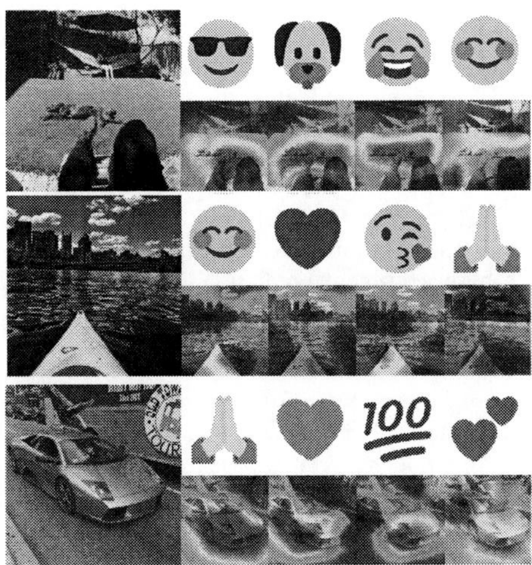

Figure 2: Three test pictures. From left to right, we show the four most likely predicted emojis and their correspondent class activation mapping heatmap.

I love being these boys' mommy!!!! *#myboys #mommy* ❤" (associated to picture of two boys wearing two blue shirts). In both examples the textual system predicts ❤. While the multimodal system correctly predicts both of them: the blue color in the picture associated to (2) helps to change the color of the heart, and the sunny/bright picture of the garden in (1) helps to correctly predict ☀.

5   Related Work

Modeling the semantics of emojis, and their applications, is a relatively novel research problem with direct applications in any social media task. Since emojis do not have a clear grammar, it is not clear their role in text messages. Emojis are considered function words or even affective markers (Na'aman et al., 2017), that can potentially affect the overall semantics of a message (Donato and Paggio, 2017).

Emojis can encode different meanings, and they can be interpreted differently. Emoji interpretation has been explored user-wise (Miller et al., 2017), location-wise, specifically in countries (Barbieri et al., 2016b) and cities (Barbieri et al., 2016a), and gender-wise (Chen et al., 2017) and time-wise (Barbieri et al., 2018).

Emoji sematics and usage have been studied with distributional semantics, with models trained on Twitter data (Barbieri et al., 2016c), Twitter data together with the official unicode description (Eisner et al., 2016), or using text from a popular keyboard app Ai et al. (2017). In the same context, Wijeratne et al. (2017a) propose a platform for exploring emoji semantics. In order to further study emoji semantics, two datasets with pairwise emoji similarity, with human annotations, have been proposed: EmoTwi50 (Barbieri et al., 2016c) and EmoSim508 (Wijeratne et al., 2017b). Emoji similarity has been also used for proposing efficient keyboard emoji organization (Pohl et al., 2017). Recently, Barbieri and Camacho-Collados (2018) show that emoji modifiers (skin tones and gender) can affect the semantics vector representation of emojis.

Emoji play an important role in the emotional content of a message. Several sentiment lexicons for emojis have been proposed (Novak et al., 2015; Kimura and Katsurai, 2017; Rodrigues et al., 2018) and also studies in the context of emotion and emojis have been published recently (Wood and Ruder, 2016; Hu et al., 2017).

During the last decade several studies have shown how sentiment analysis improves when we jointly leverage information coming from different modalities (e.g. text, images, audio, video) (Morency et al., 2011; Poria et al., 2015; Tran and Cambria, 2018). In particular, when we deal with Social Media posts, the presence of both textual and visual content has promoted a number of investigations on sentiment or emotions (Baecchi et al., 2016; You et al., 2016b,a; Yu et al., 2016; Chen et al., 2015) or emojis (Cappallo et al., 2015, 2018).

6   Conclusions

In this work we explored the use of emojis in a multimodal context (Instagram posts). We have shown that using a synergistic approach, thus relying on both textual and visual contents of social media posts, we can outperform state of the art unimodal approaches (based only on textual contents). As future work, we plan to extend our models by considering the prediction of more than one emoji per Social Media post and also considering a bigger number of labels.

Acknowledgments

We thank the anonymous reviewers for their important suggestions. Francesco B. and Horacio S. acknowledge support from the TUNER project (TIN2015-65308-C5-5-R, MINECO/FEDER, UE) and the Maria de Maeztu Units of Excellence Programme (MDM-2015-0502).

References

Wei Ai, Xuan Lu, Xuanzhe Liu, Ning Wang, Gang Huang, and Qiaozhu Mei. 2017. Untangling emoji popularity through semantic embeddings. In *ICWSM*. pages 2–11.

Claudio Baecchi, Tiberio Uricchio, Marco Bertini, and Alberto Del Bimbo. 2016. A multimodal feature learning approach for sentiment analysis of social network multimedia. *Multimedia Tools and Applications* 75(5):2507–2525.

Miguel Ballesteros, Chris Dyer, and Noah A. Smith. 2015. Improved transition-based parsing by modeling characters instead of words with lstms. In *Proceedings of the 2015 Conference on Empirical Methods in Natural Language Processing*. Association for Computational Linguistics, Lisbon, Portugal, pages 349–359.

Francesco Barbieri, Miguel Ballesteros, and Horacio Saggion. 2017. Are emojis predictable? In *Proceedings of the 2017 Conference of the European Chapter of the Association for Computational Linguistics*. Association for Computational Linguistics, Valencia, Spain.

Francesco Barbieri and Jose Camacho-Collados. 2018. How Gender and Skin Tone Modifiers Affect Emoji Semantics in Twitter. In *Proceedings of the 7th Joint Conference on Lexical and Computational Semantics (*SEM 2018)*. New Orleans, LA, United States.

Francesco Barbieri, Luis Espinosa-Anke, and Horacio Saggion. 2016a. Revealing patterns of Twitter emoji usage in Barcelona and Madrid. *Frontiers in Artificial Intelligence and Applications. 2016;(Artificial Intelligence Research and Development) 288: 239-44.* .

Francesco Barbieri, German Kruszewski, Francesco Ronzano, and Horacio Saggion. 2016b. How Cosmopolitan Are Emojis? Exploring Emojis Usage and Meaning over Different Languages with Distributional Semantics. In *Proceedings of the 2016 ACM on Multimedia Conference*. ACM, Amsterdam, Netherlands, pages 531–535.

Francesco Barbieri, Luis Marujo, William Brendel, Pradeep Karuturim, and Horacio Saggion. 2018. Exploring Emoji Usage and Prediction Through a Temporal Variation Lens. In *1st International Workshop on Emoji Understanding and Applications in Social Media (at ICWSM 2018)*.

Francesco Barbieri, Francesco Ronzano, and Horacio Saggion. 2016c. What does this emoji mean? a vector space skip-gram model for twitter emojis. In *LREC*.

Spencer Cappallo, Thomas Mensink, and Cees GM Snoek. 2015. Image2emoji: Zero-shot emoji prediction for visual media. In *Proceedings of the 23rd ACM international conference on Multimedia*. ACM, pages 1311–1314.

Spencer Cappallo, Stacey Svetlichnaya, Pierre Garrigues, Thomas Mensink, and Cees GM Snoek. 2018. The new modality: Emoji challenges in prediction, anticipation, and retrieval. *arXiv preprint arXiv:1801.10253* .

Fuhai Chen, Yue Gao, Donglin Cao, and Rongrong Ji. 2015. Multimodal hypergraph learning for microblog sentiment prediction. In *Multimedia and Expo (ICME), 2015 IEEE International Conference on*. IEEE, pages 1–6.

Zhenpeng Chen, Xuan Lu, Sheng Shen, Wei Ai, Xuanzhe Liu, and Qiaozhu Mei. 2017. Through a gender lens: An empirical study of emoji usage over large-scale android users. *arXiv preprint arXiv:1705.05546* .

J. Deng, W. Dong, R. Socher, L.-J. Li, K. Li, and L. Fei-Fei. 2009. ImageNet: A Large-Scale Hierarchical Image Database. In *CVPR09*.

Giulia Donato and Patrizia Paggio. 2017. Investigating redundancy in emoji use: Study on a twitter based corpus. In *Proceedings of the 8th Workshop on Computational Approaches to Subjectivity, Sentiment and Social Media Analysis*. pages 118–126.

Ben Eisner, Tim Rocktäschel, Isabelle Augenstein, Matko Bošnjak, and Sebastian Riedel. 2016. emoji2vec: Learning emoji representations from their description. *arXiv preprint arXiv:1609.08359* .

Bjarke Felbo, Alan Mislove, Anders Søgaard, Iyad Rahwan, and Sune Lehmann. 2017. Using millions of emoji occurrences to learn any-domain representations for detecting sentiment, emotion and sarcasm. *EMNLP* .

Kaiming He, Xiangyu Zhang, Shaoqing Ren, and Jian Sun. 2016. Deep residual learning for image recognition. In *Proceedings of the IEEE Conference on Computer Vision and Pattern Recognition*. pages 770–778.

Andrew G Howard. 2013. Some improvements on deep convolutional neural network based image classification. *arXiv preprint arXiv:1312.5402* .

Tianran Hu, Han Guo, Hao Sun, Thuy-vy Thi Nguyen, and Jiebo Luo. 2017. Spice up Your Chat: The Intentions and Sentiment Effects of Using Emoji. In *In Proceeding of the International AAAI Conference on Web and Social Media (ICWSM)*. AAAI.

Armand Joulin, Edouard Grave, Piotr Bojanowski, and Tomas Mikolov. 2017. Bag of tricks for efficient text classification. In *Proceedings of the 2017 Conference of the European Chapter of the Association for Computational Linguistics*. Association for Computational Linguistics, Valencia, Spain.

Douwe Kiela and Stephen Clark. 2015. Multi-and cross-modal semantics beyond vision: Grounding in auditory perception. In *EMNLP*. pages 2461–2470.

Mayu Kimura and Marie Katsurai. 2017. Automatic construction of an emoji sentiment lexicon. In *Proceedings of the 2017 IEEE/ACM International Conference on Advances in Social Networks Analysis and Mining 2017*. ACM, pages 1033–1036.

Min Lin, Qiang Chen, and Shuicheng Yan. 2013. Network in Network. In *International Conference on Learning Representations*.

Tsung-Yi Lin, Michael Maire, Serge Belongie, James Hays, Pietro Perona, Deva Ramanan, Piotr Dollár, and C Lawrence Zitnick. 2014. Microsoft coco: Common objects in context. In *European Conference on Computer Vision*. Springer, pages 740–755.

Wang Ling, Chris Dyer, Alan W Black, Isabel Trancoso, Ramon Fermandez, Silvio Amir, Luis Marujo, and Tiago Luis. 2015. Finding function in form: Compositional character models for open vocabulary word representation. In *Proceedings of the 2015 Conference on Empirical Methods in Natural Language Processing*. Association for Computational Linguistics, Lisbon, Portugal, pages 1520–1530.

Tomas Mikolov, Kai Chen, Greg Corrado, and Jeffrey Dean. 2013. Efficient estimation of word representations in vector space. *arXiv preprint arXiv:1301.3781* .

Hannah Miller, Daniel Kluver, Jacob Thebault-Spieker, Loren Terveen, and Brent Hecht. 2017. Understanding emoji ambiguity in context: The role of text in emoji-related miscommunication. In *11th International Conference on Web and Social Media, ICWSM 2017*. AAAI Press.

Louis-Philippe Morency, Rada Mihalcea, and Payal Doshi. 2011. Towards multimodal sentiment analysis: Harvesting opinions from the web. In *Proceedings of the 13th international conference on multimodal interfaces*. ACM, pages 169–176.

Noa Na'aman, Hannah Provenza, and Orion Montoya. 2017. Varying linguistic purposes of emoji in (twitter) context. In *Proceedings of ACL 2017, Student Research Workshop*. pages 136–141.

Petra Kralj Novak, Jasmina Smailović, Borut Sluban, and Igor Mozetič. 2015. Sentiment of emojis. *PloS one* 10(12):e0144296.

Henning Pohl, Christian Domin, and Michael Rohs. 2017. Beyond just text: Semantic emoji similarity modeling to support expressive communication. *ACM Transactions on Computer-Human Interaction (TOCHI)* 24(1):6.

Soujanya Poria, Erik Cambria, and Alexander Gelbukh. 2015. Deep convolutional neural network textual features and multiple kernel learning for utterance-level multimodal sentiment analysis. In *Proceedings of the 2015 conference on empirical methods in natural language processing*. pages 2539–2544.

David Rodrigues, Marília Prada, Rui Gaspar, Margarida V Garrido, and Diniz Lopes. 2018. Lisbon emoji and emoticon database (leed): Norms for emoji and emoticons in seven evaluative dimensions. *Behavior research methods* pages 392–405.

Olga Russakovsky, Jia Deng, Hao Su, Jonathan Krause, Sanjeev Satheesh, Sean Ma, Zhiheng Huang, Andrej Karpathy, Aditya Khosla, Michael Bernstein, Alexander C. Berg, and Li Fei-Fei. 2015. ImageNet Large Scale Visual Recognition Challenge. *International Journal of Computer Vision (IJCV)* 115(3):211–252.

Pierre Sermanet and Yann LeCun. 2011. Traffic sign recognition with multi-scale convolutional networks. In *Neural Networks (IJCNN), The 2011 International Joint Conference on*. IEEE, pages 2809–2813.

Christian Szegedy, Wei Liu, Yangqing Jia, Pierre Sermanet, Scott Reed, Dragomir Anguelov, Dumitru Erhan, Vincent Vanhoucke, and Andrew Rabinovich. 2015. Going deeper with convolutions. In *Proceedings of the IEEE Conference on Computer Vision and Pattern Recognition*. pages 1–9.

Ha-Nguyen Tran and Erik Cambria. 2018. Ensemble application of elm and gpu for real-time multimodal sentiment analysis. *Memetic Computing* 10(1):3–13.

Sanjaya Wijeratne, Lakshika Balasuriya, Amit Sheth, and Derek Doran. 2017a. Emojinet: An open service and api for emoji sense discovery. *International AAAI Conference on Web and Social Media (ICWSM 2017). Montreal, Canada* .

Sanjaya Wijeratne, Lakshika Balasuriya, Amit Sheth, and Derek Doran. 2017b. A semantics-based measure of emoji similarity. *International Conference on Web Intelligence (Web Intelligence 2017). Leipzig, Germany* .

Ian Wood and Sebastian Ruder. 2016. Emoji as emotion tags for tweets. In *Emotion and Sentiment Analysis Workshop, LREC*.

Quanzeng You, Liangliang Cao, Hailin Jin, and Jiebo Luo. 2016a. Robust visual-textual sentiment analysis: When attention meets tree-structured recursive neural networks. In *Proceedings of the 2016 ACM on Multimedia Conference*. ACM, pages 1008–1017.

Quanzeng You, Jiebo Luo, Hailin Jin, and Jianchao Yang. 2016b. Cross-modality consistent regression for joint visual-textual sentiment analysis of social multimedia. In *Proceedings of the Ninth ACM International Conference on Web Search and Data Mining*. ACM, pages 13–22.

Yuhai Yu, Hongfei Lin, Jiana Meng, and Zhehuan Zhao. 2016. Visual and textual sentiment analysis of a microblog using deep convolutional neural networks. *Algorithms* 9(2):41.

Bolei Zhou, Aditya Khosla, Agata Lapedriza, Aude
Oliva, and Antonio Torralba. 2016. Learning deep
features for discriminative localization. In *Proceedings of the IEEE Conference on Computer Vision
and Pattern Recognition.* pages 2921–2929.

Higher-order Coreference Resolution with Coarse-to-fine Inference

Kenton Lee **Luheng He** **Luke Zettlemoyer**
Paul G. Allen School of Computer Science & Engineering
University of Washington, Seattle WA
`{kentonl, luheng, lsz}@cs.washington.edu`

Abstract

We introduce a fully differentiable approximation to higher-order inference for coreference resolution. Our approach uses the antecedent distribution from a span-ranking architecture as an attention mechanism to iteratively refine span representations. This enables the model to softly consider multiple hops in the predicted clusters. To alleviate the computational cost of this iterative process, we introduce a coarse-to-fine approach that incorporates a less accurate but more efficient bilinear factor, enabling more aggressive pruning without hurting accuracy. Compared to the existing state-of-the-art span-ranking approach, our model significantly improves accuracy on the English OntoNotes benchmark, while being far more computationally efficient.

1 Introduction

Recent coreference resolution systems have heavily relied on first order models (Clark and Manning, 2016a; Lee et al., 2017), where only pairs of entity mentions are scored by the model. These models are computationally efficient and scalable to long documents. However, because they make independent decisions about coreference links, they are susceptible to predicting clusters that are locally consistent but globally inconsistent. Figure 1 shows an example from Wiseman et al. (2016) that illustrates this failure case. The plurality of **[you]** is underspecified, making it locally compatible with both **[I]** and **[all of you]**, while the full cluster would have mixed plurality, resulting in global inconsistency.

We introduce an approximation of higher-order inference that uses the span-ranking architecture from Lee et al. (2017) in an iterative manner. At each iteration, the antecedent distribution is used as an attention mechanism to optionally update existing span representations, enabling later corefer-

> *Speaker 1*: Um and **[I]** think that is what's - Go ahead Linda.
> *Speaker 2*: Well and uh thanks goes to **[you]** and to the media to help us... So our hat is off to **[all of you]** as well.

Figure 1: Example of consistency errors to which first-order span-ranking models are susceptible. Span pairs (**I**, **you**) and (**you**, **all of you**) are locally consistent, but the span triplet (**I**, **you**, **all of you**) is globally inconsistent. Avoiding this error requires modeling higher-order structures.

ence decisions to softly condition on earlier coreference decisions. For the example in Figure 1, this enables the linking of **[you]** and **[all of you]** to depend on the linking of **[I]** and **[you]**.

To alleviate computational challenges from this higher-order inference, we also propose a coarse-to-fine approach that is learned with a single end-to-end objective. We introduce a less accurate but more efficient coarse factor in the pairwise scoring function. This additional factor enables an extra pruning step during inference that reduces the number of antecedents considered by the more accurate but inefficient fine factor. Intuitively, the model cheaply computes a rough sketch of *likely* antecedents before applying a more expensive scoring function.

Our experiments show that both of the above contributions improve the performance of coreference resolution on the English OntoNotes benchmark. We observe a significant increase in average F1 with a second-order model, but returns quickly diminish with a third-order model. Additionally, our analysis shows that the coarse-to-fine approach makes the model performance relatively insensitive to more aggressive antecedent pruning, compared to the distance-based heuristic pruning from previous work.

Proceedings of NAACL-HLT 2018, pages 687–692
New Orleans, Louisiana, June 1 - 6, 2018. ©2018 Association for Computational Linguistics

2   Background

Task definition   We formulate the coreference resolution task as a set of antecedent assignments y_i for each of span i in the given document, following Lee et al. (2017). The set of possible assignments for each y_i is $\mathcal{Y}(i) = \{\epsilon, 1, \ldots, i - 1\}$, a dummy antecedent ϵ and all preceding spans. Non-dummy antecedents represent coreference links between i and y_i. The dummy antecedent ϵ represents two possible scenarios: (1) the span is not an entity mention or (2) the span is an entity mention but it is not coreferent with any previous span. These decisions implicitly define a final clustering, which can be recovered by grouping together all spans that are connected by the set of antecedent predictions.

Baseline   We describe the baseline model (Lee et al., 2017), which we will improve to address the modeling and computational limitations discussed previously. The goal is to learn a distribution $P(y_i)$ over antecedents for each span i :

$$P(y_i) = \frac{e^{s(i, y_i)}}{\sum_{y' \in \mathcal{Y}(i)} e^{s(i, y')}} \qquad (1)$$

where $s(i, j)$ is a pairwise score for a coreference link between span i and span j. The baseline model includes three factors for this pairwise coreference score: (1) $s_\mathrm{m}(i)$, whether span i is a mention, (2) $s_\mathrm{m}(j)$, whether span j is a mention, and (3) $s_\mathrm{a}(i, j)$ whether j is an antecedent of i:

$$s(i, j) = s_\mathrm{m}(i) + s_\mathrm{m}(j) + s_\mathrm{a}(i, j) \qquad (2)$$

In the special case of the dummy antecedent, the score $s(i, \epsilon)$ is instead fixed to 0. A common component used throughout the model is the vector representations g_i for each possible span i. These are computed via bidirectional LSTMs (Hochreiter and Schmidhuber, 1997) that learn context-dependent boundary and head representations. The scoring functions s_m and s_a take these span representations as input:

$$s_\mathrm{m}(i) = w_\mathrm{m}^\top \mathrm{FFNN}_\mathrm{m}(g_i) \qquad (3)$$
$$s_\mathrm{a}(i, j) = w_\mathrm{a}^\top \mathrm{FFNN}_\mathrm{a}([g_i, g_j, g_i \circ g_j, \phi(i, j)]) \qquad (4)$$

where $\circ$ denotes element-wise multiplication, FFNN denotes a feed-forward neural network, and the antecedent scoring function $s_\mathrm{a}(i, j)$ includes explicit element-wise similarity of each span $g_i \circ g_j$ and a feature vector $\phi(i, j)$ encoding speaker and genre information from the metadata and the distance between the two spans.

The model above is factored to enable a two-stage beam search. A beam of up to M potential mentions is computed (where M is proportional to the document length) based on the spans with the highest mention scores $s_\mathrm{m}(i)$. Pairwise coreference scores are only computed between surviving mentions during both training and inference.

Given supervision of gold coreference clusters, the model is learned by optimizing the marginal log-likelihood of the possibly correct antecedents. This marginalization is required since the best antecedent for each span is a latent variable.

3   Higher-order Coreference Resolution

The baseline above is a first-order model, since it only considers pairs of spans. First-order models are susceptible to consistency errors as demonstrated in Figure 1. Unlike in sentence-level semantics, where higher-order decisions can be implicitly modeled by the LSTMs, modeling these decisions at the document-level requires explicit inference due to the potentially very large surface distance between mentions.

We propose an inference procedure that allows the model to condition on higher-order structures, while being fully differentiable. This inference involves N iterations of refining span representations, denoted as g_i^n for the representation of span i at iteration n. At iteration n, g_i^n is computed with an attention mechanism that averages over previous representations g_j^{n-1} weighted according to how likely each mention j is to be an antecedent for i, as defined below.

The baseline model is used to initialize the span representation at g_i^1. The refined span representations allow the model to also iteratively refine the antecedent distributions $P_n(y_i)$:

$$P_n(y_i) = \frac{e^{s(g_i^n, g_{y_i}^n)}}{\sum_{y \in \mathcal{Y}(i)} e^{s(g_i^n, g_y^n))}} \qquad (5)$$

where s is the coreference scoring function of the baseline architecture. The scoring function uses the same parameters at every iteration, but it is given different span representations.

At each iteration, we first compute the expected antecedent representation a_i^n of each span i by using the current antecedent distribution $P_n(y_i)$ as an attention mechanism:

$$\boldsymbol{a}_i^n = \sum_{y_i \in \mathcal{Y}(i)} P_n(y_i) \cdot \boldsymbol{g}_{y_i}^n \qquad (6)$$

The current span representation $\boldsymbol{g}_i^n$ is then updated via interpolation with its expected antecedent representation $\boldsymbol{a}_i^n$:

$$\boldsymbol{f}_i^n = \sigma(\mathbf{W}_f[\boldsymbol{g}_i^n, \boldsymbol{a}_i^n]) \qquad (7)$$

$$\boldsymbol{g}_i^{n+1} = \boldsymbol{f}_i^n \circ \boldsymbol{g}_i^n + (\mathbf{1} - \boldsymbol{f}_i^n) \circ \boldsymbol{a}_i^n \qquad (8)$$

The learned gate vector $\boldsymbol{f}_i^n$ determines for each dimension whether to keep the current span information or to integrate new information from its expected antecedent. At iteration n, $\boldsymbol{g}_i^n$ is an element-wise weighted average of approximately n span representations (assuming $P_n(y_i)$ is peaked), allowing $P_n(y_i)$ to softly condition on up to n other spans in the predicted cluster.

Span-ranking can be viewed as predicting latent antecedent trees (Fernandes et al., 2012; Martschat and Strube, 2015), where the predicted antecedent is the parent of a span and each tree is a predicted cluster. By iteratively refining the span representations and antecedent distributions, another way to interpret this model is that the joint distribution $\prod_i P_N(y_i)$ implicitly models every directed path of up to length $N + 1$ in the latent antecedent tree.

4 Coarse-to-fine Inference

The model described above scales poorly to long documents. Despite heavy pruning of potential mentions, the space of possible antecedents for every surviving span is still too large to fully consider. The bottleneck is in the antecedent score $s_a(i, j)$, which requires computing a tensor of size $M \times M \times (3|\boldsymbol{g}| + |\phi|)$.

This computational challenge is even more problematic with the iterative inference from Section 3, which requires recomputing this tensor at every iteration.

4.1 Heuristic antecedent pruning

To reduce computation, Lee et al. (2017) heuristically consider only the nearest K antecedents of each span, resulting in a smaller input of size $M \times K \times (3|\boldsymbol{g}| + |\phi|)$.

The main drawback to this solution is that it imposes an a priori limit on the maximum distance of a coreference link. The previous work only considers up to $K = 250$ nearest mentions, whereas coreference links can reach much further in natural language discourse.

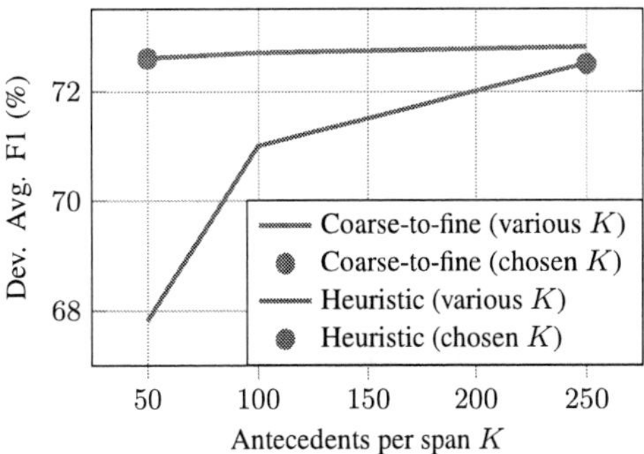

Figure 2: Comparison of accuracy on the development set for the two antecedent pruning strategies with various beams sizes K. The distance-based heuristic pruning performance drops by almost 5 F1 when reducing K from 250 to 50, while the coarse-to-fine pruning results in an insignificant drop of less than 0.2 F1.

4.2 Coarse-to-fine antecedent pruning

We instead propose a coarse-to-fine approach that can be learned end-to-end and does not establish an a priori maximum coreference distance. The key component of this coarse-to-fine approach is an alternate bilinear scoring function:

$$s_c(i, j) = \boldsymbol{g}_i^{\top} \mathbf{W}_c \, \boldsymbol{g}_j \qquad (9)$$

where $\mathbf{W}_c$ is a learned weight matrix. In contrast to the concatenation-based $s_a(i, j)$, the bilinear $s_c(i, j)$ is far less accurate. A direct replacement of $s_a(i, j)$ with $s_c(i, j)$ results in a performance loss of over 3 F1 in our experiments. However, $s_c(i, j)$ is much more efficient to compute. Computing $s_c(i, j)$ only requires manipulating matrices of size $M \times |\boldsymbol{g}|$ and $M \times M$.

Therefore, we instead propose to use $s_c(i, j)$ to compute a rough sketch of *likely* antecedents. This is accomplished by including it as an additional factor in the model:

$$s(i, j) = s_m(i) + s_m(j) + s_c(i, j) + s_a(i, j) \qquad (10)$$

Similar to the baseline model, we leverage this additional factor to perform an additional beam pruning step. The final inference procedure involves a three-stage beam search:

First stage Keep the top M spans based on the mention score $s_m(i)$ of each span.

Second stage Keep the top K antecedents of each remaining span i based on the first three factors, $s_m(i) + s_m(j) + s_c(i, j)$.

	MUC			B^3			CEAF$_{\phi_4}$			
	Prec.	Rec.	F1	Prec.	Rec.	F1	Prec.	Rec.	F1	Avg. F1
Martschat and Strube (2015)	76.7	68.1	72.2	66.1	54.2	59.6	59.5	52.3	55.7	62.5
Clark and Manning (2015)	76.1	69.4	72.6	65.6	56.0	60.4	59.4	53.0	56.0	63.0
Wiseman et al. (2015)	76.2	69.3	72.6	66.2	55.8	60.5	59.4	54.9	57.1	63.4
Wiseman et al. (2016)	77.5	69.8	73.4	66.8	57.0	61.5	62.1	53.9	57.7	64.2
Clark and Manning (2016b)	79.9	69.3	74.2	71.0	56.5	63.0	63.8	54.3	58.7	65.3
Clark and Manning (2016a)	79.2	70.4	74.6	69.9	58.0	63.4	63.5	55.5	59.2	65.7
Lee et al. (2017)	78.4	73.4	75.8	68.6	61.8	65.0	62.7	59.0	60.8	67.2
+ ELMo (Peters et al., 2018)	80.1	77.2	78.6	69.8	66.5	68.1	66.4	62.9	64.6	70.4
+ hyperparameter tuning	80.7	78.8	79.8	71.7	68.7	70.2	67.2	66.8	67.0	72.3
+ coarse-to-fine inference	80.4	**79.9**	80.1	71.0	**70.0**	70.5	67.5	**67.2**	67.3	72.6
+ second-order inference	**81.4**	79.5	**80.4**	**72.2**	69.5	**70.8**	**68.2**	67.1	**67.6**	**73.0**

Table 1: Results on the test set on the English CoNLL-2012 shared task. The average F1 of MUC, B^3, and CEAF$_{\phi_4}$ is the main evaluation metric. We show only non-ensembled models for fair comparison.

Third stage The overall coreference $s(i, j)$ is computed based on the remaining span pairs. The soft higher-order inference from Section 3 is computed in this final stage.

While the maximum-likelihood objective is computed over only the span pairs from this final stage, this coarse-to-fine approach expands the set of coreference links that the model is capable of learning. It achieves better performance while using a much smaller K (see Figure 2).

5 Experimental Setup

We use the English coreference resolution data from the CoNLL-2012 shared task (Pradhan et al., 2012) in our experiments. The code for replicating these results is publicly available.[1]

Our models reuse the hyperparameters from Lee et al. (2017), with a few exceptions mentioned below. In our results, we report two improvements that are orthogonal to our contributions.

- We used embedding representations from a language model (Peters et al., 2018) at the input to the LSTMs (ELMo in the results).

- We changed several hyperparameters:

  1. increasing the maximum span width from 10 to 30 words.

  2. using 3 highway LSTMs instead of 1.

  3. using GloVe word embeddings (Pennington et al., 2014) with a window size

of 2 for the head word embeddings and a window size of 10 for the LSTM inputs.

The baseline model considers up to 250 antecedents per span. As shown in Figure 2, the coarse-to-fine model is quite insensitive to more aggressive pruning. Therefore, our final model considers only 50 antecedents per span.

On the development set, the second-order model ($N = 2$) outperforms the first-order model by 0.8 F1, but the third order model only provides an additional 0.1 F1 improvement. Therefore, we only compute test results for the second-order model.

6 Results

We report the precision, recall, and F1 of the the MUC, B^3, and CEAF$_{\phi_4}$ metrics using the official CoNLL-2012 evaluation scripts. The main evaluation is the average F1 of the three metrics.

Results on the test set are shown in Table 1. We include performance of systems proposed in the past 3 years for reference. The baseline relative to our contributions is the span-ranking model from Lee et al. (2017) augmented with both ELMo and hyperparameter tuning, which achieves 72.3 F1. Our full approach achieves 73.0 F1, setting a new state of the art for coreference resolution.

Compared to the heuristic pruning with up to 250 antecedents, our coarse-to-fine model only computes the expensive scores $s_a(i, j)$ for 50 antecedents. Despite using far less computation, it outperforms the baseline because the coarse scores

---

[1] https://github.com/kentonl/e2e-coref

$s_c(i, j)$ can be computed for all antecedents, enabling the model to potentially predict a coreference link between any two spans in the document. As a result, we observe a much higher recall when adopting the coarse-to-fine approach.

We also observe further improvement by including the second-order inference (Section 3). The improvement is largely driven by the overall increase in precision, which is expected since the higher-order inference mainly serves to rule out inconsistent clusters. It is also consistent with findings from Martschat and Strube (2015) who report mainly improvements in precision when modeling latent trees to achieve a similar goal.

7 Related Work

In addition to the end-to-end span-ranking model (Lee et al., 2017) that our proposed model builds upon, there is a large body of literature on coreference resolvers that fundamentally rely on scoring span pairs (Ng and Cardie, 2002; Bengtson and Roth, 2008; Denis and Baldridge, 2008; Fernandes et al., 2012; Durrett and Klein, 2013; Wiseman et al., 2015; Clark and Manning, 2016a).

Motivated by structural consistency issues discussed above, significant effort has also been devoted towards cluster-level modeling. Since global features are notoriously difficult to define (Wiseman et al., 2016), they often depend heavily on existing pairwise features or architectures (Björkelund and Kuhn, 2014; Clark and Manning, 2015, 2016b). We similarly use an existing pairwise span-ranking architecture as a building block for modeling more complex structures. In contrast to Wiseman et al. (2016) who use highly expressive recurrent neural networks to model clusters, we show that the addition of a relatively lightweight gating mechanism is sufficient to effectively model higher-order structures.

8 Conclusion

We presented a state-of-the-art coreference resolution system that models higher order interactions between spans in predicted clusters. Additionally, our proposed coarse-to-fine approach alleviates the additional computational cost of higher-order inference, while maintaining the end-to-end learnability of the entire model.

Acknowledgements

The research was supported in part by DARPA under the DEFT program (FA8750-13-2-0019), the ARO (W911NF-16-1-0121), the NSF (IIS-1252835, IIS-1562364), gifts from Google and Tencent, and an Allen Distinguished Investigator Award. We also thank the UW NLP group for helpful conversations and comments on the work.

References

Eric Bengtson and Dan Roth. 2008. Understanding the value of features for coreference resolution. In *EMNLP*.

Anders Björkelund and Jonas Kuhn. 2014. Learning structured perceptrons for coreference resolution with latent antecedents and non-local features. In *ACL*.

Kevin Clark and Christopher D. Manning. 2015. Entity-centric coreference resolution with model stacking. In *ACL*.

Kevin Clark and Christopher D. Manning. 2016a. Deep reinforcement learning for mention-ranking coreference models. In *EMNLP*.

Kevin Clark and Christopher D. Manning. 2016b. Improving coreference resolution by learning entity-level distributed representations. In *ACL*.

Pascal Denis and Jason Baldridge. 2008. Specialized models and ranking for coreference resolution. In *EMNLP*.

Greg Durrett and Dan Klein. 2013. Easy victories and uphill battles in coreference resolution. In *EMNLP*.

Eraldo Rezende Fernandes, Cícero Nogueira Dos Santos, and Ruy Luiz Milidiú. 2012. Latent structure perceptron with feature induction for unrestricted coreference resolution. In *CoNLL*.

Sepp Hochreiter and Jürgen Schmidhuber. 1997. Long Short-term Memory. *Neural computation*.

Kenton Lee, Luheng He, Mike Lewis, and Luke S. Zettlemoyer. 2017. End-to-end neural coreference resolution. In *EMNLP*.

Sebastian Martschat and Michael Strube. 2015. Latent structures for coreference resolution. *TACL*.

Vincent Ng and Claire Cardie. 2002. Identifying anaphoric and non-anaphoric noun phrases to improve coreference resolution. *Computational linguistics*.

Jeffrey Pennington, Richard Socher, and Christopher D. Manning. 2014. Glove: Global vectors for word representation. In *EMNLP*.

Matthew E. Peters, Mark Neumann, Mohit Iyyer, Matt Gardner, Christopher Clark, Kenton Lee, and Luke Zettlemoyer. 2018. Deep contextualized word representations. In *HLT-NAACL*.

Sameer Pradhan, Alessandro Moschitti, Nianwen Xue, Olga Uryupina, and Yuchen Zhang. 2012. Conll-2012 shared task: Modeling multilingual unrestricted coreference in ontonotes. In *CoNLL*.

Sam Wiseman, Alexander M Rush, and Stuart M Shieber. 2016. Learning global features for coreference resolution. In *NAACL-HLT*.

Sam Wiseman, Alexander M. Rush, Stuart M. Shieber, and Jason Weston. 2015. Learning anaphoricity and antecedent ranking features for coreference resolution. In *ACL*.

Non-Projective Dependency Parsing with Non-Local Transitions

Daniel Fernández-González and **Carlos Gómez-Rodríguez**
Universidade da Coruña
FASTPARSE Lab, LyS Research Group, Departamento de Computación
Campus de Elviña, s/n, 15071 A Coruña, Spain
d.fgonzalez@udc.es, carlos.gomez@udc.es

Abstract

We present a novel transition system, based on the Covington non-projective parser, introducing non-local transitions that can directly create arcs involving nodes to the left of the current focus positions. This avoids the need for long sequences of No-Arc transitions to create long-distance arcs, thus alleviating error propagation. The resulting parser outperforms the original version and achieves the best accuracy on the Stanford Dependencies conversion of the Penn Treebank among greedy transition-based parsers.

1 Introduction

Greedy transition-based parsers are popular in NLP, as they provide competitive accuracy with high efficiency. They syntactically analyze a sentence by greedily applying transitions, which read it from left to right and produce a dependency tree.

However, this greedy process is prone to error propagation: one wrong choice of transition can lead the parser to an erroneous state, causing more incorrect decisions. This is especially crucial for long attachments requiring a larger number of transitions. In addition, transition-based parsers traditionally focus on only two words of the sentence and their local context to choose the next transition. The lack of a global perspective favors the presence of errors when creating arcs involving multiple transitions. As expected, transition-based parsers build short arcs more accurately than long ones (McDonald and Nivre, 2007).

Previous research such as (Fernández-González and Gómez-Rodríguez, 2012) and (Qi and Manning, 2017) proves that the widely-used projective *arc-eager* transition-based parser of Nivre (2003) benefits from shortening the length of transition sequences by creating non-local attachments. In particular, they augmented the original transition system with new actions whose behavior entails more than one arc-eager transition and involves a context beyond the traditional two focus words. Attardi (2006) and Sartorio et al. (2013) also extended the *arc-standard* transition-based algorithm (Nivre, 2004) with the same success.

In the same vein, we present a novel unrestricted non-projective transition system based on the well-known algorithm by Covington (2001) that shortens the transition sequence necessary to parse a given sentence by the original algorithm, which becomes linear instead of quadratic with respect to sentence length. To achieve that, we propose new transitions that affect non-local words and are equivalent to one or more Covington actions, in a similar way to the transitions defined by Qi and Manning (2017) based on the arc-eager parser. Experiments show that this novel variant significantly outperforms the original one in all datasets tested, and achieves the best reported accuracy for a greedy dependency parser on the Stanford Dependencies conversion of the WSJ Penn Treebank.

2 Non-Projective Covington Parser

The original non-projective parser defined by Covington (2001) was modelled under the transition-based parsing framework by Nivre (2008). We only sketch this transition system briefly for space reasons, and refer to (Nivre, 2008) for details.

Parser configurations have the form $c = \langle \lambda_1, \lambda_2, B, A \rangle$, where λ_1 and λ_2 are lists of partially processed words, B a list (called buffer) of unprocessed words, and A the set of dependency arcs built so far. Given an input string $w_1 \cdots w_n$, the parser starts at the initial configuration $c_s(w_1 \ldots w_n) = \langle [], [], [1 \ldots n], \emptyset \rangle$ and runs transitions until a terminal configuration of the

Proceedings of NAACL-HLT 2018, pages 693–700
New Orleans, Louisiana, June 1 - 6, 2018. ©2018 Association for Computational Linguistics

$$
\begin{array}{lll}
\textit{Covington:} & \text{Shift:} & \langle \lambda_1, \lambda_2, j | B, A \rangle \Rightarrow \langle \lambda_1 \cdot \lambda_2 | j, [], B, A \rangle \\[2pt]
& \text{No-Arc:} & \langle \lambda_1 | i, \lambda_2, B, A \rangle \Rightarrow \langle \lambda_1, i | \lambda_2, B, A \rangle \\[2pt]
& \text{Left-Arc:} & \langle \lambda_1 | i, \lambda_2, j | B, A \rangle \Rightarrow \langle \lambda_1, i | \lambda_2, j | B, A \cup \{j \rightarrow i\} \rangle \\
& & \text{only if } \nexists x \mid x \rightarrow i \in A \text{ (single-head) and } i \rightarrow^* j \notin A \text{ (acyclicity).} \\[2pt]
& \text{Right-Arc:} & \langle \lambda_1 | i, \lambda_2, j | B, A \rangle \Rightarrow \langle \lambda_1, i | \lambda_2, j | B, A \cup \{i \rightarrow j\} \rangle \\
& & \text{only if } \nexists x \mid x \rightarrow j \in A \text{ (single-head) and } j \rightarrow^* i \notin A \text{ (acyclicity).} \\[8pt]
\textit{NL-Covington:} & \text{Shift:} & \langle \lambda_1, \lambda_2, j | B, A \rangle \Rightarrow \langle \lambda_1 \cdot \lambda_2 | j, [], B, A \rangle \\[2pt]
& \text{Left-Arc}_k: & \langle \lambda_1 | i_k | ... | i_1, \lambda_2, j | B, A \rangle \Rightarrow \langle \lambda_1, i_k | ... | i_1 | \lambda_2, j | B, A \cup \{j \rightarrow i_k\} \rangle \\
& & \text{only if } \nexists x \mid x \rightarrow i_k \in A \text{ (single-head) and } i_k \rightarrow^* j \notin A \text{ (acyclicity).} \\[2pt]
& \text{Right-Arc}_k: & \langle \lambda_1 | i_k | ... | i_1, \lambda_2, j | B, A \rangle \Rightarrow \langle \lambda_1, i_k | ... | i_1 | \lambda_2, j | B, A \cup \{i_k \rightarrow j\} \rangle \\
& & \text{only if } \nexists x \mid x \rightarrow j \in A \text{ (single-head) and } j \rightarrow^* i_k \notin A \text{ (acyclicity).}
\end{array}
$$

Figure 1: Transitions of the non-projective Covington (top) and NL-Covington (bottom) dependency parsers. The notation $i \rightarrow^* j \in A$ means that there is a (possibly empty) directed path from i to j in A.

form $\langle \lambda_1, \lambda_2, [], A \rangle$ is reached: at that point, A contains the dependency graph for the input.[1]

The set of transitions is shown in the top half of Figure 1. Their logic can be summarized as follows: when in a configuration of the form $\langle \lambda_1 | i, \lambda_2, j | B, A \rangle$, the parser has the chance to create a dependency involving words i and j, which we will call left and right focus words of that configuration. The Left-Arc and Right-Arc transitions are used to create a leftward ($i \leftarrow j$) or rightward arc ($i \rightarrow j$), respectively, between these words, and also move i from λ_1 to the first position of λ_2, effectively moving the focus to $i - 1$ and j. If no dependency is desired between the focus words, the No-Arc transition makes the same modification of λ_1 and λ_2, but without building any arc. Finally, the Shift transition moves the whole content of the list λ_2 plus j to λ_1 when no more attachments are pending between j and the words of λ_1, thus reading a new input word and placing the focus on j and $j + 1$. Transitions that create arcs are disallowed in configurations where this would violate the single-head or acyclicity constraints (cycles and nodes with multiple heads are not allowed in the dependency graph). Figure 3 shows the transition sequence in the Covington transition system which derives the dependency graph in Figure 2.

The resulting parser can generate arbitrary non-projective trees, and its complexity is $O(n^2)$.

3   Non-Projective NL-Covington Parser

The original logic described by Covington (2001) parses a sentence by systematically traversing

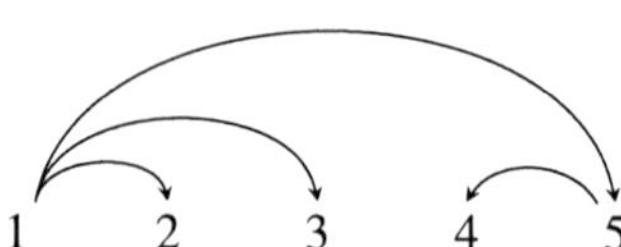

Figure 2: Dependency tree for an input sentence.

Tran.	λ_1	λ_2	Buffer	Arc
	[ ]	[ ]	[1, 2, 3, 4, 5]	
SH	[1]	[ ]	[2, 3, 4, 5]	
RA	[ ]	[1]	[2, 3, 4, 5]	$1 \rightarrow 2$
SH	[1, 2]	[ ]	[3, 4, 5]	
NA	[1]	[2]	[3, 4, 5]	
RA	[ ]	[1, 2]	[3, 4, 5]	$1 \rightarrow 3$
SH	[1, 2, 3]	[ ]	[4, 5]	
SH	[1, 2, 3, 4]	[ ]	[5]	
LA	[1, 2, 3]	[4]	[5]	$4 \leftarrow 5$
NA	[1, 2]	[3, 4]	[5]	
NA	[1]	[2, 3, 4]	[5]	
RA	[ ]	[1, 2, 3, 4]	[5]	$1 \rightarrow 5$
SH	[1, 2, 3, 4, 5]	[ ]	[ ]	

Figure 3: Transition sequence for parsing the sentence in Figure 2 using the Covington parser (LA=LEFT-ARC, RA=RIGHT-ARC, NA=NO-ARC, SH=SHIFT).

every pair of words. The Shift transition, introduced by Nivre (2008) in the transition-based version, is an optimization that avoids the need to apply a sequence of No-Arc transitions to empty the list λ_1 before reading a new input word.

However, there are still situations where sequences of No-Arc transitions are needed. For example, if we are in a configuration C with focus words i and j and the next arc we need to create

---

[1] Note that, in general, A is a forest, but it can be converted to a tree by linking headless nodes as dependents of an artificial root node at position 0.

goes from j to $i - k$ $(k > 1)$, then we will need $k - 1$ consecutive No-Arc transitions to move the left focus word to i and then apply Left-Arc. This could be avoided if a non-local Left-Arc transition could be undertaken directly at C, creating the required arc and moving k words to λ_2 at once. The advantage of such approach would be twofold: (1) less risk of making a mistake at C due to considering a limited local context, and (2) shorter transition sequence, alleviating error propagation.

We present a novel transition system called *NL-Covington* (for "non-local Covington"), described in the bottom half of Figure 1. It consists in a modification of the non-projective Covington algorithm where: (1) the Left-Arc and Right-Arc transitions are parameterized with k, allowing the immediate creation of any attachment between j and the kth leftmost word in λ_1 and moving k words to λ_2 at once, and (2) the No-Arc transition is removed since it is no longer necessary.

This new transition system can use some restricted global information to build non-local dependencies and, consequently, reduce the number of transitions needed to parse the input. For instance, as presented in Figure 4, the NL-Covington parser will need 9 transitions, instead of 12 traditional Covington actions, to analyze the sentence in Figure 2.

In fact, while in the standard Covington algorithm a transition sequence for a sentence of length n has length $O(n^2)$ in the worst case (if all nodes are connected to the first node, then we need to traverse every node to the left of each right focus word); for NL-Covington the sequence length is always $O(n)$: one Shift transition for each of the n words, plus one arc-building transition for each of the $n - 1$ arcs in the dependency tree. Note, however, that this does not affect the parser's time complexity, which is still quadratic as in the original Covington parser. This is because the algorithm has $O(n)$ possible transitions to be scored at each configuration, while the original Covington has $O(1)$ transitions due to being limited to creating local leftward/rightward arcs between the focus words.

The completeness and soundness of NL-Covington can easily be proved as there is a mapping between transition sequences of both parsers, where a sequence of $k - 1$ No-Arc and one arc transition in Covington is equivalent to a Left-Arc$_k$ or Right-Arc$_k$ in NL-Covington.

Tran.	λ_1	λ_2	Buffer	Arc
	[ ]	[ ]	[1, 2, 3, 4, 5]	
SH	[1]	[ ]	[2, 3, 4, 5]	
RA$_1$	[ ]	[1]	[2, 3, 4, 5]	$1 \rightarrow 2$
SH	[1, 2]	[ ]	[3, 4, 5]	
RA$_2$	[ ]	[1, 2]	[3, 4, 5]	$1 \rightarrow 3$
SH	[1, 2, 3]	[ ]	[4, 5]	
SH	[1, 2, 3, 4]	[ ]	[5]	
LA$_1$	[1, 2, 3]	[4]	[5]	$4 \leftarrow 5$
RA$_3$	[ ]	[1, 2, 3, 4]	[5]	$1 \rightarrow 5$
SH	[1, 2, 3, 4, 5]	[ ]	[ ]	

Figure 4: Transition sequence for parsing the sentence in Figure 2 using the NL-Covington parser (LA=LEFT-ARC, RA=RIGHT-ARC, SH=SHIFT).

4 Experiments

4.1 Data and Evaluation

We use 9 datasets[2] from the CoNLL-X (Buchholz and Marsi, 2006) and all datasets from the CoNLL-XI shared task (Nivre et al., 2007). To compare our system to the current state-of-the-art transition-based parsers, we also evaluate it on the Stanford Dependencies (de Marneffe and Manning, 2008) conversion (using the Stanford parser v3.3.0)[3] of the WSJ Penn Treebank (Marcus et al., 1993), hereinafter PT-SD, with standard splits. Labelled and Unlabelled Attachment Scores (LAS and UAS) are computed excluding punctuation only on the PT-SD, for comparability. We repeat each experiment with three independent random initializations and report the average accuracy. Statistical significance is assessed by a paired test with 10,000 bootstrap samples.

4.2 Model

To implement our approach we take advantage of the model architecture described in Qi and Manning (2017) for the *arc-swift* parser, which extends the architecture of Kiperwasser and Goldberg (2016) by applying a biaffine combination during the featurization process. We implement both the Covington and NL-Covington parsers under this architecture, adapt the featurization process with biaffine combination of Qi and Manning (2017) to these parsers, and use their same training

---

[2]We excluded the languages from CoNLL-X that also appeared in CoNLL-XI, i.e., if a language was present in both shared tasks, we used the latest version.

[3]`https://nlp.stanford.edu/software/lex-parser.shtml`

Language	Covington		NL-Covington	
	UAS	LAS	UAS	LAS
Arabic	66.67	53.24	**68.69**	**54.59**
Basque	74.31	66.18	**75.45**	**67.61**
Catalan	91.93	86.12	**92.60**	**86.99**
Chinese	83.87	76.19	**85.25**	**77.56**
Czech	84.27	77.91	**86.26**	**79.95**
English	89.94	88.74	**91.51**	**90.47**
Greek	79.91	72.65	**80.61**	**73.41**
Hungarian	76.80	65.21	**78.57**	**67.51**
Italian	82.03	75.87	**83.63**	**78.03**
Turkish	80.29	70.68	**81.30**	**71.28**
Bulgarian	81.78	76.23	**83.65**	**78.40**
Danish	86.56	81.18	**88.40**	**82.77**
Dutch	86.19	82.24	**87.45**	**83.76**
German	85.72	82.28	**87.24**	**83.92**
Japanese	92.20	90.41	**93.63**	**91.65**
Portuguese	86.69	82.19	**87.89**	**83.69**
Slovene	76.07	66.81	**77.83**	**69.74**
Spanish	74.67	69.41	**76.58**	**71.60**
Swedish	74.65	64.67	**75.62**	**65.95**
Average	81.82	75.17	**83.27**	**76.78**

Table 1: Parsing accuracy (UAS and LAS, including punctuation) of the Covington and NL-Covington non-projective parsers on CoNLL-XI (first block) and CoNLL-X (second block) datasets. Best results for each language are shown in bold. All improvements in this table are statistically significant ($\alpha = .05$).

setup. More details about these model parameters are provided in Appendix A.

Since this architecture uses batch training, we train with a static oracle. The NL-Covington algorithm has no spurious ambiguity at all, so there is only one possible static oracle: canonical transition sequences are generated by choosing the transition that builds the shortest pending gold arc involving the current right focus word j, or Shift if there are no unbuilt gold arcs involving j.

We note that a dynamic oracle can be obtained for the NL-Covington parser by adapting the one for standard Covington of Gómez-Rodríguez and Fernández-González (2015). As NL-Covington transitions are concatenations of Covington ones, their loss calculation algorithm is compatible with NL-Covington. Apart from error exploration, this also opens the way to incorporating non-monotonicity (Fernández-González and Gómez-Rodríguez, 2017). While these approaches have shown to improve accuracy under online training settings, here we prioritize homogeneous comparability to (Qi and Manning, 2017), so we use batch training and a static oracle, and still obtain state-of-the-art accuracy for a greedy parser.

Parser	Type	UAS	LAS
(Chen and Manning, 2014)	gs	91.8	89.6
(Dyer et al., 2015)	gs	93.1	90.9
(Weiss et al., 2015) greedy	gs	93.2	91.2
(Ballesteros et al., 2016)	gd	93.5	91.4
(Kiperwasser and Goldberg, 2016)	gd	93.9	91.9
(Qi and Manning, 2017)	gs	94.3	92.2
This work	gs	**94.5**	**92.4**
(Weiss et al., 2015) beam	b(8)	94.0	92.1
(Alberti et al., 2015)	b(32)	94.2	92.4
(Andor et al., 2016)	b(32)	94.6	92.8
(Shi et al., 2017)	dp	94.5	-
(Kuncoro et al., 2017) (constit.)	c	95.8	94.6

Table 2: Accuracy comparison of state-of-the-art transition-based dependency parsers on PT-SD. The "Type" column shows the type of parser: *gs* is a greedy parser trained with a static oracle, *gd* a greedy parser trained with a dynamic oracle, *b(n)* a beam search parser with beam size n, *dp* a parser that employs global training with dynamic programming, and *c* a constituent parser with conversion to dependencies.

4.3 Results

Table 1 presents a comparison between the Covington parser and the novel variant developed here. The NL-Covington parser outperforms the original version in all datasets tested, with all improvements statistically significant ($\alpha = .05$).

Table 2 compares our novel system with other state-of-the-art transition-based dependency parsers on the PT-SD. Greedy parsers are in the first block, beam-search and dynamic programming parsers in the second block. The third block shows the best result on this benchmark, obtained with constituent parsing with generative re-ranking and conversion to dependencies. Despite being the only non-projective parser tested on a practically projective dataset,[4] our parser achieves the highest score among greedy transition-based models (even above those trained with a dynamic oracle).

We even slightly outperform the arc-swift system of Qi and Manning (2017), with the same model architecture, implementation and training setup, but based on the projective arc-eager transition-based parser instead. This may be because our system takes into consideration any permissible attachment between the focus word j and any word in λ_1 at each configuration, while their approach is limited by the arc-eager logic: it al-

---

[4]Only 41 out of 39,832 sentences of the PT-SD training dataset present some kind of non-projectivity.

Language	Arc-swift		NL-Covington	
	UAS	LAS	UAS	LAS
Arabic	67.54	53.65	**68.69***	**54.59***
Basque	74.88	67.44	**75.45**	**67.61**
Catalan	**92.98**	**87.51***	92.60	86.99
Chinese	84.96	77.34	**85.25**	**77.56**
Czech	85.92	79.82	**86.26**	**79.95**
English	91.41	90.43	**91.51**	**90.47**
Greek	**81.64***	**74.56***	80.61	73.41
Hungarian	**78.70**	**69.27***	78.57	67.51
Italian	83.29	**78.60***	**83.63**	78.03
Turkish	79.56	70.22	**81.30***	**71.28***
Bulgarian	83.28	78.19	**83.65**	**78.40**
Danish	87.86	82.58	**88.40***	**82.77**
Dutch	83.27	80.14	**87.45***	**83.76***
German	86.28	82.97	**87.24***	**83.92***
Japanese	**93.64**	**91.92**	93.63	91.65
Portuguese	87.01	83.09	**87.89***	**83.69***
Slovene	**77.89**	69.37	77.83	**69.74**
Spanish	75.55	70.62	**76.58***	**71.60***
Swedish	75.00	65.66	**75.62**	**65.95**
Average	82.67	76.49	**83.27**	**76.78**

Table 3: Parsing accuracy (UAS and LAS, with punctuation) of the arc-swift and NL-Covington parsers on CoNLL-XI (1st block) and CoNLL-X (2nd block) datasets. Best results for each language are in bold. * indicates statistically significant improvements ($\alpha = .05$).

Language	Covington trans./sent.	NL-Covington trans./sent.
Arabic	194.80	**78.22**
Basque	46.74	**30.13**
Catalan	117.35	**60.07**
Chinese	19.12	**14.95**
Czech	60.62	**33.03**
English	78.01	**46.75**
Greek	89.23	**48.77**
Hungarian	68.54	**37.66**
Italian	63.67	**40.93**
Turkish	53.53	**30.08**
Bulgarian	51.35	**29.81**
Danish	66.77	**36.34**
Dutch	42.78	**28.93**
German	61.16	**31.89**
Japanese	24.30	**16.11**
Portuguese	76.14	**40.74**
Slovene	56.15	**31.79**
Spanish	109.70	**55.28**
Swedish	48.59	**29.07**
PTB-SD	81.65	**46.92**
Average	70.51	**38.37**

Table 4: Average transitions executed per sentence (trans./sent.) when analyzing each dataset by the original Covington and NL-Covington algorithms.

lows all possible rightward arcs (possibly fewer than our approach as the arc-eager stack usually contains a small number of words), but only one leftward arc is permitted per parser state. It is also worth noting that the arc-swift and NL-Covington parsers have the same worst-case time complexity, ($O(n^2)$), as adding non-local arc transitions to the arc-eager parser increases its complexity from linear to quadratic, but it does not affect the complexity of the Covington algorithm. Thus, it can be argued that this technique is better suited to Covington than to arc-eager parsing.

We also compare NL-Covington to the arc-swift parser on the CoNLL datasets (Table 3). For fairness of comparison, we projectivize (via maltparser[5]) all training datasets, instead of filtering non-projective sentences, as some of the languages are significantly non-projective. Even doing that, the NL-Covington parser improves over the arc-swift system in terms of UAS in 14 out of 19 datasets, obtaining statistically significant improvements in accuracy on 7 of them, and statistically significant decreases in just one.

Finally, we analyze how our approach reduces the length of the transition sequence consumed by

the original Covington parser. In Table 4 we report the transition sequence length per sentence used by the Covington and the NL-Covington algorithms to analyze each dataset from the same benchmark used for evaluating parsing accuracy. As seen in the table, NL-Covington produces notably shorter transition sequences than Covington, with a reduction close to 50% on average.

5 Conclusion

We present a novel variant of the non-projective Covington transition-based parser by incorporating non-local transitions, reducing the length of transition sequences from $O(n^2)$ to $O(n)$. This system clearly outperforms the original Covington parser and achieves the highest accuracy on the WSJ Penn Treebank (Stanford Dependencies) obtained to date with greedy dependency parsing.

Acknowledgments

This work has received funding from the European Research Council (ERC), under the European Union's Horizon 2020 research and innovation programme (FASTPARSE, grant agreement No 714150), from the TELEPARES-UDC (FFI2014-51978-C2-2-R) and ANSWER-ASAP (TIN2017-85160-C2-1-R) projects from MINECO, and from Xunta de Galicia (ED431B 2017/01).

[5] http://www.maltparser.org/

References

Chris Alberti, David Weiss, Greg Coppola, and Slav Petrov. 2015. Improved transition-based parsing and tagging with neural networks. In *Proceedings of the 2015 Conference on Empirical Methods in Natural Language Processing, EMNLP 2015, Lisbon, Portugal, September 17-21, 2015*. pages 1354–1359. http://aclweb.org/anthology/D/D15/D15-1159.pdf.

Daniel Andor, Chris Alberti, David Weiss, Aliaksei Severyn, Alessandro Presta, Kuzman Ganchev, Slav Petrov, and Michael Collins. 2016. Globally normalized transition-based neural networks. In *Proceedings of the 54th Annual Meeting of the Association for Computational Linguistics, ACL 2016, August 7-12, 2016, Berlin, Germany, Volume 1: Long Papers*. http://aclweb.org/anthology/P/P16/P16-1231.pdf.

Giuseppe Attardi. 2006. Experiments with a multilanguage non-projective dependency parser. In *Proceedings of the 10th Conference on Computational Natural Language Learning (CoNLL)*. pages 166–170.

Miguel Ballesteros, Yoav Goldberg, Chris Dyer, and Noah A. Smith. 2016. Training with exploration improves a greedy stack-lstm parser. *CoRR* abs/1603.03793. http://arxiv.org/abs/1603.03793.

Piotr Bojanowski, Edouard Grave, Armand Joulin, and Tomas Mikolov. 2016. Enriching word vectors with subword information. *arXiv preprint arXiv:1607.04606* .

Sabine Buchholz and Erwin Marsi. 2006. CoNLL-X shared task on multilingual dependency parsing. In *Proceedings of the 10th Conference on Computational Natural Language Learning (CoNLL)*. pages 149–164. http://www.aclweb.org/anthology/W06-2920.

Danqi Chen and Christopher Manning. 2014. A fast and accurate dependency parser using neural networks. In *Proceedings of the 2014 Conference on Empirical Methods in Natural Language Processing (EMNLP)*. Doha, Qatar, pages 740–750. http://www.aclweb.org/anthology/D14-1082.

Michael A. Covington. 2001. A fundamental algorithm for dependency parsing. In *Proceedings of the 39th Annual ACM Southeast Conference*. ACM, New York, NY, USA, pages 95–102.

Marie-Catherine de Marneffe and Christopher D. Manning. 2008. The stanford typed dependencies representation. In *Coling 2008: Proceedings of the Workshop on Cross-Framework and Cross-Domain Parser Evaluation*. Association for Computational Linguistics, Stroudsburg, PA, USA, CrossParser '08, pages 1–8. http://dl.acm.org/citation.cfm?id=1608858.1608859.

Chris Dyer, Miguel Ballesteros, Wang Ling, Austin Matthews, and Noah A. Smith. 2015. Transition-based dependency parsing with stack long short-term memory. In *Proceedings of the 53rd Annual Meeting of the Association for Computational Linguistics and the 7th International Joint Conference on Natural Language Processing of the Asian Federation of Natural Language Processing, ACL 2015, July 26-31, 2015, Beijing, China, Volume 1: Long Papers*. pages 334–343. http://aclweb.org/anthology/P/P15/P15-1033.pdf.

Daniel Fernández-González and Carlos Gómez-Rodríguez. 2012. Improving transition-based dependency parsing with buffer transitions. In *Proceedings of the 2012 Joint Conference on Empirical Methods in Natural Language Processing and Computational Natural Language Learning*. Association for Computational Linguistics, pages 308–319. http://aclweb.org/anthology/D/D12/D12-1029.pdf.

Daniel Fernández-González and Carlos Gómez-Rodríguez. 2017. A full non-monotonic transition system for unrestricted non-projective parsing. In *Proceedings of the 55th Annual Meeting of the Association for Computational Linguistics (Volume 1: Long Papers)*. Association for Computational Linguistics, Vancouver, Canada, pages 288–298. http://aclweb.org/anthology/P17-1027.

Carlos Gómez-Rodríguez and Daniel Fernández-González. 2015. An efficient dynamic oracle for unrestricted non-projective parsing. In *Proceedings of the 53rd Annual Meeting of the Association for Computational Linguistics and the 7th International Joint Conference on Natural Language Processing (ACL-IJCNLP 2015). Volume 2: Short Papers*. Association for Computational Linguistics, Beijing, China, pages 256–261. http://www.aclweb.org/anthology/P15-2042.

Alex Graves and Jürgen Schmidhuber. 2005. Framewise phoneme classification with bidirectional lstm and other neural network architectures. *Neural Networks* pages 5–6.

Eliyahu Kiperwasser and Yoav Goldberg. 2016. Simple and accurate dependency parsing using bidirectional LSTM feature representations. *TACL* 4:313–327. https://transacl.org/ojs/index.php/tacl/article/view/885.

Adhiguna Kuncoro, Miguel Ballesteros, Lingpeng Kong, Chris Dyer, Graham Neubig, and Noah A. Smith. 2017. What do recurrent neural network grammars learn about syntax? In *Proceedings of the 15th Conference of the European Chapter of the Association for Computational Linguistics: Volume 1, Long Papers*. Association for Computational Linguistics, pages 1249–1258. http://aclanthology.coli.uni-saarland.de/pdf/E/E17/E17-1117.pdf.

Mitchell P. Marcus, Beatrice Santorini, and Mary Ann Marcinkiewicz. 1993. Building a large annotated corpus of English: The Penn Treebank. *Computational Linguistics* 19:313–330.

Ryan McDonald and Joakim Nivre. 2007. Characterizing the errors of data-driven dependency parsing models. In *Proceedings of the 2007 Joint Conference on Empirical Methods in Natural Language Processing and Computational Natural Language Learning (EMNLP-CoNLL)*. pages 122–131.

Joakim Nivre. 2003. An efficient algorithm for projective dependency parsing. In *Proceedings of the 8th International Workshop on Parsing Technologies (IWPT 03)*. ACL/SIGPARSE, pages 149–160.

Joakim Nivre. 2004. Incrementality in deterministic dependency parsing. In *Proceedings of the Workshop on Incremental Parsing: Bringing Engineering and Cognition Together (ACL)*. pages 50–57.

Joakim Nivre. 2008. Algorithms for Deterministic Incremental Dependency Parsing. *Computational Linguistics* 34(4):513–553. https://doi.org/10.1162/coli.07-056-R1-07-027.

Joakim Nivre, Johan Hall, Sandra Kübler, Ryan McDonald, Jens Nilsson, Sebastian Riedel, and Deniz Yuret. 2007. The CoNLL 2007 shared task on dependency parsing. In *Proceedings of the CoNLL Shared Task Session of EMNLP-CoNLL 2007*. pages 915–932. http://www.aclweb.org/anthology/D/D07/D07-1096.pdf.

Jeffrey Pennington, Richard Socher, and Christopher D. Manning. 2014. Glove: Global vectors for word representation. In *Empirical Methods in Natural Language Processing (EMNLP)*. pages 1532–1543. http://www.aclweb.org/anthology/D14-1162.

Peng Qi and Christopher D. Manning. 2017. Arc-swift: A novel transition system for dependency parsing. In *Proceedings of the 55th Annual Meeting of the Association for Computational Linguistics, ACL 2017, Vancouver, Canada, July 30 - August 4, Volume 2: Short Papers*. pages 110–117. https://doi.org/10.18653/v1/P17-2018.

Francesco Sartorio, Giorgio Satta, and Joakim Nivre. 2013. A transition-based dependency parser using a dynamic parsing strategy. In *Proceedings of the 51st Annual Meeting of the Association for Computational Linguistics (Volume 1: Long Papers)*. Association for Computational Linguistics, pages 135–144. http://aclanthology.coli.uni-saarland.de/pdf/P/P13/P13-1014.pdf.

Tianze Shi, Liang Huang, and Lillian Lee. 2017. Fast(er) exact decoding and global training for transition-based dependency parsing via a minimal feature set. *CoRR* abs/1708.09403. http://arxiv.org/abs/1708.09403.

David Weiss, Chris Alberti, Michael Collins, and Slav Petrov. 2015. Structured training for neural network transition-based parsing. In *Proceedings of*

the 53rd Annual Meeting of the Association for Computational Linguistics and the 7th International Joint Conference on Natural Language Processing of the Asian Federation of Natural Language Processing, ACL 2015, July 26-31, 2015, Beijing, China, Volume 1: Long Papers. pages 323–333. http://aclweb.org/anthology/P/P15/P15-1032.pdf.

A Model Details

We provide more details of the neural network architecture used in this paper, which is taken from Qi and Manning (2017).

The model consists of two blocks of 2-layered bidirectional long short-term memory (BiLSTM) networks (Graves and Schmidhuber, 2005) with 400 hidden units in each direction. The first block is used for POS tagging and the second one, for parsing. As the input of the tagging block, we use words represented as word embeddings, and BiLSTMs are employed to perform feature extraction. The resulting output is fed into a multi-layer perceptron (MLP), with a hidden layer of 100 rectified linear units (ReLU), that provides a POS tag for each input token in a 32-dimensional representation. Word embeddings concatenated to these POS tag embeddings serve as input of the second block of BiLSTMs to undertake the parsing stage. Then, the output of the parsing block is fed into a MLP with two separate ReLU hidden layers (one for deriving the representation of the head, and the other for the dependency label) that, after being merged and by means of a softmax function, score all the feasible transitions, allowing to greedily choose and apply the highest-scoring one.

Moreover, we adapt the featurization process with biaffine combination described in Qi and Manning (2017) for the arc-swift system to be used on the original Covington and NL-Covington parsers. In particular, arc transitions are featurized by the concatenation of the representation of the head and dependent words of the arc to be created, the No-Arc transition is featurized by the rightmost word in λ_1 and the leftmost word in the buffer B and, finally, for the Shift transition only the leftmost word in B is used. Unlike Qi and Manning (2017) do for baseline parsers, we do not use the featurization method detailed in Kiperwasser and Goldberg (2016)[6] for the original Covington parser, as we observed that this results in lower

---

[6]For instance, Kiperwasser and Goldberg (2016) featurize all transitions of the arc-eager parser in the same way by concatenating the representations of the top 3 words on the stack and the leftmost word in the buffer.

scores and then the comparison would be unfair
in our case. We implement both systems under
the same framework, with the original Covington
parser represented as the NL-Covington system
plus the No-Arc transition and with k limited to
1. A thorough description of the model architecture and featurization mechanism can be found in
Qi and Manning (2017).

Our training setup is exactly the same used by
Qi and Manning (2017), training the models during 10 epochs for large datasets and 30 for small
ones. In addition, we initialize word embeddings
with 100-dimensional GloVe vectors (Pennington
et al., 2014) for English and use 300-dimensional
Facebook vectors (Bojanowski et al., 2016) for
other languages. The other parameters of the
neural network keep the same values.

The parser's source code is freely available at `https://github.com/danifg/`
`Non-Local-Covington`.

Detecting Linguistic Characteristics of Alzheimer's Dementia by Interpreting Neural Models

Sweta Karlekar   **Tong Niu**   **Mohit Bansal**

UNC Chapel Hill

{swetakar, tongn, mbansal}@cs.unc.edu

Abstract

Alzheimer's disease (AD) is an irreversible and progressive brain disease that can be stopped or slowed down with medical treatment. Language changes serve as a sign that a patient's cognitive functions have been impacted, potentially leading to early diagnosis. In this work, we use NLP techniques to classify and analyze the linguistic characteristics of AD patients using the DementiaBank dataset. We apply three neural models based on CNNs, LSTM-RNNs, and their combination, to distinguish between language samples from AD and control patients. We achieve a new independent benchmark accuracy for the AD classification task. More importantly, we next interpret what these neural models have learned about the linguistic characteristics of AD patients, via analysis based on activation clustering and first-derivative saliency techniques. We then perform novel automatic pattern discovery inside activation clusters, and consolidate AD patients' distinctive grammar patterns. Additionally, we show that first derivative saliency can not only rediscover previous language patterns of AD patients, but also shed light on the limitations of neural models. Lastly, we also include analysis of gender-separated AD data.

1   Introduction

Alzheimer's dementia is the most common form of dementia, caused by Alzheimer's disease (AD). AD cannot be cured or reversed (Glenner, 1990). However, medication can be used to slow or halt degeneration especially when detected at an early stage. Current diagnoses often involve lengthy medical evaluations. One of the early symptoms of AD, cognitive impairment—which can be evidenced by issues with word-finding, impaired reasoning or judgment, and changes in language (McKhann et al., 1984)—is motivating linguists and computer scientists to help quickly diagnose people afflicted by this disease.

This task is challenging because it requires diverse linguistic and world knowledge. For example, the sentence "Well...there's a mother standing there uh uh washing the dishes and the sink is overspilling...overflowing" is AD-positive. To distinguish this from a control sample, one needs to know that the word "overspill" is not common in American English (Davies, 2009), and the speaker is correcting themselves by saying "overspilling...overflowing", which hints on signs of confusion and memory loss (Duke et al., 2002). Moreover, different grammar patterns emerge based on the scenario at hand. In addition, the characteristics of AD-affected speech vary between stages of disease progression (König et al., 2015), making it harder for feature-based approaches to adapt.

Motivated by the shortcomings of manual feature-engineering for such a diverse and complex task, we first present three end-to-end neural models to address it. The first two are the widely adopted CNN and LSTM-RNN models, and the third is a stronger joint CNN-LSTM architecture. Our best-performing model requires only minimal feature engineering (namely automatic, commonly-used POS tags that are already present in the dataset) and establishes a new independent benchmark that outperforms previous AD classification scores.

More importantly, we next present interpretation results to explain what AD-relevant linguistic features these neural models are learning, via two visualization techniques: Activation Clustering (Girshick et al., 2014) and First Derivative Saliency (Simonyan et al., 2013), plus our novel approach of automatically discovering grammatical patterns common in different activation clusters. Furthermore, we split our dataset by gen-

701

Proceedings of NAACL-HLT 2018, pages 701–707

New Orleans, Louisiana, June 1 - 6, 2018. ©2018 Association for Computational Linguistics

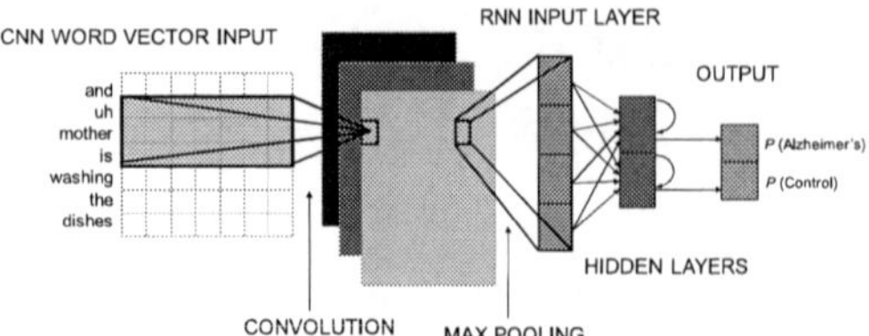

Figure 1: Our CNN-LSTM hybrid neural network.

der and analyze the performance of our model on each subsample of the data to illustrate that the features we find are not gender-specific. These methods not only help rediscover AD linguistic features that have been found by previous works—including short answers, bursts of speech, repeated requests for clarification, and starting with interjections—but also lead to new insights in AD characteristics via our automatic speech pattern extraction method. These findings could potentially help improve the accuracy and speed of medical diagnoses.

2 Related Works

Language-based Alzheimer's Detection: Previous works using language to detect AD relied mainly on hand-crafted features from transcripts (Orimaye et al., 2017, 2015), occasionally using acoustic data (König et al., 2015; Rudzicz et al., 2014). The challenge with feature-based approaches is that they rely heavily on the researchers' linguistics and medical expertise, and are also hard to generalize to other progression stages and disease types, which may correspond to different linguistic features. Hand-picked features may also become outdated as language and culture evolves. Moreover, some features may be too nuanced for humans to detect, especially at early stages of AD. In order to address these issues, Orimaye et al. (2016) adopted a deep neural network language model. However, a neural approach is usually a black-box and it is hard to interpret its reasoning for the final classification decisions. To make our approaches more interpretable while harvesting the benefits of neural approaches, we present three accurate neural models and include multiple visualization techniques to illustrate both their effectiveness and limitations.

CNN-LSTM on NL Classification: CNN and LSTM (Hochreiter and Schmidhuber, 1997) have both been leveraged extensively for extracting features in natural language. Our best performing model CNN-LSTM is closely related to C-LSTM by Zhou et al. (2015), where an LSTM is laid on

top of a CNN model. This model has been shown to perform better at sentiment classification than either of its integral parts alone.

Visualization Techniques for Neural Models: There have been various visualization techniques proposed for neural networks in both Computer Vision (Krizhevsky et al., 2012; Simonyan et al., 2013; Zeiler and Fergus, 2014; Samek et al., 2017; Mahendran and Vedaldi, 2015) and NLP (Li et al., 2015; Kádár et al., 2017). In this work, we adopt two visualization techniques: Activation Clustering (Girshick et al., 2014) following the politeness interpretation work of Aubakirova and Bansal (2016), which leads to insight on sentence-level patterns, and First Derivative Saliency (Simonyan et al., 2013) following Li et al. (2015) and Aubakirova and Bansal (2016), which provides insight to the importance of each word in deciding the final classification label.

3 Classification Models

CNN: For each sentence, we apply an embedding and a convolutional layer, followed by a max-pooling layer (Collobert et al., 2011). The convolution features are obtained by applying filters of varying window sizes to each window of words. The result is then passed to a softmax layer that outputs probabilities over two classes.

LSTM-RNN: CNNs are not specialized for capturing long-range sequential correlations (Pascanu et al., 2013a). We thus also experimented with an LSTM-RNN model, which consists of an embedding layer followed by an LSTM layer. The final state, containing information from the entire sentence, is fed to a fully-connected layer followed by a softmax layer to obtain the output probabilities.

CNN-LSTM: Observing that both models achieve results comparable to previous best performing approach, and considering that they each have their own complementary strengths, we experimented with a combined architecture, laying an LSTM layer on top of CNN (See Figure 1). This CNN layer is identical to the vanilla CNN before the max-pooling layer, and the LSTM layer is identical to the vanilla LSTM-RNN after the embedding layer. More details are provided in the appendix.

4 Experimental Setup

Dataset This study utilizes Dementia-Bank (Boller and Becker, 2005), the largest publicly available dataset of transcripts and

Figure 2: Boston cookie theft description task. Participants were asked to describe all events in the image.

audio recordings of AD (and control) patient interviews.[1] Patients were asked to perform various tasks; for example, in the "Boston Cookie Theft" description task, patients were shown an image and asked to describe what they see (See Figure 2). Other tasks include the 'Recall Test' in which patients were asked to recall attributes of a story they had been told previously. Each transcript in DementiaBank comes with automatic morphosyntactic analysis, such as standard part-of-speech tagging, description of tense, and repetition markers.[2] Note that these features are generic, automatically-extracted linguistic properties and are not AD-specific. We broke each transcript into individual utterances to use as data samples. Note that we also removed utterances that did not have accompanying POS tags. This balancing reduced the amount of data but ensured fair comparison between models with tagged and untagged setups.

Training Details Our CNN model was a 2-D convolutional neural network. Filter sizes of [3, 4, 5] were used. Our LSTM-RNN had 2 layers. The CNN-LSTM model had filter sizes [3, 4, 5, 6] and 1 LSTM hidden layer. For each model, all hyperparameters were tuned using the dev set.

See appendix for dataset and training details.

5   Results

With untagged data, our CNN, LSTM and CNN-LSTM models achieved an accuracy of 82.8%, 83.7% and 84.9%, respectively. When fed with the given POS-tagged data, our best-performing CNN-LSTM model achieved 91.1% in accuracy, setting a new benchmark accuracy for this task

Model	Details	Accuracy
2D-CNN	Non-Tagged Utterances	82.8
LSTM	Non-Tagged Utterances	83.7
CNN-RNN	Non-Tagged Utterances	84.9
CNN-RNN	POS-tagged Utterances	**91.1**

Table 1: Accuracy results of models. Note that we downsampled the data to remove utterances that did not have accompanying POS tags, so as to allow fair comparison between the tagged and untagged models.

(see Table 1 for more details).[3] Compared to other related works, Orimaye et al. (2015, 2017) used AUC instead of accuracy, and König et al. (2015) did not use DementiaBank data. Rudzicz et al. (2014) achieved an accuracy of 67.0% on the DementiaBank dataset using audio features as well as transcripts. Orimaye et al. (2016) achieved an accuracy of 87.5% but only used 36 transcripts. Their test set is thus different from ours, leading to very little data and high variance. To the best of our knowledge, Orimaye et al. (2016) used the original transcripts, which include POS tags. Hence, most previous works on this topic are not directly comparable to our work, but we aim to establish a new independent, strong neural benchmark and then more importantly focus on visualization and interpretability of neural models.

Based on error analysis of the POS-based CNN/RNN model's classification result, we found that almost all AD-positive results are classified correctly as AD-positive. However, there is more error in classifying non-AD samples, which could be due to the fact that DementiaBank includes patients with probable and possible AD, each exhibiting various degrees of symptoms. Patients who are AD-positive may still have partially unaffected speech (similar to non-AD control patients' speech). However, because all utterances from AD-positive interviews are tagged as AD-positive, these seemingly unaffected utterances are still tagged AD-positive. To further understand the errors of our model, 10% of the wrongly classified non-AD examples were randomly selected and analyzed. Of this smaller sample, 36.3% were short utterances such as *"okay"*, *"alright"*, *"oh my"*, etc. These forms of speech are utterances that are present in both classes, but more commonly found in AD-positive cases. The remaining 63.7% were examples of speech that could be classified either way without surrounding context, such as *"she's*

---

[3]We also tried using a bidirectional RNN, which gave 84.7%, 86.2% and 91.1% accuracies for our LSTM-RNN, CNN-RNN, and CNN-RNN-tagged models, respectively.

Non-AD Clusters - Cookie Task

POS	Freq	POS	Freq	POS	Freq
n	0.15	*n*	0.13	*n*	0.15
det	0.13	*det*	0.13	*det*	0.13
presp	0.07	*part*	0.09	*part*	0.10
part	0.05	*presp*	0.09	*presp*	0.10

Table 2: Top POS tags and frequencies for three non-AD clusters for the Cookie task.

AD		Non-AD	
POS	Frequency	POS	Frequency
n	0.20	*n*	0.15
det	0.14	*det*	0.13
adj	0.05	*presp*	0.07
adv	0.04	*part*	0.05

Table 3: Top POS tags in AD cluster and non-AD cluster for Cookie task.

drying dishes" and "*stool's tipping over*". Hence, future work could incorporate context from surrounding samples in each interview to help distinguish between temporarily unaffected speech patterns in AD-positive patients and the continually unaffected speech of non-AD control patients.

6 Analysis and Visualization

We first present gender analysis of our results and then present interpretation of the linguistic cues our CNN-LSTM model identified via two visualization strategies: activation clustering (Girshick et al., 2014) and first-derivative saliency heat maps (Simonyan et al., 2013).

6.1 Gender Differences

Many previous works have debated on the difference in language for male versus female patients with Alzheimer's (Bayles et al., 1999; McPherson et al., 1999; Buckwalter et al., 1996; Ripich et al., 1995; Hebert et al., 2000; Heun and Kockler, 2002). In agreement with some of these previous works, we found that the sets of the top ten most common POS-tags for both AD-positive men and women are the same, i.e., we did not detect a significant difference in the language complexity or syntax of male and female patients with AD in our dataset. Moreover, our best performing model achieved 86.6% classification accuracy on solely the male data and 86.2% accuracy on solely the female data, demonstrating that it found no statistically significant difference between the AD-positive language of men versus women.[4]

6.2 Activation Clusters

Activation clustering (Girshick et al., 2014) treats the activation values of n neurons per input as coordinates in an n-dimensional space. K-means clustering is then performed to group together inputs that maximally activate similar neurons.

6.2.1 Rediscovering Existing Strategies

Our activation clusters corroborated previous studies, forming clusters around known linguistic characteristics of Alzheimer's disease (Watson, 1999; Rudzicz et al., 2014).

Short Answers and Bursts of Speech Clusters formed around short answers, which have been split up by natural pauses in speech. {*'okay', 'and', 'yes', 'oh !', 'yes', 'fine'*}

Repeated Requests for Clarification Another cluster formed around clarification questions and confusion about the task, specifically in the past tense. {*'Did I say facts ?', 'Did I get any ?', 'Did I say elephant ?'*}

Starting with Interjections Many clusters contain utterances that start with interjections such as "oh", "well", "so", and "right". {*'Well I gotta see it', 'Oh I just see a lot of uh...', 'So all the words that you can...'*}

6.2.2 Automatic Cluster Pattern Analysis

Next, we extend activation clustering to perform novel automatic pattern discovery inside different clusters, as opposed to manually looking for patterns as in Aubakirova and Bansal (2016). Finding the most common POS tags in each cluster allows us to better understand which grammatical structures are favored. No two clusters had exactly the same most-common POS tags, but many clusters shared similar top POS-tags on the same task.

Control Clusters An example unaffected speech cluster for the Cookie task has the following as the most common POS tags: [(*'n'*, .15), (*'det'*, .13), (*'presp'*, .07), (*'part'*, .05)].[5] This pattern follows other clusters of unaffected speech, with nouns, determiners, and participles always found in the most-used POS tags. To illustrate this, two other control clusters found for the Cookie task have very similar top POS tags and frequencies: [(*'n'*, .13), (*'det'*, .13),

---

[4]Statistical insignificance calculated using the bootstrap test (Noreen, 1989; Efron and Tibshirani, 1994). We split our dataset based on gender and down-sampled the female data subset such that it had the same data-size and non-AD to AD data-ratio as the male data subset.

[5]POS tags used in this paper: v=verb, n=noun, pro=pronoun, adv=adverb, det=determiner, aux=auxiliary verb, prep=preposition, co=interjection, part=participle, presp=present participle. The frequencies of each POS tag are scaled based on the total number of tags in each cluster.

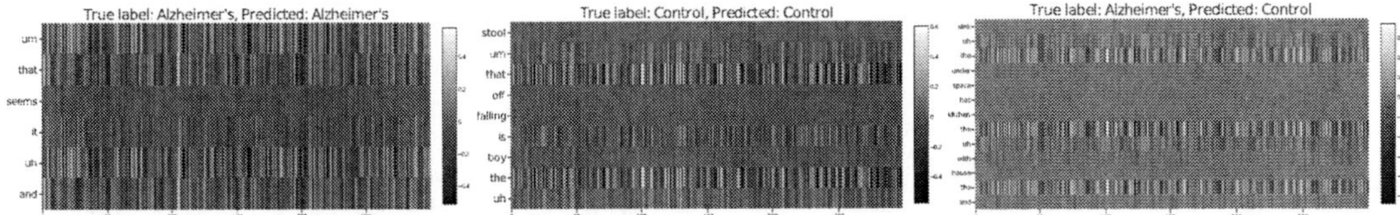

Figure 3: **Left + Middle**: first derivative saliency heat maps for correctly classified Alzheimer's and control examples. **Right**: first derivative heat saliency maps for incorrectly classified Alzheimer's example.

(*'part'*, .09), (*'presp'*, .09)] and [(*'n'*, .15), (*'det'*, .13), (*'part'*, .10), (*'presp'*, .10)] (see Table 2 for side-by-side comparison of these clusters). For the same task, non-AD clusters contain the same top four POS tags.

AD Clusters For the Recall task, one cluster of AD patients' speech shows that the most common POS tags are [(*'n'*, .15), (*'co'*, .15), (*'v'*, .06), (*'pro'*, .06)]. Across samples from the Recall task, AD-marked clusters contained frequent interjections and verbs. On the other hand, in regards to the Cookie task, the most common POS tags for the AD cluster found are [(*'n'*, .20), (*'det'*, .14), (*'adj'*, .05), (*'adv'*, .04)], i.e., more adjectives and adverbs. Hence, between different tasks such as Cookie and Recall, the most commonly used POS tags for AD clusters are distinct.

Moreover, qualitative analysis shows dissimilarities in the most common POS tags between the Cookie task's AD and non-AD cluster(s). Table 3 shows the comparison between representative AD and non-AD clusters for the Cookie task. The AD-positive cluster has only 2 most-used POS tags in common with the non-AD cluster. In fact, none of the 3 non-AD clusters found in Table 2 have adjectives or adverbs in their most-used POS tags list, unlike the AD cluster in Table 3.

6.3 First Derivative Saliency Heat Maps

Saliency heat maps (Simonyan et al., 2013) illustrate which words in an input had the biggest impact on the classification of the whole sentence. This is done by taking the gradient of the final scores w.r.t. the word embeddings of the inputs.

Heat Map Analysis The filler words "uh" and "um" are emphasized in Figure 3 (left), showing that they have a lot of influence on classification. The initial "and" is highlighted as well, corroborating the results of the activation clusters in that starting with a coordinating conjunction is a trait of Alzheimer's speech. However, in Figure 3 (middle), the "uh" filler word is not highlighted, showing that most control patients do not use filler words as heavily as Alzheimer's patients. Instead, words that give structure to a sentence have the biggest impact on classification, such as definite articles and determiners (e.g., "the" and "that"). Figure 3 (middle) shows that the most highlighted words are "the", "that" and "is".

Visualizing Limitations Furthermore, by visualizing an incorrectly classified example, we can learn about the limitations of our neural network. Figure 3 (right) illustrates a map of an incorrectly predicted sample. The model misclassified it due to the length of the utterance (activation clustering showed that AD patients tend to have short bursts of speech, see Section 6.2.1) and the heavy use of determiners. However, the repeated "um"s and starting with a coordinating conjunction strongly indicated AD, which confused our model. From Figure 3, the repeated use of filler words (i.e. "uh") had the second most influence on classification. In future work, with more context data and advanced neural methods, our model's next steps will be to learn how to better classify samples that strongly exhibit both AD and control features.

7 Conclusion

We applied three models to the AD classification task, and our CNN-LSTM model achieves a new benchmark accuracy in classifying AD using neural models. We illustrate with two visualization techniques how these models capture unique linguistic features present in AD patients. We also discussed gender analysis. Potential future work includes using more conversational context and implementing multi-class classification to differentiate among stages of AD. We also plan to apply this generalizable model to other similar neurological diseases, such as Diffuse Lewy Body disease and Huntington's disease (Heindel et al., 1989).

Acknowledgments

We thank the anonymous reviewers for their helpful comments. This work was supported by a Google Faculty Research Award, a Bloomberg Data Science Research Grant, an IBM Faculty Award, and NVidia GPU awards.

References

Malika Aubakirova and Mohit Bansal. 2016. Interpreting neural networks to improve politeness comprehension. In *Proceedings of EMNLP*.

Kathryn A Bayles, T Azuma, RF Cruz, CK Tomoeda, JA Wood, and Jr EB Montgomery. 1999. Gender differences in language of alzheimer disease patients revisited. *Alzheimer disease and associated disorders*, 13(3):138–146.

Francois Boller and James Becker. 2005. Dementiabank database guide. *University of Pittsburgh*.

J Galen Buckwalter, Albert A Rizzo, Richard McCleary, Rodman Shankle, Malcolm Dick, and Victor W Henderson. 1996. Gender comparisons of cognitive performances among vascular dementia, alzheimer disease, and older adults without dementia. *Archives of Neurology*, 53(5):436–439.

Ronan Collobert, Jason Weston, Léon Bottou, Michael Karlen, Koray Kavukcuoglu, and Pavel Kuksa. 2011. Natural language processing (almost) from scratch. *Journal of Machine Learning Research*, 12(Aug):2493–2537.

Mark Davies. 2009. The 385+ million word corpus of contemporary american english (1990–2008+): Design, architecture, and linguistic insights. *International journal of corpus linguistics*, 14(2):159–190.

Lisa M Duke, Ben Seltzer, Jennifer E Seltzer, and Jennifer J Vasterling. 2002. Cognitive components of deficit awareness in alzheimer's disease. *Neuropsychology*, 16(3):359.

Yarin Gal and Zoubin Ghahramani. 2016. A theoretically grounded application of dropout in recurrent neural networks. In *Advances in neural information processing systems*, pages 1019–1027.

Ross Girshick, Jeff Donahue, Trevor Darrell, and Jitendra Malik. 2014. Rich feature hierarchies for accurate object detection and semantic segmentation. In *Proceedings of the IEEE conference on computer vision and pattern recognition*, pages 580–587.

George G Glenner. 1990. Alzheimers disease. In *Biomedical Advances in Aging*, pages 51–62. Springer.

Alex Graves. 2013. Generating sequences with recurrent neural networks. *arXiv preprint arXiv:1308.0850*.

Liesi E Hebert, Robert S Wilson, David W Gilley, Laurel A Beckett, Paul A Scherr, David A Bennett, and Denis A Evans. 2000. Decline of language among women and men with alzheimer's disease. *The Journals of Gerontology Series B: Psychological Sciences and Social Sciences*, 55(6):P354–P361.

William C Heindel, David P Salmon, Clifford W Shults, Patricia A Walicke, and Nelson Butters. 1989. Neuropsychological evidence for multiple implicit memory systems: A comparison of alzheimer's, huntington's, and parkinson's disease patients. *Journal of Neuroscience*, 9(2):582–587.

R Heun and M Kockler. 2002. Gender differences in the cognitive impairment in alzheimer's disease. *Archives of Women's Mental Health*, 4(4):129–137.

Sepp Hochreiter and Jürgen Schmidhuber. 1997. Long short-term memory. *Neural computation*, 9(8):1735–1780.

Akos Kádár, Grzegorz Chrupała, and Afra Alishahi. 2017. Representation of linguistic form and function in recurrent neural networks. *Computational Linguistics*, 43(4):761–780.

Diederik Kingma and Jimmy Ba. 2014. Adam: A method for stochastic optimization. *arXiv preprint arXiv:1412.6980*.

Alexandra König, Aharon Satt, Alexander Sorin, Ron Hoory, Orith Toledo-Ronen, Alexandre Derreumaux, Valeria Manera, Frans Verhey, Pauline Aalten, Phillipe H Robert, et al. 2015. Automatic speech analysis for the assessment of patients with predementia and alzheimer's disease. *Alzheimer's & Dementia: Diagnosis, Assessment & Disease Monitoring*, 1(1):112–124.

Alex Krizhevsky, Ilya Sutskever, and Geoffrey E Hinton. 2012. Imagenet classification with deep convolutional neural networks. In *Advances in neural information processing systems*, pages 1097–1105.

Jiwei Li, Xinlei Chen, Eduard Hovy, and Dan Jurafsky. 2015. Visualizing and understanding neural models in nlp. *arXiv preprint arXiv:1506.01066*.

Aravindh Mahendran and Andrea Vedaldi. 2015. Understanding deep image representations by inverting them. In *Proceedings of the IEEE conference on computer vision and pattern recognition*, pages 5188–5196.

Guy McKhann, David Drachman, Marshall Folstein, Robert Katzman, Donald Price, and Emanuel M Stadlan. 1984. Clinical diagnosis of alzheimer's disease report of the nincds-adrda work group* under the auspices of department of health and human services task force on alzheimer's disease. *Neurology*, 34(7):939–939.

Susan McPherson, Carla Back, J Galen Buckwalter, and Jeffrey L Cummings. 1999. Gender-related cognitive deficits in alzheimer's disease. *International Psychogeriatrics*, 11(2):117–122.

Sylvester O Orimaye, Jojo SM Wong, Karen J Golden, Chee P Wong, and Ireneous N Soyiri. 2017. Predicting probable alzheimers disease using linguistic deficits and biomarkers. *BMC bioinformatics*, 18(1):34.

Sylvester Olubolu Orimaye, Kah Yee Tai, Jojo Sze-Meng Wong, and Chee Piau Wong. 2015. Learning linguistic biomarkers for predicting mild cognitive impairment using compound skip-grams. *arXiv preprint arXiv:1511.02436*.

Sylvester Olubolu Orimaye, Jojo Sze-Meng Wong, and Judyanne Sharmini Gilbert Fernandez. 2016. Deepdeep neural network language models for predicting mild cognitive impairment. In *BAI@ IJCAI*, pages 14–20.

Razvan Pascanu, Caglar Gulcehre, Kyunghyun Cho, and Yoshua Bengio. 2013a. How to construct deep recurrent neural networks. *arXiv preprint arXiv:1312.6026*.

Razvan Pascanu, Tomas Mikolov, and Yoshua Bengio. 2013b. On the difficulty of training recurrent neural networks. In *International Conference on Machine Learning*, pages 1310–1318.

Danielle N Ripich, Stephen A Petrill, Peter J Whitehouse, and Elaine W Ziol. 1995. Gender differences in language of ad patients a longitudinal study. *Neurology*, 45(2):299–302.

Frank Rudzicz, Leila Chan Currie, Andrew Danks, Tejas Mehta, and Shunan Zhao. 2014. Automatically identifying trouble-indicating speech behaviors in alzheimer's disease. In *Proceedings of the 16th international ACM SIGACCESS conference on Computers & accessibility*, pages 241–242. ACM.

Wojciech Samek, Alexander Binder, Grégoire Montavon, Sebastian Lapuschkin, and Klaus-Robert Müller. 2017. Evaluating the visualization of what a deep neural network has learned. *IEEE transactions on neural networks and learning systems*.

Karen Simonyan, Andrea Vedaldi, and Andrew Zisserman. 2013. Deep inside convolutional networks: Visualising image classification models and saliency maps. *arXiv preprint arXiv:1312.6034*.

Nitish Srivastava, Geoffrey E Hinton, Alex Krizhevsky, Ilya Sutskever, and Ruslan Salakhutdinov. 2014. Dropout: a simple way to prevent neural networks from overfitting. *Journal of machine learning research*, 15(1):1929–1958.

Caroline M Watson. 1999. An analysis of trouble and repair in the natural conversations of people with dementia of the alzheimer's type. *Aphasiology*, 13(3):195–218.

Matthew D Zeiler and Rob Fergus. 2014. Visualizing and understanding convolutional networks. In *European conference on computer vision*, pages 818–833. Springer.

Chunting Zhou, Chonglin Sun, Zhiyuan Liu, and Francis Lau. 2015. A c-lstm neural network for text classification. *arXiv preprint arXiv:1511.08630*.

A   Supplementary Materials

A.1   Training Details

All models had a vocabulary size of 2396, and used an Adam optimizer (Kingma and Ba, 2014) with a learning rate of $1e^{-4}$. All gradient norms were clipped to 2.0 (Pascanu et al., 2013b; Graves, 2013). For each model, the hyperparameters were tuned using the development set.

CNN   We used a 2-D CNN. Filter sizes of [3, 4, 5] were used with 128 filters per filter size. Batch size was set to 128, and a dropout (Srivastava et al., 2014) of 0.80 was applied.

LSTM   Our LSTM had 2 layers with 128 hidden units. Batch size was 32, and a dropout of 0.70 was used.

CNN-LSTM   Our CNN-LSTM model consisted of an LSTM on top of a CNN. The CNN had 100 filters per filter size of [3, 4, 5, 6]. Embedding dimensions of 300 were used. An LSTM with 300 hidden units was used. Both dropout on the CNN and recurrent dropout (Gal and Ghahramani, 2016) on the LSTM used a dropout rate of 0.65.

A.2   Dataset Details

Each transcript in DementiaBank comes with automatic morphosyntactic analysis, such as standard part-of-speech tagging, description of tense, and markers for repetitions. This automatic tagging is identical to that done on other datasets, such as the CHILDES TalkBank, and is thus not specific to DementiaBank. This dataset features transcripts of 104 different control patients, and 208 different diagnosed dementia patients. There is a total of 1017 Alzheimer's transcripts and 243 control transcripts. Each of these transcripts were then broken down by sentences and interruptions by the interviewer. We used each utterance by the patient as a data sample. Within the 14362 utterance samples, 11458 come from transcripts of Alzheimer's-diagnosed interviewees and 2904 from those of control patients. Therefore, a majority-baseline classifier that always guesses *AD-positive* will achieve an accuracy of 79.8% in our dataset. Each utterance has a POS-tagged counterpart in the dataset. A 80/10/10 train/dev/test split was used for each setting.

Deep Dungeons and Dragons: Learning Character-Action Interactions from Role-Playing Game Transcripts

Annie Louis
University of Edinburgh
10 Crichton Street
Edinburgh EH8 9AB
alouis@inf.ed.ac.uk

Charles Sutton
University of Edinburgh
10 Crichton Street
Edinburgh EH8 9AB
sutton@inf.ed.ac.uk

Abstract

An essential aspect to understanding narratives is to grasp the interaction between characters in a story and the actions they take. We examine whether computational models can capture this interaction, when both character attributes and actions are expressed as complex natural language descriptions. We propose role-playing games as a testbed for this problem, and introduce a large corpus[1] of game transcripts collected from online discussion forums. Using neural language models which combine character and action descriptions from these stories, we show that we can learn the latent ties. Action sequences are better predicted when the character performing the action is also taken into account, and vice versa for character attributes.

1 Introduction

Imagine a giant, a dwarf, and a fairy in a combat situation. We would expect them to act differently, and conversely, if we are told of even a few actions taken by a character in a story, we naturally start to draw inferences about that character's personality. Communicating narrative is a fundamental task of natural language, and understanding narrative requires modelling the interaction between events and characters.[2]

In this paper, we propose that collaboratively-told stories that arise in certain types of games provide a natural test bed for the problem of inferring interactions between characters and actions in narratives. We present a corpus of role-playing game (RPG) transcripts where characters and action sequences are described with complex natural language texts. Table 1 shows an example character

---

[1] http://groups.inf.ed.ac.uk/cup/ddd/

[2] In this paper, the word *character* will always be used in the sense of "character in a story" rather than the sense of "character in a token".

Character description
Name: Ana Blackclaw; Age: 27; Gender: Female Appearance: Standing at a mighty 6'5, she is a giant among her fellow humans. Her face is light, though paler than the average man or woman's, and is marked by scars. ... Her body is muscular, as it would have to be to carry both her armor and the hammer. Her light grey eyes nearly always keep a bored expression. Her canines seem a tad larger than the normal person's. Preferred Weapon: Hammer. Preferred Armor: Heavy. Gift: Binoculars. Darksign: No.
Action description
She stopped dead in her tracks as the hissing began. A grumble escaped her as it did so, and she looked over to make sure the other woman was doing fine. Seeing that all was not entirely well, she allowed herself to slide down, her hand gripping the slope side once more to slow herself. Once that was accomplished, she reached out and grabbed the back of the girl's neck, pulling her back to steady herself. The giant remained silent as she did so, and then glanced over to the nearby skeletons. They would be upon them soon. Her grip tightened on the hammer as she glanced from side to side. It would not be a fun fight.

Table 1: Example descriptions from our RPG corpus

description, and an action text for the same character. This example shows how the ties between characters and their actions are subtly present in the text descriptions, and learning the latent ties between them is a difficult task. Based on our corpus, and using neural language models, this work demonstrates an initial success on this problem.

The ability to understand and generate narratives is a useful skill for natural language systems, for example, to plan a coherent answer to a question, or to generate a summary of a document. Prior work on narrative processing has focused on inducing disjoint sets of character and event types (as topic models), capturing the relationship between characters in the same story, or extracting character-action pairs as low level noun-verb tuples. However, these models do not aim to match or infer characters and actions from each other.

We make two contributions towards closing this gap. We introduce a corpus of thousands of RPG

Proceedings of NAACL-HLT 2018, pages 708–713
New Orleans, Louisiana, June 1 - 6, 2018. ©2018 Association for Computational Linguistics

transcripts and demonstrate predictive cues between characters and actions by building neural language models with facility for adding side information. We show that a language model over action text obtains lower perplexity when we also make available a representation of the character who produced each token. Likewise, a language model for character descriptions benefits from information about the actions the character made. Our findings open up new possibilities for making sophisticated inference over narrative texts.

2 Related work

In work on narratives, both characters and actions have received significant attention, albeit separately. There is work on inducing *types* of characters (Bamman et al., 2013, 2014) or relationships between characters (Chang et al., 2009; Elson et al., 2010; Chaturvedi et al., 2016; Iyyer et al., 2016). Often these approaches are based on probabilistic topic models or more recently distributed word representations computed by neural networks. Others focus on learning regular and repetitive event sequences in stories (Chambers and Jurafsky, 2009; McIntyre and Lapata, 2009), together with some information about the agent of the actions. These extractions are fairly low-level, in the form of noun-verb pairs. There are also models for clustering stories either based on their characters (Frermann and Szarvas, 2017), or sentiment and topic (Elsner, 2012, 2015).

The above approaches mine *types* of actions or characters. This work focuses on infering the latent ties between actions and characters, and whether one aspect can help predict the other. Flekova and Gurevych (2015) present recent work related to this latter idea. They classify characters based on their speech and actions into an introvert or extrovert class. In contrast, we focus on attributes of characters and actions beyond such coarse traits, and when these attributes are expressed as complex descriptions.

3 A corpus of RPG transcripts

Traditionally, RPGs are played orally with players seated around a table. But there are also online forums where users play RPGs by posting text descriptions instead.

We collected a corpus of RPG threads from one such website `roleplayerguild.com`. Here each game play is recorded in two threads. In one of these, each player posts a detailed text description of the role (character) she is going to play in the game, which we call a *character description*. This description includes the character's physical appearance, personality, family background, as well as special and supernatural powers, and possessions. A second thread consists of the actual game play where each player contributes a post when his turn comes. Each post describes how the character that is assumed by that specific player responds to the game situation. Thus the story develops collaboratively. We call each post in the story thread an *action description*. An example from our corpus of a character description and an action description is shown in Table 1.

A noteworthy aspect of these RPGs is that character attributes are determined by writing the descriptions before the game starts. The story thread itself then focuses predominantly on the actions and does not reiterate character attributes. Moreover, we know unambiguously which character is associated with each action post. Such mapped pairs of clean character descriptions and associated actions would be difficult to obtain from novels or other stories without sophisticated analysis.

Our corpus contains 1,544 RPGs spanning a variety of themes—fantasy, apocalyptic, romance, anime, military, horror, and adventure. There are a total of 56,576 posts, comprising of 25.3M tokens. The maximum number of posts in a story is 753, minimum 2, and the average is 26. Note that many stories are in progress and some are long running. There are 9,771 unique characters in the corpus, and their descriptions amount to 8.5M tokens. There is a minimum of 1, average 6, and maximum 24 characters in a single story.

Even though each character or action description focuses on a single character, it nevertheless contains descriptions of background settings of the scene, and interactions of other characters (eg. descriptions of the parents of a character). Hence we preprocess the texts to only retain parts most related to the *character in focus*. To this end, in character descriptions, we only keep those sentences which mention the character's name or the personal pronouns 'he' or 'she'. The use of pronouns reflects an intuition that since the description is of one key character, the pronoun is most likely to refer to this salient entity. We also take sentences which mention personality describing words such as 'personality', 'skill', 'specialize', 'ability', 'profile', 'talent', etc., even when they do not contain the name. For action descriptions, we only keep sentences which start with the character's name. We do not use pronouns since action text may refer to other salient characters as well.

Finally, we replace the main character (contributor) of a post with an "ENT" (for entity) token. Other proper names in a post are replaced with a "NAME" token and numbers with a "NUM" token. We drop all punctuation and any text with less than 5 tokens. After these preprocessing steps, we have 1,439 stories containing 1.48M tokens for action descriptions and 2.95M for characters.

4 Learning character-action interactions

We examine the feasibility of inferring character-action interactions from text using neural language models (LM) with side information.

4.1 ACTION and CHAR language models

The *story line*, that is, the full text of a story is the token sequence $X = x_1...x_K$ created by concatenating the tokens across all the action descriptions of the story. The posts are taken in time order without any mark for post boundaries. Let C be the set of all characters in a story. For each character j, we denote the character description as the token sequence $C_j = c_{j1} \ldots c_{jm}$.

We build separate language models for action sequences and for character descriptions. The action sequence model is over the story lines (the sequence of all action descriptions in a story), i.e. X as defined above. The character description model is over individual character descriptions i.e., C_j.

First we describe the language model $P(X)$ for the story line. We hypothesize in this work that a better model of X can be built by taking into account the character in focus for each individual action description. First, a baseline recurrent neural network (RNN) language model, which we denote ACTION-LM, would be

$$\mathbf{h}_i = LSTM(\mathbf{h}_{i-1}, \mathbf{x}_{i-1})$$
$$P(x_i|x_1 \ldots x_{i-1}) = softmax(W_{hv}\mathbf{h}_i + b_v)$$

Here $\mathbf{x}_{i-1}$ is the embedding of the input token x_{i-1}, and $\mathbf{h}_{i-1}$ is the hidden state which summarizes the token sequence $x_1 \ldots x_{i-2}$. $LSTM$ computes the next hidden state using an LSTM cell (Hochreiter and Schmidhuber, 1997). The output layer produces a probability distribution over the LM vocabulary using weight matrix $W_{hv} \in$

$\mathbb{R}^{|V|*|h|}$ where $|h|$ is the hidden size and $|V|$ is the vocabulary size; b_v is the bias vector.

To take the character descriptions into account when generating actions, we define a second model ACTION-LMS which estimates

$$P(X|C) = \prod_{i=1}^{K} p(x_i|z_i, x_1...x_{i-1}, z_1...z_{i-1}),$$

where z_l is a variable indicating which character produced the token x_l. For this model, we essentially augment the RNNs with the character descriptions as side information. For each token x_l, the side information is the character description indicated by z_l, i.e, C_{z_l}. We follow the approach by Mikolov and Zweig (2012), and Hoang et al. (2016), where a feature embedding vector e representing side information is input to both the RNN's hidden and output layers, or to one of them. During development, we found that concatenating the feature embedding with the token embedding at the input layer, and with the hidden state at output layer gave the best performance. More formally, ACTION-LMS computes:

$$\mathbf{h}_i = LSTM\left(\mathbf{h}_{i-1}, \begin{bmatrix}\mathbf{x}_{i-1}\\ \mathbf{e}_i\end{bmatrix}\right)$$
$$P(\mathbf{x}_i|\mathbf{x}_1 \ldots \mathbf{x}_{i-1}) = softmax\left(W_{rv}\begin{bmatrix}\mathbf{h}_i\\ \mathbf{e}_i\end{bmatrix} + b_v\right)$$

where $\mathbf{e}_i$ is a representation of the character which produced the token x_i. The hidden state $\mathbf{h}_{i-1}$ now summarizes both the action tokens up to $i - 2$ and the character information up to $i - 1$. The output layer weight matrix is $W_{rv} \in \mathbb{R}^{|V|*(|h|+|e|)}$ where $|h|$ is the size of the RNN hidden unit, and $|e|$ the feature embedding size.

In our work, the feature embedding itself comes from a feedforward neural network trained jointly within the LM. This feature network takes as input the average value of pretrained embeddings[3] for the tokens in the character description (we remove stopwords[4]). This initial vector is passed through hidden layers to yield the feature embedding e (reminiscent of deep averaging networks by Iyyer et al. (2015)).

The language models for character descriptions are similar in structure. First, we call the unconditioned model $P(C_i)$ for a character description C_i as CHAR-LM; this is again an LSTM language model. Second, we implement CHAR-LMS

---

[3] 300 dimension *word2vec* (Mikolov et al., 2013) embeddings trained on the 1 billion word Google News Corpus.

[4] We remove stopwords for side information only

which estimates $P(C_i|X_{C_i})$, where X_{C_i} is the subsequence of X only containing the tokens produced by C_i. We obtain this conditional probability based on the same architecture as ACTION-LMS. Here the input to the feature neural network is the average pretrained embeddings of the tokens (without stopwords) in X_{C_i}.

4.2 Experiments

We randomly divide our corpus into 100 stories for testing, 20 for development, and the rest, 1319 for training. We compare the two ACTION language models, based on a vocabulary size of 20,000, and the CHAR models have a vocabulary of 10,000.

Some posts are long even after our filtering steps, and create a winding story line when concatenated. So we also explore whether limits on description lengths is useful. In ACTION models, a limit of g means that only the first g words of each post are concatenated to form X. For CHAR models, only the first g words of the description C_i is used as the sequence for the LM. The same limit g is given to both the models with and without side information. When using side information, we can restrict the conditioning text as well, to a maximum of h words. We tune these limit parameters, as well as the number of hidden layers, hidden unit sizes and dropout probability on a development set.

For the ACTION models, we set g to 100 words. ACTION-LM uses 2 layers with 256 hidden units each. ACTION-LMS has 1 layer with 256 hidden units for the feature network with h set to 25 words, and 1 layer with 50 units for the RNN part. For the CHAR models, $g = 200$ words. CHAR-LM has one hidden layer with 100 units. For CHAR-LMS, the best network was the same as ACTION-LMS but with $h = 100$ (the first 100 words of all the action posts by that character are combined as the side information). We apply a dropout probability of 0.65, clip gradients at 5.0, and use the Adam algorithm (Kingma and Ba, 2015) for optimization. All our models can trained in an hour, ACTION-LM with 14 epochs, CHAR-LM 62, ACTION-LMS 60 and CHAR-LMS 91 epochs. We implemented the models in TensorFlow[5].

4.3 Results

First, we provide examples of the patterns captured by ACTION-LMS and CHAR-LMS by sam-

---

[5] https://www.tensorflow.org

Action-LMS Model	
Prime text: ⟨bos⟩ **ENT** called …	
Char. context	Generated continuation
small girl cheerful	…her name ⟨eos⟩
bulky male	…out to the group ⟨eos⟩
hunter bow forest	…over and walked over to the large king had been making sure
fear afraid	…her her brother ⟨eos⟩
angry irritated	…back at name with her thick road with disappointment ⟨eos⟩
brutal violent	…out of **ENT** hard to help **ENT** help **ENT** help **ENT** help ⟨eos⟩
school student romantic	…out in the way of the conversation ⟨eos⟩

Char-LMS Model	
Prime text: ⟨bos⟩ **ENT** is …	
Action context	Generated continuation
appeared disappeared flew	…a very young man who has a few scars on his body ⟨eos⟩
walked looked stayed	…a very friendly person ⟨eos⟩
waited	…a little girl who is a little girl who is a little
pause stare	…a very very young woman ⟨eos⟩
strike slap	…a bad boy ⟨eos⟩
follow creep	…a slim and slim but slim physique ⟨eos⟩

Table 2: Samples from our language models

Model	Train	Dev	Test
ACTION-LM	82.56	106.83	105.06
ACTION-LMS	57.38	94.95	96.91
CHAR-LM	69.45	118.78	106.12
CHAR-LMS	61.84	110.13	100.86

Table 3: Perplexities of our models

pling from the models (Table 2). For side information, we use simple words (taken from the descriptions in our test corpus) for closer examination.

For ACTION-LMS, we seed the story line with the priming text "⟨bos⟩ **ENT** called", where **ENT** is the token in our vocabulary referring to the main character of a post. ⟨bos⟩ is a beginning of sentence marker. Different inputs for the conditioning character description are shown under "Char. context". We then sample from the LM following a greedy approach taking the most likely token at each step until either the end token ⟨eos⟩ or a maximum of 12 tokens is reached. The sample is shown under "generated continuation". Similarly, we sample from CHAR-LMS where the sequence is first primed with "**ENT** is a". We find that both models capture interesting ties between character attributes and actions. However, there is much scope for improved models of generation.

In this work, we have focused on the possibility of capturing the interactions. For that, we compare the impact of side information using perplexity on held-out data (Table 3). For both character and action LMs, adding side information leads to a significant decrease in perplexity showing that the interdependence between the two aspects can be learned computationally. Again, there is a lot of scope for improving the language models given that the development and test perplexities are much higher than those during training.

5 Conclusions

We have proposed and demonstrated the feasibility of capturing interactions between characters and their actions in stories. While our neural models show that the data can be better modeled by combining both aspects, one might eventually want to infer a missing modality by sampling or generation from the model. We plan to work on these improvements for future work, and also explore evaluation methods which go beyond language model perplexities, and capture model aspects closer to the task and domain.

References

David Bamman, Brendan O'Connor, and Noah A. Smith. 2013. Learning latent personas of film characters. In *Proceedings of the 51st Annual Meeting of the Association for Computational Linguistics*. pages 352–361.

David Bamman, Ted Underwood, and Noah A. Smith. 2014. A bayesian mixed effects model of literary character. In *Proceedings of the 52nd Annual Meeting of the Association for Computational Linguistics*. pages 370–379.

Nathanael Chambers and Dan Jurafsky. 2009. Unsupervised learning of narrative schemas and their participants. In *Proceedings of the Joint Conference of the 47th Annual Meeting of the ACL and the 4th International Joint Conference on Natural Language Processing of the AFNLP*. pages 602–610.

Jonathan Chang, Jordan Boyd-Graber, and David M. Blei. 2009. Connections between the lines: Augmenting social networks with text. In *Proceedings of the 15th ACM SIGKDD International Conference on Knowledge Discovery and Data Mining*. pages 169–178.

Snigdha Chaturvedi, Shashank Srivastava, Hal Daumé III, and Chris Dyer. 2016. Modeling evolving relationships between characters in literary novels. In *Proceedings of the Thirtieth AAAI Conference on Artificial Intelligence*. pages 2704–2710.

Micha Elsner. 2012. Character-based kernels for novelistic plot structure. In *Proceedings of the 13th Conference of the European Chapter of the Association for Computational Linguistics*. pages 634–644.

Micha Elsner. 2015. Abstract representations of plot structure. *Linguistic Issues in Language Technology* 12(5):1–31.

David K. Elson, Nicholas Dames, and Kathleen R. McKeown. 2010. Extracting social networks from literary fiction. In *Proceedings of the 48th Annual Meeting of the Association for Computational Linguistics*. pages 138–147.

Lucie Flekova and Iryna Gurevych. 2015. Personality profiling of fictional characters using sense-level links between lexical resources. In *Proceedings of the Conference on Empirical Methods in Natural Language Processing*. pages 1805–1816.

Lea Frermann and György Szarvas. 2017. Inducing semantic micro-clusters from deep multi-view representations of novels. In *Proceedings of the Conference on Empirical Methods in Natural Language Processing*. pages 1873–1883.

Cong Duy Vu Hoang, Trevor Cohn, and Gholamreza Haffari. 2016. Incorporating side information into recurrent neural network language models. In *Proceedings of the 2016 Conference of the North American Chapter of the Association for Computational Linguistics: Human Language Technologies*. pages 1250–1255.

Sepp Hochreiter and Jürgen Schmidhuber. 1997. Long short-term memory. *Neural Computation* 9(8):1735–1780.

Mohit Iyyer, Anupam Guha, Snigdha Chaturvedi, Jordan Boyd-Graber, and Hal Daumé III. 2016. Feuding families and former friends: Unsupervised learning for dynamic fictional relationships. In *Proceedings of the Conference of the North American Chapter of the Association for Computational Linguistics: Human Language Technologies*. pages 1534–1544.

Mohit Iyyer, Varun Manjunatha, Jordan Boyd-Graber, and Hal Daumé III. 2015. Deep unordered composition rivals syntactic methods for text classification. In *Proceedings of the 53rd Annual Meeting of the Association for Computational Linguistics and the 7th International Joint Conference on Natural Language Processing*. pages 1681–1691.

Diederik P. Kingma and Jimmy Ba. 2015. Adam: A method for stochastic optimization. In *Proceedings of the International Conference on Learning Representations*.

Neil McIntyre and Mirella Lapata. 2009. Learning to tell tales: A data-driven approach to story generation. In *Proceedings of the Joint Conference of the 47th Annual Meeting of the ACL and the 4th International Joint Conference on Natural Language Processing of the AFNLP*. pages 217–225.

Tomas Mikolov, Ilya Sutskever, Kai Chen, Greg Corrado, and Jeffrey Dean. 2013. Distributed representations of words and phrases and their compositionality. In *Proceedings of the Conference on Neural Information Processing Systems*.

Tomas Mikolov and Geoffrey Zweig. 2012. Context dependent recurrent neural network language model. In *Proceedings of IEEE Spoken Language Technology Workshop*. pages 234–239.

Feudal Reinforcement Learning for Dialogue Management in Large Domains

Iñigo Casanueva[1*], Paweł Budzianowski[1], Pei-Hao Su[2],
Stefan Ultes[1], Lina Rojas-Barahona[1], Bo-Hsiang Tseng[1] and Milica Gašić[1]
[1]Department of Engineering, University of Cambridge, UK
[2]PolyAI Limited, London, UK
`ic340@cam.ac.uk`

Abstract

Reinforcement learning (RL) is a promising approach to solve dialogue policy optimisation. Traditional RL algorithms, however, fail to scale to large domains due to the curse of dimensionality. We propose a novel Dialogue Management architecture, based on Feudal RL, which decomposes the decision into two steps; a first step where a master policy selects a subset of primitive actions, and a second step where a primitive action is chosen from the selected subset. The structural information included in the domain ontology is used to abstract the dialogue state space, taking the decisions at each step using different parts of the abstracted state. This, combined with an information sharing mechanism between slots, increases the scalability to large domains. We show that an implementation of this approach, based on Deep-Q Networks, significantly outperforms previous state of the art in several dialogue domains and environments, without the need of any additional reward signal.

1 Introduction

Task-oriented Spoken Dialogue Systems (SDS), in the form of personal assistants, have recently gained much attention in both academia and industry. One of the most important modules of a SDS is the Dialogue Manager (DM) (or policy), the module in charge of deciding the next action in each dialogue turn. Reinforcement Learning (RL) (Sutton and Barto, 1999) has been studied for several years as a promising approach to model dialogue management (Levin et al., 1998; Henderson et al., 2008; Pietquin et al., 2011; Young et al., 2013; Casanueva et al., 2015; Su et al., 2016). However, as the dialogue state space increases, the number of possible trajectories needed to be ex-

plored grows exponentially, making traditional RL methods not scalable to large domains.

Hierarchical RL (HRL), in the form of temporal abstraction, has been proposed in order to mitigate this problem (Cuayáhuitl et al., 2010, 2016; Budzianowski et al., 2017; Peng et al., 2017). However, proposed HRL methods require that the task is defined in a hierarchical structure, which is usually handcrafted. In addition, they usually require additional rewards for each subtask. Space abstraction, instead, has been successfully applied to dialogue tasks such as Dialogue State Tracking (DST) (Henderson et al., 2014b), and policy transfer between domains (Gašić et al., 2013, 2015; Wang et al., 2015). For DST, a set of binary classifiers can be defined for each slot, with shared parameters, learning a general way to track slots. The policy transfer method presented in (Wang et al., 2015), named Domain Independent Parametrisation (DIP), transforms the belief state into a slot-dependent fixed size representation using a handcrafted feature function. This idea could also be applied to large domains, since it can be used to learn a general way to act in any slot.

In slot-filling dialogues, a HRL method that relies on space abstraction, such as Feudal RL (FRL) (Dayan and Hinton, 1993), should allow RL scale to domains with a large number of slots. FRL divides a task spatially rather than temporally, decomposing the decisions in several steps and using different abstraction levels in each sub-decision. This framework is especially useful in RL tasks with large discrete action spaces, making it very attractive for large domain dialogue management.

In this paper, we introduce a Feudal Dialogue Policy which decomposes the decision in each turn into two steps. In a first step, the policy decides if it takes a slot independent or slot dependent action. Then, the state of each slot sub-policy is abstracted to account for features related to that slot,

Proceedings of NAACL-HLT 2018, pages 714–719
New Orleans, Louisiana, June 1 - 6, 2018. ©2018 Association for Computational Linguistics

---

*Currently at PolyAI, `inigo@poly-ai.com`

and a primitive action is chosen from the previously selected subset. Our model does not require any modification of the reward function and the hierarchical architecture is fully specified by the structured database representation of the system (i.e. the ontology), requiring no additional design.

2 Background

Dialogue management can be cast as a continuous MDP (Young et al., 2013) composed of a continuous multivariate belief state space $\mathcal{B}$, a finite set of actions $\mathcal{A}$ and a reward function $R(b_t, a_t)$. At a given time t, the agent observes the belief state $b_t \in \mathcal{B}$, executes an action $a_t \in \mathcal{A}$ and receives a reward $r_t \in \mathbb{R}$ drawn from $R(b_t, a_t)$. The action taken, a, is decided by the *policy*, defined as the function $\pi(b) = a$. For any policy π and $b \in \mathcal{B}$, the Q-value function can be defined as the expected (discounted) return R, starting from state b, taking action a, and then following policy π until the end of the dialogue at time step T:

$$Q^{\pi}(b, a) = \mathbb{E}\{R|b_t = b, a_t = a\} \qquad (1)$$

where $R = \sum_{\tau=t}^{T-1} \gamma^{(\tau-t)} r_{\tau}$ and γ is a discount factor, with $0 \leq \gamma \leq 1$.

The objective of RL is to find an optimal policy π^*, i.e. a policy that maximizes the expected return in each belief state. In *Value-based* algorithms, the optimal policy can be found by greedily taking the action which maximises $Q^{\pi}(b, a)$.

In slot-filling SDSs the belief state space $\mathcal{B}$ is defined by the *ontology*, a structured representation of a database of entities that the user can retrieve by talking to the system. Each entity has a set of properties, refereed to as *slots $\mathcal{S}$*, where each of the slots can take a value from the set $\mathcal{V}_s$. The belief state b is then defined as the concatenation of the probability distribution of each slot, plus a set of general features (e.g. the communication function used by the user, the database search method...) (Henderson et al., 2014a). The set $\mathcal{A}$ is defined as a set of *summary actions*, where the actions can be either slot dependent (e.g. *request*(food), *confirm*(area)...) or slot independent[1] (e.g. *hello*(), *inform*()...).

The belief space $\mathcal{B}$ is defined by the ontology, therefore belief states of different domains will have different shapes. In order to transfer

---

[1] We include the summary actions dependent on all the slots, such as *inform*(), in this group.

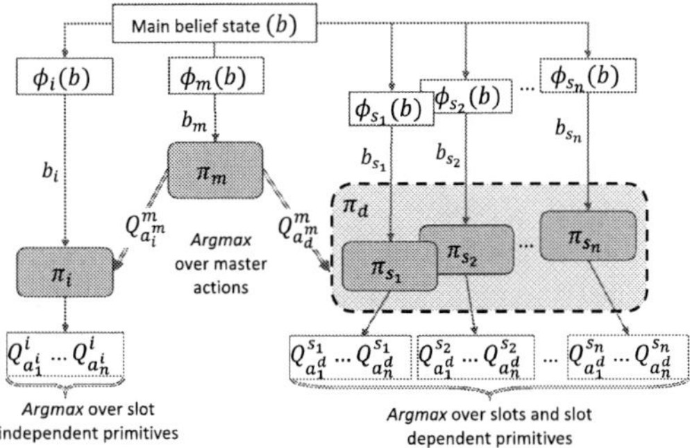

Figure 1: Feudal dialogue architecture used in this work. The sub-policies surrounded by the dashed line have shared parameters. The simple lines show the data flow and the double lines the sub-policy decisions.

knowledge between domains, Domain Independent Parametrization (DIP) (Wang et al., 2015) proposes to abstract the belief state b into a fixed size representation. As each action is either slot independent or dependent on a slot s, a feature function $\phi_{dip}(b, s)$ can be defined, where $s \in \mathcal{S} \cup s_i$ and s_i stands for slot independent actions. Therefore, in order to compute the policy, $Q(b, a)$ can be approximated as $Q(\phi_{dip}(b, s), a)$, where s is the slot associated to action a.

Wang et al. (2015) presents a handcrafted feature function $\phi_{dip}(b, s)$. It includes the slot independent features of the belief state, a summarised representation of the joint belief state, and a summarised representation of the belief state of the slot s. Section 4 gives a more detailed description of the $\phi_{dip}(b, s)$ function used in this work.

3 Feudal dialogue management

FRL decomposes the policy decision $\pi(b) = a$ in each turn into several sub-decisions, using different abstracted parts of the belief state in each sub-decision. The objective of a task oriented SDS is to fulfill the users goal, but as the goal is not observable for the SDS, the SDS needs to gather enough information to correctly fulfill it. Therefore, in each turn, the DM can decompose its decision in two steps: first, decide between taking an action in order to gather information about the user goal (information gathering actions) or taking an action to fulfill the user goal or a part of it (information providing actions) and second, select a (primitive) action to execute from the previously selected subset. In a slot-filling dialogue, the set of information gathering actions can be defined as the set of slot dependent actions, while the set of information providing actions can be defined as the remaining actions.

The architecture of the feudal policy proposed by this work is represented schematically in Figure 1. The (primitive) actions are divided between two subsets; slot independent actions $\mathcal{A}_i$ (e.g. hello(), inform()); and slot dependent actions $\mathcal{A}_d$ (e.g. request(), confirm())[2]. In addition, a set of master actions $\mathcal{A}_m = (a_i^m, a_d^m)$ is defined, where a_i^m corresponds to taking an action from $\mathcal{A}_i$ and a_d^m to taking an action from $\mathcal{A}_d$. Then, a feature function $\phi_s(b) = b_s$ is defined for each slot $s \in \mathcal{S}$, as well as a slot independent feature function $\phi_i(b) = b_i$ and a master feature function $\phi_m(b) = b_m$. These feature functions can be handcrafted (e.g. the DIP feature function introduced in section 2) or any function approximator can be used (e.g. neural networks trained jointly with the policy).

Finally, a master policy $\pi_m(b_m) = a^m$, a slot independent policy $\pi_i(b_i) = a^i$ and a set of slot specific policies $\pi_s(b_s) = a^d$, one for each $s \in \mathcal{S}$, are defined, where $a^m \in \mathcal{A}_m$, $a^i \in \mathcal{A}_i$ and $a^d \in \mathcal{A}_d$. Contrary to other feudal policies, the slot specific sub-policies have shared parameters, in order to generalise between slots (following the idea used by Henderson et al. (2014b) for DST). The differences between the slots (size, value distribution...) are accounted by the feature function $\phi_s(b)$. Therefore $\pi_m(b_m)$ is defined as:

$$\pi_m(b_m) = \underset{a^m \in \mathcal{A}_m}{\mathrm{argmax}} \, Q^m(b_m, a^m) \qquad (2)$$

If $\pi_m(b_m) = a_i^m$, the sub-policy run is π_i:

$$\pi_i(b_i) = \underset{a^i \in \mathcal{A}_i}{\mathrm{argmax}} \, Q^i(b_i, a^i) \qquad (3)$$

Else, if $\pi_m(b_m) = a_d^m$, π_d is selected. This policy runs each slot specific policy, π_s, for all $s \in \mathcal{S}$, choosing the action-slot pair that maximises the Q function over all the slot sub-policies.

$$\pi_d(b_s | \forall s \in \mathcal{S}) = \underset{a^d \in \mathcal{A}_d, s \in \mathcal{S}}{\mathrm{argmax}} \, Q^s(b_s, a^d) \qquad (4)$$

Then, the summary action a is constructed by joining a^d and s (e.g. if a^d=*request()* and *s=food*, then the summary action will be *request(food)*). A pseudo-code of the Feudal Dialogue Policy algorithm is given in Appendix A.

---

[2]Note that the actions of this set are composed just by the communication function of the slot dependent actions, thus reducing the number of actions compared to $\mathcal{A}$.

Domain	Code	# constraint slots	# requests	# values
Cambridge Restaurants	CR	3	9	268
San Francisco Restaurants	SFR	6	11	636
Laptops	LAP	11	21	257

	Env. 1	Env. 2	Env. 3	Env. 4	Env. 5	Env. 6
SER	0%	0%	15%	15%	15%	30%
Masks	on	off	on	off	on	on
User	Std.	Std.	Std.	Std.	Unf.	Std.

Table 1: Sumarised description of the domains and environments used in the experiments. Refer to (Casanueva et al., 2017) for a detailed description.

4 Experimental setup

The models used in the experiments have been implemented using the PyDial toolkit (Ultes et al., 2017)[3] and evaluated on the PyDial benchmarking environment (Casanueva et al., 2017). This environment presents a set of tasks which span different size domains, different Semantic Error Rates (SER), and different configurations of action masks and user model parameters (Standard (Std.) or Unfriendly (Unf.)). Table 1 shows a summarised description of the tasks. The models developed in this paper are compared to the state-of-the-art RL algorithms and to the handcrafted policy presented in the benchmarks.

4.1 DIP-DQN baseline

An implementation of DIP based on Deep-Q Networks (DQN) (Mnih et al., 2013) is implemented as an additional baseline (Papangelis and Stylianou, 2017). This policy, named DIP-DQN, uses the same hyperparameters as the DQN implementation released in the PyDial benchmarks. A DIP feature function based in the description in (Wang et al., 2015) is used, $\phi_{dip}(b, s) = \psi_0(b) \oplus \psi_j(b) \oplus \psi_d(b, s)$, where:
- $\psi_0(b)$ accounts for general features of the belief state, such as the database search method.
- $\psi_j(b)$ accounts for features of the joint belief state, such as the entropy of the joint belief.
- $\psi_d(b, s)$ accounts for features of the marginal distribution of slot s, such as the entropy of s.

Appendix B shows a detailed description of the DIP features used in this work.

4.2 Feudal DQN policy

A Feudal policy based on the architecture described in sec. 3 is implemented, named FDQN. Each sub-policy is constructed by a DQN policy

---

[3]The implementation of the models can be obtained in www.pydial.org

	Task	Feudal-DQN		DIP-DQN		Bnch.	Hdc.
		Suc.	Rew.	Suc.	Rew.	Rew.	Rew.
Env. 1	CR	89.3%	11.7	48.8%	-2.8	13.5	**14.0**
Env. 1	SFR	71.1%	7.1	25.8%	-7.4	11.7	**12.4**
Env. 1	LAP	65.5%	5.7	26.6%	-8.8	10.5	**11.7**
Env. 2	CR	97.8%	13.1	85.5%	9.6	12.2	**14.0**
Env. 2	SFR	95.4%	**12.4**	85.7%	8.4	9.6	**12.4**
Env. 2	LAP	94.1%	**12.0**	89.5%	9.7	7.3	11.7
Env. 3	CR	92.6%	11.7	86.1%	8.9	**11.9**	11.0
Env. 3	SFR	90.0%	**9.7**	59.3%	0.2	8.6	9.0
Env. 3	LAP	89.6%	**9.4**	71.5%	3.1	6.7	8.7
Env. 4	CR	91.4%	**11.2**	82.6%	8.7	10.7	11.0
Env. 4	SFR	90.3%	**10.2**	86.1%	9.2	7.7	9.0
Env. 4	LAP	88.7%	**9.8**	74.8%	6.0	5.5	8.7
Env. 5	CR	96.3%	**11.5**	74.4%	2.9	10.5	9.3
Env. 5	SFR	88.9%	**7.9**	75.5%	3.2	4.5	6.0
Env. 5	LAP	78.8%	5.2	64.4%	-0.4	4.1	**5.3**
Env. 6	CR	90.6%	**10.4**	83.4%	8.1	10.0	9.7
Env. 6	SFR	83.0%	**7.1**	71.9%	3.9	3.9	6.4
Env. 6	LAP	78.5%	**6.0**	66.5%	2.7	3.6	5.5

Table 2: Success rate and reward for Feudal-DQN and DIP-DQN in the 18 benchmarking tasks, compared with the reward of the best performing algorithm in each task (Bnch.) and the handcrafted policy (Hdc.) presented in (Casanueva et al., 2017).

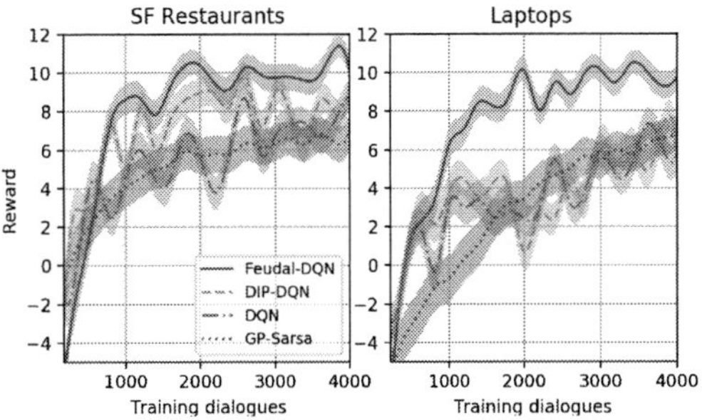

Figure 2: Learning curves for Feudal-DQN and DIP-DQN in Env. 4, compared to the two best performing algorithms in (Casanueva et al., 2017) (DQN and GP-Sarsa). The shaded area depicts the mean $\pm$ the standard deviation over ten random seeds.

(Su et al., 2017). These policies have the same hyperparameters as the baseline DQN implementation, except for the two hidden layer sizes, which are reduced to 130 and 50 respectively. As feature functions, subsets of the DIP features are used:

$$\phi_m(b) = \phi_i(b) = \psi_0(b) \oplus \psi_j(b)$$
$$\phi_s(b) = \psi_0(b) \oplus \psi_j(b) \oplus \psi_d(b, s) \, \forall s \in \mathcal{S}$$

The original set of summary actions of the benchmarking environment, $\mathcal{A}$, has a size of $5 + 3 * |\mathcal{S}|$, where $|\mathcal{S}|$ is the number of slots. This set is divided in two subsets[4]: $\mathcal{A}_i$ of size 6 and $\mathcal{A}_d$ of size 4. Each sub-policy (including π_m) is trained with the same sparse reward signal used in the baselines, getting a reward of 20 if the dialogue is successful or 0 otherwise, minus the dialogue length.

5   Results

The results in the 18 tasks of the benchmarking environment after 4000 training dialogues are presented in Table 2. The same evaluation procedure of the benchmarks is used, presenting the mean over 10 different random seeds and testing every seed for 500 dialogues. The FDQN policy substantially outperforms every other other policy in all the environments except Env. 1. The

performance increase is more considerable in the two largest domains (SFR and LAP), with gains up to 5 points in accumulated reward in the most challenging environments (e.g. Env. 4 LAP), compared to the best benchmarked RL policies (Bnch.). In addition, FDQN consistently outperforms the handcrafted policy (Hdc.) in environments 2 to 6, which traditional RL methods could not achieve. In Env. 1, however, the results for FDQN and DIP-DQN are rather low, specially for DIP-DQN. Surprisingly, the results in Env. 2, which only differs from Env. 1 in the absence of action masks (thus, in principle, is a more complex environment), outperform every other algorithm. Analysing the dialogues individually, we could observe that, in this environment, both policies are prone to "overfit" to an action [5]. The performance of FDQN and DIP-DQN in Env. 4 is also better than in Env. 3, while the difference between these environments also lies in the masks. This suggests that an specific action mask design can be helpful for some algorithms, but can harm the performance of others. This is especially severe in the DIP-DQN case, which shows good performance in some challenging environments, but it is more unstable and prone to overfit than FDQN.

However, the main purpose of action masks is to reduce the number of dialogues needed to train a policy. Observing the learning curves shown in Figure 2, the FDQN model can learn a near-optimal policy in large domains in about 1500 dialogues, even if no additional reward is used, making the action masks unnecessary.

---

[4]An additional *pass()* action is added to each subset, which is taken whenever the other sub-policy is executed. This simplifies the training algorithm.

[5]The model overestimates the value of an incorrect action, continuously repeating it until the user runs out of patience.

6 Conclusions and future work

We have presented a novel dialogue management architecture, based on Feudal RL, which substantially outperforms the previous state of the art in several dialogue environments. By defining a set of slot dependent policies with shared parameters, the model is able to learn a general way to act in slots, increasing its scalability to large domains.

Unlike other HRL methods applied to dialogue, no additional reward signals are needed and the hierarchical structure can be derived from a flat ontology, substantially reducing the design effort.

A promising approach would be to substitute the handcrafted feature functions used in this work by neural feature extractors trained jointly with the policy. This would avoid the need to design the feature functions and could be potentially extended to other modules of the SDS, making text-to-action learning tractable. In addition, a single model can be potentially used in different domains (Papangelis and Stylianou, 2017), and different feudal architectures could make larger action spaces tractable (e.g. adding a third subpolicy to deal with actions dependent on 2 slots).

Acknowledgments

This research was funded by the EPSRC grant EP/M018946/1 Open Domain Statistical Spoken Dialogue Systems.

References

Paweł Budzianowski, Stefan Ultes, Pei-Hao Su, Nikola Mrkšić, Tsung-Hsien Wen, Inigo Casanueva, Lina M. Rojas Barahona, and Milica Gašić. 2017. Subdomain modelling for dialogue management with hierarchical reinforcement learning. In *Proc of SIGDIAL*.

Iñigo Casanueva, Paweł Budzianowski, Pei-Hao Su, Nikola Mrkšić, Tsung-Hsien Wen, Stefan Ultes, Lina Rojas-Barahona, Steve Young, and Milica Gašić. 2017. A benchmarking environment for reinforcement learning based task oriented dialogue management. *arXiv preprint arXiv:1711.11023* .

Inigo Casanueva, Thomas Hain, Heidi Christensen, Ricard Marxer, and Phil Green. 2015. Knowledge transfer between speakers for personalised dialogue management. In *Proceedings of the 16th Annual Meeting of the Special Interest Group on Discourse and Dialogue*. pages 12–21.

Heriberto Cuayáhuitl, Steve Renals, Oliver Lemon, and Hiroshi Shimodaira. 2010. Evaluation of a hierarchical reinforcement learning spoken dialogue system. *Computer Speech & Language* 24(2):395–429.

Heriberto Cuayáhuitl, Seunghak Yu, Ashley Williamson, and Jacob Carse. 2016. Deep reinforcement learning for multi-domain dialogue systems. *NIPS Workkshop* .

Peter Dayan and Geoffrey E Hinton. 1993. Feudal reinforcement learning. In *Advances in neural information processing systems*. pages 271–278.

Milica Gašić, Catherine Breslin, Matthew Henderson, Dongho Kim, Martin Szummer, Blaise Thomson, Pirros Tsiakoulis, and Steve Young. 2013. Pomdp-based dialogue manager adaptation to extended domains. In *Proceedings of the SIGDIAL Conference*.

Milica Gašić, Nikola Mrkšić, Pei-hao Su, David Vandyke, Tsung-Hsien Wen, and Steve Young. 2015. Policy committee for adaptation in multi-domain spoken dialogue systems. In *Automatic Speech Recognition and Understanding (ASRU), 2015 IEEE Workshop on*. IEEE, pages 806–812.

James Henderson, Oliver Lemon, and Kallirroi Georgila. 2008. Hybrid reinforcement/supervised learning of dialogue policies from fixed data sets. *Computational Linguistics* 34(4):487–511.

M. Henderson, B. Thomson, and J. Williams. 2014a. The Second Dialog State Tracking Challenge. In *Proc of SIGdial*.

M. Henderson, B. Thomson, and S. J. Young. 2014b. Word-based Dialog State Tracking with Recurrent Neural Networks. In *Proc of SIGdial*.

Esther Levin, Roberto Pieraccini, and Wieland Eckert. 1998. Using markov decision process for learning dialogue strategies. In *Acoustics, Speech and Signal Processing, 1998. Proceedings of the 1998 IEEE International Conference on*. IEEE, volume 1, pages 201–204.

Volodymyr Mnih, Koray Kavukcuoglu, David Silver, Alex Graves, Ioannis Antonoglou, Daan Wierstra, and Martin Riedmiller. 2013. Playing atari with deep reinforcement learning. *arXiv preprint arXiv:1312.5602* .

Alexandros Papangelis and Yannis Stylianou. 2017. Single-model multi-domain dialogue management with deep learning. In *International Workshop for Spoken Dialogue Systems*.

B. Peng, X. Li, L. Li, J. Gao, A. Celikyilmaz, S. Lee, and K.-F. Wong. 2017. Composite Task-Completion Dialogue System via Hierarchical Deep Reinforcement Learning. *ArXiv e-prints* .

Olivier Pietquin, Matthieu Geist, Senthilkumar Chandramohan, and Hervé Frezza-Buet. 2011. Sample-efficient batch reinforcement learning for dialogue management optimization. *ACM Transactions on Speech and Language Processing (TSLP)* 7(3):7.

Pei-Hao Su, Pawel Budzianowski, Stefan Ultes, Milica Gasic, and Steve Young. 2017. Sample-efficient actor-critic reinforcement learning with supervised data for dialogue management. *Proceedings of SigDial* .

Pei-Hao Su, Milica Gasic, Nikola Mrksic, Lina Rojas-Barahona, Stefan Ultes, David Vandyke, Tsung-Hsien Wen, and Steve Young. 2016. Continuously learning neural dialogue management. *arXiv preprint arXiv:1606.02689* .

Richard S. Sutton and Andrew G. Barto. 1999. *Reinforcement Learning: An Introduction*. MIT Press.

Stefan Ultes, Lina M. Rojas-Barahona, Pei-Hao Su, David Vandyke, Dongho Kim, Iñigo Casanueva, Paweł Budzianowski, Nikola Mrkšić, Tsung-Hsien Wen, Milica Gašić, and Steve J. Young. 2017. Pydial: A multi-domain statistical dialogue system toolkit. In *ACL Demo*. Association of Computational Linguistics.

Zhuoran Wang, Tsung-Hsien Wen, Pei-Hao Su, and Yannis Stylianou. 2015. Learning domain-independent dialogue policies via ontology parameterisation. In *SIGDIAL Conference*. pages 412–416.

Steve Young, Milica Gašić, Blaise Thomson, and Jason D Williams. 2013. Pomdp-based statistical spoken dialog systems: A review. *Proceedings of the IEEE* 101(5):1160–1179.

A Feudal Dialogue Policy algorithm

Algorithm 1 Feudal Dialogue Policy

1: **for** each dialogue turn **do**
2:      observe b
3:      $b_m = \phi_m(b)$
4:      $a^m = \underset{a^m \in \mathcal{A}_m}{\mathrm{argmax}}\, Q^m(b_m, a^m)$
5:      **if** $a^m == a_i^m$ **then**   ▷ drop to π_i
6:          $b_i = \phi_i(b)$
7:          $a = \underset{a^i \in \mathcal{A}_i}{\mathrm{argmax}}\, Q^i(b_i, a^i)$
8:      **else** $a^m == a_d^m$ **then**   ▷ drop to π_d
9:          $b_s = \phi_s(b)\,\forall s \in \mathcal{S}$
10:          $slot, act = \underset{s \in \mathcal{S}, a^d \in \mathcal{A}_d}{\mathrm{argmax}}\, Q^s(b_s, a^d)$
11:          $a = join(slot, act)$
12:      **end if**
13:      execute a
14: **end for**

B DIP features

This section gives a detailed description of the DIP feature functions $\phi_{dip}(b, s) = \psi_0(b) \oplus \psi_j(b) \oplus \psi_d(b, s)$ used in this work. The differences with the features used in (Wang et al., 2015) and (Papangelis and Stylianou, 2017) are the following:

- No *priority* or *importance* features are used.

- No *Potential contribution to DB search* features are used.

- The joint belief features $\psi_j(b)$ are extended to account for large-domain aspects.

Feature function	Feature description	Feature size
$\psi_0(b)$	last user dialogue act (bin) *	7
	DB search method (bin) *	6
	# of requested slots (bin)	5
	offer happened *	1
	last action was *Inform no venue* *	1
	normalised # of slots (1/# of slots)	1
	normalised avg. slot length (1/avg. # of values)	1
$\psi_j(b)$	prob. of the top 3 values of b_j	3
	prob. of *NONE* value of b_j	1
	entropy of b_j	1
	diff. between top and 2nd value probs. (bin)	5
	# of slots with top value not *NONE* (bin)	5
$\psi_d(b, s)$	prob. of the top 3 values of s	3
	prob. of *NONE* value of s	1
	diff. between top and 2nd value probs. (bin)	5
	entropy of s	1
	# of values of s with prob. > 0 (bin)	5
	normalised slot length (1/# of values)	1
	slot length (bin)	10
	entropy of the distr. of values of s in the DB	1
	total	64

Table 3: List of features composing the DIP features. the tag (bin) denotes that a binary encoding is used for this feature. Some of the joint features $\psi_j(b)$ are extracted from the joint belief b_j, computed as the Cartesian product of the beliefs of the individual slots. * denotes that these features exist in the original belief state b.

Evaluating historical text normalization systems:
How well do they generalize?

Alexander Robertson
School of Informatics
University of Edinburgh
`alexander.robertson@ed.ac.uk`

Sharon Goldwater
School of Informatics
University of Edinburgh
`sgwater@inf.ed.ac.uk`

Abstract

We highlight several issues in the evaluation of historical text normalization systems that make it hard to tell how well these systems would actually work in practice—i.e., for new datasets or languages; in comparison to more naïve systems; or as a preprocessing step for downstream NLP tools. We illustrate these issues and exemplify our proposed evaluation practices by comparing two neural models against a naïve baseline system. We show that the neural models generalize well to unseen words in tests on five languages; nevertheless, they provide no clear benefit over the naïve baseline for downstream POS tagging of an English historical collection. We conclude that future work should include more rigorous evaluation, including both intrinsic and extrinsic measures where possible.

1 Introduction

Historical text normalization systems aim to convert historical wordforms to their modern equivalents, in order to make historical documents more searchable or to improve the performance of downstream NLP tools. In historical texts, a single word type may be realized with several different orthographic forms, which may not correspond to the modern form. For example, the modern English word *said* might be realized as *sayed, seyd, said, sayd*, etc. Spellings change over time, but also vary within a single time period and even within a single author, since orthography only became standardized in many languages fairly recently.

Over the years, researchers have proposed normalization methods based on rules and/or edit distances (Baron and Rayson, 2008; Bollmann, 2012; Hauser and Schulz, 2007; Bollmann et al., 2011; Pettersson et al., 2013a; Mitankin et al., 2014; Pettersson et al., 2014), statistical machine translation (Pettersson et al., 2013b; Scherrer and Erjavec,

2013), and most recently neural network models (Bollmann and Søgaard, 2016; Bollmann et al., 2017; Korchagina, 2017). However, most of these systems have been developed and tested on a single language (or even a single corpus), and many have not been compared to the naïve but strong baseline that only changes words seen in the training data, normalizing each to its most frequent modern form observed during training.[1] These issues make it hard to tell which methods generalize across languages and corpora, and how they compare to each other. Moreover, researchers have rarely examined whether their systems actually improve performance on downstream tasks.

This paper brings together best practices for evaluating historical text normalization systems, highlighting in particular the need to report results on unseen tokens and to consider the naïve baseline. We focus our evaluation on two recent neural models: one that has been previously tested only on a German collection that is not widely available (Bollmann et al., 2017), and one that is adapted from work on morphological re-inflection, but has not been used for historical text normalization (Aharoni et al., 2017). Both are encoder-decoder models; the former with soft attention, and the latter with hard monotonic attention.

We present results on five languages, for both seen and unseen words and for various amounts of training data. The soft attention model performs surprisingly poorly on seen words, so that its overall performance is worse than the naïve baseline and several earlier models (Pettersson et al., 2014). However, on unseen words (which we argue are what matters), both neural models do well.

Unfortunately, these positive results did not

---

[1] Some authors have focussed on *unsupervised* normalization, where the naïve baseline is to leave words unchanged (Mitankin et al., 2014; Hauser and Schulz, 2007). We consider only *supervised* systems in the remainder of this paper.

Proceedings of NAACL-HLT 2018, pages 720–725
New Orleans, Louisiana, June 1 - 6, 2018. ©2018 Association for Computational Linguistics

translate into improvements when we tested the English-trained models on a downstream POS tagging task using a different historical collection spanning a similar time range. Normalizing the text gave better tag accuracy than not normalizing, but neither neural model convincingly outperformed the naïve normalizer. Although these results are disappointing, the clear evaluation standards laid out here should benefit future work in this area.

2 Task setting and issues of evaluation

We follow previous work in training our systems on pairs (h, m) of historical tokens and their gold standard modern forms.[2] Note that at test time, most of the h tokens will have been seen before in the training data (due to Zipf's law), and for these tokens it is very difficult to beat a baseline that normalizes each h to the most common m seen for it in training.[3] Thus, in practice, normalization systems should typically only be applied to *unseen* tokens. It is therefore critical to report both dataset statistics and experimental results for unseen tokens.

Unfortunately, some recent papers have only reported accuracy on all tokens, and only in comparison to other (non-baseline) systems (Bollmann and Søgaard, 2016; Bollmann et al., 2017; Korchagina, 2017). These figures can be misleading if systems underperform the naïve baseline on seen tokens (which we show does happen in practice). To see why, suppose 80% of test tokens were seen in training, and the baseline gets 90% of them right, while system A gets 80% and system B gets only 70%. Meanwhile the baseline gets only 50% of unseen tokens right, whereas systems A and B get 70% and 90%, respectively. A's accuracy is higher *overall* than B's (78% vs 74%), but *both* systems underperform the baseline (82%). More importantly, the best system (90% accuracy overall) is achieved by applying the baseline to seen tokens, and the system that generalizes best (B) to unseen tokens; it is irrelevant that A scores higher overall than B.

Stemming from the reasoning above, we argue that a full evaluation of any spelling normalization system requires more complete dataset statistics and experimental results. In describing the training and test sets, researchers should not only report the number of **types** and **tokens**, but also the per-

centage of **unseen tokens** in the test (or dev) set and the percentage of **training items** (h, m) **where** $h = m$. This last statistic measures the degree of spelling variation, which varies considerably between corpora.

As for reporting results, we have argued that accuracy should be reported separately for **seen vs unseen tokens**, and overall results compared to the **naïve memorization baseline**. Since historical spelling normalization is typically a low-resource task, systems should also ideally be tested with **varying amounts of training data** to assess how much annotation might be required for a new corpus (Pettersson et al., 2014; Bollmann and Søgaard, 2016; Korchagina, 2017). Finally, since these systems may be deployed on corpora other than those they were trained on, and used as preprocessing for other tasks, we advocate reporting **performance on a downstream task and/or different corpus**. To our knowledge the only previous supervised learning system to do so is Pettersson et al. (2013b).

3 Models

We focus on two neural encoder-decoder models for spelling normalization, comparing them against the memorization baseline and to previous results from Pettersson et al. (2014). The first model (Bollmann et al., 2017)[4] uses a fairly standard architecture with a bi-directional LSTM encoder and an LSTM decoder with soft attention (Xu et al., 2015), and is trained using cross-entropy loss.

The second model is a new approach to spelling normalization, which adapts the morphological re-inflection system of Aharoni et al. (2017).[5] The reinflection model generates the characters in an inflected wordform $(y_{1:n})$, given the characters of its lemma $(x_{1:m})$ and a set of corresponding morphological features (f). Rather than using a soft attention mechanism that computes a weight vector over the entire sequence, this model exploits the generally monotonic character alignment between $x_{1:m}$ and $y_{1:n}$ and attends to only a single encoded input character at a time during decoding.

Architecturally, the model uses a standard bi-directional encoder. The decoder steps through the characters of the input and considers jointly the output of the previous step, the morphological features, and the currently attended encoded input. It outputs

---

[2] It would be possible to train on full texts rather than isolated tokens, which could improve results for ambiguous forms. However, previous models have not addressed this setting, nor do we, leaving this for future work.

[3] Our version breaks ties by choosing the first m observed.

[4] https://bitbucket.org/mbollmann/acl2017

[5] https://github.com/roeeaharoni/morphological-reinflection

	Tokens	h typ	m typ	%nc	%uns
Eng	148/16/17k	19.4k	10.6k	73.9	8.6
Ger	39/5/5k	9.0k	8.4k	84.8	14.8
Hun	137/17/17k	45.5k	25.8k	15.4	24.1
Ice	52/6/6k	9.7k	8.5k	48.0	11.3
Swe	28/2/34k	8.3k	6.5k	65.9	22.4

Table 1: Dataset statistics: the number of tokens in train/dev/test sets; *historical* and *modern* word types and % of "no-change" tokens ($h = m$) in the training sets; and the % of dev set tokens that are unseen in training.

either a character or an advance symbol (to advance the focus of attention for the next time step). It is trained on an oracle sequence of write/advance actions $s_{1:q}$ which are generated from an automatic alignment of the input and output sequences. The model maximizes $p(s_{1:q}|x_{1:m}, f)$. For details, see Aharoni et al. (2017).

We adapt the model to our purpose by removing the morphological features f, maximising only $p(s_{1:q}|x_{1:m})$. The monotonic assumption is well-suited to our task, since fewer than 0.4% of edit operations require non-monotonic alignments (i.e. character transpositions) in any of our datasets.

Other than removing the need for morphological features from the hard attention model, and increasing the number of training epochs to 50 for both models, we did no further hyperparameter tuning, since our goal was to assess the "off-the-shelf" performance of these systems.

4 Experiments

We use the same datasets as Pettersson et al. (2014), with data from five languages over a range of historical periods.[6] We use the same train/dev/test splits as Pettersson; dataset statistics are shown in Table 1. Because we do no hyperparameter tuning, we do not use the development sets, and all results are reported on the test sets.

Each system was tested as recommended above, with accuracy reported separately on seen and unseen items, and for different training data sizes. To evaluate the downstream effects of normalization, we applied the models to a collection of unseen documents and then tagged them with the Stan-

ford POS tagger, which comes pre-trained on modern English. The documents are from the Parsed Corpus of Early English Correspondence (PCEEC) (Taylor et al., 2006), comprised of 84 letter collections from the 15th-17th centuries. (Our English normalization training data is from the 14th-17th centuries.) PCEEC contains roughly 2.2m manually POS-tagged tokens but no spelling annotation. Because it uses a large and somewhat idiosyncratic set of POS tags, we converted these to better match the Stanford tags before evaluating (though the match still isn't perfect; accuracy would be higher in all cases if the tag sets were identical). Baselines are provided by tagging the unnormalized text and the output of the naïve normalization baseline.

Results: normalization accuracy Table 2 gives test set results for all models, broken down into seen and unseen items where possible. [7] The split into seen/unseen highlights the fact that neither of the neural models does as well on seen items as the baseline; indeed the soft attention model is considerably worse in English and Hungarian, the two largest datasets.[8] The result is that this model actually underperforms the baseline when applied to all tokens, although a hybrid model (baseline for seen, soft attention for unseen) would outperform the baseline. Nevertheless, the hard attention model performs best on unseen tokens in all cases, often by a wide margin, and also yields competitive overall performance.

We also compared the accuracy of the two neural models at different training data sizes starting from 1k tokens. On *seen* tokens, the baseline was best in all cases except for 1k tokens in Hungarian and Icelandic (where the soft attention model was slightly better) and the largest two data sizes in German (where the hard attention model was slightly better). This supports our claim that learned models should typically only be applied to *unseen* tokens.

Accuracy on unseen tokens is shown in Figure 1. Note that the set of unseen items gets smaller

---

[6]English: Markus (1999); German: Scheible et al. (2011); Hungarian: Simon (2014); Icelandic: Rögnvaldsson et al. (2012); Swedish: Fiebranz et al. (2011). For details of their dates and contents, see Pettersson et al. (2014).

[7]We obtained our datasets from Pettersson et al. but our baseline results are slightly different from what they report. The differences (theirs–ours) are -0.1, 0.2, 0.4, 1.2, 0.6 for Eng, Ger, Hun, Ice, Swe respectively. This could be due to differences in tie-breaking methods, or to another unknown factor. These differences suggest using caution in directly comparing their non-baseline results to ours.

[8]When we varied the training data sizes, we found that the soft attention model actually gets *worse* on seen tokens in all languages as the training data increases beyond a relatively small size. We have no good explanation for this, and it's possible that tuning the parameters would help.

	English			German			Hungarian			Icelandic			Swedish		
	A	S	U	A	S	U	A	S	U	A	S	U	A	S	U
Hybrid	92.9			95.1			76.4			**84.6**			90.8		
GIZA++ un	**94.3**			**96.6**			79.9			71.8			**92.9**		
GIZA++ bi	92.4			95.5			80.1			71.5			92.5		
Mem. baseline	91.5	**96.9**	30.5	94.1	96.9	30.5	73.6	**96.0**	2.9	80.3	**86.8**	28.3	85.4	**98.1**	41.4
Soft attention	89.9	93.7	46.9	94.3	98.1	72.4	79.8	89.4	49.6	83.1	85.9	60.1	89.7	97.2	63.8
Hard attention	93.0	96.6	**52.4**	96.5	**99.3**	**80.5**	**88.0**	95.3	**65.0**	83.5	86.2	**61.4**	90.7	97.9	**65.7**

Table 2: Tokens normalized correctly (%) for each dataset. Upper half: results on (A)ll tokens reported by Pettersson et al. (2014) for a hybrid model (apply memorization baseline to seen tokens and an edit-distance-based model to unseen tokens) and two SMT models (which align character unigrams and bigrams, respectively). Lower half: results from our experiments, including accuracy reported separately on (S)een and (U)nseen tokens.

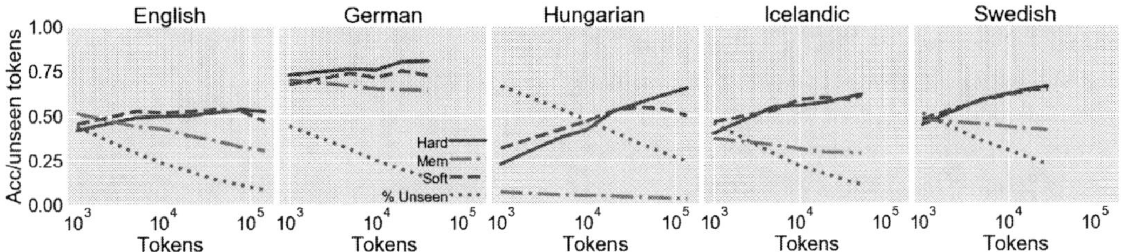

Figure 1: Proportion of unseen tokens, and normalization accuracy on those tokens, as training data size is varied.

and presumably more difficult as training data size increases, so the baseline gets worse. In contrast, the neural models are able to maintain or increase performance on this set. We expected that the bias toward monotonic alignments would help the hard attention model at smaller data sizes, but it is the soft attention model that seems to do better there, while the hard attention model does better in most cases at the larger data sizes. Note that Bollmann et al. (2017) trained their model on individual manuscripts, with no training set containing more than 13.2k tokens. The fact that this model struggles with larger data sizes, especially for seen tokens, suggests that the default hyperparameters may be tuned to work well with small training sets at the cost of underfitting the larger datasets.

Results: POS tagging Based on our results above, we tested the neural models by applying them only to unseen tokens in the PCEEC, and normalizing seen tokens using the naïve baseline in all cases. The PCEEC is a heterogeneous collection, so baseline tagger accuracy on the unnormalized text ranges from 52.0% to 82.6%, with an average of 71.0% (σ: 6.8). Figure 2 shows the effects of normalizing using the different methods.

Although normalizing provides a clear benefit, in most cases the neural models are no better than normalizing using the baseline method. The exception

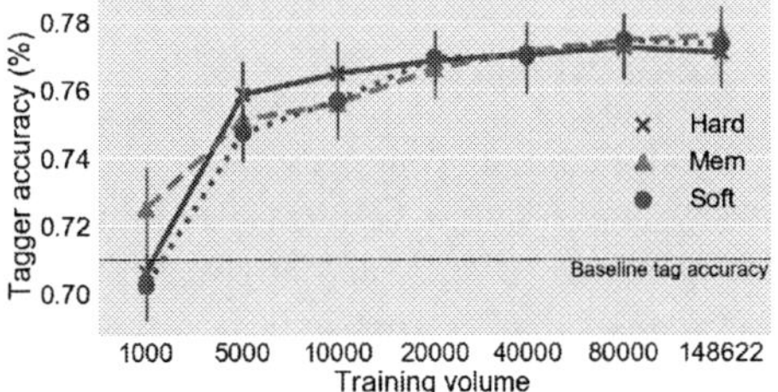

Figure 2: Average POS tagging accuracy on the unnormalized PCEEC texts (bottom of plot) and using three different normalization methods, as a function of the amount of data used to train the normalization systems.

is at 5k and 10k training items, where a two-tailed t-test shows that the hard attention model is significantly better than the other methods ($p < 0.01$). We also tried preprocessing both the normalization and tagging datasets by lowercasing all tokens; this resulted in small improvements in most cases (about 1 point) but any remaining differences were to the benefit of the baseline method.

Our findings differ from those of Pettersson et al. (2013b), who reported that their SMT-based system did work better than the baseline normalizer for POS tagging in Icelandic and verb identification in Swedish. Our contrasting findings could derive either from our use of different models or different datasets; nevertheless, they highlight the fact that intrinsic improvements do not always translate into extrinsic ones.

5   Conclusion

We have highlighted some important issues in the evaluation of historical text normalization systems: in particular, the need to report accuracy on unseen tokens and to compare performance to a naïve memorization baseline. Following these recommendations, we evaluated two neural models, one of which is new to this task. Across five languages, both models greatly outperformed the baseline on unseen tokens, with the soft attention model doing a bit better for smaller data sizes, and the hard attention model doing a bit better for larger ones. However, these improvements did not translate into clearly better POS tagging downstream.

Despite these mixed results, we hope that the evaluation guidelines presented here will help promote work in this area, in order to eventually provide better tools for working with historical text collections.

6   Acknowledgements

We thank Pettersson, Megyesi, and Nivre for the datasets, and Aharoni, Goldberg, and Ramat-Gan and Bollmann, Bingel, and Søgaard for making their code available. This work was supported in part by the EPSRC Centre for Doctoral Training in Data Science, funded by the UK Engineering and Physical Sciences Research Council (grant EP/L016427/1) and the University of Edinburgh.

References

Roee Aharoni, Yoav Goldberg, and Israel Ramat-Gan. 2017. Morphological inflection generation with hard monotonic attention. In *Proceedings of ACL*.

Alistair Baron and Paul Rayson. 2008. VARD2: A tool for dealing with spelling variation in historical corpora. In *Postgraduate Conference in Corpus Linguistics*.

Marcel Bollmann. 2012. Automatic normalization of historical texts using distance measures and the Norma tool. In *Proceedings of the Second Workshop on Annotation of Corpora for Research in the Humanities (ACRH-2), Lisbon, Portugal*.

Marcel Bollmann, Joachim Bingel, and Anders Søgaard. 2017. Learning attention for historical text normalization by learning to pronounce. In *Proceedings of ACL 2017*.

Marcel Bollmann, Florian Petran, and Stefanie Dipper. 2011. Applying rule-based normalization to different types of historical texts - an evaluation. In *Language and Technology Conference*. Springer, pages 166–177.

Marcel Bollmann and Anders Søgaard. 2016. Improving historical spelling normalization with bi-directional LSTMs and multi-task learning. In *Proceedings of COLING 2016, the 26th International Conference on Computational Linguistics*.

Rosemarie Fiebranz, Erik Lindberg, Jonas Lindström, and Maria Ågren. 2011. Making verbs count: the research project "Gender and Work" and its methodology. *Scandinavian Economic History Review* 59(3):273–293.

Andreas W Hauser and Klaus U Schulz. 2007. Unsupervised learning of edit distance weights for retrieving historical spelling variations. In *Proceedings of the First Workshop on Finite-State Techniques and Approximate Search*. pages 1–6.

Natalia Korchagina. 2017. Normalizing Medieval German texts: from rules to deep learning. In *Proceedings of the NoDaLiDa 2017 Workshop on Processing Historical Language*. Linköping University Electronic Press, 133, pages 12–17.

Manfred Markus. 1999. *Manual of ICAMET (Innsbruck Computer Archive of Machine-Readable English Texts)*. Leopold-Franzens-Universitat Innsbruck.

Petar Mitankin, Stefan Gerdjikov, and Stoyan Mihov. 2014. An approach to unsupervised historical text normalisation. In *Proceedings of the First International Conference on Digital Access to Textual Cultural Heritage*. ACM, New York, NY, USA, DATeCH '14, pages 29–34.

Eva Pettersson, Beáta Megyesi, and Joakim Nivre. 2013a. Normalisation of historical text using context-sensitive weighted Levenshtein distance and compound splitting. In *Proceedings of the 19th Nordic Conference of Computational Linguistics (NoDaLiDa 2013); Oslo University; Norway. NEALT Proceedings Series 16*. Linköping University Electronic Press, 085, pages 163–179.

Eva Pettersson, Beáta Megyesi, and Joakim Nivre. 2014. A multilingual evaluation of three spelling normalisation methods for historical text. In *LaTeCH@ EACL*. pages 32–41.

Eva Pettersson, Beáta Megyesi, and Jörg Tiedemann. 2013b. An SMT approach to automatic annotation of historical text. In *Proceedings of the Workshop on Computational Historical Linguistics at NoDaLiDa 2013; Oslo; Norway. NEALT Proceedings Series 18*. Linköping University Electronic Press, 087, pages 54–69.

Eiríkur Rögnvaldsson, Anton Karl Ingason, Einar Freyr Sigurðsson, and Joel Wallenberg. 2012. The Icelandic parsed historical corpus (IcePaHC). In *LREC*. pages 1977–1984.

Silke Scheible, Richard J Whitt, Martin Durrell, and Paul Bennett. 2011. A gold standard corpus of Early Modern German. In *Proceedings of the 5th linguistic annotation workshop*. Association for Computational Linguistics, pages 124–128.

Yves Scherrer and Tomaž Erjavec. 2013. Modernizing historical Slovene words with character-based SMT. In *Proceedings of the 4th Biennial International Workshop on Balto-Slavic Natural Language Processing*. Association for Computational Linguistics, Sofia, Bulgaria, pages 58–62.

Eszter Simon. 2014. Corpus building from Old Hungarian codices .

Ann Taylor, Arja Nurmi, Anthony Warner, Susan Pintzuk, and Terttu Nevalainen. 2006. The York-Helsinki Parsed Corpus of Early English Correspondence (PCEEC). Department of Linguistics, University of York.

Kelvin Xu, Jimmy Ba, Ryan Kiros, Kyunghyun Cho, Aaron Courville, Ruslan Salakhudinov, Rich Zemel, and Yoshua Bengio. 2015. Show, attend and tell: Neural image caption generation with visual attention. In *International Conference on Machine Learning*. pages 2048–2057.

Gated Multi-Task Network for Text Classification

Liqiang Xiao and **Honglun Zhang** and **Wenqing Chen**
State Key Lab of Advanced Optical Communication System and Network,
Shanghai Jiao Tong University
Artificial Intelligence Institute, Shanghai Jiao Tong University
800 Dongchuan Road, Shanghai, China
{xiaoliqiang,zhanghonglun,wenqingchen}@sjtu.edu.cn

Abstract

Multi-task learning with Convolutional Neural Network (CNN) has shown great success in many Natural Language Processing (NLP) tasks. This success can be largely attributed to the feature sharing by fusing some layers among tasks. However, most existing approaches just fully or proportionally share the features without distinguishing the helpfulness of them. By that the network would be confused by the helpless even harmful features, generating undesired interference between tasks. In this paper, we introduce gate mechanism into multi-task CNN and propose a new Gated Sharing Unit, which can filter the feature flows between tasks and greatly reduce the interference. Experiments on 9 text classification datasets shows that our approach can learn selection rules automatically and gain a great improvement over strong baselines.

1 Introduction

The combination of multi-task learning and neural networks has shown its advantages in many tasks, ranging from computer vision (Misra et al., 2016; Ruder et al., 2017) to natural language processing (Collobert and Weston, 2008). Multi-task learning (MTL) has the ability to share the knowledge among the joint tasks, which implicitly increases the training materials (Caruana, 1997). The shared knowledge help the network learn a more universal representation for the inputs. Inspired by this, more DNN-based approaches (Liu et al., 2015; Zhang et al., 2017) utilize multi-task learning to improve their performance.

The scheme for information sharing is the linchpin for designing an elaborate multi-task network. Most existing work attempts to find a appropriate proportion to sharing the layers between tasks, despite they entirely reuse the shallow layers (Liu et al., 2015; Caruana, 1993) or add the layers up at a ratio (Fang et al., 2017). And recently, the latter one shows its advantages for controlling relational intensity among tasks and become prevailing. More models adopt this thought to enhance the performance (Liu et al., 2015, 2016).

However, under the scheme of proportional addition (Ruder et al., 2017; Misra et al., 2016), all the features are shared with the same weight between every pair of tasks. Helpless or harmful features may be transported between tasks with the same importance as helpful ones, namely, the interference is generated. This would burden the network for distinguishing the helpful features and even mislead the predictions.

To solve above problem, we propose a new CNN-based architecture for multi-task learning, which can share features in a selective way. Our model allocates a private subnet to each task and transport the features between the subnets with a well-designed module—*Gated Sharing Unit*. It has the ability to filter features with gate mechanism (Chung et al., 2014; Srivastava et al., 2015) and select the helpful ones to benefit the tasks in hand, which expands the feature spaces and provides more evidence for right predictions. Our model is an end-to-end method and the proposed Gated Sharing Unit is easy to train.

We conduct extensive experiments on 9 benchmark datasets for text classification. The results show that our model greatly improves the performance and surpasses the single-task models and other competitors.

2 Gated Multi-Task Network

To make full use of multiple datasets and, meanwhile, avoid the interference, we introduce a new structure for multi-task learning in this section. The new structure is designed in a separative way—every task owns a private subnet. To share

726

Proceedings of NAACL-HLT 2018, pages 726–731
New Orleans, Louisiana, June 1 - 6, 2018. ©2018 Association for Computational Linguistics

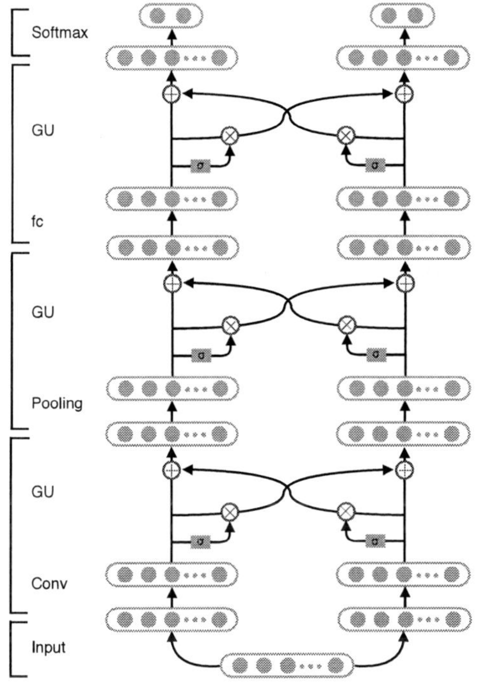

Figure 1: Illustration of the architecture for Gated Multi-Task CNN .

features across the subnets, gate mechanism is designed to selectively allow the features been exchanged. Our new model can be trained end-to-end, needing no extra supervision or handcraft hyperparameters. And it can be easily transferred to other networks such as DNN, RNN, LSTM, etc. Figure 1 illustrates the design of model structure and other details.

2.1 Model Architecture

Multi-task model with deeper layers shared can augment deeper knowledge and greatly increase the feature space (Zhang et al., 2017). But undesirable interference inevitably and simultaneously comes with the benefits, especially between less-related tasks. This would burden the models with the overhead on distinguishing helpful features. To overcome this problem, we assign each task a private subnet as illustrated in Figure 1. Tasks are relatively separated and can borrow the useful information from others through a bridge, Gated Sharing Unit (GSU). The weight of each feature in this unit is automatically learned from previous layers, needing no extra supervision, so there is more selectivity across the tasks. By filtering out useless features, tasks receive less interference

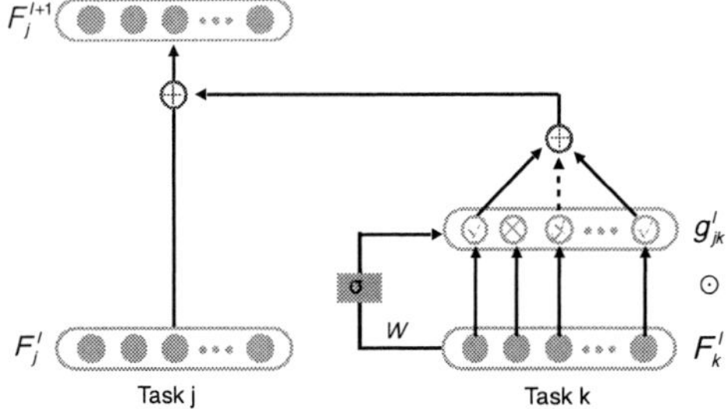

Figure 2: Illustration of Gated Sharing Unit

from each other.

2.2 Gated Sharing Unit

For reducing interference, it important to filter the information flows among the tasks. Hence, in this section, we introduce the mechanism of gate, which originates from the cells of recurrent neural networks like Long-Short Term Memory (LSTM) (Hochreiter and Schmidhuber, 1997), Gated Recurrent Unit (GRU) (Chung et al., 2014). Gated mechanism in existing studies not only shows its convenience for training (Srivastava et al., 2015), but also behaves as tool to route the information (He et al., 2016).

Inspirited by gate mechanism, we propose a new module GSU to control the information flows and selectively share the features among tasks. The details of this module is shown in Figure 2. For notation, we refer to C as the collection of N tasks and $C = \{1, 2, \cdots, N\}$. For a sample from arbitrary task j, a series of feature maps are generated in subnets. When task j borrows the features from task k, a gate $\mathbf{g}$ is inserted to select the helpful ones, which is calculated from the prior layer by

$$\mathbf{g}_{jk}^l = \sigma(\mathbf{W}_{jk}^l \cdot \mathbf{F}_k^l + \mathbf{b}_{jk}^l) \qquad (1)$$

where l means the level of the layers and σ denotes the nonlinear activation of sigmoid, which guarantees the values of $\mathbf{g}$ in the $[0, 1]$. Note that the gate $\mathbf{g}_{jk}^l$ is vector. Each component in it controls the pass of a corresponding feature. Their states move between pass and interception, or choose a middle ground if needed.

For task j, the output $\mathbf{F}_j^{l+1}$ of gates is calculated by fusing the lower layers $\mathbf{F}^l$ from all the tasks by

$$\mathbf{F}_j^{l+1} = \sum_{k \in C, k \neq j} \mathbf{g}_{jk}^l \odot \mathbf{F}_k^l + \mathbf{F}_j^l \qquad (2)$$

where $\odot$ denotes element-wise multiplication. To

represent the output for all the tasks C, we can stack Eq. (2) in matrix form

$$\begin{bmatrix} \mathbf{F}_1^{l+1} \\ \mathbf{F}_2^{l+1} \\ \vdots \\ \mathbf{F}_N^{l+1} \end{bmatrix} = \begin{bmatrix} 1 & g_{12}^l & \cdots & g_{1N}^l \\ g_{21}^l & 1 & \cdots & g_{2N}^l \\ \vdots & \vdots & \ddots & \vdots \\ g_{N1}^l & g_{N2}^l & \cdots & 1 \end{bmatrix} \begin{bmatrix} \mathbf{F}_1^l \\ \mathbf{F}_2^l \\ \vdots \\ \mathbf{F}_N^l \end{bmatrix} \quad (3)$$

From Eq. (2) and (3), we know that, in the GSU, the feature map for current task directly passes into the next layer. But the features from other tasks are merged into current task after the selection by gates. In this way, the shared features tend to be pure and helpful for current task, which avoids the harmful interference existing in conventional models.

For comparison, here we briefly introduce the methods that share the features by proportional addition (Misra et al., 2016; Ruder et al., 2017; Fang et al., 2017). They can be constructed by inserting a scaler weight α_{jk}^l between every two tasks i, j. α_{jk}^l is updated by back-propagation and reflects the degree of association between tasks, but do not select the features. In this paper, this kind of models is alluded to as PA-CNN.

2.3 Output Layer and Loss

In the last layer of task j, vector representations $\hat{\mathbf{F}}_j$ of input sequences are ultimately fed into corresponding softmax layers to fit the number of classes, which emits the prediction of probability distribution for the task j

$$\hat{y}_j = softmax(\mathbf{W}_j\hat{\mathbf{F}}_j + b_j) \quad (4)$$

where $\hat{y}_j$ is predictive result; $\mathbf{W}_j$ is the weight of the full-connected layer; and b_j is the bias term.

Given the prediction of all tasks, a global loss function forces the model to minimize the cross-entropy of prediction and true distribution for all the tasks:

$$\Phi = \sum_{j=1}^{N} \lambda_j L(\hat{y}_j, y_j) \quad (5)$$

where λ_j is the weight for the task j. In this paper, we set λ_j to $1/N$ for all N tasks to make a balance.

3 Experiments

In this section, we demonstrate the empirical performance of our model on 9 related benchmark tasks for text classification. And the results are compared with the state-of-the-art models.

Dataset	Train	Dev.	Test	V	L
Books	1398	200	400	22K	159
Electronics	1398	200	400	11K	111
DVDs	1400	200	400	22K	189
Kitchen	1400	200	400	10K	93
Apparel	1400	200	400	8K	64
Baby	1300	200	400	9K	173
RN	7860	1122	2246	29K	147
SUBJ	8000	1000	1000	21K	23
TREC	4907	545	500	10K	10

Table 1: Statistics of the text classification datasets. Train, Dev. and Test denote the size of train, development and test set respectively; C: Vocabulary size; L: Average sentence length.

3.1 Datasets

As Table 1 shows, we select 9 related benchmark datasets for text classification.

The first 6 datasets are all about product reviews, which are comprised of Amazon product reviews in 6 domains, including books, DVDs, cameras, etc. These corpora are classified according to the sentiment of positiveness or negativeness. They are collected from the raw data published by (Blitzer et al., 2007).

The rest 3 datasets are RN, SUBJ and TREC. RN is a dataset about news topic classification, which is collected from Reuters Newswire and published by (Velasco et al., 1994); SUBJ is a subjectivity dataset, whose task is to classify a sentence level text as being subjective or objective (Pang et al., 2004); TREC dataset has the task of classifying a question into 6 types (the questions are about location, person, numeric information, etc.)(Li and Roth, 2002).

3.2 Hyperparameters and Training

For all the experiments, we employ Word2Vec (Mikolov et al., 2013) to initialized the word vectors, which is trained on Google News with 100 billion words. The vectors have dimensionality of 300 and are trained by continuous bag-of-words architecture. All the other parameters are initialized with random values from uniform distribution in [-0.1, 0.1]. For every subnet we use: rectified linear units, filter windows of 3,4,5 with 100 feature maps each, mini-batch size of 50, dropout rate of 0.5, l_2 constrain of 3, learning rate of 10^{-3}. All the hyper-parameters are chosen via a small grid search on dev set. For the dataset without a stan-

Dataset	Single-Task (%)			Multi-Task (%)				
	DCNN	LSTM	BiLSTM	MT-DNN	MT-RNN	MT-CNN	PA-CNN	GMT-CNN
Books	80.7	79.5	81.0	82.3	83.3	84.0	82.2	**84.4**
Electronics	78.3	80.5	78.5	81.6	84.6	83.1	84.8	**86.9**
DVDs	80.6	81.7	80.5	83.8	84.2	84.0	83.7	**85.4**
Kitchen	79.8	78.0	81.2	80.8	**86.0**	83.4	85.1	85.9
Apparel	84.2	83.2	86.0	85.1	86.3	83.6	**87.2**	87.0
Baby	84.1	84.7	84.5	88.0	87.6	87.8	86.5	**88.3**
RN	83.6	83.5	83.7	83.9	84.2	84.3	83.6	**85.0**
SUBJ	93.0	93.1	93.2	92.7	**94.1**	92.9	93.1	94.0
TREC	93.0	92.7	93.0	93.2	93.5	93.7	93.3	**94.2**
Avg.	84.1	84.1	84.6	$85.7_{(+1.1)}$	$87.0_{(+2.4)}$	$86.3_{(+1.7)}$	$86.6_{(+2.0)}$	$\mathbf{87.9}_{(+3.3)}$

Table 2: Accuracies of our model against other state-of-the-art methods. Single-Task column shows the results of plain DCNN(Kalchbrenner et al., 2014), LSTM(Jozefowicz et al., 2015) and BiLSTM. First 3 models in the Multi-Task column shows the results of multi-task models: MT-DCNN (Liu et al., 2015), MT-RNN (Zhang et al., 2017), MT-CNN (Collobert and Weston, 2008). The remaining columns of PA-CNN and GMT-CNN shows the performance of proportional addition or gate mechanism. Number in round bracket denotes the average improvement over BiLSTM.

dard dev set we randomly select 10% as dev set. The whole network is trained through stochastic gradient decent using Adadelta update rule (Zeiler, 2012).

3.3 Performance of Multi-task CNN

Table 2 shows the comparison of the accuracies. All the results for multi-task learning models are achieved by training simultaneously on 9 datasets. From the table, we can see that the models employing multi-task learning improve the performance on most tasks beyond the single-task models, in which our model achieves the highest accuracies. Specifically, our model boosts the performance by 3.3% over the best single-task model BiLSTM, outstripping other multi-task models by at least 0.9%. Additionally, we also compare our model with the PA-CNN, a variant keeps the structure of GMT-CNN but shares the features by proportional additions. For PA-CNN, performance on several datasets is decreased than single-task due to the interference. In contract, our model shows steady improvement in all the datasets and surpasses PA-CNN by 1.3%, which indicates the effectiveness of gate mechanism.

3.4 Visualization

To intuitively show the selection process, we design an experiment to show the values of gates and how they block the useless features. For the first convolutional layer and GSU, we visualize the activations $\mathbf{F}_j^1$ of the filters with normalized values and show their corresponding weights $\mathbf{g}_{jk}^1$ in the

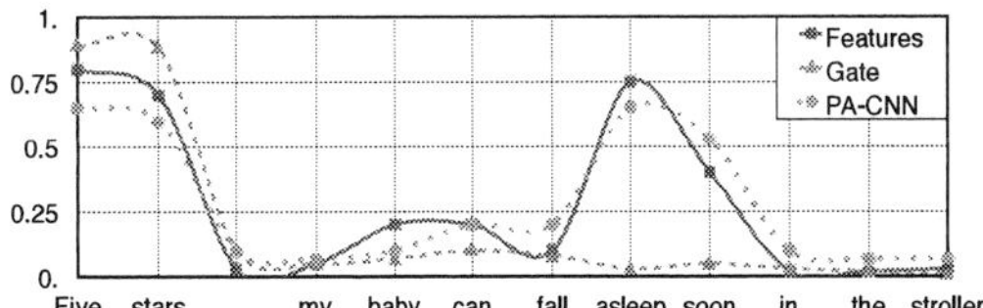

Figure 3: Features line illustrates feature weights in $\mathbf{F}_{dvds}^1$ in DVDs subnet. And Gate line shows the value of $\mathbf{g}_{baby \leftarrow dvds}^1$ that filters the features from DVDs subnet to Baby subnet. PA-CNN line visualizes the feature weights in the first layer of PA-CNN.

gate units. By that we can easily find what kind of features are discarded as interference.

Figure 3 illustrates the behavior of GSU on a random selected sentence from Baby task. We visualize the results of the first feature map for DVDs subnet and the gate unit that filters the features from DVDs to Baby task. For the positive sentence "Five stars, my baby can fall asleep soon in the stroller", we can see that subnet for DVDs task focuses on two critical positions "Five stars" and "asleep". The word "asleep" is negative for DVDs task, but actually neutral for Baby task. Successfully, our gated unit lowers the intensity of the interference "asleep", making a correct prediction. However, PA-CNN wrongly makes a negative prediction for lacking resistance to interference. This indicates the effectiveness of our gate mechanism for the feature selection in MTL.

4   Conclusion and Future Work

In this paper, we introduce gate mechanism in multi-task CNN to reduce the interference. The proposed model has an ability to select the potentially useful features, which can reduce the interference among tests. The effectiveness of our method is fully validated on 9 datasets for text classification and further illustrated by visualization experiment.

In future work, we would like to investigate the effect of memory mechanism for multi-task learning, which is similar to gate mechanism but more complex. It originates from recurrent neural network and have been proven effective for feature selection.

5   Acknowledge

We would like to thank Yaohui Jin and Yongkun Wang for their careful guidance. Besides, we appreciate the constructive advices from Naoki Yoshinaga and the valuable comments from anonymous reviewers. This research was funded by National Natural Science Foundation of China under Grant No. 61371048.

References

John Blitzer, Mark Dredze, and Fernando Pereira. 2007. Biographies, bollywood, boom-boxes and blenders: Domain adaptation for sentiment classification. In *ACL 2007, Proceedings of the 45th Annual Meeting of the Association for Computational Linguistics, June 23-30, 2007, Prague, Czech Republic.* http://aclweb.org/anthology/P07-1056.

Rich Caruana. 1993. Multitask learning: A knowledge-based source of inductive bias. In *Machine Learning, Proceedings of the Tenth International Conference, University of Massachusetts, Amherst, MA, USA, June 27-29, 1993.* pages 41–48.

Rich Caruana. 1997. Multitask learning. *Machine Learning* 28(1):41–75.

Junyoung Chung, Çaglar Gülçehre, KyungHyun Cho, and Yoshua Bengio. 2014. Empirical evaluation of gated recurrent neural networks on sequence modeling. *CoRR* abs/1412.3555. http://arxiv.org/abs/1412.3555.

Ronan Collobert and Jason Weston. 2008. A unified architecture for natural language processing: deep neural networks with multitask learning. In *Machine Learning, Proceedings of the Twenty-Fifth International Conference (ICML 2008), Helsinki, Finland, June 5-9, 2008.* pages 160–167. https://doi.org/10.1145/1390156.1390177.

Yuchun Fang, Zhengyan Ma, Zhaoxiang Zhang, Xu-Yao Zhang, and Xiang Bai. 2017. Dynamic multi-task learning with convolutional neural network. In *Proceedings of the Twenty-Sixth International Joint Conference on Artificial Intelligence, IJCAI 2017, Melbourne, Australia, August 19-25, 2017.* pages 1668–1674. https://doi.org/10.24963/ijcai.2017/231.

Kaiming He, Xiangyu Zhang, Shaoqing Ren, and Jian Sun. 2016. Deep residual learning for image recognition. In *2016 IEEE Conference on Computer Vision and Pattern Recognition, CVPR 2016, Las Vegas, NV, USA, June 27-30, 2016.* pages 770–778. https://doi.org/10.1109/CVPR.2016.90.

Sepp Hochreiter and Jürgen Schmidhuber. 1997. Long short-term memory. *Neural Computation* 9(8):1735–1780. https://doi.org/10.1162/neco.1997.9.8.1735.

Rafal Jozefowicz, Wojciech Zaremba, and Ilya Sutskever. 2015. An empirical exploration of recurrent network architectures. In *International Conference on International Conference on Machine Learning.* pages 2342–2350.

Nal Kalchbrenner, Edward Grefenstette, and Phil Blunsom. 2014. A convolutional neural network for modelling sentences. In *Proceedings of the 52nd Annual Meeting of the Association for Computational Linguistics, ACL 2014, June 22-27, 2014, Baltimore, MD, USA, Volume 1: Long Papers.* pages 655–665. http://aclweb.org/anthology/P/P14/P14-1062.pdf.

Xin Li and Dan Roth. 2002. Learning question classifiers. *Coling* 12(24):556–562.

Pengfei Liu, Xipeng Qiu, and Xuanjing Huang. 2016. Recurrent neural network for text classification with multi-task learning .

Xiaodong Liu, Jianfeng Gao, Xiaodong He, Li Deng, Kevin Duh, and Ye Yi Wang. 2015. Representation learning using multi-task deep neural networks for semantic classification and information retrieval. In *Conference of the North American Chapter of the Association for Computational Linguistics: Human Language Technologies.* pages 912–921.

Tomas Mikolov, Ilya Sutskever, Kai Chen, Greg Corrado, and Jeffrey Dean. 2013. Distributed representations of words and phrases and their compositionality. *Advances in Neural Information Processing Systems* 26:3111–3119.

Ishan Misra, Abhinav Shrivastava, Abhinav Gupta, and Martial Hebert. 2016. Cross-stitch networks for multi-task learning. In *The IEEE Conference on Computer Vision and Pattern Recognition (CVPR).*

Pang, Bo, Lee, and Lillian. 2004. A sentimental education: sentiment analysis using subjectivity summarization based on minimum cuts. *Proceedings of Acl* pages 271–278.

Sebastian Ruder, Joachim Bingel, Isabelle Augenstein, and Anders Sgaard. 2017. Sluice networks: Learning what to share between loosely related tasks .

Rupesh Kumar Srivastava, Klaus Greff, and Jürgen Schmidhuber. 2015. Highway networks. *CoRR* abs/1505.00387. http://arxiv.org/abs/1505.00387.

E Velasco, L. C. Thuler, C. A. Martins, L. M. Dias, and V. M. Gonalves. 1994. Automated learning of decision rules for text categorization. *Acm Transactions on Information Systems* 12(3):233–251.

Matthew D. Zeiler. 2012. Adadelta: An adaptive learning rate method. *Computer Science* .

Honglun Zhang, Liqiang Xiao, Yongkun Wang, and Yaohui Jin. 2017. A generalized recurrent neural architecture for text classification with multi-task learning. In *Proceedings of the Twenty-Sixth International Joint Conference on Artificial Intelligence, IJCAI 2017, Melbourne, Australia, August 19-25, 2017*. pages 3385–3391. https://doi.org/10.24963/ijcai.2017/473.

Natural Language to Structured Query Generation via Meta-Learning

Po-Sen Huang*, Chenglong Wang[†], Rishabh Singh*, Wen-tau Yih[‡], Xiaodong He*◇
*Microsoft Research, [†]University of Washington,
[‡]Allen Institute for Artificial Intelligence, ◇JD AI Research
pshuang@microsoft.com, clwang@cs.washington.edu,
rishabh.iit@gmail.com, scottyih@allenai.org, xiaodong.he@jd.com

Abstract

In conventional supervised training, a model is trained to fit all the training examples. However, having a monolithic model may not always be the best strategy, as examples could vary widely. In this work, we explore a different learning protocol that treats each example as a unique *pseudo-task*, by reducing the original learning problem to a few-shot meta-learning scenario with the help of a domain-dependent *relevance function*. When evaluated on the WikiSQL dataset, our approach leads to faster convergence and achieves 1.1%–5.4% absolute accuracy gains over the non-meta-learning counterparts.

1 Introduction

Conventional supervised training is a pervasive paradigm for NLP problems. In this setting, a model is trained to fit all the training examples and their corresponding targets. However, while sharing the same surface form of the prediction task, examples of the same problem may vary widely. For instance, *recognizing textual entailment* is a binary classification problem on whether the hypothesis follows a given textual statement, but the challenge datasets consist of a huge variety of inference categories and genres (Dagan et al., 2013; Williams et al., 2017). Similarly, for a semantic parsing problem that maps natural language questions to SQL statements, the number of conditions in a SQL query or the length of a question can vary substantially (Zhong et al., 2017).

The inherently high variety of the examples suggests an alternative training protocol: instead of learning a monolithic, one-size-fits-all model, it could be more effective to learn multiple models, where each one is designed for a specific "task" that covers a group of *similar* examples. How-

ever, this strategy is faced with at least two difficulties. As the number of tasks increases, each task will have much fewer training examples for learning a robust model. In addition, the notion of "task", namely the group of examples, is typically not available in the dataset.

In this work, we explore this alternative learning setting and address the two difficulties by adapting the *meta-learning* framework. Motivated by the few-shot learning scenario (Andrychowicz et al., 2016; Ravi and Larochelle, 2016; Vinyals et al., 2016), meta-learning aims to learn a general model that can quickly adapt to a new task given very few examples without retraining the model from scratch (Finn et al., 2017). We extend this framework by effectively creating *pseudo-tasks* with the help of a *relevance function*. During training, each example is viewed as the test example of an individual "task", where its top-K relevant instances are used as training examples for this specific task. A general model is trained for all tasks in aggregation. Similarly during testing, instead of applying the general model directly, the top-K relevant instances (in the training set) to the given test example are first selected to update the general model, which then makes the final prediction. The overview of the proposed framework is shown in Figure 1.

When empirically evaluated on a recently proposed, large semantic parsing dataset, WikiSQL (Zhong et al., 2017), our approach leads to faster convergence and achieves 1.1%–5.4% absolute accuracy gain over the non-meta-learning counterparts, establishing a new state-of-the-art result. More importantly, we demonstrate how to design a relevance function to successfully reduce a regular supervised learning problem to a meta-learning problem. To the best of our knowledge, this is the first successful attempt in adapting meta-learning to a semantic task.

---

*Work performed while XH was at Microsoft Research.

Proceedings of NAACL-HLT 2018, pages 732–738
New Orleans, Louisiana, June 1 - 6, 2018. ©2018 Association for Computational Linguistics

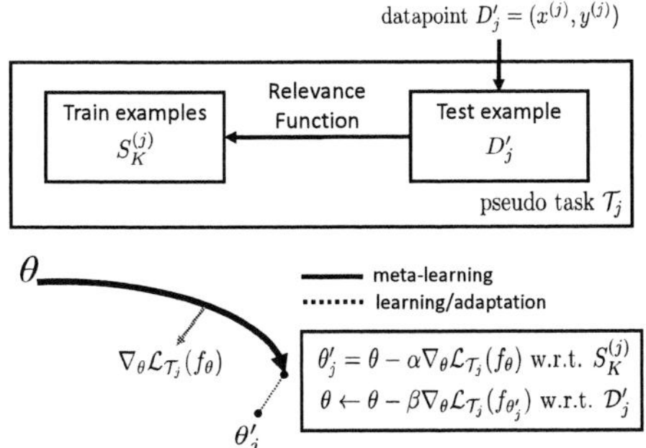

Figure 1: Diagram of the proposed framework. (Upper) we propose using a relevant function to find a support set $S_K^{(j)}$ from all training datapoints given a datapoint D'_j for constructing a pseudo-task $\mathcal{T}_j$ as in the few-shot meta-learning setup. (Bottom) We optimize the model parameters θ such that the model can learn to adapt a new task with parameters θ'_j via a few gradient steps on the training examples of the new task. The model is updated by considering the test error on the test example of the new task. See Section 2 for detail.

2 Background: Meta-Learning

Our work is built on the recently proposed Model-Agnostic Meta-Learning (MAML) framework (Finn et al., 2017), which we describe briefly here. MAML aims to learn the *learners* (for the tasks) and the *meta-learner* in the few-shot meta-learning setup (Vinyals et al., 2016; Andrychowicz et al., 2016; Ravi and Larochelle, 2016). Formally, it considers a model that is represented by a function f_θ with parameters θ. When the model adapts to a new task $\mathcal{T}_i$, the model changes parameters θ to θ'_i, where a task contains K training examples and one or more test examples (K-shot learning). MAML updates the parameters θ'_i by one or a few rounds of gradient descent based on the training examples of task $\mathcal{T}_i$. For example, with one gradient update,

$$\theta'_i = \theta - \alpha \nabla_\theta \mathcal{L}_{\mathcal{T}_i}(f_\theta),$$

where the step size α is a hyper-parameter; $\mathcal{L}_{\mathcal{T}_i}(f_\theta)$ is a loss function that evaluates the error between the prediction $f_\theta(\mathbf{x}^{(j)})$ and target $\mathbf{y}^{(j)}$, where $\mathbf{x}^{(j)}, \mathbf{y}^{(j)}$ are an input/output pair sampled from the training examples of task $\mathcal{T}_i$. Model parameters θ are trained to optimize the performance of $f_{\theta'_i}$ on the unseen test examples from $\mathcal{T}_i$ across tasks. The meta-objective is:

$$\min_\theta \sum_{\mathcal{T}_i \sim p(\mathcal{T})} \mathcal{L}_{\mathcal{T}_i}(f_{\theta'_i}) = \sum_{\mathcal{T}_i \sim p(\mathcal{T})} \mathcal{L}_{\mathcal{T}_i}(f_{\theta - \alpha \nabla_\theta \mathcal{L}_{\mathcal{T}_i}(f_\theta)})$$

The goal of MAML is to optimize the model parameters θ such that the model can learn to adapt new tasks with parameters θ'_i via a few gradient steps on the training examples of new tasks. The model is improved by considering how the test error on unseen test data from $\mathcal{T}_i$ changes with respect to the parameters.

The meta-objective across tasks is optimized using stochastic gradient descent (SGD). The model parameters θ are updated as follows:

$$\theta \leftarrow \theta - \beta \nabla_\theta \sum_{\mathcal{T}_i \sim p(\mathcal{T})} \mathcal{L}_{\mathcal{T}_i}(f_{\theta'_i}),$$

where β is the meta step size.

3 Approach

As discussed in Section 1, to reduce traditional supervised learning to a few-shot meta-learning problem, we introduce a *relevance function*, which effectively helps group examples to form *pseudo-tasks*. Because the relevance function is problem-dependent, we first describe the semantic parsing problem below, followed by the design of our relevance function and the complete algorithm.

3.1 The Semantic Parsing Task

The specific semantic parsing problem we study in this work is to map a natural language question to a SQL query, which can be executed against a given table to find the answer to the original question. In particular, we use the currently largest natural language questions to SQL dataset, WikiSQL (Zhong et al., 2017), to develop our model and to conduct the experiments.

3.2 Relevance Function

The intuition behind the design of a relevance function is that examples of the same type should have higher scores. For the questions to SQL problem, we design a simple relevance function that depends on (1) the predicted type of the corresponding SQL query and (2) the question length.

There are five SQL types in the WikiSQL dataset: {Count, Min, Max, Sum, Avg, Select}. We train a SQL type classifier f_{sql} using SVMs with bag-of-words features of the input question, which achieves 93.5% training accuracy and 88% test accuracy in SQL type prediction. Another soft indication on whether two questions can be viewed as belonging to the same "task" is their lengths, as they correlate to the lengths of the mapped SQL queries. The length of a question is the number of tokens in it after normal-

---

Algorithm 1 Pseudo-Task MAML (PT-MAML)

Require: Training Datapoints $\mathcal{D} = \{\mathbf{x}^{(j)}, \mathbf{y}^{(j)}\}$
Require: α, β: step size hyperparameters
Require: K: support set size hyperparameter
1: Construct a task $\mathcal{T}_j$ with training examples using a support set $\mathcal{S}_K^{(j)}$ and a test example $\mathcal{D}_j' = (\mathbf{x}^{(j)}, \mathbf{y}^{(j)})$.
2: Denote $p(\mathcal{T})$ as distribution over tasks
3: Randomly initialize θ
4: **while** not done **do**
5:     Sample batch of tasks $\mathcal{T}_i \sim p(\mathcal{T})$
6:     **for all** $\mathcal{T}_i$ **do**
7:        Evaluate $\nabla_\theta \mathcal{L}_{\mathcal{T}_i}(f_\theta)$ using $\mathcal{S}_K^{(j)}$
8:        Compute adapted parameters with gradient descent: $\theta_i' = \theta - \alpha \nabla_\theta \mathcal{L}_{\mathcal{T}_i}(f_\theta)$
9:     **end for**
10:    Update $\theta \leftarrow \theta - \beta \nabla_\theta \sum_{\mathcal{T}_i \sim p(\mathcal{T})} \mathcal{L}_{\mathcal{T}_i}(f_{\theta_i'})$ using each $\mathcal{D}_i'$ from $\mathcal{T}_i$ and $\mathcal{L}_{\mathcal{T}_i}$ for the meta-update
11: **end while**

---

izing entity mentions to single tokens.[1] Our relevance function only considers examples of the same predicted SQL types. If examples $\mathbf{x}^{(i)}$ and $\mathbf{x}^{(j)}$ have the same SQL type, then their relevance score is $1 - |q_{len}(\mathbf{x}^{(i)}) - q_{len}(\mathbf{x}^{(j)})|$, where q_{len} calculates the question length. Notice that the relevance function does not need to be highly accurate as there is no formal definition on which examples should be grouped in the same pseudo-task. A heuristic-based function that encodes some domain knowledge typically works well based on our preliminary study. In principle, the relevance function can also be jointly learned with the meta-learning model, which we leave for future work.

3.3 Algorithm

Given a relevance function, the adaptation of the meta-learning using the MAML framework can be summarized in Algorithm 1, called Pseudo-Task MAML (PT-MAML). For each training example $\mathbf{x}^{(j)}$, we create a pseudo-task $\mathcal{T}_j$ using the top-K relevant examples as the support set $\mathcal{S}_K^{(j)}$ (Step 1). The remaining steps of the algorithm mimics the original MAML design, update task-level models (Step 8) and the meta-level, general model (Step 10) using gradient descent.

---

[1]Phrases in questions that can match some table cells are treated as entities.

4 Experiments

In this section, we introduce the WikiSQL dataset and preprocessing steps, the learner model in our meta-learning setup, and the experimental results.

4.1 Dataset

We evaluate our model on the WikiSQL dataset (Zhong et al., 2017). We follow the data preprocessing in (Wang et al., 2017). Specifically, we first preprocess the dataset by running both tables and question-query pairs through Stanford Stanza (Manning et al., 2014) using the script included with the WikiSQL dataset, which normalizes punctuations and cases of the dataset. We further normalize each question based on its corresponding table: for table entries and columns occurring in questions or queries, we normalize their format to be consistent with the table. After preprocessing, we filter the training set by removing pairs whose ground truth solution contains constants not mentioned in the question, as our model requires the constants to be copied from the question. We train and tune our model only on the filtered training and filtered development set, but we report our evaluation on the full development and test sets. We obtain 59,845 (originally 61,297) training pairs, 8,928 (originally 9,145) development pairs and 17,283 test pairs (the test set is not filtered).

4.2 Learner Model

We use the model of Wang et al. (2017) as the *learner* in our meta-learning setup. The model is a grammar-aware Seq2Seq encoder-decoder model with attention (Cho et al., 2014; Bahdanau et al., 2014). The encoder is a bidirectional LSTM, which takes the concatenation of the table header (column names) of the queried table and the question as input to learn a joint representation. The decoder is another LSTM with attention mechanism. There are three output layers corresponding to three decoding types, which restricts the vocabulary it can sample from at each decoding step. The three decoding types are defined as follows:

- τ_V (SQL operator): The output has to be a SQL operator, i.e., a terminal from $V = \{$`Select, From, Where, Id, Max, Min, Count, Sum, Avg, And`, $=, >, \geq, <, \leq,$ `<END>, <GO>`$\}$.
- τ_C (column name): The output has to be a column name, which will be copied from either the table header or the query section of

Model	Dev		Test	
	Acc_{lf}	Acc_{ex}	Acc_{lf}	Acc_{ex}
PointerNet (2017)	44.1%	53.8%	43.3%	53.3%
Seq2SQL (2017)	49.5%	60.8%	48.3%	59.4%
Pointer loss (2017)	46.8%	52.1%	46.1%	51.8%
Meta + Pointer loss	**52.0%**	**57.7%**	**51.4%**	**57.2%**
Max loss (2017)	61.3%	66.9%	60.5%	65.8%
Meta + Max loss	**62.1%**	**67.3%**	**61.6%**	**67.0%**
Sum loss (2017)	62.0%	67.1%	61.5%	66.8%
Meta + Sum loss	**63.1%**	**68.3%**	**62.8%**	**68.0%**

Table 1: Experimental Results on the WikiSQL dataset, where Acc_{lf} represents the logical form accuracy and Acc_{ex} represents the SQL execution accuracy. "Pointer loss", "Max loss", and "Sum loss" are the non-meta-learning counterpart from Wang et al. (2017). "Meta + X" denotes the meta-learning model with learner "X".

the input sequence. Note that the column required for the correct SQL output may or may not be mentioned explicitly in the question.

- τ_Q (constant value): The output is a constant that would be copied from the question section of the input sequence.

The grammar of SQL expressions in the the WikiSQL dataset can be described in regular expression as "`Select` f c `From` t `Where` (c op v)*" (f refers to an aggregation function, c refers to a column name, t refers to the table name, op refers an comparator and v refers to a value). The form can be represented by a decoding-type sequence $\tau_V \tau_V \tau_C \tau_V \tau_C \tau_V (\tau_C \tau_V \tau_Q)^*$, which will ensure only decoding-type corrected tokens can be sampled at each decoding step.

Wang et al. (2017) propose three cross-entropy based loss functions: "Pointer loss", which is the cross-entropy between target index and the chosen index, "Max loss", which computes the probability of copying a token v in the input as the maximum probability of pointers that point to token v, and "Sum loss", which computes the probability of copying a token v in the input as the sum of probabilities of pointers that point to token v. See (Wang et al., 2017) for more detail.

4.3 Model Hyperparameters

We use the pre-trained n-gram embeddings by Hashimoto et al. (2017) (100 dimension) and the GloVe word embedding (100 dimension) by Pennington et al. (2014); each token is embedded into a 200 dimensional vector. The encoder is a 3-layer bidirectional LSTM with hidden states of size 100, and the decoder is a 3-layer unidirectional LSTM with hidden states of size 100. The model is trained with question-query pairs with a

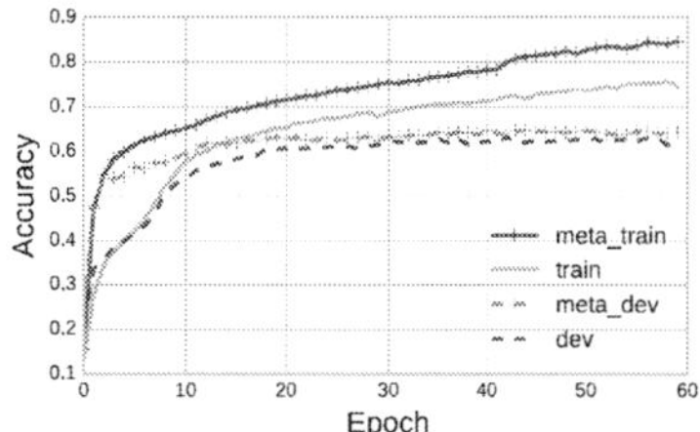

Figure 2: Logical form accuracy comparison, where "meta_train" and "meta_dev" are the train and development set accuracy using the "Meta + Sum loss" model, "train" and "dev" are the train and development set accuracy using the "Sum loss" model (Wang et al., 2017).

batch size of 200 for 100 epochs. During training, we clip gradients at 5 and add gradient noise with $\eta = 0.3$, $\gamma = 0.55$ to stabilize training (Neelakantan et al., 2015). We found the meta-learning model is trained stably without back-propagating to second order gradients. We select the support set size K to be 2 based on the development set. Empirically, the performance does not improve when we use a larger K. We set the learning rates $\alpha = 0.001$ and $\beta = 0.1$ based on the development set. The model is implemented in Tensorflow and trained using Adagrad (Duchi et al., 2011).

4.4 Results

Table 1 shows the experimental results of our model on the WikiSQL dataset. We select the model based on the best logical form accuracy on the development set, and compare our results to augmented pointer network and the Seq2SQL model (with RL) in (Zhong et al., 2017). Both logical form accuracy (denoted by Acc_{lf}) that compares the exact SQL syntax match, and the SQL execution results (denoted by Acc_{ex}) are reported. We compare our approach with its non-meta-learning counterpart using "Pointer loss", "Max loss", and "Sum loss" losses from (Wang et al., 2017). Our model achieves 1.1%–5.3% and 1.2%–5.4% gains on the test set logical form and execution accuracy, respectively.

We also investigate the training and development set logical form accuracy over different epochs by "Meta + Sum loss" and "Sum loss" models. The results are shown in Figure 2. One interesting observation is that the "Meta + Sum loss" model converges much faster than the "Sum loss" model especially in the first 10 epochs. We attribute this improvement to the ability to adapt to new tasks even with a small number of training examples.

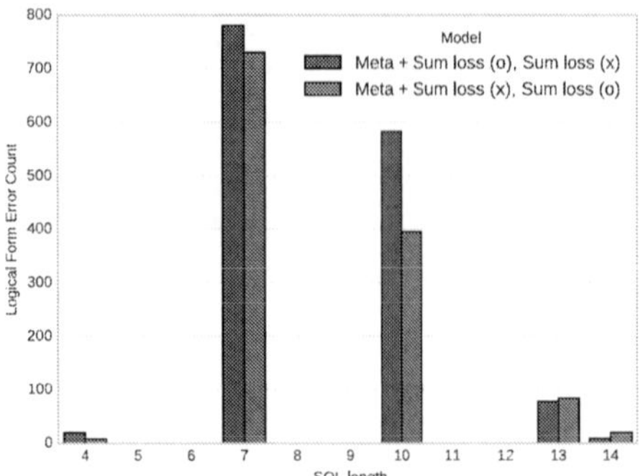

Figure 3: Logical form accuracy comparison. "Meta + Sum loss (o), Sum loss (x)" indicates the generated SQL is incorrect by the "Sum loss" model and is correct by the "Meta + Sum loss" model. Similarly, "Meta + Sum loss (x), Sum loss (o)" indicates the generated SQL is incorrect by the "Meta + Sum loss" model and is correct by the "Sum loss" model.

We compare the logical form error on the test set between the "Sum loss" model (Wang et al., 2017) and the proposed "Meta + Sum loss" model. Among the 17,283 test examples, there are 6,661 and 6,428 errors by the "Sum loss" and the "Meta + Sum loss", respectively. There are 5,190 common errors by both models. We examine the test examples where "Sum loss" is correct while "Meta + Sum loss" is not and vice versa, shown in Figure 3. We observe that the differences are mainly in ground truth SQL length = 7 and 10, where the "Meta + Sum loss" model outperforms "Sum loss" model by a large margin. We show some examples for the two cases in the supplementary material.

5   Related Work

Meta Learning One popular direction of meta-learning (Thrun and Pratt, 1998; Schmidhuber, 1987; Naik and Mammone, 1992) is to train a meta-learner that learns how to update the parameters of the learners model (Bengio et al., 1992; Schmidhuber, 1992). This direction has been applied to learning to optimize deep neural networks (Hochreiter et al., 2001; Andrychowicz et al., 2016; Li and Malik, 2017; Ha et al., 2017). Few-shot learning methods have also adapted meta-learning approaches for image recognition (Koch, 2015; Ravi and Larochelle, 2016; Vinyals et al., 2016) and reinforcement learning (Finn et al., 2017). Given that the few-shot learning setup cannot directly work in standard supervised learning problems, we explore reducing a regular supervised learning problem to the few-shot meta-learning scenario by creating pseudo-tasks with a relevance function.

Semantic Parsing Mapping natural language to logic forms has been actively studied in natural language processing research (Zettlemoyer and Collins, 2005; Giordani and Moschitti, 2010; Artzi and Zettlemoyer, 2011; Berant et al., 2013; Vlachos and Clark, 2014; Yih et al., 2014, 2015; Wang et al., 2015; Golub and He, 2016; Iyer et al., 2017; Krishnamurthy et al., 2017). However, unlike conventional approaches, which fit one model for all training examples, the proposed approach learns to adapt to new tasks. By using the support set based on the relevance function, the proposed model can adapt to a unique model for each example.

Program Induction / Synthesis Program induction (Reed and De Freitas, 2016; Neelakantan et al., 2015; Graves et al., 2014; Yin et al., 2015; Devlin et al., 2017) aims to infer latent programs given input/output examples, while program synthesis models (Zhong et al., 2017; Parisotto et al., 2017) aim to generate explicit programs and then execute them to get output. The learner model we used in this work follows the line of program synthesis models and trains on pairs of natural language (question) and program (SQL) directly.

6   Conclusion

In this paper, we propose a new learning protocol that reduces a regular supervised learning problem to the few-shot meta-learning scenario. This is done by effectively creating *pseudo-tasks* with the help of a *relevance function*. When evaluated on the newly released, large semantic parsing dataset, WikiSQL, our approach leads to faster convergence and enjoys 1.1%–5.4% absolute accuracy gains over the non-meta-learning counterparts, achieving a new state-of-the-art result.

While the initial finding is encouraging, we believe the potential of this meta-learning framework has not yet been fully realized. In the future, we plan to explore more variations of the meta-learning setup, such as using different relevance functions, including the ones that are jointly learned. We also would like to understand this approach better by testing it on more natural language processing tasks.

Acknowledgments

We thank Chelsea Finn and Eugene Brevdo for helpful discussions in meta-learning, and Adith Swaminathan, Asli Celikyilmaz, and anonymous reviewers for their valuable feedback.

References

Marcin Andrychowicz, Misha Denil, Sergio Gomez, Matthew W Hoffman, David Pfau, Tom Schaul, and Nando de Freitas. 2016. Learning to learn by gradient descent by gradient descent. In *Advances in Neural Information Processing Systems*. pages 3981–3989.

Yoav Artzi and Luke Zettlemoyer. 2011. Bootstrapping semantic parsers from conversations. In *Proceedings of the Conference on Empirical Methods in Natural Language Processing*. pages 421–432.

Dzmitry Bahdanau, Kyunghyun Cho, and Yoshua Bengio. 2014. Neural machine translation by jointly learning to align and translate. *arXiv preprint arXiv:1409.0473* .

Samy Bengio, Yoshua Bengio, Jocelyn Cloutier, and Jan Gecsei. 1992. On the optimization of a synaptic learning rule. In *Preprints Conf. Optimality in Artificial and Biological Neural Networks*. Univ. of Texas, pages 6–8.

Jonathan Berant, Andrew Chou, Roy Frostig, and Percy Liang. 2013. Semantic parsing on Freebase from question-answer pairs. In *Proceedings of the Conference on Empirical Methods in Natural Language Processing*.

Kyunghyun Cho, Bart Van Merriënboer, Caglar Gulcehre, Dzmitry Bahdanau, Fethi Bougares, Holger Schwenk, and Yoshua Bengio. 2014. Learning phrase representations using RNN encoder-decoder for statistical machine translation. *arXiv preprint arXiv:1406.1078* .

Ido Dagan, Dan Roth, Mark Sammons, and Fabio Massimo Zanzotto. 2013. *Recognizing Textual Entailment: Models and Applications*. Morgan and Claypool.

Jacob Devlin, Rudy R. Bunel, Rishabh Singh, Matthew J. Hausknecht, and Pushmeet Kohli. 2017. Neural program meta-induction. In *NIPS*. pages 2077–2085.

John Duchi, Elad Hazan, and Yoram Singer. 2011. Adaptive subgradient methods for online learning and stochastic optimization. *Journal of Machine Learning Research* 12(Jul):2121–2159.

Chelsea Finn, Pieter Abbeel, and Sergey Levine. 2017. Model-agnostic meta-learning for fast adaptation of deep networks. In *ICML*.

Alessandra Giordani and Alessandro Moschitti. 2010. Semantic mapping between natural language questions and SQL queries via syntactic pairing. In *Proceedings of the 14th International Conference on Applications of Natural Language to Information Systems*. pages 207–221.

David Golub and Xiaodong He. 2016. Character-level question answering with attention. In *Proceedings of the Conference on Empirical Methods in Natural Language Processing (EMNLP)*.

Alex Graves, Greg Wayne, and Ivo Danihelka. 2014. Neural Turing machines. *arXiv preprint arXiv:1410.5401* .

David Ha, Andrew Dai, and Quoc V Le. 2017. Hypernetworks. In *International Conference on Learning Representations*.

Kazuma Hashimoto, Caiming Xiong, Yoshimasa Tsuruoka, and Richard Socher. 2017. A joint many-task model: Growing a neural network for multiple NLP tasks. In *Empirical Methods in Natural Language Processing (EMNLP)*.

Sepp Hochreiter, A Steven Younger, and Peter R Conwell. 2001. Learning to learn using gradient descent. In *International Conference on Artificial Neural Networks*. pages 87–94.

Srinivasan Iyer, Ioannis Konstas, Alvin Cheung, Jayant Krishnamurthy, and Luke Zettlemoyer. 2017. Learning a neural semantic parser from user feedback. *arXiv preprint arXiv:1704.08760* .

Gregory Koch. 2015. Siamese neural networks for one-shot image recognition. In *ICML Deep Learning Workshop*.

Jayant Krishnamurthy, Pradeep Dasigi, and Matt Gardner. 2017. Neural semantic parsing with type constraints for semi-structured tables. In *Proceedings of the 2017 Conference on Empirical Methods in Natural Language Processing*. pages 1517–1527.

Ke Li and Jitendra Malik. 2017. Learning to optimize neural nets. In *International Conference on Learning Representations*.

Christopher D Manning, Mihai Surdeanu, John Bauer, Jenny Rose Finkel, Steven Bethard, and David McClosky. 2014. The Stanford CoreNLP natural language processing toolkit. In *Association for Computational Linguistics (ACL) System Demonstrations*.

Devang K Naik and RJ Mammone. 1992. Meta-neural networks that learn by learning. In *International Joint Conference on Neural Networks*. IEEE, volume 1, pages 437–442.

Arvind Neelakantan, Luke Vilnis, Quoc V Le, Ilya Sutskever, Lukasz Kaiser, Karol Kurach, and James Martens. 2015. Adding gradient noise improves learning for very deep networks. *arXiv preprint arXiv:1511.06807* .

Emilio Parisotto, Abdel-rahman Mohamed, Rishabh Singh, Lihong Li, Dengyong Zhou, and Pushmeet Kohli. 2017. Neuro-symbolic program synthesis. In *International Conference on Learning Representations (ICLR)*.

Jeffrey Pennington, Richard Socher, and Christopher Manning. 2014. GloVe: Global vectors for word representation. In *Proceedings of the Conference on Empirical Methods in Natural Language Processing (EMNLP)*. pages 1532–1543.

Sachin Ravi and Hugo Larochelle. 2016. Optimization as a model for few-shot learning. In *International Conference on Learning Representations (ICLR)*.

Scott Reed and Nando De Freitas. 2016. Neural programmer-interpreters. In *International Conference on Learning Representations (ICLR)*.

Jurgen Schmidhuber. 1987. *Evolutionary Principles in Self-Referential Learning. On Learning now to Learn: The Meta-Meta-Meta...-Hook*. Diploma thesis, Technische Universitat Munchen, Germany.

Jürgen Schmidhuber. 1992. Learning to control fast-weight memories: An alternative to dynamic recurrent networks. *Neural Computation* 4(1):131–139.

Sebastian Thrun and Lorien Pratt, editors. 1998. *Learning to Learn*. Kluwer Academic Publishers.

Oriol Vinyals, Charles Blundell, Tim Lillicrap, Daan Wierstra, et al. 2016. Matching networks for one shot learning. In *Advances in Neural Information Processing Systems*. pages 3630–3638.

Andreas Vlachos and Stephen Clark. 2014. A new corpus and imitation learning framework for context-dependent semantic parsing. *Transactions of the Association for Computational Linguistics* 2:547–559.

Chenglong Wang, Marc Brockschmidt, and Rishabh Singh. 2017. Pointing out SQL queries from text. Technical Report MSR-TR-2017-45. https://www.microsoft.com/en-us/research/publication/pointing-sql-queries-text/.

Yushi Wang, Jonathan Berant, and Percy Liang. 2015. Building a semantic parser overnight. In *Association for Computational Linguistics (ACL)*.

Adina Williams, Nikita Nangia, and Samuel R. Bowman. 2017. A broad-coverage challenge corpus for sentence understanding through inference. *CoRR* abs/1704.05426.

Wen-tau Yih, Ming-Wei Chang, Xiaodong He, and Jianfeng Gao. 2015. Semantic parsing via staged query graph generation: Question answering with knowledge base. In *ACL-IJCNLP*.

Wen-tau Yih, Xiaodong He, and Chris Meek. 2014. Semantic parsing for single-relation question answering. In *ACL*.

Pengcheng Yin, Zhengdong Lu, Hang Li, and Ben Kao. 2015. Neural enquirer: Learning to query tables with natural language. *arXiv preprint arXiv:1512.00965* .

Luke S. Zettlemoyer and Michael Collins. 2005. Learning to map sentences to logical form: Structured classification with probabilistic categorial grammars. In *Proceedings of the Twenty-First Conference on Uncertainty in Artificial Intelligence*. pages 658–666.

Victor Zhong, Caiming Xiong, and Richard Socher. 2017. Seq2SQL: Generating structured queries from natural language using reinforcement learning. *CoRR* abs/1709.00103.

Smaller Text Classifiers with Discriminative Cluster Embeddings

Mingda Chen   **Kevin Gimpel**

Toyota Technological Institute at Chicago, Chicago, IL, 60637, USA

{mchen,kgimpel}@ttic.edu

Abstract

Word embedding parameters often dominate overall model sizes in neural methods for natural language processing. We reduce deployed model sizes of text classifiers by learning a hard word clustering in an end-to-end manner. We use the Gumbel-Softmax distribution to maximize over the latent clustering while minimizing the task loss. We propose variations that selectively assign additional parameters to words, which further improves accuracy while still remaining parameter-efficient.

1 Introduction

Word embeddings (Bengio et al., 2003) form the foundation of most neural methods for natural language processing (NLP). However, embeddings typically comprise a large fraction of the total parameters learned by a model, especially when large vocabularies and high dimensions are used. This can become problematic when seeking to deploy NLP systems on mobile devices where memory and computation time are limited.

We address this issue by proposing alternative parameterizations for word embeddings in text classifiers. We introduce a latent variable for each word type that represents the (hard) cluster to which it belongs. An embedding is learned for each cluster. All parameters (including cluster assignment probabilities for each word and the cluster embeddings themselves) are learned jointly in an end-to-end manner.

This idea is based on the conjecture that most words do not need their own unique embedding parameters, due both to the focused nature of particular text classification tasks and also due to the power law characteristics of word frequen-

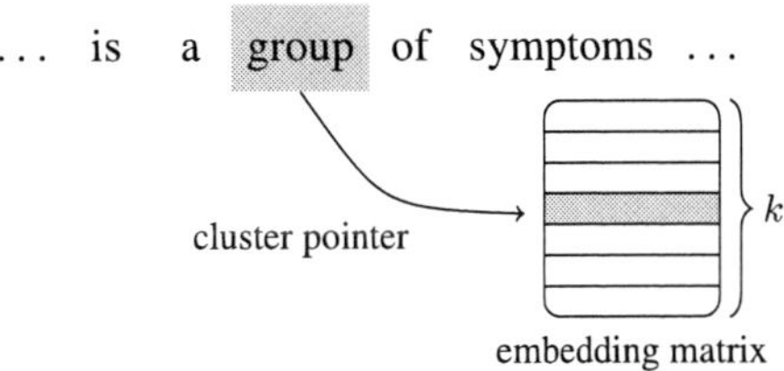

Figure 1: Schematic of deployed cluster embedding model with k clusters; cluster probabilities can be replaced by pointers at test time.

cies. For a particular task, many word embeddings would be essentially identical, so using clusters lets us avoid learning redundant embedding vectors, making parameter usage more efficient. For sentiment analysis, for example, the procedure can learn to place all sentiment-neutral words in a single cluster, and then learn distinct clusters for positive and negative words.

During learning, we minimize log loss of the correct classification label while maximizing over the latent variables. To do so, we use the Gumbel-Softmax distribution (Jang et al., 2016; Maddison et al., 2016) as a continuous approximation to hard clustering. After training, we compute the argmax over cluster assignments for each word type and replace the cluster assignment probabilities with pointers to clusters; see Figure 1. This leads to a large reduction in model size at test time.

We consider two variations of the above idea which introduce a small number of additional word-specific parameters. The best variation learns unique embeddings for only the most frequent words and uses hard clustering for the rest. We evaluate our methods on five text classification datasets, comparing them at several model size budgets. Our results demonstrate that clustering can maintain or improve performance while offering extremely small deployed models.

739

Proceedings of NAACL-HLT 2018, pages 739–745
New Orleans, Louisiana, June 1 - 6, 2018. ©2018 Association for Computational Linguistics

2 Related Work

Several methods have been proposed for reducing the memory requirements of models that use word embeddings. One is based on quantization (Botha et al., 2017; Han et al., 2016), which changes the way parameters are stored. In particular, it seeks to find shared weights among embedding vectors and only keeps scale factors for each word.

Another family of methods uses hashing functions to replace dictionaries (Tito Svenstrup et al., 2017; Joulin et al., 2017). This can save storage space, but still requires the model to have roughly the same size embedding matrix. Network pruning has also been used to compress neural networks. Han et al. (2015) pruned weights iteratively by removing weights below a threshold and then retraining the network.

Our work is also related to prior work using hard word clustering for NLP tasks (Botha et al., 2017; Brown et al., 1992). The primary difference is that we cluster words to minimize the task loss rather than doing so beforehand.

Recently, Shu and Nakayama (2018) also found clustering helpful for compressing the word embedding matrix for NLP tasks. Their method follows the intuition of product quantization (Jegou et al., 2011; Joulin et al., 2017). Our methods differ from theirs in two ways. First, our methods are trained end-to-end instead of relying on pretrained word embeddings. Since our embeddings are trained for each task, we can use much smaller embedding dimensionalities, which saves a lot of parameters. Second, our method is faster at test time because it does not use multiple code books.

3 Embedding Parameterizations

Our text classifiers use long short-term memory (LSTM; Hochreiter and Schmidhuber, 1997) networks to embed sequences of word embeddings and then use the final hidden state as input to a softmax layer to generate label predictions. The standard cross entropy loss is used for training. We use this same architecture throughout and vary the method of parameterizing the word embedding module among the four options listed below.

Standard Embeddings (SE). This is the standard setting in which each word type in the vocabulary has a unique embedding. Given a vocabulary $V = \{w_1, w_2, \cdots, w_v\}$ and embedding dimensionality m, this yields vm word embedding pa-

rameters. In our experiments, we limit the vocabulary to various sizes v, always keeping the most frequent v words and replacing the rest with an unknown word symbol.

Cluster Embeddings (CE). We next propose a method in which each word is placed into a single cluster ("hard clustering") and we learn a unique embedding vector for each cluster. We refer to this setting as using cluster embeddings (CE). We denote the embedding matrix $W \in \mathbb{R}^{k \times m}$ where k is the number of clusters and m is again the embedding dimensionality. Each word w_i now has a vector of parameters $\vec{a_i} = (a_{i1}, \cdots, a_{ik})$ which are interpreted as cluster probabilities. So this method requires learning vk cluster probabilities in addition to the km parameters for the cluster embeddings themselves.

We treat the cluster membership of each word w_i as a latent variable h_i during training. All parameters are optimized jointly to minimize cross entropy while maximizing over the latent variables. This poses difficulty in practice due to the discrete nature of the clustering. That is, maximizing over the latent variables involves non-differentiable argmax operations:

$$h_i = \arg\max_{1 \leq j \leq k} a_{ij}$$

To tackle this problem, we use the recently proposed Gumbel-Softmax to approximate the clustering decision during training. Gumbel-Softmax is a temperature-modulated continuous relaxation for the categorical distribution. When the temperature approaches 0, samples from Gumbel-Softmax will become identical to those from the categorical distribution. During training, we have a sample $\vec{t_i} = (t_{i1}, \cdots, t_{ik})$ for every instance of a word w_i. The vector $\vec{t_i}$ is a non-sparse approximation to the one-hot vector indicated by the latent variable value h_i. It is parameterized as:

$$t_{ij} = \frac{\exp\left((a_{ij} + g_j)/\tau\right)}{\sum_{l=1}^{k} \exp\left((a_{il} + g_l)/\tau\right)}$$

where the g_j are samples from a Gumbel(0,1) distribution and τ is the temperature. The embedding vector $\vec{e_i}$ for word w_i is calculated by $\vec{e_i} = W^\top \vec{t_i}$.

Even when merely using this method in a soft clustering setting, it can save parameters when $vk + km < vm$. But with hard clustering, we can reduce this further by assuming we will again

Dataset	# Classes	Train	Dev.	Test
AG News	4	115,000	5,000	7,600
DBpedia	14	560,000	5,000	70,000
Yelp Review Polarity	2	555,000	5,000	38,000
Yelp Review Full	5	645,000	5,000	50,000
IMDB Movie Reviews	2	23,000	2,000	25,000

Table 1: Dataset statistics.

maximize over latent variables at test time. In this case, the cluster for word w_i at test time is

$$\vec{t_i} = \text{one\_hot}\left(\arg\max_{1 \le j \le k} a_{ij}\right)$$

where the function one_hot returns a one-hot vector of length k with a 1 in the index given by its argument. These argmax operations can be precomputed for all words in V, permitting us to discard the vk cluster probabilities and instead just store a cluster pointer for each word, each of which will only take $O(\log_2 k)$ space.

Cluster Adjustment Embeddings (CAE). While the cluster embedding model can lead to large savings in parameters, it loses the ability to model subtle distinctions among words, especially as k decreases. We propose a modification (cluster adjustment embeddings; CAE) that represents a word by concatenating its cluster embedding with a short unique vector for the word. If we think of cluster embeddings as centroids for each cluster, this model provides a way to adjust or correct the cluster embedding for each word, while still leveraging parameter sharing via the cluster embeddings. For all CAE experiments below, we use a 1-dimensional vector (i.e., a scalar) as the unique vector for each word that gets concatenated to the cluster embedding.

Mixture Embeddings (ME). Finally, we consider a variation (mixture embeddings; ME) in which the most frequent u words use unique embeddings and the remaining words use cluster embeddings. The words with unique embeddings are selected based on word frequency in the training data, with the intuition that frequent words are potentially useful for the task and contain enough instances to learn unique embedding parameters.

4 Experimental setup

We evaluate our embedding models on five text classification datasets: AG News, DBpedia, Yelp Review Polarity, Yelp Review Full (Zhang et al.,

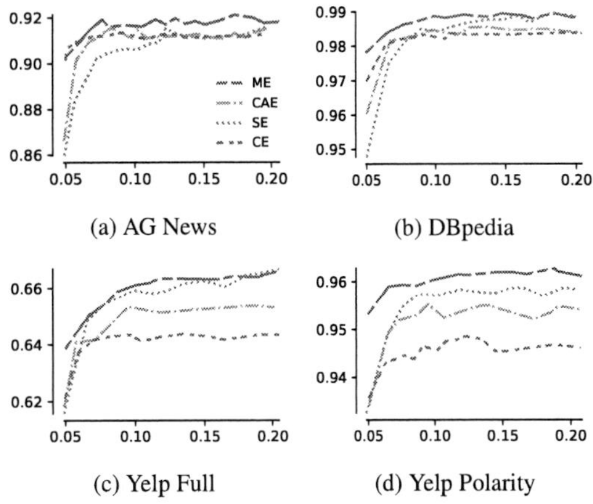

Figure 2: Development accuracy vs model size (MB) on four datasets. ME consistently outperforms other models under various size budgets.

2015), and the IMDB movie review dataset (Maas et al., 2011). We randomly sample 5,000 instances from the training set to use as development data for all datasets except for IMDB, where we sample 2,000. Table 1 shows dataset statistics. For IMDB, to make our results comparable to Shu and Nakayama (2018), we follow their experimental setup: We tokenize and lowercase the IMDB data using NLTK and truncate each review to be at most 400 words. For the other datasets, we lowercase and tokenize the sentences using regular expressions based on Kim (2014).

For optimization, we use Adam (Kingma and Ba, 2015) with learning rate 0.001. Embedding matrices are randomly initialized for all models. To reduce the hyperparameter search space, the LSTM hidden vector size is set to 50 for all experiments and the Gumbel-Softmax temperature is fixed to 0.9. When a single result is reported, all other hyperparameters (vocabulary size v, embedding dimension m, number of clusters k, and number of unique vectors u) are tuned based on the development sets. Our code is implemented in TensorFlow (Abadi et al., 2015) and is available at `https://github.com/mingdachen/word-cluster-embedding`.

5 Results

When evaluating our models, we are concerned with both accuracy and model size. We vary hyperparameters to obtain a range of model sizes for each embedding parameterization, then train models for each set of hyperparameter values. In Fig-

	AG News		DBPedia		Yelp Full		Yelp Polarity	
size	0.05	0.1	0.05	0.1	0.05	0.1	0.05	0.1
SE	84.8	90.4	95.3	98.1	59.2	62.6	93.4	95.5
CE	89.2	90.7	96.9	97.9	60.3	61.0	93.9	94.4
CAE	86.3	90.7	96.1	98.1	61.2	62.3	93.7	95.3
ME	**90.3**	**91.5**	**97.5**	**98.3**	**61.4**	**63.4**	**95.2**	**95.8**

Table 2: Test results. Model sizes are in MB.

ure 2, we plot development accuracies across the range of model sizes on four datasets. Model sizes are calculated using the formula given in the appendix.

When the model size is extremely small (e.g., less than 0.1 MB in AG News), our cluster models outperform the standard parameterization (SE). As model size increases, the standard model becomes better and better, though it does not outperform ME. While CE is weak on the Yelp tasks, which could be attributed to the difficulty of 5-way sentiment classification, we see clear improvements by adding small amounts of word-specific information via CAE and ME. ME consistently performs well compared to the others across model sizes.

We report test results in Table 2. The test results are reported based on model performance on the development set for different model sizes. The models are consistent between development and test, as our cluster models with max size 0.05MB outperform SE across datasets, with ME having the highest accuracies.

On IMDB, we compare our methods to compositional coding (Shu and Nakayama, 2018). This method learns an efficient coding of word embeddings via the summation of embeddings from multiple clusterings. The clusterings and cluster embeddings are learned offline to reconstruct pre-trained GloVe vectors (Pennington et al., 2014). We recalculated the embedding sizes from Shu and Nakayama (2018) using our formula (in the appendix). We also reimplemented their compositional coding as another embedding model and trained it in an end-to-end fashion. We use the best model configuration from Shu and Nakayama (2018) and do grid search for the embedding dimension. As for the vocabulary size v, we find models perform better with small values, and thus we fix it to $v = 3000$.

Results are shown in Table 3. Compared with compositional coding, our models perform much better with a much smaller set of embedding parameters even when we use a smaller number of cluster embeddings (e.g., compare 8×8 coding

	embedding size (MB)	model size (MB)	acc. (%)
GloVe baseline	85.947	-	87.18
8×8 coding	0.288	-	82.84
16×32 coding	1.302	-	87.37
64×8 coding	2.305	-	88.15
64×8 coding ($m = 90$)	0.245	0.353	83.43
SE ($|V| = 3000, m = 8$)	0.092	0.137	86.84
CE ($k = 50, m = 5$)	**0.004**	0.046	85.58
CAE ($k = 50, m = 5$)	0.016	0.058	86.94
ME ($k = 50, u = 300, m = 5$)	0.009	0.051	**88.22**

Table 3: IMDB test results. The four rows above the dashed line are from Shu and Nakayama (2018); our results are below it.

	words
1	million week third percent which 000 ago reports once
2	are after from has another down home than but end
3	official security china international country court city
4	heavyweights operational coordinated healing rewarded
5	com internet technology ibm google research windows
6	market quarter sales deals bid growth trade economic
7	championship yankees defense player contract football
8	troops press attack forces peace iran led army killing

Table 4: Word clusters learned using CE model on AG News. Each row is a different cluster.

to CE; both use a comparable number of cluster embedding vectors, while CE works better). ME (with $k = 50$ clusters and unique embeddings for the $u = 300$ most frequent words) outperforms all other models while retaining a small model size. CAE performs better than SE, but uses more parameters than CE. We find a better trade-off with ME, which only adds parameters to the most frequent words.

6 Discussion

6.1 Cluster Analysis

Table 4 shows clusters learned via CE on the AG News dataset. Cluster 1 appears to contain words that are related to quantities such as times and numbers while cluster 2 mostly contains prepositions and other function words. The connection to the AG News labels (World, Sports, Business, and Sci/Tech) is more clear in the subsequent clusters. Clusters 3 and 8 are related to World, cluster 4 may relate to World or Sports, clusters 5 and 6 are related to Sci/Tech, and cluster 7 is related to Sports.

6.2 Impact of Hyperparameters

Figure 3 shows the relationship between accuracy and several hyperparameters. Figure 3a shows the effect of embedding dimension on SE models. One-dimensional embeddings work reason-

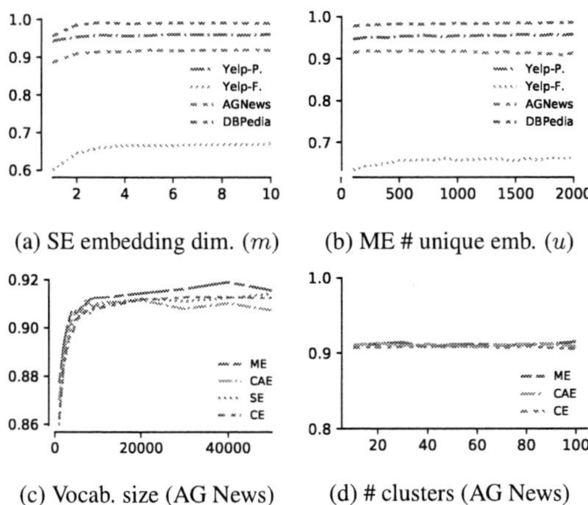

(a) SE embedding dim. (m) (b) ME # unique emb. (u)

(c) Vocab. size (AG News) (d) # clusters (AG News)

Figure 3: Dev. accuracy vs. hyperparameters.

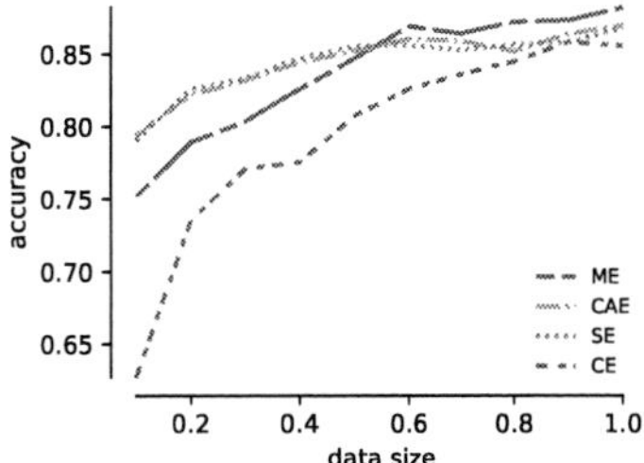

Figure 4: Varying the fraction of training data used on the IMDB task.

ably well, but the largest accuracy gains occur when increasing dimensionality from 1 to 2. Consider the LSTM gating functions, which consist of a nonlinearity applied to $U_1 \mathbf{x} + U_2 \mathbf{h}$, where $\mathbf{x}$ is a word embedding, $\mathbf{h}$ is a hidden state, and U_1, U_2 are parameters. We can think of these functions as doing affine transformations on the hidden state. So, in the one-dimensional case, the transformations that a word vector can do are restricted to translation. However, when word vectors have more than two dimensions, they can do almost any affine transformation. To further investigate this, we experimented with simple recurrent neural networks (RNNs) with very small word embedding dimensionalities in the appendix.

Figure 3b shows that for most datasets, increasing the number of unique embedding vectors (u) in ME helps for the Yelp datasets, especially early on, but $u = 500$ appears sufficient to capture most of the accuracy. Since similar trends are observed across different datasets, we only plot results for AG News in the final two plots. In Figure 3c, there is a clear boundary after which vocabulary size has minimal effect on accuracy. In Figure 3d, we observe that the number of clusters does not have much impact.

The main differences among CE, CAE, and ME are the ways they balance precision of embedding vectors and overall model size. CE forgets word identities and uses common parameters for all words in a cluster. Therefore it is expected that it should perform best only when all models are restricted to be extremely small. CAE adds parameters evenly across all words in the vocabulary while ME focuses its additional parameters

on the most frequent words. Our results show that devoting parameters to the most frequent words achieves the best balance and consistently strong results. The most frequent words in the training set are likely to be those most closely related to the task. Higher frequency also means more training data for the word's embedding parameters.

6.3 Impact of Training Data Size

Figure 4 shows test accuracies when varying the size of the training set for the IMDB task. The clustering models need relatively large amounts of training data, because they actually may have more parameters to learn during training due to the cluster membership probabilities for each word. We suspect this is why ME underperforms SE and CAE with small training sets. Even though ME permits very small deployed models, it still requires a substantial training set to learn its cluster membership probabilities.

7 Conclusions and Future Work

We proposed word embedding parameterizations that dramatically reduce the number of parameters at test time while achieving comparable or better performance. Our methods are applicable to other neural methods that use word embeddings or any kind of parameter lookup data structure. Future work will incorporate pretrained word embeddings into these cluster parameterizations and apply them to additional tasks.

Acknowledgments

We thank Qingming Tang for helpful discussions and the anonymous reviewers for their comments.

References

Martín Abadi, Ashish Agarwal, Paul Barham, Eugene Brevdo, Zhifeng Chen, Craig Citro, Greg S. Corrado, Andy Davis, Jeffrey Dean, Matthieu Devin, Sanjay Ghemawat, Ian Goodfellow, Andrew Harp, Geoffrey Irving, Michael Isard, Yangqing Jia, Rafal Jozefowicz, Lukasz Kaiser, Manjunath Kudlur, Josh Levenberg, Dandelion Mané, Rajat Monga, Sherry Moore, Derek Murray, Chris Olah, Mike Schuster, Jonathon Shlens, Benoit Steiner, Ilya Sutskever, Kunal Talwar, Paul Tucker, Vincent Vanhoucke, Vijay Vasudevan, Fernanda Viégas, Oriol Vinyals, Pete Warden, Martin Wattenberg, Martin Wicke, Yuan Yu, and Xiaoqiang Zheng. 2015. Tensor-Flow: Large-scale machine learning on heterogeneous systems. Software available from tensorflow.org. https://www.tensorflow.org/.

Yoshua Bengio, Réjean Ducharme, Pascal Vincent, and Christian Jauvin. 2003. A neural probabilistic language model. *Journal of machine learning research* 3(Feb):1137–1155.

Jan A. Botha, Emily Pitler, Ji Ma, Anton Bakalov, Alex Salcianu, David Weiss, Ryan McDonald, and Slav Petrov. 2017. Natural language processing with small feed-forward networks. In *Proceedings of the 2017 Conference on Empirical Methods in Natural Language Processing*. Association for Computational Linguistics, pages 2879–2885. http://aclweb.org/anthology/D17-1309.

Peter F. Brown, Peter V. deSouza, Robert L. Mercer, T. J. Watson, Vincent J. Della Pietra, and Jenifer C. Lai. 1992. Class-based n-gram models of natural language. *Computational Linguistics* 18(4). http://www.aclweb.org/anthology/J92-4003.

Song Han, Huizi Mao, and William J Dally. 2016. Deep compression: Compressing deep neural networks with pruning, trained quantization and huffman coding. In *International Conference on Learning Representations*.

Song Han, Jeff Pool, John Tran, and William Dally. 2015. Learning both weights and connections for efficient neural network. In C. Cortes, N. D. Lawrence, D. D. Lee, M. Sugiyama, and R. Garnett, editors, *Advances in Neural Information Processing Systems 28*, Curran Associates, Inc., pages 1135–1143. http://papers.nips.cc/paper/5784-learning-both-weights-and-connections-for-efficient-neural-network.pdf.

Sepp Hochreiter and Jürgen Schmidhuber. 1997. Long short-term memory. *Neural computation* 9(8):1735–1780.

Eric Jang, Shixiang Gu, and Ben Poole. 2016. Categorical reparameterization with Gumbel-softmax. In *International Conference on Learning Representations*.

Herve Jegou, Matthijs Douze, and Cordelia Schmid. 2011. Product quantization for nearest neighbor search. *IEEE Transactions on Pattern Analysis and Machine Intelligence* 33(1):117–128.

Armand Joulin, Edouard Grave, Piotr Bojanowski, Matthijs Douze, Hervé Jégou, and Tomas Mikolov. 2017. Fasttext.zip: Compressing text classification models. In *International Conference on Learning Representations*.

Yoon Kim. 2014. Convolutional neural networks for sentence classification. In *Proceedings of the 2014 Conference on Empirical Methods in Natural Language Processing (EMNLP)*. Association for Computational Linguistics, pages 1746–1751. https://doi.org/10.3115/v1/D14-1181.

Diederik Kingma and Jimmy Ba. 2015. Adam: A method for stochastic optimization. In *International Conference on Learning Representations*.

Andrew L. Maas, Raymond E. Daly, Peter T. Pham, Dan Huang, Andrew Y. Ng, and Christopher Potts. 2011. Learning word vectors for sentiment analysis. In *Proceedings of the 49th Annual Meeting of the Association for Computational Linguistics: Human Language Technologies*. Association for Computational Linguistics, pages 142–150. http://www.aclweb.org/anthology/P11-1015.

Chris J Maddison, Andriy Mnih, and Yee Whye Teh. 2016. The concrete distribution: A continuous relaxation of discrete random variables. In *International Conference on Learning Representations*.

Jeffrey Pennington, Richard Socher, and Christopher Manning. 2014. GloVe: Global vectors for word representation. In *Proceedings of the 2014 Conference on Empirical Methods in Natural Language Processing (EMNLP)*. Association for Computational Linguistics, pages 1532–1543. https://doi.org/10.3115/v1/D14-1162.

Raphael Shu and Hideki Nakayama. 2018. Compressing word embeddings via deep compositional code learning. In *International Conference on Learning Representations*.

Dan Tito Svenstrup, Jonas Hansen, and Ole Winther. 2017. Hash embeddings for efficient word representations. In I. Guyon, U. V. Luxburg, S. Bengio, H. Wallach, R. Fergus, S. Vishwanathan, and R. Garnett, editors, *Advances in Neural Information Processing Systems 30*, Curran Associates, Inc., pages 4928–4936. http://papers.nips.cc/paper/7078-hash-embeddings-for-efficient-word-representations.pdf.

Xiang Zhang, Junbo Zhao, and Yann LeCun. 2015. Character-level convolutional networks for text classification. In C. Cortes, N. D. Lawrence, D. D. Lee, M. Sugiyama, and R. Garnett, editors, *Advances in Neural Information Processing Systems 28*, Curran Associates, Inc., pages 649–657. http://papers.nips.cc/paper/5782-character-level-convolutional-networks-for-text-classification.pdf.

Embedding Dimension	1	2	3
Accuracy	0.82	0.78	0.84

Table 5: IMDB test results for RNN with different embedding dimensions.

A Model Size Calculation

Let the model have vocabulary size v, k embedding vectors, embedding dimension m, and o other parameters. To compute model sizes, we assume each cluster pointer is stored using $\lceil \log_2 k \rceil$ bits and that other parameters are stored using 32 bits. For the CE model, for example, model size can be calculated based on the following formula:

$$v * \lceil \log_2 k \rceil + k * m * 32 + o * 32$$

B Impact of Word Embedding Dimension

increases, the hidden states become more spread out. To evaluate this phenomena quantitatively, we calculate the area ratio that hidden states have covered, which is shown in Figure 5d. The area ratio increases monotonically with increasing embedding dimension. We also report the corresponding test accuracies in Table 5. The classification accuracy does not necessarily improve from larger usage of space. The reason for this could be the vanishing gradient problem in simple RNNs.

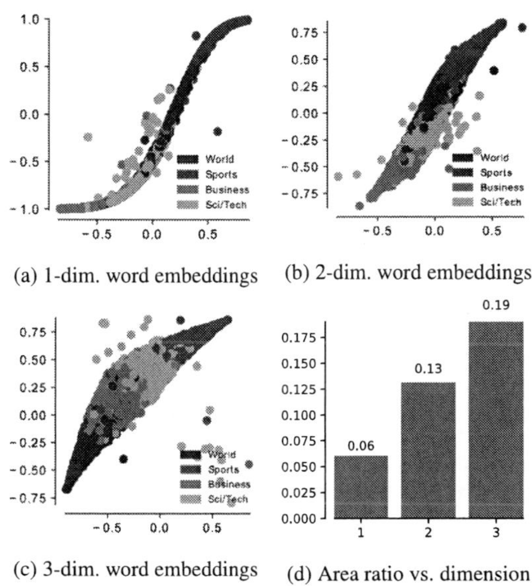

(a) 1-dim. word embeddings　(b) 2-dim. word embeddings

(c) 3-dim. word embeddings　(d) Area ratio vs. dimension

Figure 5: Plots of 2-dimensional RNN hidden states when varying word embedding dimensionality.

In order to look into the impact of word embedding dimension, we run experiments on AG News using an RNN with 2-dimensional hidden states instead of an LSTM. Figure 5 plots the final hidden states of the RNN with various embedding dimensions.

When embeddings have one dimension (Figure 5a), most of the hidden states roughly lie on a line, which is expected considering the limited transformation a scalar can do. As the dimension

Role-specific Language Models for
Processing Recorded Neuropsychological Exams

Tuka Alhanai[†], Rhoda Au[‡§], and James Glass[†]
[†]Computer Science and Artificial Intelligence Laboratory,
Massachusetts Institute of Technology, Cambridge MA, USA
[‡]Departments of Anatomy & Neurobiology, Neurology, and Epidemiology,
Boston University School of Medicine and Public Health, Boston MA, USA
[§]The Framingham Heart Study, Framingham MA, USA
`tuka@mit.edu, rhodaau@bu.edu, glass@mit.edu`

Abstract

Neuropsychological examinations are an important screening tool for the presence of cognitive conditions (e.g. Alzheimer's, Parkinson's Disease), and require a trained tester to conduct the exam through spoken interactions with the subject. While audio is relatively easy to record, it remains a challenge to automatically diarize (who spoke when?), decode (what did they say?), and assess a subject's cognitive health. This paper demonstrates a method to determine the cognitive health (impaired or not) of 92 subjects, from audio that was diarized using an automatic speech recognition system trained on TED talks and on the structured language used by testers and subjects. Using leave-one-out cross validation and logistic regression modeling we show that even with noisily decoded data (81% WER) we can still perform accurate enough diarization (0.02 % confusion rate) to determine the cognitive state of a subject (0.76 AUC).

1   Introduction

Cognitive impairment is a decline in mental abilities that is severe enough to interfere with daily life (Nussbaum and Ellis, 2003). Such conditions are particularly debilitating, with costs of up to $200 billion in the USA alone (Prince et al., 2011; Leifer, 2003; Alzheimers, 2015), and come second only to spinal-cord injuries and terminal cancer in the severity of their effects (Organization, 2003; Ferri et al., 2006).

Several methods exist to screen for cognitive conditions (e.g. Alzheimer's, Parkinson's), ranging from laboratory measures to brain imaging scans (Quadri et al., 2004; Van Himbergen et al., 2012), with the baseline being set by neuropsychological examinations. These exams are composed of multiple components that measure a specific domain of cognition such as: thinking, recall, speech, and physical movement. Each exam component is assigned a score by the tester according to the established rubric. While this exam can be comprehensive, there is an additional dimension of information that can be passively recorded - the audio of the spoken interactions. Utilizing such data would allow for the identification of spoken language biomarkers of cognitive impairment.

However, with richer information comes additional complexity (Fitch et al., 2016). The application of automatic speech processing technologies to medical domains requires a pipeline with multiple stages. Such a system requires audio pre-processing to locate speech and speaker segments (i.e. diarization) (Anguera et al., 2012), the transcription of spoken utterances (Besacier et al., 2014), and feature representation and modeling of the speaker's latent condition to determine disease biomarkers for classification purposes (Cummins et al., 2015).

Research in this domain can be categorized into two areas. First is the utilization of acoustic and linguistic information to perform speaker diarization and verification using standard corpora (e.g. Switchboard, NIST) (Stolcke et al., 2006; Reynolds et al., 2003). The second category of work seeks to evaluate speech and language biomarkers for the detection of cognitive impairment utilizing measures such as speaking rate, pauses, n-grams, and Word Error Rates (WERs) (Pakhomov et al., 2010; Lehr et al., 2012; Fraser et al., 2014; Pakhomov and Hemmy, 2014; Vincze et al., 2016), as well as Automatic Speech Recognition (ASR) for phonetic alignment and acoustic feature extraction (Tóth et al., 2015). However, systems from the speech community are developed using well-curated data with healthy speakers, while the clinical community develops systems using manually transcribed data, with some exceptions (Tóth et al., 2015; Weiner et al., 2016).

Proceedings of NAACL-HLT 2018, pages 746–752
New Orleans, Louisiana, June 1 - 6, 2018. ©2018 Association for Computational Linguistics

Our paper seeks to bridge the two areas by automating data curation for clinical use.

We hypothesize that it is possible to automate data curation for clinical use by conditioning on speaker roles, because speakers (subject/tester) during neuropsychological exams have different word usage and speaking patterns due to the question and answer nature of the evaluation. We also hypothesize that not all segments of the exam will be equally valuable in evaluating for cognitive conditions, due to potential confusion between speakers when automatically annotating speaker segments, polluting the features used for modeling cognitive conditions.

Our study differentiates itself from prior work by combining speaker-specific language modeling and ASR for speaker diarization, with the ultimate goal of assessing the cognitive condition of the subjects using the acoustic information contained in the hypothesized (and less than ideal) segments. This is an extension of work by Alhanai *et al.* that used gold standard speaker segmentations and transcriptions to evaluate cognitive outcomes. Further details on feature selection, modeling, and the relation to previous work in that domain are described in (Alhanai et al., 2017). This approach captures real-world scenarios where automatically diarized and transcribed data may not be at human parity but its usage is necessary for deploying screening technologies at scale. Moreover, audio recordings are often sub-optimal, using digital recorders on a desk, which is the case of the data used in this study. Therefore the ability to detect cognitive conditions must accommodate the presence of noisy data, of which we sought to evaluate.

1.1 Objectives

Our objectives were to (1) automatically extract and identify segments of speech that were most likely to belong to the subject, and (2) to evaluate the type of segments that were most predictive of a subject's cognitive condition.

2 Methods

2.1 Data

The data used in this work was collected from the Framingham Heart Study, an on-going longitudinal population study of 15,447 subjects from 1948 to the present (Mahmood et al., 2014). Since 1999 a subset of subjects have undergone neuropsycho-

logical examinations (Satizabal et al., 2016), and as of 2005, it became standard to record audio of these examinations. The neuropsychological examinations include multiple components to assess memory, attention, executive function, language, reasoning, visuoperceptual skills, and premorbid intelligence. All participants provided written informed consent, with study protocols and consent forms approved by the institutional review board at the Boston University Medical Center.

Our study used 92 mono-channel audio recordings of neuropsychological examinations that had available text transcripts. The exams were composed of several tests measuring memory, recall, logical and thinking. Further details and a full example are found in (Satizabal et al., 2016). The recordings were on average, 65 minutes in duration, contained 2,496 words, with a vocabulary size of 527 words.

Transcripts for each audio file were generated manually. Transcribers were instructed to include timestamps for each speaker turn (subject/tester), indicate who spoke when, transcribe speech orthographically (e.g. nineteen dollars instead of $19), include tags to highlight moments such as filled pauses (<um>), and to insert punctuation.

2.2 Outcome of Interest

Our overarching goal was to determine whether the subject being evaluated was cognitively impaired, but we also needed to determine who spoke when (subject or tester). To this end, we modeled two levels of outcomes. Our first outcome of interest was a binary indicator of the speaker type (subject or tester), with the subject coded as 1.

Our second outcome of interest was a binary indicator of cognitive impairment, with impairment coded as 1. We labeled subjects as cognitively impaired if the date of impairment (as concluded by the dementia diagnostic review panel (Seshadri et al., 2006) was on or before the date of the neuropsychological examination where the audio recording took place. Using this criteria, 21 subjects (22.8%) were cognitively impaired. Ten of these subjects had a severity rating less than mild, six were mild, five were moderate, and none were severe . Fourteen subject were diagnosed as having Alzheimer's disease using the NINCDS-ADRDA criteria (McKhann et al., 2011), and five were diagnosed with Vascular dementia based on the NINCDS-AIRENS criteria (Román et al.,

1993).

2.3 Model Choice and Evaluation Metrics

To evaluate speaker diarization we used the Diarization Error Rate (DER) metric, as well as the percentage of speech classified as non-speech (Miss), the percentage of non-speech classified as speech (False Alarm), and the percentage of speech misclassified as belonging to the other speaker (Confusion Rate) (Tranter and Reynolds, 2006). We used a time-based diarization approach, ignoring segments less than 250ms in duration. To evaluate the performance of the ASR system we used the Word Error Rate (WER) metric. Given the importance of model interpretability for detecting spoken language biomarkers, logistic regression was chosen as our modeling framework. The evaluation metrics we used for detecting cognitive impairment was the Area Under the Receiver Operating Characteristic Curve (AUC) which has the advantage of evaluating model performance across the whole range of probability cutoffs, rather than a single point estimate such as accuracy or F1 score (Huang and Ling, 2005). To assess the generalizability and robustness of our modeling techniques, we performed leave-one-out cross-validation.

3 Experiment 1: Speaker ID from Text

We first investigated the language patterns of speakers to determine whether a subject or tester was speaking (i.e., a 2 class problem). We started with the segmentation from the speaker turns labeled in the transcripts. We trained a trigram language model with Knesser Ney discounting for each speaker type. The language models were then used to generate the language perplexity of the spoken (text) segment. The training and testing was performed with leave-one-out validation (i.e. 92 folds, one fold for each of the 92 subject-tester interactions). Six features were used in the logistic regression model:

- **OOV-rate** (x2): The Out-of-Vocabulary rate of the subjects' and testers' vocabulary (from their respective training sets).

- **Perplexity** (x2): The language model perplexity for the subjects and testers.

- **Perplexity sans** <s> (x2): The language model perplexity for the subjects and testers, excluding the start and end of sentence tags (<s>,</s>).

This resulted in a classification accuracy of 84% ($\pm$0.06), and an AUC of 0.93 ($\pm$0.07) These results motivated further investigation into classifying speakers from the audio directly.

4 Experiment 2: Speaker ID from ASR

For this experiment, we decoded the audio using an Automatic Speech Recognition (ASR) system with a language model trained on each speaker (subject/tester), and an acoustic model trained on the TEDLIUM corpus. Each component of the ASR system was developed as follows:

- **Acoustic Model:** The TEDLIUM corpus contains over 1,400 audio recordings and text transcription of TED talks, for a total of 120 hours of data and 1.7M words (Rousseau et al., 2012). Using this corpus, we trained the acoustic model as a feedforward Neural Network (6 layers x 2048 hidden units) with the Minimum Bayes Risk (MBR) criterion using 40 mel filterbank features, via the Kaldi speech recognition toolkit using the 's5' TEDLIUM recipe (Povey et al., 2011; Rousseau et al., 2012).

- **Language Model:** A tri-gram language model was trained for each of the speaker and tester using the SRILM toolkit (Stolcke et al., 2002).

- **Lexicon:** We generated the word pronunciations using the LOGIOS lexical tool[1].

We decoded the audio in three ways:

1. **Oracle:** A language model was trained across all 92 transcripts, and utterances were segmented according to manually generated speaker turns.

2. **Leave-one-out:** A language model was trained on all transcripts *excluding* the transcript of the audio being decoded. Utterances were segmented according to manually generated speaker turns.

3. **Leave-one-out + automatic segmentation:** A language model was trained on all transcripts *excluding* the transcript of the audio

---

[1] http://www.speech.cs.cmu.edu/tools/lextool.html

being decoded. Utterances were *not* segmented by speaker turns, the full audio was decoded as a single segment.

The results are displayed in Table 4. Our Oracle system performed with a WER of 66.7%, while decoding without language modeling information (of the audio being decoded) resulted in a WER of 68.6%. This relatively small difference in performance (68.6% vs. 66.7%) indicated that the language usage across the audio recordings was consistent.

We also compared the Diariziation Error Rate (DER) across the different setups (Table 4). This helped us evaluate how well a speaker could be identified given various levels of information about the underlying segments being decoded.

ALL SEGMENTS

	Oracle	Loocv	Loocv auto seg.
WER (%)	66.7	68.6	81.3
DER (%)	35.8 ($\pm$ 5.9)	37.2 ($\pm$ 5.5)	40.5 ($\pm$ 05.4)
Miss	00.2 ($\pm$ 0.4)	00.2 ($\pm$ 0.4)	00.2 ($\pm$ 15.3)
False Alarm	03.9 ($\pm$ 1.2)	04.1 ($\pm$ 1.3)	03.7 ($\pm$ 01.3)
Confusion	31.7 ($\pm$ 5.9)	32.9 ($\pm$ 5.5)	36.7 ($\pm$ 05.3)
Cognitive ID			
AUC	0.72	0.70	0.68

OPTIMUM SEGMENTS

	95% subj. & 10+ words	Top 9 longest
DER (%)	-	98.2 ($\pm$ 1.6)	99.9 ($\pm$ 0.2)
Miss	-	97.9 ($\pm$ 2.1)	99.9 ($\pm$ 0.4)
False Alarm	-	00.0 ($\pm$ 0.0)	00.0 ($\pm$ 0.0)
Confusion	-	00.3 ($\pm$ 0.6)	0.02 ($\pm$ 0.2)
Cognitive ID		
AUC	-	0.75	0.76

Table 1: ASR, Speaker ID, and Cognitive ID

5 Experiment 3: Cognitive ID

Using the classified speaker segments, we were interested in determining the subject's cognitive condition (impaired or not). We modeled each segment using logistic regression and 220 acoustic features capturing prosody (pitch, zero-crossing rate, jitter, harmonic-to-noise ration) and energy in the speech (energy, spectral energy, shimmer). Full details on the acoustic feature set, and method for extraction can be found in (Alhanai et al., 2017). To calculate model performance, we took the mean predicted probability across all segments as a single value representing the probability of a subject's cognitive impairment. For this experiment, we performed leave-one-out cross-validation.

5.0.1 Speaker Turn Segmentations

For the experimental setup that used segmentations by speaker turn, we modeled cognitive impairment within a grid search space along two dimensions: (a) the total number of words that were decoded, and (b) by the percentage of words decoded that were hypothesized to belong to the subject. The results of evaluating cognitive impairment in this search space can be viewed in Figure 1. The highest AUC (of 0.75) was found when modeling with segments that had been decoded with at least 10 words, and 95% of which were hypothesized to belong to the subject.

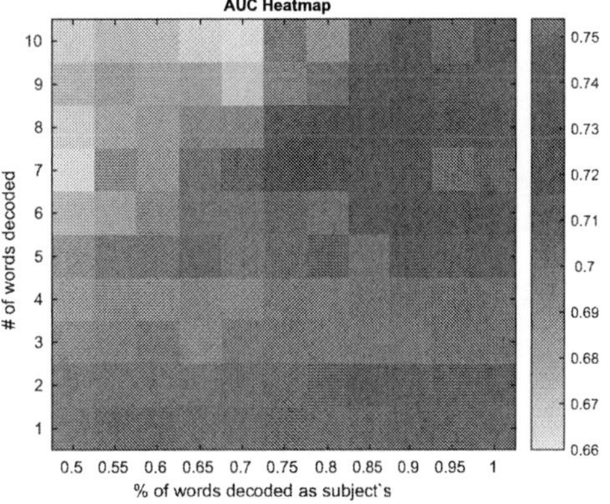

Figure 1: Cognitive ID Heatmap. Heatmap of Subject AUC across two thresholds, (y-axis) minimum number of words decoded, and (x-axis) percentage of words in a segment classified as the subject's.

5.0.2 Discarding Speaker Segmentations

For the experimental setup that was decoded without oracle speaker turn segmentation, we first segmented the decoded hypothesis along silences that were longer than 1.5 seconds, and then segmented according to the hypothesized speaker. For modeling, we selected the top N longest segments that were hypothesized to be the subject's, where N was evaluated from 1 to 15. 99% of segments hypothesized were under 25 seconds in duration, and as a pre-processing step we discarded the longest 1% of hypothesized segments, which were many minutes long and several standard deviations beyond the mean (i.e. spurious decodings). The highest AUC (of 0.76) was found when modeling the 9 longest segments hypothesized as the subject's. This was an average of 150 seconds (± 20 sec) of audio per subject, or 7% of a subject's total audio duration.

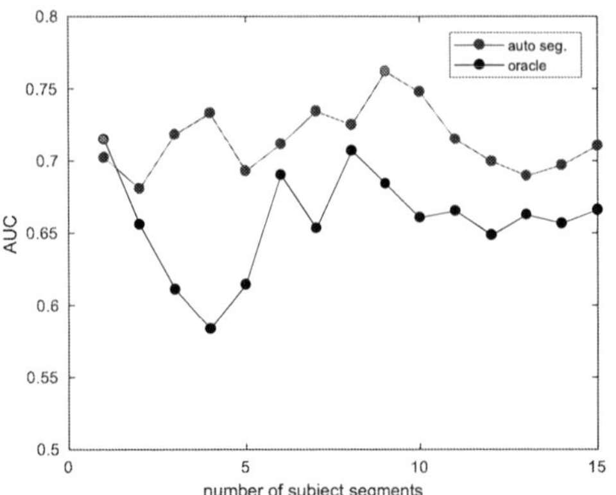

Figure 2: Cognitive ID by Number of Segments. Plot of AUC (y-axis) with respect to the number of segments per-subject (by descending order of length) used for modeling their cognitive impairment (x-axis). Red points indicate best performance (AUC 0.72 and 0.75 for oracle and automatic segmentation systems respectively).

6   Discussion

Utilizing audio recordings of spoken interactions between subjects and tester, the work in this paper sought to: (1) automatically extract and identify segments of speech that were most likely to belong to the subject, and (2) to evaluate the type of segments that were most predictive of a subject's cognitive condition.

6.1   Experiment 1: Speaker ID from Text

Our results from the first experiment showed that language usage between the subject and tester differed significantly, and that each speaker's language style was consistent across recordings (i.e. subjects consistently spoke like other subjects, and testers consistently spoke like other testers). Therefore, with the availability of highly accurate transcriptions of the same structure (neuropsychological exams), a highly accurate text-based speaker diarization can be conducted.

6.2   Experiment 2: Speaker ID from ASR

Our second set of experiments validated the observation from the previous experiment on language usage patterns across speaker roles (i.e. subjects consistently spoke like other subjects, testers consistently spoke like other testers, and subjects and testers did not speak like each other). Also, seemingly high WERs (between 66.7% and 81.3%) still contained information that was robust enough for further usage in diarization and modeling of cognitive impairment.

6.3   Experiment 3: Cognitive ID

Our last experiment showed that it was possible to perform modeling of cognitive impairment utilizing automatically segmented subject speaker turns that was on par with the oracle speaker segmentation, and that 9 segments was sufficient for evaluation. As shown in Figure 2, we also found that not all diarization was equal, nor were all segment lengths equally powerful at modeling subjects' cognitive state. In the case where no oracle segmentation was available, and automatic segmentation was utilized, longer segments contained information that was more discriminative (AUC 0.68 vs. 0.76). For the oracle system, the longest system was the most and equally predictive of cognitive impairment, as all segments taken together. This highlights that tests that elicited longer responses allowed for more robust diarization, were evaluating cognitive performance that was (via speech) most strongly associated with the outcome, and/or that longer spoken segments provided more opportunity to capture patterns associated with cognitive impairment.

Furthermore, the modeling paradigm we explored was robust enough that neither the underlying neuropsychological test need be explicitly modeled (Lehr et al., 2012), nor do the features utilized require word or phone alignments (alignments which require accurate transcriptions in order to generate) (Tóth et al., 2015).

Acknowledgments

The authors thank David Stuck, Maggie Sandoval, Alessio Signorini, and Christine Lemke from Evidation Health Inc., and Ida Xu, Brynna Wasserman, Maulika Kohli, Nancy Heard-Costa, Yulin Liu, Karen Mutalik, Mia Lavallee, Christina Nowak, Alvin Ang, and Spencer Hardy from Boston University and The Framingham Heart Study. Data curation was sponsored by DARPA and NIH grants AG016495, AG008122, AG033040. T. Alhanai thanks the Abu Dhabi Education Council for sponsoring her studies.

References

Tuka Alhanai, Rhoda Au, and James Glass. 2017. Spoken language biomarkers for detecting cognitive impairment.

Association Alzheimers. 2015. 2015 alzheimer's disease facts and figures. *Alzheimer's & dementia: the journal of the Alzheimer's Association* 11(3):332.

Xavier Anguera, Simon Bozonnet, Nicholas Evans, Corinne Fredouille, Gerald Friedland, and Oriol Vinyals. 2012. Speaker diarization: A review of recent research. *IEEE Transactions on Audio, Speech, and Language Processing* 20(2):356–370.

Laurent Besacier, Etienne Barnard, Alexey Karpov, and Tanja Schultz. 2014. Automatic speech recognition for under-resourced languages: A survey. *Speech Communication* 56:85–100.

Nicholas Cummins, Stefan Scherer, Jarek Krajewski, Sebastian Schnieder, Julien Epps, and Thomas F Quatieri. 2015. A review of depression and suicide risk assessment using speech analysis. *Speech Communication* 71:10–49.

Cleusa P Ferri, Martin Prince, Carol Brayne, Henry Brodaty, Laura Fratiglioni, Mary Ganguli, Kathleen Hall, Kazuo Hasegawa, Hugh Hendrie, Yueqin Huang, et al. 2006. Global prevalence of dementia: a delphi consensus study. *The lancet* 366(9503):2112–2117.

W Tecumseh Fitch, Bart de Boer, Neil Mathur, and Asif A Ghazanfar. 2016. Monkey vocal tracts are speech-ready. *Science advances* 2(12):e1600723.

Kathleen C Fraser, Jed A Meltzer, Naida L Graham, Carol Leonard, Graeme Hirst, Sandra E Black, and Elizabeth Rochon. 2014. Automated classification of primary progressive aphasia subtypes from narrative speech transcripts. *cortex* 55:43–60.

Jin Huang and Charles X Ling. 2005. Using auc and accuracy in evaluating learning algorithms. *IEEE Transactions on knowledge and Data Engineering* 17(3):299–310.

Maider Lehr, Emily Prud'hommeaux, Izhak Shafran, and Brian Roark. 2012. Fully automated neuropsychological assessment for detecting mild cognitive impairment. In *Thirteenth Annual Conference of the International Speech Communication Association*.

Bennett P Leifer. 2003. Early diagnosis of alzheimer's disease: clinical and economic benefits. *Journal of the American Geriatrics Society* 51(5s2).

Syed S Mahmood, Daniel Levy, Ramachandran S Vasan, and Thomas J Wang. 2014. The framingham heart study and the epidemiology of cardiovascular disease: a historical perspective. *The Lancet* 383(9921):999–1008.

Guy M McKhann, David S Knopman, Howard Chertkow, Bradley T Hyman, Clifford R Jack, Claudia H Kawas, William E Klunk, Walter J Koroshetz, Jennifer J Manly, Richard Mayeux, et al. 2011. The diagnosis of dementia due to alzheimers disease: Recommendations from the national institute on aging-alzheimers association workgroups on diagnostic guidelines for alzheimer's disease. *Alzheimer's & dementia* 7(3):263–269.

Robert L Nussbaum and Christopher E Ellis. 2003. Alzheimer's disease and parkinson's disease. *New England Journal of Medicine* 348(14):1356–1364.

World Health Organization. 2003. *The world health report 2003: shaping the future.* World Health Organization.

Serguei VS Pakhomov and Laura S Hemmy. 2014. A computational linguistic measure of clustering behavior on semantic verbal fluency task predicts risk of future dementia in the nun study. *Cortex* 55:97–106.

Serguei VS Pakhomov, Glenn E Smith, Susan Marino, Angela Birnbaum, Neill Graff-Radford, Richard Caselli, Bradley Boeve, and David S Knopman. 2010. A computerized technique to assess language use patterns in patients with frontotemporal dementia. *Journal of neurolinguistics* 23(2):127–144.

Daniel Povey, Arnab Ghoshal, Gilles Boulianne, Lukas Burget, Ondrej Glembek, Nagendra Goel, Mirko Hannemann, Petr Motlicek, Yanmin Qian, Petr Schwarz, et al. 2011. The kaldi speech recognition toolkit. In *IEEE 2011 workshop on automatic speech recognition and understanding*. IEEE Signal Processing Society, EPFL-CONF-192584.

Martin Prince, Renata Bryce, and Cleusa Ferri. 2011. *World Alzheimer Report 2011: The benefits of early diagnosis and intervention.* Alzheimer's Disease International.

Pierluigi Quadri, Claudia Fragiacomo, Rita Pezzati, Enrica Zanda, Gianluigi Forloni, Mauro Tettamanti, and Ugo Lucca. 2004. Homocysteine, folate, and vitamin b-12 in mild cognitive impairment, alzheimer disease, and vascular dementia. *The American journal of clinical nutrition* 80(1):114–122.

Douglas Reynolds, Walter Andrews, Joseph Campbell, Jiri Navratil, Barbara Peskin, Andre Adami, Qin Jin, David Klusacek, Joy Abramson, Radu Mihaescu, et al. 2003. The supersid project: Exploiting high-level information for high-accuracy speaker recognition. In *Acoustics, Speech, and Signal Processing, 2003. Proceedings.(ICASSP'03). 2003 IEEE International Conference on*. IEEE, volume 4, pages IV–784.

Gustavo C Román, Thomas K Tatemichi, T Erkinjuntti, JL Cummings, JC Masdeu, JHet al Garcia, L Amaducci, J-M Orgogozo, A Brun, Aea Hofman, et al.

1993. Vascular dementia diagnostic criteria for research studies: Report of the ninds-airen international workshop. *Neurology* 43(2):250–250.

Anthony Rousseau, Paul Deléglise, and Yannick Esteve. 2012. Ted-lium: an automatic speech recognition dedicated corpus. In *LREC*. pages 125–129.

Claudia L Satizabal, Alexa S Beiser, Vincent Chouraki, Geneviève Chêne, Carole Dufouil, and Sudha Seshadri. 2016. Incidence of dementia over three decades in the framingham heart study. *New England Journal of Medicine* 374(6):523–532.

Sudha Seshadri, Alexa Beiser, Margaret Kelly-Hayes, Carlos S Kase, Rhoda Au, William B Kannel, and Philip A Wolf. 2006. The lifetime risk of stroke. *Stroke* 37(2):345–350.

Andreas Stolcke, Klaus Ries, Noah Coccaro, Elizabeth Shriberg, Rebecca Bates, Daniel Jurafsky, Paul Taylor, Rachel Martin, Carol Van Ess-Dykema, and Marie Meteer. 2006. Dialogue act modeling for automatic tagging and recognition of conversational speech. *Dialogue* 26(3).

Andreas Stolcke et al. 2002. Srilm-an extensible language modeling toolkit. In *Interspeech*. volume 2002, page 2002.

Laszló Tóth, Gábor Gosztolya, Veronika Vincze, Ildikó Hoffmann, Gréta Szatlóczki, Edit Biró, Fruzsina Zsura, Magdolna Pákáski, and János Kálmán. 2015. Automatic detection of mild cognitive impairment from spontaneous speech using asr. In *Sixteenth Annual Conference of the International Speech Communication Association*.

Sue E Tranter and Douglas A Reynolds. 2006. An overview of automatic speaker diarization systems. *IEEE Transactions on audio, speech, and language processing* 14(5):1557–1565.

Thomas M Van Himbergen, Alexa S Beiser, Masumi Ai, Sudha Seshadri, Seiko Otokozawa, Rhoda Au, Nuntakorn Thongtang, Philip A Wolf, and Ernst J Schaefer. 2012. Biomarkers for insulin resistance and inflammation and the risk for all-cause dementia and alzheimer disease: results from the framingham heart study. *Archives of neurology* 69(5):594–600.

Veronika Vincze, Gabor Gosztolya, Laszlo Toth, Ildiko Hoffmann, Greta Szatloczki, Zoltan Banreti, Magdolna Pakaski, and Janos Kalman. 2016. Detecting mild cognitive impairment by exploiting linguistic information from transcripts. In *Proceedings of the 54th Annual Meeting of the Association for Computational Linguistics*. volume 2, pages 181–187.

Jochen Weiner, Christian Herff, and Tanja Schultz. 2016. Speech-based detection of alzheimer's disease in conversational german. In *INTERSPEECH*. pages 1938–1942.

Slot-Gated Modeling for Joint Slot Filling and Intent Prediction

Chih-Wen Goo[†]   **Guang Gao**[†]   **Yun-Kai Hsu**[⋆]   **Chih-Li Huo**[⋆]
Tsung-Chieh Chen[⋆]   **Keng-Wei Hsu**[⋆]   **Yun-Nung Chen**[†]
[†]National Taiwan University
[⋆]Institute for Information Industry
`r05944049@ntu.edu.tw` `y.v.chen@ieee.org`

Abstract

Attention-based recurrent neural network models for joint intent detection and slot filling have achieved the state-of-the-art performance, while they have independent attention weights. Considering that slot and intent have the strong relationship, this paper proposes a slot gate that focuses on learning the relationship between intent and slot attention vectors in order to obtain better semantic frame results by the global optimization. The experiments show that our proposed model significantly improves sentence-level semantic frame accuracy with 4.2% and 1.9% relative improvement compared to the attentional model on benchmark ATIS and Snips datasets respectively[1].

1   Introduction

Spoken language understanding (SLU) is a critical component in spoken dialogue systems. SLU is aiming to form a semantic frame that captures the semantics of user utterances or queries. It typically involves two tasks: intent detection and slot filling (Tur and De Mori, 2011). These two tasks focus on predicting speakers intent and extracting semantic concepts as constraints for the natural language. Take a movie-related utterance as an example, *"find comedies by James Cameron"*, as shown in Figure 1. There are different slot labels for each word in the utterance, and a specific intent for the whole utterance.

Slot filling can be treated as a sequence labeling task that maps an input word sequence $\mathbf{x} = (x_1, \cdots, x_T)$ to the corresponding slot label sequence $\mathbf{y}^S = (y_1^S, \cdots, y_T^S)$, and intent detection can be seen as a classification problem to decide the intent label y^I. Popular approaches for slot filling include conditional random fields (CRF) (Ray-

W	find	comedies	by	james	cameron
	↓	↓	↓	↓	↓
S	O	B-genre	O	B-dir	I-dir
I	find_movie				

Figure 1: An example utterance with annotations of semantic slots in IOB format (S) and intent (I), B-dir and I-dir denote the director name.

mond and Riccardi, 2007) and recurrent neural network (RNN) (Yao et al., 2014), and different classification methods, such as support vector machine (SVM) and RNN, have been applied to intent prediction.

Considering that pipelined approaches usually suffer from error propagation due to their independent models, the joint model for slot filling and intent detection has been proposed to improve sentence-level semantics via mutual enhancement between two tasks (Guo et al., 2014; Hakkani-Tür et al., 2016; Chen et al., 2016). In addition, the attention mechanism (Bahdanau et al., 2014) was introduced and leveraged into the model in order to provide the precise focus, which allows the network to learn where to pay attention in the input sequence for each output label (Liu and Lane, 2015, 2016). The attentional model proposed by Liu and Lane (2016) achieved the state-of-the-art performance for joint slot filling and intent prediction, where the parameters for slot filling and intent prediction are learned in a single model with a shared objective. However, the prior work did not "explicitly" model the relationships between the intent and slots; instead, it applied a joint loss function to "implicitly" consider both cues. Because the slots often highly depend on the intent, this work focuses on how to model the explicit relationships between slots and intent vectors by introducing a slot-gated mechanism. The contributions are three-fold: 1) the proposed slot-

---

[1]The code is available at: `https://github.com/MiuLab/SlotGated-SLU`.

Proceedings of NAACL-HLT 2018, pages 753–757
New Orleans, Louisiana, June 1 - 6, 2018. ©2018 Association for Computational Linguistics

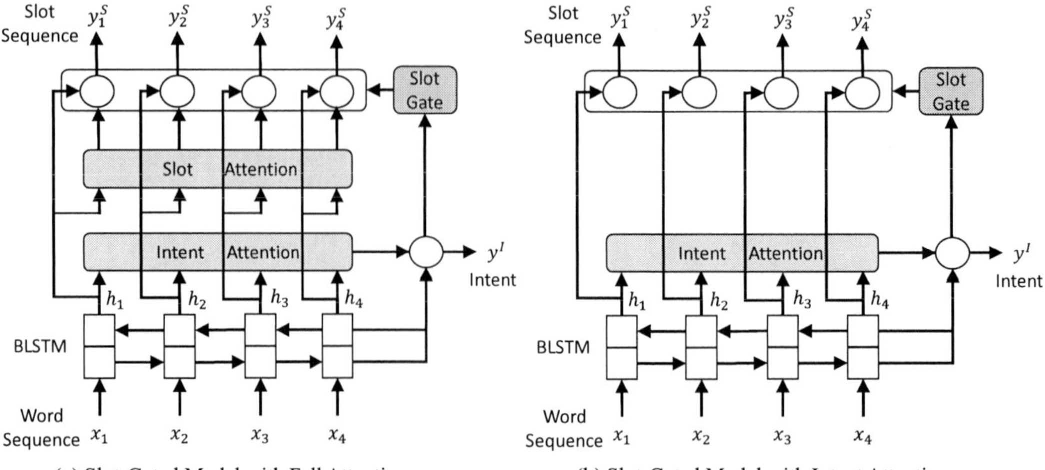

(a) Slot-Gated Model with Full Attention   (b) Slot-Gated Model with Intent Attention

Figure 2: The architecture of the proposed slot-gated models.

gated approach achieves better performance than the attention-based models; 2) the experiments on two SLU datasets show the generalization and the effectiveness of the proposed slot gate; 3) the gating results help us analyze the slot-intent relations.

2 Proposed Approach

This section first explains our attention-based RNN model and then introduces the proposed slot gate mechanism for joint slot filling and intent prediction. The model architecture is illustrated in Figure 2, where there are two different model. (a) is one with both slot attention and intent attention and (b) is another with only intent attention.

2.1 Attention-Based RNN Model

The bidirectional long short-term memory (BLSTM) model (Mesnil et al., 2015) takes a word sequence $\mathbf{x} = (x_1, \ldots, x_T)$ as input, and then generates forward hidden state $\overrightarrow{h_i}$ and backward hidden state $\overleftarrow{h_i}$. The final hidden state h_i at time step i is a concatenation of $\overrightarrow{h_i}$ and $\overleftarrow{h_i}$, i.e. $h_i = [\overrightarrow{h_i}, \overleftarrow{h_i}]$.

Slot Filling For slot filling, $\mathbf{x}$ is mapping to its corresponding slot label sequence $\mathbf{y} = (y_1^S, \ldots, y_T^S)$. For each hidden state h_i, we compute the slot context vector c_i^S as the weighted sum of LSTM's hidden states, $h_1, \ldots, h_T$, by the learned attention weights $\alpha_{i,j}^S$:

$$c_i^S = \sum_{j=1}^{T} \alpha_{i,j}^S h_j, \qquad (1)$$

where the slot attention weights are computed as below.

$$\alpha_{i,j}^S = \frac{\exp(e_{i,j})}{\sum_{k=1}^{T} \exp(e_{i,k})}, \qquad (2)$$

$$e_{i,k} = \sigma(W_{he}^S h_k), \qquad (3)$$

where σ is the activation function, and W_{he}^S is the weight matrix of a feed-forward neural network. Then the hidden state and the slot context vector are utilized for slot filling:

$$y_i^S = \texttt{softmax}(W_{hy}^S(h_i + c_i^S)), \qquad (4)$$

where y_i^S is the slot label of the i-th word in the input, and W_{hy}^S is the weight matrix. The slot attention is shown as the blue component in Figure 2(a).

Intent Prediction The intent context vector c^I can also be computed in the same manner as c^S, but the intent detection part only takes the last hidden state of BLSTM. The intent prediction is modeled similarly:

$$y^I = \texttt{softmax}(W_{hy}^I(h_T + c^I)). \qquad (5)$$

2.2 Slot-Gated Mechanism

This section describes the proposed slot-gated mechanism illustrated in the red part of Figure 2. The proposed slot-gated model introduces an additional gate that leverages intent context vector for modeling slot-intent relationships in order to improve slot filling performance. First, slot context vector c_i^S and intent context vector c^I are combined (c^I broadcasts in time dimension to have the

754

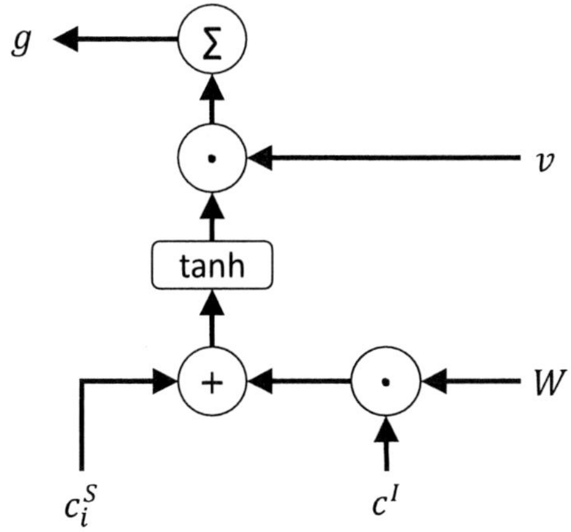

Figure 3: Illustration of the slot gate.

same shape with c_i^S) to pass through a slot gate illustrated in Figure 3:

$$g = \sum v \cdot \tanh(c_i^S + W \cdot c^I) \qquad (6)$$

where v and W are trainable vector and matrix respectively. The summation is done over elements in one time step. g can be seen as a weighted feature of the joint context vector (c_i^S and c^I). We use g to weight between h_i and c_i^S to derive y_i^S and replace (4) as below:

$$y_i^S = \texttt{softmax}(W_{hy}^S(h_i + c_i^S \cdot g)). \qquad (7)$$

A larger g indicates that the slot context vector and the intent context vector pay attention to the same part of the input sequence, which also infers that the correlation between the slot and the intent is stronger and the context vector is more "reliable" for contributing the prediction results.

To compare the power of the slot gate with attention mechanism, we also propose a slot-gated model with only intent attention in which (6) and (7) are reformed as (8) and (9) respectively (shown in Figure 2(b)):

$$g = \sum v \cdot \tanh(h_i + W \cdot c^I) \qquad (8)$$

$$y_i^S = \texttt{softmax}(W_{hy}^S(h_i + h_i \cdot g)) \qquad (9)$$

This version allows the slots and intent to share the attention mechanism.

2.3 Joint Optimization

To obtain both slot filling and intent prediction jointly, the objective is formulated as

$$p(y^S, y^I \mid \mathbf{x}) \qquad (10)$$

	ATIS	Snips
Vocabulary Size	722	11,241
#Slots	120	72
#Intents	21	7
Training Set Size	4,478	13,084
Development Set Size	500	700
Testing Set Size	893	700

Table 1: Statistics of ATIS and Snips datasets.

$$= p(y^I \mid \mathbf{x}) \prod_{t=1}^{T} p(y_t^S \mid \mathbf{x})$$

$$= p(y^I \mid x_1, \cdots, x_T) \prod_{t=1}^{T} p(y_t^S \mid x_1, \cdots, x_T),$$

where $p(y^S, y^I \mid \mathbf{x})$ is the conditional probability of the understanding result (slot filling and intent prediction) given the input word sequence and is maximized for SLU.

3 Experiment

To evaluate the proposed model, we conduct experiments on the benchmark datasets, ATIS (Airline Travel Information System) and Snips. The statistics are shown in Table 1.

3.1 Setup

The ATIS (Airline Travel Information Systems) dataset (Tur et al., 2010) is widely used in SLU research. The dataset contains audio recordings of people making flight reservations. The training set contains 4,478 utterances and the test set contains 893 utterances. We use another 500 utterances for development set. There are 120 slot labels and 21 intent types in the training set.

To justify the generalization of the proposed model, we use another NLU dataset custom-intent-engines[2] collected by Snips for model evaluation. This dataset is collected from the Snips personal voice assistant, where the number of samples for each intent is approximately the same. The training set contains 13,084 utterances and the test set contains 700 utterances. We use another 700 utterances as the development set. There are 72 slot labels and 7 intent types.

Compared to single-domain ATIS dataset, Snips is more complicated mainly due to the intent diver-

---

[2]https://github.com/snipsco/
nlu-benchmark/tree/master/
2017-06-custom-intent-engines

Intent	Utterance Example
SearchCreativeWork	Find me the I, Robot television show
GetWeather	Is it windy in Boston, MA right now?
BookRestaurant	I want to book a highly rated restaurant tomorrow night
PlayMusic	Play the last track from Beyonc off Spotify
AddToPlaylist	Add Diamonds to my roadtrip playlist
RateBook	Give 6 stars to Of Mice and Men
SearchScreeningEvent	Check the showtimes for Wonder Woman in Paris

Table 2: Intents and examples in Snips dataset.

Model		ATIS Dataset			Snips Dataset		
		Slot (F1)	Intent (Acc)	Sentence (Acc)	Slot (F1)	Intent (Acc)	Sentence (Acc)
Joint Seq. (Hakkani-Tür et al., 2016)		94.3	92.6	80.7	87.3	96.9	73.2
Atten.-Based (Liu and Lane, 2016)		94.2	91.1	78.9	87.8	96.7	74.1
Proposed	Slot-Gated (Full Atten.)	$94.8^\dagger$	$93.6^\dagger$	$82.2^\dagger$	$\mathbf{88.8^\dagger}$	**97.0**	$\mathbf{75.5^\dagger}$
	Slot-Gated (Intent Atten.)	$\mathbf{95.2^\dagger}$	$\mathbf{94.1^\dagger}$	$\mathbf{82.6^\dagger}$	88.3	96.8	74.6

Table 3: SLU performance on ATIS and Snips datasets (%). † indicates the significant improvement over all baselines ($p < 0.05$).

sity and large vocabulary. Table 2 shows the intents and associated utterance examples. Regarding the intent diversity, for example, *GetWeather* and *BookRestaurant* in Snips are from different topics, resulting larger vocabulary. In the other hand, intents in ATIS are all about flight information with similar vocabularies across them. Moreover, intents in ATIS are highly unbalanced, where *atis_flight* accounts for about 74% of training data while *atis_cheapest* appears only once. The comparison between two datasets can be found in Table 1.

In all experiments, we set the size of hidden vectors to 64, the optimizer is adam, the reported numbers are averaged over 20 runs, and the maximum epoch is set to 10 and 20 on ATIS and Snips respectively with an early-stop strategy.

3.2 Results and Analysis

We evaluate the SLU performance about slot filling using F1 score, intent prediction using accuracy, and sentence-level semantic frame parsing using whole frame accuracy. The experimental results are shown in Table 3, where the compared baselines for joint slot filling and intent prediction include the state-of-the-art sequence-based joint model using bidirectional LSTM (Hakkani-Tür et al., 2016) and attention-based model (Liu and Lane, 2016). We validate the performance improvement with statistical significance test for

all experiments, where single-tailed t-test is performed to measure whether the results from the proposed model are significant better than ones from baselines. The numbers with star markers indicate that the improvement is significant with $p < 0.05$.

Table 3 shows that the proposed slot-gated mechanism with full attention significantly outperforms the baselines for both datasets, where almost all tasks (slot filling, intent prediction, and semantic frame) obtain the improvement, demonstrating that explicitly modeling strong relationships between slots and intent can benefit SLU effectively. In ATIS dataset, the proposed slot-gated model with only intent attention achieves slightly better performance with fewer parameters (from 284K to 251K). However, it does not achieve better results in Snips dataset. Considering different complexity of these datasets, the probable reason is that a simpler SLU task, such as ATIS, does not require additional slot attention to achieve good results, and the slot gate is capable of providing enough cues for slot filling. On the other hand, Snips is more complex, so that the slot attention is needed in order to model slot filling better (as well as the semantic frame results).

It is obvious that our proposed model performs better especially on sentence-level semantic frame results, where the relative improvement is around 4.1% and 1.9% for ATIS and Snips respectively.

It may credit to the proposed slot gate that learns the slot-intent relations to provide helpful information for global optimization of the joint model. In sum, for joint slot filling and intent prediction, the experiments show that leveraging explicit slot-intent relations controlled by the slot-gated mechanism can effectively achieve better sentence-level semantic frame performance due to global consideration.

4 Conclusion

This paper focuses on learning the explicit slot-intent relations by introducing a slot-gated mechanism into the state-of-the-art attention model, which allows the slot filling can be conditioned on the learned intent result in order to achieve better SLU (joint slot filling and intent detection). The experiments show that the proposed approach outperforms the baselines and can be generalized to different datasets. Also, the slot-gated model is more useful for a simple understanding task, because the slot-intent relations are stronger and easily modeled, and this paper provides the guidance of model design for future SLU work.

Acknowledgements

We would like to thank reviewers for their insightful comments on the paper. The authors are supported by the Institute for Information Industry, Ministry of Science and Technology of Taiwan, Google Research, Microsoft Research, and MediaTek Inc..

References

Dzmitry Bahdanau, Kyunghyun Cho, and Yoshua Bengio. 2014. Neural machine translation by jointly learning to align and translate. *arXiv preprint arXiv:1409.0473*.

Yun-Nung Chen, Dilek Hakanni-Tür, Gokhan Tur, Asli Celikyilmaz, Jianfeng Guo, and Li Deng. 2016. Syntax or semantics? knowledge-guided joint semantic frame parsing. In *Proceedings of 2016 IEEE Spoken Language Technology Workshop*, pages 348–355. IEEE.

Daniel Guo, Gokhan Tur, Wen-tau Yih, and Geoffrey Zweig. 2014. Joint semantic utterance classification and slot filling with recursive neural networks. In *Proceedings of 2014 IEEE Spoken Language Technology Workshop*, pages 554–559. IEEE.

Dilek Hakkani-Tür, Gökhan Tür, Asli Celikyilmaz, Yun-Nung Chen, Jianfeng Gao, Li Deng, and Ye-Yi Wang. 2016. Multi-domain joint semantic frame parsing using bi-directional rnn-lstm. In *Proceedings of INTERSPEECH*, pages 715–719.

Bing Liu and Ian Lane. 2015. Recurrent neural network structured output prediction for spoken language understanding. In *Proc. NIPS Workshop on Machine Learning for Spoken Language Understanding and Interactions*.

Bing Liu and Ian Lane. 2016. Attention-based recurrent neural network models for joint intent detection and slot filling. In *Proceedings of INTERSPEECH*.

Grégoire Mesnil, Yann Dauphin, Kaisheng Yao, Yoshua Bengio, Li Deng, Dilek Hakkani-Tur, Xiaodong He, Larry Heck, Gokhan Tur, Dong Yu, et al. 2015. Using recurrent neural networks for slot filling in spoken language understanding. *IEEE/ACM Transactions on Audio, Speech and Language Processing (TASLP)*, 23(3):530–539.

Christian Raymond and Giuseppe Riccardi. 2007. Generative and discriminative algorithms for spoken language understanding. In *Eighth Annual Conference of the International Speech Communication Association*.

Gokhan Tur and Renato De Mori. 2011. *Spoken language understanding: Systems for extracting semantic information from speech*. John Wiley & Sons.

Gokhan Tur, Dilek Hakkani-Tür, and Larry Heck. 2010. What is left to be understood in ATIS? In *Proceedings of 2010 IEEE Spoken Language Technology Workshop (SLT)*, pages 19–24. IEEE.

Kaisheng Yao, Baolin Peng, Yu Zhang, Dong Yu, Geoffrey Zweig, and Yangyang Shi. 2014. Spoken language understanding using long short-term memory neural networks. In *Proceedings of 2014 IEEE Spoken Language Technology Workshop*, pages 189–194. IEEE.

An Evaluation of Image-based Verb Prediction Models against Human Eye-tracking Data

Spandana Gella and **Frank Keller**
School of Informatics, University of Edinburgh
10 Crichton Street, Edinburgh EH8 9AB, UK
spandana.gella@ed.ac.uk, keller@inf.ed.ac.uk

Abstract

Recent research in language and vision has developed models for predicting and disambiguating verbs from images. Here, we ask whether the predictions made by such models correspond to human intuitions about visual verbs. We show that the image regions a verb prediction model identifies as salient for a given verb correlate with the regions fixated by human observers performing a verb classification task.

1 Introduction

Recent research in language and vision has applied fundamental NLP tasks in a multimodal setting. An example is word sense disambiguation (WSD), the task of assigning a word the correct meaning in a given context. WSD traditionally uses textual context, but disambiguation can be performed using an image context instead, relying on the fact that different word senses are often visually distinct. Early work has focused on the disambiguation of nouns (Loeff et al., 2006; Saenko and Darrell, 2008; Chen et al., 2015), but more recent research has proposed visual sense disambiguation models for verbs (Gella et al., 2016). This is a considerably more challenging task, as unlike objects (denoted by nouns), actions (denoted by verbs) are often not clearly localized in an image. Gella et al. (2018) propose a two-stage approach, consisting of a verb prediction model, which labels an image with potential verbs, followed by a visual sense disambiguation model, which uses the image to determine the correct verb senses.

While this approach achieves good verb prediction and sense disambiguation accuracy, it is not clear to what extend the model captures human intuitions about visual verbs. Specifically, it is interesting to ask whether the image regions that the model identifies as salient for a given verb correspond to the regions a human observer relies on when determining which verb is depicted. The output of a verb prediction model can be visualized as a heatmap over the image, where hot colors indicate the most salient areas for a given task (see Figure 2 for examples). In the same way, we can determine which regions a human observes attends to by eye-tracking them while viewing the image. Eye-tracking data consists a stream of gaze coordinates, which can also be turned into a heatmap. Model predictions correspond to human intuitions if the two heatmaps correlate.

In the present paper, we show that the heatmaps generated by the verb prediction model of Gella et al. (2018) correlate well with heatmaps obtained from human observers performing a verb classification task. We achieve a higher correlation than a range of baselines (center bias, visual salience, and model combinations), indicating that the verb prediction model successfully identifies those image regions that are indicative of the verb depicted in the image.

2 Related Work

Most closely related is the work by Das et al. (2016) who tested the hypothesis that the regions attended to by neural visual question answering (VQA) models correlate with the regions attended to by humans performing the same task. Their results were negative: the neural VQA models do not predict human attention better than a baseline visual salience model (see Section 3). It is possible that this result is due to limitations of the study of Das et al. (2016): their evaluation dataset, the VQA-HAT corpus, was collected using mouse-tracking, which is less natural and less sensitive than eye-tracking. Also, their participants did not actually perform question answering, but were given a question and its answer, and then had to mark up the relevant image regions. Das et al. (2016) report a human-

Proceedings of NAACL-HLT 2018, pages 758–763
New Orleans, Louisiana, June 1 - 6, 2018. ©2018 Association for Computational Linguistics

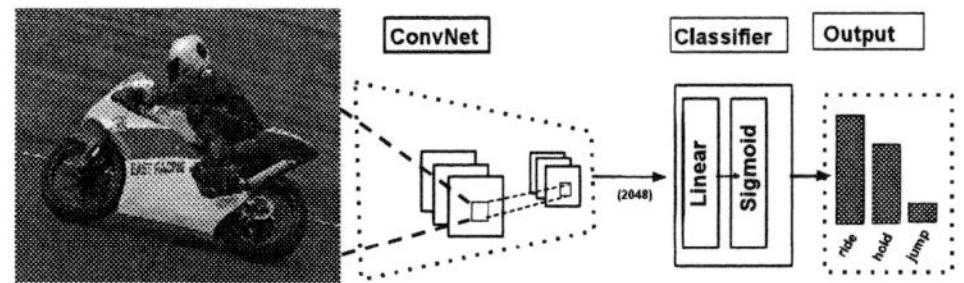

Figure 1: A schematic view of our multilabel verb classification model.

human correlation of 0.623, which suggests low task validity.

Qiao et al. (2017) also use VQA-HAT, but in a supervised fashion: they train the attention component of their VQA model on human attention data. Not surprisingly, this results in a higher correlation with human heatmaps than Das et al.'s (2016) unsupervised approach. However, Qiao et al. (2017) fail to compare to a visual salience model (given their supervised setup, such the salience model would also have to be trained on VQA-HAT for a fair comparison).

The work that is perhaps closest to our own work is Hahn and Keller (2016), who use a reinforcement learning model to predict eye-tracking data for text reading (rather than visual processing). Their model is unsupervised (there is no use of eye-tracking data at training time), but achieves a good correlation with eye-tracking data at test time.

Furthermore, a number of authors have used eye-tracking data for training computer vision models, including zero shot image classification (Karessli et al., 2017), object detection (Papadopoulos et al., 2014), and action classification in still images (Ge et al., 2015; Yun et al., 2015) and videos (Dorr and Vig, 2017). In NLP, some authors have used eye-tracking data collected for text reading to train models that perform part-of-speech tagging (Barrett et al., 2016a,b), grammatical function classification (Barrett and Søgaard, 2015), and sentence compression (Klerke et al., 2016).

3 Fixation Prediction Models

Verb Prediction Model (M) In our study, we used the verb prediction model proposed by Gella et al. (2018), which employs a multilabel CNN-based classification approach and is designed to simultaneously predict all verbs associated with an image. This model is trained over a vocabulary that consists of the 250 most common verbs in the TUHOI, Flickr30k, and COCO image description datasets. For each image in these datasets, we obtained a set of verb labels by extracting all the verbs from the ground truth descriptions of the image (each image comes with multiple descriptions, each of which can contribute one or more verbs).

Our model uses a sigmoid cross-entropy loss and the ResNet 152-layer CNN architecture. The network weights were initialized with the publicly available CNN pretrained on ImageNet[1] and fine-tuned on the verb labels. We used stochastic gradient descent and trained the network with a batch size of one for three epochs. The model architecture is shown schematically in Figure 1.

To derive fixation predictions, we turned the output of the verb prediction model into heatmaps using the class activation mapping (CAM) technique proposed by Zhou et al. (2016). CAM uses global average pooling of convolution feature maps to identify the important image regions by projecting back the weights of the output layer onto the convolutional feature maps. This technique has been shown to achieve competitive results on both object localization and localizing the discriminative regions for action classification.

Center Bias (CB) We compare against a center bias baseline, which simulates the task-independent tendency of observers to make fixations towards the center of an image. This is a strong baseline for most eye-tracking datasets (Tatler, 2007). We follow Clarke and Tatler (2014) and compute a heatmap based on a zero mean Gaussian with a co-variance matrix of $\begin{pmatrix} \sigma^2 & 0 \\ 0 & v\sigma^2 \end{pmatrix}$, where $\sigma^2 = 0.22$ and $v = 0.45$ (the values suggested by Clarke and Tatler 2014).

Visual Salience (SM) Models of visual salience are meant to capture the tendency of the human visual system to fixate the most prominent parts of a scene, often within a few hundred milliseconds of exposure. A large number of salience models have been proposed in the cognitive literature, and we choose the model of Liu and Han (2016), as it currently achieves the highest correlation with human fixations on the MIT300 benchmark out of 77 models (Bylinskii et al., 2016).

The deep spatial contextual long-term recurrent convolutional network (DSCLRCN) of Liu and Han (2016) is trained on SALICON (Jiang et al., 2015), a large human attention dataset, to infer salience for arbitrary images. DSCLRCN learns powerful local feature representations while simul-

---

[1] `https://github.com/KaimingHe/deep-residual-networks`

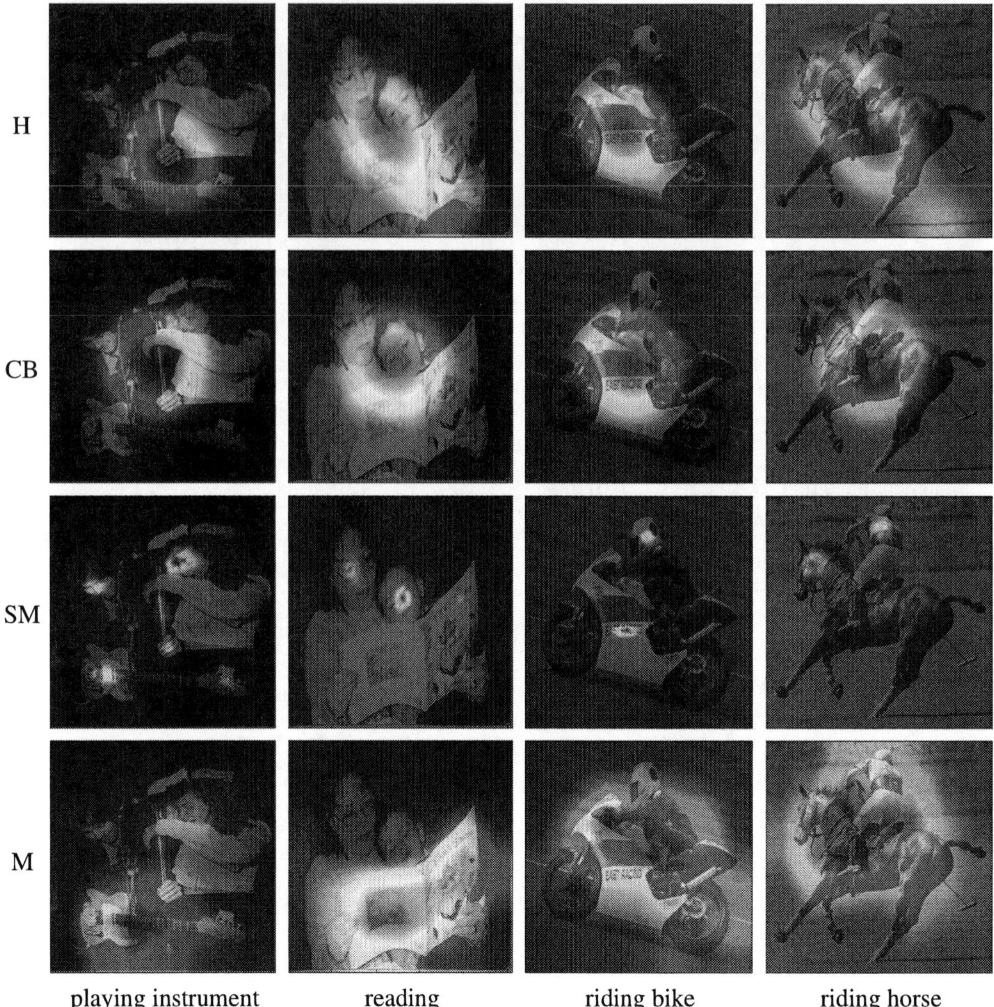

Figure 2: Heatmaps visualizing human fixations (H), Center Bias (CB), salience model (SM) predictions, and verb model (M) prediction for randomly picked example images. The SM heatmaps are very focused, which is a consequence of that model being trained on SALICON, which contains focused human attention maps. However, our evaluation uses rank correlation, rather than correlation on absolute attention scores, and is therefore unaffected by this issue.

taneously incorporating global context and scene context to compute a heatmap representing visual salience. Note that salience models are normally tested using free viewing tasks or visual search tasks, not verb prediction. However, salience can be expected to play a large role in determining fixation locations independent of task, so DSCLRCN is a good baseline to compare to.

4 Eye-tracking Dataset

The PASCAL VOC 2012 Actions Fixation dataset (Mathe and Sminchisescu, 2013) contains 9,157 images covering 10 action classes (phoning, reading, jumping, running, walking, riding bike, riding horse, playing instrument, taking photo, using computer). Each image is annotated with the eye-fixations of eight human observers who, for each image, were asked to recognize the action depicted and respond with one of the class labels. Participants were given three seconds to freely view an image while the x- and y-coordinates of their gaze positions were recorded. (Note that the original dataset also contained a control condition in which four participants performed visual search; we do not use the data from this control condition.) In Figure 2 (row H) we show examples of heatmaps generated from the human fixations in the Mathe and Sminchisescu (2013) dataset. For details on

Verb	Images	Rank correlations							
		H	CB	SM	M	CB+SM	CB+M	M+SM	M+CB+SM
phoning	221	0.911	0.599	0.361	0.562	0.598	**0.654**	0.569	0.652
reading	231	0.923	0.589	0.404	0.544	0.598	**0.655**	0.558	0.655
jumping	201	0.930	0.612	0.300	0.560	0.609	**0.650**	0.561	0.647
running	154	0.934	0.548	0.264	0.536	0.545	**0.604**	0.536	0.602
walking	195	0.938	0.553	0.311	0.535	0.552	**0.611**	0.537	0.609
riding bike	199	0.925	0.580	0.329	0.518	0.578	**0.622**	0.527	0.621
riding horse	206	0.910	0.593	0.351	0.532	0.588	**0.604**	0.532	0.601
playing instrument	229	0.925	0.571	0.350	0.478	0.568	**0.596**	0.484	0.593
taking photo	205	0.925	**0.656**	0.354	0.508	0.647	0.630	0.514	0.628
using computer	196	0.916	0.633	0.389	0.525	0.626	**0.655**	0.533	0.652
overall	2037	0.923	0.592	0.344	0.529	0.591	**0.628**	0.535	0.626

Table 1: Table of average rank correlation scores for the verb prediction model (M), compared with the upper bound of average human-human agreement (H), center bias (CB) baseline (Clarke and Tatler, 2014), and salience map (SM) baseline (Liu and Han, 2016). Results are reported on the validation set of the PASCAL VOC 2012 Actions Fixation data (Mathe and Sminchisescu, 2013). The best score for each class is shown in **bold** (except upper bound). Model combination are by mean of heatmaps.

the eye-tracking setup used, including information on measurement error, please refer to Mathe and Sminchisescu (2015), who used the same setup as Mathe and Sminchisescu (2013).

While actions and verbs are distinct concepts (Ronchi and Perona, 2015; Pustejovsky et al., 2016; Gella and Keller, 2017), we can still use the PASCAL Actions Fixation data to evaluate our model. When predicting a verb, the model presumably has to attend to the same regions that humans fixate on when working out which action is depicted – all the actions in the dataset are verb-based, hence recognizing the verb is part of recognizing the action.

5 Results

To evaluate the similarity between human fixations and model predictions, we first computed a heatmap based on the human fixations for each image. We used the PyGaze toolkit (Dalmaijer et al., 2014) to generate Gaussian heatmaps weighted by fixation durations. We then computed the heatmap predicted by our model for the top-ranked verb the model assigns to the image (out of its vocabulary of 250 verbs). We used the rank correlation between these two heatmaps as our evaluation measure. For this, both maps are converted into a 14×14 grid, and each grid square is ranked according to its average attention score. Spearman's ρ is then computed between these two sets of ranks. This is the same evaluation protocol that Das et al. (2016) used to evaluate the heatmaps generated by two question answering models with unsupervised attention, viz.,

the Stacked Attention Network (Yang et al., 2016) and the Hierarchical Co-Attention Network (Lu et al., 2016). This makes their rank correlations and ours directly comparable.

In Table 1 we present the correlations between human fixation heatmaps and model-predicted heatmaps. All results were computed on the validation portion of the PASCAL Actions Fixation dataset. We average the correlations for each action class (though the class labels were not used in our evaluation), and also present overall averages. In addition to our model results, we also give the correlations of human fixations with (a) the center bias baseline, and (b) the salience model. We also report the correlations obtained by all combinations of our model and these baselines. Finally, we report the human-human agreement averaged over the eight observes. This serves as an upper bound to model performance.

The results show a high human-human agreement for all verbs, with an average of 0.923. This is considerably higher than the human-human agreement of 0.623 that Das et al. (2016) report for their question answering ask, indicating that verb classification is a task that can be performed more reliably than Das et al.'s (2016) VQA region markup task (they also used mouse-tracking rather than eye-tracking, a less sensitive experimental method).

We also notice that the center baseline (CB) generally performs well, achieving an average correlation of 0.592. The salience model (SM) is less convincing, averaging a correlation of 0.344. This is likely due to the fact that SM was trained on the SALICON dataset; a higher correlation can probably be achieved by fine-tuning the salience model on the PASCAL Actions Fixation data. However, this would no longer be fair comparison with our verb prediction model, which was not trained on fixation data (it only uses image description datasets at training time, see Section 3). Adding SM to CB does not lead to an improvement over CB alone, with an average correlation of 0.591.

Our model (M) on its own achieves an average correlation of 0.529, rising to 0.628 when combined with center bias, clearly outperforming center bias alone. Adding SM does not lead to a further improvement (0.626). The combination of our model with SM performs only slightly better than the model on its own.

In Figure 2, we visualize samples of heatmaps generated from the human fixations, the center-bias, the salience model, and the predictions of our model. We observe that human fixations and center bias exhibit high overlap. The salience model attends to regions that attract human attention independent of task (e.g., faces), while our model mimics human observers in attending to regions that are associated with the verbs depicted in the image. In Figure 2 we can observe that our model predicts fixations that vary with the different uses of a given verb (riding bike vs. riding horse).

6 Conclusions

We showed that a model that labels images with verbs is able to predict which image regions humans attend when performing the same task. The model therefore captures aspects of human intuitions about how verbs are depicted. This is an encouraging result given that our verb prediction model was not designed to model human behavior, and was trained on an unrelated image description dataset, without any access to eye-tracking data. Our result contradicts the existing literature (Das et al., 2016), which found no above-baseline correlation between human attention and model attention in a VQA task.

References

Maria Barrett, Joachim Bingel, Frank Keller, and Anders Søgaard. 2016a. Weakly supervised part-of-speech tagging using eye-tracking data. In *Proceedings of the 54th Annual Meeting of the Association for Computational Linguistics, Volume 2: Short Papers*. Berlin, pages 579–584.

Maria Barrett, Frank Keller, and Anders Søgaard. 2016b. Cross-lingual transfer of correlations between parts of speech and gaze features. In *Proceedings of the 26th International Conference on Computational Linguistics*. Osaka, pages 1330–1339.

Maria Barrett and Anders Søgaard. 2015. Using reading behavior to predict grammatical functions. In *EMNLP Workshop on Cognitive Aspects of Computational Language Learning*. Lisbon, Portugal.

Zoya Bylinskii, Tilke Judd, Ali Borji, Laurent Itti, Frédo Durand, Aude Oliva, and Antonio Torralba. 2016. Mit saliency benchmark. http://saliency.mit.edu/.

Xinlei Chen, Alan Ritter, Abhinav Gupta, and Tom M. Mitchell. 2015. Sense discovery via co-clustering on images and text. In *IEEE Conference on Computer Vision and Pattern Recognition, CVPR 2015, Boston, MA, USA, June 7-12, 2015*. pages 5298–5306.

Alasdair DF Clarke and Benjamin W Tatler. 2014. Deriving an appropriate baseline for describing fixation behaviour. *Vision research* 102:41–51.

Edwin S Dalmaijer, Sebastiaan Mathôt, and Stefan Van der Stigchel. 2014. Pygaze: An open-source, cross-platform toolbox for minimal-effort programming of eyetracking experiments. *Behavior research methods* 46(4):913–921.

Abhishek Das, Harsh Agrawal, Larry Zitnick, Devi Parikh, and Dhruv Batra. 2016. Human attention in visual question answering: Do humans and deep networks look at the same regions? In *Proceedings of the 2016 Conference on Empirical Methods in Natural Language Processing, EMNLP 2016, Austin, Texas, USA, November 1-4, 2016*. pages 932–937.

Michael Dorr and Eleonora Vig. 2017. Saliency prediction for action recognition. In *Visual Content Indexing and Retrieval with Psycho-Visual Models*, Springer, pages 103–124.

Gary Ge, Kiwon Yun, Dimitris Samaras, and Gregory J Zelinsky. 2015. Action classification in still images using human eye movements. In *Proceedings of the IEEE Conference on Computer Vision and Pattern Recognition Workshops*. pages 16–23.

Spandana Gella and Frank Keller. 2017. An analysis of action recognition datasets for language and vision tasks. In *Proceedings of the 55th Annual Meeting of the Association for Computational Linguistics, Volume 2: Short Papers*. Vancouver, pages 64–71.

Spandana Gella, Frank Keller, and Mirella Lapata. 2018. Disambiguating visual verbs. *IEEE Trans. Pattern Anal. Mach. Intell.* .

Spandana Gella, Mirella Lapata, and Frank Keller. 2016. Unsupervised visual sense disambiguation for verbs using multimodal embeddings. In *NAACL HLT 2016, The 2016 Conference of the North American Chapter of the Association for Computational Linguistics: Human Language Technologies, San Diego California, USA, June 12-17, 2016*. pages 182–192.

Michael Hahn and Frank Keller. 2016. Modeling human reading with neural attention. In *Proceedings of the 2016 Conference on Empirical Methods in Natural Language Processing, EMNLP 2016, Austin, Texas, USA, November 1-4, 2016*. pages 85–95.

Ming Jiang, Shengsheng Huang, Juanyong Duan, and Qi Zhao. 2015. Salicon: Saliency in context. In *Proceedings of the IEEE conference on computer vision and pattern recognition*. pages 1072–1080.

Nour Karessli, Zeynep Akata, Bernt Schiele, and Andreas Bulling. 2017. Gaze embeddings for zero-shot image classification. In *2017 IEEE Conference on Computer Vision and Pattern Recognition, CVPR 2017, Honolulu, HI, USA, July 21-26, 2017*. pages 6412–6421.

Sigrid Klerke, Yoav Goldberg, and Anders Søgaard. 2016. Improving sentence compression by learning to predict gaze. In *Proceedings of the Conference of the North American Chapter of the Association for Computational Linguistics*. San Diego, CA.

Nian Liu and Junwei Han. 2016. A deep spatial contextual long-term recurrent convolutional network for saliency detection. *CoRR abs/1610.01708*.

Nicolas Loeff, Cecilia Ovesdotter Alm, and David A. Forsyth. 2006. Discriminating image senses by clustering with multimodal features. In *ACL 2006, 21st International Conference on Computational Linguistics and 44th Annual Meeting of the Association for Computational Linguistics, Proceedings of the Conference, Sydney, Australia, 17-21 July 2006*. Association for Computational Linguistics, pages 547–554.

Jiasen Lu, Jianwei Yang, Dhruv Batra, and Devi Parikh. 2016. Hierarchical question-image co-attention for visual question answering. In D. D. Lee, M. Sugiyama, U. V. Luxburg, I. Guyon, and R. Garnet t, editors, *Advances in Neural Information Processing Systems 29*, Curran Associates, Inc., pages 289–297.

Stefan Mathe and Cristian Sminchisescu. 2013. Action from still image dataset and inverse optimal control to learn task specific visual scanpaths. In *Advances in neural information processing systems*. pages 1923–1931.

Stefan Mathe and Cristian Sminchisescu. 2015. Actions in the eye: Dynamic gaze datasets and learnt saliency models for visual recognition. *IEEE Transactions on Pattern Analysis and Machine Intelligence* 37.(7):1408–1424.

Dim P Papadopoulos, Alasdair DF Clarke, Frank Keller, and Vittorio Ferrari. 2014. Training object class detectors from eye tracking data. In *European Conference on Computer Vision*. Springer, pages 361–376.

James Pustejovsky, Tuan Do, Gitit Kehat, and Nikhil Krishnaswamy. 2016. The development of multimodal lexical resources. In *Proceedings of the Workshop on Grammar and Lexicon: interactions and interfaces (GramLex)*. pages 41–47.

Tingting Qiao, Jianfeng Dong, and Duanqing Xu. 2017. Exploring human-like attention supervision in visual question answering. ArXiv:1709.06308.

Matteo Ruggero Ronchi and Pietro Perona. 2015. Describing common human visual actions in images. In *Proceedings of the British Machine Vision Conference (BMVC 2015)*. BMVA Press, pages 52.1–52.12.

Kate Saenko and Trevor Darrell. 2008. Unsupervised learning of visual sense models for polysemous words. In *Advances in Neural Information Processing Systems 21, Proceedings of the Twenty-Second Annual Conference on Neural Information Processing Systems, Vancouver, British Columbia, Canada, December 8-11, 2008*. pages 1393–1400.

Benjamin W. Tatler. 2007. The central fixation bias in scene viewing: selecting an optimal viewing position independently of motor biases and image feature distributions. *Journal of Vision* 7(14):1–17.

Zichao Yang, Xiaodong He, Jianfeng Gao, Li Deng, and Alexander J. Smola. 2016. Stacked attention networks for image question answering. In *IEEE Conference on Computer Vision and Pattern Recognition*. Las Vegas, NV.

Kiwon Yun, Gary Ge, Dimitris Samaras, and Gregory Zelinsky. 2015. How we look tells us what we do: Action recognition using human gaze. *Journal of vision* 15(12):121–121.

Bolei Zhou, Aditya Khosla, Agata Lapedriza, Aude Oliva, and Antonio Torralba. 2016. Learning deep features for discriminative localization. In *Computer Vision and Pattern Recognition*.

Learning to Color from Language

Varun Manjunatha[★♠○]   Mohit Iyyer[★†‡]   Jordan Boyd-Graber[♠♣○◇]   Larry Davis[♠○]

University of Maryland : Computer Science[♠], Language Science[◇], iSchool[♣], UMIACS[○]
Allen Institute of Artificial Intelligence[†]   University of Massachusetts, Amherst[‡]
{varunm@cs, jbg@umiacs, lsd@umiacs}.umd.edu   miyyer@cs.umass.edu

Abstract

Automatic colorization is the process of adding color to greyscale images. We condition this process on language, allowing end users to manipulate a colorized image by feeding in different captions. We present two different architectures for language-conditioned colorization, both of which produce more accurate and plausible colorizations than a language-agnostic version. Through this language-based framework, we can dramatically alter colorizations by manipulating descriptive color words in captions.

1 Introduction

Automatic image colorization (Cheng et al., 2015; Larsson et al., 2016; Zhang et al., 2016; Iizuka et al., 2016; Deshpande et al., 2017)—the process of adding color to a greyscale image—is inherently underspecified. Unlike background scenery such as sky or grass, many common foreground objects could plausibly be of any color, such as a person's clothing, a bird's feathers, or the exterior of a car. Interactive colorization seeks human input, usually in the form of clicks or strokes on the image with a selected color, to reduce these ambiguities (Levin et al., 2004; Huang et al., 2005; Endo et al., 2016; Zhang et al., 2017). We introduce the task of colorization from natural language, a previously unexplored source of color specifications.

Many use cases for automatic colorization involve images paired with language. For example, comic book artwork is normally first sketched in black-and-white by a penciller; afterwards, a colorist selects a palette that thematically reinforces the written script to produce the final colorized art. Similarly, older black-and-white films are often colorized for modern audiences based on cues from dialogue and narration (Van Camp, 1995).

Language is a weaker source of supervision for colorization than user clicks. In particular, language lacks ground-truth information about the colored image (e.g., the exact color of a pixel or region). Given a description like *a blue motorcycle parked next to a fleet of sedans*, an automatic colorization system must first localize the motorcycle within the image before deciding on a context-appropriate shade of blue to color it with. The challenge grows with abstract language: a red color palette likely suits an artistic rendering of *the boy threw down his toy in a rage* better than it does *the boy lovingly hugged his toy*.

We present two neural architectures for language-based colorization that augment an existing fully-convolutional model (Zhang et al., 2016) with representations learned from image captions. As a sanity check, both architectures outperform a language-agnostic model on an accuracy-based colorization metric. However, we are more interested in whether modifications to the caption properly manifest themselves in output colorizations (e.g., switching one color with another); crowdsourced evaluations confirm that our models properly localize and color objects based on captions (Figure 1).

2 Model

This section provides a quick introduction to color spaces (Sec. 2.1) and then describes our baseline colorization network (Sec. 2.2) alongside two models (Sec. 2.3) that colorize their output on representations learned from language.

2.1 Images and color spaces

An image is usually represented as a three dimensional tensor with red, green and blue (RGB) channels. Each pixel's color and intensity (i.e., lightness) are *jointly* represented by the values of these three channels. However, in applications such as

---

★Authors contributed equally

Proceedings of NAACL-HLT 2018, pages 764–769
New Orleans, Louisiana, June 1 - 6, 2018. ©2018 Association for Computational Linguistics

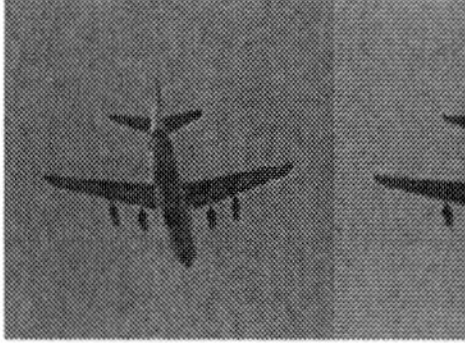

Figure 1: Three pairs of images whose colorizations are conditioned on corresponding captions by our **FILM** architecture. Our model can localize objects mentioned by the captions and properly color them.

colorization, it is more convenient to use representations that separately encode lightness and color. These *color spaces* can be obtained through mathematical transformations of the RGB color space; in this work, following Zhang et al. (2016), we use the CIE *Lab* space (Smith and Guild, 1931). Here, the first channel (L) encodes only lightness (i.e., black-and-white). The two color channels a and b represent color values between green to red and blue to yellow, respectively. In this formulation, the task of colorization is equivalent to taking the lightness channel of an image as input and predicting the two missing color channels.

2.2 Fully-convolutional networks for colorization

Following Zhang et al. (2016), we treat colorization as a classification problem in CIE *Lab* space: given only the lightness channel L of an image (i.e., a greyscale version), a fully-convolutional network predicts values for the two color channels a and b. For efficiency, we deviate from Zhang et al. (2016) by quantizing the color channels into a 25×25 grid, which results in 625 labels for classification. To further speed up training, we use a one-hot encoding for the ab channels instead of soft targets as in Zhang et al. (2016); preliminary experiments showed no qualitative difference in colorization quality with one-hot targets. The contribution of each label to the loss is downweighted by a factor inversely proportional to its frequency in the training set, which prevents desaturated ab values. Our baseline network architecture (**FCNN**) consists of eight convolutional blocks, each of which contains multiple convolutional layers followed by batch normalization (Ioffe and Szegedy, 2015).[1] Next, we propose two ways to integrate additional *text*

---

[1]See Zhang et al. (2016) for complete architectural details. Code and pretrained models are available at `https://github.com/superhans/colorfromlanguage`.

	ab Accuracy		Human Experiments		
Model	acc@1	acc@5	plaus.	qual.	manip.
FCNN	15.4	45.8	20.4	32.6	N/A
CONCAT	17.9	50.3	39.0	**34.1**	77.4
FILM	**23.7**	**60.5**	**40.6**	32.1	**81.2**

Table 1: While **FILM** is the most accurate model in *ab* space, its outputs are about as contextually plausible as **CONCAT**'s according to our *plausibility* task, which asks workers to choose which model's output best depicts a given caption (however, both models significantly outperform the language-agnostic **FCNN**). This additional plausibility does not degrade the output, as shown by our *quality* task, which asks workers to distinguish an automatically-colorized image from a real one. Finally, our caption *manipulation* experiment, in which workers are guided by a caption to select one of three outputs generated with varying color words, shows that modifying the caption significantly affects the outputs of **CONCAT** and **FILM**.

input into **FCNN**.

2.3 Colorization conditioned on language

Given an image I paired with a unit of text T, we first encode T into a continuous representation h using the last hidden state of a bi-directional LSTM (Hochreiter and Schmidhuber, 1997). We integrate h into every convolutional block of the **FCNN**, allowing language to influence the computation of all intermediate feature maps.

Specifically, say $\mathbf{Z}_n$ is the feature map of the nth convolutional block. A conceptually simple way to incorporate language into this feature map is to concatenate h to the channels at each spatial location i, j in $\mathbf{Z}_n$, forming a new feature map

$$\mathbf{Z}'_{n_{i,j}} = [\mathbf{Z}_{n_{i,j}}; h]. \qquad (1)$$

While this method of integrating language with images (**CONCAT**) has been successfully used for other vision and language tasks (Reed et al., 2016;

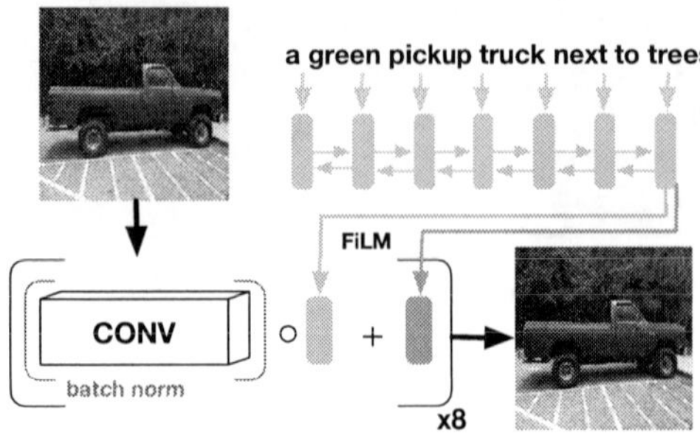

Figure 2: **FILM** applies feature-wise affine transformations (conditioned on language) to the output of each convolutional block in our architecture.

Feichtenhofer et al., 2016), it requires considerably more parameters than the **FCNN** due to the additional language channels.

Inspired by recent work on visual question answering, we also experiment with a less parameter-hungry approach, feature-wise linear modulation (Perez et al., 2018, **FILM**), to fuse the language and visual representations. Since the activations of **FILM** layers have attention-like properties when trained on **VQA**, we also might expect **FILM** to be better at localizing objects from language than **CONCAT** on colorization (see Figure 4 for heatmap visualizations).

FILM applies a feature-wise affine transformation to the output of each convolutional block, where the transformation weights are conditioned on language (Figure 2). Given $\mathbf{Z}_n$ and h, we first compute two vectors γ_n and β_n through linear projection,

$$\gamma_n = \mathbf{W}_{n_\gamma} h \qquad \beta_n = \mathbf{W}_{n_\beta} h, \qquad (2)$$

where $\mathbf{W}_{n_\gamma}$ and $\mathbf{W}_{n_\beta}$ are learned weight matrices. The modulated feature map then becomes

$$\mathbf{Z}'_{n_{i,j}} = (1 + \gamma_n) \circ \mathbf{Z}_{n_{i,j}} + \beta_n, \qquad (3)$$

where $\circ$ denotes the element-wise product. Compared to **CONCAT**, **FILM** is parameter-efficient, requiring just two additional weight matrices per feature map.

3 Experiments

We evaluate **FCNN**, **CONCAT**, and **FILM** using accuracy in ab space (shown by Zhang et al. (2016) to be a poor substitute for plausibility) and with crowdsourced experiments that ask workers to judge colorization *plausibility*, *quality*, and the

colorization flexibly reflects language *manipulations*. Table 1 summarizes our results; while there is no clear winner between **FILM** and **CONCAT**, both rely on language to produce higher-quality colorizations than those generated by **FCNN**.

3.1 Experimental setup

We train all of our models on the 82,783 images in the MSCOCO (Lin et al., 2014) training set, each of which is paired with five crowdsourced captions. Training from scratch on MSCOCO results in poor quality colorizations due to a combination of not enough data and increased image complexity compared to ImageNet (Russakovsky et al., 2015). Thus, for our final models, we initialize all convolutional layers with a **FCNN** pretrained on ImageNet; we finetune both **FILM** and **CONCAT**'s convolutional weights during training. To automatically evaluate the models, we compute top-1 and top-5 accuracy in our quantized ab output space[2] on the MSCOCO validation set. While **FILM** achieves the highest ab accuracy, **FILM** and **CONCAT** do not significantly differ on crowdsourced evaluation metrics.

3.2 Human experiments

We run three human evaluations of our models on the Crowdflower platform to evaluate their plausibility, overall quality, and how well they condition their output on language. Each evaluation is run using a random subset of 100 caption/image pairs from the MSCOCO validation set,[3] and we obtain five judgments per pair.

Plausibility **given caption:** We show workers a caption along with three images generated by **FCNN**, **CONCAT**, and **FILM**. They choose the image that best depicts the caption; if multiple images accurately depict the caption, we ask them to choose the most realistic. **FCNN** does not receive the caption as input, so it makes sense that its output is only chosen 20% of the time; there is no significant difference between **CONCAT** and **FILM** in plausibility given the caption.

Colorization *quality***:** Workers receive a pair of images, a ground-truth MSCOCO image and a generated output from one of our three architectures,

---

[2] We evaluate accuracy at the downsampled 56×56 resolution at which our network predicts colorizations. For human experiments, the prediction is upsampled to 224×224.

[3] We only evaluate on captions that contain one of ten "color" words (e.g., red, blue purple).

Figure 3: The top row contains successes from our caption manipulation task generated by FILM and CONCAT, respectively. The second row shows examples of how captions guide FILM to produce more accurate colorizations than FCNN (failure cases outlined in red). The final row contains, from left to right, particularly eye-catching colorizations from both CONCAT and FILM, a case where FILM fails to localize properly, and an image whose unnatural caption causes artifacts in CONCAT.

and are asked to choose the image that was *not* colored by a computer. The goal is to fool workers into selecting the generated images; the "fooling rates" for all three architectures are comparable, which indicates that we do not reduce colorization quality by conditioning on language.

Caption *manipulation*: Our last evaluation measures how much influence the caption has on the CONCAT and FILM models. We generate three different colorizations of a single image by swapping out different colors in the caption (e.g., *blue car*, *red car*, *green car*). Then, we provide workers with a single caption (e.g., *green car*) and ask them to choose which image best depicts the caption. If our models cannot localize and color the appropriate object, workers will be unable to select an appropriate image. Fortunately, CONCAT and FILM are both robust to caption manipulations (Table 1).

4 Discussion

Both CONCAT and FILM can manipulate image color from captions (further supported by the top row of Figure 3). Here, we qualitatively examine model outputs and identify potential directions for improvement.

Language-conditioned colorization depends on correspondences between language and color statistics (*stop signs* are always red, and *school buses* are always yellow). While this extra information helps us produce more plausible colorizations compared to language-agnostic models (second row of Figure 3), it biases models trained on natural images against unnatural colorizations. For example, the yellow sky produced by CONCAT in the bottom right of Figure 3 contains blue artifacts because skies are usually blue in MSCOCO. Additionally, our models are limited by the lightness channel L of the greyscale image, which prevents dramatic color shifts like black-to-white. Smaller objects are also problematic; often, colors will "leak"

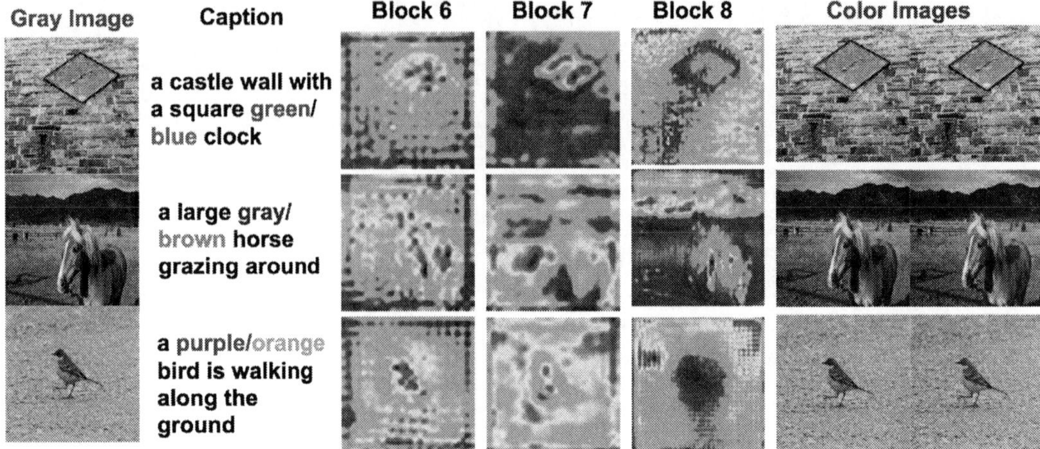

Figure 4: Examples of intermediate layer activations while generating colorized images using the **FILM** network. These activation maps correspond to the mean activation immediately after the **FILM** layers of the sixth, seventh, and eighth blocks. Interestingly, the activations after the **FILM** layer of Block 6 always seems to focus on the object that is to be colorized, while those of Block 8 focus almost exclusively on the background. The activation maps do not significantly differ when color words in the caption are manipulated; therefore, we show maps only for the first color word in these examples.

into smaller objects from larger ones, as shown by **FILM**'s colorizations of purple plants (Figure 3, bottom-middle) and yellow tires (middle-left).

Figure 4 shows activation maps from intermediate layers generated while colorizing images using the **FILM** network. Each intermediate layer is captured immediately after the **FILM** layer and is of dimension $h \times w \times c$ (e.g., $112 \times 112 \times 64$, $28 \times 28 \times 512$, etc.), where h is the height of the feature map, w is its width, and c is the number of channels.[4] On inspection, the first few activation maps correspond to edges and are not visually interesting. However, we notice that the sixth activation map usually focuses on the principal subject of the image (such as a car or a horse), while the eighth activation map focused everywhere but on that subject (i.e., entirely on the background). This analysis demonstrates that the **FILM** layer emulates visual attention, reinforcing similar observations on visual QA datasets by Perez et al. (2018).

5 Future Work

While these experiments are promising, that there are many avenues to improve language-conditioned colorization. From a vision perspective, we would like to more accurately colorize parts of objects (e.g., a person's shoes); moving to more complex ar-

chitectures such as variational autoencoders (Deshpande et al., 2017) or PixelCNNs (Guadarrama et al., 2017) might help here, as could increasing training image resolution. We also plan on using refinement networks (Shrivastava et al., 2017) to correct for artifacts in the colorized output image. On the language side, moving from explicitly specified colors to abstract or emotional language is a particularly interesting. We plan to train our models on dialogue/image pairs from datasets such as COMICS (Iyyer et al., 2017) and visual storytelling (Huang et al., 2016); these models could also help learn powerful joint representations of vision and language to improve performance on downstream prediction tasks.

Acknowledgement

Manjunatha and Davis are partially supported by the Office of Naval Research under Grant N000141612713: Visual Common Sense Reasoning. Boyd-Graber is supported by NSF Grant IIS-1652666. We thank Richard Zhang for helpful comments on our ideas to make training the colorization more efficient.

---

[4]We compute the mean across the c dimension and scale the resulting $h \times w$ feature map between the limits [0, 255].

References

Zezhou Cheng, Qingxiong Yang, and Bin Sheng. 2015. Deep colorization. In *International Conference on Computer Vision*.

Aditya Deshpande, Jiajun Lu, Mao-Chuang Yeh, Min Jin Chong, and David Forsyth. 2017. Learning diverse image colorization. In *Computer Vision and Pattern Recognition*.

Yuki Endo, Satoshi Iizuka, Yoshihiro Kanamori, and Jun Mitani. 2016. Deepprop: Extracting deep features from a single image for edit propagation. In *Eurographics*.

Christoph Feichtenhofer, Axel Pinz, and Andrew Zisserman. 2016. Convolutional two-stream network fusion for video action recognition. In *Computer Vision and Pattern Recognition*.

Sergio Guadarrama, Ryan Dahl, David Bieber, Mohammad Norouzi, Jonathon Shlens, and Kevin Murphy. 2017. Pixcolor: Pixel recursive colorization. *arXiv preprint arXiv:1705.07208* .

Sepp Hochreiter and Jürgen Schmidhuber. 1997. Long short-term memory. *Neural computation* 9:1735–1780.

Ting-Hao Kenneth Huang, Francis Ferraro, Nasrin Mostafazadeh, Ishan Misra, Aishwarya Agrawal, Jacob Devlin, Ross Girshick, Xiaodong He, Pushmeet Kohli, Dhruv Batra, et al. 2016. Visual storytelling. In *Conference of the North American Chapter of the Association for Computational Linguistics*.

Yi-Chin Huang, Yi-Shin Tung, Jun-Cheng Chen, Sung-Wen Wang, and Ja-Ling Wu. 2005. An adaptive edge detection based colorization algorithm and its applications. In *Proceedings Annual ACM International Conference on Multimedia*.

Satoshi Iizuka, Edgar Simo-Serra, and Hiroshi Ishikawa. 2016. Let there be Color!: Joint End-to-end Learning of Global and Local Image Priors for Automatic Image Colorization with Simultaneous Classification. In *ACM Transactions on Graphics*.

Sergey Ioffe and Christian Szegedy. 2015. Batch normalization: Accelerating deep network training by reducing internal covariate shift. In *Proceedings of the International Conference of Machine Learning*.

Mohit Iyyer, Varun Manjunatha, Anupam Guha, Yogarshi Vyas, Jordan Boyd-Graber, Hal Daumé III, and Larry Davis. 2017. The amazing mysteries of the gutter: Drawing inferences between panels in comic book narratives. In *Computer Vision and Pattern Recognition*.

Gustav Larsson, Michael Maire, and Gregory Shakhnarovich. 2016. Learning representations for automatic colorization. In *Proceedings of the European Conference on Computer Vision*.

Anat Levin, Dani Lischinski, and Yair Weiss. 2004. Colorization using optimization. In *ACM Transactions on Graphics*.

Tsung-Yi Lin, Michael Maire, Serge J. Belongie, Lubomir D. Bourdev, Ross B. Girshick, James Hays, Pietro Perona, Deva Ramanan, Piotr Dollár, and C. Lawrence Zitnick. 2014. Microsoft COCO: Common objects in context. In *Proceedings of the European Conference on Computer Vision*.

Ethan Perez, Florian Strub, Harm de Vries, Vincent Dumoulin, and Aaron C. Courville. 2018. FiLM: Visual reasoning with a general conditioning layer. In *Association for the Advancement of Artificial Intelligence*.

Scott E Reed, Zeynep Akata, Santosh Mohan, Samuel Tenka, Bernt Schiele, and Honglak Lee. 2016. Learning what and where to draw. In *Advances in Neural Information Processing Systems*.

Olga Russakovsky, Jia Deng, Hao Su, Jonathan Krause, Sanjeev Satheesh, Sean Ma, Zhiheng Huang, Andrej Karpathy, Aditya Khosla, Michael Bernstein, Alexander C. Berg, and Li Fei-Fei. 2015. Imagenet large scale visual recognition challenge. *International Journal of Computer Vision* .

Ashish Shrivastava, Tomas Pfister, Oncel Tuzel, Joshua Susskind, Wenda Wang, and Russell Webb. 2017. Learning from simulated and unsupervised images through adversarial training. In *Computer Vision and Pattern Recognition*.

Thomas Smith and John Guild. 1931. The C.I.E. colorimetric standards and their use. *Transactions of the Optical Society* 33(3):73.

Julie Van Camp. 1995. The colorization controversy. *The Journal of Value Inquiry* 29(4).

Richard Zhang, Phillip Isola, and Alexei A Efros. 2016. Colorful image colorization. In *Proceedings of the European Conference on Computer Vision*.

Richard Zhang, Jun-Yan Zhu, Phillip Isola, Xinyang Geng, Angela S Lin, Tianhe Yu, and Alexei A Efros. 2017. Real-time user-guided image colorization with learned deep priors. *ACM Transactions on Graphics* 9(4).

Punny Captions: Witty Wordplay in Image Descriptions

Arjun Chandrasekaran[1]   **Devi Parikh**[1,2]   **Mohit Bansal**[3]
[1]Georgia Institute of Technology   [2]Facebook AI Research   [3]UNC Chapel Hill
{carjun, parikh}@gatech.edu   mbansal@cs.unc.edu

Abstract

Wit is a form of rich interaction that is often grounded in a specific situation (e.g., a comment in response to an event). In this work, we attempt to build computational models that can produce witty descriptions for a given image. Inspired by a cognitive account of humor appreciation, we employ linguistic wordplay, specifically puns, in image descriptions. We develop two approaches which involve retrieving witty descriptions for a given image from a large corpus of sentences, or generating them via an encoder-decoder neural network architecture. We compare our approach against meaningful baseline approaches via human studies and show substantial improvements. We find that when a human is subject to similar constraints as the model regarding word usage and style, people vote the image descriptions generated by our model to be slightly wittier than human-written witty descriptions. Unsurprisingly, humans are almost always wittier than the model when they are free to choose the vocabulary, style, etc.

1 Introduction

"Wit is the sudden marriage of ideas which before their union were not perceived to have any relation." – Mark Twain. Witty remarks are often contextual, i.e., grounded in a specific situation. Developing computational models that can emulate rich forms of interaction like contextual humor, is a crucial step towards making human-AI interaction more natural and more engaging (Yu et al., 2016). E.g., witty chatbots could help relieve stress and increase user engagement by being more personable and human-like. Bots could automatically post witty comments (or suggest witty responses) on social media, chat, or messaging.

The absence of large scale corpora of witty captions and the prohibitive cost of collecting such a dataset (being witty is harder than just describing

(a) **Generated**: a poll (pole) on a city street at night.
Retrieved: the light knight (night) chuckled.
Human: the knight (night) in shining armor drove away.

(b) **Generated**: a bare (bear) black bear walking through a forest.
Retrieved: another reporter is standing in a bare (bear) brown field.
Human: the bear killed the lion with its bare (bear) hands.

Figure 1: Sample images and witty descriptions from 2 models, and a human. The words inside '()' (e.g., pole and bear) are the puns associated with the image, i.e., the source of the unexpected puns used in the caption (e.g., poll and bare).

an image) makes the problem of producing contextually witty image descriptions challenging.

In this work, we attempt to tackle the challenging task of producing witty (pun-based) remarks for a given (possibly boring) image. Our approach is inspired by a two-stage cognitive account of humor appreciation (Suls, 1972) which states that a perceiver experiences humor when a stimulus such as a joke, captioned cartoon, etc., causes an *incongruity*, which is shortly followed by *resolution*.

We introduce an incongruity in the perceiver's mind while describing an image by using an unexpected word that is phonetically similar (pun) to a concept related to the image. E.g., in Fig. 1b, the expectations of a perceiver regarding the image (bear, stones, etc.) is momentarily disconfirmed by the (phonetically similar) word 'bare'. This incongruity is resolved when the perceiver parses the entire image description. The incongruity followed by resolution can be perceived to be witty.[1]

---

[1]Indeed, a perceiver may fail to appreciate wit if the pro-

Proceedings of NAACL-HLT 2018, pages 770–775
New Orleans, Louisiana, June 1 - 6, 2018. ©2018 Association for Computational Linguistics

We build two computational models based on this approach to produce witty descriptions for an image. First, a model that retrieves sentences containing a pun that are relevant to the image from a large corpus of stories (Zhu et al., 2015). Second, a model that generates witty descriptions for an image using a modified inference procedure during image captioning which includes the specified pun word in the description.

Our paper makes the following contributions: To the best of our knowledge, this is the first work that tackles the challenging problem of producing a witty natural language remark in an everyday (boring) context. We present two novel models to produce witty (pun-based) captions for a novel (likely boring) image. Our models rely on linguistic wordplay. They use an unexpected pun in an image description during inference/retrieval. Thus, they do not require to be trained with witty captions. Humans vote the descriptions from the top-ranked *generated* captions 'wittier' than three baseline approaches. Moreover, in a Turing test-style evaluation, our model's best image description is found to be wittier than a witty human-written caption[2] 55% of the time when the human is subject to the same constraints as the machine regarding word usage and style.

2   Related Work

Humor theory. General Theory of Verbal Humor (Attardo and Raskin, 1991) characterizes linguistic stimuli that induce humor but implementing computational models of it requires severely restricting its assumptions (Binsted, 1996).

Puns. Zwicky and Zwicky (1986) classify puns as *perfect* (pronounced exactly the same) or *imperfect* (pronounced differently). Similarly, Pepicello and Green (1984) categorize riddles based on the linguistic ambiguity that they exploit – phonological, morphological or syntactic. Jaech et al. (2016) learn phone-edit distances to predict the counterpart, given a pun by drawing from automatic speech recognition techniques. In contrast, we augment a web-scraped list of puns using an existing model of pronunciation similarity.

Generating textual humor. JAPE (Binsted and Ritchie, 1997) also uses phonological ambiguity to generate pun-based riddles. While our task involves producing free-form responses to a novel

stimulus, JAPE produces stand-alone "canned" jokes. HAHAcronym (Stock and Strapparava, 2005) generates a funny expansion of a given acronym. Unlike our work, HAHAcronym operates on text, and is limited to producing sets of words. Petrovic and Matthews (2013) develop an unsupervised model that produces jokes of the form, *"I like my X like I like my Y, Z"* .

Generating multi-modal humor. Wang and Wen (2015) predict a meme's text based on a given funny image. Similarly, Shahaf et al. (2015) and Radev et al. (2015) learn to rank cartoon captions based on their funniness. Unlike typical, boring images in our task, memes and cartoons are images that are already funny or atypical. E.g., "LOL-cats" (funny cat photos), "Bieber-memes" (modified pictures of Justin Bieber), cartoons with talking animals, etc. Chandrasekaran et al. (2016) alter an abstract scene to make it more funny. In comparison, our task is to generate witty natural language remarks for a novel image.

Poetry generation. Although our tasks are different, our generation approach is conceptually similar to Ghazvininejad et al. (2016) who produce poetry, given a topic. While they also generate and score a set of candidates, their approach involves many more constraints and utilizes a finite state acceptor unlike our approach which enforces constraints during beam search of the RNN decoder.

3   Approach

Extracting tags. The first step in producing a contextually witty remark is to identify concepts that are relevant to the context (image). At times, these concepts are directly available as e.g., tags posted on social media. We consider the general case where such tags are unavailable, and automatically extract tags associated with an image.

We extract the top-5 object categories predicted by a state-of-the-art Inception-ResNet-v2 model (Szegedy et al., 2017) trained for image classification on ImageNet (Deng et al., 2009). We also consider the words from a (boring) image description (generated from Vinyals et al. (2016)). We combine the classifier object labels and words from the caption (ignoring stopwords) to produce a set of tags associated with an image, as shown in Fig. 2. We then identify concepts from this collection that can potentially induce wit.

Identifying puns. We attempt to induce an incongruity by using a pun in the image description. We identify candidate words for linguistic wordplay

---

cess of 'solving' (resolution) is trivial (the joke is obvious) or too complex (they do not 'get' the joke).

[2] This data is available on the author's webpage.

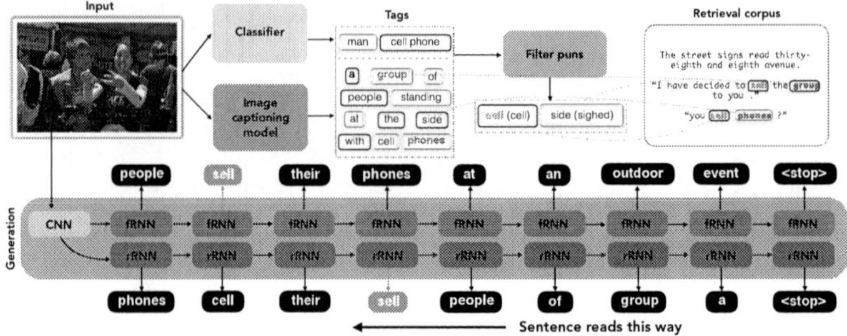

Figure 2: Our models for generating and retrieving image descriptions containing a pun (see Sec. 3).

by comparing image tags against a list of puns.

We construct the list of puns by mining the web for differently spelled words that sound exactly the same (heterographic homophones). We increase coverage by also considering pairs of words with 0 edit-distance, according to a metric based on fine-grained articulatory representations (AR) of word pronunciations (Jyothi and Livescu, 2014). Our list of puns has a total of 1067 unique words (931 from the web and 136 from the AR-based model).

The pun list yields a set of puns that are associated with a given image and their phonologically identical counterparts, which together form the *pun vocabulary* for the image. We evaluate our approach on the subset of images that have non-empty pun vocabularies (about 2 in 5 images).

Generating punny image captions. We introduce an incongruity by forcing a vanilla image captioning model (Vinyals et al., 2016) to decode a *phonological counterpart* of a pun word associated with the image, at a specific time-step during inference (e.g., 'sell' or 'sighed', showed in orange in Fig. 2). We achieve this by limiting the vocabulary of the decoder at that time-step to only contain counterparts of image-puns. In following time-steps, the decoder generates new words conditioned on all previously decoded words. Thus, the decoder attempts to generate sentences that flow well based on previously uttered words.

We train two models that decode an image description in forward (start to end) and reverse (end to start) directions, depicted as 'fRNN' and 'rRNN' in Fig. 2 respectively. The fRNN can decode words after accounting for the incongruity that occurs early in the sentence and the rRNN is able to decode the early words in the sentence after accounting for the incongruity that can occur later. The forward RNN and reverse RNN generate sentences in which the pun appears in each of

the first T and last T positions, respectively.[3]

Retrieving punny image captions. As an alternative to our approach of *generating* witty remarks for the given image, we also attempt to leverage natural, human-written sentences which are relevant (yet unexpected) in the given context. Concretely, we retrieve natural language sentences[4] from a combination of the Book Corpus (Zhu et al., 2015) and corpora from the NLTK toolkit (Loper and Bird, 2002). The retrieved sentences each (a) contains an incongruity (pun) whose counterpart is associated with the image, and (b) has support in the image (contains an image tag). This yields a pool of candidate captions that are perfectly grammatical, a little unexpected, and somewhat relevant to the image (see Sec. 4).

Ranking. We rank captions in the candidate pools from both generation and retrieval models, according to their log-probability score under the image captioning model. We observe that the higher-ranked descriptions are more relevant to the image and grammatically correct. We then perform non-maximal suppression, i.e., eliminate captions that are similar[5] to a higher-ranked caption to reduce the pool to a smaller, more diverse set. We report results on the 3 top-ranked captions. We describe the effect of design choices in the supplementary.

4   Results

Data. We evaluate witty captions from our approach via human studies. 100 random images (having associated puns) are sampled from the val-

---

[3]For an image, we choose $T = \{1, 2, ..., 5\}$ and beam size = 6 for each decoder. This generates a pool of 5 (T) $*$ 6 (beam size) $*$ 2 (forward + reverse decoder) = 60 candidates.

[4]To prevent the context of the sentence from distracting the perceiver, we consider sentences with < 15 words. Overall, we are left with a corpus of about 13.5 million sentences.

[5]Two sentences are similar if the cosine similarity between the average of the Word2Vec (Mikolov et al., 2013) representations of words in each sentence is ≥ 0.8.

idation set of COCO (Lin et al., 2014).

Baselines. We compare the wittiness of descriptions generated by our model against 3 qualitatively different baselines, and a human-written witty description of an image. Each of these evaluates a different component of our approach. **Regular inference** generates a fluent caption that is relevant to the image but is not attempting to be witty. **Witty mismatch** is a human-written witty caption, but for a different image from the one being evaluated. This baseline results in a caption that is intended to be witty, but does not attempt to be relevant to the image. **Ambiguous** is a 'punny' caption where a pun word in the boring (regular) caption is replaced by its counterpart. This caption is likely to contain content that is relevant to the image, *and* it contains a pun. However, the pun is not being used in a fluent manner.

We evaluate the **image-relevance** of the top witty caption by comparing against a boring machine caption and a random caption (see supplementary).

Evaluation annotations. Our task is to generate captions that a layperson might find witty. To evaluate performance on this task, we ask people on Amazon Mechanical Turk (AMT) to vote for the wittier among the given pair of captions for an image. We collect annotations from 9 unique workers for each relative choice and take the majority vote as ground-truth. For each image, we compare each of the generated 3 top-ranked and 1 low-ranked caption against 3 baseline captions and 1 human-written witty caption.[6]

Constrained human-written witty captions. We evaluate the ability of humans and automatic methods to use the given context *and pun words* to produce a caption that is perceived as witty. We ask subjects on AMT to describe a given image in a witty manner. To prevent observable *structural* differences between machine and human-written captions, we ensure consistent pun vocabulary (utilization of pre-specified puns for a given image). We also ask people to avoid first person accounts or quote characters in the image.

Metric. 3, we report performance of the generation approach using the Recall@K metric. For

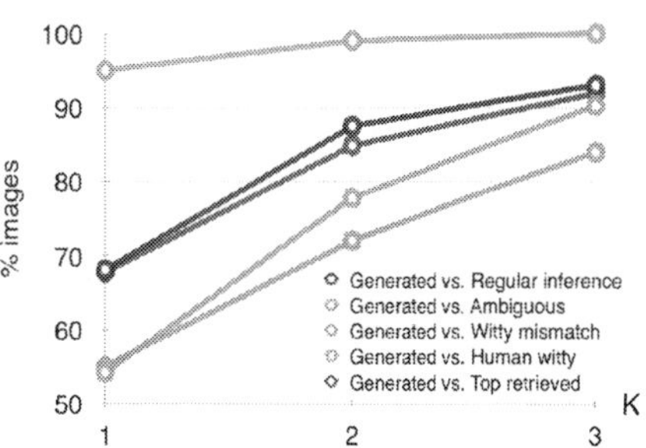

Figure 3: Wittiness of top-3 generated captions vs. other approaches. y-axis measures the % images for which at least one of K captions from our approach is rated wittier than other approaches. Recall steadily increases with the number of generated captions (K).

$K = 1, 2, 3$, we plot the percentage of images for which at least one of the K 'best' descriptions from our model outperformed another approach.

Generated captions vs. baselines. As we see in Fig. 3, the top generated image description (top-1G) is perceived as wittier compared to all baseline approaches more often than not (the vote is $>50\%$ at $K = 1$). We observe that as K increases, the recall steadily increases, i.e., when we consider the top K generated captions, increasingly often, humans find at least one of them to be wittier than captions produced by baseline approaches. People find the top-1G for a given image to be wittier than mismatched human-written image captions, about 95% of the time. The top-1G is also wittier than a naive approach that introduces ambiguity about 54.2% of the time. When compared to a typical, boring caption, the generated captions are wittier 68% of the time. Further, in a head-to-head comparison, the generated captions are wittier than the retrieved captions 67.7% of the time. We also validate our choice of ranking captions based on the image captioning model score. We observe that a 'bad' caption, i.e., one ranked lower by our model, is significantly less witty than the top 3 output captions.

Surprisingly, when the human is constrained to use the same words and style as the model, the generated descriptions from the model are found to be wittier for 55% of the images. Note that in a Turing test, a machine would equal human performance at 50%[7]. This led us to speculate if the con-

---

[6]This results in a total of 4 (captions) $*2$ (generation + retrieval) $*4$ (baselines + human caption) $= 32$ comparisons of our approach against baselines. We also compare the wittiness of the 4 generated captions against the 4 retrieved captions (see supplementary) for an image (16 comparisons). In total, we perform 48 comparisons per image, for 100 images.

[7]Recall that this compares how a witty description is constructed, given the image *and* specific pun words. A Turing test-style evaluation that compares the overall wittiness of a machine and a human would refrain from constraining the human in any way.

(a) **Generated**: a bored (board) bench sits in front of a window.
Retrieved: Wedge sits on the bench opposite Berry, bored (board).
Human: could you please make your pleas (please)!

(b) **Generated**: a loop (loupe) of flowers in a glass vase.
Retrieved: the flour (flower) inside teemed with worms.
Human: piece required for peace (piece).

(c) **Generated**: a woman sell (cell) her cell phone in a city.
Retrieved: Wright (right) slammed down the phone.
Human: a woman sighed (side) as she regretted the sell.

(d) **Generated**: a bear that is bare (bear) in the water.
Retrieved: water glistened off her bare (bear) breast.
Human: you won't hear a creak (creek) when the bear is feasting.

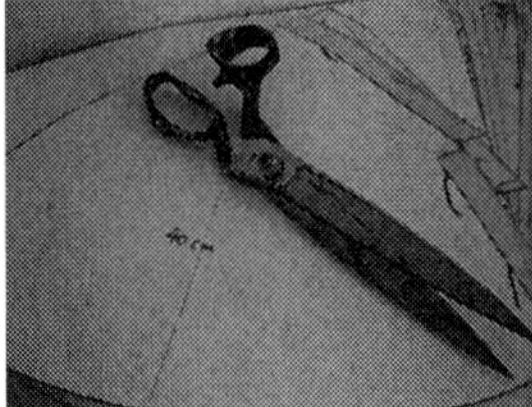   

(e) **Generated**: a loop (loupe) of scissors and a pair of scissors.
Retrieved: i continued slicing my pear (pair) on the cutting board.
Human: the scissors were near, but not clothes (close).

(f) **Generated**: a female tennis player caught (court) in mid swing.
Retrieved: i caught (court) thieves on the roof top.
Human: the man made a loud bawl (ball) when she threw the ball.

(g) **Generated**: a bored (board) living room with a large window.
Retrieved: anya sat on the couch, feeling bored (board).
Human: the sealing (ceiling) on the envelope resembled that in the ceiling.

(h) **Generated**: a parking meter with rode (road) in the background.
Retrieved: smoke speaker sighed (side).
Human: a nitting of color didn't make the poll (pole) less black.

Figure 4: The top row contains selected examples of human-written witty captions, and witty captions generated and retrieved from our models. The examples in the bottom row are randomly picked.

straints placed on language and style might be restricting people's ability to be witty. We confirmed this by evaluating free-form human captions.

Free-form Human-written Witty Captions. We ask people on AMT to describe an image (using any vocabulary) in a manner that would be perceived as funny. As expected, when compared against automatic captions from our approach, human evaluators find free-form human captions to be wittier about 90% of the time compared to 45% in the case of constrained human witty captions. Clearly, human-level creative language with unconstrained sentence length, style, choice of puns, etc., makes a significant difference in the wittiness of a description. In contrast, our automatic approach is constrained by caption-like language, length, and a word-based pun list. Training models to intelligently navigate this creative freedom is an exciting open challenge.

Qualitative analysis. The generated witty captions exhibit interesting features like alliteration ('a bare black bear ...') in Fig. 1b and 4c. At times, both the original pun (pole) and its counterpart (poll) make sense for the image (Fig. 1a). Occasionally, a pun is naively replaced by its counterpart (Fig. 4a) or rare puns are used (Fig. 4b). On the other hand, some descriptions (Fig. 4e and 4h) that are forced to utilize puns do not make sense. See supplementary for analysis of retrieval model.

5 Conclusion

We presented novel computational models inspired by cognitive accounts to address the challenging task of producing contextually witty descriptions for a given image. We evaluate the models via human-studies, in which they significantly outperform meaningful baseline approaches.

Acknowledgements

We thank Shubham Toshniwal for his advice regarding the automatic speech recognition model. This work was supported in part by: a NSF CAREER award, ONR YIP award, ONR Grant N00014-14-12713, PGA Family Foundation award, Google FRA, Amazon ARA, DARPA XAI grant to DP and NVIDIA GPU donations, Google FRA, IBM Faculty Award, and Bloomberg Data Science Research Grant to MB.

References

Salvatore Attardo and Victor Raskin. 1991. Script theory revis (it) ed: Joke similarity and joke representation model. *Humor-International Journal of Humor Research* 4(3-4):293–348.

Kim Binsted. 1996. Machine humour: An implemented model of puns. *PhD Thesis, University of Edinburgh* .

Kim Binsted and Graeme Ritchie. 1997. Computational rules for generating punning riddles. *Humor: International Journal of Humor Research* .

Arjun Chandrasekaran, Ashwin Kalyan, Stanislaw Antol, Mohit Bansal, Dhruv Batra, C. Lawrence Zitnick, and Devi Parikh. 2016. We are humor beings: Understanding and predicting visual humor. In *CVPR*.

Jia Deng, Wei Dong, Richard Socher, Li-Jia Li, Kai Li, and Li Fei-Fei. 2009. Imagenet: A large-scale hierarchical image database. In *Computer Vision and Pattern Recognition, 2009. CVPR 2009. IEEE Conference on*. IEEE, pages 248–255.

Marjan Ghazvininejad, Xing Shi, Yejin Choi, and Kevin Knight. 2016. Generating topical poetry. In *EMNLP*.

Aaron Jaech, Rik Koncel-Kedziorski, and Mari Ostendorf. 2016. Phonological pun-derstanding. In *HLT-NAACL*.

Preethi Jyothi and Karen Livescu. 2014. Revisiting word neighborhoods for speech recognition. *ACL 2014* page 1.

Tsung-Yi Lin, Michael Maire, Serge Belongie, James Hays, Pietro Perona, Deva Ramanan, Piotr Dollár, and C Lawrence Zitnick. 2014. Microsoft coco: Common objects in context. In *European Conference on Computer Vision*. Springer, pages 740–755.

Edward Loper and Steven Bird. 2002. Nltk: The natural language toolkit. In *Proceedings of the ACL-02 Workshop on Effective Tools and Methodologies for Teaching Natural Language Processing and Computational Linguistics - Volume 1*. Association for Computational Linguistics, ETMTNLP '02.

Tomas Mikolov, Ilya Sutskever, Kai Chen, Greg S Corrado, and Jeff Dean. 2013. Distributed representations of words and phrases and their compositionality. In *Advances in neural information processing systems*.

William J Pepicello and Thomas A Green. 1984. *Language of riddles: new perspectives*. The Ohio State University Press.

Sasa Petrovic and David Matthews. 2013. Unsupervised joke generation from big data. In *ACL*.

Dragomir Radev, Amanda Stent, Joel Tetreault, Aasish Pappu, Aikaterini Iliakopoulou, Agustin Chanfreau, Paloma de Juan, Jordi Vallmitjana, Alejandro Jaimes, Rahul Jha, et al. 2015. Humor in collective discourse: Unsupervised funniness detection in the new yorker cartoon caption contest. *arXiv preprint arXiv:1506.08126* .

Dafna Shahaf, Eric Horvitz, and Robert Mankoff. 2015. Inside jokes: Identifying humorous cartoon captions. In *Proceedings of the 21th ACM SIGKDD International Conference on Knowledge Discovery and Data Mining*. ACM, pages 1065–1074.

Oliviero Stock and Carlo Strapparava. 2005. HAHAcronym: A computational humor system. In *ACL*.

Jerry M Suls. 1972. A two-stage model for the appreciation of jokes and cartoons: An information-processing analysis. *The Psychology of Humor: Theoretical Perspectives and Empirical Issues* .

Christian Szegedy, Sergey Ioffe, Vincent Vanhoucke, and Alexander A Alemi. 2017. Inception-v4, inception-resnet and the impact of residual connections on learning. In *AAAI*. pages 4278–4284.

Oriol Vinyals, Alexander Toshev, Samy Bengio, and Dumitru Erhan. 2016. Show and tell: Lessons learned from the 2015 mscoco image captioning challenge. *IEEE transactions on pattern analysis and machine intelligence* .

William Yang Wang and Miaomiao Wen. 2015. I can has cheezburger? a nonparanormal approach to combining textual and visual information for predicting and generating popular meme descriptions. In *NAACL*.

Zhou Yu, Leah Nicolich-Henkin, Alan W Black, and Alex I Rudnicky. 2016. A wizard-of-oz study on a non-task-oriented dialog systems that reacts to user engagement. In *17th Annual Meeting of the Special Interest Group on Discourse and Dialogue*. page 55.

Yukun Zhu, Ryan Kiros, Rich Zemel, Ruslan Salakhutdinov, Raquel Urtasun, Antonio Torralba, and Sanja Fidler. 2015. Aligning books and movies: Towards story-like visual explanations by watching movies and reading books. In *Proceedings of the IEEE International Conference on Computer Vision*. pages 19–27.

Arnold Zwicky and Elizabeth Zwicky. 1986. Imperfect puns, markedness, and phonological similarity: With fronds like these, who needs anemones. *Folia Linguistica* 20(3-4):493–503.

The Emergence of Semantics in Neural Network Representations of Visual Information

Dhanush Dharmaretnam
University of Victoria
Department of Computer Science,
3800 Finnerty Rd, Victoria, Canada
dhanushd@uvic.ca

Alona Fyshe
University of Victoria
Department of Computer Science,
3800 Finnerty Rd, Victoria, Canada
afyshe@uvic.ca

Abstract

Word vector models learn about semantics through corpora. Convolutional Neural Networks (CNNs) can learn about semantics through images. At the most abstract level, some of the information in these models must be shared, as they model the same real-world phenomena. Here we employ techniques previously used to detect semantic representations in the human brain to detect semantic representations in CNNs. We show the accumulation of semantic information in the layers of the CNN, and discover that, for misclassified images, the correct class can be recovered in intermediate layers of a CNN.

1 Introduction

As we study semantics through the lens of a corpus, it can be easy to forget that concepts exist independently of language. Animals with no language system still form representations of concepts, based on their interactions with the world (e.g. vision, touch, taste). In this paper, we bridge the gap between the study of semantics in computer vision and computational linguistics. We take inspiration from previous work on brain-based representations of meaning, and measure the semantic information through the layers of a Convolutional Neural Network (CNN) trained to detect objects in images.

Our work is not the first to draw connections between computer vision and distributional semantics. Indeed, joint models of semantics based on images and text have been developed, and word vectors have been grounded in the visual space (Silberer and Lapata, 2012, 2014; Bruni and Baroni, 2013). However, we believe that our work is the first to explore the convergence of semantic embeddings built from text and images, specifically studying the hidden representations of

CNNs, and how the accumulation of semantic evidence builds as a function of network depth.

2 Methods

The representations created by CNNs have differing numbers of dimensions, and even within a CNN, the size of layers may differ (see Section 2.2 for more details on CNNs). In addition, the size of word vectors also varies. We need a method to detect similarities across embedding spaces, regardless of their dimensionality.

A solution, *similarity-encoding*, was proposed in parallel by two recent papers (Anderson et al., 2016; Xu et al., 2016), which calculates the similarity of embedding spaces using the *correlation* of elements within a space, rather than directly comparing the embeddings between spaces.

Similarity-encoding compares the correlation matrices of embedding spaces. For example, if the word vectors have dimension p, our matrix of word vectors will be $\mathbb{R}^{k \times p}$ (where k is the number of concepts). The resulting correlation matrix will be $W \in \mathbb{R}^{k \times k}$, and will represent the pairwise correlation of all concepts in word space. Similarly, for a given layer of a CNN with dimension q, we can create a matrix of embeddings for the same k concepts ($\mathbb{R}^{k \times q}$), and compute a correlation matrix in image space: $I \in \mathbb{R}^{k \times k}$. Thus, we have taken embedding spaces for the same set of k concepts and created new spaces of dimension k based on the correlation between concepts. Because the correlation spaces share the same dimension, we can directly compare the correlation matrices of word vectors (W) with the correlation matrices of image embeddings (I).

To compare the correlation spaces, we could simply calculate the correlation between matrices W and I, which would be a Representational Similarity Analysis (RSA), as proposed by Kriegeskorte et al. (2008). RSA has the advantage of being a

776

Proceedings of NAACL-HLT 2018, pages 776–780
New Orleans, Louisiana, June 1 - 6, 2018. ©2018 Association for Computational Linguistics

fairly simple and straightforward method for comparing the representations across two embedding spaces. However, RSA has the disadvantage that it produces one aggregate number for a pair of correlation matrices, and does not show which concepts contributed most to a high or low score. We will need this added flexibility to explore misclassified images in Section 3.3.

Both Anderson et al. (2016) and Xu et al. (2016) extend RSA with an additional analysis step, inspired by some of the first work searching for semantics in the brain (Mitchell et al., 2008). Anderson et al. (2016) present a pictorial overview of the procedure in Figure 2 of their paper.

In similarity-encoding, we choose two elements from the concept list (c_1 and c_2), and calculate the correlation of their embeddings to every other $k-2$ concept in each embedding space (word or image). This creates a vector for each of the two held out concepts with length $k - 2$, and is equivalent to selecting the corresponding rows of the full correlation matrices W and I, but omitting the columns which correspond to c_1 and c_2. We then compare the correlation patterns of c_1 and c_2 in word space (vectors w_{c_1} and w_{c_2}) to the correlations in image space (vectors i_{c_1} and i_{c_2}) by checking if:

$$\text{corr}(w_{c_1}, i_{c_1}) + \text{corr}(w_{c_2}, i_{c_2}) \quad (1)$$

(the correlation of correctly matched concepts: c_1 to c_1 and c_2 to c_2) is greater than:

$$\text{corr}(w_{c_1}, i_{c_2}) + \text{corr}(w_{c_2}, i_{c_1}) \quad (2)$$

(the correlation of incorrectly matched concepts). Xu et al. (2016) call this the **2 vs. 2 test**. If the correctly matched vectors are more correlated than the incorrectly matched vectors, then the test is considered to have passed. We perform the 2 vs. 2 test for all possible pairs of concepts, 13,695 tests in total. The **2 vs. 2 accuracy** is the percentage of 2 vs. 2 tests passed, and chance 2 vs. 2 accuracy is 50%. We compute significance for the 2 vs. 2 test by performing a permutation test: permuting the rows of embeddings in one space, and re-running the full similarity-encoding methodology.

2.1 Word Vectors

We chose four word vector models from recent work. **SkipGram** vectors are from a neural network trained to predict co-occurring words. We used the 300 dimensional model trained on Google news (English) (Mikolov et al., 2013). **RNN** is a recurrent neural network trained to predict the next word in a sequence. It has 640 dimensions, and was trained on transcriptions of English broadcast news(Mikolov et al., 2011). **Glove** is a regression-based model that incorporates both local and global co-occurrence information. This 300-dimensional model was trained on the English Wikipedia and Gigaword 5 corpora combined (Pennington et al., 2014). **Cross-lingual** word vectors project embeddings from multiple languages into a shared space. We used the German-English model (512 dimensions), trained on WMT-2011 (Faruqui and Dyer, 2014).

2.2 Convolutional Neural Networks

Convolutional Neural Networks (CNNs) can be trained to perform image classification (Goodfellow et al., 2016). In general, the input is three continuous valued matrices, representing the RGB values of an image. The network convolves the input with a set of learned filters (typically 2D). The output of the convolution is fed to another layer of the network, which performs additional operations (e.g. more convolutions, pooling). Each layer of the network produces a hidden representation that is used by subsequent layers, ending in a final classification layer.

There has been a proliferation of neural network architectures for image classification; we explore three CNNs: VGG 16, ResNet 50 and Inception V3. We chose these networks based on availability (pre-trained models are readily downloadable), for their performance on image classification tasks, and for their diversity in structural complexity. All CNNs used here were trained on ImageNet (Deng et al., 2009).

VGG 16 is one of the two deepest networks described in Simonyan and Zisserman (2014). It has a very simple linear architecture. We measured the 2 vs. 2 accuracy against all convolutional and dense layers of the network. **Inception V3** (Szegedy et al., 2015), has a more complicated architecture, including Inception blocks which act as multi-resolution feature extractors, applying differently sized filters in parallel. We measured the 2 vs. 2 accuracy at the concat (mixed) layers, which appear at the end of inception blocks. **ResNet 50** (He et al., 2015) uses residual modules, which use linear shortcut connections to allow earlier representations to filter up as required. Residual modules allow the networks to become very deep without the typical problems in training associated with deep networks. We measured the 2 vs. 2 accuracy at the activation layers both within and at the end of residual blocks.

Illustrations of the architectures for each of these networks appear in the supplementary material (Figures 1-3), annotated to show the layers we used for our experiments. We used the Keras implementation of all networks (Chollet et al., 2015).

2.3 Concept Selection

Each of the CNNs described in Section 2.2 was trained on ImageNet, a collection of over a million images, each annotated for the presence of one of 1000 concepts. These concepts can be fairly high-level single words (e.g. stove, sandwich) or extremely specific multi-word concepts (e.g. German short-haired pointer, tobacco shop). We selected all concepts for which a match was found in all four of the word vector models from Section 2.1, resulting in 166 concepts. From this set of 166 concepts, we randomly chose 5 images annotated with the given concept in the ImageNet validation set, for a total of 830 images.

We then computed each network's activation on each of the 830 images. These images are divided into 5 groups, such that each of the 166 concepts occurs exactly once per group. We ran the 2 vs. 2 test separately for each of the 5 groups, and report the average across the 5 runs to account for variability across images.

3 Results

3.1 Word Vector Comparison

Figure 1 shows the performance of several word vector models against the layers of VGG 16. The first point represents the performance using correlation at the pixel level only, and no CNN-derived representation. The performance of SkipGram, Glove and the Cross-lingual vectors are very similar, and are within a percentage or two across all layers. The RNN model we tested did not perform as well, on average about 5% lower in the first convolutional layers, and 10% lower in the highest hidden layers. These results are similar to those seen in Xu et al. (2016) when comparing word vectors to brain activity. Because the performance is very similar for the three top performing word vectors, our analyses proceeds with SkipGram vectors only.

Note that the 2 vs. 2 accuracy improves as we move up the layers of the CNN. This is evidence that, though trained on very different data sources,

the semantic representations in CNNs and word vectors are quite similar, and the similarities grow stronger as the CNN gets closer to its final classification layer. Though the starting points are different (text vs. images) the final result of the CNN is similar to word vectors built from corpora, implying that a shared embedding space can emerge from each data source independently.

The very early layers of CNNs have been shown to represent low level features like edges, curves and other simple shapes (Mahendran and Vedaldi, 2016), so we did not expect early layers to have any significant relation to word vectors. We were surprised to find that even the very first layer of the VGG 16 gives above chance 2 vs. 2 accuracy using SkipGram vectors ($p < 0.001$). Upon inspection, we found that the correlation for matched vectors (the value for Eq. 1) was just slightly larger than the correlation for mismatched vectors (the value of Eq. 2), implying that the network has only weak evidence for semantic relationships at the early layers of the CNN. Figure 4 in the supplementary material shows this effect in greater detail. Note that the first layer of VGG 16 improves upon the pixel level accuracy, implying that even simple CNN features provide useful signal.

We also noted that some macroscopic distinctions between the concepts can likely be inferred from the low level features of images alone. For example, man made objects tend to have more straight lines and natural objects are more curved. Thus, it is logical that the early layers of a CNN could distinguish between some pairs of objects using only the most basic of visual features.

3.2 CNN Comparison

Figures 1-3 show 2 vs. 2 accuracy for SkipGram vectors against the layers of VGG 16, ResNet 50 and Inception V3 networks. In general, the pattern is similar: as the depth of the layers increases, so too does the 2 vs. 2 accuracy. However, there are a few interesting exceptions to this pattern. In ResNet 50 we see a drop in accuracy in several places, most notably between activation layers 16 and 17. Upon inspection of the architecture diagram, we noted that several of the early residual blocks were not improving 2 vs. 2 accuracy, and relied mostly on residual connections (see Supp. Figure 3), implying some of the depth in ResNet 50 may be unnecessary.

We see maximum 2 vs. 2 accuracy in later layers of CNNs, but not always at the last layer. Incep-

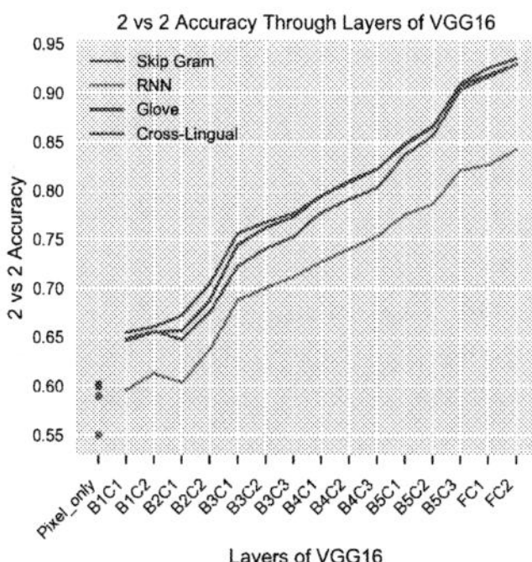

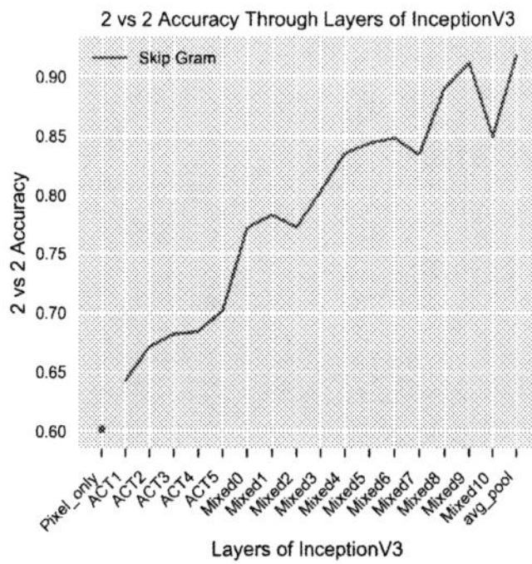

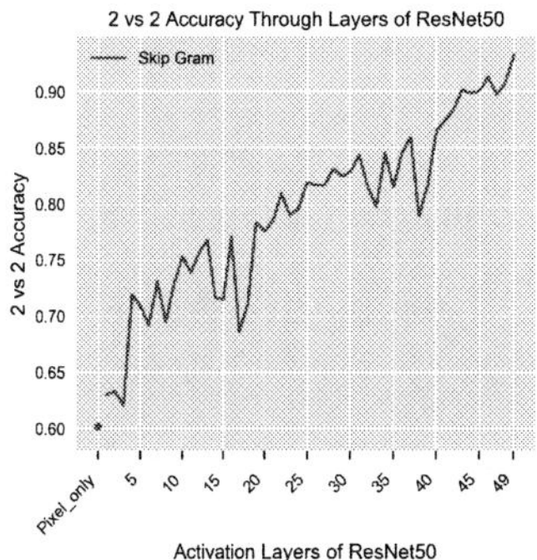

Figure 1: 2 vs. 2 accuracy for 4 word vector models and layers of VGG 16. BnCm: mth conv. layer of the nth block.

Figure 2: 2 vs. 2 accuracy for SkipGram and layers of Inception V3.

Figure 3: 2 vs. 2 accuracy for SkipGram and layers of ResNet 50.

tion V3 shows maximum accuracy of 0.90 at layer Mixed9, several layers before the final classification layer. ResNet 50 has maximum accuracy of 0.93 at the last layer, and VGG 16 peaks at the final layer with 0.94 accuracy. This implies that there may be a way to improve Inception V3 using, for example, a skip connection from the highest scoring layer to the final classification layer.

3.3 Misclassifications

We wondered if mistakes made in the ImageNet classification task could be detected, or even compensated for, using word vectors. Within one set of 166 images, we selected those images misclassified by VGG 16 such that they were misclassified into classes with a matching word vector (36 images). Could word vectors determine where in the network these misclassifications emerge? For this, we developed a variant of the 2 vs. 2 test: the **1 vs. 2 test**. For every misclassified image, there is a true and a predicted concept class (c_{true} and $c_{predicted}$, guaranteed to be different, since the image was misclassified). We selected the word vectors corresponding to c_{true} and $c_{predicted}$ and compute their correlation to all word vectors for which there was a corresponding correctly classified image. This creates vectors w_{true} and $w_{predicted}$ which represent correlations in word space. We also compute the correlations of the hidden representations for the misclassified image to the hidden representations of the correctly classified images to create a vector $i_{misclassified}$. The 1 vs. 2 test is considered to have passed if $i_{misclassified}$ is more correlated to w_{true} than to $w_{predicted}$. The 1 vs. 2 accuracy is the fraction of 1 vs. 2 tests passed, and chance is again 50%. The 1 vs. 2 test allows us to test if the classification mistake made at the final layer of the CNN is present through all of the hidden layers of the CNN.

Figure 4 shows the results for this experiment using layers from VGG 16. We see that in B4C1 and B5C1, the correlation of the hidden representations are, on average, significantly closer to the correlations of the correct rather than the predicted word vector ($p = 0.048$). But, during the last fully connected layer, this difference disappears, leading to the misclassification of the image. This implies that, for at least some of the misclassified images, the information required to make the correct prediction exists in the hidden representations, but the classification layer is not using it for the final prediction.

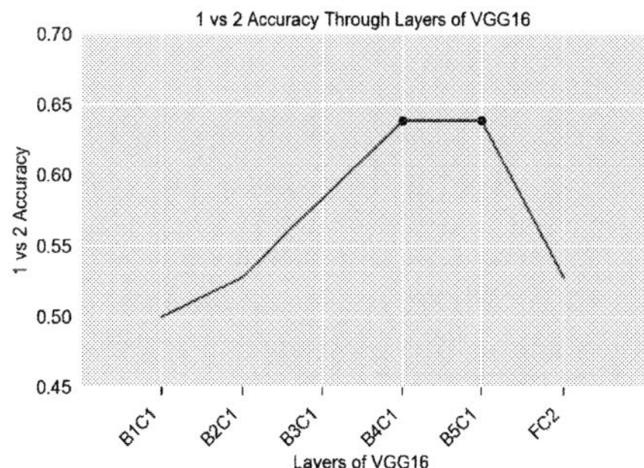

Figure 4: Results for the 1 vs. 2 test. For some layers of VGG 16, the correct class of misclassified images can be recovered (black dots).

4   Conclusion and Future Work

In this paper, we used methodology originally developed to analyze brain images to study semantic representations in CNNs. Our results point to several interesting possibilities for future work. The techniques explored here could be use to combat adversarial attacks on CNNs, detect misclassifications, or possibly guide the improvement of CNN architectures, and eventually help to unite the study of semantics in computer vision and computational linguistics.

5 Acknowledgments

This research was supported by CIFAR (Canadian Institute for Advanced Research) and NSERC (Natural Sciences and Engineering Research Council). This research was enabled in part by support provided by WestGrid (`https://www.westgrid.ca/`) and Compute Canada (`www.computecanada.ca`).

References

Andrew James Anderson, Benjamin D. Zinszer, and Rajeev D.S. Raizada. 2016. Representational similarity encoding for fMRI: Pattern-based synthesis to predict brain activity using stimulus-model-similarities. *NeuroImage* 128:44–53.

Elia Bruni and Marco Baroni. 2013. Multimodal Distributional Semantics. *Journal of Artificial Intelligence Research* 48.

François Chollet et al. 2015. Keras. `https://github.com/fchollet/keras`.

Jia Deng, Wei Dong, R. Socher, Li-Jia Li, Kai Li, and Li Fei-Fei. 2009. ImageNet: A large-scale hierarchical image database. *2009 IEEE Conference on Computer Vision and Pattern Recognition* pages 2–9.

Manaal Faruqui and Chris Dyer. 2014. Improving vector space word representations using multilingual correlation. *Proceedings of the European Association for Computational Linguistics* pages 462–471.

Ian Goodfellow, Yoshua Bengio, and Aaron Courville. 2016. *Deep Learning*. MIT Press. `http://www.deeplearningbook.org`.

Kaiming He, Xiangyu Zhang, Shaoquing Ren, and Jian Sun. 2015. Deep Residual Learning for Image Recognition. *arXiv preprint arXiv:1512.03385* pages 1–17.

Nikolaus Kriegeskorte, Marieke Mur, and Peter Bandettini. 2008. Representational similarity analysis - connecting the branches of systems neuroscience. *Frontiers in systems neuroscience* 2(November):4.

Aravindh Mahendran and Andrea Vedaldi. 2016. Visualizing Deep Convolutional Neural Networks Using Natural Pre-images. *International Journal of Computer Vision* 120(3):233–255.

Tomas Mikolov, Greg Corrado, Kai Chen, and Jeffrey Dean. 2013. Efficient Estimation of Word Representations in Vector Space. *Proceedings of the International Conference on Learning Representations (ICLR 2013)* pages 1–12.

Tomáš Mikolov, Stefan Kombrink, Anoop Deoras, Lukáš Burget, and Jan Černocký. 2011. RNNLM — Recurrent Neural Network Language Modeling Toolkit. In *Proceedings of Automatic Speech Recognition and Understanding (ASRU)*. pages 1–4.

Tom M Mitchell, Svetlana V Shinkareva, Andrew Carlson, Kai-Min Chang, Vicente L Malave, Robert A Mason, and Marcel Adam Just. 2008. Predicting human brain activity associated with the meanings of nouns. *Science (New York, N.Y.)* 320(5880):1191–5.

Jeffrey Pennington, Richard Socher, and Christopher D Manning. 2014. GloVe : Global Vectors for Word Representation. In *Conference on Empirical Methods in Natural Language Processing*. Doha, Qatar.

Carina Silberer and Mirella Lapata. 2012. Grounded models of semantic representation. In *Proceedings of the 2012 Joint Conference on Empirical Methods in Natural Language Processing and Computational Natural Language Learning*. pages 1423–1433.

Carina Silberer and Mirella Lapata. 2014. Learning Grounded Meaning Representations with Autoencoders. *Proceedings of the 52nd Annual Meeting of the Association for Computational Linguistics (Volume 1: Long Papers)* pages 721–732.

Karen Simonyan and Andrew Zisserman. 2014. Very Deep Convolutional Networks for Large-Scale Image Recognition. *arXiv preprint* pages 1–14.

Christian Szegedy, Vincent Vanhoucke, Sergey Ioffe, Jonathon Shlens, and Zbigniew Wojna. 2015. Rethinking the Inception Architecture for Computer Vision. *arXiv preprint* .

Haoyan Xu, Brian Murphy, and Alona Fyshe. 2016. BrainBench : A Brain-Image Test Suite for Distributional Semantic Models. *Proceedings of the 2016 Conference on Empirical Methods in Natural Language Processing (EMNLP-16)* pages 2017–2021.

Visual Referring Expression Recognition:
What Do Systems Actually Learn?

Volkan Cirik, Louis-Philippe Morency, Taylor Berg-Kirkpatrick
Carnegie Mellon University
{vcirik,morency,tberg}@cs.cmu.edu

Abstract

We present an empirical analysis of state-of-the-art systems for referring expression recognition – the task of identifying the object in an image referred to by a natural language expression – with the goal of gaining insight into how these systems reason about language and vision. Surprisingly, we find strong evidence that even sophisticated and linguistically-motivated models for this task may ignore linguistic structure, instead relying on shallow correlations introduced by unintended biases in the data selection and annotation process. For example, we show that a system trained and tested on the input image *without the input referring expression* can achieve a precision of 71.2% in top-2 predictions. Furthermore, a system that predicts only the *object category* given the input can achieve a precision of 84.2% in top-2 predictions. These surprisingly positive results for what should be deficient prediction scenarios suggest that careful analysis of what our models are learning – and further, how our data is constructed – is critical as we seek to make substantive progress on grounded language tasks.

1 Introduction

There has been increasing interest in modeling natural language in the context of a visual grounding. Several benchmark datasets have recently been introduced for describing a visual scene with natural language (Chen et al., 2015), describing or localizing specific objects in a scene (Kazemzadeh et al., 2014; Mao et al., 2016), answering natural language questions about the scenes (Antol et al., 2015), and performing visually grounded dialogue (Das et al., 2016). Here, we focus on referring expression recognition (RER) – the task of identifying the object in an image that is referred to by a natural language expression produced by a human (Kazemzadeh et al., 2014; Mao et al., 2016; Hu et al., 2016; Rohrbach et al., 2016; Yu et al., 2016; Nagaraja et al., 2016; Hu et al., 2017).

Recent work on RER has sought to make progress by introducing models that are better capable of reasoning about linguistic structure (Hu et al., 2017; Nagaraja et al., 2016) – however, since most of the state-of-the-arts systems involve complex neural parameterizations, what these models actually learn has been difficult to interpret. This is concerning because several post-hoc analyses of related tasks (Zhou et al., 2015; Devlin et al., 2015; Agrawal et al., 2016; Jabri et al., 2016; Goyal et al., 2016) have revealed that some positive results are actually driven by superficial biases in datasets or shallow correlations without deeper visual or linguistic understanding. Evidently, it is hard to be completely sure if a model is performing well for the right reasons.

To increase our understanding of how RER systems function, we present several analyses inspired by approaches that probe systems with perturbed inputs (Jia and Liang, 2017) and employ simple models to exploit and reveal biases in datasets (Chen et al., 2016a). First, we investigate whether systems that were designed to incorporate linguistic structure actually require it and make use of it. To test this, we perform perturbation experiments on the input referring expressions. Surprisingly, we find that models are robust to shuffling the word order and limiting the word categories to nouns and adjectives. Second, we attempt to reveal shallower correlations that systems might instead be leveraging to do well on this task. We build two simple systems called Neural Sieves: one that completely *ignores* the input referring expression and another that only predicts the category of the referred object from the input expression. Again, surprisingly, both sieves are able to identify the correct object with surprising precision in top-2 and top-3 predictions. When these two simple systems are com-

Proceedings of NAACL-HLT 2018, pages 781–787
New Orleans, Louisiana, June 1 - 6, 2018. ©2018 Association for Computational Linguistics

bined, the resulting system achieves precisions of 84.2% and 95.3% for top-2 and top-3 predictions, respectively. These results suggest that to make meaningful progress on grounded language tasks, we need to pay careful attention to what and how our models are learning, and whether our datasets contain exploitable bias.

2 Related Work

Referring expression recognition and generation is a well studied problem in intelligent user interfaces (Chai et al., 2004), human-robot interaction (Fang et al., 2012; Chai et al., 2014; Williams et al., 2016), and situated dialogue (Kennington and Schlangen, 2017). Kazemzadeh et al. (2014) and Mao et al. (2016) introduce two benchmark datasets for referring expression recognition. Several models that leverage linguistic structure have been proposed. Nagaraja et al. (2016) propose a model where target and supporting objects (i.e. objects that are mentioned in order to disambiguate the target object) are identified and scored jointly. The resulting model is able to localize supporting objects without direct supervision. Hu et al. (2017) introduce a compositional approach for the RER task. They assume that the referring expression can be decomposed into a triplet consisting of the target object, the supporting object, and their spatial relationship. This structured model achieves state-of-the-art accuracy on the Google-Ref dataset. Cirik et al. (2018) propose a type of neural modular network (Andreas et al., 2016) where the computation graph is defined in terms of a constituency parse of the input referring expression.

Previous studies on other tasks have found that state-of-the-art systems may be successful for reasons different than originally assumed. For example, Chen et al. (2016b) show that a simple logistic regression baseline with carefully defined features can achieve competitive results for reading comprehension on CNN/Daily Mail datasets (Hermann et al., 2015), indicating that more sophisticated models may be learning realtively simple correlations. Similarly, Gururangan et al. (2018) reveal bias in a dataset for semantic inference by demonstrating a simple model that achieves competitive results *without looking at the premise*.

3 Analysis by Perturbation

In this section, we would like to analyze how the state-of-the-art referring expression recognition systems utilize linguistic structure. We conduct experiments with perturbed referring expressions where various aspects of linguistic structure are obscured. We perform three types of analyses: the first one studying syntactic structure (Section 3.2), the second focusing on the importance of word categories (Section 3.3), and the final one analyzing potential biases in the dataset (Section 3.4).

3.1 Analysis Methodology

To perform our analysis, we take two state-of-the-art systems CNN+LSTM-MIL (Nagaraja et al., 2016) and CMN (Hu et al., 2017) and train them from scratch with perturbed referring expressions. We note that the perturbation experiments explained in next subsections are performed on all train and test instances. All experiments are done on the standard train/test splits for the Google-Ref dataset (Mao et al., 2016). Systems are evaluated using the precision@k metric, the fraction of test instances for which the target object is contained in the model's top-k predictions. We provide further details of our experimental methodology in Section 4.1.

3.2 Syntactic Analysis by Permuting Word Order

In English, word order is important for correctly understanding the syntactic structure of a sentence. Both models we analyze use Recurrent Neural Networks (RNN) (Elman, 1990) with Long Short-Term Memory (LSTM) cells (Hochreiter and Schmidhuber, 1997). Previous studies have shown that reccurrent architectures can perform well on tasks where word order and syntax are important: for example, tagging (Lample et al., 2016), parsing (Sutskever et al., 2014), and machine translation (Bahdanau et al., 2014). We seek to determine whether recurrent models for RER depend on syntactic structure.

Premise 1: *Randomly permuting the word order of an English referring expression will obscure its syntactic structure.*

We train CMN and CNN+LSTM-MIL with shuffled referring expressions as input and evaluate their performance.

Model	No Perturbation	Shuffled	Δ
CMN	.705	.675	-.030
LSTM+CNN-MIL	.684	.630	-.054

Table 1: Results for Shuffling Word Order for Referring Expressions. Δ is the difference between no perturbation and shuffled version of the same system.

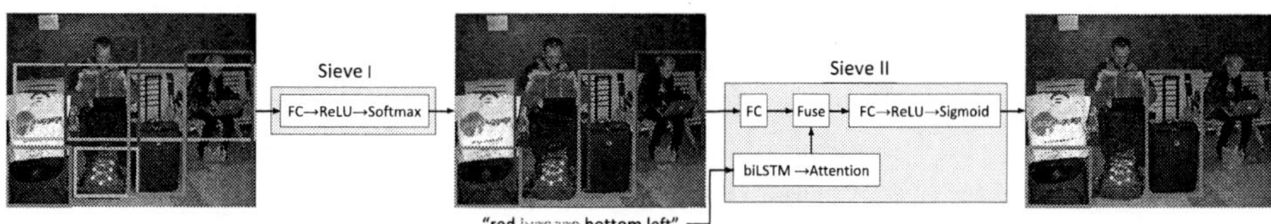

Figure 1: Overview of Neural Sieves. Sieve I filters object types having multiple instances. Sieve II filters objects of one category mentioned in referring expression. Objects of the same category have the same color frames. Best seen in color.

Table 1 shows accuracies for models with and without shuffled referring expressions. The column with Δ shows the difference in accuracy compared to the best performing model without shuffling. The drop in accuracy is surprisingly low. Thus, we conclude that these models do not stongly depend on the syntactic structure of the input expression and may instead leverage other, shallower, correlations.

3.3 Lexical Analysis by Discarding Words

Following the analysis presented in Section 3.2, we are curious to study what other aspects of the input referring expression may be essential for state-of-the-art performance. If syntactic structure is largely unimportant, it may be that spatial relationships can be ignored. Spatial relationships between objects are usually represented by prepositional phrases and verb phrases. In contrast, simple descriptors (e.g. green) and object types (e.g. table) are most often represented by adjectives and nouns, respectively. By discarding all words in the input that are not nouns or adjectives, we hope to test whether spatial relationships are actually important to state-of-the-art models. Notably, both systems we test were specifically designed to model object relationships.

Premise 2: *Keeping only nouns and adjectives from the input expression will obscure the relationships between objects that the referring expression describes.*

Table 2 shows accuracies resulting from training and testing these models on only the nouns and adjectives in the input expression. Our first observation is that the accuracies of models drop the most when we discard the nouns (the rightmost column in Table 2). This is reasonable since nouns

Models	Noun & Adj (Δ)	Noun (Δ)	Adj (Δ)
CMN	.687 (-.018)	.642 (-.063)	.585 (-.120)
LSTM+CNN-MIL	.644 (-.040)	.597 (-.087)	.533 (-.151)

Table 2: Results with discarded word categories. Numbers in parentheses are Δ, the difference between the best performing version of the original model.

define the types of the objects referred to in the expression. Without nouns, it is extremely difficult to identify which objects are being described. Second, although both systems we analyze model the relationship between objects, discarding verbs and prepositions, which are essential in determining the relationship among objects, does not drastically effect their performance (the second column in Table 2). This may indicate the superior performance of these systems does not specifically come from their modeling approach for object relationships.

3.4 Bias Analysis by Discarding Referring Expressions

Goyal et al. (2016) show that some language and vision datasets have exploitable biases. Could there be a dataset bias that is exploited by the models for RER?

Premise 3: *Discarding the referring expression entirely and keeping only the input image creates a deficient prediction problem: achieving high-peformance on this task indicates dataset bias.*

We train CMN by removing all referring expressions from train and test. We call this model "image-only" since it ignores the referring expression and will only use the input image. We compare the CMN "image-only" model with the state-of-the-art configuration of CMN and a *random baseline*. Table 3 shows precision@k results. The "image-

Model	P@1	P@2	P@3	P@4	P@5
CMN	.705	.926	.979	.993	.998
CMN "image-only"	.411	.731	.885	.948	.977
Random Baseline	.204	.403	.557	.669	.750

Table 3: Results with discarded referring expressions. Surprisingly, the top-2 prediction (73.1%) of the "image-only" model is better than the top prediction of the state-of-the-art (70.5%).

only" model is able to surpass the random baseline by a large margin. This result indicates that the dataset is biased, likely as a result of the data selection and annotation process. During the construction of the dataset, Mao et al. (2016) annotate an object box only if there are at least 2 to 4 objects of the same type in the image. Thus, only a subset of object categories ever appear as targets because some object types rarely occur multiple times in an image. In fact, out of 90 object categories in MSCOCO, 43 of the object categories are selected as target objects less than 1% of the time they occur in images. This potentially explains the relative high performance of the "image-only" system.

3.5 Discussion

The previous analyses indicate that exploiting bias in the data selection process and leveraging shallow linguistic correlations with the input expression may go a long way towards achieving high performance on this dataset. First, it may be possible to simplify the decision of picking an object to a much smaller set of candidates without even considering the referring expression. Second, because removing all words except for nouns and adjectives only marginally hurt performance for the systems tested, it may be possible to further reduce the set of candidates by focusing only on simple properties like the category of the target object rather than its relations with the environment or with adjacent objects.

4 Neural Sieves

We introduce a simple pipeline of neural networks, Neural Sieves, that attempt to reduce the set of candidate objects down to a much smaller set that still contains the target object given an image, a set of objects, and the referring expression describing one of the objects.

Sieve I: Filtering Unlikely Objects. Inspired by the results from Section 3.4, we design an "image-only" model as the first sieve for filtering *unlikely* objects. For example in Figure 1, Sieve I filters out the backpack and the bench from the list of bounding boxes since there is only one instance of these object types. We use a similar parameterization of one of the baselines (CMN$_{LOC}$) proposed by Hu et al. (2017) for Sieve I and train it by only providing spatial and visual features for the boxes, ignoring the referring expression. More specifically, for visual features r^{vis} of a bounding boxes of an object, we use Faster-RCNN (Ren et al., 2015). We use 5-dimensional vectors for spatial features $r^{spat} = [\frac{x_{min}}{W_V}, \frac{y_{min}}{H_V}, \frac{x_{max}}{W_V}, \frac{y_{max}}{W_V}, \frac{A_r}{A_V}]$ where A_r is the size and $[x_{min}, y_{min}, x_{max}, y_{max}]$ are coordinates for bounding box r and A_V, W_V, H_V are the area, the width, and the height of the input image

V. These two representations are concatenated as $r^{vis,spat} = [r^{vis}r^{spat}]$ for a bounding box r.

We parameterize Sieve I with a list of bounding boxes R as the input with parameter set Θ_I as follows:

$$s_I = W_I^{score} r^{vis,spat} \tag{1}$$
$$f_I(R; \Theta_I) = softmax(s_I) \tag{2}$$

Each bounding box is scored using a matrix W_I^{score}. Scores for all bounding boxes are then fed to softmax to get a probability distribution over boxes. The learned parameter Θ_I is the scoring matrix W_I^{score}.

Sieve II: Filtering Based on Objects Categories After filtering *unlikely* objects based only on the image, the second step is to determine which object category to keep as a candidate for prediction, filtering out the other categories. For instance, in Figure 1, only instances of suitcases are left as candidates after determining which type of object the input expression is talking about. To perform this step, Sieve II takes the list of object candidates from Sieve I and keeps objects having the same object category as the referred object. Unlike Sieve I, Sieve II uses the referring expression to filter bounding boxes of objects. We again use the baseline model of CMN$_{LOC}$ from the previous work (Hu et al., 2017) for the parametrization of Sieve II with a minor modification: instead of predicting the referred object, we make a binary decision for each box of whether the object in the box is the same category as the target object.

More specifically, we parameterize Sieve II as follows:

$$\hat{r}^{vis,spat} = W_{II}^{vis,spat} r^{vis,spat} \tag{3}$$
$$z_{II} = \hat{r}^{vis,spat} \odot f_{att}(T) \tag{4}$$
$$\hat{z}_{II} = z_{II} / \parallel z_{II} \parallel_2 \tag{5}$$
$$s_{II} = W_{II}^{score} \hat{z}_{s2} \tag{6}$$
$$f_{II}(T, R; \Theta_{II}) = sigmoid(s_{II}) \tag{7}$$

We encode the referring expression T into an embedding with $f_{att}(T)$ which uses an attention mechanism (Bahdanau et al., 2014) on top of a 2-layer bidirectional LSTM (Schuster and Paliwal, 1997).

We project bounding box features $r^{vis,spat}$ to the same dimension as the embedding of referring expression (Eq 3). Text and box representations are element-wise multiplied to get z_{II} as a joint representation of the text and bounding box (Eq 4). We L2-normalize to produce $\hat{z}_{II}$ (Eq 5, 6). Box scores

Model	precision@k	Accuracy
CMN	1	.705
CMN	2	.926
CMN	3	.979
LSTM+CNN-MIL	1	.684
LSTM+CNN-MIL	2	.907
LSTM+CNN-MIL	3	.972
Neural Sieve I	1	.401
Neural Sieve I	2	.712
Neural Sieve I	3	.866
Neural Sieve I + II	1	.488
Neural Sieve I + II	2	.842
Neural Sieve I + II	3	.953

Table 4: Precision@k accuracies for Neural Sieves and state-of-the-art systems. Note that even without using the referring expression, Sieve I is able to reduce the number of candidate boxes to 3 for 86.6% of the instances. When we further predict the type of objects with Sieve II, the number of candidate boxes is reduced to 2 for 84.2% of the instances.

s_{II} are calculated with a linear projection of the joint representation (Eq 6) and fed to the sigmoid function for a binary prediction for each box. The learned parameters Θ_{II} are $W_{II}^{vis,spat}$, W_{II}^{score}, and parameters of the encoding module f_{att}.

4.1 Filtering Experiments

We are interested in determining how accurate these simple nueral sieves can be. High accuracy here would give a possible explanation for the high performance of more complex models.

Dataset. For our experiments, we use Google-Ref (Mao et al., 2016) which is one of the standard benchmarks for referring expression recognition. It consists of around 26K images with 104K annotations. We use their Ground-Truth evaluation setup where the ground truth bounding box annotations from MSCOCO (Lin et al., 2014) are provided to the system as a part of the input. We used the split provided by Nagaraja et al. (2016) where splits have disjoint sets of images. We use precision@k for evaluating the performance of models.

Implementation Details. To train our models, we used stochastic gradient descent for 6 epochs with an initial learning rate of 0.01 and multiplied by 0.4 after each epoch. Word embeddings were initialized using GloVe (Pennington et al., 2014) and finetuned during training. We extracted features for bounding boxes using the fc7 layer output of Faster-RCNN VGG-16 network (Ren et al., 2015) pre-trained on MSCOCO dataset (Lin et al., 2014). Hyperparameters such as hidden layer size of LSTM networks were picked based on the best

validation score. For perturbation experiments, we did not perform any grid search for hyperparameters. We used hyperparameters of the previously reported best performing model in the literature. We released our code for public use[1].

Baseline Models. We compare Neural Sieves to the state-of-the-art models from the literature. **LSTM + CNN - MIL** Nagaraja et al. (2016) score *target object-context object* pairs using LSTMs for processing the referring expression and CNN features for bounding boxes. The pair with the highest score is predicted as the referred object. They use Multi-Instance Learning for training the model. **CMN** (Hu et al., 2017) is a neural module network with a tuple of object-relationship-subject nodes. The text encoding of tuples is calculated with a two-layer bi-directional LSTM and an attention mechanism (Bahdanau et al., 2014) over the referring expression.

4.2 Results

Table 4 shows the precision scores. The referred object is in the top-2 candidates selected by Sieve I 71.2% of the time and in the top-3 predictions 86.6% of the time. Combining both sieves into a pipeline, these numbers further increase to 84.2% for top-2 predictions and to 95.3% for top-3 predictions. Considering the simplicity of Neural Sieve approach, these are surprising results: two simple neural network systems, the first one ignoring the referring expression, the second predicting only object type, are able to reduce the number of candidate boxes down to 2 on 84.2% of instances.

5 Conclusion

We have analyzed two RER systems by variously perturbing aspects of the input referring expressions: shuffling, removing word categories, and finally, by removing the referring expression entirely. Based on this analysis, we proposed a pipeline of simple neural sieves that captures many of the easy correlations in the standard dataset. Our results suggest that careful analysis is important both while constructing new datasets and while constructing new models for grounded language tasks. The techniques used here may be applied more generally to other tasks to give better insight into what our models are learning and whether our datasets contain exploitable bias.

---

[1]https://github.com/volkancirik/neural-sieves-refexp

References

Aishwarya Agrawal, Dhruv Batra, and Devi Parikh. 2016. Analyzing the behavior of visual question answering models. In *Proceedings of the 2016 Conference on Empirical Methods in Natural Language Processing*. Association for Computational Linguistics, pages 1955–1960. https://doi.org/10.18653/v1/D16-1203.

Jacob Andreas, Marcus Rohrbach, Trevor Darrell, and Dan Klein. 2016. Neural module networks. In *Proceedings of the IEEE Conference on Computer Vision and Pattern Recognition (CVPR)*. pages 39–48.

Stanislaw Antol, Aishwarya Agrawal, Jiasen Lu, Margaret Mitchell, Dhruv Batra, C Lawrence Zitnick, and Devi Parikh. 2015. Vqa: Visual question answering. In *Proceedings of the IEEE International Conference on Computer Vision*. pages 2425–2433.

Dzmitry Bahdanau, Kyunghyun Cho, and Yoshua Bengio. 2014. Neural machine translation by jointly learning to align and translate. *arXiv preprint arXiv:1409.0473* .

Joyce Y Chai, Pengyu Hong, and Michelle X Zhou. 2004. A probabilistic approach to reference resolution in multimodal user interfaces. In *Proceedings of the 9th international conference on Intelligent user interfaces*. ACM, pages 70–77.

Joyce Y Chai, Lanbo She, Rui Fang, Spencer Ottarson, Cody Littley, Changsong Liu, and Kenneth Hanson. 2014. Collaborative effort towards common ground in situated human-robot dialogue. In *Proceedings of the 2014 ACM/IEEE international conference on Human-robot interaction*. ACM, pages 33–40.

Danqi Chen, Jason Bolton, and Christopher D. Manning. 2016a. A thorough examination of the cnn/daily mail reading comprehension task. In *Proceedings of the 54th Annual Meeting of the Association for Computational Linguistics (Volume 1: Long Papers)*. Association for Computational Linguistics, pages 2358–2367. https://doi.org/10.18653/v1/P16-1223.

Danqi Chen, Jason Bolton, and Christopher D. Manning. 2016b. A thorough examination of the cnn/daily mail reading comprehension task. In *Proceedings of the 54th Annual Meeting of the Association for Computational Linguistics (Volume 1: Long Papers)*. Association for Computational Linguistics, Berlin, Germany, pages 2358–2367. http://www.aclweb.org/anthology/P16-1223.

Xinlei Chen, Hao Fang, Tsung-Yi Lin, Ramakrishna Vedantam, Saurabh Gupta, Piotr Dollár, and C Lawrence Zitnick. 2015. Microsoft coco captions: Data collection and evaluation server. *arXiv preprint arXiv:1504.00325* .

Volkan Cirik, Taylor Berg-Kirkpatrick, and Louis-Phillippe Morency. 2018. Using syntax to ground referring expressions in natural images. In *32nd AAAI Conference on Artificial Intelligence (AAAI-18)*.

Abhishek Das, Satwik Kottur, Khushi Gupta, Avi Singh, Deshraj Yadav, José MF Moura, Devi Parikh, and Dhruv Batra. 2016. Visual dialog. *arXiv preprint arXiv:1611.08669* .

Jacob Devlin, Saurabh Gupta, Ross Girshick, Margaret Mitchell, and C Lawrence Zitnick. 2015. Exploring nearest neighbor approaches for image captioning. *arXiv preprint arXiv:1505.04467* .

Jeffrey L Elman. 1990. Finding structure in time. *Cognitive science* 14(2):179–211.

Rui Fang, Changsong Liu, and Joyce Yue Chai. 2012. Integrating word acquisition and referential grounding towards physical world interaction. In *Proceedings of the 14th ACM international conference on Multimodal interaction*. ACM, pages 109–116.

Yash Goyal, Tejas Khot, Douglas Summers-Stay, Dhruv Batra, and Devi Parikh. 2016. Making the v in vqa matter: Elevating the role of image understanding in visual question answering. *arXiv preprint arXiv:1612.00837* .

Suchin Gururangan, Swabha Swayamdipta, Omer Levy, Roy Schwartz, Samuel R Bowman, and Noah A Smith. 2018. Annotation artifacts in natural language inference data. In *Proceedings of the 2018 Conference of the North American Chapter of the Association for Computational Linguistics: Human Language Technologies*. Association for Computational Linguistics.

Karl Moritz Hermann, Tomas Kocisky, Edward Grefenstette, Lasse Espeholt, Will Kay, Mustafa Suleyman, and Phil Blunsom. 2015. Teaching machines to read and comprehend. In *Advances in Neural Information Processing Systems*. pages 1693–1701.

Sepp Hochreiter and Jürgen Schmidhuber. 1997. Long short-term memory. *Neural computation* 9(8):1735–1780.

Ronghang Hu, Marcus Rohrbach, Jacob Andreas, Trevor Darrell, and Kate Saenko. 2017. Modeling relationships in referential expressions with compositional modular networks .

Ronghang Hu, Huazhe Xu, Marcus Rohrbach, Jiashi Feng, Kate Saenko, and Trevor Darrell. 2016. Natural language object retrieval. In *Proceedings of the IEEE Conference on Computer Vision and Pattern Recognition*. pages 4555–4564.

Allan Jabri, Armand Joulin, and Laurens van der Maaten. 2016. Revisiting visual question answering baselines. In *European conference on computer vision*. Springer, pages 727–739.

Robin Jia and Percy Liang. 2017. Adversarial examples for evaluating reading comprehension systems. *arXiv preprint arXiv:1707.07328* .

Sahar Kazemzadeh, Vicente Ordonez, Mark Matten, and Tamara L. Berg. 2014. Referit game: Referring to objects in photographs of natural scenes. In *EMNLP*.

Casey Kennington and David Schlangen. 2017. A simple generative model of incremental reference resolution for situated dialogue. *Computer Speech & Language* 41:43–67.

Guillaume Lample, Miguel Ballesteros, Sandeep Subramanian, Kazuya Kawakami, and Chris Dyer. 2016. Neural architectures for named entity recognition. *arXiv preprint arXiv:1603.01360* .

Tsung-Yi Lin, Michael Maire, Serge Belongie, James Hays, Pietro Perona, Deva Ramanan, Piotr Dollár, and C Lawrence Zitnick. 2014. Microsoft coco: Common objects in context. In *European Conference on Computer Vision*. Springer, pages 740–755.

Junhua Mao, Jonathan Huang, Alexander Toshev, Oana Camburu, Alan L Yuille, and Kevin Murphy. 2016. Generation and comprehension of unambiguous object descriptions. In *Proceedings of the IEEE Conference on Computer Vision and Pattern Recognition (CVPR)*. pages 11–20.

Varun Nagaraja, Vlad Morariu, and Larry Davis. 2016. Modeling context between objects for referring expression understanding. In *ECCV*.

Jeffrey Pennington, Richard Socher, and Christopher D Manning. 2014. Glove: Global vectors for word representation. In *EMNLP*. volume 14, pages 1532–1543.

Shaoqing Ren, Kaiming He, Ross Girshick, and Jian Sun. 2015. Faster r-cnn: Towards real-time object detection with region proposal networks. In *Advances in neural information processing systems*. pages 91–99.

Anna Rohrbach, Marcus Rohrbach, Ronghang Hu, Trevor Darrell, and Bernt Schiele. 2016. Grounding of textual phrases in images by reconstruction. In *European Conference on Computer Vision*. Springer, pages 817–834.

Mike Schuster and Kuldip K Paliwal. 1997. Bidirectional recurrent neural networks. *IEEE Transactions on Signal Processing* 45(11):2673–2681.

Ilya Sutskever, Oriol Vinyals, and Quoc V Le. 2014. Sequence to sequence learning with neural networks. In *Advances in neural information processing systems*. pages 3104–3112.

Tom Williams, Saurav Acharya, Stephanie Schreitter, and Matthias Scheutz. 2016. Situated open world reference resolution for human-robot dialogue. In *The Eleventh ACM/IEEE International Conference on Human Robot Interaction*. IEEE Press, pages 311–318.

Licheng Yu, Patrick Poirson, Shan Yang, Alexander C Berg, and Tamara L Berg. 2016. Modeling context in referring expressions. In *European Conference on Computer Vision*. Springer, pages 69–85.

Bolei Zhou, Yuandong Tian, Sainbayar Sukhbaatar, Arthur Szlam, and Rob Fergus. 2015. Simple baseline for visual question answering. *arXiv preprint arXiv:1512.02167* .

Visually Guided Spatial Relation Extraction from Text

Taher Rahgooy* Umar Manzoor* Parisa Kordjamshidi*†
*Tulane University, Computer Science Department, New Orleans, LA, USA
†Florida Institute for Human and Machine Cognition (IHMC), Pensacola, FL, USA
{trahgooy,umanzoor,pkordjam}@tulane.edu

Abstract

Extraction of spatial relations from sentences with complex/nesting relationships is very challenging as often needs resolving inherent semantic ambiguities. We seek help from visual modality to fill the information gap in the text modality and resolve spatial semantic ambiguities. We use various recent vision and language datasets and techniques to train inter-modality alignment models, visual relationship classifiers and propose a novel global inference model to integrate these components into our structured output prediction model for spatial role and relation extraction. Our global inference model enables us to utilize the visual and geometric relationships between objects and improves the state-of-art results of spatial information extraction from text.

1 Introduction

Significant progress has been made in spatial language understanding by mapping natural language text to spatial ontologies (Kordjamshidi and Moens, 2015). The research results show that spatial entities can be extracted with a good accuracy, however, spatial relation extraction is still challenging (Kordjamshidi et al., 2017a; Pustejovsky et al., 2015). Particularly, when the sentences convey more than one relationship, finding the right links between the spatial objects and spatial prepositions becomes difficult. For example, the spatial meaning of *There is a car in front of the house on the left*, can be interpreted in different ways: *(A car in front of the house) on the left* or *A car in front of (the house on the left)*. This issue is related to the well-known *prepositional phrase attachments* (pp-attachments) syntactic ambiguity which is problematic for our goal of spatial semantic extraction too. The previous research shows some of these ambiguities can be resolved by simultaneously reasoning from the associated image (Christie et al., 2016; Delecraz et al., 2017). Consider the scene in Figure 1, we can easily resolve the ambiguity and choose the correct interpretation with the help of the associated image.

Although we do not directly tackle the task of pp-attachment here, resolving this issue will help our task to find the accurate link between the spatial prepositions (i.e. *spatial indicators*) and spatial objects/roles (*trajector* and *landmark*). The spatial semantic links can go beyond the syntactic links/attachments, therefore merely fixing the preposition attachments is not sufficient for our task. We exploit the image to find the right preposition that describes the relationships between the spatial roles, for example *on the left* can be a relationship between *the house* and implicit landmark *picture* as well as *a car* and implicit landmark *picture*. There are many recent works on combining vision and language for domains such as image captioning (Karpathy and Fei-Fei, 2017), visual image retrieval (Hu et al., 2016), visual question answering (Krishna et al., 2017; Faghri et al., 2017), activity recognition (Gupta and Malik, 2015; Yatskar et al., 2016; Yang et al., 2016), visual relation extraction (Lu et al., 2016; Xu et al., 2017; Haldekar et al., 2017; Peyre et al., 2017; Liao et al., 2017) and object localization (Kazemzadeh et al., 2014; Schlangen et al., 2016). We aim at exploiting models from visual modality to boost the models trained by the text modality and improve spatial role labeling task (SpRL) (Kordjamshidi et al., 2011). The most related work to ours is (Kordjamshidi et al., 2017a) in which they connected phrases to ground-truth labeled segments using word embedding similarity to generate additional visual features, whereas, in this work, we train actual inter-modality alignment models to include visual information in our model. The challenges are 1) existing textual datasets for SpRL does not have enough examples to train such

788

Figure 1: A captioned scene from CLEF IAPR TC-12 dataset: *There is a car in front of the house on the left.*

visual models, therefore, such models need to be trained on external datasets and later incorporated in our multi-modal setting, 2) Aligning text entities with image entities is a complex and challenging task itself. Each modality in isolation represents spatial relations imperfectly, however, each one can reflect different types of spatial relation better than the other. If we can handle the mentioned challenges and combine the two modalities then vision modality fills the information gap of the text modality and improves the information extraction.

To overcome the above challenges, we 1) trained two visual models namely word-segment alignment, trained on ImageClef Referring Expression Dataset[1] to connect the two modalities, and preposition classifier, trained on Visual Genome dataset (Krishna et al., 2017) to help in link disambiguation, and 2) generated a unified graph, based on both image and text data and proposed a global machine learning model to exploit the information from the companion images.

The contribution of this paper includes a) exploiting the visual information to solve the SpRL task and improving the state-of-the-art results significantly b) forming a global inference model that imposes the consistency constraints on the decisions made based on the two modalities c) exploiting external vision and language datasets to inject external knowledge into our models d) augmenting an existing dataset which is annotated by spatial semantics with the image segment alignments, this dataset will help the evaluation of the existing methods for combining vision and language for fine-grained spatial semantic extractions.

2 Model Description

Given a piece of text, S, here a sentence - split into number of phrases, and an accompanying image,

I segmented into number of segments represented by bounding boxes, the goal is to identify the textual phrases that have spatial roles and detect the relationships between them. The spatial roles included in this task are defined as:

(a) **Spatial indicators (sp):** these are triggers indicating the existence of spatial information in a sentence;

(b) **Trajectors (tr):** these are the entities whose location are described;

(c) **Landmarks (lm):** these are the reference objects for describing the location of the trajectors.

In the textual description of Figure 1, the location of *car (trajector)* has been described with respect to *house (landmark)* using the preposition *in front of*. Furthermore, spatial relationships and their types are defined as follows:

(a) **Spatial relations:** these indicate a link between the three above mentioned roles $(sp.tr.lm)$, forming spatial triplets.

(b) **Coarse-grained relation types:** these indicate the coarse-grained type of relations in terms of spatial calculi formalisms including *region*, *direction*, and *distance* types.

(c) **Fine-grained relation types:** these indicate the fine-grained type of relations in terms of each specific spatial calculi formalism. *Region connection calculi (RCC8)* types (e.g. disconnected (DC), externally connected (EC), etc.), a closed set of directional relations (e.g. left, right), and an open set of distal relations (e.g. close, far) are defined for regional, directional, and distal relationships respectively.

For example, given the sentence and its accompanying image in Figure 1, the goal is to identify the spatial relations, $\langle [A\ car]_{tr}, [in\ front\ of]_{sp}, [the\ house]_{lm}\rangle$ and $\langle [the\ house]_{tr}, [on\ the\ left]_{sp}, [None]_{lm}\rangle$ and also determine their coarse-grained types (*direction* and *direction* respectively) and fine-grained types (*front* and *left* respectively).

We formulate this problem as a structured output prediction problem. Given a set of input-out pairs as training examples, $E = \{(x^i, y^i) \in \mathcal{X} \times \mathcal{Y} : i = 1..N\}$, a scoring function $g(x, y; W) = \langle W, \phi(x, y)\rangle$ will be learned. Where W is the weight vector and $\langle, \rangle$ is dot product between two vectors. This function is a linear discriminant function defined over combined feature representation of inputs and outputs denoted by $\phi(x, y)$

[1]http://tamaraberg.com/referitgame/

(Tsochantaridis et al., 2005). However, for this work we use a piece-wise training model in which independent models are trained per concepts in the output and the predictions are done based on global inference (Punyakanok et al., 2005).

We construct a graph using the phrases $\{p_1, ..., p_n\}$ and bounding boxes $\{b_1...b_m\}$, and link these nodes to make composed concepts (like relations, roles, etc.). We associate a classifier to each concept in the graph and encode the domain knowledge as global constraints over these concepts. We use global reasoning by imposing these constraints over various (node and edge) classifiers to produce the final outputs. The input of our structured output prediction model is the aforementioned graph and the output is the concepts assigned to the nodes and edges of this graph. In the following we describe the information that we use from each modality (i.e. text and image) and from inter-modality relationships and describe the relevant classifiers, features and constraints.

2.1 Text

We use binary classifiers to identify spatial roles and relations. The spatial roles of trajector, landmark and spatial indicator are denoted by tr, lm, and sp. $sp.tr.lm$, $sp.tr.lm.\gamma$, and $sp.tr.lm.\lambda$ denote spatial relations, coarse-grained relation types, and fine-grained relation types respectively. Additionally, we denote candidate fine-grained types related to coarse-grained type γ by Λ_γ.

Features: We use phrase-based features $\phi_{phrase}(p_i)$ for role classifiers in which p_i is the identifier of ith phrase in the sentence which include several linguistically motivated features such as lexical form of the words in the phrases, lemmas, pos-tags, etc. In addition, motivated by features used in (Roberts and Harabagiu, 2012) and (Kordjamshidi et al., 2017a), we use a combination of phrase-based features like concatenation of headwords of the roles, concatenation of their pos, and other relative features such as distance between roles, dependency relations, sub-categorization, etc., to represent the relations and this is referred to as $\phi_{triplet}^{text}(p_i, p_j, p_k)$.

Constraints: The constraints over spatial concepts expressed in text are as follows,

$$\sum_i \sum_k sp_i tr_j lm_k \geq tr_j$$

Each tr candidate at least should appear in one relation

$$\sum_i \sum_j sp_i tr_j lm_k \geq lm_k$$

Each lm candidate at least should appear in one relation

$$\sum_j \sum_k sp_i tr_j lm_k = sp_i$$

Each sp candidate should appear in one relation

$$\sum_j tr_j \geq sp_i$$

For each sp we should have at-least one tr

$$\sum_k lm_k \geq sp_i$$

For each sp we should have at-least one lm. Including null landmarks

$$sp_i tr_j lm_k \gamma \leq sp_i tr_j lm_k$$

is-a constraints between relations and coarse-grained types

$$sp_i tr_j lm_k \lambda \leq sp_i tr_j lm_k \gamma \quad \lambda \in \Lambda_\gamma$$

is-a constraints between coarse-grained and corresponding fine-grained types.

2.2 Image

In the image modality, we have two types of classifiers, 1) for localization of an object in the image given a referring expression, and 2) for extraction of spatial relations, called *Word-Segment Alignment* and *Preposition Classifier* respectively.

Word-Segment alignment: motivated by (Schlangen et al., 2016), we trained a set of binary object localization classifiers to link words and image segments. These per word classifiers are trained using *ImageClef Referring Expression Dataset*.

Preposition classifier: is a multi-class classifier that takes two bounding boxes and returns the spatial relation (preposition here) between them. This classifier is trained on a subset of visual genome dataset (Krishna et al., 2017) described in section 3.1, this classifier provides the external knowledge from visual resources and help in disambiguation of ambiguous links (i.e. finding the correct link between spatial preposition and spatial roles).

Features: A deep convolutional neural network, "GoogLeNet" is used to extract features for bounding boxes that are used by *Word-Segment Alignment*, for details see (Schlangen et al., 2016). For the *Preposition Classifier* we use bounding box features $\phi_{box}(b) = [l, x_{min}, y_{min}, w_b, h_b]$ where l is the label of the box, (x_{min}, y_{min}) is the top-left point of the box, w_b, h_b are the width and height of the box respectively. In addition we use pair features $\phi_{pair}^{visual}(b_i, b_j)$ including, label of each box, distance between the center of the two boxes, a vector from the center of first box to the center of second box, aspect ratio of each box, word to vector representation of each box's label, the normalized area of each box, intersection, union, intersection over union of the two boxes, and four directional (above, below, left and right) features calculated with reference to the two boxes. Box and pair features are adopted from (Ramisa et al., 2015).

2.3 Inter-Modality

An essential part of having a global inference over multimodal data is to have the connections between the two modalities. *Word-Segment Alignment* classifier is used to align the headword of each phrase p in the sentence to its corresponding bounding box b in the image and this alignment is denoted by $p \rightarrow b$. A binary feature $isAligned$ (that indicates if the phrase is connected to an object in the image) is added to the features of classifiers in the text side.

Constraints: Given two bounding boxes b_1 and b_2 we say that the preposition α is supported by the image and write $iSup^{\alpha}_{b_1 b_2}$ if α is ranked among top N prepositions according to *Preposition Classifier* scores. Using this indicator we define the following inter-modality constraint.

$$iSup^{\alpha}_{b_1 b_2} \leq sp_i tr_j lm_k$$
$$p_i \rightarrow b_1, p_j \rightarrow b_2, \alpha = p_i$$

For aligned pairs, the visual relation should support the textual relation

2.4 Global Reasoning

We obtain the output of each classifier in the model holistically by global reasoning that is by considering global correlations among classifiers, when calculating outputs. This goal is achieved by optimizing an objective function that is the summation of classifiers' discriminant functions,

$$\sum_{i \in C_{sp}} \langle W_{sp}, \phi_{sp_i} \rangle . sp_i + \sum_{i \in C_{tr}} \langle W_{tr}, \phi_{tr_i} \rangle . tr_i +$$

$$\sum_{i \in C_{lm}} \langle W_{lm}, \phi_{lm_i} \rangle . lm_i +$$

$$\sum_{i \in C_{sp}} \sum_{j \in C_{tr}} \sum_{k \in C_{lm}} \langle W_{sptrlm}, \phi_{sp_i tr_j lm_k} \rangle . sp_i tr_j lm_k +$$

$$\sum_{\gamma \in \Gamma} \sum_{i \in C_{sp}} \sum_{j \in C_{tr}} \sum_{k \in C_{lm}} \langle W_{sptrlm}, \phi_{sp_i tr_j lm_k \gamma} \rangle . sp_i tr_j lm_k \gamma +$$

$$\sum_{\lambda \in \Lambda} \sum_{i \in C_{sp}} \sum_{j \in C_{tr}} \sum_{k \in C_{lm}} \langle W_{sptrlm}, \phi_{sp_i tr_j lm_k \lambda} \rangle . sp_i tr_j lm_k \lambda +$$

$$\sum_{\alpha \in Prep} \sum_{(i,j) \in C_{iSup}} \langle W_{iSup^{\alpha}}, \phi_{iSup^{\alpha}_{ij}} \rangle . iSup^{\alpha}_{ij}.$$

Each classifier is shown as a binary variable (e.g. tr_i for trajector classifier). $\Lambda, \Gamma, Prep$ are the candidates for fine-grained relations, coarse-grained relations, and prepositions from text respectively. C_l denotes the candidates for label l.

The following model variations are designed using combination of text and image modalities for experimentation.

Baseline Model (BM): Independent classifiers are trained only on the textual features described in Section 2.1. This is a learning only model and each classifier makes independent predictions.

Baseline + Constraints (BM+C): The output of the classifiers obtained from the BM model are adjusted by global inference over textual constraints defined in Section 2.1.

Ground-truth alignments (GT): This setting is very similar to the $BM + C$ model except the $isAligned$ feature (see Section 2.3) added to consider the ground-truth alignments.

Alignment Classifier (AC): Similar to the GT model, but instead of ground-truth information we use *Word-Segment Alignment* classifier to align bounding boxes with the phrases in the sentence.

GT + Preposition (GT+P): In this setting, ground-truth alignments alongside *Preposition classifier* is used to enforce all constraints in the global inference over the two modalities.

AC + Preposition (AC+P): Same as GT+P model but with *Word-Segment Alignment* classifiers instead of ground-truth alignments.

3 Experimental Setup

We report the experimental results of our model and compare it with the state-of-the-art (Kordjamshidi et al., 2017a) model, referred here as *M0* model. A role prediction is considered correct if there is a phrase overlap between the ground-truth and predicted roles and each relation is counted as correct when all three arguments are correct. All the base classifiers described in Section 2.1 are sparse perceptrons. We use *Saul* (Kordjamshidi et al., 2015, 2016) to implement the models and solve the global inference of Section 2.4. The code is publicly available here. [2]

3.1 DataSets

CLEF 2017 mSpRL dataset: This dataset is a subset of IAPR TC-12[3] Benchmark which is annotated for the SpRL task (Kordjamshidi et al., 2017c, 2012). It contains 613 images with descriptions including $1,213$ sentences. The standard split of the dataset contains 761 training and 939 testing spatial relations (Kordjamshidi et al., 2017b). Furthermore, we added new annotations

---

[2]https://github.com/HetML/SpRL/tree/paper2
[3]http://www.imageclef.org/SIAPRdata

	Visual Genome			CLEF		
	P	R	F1	P	R	F1
above	47.24	21.59	29.63	87.50	22.58	35.90
behind	65.02	22.65	33.56	80.00	22.22	34.78
in	80.99	54.96	65.48	83.80	79.87	81.79
in front of	31.65	6.67	11.02	80.00	16.33	27.12
on	79.76	95.75	87.03	38.39	91.49	54.09

(a) Preposition classifier results on Visual genome and CLEF datasets

	P	R	F1
M0	68.34	57.93	62.71
BM	65.64	60.23	62.82
BM+C	70.04	66.55	68.25
GT	66.37	75.14	70.48
GT+P	67.14	74.80	70.76
AC	71.39	66.55	68.89
AC+P	71.69	66.10	68.78

(b) Spatial relations results on CLEF test set

Table 1: Experimental results, where P and R denote precision and recall respectively.

to this dataset to align phrases in the text with the segments of the related images using brat tool.[4] The alignments are used only for evaluations and are publicly available. [5]

Visual Genome dataset (VG): Visual Genome dataset has seven main components (Krishna et al., 2017), one of them is relationships component which contains the relationships (prepositions) between two bounding boxes. The dataset contains 108077 images and the relationships component contains 2316104 relation instances. We used a subset the relationships that correspond to the most frequent prepositions in CLEF dataset. We used 80% for training (811661 instances) and 20% for testing (202916 instances).

ReferItGame Dataset: It contains $120,000$ referring expressions and covers 99.5 percent of the regions of SAIAPRTC-12 dataset which is a segmented and annotated version of the IAPR TC-12 dataset (Kazemzadeh et al., 2014).

3.2 Experimental Results

Word-Segment Alignment: We implemented and trained classifiers per words as described in Section 2.2 for the most frequent words in ReferItGame dataset using (Schlangen et al., 2016) approach. We evaluated the trained model on both ReferitGame and CLEF testset, and obtained 64% and 45% accuracy respectively. This trained model is used to align words and segments in CLEF dataset. The end-to-end evaluation results show that the models trained by this external dataset are helpful though those are not highly accurate for every referring word.

Preposition Classifier: As described in Section 2.2, these are trained on a subset of Visual Genome dataset described in Section 3.1 and evaluated on both Visual Genome and CLEF test sets. Table 1a shows five best prepositions result whereas the result for other prepositions is less

than 20% F1.

Spatial Relations: The experimental results in Table 1b show that our baseline model (BM) is as good as the state-of-the-art model (M0). Incorporating $isAligned$ feature (in GT and AC models) further improves the results because having the phrases visualized in the image increases the confidence scores of the spatial role and relation classifiers and leads to a higher recall. The global inference over constraints in $BM+C$ significantly improves the performance of BM (about 5% F1). $GT+P$ results show that inter-modality constraints help in improving the results (about 2% F1) which indicates some of the visual relations successfully confirmed and boosted their corresponding relations in the text modality. However, this improvement is limited which is expected considering the low performance of *Preposition Classifier*. The $GT+P$ results indicate the significance of the visual information in our model when the correct alignments are provided. The alignment classifiers in the AC model also slightly improve the $BM+C$. However, as it is visible in $AC+P$ results, when we have both noisy alignments and noisy visual relations the results drop slightly compared to AC.

4 Conclusion

Our global inference model exploits visual modality classifiers including object localization by referring expressions and spatial relation classifiers between visual objects, as well as classifiers that extract spatial roles and relation from text. The global inference imposes consistency over the two modalities and identifies the spatial relations in text in accordance with their counterparts in the image. The experimental results show the effectiveness of the visual information in resolving the ambiguity of spatial semantics of text. There is still a large room to improve the modality alignments and relation extraction from images to obtain better gains from visual information.

---

[4]http://brat.nlplab.org/
[5]http://www.cs.tulane.edu/~pkordjam/
SpRL.htm#data

References

Gordon Christie, Ankit Laddha, Aishwarya Agrawal, Stanislaw Antol, Yash Goyal, Kevin Kochersberger, and Dhruv Batra. 2016. Resolving language and vision ambiguities together: Joint segmentation & prepositional attachment resolution in captioned scenes. In *Proceedings of the 2016 Conference on Empirical Methods in Natural Language Processing*. pages 1493–1503.

Sebastien Delecraz, Alexis Nasr, Frederic Bechet, and Benoit Favre. 2017. Correcting prepositional phrase attachments using multimodal corpora. In *Proceedings of the 15th International Conference on Parsing Technologies*. pages 72–77.

Fartash Faghri, David J. Fleet, Ryan Kiros, and Sanja Fidler. 2017. VSE++: improved visual-semantic embeddings. *CoRR* abs/1707.05612. http://arxiv.org/abs/1707.05612.

Saurabh Gupta and Jitendra Malik. 2015. Visual semantic role labeling. *CoRR* abs/1505.04474. http://arxiv.org/abs/1505.04474.

Mandar Haldekar, Ashwinkumar Ganesan, and Tim Oates. 2017. Identifying spatial relations in images using convolutional neural networks. In *Neural Networks (IJCNN), 2017 International Joint Conference on*. IEEE, pages 3593–3600.

Ronghang Hu, Huazhe Xu, Marcus Rohrbach, Jiashi Feng, Kate Saenko, and Trevor Darrell. 2016. Natural language object retrieval. In *Computer Vision and Pattern Recognition (CVPR), 2016 IEEE Conference on*. IEEE, pages 4555–4564.

Andrej Karpathy and Li Fei-Fei. 2017. Deep visual-semantic alignments for generating image descriptions. *IEEE Trans. Pattern Anal. Mach. Intell.* 39(4):664–676. https://doi.org/10.1109/TPAMI.2016.2598339.

Sahar Kazemzadeh, Vicente Ordonez, Mark Matten, and Tamara L. Berg. 2014. Referit game: Referring to objects in photographs of natural scenes. In *EMNLP*.

P. Kordjamshidi, D. Roth, and H. Wu. 2015. Saul: Towards declarative learning based programming. In *Proc. of the International Joint Conference on Artificial Intelligence (IJCAI)*. http://cogcomp.cs.illinois.edu/papers/KordjamshidiRoWu15.pdf.

Parisa Kordjamshidi, Steven Bethard, and Marie-Francine Moens. 2012. SemEval-2012 task 3: Spatial role labeling. In *Proceedings of the First Joint Conference on Lexical and Computational Semantics: Proceedings of the Sixth International Workshop on Semantic Evaluation (SemEval)*. volume 2, pages 365–373.

Parisa Kordjamshidi, Daniel Khashabi, Christos Christodoulopoulos, Bhargav Mangipudi, Sameer Singh, and Dan Roth. 2016. Better call saul: Flexible programming for learning and inference in nlp. In *Proceedings of COLING 2016, the 26th International Conference on Computational Linguistics: Technical Papers*. pages 3030–3040.

Parisa Kordjamshidi and Marie-Francine Moens. 2015. Global machine learning for spatial ontology population. *Web Semantics: Science, Services and Agents on the World Wide Web* 30:3–21.

Parisa Kordjamshidi, Taher Rahgooy, and Umar Manzoor. 2017a. Spatial language understanding with multimodal graphs using declarative learning based programming. In *Proceedings of the 2nd Workshop on Structured Prediction for Natural Language Processing*. pages 33–43.

Parisa Kordjamshidi, Taher Rahgooy, Marie-Francine Moens, James Pustejovsky, Umar Manzoor, and Kirk Roberts. 2017b. Clef 2017: Multimodal spatial role labeling (msprl) task overview. In *International Conference of the Cross-Language Evaluation Forum for European Languages*. Springer, pages 367–376.

Parisa Kordjamshidi, Martijn van Otterlo, and Marie-Francine Moens. 2011. Spatial role labeling: towards extraction of spatial relations from natural language. *ACM - Transactions on Speech and Language Processing* 8:1–36.

Parisa Kordjamshidi, Martijn van Otterlo, and Marie-Francine Moens. 2017c. Spatial role labeling annotation scheme. In N. Ide James Pustejovsky, editor, *Handbook of Linguistic Annotation*, Springer Verlag.

Ranjay Krishna, Yuke Zhu, Oliver Groth, Justin Johnson, Kenji Hata, Joshua Kravitz, Stephanie Chen, Yannis Kalantidis, Li-Jia Li, David A Shamma, et al. 2017. Visual genome: Connecting language and vision using crowdsourced dense image annotations. *International Journal of Computer Vision* 123(1):32–73.

Wentong Liao, Shuai Lin, Bodo Rosenhahn, and Michael Ying Yang. 2017. Natural language guided visual relationship detection. *CoRR* abs/1711.06032. http://arxiv.org/abs/1711.06032.

Cewu Lu, Ranjay Krishna, Michael Bernstein, and Li Fei-Fei. 2016. Visual relationship detection with language priors. In *European Conference on Computer Vision*. Springer, pages 852–869.

Julia Peyre, Josef Sivic, Ivan Laptev, and Cordelia Schmid. 2017. Weakly-supervised learning of visual relations. In *Proceedings of the IEEE Conference on Computer Vision and Pattern Recognition*. pages 5179–5188.

V. Punyakanok, D. Roth, W. Tau Yih, and D. Zimak. 2005. Learning and inference over constrained output. In *IJCAI'05*. pages 1124–1129. http://dl.acm.org/citation.cfm?id=1642293.1642473.

James Pustejovsky, Parisa Kordjamshidi, Marie-Francine Moens, Aaron Levine, Seth Dworman, and Zachary Yocum. 2015. Semeval-2015 task 8: Spaceeval. In *Proc. of the Annual Meeting of the Association for Computational Linguistics (ACL)*. ACL, pages 884–894. http://cogcomp.org/papers/PustejovskyetalSemEval2015.pdf.

Arnau Ramisa, Josiah Wang, Ying Lu, Emmanuel Dellandrea, Francesc Moreno-Noguer, and Robert Gaizauskas. 2015. Combining geometric, textual and visual features for predicting prepositions in image descriptions. In *Proceedings of the 2015 Conference on Empirical Methods in Natural Language Processing*. Association for Computational Linguistics, Lisbon, Portugal, pages 214–220. http://aclweb.org/anthology/D15-1022.

Kirk Roberts and Sanda M Harabagiu. 2012. Utd-sprl: A joint approach to spatial role labeling. In *Proceedings of the First Joint Conference on Lexical and Computational Semantics-Volume 1: Proceedings of the main conference and the shared task, and Volume 2: Proceedings of the Sixth International Workshop on Semantic Evaluation*. Association for Computational Linguistics, pages 419–424.

David Schlangen, Sina Zarrieß, and Casey Kennington. 2016. Resolving references to objects in photographs using the words-as-classifiers model. In *Proceedings of the 54th Annual Meeting of the Association for Computational Linguistics (Volume 1: Long Papers)*. volume 1, pages 1213–1223.

Ioannis Tsochantaridis, Thorsten Joachims, Thomas Hofmann, and Yasemin Altun. 2005. Large margin methods for structured and interdependent output variables. In *Journal of Machine Learning Research (JMLR)*. pages 1453–1484.

Danfei Xu, Yuke Zhu, Christopher B Choy, and Li Fei-Fei. 2017. Scene graph generation by iterative message passing. *arXiv preprint arXiv:1701.02426* .

Shaohua Yang, Qiaozi Gao, Changsong Liu, Caiming Xiong, Song-Chun Zhu, and Joyce Y Chai. 2016. Grounded semantic role labeling. In *HLT-NAACL*. pages 149–159.

Mark Yatskar, Luke Zettlemoyer, and Ali Farhadi. 2016. Situation recognition: Visual semantic role labeling for image understanding. In *Proceedings of the IEEE Conference on Computer Vision and Pattern Recognition*. pages 5534–5542.

Watch, Listen, and Describe: Globally and Locally Aligned Cross-Modal Attentions for Video Captioning

Xin Wang and **Yuan-Fang Wang** and **William Yang Wang**
University of California, Santa Barbara
{xwang,yfwang,william}@cs.ucsb.edu

Abstract

A major challenge for video captioning is to combine audio and visual cues. Existing multi-modal fusion methods have shown encouraging results in video understanding. However, the temporal structures of multiple modalities at different granularities are rarely explored, and how to selectively fuse the multi-modal representations at different levels of details remains uncharted. In this paper, we propose a novel hierarchically aligned cross-modal attention (HACA) framework to learn and selectively fuse both global and local temporal dynamics of different modalities. Furthermore, for the first time, we validate the superior performance of the deep audio features on the video captioning task. Finally, our HACA model significantly outperforms the previous best systems and achieves new state-of-the-art results on the widely used MSR-VTT dataset.

1 Introduction

Video captioning, the task of automatically generating a natural-language description of a video, is a crucial challenge in both NLP and vision communities. In addition to visual features, audio features can also play a key role in video captioning. Figure 1 shows an example where the caption system made a mistake analyzing only visual features. In this example, it could be very hard even for a human to correctly determine if the girl is singing or talking by only watching without listening. Thus to describe the video content accurately, a good understanding of the audio signature is a must.

In the multi-modal fusion domain, many approaches attempted to jointly learn temporal features from multiple modalities (Wu et al., 2014a), such as feature-level (early) fusion (Ngiam et al., 2011; Ramanishka et al., 2016), decision-level (late) fusion (He et al., 2015), model-level fusion (Wu et al., 2014b), and attention fusion (Chen

Figure 1: A video captioning example.

and Jin, 2016; Yang et al., 2017), etc. But these techniques do not learn the cross-modal attention and thus fail to selectively attend to a certain modality when producing the descriptions.

Another issue is that little efforts have been exerted on utilizing temporal transitions of the different modalities with varying analysis granularities. The temporal structures of a video are inherently layered since the video usually contains temporally sequential activities (*e.g.* a video where *a person reads a book, then throws it on the table. Next, he pours a glass of milk and drinks it*). There are strong temporal dependencies among those activities. Meanwhile, to understand each of them requires understanding many action components (e.g., *pouring a glass of milk* is a complicated action sequence). Therefore we hypothesize that it is beneficial to learn and align both the high-level (global) and low-level (local) temporal transitions of multiple modalities.

Moreover, prior work only employed hand-crafted audio features (*e.g.* MFCC) for video captioning (Ramanishka et al., 2016; Xu et al., 2017; Hori et al., 2017). While deep audio features have shown superior performance on some audio processing tasks like audio event classification (Hershey et al., 2017), their use in video captioning needs to be validated.

795

Proceedings of NAACL-HLT 2018, pages 795–801
New Orleans, Louisiana, June 1 - 6, 2018. ©2018 Association for Computational Linguistics

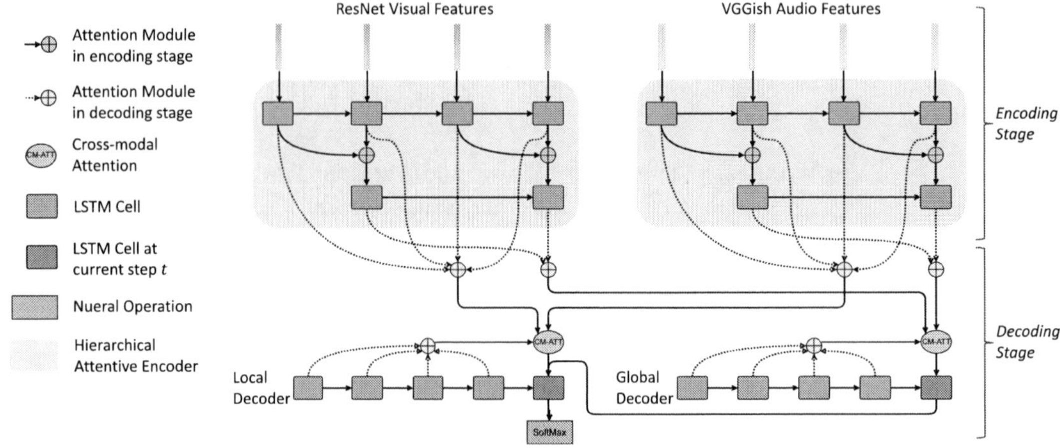

Figure 2: Overview of our HACA framework. Note that in the encoding stage, for the sake of simplicity, the step size of high-level LSTM in both hierarchical attentive encoders is 2 here, but in practice usually they are set much longer. In the decoding stage, we only show the computations of the time step t (the decoders have the same behavior at other time steps).

In this paper, we propose a novel hierarchically aligned cross-modal attentive network (HACA) to learn and align both global and local contexts among different modalities of the video. The goal is to overcome the issues mentioned above and generate better descriptions of the input videos. Our contributions are fourfold: (1) we invent a hierarchical encoder-decoder network to adaptively learn the attentive representations of multiple modalities, including visual attention, audio attention, and decoder attention; (2) our proposed model is capable of aligning and fusing both the global and local contexts of different modalities for video understanding and sentence generation; (3) we are the first to utilize deep audio features for video captioning and empirically demonstrate its effectiveness over hand-crafted MFCC features; and (4) we achieve the new state of the art on the MSR-VTT dataset.

Among the network architectures for video captioning (Yao et al., 2015; Venugopalan et al., 2015b), sequence-to-sequence models (Venugopalan et al., 2015a) have shown promising results. Pan et al. Pan et al. (2016) introduced a hierarchical recurrent encoder to capture the temporal visual features at different levels. Yu et al. (2016) proposed a hierarchical decoder for paragraph generation, and most recently Wang et al. (2018) invented a hierarchical reinforced framework to generate the caption phrase by phrase. But none had tried to model and align the global

and local contexts of different modalities as we do. Our HACA model does only learn the representations of different modalities at different granularities, but also align and dynamically fuse them both globally and locally with hierarchically aligned cross-modal attentions.

2 Proposed Model

Our HACA model is an encoder-decoder framework comprising multiple hierarchical recurrent neural networks (see Figure 2). Specifically, in the encoding stage, the model has one hierarchical attentive encoder for each input modality, which learns and outputs both the local and global representations of the modality. (In this paper, visual and audio features are used as the input and hence there are two hierarchical attentive encoders as shown in Figure 2; it should be noted, however, that the model seamlessly extends to more than two input modalities.)

In the decoding stage, we employ two cross-modal attentive decoders: the *local decoder* and the *global decoder*. The global decoder attempts to align the global contexts of different modalities and learn the global cross-modal fusion context. Correspondingly, the local decoder learns a local cross-modal fusion context, combines it with the output from the global decoder, and predicts the next word.

2.1 Feature Extractors

To exploit visual and audio cues, we use the pre-trained convolutional neural network (CNN) models to extract deep visual features and deep audio features correspondingly. More specifically, we utilize the ResNet model for image classification (He et al., 2016) and the VGGish model for audio classification (Hershey et al., 2017).

2.2 Attention Mechanism

For a better understanding of the following sections, we first introduce the soft attention mechanism. Given a feature sequence $(\mathbf{x}_1, \mathbf{x}_2, ..., \mathbf{x}_n)$ and a running recurrent neural network (RNN), the context vector $\mathbf{c}_t$ at time step t is computed as a weighted sum over the sequence:

$$\mathbf{c}_t = \sum_{k=1}^{n} \alpha_{tk}\mathbf{x}_k \quad , \tag{1}$$

These attention weights $\{\alpha_{tk}\}$ can be learned by the attention mechanism proposed in (Bahdanau et al., 2014), which gives higher weights to certain features that allow better prediction of the system's internal state.

2.3 Hierarchical Attentive Encoder

Inspired by Pan et al. (2016), the hierarchical attentive encoder consists of two LSTMs and the input to the low-level LSTM is a sequence of temporal features $\{\mathbf{f}_i^{e_L}\}$ and $i \in \{1, ..., n\}$:

$$\mathbf{o}_i^{e_L}, \mathbf{h}_i^{e_L} = e_L(\mathbf{f}_i^{e_L}, \mathbf{h}_{i-1}^{e_L}) \quad , \tag{2}$$

where e_L is the low-level encoder LSTM, whose output and hidden state at step i are $\mathbf{o}_i^{e_L}$ and $\mathbf{h}_i^{e_L}$ respectively. As shown in Figure 2, different from a stacked two-layer LSTM, the high-level LSTM here operates at a lower temporal resolution and runs one step every s time steps. Thus it learns the temporal transitions of the segmented feature chunks of size s. Furthermore, an attention mechanism is employed between the connection of these two LSTMs. It learns the context vector of the low-level LSTM's outputs of the current feature chunk, which is then taken as the input to the high-level LSTM at step j. In formula,

$$\mathbf{f}_j^{e_H} = \sum_{k=s(j-1)+1}^{sj} \alpha_{jk}\mathbf{o}_k^{e_L} \quad , \tag{3}$$

$$\mathbf{o}_j^{e_H}, \mathbf{h}_j^{e_H} = e_H(\mathbf{f}_j^{e_H}, \mathbf{h}_{j-1}^{e_H}) \quad , \tag{4}$$

where e_H denotes the high-level LSTM whose output and hidden state at j are $\mathbf{o}_j^{e_H}$ and $\mathbf{h}_j^{e_H}$.

Since we are utilizing both the visual and audio features, there are two hierarchical attentive encoders (v for visual features and a for audio features). Hence four sets of representations are learned in the encoding stage: high-level and low-level visual feature sequences ($\{\mathbf{o}_j^{v_H}\}$ and $\{\mathbf{o}_i^{v_L}\}$), and high-level and low-level audio feature sequences ($\{\mathbf{o}_j^{a_H}\}$ and $\{\mathbf{o}_i^{a_L}\}$).

2.4 Globally and Locally Aligned Cross-modal Attentive Decoder

In the decoding stage, the representations of different modalities at the same granularity are aligned separately with individual attentive decoders. That is, one decoder is employed to align those high-level features and learn a high-level (global) cross-modal embedding. Since the high-level features are the temporal transitions of larger chunks and focus on long-range contexts, we call the corresponding decoder as *global decoder* (d_G). Similarly, the companion *local decoder* (d_L) is used to align the low-level (local) features that attend to fine-grained and local dynamics.

At each time step t, the attentive decoders learn the corresponding visual and audio contexts using the attention mechanism (see Figure 2). In addition, our attentive decoders also uncover the attention over their own previous hidden states and learn aligned decoder contexts $\mathbf{c}_t^{d_L}$ and $\mathbf{c}_t^{d_G}$:

$$\mathbf{c}_t^{d_L} = \sum_{k=1}^{t-1} \alpha_{tk}^{d_L}\mathbf{h}_k^{d_L}, \quad \mathbf{c}_t^{d_G} = \sum_{k=1}^{t-1} \alpha_{tk}^{d_G}\mathbf{h}_k^{d_G}. \tag{5}$$

Paulus et al. (2017) also show that decoder attention can mitigate the phrase repetition issue.

Each decoder is equipped with a *cross-modal attention*, which learns the attention over contexts of different modalities. The cross-modal attention module selectively attends to different modalities and outputs a fusion context $\mathbf{c}_t^f$:

$$\mathbf{c}_t^f = \tanh(\beta_{tv}\mathbf{W}_v\mathbf{c}_t^v + \beta_{ta}\mathbf{W}_a\mathbf{c}_t^a + \beta_{td}\mathbf{W}_d\mathbf{c}_t^d + b), \tag{6}$$

where $\mathbf{c}_t^v$, $\mathbf{c}_t^a$, and $\mathbf{c}_t^d$ are visual, audio and decoder contexts at step t respectively; $\mathbf{W}_v$, $\mathbf{W}_a$ and $\mathbf{W}_d$ are learnable matrices; β_{tv}, β_{ta} and β_{td} can be learned in a similar manner of the attention mechanism in Section 2.2.

The global decoder d_G directly takes as the input the concatenation of the global fusion context $\mathbf{c}_t^{f_G}$ and the word embedding of the generated word w_{t-1} at previous time step:

$$\mathbf{o}_t^{d_G}, \mathbf{h}_t^{d_G} = d_G([\mathbf{c}_t^{f_G}, emb(w_{t-1})], \mathbf{h}_{t-1}^{d_G}). \quad (7)$$

The global decoder's output $\mathbf{o}_t^{d_G}$ is a latent embedding which represents the aligned global temporal transitions of multiple modalities. Differently, the local decoder d_L receives the latent embedding $\mathbf{o}_t^{d_G}$, mixes it with the local fusion context $c_t^{f_L}$, and then learns a uniform representation $\mathbf{o}_t^{d_L}$ to predict the next word. In formula,

$$\mathbf{o}_t^{d_L}, \mathbf{h}_t^{d_L} = d_L([\mathbf{c}_t^{f_L}, emb(w_{t-1}), \mathbf{o}_t^{d_G}], \mathbf{h}_{t-1}^{d_L}). \quad (8)$$

2.5 Cross-Entropy Loss Function

The probability distribution of the next word is

$$p(w_t|w_{1:t-1}) = softmax(\mathbf{W}_p[\mathbf{o}_t^{d_L}]), \quad (9)$$

where $\mathbf{W}_p$ is the projection matrix. $w_{1:t-1}$ is the generated word sequence before step t. θ be the model parameters and $w_{1:T}^*$ be the ground-truth word sequence, then the cross entropy loss

$$\mathcal{L}(\theta) = -\sum_{t=1}^{T} \log p(w_t^*|w_{1:t-1}^*, \theta). \quad (10)$$

3 Experimental Setup

Dataset and Preprocessing We evaluate our model on the MSR-VTT dataset (Xu et al., 2016), which contains 10,000 videos clips (6,513 for training, 497 for validation, and the remaining 2,990 for testing). Each video contains 20 human annotated reference captions collected by Amazon Mechanical Turk. To extract the visual features, the pretrained ResNet model (He et al., 2016) is used on the video frames which are sampled at $3fps$. For the audio features, we process the raw WAV files using the pretrained VGGish model as suggested in Hershey et al. (2017)[1].

Evaluation Metrics We adopt four diverse automatic evaluation metrics: BLEU, METEOR, ROUGE-L, and CIDEr-D, which are computed using the standard evaluation code from MS-COCO server (Chen et al., 2015).

---

[1] https://github.com/tensorflow/models/tree/master/research/audioset

Models	BLEU-4	METEOR	ROUGE-L	CIDEr
Top-3 Results from MSR-VTT Challenge 2017				
v2t_navigator	40.8	28.2	60.9	44.8
Aalto	39.8	26.9	59.8	45.7
VideoLAB	39.1	27.7	60.6	44.1
State Of The Arts				
CIDEnt-RL	40.5	28.4	61.4	**51.7**
Dense-Cap	**41.4**	28.3	61.1	48.9
HRL	41.3	**28.7**	**61.7**	48.0
Our Models				
ATT(v)	39.6	27.4	59.7	45.8
CM-ATT(va)	41.7	28.6	61.2	48.2
CM-ATT(vad)	41.9	29.1	61.5	48.0
HACA(w/o align)	42.8	29.0	**61.8**	48.9
HACA	**43.4**	**29.5**	**61.8**	**49.7**

Table 1: Results on the MSR-VTT dataset.

Training Details All the hyperparameters are tuned on the validation set. The maximum number of frames is 50, and the maximum number of audio segments is 20. For the visual hierarchical attentive encoders (HAE), the low-level encoder is a bidirectional LSTM with hidden dim 512 (128 for the audio HAE), and the high-level encoder is an LSTM with hidden dim 256 (64 for the audio HAE), whose chunk size s is 10 (4 for the audio HAE). The global decoder is an LSTM with hidden dim 256 and the local decoder is an LSTM with hidden dim 1024. The maximum step size of the decoders is 16. We use word embedding of size 512. Moreover, we adopt Dropout (Srivastava et al., 2014) with a value 0.5 for regularization. The gradients are clipped into the range [-10, 10]. We initialize all the parameters with a uniform distribution in the range [-0.08, 0.08]. Adadelta optimizer (Zeiler, 2012) is used with batch size 64. The learning rate is initially set as 1 and then reduced by a factor 0.5 when the current CIDEr score does not surpass the previous best for 4 epochs. The maximum number of epochs is set as 50, and the training data is shuffled at each epoch. Schedule sampling (Bengio et al., 2015) is employed to train the models. Beam search of size 5 is used during the test time inference.

4 Results

4.1 Comparison with State Of The Arts

In Table 1, we first list the top-3 results from the MSR-VTT Challenge 2017: v2t_navigator (Jin et al., 2016), Aalto (Shetty and Laaksonen, 2016), and VideoLAB (Ramanishka et al., 2016). Then we compare with the state-of-the-art methods on the MSR-VTT dataset: CIDEnt-RL (Pasunuru and

Features	BLEU-4	METEOR	ROUGE-L	CIDEr
video only	39.6	27.4	59.7	45.8
video + MFCC	40.3	28.5	60.8	47.5
video + VGGish	**41.7**	**28.6**	**61.2**	**48.2**

Table 2: Performance of the cross-modal attention model with various audio features.

Bansal, 2017), Dense-Cap (Shen et al., 2017), and HRL (Wang et al., 2018). Our HACA model significantly outperforms all the previous methods and achieved the new state of the art on BLEU-4, METEOR, and ROUGE-L scores. Especially, we improve the BLEU-4 score from 41.4 to 43.1. The CIDEr score is the second best and only lower than that of CIDEnt-RL which directly optimizes the CIDEr score during training with reinforcement learning. Note that all the results of our HACA method reported here are obtained by supervised learning only.

4.2 Result Analysis

We also evaluate several baselines to validate the effectiveness of the components in our HACA framework (see Our Models in Table 1). *ATT(v)* is a generic attention-based encoder-decoder model that specifically attends to the visual features only. *CM-ATT* is a cross-modal attentive model, which contains one individual encoder for each input modality and employs a cross-modal attention module to fuse the contexts of different modalities. *CM-ATT(va)* denotes the CM-ATT model consisting of visual attention and audio attention, while *CM-ATT(vad)* has an additional decoder attention.

As presented in Table 1, our ATT(v) model achieves comparable results with the top-ranked results from MSR-VTT challenge. Comparing between ATT(v) and CM-ATT(va), we observe a substantial improvement by exploiting the deep audio features and adding cross-modal attention. The results of CM-ATT(vad) further demonstrates that decoder attention was beneficial for video captioning. Note that to test the strength of the aligned attentive decoders, we provide the results of *HACA(w/o align)* model, which shares almost same architecture with the HACA model, except that it only has one decoder to receive both the global and local contexts. Apparently, our HACA model obtains superior performance, which therefore proves the effectiveness of the context alignment mechanism.

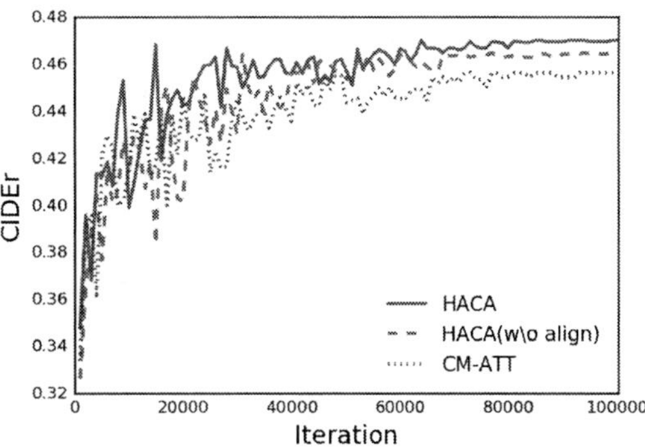

Figure 3: Learning curves of the CIDEr scores on the validation set. Note that greedy decoding is used during training, while beam search is employed at test time, thus the testing scores are higher than the validation scores here.

4.3 Effect of Deep Audio Features

In order to validate the superiority of the deep audio features in video captioning, we illustrate the performance of different audio features applied in the CM-ATT model in Table 2. Evidently, the deep VGGish audio features work better than the hand-crafted MFCC audio features for the video captioning task. Besides, it also shows the importance of understanding and describing a video with the help of audio features.

4.4 Learning Curves

For a more intuitive view of the model capacity, we plot the learning curves of the CIDEr scores on the validation set in Figure 3. Three models are presented: HACA, HACA(w/o align), and CM-ATT. They are trained on same input modalities and all paired with visual, audio and decoder attentions. We can observe that the HACA model performs consistently better than others and has the largest model capacity.

5 Conclusion

We introduce a generic architecture for video captioning which learns the aligned cross-modal attention globally and locally. It can be plugged into the existing reinforcement learning methods for video captioning to further boost the performance. Moreover, in addition to the deep visual and audio features, features from other modalities can also be incorporated into the HACA framework, such as optical flow and C3D features.

References

Dzmitry Bahdanau, Kyunghyun Cho, and Yoshua Bengio. 2014. Neural machine translation by jointly learning to align and translate. *arXiv preprint arXiv:1409.0473* .

Samy Bengio, Oriol Vinyals, Navdeep Jaitly, and Noam Shazeer. 2015. Scheduled sampling for sequence prediction with recurrent neural networks. In *Advances in Neural Information Processing Systems*. pages 1171–1179.

Shizhe Chen and Qin Jin. 2016. Multi-modal conditional attention fusion for dimensional emotion prediction. In *Proceedings of the 2016 ACM on Multimedia Conference*. ACM, pages 571–575.

Xinlei Chen, Hao Fang, Tsung-Yi Lin, Ramakrishna Vedantam, Saurabh Gupta, Piotr Dollár, and C Lawrence Zitnick. 2015. Microsoft coco captions: Data collection and evaluation server. *arXiv preprint arXiv:1504.00325* .

Kaiming He, Xiangyu Zhang, Shaoqing Ren, and Jian Sun. 2016. Deep residual learning for image recognition. In *Proceedings of the IEEE conference on computer vision and pattern recognition*. pages 770–778.

Lang He, Dongmei Jiang, Le Yang, Ercheng Pei, Peng Wu, and Hichem Sahli. 2015. Multimodal affective dimension prediction using deep bidirectional long short-term memory recurrent neural networks. In *Proceedings of the 5th International Workshop on Audio/Visual Emotion Challenge*. ACM, pages 73–80.

Shawn Hershey, Sourish Chaudhuri, Daniel PW Ellis, Jort F Gemmeke, Aren Jansen, R Channing Moore, Manoj Plakal, Devin Platt, Rif A Saurous, Bryan Seybold, et al. 2017. Cnn architectures for large-scale audio classification. In *Acoustics, Speech and Signal Processing (ICASSP), 2017 IEEE International Conference on*. IEEE, pages 131–135.

Chiori Hori, Takaaki Hori, Teng-Yok Lee, Ziming Zhang, Bret Harsham, John R. Hershey, Tim K. Marks, and Kazuhiko Sumi. 2017. Attention-based multimodal fusion for video description. In *The IEEE International Conference on Computer Vision (ICCV)*.

Qin Jin, Jia Chen, Shizhe Chen, Yifan Xiong, and Alexander Hauptmann. 2016. Describing videos using multi-modal fusion. In *Proceedings of the 2016 ACM on Multimedia Conference*. ACM, pages 1087–1091.

Jiquan Ngiam, Aditya Khosla, Mingyu Kim, Juhan Nam, Honglak Lee, and Andrew Y Ng. 2011. Multimodal deep learning. In *Proceedings of the 28th international conference on machine learning (ICML-11)*. pages 689–696.

Pingbo Pan, Zhongwen Xu, Yi Yang, Fei Wu, and Yueting Zhuang. 2016. Hierarchical recurrent neural encoder for video representation with application to captioning. In *Proceedings of the IEEE Conference on Computer Vision and Pattern Recognition*. pages 1029–1038.

Ramakanth Pasunuru and Mohit Bansal. 2017. Reinforced video captioning with entailment rewards. In *Proceedings of the 2017 Conference on Empirical Methods in Natural Language Processing*. Association for Computational Linguistics, Copenhagen, Denmark, pages 979–985.

Romain Paulus, Caiming Xiong, and Richard Socher. 2017. A deep reinforced model for abstractive summarization. *arXiv preprint arXiv:1705.04304* .

Vasili Ramanishka, Abir Das, Dong Huk Park, Subhashini Venugopalan, Lisa Anne Hendricks, Marcus Rohrbach, and Kate Saenko. 2016. Multimodal video description. In *Proceedings of the 2016 ACM on Multimedia Conference*. ACM, pages 1092–1096.

Zhiqiang Shen, Jianguo Li, Zhou Su, Minjun Li, Yurong Chen, Yu-Gang Jiang, and Xiangyang Xue. 2017. Weakly supervised dense video captioning. In *The IEEE Conference on Computer Vision and Pattern Recognition (CVPR)*.

Rakshith Shetty and Jorma Laaksonen. 2016. Frame- and segment-level features and candidate pool evaluation for video caption generation. In *Proceedings of the 2016 ACM on Multimedia Conference*. ACM, pages 1073–1076.

Nitish Srivastava, Geoffrey E Hinton, Alex Krizhevsky, Ilya Sutskever, and Ruslan Salakhutdinov. 2014. Dropout: a simple way to prevent neural networks from overfitting. *Journal of machine learning research* 15(1):1929–1958.

Subhashini Venugopalan, Marcus Rohrbach, Jeffrey Donahue, Raymond Mooney, Trevor Darrell, and Kate Saenko. 2015a. Sequence to sequence-video to text. In *Proceedings of the IEEE international conference on computer vision*. pages 4534–4542.

Subhashini Venugopalan, Huijuan Xu, Jeff Donahue, Marcus Rohrbach, Raymond Mooney, and Kate Saenko. 2015b. Translating videos to natural language using deep recurrent neural networks. In *Proceedings of the 2015 Conference of the North American Chapter of the Association for Computational Linguistics: Human Language Technologies*.

Xin Wang, Wenhu Chen, Jiawei Wu, Yuan-Fang Wang, and William Yang Wang. 2018. Video captioning via hierarchical reinforcement learning. In *The IEEE Conference on Computer Vision and Pattern Recognition (CVPR)*.

Chung-Hsien Wu, Jen-Chun Lin, and Wen-Li Wei. 2014a. Survey on audiovisual emotion recognition:

databases, features, and data fusion strategies. *AP-SIPA transactions on signal and information processing* 3.

Zuxuan Wu, Yu-Gang Jiang, Jun Wang, Jian Pu, and Xiangyang Xue. 2014b. Exploring inter-feature and inter-class relationships with deep neural networks for video classification. In *Proceedings of the 22nd ACM international conference on Multimedia*. ACM, pages 167–176.

Jun Xu, Tao Mei, Ting Yao, and Yong Rui. 2016. Msr-vtt: A large video description dataset for bridging video and language. In *Proceedings of the IEEE Conference on Computer Vision and Pattern Recognition*. pages 5288–5296.

Jun Xu, Ting Yao, Yongdong Zhang, and Tao Mei. 2017. Learning multimodal attention lstm networks for video captioning. In *Proceedings of the 2017 ACM on Multimedia Conference*. ACM, pages 537–545.

Xitong Yang, Palghat Ramesh, Radha Chitta, Sriganesh Madhvanath, Edgar A. Bernal, and Jiebo Luo. 2017. Deep multimodal representation learning from temporal data. In *The IEEE Conference on Computer Vision and Pattern Recognition (CVPR)*.

Li Yao, Atousa Torabi, Kyunghyun Cho, Nicolas Ballas, Christopher Pal, Hugo Larochelle, and Aaron Courville. 2015. Describing videos by exploiting temporal structure. In *Proceedings of the IEEE international conference on computer vision*. pages 4507–4515.

Haonan Yu, Jiang Wang, Zhiheng Huang, Yi Yang, and Wei Xu. 2016. Video paragraph captioning using hierarchical recurrent neural networks. In *Proceedings of the IEEE conference on computer vision and pattern recognition*. pages 4584–4593.

Matthew D Zeiler. 2012. Adadelta: an adaptive learning rate method. *arXiv preprint arXiv:1212.5701* .

Author Index